Number One in Heaven

Number in

One Heaven

The Heroes Who Died for Rock 'n' Roll

Jeremy Simmonds

PENGUIN BOOKS

This book is dedicated to the memory of my father

Penguin Books

Published by the Penguin Group
Penguin Books Ltd, 80 Strand, London WC2R 0RL, England
Penguin Group (USA) Inc., 375 Hudson Street, New York, New York 10014, USA
Penguin Group (Canada), 90 Eglinton Avenue East, Suite 700, Toronto, Ontario, Canada M4P 2Y3
(a division of Pearson Penguin Canada Inc.)
Penguin Ireland, 25 St Stephen's Green, Dublin 2, Ireland
(a division of Penguin Books Ltd)
Penguin Group (Australia), 250 Camberwell Road, Camberwell, Victoria 3124, Australia
(a division of Pearson Australia Group Pty Ltd)
Penguin Books India Pvt Ltd, 11 Community Centre, Panchsheel Park, New Delhi – 110 017, India
Penguin Group (NZ), cnr Airborne and Rosedale Roads, Albany, Auckland 1310, New Zealand
(a division of Pearson New Zealand Ltd)
Penguin Books (South Africa) (Pty) Ltd, 24 Sturdee Avenue, Rosebank, Johannesburg 2196, South Africa

Penguin Books Ltd, Registered Offices: 80 Strand, London WC2R 0RL, England

www.penguin.com

First published 2006
1

Copyright © Jeremy Simmonds, 2006
All rights reserved
The moral right of the author has been asserted

Designed by Richard Marston
Printed in England by Butler and Tanner, Frome

ISBN-13: 978–0–141–02287–1
ISBN-10: 0–141–02287–6

'Once you're dead you're made for life – you have to die before they think you're worth anything' Jimi Hendrix

Robert Johnson: Sold his soul but couldn't buy it back

Through the haze of cigarette smoke and honest sweat, the whiskey didn't so much look good as essential. Just one or two before sleep would do it for the guitar-slinger, already weary from a day's labour, the musician now pushed to the limit by the roadhouse-owner's demands. But though the atmosphere was tense, he was oblivious to anything that may have been afoot that night. He'd not noticed the stale, sour tinge upon the bottle's rim – escaping the lights, the noise and the people was his only wish at this late hour. The faces of those who'd shared his performance that night were ecstatic yet strange. Then their eager voices began to waver, distort and finally become incoherent as the 27-year-old bluesman began to slump . . .

Thus, the night of 16 August 1938 kick-starts a timeline of death in popular music – with the strychnine-poisoning of **Robert Johnson**, the Delta-blues pioneer considered by many the finest of them all. The likelihood is that his end came at the Three Forks roadhouse in Greenwood, Mississippi, belonging to his lover's jealous husband; it is also highly probable that Johnson (born in Hazlehurst, Mississippi, on 8 May 1911) had been with the woman in question that very evening – and it is beyond any doubt that the agony in which the writer of classics like 'Sweet Home Chicago' and 'Come on in My Kitchen' ended his days forty-eight hours later caused him to denounce the 'evil blues' and give his dying soul to Christianity.

So, with a holler to the devil himself, what better way to summon up a roll-call of the deceased? The sentiments uttered and spluttered by Johnson as he crawled back to the crossroads two nights later might equally apply to the further ungodliness that was to emerge in his wake. Upon its arrival in the fifties, rock

'n' roll was tagged 'the music of the devil' by the same God-fearing folk who dubbed the secular world of soul and R & B also inherently 'wrong' – particularly when its delights had tempted some of their own to wander. Similarly, folk, punk, dance music and hip hop have all incurred the wrath of the puritans at some point. All of which leads one to suspect that things might be getting a tad crowded 'downstairs'.

But no matter where he is now, Robert Johnson's in fine company. The above dramatization of his demise serves only to preface *Number One in Heaven* – the ultimate chronology of pop's dead. What lies before you is the definitive register of those who arrived, rocked and pegged out over the past forty or so years. Space demands that details in some cases might read like a perverse end-of-term report, highlighting where the subject performed admirably – and underlining specifically where he failed, and ultimately fell. In this school of rock, you have to be absent to attend – those who make it are those who *didn't* make it.

Who is included?

Naturally, there'll be readers who'll feel certain names have been unfairly brushed over (or, worse still, ignored completely), but the criteria for inclusion are simple. If an artist had a short but 'unusual' life, he's in (step forward, Mr G G Allin); if he had an extraordinary demise, he's *definitely* in (take a bow, Sam Cooke); if he made a significant contribution to his art, he'll also get a paragraph (not you, Baltimora . . .).

Who isn't included?

Well, 1938 was one hell of a long time ago and to list *all* demises in popular music before 1965 would (given the field's infancy) be virtually impossible. Genres are blurred and embryonic at this point, thus *Number One in Heaven*'s apparent ban on certain musical styles is instigated for no other reason than that rock 'n' roll was supposedly sent to destroy them. (Until they cross over, of course.) Gospel, for example, manifests itself via such fabulous performers as the aforementioned Cooke and Mahalia Jackson – though one might have to scroll the small print pretty carefully for the lesser names. As one must also do to find those for whom detail is sketchy, those who enjoyed only the merest flirtation with musical success, or indeed those who survived beyond a completely arbitrary threshold of sixty-five years – apart from that special bunch who make up the book's thirty Golden Oldies. For these, *Number One in Heaven* offers the safety net known as Lest We Forget, which each year will scoop up the old and the also-rans alike.

Peripherals

Mortality can be a tricky subject, so should this unrelenting parade of the deceased cause one to pause for breath and check one's own pulse, then relief is at hand. The expansive chronology section is broken by a smorgasbord of intriguing, lighter-hearted facts (Dead Interesting!) and lucky escapes (Close . . . Closer!), as well as a parade of completely subjective Top Tens (The Death Toll) featuring the most morbid tunes pop music has ever seen. So, not that much of a respite, it's true.

But the chronicle cannot begin in earnest without first cataloguing those major names who fell during pop's monochrome years . . .

Shameless disclaimer

This book isn't really designed to carry exhaustive biographies of every entrant, so readers desiring such are encouraged to look elsewhere. It's also fair to say that with thousands of dates to consider, one or two small errors may creep in – so do inform Number One in Heaven *(www.numberoneinheaven. com) if a mistake becomes apparent. (Similarly, any new information is also gratefully received.)*

Pre-1965

Despite Johnson's apparent condemnation of his own lifestyle (he *was* painfully sick, remember), his earlier words and actions were set to inspire. Without his scratchy musings there'd be no Muddy Waters, no Hendrix, no Stones and – heaven forbid – no Gun Club. Similarly influential was Huddie Ledbetter – the Cajun-blues guitarist known as **Leadbelly** who, in 1949, finally submitted to amyotrophic lateral sclerosis, a crippling condition known as Lou Gehrig's disease (after the New York baseball star who'd died from the disease eight years previously). Ledbetter (born in Mooringsport, Louisiana, on 29 January 1889 (or 1885)) had been imprisoned regularly for violent crimes – including a thirty-year term for homicide. The abiding myth about the man is that he was pardoned from incarceration in 1925 when a recording of his musical plea for freedom found its way into the hands of the serving governor. Remarkable, if true; more likely is that standard parole terms were considerably more lenient then than they are now. Leadbelly, however, left behind a host of standards, including 'Black Betty', and a long-suffering wife.

But in those less-enlightened (and pre-AIDS) times, the unhealthy were picked off by a host of unlikely ailments. With little public health awareness, conditions now more associated with maturity were far more prevalent among the young. Of course, added to this

Hank Williams: There was a tear in his beer

was an increased availability of drugs and alcohol to the newly rich. In 1953, country music lost its finest ever exponent to a heart condition – or so it initially seemed. A defining figure of contemporary music per se, **Hank Williams** (born Hiram King Williams in Mount Olive, Alabama, on 17 September 1923) would blueprint rock 'n' roll behaviour, his drinking and womanizing colouring the 'Hillbilly Shakespeare''s lyric-writing but also severely curtailing his relationship with the country-music establishment. He had not even reached his thirties by New Year's Eve 1952, when the increasingly wayward and by-now out-of-favour star had been due to play a rare concert in Ohio. With bad weather cancelling all flights out of Tennessee, Williams – not wishing to miss out on one of the few opportunities still coming his way – travelled to the gig in a chauffeured Cadillac and attempted to sleep off the effects of alcohol, wrongly prescribed tablets and two shots of morphine. Stopping the singer's young driver for speeding, a concerned police officer remarked that his passenger 'looked dead'. On closer inspection it was discovered to be more than appearance: the man who'd declared 'I'll Never Get out of This World Alive' was affirmed deceased from heart failure at 7 am on New Year's Day 1953. Williams's burial three days later at Montgomery, Alabama, drew the largest recorded US crowd since the inauguration of Confederate President Jefferson Davis, almost a century before.

Billie Holiday (born Eleanora Fagan Gough in Baltimore, Maryland, on 7 April 1915), on the other hand, combined her heart failure with cirrhosis of the liver when she entered the eternal nightclub. Holiday had had a shockingly hard life from day one, raped by a neighbour at eleven, forced into prostitution before she was out of her teens and preyed upon by countless parasites throughout her otherwise glorious career. A natural singer, Holiday oddly described her gift as 'no more work than sitting down and eating roast duck', though 'cold turkey' was more often on the Holiday menu. Her dependency upon heroin and alcohol precipitated a disturbing decline in her health that led ultimately to her death on 17 July 1959.[1] Four years down the line, a similar fate befell another blues/swing artist often overlooked in Holiday's favour – **Dinah Washington** (born Ruth Lee Jones in Tuscaloosa, Alabama, on 29 August 1924). Her personal life was, correspondingly, also far from a bed of roses: Washington's rapacious drinking hardly helping matters, she recorded seven failed marriages over the years and hid an obsession with weight loss that caused her to consume dietary tablets in frightening quantities. Adding a bizarre spate of mercury injections into the mix, inevitably this combined mania finished her off, on 5 December 1963.

There were, of course, uncomplicated drug deaths. On 21 May 1964, **Rudy Lewis** became the first of numerous Drifters to soft-shoe-shuffle off doo-wop's mortal coil over the next few decades (➳ *Dead Interesting!*). Lewis (heroin overdose) had been the third lead – Johnny Williams (homesickness) and James Poindexter (stage fright) having proved unworkable – in an apparently unending search to replace Ben E King (cash dispute). Although the otherwise-healthy Lewis (born in Philadelphia on 23 August 1936) was found in a hotel room with a needle in his arm, his death was diplomatically put down to 'asphyxiation after a particularly large supper' by senior Drifter and spokesman Johnny Moore – who was to join him in an ever-growing celestial version of the band thirty-four years on (➳ *December 1998*).

The first bona fide rock 'n' roll death was probably the massive heart attack that finished off **Danny Cedrone** (born Donato Cedrone, 20 June 1920) on 18 June 1954. This young guitarist's best-known solo will remain familiar to pretty much everyone as it continues to chime out across rock revival nights and wedding receptions alike, from the middle eight of Bill Haley & His Comets' 'Rock around the Clock'. Slide-guitar ground-breaker **Elmore James** (born in Richland, Mississippi, on 27 January 1918) was similarly dogged with a dodgy ticker throughout his life; the frenetic Chicago-blues and boogie-woogie man checked out after a third coronary on 5 May 1963.

Making history in such a way and not living to see it must surely frustrate those on the other side. What of **Stuart Sutcliffe**, the 'fifth Beatle' and already a part of that phenomenon's history before his death from a

[1]At the time of her death, the bedridden Billie Holiday had been placed under house arrest for possession of narcotics. It is believed she had $700 strapped to her leg, the advance for her autobiography, *Lady Sings the Blues*.

DEAD INTERESTING!

SIX FEET UNDER THE BOARDWALK

With at least fifteen dead members from their various incarnations, The Drifters are definitely among the front-runners in *Number One in Heaven*'s Deceased Members Hit Parade. The names of those we know to be confined to vocal history are:

Al Banks (lead, 26/7/1937–7/1977)
Little David Baughan (tenor, 1938–70)
Fred Below (drummer, 16/9/1926–14/8/1988)
Marcel Evans (tenor, d 28/10/2005)
Doc Green (baritone, 8/10/1934–10/3/1989)
Bill Fredericks (baritone/lead, no dates available)
Elsbeary Hobbs (bass, 4/8/1936–31/5/1996)
Rudy Lewis (lead, 23/8/1936–21/5/1964)
Clyde McPhatter (tenor, 15/11/1932–13/6/1972)
Johnny Moore (tenor/lead, 15/12/1934–30/12/1998)
Lover Patterson (manager/singer, 1930–65)
Eugene Pearson (baritone, 1935–6/4/2000)
Bobby Warren (singer, d 29/4/2000)
Johnny Williams (tenor/lead, 27/10/1940–19/12/2004)
Vernon Young (lead, 13/1/1949–17/2/2005)

(Real completists might like to add journeyman sax-player Earle Warren (d 1994), singer 'Pico' Payne (d 2002) and even one-time Sex Pistols producer Dave Goodman (d 2005), who apparently played bass with The Drifters at their London shows during the early seventies.)

Stuart Sutcliffe: Brushed with fame, brushed with death

brain haemorrhage in the spring of 1962? A talented painter, who should perhaps never have strayed from his original calling, struggling guitarist Sutcliffe (born in Edinburgh on 23 June 1940) found himself the victim of one of many regular attacks on The Silver Beetles (as he'd once named them), in which he was knocked to the ground and kicked in the head. Although bleeding profusely from the resultant gash, he refused to allow his mother to call an ambulance. The Beatles then decamped to Hamburg, where Sutcliffe experienced headaches and mood swings, which he attributed to his new lifestyle. Abandoning music to return to art, Sutcliffe (much to John Lennon's disappointment) remained in Germany to shack up with lover Astrid Kirchherr – but, sadly, it was to be only a short-lived arrangement. Despite doctors diagnosing nothing, Sutcliffe was virtually confined to his bed by April, collapsing unconscious on the 10th and – despite attempts to revive him – dying on the way to hospital. A post mortem finally revealed the tumour beneath his skull exactly where he had been kicked two years previously.[1] When The Beatles returned to Hamburg the next day, a heartbroken Kirchherr met them at the airport: 'When they asked me, "Where's Stu?", with tears rolling down my face I told them the news. John cried hysterically while Paul [McCartney] and Pete [Best] wept unashamedly.'

Sutcliffe's insidious injury all too eerily echoed that of **Jay Perkins** four years before. In the spring of 1956, Perkins (born James Buck Perkings in Tiptonville, Tennessee, in 1930) had travelled to New York as one of the three guitar-picking Perkins Brothers to perform better-known sibling Carl's 'Blue Suede Shoes' on that cutting-edge music showcase *The Perry Como Show*. Their driver, clearly struggling to contain his excitement, fell asleep at the wheel, and the group's luxury Chrysler slammed into a poultry pick-up. Suffering a fractured neck, Jay could only watch on television as

---

[1]Some (Stuart Sutcliffe's mother among them) suggest that his death was actually promoted by a recent fall downstairs, belying the obvious fact that he'd experienced medical problems earlier than 1962. Others point to genetic disorders. Both beliefs are considerably less likely.

young Elvis Presley debuted the soon-to-be-classic song in their absence, stealing the show as he did so. Jay Perkins suffered massive repercussions from his injuries, becoming ill on tour two years later and dying on 21 October 1958. But his was not the first car accident in our survey . . .

If Cedrone was likely the first rocker to go, then it's beyond much doubt that distinctive, pencil-moustachioed **Tommy Gaither** (born in 1927) of Baltimore sensations The Orioles was the first 'name' singer to die in one of the era's increasingly prevalent motor accidents. After a New York show on 5 November 1950, Gaither took the concept of a drive-in restaurant rather too literally: the over-tired singer steered his band's yellow Dodge into the establishment's front wall. More sinister was R & B singer **Jesse Belvin**'s demise on 6 February 1960. Appearing at an early integrated-audience concert at Little Rock, Arkansas, Belvin (born in San Antonio, Texas, on 15 December 1932) and illustrious co-stars Sam Cooke (who was to survive him by under five years), Jackie Wilson, Marv Johnson and Little Willie John were subjected to dismal barracking from white supremacists. Four hours after the performance, Belvin, his wife/manager, JoAnn (who died a week later), and his driver, Charles Shackleford, lay shattered on Highway 67. The tyres of the hired vehicle had, according to state troopers at the scene, 'obviously been tampered with'. Many felt that this was very likely the work of the same race-hate group that had disrupted the show, though no investigation was ever carried out.[1] (Spare a thought, also, for young **Vernon Isley** – boy prodigy and fourth-oldest of soul giants-to-be The Isley Brothers: he and his bicycle careered into a lorry in 1955, when Vernon was just eleven.)

Aircraft-fearing, non-driving **Eddie Cochran** had been nursing a premonition that he would die dramatically for some time, troubled as he was by the death of his friend Buddy Holly (of whom more shortly). As Cochran (born Ray Edward Cochrane in Albert Lea, Minnesota, on 18 October 1938) travelled to Heathrow Airport from Bristol, the Ford Consul that carried him and fellow touring rock 'n' roll great Gene Vincent had a high-speed blow-out on the A4 near Chippenham, Wiltshire. Cochran was thrown through a door after the car skidded 150 yards on the wet road, striking a concrete lamp-post; the singer received a massive blow to his skull as he landed. While 19-year-old chauffeur George Martin[2] escaped uninjured, Vincent suffered a fractured collarbone and severe injuries to his legs. Cochran's girlfriend, Sharon Sheeley, and tour manager, Pat Tomkins, also suffered minor damage. Cochran himself was less fortunate. Admitted to a Bath hospital, he died at 4 pm on Easter Day, 17 April 1960, from extensive brain lacerations, instantly assuming the status of rock 'n' roll's second martyr. (His death attracted more attention in Britain than back at home, and Cochran's 'Three Steps to Heaven' was number one there a month later.)

It was water that saw the demise of another key early rocker, Rock 'n' Roll Trio frontman **Johnny Burnette** (born in Memphis, Tennessee, on 25 March 1934), who met a premature end during a fishing accident: Burnette drowned in Clearlake, California, after his unlit craft was struck by a larger vessel on 1 August 1964. But it's fair to say that the inability of the touring musician to

---

[1] Belvin, who had notified his family of the hostile reception he and other artists had encountered on the tour, had reportedly received at least six death threats from anti-black organizations. The truth behind the crash was fudged for ever, though, when it emerged that Shackleford may have fallen asleep at the wheel and indeed that another car had been involved – in which at least two passengers were also killed.

[2] It was reported in the early nineties that Martin – dubbed 'the man who killed Eddie' – was *still* regularly being roughed up by Teds in his West Country home town.

The late, great Rock 'n' Roll Trio – Johnny Burnette (centre), flanked by Paul Burlison (who died in 2003) and Dorsey Burnette (✝ *August 1979*)

master his transportation was commonplace: if a hired car or boat seemed potential bad news, then agreeing to ride in a twin-engine plane must have been akin to assigning one's spirit there and then to the hereafter. Gospel figurehead **Ronald 'R W' Blackwood** (born in Ackerman, Mississippi, on 23 October 1921) – of the Elvis-approved Blackwood Brothers Quartet – thought he was on to a good thing when he bought such a craft to ease his troupe's travelling commitments. Ahead of test-flying his new toy, though, supposedly experienced pilot Blackwood critically forgot to re-trim the plane's tabs (whatever that means), and the Beechcraft plummeted to the ground, taking him, his bass-singer Bill

Lyles and their buddy John Ogburn Jr to an unexpectedly early date with inspiration on 30 June 1954.

Likewise, **Patsy Cline** (born Virginia Patterson Hensley in Winchester, Virginia, on 8 September 1932) seemed fated. The Queen of Country had survived a head-on car crash just a year before, but on 5 March 1963, her lover/manager, Randy Hughes, decided they should travel from Kansas City to Nashville in his private Piper Comanche. Shunning sensible advice, Hughes flew Cline and fellow country stars Hawkshaw Hawkins and Cowboy Copas (his father-in-law) into a storm. With conditions worsening by the second, his hopelessly lost craft hit trees at Fatty Bottom,

Tennessee. All on board perished; Patsy Cline, it is said, could only be identified by the back-upper-half of her torso.[1] A year on, country lyricists gained yet more material with the death of **'Gentleman' Jim Reeves** (born in Panola County, Texas, on 20 August 1923). By all accounts a far more experienced pilot than Randy Hughes, Reeves nonetheless perished when his Beechcraft Debonair planted itself, him and road manager/pianist 'Docky' Dean Manuel in private land on 31 July 1964. A search party of 700 – mostly country singers – attempted to track down the aircraft, only to be beaten to it by a somewhat blunt Tennessee patrolman who described the scene as looking as though 'someone had dumped a load o' trash'.

There's been little before or since, though, to match the dramatic end to the eighteen-month career of **Buddy Holly**. The true original of rock 'n' roll was, of course, killed alongside **J P 'Big Bopper' Richardson** and **Ritchie Valens** on 3 February 1959 – 'the day the music died' (or, perhaps more accurately, the end of rock 'n' roll's age of innocence). Perversely, the chances are that Holly et al could have avoided pop music's first, and most infamous, major disaster simply by mending a faulty heater in their tour bus. With a sharp north-easterly cutting through them, Holly (born Charles Hardin Holley in Lubbock, Texas, on 7 September 1936) and his new back-up musicians were wearying as the 24-city Winter Dance Party tour dragged on. Other artists on the mammoth bill included new sensation Valens (born Richard Valenzuela in Los Angeles, California, on 13 May 1941), old sensation the Big Bopper (born Jiles Perry Richardson in Sabine Pass, Texas, on 24 October 1930), The Crickets, with whom Holly had recently parted company, Dion & The Belmonts, and Frankie Sardo. Budget restrictions meant all the acts travelled in a rickety old bus, and on one occasion, when its heater broke down, passengers had to burn newspapers to keep from freezing in temperatures below −30° (Holly's drummer, Carl Bunch, was hospitalized with frostbite as a result). After the 2 February performance at Clearlake, Iowa, Buddy Holly decided he'd had enough and announced his decision to charter an aircraft to the next venue in Fargo, North Dakota. He wanted to arrive in relative comfort, relaxed and with time to spare to launder clothes rendered filthy by the bus. The plane (yes, a 1947 Beechcraft) and pilot were duly hired, though the craft's small capacity meant spaces were restricted. Holly's idea, naturally, had been to cater for his own band, but with Richardson running a fever, bassist Waylon Jennings generously gave up his seat to the stocky performer, who was barely accommodated by the coach seating anyway. Holly quipped to his close friend, 'I hope your ol' bus freezes over!', to which Jennings riposted, 'Well, I hope your plane crashes!' Both events *did* occur – and this apparently throwaway banter was to haunt Jennings until his death (☞ *February 2002*). Valens persuaded Holly's guitarist, Tommy Allsup, to toss a coin for the remaining seat. 'Heads' it was: Valens won the seat, Allsup his life.[2]

With fog and a blanket of snow following the harsh winds, the Beechcraft took off unsteadily just before 1 am. Visibility would have been poor as it climbed to an altitude of around 800 feet – there were subsequent rumours that the pilot, 21-year-old Roger Petersen, was insufficiently experienced with the craft's instrumentation in such conditions – and it disappeared from the radar less than five miles out of Mason City Municipal Airport. Once the fog had cleared, at around 9.30, the wreckage of the aircraft was found fifteen miles away in a remote field belonging to farmer Albert Juhl, its right wing having apparently hit the ground, causing it to corkscrew out of control and break up. All three musicians were dead, having been thrown from the plane, itself now little more than a twisted ball of metal. The pilot, also deceased, had somehow remained inside the cockpit. All had suffered injuries so traumatizing that their bodies were virtually unrecognizable: Buddy Holly's injuries included fractures to virtually every

---

[1] A Virginian country DJ was severely reprimanded for clumsily playing Cline's 'I Fall to Pieces' in her honour following the breaking news. Meanwhile, not-to-be-outdone country star Jack Anglin was killed in a car crash as he made his way to her funeral.

[2] Allsup opened a club in Texas named 'The Heads-Up Saloon' in tribute to his extreme good fortune that day.

bone, his skull split in two by the impact. Holly's personal effects retrieved included $193 in cash – from which the coroner reportedly helped himself to his $11.65 fee.[1] The mercurial performer was buried in the City of Lubbock Cemetery, with more than a thousand mourners paying their respects to the young legend. However, they included neither the band members (offered bonuses to remain on the tour, though allegedly they never received the money), nor Holly's shattered young wife, Maria Elena Santiago, who had also lost his unborn baby. An early indication of rock's ability to brush aside such tragedy came with the immediate continuation of the Winter Dance Party, Fargo teenager Bobby Vee stepping into the breach on 3 February, and The Crickets somehow managed to complete the tour.[2] As for Farmer Juhl, for many years he'd be more than happy to show thousands of paying visitors the exact spot where 'the music died'.

Rumour circulated briefly that a gunshot on board (possibly fired by Holly) might have killed the pilot, but this ludicrous theory has generally been dismissed due to lack of real evidence or, indeed, any motive whatsoever. But there again, what motive did R & B singer **Johnny Ace** have when he put a .22 handgun to his head and pulled the trigger on Christmas Eve 1954? Little more, it seems, than a desire to impress his girlfriend, Olivia, and blues singer 'Big Mama' Thornton, his guests backstage as he took a break from the Houston crowd. Olivia on his lap, he put the gun to his head and, chancing upon the one bullet in the chamber, proceeded to blow his brains out. Johnny Ace (born John Marshall Alexander in Memphis, Tennessee, on 9 June 1929) was certified dead on Christmas morning.

Cut to December 1964 – and the darkest tale of pop music's nascent history. After his initial spate of international hits, soul's first and brightest talent **Sam Cooke** narrowly escaped death with guitarist Cliff White and young singer Lou Rawls[3] in a 1958 car accident, which had killed their driver, Eddie Cunningham; just months later, his first wife, Dolores, had mysteriously committed suicide at the wheel of her own car. Though these distressing events led to a fracturing of

Johnny Ace: Make that one less for Christmas dinner ...

[1] In 1980, Holly's other retrieved belongings, his spectacles and poker dice, along with the Big Bopper's watch, were returned to their families after turning up in an envelope at the county courthouse where they had remained for over twenty years. The glasses now reside in the Buddy Holly Center, Lubbock – which also contains artefacts like the public telephone from which all three deceased performers made final calls.

[2] In the wake of Holly's death, the next two Crickets' singers also suffered horrific fatalities. His replacement for the tour, Ronnie Smith (born in 1935), hanged himself in October 1962; next, David Box (born in Sulphur Springs, Texas, on 11 August 1943) would die along with a later band in an air crash morbidly reminiscent of Holly's, on 23 October 1964. (A man often touted as a future Cricket – he'd recorded both one of their songs and one of Holly's – was garage rocker Bobby Fuller. He died in extremely suspicious circumstances (☞ *July 1966*).)

[3] Grammy-winning singer Lou Rawls died of cancer in the second week of 2006.

The legendary Sam Cooke: He sent us – we sent him back too soon

his previously impeccable cool, the 1963 drowning of his baby son, Vincent, in the family swimming pool was to cripple Cooke. It came as relief to many that, back home for Christmas the year after, Sam Cooke (born in Clarksdale, Mississippi, on 22 January 1931) appeared to be in brighter spirits than he had been in months. On 11 December, he and producer Al Schmitt and Schmitt's wife, Joan, sipped cocktails, waiting for dinner at Martoni's restaurant in LA, when they were approached by a record-label PR – and a slim 22-year-old Eurasian woman called Elisa Boyer, initially thought by the party to be a young singer. (It transpired, of course, that she was in a somewhat different line of 'entertainment'.) Their table ready, Cooke turned to pay for the drinks, giving Boyer an opportunity to observe the large amount of cash he had on his person – perhaps five thousand dollars. It became obvious that Cooke was taken with this girl, and he picked distractedly at his starter, disappearing from the table before his main course could be served. By 10.45 pm, Schmitt and his wife had written Cooke off but, spotting him in a private booth with Boyer, suggested that they all met later at PJ's Club on Sunset Boulevard – by 1.30 am, Cooke hadn't shown, and they headed home. Finally arriving at the nightspot, Cooke was intoxicated and brash, eventually threatening a man he felt was fraternizing too closely with Boyer; she, disturbed by his behaviour, allegedly then asked him to drive her home. Cooke obliged, though he was clearly in no condition to drive, frightening the girl further by putting his foot down and taking them on to the freeway in his Ferrari. At 2.35 am, the couple arrived at the Hacienda Motel in Figueroa Street, Watts, an inexpensive hostelry that (unlike many of its time) allowed black customers and – crucially – was known as a joint for working girls to take their clients. Equally crucially, Elisa Boyer – according to 55-year-old maître d' Bertha Franklin (soon to become the significant figure in this unfolding tale) – seemed quiet and unconcerned as she and Cooke entered the establish-ment. (Indeed, she had waited alone in the car park as Cooke checked for an available room.) Franklin,

having put two and two together, suggested the pair check in as husband and wife, and 'Mr and Mrs Cooke' repaired to their room. Although details of the rest of the night's incidents have remained cloudy ever since, Elisa Boyer would insist that Sam Cooke had led her in against her will.[1] She would also attest that he had locked her into their room, had physically restrained her and attempted to remove her clothing. Whether a sexual assault took place is uncertain – no examination of Boyer was ever made – though Cooke's apparent desperation still allowed both to use the bathroom, from which Boyer claimed she attempted to climb out via a window. While Cooke was in the bathroom, she made good her escape via the room door, grabbing her own and Cooke's clothes as she ran, first to Franklin's connecting apartment and then, failing to rouse the manageress (in deep telephone conversation with the motel's owner), out on to the street. Sam Cooke, believing Boyer to be hiding in Franklin's apartment, arrived soon after in just his overcoat, wearing one shoe. When Bertha Franklin understandably refused him entry, Cooke barged the door down and, perhaps believing the maître d' was in on the scam, demanded to know where Boyer was. The manageress now reportedly escaped his clutches and reached for the pistol she kept on her TV set for 'such eventualities'. Firing three times at close range, she hit him between two ribs, the fatal bullet passing through his heart and both lungs. Cooke's final words were, 'Lady! You shot me!' The police received two calls, from Elisa Boyer, still on the street and unaware of events since she fled, and from motel-owner Evelyn Carr, who had heard the entire fracas over the phone. But by the time LAPD law-enforcers had arrived at the motel, Sam Cooke was dead.

Within days, a seven-member coroner's jury ruled that the shooting constituted 'justifiable homicide'

[1]Boyer – who had told the police she was 'unemployed' – also attested that she had never visited the motel before. This was proven untrue, as evidence showed that she had used the joint regularly with her clients. She was also found to be in possession of a 'black book' containing the numbers of various Hollywood bigwigs, precipitating talk of a much-less-likely 'set-up' conspiracy.

– and the case itself open and shut. Various details had been sketchy, many more glossed over from the start, prompting riots outside the motel and in other parts of the city. Why had Boyer fled with Cooke's clothes? What had become of the considerable amount of money in his possession? Following her husband's death, Barbara Cooke – perhaps controversially – chose not to pursue any further investigation, according to her, in deference to her young family; according to others, to protect long-term posthumous record sales, should the story become even less savoury. At her husband's enormously attended Los Angeles funeral, Barbara showed up with his friend, singer Bobby Womack – and had dressed her new beau entirely from Cooke's wardrobe. Although the full facts will never be unearthed, Sam Cooke's is perhaps an appropriately murky saga to set us up for the battered pages to follow from rock's diary of disasters . . .

Guide to Main Entries

MONTH
Day/date

Artist
(details of birth)
Band*
(Other main acts where artist appeared)*
Symbol – see below

The body of the text contains the artist's biography and details of the story behind his/her death. Arrows within the text indicate connected artists (◀ *past entry*) or (*future entry* ▶). (Lest We Forget dates are in British format ie, date/month/year.)

* if applicable

KEY TO SYMBOLS

- Accidental
- Air crash
- Alcohol abuse
- Car/vehicle crash
- Choking
- Crime-related
- Destitution/poor maintenance
- Disappearance
- Drowning/water-related
- Drug-related
- Eating disorder
- Electrocution
- Fire
- General ill health
- Gun-related
- Heart-related
- Murder/unlawful killing
- Natural causes
- On stage
- Poisoning
- Rail accident
- Recreational/misadventure
- Suicide
- Unsolved

1965

JANUARY

Wednesday 20

Alan Freed

(Johnstown, Pennsylvania, 15 December 1921)

The DJ widely believed to have coined the phrase 'rock 'n' roll' actually began as a jazz trombonist with a band called Sultans of Swing (thereby also providing a name for a much-later Dire Straits hit). Freed became the first broadcaster to break down the obvious barriers and play so-called 'race' music to a largely white audience when he took to the air full-time with an R & B show for the WJW station in Cleveland. Moving to the more upbeat WINS in New York, Freed – now restyled as 'Moondog' – exposed young teenagers to the likes of Chuck Berry and Bo Diddley, while bravely refusing to play the white covers of black hits his programmers suggested. This forward thinking made him a sitting target for the prejudices of the era's conservatives and racists.

However, Freed proved a flawed individual, and this cost him dearly in his working life. Initially, problems were not necessarily of his own making: appearing in movies such as *Rock around the Clock*, the thirty-something appeared older than his years, alienating a large section of his young audience overnight as a result. Then, when he moved to television, Freed's ABC *Rock 'n' Roll Dance Party* also ended abruptly after a scandal (which seems risible now) erupted when black singer Frankie Lymon (☞ *January 1968*) was caught on camera dancing with a white girl, outraging Southern station affiliates. Worse still, when a live event at the Boston Arena in 1958 ended in a riot, WINS cancelled his radio contract despite the fact that any charges of incitement against Freed were soon dropped. A year later, the even greater 'payola' (money for airplay) scandal displayed his dubious business practices openly and effectively ended Freed's broadcasting career; he was found guilty on two counts of accepting commercial bribery a couple of years later and made 'industry scapegoat' for what pretty much everybody else in the game had been doing for years.

An internal injury sustained in a car accident in 1953 returned to haunt Alan Freed – by 1965 a shadow of his

Alan Freed: Payola was on the menu

> '**Live fast, die young, make a good-looking corpse.**'
> **Alan Freed**

former self and ostracized by many of his former acolytes. As he drifted from satellite town to satellite town in search of broadcasting work, Freed's health began to fail. Virtually bankrupted by his legal debts and drinking heavily, he checked into a hospital in Palm Springs on 15 January 1965 – just as charges of tax evasion were levied against him. Freed died five days later from uraemia and cirrhosis of the liver before he could answer any of those charges. He went to the grave penniless – a far cry from just a few years before, when he had been able to claim thousands of dollars a day for his services.

Despite the (arguably heavy-handed) treatment Freed received towards the end of his life, the Rock 'n' Roll Hall of Fame Museum, which opened in 1986, was nevertheless situated in Cleveland in honour of one of its sons' great achievements.

FEBRUARY

Monday 15

Nat 'King' Cole
(Nathaniel Coles – Montgomery, Alabama, 17 March (most likely) 1917)

Those rich, velveteen tones that seemed the aural equivalent of melting Bournville were actually the result of sixty smokes a day. His millions of fans may have thanked him for this concession to vocal gravitas, but his lungs did not: Nat Cole succumbed to cancer before he was fifty. Remembered as one of the twentieth century's finest interpreters of a song, Cole was also a gifted pianist, playing 'Yes, We Have No Bananas' at the age of four to anyone who would listen. A few years on, Cole landed a residency with his older brother, Eddie,

at the Panama Club, Chicago – and had not left his teens behind by the time they had recorded their first side. Promotion of his renamed 'King Cole Trio' by Lionel Hampton subsequently set Cole on a more upwardly mobile path, and before long Capitol were ready to offer a major-label contract. Their new charge was shortly the most successful artist the label had ever known, their premises on Hollywood and Vine thereafter referred to as 'The House That Nat Built'. Cole could even claim the distinction of placing the first ever number-one LP on Billboard's charts. If the King Cole Trio had been a success, Cole's solo career, with the band now very much his back-up, was the stuff of legend: in the latter half of 1947, Cole recorded some eighty songs – more than most artists manage in a career. Many of these became hits, though the most sublime was surely Eden Ahbez's 'Nature Boy', an uplifting minor chord air that stirs the soul to this day. It sat at number one for two months in 1948, while Cole was on honeymoon with his second wife, singer Maria Ellington. Cole hit 50 million sales sometime in 1960 – many recordings backed by The Four Knights (three of whom – Gene Alford, John Wallace and Clarence Dixon – have also since died) – and became the first black artist to front his own television showcase. During this time he would still periodically moonlight at the piano.

By 1964, Cole began to notice a sinister loss in weight as he toured with his band. This made him irritable, the change only too noticeable in this man of otherwise impeccable manner and mood. Always a heavy smoker, Cole was informed of a malignant tumour discovered in his lung; it was then only a matter of time. Following a walk on the beach with his wife early in 1965, Cole died quietly in his sleep – giving the lie to all the trade papers' notices that he was 'doing fine'.

MARCH

Monday 12

Fraser Calder
(Glasgow)

James Giffen
(Glasgow)

The Blues Council

With a vibrant British blues scene fragmenting in the early sixties, one of the most impressive (if short-lived) line-ups must have been that of Glasgow's Blues Council. This hard-touring band revolved around noted saxophonist Bill Patrick, raw young guitarist Leslie Harvey (the latter doubtless encouraged by the already raucous lifestyle and reputation of his better-known brother, Alex), drummer Billy Adamson, sax-player Larry Quinn and pianist John McGinnis, and was completed by bassist James Giffen and singer and frontman Fraser Calder. Parlophone issued their dynamic debut single, 'Baby Don't Look Down', to extensive local airplay in late 1964, and, as the year turned, all appeared rosy.

Theirs was very much a name known only in Scotland, though, and events sadly did not allow their reputation to spread further. On the way home from a gig in Edinburgh, the band's tour van crashed outside Glasgow, killing Calder and Giffen instantly. Despite Patrick's drafting-in of yet another saxophonist, Bobby Wishart, to the despondent survivors there was no way The Blues Council could continue, and before the summer they had gone their separate ways: Bill Patrick hooked up with The Sensational Alex Harvey Band, John McGinnis started Sock 'Em JB and Les Harvey eventually joined Stone the Crows. For Harvey, however, the tragedy would prove merely a precursor to one of the most dramatic deaths in rock history, seven years later (☛ *May 1972*).

See also *Alex Harvey (☛ February 1982)*

MAY

Tuesday 25

Sonny Boy Williamson II

(Aleck Ford 'Rice' Miller – Mississippi, 12 March 1905 (or 1908, or 12 December 1899))

As the title of his 1953 album suggested, Sonny Boy Williamson 'II' was always 'clownin'' with the world'. With more front than a hundred wooden porches, the blues harmonica-player 'borrowed' his assumed name from that of contemporary blues harpist John Lee Williamson, towards the end of his life hoodwinking many into believing he was indeed the original 'Sonny Boy'.

A gifted performer in his own right, Williamson was born into a sharecropper's family, and lived the familiar bluesman's life of a wandering minstrel, playing every juke joint in town, trying to scratch a living. It was, however, a regular Arkansas radio-station KFFA slot presenting *King Biscuit Time* (sponsored by King Biscuit flour) that made him a star locally and an influence on other Delta-blues players. Among his self-written pieces were 'One Way Out' (later a hit for The Allman Brothers) and 'Nine Below Zero'. When he signed, as late as 1950, to Lillian McMurry's Trumpet label (and thereafter Chess), many of his minimalist harmonica workouts found their way on to disc at last. Williamson's talent didn't go unnoticed by the new breed either and, before he died, this excellent craftsman

visited Europe and recorded with The Animals and The Yardbirds. (Such was Williamson's history of telling tall stories, many back home refused to believe he had travelled to Britain, let alone played with its top rock musicians.)

Williamson returned to the USA to resume *King Biscuit Time* in 1964, his alcoholism now exacerbated by the tuberculosis he knew was killing him. Struggling not to cough up blood during his performances, he played an impromptu jam, now the stuff of folklore, with the group Levon & The Hawks (who went on to become Bob Dylan's back-up unit The Band) just a fortnight before he passed away. Williamson's failure to show up to present his radio show in May 1965 prompted KFFA to send someone to rouse him – but it was too late. Williamson had died in his sleep at his boarding house in Helena, Arkansas. Stonemasons wrongly engraved the date of death on Williamson's headstone as '23 June'. Despite obvious discrepancies over his birth date, this *is* an error.

AUGUST

Saturday 14

Charles Fizer

(Shreveport, Louisiana, 3 June 1940)
The Olympics

One of the more versatile of the era's slew of vocal quartets, The Olympics began in 1954 as The Challengers while still at high school in Compton, California. Initially, this group was moulded more in the style of The Coasters than the standard doo-wop unit, onstage schtick between members setting up novelty tunes such as their popular debut, US number-eight

hit 'Western Movies' (Demon, 1958 – a witty number in which the narrator bemoans his girlfriend's addiction to cowboy pictures), which also made the UK Top Twenty. The group's first line-up comprised Walter 'Sleepy' Ward (lead), Eddie Lewis (tenor), Walter Hammond (baritone) and – often at the heart of the operation – Charles Fizer (tenor/baritone), who joined following a talent contest. Fizer was certainly a larger-than-life character, finding himself in the hands of the law more than once in his short life; just as The Olympics were enjoying their biggest success he found himself on an enforced 'sabbatical' from the band when a prison sentence for drugs possession kept him away for a year (he was replaced by Melvin King).

Cut to 11 August 1965: days after masses of black music fans had chanted the positive slogan 'Burn, baby, burn!' at the Stax Revue in Watts, Los Angeles, the phrase itself was to take on a darker hue. As black brothers Marquette and Ronald Frye travelled into South Central in their 1950 Buick, they were stopped by a California Highway Patrol, who believed the driver to be intoxicated. With little apparent motive, the police hauled Marquette from the car and set about punching and kicking him and slamming him in his own car door; even the Fryes' mother found herself handcuffed, slapped and hit when she attempted to intervene. Within an hour, South LA was in the middle of the most violent racial uprising it had ever witnessed, with Watts at the very epicentre. Following early altercations, the *Los Angeles Times* talked of 'rocks flying, then wine and whiskey bottles, concrete, pieces of wood – the targets anything strange to the neighbourhood'.

By the weekend, Lyndon B Johnson described a 'disaster area', and the LAPD admitted that the situation was out of their control; there would inevitably be casualties as they stepped up attempts to regain the township. The majority of these would be innocents, in the wrong place at the wrong time, most of them black. One such was Charles Fizer. On 14 August, day three of the uprising, Fizer – very much a reformed character since his incarceration – was making his way innocently to an Olympics rehearsal when he was hit by National Guard bullets and died on the street. He was just one of thirty-four to die that week; Melvin King's sister was another, on the very same afternoon. A further thousand were injured and four times that many arrested as Watts was razed to the ground over six days. A neglected suburb for years – and with a particularly poor record for police brutality – it lay desolate, a charred monument to years of oppression. Devastated by the events of 14 August, Melvin King played just one more performance before throwing in the towel with The Olympics. His replacement, Mack Starr, died equally tragically following a motorcycle accident in Los Angeles (☞ *June 1981*).

OCTOBER

Thursday 21

Bill Black

(William Patton Black Jr – Memphis, Tennessee, 17 September 1926)
Bill Black's Combo
Scotty & Bill
Doug Poindexter & The Starlight
Wranglers

Guitarist Bill Black was well situated to join up with the biggest star popular music had ever seen, though ironically his time as bass-player behind Elvis Presley proved far less lucrative – or artistically rewarding – than working with his own band,

Bill Black's Combo. Sam Phillips was fast to spot Black's potential, prising him and guitarist cohort Scotty Moore away from his own hoedown act Doug Poindexter & The Starlight Wranglers before lining them up to record with the young Presley at Sun Records. Over four years, the pair cut some hugely influential sides with the King, 'That's All Right Mama' (1954), 'All Shook Up' and 'Jailhouse Rock' (both 1957) among them. One problem, however, was the sharp practice of Colonel Tom Parker as Elvis's star went supernova. Believing his charge to be a level above the others (and more than a little concerned at Black's often commanding stage presence), Parker was not prepared to pay Scotty and Bill much more than a basic union wage. By 1958 the pair had cut and run. As frontman for Bill Black's Combo, Black – strangely forgotten by many today – was as prolific as he was successful: in six years he recorded a remarkable fourteen albums, shifting 5 million units.

Early in 1965, Bill Black was diagnosed with a brain tumour. Devastated, and feeling his time was limited, he signed over responsibilities for the band to guitarist Bob Tucker (who would front them into the 1980s) before undergoing the first of three operations. On 8 October, after the third operation, Black slipped into a coma from which he did not recover, and died two weeks later at the Baptist Memorial Hospital in Memphis – the very same hospital at which Presley himself was pronounced dead, nearly twelve years later (☞ *August 1977*). Although visiting Black's widow, Evelyn, and three children, a saddened Elvis Presley did not attend his former friend's funeral, fearing that his presence would 'turn it into a circus'.

DECEMBER

Thursday 9

Eddie Sulik

(Sagamore, Pennsylvania, 1929)
The Echoes

Rockabilly has never been noted as a genre for throwing up heart-throbs, but Eddie Sulik, with his immaculate hair, cleft chin and composed off-camera gaze when on photo duty, was surely one of the few. A comparative latecomer to fame, Sulik was, in his early career, one half of The Echoes, a popular Nashville vocal duo who scored a few minor hits with Columbia. A return to solo work and a seemingly endless schedule of club dates kept Sulik's clear vocal tones in the public ear during the early sixties, his oeuvre drawn from rock 'n' roll, country, pop and Latin. His success was still fairly regional, but in 1965, a recording/publishing deal with guitar-giant Chet Atkins and Archie Bleyer of Cadence Records looked to be on the cards.

Eddie Sulik never made the meeting that would probably have changed his life. The night before the conference in New York City, Sulik was killed in an automobile crash near his home in Connecticut; the songs he had prepared on tape for Atkins and Bleyer remained unheard until released by Sulik's son, Eddie Jr, as *A Farewell Legacy* some thirty-four years later.

Lest We Forget

Other notable deaths that occurred sometime during 1965:

Carl Adams (US rockabilly guitarist who played with three fingers after losing two in a shooting accident; born Louisiana, 7/11/1935; kidney failure, 25/2)

Dave Barbour (US guitarist/composer; born Long Island, New York, 1912; divorced from singer Peggy Lee, he had asked her to remarry four days before dying from an undiagnosed heart condition, 11/12)

Earl Bostic (US jazz/R & B saxophonist; born Oklahoma, 25/4/1913; heart attack, 28/10)

Dorothy Dandridge (popular US actress/singer; born Ohio, 9/11/1922; overdose – possibly suicide, 8/9)

Spike Jones (eccentric US comic/percussionist who formed The City Slickers and influenced the likes of The Bonzo Dog Doo-Dah Band; born Lindley Armstrong Jones, California, 14/12/1911; emphysema 1/5)

Peter LaFarge (Native American (Nargaset) folk singer/writer who worked with Johnny Cash and hung with the young Bob Dylan; born 1931; stroke/suicide, depending upon your source, 27/10)

Ira Louvin (US bluegrass singer with The Louvin Brothers; born Lonnie Ira Loudermilk, Alabama, 21/4/1921; having survived a near-fatal fight with his third wife, he died in a car crash, 20/6)

Todd Rhodes (US jazz/R & B pianist; born Kentucky, 31/8/1900; having already lost a leg, he died from complications arising from inept hospital treatment for his diabetes, 4/6)

Terry Thompson (US R & B/rock guitarist who penned 'A Shot of Rhythm and Blues' and played with the Muscle Shoals FAME Studio Rhythm Section; born Mississippi, 1941; alcohol/drug overdose, 10/11)

Harrison Verrett (US jazz guitarist and brother-in-law of Fats Domino; born Los Angeles, 26/2/1907; undisclosed, 10/1965)

For a complete list of fallen artists, visit

www.numberoneinheaven.com

MARCH

Monday 7

Mike Millward

(Bromborough, Merseyside, 9 May 1942)

The Fourmost
(Kingsize Taylor & The Dominoes)

Millward – formerly of the intriguingly named Kingsize Taylor & The Dominoes – was singer/rhythm guitarist with early Brian Epstein discoveries The Fourmost. In an era overrun with quartets, the band underwent almost as many changes of identity as personnel: in their brief history they were known as The Blue Jays, The Four Jays and even the extremely clunky Four Mosts when it transpired that an American band had the same name. No matter, the group – Millward, Brian O'Hara (vocals/guitar), Billy Hatton (bass) and Dave Lovelady (drums) – enjoyed a number of Top Forty singles (the first two Lennon and McCartney songs) while Merseybeat was the hot phenomenon. The pinnacle for the group was the UK number-six hit 'A Little Loving' (April 1964) and an appearance alongside Liverpool contemporaries in the film *Ferry across the Mersey*. It was at this point that Mike Millward was diagnosed with

throat cancer, which by and large put paid to his singing career. On recovery, Millward learned that he had leukaemia, which forced him into complete retirement. The most popular member of the group, Millward died at just twenty-three, and The Fourmost rapidly settled for a career as a cabaret turn, with the hits drying up. O'Hara fronted regular reunions for the group until his own unfortunate suicide (☞ *June 1999*).

APRIL

Saturday 30

Richard Fariña

(Brooklyn, New York, 8 March 1937)

Richard & Mimi Fariña

Described variously as 'America's least-known superstar' or 'a scattered mind with a death wish', Richard Fariña had a short and eventful life. Born to a Cuban engineer and his Northern Irish wife, it was Fariña's mother's background that would become the source of his early interests: a visit to her homeland in 1953 saw him affiliate himself with the IRA. But, believing statistics were 'not as much fun as

stories', Fariña became an archetypal anti-authority writer and musician, the dulcimer being his unlikely instrument of choice. A young man with opinions and wild oats to sow, Fariña made the 'oppressive regime' of his university's segregation policy the target of early protests – his actions causing his suspension and high-profile police intervention. Ever a restless soul, Fariña dropped out of studies, short-term employment at an advertising agency and a doomed marriage to established musician Carolyn Hester. While performing in Greenwich Village, he met his second wife and ultimate musical collaborator, Mimi, a dance student, guitarist and 17-year-old sister of Joan Baez. The pair were immediately accepted into the folk community, debuting at the 1964 Big Sur Festival and shortly thereafter signing with Vanguard, who released an eponymous debut album (1965) and a rated follow-up, *Reflections in a Crystal Wind*, early the following year.

Now a respected poet, playwright, columnist and author, Fariña's *Been down So Long It Looks Like up to Me* – a novel inspired by college experiences – was published in New York. It was clearly a time for celebration, especially as the day of the book launch in Carmel coincided with Mimi's twenty-first birthday. Following the launch, a number of friends accompanied Richard and Mimi to her sister's house for a surprise party; one of these was Willie Hinds, an inexperienced biker who sometime during the course of the evening offered Fariña a ride on his newly acquired Harley Davidson. As the pair reached 100 mph weaving through the rolling hills on the winding roads of Carmel, Hinds failed to make a bend, skidded and lost control of his bike. Hinds survived the wipe-out with minor injuries but Fariña was hurled across two fences into an embankment and died immediately.

See also *Mimi Fariña (* July 2001)*

JULY

Monday 18

Bobby Fuller
(Goose Creek, Texas, 22 October 1942)
The Bobby Fuller Four

Bobby Fuller (*second left*) with The Bobby Fuller Four: 'The Law' simply wasn't interested

The true spirit of rock 'n' roll lived and died in Bobby Fuller – but was the Texas-born guitarist the genre's first genuine murder victim? When his mother, Lorraine, discovered her son's lifeless corpse propped up against the steering wheel of her car, she noticed not just the acrid smell of blood but also the distinctive fumes of petrol.

Like most young Texans, Fuller and his older brother, Randy, were fans of local-boy-made-good Buddy Holly and sought to emulate his success (if not his virtuosity) as soon as they could learn a few basic chords. This they would have achieved, had several events not put paid to The Bobby Fuller Four during their 1966 peak. All had begun well enough, with the teenage Fuller not only running a basic studio set-up in his basement but also graduating from music school; he made various recordings with

independent labels before the local-airplay hit 'King of the Wheels' (1965) elevated him to the position of cult hero to the growing El Paso garage-rock 'n' roll crowd. Settling on a Bobby Fuller Four line-up of himself as lead guitarist/vocalist, Randy Fuller (bass), Jim Reese (guitars) and Dwayne Quirico (the first of four short-term drummers, another of whom would be the studio-based Barry White – yes, *that* Barry White), the ambitious front-man relocated his band to the more happening LA. The result was a series of raunchy, stripped-down singles on Mustang, 'Let Her Dance', 'Love's Made a Fool of You' and ex-Cricket Sonny Curtis's seminal 'I Fought the Law' – a massive US hit at the

beginning of 1966 and, of course, a much-covered standard for decades to follow. But fame was to be short-lived, recording sessions all but capsized by feuding between the two brothers. That summer, Fuller had pretty much made up his mind to dissolve the band and was due to meet with his musicians to tell them of his solo plans, but the meeting never took place. On the afternoon of 18 July, Lorraine Fuller's missing Oldsmobile suddenly 'turned up' in a field next to her apartment on Sunset Strip, Hollywood. In it she found her son Bobby – missing for some fourteen hours – not just dead but in rigor mortis, badly beaten and doused in fuel. Rumours had abounded about Fuller's mental state – he had recently become mildly depressed with the state of affairs with his band and his relationships (he had fathered a son whom he was not allowed to see) and had also experimented frequently with the then currently popular LSD – and the coroner returned a verdict of suicide by asphyxiation (the suggestion being that he'd 'drunk' the petrol), later changed to accidental death. A Hollywood police officer had, for some inconceivable reason, destroyed crucial evidence at the scene such as the gasoline canister. Although officials seemed keen to close the case as soon as possible, Lorraine and Randy Fuller were desperate to pursue what they felt was surely foul play. After all, the brothers weren't strangers to murder: on a shooting trip in the early sixties, the Fullers' half-brother Jack had been gunned down by a purported 'friend'. But despite apparent oddities in the case, the official statement of 'no evidence to suggest foul play' has never been altered. Randy Fuller's continued pleas – even appearing on NBC's *Unsolved Mysteries* series – have fallen on deaf ears ever since.

SEPTEMBER

Thursday 1

Leroy Griffin

(New Haven, Connecticut, 5 April 1934)

The Nutmegs

Hailing from New Haven, The Nutmegs were the latest in a seemingly endless line of vocal groups from the area, but they did at least have the distinctive tones of Leroy Griffin at the helm. Griffin fronted the band (alongside his brother Sonny and, for a while, another singer bizarrely also named Leroy Griffin), which enjoyed big US R & B hits with 'Story Untold' and the best-known Nutmegs song 'Ship of Love' (both 1955) – the latter of which was only prevented from becoming a national pop hit when a simultaneous version emerged by The Crew Cuts.

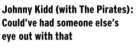

**Johnny Kidd (with The Pirates):
Could've had someone else's
eye out with that**

Griffin's death in September 1966 will forever remain mysterious. It seems that he and a work colleague had an altercation at a Koppers coke plant where Griffin still occasionally laboured to earn a living. Horrifically, Griffin either fell or was pushed into one of the factory's giant furnaces, where he was quickly burned to death.

OCTOBER

Friday 7

Johnny Kidd

(Frederick Heath – Willesden, London,
23 December 1939)

**Johnny Kidd & The Pirates
(The Five Nutters)**

Whether he was an influence on Adam Ant is open to conjecture, but Johnny Kidd was the first performer in British pop music to don the panto gear. An early skiffle convert, he formed his own band, The Five Nutters, while still a teenager. When rock 'n' roll kicked in, his interest in Lonnie Donegan et al dipped somewhat and he sought a new image – that of seventeenth-century buccaneer Captain William Kidd. The look presaged a name change, too, and had immediate appeal, particularly to HMV, who issued the first Johnny Kidd single, the excellent 'Please Don't Touch' in May 1959. Its Top Thirty placing was a solid but not earth-shattering start, but the label's next move – to sack the band and bring in experienced hands – was less effective, a series of covers by and large failing to dent the listings. Kidd's co-written 'Shakin' All Over' (1960), though, was a genuine 'moment' in pop-music history and is rightly viewed as the classic British pre-Beatles rock 'n' roll record; this infectious stop/start rocker duly took Kidd – now with The Pirates,

Alma Cogan: Her 'ostrich look' never caught on

the accident, continued touring as The Pirates, and bass-player Nick Simper went on to join Deep Purple in the seventies.

See also *Alan Caddy (August 2000)*

Wednesday 26

Alma Cogan

(Alma Angela Cohen – Stepney, London, 19 May 1932)

If there weren't many British pop and rockabilly acts around during the fifties, female artists were in even shorter supply. But Alma Cogan was one such artist who positively thrived in this era, her voice equally at home in both adult and teenage markets. Brought up in Worthing, Sussex, Cogan attended art school, though it was her singing that caught the attention of Ted Heath (the bandleader) before HMV gave her an opportunity to record in 1952. Cogan's stage presence was also quickly noted, earning her a residency on the BBC radio show *Take It from Here*. The singer's soon-widely-recognized love of garish clothing would be acknowledged in her first hit record, the Top Five 'Bell Bottom Blues' (1954), which began an impressive run of twenty-two chart successes, culminating with 'Dreamboat', a chart-topper from 1955. Cogan's hits – which had pretty much descended into pop novelties by the start of the next decade – dried up by 1961, as acts such as the younger Helen Shapiro began to come through. There was still the staple cabaret circuit, which she pursued for several years, and it was at one such date in Sweden in the autumn of 1966 that Cogan mysteriously collapsed. Rushed to hospital, the 34-year-old vocalist was diagnosed with throat cancer; within weeks she was admitted to the Middlesex Hospital, where, shortly thereafter, she passed away.

including top guitarists Alan Caddy and Joe Moretti – to number one that summer. From this, the only direction for a working unit on the label payroll to go was likely to be downwards, and tunes that disappointingly pushed this distinctive band into a 'Merseybeat' direction were largely misses (1963's 'I'll Never Get Over You' a notable exception). Kidd was a hard-worker, however, and he and his group would still kick up something of a storm on their exhaustive live schedule, with

occasional support from The Who – a band that has consistently cited him as an influence.

With a fresh line-up, Johnny Kidd & The New Pirates were on the road again in October 1966 when tragedy – or, more truthfully, a skidding lorry – struck. The recently married Kidd was travelling in the tour van to an engagement when he was killed in the crash on the M1 near Radcliffe, just outside Bury, Lancashire. The remainder of the band, all of whom survived

Lest We Forget

Other notable deaths that occurred sometime during 1966:

Henry Booth (US tenor vocalist with R & B acts The Royals – alongside Jackie Wilson – and The Midnighters; born Alabama, 7/3/1934; believed shot dead during a fight)

Bill Gillum (US bluesman; born William McGinlay Gillum, Mississippi, 11/9/1904; shot in the head during an argument in Chicago, 29/3)

Mississippi John Hurt (US bluesman; born Mississippi (obviously), 3/7/1893; heart attack, 2/11)

Helen Kane (US singer/writer/actress/costumier, best known as the Queen of Boop-boop-a-doop and a likely influence on Marilyn Monroe; born New York, 4/8/1903; unknown, 26/9)

Harry C McAuliffe (US country/crossover singer known as 'Big Slim the Lone Cowboy'; born in West Virginia, 9/5/1903; unknown, 13/10)

Lucius Millinder (influential US jump-blues bandleader; born Alabama, 8/8/1900; liver failure, 28/9)

Billy Rose (US songwriter/composer who wrote 'Does the Spearmint Lose Its Flavour?' among other such delights; born William Rosenberg, New York, 6/9/1899; contracted pneumonia in Jamaica, and died 10/2)

Will Shade (US bluesman and part of The Memphis Jug Band; born Will Brimmer, Mississippi, 5/2/1898; pneumonia, 18/9)

Carter Stanley (US bluegrass singer with The Carter Brothers; born Virginia, 27/8/1925; cirrhosis of the liver, 1/12)

Washboard Sam (US bluesman; born Robert Brown, Arkansas, 15/7/1910; heart disease, 6/11)

Slim Willet (US country guitarist/writer whose 'Don't Let the Stars (Get in Your Eyes)' was a chart-topper for Perry Como in 1953; born Texas, 1/12/1919; heart failure, 1/7)

For a complete list of fallen artists, visit

www.numberoneinheaven.com

1967

JANUARY

Tuesday 27

Luigi Tenco
(Cassine, Italy, 21 March 1938)

Luigi Tenco wanted success, whatever the cost, but he was a troubled man who suffered at the hands of the critics as well as in his brief personal life. Tenco never knew his father, who died months before his birth, leaving his mother to bring up both Luigi and his older brother alone. He struggled to settle in his studies and early career before his love of singing drove him to form bands with his friends. Tenco was never the strongest vocal performer in the pop/jazz/ballad arena in which he worked, thus it was his more marked talent as a *cantautore* ('singing author') and arranger that eventually brought him some attention on the Italian music scene. Tenco was also classically handsome, his dark, moody charm eventually wooing former Miss Egypt and, by then, highly rated singer Dalida; in 1966, their mutual label RCA introduced the pair as potential duet partners. Tenco and Dalida fell hopelessly in love and decided on a unique performance for the upcoming San Remo Festival, an annual contest to determine Italy's finest popular songs and writers: they were to perform together, each offering a version of the chosen ballad, Tenco's own '*Ciao, Amore, Ciao*'. The couple even announced an April wedding to garner maximum press interest. He was a passionate, ambitious newcomer; she a beautiful, talented songstress – how could they fail?

Well, the answer perhaps lies in Luigi Tenco's misplaced self-belief. He had talent for sure, but his temperament and high opinion of his mediocre voice would ultimately cost him. While Dalida's rendition of the song won her applause, Tenco's did not; Tenco, Dalida and the song were eliminated in the first round. The by-now totally wired Tenco – who had drunk heavily and taken a number of tranquilizers before his performance – flew into a rage and, against Dalida's wishes, began berating the judges as corrupt and the whole festival as meaningless. Unable to deal with such public rejection, Tenco snubbed the subsequent dinner, stormed back to their room at the Hotel Savoja and locked himself in. By 2.15 am Dalida, who *had* attended the celebrations, returned, concerned that she was unable to summon her lover. She found Tenco splayed out across the floor, with a gun at his side. An almost illegible note 'explained' his frustration at the world and his desire to 'show them all' – but Dalida wasn't convinced by the handwriting. Why would Tenco take his own life because of what to her seemed little more than a setback? Until her own death, Dalida remained convinced that he had been the victim of a conspiracy; indeed, she was to suffer an extraordinary series of partner suicides, three of her lovers taking their own lives before, sadly, she too followed suit (☛ *May 1987*).

FEBRUARY

Friday 3

Joe Meek
(Robert George Meek – Newent, Gloucestershire, 5 April 1929)

How a producer with the vision of Joe Meek made it happen in the staid world of late-fifties UK recording is nothing short of a miracle. That this maverick's life ended in the shocking, dramatic way that it did is, however, more in keeping with the script.

One of three brothers brought up in rural Newent, Robert George 'Joe' Meek was not an outdoor type like his older siblings, preferring to spend time in a garden shed dabbling with wireless sets and gramophone equipment than climb trees. A boy with tastes that generally separated him from his peers, Meek – perhaps showing more business nous than at times during his adult life – would charge locals to watch him perform musical plays as a variety of characters, both male and female. The knock-on from these interests saw him engineering hit records at IBC for Lonnie Donegan ('Cumberland Gap') and Frankie Vaughan ('Green Door') by the age of twenty-five – despite being completely tone deaf. Wishing in vain to utilize effects such as homemade instrumentation, foot-stomps instead of bass drums and reverb in his records, Meek left IBC to become the first notable producer to lease his tapes to a variety of major labels. Few at this time realized he was recording many acts at his flat – merely a few rooms above a leather-goods outlet on North London's Holloway Road. Despite this, a 1960 Top Ten hit with Michael Cox's whimsical 'Angela Jones' on his short-lived Triumph Records was just a precursor to some extraordinary successes; British pop music was on the verge of major transformation and Meek was responsible for much of it in this pre-Beatles era. If the glorious 'Johnny Remember Me' by actor John Leyton was a pioneering 1961 effort that brought considerable attention, The Tornados' 1962 communication-satellite overture 'Telstar' appeared to seal matters globally. This record was the first British hit to top the US chart – despite being dismissed by German-born bassist Heinz Burt as 'crap' on first playback. (It was later dubiously honoured as a favourite of Margaret Thatcher.)

Joe Meek's personal world was seldom functional, however. An unseemly incident and arrest for 'importuning' (the term then used for 'soliciting') broke the news of Meek's sexuality to his family in 1963, although it had been an open secret within the industry for some time.

The brilliant Joe Meek: Often a little behind with his rent

A series of blackmail attempts by previous partners resulted, which only fired the latent paranoia of a man who was now experimenting with pills and hallucinogenics which intensified his belief that others were pilfering his gimmicks. One of his charges – Screaming Lord Sutch, whose schoolboy schlock-horror set pieces were ideal vehicles for the producer's whims – was taken into a corridor to discuss business because Meek thought the entire flat had been bugged in his absence. In the event, none of Sutch's records ever gave Meek a hit anyway, and it was French composer Jean Ledrut who threatened *him* with legal action, claiming he'd pilfered the melody for 'Telstar' (though Meek's family were to win the legal battle for ownership of the song in 1968). It made little difference: Meek's business acumen was virtually non-existent, and as the decade grew he was owed money, in debt and falling behind the twin stables of The Beatles/The Stones and their various coat-tailers. By 1967, a long, long time since his last major hit (The Honeycombs' rousing 1964 number one 'Have I the Right?'), Meek was fast becoming an anachronism in an industry that was picking up pace at frightening speed. His moods began to fluctuate wildly, and he was soon taking prescription medication for depression.

On the morning of the eighth anniversary of Buddy Holly's death (➤ *Pre-1965*), Joe Meek was in a belligerent mood. He was standing in the kitchen of his flat, studying unopened letters, when studio assistant Patrick Pink – who Meek was set to record – arrived for the day's activities. Meek finished his breakfast in silence before disappearing to the upstairs studio. Pink was shortly joined by Meek's landlady, Violet Shenton, who, observing the studio hand's plight, offered to 'talk Meek round' (she had frequently dealt with Meek in the past, usually by banging a broom handle against her ground-floor ceiling). This time,

though, an argument – apparently about Meek's rent book – began to escalate in the room above Pink's head. As he moved to investigate, a gunshot rang out. Shenton fell from the doorway, down the staircase and into his arms: she had been shot in the back. In utter shock and bemusement, Pink had barely mouthed the words, 'She's dead,' when a second shot stopped him in his tracks. He looked up to see his boss prone on the studio floor, a gun by his body. Joe Meek died instantly, while 52-year-old Violet Shenton died on arrival at hospital. Police at the scene were quick to charge first Patrick Pink, then Heinz Burt, the gun's owner (and for many years the target of Meek's attentions), who, having kept the weapon at the flat where he'd until recently been staying, had left his fingerprints all over it. Various lurid tales have been linked to Meek's world during the last months of his life – including one truly horrific story of the Suffolk murder and mutilation of 17-year-old Bernard Oliver, a gay youth known to Meek, weeks before his death, though no fast connection was ever made. Before long, though, it became apparent to all that there was no third-party involvement in the events of 3 February – it was simply a tragic and unnecessary end to the lives of two people.

One of his last productions, The Cryin' Shames' 'Nobody Waved Goodbye' (1967), played at Joe Meek's Newent funeral as 200 mourners did just that to a man who had given much to many in a brief but potent period for British culture.

'His suicide was a logical end to the pressure he put himself under.'

Geoff Goddard, composer of 'Johnny Remember Me'

Brian Epstein

(Liverpool, 19 September 1934)

Brian Epstein (*far right*) with The Beatles: Curtains for the manager?

Brian Epstein was both Jewish and gay, when to admit to either might have been to compromise oneself. But this apparent outsider – in his adult life the music world's best-known impresario – was born into a middle-class back-ground, relatively secure in a series of private schools while Europe waged war for a second time.

While on National Service, Epstein underwent cruel (though at the time compulsory) army psychiatric treat-ment for his homosexuality and the inevitable discharge – with all the stigma that entailed. Epstein's restlessness and below-the-surface flamboyance saw him spend three terms at London's RADA before returning to a more modest retail position at his father's Liverpool furniture business. Seeking relief from such mundane activity, Brian Epstein opened a record section in the music department, which to the great surprise and delight of his father proved a big success – so much so that the young entrepreneur soon opened his own separate branch (North East Music Stores – later an enor-mous music-business empire). His new-found position won Epstein a record review column in new local paper *Mersey Beat*, although he used it mainly as an advertisement for the store, which, of course, was also conveniently positioned near Liverpool's most 'happening' venue, The Cavern Club. Although he most likely knew of The Beatles before spend-ing a lunchtime checking them out, Epstein met the band here on 9 November 1961, kick-starting the most famous story in popular music.

Brian Epstein was suddenly thrown headlong into an industry pretty much inventing itself around him. Perhaps a little harshly, he's recalled just as often now as the man who *mis*managed The Beatles, the group allegedly receiving almost no money for performances, records and licensing in the early days. Much of this may be true, but Epstein had soon become more than a manager, in the sense understood at the time: he oversaw The Beatles' image, clothes, publicity and overall professionalism (which immediately prompted the sacking of drummer Pete Best and the poaching of Ringo Starr from Rory Storm & The Hurricanes) as the group began to make serious progress. At the start, much was based on trust – Epstein didn't officially sign the band

'After Brian died – we *collapsed.*'

John Lennon, 1970

until almost a year after the Cavern gig, by which time they had (after numerous rejections) been picked up by George Martin at Parlophone, an otherwise spoken-word label. The Beatles agreed for Epstein to take 25 per cent of their earnings, which, had he lived longer, would have placed him among the wealthiest Svengalis in the world. As it was, a lack of appreciation for the importance royalties would play as the sixties progressed was to cost Epstein dearly.

However, during 1963–4 The Beatles became the biggest-selling group in Britain's history, while Epstein's expanding stable achieved a strike-rate which has never been matched: his new charges Gerry & The Pacemakers, Billy J Kramer & The Dakotas and Cilla Black managed seven number-one singles between them, while the all-conquering Beatles topped the charts six times on their own. In the USA, the Fab Four's utter blitzing of the American market brought an unprecedented *fifteen* hit records in 1964 alone – six of which hit the summit. There would not be much let-up for the next three years, either. While The Beatles (particularly John Lennon and Paul McCartney) continued to build as the most potent creative force popular music had seen, Brian Epstein began to find himself losing control of the reins. His world was now a circus and he would turn to artificial means to deal with the increasing pressures of being ring-master to such a phenomenon. On top of his growing substance use, the world's best-known manager found himself in and out of clandestine relationships – generally with partners unlikely to forge anything else – at an alarming rate. His contract with the group due to end in 1967, Epstein had one last ground-breaking creative card to play – to put The Beatles on at several US stadia, culminating with Candlestick Park in August 1966, thus pre-empting 'arena' rock by several years. This, however, had an unforeseen consequence: the band unanimously agreed after Candlestick Park to retire from exhausting live work – which left Epstein with little more to do for them. Alarmed that The Beatles might not re-employ him, Epstein merged NEMS with the Robert Stigwood Organization in January 1967. Although this made for a mighty stable of talent (Stigwood had Hendrix, Cream, The Who, The Bee Gees and The Moody Blues), it smacked of desperation to those who knew Epstein. The news was not well received by The Beatles, either.

Clearly now lost to a twilight world, Brian Epstein gave his last ever interview to the *Melody Maker* three weeks before he died. In it, he spoke of the desolation and loneliness he felt in his spiralling situation; his father, who had encouraged him from the start, had died just a week before, exacerbating his depression. He also admitted to recreational drug use and, as was widely known, that he was taking vast quantities of pills to sleep (Epstein often didn't emerge until late afternoon, whether for work or to be present at Beatles' sessions – the last one he attended was on 23 August 1967. Four mornings later, the butler and housekeeper at Epstein's Belgravia home were unable to rouse him from behind his locked door. Forcing the bedroom door open, a quickly summoned doctor discovered Epstein's lifeless body lying on his bed, surrounded by bottles of pills. There was no suicide note – although he had considered this solution in the recent past, as letters found by his assistant, Joanna Newfield, later corroborated – so a verdict of accidental death was returned by the coroner. Brian Epstein had over-dosed on Carbitral at the age of thirty-two. The band that he had helped turn into world-beaters learned the shocking news in Wales, where they had an audience with the visiting Maharishi; they returned immediately, and Jimi Hendrix cancelled a show in London as a mark of respect. Epstein's brother, Clive, made plans for NEMS.

A small service in Liverpool was not attended by the devastated Beatles – Epstein's mother, Queenie (having only just buried her husband), decided on a small, family affair. Offering an ounce of light relief to an otherwise sombre occasion, a traffic delay holding up the hearse's passage to the cemetery prompted Gerry Marsden to remark, 'Trust Brian to be late for his own bloody funeral.'

See also *Stuart Sutcliffe (* Pre-1965); Mal Evans (* January 1976); John Lennon (* December 1980); George Harrison (* November 2001)*

OCTOBER

Tuesday 3

Woody Guthrie
(Okemah, Oklahoma, 14 July 1912)

Woody Guthrie could always be guaranteed to find wry, witty and urbane words to accompany life's tragedies, whatever form they might take; sadly, all accolades for his work were to be posthumous. He saw much of life's downside when young: his older sister, Clara, died in a fire when he was a boy, his devoted mother became terminally ill and his father's land dealings – in what had been one of the first of the oil-boom towns – went belly up. Guthrie hit the road for Texas in 1931, his guitar at his side (initially composing new words to old tunes), but found success a long time in coming as a musician. Guthrie's broad array of creative talents – he made a living as a signwriter – meant he could still just about support his young wife (and soon three children) as the Depression kicked in. However, just as workers had begun to fight their way out of this lean period, the Great Dust Bowl Storm of 1935 stripped them of homes and land, taking many lives as it travelled across the Great Plains. These days were recounted in Guthrie's semi-autobiographical novel, *Bound For Glory* (1943).

Woody Guthrie was the archetypal wandering minstrel who developed a relationship with the open road, hitchhiking, stowing himself away and riding freight cars to find the action. When he arrived in California, the poor reception he got from insular types fearful of a post-storm influx of outsiders (and suspicious of an apparent Commie in their midst) only strengthened the resolve of a man fast becoming the first notable white protest singer. Another shift saw the restless Guthrie take his 'songs of the people' to New York, where he befriended the likes of Leadbelly (*Pre-1965*), Pete Seeger and Cisco Houston and took up a distinctly 'leftist' stance – his 'This Machine Kills Fascists' guitar slogan was a prominent feature of the act. The limitations of New York radio caused the too-often-snubbed Guthrie to move on again, although he returned, after a stint in the navy, with a second wife and three more children – one of whom, Cathy, died tragically in another domestic fire when just four; another, Arlo, of course, followed him into the music business. (Ever restless, Guthrie would later marry a third time and father a seventh child.)

The last thirteen years of Guthrie's life were spent in chronic ill health. Doctors offered conflicting diagnoses, though schizophrenia was suggested more than once. In fact, it was Huntington's chorea – a degenerative disease that had seen his mother institutionalized thirty years earlier – that robbed this talent of virtually all his faculties and eventually took his life.

Otis Redding
(Dawson, Georgia, 9 September 1941)
(Various acts)

Ronnie Caldwell
(Memphis, Tennessee, 1948)
Carl Lee Cunningham
(Memphis, Tennessee, 1948)
Phalon Jones
(Memphis, Tennessee, 1948)
Jimmie King
(Memphis, Tennessee, 8 June 1949)
The Bar-Kays

The second 'day the music died' was a cold, foggy December afternoon in Wisconsin and – like Buddy Holly almost nine years before (*Pre-1965*) – a ground-breaking stylist, equally at home with the gentle and the uptempo, was taken at the absolute height of his powers.

A minister's son, Redding was singing gospel in Macon, Georgia, as a child, his voice already a powerful gift at five years old. Then, dropping out of his studies to help his financially strapped family, Redding earned a small amount of money singing with Little Richard's Upsetters before taking the post of lead vocalist with Johnny Jenkins's Pinetoppers (both much against his sick father's devout preferences). The Pinetoppers were signed to Atlantic but recorded much of their material at the hallowed Stax-Volt Studios in Memphis, the label's trademark call-and-response sound evident in their output; in spite of this coup, the hits were confined to Georgia. Redding's own solo recordings – backed by Booker T & The MGs – included the US R & B hit, 'These Arms of Mine' (1962), originally mooted as a B-side. 1965 brought the splendid *Otis Blue*, an album full of Stax trickery that included the first classic Redding soul composition, 'Respect', which became a bigger hit for Aretha Franklin. His own crossover chart success still proved elusive at home – where he didn't reach the Top Twenty until his death – though a couple of covers were picking up overseas interest. Redding's rendition of 'My Girl' narrowly missed the UK Top Ten in 1965, while his

1966 version of 'Satisfaction' gained European airplay and was later rated by Mick Jagger as the best Stones cover he'd ever heard.

Although tragedy eventually made them world famous, little is known about the personal lives of the young men who made up the funky soul six-piece that backed Redding through his winter 1967 tour. Put together by Booker T & The MGs' Al Jackson in Memphis a year before the tragedy, they began as The Imperials. Becoming The Bar-Kays (apparently a slang term for Bacardi, their preferred brand of rum), Jimmie King (guitars), Ben Cauley (trumpet), Ronnie Caldwell (organ), Phalon Jones (saxophone), James Alexander (bass) and Carl Lee Cunningham (drums) enjoyed a sizeable hit with the catchy, upbeat 'Soul Finger' during the summer of 1967. Their promising outlook was fused when the man who had wowed all at the Monterey Festival selected them as his next touring band.

Redding was, at this point, staying on a houseboat off Sausalito, near San Francisco, while he performed at the Fillmore Auditorium. As he sat gazing into the waters, he was inspired to write the timeless 'Dock of the Bay', taking the song to MGs' guitarist Steve Cropper, who assisted him in completing the haunting piece. On 6 December, the track was committed to tape: Redding, however, was never to hear the final mix, an unrecorded final verse replaced by the song's now-distinctive whistle.

Otis Redding believed in wise investment and, now a performer of some means, he had recently put his money into a ranch and a twin-engine Beechcraft H18. After a television special and three evening shows in Cleveland, hopping by plane over to Madison, Wisconsin, for the next leg of the tour seemed a good idea. Conditions, however, were worsening, with freezing fog descending, and it was suggested to Redding that he rethink the journey; the super-conscientious performer would hear none of it and so, early in the afternoon, the Beechcraft took to the skies with eight on board. Just three miles south of Madison's Municipal Airport the plane began to lose power, and pulled up to circle and make another approach. Then – tragedy: at 3.28 pm, the craft went into a tailspin and plummeted into the icy depths of Lake Monoma, where it broke apart. With all on board exposed to the freezing water, it was sadly only a matter of time before they perished from the impact, drowning or hypothermia. Apart from Redding, Caldwell, Cunningham and King, the musicians' valet, Matthew Kelly, and pilot Richard Fraser (both twenty-six) were also killed in the accident. The lone survivor pulled from the waters was Ben Cauley, who, unable to do anything for his colleagues, later described the trauma of hearing their calls of distress as they tried to swim to safety. The body of Phalon Jones was not recovered for several days. Cauley – along with Alexander, who hadn't

Otis Redding: He fell short of the dock

been on the plane – returned with a new line-up of The Bar-Kays in 1968.

One week later, Otis Redding's Macon City Auditorium memorial attracted 4,500 visitors; Joe Tex, Sam Moore, Johnnie Taylor, Don Covay, Joe Simon, Percy Sledge and Solomon Burke were the soul luminaries selected as pallbearers. Redding, who was buried in the grounds of the family's estate, the Big O Ranch, was commemorated by a bronze statue erected in Macon. 'Dock of the Bay' – like its 4-million-selling parent album – made Redding the latest in a line of posthumous chart-toppers within four months. The record stalled just short of the UK summit, but there was love for Redding in Britain as well, where he replaced Elvis Presley as 'World's Best Singer' in a *Melody Maker* poll just after his death.

Rockin' Robin Roberts

(Lawrence Fewell Roberts – New York,
23 November 1940)

The Wailers

Dynamic singer and performer Robin Roberts's main claim to rock 'n' roll fame was a brief moment of improvised inspiration on an early version of the song that would become a pop-music staple: 'Louie Louie'.

The version in question was that of The Wailers, a Seattle band who could claim to be not only one of the first garage acts to gain attention, inspiring The Sonics and The Kingsmen (whose rendition of 'Louie' is better known), but also direct ancestors to the city's grunge scene of the early nineties. Originally an instrumental combo, The Wailers chanced upon former Little Bill & The Bluenotes' leader Rockin' Robin Roberts as he performed a capella atop a bench to passing visitors at the 1959 Washington State Fair. An immediate hit as their new singer, Roberts recorded the seminal track in 1961, adding the now-familiar R & B whoops that turned the song around. A lack of commercial interest, however, curtailed his involvement with the group; he continued his studies in Oregon but, having failed to gain a degree, he retired from music and joined the Marine Reserves.

The Wailers were a distant memory by 22 December 1967. Roberts – a passenger in a car travelling the wrong way on a San Mateo County freeway – was killed at 1.50 am when the vehicle collided with opposing traffic.

Lest We Forget

Other notable deaths that occurred sometime during 1967:

Laverne Andrews (US pop/boogie-woogie singer with the popular Andrews Sisters; born Minnesota, 6/7/1915; cancer, 8/5)

Alan Avick (US guitarist who played alongside a pre-Blondie Chris Stein in psychedelic garage band First Crow to the Moon; leukaemia)

Bert Berns (revered US singer, songwriter and early Drifters producer who also founded Bang Records; born New York, 8/11/1929; sick during childhood, he died of heart failure in a New York hotel, 30/12)

Charles 'Ty' Brian (UK guitarist with Merseybeat act Rory Storm & The Hurricanes; born Liverpool, 1941; following an appendectomy, he was taken ill during a gig and died in hospital from complications)

John Coltrane (US avant-garde jazz legend; born North Carolina, 23/9/1926; cancer, 17/7)

Ida Cox (US unofficial Queen of the Blues; born Georgia, 25/2/1896; cancer, 11/10)

J B Lenoir (US blues guitarist/harmonica-player; born Mississippi, 5/3/1929; heart attack following a car accident in Illinois, 29/4)

Jayne Mansfield (popular US actress who recorded with Jimi Hendrix (!); born Vera Jayne Palmer, Pennsylvania, 19/4/1933; she died in a car crash, but was not decapitated as is widely believed, 29/6)

Moon Mullican (US country/hillbilly pianist, who influenced Jerry Lee Lewis among others; born Aubrey Mullican, Texas, 27/3/1909; heart attack, 1/1)

Robert Nighthawk (revered US blues slide-guitarist who influenced many early rock performers; born Robert McCollum, Arkansas, 30/11/1909; heart failure, 5/11)

For a complete list of fallen artists, visit
www.numberoneinheaven.com

1968

FEBRUARY

Frankie Lymon

(Washington Heights, New York,
30 September 1942)

Frankie Lymon & The Teenagers

The Premiers – Bronx singers Jimmy
Merchant, Sherman Garnes, Herman
Santiago and Joey Negroni – were a
band without real focus. Then, one
afternoon, they chanced upon a 12-
year-old would-be vocalist named
Frankie Lymon, who worked at the
grocery store below producer Richard
Barrett's flat; his cash-strapped family lived in cramped surroundings,
prompting the streetwise, shrewd
youngster to seek employment.

Encouraged by manager George
Goldner (who signed the act to his Gee
label), Lymon's pre-pubescent soprano
took centre stage, replacing Santiago's
deeper tones. Further change
occurred: the group's name became
The Teenagers at the behest of studio
sax-man Jimmy Wright, and, perhaps
most significantly, Lymon himself suggested changing the words and melody
to the group's best number, 'Why Do
Birds Sing So Gay?', which henceforth
became 'Why Do Fools Fall in Love?'

**Frankie Lymon (*second right*) with Negroni, Santiago, Merchant and Garnes:
A teenager's life?**

– though his input has been greatly disputed since. No matter, in February 1956, the recorded version of this song soared into the US Top Ten, shifting a million copies; in the UK, it went to number one. With Johnny Ace dead (◂ *Pre-1965*), Lymon became the top black teen pin-up, dropped out of his schooling and toured with the band, scoring further US hits with 'I Want You to be My Girl' (1956) and 'Goody Goody' (1957), while 'Baby Baby' and '(I'm Not a) Juvenile Delinquent' (both 1957) continued their success in Britain. The latter title, though, was to prove depressingly ironic ...

Lymon had already had an affair with Platters singer Zola Taylor at just thirteen, but his world began to fall apart when he reached full maturity. The singer's attempted solo career faltered, after he was shown dancing with a white girl on television's *Dance Party*, which many believed – however ludicrous it might now sound – effectively ended his chances. Having experimented with drugs even before his brief fame, Lymon entered rehab in 1961, but in 1966 was charged with narcotics possession (he allegedly sold the rights to 'Why Do Fools?' to buy drugs). To avoid a custodial sentence, Lymon joined the army; his discharge from the forces (for repeatedly going AWOL) followed by a short-lived marriage to teacher Emira Eagle then took him to Georgia.

In mid February 1968, the recently recontracted Lymon told Emira he had a 'weekend job' back in New York, but when he failed to return, she became suspicious. Two weeks later, his body was found in the bathroom of his grandmother's Harlem apartment – the home in which he had been brought up two decades before – an emptied needle next to his body. The Teenagers (now seriously contravening the Trade Descriptions Act) struggled to create any momentum without the singer; Garnes (▸ *February 1977*) and Negroni (▸ *September 1978*) also died young, a decade after Lymon.

Little Willie John
(Cullendale, Arkansas, 15 November 1937)

The resonant tenor voice of William Edward John belied its perpetrator's small stature. Alongside Sam Cooke – though without ever being as commercially popular – John was one of the best-loved practitioners of proto-soul, working with legends like Count Basie and Johnny Otis from the age of fourteen. Part of a musically gifted family (his sister Mabel became one of Ray Charles's Raelettes), John was signed to King Records at eighteen, enjoying sporadic crossover hits starting with 'Fever' (1956), which, like many black records of the era, became a bigger hit for a white artist (in this case, Peggy Lee), while another was later picked up by The Beatles. Willie John's last and biggest hit was 'Sleep' (1960), and King decided to drop him when it became apparent his moment had passed. This did not sit well with John, as noted for his unstable personality as for his music: in 1964, he was charged with assault in Miami but jumped bail and headed to Seattle where, during an after-hours lock-in at one of his infrequent live engagements, John returned from the lavatory to discover a patron, Kendall Roundtree, had helped himself to his seat. When he refused to move, a scuffle inevitably broke out, Roundtree somehow sustaining a fatal injury. Many sources claim that this was from a blow to the head, while some state that John – who often carried a weapon – had used a knife. Despite the charges against him (and the fact that he had already breached bail), John continued to perform while he awaited trial. In the event, he only avoided a conviction for murder when his defence lawyer pointed out that Roundtree was the much bigger man; even so, on 18 May 1966, he was facing eight to twenty years at Washington State Penitentiary.

Then, having completed just two years of his sentence, Willie John died mysteriously. Keen to put the case behind them, authorities returned a verdict of 'heart attack', though there have been unsubstantiated tales over the years of mistreatment by both staff and inmates, possibly resulting in asphyxiation.

JUNE
Friday 14

Ken Errair
(Detroit, Michigan, 23 January 1928)

The Four Freshmen

In May 1953, Ken Errair was recruited as replacement for tour-tired Hal Kratzsch in the jazz-styled vocal four-piece The Four Freshmen – an acclaimed vocal harmony troupe formed by brothers Don and Ross Barbour while at the Arthur Jordan Conservatory of Music in Indianapolis. Before Errair joined, the group had had several sheet-music hits, but his first recording session that July spawned a radio-airplay hit in 'Holiday/It Happened Once Before' (1953). Success for Errair was brief – he had married actress Jane Withers (soon to be seen in the epic movie *Giant*) just ahead of joining the group, and, like his predecessor, found constant touring detrimental to his domestic life. The decisive Barbours were quick to give Errair his marching orders (replacing him with Ken Albers), preventing him from enjoying the US Top Twenty hit 'Graduation' in June 1956.

Ken Errair attempted to crack the market on his own with the self-explanatory *Solo Session* album for Capitol a year later but, now a settled man with a wife and two children, found a seemingly more stable future in real estate instead. Sadly, travelling to a California development, he was killed instantly when his light aircraft crashed in bad weather. His colleague Don Barbour had died in a Los Angeles car crash in 1961, while Kratzsch succumbed to cancer in 1970.

JULY

Wednesday 24

Nervous Norvus

(James Drake – Memphis, Tennessee, 13 May 1912)

One of the more idiosyncratic characters to emerge from early pop culture, Nervous Norvus initially pushed himself as working musician/writer Singing Jimmy Drake before finally earning notoriety with a brace of novelty hits that baffled US radio listeners in the fifties – that is, once the authorities had given the go-ahead to let them be heard. With the combined restrictions of the Depression and crippling asthmatic and heart conditions, Drake endured a housebound upbringing. However, having learned the ukulele while young, he set off as a young man to busk in sub-Woody Guthrie style around the country between jobs. Having been excused military service during the war due to his various ailments, Drake worked the shipyards, eventually taking a peacetime job as a truck driver, which prompted his best-known song, the curious 'Transfusion' (1956) – a dark tune telling of a trucker who in his career had caused

countless accidents and now sought assistance from the local blood bank as he lay on his death bed.

Drake was largely inspired by the fifties Bay Area broadcaster Red Blanchard, a DJ who had cut an album or two of mildly comic novelties with a teenage audience in mind. Changing his name to Nervous Norvus – this time in homage to one of Blanchard's tunes – Drake, now in his forties, began peddling his somewhat derivative songs like pizza, i.e., one for seven bucks, two for eleven, etc. It was only once he'd hit upon the genuinely different 'Transfusion' that folk began to take notice. After some delay, the record – replete with 'crashes' and 'skids' inserted by Blanchard – unexpectedly made the US Top Ten, its follow-up 'Ape Call' further confounding critics by also making the Billboard chart a couple of months later. Briefly, 'Norvus Fever' was in (or at least on) the air. Although his success meant he was now able to take up music full-time, Drake's reluctance to perform the songs publicly would foreshorten his moment in the spotlight.

Various stories about Drake's life suggest a solitary 'mummy's boy' type who'd never had a relationship (odd, given that he had supposedly been married in 1942) and who drank himself to a premature death. The latter is, however, fairly likely: Drake died from cirrhosis of the liver at Almeida County Hospital. In good 'Transfusion' style, he donated his body to the University of California's anatomy department.

Alexandra Nebedov

(Doris Nebedov – Heydekrug, Prussia (Lithuania), 19 May 1942)

Sensibly shedding her given name, Alexandra Nebedov was something of a prodigy – a gifted artist, actress, dancer and singer, as well as being fluent in several languages. The latter skills proved significant as she scored hit records in French, Russian, Spanish and Hebrew, her best-known English-language song being 1967's 'Golden Earrings'. Nebedov was to prove a popular draw in France: within two years of being discovered she had recorded with MOR stars Gilbert Bécaud and Yves Montand. She settled, however, in Munich with her young son.

Constantly on tour, Nebedov was taking a rare vacation in Schleswig-Holstein with her family when her and her mother's lives were ended by a collision with a truck they were attempting to pass in her Mercedes. What seemed like a tragic and unavoidable accident was soon shrouded in mystery: it transpired that Nebedov had taken out life insurance that same week and that her son – who survived the crash – had had a year's schooling pre-paid. The case was reopened in 2004, when reports emerged that the singer might have committed suicide because it had become known that her then-current lover, Pierre Lafaire, had been a US spy.

AUGUST

Monday 5

Luther Perkins
(Tennessee, 8 January 1928)

The Tennessee Two

Guitar-pickin' Luther Perkins and bassist Marshall Grant formed The Tennessee Two, a struggling but cheery country duo that moonlighted in Memphis bars and cathouses while holding down motor-sales jobs by day. Their major break came along in the shape of showroom-colleague Roy Cash's younger brother Johnny, who fronted their act. The group was aware of its musical shortcomings, but Sam Phillips at Sun Records could hear a whole new sound in their apparent sparseness. Thus, throughout the late fifties and early sixties, as Johnny Cash's reputation grew, Perkins and the band – latterly augmented by (unrelated) Carl Perkins – toured the US in Cash's Plymouth, their genial rough 'n' ready style complementary to the singer's deeply laconic tones.

Luther Perkins's performance at Cash's famous Folsom Prison gig proved his last: he died from burns and smoke inhalation a couple of days after falling asleep with a lit cigarette in his hand. Perkins – who had also played with Jerry Lee Lewis – was buried in Henderson, Tennessee. He'd been a good friend to Cash, who was so moved by his death that he eulogized him in song and continued to issue the guitarist's pay cheque to his widow for at least six months afterwards. Perkins's singing brother, Thomas Wayne Perkins, died equally tragically three years later.

See also *Johnny Cash (*✒ *Golden Oldies #16)*

SEPTEMBER

Saturday 28

Dewey Phillips
(Crump, Tennessee, 13 May 1926)

If Alan Freed was the DJ who made rock 'n' roll popular, largely unsung hero Dewey Phillips was the first to introduce his mainly white listeners to black (so-called race) music – and was almost certainly the first broadcaster to play and interview Elvis Presley. Taking over WHBQ's *Red Hot & Blue* show in 1949 and introducing a mid-South audience to a different kind of music, Phillips pre-dated John Peel by several decades with wrong speeds, sides, etc., but the man was no slouch either: what had begun as a 15-minute weekly show became three hours, five nights a week, under his guidance. His playing of an acetate of Presley's 'That's All Right, Mama' in July 1954 was the high point – though a later unauthorized pre-release on his show damaged his relationship with The King.

The 'formatting' of radio programmes is not a new phenomenon: following the payola scandal of the late fifties which so damaged Freed, Phillips found himself out of sorts with new-style playlisting, and lost his slot in the shake-up. Ever more reliant on prescription painkillers following a car accident when he was younger, he slipped into decline and, despite finding other radio openings, Phillips's on-air tomfoolery became harsh and cynical – he was, by the mid sixties, a broken man. He died in his sleep, aged forty-two.

See also *Alan Freed (*✒ *January 1965)*

OCTOBER

Thursday 31

Malcolm Hale
(Butte, Montana, 17 May 1941)

Spanky & Our Gang

Formed in Illinois in 1965, Spanky & Our Gang were occasionally looked upon as a poor man's Mamas & The Papas, the group's disciplined harmonies more than reminiscent of their better-known Californian contemporaries. Hale was a working singer/multi-instrumentalist when he met Chicago-based Oz Bach (bass), Nigel Pickering (guitar) and Elaine 'Spanky' McFarlane, the latter a washboard-toting singer who had performed with jazz/folk/protest act The New Wine Singers. As if that name weren't awful enough, the new group had become Spanky & Our Gang by the time they recruited Hale as a guitarist and drummer. A brief flurry of hits on Mercury began with 'Sunday Will Never Be the Same Again' (1967), a US Top Ten single rejected originally by rival bands The Left Banke and – yes – The Mamas & The Papas.

Malcolm Hale, who arranged much of the group's work, died suddenly at his Chicago apartment at the age of twenty-seven. There have been conflicting verdicts of 'walking' pneumonia or cirrhosis of the liver, though some reports also suggest that he may have died as a result of carbon-monoxide poisoning due to a faulty heater. Either way, it proved pretty much the end of the line for the group. McFarlane left to have a baby (though she reformed the group in 1975), and later member Lefty Baker died just three years later (✒ *August 1971*), Bach some decades after (✒ *September 1998*).

Lest We Forget

Other notable deaths that occurred sometime during 1968:

Bruce Cloud (US second tenor with vocal group Billy Ward & The Dominoes; born *c* 1932; when his solo career failed to take off, tragically he killed his wife and child before committing suicide)

Red Foley (US country singer who recorded 'Old Shep' and was father-in-law to Pat Boone; born Clyde Julian Foley, Kentucky, 16/7/1910; heart attack, 19/9)

Little Walter (US bluesman; born Marion Walter Jacobs, Louisiana, 1/5/1930; died from a blood clot promoted by injuries sustained in a Chicago street fight, 15/2)

Skeets McDonald (US honky-tonk singer; born Enos McDonald, Arkansas, 1/10/1915; heart attack, 31/3)

Wes Montgomery (celebrated jazz/blues guitarist; born Indiana, 6/3/1925; heart attack, 15/6)

Syd Nathan (US founder of R & B label King Records, the home of many early top vocal acts; born Ohio, 27/4/1904; heart disease/pneumonia, 5/3)

Phill Pill (US showband pianist with Brandi Perry & The Bubble Machine; born California; ambushed and shot in Vietnam, 5/7)

George 'King' Scott (US tenor with gospel acts The Hesitations and Five Blind Boys of Alabama; born Alabama, 18/3/1929; like Blind Boy Vel Taylor in 1947, he died from an accidental gunshot wound, 2/1968)

Benny Treiber (US bassist with The Mind's Eye, who were briefly produced by The Monkees, until Davy Jones removed him from the band; drowned when his boat capsized on McQueeney Lake, Texas)

Cathy Wayne (Australian show singer; born Cathy Warne; shot on stage performing in Vietnam – allegedly by US fire)

Curt Willis (US showband drummer with Brandi Perry & The Bubble Machine; blood loss following the ambush that killed Phil Pill, 5/7)

For a complete list of fallen artists, visit

www.numberoneinheaven.com

MARCH

Wednesday 26

Dickie Pride

(Richard Knellar – Thornton Heath, Surrey,
21 October 1941)

The Cliftons

Dickie Pride – 'The Sheikh of Shake' – looked to be the latest in a long line of Larry Parnes success stories when picked out at just seventeen years of age. Pride had originally been spotted by Russ Conway in a pub in Tooting, South London; on witnessing his performance, Parnes signed him on the spot. Something of a handful on the road, Pride soon demanded alterations to the repetitive nightly set that Parnes insisted he perform. Within a couple of years, his increasingly maverick behaviour saw him dropped from Parnes's popular touring showcases, wherein the likes of Billy Fury flourished. Although he still fronted a band called The Cliftons (with, at one point, future Rolling Stone Bill Wyman on bass), the rot had set in.

Once optimistically billed as 'Britain's answer to Little Richard', Pride could buck the system no more: a dramatic plunge from the limelight to which he'd become accustomed saw him working as a storeman by the end of 1962 and gradually becoming addicted to various drugs. In 1967, Pride was referred to a mental hospital, where it was somehow ruled that he should undergo a lobotomy. At the start of 1969, he attempted an ill-fated comeback, but was found dead in his bed, having accidentally overdosed on sleeping tablets, leaving a widow and four-year-old son.

See also *Larry Parnes (☞ August 1989).*

MAY

Friday 2

'Benny' Benjamin

(William Benjamin – Detroit, Michigan,
15 July 1925)

The 'Funk Brothers'

William 'Benny' Benjamin was the house drummer at Motown, his distinctive rhythms backing dozens of the best-known records to emerge from the stable. Known also as 'Papa Zita', Benjamin had been an employee at Berry Gordy's label before he was committed to vinyl as one of the original 'Funk Brothers', but despite playing on hits by The Supremes, Stevie Wonder, The Four Tops and Marvin Gaye, Benjamin remained unknown to those who bought the records. Struggling with a drink problem, he died of a stroke at home shortly after his premature retirement. Among other 'Funk Brothers', Benjamin's main partners in crime were James 'Jamie' Jamerson (☞ *August 1983*) and Earl Van Dyke (☞ *September 1992*).

See also *Robert White (☞ October 1994). Other occasional 'Funk Brothers' 'Pistol' Allen and Johnny Griffith both passed away in 2002.*

Tuesday 6

Don Drummond

(Jamaica, 1943)

The Skatalites

Forming the seminal Skatalites with Roland Alphonso in 1963, instinctive talent Drummond wrote much of the ska group's material and became recognized for his trombone sound – best recalled on the standard 'Guns of Navarone'. Drummond, under the early guidance of influential producer Clement 'Coxsone' Dodd, went on to work with both Bob Marley & The Wailers and Toots & The Maytals.

But, despite his prowess as a musician and performer, Drummond had severe mental-health issues not helped by his excessive marijuana use, lack of financial reward or indeed recognition while he was alive. His problems came to a tragic head on 31 December 1964, when his girlfriend, Anita 'Margarita' Mahfood, administered him the wrong drugs, causing Drummond to sleep through a scheduled concert appearance for The Skatalites, apparently a genuine mistake on her part. On discovering some hours later, however, that Mahfood – an exotic dancer – had deliberately given him the wrong medication in order to spend New Year's Eve performing herself, he flew into a rage. When she returned to his East Kingston home at 3.30 am, an argument ensued, during which Mahfood was stabbed four times in the chest. Entering the Rockfort police station an hour later, Drummond apparently muttered, 'A woman in de yard stab herself – an' I would like de police to come and see her.' Two officers accompanied him back home to discover Anita Mahfood dead on their bed. The murder weapon still protruded from her body, now covered in a chamois; Drummond then tried to claim Mahfood had inflicted the wounds herself. What quickly confirmed his guilt was the position of his beloved trombone, by the bed with his girlfriend's hand strangely thrust far into the bell. Drummond was deemed legally insane and sentenced to imprisonment at the Bellevue (a notorious Jamaican psychiatric unit). While he was incarcerated his band fell apart – that 'Guns of Navarone' went on to become a massive international hit in 1967 is little more than a sad footnote. The causes of Drummond's own death while institutionalized remain speculative: the majority accept the given verdict of suicide, though suggestions of intervention by members of Mahfood's family – or even a beating by guards at the unit – were dramatically brought to the fore by Drummond's contemporary

Hugh Malcolm (drummer with The Supersonics), who symbolically ripped up his friend's death certificate at a memorial service for the musician.

See also *Jackie Mittoo (☞ December 1990); Tommy McCook (☞ Golden Oldies #6); Roland Alphonso (☞ Golden Oldies #8). Occasional Skatalites singer Vic Taylor passed away in 2003.*

Wednesday 14

Martin Lamble
(London, 28 August 1948)
Fairport Convention

Martin Lamble was only twenty when he died. The cocksure drummer had been so convinced of his own ability that his heckling of original Fairport Convention percussionist Shaun Frater resulted in the latter getting the push and Lamble securing the job at only seventeen. At various times boasting the now-revered Sandy Denny, Richard Thompson and Ian Matthews among its ranks, Fairport found crossover success fairly rapidly.

With two albums cementing their position at the fore of Britain's folk-rock scene, Fairport Convention were touring the third, *Unhalfbricking* (1969), when disaster struck. Travelling back to London from a Birmingham concert, the band's van was involved in a crash near Mill Hill; while other members were shaken up, Thompson was badly injured – and Martin Lamble was killed instantly. As a mark of respect to their young drummer, Fairport Convention decided to continue, issuing in July what would be their only UK hit single, '*Si tu dois partir*', in his memory. The band was to endure a fractured career until further tragedy claimed singer Sandy Denny less than a decade later (☞ *April 1978*); her partner and some-time Fairport member, Trevor Lucas, also died prematurely (☞ *February 1989*).

Brian Jones: Turned his back on one or two over the years

'Of course Brian was being set up. First the police would be tipped off that he was holding drugs and a few minutes later the tip-off would come to me. I think that someone in The Stones' organization wanted him out of the way.'

Trevor Kempson, journalist, *News of the World*

Brian Jones

(Lewis Brian Hopkin-Jones – Cheltenham, England, 28 February 1942)

The Rolling Stones

Although Jagger and Richards were inevitably to become the focal point, The Rolling Stones were Brian Jones's band. Although the founder's playing was inspired by the traditional arrangements of his heroes, it was his own wayward, maverick behaviour that informed The Stones' enduring attitude and stance. At the age of twenty-seven, a whirl-wind life – involving much mistrust and betrayal – yielded to a shocking and needless death. Shortly before he died, Brian Jones had seemed to his many friends reconciled and focused for the first time in years. He had a new partner – Swedish student Anna Wohlin – with whom he seemed content, plus an enviable home that he loved at Cotchford Farm.

In the years prior to his death, Jones had been impetu-ous, not one for continuity, flitting between addresses and girlfriends like a butterfly among flowers. As a result, he fathered six sons by different women (the first when he was just fifteen), and faced paternity suits for at least three. That was his way: Jones, popularly viewed as sensitive and engaging, always managed to upset those whose lives he touched with a series of selfish and thoughtless deeds. (Erstwhile partner Pat Andrews was dismayed when the musician christened a later child Julian Mark, a reversal of their son's name.) Responsibility never high in his priori-ties, an already-fractious relationship with his parents had virtually petered out before Jones reached his twenties. But, whatever they may have felt about his morals, many were surprised by the sheer magnitude of Jones's success: he met, played with and bowled over many of the heroes of his youth, including Bo Diddley and Alexis Korner, before a young Mick Jagger and Keith Richards were seduced by his stinging slide guitar, and hooked up with him in 1962, even agreeing to be 'The Rolling Stones', a name they both plainly disliked. Soon headlining at London's Crawdaddy Club, The Stones (completed by rhythm section Bill Wyman and Charlie Watts) became the tightest unit in town within a couple of years, presenting a serious threat to the global domination of their 'politer' northern friends, The Beatles. With whizz-kid manager Andrew Loog Oldham orchestrating their misbehaviour, the band set about becoming the most talked-about rock 'n' roll rebels the industry had yet seen. Brian Jones – seemingly shy, precociously talented and boy-next-door handsome – was the most popular member. He also nurtured a sense of style that blueprinted 'pop star flair' for years to come.

Outside The Stones' music, there were two particularly significant developments as the band grew to become the world's second biggest: their management's apparent insistence on employing dubious 'hard cases' and Brian Jones's rapidly increasing paranoia. The guitarist, having had the means from a young age, was already a heavy drinker when stardom opened his world up to drugs. According to those who were there, it was common to witness him mixing beer with wine with whisky, amphetamines with hash with acid. Once the press got hold of this information, Jones's life became increasingly intolerable. He was not 'good' on drugs, falling into zombified states and questioning the motives behind everyone's actions. Like many paranoiacs, however, his rawest fears were not unfounded. In early 1967, the latest love of Jones's life was Anita Pallenberg, a stunning German-Italian model who appeared to share and understand all his hopes and ambitions. To her, he could discharge his deepest fears – which at the time consisted largely of Jagger, Richards and Oldham attempting to undermine his leadership of The Stones. Although there was some truth in this summation, it was mostly Jones's drug habits that were fuelling his apprehension, as well as causing him to be less than efficient during studio time. Gradually, Pallenberg helped his confidence to return – that is, until their arguments and his violent conduct precipitated an affair with Keith Richards on a trip to Morocco. Needless to say, Jones was devastated. His chronic mental condition was soon compounded by an alleged drug 'plant' at his flat; only his ill health prevented him receiving a similar jail sentence to those handed to Jagger and Richards that year.

By this time, Brian Jones had been assigned a minder – the first of the 'hard cases' to enter the guitarist's world. Tom Keylock was a thick-set ex-paratrooper whose task it was to keep the meandering musician on the straight and narrow, which, for the most part, he did. The Rolling Stones was now a vast company of players, having been taken over by ruthless American businessman Allen Klein. Keylock was to move quickly up The Stones' ladder, soon becoming the band's tour manager, and was to elevate one or two of his old friends with him. One of these was builder Frank Thorogood, who had created his own niche by building a security wall at Mick Jagger's Elizabethan mansion. But, when Thorogood's pilfering of a valuable guitar put paid to doing major building work for Keith Richards, Keylock was at pains to find his pal another position within Rolling Stones Inc.

Towards the end of 1968, Jones – possibly playing 'keep up' with Jagger, Richards and their country retreats – purchased a farmhouse in Sussex. Cotchford Farm seemed the perfect spot for the troubled guitarist to ground himself and start afresh. It was the former home of A A Milne, the setting for his enchanting Winnie-the-Pooh tales and – to Jones's obvious delight – boasted a lifesize Christopher Robin statue in honour of the writer's son, the hero of his stories. Finding himself less and less involved with The Stones, Brian Jones had new aspirations and wanted his home to reflect this. He was, however, not the only person to harbour ambitions for the house: Thorogood, who 'conveniently' moved on to the renovation of this property, also had ideas of his own. Suggesting that it would be most efficient for him to live in the adjoining flat during the week, the married Thorogood moved himself in with a girlfriend (nurse Janet Lawson) before Jones had much chance to object. To the musician's chagrin, Thorogood then moved them both into the house proper, claiming the flat was not big enough. Although pretty much everyone at The Stones' office (and a couple of their girlfriends) harboured a thorough dislike and mistrust of this man, somehow no one saw fit to keep him away from the fragile Brian Jones. Thorogood – not to mention the handful of devious labourers now under his charge – felt he had the measure of Jones; the builder couldn't get away with his tricks at

the expense of the wilier Richards, but soon found ways to take advantage of his new boss. Possessions inevitably went missing, furniture was mysteriously ordered on Jones's account and work-days fast became extended boozing sessions. Any work that *was* completed was botched.

Early in June 1969, the other Stones called round to inform their 'unmanageable' guitarist that his time was finally up. Although he felt some relief at relinquishing something that had become a chore to him, Jones still felt shunned by the band he himself had begun. Partly to quell these feelings, Jones began making serious plans with a number of top musician friends, including Steve Winwood, Steve Marriott and even Jimi Hendrix, Bob Dylan and John Lennon, planning a supergroup line-up to put all of their previous bands in the shade. The 'plan' had a consolidating effect. On 2 July, a revitalized Jones finally decided that the workmen must all go, which inevitably caused ructions with Thorogood. Because he had (unsurprisingly) given Keylock the task of breaking the news, Jones felt it would soften the blow to invite Thorogood and Lawson to join him and Anna Wohlin for a final drink and a swim in his pool. By the beginning of the evening, Brian Jones was already well over the limit.

The statement given to the police by Thorogood on 3 July was to the effect that he and Jones had been bathing late at night, while the girlfriends were indoors. The builder claimed to have disappeared to find a cigarette, leaving Jones alone in the pool. On his return, he found Jones floating on the water – apparently having drowned while unsupervised. He, Lawson and Wohlin had attempted to revive the musician, but to no avail. It seemed plausible: Jones was an asthmatic, a known drug-user, heavily under the influence of alcohol at the time, and it had been dark. By the end of that week an official verdict of misadventure had been filed. However, the strongly held belief that there had been others at Jones's 'party' and eyewitness allegations from people as diverse as Gary Scott of The Walker Brothers and Jones's socialite friend Nicholas Fitzgerald, suggested otherwise.

Just before he died in November 1993, Frank Thorogood made this depressing revelation to a shocked Tom Keylock: 'It was me that did Brian. I just finally snapped – it just happened.' Belated interviews with two anonymous members of the builder's team appear to substantiate this confession. Both 'Marty' and 'Joe' documented the tale of how the group – jealous of Brian Jones's fame, popularity and, most crucially, his swimming ability – had drunkenly rounded on the 'fucking ponce' and forced him under the water. Despite Brian's pleas, the 'game' continued to its tragic conclusion. Both men suggested that it was the scorned Thorogood who had been holding Brian Jones down when he drowned, though it seemed all bore considerable malice towards their employer, this 'ponce', a celebrity with a host of attractive women hanging off his every word – forgetting that a) this young man's wealth had been self-made with no small amount of hard work, and b) it was paying for the lifestyle which they had suddenly co-opted. The evidence may seem damning, but the case has never been reopened and at least one of Jones's alleged killers remains at large thirty-seven years later. According to his friend Pamela des Barres, Jones had been presented during a trip to Ceylon at the end of 1968 with his astrological chart, which had apparently read: 'Be careful swimming in the coming year. Don't go into the water without a friend.'

Jones was buried in Cheltenham on 10 July 1969; only Bill Wyman and Charlie Watts from the band attended his funeral. Two days later, 250,000 fans showed up at The Rolling Stones' free concert at Hyde Park – rebilled in tribute to their former guitarist.

'The sadness of his dying is somehow not so bad as the sadness of seeing him trying to live.'

Shirley Arnold, The Rolling Stones' secretary.

Sunday 20

Roy Hamilton

(Leesburg, Georgia, 16 April 1929)

The Searchlight Gospel Singers

Although little spoken of nowadays, the distinctive soul/doo-wop voice of Roy Hamilton graced many Epic and Columbia releases during the fifties and sixties. He was originally a vocalist with The Searchlight Gospel Singers, having practised with his local church choir from the age of six and won several talent contests during his teens. Known as 'The Golden Boy with the Golden Voice', Hamilton made his name with such standards as 'You'll Never Walk Alone', 'Ebb Tide' and 'Unchained Melody', recording some eighty songs in a short career. At one point he was a close friend of Elvis Presley, who, according to some, emulated his vocal style.

Hamilton's death has remained something of a mystery: the general consensus seems to be that he died following a stroke, clearly rare for a man under forty. Despite his posthumous induction into the Georgia Music Hall of Fame, Hamilton's standing in the business had faltered during the late sixties, making suicide also a distinct possibility.

OCTOBER

Wednesday 22

Tommy Edwards

(Richmond, Virginia, 17 February 1922)

Another velvet-voiced singer in the style of Nat 'King' Cole, Edwards was a favourite around Richmond before his songwriting prowess sent him to New York City in 1949. One song in particular had cemented his reputation: the bizarrely titled 'That Chick's Too Young to Fry', a sizeable 1946 hit for Louis Jordan. Also an accomplished pianist, Edwards's own biggest record would be 1958's 'It's All in the Game' – possibly the only number-one hit written by a former US vice-president (Charles Gates Dawes). Tommy Edwards's success was a distant memory by the time he died of an undetected brain aneurysm at the age of forty-seven.

DECEMBER

Monday 1

Magic Sam

(Samuel Gene Maghett – Grenada, Mississippi, 14 February 1937)

The popular songwriter, guitarist and King of West-Side Blues died of a heart attack at the age of thirty-two. After briefly serving time for army desertion in 1961, Magic Sam became a prime mover in Chicago's electric-blues scene, recording two well-received albums, and was on the verge of a deal with Stax – and major stardom – at the time of his death:

a triumphant performance at Michigan's 1969 Ann Arbor Blues Festival proved to be his critical zenith. Then, complaining of heartburn, the mercurial musician collapsed one morning in Chicago, never to recover.

Close...
Nancy Nevins
Sweetwater

While many high-profile stars of Woodstock 1969 were to fall over the next decade or so, one name seldom mentioned is that of Sweetwater. This Latin-styled band (who regularly opened for acts like The Doors and Janis Joplin) were the first to play the legendary festival – but after that distinction, their luck was decidedly out. Lead singer Nancy Nevins very nearly became the first to perish when her car was struck by a drunk driver in December 1969; the accident left her in a coma and brain-damaged. Although she recovered, her vocal chords were permanently damaged, a disability that effectively ended Sweetwater as a going concern until a brief reconvening in 1997. But by this time few original members were around to join her: drummer Alan Malarowitz had been less fortunate than Nevins, dying in a car crash in 1981, while cellist August Burns succumbed to pneumonia after a bizarre accident the following year. Flautist Albert Moore passed away from lung cancer in 1994.

Lest We Forget

Other notable deaths that occurred sometime during 1969:

Paul Chambers (US bassist with The Miles Davis Quintet; born Pittsburgh, 22/4/35; tuberculosis, 4/1)

Leonard Chess (Polish-born founder of Chess Records; born Lazer Schmuel Chez, Motol, 12/3/1917; heart attack, 16/10)

Judy Garland (celebrated US musical actress/singer; born Frances Ethel Gumm, Minnesota, 10/6/1922; overdose of barbiturates, 22/6)

Gary Allen Hinman (US musician/teacher and 'friend to the stars'; born Colorado, 24/12/1934; selling Manson Family member Bobby Beausoleil dodgy mescaline, he was stabbed twice by the buyer, 27/7)

Meredith Hunter (US Rolling Stones fan murdered at the Altamont concert; born 1951; stabbed to death by Hell's Angels employed as security guards, 6/12)

Skip James (US blues musician; born Nehemiah James, Bentonia, Mississippi; cancer, 3/10)

Frederick Earl 'Shorty' Long (US R & B singer who hit with 'Here Comes the Judge' in 1968; born Alabama, 20/5/1940; drowned after his boat capsized, 29/6)

Johnny Moore (US lead with pioneering vocal act The Blazers; born Texas, 20/10/1906; unknown, 6/1)

Jimmy McHugh (revered US composer/songwriter; born Massachusetts, 10/7/1894; unknown, 23/5)

Lemon 'Banjo Boy' Nash (US blues guitarist/banjo-player; born Louisiana, 22/4/1898; unknown)

Josh White (US folk/blues guitarist who worked with Blind Joe Taggart; born North Carolina, 11/2/1914; died during heart surgery, 5/9)

For a complete list of fallen artists, visit

www.numberoneinheaven.com

1970

JANUARY

Saturday 17

Billy Stewart
(William Larry Stewart – Washington, DC, 24 March 1937)

William Cathey
(1937)

Rico Hightower
(1947)

Norman P Rich
(26 February 1930)
The Soul Kings

Known in the industry as 'Fat Boy', the formidable Billy Stewart enjoyed a measure of US success during the sixties with his R & B-flavoured Soul Kings, the band he formed after spending some time under the wing of admirer Bo Diddley. The jovial musician's background and upbringing in gospel – his family had performed as The Stewart Gospel Singers – had given him an enviable voice as well as considerable talent at the piano. Stewart's move to secular music was marked by his fondness for updating show tunes: his barn-storming take on George Gershwin's 'Summertime' produced a big-selling US Top Ten

single for Chess Records in August 1966. In the late fifties, as a member of The Rainbows, Stewart shared the limelight with future star Don Covay and the legendary Marvin Gaye (☞ *April 1984*).

The writing appeared to be on the wall for Stewart and his associates well before their fateful crash in January 1970: in 1968, a horrific coach accident and explosion had all but wiped out his road crew, while Stewart himself had narrowly escaped death in a motorbike smash one year later. But popular music suffered its second major band wipe-out when Stewart's brand-new Ford Thunderbird developed a wheel-lock fault as he and his band travelled towards Smithfield, North Carolina, on Interstate 95. Hitting a bridge, the vehicle careered down a bank, coming to rest in the Neuse River; all four band members – Stewart, William Cathey, Rico Hightower and Norman P Rich – were killed. Stewart's bereaved family went on to take legal action against Ford, reaching an out-of-court settlement.

Saturday 24

James 'Shep' Sheppard
(Queens, New York, 24 September 1935)
The Heartbeats
Shep & The Limelites

Hard-working and distinctive leader 'Shep' Sheppard fronted highly polished New York doo-wop group The Heartbeats before he hit his twenties. Writing songs in his bathtub, Sheppard composed the sumptuous 'Crazy For You', the 1955 airplay hit that brought his band overdue wider attention. Carrying an ego the size of a small continent, Sheppard was keen to grab as much limelight as he could (hence his second band's name), which caused some resentment in the group, who eventually abandoned him: The Heartbeats' patience finally ran out after a Philadelphia gig during which the singer somehow managed to fall asleep in the middle of the group's 'A Thousand Miles Away'! With The Limelites, Sheppard went on to compose such standards as the US 1961 number two 'Daddy's Home' (better remembered in the UK as a schmaltzy Christmas runner-up for Cliff Richard twenty years later). Disbanding the group in 1966, Sheppard reunited The Limelites to play the cabaret circuit three years later; however, following one such show, the singer was discovered robbed, stabbed and bludgeoned to death in his car on the Long Island Expressway. Sheppard was known to be heavily in debt at the time, and his killers were most likely loan sharks who had been tailing him for months.

Saturday 31
Slim Harpo
(James Isaac Moore – Lobdell, Louisiana, 11 January 1924)

James Moore, orphaned in tenth grade, dropped out of school to follow a familiar blues path working the juke joints and picnics until he'd cemented a reputation as the fastest-rising guitarist/harmonica-player in Baton Rouge. By his twenties, and under the guidance of wily bluesman Lightnin' Slim, Moore's languid style had garnered him the attention of Nashville-based Excello Records boss, Jay Miller. (At this time, he was known as 'Harmonica Slim', a name that had to be dropped in favour of 'Slim Harpo', as it already had an owner.) Miller saw the young musician as ideal accompaniment to Lightnin' Slim, later recording his own single, 'I'm a King Bee', in 1957. Flirting with rock 'n' roll, Slim Harpo scored an unexpected US Top Forty entry with 'Rainin' in My Heart' (1961); returning the favour on this hit was none other than Lightnin' Slim. Playing together, the pair enjoyed a string of R & B hits, while a number of Harpo songs were later covered by blues-influenced white British acts such as The Yardbirds, The Pretty Things and, naturally, The Rolling Stones.

Slim Harpo had been a hale and healthy man all his life, somehow juggling a music career with his own trucking business during the sixties. His inexplicable, untimely death from a heart attack at forty-six saddened many.

FEBRUARY

Tuesday 24
Darrell Banks
(Darrell Eubanks – Mansfield, Ohio, 25 July 1937)
(Various acts)

Brought up in Buffalo, New York, Darrell Banks's gospel training nurtured the rounded vocal increasingly associated with the Northern soul genre. His first secular groups were little-known club acts The Daddy B Combo and Grand Prix, his dominant voice and presence enough to encourage manager Doc Murphy – who was also Eubanks's dentist – to take a chance on the singer. All appeared to be going well for the newly renamed Banks when his first single for the Revilot label, 'Open the Door to Your Heart' (1966), achieved an R & B number two and a very respectable twenty-seven in the national pop charts. His following 45s would be equally competent, but in his search for consistent success, Banks was to be disappointed.

Just weeks after Darrell Banks's final record release (and his final stab at stardom), he was to find himself in the middle of a grim domestic scenario in his then home town, Detroit. A patrolman named Aaron Bullock had just dropped his girlfriend, barmaid Marjorie Bozeman, at her home, when Banks – who, it transpired, had also been seeing her – emerged from a stationary car and grabbed Bozeman by her coat, stating angrily that they 'needed to talk'. According to the many witnesses present, Bullock then made himself known as an officer of the law and ordered Banks to release Bozeman. At this point, Banks produced a .22 revolver from his jacket; Bullock

responded as per his police training by ducking, pulling his own gun and shooting Banks – fatally – in the neck and chest. Darrell Banks died at 12.10 pm at the New Grace Hospital, his distraught lover explaining that she had been trying to end the relationship with the patrolman in order to settle down with the singer. Although Banks's death certificate declares a 'homicide', no case was ever brought. Banks – who was divorced and survived by a son and a daughter – was interred at the Detroit Memorial Park Cemetery. His grave remained unmarked for over thirty years until a group of fans financed a headstone in his honour in July 2004.

MARCH

Saturday 14
Mary Ann Ganser
(Queens, New York, 4 February 1948)
The Shangri-Las

The Shangri-Las had us believe that they were two pairs of misunderstood teenage sisters with homework, unsuitable boyfriends and angst-ridden parental relationships, their lurid tales of adolescent woe seemingly torn directly from discarded romance comics. Under the guiding hand of lauded producer George 'Shadow' Morton, the group pumped out a series of punchy three-minute slices of emotionally draining suburban pop that couldn't fail to resonate. Tragically, singer Mary Ann Ganser's own life was as short and dramatic as a Shangri-Las mini epic.

Mary Ann and Margie (Marguerite) Ganser were two of five children born to a middle-class New York physician and his nightclub-singer wife, twins who sadly lost their father when still young. They lived just one block from Andrew Jackson High School colleagues Mary and Liz 'Betty' Weiss, and the two pairs of sisters became firm friends in 1963, when a mutual love of singing pulled their worlds together. Honing a nasal-sounding harmonic style (Mary Weiss took lead), The Shangri-Las were playing the hops before the high-school year was out. Artie Ripp – sinisterly named head honcho at Kama Sutra – was quick to sign the group after witnessing an early performance: rock 'n' roll may still have been young, but girl groups were very much 'happening'. A few minor recordings were made before producer/writer George 'Shadow' Morton appeared on the scene with the cool, disquieting 'Remember (Walkin' in the Sand)' (1964) – which would change the girls' lives and fortunes for ever. The Shangri-Las (who had now joined the short-lived Red Bird label as minors, their contracts signed by their parents) found themselves with an unexpected Top Five hit. This was followed by an undisputed classic, 'Leader of the Pack', which, by the end of the fall, saw The Shangri-Las dramatically displace The Supremes at the top of the US charts. For a time, the US was hip to The Shangri-Las' groove and a series of 'teen angst' vignettes followed (🖛 *The Death Toll #1*).

Inevitably, after a unique moment like 'Leader', it was to be downhill for the group. The less-successful further songs prompted a 'tougher' image for The Shangri-Las, the flouncy dresses and sequins abandoned for catsuits or jeans, but their moment rapidly appeared to be over. Although they moved to the much larger Mercury label, The Shangri-Las' record sales continued to fall while early contract mishandling meant that the girls saw little of the money due to them from the bigger hits of yore. Margie quit the band in 1966 for this reason (and her group's incessant partying); The Shangri-Las – bar the odd reissue – were a spent brand by 1969.

The facts behind Mary Ann's sudden death in 1970 still, to this day, divide her fans, friends and family. For a long time, it was believed that she might have suffered from encephalitis brought on by a malignant mosquito bite, and that she died following an untreated seizure while visiting a friend. Others – including, allegedly, the Gansers' mother – suggest that Mary Ann had battled heroin addiction for the last two years of her life, an overdose of barbiturates causing her death at just twenty-two.

See also *Margie Ganser Dorste (🖛 July 1996)*

Monday 16

Tammi Terrell

(Thomasina Montgomery – Philadelphia, Pennsylvania, 29 April 1945)

The tale of soul vocalist Tammi Terrell is almost as tragic for her lack of real recognition during her short life as for her early death. A regular talent-show victor as a girl, the young Tammy Montgomery moved her audiences with a series of sublime, sensual performances and a voice that could melt the hardest heart touring with the prestigious James Brown Revue during the early sixties. Tammi Montgomery somehow still found time for her studies and, although romantically linked to Brown (and also to Temptation David Ruffin), she was believed to have married boxer Ernie Terrell (whose sister Jean replaced Diana Ross as a Supreme in 1970) while still a student at the University of Pennsylvania – though it's more likely that she took his name as it was easier to remember than her own. Brief stints with Brown's label and then with Checker were followed by a move to Berry Gordy's Tamla Motown in 1965, where Terrell was 'coupled' with

Marvin Gaye, the duo's voices proving an instant, magical hit: a series of classic takes followed, among them the 1967–8 international smashes 'Precious Love', 'You're All I Need to Get By' and 'Ain't Nothin' Like the Real Thing'.

It was on tour with Gaye in 1967, though, that Terrell learned the grave news of her physical condition. After collapsing on stage at Virginia's Hampton-Sydney College, she was diagnosed with a malignant brain tumour. Terrell continued to work until her death, recording her own (still greatly underrated) solo album, *Irresistible*, in 1968, but, following many operations, her health had deteriorated so profoundly that later duets with Gaye, such as 'The Onion Song' (1969), had to be rerecorded by writer/vocalist Valerie Simpson (of Ashford & Simpson). In her final months, Tammi Terrell was partially paralysed, blind and wheelchair-bound, her weight dropping to around 85 lbs. After her death, a month short of her twenty-fifth birthday, she was remembered by a devastated Marvin Gaye on his landmark 1971 album, the sombre and studied *What's Going On?*

See also *Marvin Gaye (🖛 April 1984)*

APRIL
Monday 13

Kid Thomas

(Lou Thomas Watts – Sturgis, Mississippi, 20 June 1934)

(The Rhythm Rockers)

Another prodigious practitioner of the harmonica, Lou Thomas Watts had moved to Chicago with his parents in 1941 and learned the instrument from bluesman Little Walter Smith;

in lieu of the payment he didn't have, 'Kid Thomas' traded his teacher the basics of drumming – his own early musical specialization! While still a boy, the increasingly wayward Thomas frequented adult environments, blowing the harp for the likes of Chicago greats Elmore James, Muddy Waters and Bo Diddley. By the late fifties he was recording for King-Federal, his raucous stylings often compared with those of Little Richard. The Kid's reputation was fast growing out of hand, however, the young blues prodigy pulling stunts such as stealing cars so that he and his band might make their gigs.

Thomas eventually settled in Los Angeles in 1960, forming a new band, The Rhythm Rockers, and cutting sides with Muriel Records. Sadly, these achieved no commercial recognition, and he returned to the gardening business he had started when younger, a well-stocked Beverley Hills-based address book keeping the wolf from the door. On 10 September 1969, however, his van struck and killed a 10-year-old cyclist, who died shortly after. Thomas – whose driving licence had already been revoked – was arrested and charged with manslaughter. When the case was controversially thrown out of court, though, the boy's father decided to take matters into his own hands. As the rest of the world was engaged in the unfolding drama of Apollo 13, Thomas waited outside a courtroom to face his licence aberration. Without warning, the bereaved parent appeared, pulled a gun from his jacket and shot the musician at close range. Kid Thomas died at 9.20 am at the Beverley Hills UCLA Medical Center – leaving a wife and his own young children.

JUNE

Thursday 11

Earl Grant
(Oklahoma City, Oklahoma, 20 January 1933)

Briefly the hottest property in lounge/R & B, organist Earl Grant also played trumpet and drums, and possessed a voice so dusky but pure it was assumed in many quarters that he must be related to Nat 'King' Cole. The truth is that Grant had had to work hard at his delivery, studying music at three universities where his specialization in keyboards developed. Scoring a 1958 Top Ten US hit with the single 'The End', Earl Grant then managed a half-million seller with his debut album for Decca, *Ebb Tide* (1961). He also featured in a number of movies, including Henry King's *Tender is the Night* (1962). On returning from a performance in Juarez, Mexico, Earl Grant was killed in a road accident as he passed through Lordsburg, New Mexico.

Tuesday 23

Grady Pannel
(Tennessee, 15 December 1949)
Electric Toilet
(The Herdsmen)

Wayne Reynolds
(Tennessee, 1949)
Electric Toilet

Vocalist and Wurlitzer/Moog-master Grady Pannel had been a member of The Herdsmen when he teamed up with songwriter/guitarist Dave Hall. The latter's brainchild, Memphis-based Electric Toilet, was completed by the addition of another guitarist, Wayne

Reynolds, the band's pulsating sound distinctive among early Southern US psychedelia. A suitably hippy-esque debut album, *In the Hands of Karma* (1969), was recorded for Nasco, picking up local airplay on Tennessee radio as the band began to develop some momentum. This impetus was sadly stopped in its tracks by the deaths of Pannel and Reynolds in a car crash the following year, Hall choosing to disband rather than continue the project. The only mystery remaining is how they ever decided on that name.

SEPTEMBER

Thursday 3

Alan 'Blind Owl' Wilson
(Boston, Massachusetts, 4 August 1943)
Canned Heat

A dark couple of months for US rock 'n' roll saw three of the key players at the 1967 Monterey Pop Festival die in 1970 – beginning with the shock suicide of Canned Heat vocalist Alan Wilson, a living, breathing blues/roots fanatic who existed solely for the music and his vast record collection. Wilson, brought up in Arlington, was a guitar/harmonica virtuoso from his youth who became so hell-bent on mastering his craft that he even accompanied Son House on his comeback album, *Father of the Blues* (1965). Recruiting fellow blues-obsessive, the redoubtable Bob 'The Bear' Hite, Wilson began a jug band of his own in 1966, while at college in Los Angeles. In came ex-Mothers of Invention guitarist Henry 'Sunflower' Vestine (another blues aficionado), bassist Larry 'The Mole' Taylor and drummer Frank Cook. Thus Canned Heat (the name lifted by Hite from a 1928 Tommy Johnson tune) was born. Co-led by Wilson's winsome falsetto and Hite's giant, rasping bass, the young band wowed the fans at Monterey the following year, surprising many by becoming the first white blues act to score a chart hit, the evocative 'On the Road Again' (1968) – a Wilson-reworked blues standard. This was quickly followed by a big-selling second album, *Boogie with Canned Heat*, by which time Cook had been replaced on percussion by Mexican Adolfo 'Fito' de la Parra. More hit records followed in the shape of the anthemic 'Going Up Country' (1968) and – following a triumphant headlining performance at Woodstock – Wilbert Harrison's more commercial 'Let's Work Together' (1970), which very nearly gave the world the unlikely sight of the Heat at UK number one.

But beneath success and critical acclaim there lay turmoil. While Detroit guitarist Harvey Mandel stepped in for the errant Vestine (who would later rejoin the band), Alan Wilson's health was causing the frontman concern. His bluesy nickname was no joke: Wilson's sight was so heavily impaired that it caused him frequent bouts of depression, for which he often sought pharmaceutical relief. Shortly before his death, Wilson had been admitted to a psychiatric clinic, but to no avail: on 3 September 1970, his body was discovered in a sleeping bag outside Bob Hite's California residence at Topanga Canyon, an empty bottle of tranquillizers by his side. Friends claimed he may have attempted suicide on at least three previous occasions. Canned Heat continued in various forms for the next thirty-plus years (Joe Scott Hill was Wilson's immediate replacement), clocking up a remarkable thirty-six studio albums in that time, though Wilson's original partner, Hite, died in his thirties (☛ *April 1981*), and Vestine later succumbed to one of the most rock 'n' roll deaths imaginable (☛ *October 1997*).

Jimi Hendrix

(Johnny Allen Hendrix – Seattle, Washington, 27 November 1942)
The Jimi Hendrix Experience
The Band of Gypsys
(Various acts)

'It's funny how most people love death. Once you're dead, you're made for life – you have to die before they think you're worth anything.' Jimi Hendrix, 1968

Whether in the guise of blues guitarist, psychedelic icon or smouldering ladies' man, we'll never see the like of James Marshall Hendrix again. The man trucked on in, lit a real big fire and then checked out before he'd had a chance to see what those flames might attract or indeed where they might catch next. Hendrix's own little inferno died there and then, music's loss now mythology's gain.

Despite Hendrix's denial of the fact (and even his occasional claim that the man wasn't his biological parent), his father loved both him and his body of work; the musician's estranged mother had died early, a victim of alcoholism. Al Hendrix – who had given his son his guitar and thus the identity that would capture the imagination of generations – was a pretty mean saxophone-player himself, accompanying the fledgling musician at home. Childish drawings of Elvis Presley showed from where Jimi Hendrix's love for rock 'n' roll stemmed, but he was also well educated in the blues, forming his own rhythm bands in Seattle while a teen. In his youth, he'd displayed many of the hallmarks of his future rock lifestyle, finding himself in trouble with the law and then earning a 'generous' medical discharge when a spell with the Kentucky-based 101st Airborne Division didn't quite work out (the tell-tale criticisms were that Hendrix 'was either asleep or thinking about his guitar'). The dismissal also meant that Hendrix was ineligible for combat when Vietnam reared its ugly head three years later; his work, however, was to be of considerable comfort to soldiers stationed there over the coming months. Hunting out the R & B scene in nearby Nashville, Hendrix moved there to play alongside heroes like Curtis Knight – the man generally accepted to have discovered Hendrix – and Little Richard.

Jimi Hendrix: In the studio, and out of it

Just ahead of his twenty-third birthday, Hendrix signed a three-year contract with Ed Chalpin that was later to cause him problems. As Jimmy James & The Blue Flames (originally The Rainflowers), Hendrix and his band – which featured a young Randy California, later of rock band Spirit – gained a residency at New York's Café Wha?, a Greenwich Village venue where his talent was at last likely to be unearthed by musicians who had the means to make a difference. Via a tip-off from Linda Keith (Rolling Stone Keith Richards's girlfriend), Hendrix met Animals bassist Chas Chandler, who offered him the chance to record 'Hey Joe', a song coincidentally already in the guitarist's oeuvre. Back in London – where Hendrix was to make his name first – word spread quickly among the heavyweights of rock and blues about this freaky US prodigy: a 'table napkin' deal was duly signed with Kit Lambert's Track label. Before 'Hey Joe' (1966) became a UK Top Ten hit, a jam session saw Hendrix wipe the floor with Eric Clapton; the Cream legend was initially nonplussed and muttered to his band-mates: 'You never told me he was *this* fucking good!' And Clapton was to be trumped once again – just a few months later, The Jimi Hendrix Experience's debut album, *Are You Experienced?* (1967), blew Cream's *Disraeli Gears* clean out of sight in Britain. In the States, the ride was not to be quite so smooth: on tour with fans The Monkees, Hendrix was heckled off stage, but, as a live act, The Experience were unlike anything rock 'n' roll had yet seen – and certainly *not* intended for teenyboppers. The stoic Noel Redding (bass) played straight man to the crazed antics of drummer Mitch Mitchell and, of course, the man at the centre of the fire. But, despite the mythologizing, Hendrix only performed the 'flaming guitar' trick three times, most famously at Monterey in 1967 – for many, the summit of Hendrix's live achievements.

Following this triumphant period there was inevitably a backlash; suffice to say, it began around mid 1967 and never let up. If the resurfacing of the Chalpin contract (about

which Lambert and Chandler knew nothing) was one small problem, the increased presence of drugs in Hendrix's daily routine was a greater one. Although he was a very likeable, unassuming person in the main, Hendrix soon revealed that he had much rage lurking within him. After a fraught tour of Scandinavia, the frontman fell out with the somewhat disapproving Redding, losing his temper, trashing a hotel room and getting himself busted for the first time. Things weren't much better back in London, either. Although most still found the music great – follow-up albums *Axis: Bold As Love* (1967) and the double *Electric Ladyland* (1968) were also astonishingly innovative – in the studio, Hendrix became more and more self-indulgent the more he used. Mentor and producer Chas Chandler finally quit when the guitarist was demanding as many as forty takes for a song and was still unsatisfied. A further split then occurred, from business partner Mike Jeffrey, a man believed by many to have embezzled much of Hendrix's money and to be linked to the Mafia.

In 1969, Hendrix's infamously 'arrogant' appearance on BBC television's *Happening For Lulu* show was followed by yet another highly publicized bust (heroin, this time) and a final split with Redding. Billy Cox took over bass in time for another landmark performance at Woodstock – the festival's loose organization left Hendrix and his new band, Gypsy Sun & Rainbows, playing to just 30,000 at 8 am on 18 August. Those who saw and heard the event witnessed something remarkable, however: Hendrix objected vehemently to the continued US presence in Vietnam, but instead of voicing his disapproval – as many had in the days preceding – he treated the audience to the most surreal, distorted version of 'The Star-Spangled Banner' on his prized Strat. Rumours persist that he had been spiked with powerful acid just ahead of the gig; whether this was or was not the case, it proved a chilling precursor to the sad, final events of the following year.

With Mitch Mitchell also gone, Hendrix began another short-lived project, The Band of Gypsys, with old pal Buddy Miles on drums; despite a memorable New Year gig at Fillmore East (documented on his last authorized album, issued in May 1970), they too went the way of all flesh before the end of January 1970. Although Mitchell returned to the fold, a European tour folded because Cox suffered a breakdown. Time, it seemed, was all but up. On the back of these problems, plus a commercial direction he felt was stifling his creativity, Hendrix began snorting heroin that summer. One of the last to see Jimi Hendrix alive was The Move's Trevor Burton, who described the star as 'out of it, with no one to look out for him': this appeared to be the case on 18 September. Monika Dannemann, an obsessive German 'fan' who had become more than just an acquaintance to Hendrix, had given him a handful of Vesperax sleeping pills, *nine* of which he foolishly ingested, with alcohol. The story from hereon is confused. Dannemann maintained for many years that Hendrix was still alive when she accompanied him in the ambulance to hospital – a claim refuted by another of the star's noted affiliates, Kathy Etchingham, who started legal action against Dannemann in the nineties. (As a result, the distraught Danneman committed suicide in 1996.) Police arriving at London's Samarkand Hotel the following morning definitely found Hendrix alone, lying dead in a pool of his own vomit. Perhaps the greatest musical talent of his generation was gone, in the saddest, most squalid way, the circumstances of which have been the subject of endless conjecture in the decades since, taking in suicide, medical incompetence – and even murder. But Jimi Hendrix was far from the drug-crazed control freak that some would have him, more a sensitive, misguided soul frustrated and finally slain by the myth that had been encircling him for some time – when all he wanted to do was play.

Hendrix was interred in Renton, Washington; friends held an impromptu jam session beside the open casket at his wake. In the UK, Hendrix became the latest post-humous chart-topper when his 'Voodoo Chile' went to number one two months after his death. Hendrix's estate, estimated at $80 million, was at the centre of an unseemly court battle: the singer's brothers – left out of the will – failed to secure any of the estate after Al Hendrix's death in 2002. Indeed, no relative on his mother's side has ever benefited, individuals unable even to agree where his casket rests, it having been 'moved' by his sister that year.

See also *Noel Redding (☞ May 2003)*

'People – whether they know it or not – like their blues singers miserable. Then they like them to die afterwards.'

Janis Joplin

Janis Joplin

(Port Arthur, Texas, 19 January 1943)

Big Brother & The Holding Company

Whether it was in her music, her beliefs or indeed in her sexual predilections, Janis Joplin always had another new barrier to break down. Despite its supposed manifesto of freedom for all, the hippy culture of the late sixties could be sexist and challenging; Joplin was one female figure who cut through this – just as her pure, strident tones had cut through the suffocating industrial air of her oil-refining home town all those years before.

'Don't compromise yourself – you are all you've got.' An unreconstructed rebel, Janis Joplin destroyed many of her own personal demons while railing against the wrongs she saw elsewhere. She hated segregation: one of her last actions was to buy a headstone to commemorate her heroine Bessie Smith – the blues singer refused access to a whites-only hospital when she was dying in 1937. The powerful tones of Smith were what initially drew Joplin to the blues, coming as she did from a background of, on the one hand, the country music played by her siblings, and on the other, the opera preferred by her parents. Joplin heard in Smith's a voice that could precipitate change (in whatever form), and set about exorcizing her 'sweet little chorister' image.

Janis Joplin's first battle, though, was with her own identity: she was an 'unlucky' teenager in that she was smitten with acne and developed what she felt was an unflattering figure. An outcast, she tended to fraternize with an unseemly element with which her burgeoning tearaway image made her popular. Joplin frequently flitted across the Texas border to Louisiana's forbidden world of cheap road-houses and live music (two of the four pastimes that would always remain her favourites). University days brought a second battle: although she joined her first band, she found herself voted 'Ugliest Man on Campus' by some basic types at Austin's University of Texas. The end result of such humiliating, low-rent sexism was that Joplin dropped out to work as a singer, her first step towards becoming the biggest female star in US rock – and, for many, the greatest white blues songstress of all time. Yet it very nearly didn't happen. Having lost an alarming amount of weight

Janis Joplin: Just caffeine and nicotine, this time, with since-departed friends Andy Warhol and Tim Buckley (➤ *June 1975*)

(mainly due to her use of amphetamines), Joplin returned to her parents' home in 1964, to try to neutralize her increasingly ripped-away lifestyle. Hard to imagine, but she tidied herself up, bought some dresses and even considered marriage and secretarial work. Two years later, though, Joplin was back on the scene: musician, poet and friend Chet Helms caught one of her ragged live performances and took the singer to San Francisco to meet Big Brother & The Holding Company, a so-so Bay Area band needing a vocalist (Joplin had already turned down The Thirteenth Floor Elevators). Big Brother guitarist Sam Andrews, who was to accompany Joplin through the remaining phases of her career, stated: 'It took her a year to learn to sing with us, and a year to dress the part. She was always gonna be one of the boys.' In spite of a largely forgettable first album, Big Brother featuring Janis Joplin knew how to party on stage, and – like Jimi Hendrix – were an absolute smash at Monterey in June 1967. One who thought so was Bob Dylan's manager, Albert Grossman, who managed them as a result, securing a deal with Columbia. A second album, under the abbreviated title of *Cheap Thrills* (originally *Dope, Sex and . . .*), crashed into the US charts, astonishingly topping them for two months – while spawning the huge hit single 'Piece of My Heart' (originally recorded by another of Joplin's inspirations, Etta Franklin). By now, however, Joplin had moved on. Encouraged to go solo by those who felt she was carrying Big Brother, she made a couple of

attempts at fashioning her own backing band, first with the sprawling Kozmic Blues Band and then, with greater success, the somewhat stripped-down but musically much-improved Full Tilt Boogie Band: John Till (guitars), Richard Bell (piano), Brad Campbell (aka Keith Cherry, bass), Ken Pearson (organ) and Clark Pierson (drums).

'On stage, I make love to 25,000 people. Then I go home alone.' As she became a major star in America, Joplin's performances became ever more explosive, more rampant, more sexually charged and more confrontational. Her renewed lifestyle of full-on sex, drugs and rock 'n' roll similarly showed little sign of letting up. Joplin had affairs and relationships with both men and women (not least Peggy Caserta, who documented most of their activities in her 'fuck and tell' journal, *Going down with Janis*). She drank to excess – usually tequila or Southern Comfort – and was described by stalwart Andrews as 'more aggressive, loud and belligerent than ever before' when inebriated. Given her caustic wit, this made for some interesting moments, one such being a stand-up fight with a female Hell's Angel (which she won, obviously), another her clouting of Jim Morrison with an empty bottle of Jim Beam and a third her appearance on NBC's *Dick Cavett Show*, where she warned former schoolmates of her imminent return for a tenth-year reunion: 'They laughed me out of class, out of town and out of state – so I'm goin' back!' In the event, it was to be her last visit to her family home.

It was Janis Joplin's voracious heroin intake that caused most disquiet among her colleagues. She was shooting up junk and had already overdosed non-fatally five times, but she found kicking the habit too much like painfully hard work and by mid September she was once again on the needle. On the evening of 3 October 1970, Janis Joplin returned from an arduous day at the LA studio where she was recording vocals with Doors producer Paul Rothchild for her latest, as yet untitled album. A track, 'Buried Alive in the Blues', was all set for her magic touch the following day. She needed to make up some ground following the less-than-ecstatically received *I Got Dem Ol' Kozmic Blues Again, Mama*, her last long-player. After leaving the studio, Joplin chugged down several Screwdrivers (by way of a change) with Pearson at Barney's Beanery on Santa Monica Boulevard before returning to Room 105 at the Landmark Hotel, Franklin Avenue, a well-known place for rock stars to hook up with their dealers. On this occasion, Joplin's supplier, George (her preferred dealer, for fear of receiving cut drugs), was, unbeknown to her, out of town and the heroin she picked up had not been pharmaceutically checked – at least, not by anyone she knew or trusted. Joplin bought a vending pack of cigarettes, took her change and returned to her room: she chose to skin-pop the drug, a method of injection that gives a delayed hit. Joplin was found, sixteen hours later, by her road manager, John Cooke: she was clearly dead, clad only in a blouse and underwear, with the change from the cigarette machine still clasped in her hand. Although Joplin appeared to have collapsed and hit her head on a nightstand, the likelihood is that the heroin (according to doctors, close to 40 per cent pure, as opposed to the street 'norm' of 1–2 per cent) killed her outright. Also found in the room was Joplin's 'hype kit' – gauze, cotton wool, a towel and syringe. Finally, a red balloon was 'returned' to Room 105: inevitably, it contained heroin.

The next evening, the numbed survivors of The Full Tilt Boogie Band retired to Clark Pierson's house to remember Janis Joplin and smoke a few joints in her name. With the extracted cut 'Me and Bobby McGee' making Janis Joplin the latest dead idol to have a number-one single, their album would be released, incomplete, as *Pearl*, Joplin's lifelong nickname. And it, too, would hold the US top slot – for nine weeks – with the track 'Buried Alive in the Blues' included as an instrumental.

Surviving Jimi Hendrix by just two weeks (☛ *September 1970*), Joplin had mused whether she might receive similar press coverage if she were to die. That said, there is no evidence to suggest her death was anything other than misadventure, thus suicide speculation and conspiracies should be ruled out.

The hotel, now known as the Highland Gardens, maintains that the ghost of Janis Joplin still inhabits Room 105.

Baby Huey

(James Ramey – Richmond, Indiana, 1944)
Baby Huey & The Babysitters

Never likely to see his old age, James Ramey was a huge presence in every sense: a glandular problem he suffered since childhood meant his weight was seldom below 350 lbs once he reached adulthood. Despite this, he was a tremendous soul performer in the Otis Redding tradition, loved locally in his adopted Chicago and nicknamed 'Baby Huey', after the giant cartoon duck popular in the fifties. Ramey was certainly a one-off, dressing as a schoolboy for some early Babysitters performances, while the Afro-sporting 6'1" giant was so incendiary on stage that a 1966 concert in Notre Dame had to be broken up by riot police. Ramey's career saw him shift from hard-line R & B into acid-laced soul as the sixties progressed, and The Babysitters' debut album for Curtis Mayfield's Curtom record label was finally recorded early in 1970. Ramey's heroin-related heart attack in Chicago's Roberts Motel meant that the singer never saw his first record issued, however: his body just wasn't able to stand the combination of his size and his appetite for illegal substances. Nevertheless, The Babysitters released *The Baby Huey Story – The Living Legend* and continued briefly with none other than a teenage Chaka Khan (whose husband was the group's bassist) as Ramey's replacement on vocals.

The Baby Huey rendition of Mayfield's 'Hard Times' has been sampled widely in recent years by, among others, A Tribe Called Quest on their 1991 hit 'Can I Kick It?'

DECEMBER

Wednesday 16

George 'Smitty' Smith

(Florida, 18 December 1939)

The Manhattans

Success didn't arrive for second-wave doo-wop/soul outfit The Manhattans until some years after the death of original lead vocalist, George 'Smitty' Smith. The group had evolved in 1960 from another Newark vocal unit called The Statesmen, developing a strong visual image that incorporated matching suits and white gloves accompanied by simple, synchronized dance movements. In New York, they were considered every bit as good as the more nationally revered Temptations and Spinners – and they boasted two great frontmen in Smith and Winfred 'Blue' Lovett. While Lovett co-wrote many of the group's hits, it was more often than not Smith's vocal that lifted the work a level above that of the era's scores of other vocal acts.

Perhaps pre-empting (or documenting) his own crippling illness, Smith utilized his extraordinary voice, awash with rich emotion and despair, on such early Manhattans sides as 'I'm the One That Love Forgot' and 'Follow Your Heart' (both 1965). His condition an open secret for some time, Smith died of spinal meningitis two days before his thirty-first birthday as The Manhattans began to fade from the spotlight. They returned with Gerald Alston assuming lead vocals, presaging a number of mid-seventies pop hits, including the US number one 'Kiss and Say Goodbye' (1976).

See also *Richard Taylor (➜ December 1987)*

Lest We Forget

Other notable deaths that occurred sometime during 1970:

Little David Baughan (US tenor vocalist who deputized for the drafted Clyde McPhatter in the original line-up of The Drifters; born in 1938; unknown)

George Bean (UK folk/rock singer with Trifle and the shamefully named George Bean & The Runners, who covered both Bob Dylan and The Rolling Stones, backing Lulu and Cat Stevens; unknown)

Neil Boland (UK chauffeur to The Who's Keith Moon; run over by his own car when non-driver Moon attempted to use it to escape angry skinheads, 4/1)

Tony Clarke (US soul singer signed to Chess Records; born New York, *c* 1944; believed murdered)

Ruth 'Baby Sis' Davis (US lead with gospel act The Davis Sisters; born 1927; despite a lifetime's devotion to their faith, four of the sisters died tragically, Ruth falling victim to diabetes/liver disease, 2/1)

George Goldner (US record boss who formed the labels Red Bird, End, Gee and Gone and worked with Little Richard and The Shangri-Las, among others; born New York, 1918; heart attack, 15/5)

Earl Hooker (US R & B/rock 'n' roll guitarist, second cousin to John Lee Hooker; born Mississippi, 15/1/1930; tuberculosis, 21/4)

Lonnie Johnson (US blues/jazz musician; born Louisiana, 8/2/1889; stroke, 16/6)

Alexander Sharp (US first tenor with pioneering vocal groups The Orioles and The Ink Spots; born 1919; surviving two Orioles car-crash incidents, he eventually succumbed to a heart attack, 1/1970)

Otis Spann (US blues pianist, Muddy Waters collaborator and house musician at Chess Records; born Mississippi, 21/3/1930; cancer 24/4)

For a complete list of fallen artists, visit

www.numberoneinheaven.com

The Death Toll #1

TUNING TO THE OTHER SIDE

'Mawk pop', 'death ditties', 'tearjerkers' – during the sixties, you simply had to have a cool young thing pop his or her clogs within your lyric. Better than any mentholated sweet, these tunes *really* cleared the sinuses all those years ago:

1 'Leader of the Pack'
The Shangri-Las (1965)

Finishing top of the pile can only be 'Betty's Jimmy' – though the leather-clad bad lad sounded more like he finished bottom of the pile, thanks to some highly melodramatic production from the legendary George 'Shadow' Morton. The four-way nasal whine of the fabby Shangri-Las – who became the genre's gurus – only added to the song's overall heart-wrenchingness, many listeners probably having experienced genuine motorbike crashes that were less traumatic. A bona fide classic – but you knew that.

2 'Johnny, Remember Me'
John Leyton (1961)

Many might remember Johnny's lover, but fewer recall *Harpers West One*, the ITV soap opera that launched actor/singer John Leyton on an unsuspecting public with this tie-in hit. Another belter, this record showcased the considerable talents of Joe Meek – very much the UK's own 'Shadow' Morton. Meek and composer Geoff Goddard claimed to have spoken to the late Buddy Holly in a séance – their bespectacled hero told them the song would go to number one. Which it did.

3 'Tell Laura I Love Her'
Ricky Valance/Ray Peterson (1960)

Despite US Top Ten status, Ray Peterson's version of Jeff Barry's seminal pile-up sob-inducer drew the ire of Christian groups, who thought it 'ungodly'. For young Welsh crooner David Spencer (recently renamed in deference to late singer Ritchie Valens), the stuff started to hit the fan when the BBC placed a ban on it after several

motorsport deaths that year – but it still lapped all opposition, ending the year in pole position. The song also spawned the first 'answer' record in the shape of Laura Lee's 'Tell Tommy I Miss Him' (1961) – another Meek production.

4 'Running Bear'
Johnny Preston (1960)

This transatlantic chart-topper – complete with ersatz whoops – recounted the melodramatic tale of the young brave and the target of his affections (a rival tribe's Little White Dove) who were pulled underwater as they attempted to consummate their love. Another story of Native American love came in the shape of Roy Orbison's 'Indian Wedding', whose tragic couple disappeared in the snow (yes, really) in lyrics too trite to bear repetition here.

5 'Teen Angel'
Mark Dinning (1960)

Shock, horror – Dinning's deceased driver was a *lady* – bringing another BBC ban for a record that had shifted over a million copies in the States. Boasting (if that's the correct verb) yet more of the crassest verses seen in pop music, 'Teen Angel' was co-written by Dinning's sister Jean – formerly of forties vocal sensations the imaginatively named Dinning Sisters. To those who know their work, this will make complete sense.

6 'Honey'
Bobby Goldsboro (1968)

Replete with heavenly choirs of angels, Goldsboro's US chart-topper (and twice UK runner-up) shifted mawk on some way technologically but never quite got around to telling us how Honey snuffed it. She'd already wrecked Bobby's car – so it couldn't have been that. I mean, *twice* would have been plain stupid.

7 'Ebony Eyes'
The Everly Brothers (1961)

The spin here was that 'Ebony Eyes' was a young bride-to-be killed in an air crash as she flew to marry her GI groom unable to secure leave for a ceremony at home. This

overly emotional sentimental fantasy was originally the B-side to the Brothers' 'Walk Right Back'.

8 'Terry'
Twinkle (1964)

Before The Shangri-Las, there was cute little Lynne Ripley – aka British vocalist Twinkle. Just ahead of the 'Leader of the Pack', a grease-stained, DA-sporting British biker arrived in the shape of 'Terry'. Like 'The Leader', Twinkle's fella rode his bike into oblivion – and he too left a less-than-adept chanteuse to cry at his graveside.

9 'And the Water Turned Red'
Johnny Cymbal (1963)

So to the murky depths of the chart. Popular crooner Johnny Cymbal (possibly not his real name) surfaced in 1963 with one of the most bizarre tearjerkers, the utterly over-the-top 'And the Water Turned Red'. A dozen years before *Jaws*, this song dared to describe the bloodied waves following a girl's death at the hands (teeth?) of a shark – and even had its bereft hero return to his dead girl's graveside with the creature's severed fin! It distinguished itself by reaching US #108 in 1963.

10 'I Want My Baby Back'
Jimmy Cross (1965)

Finally, a crude but nonetheless amusing 1965 pastiche of the death-ditty genre that saw its lead attempt to reunite with his dead girlfriend by jemmying open her coffin. The pair had crashed on the way home from a Beatles gig; Cross's baby was found 'over there' and 'over there' and 'over there' – you get the idea. The record's most notable airing was as chart-topper of Kenny Everett's Capital Radio *Bottom Thirty* (a hilarious 'worst records' countdown) more than a decade after issue.

1971

MARCH

Saturday 13

Arlester 'Dyke' Christian

(Buffalo, New York, 13 June 1943)

Dyke & The Blazers

(The Odd Squad)

'Funky Broadway' – as chunky a piece of New York soul as could be found in 1967 – was the catalyst record for the brief notoriety of Arlester 'Dyke' Christian's band, Dyke & The Blazers, the East Side's prime funk unit at the end of the sixties. When discovered, 'Dyke' Christian was merely a bean-pole street-gang kid who somehow just had the brass neck to carry it all off. Under the guidance of mas-termind Carl La Rue, Dyke & The Blazers stormed the chitlin circuit (New York's soul- and sleaze-loving clubs and bars), and with the steamy 'We Got Soul' and the of-its-time 'Let a Woman be a Woman, Let a Man be a Man' even managed a brace of national Top Forty hits in 1969. But Christian's street habits were hard to kick: though he had purchased a ranch house in Phoenix, he'd often be found hanging out or gambling with acquaintances from those days – and would in time develop something of a heroin dependency. Eventually, this caused the indirect dissolution of The Blazers.

Just ahead of a European tour with a new band, The Odd Squad, Arlester Christian found himself back on Broadway (Phoenix, this time) – and somehow in a disagreement with a man named Clarence Daniels. Rumour had it that Christian believed this man to be a police nark, though more likely he was a dealer to whom the soul man owed a lot of money. As their debate became more and more heated, Christian grabbed Daniels through the window of his 1963 Falcon; the driver then pulled a pistol, shooting the singer twice in the chest, once in the thigh and once in the temple. Arlester Christian was pronounced dead at around 3 pm. Despite the ferocity of Daniels's shooting, the gunman was acquitted of all charges that December, having 'acted in self-defence'.

Jim Morrison

(Melbourne, Florida, 8 December 1943)
The Doors

Jim Morrison: Back off, cop – it's just a microphone

From the lithe, barefoot nomad walking California's beaches to the ravaged figure found in his Paris bathtub just six years later, Jim Morrison was the complete artist. He wore rebellion as a badge, was obsessed with chaos and disorder, urgently compelled to push it all just that one stage further. Morrison was wilful, selfish and goading – yet at times the self-styled 'Lizard King' displayed deep integrity, warmth, no small love for others and a knowledge of what they had to offer. Morrison's unusual death only compounded a legend already close to fully grown.

Born into a military family that insisted upon achievement through strict discipline, James Douglas Morrison was a war baby; his father, Steve – who was to become the youngest admiral in the US navy – was away much of the time. Morrison's father disapproved of his son's diametrically opposed ideals, and the boy drifted away, never to return to the family fold. Indeed, as The Doors hit their stride and his mother, Clara, and brother, Andy, attempted to see the estranged star after a Washington concert, Morrison openly snubbed them. Morrison's world was his and his only, but even before fame allowed him the luxury of picking and choosing companions, he was making this kind of decision as a matter of course.

Much, however, has been made of one particular family experience spoken of by the singer. As a 4-year-old, Morrison travelled with his family from Santa Fe to Albuquerque (one of many addresses he knew growing up). On the journey, their car encountered an overturned truck and a group of injured and dying Pueblo Native Americans. Morrison was overwhelmed by the harrowing spectacle, claiming that the soul of one of the dead Pueblos had passed into his body at that moment. He believed that this event above all others gifted him his freedom of spirit, his desire to reach inside the soul and his urge to spread the values he felt were as essential as they were inflammatory. As a student at Florida State University, Morrison read Nietzsche, Rousseau and Sartre – though the texts that perhaps fired his imagination the most were those of French surrealist Antonin Artaud (who believed in the cathartic purification of man through adversity) and Norman O Brown, whose *Life Against Death* inspired Morrison with its Freudian reinterpretation of history as the result of man's hostility to life. Morrison believed one had to stretch one's own personal boundaries and to reject authority without qualm. His method of getting himself to the abyss was through his poetry and his performances, certainly – but the combined assistance of mind-altering substances and no shortage of people to help him indulge his every whim greatly hastened this achievement.

The name of his ground-breaking band came via two other Morrison gurus: borrowing from a William Blake couplet, writer Aldous Huxley called the account of his own drug experiences *The Doors of Perception*. This title gave Morrison a tag; he was after all, already a big hash-consumer and had experimented with hallucinogens. One of the friends he had made at UCLA while studying film was musician Ray Manzarek; the keyboard-player was bowled over by the intensity of this wayward spirit and his no-holds-barred poetry when Morrison knelt before him on Venice Beach spilling what would become 'Moonlight Drive'. Manzarek introduced Morrison to guitarist Robby Krieger and drummer John Densmore (of The Psychedelic Rangers). Bar mitzvahs and party shows became gigs at local bars, these giving way to a residence at the Whisky A Go-Go, the fabled venue on Sunset Boulevard, in 1966 just a year or two old itself. The Doors, as Morrison had desired, were well and truly 'open'. But this was no one-man show: the singer himself made it apparent to anyone who would listen that although he may have been the focal point The Doors were very much 'a group'. Manzarek was to prove a versatile keyboardist who drew inspiration from jazz and dance styles (the opening salvo of 'Break On Through' is pure bossa nova), while Krieger pretty much wrote early Doors' classic 'Light My Fire' on his own, and Densmore was an able pianist as well as percussionist. (Nevertheless, Manzarak and Krieger were to lose a legal battle with Morrison's family over use of the band name after they unveiled a new line-up – with former Cult vocalist Ian Astbury – three decades after the original singer's death.)

However, it was Morrison's stage antics that were most talked about by The Doors' increasing following. Relations were 'up and down' at the Whisky, where the singer often performed drunk – occasionally with his back to the crowd. But Elektra saw the potential in this extraordinary shaman who dominated the stage with three decidedly leftfield-looking musicians improvising around him. By 1967, The Doors were dubbed America's Rolling Stones, though this band was to add a dimension of 'art academia' to the familiar pattern of sleaze-soaked rhythm and blues. As first album *The Doors* began to climb the charts (the sleeve notes claimed his family were 'dead'), Morrison was courted by the press, who found the 'erotic politician' (his words) good for a quote. Produced by the highly rated Paul Rothchild, this debut eventually hit number two across the USA, selling a million copies in the process. Its second single, 'Light My Fire', went to Billboard number one in July 1967 (a trick they pulled off a second time with 'Hello, I Love You' the following summer). As unlikely as it seemed, Los Angeles' most uncompromising band were now stars; Morrison marked the occasion by getting royally drunk and buying the tightest black-leather outfit in California, but his apparent disaffection with pop stardom was already evident as Doors-mania caught on around him like a forest fire. The one saving grace of fame, as he saw it, was the extended opportunity to antagonize authority ('I am the Lizard King – I can do anything!'). His disregard of TV host Ed Sullivan's wishes by singing the banned word 'higher' (in 'Light My Fire') on his show is just one example, the regular goading of officers at The Doors' by-now heavily policed concerts another. And more was to follow.

'If you can get a whole roomful of drunk, stoned people to actually wake up and think, you're doing something.' This was the thrust of much of Morrison's rhetoric over the years. It may well have been the case, but by 1969 Morrison was almost perpetually 'gone' himself: his indulgences hit previously unseen heights and studio sessions were wasteful; performances, similarly, started to descend into mayhem. To Morrison, though, this was all part of the deal, and a March concert in Florida proved a pivotal point in his career. He had been 'inspired' by recent performances of Artaud's work involving chaos and public nudity. He had also been drinking heavily on the flight to Miami, and, like the rest of The Doors, was angered by the venue's attempts to take money from them. As his rapidly wearying band started up the strains of 'Touch Me', Morrison apparently decided to take his own lyric a shade literally. Whirling drunkenly about the stage, Morrison taunted his audience – 'You're all a bunch of fuckin' idiots! How long you gonna be pushed around?' – who lapped it up regardless. Then, in one of rock's most infamous incidents, he tantalized the crowd further by offering to reveal his genitals. Whether he actually did this or not has never been ascertained; although he was arrested soon after the performance, the trial lasted a year and a half and Morrison was eventually sentenced to a total of eight months' hard labour and a $500 fine. Of course, he didn't live long enough to endure this punishment.

After the drawn-out trial, Jim Morrison decided The Doors' sixth studio album (*LA Woman*, 1971) was to be his last with the band. He was tired of the circus of which he'd long been ringmaster and wished to devote his time to other media projects – in particular his resonant, lurid poetry, which had already gained favourable attention. Morrison and his long-term, on-off partner, Pamela Courson (who'd adopted his name early on), moved to Paris in March. Here, the couple seemed at ease, the pressures of fame and the law, as well as their continued infidelity to one another back in California, diminishing with the late-afternoon sunlight as it played on the Seine. Sometimes they lived at the hotel where another Morrison hero, Oscar Wilde, had died – at others in an apartment at 17 rue Beautreillis.

But, by summer, Courson had become disquieted by a drop in Morrison's mood. She and Morrison's US friend Alan Ronay did their best to distract the singer during supper on the evening of 2 July, but it was clear all was far from well. After a silent meal, Morrison may have gone alone to see the Robert Mitchum movie *Pursued* at a local cinema, or perhaps to the Rock 'n' Roll Circus (a bar by the Seine), or he may have returned straight home to the apartment. One fact that seems fairly conclusive is that when he complained of 'feeling ill' Courson drew Morrison a bath – and found his dead body still immersed next morning. Whether he had overdosed on heroin remains an unanswered question: his body was already sealed in a coffin before a reliable post mortem could be performed. What seems most likely is that years of alcohol and drug abuse finally took their toll on a man who was only twenty-seven but 'felt bloated and forty-seven'. (Shortly before her own 1974 death from an overdose, Courson allegedly confessed to Morrison biographer Danny Sugerman that she had administered Morrison a 'fatal shot of heroin'.) So Morrison succumbed to the heart attack he himself had anticipated towards the end. He'd refused medical assistance that same evening.

Jim Morrison was buried privately on 7 July at Père Lachaise cemetery, alongside Edith Piaf, Oscar Wilde and Balzac. His headstone has long featured not only his name but also those of hundreds of fans from around the world (French authorities are thus keen to have it removed to the USA). Morrison's words continue to sell records, while Oliver Stone's 1991 biopic *The Doors* gives a vibrant, if distorted, view of the artist's life. (The latter also provoked The Doors' first ever UK Top Ten hit with the reissued 'Light My Fire'.)

In his later writing, Jim Morrison fantasized about faking his death and starting again as Mr Mojo Risin' – an anagram of his name. And there will always be those who maintain Mr Mojo Risin', the Lizard King, the 'erotic politician' – or just plain old Jim – cocked that ultimate snook and is still around today . . .

See also *Danny Sugerman (☞ January 2005)*

'You're drinking with Number Three.'
Jim Morrison, to friends after hearing of Hendrix and Joplin's deaths

Sunday 4

Don McPherson
(Indianapolis, Indiana, 9 July 1941)
Main Ingredient

Former Harlem school-friends Main Ingredient began their musical life as The Poets in the mid sixties, this mellow, soulful R & B act the brainchild of Don McPherson. McPherson took his place as the combo's lead singer, his passionate vocal reminiscent of that of Smokey Robinson. Signing to Red Bird, the singer and his cohorts, Cuba Gooding (briefly), Enrique Sylvester and Luther Simmons Jr enjoyed a number-two R & B hit with 'She Blew a Good Thing' before changing the band's name to The Insiders. Their ultimate name, Main Ingredient, was the choice of the label (allegedly taken from the blurb on a Coke bottle). However, after two well-received long-players, Don McPherson was diagnosed with leukaemia.

McPherson's early death preceded the flurry of US pop hits enjoyed by the group (beginning with 1972's platinum-selling 'Everybody Plays the Fool', for which lead vocals were taken by the returned Gooding). Main Ingredient split in 1976, though re-formed versions toured for a further twenty or so years.

AUGUST

Wednesday 11

Lefty Baker
(Eustace Britchforth – Miami, Florida,
7 January 1942)
Spanky & Our Gang
(The Folkers)
(The Bitter End Singers)

Spanky & Our Gang was a US har-
mony/pop group, among rock 'n'
roll's first acts to lose two members
in separate circumstances. The band
– loosely termed Chicago's Mamas &
The Papas – had been formed by blues
singer Elaine McFarlane and musicians
Oz Bach, Malcolm Hale and Nigel
Pickering. Often dressed in flowing
robes and wearing the requisite thick
moustache, guitarist Lefty Baker
replaced Bach for the group's final
chart outings for Mercury, 'Sunday
Mornin'', 'Like to Get to Know You'
and 'Give a Damn' (1968), shortly
after which Hale passed away suddenly
(◄ *October 1968*). This, and lessening
interest in them, ended Spanky & Our
Gang as a going concern.

   Baker's own untimely death from
cirrhosis of the liver in Burbank,
California, came about a year or so
after he left Spanky & Our Gang. He
had attempted to launch a couple of
new bands and was also overseeing his
own recording studio.

See also *Oz Bach (☞ September 1998)*

Friday 13

King Curtis
(Curtis Ousley – Fort Worth, Texas,
7 February 1934)
The Coasters
The Kingpins
The Noble Knights

Young prodigy 'King' Curtis Ousley
was seen as jazz saxophone's *enfant terrible* when he forced his way into Lionel
Hampton's band as a freshman; after
all, he'd hawked his tenor sax around
the streets of his home town from the
age of twelve and utterly believed his
time had come. Having turned down
a scholarship to tour with Hampton,
Ousley moved to New York, earning a good living as a session-player.
Crossing over to rock 'n' roll, Curtis
formed his own band, King Curtis &
The Noble Knights (later the Aretha
Franklin-backing Kingpins), though
Ousley's most-noted work was on the
hits of others, of which fifteen charted
on Billboard during his career. His fantastic playing with The Coasters is best
illustrated by the sax break that illu-
minates their biggest hit, 'Yakety Yak'
(1958). Before his death, King Curtis
featured prominently on the recordings of Nat 'King' Cole, Buddy Holly,
Wilson Pickett, Sam & Dave, Eric
Clapton and The Isley Brothers.

   A few months after guesting on
John Lennon's 1971 *Imagine* album,
Curtis Ousley found himself, like
most New Yorkers, suffering in a
severe August heatwave. Lugging an
air-conditioning system to his apartment on West 86th Street, Ousley's
path was blocked by two drug-using
vagrants. Asking them to move, the
musician was met with aggression and
attacked with a knife: convicted felon
Juan Montanez inexplicably stabbed
Ousley in the heart. Although he
managed to disarm Montanez – and
indeed stab him with his own weapon

King Curtis: See – it was official

– King Curtis was dead on arrival at
the Roosevelt Hospital. His funeral
was a gathering of the good and the
great – a Kingpins' set was followed
by a spiritual sung by Aretha Franklin;
also in attendance were Jesse Jackson,
Stevie Wonder and Duane Allman
(himself killed just two months later
(☞ *October 1971*)). Montanez was later
convicted of Ousley's murder.

   Despite The Coasters being the
top knockabout vocal group of their
day, many associated with them met
some truly shocking fates through the
years, among them touring vocalist
Nathaniel 'Buster' Wilson (☞ *April
1980*) and long-time frontman Cornell
Gunter (☞ *February 1990*), both of
whom were also murdered.

See also *Bob B-Soxx (☞ November 2000).
Original Coasters Will 'Dub' Jones (2000)
and Billy Guy (2002) have also passed on
– as have touring singers Randy Jones and
Darrell Reynolds (both 2002) and sometime
drummer Gerald Baxter (2003).*

Gene Vincent: Butter wouldn't melt ...

'Gene was a very sad, pathetic person. He was suicidal even before the accident. I wondered why God didn't just pick Gene then.'

Eddie Cochran's girlfriend, Sharon Sheeley, after the crash that killed her lover

OCTOBER

Tuesday 12

Gene Vincent

(Vincent Eugene Craddock – Norfolk, Virginia, 11 February 1935)

Gene Vincent & The Blue Caps

One of rock 'n' roll's first maverick pin-ups, Gene Vincent is often wrongly cast as a slighter performer than many of his contemporaries. To many though, he seemed the real McCoy, the embodiment of what their parents apparently feared. Not for him the compromise of a balladeering Elvis, or the studied melody of a Buddy Holly – Gene Vincent felt like the terse, brooding rebel who might just as likely put a knife to your upholstery as steal a kiss.

Throughout his life, Vincent was known for his changeable moods, dogged as he was by a serious leg injury incurred when he was a young naval motorbike courier in 1953. The extended lay-off while recuperating, however, honed his guitar skills and vocal styling. Gene Vincent was performing in Virginia nightclubs before he was even out of plaster – and, though he required a steel leg brace thereafter, he made the transition to rock 'n' roll star surprisingly smoothly. By 1956 he'd formed The Blue Caps (initially The Virginians) and – with the backing of Capitol, clearly hungry to land an Elvis of their own – put his *pièce de résistance*, the reverb-soaked Don Graves song 'Be-Bop-a-Lula', high into the national listings. Vincent's concurrent appearance in the classic rock 'n' roll picture *The Girl Can't Help It* and his riotous private life – he would marry four times – cemented his position as the genre's wildest boy.

Vincent continued to be in favour at home, though a storming follow-up single, 'Race with the Devil', probably failed to chart because the word 'devil' placed fear in the hearts of radio programmers. In Japan and Europe – particularly in a UK no longer content with toothsome types like Tommy Steele – moody Gene Vincent was just the ticket. A 1960 tour with his buddy and fellow rock heart-throb Eddie Cochran had Britain's faithful Teddy boys and their dolls foaming at the mouth with anticipation. But, after triumphant performances, the tour ended horrifically in Wiltshire when the car containing Cochran and Vincent crashed on 17 April 1960: Cochran died from his injuries (*Pre-1965*). Despite having broken an arm, Vincent carried Cochran to the ambulance, but further aggravated injury to his leg left him in pain and limping for the rest of his life. By 1967 Vincent had virtually retired, the hits having dried up in Britain as well. The now-ex-pat singer became more and more reliant on alcohol as well as aspirin to stem the physical pain and emotional frustration that almost constantly hindered a performer still supposedly in his prime. A quick-tempered man at the best of times, Vincent was now prone to severe outbursts of temper, though a brief revival of his career fortunes at the end of the decade saw the star tour again and befriend hard-drinking rocker Jim Morrison – a huge Vincent fan who had adopted many of his onstage mannerisms and who died the same year (*July 1971*). The pair were frequently seen at the now-infamous Shamrock Bar on LA's Santa Monica Boulevard. (When The Doors chose him as their support at the 1969 Toronto Festival, Vincent was backed by even-more-rebellious types in the shape of Alice Cooper's band.)

Vincent made his final return to the USA in the autumn of 1971, a shadow of the coolly sullen waif who had set rock 'n' roll so firmly on course over a decade before. When his concerned parents visited the singer at his California home, Vincent was still suffering the after-effects of a three-day drinking binge combined with a 'diet' of little more than the tomato juice that made up his larder; clearly distressed, he turned to allow them into his home and tripped, falling and bursting his chronic stomach ulcers. Vomiting blood, Gene Vincent was admitted to the Newhall Community Hospital where he died within an hour. Vincent's mother, Mary Craddock, later stated: 'He wore the sweetest smile – he wanted to die. He was glad to think he was getting out of the mess he was in.'

Gene Vincent was awarded a star on the Hollywood Walk of Fame (while still alive), and was finally inducted into the Rock 'n' Roll Hall of Fame in 1998. He is, of course, recalled in one of the finest tribute songs of all time: Ian Dury & The Blockheads' 'Sweet Gene Vincent' (1978).

See also *Cliff Gallup (*☞ *October 1988); Max Lipscomb (*☞ *March 1991); Willie Williams (*☞ *August 1999); Paul Peek (*☞ *April 2001). Other Blue Caps Grady Owen (1999), Jerry Lee Merritt (2001) and Juvenal Gomez (2002) have also died.*

Friday 29

Duane Allman

(Howard Duane Allman – Nashville, Tennessee, 20 November 1946)

The Allman Brothers Band
(The Hour Glass)
(Various acts)

The somewhat nebulous term 'Southern rock' covers a number of bands who played R & B/blues-based guitar music; Duane Allman and his younger brother Gregg formed the band most fondly remembered of the genre. To overcome the loss of

their father in the Korean War one Christmas when they were small, the brothers immersed themselves in the classic sounds of the blues and contemporary acts like The Beatles and Otis Redding, bored with the beach pop that soundtracked their Daytona upbringing. Though he was taught to play by his younger brother, it was Duane Allman who really had 'natural fire', his slide-guitar style unlike anything heard before, making him Muscle Shoals' top session man. By hanging with black musicians, the Allmans had broken the taboos of the era (as The Hour Glass); Duane Allman enforced this by playing behind various soul acts, not least Aretha Franklin and Wilson Pickett. He, of course, trademarked the early Allman Brothers sound, which fully came together when the band – the brothers (various instruments), Berry Oakley (bass), Dick Betts (guitar/ vocals), Butch Trucks and 'Jaimoe' Johnny Johanson (both drums) – made its way to Macon, Georgia. Promoting a 'brotherhood' ethic, the Allmans insisted each member tattoo a mushroom on his ankle, and the hallucinogenic reference soon became very evident in the music, while much of the first album was composed in a local graveyard. Their eponymous debut was eventually cut in New York to rapturous acclaim, and promoter Bill Graham installed the band at his Fillmore venues, their extraordinary, snaking jams making up a series of early live albums. Somehow, Duane Allman found time to record with others, including Eric Clapton – it is his slide work that adorns Derek & The Dominoes' 'Layla' (1971).

For the guitarist, though, it was an all-too-short session under the spotlight. During the recording of what is widely considered The Allman Brothers' artistic high, *Eat a Peach* (1972), the band took a break to celebrate the birthday of Oakley's wife. At 5.30 pm on 29 October 1971, Allman took off on his Harley

Davidson to pick up a birthday cake and gifts from his house, followed in cars by girlfriend Dixie, plus Oakley and his sister. Allman was speeding as he headed west from Macon, when the appearance of a flat-bed pipe truck caused him to swerve, skidding ninety feet across the intersection to avoid collision. Losing his helmet and falling under his bike, Allman incurred massive internal injuries, possibly exacerbated by the frantic intervention of truck-driver Charles Wertz. The musician was rushed to Macon Medical Center where, although revived twice, he died in surgery three hours after the incident.

The Allman Brothers Band played at their leader's funeral three days later, deciding to continue in his memory. Just over a year later, Oakley – who had become the band's unofficial new frontman – met an eerily similar fate just one mile from the site of Allman's crash (☞ *November 1972*); legal disputes having kept Allman's body in storage since his death, it was decided to bury the two friends side by side at the Rose Hill Military Cemetery in Macon.

See also *Lamar Williams (*☞ *January 1983); Allen Woody (*☞ *August 2000)*

The Allman Brothers Band – Trucks, Oakley, Johanson, Allman G, Allman D and Betts: Already in deep water

Lest We Forget

Other notable deaths that occurred sometime during 1971:

Louis Armstrong (formidable US jazz musician/ vocalist 'Satchmo' scored US and UK #1 pop hits with 'Hello Dolly' and 'What a Wonderful World' respectively; born Louisiana, 4/8/1901; heart attack, 6/7)

Reverend Roy Blackwood (US gospel singer and founder member of The Blackwood Brothers, who were close associates of Elvis Presley; born Mississippi, 24/12/1900; natural causes, 21/3)

Charlie Fuqua (US singer and founder member of vocal legends The Ink Spots; born Connecticut, 20/10/1910; unknown, 21/12)

Wynton Kelly (noted US jazz/R & B pianist who played with Dizzy Gillespie and later Miles Davis; born Jamaica, 2/12/1931; epileptic seizure, 12/4)

Leslie Kong (Jamaican producer who worked with Bob Marley, Jimmy Cliff, Desmond Dekker and The Melodians among others – he somehow also ran an ice-cream parlour; born 1933; heart attack, 9/8)

'Papa' George Lightfoot (US blues vocalist/ harmonica-player who worked with Fats Domino; born Mississippi, 2/3/1924; heart attack and respiratory failure, 28/11)

Harold McNair (Jamaican jazz-trained saxophonist/ flautist who played with Cressida, Donovan and Ginger Baker's Airforce; born Kingston, 5/11/1931; lung cancer, 26/3)

'Boll Weevil' Bill Moore (US bluesman; born North Carolina, 22/4/1913; bronchopneumonia, 2/5)

Herman 'Little Junior' Parker (US blues harmonica-player with The Beale Streeters, who played with Howlin' Wolf; born Arkansas, 3/3/1927; died during surgery for a brain tumour, 18/11)

Thomas Wayne Perkins (US rockabilly singer who scored in 1959 with 'Tragedy'; born Minnesota, 22/7/1940; car crash – three years after the tragic death of his guitarist brother Luther, 15/8)

Francis Wolff (German-born label executive and co-founder of New York's Blue Note Records; heart attack, 8/3)

For a complete list of fallen artists, visit

www.numberoneinheaven.com

JANUARY

Sunday 16

David Seville
(Ross S Bagdasarian Sr – Fresno, California,
27 January 1919)

Known primarily for his novelty output, Seville was a respected rockabilly musician and writer during his early music career: success for Rosemary Clooney with Seville's co-written 'Come on-a My House' (1951) then gave the artist scope to promote

David Seville & The Chipmunks: Presumably worked for peanuts

his own work. As fictitious double act Alfi & Harry, he signed with the Los Angeles label Liberty, getting an unexpected UK Top Twenty hit with 'The Trouble with Harry' (1955). Three years on, Seville hit paydirt using his own (assumed) name with a US number one, the very odd 'Witch Doctor', the first of many records to employ a double-speed vocal track. Winning three Grammy awards, Seville also acted under his real name in several movies, including Alfred Hitchcock's *Rear Window*.

Seville's most enduring commercial success, however, was with The Chipmunks – a mildly irritating rodent trio (named after three of Liberty's executives) that became popular with young television audiences. Astonishingly, Seville saw himself once again at US number one with 'The Chipmunk Song' – and the million-seller held that position for a month early in 1959. Perhaps blazing a trail for The Wombles and Smurfs to follow, the buck-toothed cartoon trio then managed a further seven Top Forty hit singles to 1963. Seville also released a good number of Chipmunks albums during the sixties (*The Chipmunks Sing The Beatles*; anyone?). By the time of his premature death from a heart attack in Hollywood, Seville had shifted over 30 million records. The characters were resurrected by Ross Bagdasarian Jr in 1980.

Mahalia Jackson
(New Orleans, Louisiana, 26 October 1911)

The undisputed Queen of Gospel was born into the family of a Southern Baptist minister; sadly her mother died when she was just five. The granddaughter of slaves, Mahalia Jackson was working full-time by age sixteen, and singing for her faith – the beauty of her rich, near-faultless contralto lifting the hearts of many during the Depression.

Relocating to Chicago in 1927, she joined the Greater Salem Baptist Church – collaborating with 'Father of Gospel' Thomas Dorsey – and toured with a quintet before carving out her own niche as a solo recording artist with Decca and Apollo. Because she refused to follow the nightclub route into the world of secular music (unlike later singers Sam Cooke and Aretha Franklin), Jackson arguably became the most influential black gospel performer to those that came afterwards, and also introduced a generation of white listeners to the genre. It should be remembered, too, that in those times gospel often sold in quantities that dwarfed sales of other musical styles: Jackson's mid-thirties hit

Mahalia Jackson: Even Aretha looked up to her

'A voice like this comes not once in a century, but once in a millennium.'

Martin Luther King

'I Will Move on up a Little Higher', for instance, shifted over a million copies. By 1954 her importance was finally recognized by large label Columbia, while her influence extended well beyond her music: Jackson was a close ally of Martin Luther King, and frequently joined the black civil rights activist on his crusades – in particular the Alabama bus boycott of 1955, at which she performed. During her career, Jackson sang before four US presidents – and her astute business acumen also saw her launch a successful chain of chicken restaurants.

Jackson's relentless work ethic had a detrimental effect during her final years. After a lifelong battle with high blood pressure, she died from heart failure in Evergreen Park, Chicago, at the age of sixty. Devotee Aretha Franklin sang 'Precious Lord, Take My Hand' at her New Orleans funeral.

MARCH

Tuesday 14

Linda Jones
(Newark, New Jersey, 14 January 1944)

Just weeks after the death of one of the genre's true giants, gospel-trained singer Linda Jones passed away at just twenty-eight. While clearly not in the same league as Mahalia Jackson, Jones was nonetheless a veritable vocal gymnast whose melodramatic performances (initially for MGM as Linda Lane) made her a favourite with soul audiences throughout the late sixties. She was also an instigator of the now-maligned practice known as 'melisma' (the spreading of a note over several syllables). Though her biggest hit was with 1967's 'Hypnotized', it's said that there was no sound reproduction equipment at the time that could withstand the awesome first thirty seconds of her 'Not on the Outside'!

Linda Jones – a noted influence on Gladys Knight, Chaka Khan and Patti Labelle – struggled to finish a concert at New York's Apollo Theater and collapsed backstage, dying later of complications arising from diabetes.

APRIL

Thursday 27

Phil King
(c 1947)
Blue Oyster Cult

Long Island heavy/prog band Blue Oyster Cult are often referred to as 'the thinking man's rock band' – which perhaps makes Phil King's death all the more unlikely.

Beginning as Soft White Underbelly in the late sixties, the group formed by influential musician and writer Sandy Pearlman at Stony Brook College would run through an enormous number of members in its lengthy history. In their formative years, Blue Oyster Cult (apply umlauts as appropriate) found the position of vocalist the hardest to fill. BOC signed, briefly, to Elektra, the label that had enjoyed enormous success with The Doors over the previous years; it was believed that singer Les Bronstein had a similar presence to that of Jim Morrison. However, Bronstein suddenly quit, leaving the door open for a series of frontmen, of whom the shortest-lived was probably Phil King.

King was not considered reliable by the other members of the group and had already left by the release of their eponymous debut for CBS (1972) – the vacant slot was taken by the band's manager, Eric Bloom. The wayward King had fallen into a twilight world of drink and gambling, and it was during such a session that he was murdered in New York, shot three times in the back of the head following an argument.

MAY

Wednesday 3

Les Harvey
(Leslie Harvey – Glasgow, 1947)
Stone the Crows
(Various acts)

The somewhat-less-flamboyant younger of the rocking Harvey brothers, Les joined his first band, The Kinning Park Ramblers, at just sixteen. By eighteen, the hard-working guitarist/songwriter was playing with The Blues Council, a touring combo

that disbanded after the tragic deaths of two of its members, singer Fraser Calder and bass player James Giffen (☞ *March 1965*). Les Harvey's demise, however, was even more dramatic.

Introduced to no-holds-barred rock/blues singer Maggie Bell by his brother, Harvey's fortunes changed when he joined Power, soon to become Stone the Crows, a popular live act managed by Led Zeppelin boss Peter Grant. Harvey's textural yet dynamic playing was as key to the act as the duelling vocals of Bell and Jimmy Dewar; his Les Paul technique had been noted elsewhere, and a touring stint with Aretha Franklin's band ensued in 1971. With a fourth album *Ontinuous Performance* [sic] for a new line-up of Stone the Crows in pre-production, the band played a low-key tour of the UK in the spring of 1972. Tuning up at the start of a performance at Swansea's Top Rank Ballroom, Les Harvey grasped a poorly grounded microphone and was electrocuted. As 1,200 expectant fans looked on, Harvey collapsed at the front of the stage in what for many years would be rock music's most public tragedy. He died in hospital, where girlfriend Bell was also receiving treatment. Catastrophe continued to haunt those connected with Harvey: replacement guitarist in Stone the Crows Jimmy McCulloch also died in tragic circumstances (☞ *September 1979*), as indeed did Les's older and better-known brother, Alex Harvey (☞ *February 1982*).

See also *James Dewarl (☞ May 2002)*

JUNE

Tuesday 13

Clyde McPhatter
(Durham, North Carolina, 15 November 1932)
The Drifters
(Billy Ward & The Dominoes)

Despite his relatively brief fame, the importance of an artist like Clyde McPhatter to later vocalists like Smokey Robinson should not be underestimated; another Baptist minister's child, McPhatter's resonant tenor was largely the result of his gospel training. He made the move to R & B, very much the flavour in 1950, fronting Billy Ward & The Dominoes at just seventeen. McPhatter (and indeed his fans) reached near-hysteria during his stage performances, so involved was he in his music, and The Dominoes quickly became a 'name', charting many songs on the US R & B listings – their racy 'Sixty-Minute Man' was 1951's number-one seller. They did not see national pop success until after his departure, however, because in 1953 – after a number of salary disputes with Ward – the popular lead upped sticks for Atlantic Records. (Legend has it that, on the very day of the split, label supremo Ahmet Ertegun telephoned every McPhatter in New York City until he found his man.) Here, McPhatter formed the soon-to-be-legendary vocal troupe The Drifters. (The Dominoes, meanwhile, consoled themselves with new boy Jackie Wilson at the helm.) Had he not been drafted in May 1954, Clyde McPhatter would probably have become a major international star with Atlantic. However, while he served in the army, the touring Drifters were fronted by 'soundalike' David Baughan, and on his return McPhatter decided to call time on the group. Several solo successes ensued with Atlantic and Mercury – including the 1958 gold disc 'A Lover's Question' – but the impetus of his earlier career had been stalled, and no hit records were forthcoming after 1962. Further labels shed the once-great singer like a hand-me-down jumper.

Clyde McPhatter's spiralling depression at his lack of longevity caused him to resort to the bottle, his health deteriorating at an alarming rate over the last years of his life. In 1972, having failed to relaunch his career, he was discovered dead by his female companion in a cheap Bronx hotel. McPhatter, already stricken with a variety of kidney and liver ailments, had suffered a heart attack in his sleep. No longer a star, McPhatter was – after Rudy Lewis and Baughan – already the third former Drifter to pass on (➤ *Pre-1965/Dead Interesting!*) though his death was shockingly overlooked by the media. Some semblance of proportion was reached, however, with his induction into the Rock 'n' Roll Hall of Fame fifteen years later.

JULY

Monday 24

Bobby Ramirez
(Mexico, 1949)
Edgar Winter's White Trash
(Various acts)

Few personal details are known of Bobby Ramirez, a young rock drummer who began playing at fourteen, performing and recording with LaCroix and Rick Derringer, as well as cutting two records with Edgar Winter's first band, White Trash. The story of his terrible death, however, has recently been made public.

White Trash were enjoying a successful US tour with British prog outfit Uriah Heep, a particularly well-attended show at Chicago's Rosemont Hall putting the bands in celebratory mood. It's unlikely the city's downtown area had seen so many long-hairs and prog-rockers in one place – although this offers little excuse for the barbaric reception given to Bobby Ramirez. After watching a performance by female rockers Bertha, Ramirez excused himself to the toilets, where a man using the facilities took exception to his coiffure, suggesting he might choose to use the ladies' room. Ramirez retorted, and the man punched him, drawing blood. While the club-owner attempted to calm the situation and usher the musicians away, the understandably incensed Ramirez wanted to involve the police. When this was refused, the young percussionist took matters into his own hands, and followed his attacker into the night. It proved a costly decision: band member Jerry LaCroix, who was also assaulted, described coming round only to see Bobby Ramirez bloody and lifeless in the arms of the band's road manager. The assailant – like Ramirez, of Mexican descent – had used a pointed, steel-tipped shoe to injure his victim, and he had not been alone, suggesting that this attack had been premeditated.

See also *Randy Jo Hobbs (➤ August 1993)*

AUGUST

Brian Cole
(Tacoma, Washington, 8 September 1944)
The Association

Originally a thirteen-piece folk/comedy unit called The Men, the 'trimmer' Association enjoyed US number-one hits and no small amount of critical acclaim. Founding member Brian Cole played a variety of instruments, including stand-up bass, which he traded for something more manageable as the band wisely ditched its knockabout routine for a more mainstream act. By 1966 The Association were among America's hottest properties, multi-instrumentalist Terry Kirkman's 'Cherish' taking the group to the chart summit in September; also a popular live draw, the five LA-based boys could do little wrong for a couple of years, also taking 'Windy' to the top in 1967.

As their favoured style of harmony rock began to fade, The Association found it harder to place themselves. A 1972 album for Columbia proved a failure – and shortly afterwards, a dejected Brian Cole's sad death from a heroin overdose at his Hollywood home appeared to be the final straw for the band. The group rallied, however, and were still performing on the circuit at the beginning of the millennium.

Rory Storm (with The Hurricanes): Kicked it while young

SEPTEMBER

Thursday 28

Rory Storm

(Alan Caldwell – Old Swan, Liverpool,
21 September 1939)

Rory Storm & The Hurricanes

'The band that Ringo left' were main players during the early sixties Merseybeat boom. They had started out in 1958 as a skiffle combo called The Texans, fronted by Caldwell as 'Al Storm', a presence whose stage dynamics masked a stutter but showed the hallmarks of a star in the making. The band's transition to rock 'n' roll, however, alienated some of the fanbase for which they had strived

– and Rory Storm & The Hurricanes (as they became) never recovered sufficiently to crack the beat market. The first to bail out was, of course, Ritchie Starkey – Ringo Starr – offered £25 a week to drum for The Beatles, who did his best to placate The Hurricanes by offering them recording time with The Beatles (this was never accepted, perhaps because of pride). Not only that, the band's second Parlophone single, 'America' (1964), was – uniquely – produced by Beatles manager Brian Epstein; even this could not turn their fortunes. Finally, the dramatic post-concert death of lead guitarist Charles 'Ty' Brian in 1967 caused the ailing band to split. Attempts to revive The Hurricanes by Storm and guitarist Johnny Byrne fell on deaf ears. Despite his speech impediment, Storm (reverting to Caldwell) took up a DJ post in Spain.

More heartbreak arrived with his father's death early in 1972; struggling to do his best by his widowed mother, the singer developed a chest infection that required medication. Just a week after his thirty-third birthday, Caldwell was discovered sprawled across his bed by his distraught mother, apparently having taken an overdose at her home. Distressed by her husband's death – and now the loss of a son – she apparently decided to take her own life there and then. The press dined out on a tale some had dubbed a suicide pact; while this was clearly not so, the intent behind Caldwell's death will remain a mystery. Asked why he hadn't attended his former bandmate's funeral, Ringo Starr's reported comment was: 'I wasn't there for his birth, either.'

See also *Johnny 'Guitar' Byrne* (☛*August 1999*)

OCTOBER

Monday 9

Slim Smith
(Keith Smith – Jamaica, 1948)
The Techniques

Although he had a fairly unstable upbringing, Slim Smith made some of the most accomplished rocksteady during his short life. Smith was blessed with the purest of falsettos, which brought to mind the voice of Curtis Mayfield rather than any reggae contemporary. As leader of the smooth band The Techniques, Smith had the rare privilege of recording sides for both Clement 'Coxsone' Dodd's Studio One ('Try Again', 'Mercy Mercy') *and* Duke Reid's Trojan labels ('Queen Majesty', 'Travelin' Man') – otherwise virtually unheard of with these great rivals. At the same time (as was fashionable in rocksteady), his group also recorded a number of standards. That Smith managed all this before his twenties is even more of a marvel.

The exact circumstances of Slim Smith's death remain uncertain, but it *is* known that he died from loss of blood after putting his hand through a pane of glass. It's possible that he took this measure because he was locked out of his home, but more likely that severe depression pushed him over the limit – it is believed that Smith had become obsessed by other performers receiving 'better' label treatment than he was.

NOVEMBER

Sunday 5

Miss Christine
(Christine Frka – San Pedro, California, 1950)
The GTOs

'Miss' Christine Frka – with partners-in-crime including Miss Cynderella (Cynthia Wells), Miss Linda (Parker), Miss Lucy, Miss Mercy (Fontentot), Miss Pamela (des Barres, *née* Miller), Miss Sandra (Leano), Miss Sparky, Miss Vicki (Budinger) and Suzi Creamcheese – created the notorious Girls Together Outrageously (Often/Only/Occasionally, etc.). This 'act', originally dance troupe The Laurel Canyon Ballet Company, seemed as hell-bent on bedding rock stars as they were on making records. The GTOs did, however, cut a 1970 album, the conceptual part-song/part-spoken-word *Permanent Damage* for Frank Zappa's Straight label, backed by a catalogue of top musicians. Frka became governess to Zappa's daughter Moon Unit, initially in payment for squatting at his home. (The GTOs' prefixes of 'Miss' had been given them by frequent visitor to the household Tiny Tim, who married Miss Vicki.) Frka kept Zappa's wife, Gail, company and also introduced Zappa to her then boyfriend, the young Alice Cooper, whom she recommended the maverick acid rocker record. Zappa's thanks to her included picturing her emerging from a tomb on the cover of his own *Hot Rats* album (1969). (The GTOs' frequent recreational drug use had to be very much hidden from non-user Zappa, however.)

Despite her notoriety, Frka, at least according to des Barres, always claimed to be frigid, a fact immortalized on the Flying Burrito Brothers' 'Christine's Tune' (1969). One possible reason for this was that throughout her life she had suffered from curvature of the spine; it is believed that her death in a hotel room was as a result of an overdose of painkillers.

See also *Frank Zappa (*☞ *December 1993); Tiny Tim (*☞ *November 1996). Miss Sandra died in 1991, Miss Lucy a year later.*

Monday 6

Billy Murcia
(Bogotá, Colombia, 1951)
**The New York Dolls
(Actress)**

Whether The New York Dolls actually invented punk rock is something of a moot point. That one of rock's most self-destructive units has become one of the genre's 'deadest' bands is beyond argument. The first to fall was unsung drummer Billy Murcia, a South American-born high-school drop-out who had travelled to New York, joining founder Dolls Johnny Thunders (*née* Genzale, lead guitar) and Arthur 'Killer' Kane (bass) in the band Actress. Murcia suggested the name-change to New York Dolls and an image-change, to cross-dressing glam punks, and the band was completed by the addition of Sylvain Sylvain (*née* Mizrahi, guitar) and Mick Jagger-aping frontman David Johansen in 1971. Despite label diffidence, The Dolls' trashy set became a cult must-see, packing the audiences in at 'cooler' New York venues like Max's Kansas City and The Mercer Arts Center.

A no-nonsense percussionist, Murcia was driving the project when The New York Dolls toured the UK with The Faces in 1972. But, at a party during the tour, Murcia imbibed so heavily of alcohol and substances (mainly Mandrax) that his girlfriend felt the best way to sober him up was to put him in a bath. What happened to the drummer next remains unclear, although it seems likely that, never fully regaining consciousness, Murcia drowned – either in the bathtub or in the black coffee he was subsequently force-fed. The Dolls – today rated as one of New York's most influential rock acts – continued for a few years without commercial success, the lives of Thunders (☞ *April 1991*), replacement drummer Jerry Nolan (☞ *January 1992*) and Kane (☞ *July 2004*) all since claimed.

Saturday 11

Berry Oakley

(Raymond Berry Oakley – Chicago, Illinois, 4 April 1948)

The Allman Brothers Band
(Tommy Roe & The Roemans)
(Various acts)

Berry Oakley was a natural musician, brought up on the blues. He'd moved to Florida as a teenager, finding himself a position in The Roemans – big-selling Tommy Roe's touring band – when their bassist was drafted. Then came Second Coming, a politically charged rock band, before he claimed bassist position with the original Allman Brothers Band. Under this banner, Oakley helped to set new standards for inspired improvised rock. However, The Allman Brothers Band were soon shattered by the loss of Duane Allman, their undisputed jewel in the crown (☞ *October 1971*). And as if this weren't enough, just over a year later, an incident of ghostly similarity befell its second self-imposed leader.

Heading for the Big House – the band's communal residence, originally rented by Oakley and his family – the bass-player and his friend roadie Kim Payne were engaging in a bit of motorcycle horseplay. The pair wove

in and out of the cars on Macon's Bartlett Avenue until Payne decided to lose his buddy by putting his foot down. As he approached an intersection, a city bus appeared from the opposite direction; Payne managed to avoid the vehicle as its driver slammed on his brakes, but Oakley's Triumph hit the bus full on. Like Duane Allman a year before, the rider skidded some sixty feet across the street, his machine landing on top of him. A rueful Payne later mused: 'I knew Berry was probably turning on the gas to catch up with me. I also knew he wasn't very good at riding.' Refusing immediate medical treatment, Berry Oakley went into shock and walked away from the scene. He died from a skull fracture later that afternoon, at the very same hospital where Allman had passed away the previous year. Position of bassist within the band proved to be unlucky: Oakley's replacement Lamar Williams also died prematurely (☞ *January 1983*), as did a third, Allen Woody (☞ *August 2000*).

Saturday 18

Danny Whitten

(New York, 1943)

Crazy Horse
(The Rockets)
(Danny & The Memories)

Talented arranger Danny Whitten's first foray into popular music was with his mid-sixties act Danny & The Memories, although given that this group performed a capella, Whitten's guitar prowess did not reveal itself until he formed The Rockets, a six-piece rock band that released one album in 1968. Though the record-buying public ignored his work, Neil Young of the soon-to-split Buffalo Springfield certainly didn't. Whitten had invited the Canadian guitarist to play with The Rockets at LA's legendary Whisky A Go-Go – now Young was convinced that Whitten was an ideal guitarist and that this was to be *his* new band. The Rockets became Crazy Horse, Whitten jousting with Young on his brilliant 1969 solo outing *Everybody Knows This is Nowhere* and its follow-up *After the Goldrush* (1970), especially on the epic 'Southern Man'.

Unfortunately, Whitten utilized this huge career upturn to support his increasing use of heroin; Neil Young viewed Crazy Horse as his Rolling Stones and was hugely dismayed to see his lead guitarist fast becoming dependent on the drug. Shortly after the release of a debut Crazy Horse album (1971), Whitten was fired from his own band. Sympathetic towards his former guitarist – not to mention afraid that an unoccupied Whitten might invite trouble – Neil Young invited him to tour again in late 1972, on condition that he kick heroin into touch. But with drugs off the menu, the guitarist relied instead on alcohol, which made him barely coherent. Another chance had gone and Young had little option other than to fly him home to LA to straighten out. Danny Whitten never made it back: using the cash with which he had been paid off, he purchased a wrap of pure heroin, overdosing on the very evening of his dismissal. Young remembered his friend in the harrowing 'Needle and the Damage Done' (1972) and 'Tonight's the Night' (1975), while Whitten's own 'I Don't Want to Talk about It' (1971) became a standard, covered by artists as diverse as Rod Stewart, Nils Lofgren and Everything but the Girl.

Lest We Forget

Other notable deaths that occurred sometime during 1972:

James C Bracken (US co-founder of the Vee-Jay R & B label; born Missouri, 23/5/1909; unknown, 20/2)

Mick Bradley (UK drummer with British blues-rock combos Methuselah and Steamhammer; undiagnosed leukaemia, 2/1972)

Maurice Chevalier (popular French singer/actor; born Menilmontant, 12/9/1888; unknown, 1/1)

Reverend Gary Davis (US blues/folk guitarist whose distinctive style influenced, among others, Jerry Garcia and Ry Cooder; born Laurens, South Carolina, 30/4/1896; heart attack, 5/5)

Charlie 'Redman' Freeman (US session guitarist/saxophonist who recorded with many great singers, particularly Jerry Lee Lewis; born Memphis, *c* 1941; a habitual drinker, he choked on his own vomit)

Mississippi Fred McDowell (US blues slide-guitarist; born Tennessee, 12/1/1904; cancer, 3/7)

Jimmy Rushing (US jazz/blues singer with The Blue Devils; born Oklahoma, 26/8/1903; leukaemia, 8/6)

Pete Watson (Australian singer/bassist with sixties bands The Phantoms and the very successful MPD Ltd; after a few years of ill health, he succumbed to chronic illness in Perth, 30/4)

Billy Williams (US pop singer, who hit with 1957's 'I'm Gonna Sit Right Down and Write Myself a Letter'; born Texas, 28/12/1910; diabetes-related illnesses, 17/10)

John 'Scarface' Williams (US musician with Huey Smith & The Clowns; stabbed to death during a fight)

For a complete list of fallen artists, visit
www.numberoneinheaven.com

MARCH

Thursday 8

Ron 'Pigpen' McKernan

(San Bruno, California, 8 September 1945)

The Grateful Dead

The genesis of The Dead can be traced to the 1962 collision of Ron McKernan's band with that of Jerry Garcia, the pair teaming up (as Second Story Men and then The Zodiacs) to create the myth that would become The Grateful Dead – not so much a rock band, more a way of life. McKernan's father was a white R & B/blues singer and DJ, so he was exposed early to the genre and encouraged to take up the harmonica. Like Garcia, he was brought up in the decidedly bohemian district of Palo Alto, both of them music archivists more at home playing the area's bars than studying for school finals. 'Pigpen' (it was a school nickname) dropped out of education by 'mutual agreement' when he started adopting a biker look as a teenager: unfortunately, his later ill health was also kick-started by the appetite for alcohol he discovered at that time.

The Grateful Dead were originally Mother McCree's Uptown Jug Champions, an unwieldy name that gave way to The Warlocks, which was already taken. Nestling comfortably into the Haight-Ashbury scene, the group had originally been the unofficial house band at Ken Kesey's notorious 'acid test' parties – a prevalent entertainment since the drug's discovery. The buzz surrounding The Dead only became audible outside of San Francisco following the band's astonishing performance at the Monterey Festival, after which they took their place at the helm of the underground, the scene's top 'live' attraction, McKernan's bluesy keyboard (and other instruments) driving the group's dense, sinewy sound. Often performing as lead singer, this somewhat fragile musician was a reluctant hero: he was reportedly much more interested in the music (and the booze, of course) than the surrounding subculture, and was an unwilling participator in LSD binges that would leave him paranoid and consequently unable to play. But McKernan's problems really started when second drummer Mickey Hart's father disappeared with several thousand dollars of the band's cash, leaving him impoverished. Then, in 1971, treatment for alcoholism revealed cirrhosis of the liver – a terminal condition which McKernan chose to keep from the rest of The Grateful Dead. His last live performance in May 1972 coincided with the questionable assistance of Keith and Donna Godchaux with keyboard duties. It was, however, clear to all that McKernan was unwell. The following month, the declining keyboardist left the band, and died from a gastrointestinal haemorrhage nine months later. Discovered alone at his Corte Madera home by a neighbour, McKernan, it transpired, had asked his long-term girlfriend to leave him two months earlier.

McKernan was buried in full biker get-up at Alta Mesa Memorial Park, and The Dead lived on, of course, dedicating that July's *Bear's Choice* LP to the unit's founding member.

See also *Keith Godchaux (☞ July 1980); Brent Mydland (☞ July 1990); Jerry Garcia (☞ August 1995). A further keyboardist, Vince Welnick, died in June 2000.*

MAY

Thursday 10

Mike Furber

(London, 26 September 1948)

The Bowery Boys

Singer Mike Furber formed The Bowery Boys in 1965 with Robbie van Delft (guitar), Paul Wade (bass), Greg

Walker (rhythm guitar) and Nevile Peard (drums), in Brisbane, Australia, where his family had moved when he was small. Furber, equally blessed and cursed by his limited but resonant voice and babyface looks, was to be mauled in the jaws of a pop industry desperate for new idols. The group were very popular on the Sydney music scene, beginning strongly enough with a series of punchy singles including 'That's When the Happiness Began' (1966), but manager Ivan Dayman's promotion of Furber over the other Bowery Boys led quickly to disharmony and conflict. By August 1966 a band expected to clean up internationally had already split.

Although he began working solo (even once opening for The Four Tops), Furber's career was scuppered when he was conscripted in the early seventies, an experience that left him high, dry and very depressed. Following his sacking from the musical *Nuclear* – in which he had pretty much invested all hope – Furber hanged himself at a garage near his apartment in Sydney.

Close ...
Robert Wyatt
(Soft Machine/Matching Mole)

Drummer Robert Wyatt had long been part of the music scene in Canterbury, England, where he had made his name with the prog/jazz Soft Machine before embarking on his own project, Matching Mole. On 1 June 1973, just after cutting a debut album, Wyatt made a drainpipe exit from a drunken party, fell four storeys from the London hotel window and broke his spine in two places. Paralysed from the waist down and wheelchair-bound, Wyatt turned to singing, enjoying critical acclaim that continues to this day.

Closer!
Don Powell
(Slade)

Slade had just become the first ever UK pop act to send two consecutive singles straight to number one when founder Powell's car turned over in July 1973. The drummer of Britain's favourite superyobs just about escaped with his neck in the motorway car smash that killed his fiancée, Angela Morris. As the band kept vigil at his bedside, singer Noddy Holder uttered: 'No Don, no more Slade – end of story.' Despite surgeons drilling into his skull, Powell went on to make a remarkable recovery – though his memory loss meant that it has never been ascertained whether he or his partner was behind the wheel that day.

JULY

Clarence White
(Lewiston, Maine, 7 June 1944)
The Byrds
(Nashville West)
(The Kentucky Colonels)
(Muleskinner)

During a traumatic year for ex-Byrds, pioneering country-rock guitarist Clarence White died just ahead of the legendary Gram Parsons (☞ *September 1973*) and three months after Scotty Stoneman, a colleague in White's early bluegrass band The Kentucky Colonels. White – born into a musical family – joined the latter aged just ten; the group, first known as The Country Boys, had been started by White's older brother Roland in 1962. After a solo spell – during which time he cut an album on Bakersfield – and a stint with the influential Nashville West, White and his Fender were invited by Roger McGuinn to join The Byrds to replace the departed Gram Parsons and Chris Hillman, playing on the untitled album of 1968. The Byrds were not, however, the force they had been in their previous incarnation and, as the group began to wind down, White worked with Randy Newman and Joe Cocker. McGuinn disbanded The Byrds three years later, after seismic line-up changes.

Continuing his session work into the seventies, the tireless White (spoken of in some quarters in the hushed tones normally reserved for Jimi Hendrix) formed the 'supergroup' Muleskinner, rejoined The Kentucky Colonels and, in 1973, was working on another solo album. After a performance in Lancaster, California, White was stacking

Byrds clustered: McGuinn, Crosby, Clarke and White

equipment into his van when he was hit by the truck of a drunk female driver; he died later from a stomach haemorrhage. White was buried in California's Joshua Memorial Park on 19 July; Gram Parsons and others sang an impromptu rendition of 'Farther Along' – a favourite country-gospel standard recorded twice by White – at his graveside.

See also *Gene Clark (☛ May 1991); Michael Clarke (☛ December 1993)*

Friday 27

Roger Durham
(Kansas City, Missouri, 14 February 1946)
Bloodstone

In 1973, Bloodstone looked to be R & B's new sensation with the single 'Natural High' shooting into the US Top Ten that June, but, with the record still high in the charts, the band was

shattered by a pair of unrelated tragedies. Bloodstone had begun in 1962, formed after a talent show at Kansas City's Central High School. By the end of the sixties the group (then a doo-wop outfit known as The Sinceres) had taken themselves off to the brighter lights of Los Angeles, where a change of style and identity invited improved fortunes. Roger Durham proved a soulful lead singer, so much so that Al Green invited the band to support him on his 1972 European tour – a lucrative deal with Decca and a subsequent hit single and album resulted.

Durham became a big fan of the UK, returning to London several times. On his last trip, though, he was thrown by an untrained horse while riding in the country. Durham's internal injuries were so extensive that he died later in hospital. A matter of months later, drummer Melvin Webb – who had shunned the tour to be with his ailing mother – also died, from diabetic complications, while founding singer/guitarist Willis Draffen Jr died in 2002.

AUGUST

Friday 17

Paul Williams
(Birmingham, Alabama, 2 July 1939)
The Temptations

An African-American baritone, Paul Williams had been friends with fellow-Temptation Eddie Kendricks since their schooldays in Birmingham; the pair were keen sportsmen as well as budding vocal performers. Moving with his colleague to Detroit, Williams found his abilities as a singer, dancer and bass guitarist in demand: completed by Kell Osbourne, their three-man doo-wop act was noted by manager and keen-eyed scout Milton Jenkins, and from thereon a bewildering sequence of name changes sealed their destiny. Jenkins named them first The Cavaliers, then The Primes, then – having amalgamated them with a band called The

Distants – The Elgins. A fruitful meeting with Motown head Berry Gordy would see that the moniker established on the front lawn was – finally – The Temptations.

Although he was also a dab hand at choreography, Williams as frontman was not making The Temptations an especially easy act to break. Fortunes changed for the better with the introduction of the younger David Ruffin in 1963. (The move did have a silver lining for Williams in that it also brought about the firing of singer Elbridge Bryant, who had physically attacked him after a show the previous Christmas.) With Ruffin pushing Williams into the background (and Smokey Robinson offering tunes to the band), the hits began, like magic, to emerge. The pinnacle for The Temptations at this stage was the enduring 1965 chart-topper 'My Girl'. Paul Williams occasionally found himself leading some of the tunes – though these were more often than not fillers rather than group standards. A lifelong sufferer from sickle cell anaemia, Williams's poor health – and consequent alcohol and drug abuse – saw him less and less involved with the group, and his final marching orders arrived in 1971. Despite The Temptations' success during the sixties, the group had been underpaid for many years because of poor business practice. A father of four, the singer thus wound up broke and depressed. He was found in his car in a deserted parking lot, just minutes from Motown's Hitsville Studios, wearing swimming trunks, the pistol in his hand a clue to the manner of his death.

The Temps naturally flourished, and in 1989 were named America's favourite soul group by the Rock 'n' Roll Hall of Fame. Within six years, however, a further three of them – David Ruffin (☞ *June 1991*), Eddie Kendricks (☞ *October 1992*) and Melvin Franklin (☞ *February 1995*) – would also be dead.

See also *Elbridge Bryant (☞ October 1975)*

Gram Parsons

(Cecil Ingram Connor III – Winter Haven, Florida, 5 November 1946)

Gram Parsons & The Fallen Angels
The Flying Burrito Brothers
The Byrds
(The International Submarine Band)
(Various acts)

Was Gram Parsons the first crossover country-rock star? Certainly, with his flowing locks and sparkling 'Nudie' suits, Parsons was the first country-influenced musician to *dress* like a rock star. Yet the word 'star' represents something of a paradox: other than during his brief spell with The Byrds, Parsons barely sold a record during his lifetime. Parsons was, however, a mightily blessed talent who had more love and enthusiasm for his musical heritage than he did for most of the individuals with whom he came into contact. Parsons's undoubted spirituality was reflected in his death in a motel room at Joshua Tree National Park – not to mention the truly odd aftermath.

Despite being born into considerable wealth, Parsons's character was moulded by tragedy met in his formative years: his father, Coon Dog, committed suicide with a .38 at Christmas in 1958 (Gram and his sister were later adopted by Bob Parsons), and his mother, Avis, died mysteriously seven years later amid alcohol problems. The young Parsons's enthusiasm for music had begun with the country strains of Merle Haggard and The Kingston Trio – not to mention the emergence of his idol Elvis Presley. His desire for a 'look' manifested itself as early as age fifteen, when Parsons and his school-friends dressed in suits to perform as The Shilos. A year later, he joined The Legends, a 'proper' band that featured future hit-makers Jim Stafford and Kent LaVoie (Lobo), as well as Parsons's future collaborator Jon Corneal.

But Gram Parsons cut an increasingly wayward figure, failing in his studies at Harvard and dropping out. Parsons had no financial insecurities, however, therefore music – initially in the shape of country-rock pioneers The International Submarine Band, whom he had met while at high school – became the single thrust of his existence. Parsons's reputation grew during time spent in New York and certainly travelled faster than any record sold by

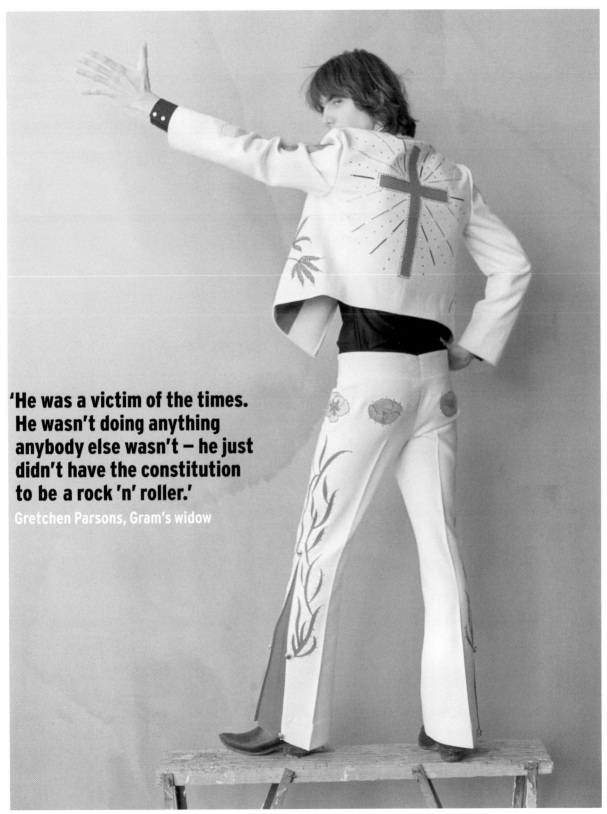

'He was a victim of the times. He wasn't doing anything anybody else wasn't – he just didn't have the constitution to be a rock 'n' roller.'
Gretchen Parsons, Gram's widow

Gram Parsons: Posing in his 'nudie'

The ISB. In LA, in 1968, he was invited to join The Byrds. Even though he was with them for less than six months, Parsons influenced their *Sweetheart of the Rodeo* album to such a degree that it halted the downturn in the fortunes of one of the States' biggest bands. (Parsons's tenure with The Byrds was ended by a disagreement with frontman Roger McGuinn over a tour of South Africa; although it appeared the country-lovin' Parsons was displaying unexpected left-wing tendencies, it is more likely that what caused him not to make the trip was his new-found friendship with Rolling Stone Keith Richards, with whom he would later spend more time than with most of his own bands.)

Parsons's most celebrated work, though, was that with The Flying Burrito Brothers – what the singer would call his Cosmic American Music. This band was formed with ex-Byrd Chris Hillman, with Sneaky Pete Kleinow (pedal steel), Chris Ethridge (bass) and Jon Corneal (drums). Their *Gilded Palace of Sin* (1969) was an album chock full of pain and beauty, Parsons's finest moment perhaps the exquisite 'Hot Burrito #1'. Its follow-up, however, was less well received, and the band were often criticized for their under-rehearsed shows. Parsons now began to wear 'Nudie' suits (the gaudy Hollywood-tailored apparel designed for some of the top artists), and to indulge his increasing penchant for drink and drugs – mainly imbibed in the sprawling outdoors he loved at Joshua Tree. The Burritos (who got their largest ever audience at the notorious Stones concert at Altamont) fell apart by 1971; Gram Parsons was fired from the band he had formed because of his increasing unreliability on and off stage.

After a summer spent in France, hanging (many thought needlessly) with The Stones as they recorded *Exile on Main Street*, Gram Parsons returned from his sabbatical to form a stunning studio band, The Fallen Angels, which featured a future star of leftfield country, Emmylou Harris, as well as members of Elvis's band. But touring a debut record proved impossible: Parsons's habits were so out of control that live events would quickly disintegrate. A highly regarded second album, *Grievous Angel*, notwithstanding, this was merely the start of Gram Parsons's descent into oblivion.

At the funeral for his friend the fine guitarist Clarence White (➤ *July 1973*), Parsons had intimated to Chris Hillman and his road manager Phil Kaufman that he wished to be cremated at Joshua Tree. Said Parsons, 'I don't want them doing this to me – I want to go out in a puff of smoke!' Just a few days later, this almost came prematurely true: his Laurel Canyon home burned down, and he and his second wife, Gretchen, were obliged to move in temporarily with the loose-living Kaufman – much against Gretchen's wishes. Perhaps traumatized by recent events (the couple had also recently returned from an unhappy cruise with his stepfather), Parsons told Gretchen that he was off once again to his favoured desert national park, this time to clean up his act once and for all. In truth, he had hired rooms at the Joshua Tree Inn for himself and three friends – road valet Michael Martin, Martin's girlfriend, Dale McElroy, and Parsons's high-school friend Margaret Fisher – for a session of 'self-medication' with alcohol and morphine. Parsons's decision that heroin should also be on the menu was to have tragic consequences.

Discovering that Parsons had overdosed in Room 8 at the motel, first Fisher then McElroy tried to revive him. By 12.15 am he was taken to the nearby Yucca Valley Hospital, but a quarter of an hour later the celebrated 26-year-old musician was declared dead from 'drug toxicity'. Wheelchair-bound Bob Parsons attempted to claim the body (possibly to help him secure the Connor family's estate), but Phil Kaufman had other plans. Remembering Parsons's wishes, he and fellow roadie Michael Martin hurried to LAX to intercept the body before it could be flown to New Orleans. Brazenly, Kaufman sold his tale to the hangar office (signing the release papers 'Jeremy Nobody'), and even managed to shake off a police officer, who observed the pair's bizarre behaviour ruefully but apparently without suspicion. Parsons's casket was then loaded into the booze-filled hearse they had borrowed. Picking up petrol on the way, they headed back to Joshua Tree; the desert cremation of Parsons's corpse could apparently be seen for five miles as the pyre burned bright and long.

The papers – almost having 'lost' the story of Parsons's death because of Jim Croce dying the very next day – were suddenly in a lather about this dramatic new twist to the tale. Kaufman and Martin turned themselves in, appearing at West LA Municipal Court on 5 November (which would have been Parsons's twenty-seventh birthday). Because the theft of a body was not a recognized crime (a corpse being of no intrinsic value), the pair were only fined around $1,300 – an amount they managed to recoup, more or less, from a wake thrown in Gram Parsons's honour, featuring an early performance by Jonathan Richman. Bob Parsons – who made no money out of the estate and died just a year later – had his stepson's remains shipped to New Orleans, where a modest service was held at the relatively staid Garden of Memories Cemetery, New Orleans.

> ## 'Gram's extraordinary life and death is something that might be in a movie, but you don't think of it happening in real life.'
> Emmylou Harris

Thursday 20

Jim Croce
(Philadelphia, Pennsylvania, 10 January 1943)

Having purchased his first guitar from a toy store, Jim Croce grew to become a major star-in-the-making during seventies America's singer/songwriter boom. It was at Villanova College, Pennsylvania, that Croce became something of a hit, playing for his frat-house buddies – and he would play mostly campus concerts until he was able to cut an album in 1969. This record failed to take off, though, and Croce returned to various jobs, including summer-camp supervisor and welder; the closest he came to a break was writing a couple of commercials for local radio, and the coffee-house circuit continued to be his only real outlet for 'proper' songs. A second album, *You Don't Mess around with Jim* (1972) – recorded after ABC invited him to New York – made a huge difference: peddling a distinctly blue-collar style of blues, he struck gold with a series of hit singles, including the million-selling 'Bad, Bad Leroy Brown' (1973).

All seemed set – but unfortunately the singer was barely around long enough to witness, let alone enjoy, his success. After commercial airlines lost his luggage and instruments, Croce thought it wise to hire his own twin-engine Beechcraft (yes, that plane again), in which he felt his belongings would remain safe. After a storming concert in front of 2,000 at Northwestern State University, Louisiana, the craft, carrying Croce and his entourage, attempted to take off from Natchitoches Airport. When pilot Robert Elliot failed to gain sufficient altitude at the end of the runway, the plane hit trees and crashed into the ground. The six aboard – Croce, his friend and lead guitarist Maury Muhleisen, publicist Kenny Cortese, road manager Dennis Rast, comedian George Stevens (who opened the singer's shows) and the pilot himself – all died in the accident. For his widow and former collaborator, Ingrid Croce, it was a massive burden to bear. Her own career had been curtailed by vocal chord damage, she had also recently lost both parents and in 1975 she was to discover that their son, Adrian – for whom Croce penned the poignant 'Time in a Bottle' (1973; a second chart-topper and one of four posthumous hits) – had a severe sight disorder. A woman of immense fortitude, Ingrid Croce won the rights to her husband's work in 1985 and opened an award-winning music-venue restaurant in his honour, while Adrian (A J) Croce is now a respected musician in his own right.

NOVEMBER

Saturday 10

David 'Stringbean' Akeman
(Annville, Kentucky, 17 June 1915)
Bill Monroe's Bluegrass Boys
(Various acts)

The cheery, frugal-livin' David Akeman was a much-loved purveyor of Kentucky bluegrass, his banjo never far from his side. Fondly dubbed 'Stringbean' by forgetful bandleader Asa Martin, Akeman also became known as 'The Kentucky Wonder' during the forties, so intricate was his picking. With Martin's band, Akeman also developed his shtick as singer and comic performer – which was to serve him well in later life when he presented popular country television hour *Hee Haw*. Akeman is best known, though, as a member of Bill Monroe's celebrated Bluegrass Boys – the definitive country pickers of their day.

The musician had no real interest in fame, however, and he and his wife, Estelle, inhabited a modest cabin in Ridgetop, Tennessee, their only luxury the vintage Cadillac parked outside. Like many older country folk of the era, the Depression had made them suspicious of banking practices, and they tended to store their money at home. Inevitably, with a name as high-profile as Akeman's, word of this got round. On the night of 10 November, cousins John and Marvin Douglas lay in wait as Mr and Mrs Akeman returned from a night on the town. The musician was shot at point-blank range and died in front of his terrified wife – who was then pursued by the men before they picked her off too. The bodies were discovered the following morning by neighbour and country performer Louis 'Grandpa' Jones, who described the home as 'stripped bare save for a chainsaw'. This crime sent shockwaves throughout Nashville, and the cousins received life sentences for the double homicide. They didn't take all the money, however: some twenty-three years later, $20K in cash was discovered rotting in a chimney breast at Akeman's former home.

Monday 26

John Rostill
(Birmingham, England, 16 June 1942)
The Shadows

John Rostill – originally guitarist with The Interns – was the longest-serving bass player with The Shadows, replacing Brian Locking (who had left for 'religious' reasons) in 1963 and even surviving a short break-up in 1968. The quiet, unassuming Rostill played on several Top Ten hits, both for the group on its own and also as back-up to Cliff Richard, while also touring extensively with Tom Jones towards the end of his life.

But Rostill died before he could know the enormous success of his compositions. In November 1973, fellow Shadow Bruce Welch called at Rostill's Hertfordshire home to work on new material. After getting no answer from his home studio, Welch and the bassist's wife were horrified to discover that he had been electrocuted. One month later, his award-winning 'Let Me be There' gave Olivia Newton-John her first gold single in the USA, and further Rostill-penned hits 'If You Love Me (Let Me Know)' and 'Please, Mr, Please' each shifted nearly a million copies for her over the next couple of years.

DECEMBER

Thursday 20

Bobby Darin

(Walden Robert Cassotto – Bronx, New York, 14 May 1936)

Life was never going to be easy for Bobby Cassotto, aka Darin: in a series of twists that would keep the sharpest *EastEnders* viewer guessing, he discovered as an adult that the 'mother' who brought him up was actually his grandmother Polly, and his 'sister' Nina his mother – his father (a small-time gangster, according to the singer) had died before he was born. Darin was so humiliated by these revelations that he offered his impoverished family almost no financial assistance once he'd hit the big time. As if all this weren't enough, the singer had been stricken with rheumatic fever as a child, weakening his heart and leaving

him in precarious health for the rest of his life. Darin somehow performed well at school. He was a versatile musician and realized quickly his dream to perform with a band, losing his 'stigmatic' Italian surname as he worked the New York clubs. With rock 'n' roll still somewhat in its infancy, though, he was pigeonholed by Decca (the first label to spot his talent): what followed was a sequence of banal ballads with a semi-quiff, carefully designed for the maximum commercial return. However, his arresting, self-penned 'Splish Splash' all but topped the US chart in 1958 – and a year later, the Kurt Weill standard 'Mack the Knife' did.

A unique artist, Darin tried acting – he won a Golden Globe Award in 1962 – and even political activism, to which end he recorded a pair of protest records following the assassination of Robert Kennedy, whose election campaign he'd supported. Darin's devotion was so complete that he chose to sleep next to the coffin all night following Kennedy's death.

Bobby Darin's inconsistent health dictated his activity after his thirtieth birthday, though. In 1971, he underwent long-overdue corrective heart surgery, which enabled the star to continue working for a while, but, at the end of 1973, an attempt to repair a faulty valve proved one operation too many. Darin died during surgery, and his body – as requested – was left to the UCLA Medical Center. Lifelong fan Kevin Spacey played the singer in the 2000 biopic *Beyond the Sea*.

Clayton Perkins

(Lloyd Clayton Perkings – Tiptonville, Tennessee, 1935)

The Perkins Brothers

Younger brother of the prodigious guitarist and songwriter Carl Perkins, bassist Clayton found himself in Carl's shadow as the group they'd formed with third sibling, Jay, began to attract attention from Sun Records. Perkins was somewhat upstaged as he strummed his upright bass, but was nonetheless excited at the thought of appearing on national television as Carl's 'Blue Suede Shoes' began to take off. In a twist of fate that was decisive for all three Perkins Brothers, a near-fatal car accident prevented them from making the trip to New York. With his career changing direction, moving into country music, Carl Perkins had no use for his brother and made the painful decision to fire the needy Clayton in 1963.

The bass-player never worked in music again. Depressed by the premature death of his brother Jay Perkins (➤ *Pre-1965*), he fell into alcoholism and left his family behind. In generally poor health, Clayton Perkins was found in his bed on Christmas Day 1973, having apparently shot himself with a .22 pistol.

See also *Carl Perkins (➤ Golden Oldies #5)*

Lowman Pauling

(North Carolina, 14 July 1926)

The '5' Royales

Although he is best known for his swooping bass vocals with doo-wop favourites The '5' Royales, Lowman Pauling was also a very versatile and forward-thinking guitarist who used distortion techniques way before most rock acts – and is cited regularly by many as an influence. Known variously by the nicknames of 'El' or 'Pete', Pauling joined his father's Carolina-based Royal Sons gospel quintet as a boy, making the transition to secular music and going on to score countless R & B chart entries (some sufficiently racy to create issue with his father) with The Royales during the 1950s. Although the vast majority of these were at least co-written by Pauling, 'Dedicated to the One I Love' twice became a million-selling tune for both The Shirelles (1961) and The Mamas & The Papas (1967). Well recognized for his guitar and songwriting skills, Pauling also found work with bigger R & B stars such as Sam & Dave.

In the middle of performing custodial duties at a Brooklyn synagogue the day after Christmas, Lowman Pauling collapsed and died suddenly from an epileptic seizure. Most of the various Royales have since joined him: Obadiah Carter, Gene Tanner, Eudell Graham and brother Clarence Pauling passed on in quick succession between 1994 and 1995, while frequent lead Johnny Tanner died in 2005.

Lest We Forget

Other notable deaths that occurred sometime during 1973:

Bruce Berry (US roadie with Crosby, Stills, Nash & Young, commemorated alongside Danny Whitten in Neil Young's 'Tonight's the Night'; several days' partying with the band resulted in his overdosing on cocaine/heroin, 6/73)

Rick Dey (US garage bassist with The Furys, The Vejtables and The Wilde Knights – who recorded the oh-so-shocking 'Beaver Patrol'; born 1948; overdosed on nitrous oxide, 5/11)

Larry Finnegan (US rockabilly artist who scored a US #11 hit with 'Dear One' in 1962 and founded his own label; born John Lawrence Finneran, New York, 10/8/38; brain tumour, 22/7)

Jerome Green (US singer/tuba- and maraca-player with Bo Diddley, influential to Mick Jagger; born 1934; unknown)

Mike Jeffreys (UK manager of The Animals and Jimi Hendrix; the DC9 in which he was returning to Britain collided with a Convair in mid-air)

Jerry Lee Lewis Jr (US son of the rock 'n' roll legend who played percussion in his father's band; born 2/11/1954; driving a jeep his father had bought him for his birthday, he collided with a car, 13/11)

Memphis Minnie (US blues singer/guitarist; born Louisiana, 3/6/1897; stroke, 6/8)

Steve Perron (US singer with The Children (Chillen) and The Mind's Eye, who also wrote ZZ Top's 'Francine'; born 26/8/1945; choked on own vomit, 9/8)

Allan Sherman (popular US singer/comedian who hit US #2 with the single 'Hello Mudduh, Hello Fadduh!' as well as scoring chart-topping albums; born Illinois, 30/11/1924; respiratory failure, 21/11)

Murry Wilson (uncompromising US manager/producer of The Beach Boys – father to Brian, Dennis and Carl. Neither Brian nor Dennis attended his funeral; heart attack, 4/6)

For a complete list of fallen artists, visit

www.numberoneinheaven.com

1974

FEBRUARY

Thursday 28

Bobby Bloom
(New York, 1946)

The term 'one-hit wonder' could have been coined for Bobby Bloom – and for him it certainly had a dark double-meaning. Although the US singer only troubled the charts once, his was the highest-profile case of accidental self-shooting since that of Johnny Ace (➤ *Pre-1965*) nearly twenty years before. Originally a member of The Imaginations, the fairly talented Bloom became a soul-influenced songwriter who could name Tommy James & The Shondells' UK number one 'Mony Mony' among his credits. His own performing career was patchy, to say the least, but, despite failed releases on many labels, the upbeat transatlantic Top Ten entry 'Montego Bay' (which, once again, fared better in Britain) saw his profile soar briefly in 1970. (Bloom also recorded as a member of animated 'bubblegum' heroes The Archies – though, unfortunately for him, not on the million-selling 'Sugar Sugar'.)

Although Bobby Bloom was despondent about the sporadic nature of his success, his early death was no suicide. It was, however, a deeply ignominious passing: Bloom was apparently cleaning a gun at his Hollywood home when it unexpectedly fired.

MARCH

Saturday 9

Harry Womack
(Harris Womack – Cleveland, Ohio, 25 June 1945)
The Valentinos
The Womack Brothers

Realizing the dream of their deeply devout father Friendly, gospel quintet The Womack Brothers – Cecil, Curtis, Bobby, Friendly Jr and tenor Harry – became a surprise draw, emerging as they did from the tough neighbourhood of Quincy, Cleveland. It all appeared to fall into place when Sam Cooke took them on tour with his Soul Stirrers in the mid fifties: to Friendly Sr's disgust, his boys opted to take the same secular route as Cooke; their father kicked them out of his house for deferring to the 'devil's music'. Signing with Cooke's SAR label, the brothers became The Valentinos, enjoying R & B hits

until their mentor's dramatic death (➤ *Pre-1965*) caused the collapse of the label. Bobby Womack attended Sam Cooke's funeral as the widow's new beau – even wearing a suit from Cooke's wardrobe. Within this detail lies a black coincidence, to emerge a decade on . . .

By the 1970s, the ambitious Bobby Womack had become something of a star, and Harry occasionally played bass for his band. Bobby would repay his brother not least with the 1972 R & B hit 'Harry Hippie' – an unlikely homage to his sibling's rather carefree existence. Harry Womack's happy-go-lucky persona was set to cause critical problems, however, with his live-in girlfriend of five years. By 1974 this jealous lover had become so suspicious of Harry's behaviour that Bobby Womack suggested he come on tour with his band, in order that the couple might sort out their domestic situation. In the event, Bobby Womack returned to his apartment one night to find his brother – who had a room there – brutally stabbed to death: Harry's girlfriend had discovered girls' clothes in his closet, and had attacked him with a kitchen knife. It transpired that the garments actually belonged to Bobby's latest love.

APRIL

Vinnie Taylor

(Chris Donald – San Salvador, Bahamas,
1948 or 1949)

Sha-Na-Na

The most unlikely participants at
Woodstock were surely rock revivalists Sha-Na-Na, whose carefully cho-
reographed prelude to Jimi Hendrix
et al proved an unexpected success
amid universal hippydom. Guitarist
Chris Donald joined them the year
after, with the group's profile then
at its highest. The son of a US State
Department employee, young buck
Donald had returned to America with
his family, and played guitar with a
series of surf-orientated bands before
Sha-Na-Na beckoned; Vinnie Taylor
(as he would become known) obliged
the group by slicking back his hair and
growing the requisite sideburns.

Although his image made him
a popular stage figure, life did not
end happily for Taylor: following a
performance at the University of
Virginia, he retired to his Holiday
Inn bedroom in Charlottesville and
overdosed, probably on heroin, during
the night. The band he left behind
descended into repetitious variety-slot
filling, a lucrative US TV series and an
appearance in the movie *Grease* (1977),
nonetheless keeping the name of Sha-
Na-Na in the public eye. The group
continued to tour until the death of
singer and bass-player 'Chico' Ryan
(🖝 *July 1998*).

MAY

Graham Bond

(John Clifton Bond – Romford, Essex,
28 October 1937)

The Graham Bond Trio/Organization
The Graham Bond Initiation
Alexis Korner's Blues Incorporated
The Don Rendell Quintet

**Graham Bond: An underground smash,
if you see what I mean ...**

Thick-set, unfashionable Graham
Bond never really wanted to be 'the
next big thing'. An Essex-born music
enthusiast, he played alto sax for Don
Rendell's jazz quintet at the age of
fifteen, finding himself earmarked as
Britain's New Jazz Star in 1961. Bond
– whose playing partners would make
up a veritable Who's Who of British
blues glitterati – made the transition
to blues rock, playing first with Alexis
Korner (the genre's godfather) and
then persuading band members Jack
Bruce and Ginger Baker to join him
in his own new project in 1963. The
Graham Bond Organization was
soon known for its leader's distinctive
Hammond organ and rasping vocal.
(A lack of hit singles – then essential
currency for any beat combo – caused

Bruce and Baker's departure to form
Cream with Eric Clapton three years
later.)

Bond struggled to reachieve the
critical heights he'd experienced in the
sixties, moving briefly to the USA with
his partner, singer Diane Stewart, to
find work, and then back to Britain,
where – despite recording with Bruce
and Baker's new projects – his slump
into self-destruction alarmed his colleagues. Increasingly obsessed with the
occult, Bond (with Stewart) formed the
band Holy Magick, and began ingesting vast amounts of drugs and alcohol

as his frustration and despondency increased. His Graham Bond Initiation music project collapsed within two years.

Near-destitute, Bond's personal problems escalated, with his two-year marriage to Stewart ending in 1972 (posthumous allegations of the sexual abuse of a stepdaughter emerged in a biography) and work impossible to find. Bond was seemingly hamstrung: his attempts to take even low-paid music jobs were met with genuine disbelief by potential employers, astonished to be approached by such a legend. Following a month in prison for a public misdemeanour (and subsequent enforced institutionalization), Graham Bond died under a tube train at London's Finsbury Park station. Although the driver of the train described Bond as having 'appeared in front of him' as he emerged from the tunnel, without a suicide note we can never know whether his death was intentional. Bond's funeral in Streatham was no more straightforward either – a vast pentagram hung behind his coffin, and Jack Bruce improvised a bluesy dirge on the church organ.

JUNE

Sunday 30

George Chase
Damon DeFeis
(1957)
Creation

Not to be confused with the British psychedelic band of a few years before, Creation was a New York funk-rock act set up by guitarist John Henderson, his singer wife, Sarita, second vocalist George Chase, Damon

DeFeis (keyboards) and Eric Carr (drums), previously playing as Salt 'n' Pepper (again, not to be confused . . .)

On the night of 29 June 1974, Creation played a packed nightspot called Gulliver's in Port Chester, New York. A young hood named Peter Leonard had burgled the bowling club next door, and decided that the best way to cover his tracks was to start a fire in the alleys themselves. The blaze spread, thick black smoke seeping through the ventilation ducts of Gulliver's, a discotheque-cum-restaurant on several floors. By the time the Port Chester and Greenwich Fire Departments had been summoned, the damage was done. Attempting to announce an evacuation, Creation were overcome with smoke. Chase and DeFeis were among twenty-four who perished in the ensuing catastrophe, though Eric Carr was something of a hero, saving the lives of both John and Sarita Henderson. Leonard served seven years for manslaughter. Creation continued under the new name Mother Nature/Father Time; Carr then went on to considerable fame as drummer with theatrical rockers Kiss in 1980, before his own premature death a decade later (☛ *November 1991*).

JULY

Tuesday 2

Jimmy Ricks
(Jackson, Florida, 6 August, 1924)
The Ravens

Among the true founders of American R & B, The Ravens were formed pretty much straight after the end of the war by Harlem waiters Jimmy Ricks and Warren Suttles. It's hard to imagine what company they

might have kept in the Billboard chart at this time, but The Ravens were there with 'Write Me a Letter' and the massive 'Old Man River' in 1947. By 1950, though, Ricks was the only original member of the group remaining as they signed with Mercury Records, and had switched to a solo career by 1956 – though The Ravens would tour the nostalgia circuit during the seventies. Ricks was one month short of his fiftieth birthday when he died from a sudden heart attack; his replacement in The Ravens, Joe van Loan, also died just two years later. Sometime lead Maithe Marshall passed on in 1989 and another member, Ollie Jones, in 1990.

Monday 29

'Mama' Cass Elliot
(Ellen Naomi Cohen – Baltimore, Maryland, 19 September 1941)
The Mamas & The Papas
(The Big Three)
(The Mugwumps)

Cass Elliot was a big lady, but, nope, contrary to one of pop music's most persistent myths, she did *not* die choking on a ham sandwich. It's believed that a flippant remark attributed to an attendant physician made it into the post mortem report, but a senior pathologist attested that although the food was present, none had blocked the singer's trachea. Elliot was just 5'5" tall but weighed in excess of 230 lbs – and it was this that brought about her early heart attack.

Among a slew of bearded guitar-noodlers, The Mamas & The Papas were the vocal leaders of the Greenwich music scene during the sixties. Having moved around constantly as a child, Ellen Cohen settled in New York in 1960, changed her name and acted in several off-Broadway shows. She joined a couple of bands, The Big

'Mama' Cass: Put everyone else in the shade

'She was fat, but cheerfully, willingly, *superbly* so.'

Michelle Phillips, The Mamas & The Papas

Three (an early example of Elliot's self-deprecating humour) with her husband – the unluckily named Jimmy Hendricks – and The Mugwumps, where she met Denny Doherty, who joined her in her best-remembered group. (The other Mugwumps, John Sebastian and Zal Yanovsky, went on to found the equally successful Lovin' Spoonful.) The Mamas & The Papas were completed by the innovative John Phillips and his wife, (Holly) Michelle Gilliam, who were initially reluctant to involve Elliot, possibly because of her size. Eventually, they had to concede that she had 'something', the four Greenwich friends finding their unique harmonies while vacationing in the Virgin Islands. Moving to Los Angeles in 1964, the quartet (originally known as The New Journeymen) met success astonishingly fast: their first two albums shifted well over a million units each, while inspiringly tuneful hits including 'California Dreamin'', 'Monday Monday', 'Dedicated to the One I Love' (all 1966) and 'Creeque Alley' (1967) were all to become standards. Cass Elliot – often at the band's fore – was an instant hit with fans and never slow with a riposte where one was appropriate.

The downfall of The Mamas & The Papas was precipitated by tense personal relationships between the members: at one point, Michelle Phillips was dismissed from the band, she and her husband parting in 1970. Ultimately, despite their rejuvenation by a triumphant Monterey Festival performance, hopes of reviving the fortunes of The Mamas & The Papas were to be dashed. Elliot – now with a daughter, Owen Vanessa (the identity of the father was never revealed) – had also divorced, but enjoyed solo success; her biggest latterday hit was the UK Top Ten 'It's Getting Better' (1969).

In terms of her health, though, things were far from improving. Inflicting a series of ill-advised crash diets on herself – reportedly allowing just one meal a week – Elliot put her heart under severe pressure as she began a two-week showcase at the London Palladium in July 1974. She was found dead at a flat in Curzon Place, Mayfair, belonging to her friend Harry Nilsson – a venue that, four years later, was to claim the life of a second rock star, Keith Moon (☞ *September 1978*).

See also *John Phillips (*☞ *Golden Oldies #11); Zal Yanovsky (*☞ *December 2002)*

AUGUST

Friday 9

Bill Chase
(William Edward Chiaiese – Squantum, Massachusetts, 20 October 1934)

Walter Clark
(1949)

John Emma
(1952)

Wally Yohn
(1947)

Chase

Chase – a powerful, nine-piece jazz-rock ensemble predicted to become as huge as Chicago (the band) – were founded in 1970 by trumpeter Bill Chase, a veteran of the business who'd gained experience and respect with jazz performers Woody Herman and Stan Kenton during the sixties. A meaningful breakthrough to the rock sector seemed a tougher nut to crack for Chase, though, and their 1971 'Get It On' was the only Top Forty hit the band were to enjoy.

In 1973, a difficult light-aircraft flight for Chase had left bassist Dartanyon Brown too scared ever to fly again – and was to prove a sinister omen for the band. A year later, having completed a week of well-received dates in Texas, Bill Chase and his band were all set for an appearance at the Jackson County Fair in Minnesota when the group's Piper Comanche fell from the sky in adverse conditions. The craft crashed just short of the runway as it attempted to land: Chase and three members of his band – Walter Clark (drums), John Emma (guitar) and Wally Yohn (keys) – were killed, as were the pilot and co-pilot. The rest of the band learned the terrible news as they awaited their contingent at the fair. With pilot error and poor radio communications given as the reason for the disaster, the bereaved families all filed successful lawsuits.

SEPTEMBER

Monday 23

Robbie McIntosh
(Dundee, Scotland, 6 May 1950)
The Average White Band
(Oblivion Express)

Beginning his career with RCA-signed Forevermore in the late sixties, percussionist Robbie McIntosh was spotted by Brian Auger (late of Trinity), who selected him for his newer band Oblivion Express – a name that later rang ironically true. McIntosh could have been called a journeyman musician, even though he was only twenty-four when he died. He eventually wound up in The Average White Band in 1972, having been one of several band members who had had a UK number one that year as back-up for Chuck Berry on his frivolous 'My Ding-a-Ling' single. AWB's own success only really began after a 1973 debut album with CBS had fared poorly. A second, eponymous record on Atlantic picked up wider attention – not least for its distinctive sleeve – with featured single 'Pick up the Pieces' mustering airplay by the end of 1974.

For Robbie McIntosh, though, it was already too late. At a Hollywood party thrown by millionaire playboy Kenneth Moss in honour of surviving Allman Brother, Gregg, the band (tired after a week-long booking at LA's Troubadour Club) were offered what they thought was cocaine. Having hoovered it all up, they discovered to their horror that the substance was, in fact, heroin laced with strychnine; attempts to eject the poison from their systems were effective for the majority of AWB, though singer/bassist Alan Gorrie had the attendant Cher (then Allman's girl-friend) to thank for making him pace the floor to prevent him slipping into a coma. Unable to force the exhausted McIntosh to stay awake – let alone vomit up the contents of his stomach – his bandmates could only watch as the young drummer slipped away. Moss later pleaded guilty to invol-untary manslaughter but served just three months. A bereft Average White Band, meanwhile, replaced McIntosh with their first black member, Steve Ferrone (who also replaced McIntosh in Oblivion Express): within two months of the tragedy, the appropri-ately titled single was on its way to topping the US charts.

Nick Drake

(Rangoon, Burma, 19 June 1948)

Was the music of Nick Drake simply too ethereal, too beautiful to be noticed in an era obsessed with the glamour of pop or the pomp and technique of prog rock? Whatever the reason, Drake was a severely underrated songwriter during his lifetime, and it took two more decades for his work to be given even adequate recognition. Perhaps many aspects of Nick Drake's world precluded pop stardom during his lifetime. He was a deeply – overly, according to some – sensitive character from a very young age, and certainly no wild man. Nor indeed was his gift the result of struggle in a conventional sense: Drake's family was distinctly upper-middle class. His father, Rodney, was an engineer, deployed abroad until his health dictated the family's return to Britain when Nick was four. A gentle, slender and good-looking man, Nick Drake found his demons came from within, at a time when such admissions were still not permitted.

Raised in Tanworth-in-Arden near Birmingham, the quiet Drake excelled at school in both studies and games, subsequently winning a Cambridge scholarship in 1966. But the creativity of making and writing music was his real love: Drake – who had learned clarinet, alto sax, piano and guitar – became, according to his mother, Molly (also a songwriter), an insomniac who sat in an orange armchair writing his melodies into the small hours. To his parents' chagrin, Drake left his studies to concentrate on his art. He was inspired by musicians like Bert Jansch and John Renbourn, but it was plain to the few who knew him that his talent was the equal or better of most of those that had gone before. Although this select band of fans was to remain select, one who took Drake seriously was Fairport Convention producer Joe Boyd (on the recommendation of bassist Ashley Hutchings), who arranged first a demo for his Witchseason imprint and then the sessions for what would become the singer/songwriter's spellbinding debut album, *Five Leaves Left* (1969). The latter – its title often wrongly interpreted as an early statement of the singer's suicidal intent – is a collection of songs both uplifting yet disquieting, their fragility enhanced by string arrangements by Drake's university friend Robert Kirby and the input of established musicians such as Richard Thompson. Its 1970 follow-up, *Bryter Layter*, was an altogether more accomplished affair, but still possessed much of the frail charm of the debut and perhaps Drake's finest composition, 'Northern Sky'. Neither record made serious headway, despite critical acclaim – a paradox that confounded the musician. Some suggested that a lack of interest in Drake's sprightlier second collection was down to his reluctance to take the album on the road: he'd played a series of dates at the time of the debut but had always been uncomfortable with performing, seldom making eye contact with his audience. Now, early signs of depression were interpreted as 'disappointment' in most quarters.

In 1971, peers could see the change in Nick Drake's personality. He was withdrawn and was prescribed the anti-depressant Tryptizol by a psychiatrist, but early on found its side effects insupportable. Chris Blackwell, head of Island Records (with whom Drake now recorded), had a better idea – he offered the artist a couple of weeks at his Spanish apartment: Drake accepted, and on his return that October announced to delighted colleagues that he was ready to go into the studio for a third album. The result, however, was a deeply personal, lonely disc, cut by the musician in just two nights. Island's first knowledge of the work was a set of tapes left at reception, so reticent had the singer become. Despite the earlier hopes of his friends and family, that all was clearly not well was borne out by the collection of sparse songs that made up *Pink Moon* (1972). When this, too, failed to make an impact, Drake's frustration turned to anger: he would accuse only-slightly-more-successful contemporaries of 'selling out', labelling friend John Martyn 'devious' and deeming Joe Boyd's decision to move to the

> ## 'I'd rather he died because he wanted to end it than it to be the result of a tragic mistake. That would seem to me to be terrible – for it to be a plea for help that nobody hears.'
> Actress Gabrielle Drake, Nick's sister

USA 'a betrayal'. Turning his back on music, Nick Drake tried a new career in computer programming, and even enlisted in the army. When these paths also proved fruitless, Drake returned to his parents' home, isolated and despondent. Having reached his lowest point, Drake – who checked himself into a psychiatric unit for a month – stated that he 'didn't see the point of living'.

Once again, an invitation to foreign soil (or, in this case, water) stemmed the startling decline of a man who should have been in his prime. Drake lived on a houseboat on the Seine for a while, reacquainting himself with chanteuse Françoise Hardy, who, having fallen in love with Drake's songs some time earlier, had expressed an interest in his writing for her. Partly invigorated by this new-found approval of his work, Drake cut four tracks for a proposed fourth album of his own while making arrangements to settle permanently in Paris, and returned home to organize this move (and to start learning French) in November 1974. It was never to happen: Nick Drake died in the early hours of the twenty-fifth – seemingly from an overdose of Tryptizol. He was discovered sprawled across his bed the following lunchtime by his mother. Suicide was the verdict, though Drake had left no note to this effect, and had even recently denounced such an action as one he could never consider. His mother believed that her son had suggested his intent to her – and lyrics to his later works seemed to support the notion that he'd been greatly unhappy for the last couple of years – but many believe Drake's death can only have been accidental. Writer Nick Kent, who covered Drake's passing for the *NME*, insisted that 'there was no great flourish that so often tends to typify the self-imposed taking of one's life'.

Nick Drake reportedly sold fewer than 30,000 records while he was alive, but times and attitudes change. Three decades on, the rock revisionists have had a field day with a series of reissues and, in the case of *Made to Love Magic* (2004), previously unreleased material finding its way on to the market. Those who have openly acknowledged Drake's influence over the years include artists as diverse as Elton John, Television's Tom Verlaine, Robert Smith of The Cure and ex-Dinosaur Jr leader J Mascis.

DECEMBER

Sunday 15

Rodd Keith

(Rodney Keith Eskelin – Baltimore, Maryland, 1937)

(Rodd & Bobbie)

Little-known talent Rodd Keith was a songwriter and multi-instrumentalist whose father's conversion to fundamentalism grounded Keith's musical skills in gospel. His upbringing had a profound effect on him, and he married another non-secular musician, the couple touring the South as keyboard duo Rodd & Bobbie, eventually securing a regular television slot in the late fifties. A hugely unpredictable figure, Keith then turned his back on religion (and on his marriage and young son) for secular music, though, initial success lacking, he resorted to stunts such as looting the music shop that employed him in order to raise capital. Moving alone to California, where he remarried, the maverick musician began recording under a variety of aliases, customers approaching him from far and wide for his unusual and seemingly effortless ability to set anything – prose, poetry, whatever – to music ('song poems').

Abusing drugs increasingly, Rodd Keith nurtured the regrettable habit of playing practical jokes in order to 'psyche out' his acquaintances. One of these was to walk along high and very narrow ledges. At 5.10 am on the morning of 15 December, Keith was indulging in this activity when he slipped and fell from a freeway overpass on Santa Monica Boulevard. Passing traffic was unable to avoid his falling body, and Keith was struck by several cars, sustaining massive injuries which killed him. The plot thickened when it was discovered that he had recently spoken of making a movie about just such an occurrence.

Lest We Forget

Other notable deaths that occurred sometime during 1974:

Pink Anderson (noted US bluesman whose name apparently inspired that of Pink Floyd; born South Carolina, 12/2/1900; heart attack, 12/10)

Charles 'Packy' Axton (much-recorded US saxophonist – the son and nephew of the founders of Stax – whose Mar-Keys evolved into Booker T & The MGs (without him); born 17/2/1941; heart attack, 1/74)

Herb Coleman (US first tenor with The Delta Rhythm Boys; born New York, 2/10/1927; shot during a visit to Cannes, he died in the arms of group leader Lee Gaines, 12/6)

Pamela Courson (US 'muse' to Jim Morrison who took his name and worked for The Doors' company; born California, 22/12/1946; heroin overdose, 25/4)

Arthur 'Big Boy' Crudup (seminal gospel/blues singer who wrote Elvis's first hit, 'That's All Right Mama'; born Mississippi, 24/8/1905; heart attack, 28/3)

Adge Cutler (popular original frontman of 'ooh-aar' scrumpy 'n' western outfit, The Wurzels; born Somerset, 1930; car crash 5/5)

Shorty Horton (US original bass-player with Link Wray's bands; born Brantley Moses Horton, Virginia, 5/6/1921; unknown, 11/11)

Lightnin' Slim (US 'swamp blues' maestro; born Otis V Hicks, Missouri, 13/3/1913; cancer, 27/6)

Bernie Nee (US one-man orchestra – 'The Five Blobs' – who charted in 1958 with the theme from the movie *The Blob*; born 4/12/1922; unknown, 2/74)

Ed Sullivan (celebrated 'stone-faced' TV host who introduced the US to The Beatles, Rolling Stones and Doors, among dozens of other artists; born New York, 28/9/1901 (or 1902); cancer, 13/10)

For a complete list of fallen artists, visit

www.numberoneinheaven.com

FEBRUARY

Monday 10

Dave Alexander

(Detroit, Michigan, 3 June 1947)

The Stooges

The somehow indestructible Iggy Pop kept on going while contemporaries of his fell by the wayside: Dave Alexander was the first such victim. As a 17-year-old Beatles/Stones fan, Alexander, having dropped out of school, dreamed of being in a band. Flying to England on a whim with his friend Ron Asheton, Alexander didn't manage to meet his heroes, but he returned to the US more determined than ever. The pair rehearsed with Ron's brother, Scott – and, in 1965, the very first inklings of The Stooges could be heard rasping from the bass guitarist's basement. All they lacked was a frontman – but then there was this weird guy who worked at the local record store . . .

The (Psychedelic) Stooges were complete in 1967 when they recruited James Jewell Osterberg (aka Iggy Pop, late of The Prime Movers), the band – effectively Ron (guitar), Scott Asheton (drums) and Alexander (bass) – a stonewall backing to the frontman

and his bizarre stage antics. In spite of their primeval sound and the singer's predilection for smearing himself with blood and peanut butter on stage, Elektra signed The Stooges in 1968. Alexander was becoming more and more interested in mysticism as the group made its first (low-selling) pair of albums: he persuaded the band to record his strange chanting for the ten-minute 'We Will Fall' for the John Cale-produced *The Stooges* (1969). His primal bass riff drove the band's best moment, 'Dirt' from *Fun House* (1970), but Alexander's particularly heavy abuse of drugs caused his unlikely firing by Iggy shortly after this record – following a performance at the Jackson Goose Lake Festival when a tripping Alexander forgot all the songs. Although he was replaced on bass by Ron Asheton (James Williamson came in on guitars), the proto-punk pioneers disbanded soon after – to return as Iggy & The Stooges two years on.

During a long-running feud with the singer in the eighties, the Asheton brothers were quoted as saying that had Iggy not sacked Alexander he might still be alive today. He died early in 1975, years of drug and alcohol abuse weakening his body until he fell victim to pneumonia in Detroit. Just months later, The Stooges lost another bass-player (and roadie) – Zeke Zettner – to a drug overdose.

But one former Stooge often believed dead by inaccurate sources is saxophonist Steve Mackay, whose playing lit up the band's second album. Mackay proved he was very much alive in 2003, playing to thousands of Stooges fans amazed to see him – and his original sax – reunited for a tour with Iggy and the Ashetons.

APRIL

Wednesday 23

Pete Ham

(Swansea, West Glamorgan, 27 April 1947)

Badfinger

Affectionately known as 'The Drunken Beatles', Badfinger's was a slower, bluesier take on the Fab Four's sound – though most of the band were gifted songwriters in their own right. Many critics believe Badfinger could have gone on to become one of Britain's biggest acts by the mid seventies – instead, theirs remains arguably the most tragic band fable of all.

It all started well for The Iveys (as they were once known). The band – eventually lead singer/guitarist/pianist Pete Ham, Tom Evans (rhythm/bass), Joey Molland (guitars) and Mike Gibbins (drums) – had been signed to The Beatles' Apple label and were developing a strong relationship with various soon-to-be-ex-Beatles. Following a name change, they began an impressive run of transatlantic Top Ten entries with 'Come and Get It' (1970, written by Paul McCartney), 'No Matter What' and 'Day After Day' (both 1971, the latter produced by George Harrison). Something of an Apple house band, Badfinger also contributed to various Beatles' solo projects – but with their own hits drying up all too quickly, it was a classic song for another artist that was to prove a particular *bête noire* for writers Ham and Evans.

The end came for Pete Ham following a series of legal problems between Badfinger's management and the label (from whom they had parted company, signing with Warner Bros after an unsuccessful fourth album in 1974). The crippling disputes prevented this talented artist from either working or earning from past successes; quite simply, he was put out of service by the music business. Had Badfinger's legal and financial dealings been better managed, Ham would have become a very wealthy man indeed – Harry Nilsson's version of his and Evans's 'Without You' topped the charts worldwide in 1972 (a 1994 mauling by Mariah Carey somehow outsold even that). This extraordinary ballad was inspired by Ham's girlfriend, Anne Herriott – as was 1975's 'Helping Hand'. In this, his last ever composition, Ham appeared to be reaching out to his lover for help during the darkest period of his life. But it was too late. Warners pulled their last two albums at the point of release; Badfinger were falling apart; Pete Ham quit the line-up that spring. Desperate and confused, he polished off a bottle and hanged himself in the garage studio of the London flat he shared with Herriott, just three days before his twenty-seventh birthday

and one month before the birth of the couple's daughter, Petera. His suicide note reportedly described Badfinger's business manager Stan Polley as a 'soulless bastard'. One of the first to the scene, his long-time friend and colleague Tom Evans never recovered from seeing Ham's body in that garage: he took his own life in similar circumstances eight years later (☛ *November 1983*).

See also *Mike Gibbins (☛ October 2005)*

Friday 25

Mike Brant

(Moshé Brandt – Cyprus, 1 February 1947)
The Chocolates

A similar tale emerged from France just days after the death of Pete Ham. Pop heart-throb Mike Brant took his own life in Paris – and, once again, it was the pressures of a hungry industry that seemed to precipitate his action. Brant (or Brandt, as he was born) didn't utter a word as a toddler; his Israeli parents feared until he turned five that he might always be mute. Far from it – their son possessed a more than decent voice and his dark looks had begun to turn heads even when working on a kibbutz as a teenager. The family had moved back to Israel, and Brant was fronting his brother's band The Chocolates (under new identity Mickaël Sela), who began to create waves on the dinner circuit. With the group reaching low-level international status, Brant was discovered by French chanteuse Sylvie Vartan – and, though he sang purely phonetically, his ticket into the glitzy world of French pop was assured. Vartan took the young singer to France in 1969, and musical director Jean Renard (the man responsible for such 'delights' as Johnny Hallyday) offered Brant a five-year contract. His

first single, *Laisse-moi t'aimer* ('Let Me Love You'), was released in 1970 – and promptly sold 1.5 million copies to eager French housewives. The image was everything one might imagine: medallion, slashed-open shirt, vacuous expression – but the formula worked and 'Mike Brant' became the biggest star French pop had seen for some time.

But Brant, unwittingly, was merely a pawn. When the singer was involved in a car accident in early 1971, Renard's first priority was to obtain photographs of him lying in hospital to sell to a national newspaper – after all, the injured singer had a new record out. The partnership was shortly dissolved. Under the new management of Charles Talar, Brant then found that the hysteria surrounding him was such that, when not performing, he had to remain locked in his room most of the time (which ended the only meaningful relationship he was to enjoy). In 1974, Brant's world began to unravel dramatically: he experienced a breakdown on stage in Boissy-Saint-Leger, then his apartment was burgled and most of his valuables stolen (including lithographs from his friend Salvador Dalí). On 21 November 1974, the increasingly unhinged singer attempted suicide for the first time, throwing himself from a hotel window. Although friends rallied for months – and hit records *still* continued to come – Brant finally completed the deed, jumping from his apartment. As the stars of French pop music made their way to Israel for their colleague's funeral, sales of Mike Brant's final album topped the million mark in his adopted land. Thirty years on, his estate still benefits from more than 200,000 sales of his records every year.

Tim Buckley: Hello and goodbye

JUNE

Sunday 29

Tim Buckley

(Timothy Charles Buckley III – Washington, DC,
14 February 1947)

(The Bohemians)

In 1965, Los Angeles music review *Cheetah* heralded three newcomers to the songwriter fold – Jackson Browne, Steve Noonan and Tim Buckley. While Noonan disappeared without much trace, Browne went on to commercial stardom during the seventies. As for Buckley, he would chart, briefly, an entirely different universe altogether, his music always marginal. His highly original style was, however, to inspire following generations, its timelessness secured by his dramatic young death.

Tim Buckley's message was unique, often emerging disguised as a series of whoops or grunts, so deeply entrenched was the singer/songwriter in his work. There were early clues: former high-school friend and co-writer Larry Beckett talked of how the young singer projected his voice to scream at buses or impersonate musical instruments. Buckley is usually referred to as a folk act, though in truth he was brought up on Johnny Cash and Hank Williams, his own music born out of gospel, jazz and soul. Buckley knew no real parameters, using his five-octave range however he chose. Commercial appreciation would always be out of reach, but Buckley – and those who had sufficient faith to record and produce his records – recognized this early in his career. Buckley and Beckett had formed a trio, The Bohemians, with another friend Jim Fielder, but it was the frontman who stood out. Buckley signed with Elektra

('I must have listened to his demo twice a day for a week' – Jac Holzman, producer), and an eponymous 1966 debut album set out his stall, but it was his second record, *Goodbye and Hello* (1967) that was his most – if not only – avowedly accessible work (even though it only managed a Billboard peak of 171). Strangely, this confident record arrived when his personal life was in crisis, his wife, Mary Guibert – and young son Jeffrey – estranged from the singer. Buckley's music was almost certainly driven by the turmoil of his upbringing. Brought up in New York, then Anaheim, California, he'd felt rejected by his military father who, injured during the Second World War, often took out his rage on the good-looking young Buckley, calling him a 'faggot'; his mother, meanwhile, believed her son would die young – because 'that's what poets do'. In 1970, American music-buyers were tuning into the gentler, near-MOR sounds of James Taylor or David Gates, leaving Buckley's sixth set, *Starsailor* – an experimental work using flugelhorns and the like – to gather dust. Those who didn't hear it missed his finest moment, 'Song to the Siren', a tune covered superbly in 1983 by This Mortal Coil.

Buckley's work became increasingly impenetrable over the next few years: some of his habits, meanwhile, are all too familiar. The singer was no junkie, but he *was* very impressionable, taking substances on the whim of others; he'd also developed a predilection for pushing as far as he could, whether this meant driving too fast or drinking too much. After a sell-out show in Dallas, Buckley arrived inebriated at the Santa Monica home of his friend, music student Richard Keeling, who clearly did not wish to be disturbed. Thrusting some powder at the musician, Keeling washed his hands of Buckley as he snorted the drug, in the mistaken belief that it was cocaine. Within a short time, the singer was in a bad way, and had to be taken home to his second wife, Judy, who, believing he would sleep it off, put him to bed. She returned to him later to discover that he had turned blue – and had slipped away. A post mortem revealed that Tim Buckley had ingested both heroin and morphine. Keeling, as the supplier, was indicted on two charges of second-degree murder but charged with involuntary manslaughter.

If the rare music of Tim Buckley was to be transcended by anyone, it was by Jeff, the son he barely knew, who like his father was taken way, way too soon (☞ *May 1997*).

JULY

Thursday 31

Tony Geraghty
(Republic of Ireland, 1952)
Brian McCoy
(Northern Ireland, 1942)
Fran O'Toole
(Republic of Ireland, 1948)
The Miami Showband

Three years after fourteen died in Derry on Bloody Sunday, a group of innocent musicians were cut down in similar scenes of senseless terrorism. A changing unit – in 1975 comprising Tony Geraghty (guitar), Des McAlea (saxophone), Brian McCoy (trumpet), Ray Millar (drums), Fran O'Toole (vocals), Dickie Rock (vocals) and Steven Travers (bass) – The Miami Showband were little more than just that: a good-time Dublin pop group with wide appeal and a number of albums to their name. They certainly posed little political threat to anyone.

The band had been visiting Banbridge, County Down, to play a concert at the Castle Ballroom, when terror struck. A splinter group of the

notorious paramilitary organization the UVF (Ulster Volunteer Force) – known as the Shankhill Butchers – had been involved in several ruthless acts before. This time they chose to frame the Catholic members of the Showband as IRA-supporters attempting to smuggle munitions across the border. Thus an ambush was carried out on the group's minibus just outside Newry; four UVF members set up a bogus army roadblock and flagged the vehicle down. When two of them tried to plant an explosive device in one of the band's amps, it detonated, killing them both instantly. In the aftermath to this already grisly scene, Geraghty, McCoy and O'Toole were taken off the bus and summarily executed by shotgun. A year later, Thomas Crozier and Rodney McDowell – the two UVF members held responsible for the killings – were each sentenced to thirty-five years in prison.

AUGUST

Wednesday 27

Bob Scholl
(Mount Vernon, Westchester, New York, 14 July 1938)
The Mello-Kings

Hailed as the 'blackest-sounding white group' of their day, The Mello-Kings deserve plaudits for being one of the first inter-racial vocal groups to achieve a level of national success. Led by first tenor Bob Scholl – along with his brother Jerry (lead) – the group fought their way out of the tough suburb of Mount Vernon to sign as teenagers with Al Silver's Herald label. In August 1957, a single, 'Tonite, Tonite', was all ready to launch the band – then known as The Mellotones – to stardom, until surly Gee Records boss George

Goldner pointed out to Silver that he already had a band in the charts with this name. Thus, The Mello-Kings were born – and the record gave them a huge R & B/airplay hit. It was in live performance that the band flourished most of all, a huge draw on the chitlin circuit during the late fifties, though they had further localized hits such as 'Valerie' (1958).

Despite no wider acceptance for The Mello-Kings, Bob Scholl managed to continue the group until 1969, finding a new outlet on the revival circuit – until his death in a New York boating accident.

OCTOBER

Wednesday 1

Al Jackson Jr
(Memphis, Tennessee, 27 November 1935)
Booker T & The MGs

Unassuming, congenial percussionist Al Jackson had the best possible start, playing the traps with his father, big-band leader Al Jackson Sr, at just five years old. His formidable style, energy and God-given ability to 'sniff out the groove' meant Jackson was seldom out of work. Beginning as a full-time member of his father's jazz/dance band during his teens, via Willie Mitchell's house band at Hi Records, he secured the enviable position of Stax house drummer with Booker T & The MGs. The latter – regularly lauded as the tightest backing band in the world – enjoyed a series of timeless international hits under their own steam, including 'Green Onions' (1962) and 'Time Is Tight' (1969). Members of the band also played on numerous hits for other artists/labels, including Eddie Floyd, Sam & Dave and Wilson Pickett.

Throughout his life, Jackson had so many friends and admirers (future MGs bassist Donald 'Duck' Dunn almost cost himself his marriage, so obsessed was he with watching the young prodigy play with Willie Mitchell every night) that it is hard to imagine the man having enemies of any description. However, the nature of his death throws this into sharp perspective.

Had Jackson not been such a keen boxing enthusiast, the first night of October would surely have ended very differently. Wanting to watch the Muhammad Ali/Joe Frazier rematch (the so-called 'Thrilla in Manila') on a giant screen (a rarity in those days) at Mid-South Coliseum, Jackson informed the Detroit studio who had hired him to produce a Major Lance session that he'd fly out from Memphis a day later. Returning home from the match in good spirits, Jackson interrupted intruders, who forced him into a prone position and tied him up before he could utter a word. Apparently, one of the gang knew of Jackson (or at least his home) and had chosen this as the venue to rendezvous after a bank robbery in Florida earlier that week. Also present

was Jackson's estranged wife, Barbara – bound and gagged, and thus unable to warn her husband. She could only watch as a gunman pulled a pistol and shot him five times in the back. By 3 am, Barbara Jackson had worked herself free and ran screaming into the street, after which the police were quickly summoned. Al Jackson, without medical attention, was already dead from his injuries. He and his wife had been working towards a divorce, and she – having that July shot him in the chest supposedly in self-defence – was among the first to be suspected. The circumstances seemed particularly suspicious given that no item of value appeared to have been removed during the break-in. On 15 July 1976, though, the gunman responsible (rumoured to be the boyfriend of singer Denise LaSalle) died in a shoot-out while resisting arrest in Seattle.

If the death of Otis Redding eight years before (December 1967) was a grave blow to Stax, this brutal slaying of one of its lynchpins saw the once-great label close its doors for good just a year afterwards, and the label finally collapsed when executive Johnny Baylor was found guilty of defrauding creditors of $2.5 million.

Al Jackson Jr, with Booker T and MGs Steve Cropper and Lewis Steinberg: Time was tight

Sunday 26

Elbridge 'Al' Bryant
(Thomasville, Georgia, 28 September 1939)
The Temptations
(Various acts)

Possessor of a fine falsetto/tenor, Elbridge Bryant moved to Detroit to become (via earlier vocal troupe The Distants) an original member of The Temptations – but is often forgotten inbiographies because he was dismissed from the group ahead of their mid-sixties chart domination. Just how many songs featured Bryant's crystal-clear tones is uncertain, as few Temptations records featured full credits, though he definitely sang lead on 'Isn't She Pretty?' (1962) and 'May I Have This Dance?' (1963) – undeniably among the act's most-favoured early numbers. Bryant, however, had a tendency towards heavy drinking and belligerence, which ultimately curtailed his time with Motown's biggest group.

Bryant, desperate to leave his day-job as a milkman, became increasingly disillusioned with the band's lack of success, and his unreliability and aggressive behaviour were the result of alcohol-promoted mood swings. Bryant attacked bandmate Paul Williams on a couple of notorious occasions – once smashing a beer bottle across the baritone's face; after the second occurrence, following a performance at the Motortown Christmas Revue in 1963, he was dismissed by The Temps and replaced by David Ruffin. Bryant spent time with lesser acts – such as the locally popular Dramatics – but his drinking did not let up and his death in Florida from cirrhosis of the liver therefore came as little surprise.

See also *Paul Williams (August 1973); David Ruffin (June 1991); Eddie Kendricks (October 1992); Melvin Franklin (February 1995)*

DECEMBER

Monday 8

Gary Thain

(Wellington, New Zealand, 15 May 1948)

Uriah Heep
The Keef Hartley Band

Gary Thain was a journeyman bassist who began his career with a number of New Zealand turns before moving to Britain when he was eighteen. Reluctant to be in the spotlight, Thain developed a reputation for his fastidious work rather than any onstage flamboyance. Although he picked up his first music-press column inches as a member of the blues-rock combo The Keef Hartley Band, it was with prog stalwarts the occasionally critically derided Uriah Heep that Thain experienced his most successful period. Playing with Uriah Heep in Dallas in September 1974, Thain received a massive electric shock on stage which caused him several months of ill health, during which time his cohorts saw fit to dismiss him from the band. The bassist understandably became reclusive and depressed; he'd had heart problems throughout his life, and now these were being exacerbated by his increasing use of heroin. The Texas experience having weakened his resistance, Gary Thain died in Norwood, London, apparently from an overdose.

See also *David Byron (☞ February 1985)*

'He was a rather weak person who never took care of himself. But still a nice guy – and a great bassist.'

Ken Hensley, leader,
Uriah Heep

Lest We Forget

Other notable deaths that occurred sometime during 1975:

Cannonball Adderley (US soul/jazz saxophonist; born Julian Adderley, Florida, 15/9/1928; stroke, 8/8)

Saul Bihari (US record executive and co-founder (with his three brothers) of early R & B label, Modern Records; born Missouri, 9/3/1918; unknown, 22/2)

Patsy Collins (giant UK roadie with Deep Purple; arguing with promoters over $750K owed to the band, he fell down a Jakarta lift shaft and died in a cab on the way to hospital – his body then 'disappeared', 4/12)

Jerry Daniels (US member of vocal pioneers The Ink Spots; born Indiana, 14/12/1915; unknown, 7/11)

Tom 'Big Daddy' Donahue (formidable US rock DJ/entrepreneur who produced The Beatles' last ever US show at Candlestick Park; born Indiana, 21/5/1928; heart attack, 28/4)

Lefty Frizzell (influential US country musician and sometime collaborator with Hank Williams; born William Orville Frizzell, Texas, 31/3/1928; stroke/haemorrhage, 19/7)

Ronnie Quinton (UK roadie with Deep Purple who was killed in a car crash – just eight months before the death of Patsy Collins, 10/4)

Arthur 'Duke' Reid (influential Jamaican reggae producer, DJ and Trojan Records founder, the main rival to Clement 'Coxsone' Dodd; born Portland, c 1915; lengthy illness)

Stephen Taylor (Jamaican singer and founder of The Ethiopians, who hit with 1967's 'Train To Skaville'; born 1944; car crash)

T-Bone Walker (fêted US blues guitarist – the first to 'plug in' – who influenced a generation of rock acts including the Allman Bros; born Aaron Thibeaux Walker, Texas, 28/5/1910; bronchial pneumonia, 16/3)

For a complete list of fallen artists, visit
www.numberoneinheaven.com

1976

JANUARY

Sunday 4

Mal Evans

(Malcolm Evans – Liverpool, 27 May 1937)

A long-time friend of The Beatles, Mal Evans became the Fab Four's driver, then roadie and even contributed to many legendary recordings. His vocals can be heard on 'Yellow Submarine' (1966) and he also played on 'You Won't See Me' (1965), 'Being for the Benefit of Mr Kite', 'A Day in the Life' (both 1967), 'Helter Skelter' and 'Dear Prudence' (both 1968). He also discovered Badfinger, among the first acts to be recorded by Apple Records.

By the mid seventies, Evans was living in Los Angeles and working on a book of his memoirs, entitled *Living with the Beatles' Legend*. His life was far from stable, though: he'd become estranged from his wife, Lili, with messy divorce proceedings pending, and appeared to be sliding into depression. On the night of 4 January, Evans's new girlfriend, Fran Hughes, returned to the apartment they shared at 8122 West 4th to find her lover very inebriated, loaded up on valium and threatening to put a 30.30 rifle in his mouth. Desperate to get him under some sort of control, Hughes called John Hoernle (his collaborator on the book) for help, but Evans became violent when Hoernle tried to remove the rifle from his clutches. Picking up the phone a second time, Hughes dialled 911. Within a short time, two officers arrived at the apartment to confront a now-calmer Mal Evans, but he panicked on seeing them, and refused to relinquish his gun, waving the weapon in their faces – at which point the officers fired at him six times. Four bullets hit the former roadie and he fell dead at their feet. As the officers had acted in self-defence, authorities declared that there was no case to answer.

John Lennon reportedly wept when he heard of the shooting and friend Harry Nilsson took responsibility for Evans's funeral arrangements and paid for his ashes to arrive back in Britain in an urn rather than in a cardboard container. Although he was uncredited at the time, a lump sum for Evans's musical contributions was paid to his estate by former Beatles during the nineties.

See also *John Lennon (➡ December 1980); Harry Nilsson (➡ January 1994)*

FEBRUARY

Thursday 5

Rudy Pompilli

(Rudolph Pompilli – Chester, Pennsylvania, 16 April 1924)

Bill Haley & His Comets

Rudy Pompilli was, for twenty years, the right-hand man of rock 'n' roll's first international star, Bill Haley, replacing original sax-player Joey d'Ambrosio in 1955. Despite the death of Danny Cedrone the previous summer (➡ *Pre-1965*), The Comets were enjoying their highest ever profile with the million-selling 'Rock around the Clock' still high in the charts. 'Rude the Dude' was a self-taught musician who had found some local fame with Ralph Martieri's jazz orchestra, and met Haley before his sudden success when the kiss-curled rocker was a radio manager in Chester. Haley wanted Pompilli for The Comets; he offered them fresh style, co-writing a number of tracks – not least his own 'Rudy's Rock', which graced the soundtrack to the *Rock around the Clock* movie. This creative input accompanied his onstage image of a clowning virtuoso who could play on his back, on the hop – you name it.

But The Comets' star began to fade; they split for the first time in 1962, before Pompilli took it upon himself to reorganize the band in the mid sixties for reunion dates. The sax-player then fell ill with what he thought was influenza during a 1974 tour in the wake of a successful British reissue of 'Rock around the Clock'. Upon his return to the States, Pompilli learned that he had lung cancer; he succumbed to the disease two years later. Haley – who was far less visible in the band at this time – was devastated by the loss of his close friend and sidekick.

See also *Bill Haley (*☛ *February 1981) plus the accompanying 'Dead Interesting!' for a complete list of fallen Comets.*

Thursday 12

Sal Mineo

(Salvatore Mineo Jr – The Bronx, New York, 10 January 1939)

Given that his upbringing was spent in and out of two-bit New York gangs, it's perhaps not surprising that actor and singer Sal Mineo – known in the movie press as 'The Switchblade Kid' – spent his last moments on the street.

A troubled child, he was arrested for robbery at the age of ten (although his family now insists that this was merely media publicity), but choosing drama and dance classes over institutionalization calmed Mineo – though it alienated him from his tough buddies. Within two years he starred opposite Yul Brynner in *The King and I*, and four years later played the young, sexually ambiguous foil to James Dean's rebellious leads in both *Rebel without a Cause* and *Giant*, securing a host of other impressive movie billings. Sal Mineo's recording career was far briefer: an obvious pin-up idol, he hit the US Top Ten with 'Start

Movin' in My Direction' (1957), but, with a number of 'proper' rock 'n' roll icons emerging – and much speculation about his sexuality – Mineo disappeared after just one more hit. His screen career was to last another decade, but by 1972 work was proving harder to come by for a child star who had, unfortunately, grown up. As the sixties progressed, increased sexual freedom meant that Mineo could edge further out of the closet (one liaison was with Rock Hudson), but though his social world was flourishing, his finances were not. By 1976 he was close to broke. Then, suddenly, a well-received role in the off-Broadway play *PS Your Cat is Dead* seemed to reverse his fortunes.

Sal Mineo's life, however, was ended senselessly in the car park of his rented West Hollywood apartment. Back from rehearsal, the actor emerged from his car and was confronted by a man wielding a hunting knife. Mineo was stabbed once – fatally – in the heart, his assailant fleeing without carrying out his intended robbery. Three years later, 21-year-old habitual criminal Lionel Williams (who, despite denying his crime in public, boasted of it while jailed on a felony charge) was convicted of second-degree murder, though many – including Mineo's friend John Lennon – still felt there might be a conspiracy surrounding his killing. An admirer of Mineo for his often-uncompromising work, Lennon, in 1980, demanded the case be reopened; just days later, he himself was murdered in New York (☛ *December 1980*).

Florence Ballard

(Detroit, Michigan, 30 June 1943)
The Supremes

Music historians have a great deal of sympathy for Florence Ballard, the 'forgotten Supreme' most believe was systematically conspired against by Diana Ross, Berry Gordy and the Motown machine itself. As the original lead singer of America's biggest ever girl group, Ballard certainly appeared to have been handed a raw deal. Often overlooked in such sweeping summaries, though, is Ballard's predominant self-destructive gene.

'Flo' was born the eighth of thirteen Ballard children. Like fellow Supremes Ross and Mary Wilson (plus Betty Travis, then Barbara Martin, neither of whom made the final cut), she was brought up in the Brewster Housing Project in Detroit, a vast estate close to Gordy's Hitsville USA Studios. Often compared to Billie Holiday, Ballard was just sixteen when she was snapped up by Gordy to join a female band to support The Primes (a prototype Temptations). The entrepreneur eventually signed Ballard's band for the newly founded Tamla Motown label in 1961, and The Primettes became The Supremes, the name suggested by Ballard, who had already assumed the role of leader and spokeswoman. After sluggish beginnings, this fresh-sounding group was coupled with the songwriting team of Holland, Dozier and Holland, and set about breaking records left, right and centre. Beginning with 'Where Did Our Love Go?' and 'Baby Love' (1964), The Supremes racked up twelve US number ones before 1970, their sales exceeding 20 million.

But if all appeared rosy for Ballard in 1964, her world was to come crashing down around her three years later.

Berry Gordy's interest in Diana Ross was apparent from the early days, and, little by little, *she* was pushed to the fore at Ballard's expense. The latter's attempts to regain control were as drastic as they were ineffective: when the outspoken singer's objections to Ross's special treatment fell on deaf ears, she ditched her trademark beehive and began drinking before live performances. Gordy quickly lost patience, seeing Ballard as little more than a thorn in his and Ross's side, and she was unceremoniously ousted from the group, replaced by the more amenable Cindy Birdsong (formerly of Patti Labelle & The Bluebells). (Officially, Motown suggested that Ballard's 'retirement' was down to 'the strain of touring'.) Ballard was paid off with a risible $140,000 for all future rights in 1968, while for 'The Supremes' one now read 'Diana Ross & The Supremes': the deed, as envisaged by Gordy and Ross, was done. Or so it appeared . . .

Her solo career with the ABC label stuttering, an increasingly desperate Ballard attempted to sue Motown in 1971 (by which time Ross had left The Supremes) for nearly $9 million, which she felt she was entitled to, describing Gordy's 'secret, subversive, malicious plotting and planning'. But the earlier settlement was declared legal and above board, and the case was thrown out of court, leaving Ballard near-destitute. Her marriage to inexperienced manager Tom Chapman subsequently collapsed, leaving her with three children to support alone. Her drinking, predictably, renewed apace, this time accompanied by an alarming increase in weight. While this destroyed her self-confidence as a performer, Ballard – who had no financial support from Chapman – still maintained sufficient pride to avoid asking for help elsewhere and, having lost her home in Buena Vista, was, in 1975, claiming welfare. To all intents and purposes, Ballard had returned to the housing-project world of her childhood.

A potential life-saver arrived in the form of a $50K pay-out from Motown (at the behest of Diana Ross, now flourishing as a solo artist). But this much-needed cash didn't reverse Florence Ballard's health problems: on the evening of 21 February, the singer – now weighing in excess of 200 lbs – checked herself into Mount Carmel Mercy Hospital, Michigan. Her limbs ached and she'd started to feel numbness in her extremities. Alarmed by these tell-tale signs, doctors worked through the night to save Ballard, but the former star died from coronary artery thrombosis at 10.05 the very next morning. A coroner later confirmed that Ballard had ingested an 'unspecified' amount of dietary pills and alcohol.

Perhaps understandably, Ross's attempts at reconciliation with Ballard had, like the handouts and menial jobs offered to her, been routinely ignored. The die had been cast: despite more than a suggestion of contrition on her part, Ross was always portrayed as the 'Judas' in Ballard's story. Five days later, Ross was roundly jeered at the well-attended but highly charged funeral service at Detroit's New Bethel Baptist Church – the crowd of some 5,000 became hysterical and snatched floral tributes and other souvenirs from the casket as it passed.

MARCH

Friday 19

Paul Koss

(Hampstead, London, 14 September 1950)
Free
(Back Street Crawler)
(Black Cat Bones)

There was a time when arguably the best blues-based rock guitarists were emanating from the British Isles:

beginning with Eric Clapton, a rich late-sixties lineage that included Jeff Beck, Jimmy Page and Mick Taylor also gave the rock world the often-underrated Paul Kossoff. With his expressive vibrato and cleverly under-stated take on the blues, it's little wonder that Kossoff – the son of British actor David Kossoff – had been classically trained as a child. What's more surprising is that he nearly gave up the guitar at fifteen, but a decent deal on a 1954 Gibson Les Paul changed his mind – and the course of his life.

In his teens, Kossoff came into contact with a number of musicians who had a profound effect on him: one was the young Jimi Hendrix, a customer of the music centre at which Kossoff worked; another was drummer Simon Kirke, with whom Kossoff formed his first band, Black Cat Bones, becoming his long-time collaborator in Free. The pair targeted Paul Rodgers after watching the vocalist entertain the patrons of a London boozer (fourth Free-man, bassist Andy Fraser, was another teenage prodigy – with John Mayall's Bluesbreakers). By 1969 the Alexis Korner-approved Free were opening for Blind Faith on their US tour. In 1970 Free were at number two in the UK and number four in the States with future party staple, the stompalong 'All Right Now'. Further hits arrived, mainly in their homeland, but the inconsistent reception of their albums prompted Fraser to leave in 1971. Free returned in 1972, but the early impetus had gone – Kossoff, still only twenty-one, had developed a concerning drug habit, a major factor towards Free's capitulation in 1973.

With Rodgers and Kirke elsewhere enjoying immense success with Bad Company, Kossoff was briefly picked up by his own project, Back Street Crawler. Commercial success, though, was not as forthcoming as it had been for his former colleagues, and Kossoff's health and spirits were noticeably declining. On 30 August

Phil Ochs

(El Paso, Texas, 19 December 1940)

He may have been a quality vocal performer and a so-so guitarist, but Phil Ochs was destined to play second fiddle to Bob Dylan during the sixties folk boom. A fan of Elvis, Buddy Holly and country music, the young Ochs was something of a daydreamer. Given his fiercely anti-military stance, it's surprising to learn that Ochs put himself forward for military academy in Staunton, but the fragile artist believed he would come away a better person from the experience. The discipline he learned didn't, however, prevent him from dropping out of his studies in Ohio, and Ochs fitted snugly into Greenwich Village's folk scene on his 1962 arrival. He had a fistful of tunes and attitude to burn, thus he was 'home'. In the wake of Dylan's early success, Elektra seemed to agree that this self-styled 'singing journalist' also had something, and released his first album, *All the News That's Fit to Sing* (1964). Subjects readily presented themselves – Cuba (he was a follower of Fidel Castro), Vietnam, civil rights – and the time seemed right for Phil Ochs. His 'Draft Dodger Rag' from the second long-player *Ain't Marching Anymore* (1965) added much-needed wry humour to the genre, and became something of an anti-'Nam anthem.

Like Dylan, Ochs also took the electric route – though many thought that the added production this necessitated on his recorded output diluted essential numbers like 'Crucifixion'. Unfazed, the singer headed to California and signed with A&M, but his constant banging on the door still failed to garner any response

Paul Kossoff: The spirit was willing, the flesh was weak

1975, the guitarist had to be revived when his heart stopped for a full half-hour – a warning sign that would have caused many to rethink their lifestyle. Not so Paul Kossoff. Still touring heavily, the guitarist was flying from Los Angeles to New York when he fell into a drug-induced coma, and died of heart failure as he slept. His father spent much of his later life campaigning against drug abuse, taking a poignant stage show about his son's death on the road in the late seventies.

greater than the mild irritation of a few Democrats. His frustration was compounded when a 1968 single seemingly bound for Billboard was pulled from radio for its length and references to pot-smoking. Later album *Rehearsals For Retirement* (1969) featured his tombstone on the sleeve, the music itself displaying growing personal despair, his attitude made ever more belligerent by his intake of alcohol. The worn-down and worn-out Ochs then released a sardonic 1970 set, *Greatest Hits*, compiling a band and decking himself out in a silver lamé suit to tour the record. Then, in 1973, Ochs was set upon in a mysterious incident in Africa, mugged and almost strangled by a band of thieves; he survived but suffered severe vocal-chord damage. Two years on, he toured under the reckless alter ego of 'John Train', a caricature of himself he claimed had 'killed Phil Ochs'. Unsurprisingly, friends, alienated during this phase, described him as suicidal. It came as little surprise when the 'reborn' Phil Ochs was found hanged at his sister's apartment in Queens, New York. He apparently thought himself a failure, of no use to anyone – and an anachronism from an age now gone for ever.

'If I could put into one word what the essence of The Yardbirds was – it would be "electricity".'

(The unfortunate words of) Keith Relf, 1975

MAY

Friday 14

Keith Relf

(William Keith Relf – Richmond, Surrey, 22 March 1943)
The Yardbirds
Renaissance
(Medicine Head)
(Various acts)

Never especially healthy, Keith Relf seemed to be living on borrowed time from his childhood. Chronic asthma almost cost him his life on three separate occasions, his choice to sing and play the harmonica perhaps not the most sensible given his talent as a guitarist and songwriter. Playing in London-based bands, the musician found fame at just twenty with The Yardbirds (originally The Metropolis Blues Quartet), still one of the most widely revered British rock bands of the mid sixties, shedding in their wake an extraordinary legacy of guitarists: Jeff Beck, Jimmy Page and Eric Clapton (the latter a former Kingston art-school friend recommended by Relf). Before their breakthrough, however, Relf suffered his first major health scare with a collapsed lung after the band's first tour of the States in 1964. Nevertheless, his renewed vocals were heard across the land just months later as The Yardbirds put together a run of five consecutive Top Ten hits – including the brilliant and evocative 'For Your Love', 'Heart Full of Soul' (both 1965) and 'Shapes Of Things' (1966). A constantly changing line-up of such auspicious musicians inevitably limited the band's lifespan, the inevitable split coming in July 1968. While Page went off to form Led Zeppelin, Relf took a statelier path, forming Together with fellow ex-Yardbird Jim McCarty, this band

becoming, with the addition of Relf's sister, Jane, Renaissance – a group that had its biggest success after the Relfs had left. A brief stint with Medicine Head continued Relf's Midas touch, as they too gained commercial acceptance, but an unlikely spell with heavy act Armageddon brought less success, and Relf had begun yet another new project, Illusion, by 1976.

On 14 May, Relf's young son, Daniel, walked into his basement studio to find him lying prone, apparently having fallen. The musician had actually been electrocuted as he stood over a hidden gas line to tune his badly earthed guitar. The shock had not been great, but Relf, who had emphysema on top of his asthma (and had been suffering personal problems) was dead.

AUGUST

Tuesday 10

Gus Gossert

(Robert Charles Gossert – Pennsylvania, 14 June 1943)

Known as the 'Curly-Headed Kid', Gossert was a law graduate turned US disc jockey brave enough to play 'street corner' doo-wop on pop radio when nobody else would touch it – a decade-plus after most of it had been released. Generally credited with coining the phrase itself, Gossert opened his *Doo-Wop Shop* on New York's WCBS, having completed rookie stints in Hawaii and San Francisco, where mainstream pop/rock was all that was on the menu. While the show itself became an indefinite fixture, Gossert – a radio-archive fanatic – took his platters to nearby WPIX, where he augmented a longer slot with segments of old radio shows from a similar era.

Gossert's use of narcotics and alleged connections with drug-trafficking rings brought about his downfall. Following a bust, the NYPD offered the DJ an early release on the condition he remained clean – and moved elsewhere. Whether this deal was carved out because he was a public figure or simply because he had 'information' will always remain unclear. One clue might come from the nature of his death: returning from a visit to Nashville to spend time with his student girlfriend (future country star Pam Tillis), Gus Gossert was gunned down in mysterious circumstances.

DECEMBER

Saturday 4

Tommy Bolin

(Sioux City, Iowa, 1 August 1951)

Deep Purple
The James Gang
(Zephyr)
(Energy)

One of the few youngsters of his era whose parents completely approved of rock 'n' roll, Bolin's mother taught music and his father took him, aged five, to see Elvis Presley. Although Bolin learned drums, his broad-minded mum and dad also saw to it that he had a guitar and a radio, to which he played along with the hits of The Beatles and Stones as a teen. Bolin was single-minded: he left school at fifteen (following an altercation regarding the length of his hair) and set about making it in music. Stints with a number of bands, including Denver act Zephyr – on whose albums he added lead vocals while playing some strikingly fluent guitar – got the young Bolin noticed by The James Gang (an interim stint with jazz-

---

Close!
Jerry Lee Lewis/'Butch' Owens

The success of rocker Jerry Lee Lewis may have endured for more than four decades, but his life has thrown up a relentless list of personal loss and close calls. For starters, there was a whole lotta head-shakin' goin' on at his birthday party on 29 September 1976, 'The Killer' very nearly validating his epithet after accidentally shooting his own bass-player, Norman 'Butch' Owens, in the chest. Twice. 'Butch' somehow survived – but there have been many associates of Jerry Lee who haven't.

At three, he'd witnessed the death of his brother Elmo, killed by a truck. In 1962 and 1973, tragic accidents took his beloved sons Steve (drowned as a toddler) and Jerry Lee Jr (drummer in his father's band who died at nineteen in a jeep crash). Of his many wives, Jaren Gunn Pate also mysteriously drowned in a swimming pool (1982), while Shawn Michelle Stevens died from a methadone overdose a year on, in which Lewis was briefly implicated. A prolific drinker, Jerry Lee himself twice narrowly escaped death from stomach haemorrhaging, though alcohol accounted for his early session-musician Charlie 'Redman' Freeman in 1972.

> ## 'He was innocent to a fault – like a charming little kid. People just let him have what he wanted. If they didn't give it to him, then he'd find someone who would.'
>
> Karen Ulibarri, Bolin's ex-girlfriend

rockers Energy having failed to land him a deal) and finally Deep Purple. The British rock pioneers saw in Bolin a natural successor to the departing Ritchie Blackmore, and the Iowa axeman became a permanent fixture for the band's final year. Despite this success, Bolin was constantly strapped for cash, rumour suggesting he was profligate with his friends and those who worked for him; just as likely is that much of his considerable income at the time was disappearing in the direction of the liquor store and his dealers.

When Deep Purple finally called it a day in 1976, the guitarist saw it as a chance to found his own band. Although more often than not 'out of it', Bolin recorded two albums in just over a year (both of which scraped into the Billboard Hot 100), impressing both his label and admirer Jeff Beck, a hero of Bolin's, who invited him to open his Jai-Alai Fronton Club gig in Miami on 3 December. Bolin was delighted and the set went well, putting him in the mood to hang with Beck and other friends after the show. Bolin and a number of colleagues retired to the Newport Hotel, where, having exhausted the bar, some of them headed to his room. The guitarist then disappeared to a bathroom with long-time friend Phillip Tolemini (apparently to discuss a limo service for the musician) and a man believed to be a supplier. Back in the main room, Bolin's behaviour grew erratic – until he slumped over in the middle

of a phone conversation. Hugely concerned, companions – including Bolin's new girlfriend, Valeria Monseglio – placed him in a shower, before putting him to bed. Although he rallied long enough to utter a few words, by 7 am, Monseglio was unable to find any sign of his pulse.

It was an unfortunate but increasingly familiar scenario: rocker shoots junk, rocker passes out, rocker comes to, rocker dies. Had an ambulance been called earlier, Tommy Bolin may well have survived; the likelihood is, though, that there were one or two in attendance who wanted to keep the authorities at bay. In the event, a Dade County coroner stated that the musician's death was caused by a massive ingestion of alcohol, cocaine, lidocaine and morphine. Bolin's accidental death followed those of two of Deep Purple's road crew the previous tour.

See also *Candy Givens (*➧ *January 1984)*

Close!
Katie Webster

She was the queen of swamp boogie, but full-throated Katie Webster (Kathryn Jewel Thorne) might have had her career curtailed by the tragedy that killed the legendary Otis Redding and most of The Bar-Kays (➧ *December 1967*). Her mastery of barrelhouse piano and earthy vocal prompted Redding to book Webster for his tours as early as 1964 – but her 1967 pregnancy prevented her being allowed to fly with his entourage three years later. Webster's devastation turned to disbelief as news broke of the terrible air crash that had taken a soul-music great. Taking a career break after the tragedy (and the birth of her child), she returned to become a force in Europe during the eighties. Katie Webster eventually passed on from heart failure in 1999.

Lest We Forget

Other notable deaths that occurred sometime during 1976:

Tom Baird (US keyboardist with sixties Pacific-Northwest act The Classics who went on to produce and arrange artists including Diana Ross; born British Columbia, 27/4/1943; boating accident, 25/2)

Anthony 'Duster' Bennett (UK blues-rock singer/musician who worked with John Mayall's Bluesbreakers and Fleetwood Mac; born Welshpool, 23/9/1946; car crash after he fell asleep at the wheel, 26/3)

Floyd Council (US bluesman known as 'Dipper Boy' who also inspired the name Pink Floyd; born North Carolina, 2/9/1911; cardiac arrest, 9/5)

Count Ossie (Jamaican leader of Mystic Revelation of Rastafari who recorded the original 'Oh Carolina' with Prince Buster; born Oswald Williams, St Thomas, 3/1928; car crash/crushed to death, 18/10)

Jesse 'Lone Cat' Fuller (US blues guitarist; born Georgia, 12/3/1896; heart disease, 29/1)

Howlin' Wolf (highly influential US Delta-blues guitarist; born Chester Arthur Bennett, Mississippi, 10/6/1910; kidney failure, 10/1)

Jimmy Reed (much-referenced US blues guitarist; born Matthias James Reed Leeland, Mississippi, 6/9/1925; respiratory failure exacerbated by epilepsy, 29/8)

Paul Robeson (legendary US gospel singer and black rights activist; born New Jersey, 9/4/1898; stroke, after living in seclusion for ten years, 23/1)

Victoria Spivey (US blues singer; born Texas, 15/10/1906; internal haemorrhaging, 3/10)

Jesse Whitten (US guitarist with popular multinational soul act Heatwave; born Chicago, 1950; as the band began to break both the UK and US, he was stabbed to death in his home town, 11/1976)

For a complete list of fallen artists, visit

www.numberoneinheaven.com

FEBRUARY

Saturday 26

Sherman Garnes

(The Bronx, New York, 8 June 1940)

Frankie Lymon & The Teenagers
(The Premiers)

Garnes was a lanky, basketball-loving *basso profundo* whose music career began when he met tenor Jimmy Merchant while the boys were ninth-graders at New York's Edward W Stitt Junior High School. Both strong singers, they formed The Earth Angels before Garnes introduced Herman Santiago (second tenor) and Joey Negroni (baritone) into the mix, creating a quartet called The Premiers (also known at various times as The Coup de Villes and The Ermines). The band only became classic vocal troupe The Teenagers once streetwise young upstart Frankie Lymon – who only just qualified – had joined the fray. The Teenagers fast-tracked to major-league success (Garnes's throaty 'doom-a-de-doom' kick-starts platinum 1956 'sig tune' 'Why Do Fools Fall in Love?') but their time in the spotlight was predictably short. Garnes – who'd not even had the chance to complete his

schooling – was offered little more than $1,000 as a pay-off at the end of 1958.

Within ten years former Teenagers had seen their lead singer die prematurely of a heroin overdose (➤ *February 1968*). By the end of the next decade two more would join him: long out of the music-business limelight, Garnes died while undergoing open heart surgery. Negroni survived him by just over eighteen months (➤ *September 1978*).

MAY

Tuesday 3

Helmut Köllen

(Cologne, Germany, 1950)

Triumvirat

Contributing one of the year's more organized departures, singer and guitarist Köllen committed suicide by carbon-monoxide poisoning, sitting in his garage listening to his band's tapes on the car stereo. Köllen had made something of a name for himself in the Euro-prog market of the early to mid seventies; Triumvirat's best-selling album was 1975's *Sparticus*

[*sic*]. He left the following year, however, to pursue a less-successful solo career, which may or may not have led to his untimely demise in his home town.

Tuesday 10

Gene Mumford

(Eugene Mumford – North Carolina, 24 June 1925)

Billy Ward & The Dominoes
The Ink Spots
The Larks
(The Jubilators/Selah Jubilee Singers)
(Golden Gate Quartet)

Despite professional prowess with a variety of gospel and doo-wop outfits (the most significant of which are named above), Gene Mumford's personal life was beset with problems: in 1945, as he prepared to turn professional as a vocalist, he was falsely accused of the attempted rape of a white woman and eventually served two years on the chain gang in Carolina before being granted a pardon in 1949. On his release, Mumford rejoined his gospel pals in the group that became The Larks, also writing a number of their works. And Mumford was very much the lead attraction of The Dominoes (where he replaced Jackie Wilson), singing with the celebrated vocal group until 1959, after which he performed with various vocal revues, including a stint fronting The Ink Spots.

Gene Mumford's troubles were not over, though. He battled with drink and general ill health before bacterial pneumonia – complicated by a combination of alcoholism and diabetes – claimed his life in Los Angeles at the age of fifty-one. Mumford survived former Larks colleague Allen Bunn by just three months, though other original members Hadie Rowe (1998), Thurmon Ruth (2002) and David McNeil (2005) survived into their seventies. (Orville Brooks, David Bowers, Isaiah Bing and Glen Burgess, members of a second line-up formed by Mumford, have also died.)

Thursday 26

William Powell Jr
(Canton, Ohio, 20 January 1942)
The O'Jays

The Triumphs was a five-piece band formed at Canton's McKinley High School by baritone William Powell and friends Eddie Levert and Walter Williams, recording for the King label as The Mascots as early as 1961. The name under which the group achieved mass acceptance was given them by modest Cleveland disc jockey Eddie O'Jay. The O'Jays were often derided by critics as playing a 'watered down' version of what Motown and Stax were putting out, but they nonetheless developed a loyal R & B following in the Midwest over the next decade, before the three original members enjoyed a string of international hits with much-loved tunes such as 'The Backstabbers' (1972) and feel-good US 1973 chart-topper 'Love Train'.

Two years later, it was all but over

for William Powell: undergoing treatment for injuries sustained in a car accident in 1975, he was diagnosed with cancer. The disease spread rapidly, and Powell was forced to retire from the million-selling soul act soon after, the O'Jays' management remarkably quick to find a replacement in former Little Anthony & The Imperials frontman Sammy Strain. Powell died at Aultman Hospital in the town of his birth.

JUNE

Wednesday 22

Peter Laughner
(Cleveland, Ohio, 22 August 1952)
Pere Ubu
(Rocket from the Tombs)
(Friction)

A founding member of celebrated Ohio avant-garde rockers Pere Ubu, Peter Laughner had already left the band to pursue his own project, Friction, at the time of his premature death – missing out on the great approval Pere Ubu were to receive in the late seventies. As the band seemed poised for critical acclaim, Laughner was making a living as a reviewer himself, with local music magazine *Scene* and the popular national journal *Creem*. His broad talent was recalled by long-time Ubu bassist Tony Maimone: 'You could give him any topic and he'd write a song in ten minutes. He was a great, great writer – and a really good journalist.'

As a guitarist, Laughner had originally hooked up with Ubu vocalist David Thomas in 1973 to form the garage-rock act Rocket from the Tombs, which was heavily influenced by the likes of The Stooges and MC5. Unfortunately, the young Laughner

also adopted their pro-drug stance, developing something of a problem with heroin in his early twenties. His continued abuse resulted in his contracting acute pancreatitis – which eventually killed him.

JULY

Monday 4

Richard Michaels
(Richard Michaels Haddad – Detroit, Michigan, 6 June 1951)
Allen Project
(SRC)

Richard Michaels appeared to have a career in rock sewn up when a demo by Alien Project – the Canadian outfit for whom he sang, wrote and played bass – was picked up by Columbia Records. Originally known by his given name of Richard Michaels Haddad, the young musician had also played with Detroit rock act SRC, where his strong writing was noted by Alien Project leader Steve Perry.

Michaels died when, driving on an East Coast freeway, his car hit a verge and flipped, killing him instantly. Having immediately disbanded Alien Project, Steve Perry thereafter went on to multi-platinum success throughout the eighties as singer with US stadium giants Journey. Perry nobly used his position to secure the release of an album of Richard Michaels's SRC and Alien Project material, dedicating the disc to his memory.

AUGUST

Ron Haydock

(Chicago, Illinois, 1940)

Ron Haydock & The Boppers

Ron Haydock was a little-known but hugely colourful character who made something of a name for himself as a singer, writer, actor and magazine editor – without ever really achieving mainstream success. In the late fifties, he formed proto-schlock band The Boppers, hitting the Chicago airwaves with the frenzied sub-classic '99 Chicks'. (One Haydock classic, 'Rollin' Danny', was efficiently covered by fan Mark E Smith of The Fall during the eighties, while The Cramps have also cited him as an influence.) At the same time, he found a niche for himself in a series of B-movies, including 1962's *The Man Who Finally Died* and 1966's cult favourite *Rat Pfink a Boo Boo*, in which Haydock played the eponymous rocker/superhero. He went on to script for the likes of Lon Chaney (allegedly no fan of Haydock's work), and also edited monster magazines and wrote risqué pulp fiction under the name Vin Saxon.

Disorientated by escalating depression, Haydock was struck and killed in a hit-and-run by an 18-wheeler truck in Victorville, California, as he negotiated an exit ramp while hitchhiking.

Elvis Presley

(Tupelo, Mississippi, 8 January 1935)

Some theories have him living incognito outdoors, jollying the inmates of nursing homes – even inhabiting a lunar camp – so perhaps Elvis is holed up somewhere in Iraq? In the spring of 2004, US intelligence couldn't direct us to any WMDs; however, they did unearth a giant portrait of popular culture's most recognizable icon among those of prominent Islamic figures. But, despite what some think, the King is dead. So – long may he live, his image (well, that of his best years) preserved for all eternity as adornment for pretty much anything one cares to choose. Even toilet seats.

In fact, Elvis Aron Presley ('Aaron' was a posthumous misspelling) believed a few unquantifiable theories himself – one such being that he had inherited the strength of his stillborn twin, Jesse Garon. Whether true or not, Elvis managed to pull himself up from the 'shotgun shack' of his childhood to realize probably the greatest international success popular music will ever know. The first good move was the one that Presley and his working parents made when he was thirteen, from Tupelo to the Lauderdale Courts housing project in Memphis, just a stone's throw from Beale Street, with its rich musical heritage. Here, Elvis dropped his *Captain Marvel* comics and picked up the guitar bought him when a bicycle was deemed too expensive by his folks. That was the second good move. Near by were Sun Studios, where, five years later, Elvis recorded a $4 acetate of popular ballads 'My Happiness' and, conversely, 'That's When Your Heartaches Begin' as a belated birthday present to his mother, Gladys. Just as impressed as Presley's doting mom was Sam Phillips, the foresighted head of Sun, who, after a couple of false starts, placed the mysterious young singer with musicians Bill Black (bass/upright bass) and Scotty Moore (guitar). 'That's All Right (Mama)' (1954) was recorded by chance, a local hit that put Presley in demand

'Every time I think I'm getting old and gradually heading to the grave – something else happens.'

Elvis Presley

Elvis and the Colonel in a rare 'role-reversal' scenario?

for live appearances. Still considered a country/rockabilly act – he never quite cut it as a gospel singer – Presley was offered regular Grand Ole Opry and *Louisiana Hayride* showcases, where the singer's unique performances proved something of an eye-opener, not least to the wily 'Colonel' Tom Parker.

By the end of 1955 Parker had lured Presley away from the limitations of Sun, contracting him to a very favourable deal (ie, favourable to Parker – though it was later renegotiated as a 50/50 split) with the promotions company Parker shared with country star Hank Snow, and Phillips signed over the burgeoning star to RCA Victor for $35K. Parker's guile has since, of course, been heavily criticized in the vast forests of press about Elvis, but it should be remembered that as a manager/entrepreneur he was second to none, seizing the moment spectacularly for his new charge: all licensing (guitars, plates, pillow cases – whatever) was sewn up from day one – remarkable, given that this kind of phenomenon had never been seen before – and a seven-picture movie deal was also unprecedented. That Elvis was unhappy with the admittedly hokum films is neither here nor there: he was under strict contract and if that meant singing 'Old Macdonald's Farm' (in 1967's *Double Trouble*), then sing it he would. His records weren't hokum, of course: all releases between the two-month chart-topper 'Heartbreak Hotel' (1956) and 'Jailhouse Rock' (1957) remain exuberant, as do many that followed – though his pin-up status inevitably demanded the somewhat more dispensable ballads. As 'Jailhouse Rock' enjoyed its fourth of seven weeks atop the charts, a more established US institution came knocking. Presley was called up for service, commencing April 1958, his now-familiar locks shorn – perhaps some of that 'strength' disappearing with them. Erstwhile fan John Lennon was just one who felt the quality of his recorded output dropped off after Elvis's return to civilian life in 1960. Commercially, he still possessed clout – though he was subsequently considered less 'essential' than, well, Lennon, for one. The so-called British Invasion pushed Presley from number one for seven years until the excellent 'Suspicious Minds' (US, 1969) and the lesser 'The Wonder of You' (UK, 1970) returned him to the top of the charts. This was a revised Elvis, however – one that had eschewed the shirts and jeans of old to deck himself out in post-Humperdinck/Jones slashed, sequinned suits and medallions for an audience that had grown up since the night they screamed at his 'unholy' gyrations on *The Ed Sullivan Show* a decade before. Now, Presley fans were content to sit quietly at cabaret venues, counting themselves lucky to receive just a glint of that distant smile.

Although in his younger days a believer in celibacy before marriage, Elvis had many noted 'unofficial' relationships, including with actresses Ann-Margret, Cybill Shepherd and Natalie Wood, plus beauty queen Linda

'Elvis? He died when he went into the army.'

John Lennon, 1980

Thompson. The love of his life, however, was his young wife, Priscilla Beaulieu. When she was just a teenager and Presley was serving his country, he had wooed Priscilla, the life he offered more attractive than the one she actually experienced while at Graceland. Although he undoubtedly worshipped her, Elvis never matured sufficiently to leave bachelorhood behind, his rough, tough, gun-packing 'Memphis Mafia' buddies sticking around even after the couple's wedding. Presley was nonetheless a good father to his daughter, Lisa Marie, born in 1968, a time when – perhaps not uncoincidentally – the singer appeared to be at physical peak. Before his dramatic decline he weighed in at 168 lbs and, reportedly, trained 'like a fighter'. During 1973, though, Presley's separation from Priscilla precipitated his legendary unhealthy eating and abuse of drugs. Sleeping mainly by day (he'd always suffered from insomnia), he became addicted to placidyls – just the start of a well-documented reliance upon pills which, as a man of no few morals (if a curtailed education), he justified on the grounds that they had been 'professionally prescribed'. By the mid seventies Elvis was frequently unable to complete live performances, so exhausted was he by his habit. By late 1976 he had a new fiancée, 20-year-old actress/model Ginger Alden – but looked a bloated distortion of his former self.

On the evening of 16 August 1977, the media sizzled like a deep-fried peanut butter and bacon sandwich. It was true: the King was dead at forty-two. That afternoon, Alden had awoken, surprised to find herself alone in the bed at Graceland. Investigating Elvis's en suite bathroom, she discovered the singer naked, slumped face down by his toilet – a hugely unflattering end to a life most glamorous. Confirmed dead on his 3.30 pm arrival at Baptist Memorial Hospital, the King's passing was initially put down to a heart attack – his mother, beside whom he was eventually interred, had died this way. This has since been discounted, the singer's death now attributed to cardiac arrhythmia and hypertensive cardiovascular disease, almost certainly precipitated by a sudden, massive intake of prescription drugs (as opposed to the 'straining a stool' verdict so beloved of the star's detractors). Within hours, several thousand had gathered outside his home; Presley's body lay in state at

Graceland for three days before the circus surrounding his funeral commenced. Tens of thousands lined the streets as a seemingly endless procession of vehicles headed to Forest Hills Cemetery after a brief service attended by few celebrity faces (according to reports, just Ann-Margret, James Brown and George Hamilton). Of course, many stars paid tribute later, Lennon breaking a self-imposed silence, though Bob Dylan reportedly fell into depression. Presley's body was returned to Graceland – at a later date, and under the cover of night, after an attempted body snatch.

Following his death, Presley's best record in ages, 'Way Down', topped the UK charts – one of thirty-seven US/ UK number ones to his name as his music continues to sell. As a corporation, 'Elvis Inc' has probably turned over in excess of $100 million since his departure: one suspects that even an improbable return from the ether couldn't increase the market domination the King continues to hold (☞ *Dead Interesting!*), though there are millions who hope – and wait . . .

See also *Bill Black (☞ October 1965); Colonel Tom Parker (☞ Golden Oldies #4); Sam Phillips (☞ Golden Oldies #15)*

SEPTEMBER

Keith Harwood

(c 1940)

Whether recording engineers can truly be legendary is perhaps a matter for debate, but London Olympic Studios wizard Keith Harwood – the man behind timeless recordings by David Bowie, Led Zeppelin, Humble Pie, The Pretty Things and Mott the Hoople – was considered so by many. His best-known work was probably the slew of albums he made with The Rolling Stones during the seventies; indeed his last sessions before he died had been on 'Love You Live' (spring, 1977), a concert recording that The Stones eventually dedicated to Harwood's memory. A further irony was that Harwood was on his way back from Olympic when his car hit the same South London tree that was to claim a much bigger name less than two weeks later . . .

DEAD INTERESTING!

YOU CAN'T TAKE IT WITH YOU

A recent survey showed that Elvis is, unsurprisingly, *still* very much popular music's big-earner six feet under. Thanks to CD/DVD sales, television rights, books, etc, the King's estate raked in almost $45 million (£25 million) in 2005, almost three decades after his death.

2005	2004			
1	1	Elvis Presley	$45m	(£25m)
2	2	John Lennon	$22m	(£12m)
3=	3=	George Harrison	$7m	(£3.8m)
3=	–	Johnny Cash	$7m	(£3.8m)
5	3=	Bob Marley	$6m	(£3.25m)
5=	–	Ray Charles	$6m	(£3.25m)
5=	5	Jimi Hendrix	$6m	(£3.25m)
8	6=	Jerry Garcia	$5m	(£2.7m)
8=	6=	Freddie Mercury	$5m	(£2.7m)
8=	6=	Tupac Shakur	$5m	(£2.7m)
8=	6=	Frank Sinatra	$5m	(£2.7m)

The figure was set to be greater still in 2006, with the reissue of *all* Presley's UK chart-toppers to commemorate what would have been his seventieth birthday the previous year.

Source: Forbes.com

Marc Bolan: The 20th century boy with his fair people 'in his hair' and (*opposite*) Tyrannosaurus wreck

Marc Bolan

(Mark Feld – Hackney, London, 30 September 1947)

T Rex/Tyrannosaurus Rex

(John's Children)

'I'll see you next week . . . same Marc time . . . same Marc channel!' The kitsch vernacular of his Granada TV pop show was indicative more of the desperation of his publicity department than of the charisma of Marc Bolan himself. Its pre-primetime slot was also a measure of how far the former idol had descended since his heady days at the start of the decade. However, it was not the budget television series that was to relaunch interest in Bolan; fate saw to it that any further success was to be posthumous. As a memorably impromptu edition fooling with old pal David Bowie aired, fans were already aware that there'd be no 'Marc time' next week – and the day's papers were publishing images of the mangled wreckage of his car being disentangled from a sycamore tree on Barnes Common.

Bolan *had* been a genuine star, of that there's no argument. Aside from Bowie's brief (if enduring) foray into the genre, T Rex represented the real talent in premier-league glam rock, artistically head and shoulders above the Slades, Sweets and Gary Glitters with whom they regularly rubbed shoulders at the business end of the UK hit parade. Having ditched the folksier, acoustic arrangements of his first band, John's Children, Bolan gave his fanbase one or two clues as to which direction he was likely to take Tyrannosaurus Rex with indulgent hippy/glam titles like *My People were Fair and Had Sky in Their Hair . . . but Now They're Content to Wear Stars on Their Brows* (1968). Bolan, under the name Toby Tyler, had previously worked as a model and knew how to exploit his undoubtedly good looks. As his 45 'Ride a White Swan' catapulted to UK number two, he seemed to have completed his reinvention as Prince of Glam while sufficiently satisfying the more serious consumers of the albums market. For the next three years, T Rex were seldom out of the British charts with a succession of records that were consistently infectious ('Hot Love', 'Telegram Sam', 'Metal Guru') and occasionally brilliant ('20th Century Boy'). In 1971 alone, the band enjoyed ten weeks at number one – though Bolan's intermittent arrogance in interview saw to it that only one US disc ('Get It On', retitled 'Bang a Gong') sold well. By 1974, though, bar a couple of sporadic moments, the buzz had gone and the glitter was fading fast. Fearing harder

times ahead, the millionaire star split the latest line-up of T Rex and took himself off to Monte Carlo to live as a tax exile, developing a cocaine habit and almost dying of a heart attack. Although he'd alienated a few UK music-biz associates, Bolan returned in 1977, now embracing a host of emerging punk faces, many of whom appeared on his TV showcase. Thus, Bolan had rechristened himself, this time as the movement's true godfather. Many of the new breed seemed happy to accommodate this whim, having grown up on Bolan's music. The latest rebirth appeared to be going to plan.

Marc Bolan loved cars, particularly the Rolls-Royces and US Oldsmobiles of his lyrics. Oddly, however, the singer had a mental block about driving himself, and had never learned: like his hero Eddie Cochran before him (➤ *Pre-1965*), Bolan believed he would die in a car accident – and, as with Cochran, so it proved. His American girlfriend, R & B singer Gloria Jones (of 'Tainted Love' fame), took the wheel of their purple Mini 1275 GT for a night out on 15 September, concluded by a midnight dinner at Morton's of Berkeley Square. Also in attendance were Jones's brother Richard (a music producer who had worked with both his sister and her boyfriend), Bolan's manager Tony Howard and promoter Eric 'Monster' Hall. As drink began to loosen the party up, Jones persuaded his sister to play and sing at the piano.

Shortly after 5 am on 16 September, as Bolan and Jones headed home, the Mini left the road at a hump-backed bridge on Queen's Ride, SW15, demolishing a fence and smashing into a tree. Richard Jones's car arrived almost immediately after the crash, and he summoned help and assisted his injured sister, lying unconscious but alive. Bolan, however, had not been so fortunate: his side of the car had taken almost 100 per cent of the impact and the singer was killed instantly, crushed and thrown into the back of the car. According to Richard Jones, both cars had

been travelling at just 30 mph as they approached this notorious black spot. Local dairy-worker Philip Evans-Lowe's was the only other vehicle on the road at the time: 'When I arrived, a girl was lying on the bonnet and a man with long, dark curly hair was stretched out in the road. There was a hell of a mess . . . I rushed to get the police.' The official cause of death was certified as 'shock and haemorrhage due to multiple injuries consistent with road traffic accident'. A copy of the *New Musical Express*, allegedly found open on the Mini's back seat, detailed Bolan's supposed comeback with the album *Dandy in the Underworld*.

Bolan is survived by his and Jones's son, Rolan, who, less than two years old at the time, has no significant memories of his father. In 2002, he unveiled a twenty-fifth anniversary plaque to commemorate Bolan at the site. Jones and her son went to the US to recover and have her jaw reset, after Howard finally broke the news of her common-law husband's death to her in hospital four days after the event. All parties having drunk 'moderately' on the fateful night, Jones faced charges of dangerous driving but somehow avoided trial, perhaps because the car had been inefficiently serviced shortly before, some of its wheel nuts reportedly not even finger-tight. Bolan's funeral at Golders Green crematorium inevitably resembled a *Who's Who* of UK pop music. Among those in attendance were Rod Stewart, Elton John, Steve Harley, Alvin Stardust and David Bowie, the latter of whom was particularly distraught, having worked with Bolan so soon before. Wreaths were forwarded by other stars, and Bolan's management arranged a floral white swan as a tribute.

Despite his achievements, Bolan's affairs were anything but straightforward following the accident. Within hours of his death, not only had fans allegedly taken valuable letters and receipts from Bolan's flat but taxmen had made a demand for some £3 million in unpaid contributions – as a final insult, Bolan's parents were invited to 'make an offer' on his bloodstained clothes.

By putting his will into the hands of his then-management in 1973, Bolan had inadvertently signed away much of his earnings before his death. Most of Bolan's royalties were tied up in a series of 'tax efficient' companies (named Wizard) set up outside the UK. No one, however, had a clue where any of these were, bar a surviving outlet in the Bahamas, which declined to comment on money it now considered its own. Sorting the mess out now is more problematic because virtually *all* noteworthy members of the various incarnations of T Rex have since died (➤ *Dead Interesting!*). In 2006, the only notable musician still living to have played with Bolan was drummer Bill Legend – who has not seen a penny of the star's estate.

DEAD INTERESTING!

T REX-TINCTION

These days, living associates of Marc Bolan are as hard to find as his band's dinosaur namesake. But before folk embark upon any DNA reincarnation, they'd best check through the following . . .

In one of pop's darker ironies, T Rex co-founder/percussionist Steve Peregrin Took died celebrating a belated royalty cheque (➤ *October 1980*); six months later, early bassist Steve Currie perished in a car accident eerily similar to Bolan's (➤ *April 1981*). Took's replacement, bongo-player Mickey Finn, was still performing under the T Rex moniker when he died from liver and kidney failure (➤ *January 2003*), and 'Dino' Dines, keyboardist between 1974 and Bolan's death, passed on a year later (➤ *January 2004*). Two of Bolan's managers, Tony Secunda (➤ *February 1995*) and Tony Howard (2001) have also died prematurely.

This apparent 'curse of T Rex' does not even end there: Bolan's first wife, June Child, died of a heart attack in 1994 during a trip to Turkey funded by selling some of his unreleased music, while Secunda's widow, Chelita – who developed Bolan's glitter look – died in 2000. Muriel Young, who produced his television show, and musician Richard Jones – the first to come to Bolan's aid – both passed away the following year.

Friday 30

Mary Ford
(Iris Colleen Summers – Pasadena, California
7 July 1928)

Discovered by her better-known husband, celebrated guitarist Les Paul, Mary Ford saw much pre-rock 'n' roll success with hits like 'How High the Moon' (1951). In 1948 – at the very start of their personal and professional partnership – the couple had survived a terrifying crash when their car skidded off the road, plummeting twenty feet into a frozen Oklahoma creek. As Paul convalesced, his close friend Bing Crosby presented him with an Ampex recorder as a get-well gift, on which he made some of Ford's earliest recordings.

After being in a diabetic coma for nearly two months, Mary Ford eventually yielded to the cancer that had brought an early end to her professional career. It was to prove a particularly difficult year for Les Paul, who also lost his manager, two members of the original Les Paul Trio and, of course, Crosby.

OCTOBER

Thursday 13

Shirley Brickley
(Philadelphia, Pennsylvania, 9 December 1944)

The Orlons

Shirley Brickley – initially alongside her two younger sisters, Audrey and Jean – formed the Philadelphia all-girl vocal group, Audrey & The Teenetts with friends Rosetta Hightower and Marlena Davis (who died in 1993).

When her sisters were pulled out of the group by their mother, Brickley, Hightower and Davis continued as The Orlons, singing at Philadelphia schools with baritone Stephen Caldwell. The hits came when Cameo Parkway Records signed them in 1961 – the best known is probably the 1962 US number-two single 'The Wah Watusi'. The Orlons consolidated their success (and royalties) by singing back-up with Bobby Rydell and Dee Dee Sharp's bands. However, once the British invasion had taken hold by the mid sixties, The Orlons disbanded, Shirley Brickley struggling to find anything other than menial or bartending work.

It is assumed that she was the unlucky victim of a failed house robbery, because – aged just thirty-two – Brickley was murdered by an intruder's gunshot in her Philadelphia home. No arrest was ever made.

Thursday 20

Cassie Gaines
(Miami, Oklahoma, 9 January 1948)

Steve Gaines
(Miami, Oklahoma, 14 September 1949)

Ronnie Van Zant
(Jacksonville, Florida, 15 January 1948)

Lynyrd Skynyrd

In the autumn of 1977, Florida giants Lynyrd Skynyrd were poised to promote their latest album, *Street Survivors*. With its strong line-up of Southern rock workouts such as death-ditty 'That Smell' – and a (soon to be pulled) lurid cover illustration depicting the band engulfed in flames – the record was set to launch them into rock's upper echelon. The appalling quirk of fate that then befell Skynyrd as they began the fifty-date 'Tour of the Survivors' resounds to this day.

Charismatic singer Ronnie Van Zant met the band in 1965, joining guitarist schoolfriends Allen Collins and Gary Rossington in My Backyard. By the seventies they had emerged as Lynyrd Skynyrd (a mutation of 'Leonard Skinner', the name of an unpopular gym teacher who'd disapproved of the length of their hair) and had signed with MCA. The first pair of albums produced the standards 'Freebird' (1973, dedicated to the late Duane Allman (◀ *October 1971*)) and US Top Ten hit 'Sweet Home Alabama' (1974). Numerous augmentations to the line-up of this sprawling combo followed, with brother/sister duo guitarist Steve Gaines and vocalist Cassie (as one of Skynyrd's female singers, The Honkettes) in place by the end of 1976. On the back of a couple of less-well-received albums, this latest upgrade ensured that the new set, *Street Survivors*, was a serious return to form for Lynyrd Skynyrd.

On 19 October 1977, Skynyrd's 1948 Convair 240 aircraft had had a small fire in its engine which sent a 20-foot jet of flame shooting into the air behind it. Cassie Gaines – never the best of flyers anyway – vowed not to set foot on that plane again. However, after much ribbing by (and persuasion from) her band colleagues, the vocalist agreed to cancel a commercial flight she had booked to continue the band's tour to Florida using the Convair. Just before 4 pm the following afternoon, Houston air traffic control received a distress call from a private aircraft in the vicinity which was low on fuel. Within minutes of the call, the craft – carrying band members Van Zant, Gaines and Gaines, Rossington, Collins, Billy Powell (keys), Artimus Pyle (drums) and Leon Wilkeson (bass) – pitched into woodland in Gillburg, Mississippi, both engines having died.

Survivor Powell takes up the harrowing story: 'Our co-pilot, John Gray, had been drinking the night before and, for all I know, may still have been

The classic Skynyrd line-up – of whom Leon Wilkeson (*left*), Allen Collins (*third left*), Steve Gaines (*second right, standing*), Ronnie Van Zant (*third right, crouching*) and Cassie Gaines (*right, seated*) are no more

drunk. He told me they were transferring oil from one wing to another . . . We hit the trees at approximately ninety miles per hour. The tail section broke off, the cockpit broke off and buckled underneath, and both wings broke off. The fuselage turned sideways and everybody was hurled forward. That's how Ronnie died: he was catapulted at about eighty miles per hour into a tree – died instantly of a massive head injury. I started walking around in a daze: I saw John Gray hanging from a tree, decapitated. Then I saw Cassie, who was cut from ear to ear. She bled to death right in front of me.' Powell, Collins and Pyle – the last with three ribs sticking through his chest – somehow

managed to summon help from local farmers. Had they not done so, the body count may have been higher than three band members, two pilots and road manager Dean Kilpatrick. Even so, rumour suggests backwood scavengers arrived at the scene long before the paramedics, looting anything that bore the band's name (or indeed any valuables at all) from the dead and survivors alike. During that long night, it is believed that as many as 3,000 people visited the crash site. By morning the carcass was all but picked clean. (Similarly, during 2000, Van Zant's and Steve Gaines's remains were reportedly desecrated by 'curious' fans.)

Rossington, Powell and Pyle had

all lost their fathers in their formative years – the latter to a plane crash that bore a chilling resemblance to this one, even down to its departure from the same Greenville airport. Though Lynyrd Skynyrd's various re-formations proved largely unsuccessful, a new line-up was revealed in time for the tenth anniversary of the accident. Butthings weren't the same without the charismatic Ronnie Van Zant, who, despite a tendency towards drinking and fighting, had often been looked upon as the father figure the others never knew.

See also *Allen Collins (✝ January 1990); Leon Wilkeson (✝ July 2001)*

Lest We Forget

Other notable deaths that occurred sometime during 1977:

Al Banks (US lead vocalist with fifties doo-wop act The Turbans before a brief stint with The Drifters; born Andrew Banks, Pennsylvania, 26/7/1937; unknown, 7/1977)

George Barnes (seminal US musician who played with The Jodimars – believed one of the first to record with electric guitar; born Chicago, 17/7/1921; heart attack, 15/9)

Bing Crosby (the world's most popular pre-rock 'n' roll crooner – 'White Christmas' is the biggest-selling record of our time; born Harry Lillis Crosby, Washington, 2/5/1904; cardiac arrest while playing golf, 14/10)

Sleepy John Estes (US blues guitarist; born Tennessee, 25/1/1904; a stroke put him to sleep for the last time, 5/6)

Peter Carl Goldmark (Hungarian-born but US-naturalized inventor of the LP record, among other little sidelines like colour TV; born Budapest, 2/12/1906; car crash, 7/12)

Willie Jones (US R & B/blues pianist; born Mississippi, 21/2/1920; cardiovascular disease, 31/12)

Gary Kellgren (UK studio engineer who worked with Jimi Hendrix, Frank Zappa, George Harrison, Ringo Starr, Sly Stone and Rod Stewart; born 1939; drowned at a Hollywood swimming party, 20/7)

Matt McGinn (UK singer/composer known as The Scottish King of Folk; born Glasgow, 17/1/1928; living in a two-room house with his family of nine, he died from smoke inhalation during a fire, 6/1)

Jimmy Stuard (US New York 'gay' disco DJ; he was one of nine people killed at the tragic Everard Bathhouse fire, 25/5)

Bukka White (US blues guitarist; born Booker T Washington White, Tennessee, 12/11/1906; cancer, 26/2)

For a complete list of fallen artists, visit

www.numberoneinheaven.com

The Death Toll #2

BOTTOM OF THE POPS

The following is a non-definitive chart of songs about genuine tragedies written *sans* consideration for such trifling issues as taste or sensitivity – plus one or two censored by authorities who didn't quite get it. Read 'em and weep.

1 'Teenybopper Death'
Michael des Barres (1974)

Recorded by cult actor and ex-Silverhead vocalist Michael des Barres (one-time husband of GTOs singer Pamela), this sweet little number dealt with the tragedy of Bernadette Whelan – the 14-year-old fan who died from asphyxiation after a David Cassidy concert at White City. Staggeringly, the track had its title changed to 'Bernadette' and was all set for release as a UK single until pulled at the last moment by (err, appropriately) Purple Records, following understandably adverse tabloid publicity.

2 'Gary Gilmore's Eyes'
The Adverts (1977)

Now accepted into the pantheon of great punk singles, TV Smith's fantasy (or nightmare) of the grimmest possible transplant gave his Adverts their only hit in 1977. Gilmore was the US murderer who'd killed at least twice before facing the death penalty in January the same year; a lesser-known fact is that two people actually *did* receive the killer's corneas upon his request.

3 'Jack the Ripper'
Screaming Lord Sutch (1963)

Often exempted from modern censure, the late David Sutch (☞ *June 1999*) was as guilty as anyone with this very early piece of sensationalism concerning London's most notorious killer and rapist (who later returned in Thin Lizzy's banned 'Killer on the Loose' in 1980). This track failed to chart despite being accompanied by a Scopitone – the earliest form of promotional film – depicting Sutch as 'Jack', replete with snarling grin. Not nice.

4 'Angel Of Death'
Slayer (1986)

Musically powerful, perhaps – but what was the California speed-metallers' message here? This 'tribute' concerned Josef Mengele – the deeply disturbed Nazi physician whose experiments on children rank among the most appalling atrocities of the twentieth century. Slayer are by no means the only band to exploit this subject area and, perhaps sensibly, they've remained tight-lipped about the track since its appearance on the album *Reign in Blood* two decades ago.

5 'I Don't Like Mondays'
Boomtown Rats (1979)

In the UK, punters and programmers didn't seem terribly bothered that the basis for 'I Don't Like Mondays' was the genuine (and very recent) story of Californian schoolgirl Brenda Spencer, who arrived at school one morning with a bad mood and a loaded pistol – killing two and injuring many more; by contrast, US radio stations weren't exactly tripping over themselves to playlist the former British chart-topper. (What price The Arctic Monkeys writing the modern-day equivalent about Columbine?) Well, quite.

6 'No One is Innocent'
Sex Pistols (1978)

The Pistols – but without Johnny. Not content with offering lead vocals to exiled train robber Ronald Biggs, Paul Cook and Steve Jones amused themselves with trite lyrics about Moors Murderers Myra Hindley and Ian Brady, while claiming that the Nazis were simply 'having fun'. Original titles 'Cosh the Driver' and 'The Biggest Blow' were considered a bridge too far, even by Sex Pistols standards. The record, already censored by the BBC, also received a possibly unique on-air ban from ITV.

7 'Tube Disasters'
Flux of Pink Indians (1980)

Songwriter Colin Birkett was at great pains to explain that his apparently distasteful lyric pertaining to the infamous 1975 Moorgate underground crash that left forty-three dead was intended as an ironic sneer at the media's lurid coverage of same. It was all the more difficult for the anarchist/pacifist/vegetarian given that his previous band, The Epileptics, had, unsurprisingly, come under fire for their choice of group moniker. Great record, though.

8 'Marie Provost'
Nick Lowe (1977)

On the other hand, of what was the genial king of pub rock thinking when he penned this wicked ditty? 'Marie Provost' told the macabre story of the fallen US silent movie actress who died alone and was eaten by her own pet dachshund. For lyrics rhyming 'winner' with 'doggie's dinner', Lowe received one fat slap on the wrist from Provost's fan club. The rest of us could only smirk.

9 'Psycho'
Leon Payne (1974)

More US firearms madness here, in the shape of ex-marine Charles Whitman, who in August 1966 chose to gun down fifteen at the University of Texas. Payne's bizarre, restless and largely spoken attention to detail is what makes this such a disquieting listen – and was what saw a universal media ban slapped on the track. (Oddly, Elvis Costello chose to cover the song during his 1981 'country' phase.)

10 'Midnight Rambler'
The Rolling Stones (1969)

Yes, even Jagger gets in on the act with this disturbing ditty about Alberto DeSalvo – the notorious Boston Strangler. The studio version of 'Midnight Rambler' was little more than incidental music under recordings of DeSalvo's confessions to the Boston police, but live performances had sick audiences joining in with wails and screams. Well, those *were* less-enlightened times, I suppose.

1978

JANUARY

Monday 23

Terry Kath
(Chicago, Illinois, 31 January 1946)
Chicago
(Various acts)

'Don't worry –
it's not loaded, see?'

Famous last words from
Terry Kath

He's the contributor of one of pop history's most-referred-to deaths by misadventure, but it should first be remembered that Terry Kath was an accomplished guitarist, even prompting praise from Jimi Hendrix, who, when his band invited Chicago Transit Authority (as Chicago then were) to join him on a European tour in 1968, confessed he felt Kath was the better guitarist.

He'd had a good start, learning Beach Boys tunes on his brother's drums and his mother's banjo during his teens. But Kath's extraordinary ability to sound as though he were playing both lead and rhythm guitar at the same time most likely came out of the lessons he took from a jazz-player before hitting the rock trail with first The Missing Links, then The Big Thing – who became CTA. Kath was very much the leader of the new band, adding vocals as well as his trademark playing, a role later shared with Peter Cetera. As Chicago – the abbreviation came about when the *real* Chicago Transit Authority threatened legal action (beware, Mull Historical Society) – the band were an enormous smash, sliding effortlessly from horny jazz rock into the laid-back afterglow of stadium AOR. Their numbered eponymous albums built a loyal fanbase over the years, while hits arrived with the regularity of Chicago buses: 'Make Me Smile' and '25 or 6 to 4' were the first of twenty Top Ten singles for the band over the next couple of decades. Their commercial zenith was reached in the autumn of 1976, when 'If You Leave Me Now' went to number one on both sides of the Atlantic.

The second phase of Chicago's success, though, occurred without Terry Kath. One week before his thirty-second birthday, the musician and his actress wife, Camelia, now living in Malibu, California, attended a party at the house of Chicago crew member Donnie Johnson, in nearby Woodland Hills. Kath and Johnson chugged a few beers and supped a few bourbons, the conversation turning – as often it would – to the subject of firearms. Casual gun-owner Johnson was not in the same league as Kath: Chicago's guitarist was an avid firearms collector, more often than not travelling armed. Seemingly, the musician was such a lover of weaponry that once the party started to break up, he took it upon himself to clean Johnson's .38 revolver. Kath's behaviour got more out of order, and Johnson's annoyance turned to extreme concern, as the clearly 'juiced' musician put the .38 to his head and pulled the trigger – the chamber was empty. What to onlookers represented plain stupidity was to Kath clearly a sign he knew what he was doing: the singer believed himself no slouch when it came to party tricks and, producing his own 9-mm pistol from nowhere, he attempted the same trick. With the immortal words recalled above, Kath once again squeezed the trigger; the gunman had forgotten (or was too inebriated to remember) that an automatic chambers a bullet, uh, automatically – ie, it does not require the magazine to remain inserted.

A verdict of accidental death under the influence of alcohol and drugs was passed, as was Kath, into pop-music folklore. Some 400 attended his interment in Forest Lawn, Glendale, including members of Chicago, who continued successfully into the 1980s – though many fans believe the band died with Terry Kath.

Vic Ames

(Victor Urick – Malden, Massachusetts,
20 May 1926)

The Ames Brothers

At pretty much the same time as
Terry Kath was playing with his
piece, Vic Ames, first tenor with
one of America's first commercially
successful white vocal bands, The
Ames Brothers, came unstuck on a
Tennessee road.

The Ames Brothers were Ed, Vic,
Gene (who died in 1997) and Joe, the
four oldest of nine musical siblings,
who became one of Boston's most
popular tight harmony units by the
early fifties. Signing first with Coral,
then with RCA, The Ames Brothers
enjoyed national hit status in 1950
with their platinum 'Rag Mop', and
1954's 'Naughty Lady of Shady Lane'
became a huge international hit. The
group were also among the first to
develop specific characters, Vic Ames
being very much the band 'clown', his
original desire to become a serious
actor having been scuppered by a
performance back in 1940 that left his
audience helpless with mirth. Ames's
comic persona proved popular as the
brothers fronted their own network
television series in 1955.

After the group split in 1961, Vic
Ames fronted his own Arkansas
TV talk show. Later, the former
singer moved to Nashville to work
as a country-music agent. It was here
that he lost his life when his car skidded on pack ice and slammed into a
streetlamp.

Greg Herbert

(Philadelphia, Pennsylvania, 19 May 1947)

Blood, Sweat & Tears
(Miles Davis Group)
(Woody Herman Orchestra)
(Thad Jones/Mel Lewis Orchestra)

It was clearly all too exciting for
Gregory Herbert. He'd been a professional alto saxophonist since the
age of sixteen (playing with Duke
Ellington, no less), but it nonetheless
took him until he was nearly thirty
to find a niche in the rock end of the
jazz market. Blood, Sweat & Tears
were already several years past their
commercial peak by the time Herbert
was drafted in as replacement for Bill
Tillman, who already felt like the ump-
teenth BST saxophonist. An impressive stylist and improviser, Herbert
shared sax duties on the Blood, Sweat
& Tears album *Brand New Day* (1977),
which diehard fans believed to be
something of a return to form.

January 1978 saw a European tour
for Blood, Sweat & Tears to try and
reignite interest there. All seemed
to be going according to plan when,
after a concert in Amsterdam, Greg
Herbert took an overdose of cocaine
– and died in his hotel room. The
remaining band members terminated
the tour there and then, returning
to the States, where they went their
separate ways.

MARCH

Saturday 11

Claude François

(Ismaïlia, Egypt, 1 February 1939)

In 1956, the growing Suez Canal crisis
caused the young singer, his French
father and Italian mother to up sticks
from their base in Egypt and move
to Monte Carlo, Claude François getting an early taste of the revue bars
that were soon to become his world.
With his father sick and unable to
work, the family found it hard to make
ends meet in Monaco, so the young
François took a job as drummer in a
nightclub band: using the opportunity
to test his singing voice, the good-
looking blond crooner quickly became
very popular. By 1960 'Clo-Clo' (as he
was dubbed) was married but nonetheless wowing a generation of young
women with his thinly disguised
impersonations of American rock 'n'
roll stars at venues in Paris and along
the Côte d'Azur. Soon, his covers of
Everly Brothers, Trini Lopez and even
Beatles hits would take François to
the upper reaches of the French hit
parade, while his own '*Belles, Belles,
Belles*' reportedly sold over 1.5 million
copies in 1962. François's composition '*Comme d'habitude*' then became
one of the most recognized tunes in
the world: with lyrics reworked by
Paul Anka, it morphed into the much-
covered and much-loved 'My Way'.

Claude François found the
British and American markets
harder to crack in the early seventies,
his showmanlike performances
considered a touch dated by the two
musical epicentres (his one British
hit, 1976's truly ghastly 'Tears on
the Telephone', barely scraped
into the Top Forty). Nevertheless,
François was a massive draw live,

Claude François: A song, a shower and a short circuit

playing a series of sell-out dates in the UK in 1975. At this period in his career, he narrowly escaped death on three separate occasions: first, collapsing from exhaustion, second, avoiding a London IRA bombing by just seconds – and finally escaping a deranged fan with a shotgun (a windmill at his home also burned down during this time). In 1978, however, Claude François braved a return to London for further shows and a TV special. Within days, his luck ran out and he became the latest in 1978's growing list of accidental pop fatalities. Having returned with his girlfriend to their Paris apartment, he prepared for another television appearance on TF1's *Rendez-vous de Dimanche* the following day. After showering, François noticed that a bulb needed changing. So, standing with his feet in the water, the singer attempted to replace it – and was instantly electrocuted; all efforts to revive him failed and François was declared deceased at 3.30 pm. Nearly 400 attended his funeral at a church in Auteuil, and many inconsolable fans mourned outside (reports suggest that at least two fans committed suicide in the aftermath). On the twenty-second anniversary of his death, Place Claude François in Paris was unveiled in the singer's memory.

APRIL

Friday 14

Hanus Berka

(Prague, Czechoslovakia, 15 December 1940)
Emergency

Hanus Berka never reached celebrity status as such, but he was nonetheless an influential figure in European orchestral rock in the early seventies. Classically trained and keen on electronica, Berka was a founder of Emergency, a unit originally put together as a house band for the Czech version of the popular (if controversial) stage musical *Hair*. A multi-instrumentalist who had a gift for arranging and organization, Berka rightly saw more potential in this group of musicians, keeping the majority of them together to record a trio of albums of jazz-flavoured rock. (One member of this line-up was singer Peter Bischof, who later earned the dubious distinction of writing hits for Milli Vanilli.)

The bad year for jazz-rock musicians continued. A sufferer of the sleeping disorder narcolepsy, Hanus Berka was killed at the wheel of his car, just yards from the front door of his house. Losing control of the vehicle, he unwittingly veered into a tree, and died in the collision.

Friday 21

Sandy Denny

(Alexandra Elene MacLean Lucas – Wimbledon, London, 6 January 1947)
Fairport Convention
Fotheringay
(The Strawbs)

Almost thirty years after her death, Sandy Denny's remains the first name on most lips when talk turns to folk divas. She was a cut above most of her contemporaries, both as a solo vocalist and as a key member of that most celebrated British group Fairport Convention. In 1968, having abandoned her studies at Kingston College of Art (where her contemporaries included guitarist Jimmy Page), Denny took her subtle soprano to the 2-year-old group – which comprised a remarkable collection of folk luminaries, Ashley Hutchings, Richard Thompson and Ian Matthews – via a couple of short stints recording with

Sandy Denny with heavy friends – in this case, three-quarters of Led Zeppelin

Led Zeppelin's fourth album (teaming up once again with Page) and there was even a brief reconciliation with Fairport during 1975, before her last solo set *Rendezvous* was finally issued in 1977. Sandy Denny's last years were both tragic and unflattering. Troubled by alcohol abuse, Denny was desperate to become a mother, believing that this would complete a world she was finding it harder and harder to deal with. The birth of her daughter, Georgia, however, only compounded a life fast unravelling. Known to have used cocaine (and possibly heroin) during gestation, Denny caused her many friends concern with her behaviour as a new mother. She frequently drove her orange VW Beetle while drunk – often with the baby aboard – and the otherwise photogenic singer had begun to look haggard in live performance.

With her marriage to her errant husband, musician Trevor Lucas, collapsing, Denny visited her parents at their holiday home in Cornwall, and suffered a calamitous fall down some steps, hitting her head on concrete. Her mother, reportedly more concerned to preserve their reputation than to acquire medical assistance, refused to have her daughter seen drunk – a huge error of judgement that came back to haunt Denny's family a month later. A concerned Lucas took their daughter to *his* family in Australia – apparently with little intention of returning – and the singer was found collapsed at the London home of her friend Miranda Ward. Four days later, Sandy Denny died at Atkinson Morley Hospital, never having regained consciousness. Doctors initially put the death down to mid-brain trauma, believing she'd suffered the injury at Ward's home: those who had seen Denny sporting a horrific wound at her final concert three weeks earlier knew that this was not the case.

See also *Trevor Lucas (☞ February 1989)*

DEAD INTERESTING!

MAIS JE NE DOIS PAS PARTIR!

You couldn't make it up – though clearly somebody did. Former Fairport Convention violinist Dave Swarbrick was amazed when the *Daily Telegraph* published his obituary on 20 April 1999. True, he'd been unwell (he underwent a double lung transplant five years later) – but *dead*? Although they offered a written apology, the newspaper failed to present any kind of explanation for the error, prompting Swarbrick to offload signed photocopies of the piece at a gig in Coventry. For which the *Telegraph* then threatened legal action for breach of copyright.

The Strawbs. Denny's vast knowledge of traditional British folk made her the group's most significant member during her admittedly brief time in the ranks, influencing a change of direction for Fairport with the album *What We Did on Our Holidays* (1969), one of three recordings in her eighteen months with the group. This honeymoon period ended tragically, however, with the death of drummer Martin Lamble as they toured *Unhalfbricking* (☞ *May 1969*). Another album, *Liege and Lief* (1969), then upset Fairport diehards because the band dared to follow American counterparts by going electric. The move also caused unrest within the ranks of Fairport Convention, Ian Matthews leaving to form Matthews Southern Comfort.

This unsettling period unsurprisingly led to Denny's departure from the group. She formed Fotheringay (named after one of her popular Fairport compositions), but again this was not to last. Denny's best work hereafter was her live, solo outings – her fragile voice generally worked better without backing. On other occasions she sang 'Battle of Evermore' on

JULY

Saturday 29

Glen Goins
(Plainfield, New Jersey, 2 January 1954)
**Parliament/Funkadelic
(Quazar/Mutiny)**

To be considered the best vocalist/ rhythm guitarist to emerge from the P-Funk stable is no mean feat, considering the sheer number of musicians that have come and gone in fifty years of Parliament/Funkadelic. Glen Goins's time in what has become a funk institution was very brief, but his soaring voice and dynamic rhythm playing is still greatly missed by the groups' followers.

America's biggest, sweatiest, most colourful combo actually had a nucleus as The Parliaments, a New Jersey barbershop vocal troupe founded by George Clinton, but that was a far cry from the glammed-up, sci-fi beast into which they would mutate twenty years later. By 1975 Clinton and co were producing the rip-roaring P-Funk classic *Mothership Connection*, the first album to feature the lead vocals of gospel-taught Goins, which housed a breakthrough US hit, 'Tear the Roof off the Sucker'. This set was followed by *The Clones of Dr Funkenstein* (1976) and *Funkentelechy vs. the Placebo Syndrome* (1977), the latter a monstrously ambitious piece of conceptual work that in its live format featured onstage spaceships and the like, as Parliament/Funkadelic became arguably the hottest concert draw in the world. But, as so many other P-Funkers were to do, Goins – disillusioned by Clinton's controlling manner – had already left the pack to pursue another project in the shape of Quazar. This new funk unit, which Goins joined with fellow Parliament-mutineer Jerome Brailey, had been formed by his brother Kevin, and would duly morph – P-Funk style – into another act called, simply, Mutiny.

A quiet man outside his work, Glen Goins experienced recurring health problems throughout his short life. In 1978, Mutiny were signed to Arista, but Goins collapsed at home in New Jersey on 27 July – and died two days later from complications arising from Hodgkin's disease. Kevin Goins completed Mutiny's 1979 debut album *Mutiny on the Mamaship*, dedicating the set to his brother's memory.

See also *'Tiki' Fulwood (➤ November 1979); Eddie Hazel (➤ December 1992); Raymond Davis (➤ Golden Oldies #26)*

AUGUST

Thursday 24

Stacy Sutherland
(Kerr County, Texas, 28 May 1946)
13th Floor Elevators

The average dark, uncompromising guitar hero would have found it hard to hold an audience when competing with spacelord frontman Roky Erickson, but Stacy Sutherland – axe-toting psychewarrior with short-lived Austin legends The 13th Floor Elevators – didn't do a bad job of being second in command. Although they remain a relatively exclusive treat for a minority of record-buyers, in their day The Elevators were the top acid-guzzling, stoner kings of over-amplified, psychedelic preach-pop. The band was the result of a collision between two Texan garage outfits, The Lingsmen (Sutherland) and The Spades (Erickson). As The 13th Floor Elevators (the new name coined as a reference to the 'floor that doesn't exist' for superstitious American hotel-goers), they embarked upon a 2-year rampage of drug-taking. Nevertheless, they created extraordinary music as they went – the expression 'psychedelic' had not been seen on an album sleeve until The Elevators' 1966 debut. With 'guru' Tommy Hall playing a 1.5-gallon 'electric' aluminium jug, the line-up was somewhat more sedately completed by Benny Thurman (bass; later replacement Danny Galindo died in 2001) and John Ike Walton (drums). As The Elevators' most talented player, Stacy Sutherland would have a big say in the band's songwriting, but it was his and Erickson's recreational habits that garnered the most column inches. Erickson became a sort of American Syd Barrett, paranoid, deluded and convinced he was a Martian with a 'third eye' – he would be in and out of institutions for years afterwards. For Sutherland, the future was even darker. The Texas Rangers were almost constantly on the band's (and especially his) tail, and he spent a jail term for drug possession in 1968. The rest of the band were put out by this development, and The Elevators dissolved some months after (Tommy Hall eventually became a Christian).

In 1977, Sutherland joined a line-up of The Elevators for a reunion show – without the unwell Erickson – but any pipe dreams that the group might one day re-form were exposed as hallucinations when the once-fried guitar man, now often strung out on heroin, was shot dead by his estranged wife in a domestic dispute in Houston. He was buried in the town of his birth.

'They didn't make any money to speak of, but they did get lots of pussy and buttloads of free drugs.'
Bob Galindo, Texan musician, Elevators fan and brother of bassist Danny

SEPTEMBER

Tuesday 5

Joey Negroni
(Harlem, New York, 9 September 1940)

Frankie Lymon & The Teenagers

The third member of the late-fifties vocal sensations to die young, Puerto Rican Joey Negroni had been a part of the set-up when it amounted to little more than a group of friends – baritone Negroni, plus his partner in The Ermines, lead/second tenor Herman Santiago, and joining members Sherman Garnes (bass) and Jimmy Merchant (tenor) – from the Edward W Stitt Junior High School, going on to perform as The Premiers. It was only with the introduction of a cocksure frontman – soprano Frankie Lymon – that the group looked and sounded ready for the big time. As The Teenagers, they hit it full-on in 1956, with the timeless 'Why Do Fools Fall in Love?' jetting into the US Top Ten (and careering all the way to UK number one). Further hits stuttered and spluttered: by the time Lymon's voice broke the game was all but up for The Teenagers.

By late 1978, 60 per cent of the youthful line-up had passed on: Frankie Lymon had developed an addiction that he couldn't beat (➤ *February 1968*), and Sherman Garnes had died during surgery (➤ *February 1977*). Similarly, Joey Negroni had critical health issues: a belatedly discovered brain tumour saw him die from a cerebral haemorrhage.

Thursday 7

Keith Moon
(Wembley, Middlesex, 23 August 1946)

The Who
(The Escorts)
(The Beachcombers)

'At first I thought he was gonna jump out the coffin and laugh at us.'
John Entwistle

'We were all set to become movie moguls. So his timing, as per usual, was a bit off.'
Pete Townshend

'If one journalist says we're not the same without Keith, I'll personally break his legs.'
Roger Daltrey

The Who 'deal' with Keith Moon's passing

No matter how unintentional it may have been, there's something vaguely apposite about the fact that Keith Moon's demise was a self-destruction of sorts. Moon's all-too-brief thirty-odd years were a riot of ruination, excess and damage documented to a value of £300K. There are also, of course, one or two white lies to keep the customer on his toes, but, regardless of their legitimacy, Moon tales have embellished rock 'n' roll folklore with head-spinning regularity.

Keith Moon *made* The Who. Before, they were tight, cohesive, musical: after the gurning showman muscled his way in, they became toxic and dangerous, a three-dimensional experience. The potent combination of Pete Townshend's disaffected lyrics and Moon's firework display behind the traps made them Britain's first and most convincing punk-rock band. The fact that Moon was a great drummer is often overlooked because of his behaviour, but during the seventies there were few to equal him. In the sixties, there were none. A fan of D J Fontana

Keith Moon: Don't mess with Uncle Ernie if you want to see your toys again ...

(Elvis's maverick original drummer), Moon claimed never to have had a drumming lesson in his life – although this is more than likely one of his yarns. Before making his debut with The Who, he'd played with The Escorts and then, improbably, with a harmony covers group named The Beachcombers. Despite Moon's well-documented love of The Beach Boys, this was no surf band and he knew he was dragging his heels with them. (So intense had his performance become that his drum kit often had to be secured to the floor with nails.) Moon was now intrigued by a brasher combo known as The Detours: according to legend, a drunken Moon rubbished the band's session percussionist, Doug Sandon, and took to the kit himself during the interval at a pub gig at his local (The Oldfield). Apocryphal or otherwise, what happened next created a blueprint for the next fifteen years of his, and The Who's, life. Moon – reportedly dressed entirely in 'ginger' (jacket, cords, the lot) – utterly wrecked the hapless player's drum kit, snapping the bass pedal in two and putting the skins through

as he rampaged through a version of 'Roadrunner'. In the stunned silence that followed, spokesman/singer Roger Daltrey, with rare, understated comedy, asked: 'What're you doing Monday, mate?'

With Moon on board, the image of the band changed accordingly. Another 1964 gig saw Townshend (who had started to use his trademark 'windmill' style) trash his instrument in a fit of pique brought on by a difficult audience: Moon continued the onstage demolition and the UK had a new benchmark in raw rock 'n' roll aggression. Their musicianship without question, The Who made records that were always remarkably melodic, beginning an early surge of UK hits with 'I Can't Explain'. 'Anyhow Anywhere Anyway' and the breathtaking high that was 'My Generation' (all 1965) suggested this phenomenon would give The Beatles and Stones a good run for their money. (Surprisingly, in America – despite consistently destroying records for live attendance and decibel output – The Who only ever enjoyed one Top Ten disc.) With music ever more ground-breaking and elaborate, the line-up of Daltrey, Townshend, Moon and his close friend for many years, bassist John 'The Ox' Entwistle, remained unbroken until 1978. The drummer's ability as an actor and comedian was no fluke either; he may have been prone to spontaneous combustion but Moon had innate talent here. His often-remarked-upon resemblance to actor Robert Newton (Long John Silver in the 1950 screen version of *Treasure Island*) was actually as lovingly manipulated as his somewhat typecast role as Uncle Ernie in the movie of Townshend's rock opera, *Tommy* (1975).

The sustained level of success The Who experienced meant money, which in turn meant fewer mundane hassles and more than sufficient space to do the things young men wanted to do. While the others enjoyed trout fishing (Daltrey) and painting (Entwistle), Moon's methods of entertaining himself were altogether less serene. (Legend has it that when his accountant told him he was technically a millionaire but would need to spend in order to claim on tax, the drummer blew the whole lot in six remarkable weeks, on a hotel, houses, cars and expensive trinkets). He developed a taste for cognac and (this being the seventies) Liebfraumilch. But most of all Keith Moon nurtured a love for mischief. His delight in pyrotechnics was brought to America's attention as The Who made that landmark 1967 appearance on *The Smothers Brothers* TV show. Rattling their way through 'My Generation', pretty much no one but the drummer knew that his drums were set to blow. Having bribed a stagehand to supply flash powder for the stunt, Moon had overdone the dose, causing the kit to explode, almost severing his leg with a cymbal and singeing the hair of Pete Townshend (who himself had already kicked over an amp), rendering the guitarist partially deaf. (Stage left, guest star Bette Davis fainted into Mickey Rooney's arms.) The list is endless: by the mid seventies 'Moon the Loon' had swung from chandeliers, disrobed completely in exclusive public venues, dressed up as Hitler or a trans-sexual, taken horse tranquillizers – and, yes, even thrown televisions out of hotel windows. On one occasion, he parked a mini-hovercraft on a railway line, disrupting train services for hours. The infamous twenty-first birthday story, in which the drummer drove a Lincoln into a Holiday Inn swimming pool during The Who's first US tour, has, however, been dismissed as fable, though Moon did indulge in a lot of horseplay with Herman's Hermits (for whom The Who had been opening).

A limitless appetite for booze and amphetamines fuelling his antics, Moon's lifestyle was fast getting out of hand by 1970, his compulsion for fooling and causing public affray now wearing thin with his bandmates (par-ticularly drug-shunning Daltrey) and also his young wife, Kim Kerrigan, whom he had married when she was just sixteen. Kerrigan, now with a young daughter, Mandy, felt

neglected – after all, her husband could barely remember his daughter's age. Perhaps the beginning of the end was when, attempting to escape a group of Hertfordshire skinheads, Moon accidentally ran over and killed his own driver, Neil Boland: the incident haunted Moon for the remainder of his life. Kerrigan divorced him three years later. But rather than change his lifestyle, Moon decamped in 1974 to the US with new girlfriend, Swedish model Annette Walter-Lax, where he was reunited with various buddies including The Beatles and Harry Nilsson. Apart from a brief visit of a few months to complete The Who's *Who By Numbers* album and his own solo effort, *Two Sides of the Moon* (1975), Keith Moon did not return to the UK until 1977 – whereupon Nilsson handed him the keys to his London flat at 9 Curzon Place, Mayfair – the selfsame apartment in which their friend Cass Elliot had died four years previously (☞ *July 1974*). The events of August 1978 prompted Nilsson to sell the property.

On the night of the 6th, Moon and Walter-Lax had partied – in relatively restrained fashion – in the company of Paul and Linda McCartney at the movie launch for *The Buddy Holly Story*. The night was short and staid: food and drink either went into mouths or remained where it was. The couple returned to Curzon Place at around midnight, and Moon collapsed asleep on his bed, to wake at 7.30 and have his girlfriend cook him up a steak breakfast as he watched a holiday showing of *The Abominable Dr Phibes* on television. With both partners still suffering the effects of the previous evening, further sleep was required; Walter-Lax, knowing that Moon snored loudly when he'd been drinking, chose to crash out on the sofa. When she awoke at 3.40 pm, however, he was making no sound at all: she attempted mouth-to-mouth resuscitation – but her lover was already dead. At the Middlesex Hospital, a post mortem found that Moon had ingested thirty-two Heminevrin tablets – one for each year of his life – that had been rashly prescribed him to combat alcoholism in a 'take as you please' supply of one hundred. Ironic that, after years of imbibing illicit substances, it should be a legal drug that called time on the drummer's behaviour.

Keith Moon's funeral attracted 120 friends from the world of rock 'n' roll, all of whom crammed into the tiny chapel at Golders Green crematorium. Among the mourn-ers were Moon's daughter and ex-wife (who reportedly lost her hair as a result of shock at his death), Annette Walter-Lax, Eric Clapton and those by-now hardy funeral-goers, Bill Wyman and Charlie Watts. Perhaps Daltrey (who, despite his apparent bravado, cried throughout the service) provided the most appropriate floral tribute – a champagne bottle embedded in a television set.

See also *Kit Lambert (☞ April 1981); John Entwistle (☞ June 2002)*

OCTOBER

Friday 6

Johnny O'Keefe
(Waverley, Sydney, 19 January 1935)

Johnny O'Keefe & The Deejays

'She's My Baby', 'Don't You Know?' (both 1960) and 'I'm Counting On You' (1961) ... If the titles mean nothing, then you should know that they were all big-selling singles, number ones for Johnny O'Keefe, an artist who, although he never once cracked the US or UK charts, had twenty-nine Top Forty hits in Australia between 1958 and 1974. O'Keefe is considered the first professional rock 'n' roller down under, and there are many who credit the clean cut but cool crooner as the man who single-handedly established the Australian recording industry, for, as well as enjoying a 16-year hit career himself, O'Keefe was widely noted for his lifelong support of Australian talent and his encouragement of radio programmers to play home-grown acts. He'd always had a flair for PR, bluffing his way into a contract with Festival Records in 1957 by telling the press he was already signed with them. But although artists like Olivia Newton-John and Helen Reddy had US chart-toppers as an indirect result of O'Keefe's influence, his own attempts at cracking this market (where he was somewhat inanely dubbed 'The Boomerang Boy') were entirely unsuccessful.

Outside the studio, Johnny O'Keefe was a popular figure all round. When he was seriously injured in 1960 – his Plymouth Belvedere was virtually written off by a truck – fans congregated around the hospital where he lay, praying for his recovery. They had a long wait, but O'Keefe pulled through after a fortnight as the nation held its breath.

Even when the hits dried up, Johnny O'Keefe's status guaranteed constant television appearances. Thus, the news that he'd died from a heart attack at his Sydney home was met with hushed astonishment from a generation of Australian fans who had grown up with and loved the star's music.

Monday 9

Jacques Brel
(Schaerbeek, Belgium, 8 April 1929)

Jacques Brel was more of a fine artist than songwriter, his compositions vignettes of hard experience, ever more full of passion, action and location as his own life progressed. Guitar always to hand, Brel took his first tentative steps towards assembling arguably the twentieth century's most essential catalogue of windswept ballads, beginning his career fitting gigs in between shifts at his father's box-making company. He relocated to Paris in his early twenties, where his innate ability to pull the heartstrings would, with increasing regularity, bowl over audiences – most notably during a stunning performance at the city's Olympia Theatre in July 1954. Brel's unique take on the *chanson* had also been observed by the Philips label, who signed him and issued his eponymous debut album that year. Although France became his adopted country, Brel never forgot his roots, vehemently declaring himself 'a Flemish singer' in interview. His first commercial breakthrough nonetheless occurred in France, with the single release of his '*Quand on n'a que l'amour*' (1956, later adapted as 'If We Only Have Love') reaching the Top Five.

Jacques Brel: Almost certainly the most interesting musician to emerge from Belgium

The UK was a little slower to catch on, but US acceptance was assured after an impressive set at New York's Carnegie Hall early in 1963, his songs now regularly rewritten for an English-speaking audience by American folk poet Rod McKuen.

As his reputation flourished, Brel diversified from love songs to social commentary, generally taking a few potshots at his native country's traditional Flemish speakers as he did so – a far cry from his earlier declarations. While the comic compositions of Brel's early work mocked the conventions of Flemish life, his later diatribes were far more politicized; he described the right-wing Flemish Movement as 'Nazis during the war and Catholics in between' in the barbed 'La, La, La' (1967). Around this time, Brel turned his back on live musical performance and didn't release a new album for nearly a decade, finding different outlets for his expression, performing as a straight actor in the French film *Les Risques du métier* and a comic turn in *L'Emmerdeur* (two of nine movies he made before 1973), while also writing and directing the translated US stage musical *Man of La Mancha* (1968). But much more than these outside projects, Brel will naturally be best remembered for his recorded works. Though his songs have been covered in English by a diverse variety of high-profile artists, from David Bowie ('Amsterdam'/'My Death') to Dionne Warwick ('If We Only Have Love') via Marc Almond ('Jackie') and Terry Jacks ('Seasons in the Sun'/'If You Go Away'), the perfect pop interpreter for Brel's songs of love and theatre was probably Scott Walker, whose debut solo album included near-definitive English-language versions of Brel's 'Jackie (*La Chanson de Jacky*)', 'My Death (*La Morte*)', 'Amsterdam' and 'Mathilde'.

A keen yachtsman, Jacques Brel was in the Canary Islands when he was diagnosed with lung cancer in October 1974. A year later, after painful surgery, he took himself to the Marquises Islands in French Polynesia, where he remained, only returning to France to release the successful 1977 album *Brel*. Sales of this final record went on to top 2 million following his death a year later. Brel died, and was buried, in Altuona, on the Polynesian island of Hiva-Oa.

Saturday 21

Mel Street
(King Malachi Street – Grundy, Virginia, 21 October 1935)
The Swing Kings

A straight-down-the-line country boy, Mel Street was tipped as one of the genre's most promising performers of the decade, but he never overcame the depression that kept him locked out of mainstream success. It had always seemed likely that Street would achieve his goal: he frequently held down more than one job in order to provide for his wife and children, while still finding time to play the clubs. After joining a band called The Swing Kings, he even found himself a regular slot on *Country Showtime* – a weekend variety half-hour on a local Virginia TV network.

Eventually signing a lucrative deal with Mercury, Street's records began to hit the country charts – but a major breakthrough eluded him, requiring the singer to tour relentlessly, which put massive pressure on this family man. On 21 October 1977, the Mel Street single 'Just Hangin' On' entered the country chart. Its title proved accurate: on the same day – the singer's forty-third birthday – he put a gun to his head and blew his brains out. After his death, demand for Street's greatest-hits package was phenomenal – it sold half a million copies.

DECEMBER

Wednesday 27

Chris Bell
(Memphis, Tennessee, 12 January 1951)
Big Star
(Ice Water/Rock City)

If the turn of phrase can be excused, there was something painfully unavoidable about Chris Bell's death. He was a character of great inner sadness, a dark, unfathomable figure who endeared and frustrated in equal measures. As a young man, he'd spend most of his time in the 'Back House', a building on his family's expansive Memphis land with one room for music and one for his other passion, photography. Friends would come and go, and the concept of Bell forming a band had been floating around since his teens.

By 1969 the guitarist/singer and Beatles devotee had a band, Ice Water (previously Rock City – a band originally formed to back singer Tom Eubanks, whom Bell had planned to produce), of whom no one had heard. That is, until his old high-school buddy Alex Chilton arrived to front the band soon known as Big Star, a unique act – completed by bassist Andy Hummel and drummer Jody Stephens – that predated the new wave by some four years to become the US's first and perhaps most interesting power-pop unit. Although the attention given this band was generally directed at his co-founder (after all, Chilton had known much success between 1967 and 1969 with The Box Tops), Bell was arguably the most passionate force behind Big Star's (at the time) overlooked recordings. Stax (of all people) took a chance on the band, releasing their 1972 debut album,

Big Star – Bell, Stephens, Hummel and Chilton: Should have emulated their name

#1 Record, a terrific set driven by Bell's lyrical (and production) input. But, because Stax were suffering financial difficulties at this time, distribution for this potentially huge record was poor, thus it sold maybe 5,000 copies. The lack of any commercial reaction was devastating to Bell, who had wanted desperately to make this record since he was a boy. His disappointment gradually giving way to acute depression, Bell decided very soon after that it just wasn't working for him – and may have attempted suicide for the first time. (Lyrics to the exquisite, sombre 'Try Again' or 'Feel' suggest Bell's mental state.) His brother David took the step of removing Bell from the scene of all his angst by taking him to Europe, though the amount of substances ingested by the brothers only deflected problems.

Big Star's second record, *Radio City* (1973) was – despite credits reading 'Bell/Chilton' – completed with the main protagonists working apart. It was sound, but scarcely in the league of its predecessor, and now critical dismissal was added to commercial shunning. Bell's reaction was to go off the rails once more, becoming addicted to heroin and attempting suicide again – this time resulting in hospitalization. His brother removed him to the château studios in France used by Elton John, and Bell – clearly rejuvenated by the experience – put together music for a solo project. *I am the Cosmos* was even more a revelation of Bell's feelings, with some 'fight' in both content and delivery. But the album did not see a release and Bell quietly threw in the towel to work in his parents' restaurant business. Then, just after Christmas 1978, he was heading home when his compact Triumph hit a kerb and skidded across a private driveway, whereupon it smashed full-on into a lamp-post. The said pole broke off at its base and collapsed on to the car, killing Chris Bell at the scene.

Perhaps the greatest tragedy of Bell's career is that while nobody took any interest in his work when he was alive, his albums with and without Big Star are now treated as the treasures they should always have been, and he and Chilton have since been cited regularly as influences by many acts, REM, Teenage Fanclub and Primal Scream among them. In 1992, this recognition prompted Big Star to re-form and Rykodisc to give *I am the Cosmos* a long-overdue release.

Lest We Forget

Other notable deaths that occurred sometime during 1978:

Larry Brownlee (US R & B/soul vocalist with The CODs, Mystique and The Lost Generation, who charted in 1970 with 'The Sly, the Slick and the Wicked'; born Illinois, 18/3/1943; murdered in Chicago)

Eddie Calvert (UK musician – 'The Man with the Golden Trumpet' – who had fifties #1s with 'Oh Mein Papa' and 'Cherry Pink & Apple Blossom White'; born Lancashire, 15/3/1922; unknown, 7/8)

Maybelle Carter (US country guitarist, mother of June Carter Cash – thus mother-in-law of Johnny Cash; born Maybelle Addington, 10/5/1909; Parkinson's disease with respiratory complications, 23/10)

Jimmy Cross (US novelty singer of unabashed death-ditty classic 'I Want My Baby Back' (– *Death Toll #1*) – also briefly a screen actor and radio producer; born 17/11/1938; heart attack, 8/10)

Don Ellis (noted US horn-player who played with both jazz and rock musicians; born California, 25/7/1934; heart attack, 17/12)

Rick Evers (US drummer/songwriting partner of Carole King, whom he married in 1977; heroin overdose)

Nancy Spungen (US punk groupie and girlfriend of Sex Pistol Sid Vicious; born Pennsylvania, 27/2/1958; stabbed to death in the Chelsea Hotel, New York – apparently by Vicious, 12/10)

Foy Willing (US country singer/founder of Riders of the Purple Sage; born Foy Willingham, Texas, 1915; unknown, 24/7)

Tom Wilson (noted US producer who worked with The Animals, Bob Dylan, Simon & Garfunkel, Velvet Underground and Frank Zappa; born Texas, 25/3/1931; heart attack, 6/9)

Gerhard Zachar (German bass guitarist with Dresden soft-rock band Lift; born 8/10/1945; died in a car crash that also killed singer Henry Pacholski, 11/1978)

For a complete list of fallen artists, visit

www.numberoneinheaven.com

1979

JANUARY

Saturday 13

Donny Hathaway

(Chicago, Illinois, 1 October 1945)

Just as 1978 had begun with the fatality of a Chicago-born musician, so would 1979 – although Donny Hathaway's death was apparently no accident. Raised by his grandmother in St Louis, Missouri, young Hathaway was considered an intellectual among the soul fraternity. Gospel-turned-cocktail-jazz singer Hathaway had started as a music-theory major, attracting the interest of Curtis Mayfield, who employed the graduate as a producer at his Curtom label. With his foot firmly in the door, Hathaway began his own recording career with the duet 'I Thank You Baby' (1969) with June Conquest, and composed sophisticated tunes both for himself and others such as Aretha Franklin. It would be, though, his work with soul-ballad queen Roberta Flack – his former classmate at Howard University, Washington, DC – that resonated most with fans: 'You've Got a Friend' (1971, written by James Taylor) and, in particular, 'Where is the Love?' (1972) were US hits and suggested there might be more between the pair than mere professional empathy.

Sadly for Hathaway, his love for Flack was – apparently – unrequited. During the seventies, the singer suffered frequent bouts of depression, not least when their working relationship began to suffer as early as 1973; on his own, Hathaway found the going tougher and retreated from the limelight, though partial reconciliation with Flack led to another album in 1977. A single, 'The Closer I Get to You' (1978), became their biggest hit together, just edged out of US number one by The Bee Gees. In January 1979, the pair recorded more songs in New York, all their earlier differences seemingly patched up – but this wasn't enough for Hathaway. Distraught that he could never be with Flack (who was happily married with children), he made a shocking decision. After a final plea to Flack, Hathaway allegedly removed the glass from a window while she was otherwise occupied, stepped out on to the ledge and dropped from the fifteenth floor of the Plaza Hotel. His body landed on a second-floor ledge.

Opinion was divided after the ensuing inquest: while the Reverend Jesse Jackson (who read Hathaway's eulogy) suggested that this was no suicide, the coroner remained adamant that 'no adult ever fell from a waist-high window'. One bizarre fact that emerged was that Hathaway apparently made a habit of preaching from hotel windows – and had been ejected from more than one hotel for doing so. Flack & Hathaway's poignantly titled 'Back Together Again' (1980) gave the singer a sizeable posthumous hit, while his surviving daughter, Lalah, enjoyed musical success during the nineties.

FEBRUARY

Sid Vicious

(Simon John Ritchie – Lewisham, London, 10 May 1957)

The Sex Pistols

'I'll die before I'm twenty-five. And when I do, I'll have lived the way I wanted to.'

Sid Vicious, in 1978

If The Ramones dumbed down punk with a cartoon-like frenzy of action, then überfan Sid's means of achieving the same were just the opposite – his sullen, deliberately self-destructive personality seemed to hit the spot as far as the nihilistic end of the market was concerned. Whether punk was ever meant to be about this is open to debate, but there's little doubt that Vicious was marketed as an icon on whom followers could impose whatever fantasy they wished. Was Vicious a mass of contradictions? Rose-tinted minority opinion paints him as a reluctant intellectual who quoted Wilde, more remember him as a volatile attention-seeker who only wanted to be a rock star – a prize for which he was prepared to die.

Stories about his young life vary from the lurid to the downright ludicrous, but there's little doubt that Simon John Ritchie, at some point or other, caused harm to old women, young women, the odd journalist and an assortment of animals. In his defence, he had a deeply unsettled upbringing: his father walked out on his bohemian mother, Anne, when Simon was just two years old, and his step-father, a middle-class Kentish man called Chris Beverley, died within months of his mother's second marriage, which placed him into a rough Tunbridge Wells secondary modern rather than the private education in which he might have ended up. At this school, the now-renamed John Beverley had few friends. For one, he was volatile and unpredictable – but, more significantly, he couldn't take friends home because his mother had used heroin since the early sixties. By the time her son was sixteen they were known to shoot up together.

Returning to London in 1974, Beverley spent time around Kingsway College and had settled sufficiently to acquire a couple of allies in two other Johns, Wardle (Jah Wobble) and former Hackney school-friend Lydon (Johnny Rotten): together they would drink copiously and get up to little more than check out each other's music collections (Beverley was, believe it or not, a fan of Brian Eno, The Pink Fairies and Weather Report, among others). But, outside this, his disturbing need for drugs was what cemented his wayward legend for the couple of years before he joined the Sex Pistols. His behaviour became increasingly malevolent as a result: in October 1975, Beverley sold some powder (which turned out to be toilet cleaner) at an Oxford party under the premiss that it was some of the amphetamine he was widely known to be taking at this time – it very nearly killed its recipient. Later, the out-of-control Beverley boasted to friends of mugging an old lady at knifepoint in an alleyway. As if that weren't enough, he then (famously) set about *NME* scribe Nick Kent with a bike chain at the 100 Club (he later blinded a girl in one eye when he threw a pint glass at another early Pistols gig there – for which he spent a paltry week in remand). So, when *was* music going to play any part in this rock 'n' roller's life?

Well, soon after – to a degree. As the Pistols – Johnny Rotten (vocals), Steve Jones (guitars), Paul Cook (drums) and, at this stage, Glen Matlock (bass) – began to gain notoriety, a jealous Beverley fashioned his own band, Flowers Of Romance, with three women, two of whom were future members of The Slits, Viv Albertine and Paloma 'Palmolive' Romero. When this fell apart after Beverley expressed a 'liking' for the Nazis, he spent some time behind the kit of the fledgling Siouxsie & The Banshees . . . until they found a proper drummer. But Vicious – as he was finally to be known – was not to be denied. Despite wide disapproval from their peers, on 3 March 1977 the Sex Pistols and manager Malcolm McLaren kicked out Glen Matlock (the man who had written most of debut single 'Anarchy in the UK') to replace him with Sid Vicious. Who had never played bass in his life. It was just one more tabloid-taunting move amid the taking of nearly £150K from three major labels inside six months as the band began its 'cash from chaos' plan in earnest. The records were admittedly great at this point – 'God Save the Queen', 'Pretty Vacant' and 'Holidays in the Sun' all went Top Ten (the first of these would probably have been a UK number one but authorities wouldn't allow that) as Britain decided between monarchy and anarchy in the heady summer of 1977.

Although he'd made cursory attempts to learn his instrument, The Sex Pistols' newest acquisition had begun to fall apart as early as April 1977, when punk's most notorious groupie, Nancy Spungen, arrived in his world. Spungen was a rebellious Pennsylvanian who had attempted suicide on at

Sid and Nancy: Punk's 'Posh and Becks'

'I'm glad he died. Nothing can hurt him any more.'

Anne Beverley, Vicious's mother

least one occasion and had used smack since her early teens; she'd even been to known to strip and sleep around for her habit. A former cashier at CBGB's, Spungen had initially come to London with the intention of bedding one of The New York Dolls, but, on being banned outright from even approaching former drummer Jerry Nolan, she turned her attention to Sid. Despite his outer bravado, Vicious was naive, weak-willed and quite possibly still a virgin: to him, with his blurred vision and increasingly warped perception of reality, Spungen probably looked like a goddess, a rock chick to out-rock-chick them all. Under her guidance, Vicious slipped into heroin meltdown as the Pistols folded in on themselves during the ill-fated 1978 US tour. By now his deranged 'act' consisted of calling American audiences 'faggots' and making himself bleed on stage, the bassist's amp generally switched off while a session-player strummed behind the scenes. Then, one afternoon in January, Vicious awoke from a drug-related coma in a New York hospital

to discover that Rotten, Cook and Jones had all called time on what they considered an increasingly wretched project. Now – he thought – he needed Spungen more than ever.

Despite the break-up of one of the most potent bands of all time, the remainder of the year was not entirely uneventful for Sid Vicious: he recorded a memorably nihilistic rendition of 'My Way', which illuminated that otherwise miserable movie *The Great Rock 'n' Roll Swindle* – and in August he moved back to New York with Spungen. The idea was to quit heroin and reignite Vicious's career (with Spungen, somehow, as his manager). He played a few gigs – with various ex-Dolls, and even Mick Jones of The Clash, as back-up – but New York remained largely unsympathetic to a performer and his muse whose reputations it remembered only too damn well.

So, with their shared heroin and methadone habit wrapping them in a warm blanket, punk's most notorious couple hid themselves away in Room 100 of the $17-a-night

'Sid actually did nothing. Excellent person, but drugs turned him into an unpleasant Mr Hyde.'

Johnny Rotten

Chelsea Hotel, West 23rd Street, New York – a once-glamorous residence that now reserved its lower floors for supposed artisans and junkies. It all came to a shocking, if predictable, climax when, sometime between 5 and 9 am on the morning of 12 October, Vicious entered the bathroom to find Spungen in her underwear, slumped by the lavatory, apparently stabbed to death. The murder weapon he recognized as his own knife – which she had recently bought him for protection from frequent attacks. Understandably in shock from the event, Vicious confessed on arrest that *he* had done it because he was a 'dirty dog' – only to deny responsibility on further questioning. It is widely known that various suppliers and users came and went from Room 100 that night – and that on top of his usual intake, Vicious had dropped as many as nine Tuinols (amphetamines) – but to this day nobody really has a firm notion of what transpired. Many believe that criminal friends of a supplier had robbed them and attacked Spungen, while others think there may have been a suicide pact; Vicious's mother – who despised her son's girlfriend – maintained until her own death (from a 1996 overdose) that Spungen stabbed herself. Vicious was charged and incarcerated at Riker's Island Prison, and although he was bailed at a cost of around $50K, he soon found himself back behind bars. Ten days after his release, he attempted suicide, which saw him placed in a psychiatric unit at the Bellevue Hospital. Vicious was clearly traumatized by the death of Spungen, but the shock of her death was still insufficient to revise his behaviour. Before his own demise, he found time to acquire a new girlfriend (actress Michelle Robinson, who herself had recently lost a partner) and to inflict another serious eye injury, this time on Patti Smith's brother Todd in January 1979. For this, he received a sentence of fifty-five days – which, of course, he was never to serve.

Celebrating his second bail in just three months, Vicious threw his last party on 2 February in the company of Robinson, various junkie friends and Anne Beverley – who had been in America for a while – at Robinson's Greenwich Village apartment. Although Vicious had been detoxified while serving time, he, his friends and his mother saw no reason not to get him a fix. The heroin was, according to its pusher, almost 100 per cent pure; on his first hit, Vicious passed out but came round. He got up, spoke to his mother,

and then – as she and Robinson slept – shot up again. His vast second dose killed him during the night, while Robinson slept beside him in ignorance. He was cremated in New York three days later. Although a verdict of suicide was passed, the blame for his (and Spungen's) death has consistently been shoved from pillar to post in the twenty-seven years since. Put simply, Sid Vicious was never going to be saved. He wanted the legacy too much.

The ashes of Sid Vicious were, according to his mother, scattered over the Pennsylvania plot where Nancy Spungen was buried – much against her family's wishes. Another widely spread story is that Anne Beverley accidentally dropped the urn at Heathrow Airport, and Vicious's remains were sucked up into the air-conditioning and subsequently blown about the building and its travellers.

DEAD INTERESTING!

'WHAT DO I GET?' (SEVERE DEPRESSION, IT SEEMS)

Very strange is the supposed 'Curse of The Buzzcocks', an extraordinary phenomenon affecting icons who have played with the celebrated Manchester punks. The Buzzcocks were one of the young punk bands who opened on several now legendary nights for The Sex Pistols: Sid Vicious died of a self-inflicted overdose (◄ *February 1979*). Then, less than a year after touring as the band's support, Joy Division singer Ian Curtis hanged himself (► *May 1980*). Most bizarrely, Nirvana's Kurt Cobain became the third new-wave legend to take his own life subsequent to touring with The Buzzcocks (► *April 1994*): a year before, the Seattle grunge gods had chosen the re-formed band to open on their European tour.

Genial Buzzcocks frontman Pete Shelley nowadays says, 'There's no need for the supports to know about this. I save it 'til after the tour.'

MARCH

Mike Patto

(Michael Thomas McCarthy – Cirencester,
Gloucestershire, 22 September 1942)

Patto (Timebox)
Spooky Tooth
(Boxer)
(Various acts)

Mike Patto's is the classic tragedy of
the man who appeared to have it all.
A talented musician/singer, Patto
played with and for so many diverse
acts in his lifetime it would take an
entire 'Rock Family Tree' to deal
adequately with them all. As a young
man, though, it was his ability on the
games field that impressed most, and
he was a county champion boxer in
Norfolk as a youth. There wasn't a lot
Patto *couldn't* do, to be honest. He'd
been a good scholar and was popular
with women because of his ability on
the dance floor (he was a champion
here, too), but it is for his musicianship that he is best remembered. (His
name-change to 'Patto' came from not
wanting to sound like 'McCartney'.)
His first band to gain wide notice was
a covers act called The Fretmen, with
whom Patto appeared on television,
while another, The Bo Street Runners
(briefly featuring Mick Fleetwood on
drums) were offered a contract with
Brian Epstein. This, incredibly, was
turned down – as was a further contract with Larry Parnes, after intervention from Patto's father. The first real
breakthrough for this dynamic guitarist and singer came in the late sixties,
with the group Timebox, who then
became Patto. Although Mike Patto
still hadn't achieved huge success, he
was invited to join Spooky Tooth in
November 1973. The band already
had two frontmen in Mick Jones (later

of Foreigner) and Gary Wright (who
became a successful solo artist); the latter unfortunately proved incompatible
with Patto – thus he was on the move
once more.

It was while performing with
Boxer that Mike Patto learned of his
illness. After collapsing during a 1976
American tour, he was diagnosed with
lymphatic leukaemia, and the band
returned to the UK so that he could
commence treatment. Less than three
years after the diagnosis, Patto passed
away and was buried in his adopted
home of Hingham, Norfolk. He is
survived by his wife and three children,
including his musician son, Michael.

See also *Ollie Halsall (☛ May 1992);
Greg Ridley (☛ November 2003)*

Roy Montrell

(Raymond Montrell – New Orleans, Louisiana,
27 February 1928)

To call him a session man would be
hugely unfair, for Roy Montrell was
one of the most sought after and
inspiring guitarists of his day, playing with Bobby Mitchell, Lloyd Price
and Little Richard, but most influen-
tially as a member of Fats Domino's
band, after his military discharge in
the early fifties. Such was the demand
for Montrell's services – the number
of well-known songs on which he
performed may well reach into the
thousands – that he only ever cut a few
sides of his own, including '(Everytime
I Hear) That Mellow Saxophone'
(1956) and 'Mudd' (1960).

Montrell's glittering career ended
tragically though, when – on tour
with Domino – he was found dead
in his room at the Sonesta Hotel,
Amsterdam, apparently from a heroin
overdose, the needle and paraphernalia
still by his side.

Zenon De Fleur

(Zenon Hierowski – Shepherd's Bush, London,
9 September 1951)
The Count Bishops
(Long Pig)

Yet another young musician
influenced by Elvis and the blues,
Zenon Hierowski built himself
a guitar in woodwork classes at
fourteen, and a few years later
founded his own band, Long Pig.
While working as an accountant,
Hierowski (who changed his moniker
to the more flamboyant 'De Fleur',
apparently after a studio engineer
had said, 'Look at Zen on de floor!')
joined the band Chrome. As The
Count Bishops – Telecaster-toting
De Fleur, Dave Tice (lead vocals,
replacing Mike Spenser), Johnny
Guitar (guitars), Steve Lewins
(bass) and Paul Balbi (drums) – the
band became one of the best on
the live circuit during the era. The
Count Bishops were the first to
join Chiswick Records ahead of
rivals The Hammersmith Gorillas
and Roogalator – but they were all
to become part of an exciting late-
seventies R & B sub-scene that
introduced folk to bands like Dr
Feelgood and Eddie & The Hot Rods.

With units refusing to shift, the
band shortened their name to The
Bishops and signed with Dutch label
Dynamite. But in March 1979, it
all ended sadly for De Fleur, when
– after a typically boisterous Bishops'
gig at The Nashville in West London
– he crashed his car into a tree, sustaining severe injuries. Although off
the critical list, and even asking about
artwork for the band's imminent
third album from his West Middlesex
Hospital bed, Zenon De Fleur
suffered a relapse and died of a heart
attack one week later. He is perhaps

best recalled for his raucous vocal on The Count Bishops' one genuine classic, 'Train Train' (1976).

JUNE

Thursday 21

Angus MacLise

(Bridgeport, Connecticut, 14 March 1938)

The Velvet Underground
(Joyous Lake)

Although he's generally referred to as the Velvet Underground drummer who left before they began recording, Angus MacLise was no avant-garde Pete Best, being highly prolific in and around world and experimental music. Having learned Haitian drumming as a boy, he was entered into the Buddy Rich School to master jazz technique throughout the fifties. Thereafter, he played with a number of free-form acts and worked with La Monte Young and a pre-Lennon Yoko Ono, as well as overseeing multimedia events of his own. The band's original drummer, Angus MacLise founded Velvet Underground when he met John Cale – then a friend of Young's – at a musicians' collective, but walked out on the group when he discovered that they would be performing their first gig for money, something a purist like MacLise would always refuse to do. Claiming that this group would likely be 'too structured' for his own tastes, he put together his own amalgamation, Joyous Lake. (Sterling Morrison was quoted as saying that even Keith Moon was considered 'too controlled' by the drummer, who was replaced in VU by Maureen 'Moe' Tucker.)

A traveller for much of his life, Angus MacLise placed little importance on financial security, his frugality partly responsible for his premature death from hypoglycaemia while hospitalized in Kathmandu, Nepal.

See also *Nico (☞ July 1988); Sterling Morrison (☞ August 1995)*

Friday 29

Lowell George

(Hollywood, California, 13 April 1945)

Little Feat
The Mothers of Invention
(The Standells)
(The Factory)

As a slide-player, Lowell George tends now to be rated in the same bracket as the late Duane Allman, but his heroin-promoted death continued a depressing litany of premature fatalities in Southern rock. As the main man behind Little Feat, though, George was far less conventional than most of his peer group, spanning the genres from gospel through R & B to country-blues and boogie-woogie.

The son of a furrier and a neighbour of actor Errol Flynn, George made his musical debut on television, playing harmonica with his brother Hampton at the age of six – but veered towards the guitar, and then the flute, during adolescence. The latter gave George scope to master the oboe, his playing of which can be heard on many Frank Sinatra recordings during the late fifties and early sixties. George's first folk-rock act was The Factory (whose work was only issued a decade after his death), but this quickly gave way to a brief few weeks as frontman for garage rockers The Standells before Frank Zappa's Mothers of Invention came calling. George played on two of The Mothers' albums, and was set to sign his own group, Little Feat, with Zappa's label until negotiations broke down in 1969. In the event, this great band signed with Warners and put out eight albums in nine years, the best of which was probably 1974's *Feats Don't Fail Me Now*. The year after, George contracted hepatitis, which would curtail his touring a great deal. But although Little Feat disbanded in

Lowell George: Thanks, I'll drink it here

'The best singer, songwriter and guitar-player I've ever heard, hands down.'
Bonnie Raitt

1978, it was not the end for George: within months of his going it alone, Warners issued *Thanks I'll Eat It Here* – a mainly covers album that had been some two years in the making – and all appeared rosy for a prolific solo career for Lowell George.

But the combination of George's tendency to obesity and his seemingly unshakeable desire to use class-A drugs had its unavoidable effect as he promoted the record. After a performance at George Washington University in DC, he overdosed on the way to a concert in Virginia – and died of a subsequent heart attack.

JULY

Friday 6

Van McCoy
(Washington, DC, 6 January 1944)
Van McCoy & The Soul City Symphony
(The Starlighters)

Washington-based session instrumentalist/writer Van McCoy was in his thirties before his theme tune, 'The Hustle', became an enormous worldwide smash in 1975. Before this, he'd been a well-respected producer/songwriter under the guidance of Leiber and Stoller, working with a number of not inconsiderable talents like Aretha Franklin and Gladys Knight. Push farther back still, and McCoy, who had sung with The Starlighters, was himself putting out records such as the near-hit 'Hey Mr DJ', on Scepter, when he was just a teenager.

That title gave a small hint of what was to come: late in 1974, McCoy – now fronting an amalgamation called The Soul City Symphony – was putting the finishing touches to his *Disco Baby* album, a professional but somewhat nondescript series of

workouts for the dance floor, when he came up with 'The Hustle', an instrumental that almost didn't make the collection. Some months later, the song was number one in the Billboard charts. Although it was his only Top Forty success in America, McCoy employed the formula well elsewhere: he helped to rework the track for the Stylistics' 'I Can't Give You Anything but My Love' (a 1975 UK number one), making the UK Top Five a second time with 'The Shuffle' (1977), a similar-sounding piece that became a BBC radio sports theme.

A Grammy winner in 1976, McCoy also wrote a top-seller for former Temptation David Ruffin and worked on soundtracks – though his real love in music was the Rachmaninov, Tchaikovsky and Dvořák his mother played him as a child. McCoy died unexpectedly from a heart attack in Englewood, New Jersey.

Thursday 12

Minnie Riperton
(Chicago, Illinois, 8 November 1947)
(The Gems)
(The Rotary Connection)

Like Van McCoy, she'll forever be associated with one all-conquering 1975 hit single, but Minnie Riperton was a singer who had studied opera until seduced by R & B. The youngest of eight children, Riperton was a gospel singer when discovered by the hawks at Chess Records, who made her a receptionist and placed her in a house vocal group called The Gems (first single: the extravagantly titled 'That's What They Put Erasers on Pencils For').

With The Gems subsequently limited to backing Chess vocalists, Riperton – for some reason then known as Andrea Davis – released the solo 'Lonely Girl', which bombed,

and joined The Rotary Connection, an altogether more sophisticated venture, between 1967 and 1970. Her extraordinary five-octave soprano then caught the attention of Stevie Wonder, who recruited her for his Wonderlove backing band – and went on to produce her big-selling second solo album for Epic, *Perfect Angel*. From this set came *that* song: written by Riperton with husband Richard Rudolph, 'Lovin' You' (US number one, UK number two) placed her on virtually every radio station in the world throughout 1975.

As she recorded her penultimate studio album in 1976, Minnie Riperton learned that she was dying from breast cancer, stunning television audiences by announcing her condition during a live chat show. As she steeled herself for a battle she would not win, Riperton became a spokeswoman for the American Cancer Society and was one of the era's highest-profile users of cannabis to alleviate her suffering. Within months of her death, a crass, rehashed album of Riperton's discarded studio work was issued to cash in. In more recent times, 'Lovin' You' has formed the basis for a concept record by The Orb – and a Burger King ad. Riperton's surviving daughter, Maya Rudolph (whose name recurs in the lyric at the end of the song), appears regularly on US television, hosting NBC's *Saturday Night Live*.

Sunday 15

Rick Garberson
(Akron, Ohio, 15 November 1950)
The Bizarros

Emerging from the same Ohio music scene as Devo and The Waitresses, post-punk misfits The Bizarros were formed at the University of Akron by singer Nick Nicholis, Terry Walker (keyboards/bass/guitars), brothers Jerry (lead guitar) and Don Parkins (bass/guitars). Rick Garberson was the band's original percussionist as they opened for local heroes like Pere Ubu and signed with Mercury imprint, Blank Records.

For Garberson, it would be a limited experience: known to be depressed, he died from carbon-monoxide poisoning in his garage just months after the group's eponymous debut album hit the shops. Surviving members of The Bizarros – having reconvened in 1998 after a sixteen-year hiatus – released a new record, *You Can't Fight Your Way Uptown from Here*, in 2003.

AUGUST

Sunday 19

Dorsey Burnette
(Memphis, Tennessee, 28 December 1932)
The (Johnny Burnette) Rock 'n' Roll Trio

Tough-kid Dorsey Burnette forever found himself in scrapes at school: he was the older brother of Johnny Burnette, and didn't like to see him getting picked on. Thus, following school, both brothers immediately took to boxing, at one point becoming Golden Gloves champions in the sport. They would tag with fellow pugilist and distinctive 'buzzsaw' guitarist Paul Burlison, who had punched his weight as a partner of Howlin' Wolf's, to form The Rock 'n' Roll Trio in 1953. The band suffered disappointment when rejected by Sam Phillips at Sun Records for sounding too similar to Elvis Presley, so all three hit New York City to better their chances of success. Surprisingly for the popular live draw, this was not forthcoming and they called it a day

when notable numbers such as 'Train Kept a-Rollin'' failed to sell with the Coral label. Although Johnny made something of a solo career for himself, in August 1964, Dorsey Burnette suffered his greatest pain when he lost his cherished younger brother (➺ *Pre-1965*). Shouldering the blame for what was clearly a terrible catastrophe, Burnette looked to drugs and alcohol to deal with the guilt he had created within himself.

For the last fifteen years of his life, Burnette cut countless flop records for some twelve labels, continued to get into fights and – eventually – found Christianity before he died. He had just cut a disc with an old rockabilly buddy, Jimmy Bowen, when he collapsed and died from a heart attack. Tanya Tucker, Kris Kristofferson and Glen Campbell were among those who played a benefit concert for his widow. Less than a year after Burnette's death, his nephew Rocky (Johnny's son) enjoyed a US hit with 'Tired of Toein' the Line', and his own guitarist son Billy became a member of Fleetwood Mac in 1987. The innovative Burlison died in 2003.

SEPTEMBER

Thursday 27

Jimmy McCulloch
(Glasgow, 4 June 1953)
Paul McCartney & Wings
Thunderclap Newman
Stone the Crows
(Various acts)

What 'Little' Jimmy McCulloch packed into his brief, young career, most musicians would be hard pushed to fit into their entire lives. He (a guitarist) and his older brother

Jack (a drummer) fronted bands in Cumbernauld at the ages of eleven and thirteen, playing the pubs well before either was legally allowed to drink. The second band was One in a Million, an accomplished four-piece that released a pair of singles and impressed Pete Townshend, who recommended the diminutive but already versatile McCulloch Jr to an old art-school mate, Andy Newman. Although the latter's trio, Thunderclap Newman, was not around for long, they did come up with 1969's 'Something in the Air', a record that made McCulloch the youngest ever guitarist to play on a credible UK number-one single. (Go on, disprove it.)

His next moves would not have disgraced an ageing session man, filling in with some heavyweight names with the bands of former Bluesbreaker John Mayall and Steve Ellis, ex of Love Affair. In 1972, the tragic death of Les Harvey (➺ *May 1972*) landed McCulloch the gig with Stone the Crows, perhaps his highest profile so far. But again, this didn't last, and by the following year he'd joined two further bands – Blue (a Glasgow act formed by Hugh Nicholson of The Marmalade) and Tundra. Bear in mind that McCulloch was only just out of his teens at this point. The final – and by far the biggest – chapter in Jimmy McCulloch's rock biography was made possible by a call from one of the world's wealthiest musicians. Helping on a Linda McCartney solo project, McCulloch was hired full-time for Wings' *Venus and Mars* (1975), at which time Paul McCartney's band was probably the biggest pop unit in the world. He stayed with Wings for three more albums, *Wings at the Speed of Sound* (1976), *Wings Over America* (1977) and *London Town* (1978), though had already left by the time 'Mull of Kintyre' was on its way to becoming the UK's best-selling 45 ever (well, until 1984).

By now, McCulloch had made far more money than most folk his age and unfortunately fell foul of one or two rock 'n' roll temptations. After a period spent with, first, the re-formed Small Faces on tour (this was just a matter of weeks), then with 'supergroups' Wild Horses and The Dukes, 26-year-old McCulloch was found dead in his London flat, having apparently suffered heart failure. It was later established that this had been brought on by a lethal mix of alcohol and morphine.

See also *Linda McCartney (☛ April 1998). Thunderclap Newman singer/ drummer 'Speedy' Keen passed away in 2002.*

NOVEMBER

Thursday 1

Judee Sill

(Judith Sill – Oakland, California, 4 October 1944)

Her name remains largely unknown, but singer/songwriter Judee Sill's life and death were extraordinarily difficult and tragic. Sill had one of the strangest, most unhappy upbringings one could imagine. Her father – who died when she was a child – made his money running illegal gambling schools at his Oakland bar, and Sill often had to hide under tables or pinball machines to avoid the frequent fights. Before her mother died from cancer when Sill was twenty-two, she also lost a brother in a car accident – and her first husband (whom she married at seventeen) in a rafting accident after they'd split. Little wonder, perhaps, that Sill developed a $150-a-day heroin habit in her teens – an addiction she supported through

Judee Sill: Somehow still smiling

'She had every problem going, but she made fantastic music.'

Andy Partridge, XTC

robbery (for which she was sent to remand school), forgery (for which she was imprisoned) and, allegedly, prostitution. The great shame was that Judee Sill had much to offer otherwise. Briefly an Asylum labelmate of Joni Mitchell, Sill described herself as influenced mainly by Pythagoras, Bach and Ray Charles, her richly harmonic songs full of the kind of imagery and symbolism that intrigued as to this outwardly religious young woman's real beliefs. Sill's best-known composition is probably 'Jesus was a Crossmaker', a track which received

radio play but didn't chart. David Geffen dropped her from his label after this failure (and that of its parent album). Sill's refusal to play support slots on rock tours that she despised effectively sank her career, though she managed to pen a minor hit for The Turtles in 'Lady-O' (1969), marrying keyboardist Bob Harris (who died in 1993).

Because she released no records after her *Heart Food* album (1973), some maintain Sill died around 1974. The most likely date, however, is November 1979, and she supposedly cut a lost album that year. Sill had apparently injured her back and refused morphine because of her addiction to heroin – which makes an overdose of the latter drug appear very probable. Rumours abound that Sill was near-destitute at the time and living in an abusive relationship.

Saturday 17

John Glascock
(Islington, London, 2 May 1951)
Jethro Tull
Chicken Shack
(Various acts)

An affable, workmanlike bassist, Glascock already had an impressive CV before beginning his four-year spell with prog-folkers Jethro Tull in 1975. He and his percussionist brother Brian (later of The Motels) originally played in a band with future Rolling Stone Mick Taylor, the left-handed Glascock greatly inspired by Paul McCartney. By the time he'd joined Tull, he had played rock with The Gods, blues/soul with Toe Fat and blues/R & B with popular live act Chicken Shack. He then rejoined his brother for a time with LA avant-garde fusionists Carmen – who were invited on a US support slot with Jethro Tull, when the latter's leader Ian Anderson was alerted to Glascock's ability. His first record with Jethro Tull was 1976's ironically titled *Too Old to Rock 'n' Roll, Too Young to Die*.

Glascock's premature death offers a stern warning to those who ignore dental problems: suffering from a neglected tooth abscess, the bass-player became seriously ill when the infection spread to his heart and damaged an already weak valve – a hereditary condition. In 1977, he underwent surgery to replace the valve, but he never totally recovered. Falling ill during the recordings,

Glascock contributed to his final album for Tull (1979's *Storm Watch*), and played his last gig exactly three years to the day of his first. On 17 November, John Glascock's replacement valve was rejected by his body, and the musician died during emergency surgery.

Thursday 29

'Tiki' Fulwood
(Ramon Fulwood – Philadelphia, Pennsylvania, 23 May 1944)
Parliament/Funkadelic

Just eighteen months after the death of rhythm guitarist Glen Goins (← *July 1978*), the P-Funk stable lost another key component to illness. 'Tiki' Fulwood had been a house drummer at Philadelphia's Uptown Theater before he was invited to join the sassiest funk conglomerate the world has yet seen; he joined Funkadelic as early as 1968 and appeared prominently on their self-titled debut album. Fulwood's career with the band was to be very fragmented, however: he developed a taste for drugs, which affected his ability as a live percussionist, and was given his marching orders after two (perhaps appropriately titled) further albums, *Free Your Mind and Your Ass Will Follow* and *Maggot Brain*. Fulwood regained control somewhat, via time spent playing sessions behind soul vocalist Tyrone Davis, and rejoined Funkadelic. But in 1971–2, Fulwood's world was disrupted when he lost both parents to stomach cancer. In 1975, he was fired again after a violent episode: he attacked

P-Funk übermeister George Clinton, demanding payment. His drumming was edited from the band's best-known song, 'Tear the Roof off the Sucker', and replaced with that of Jerome Brailey. Fulwood had on occasion had spats with Brailey: guarding his position jealously, he had allegedly pointed a gun at the P-Funk mainstay several years before, believing him to be after his job (which, of course, he was).

Three years on, 'Tiki' Fulwood was confirmed as suffering from the same condition as his parents. The disease developed quickly, killing him just a year after diagnosis.

See also *Eddie Hazel (← December 1992); Raymond Davis (← Golden Oldies #26)*

Ray Smith
(Melber, Kentucky, 30 October 1934)
Ray Smith & The Rock 'n' Roll Boys

On the same day Fulwood died, a man from a completely different musical background took his own life in Canada. For Ray Smith, there were no fancy nicknames or elaborate licks, his style was strictly down-home country-infused rockabilly – and, for a while at least, the kids loved it. Kentucky native Smith was a talent-show winner heard singing in the shower while serving with the US air force in California, and returned to Kentucky to form The Rock 'n' Roll Boys (with Raymond Jones on guitar, Dean Perkins on steel guitar, James Bardwell on bass and Henry Stevens on drums) after his discharge. They were popular, to say the least, land-

'Don't stick no fork in me – I ain't done yet!'
Ray Smith, shortly before his death

ing their own local television show in 1957 and, a year later, a contract that most early rockers would have killed for, with Sam Phillips's Sun label. For Sun, Smith recorded 'So Young' (1958, featuring a young Charlie Rich on drums) – considered by many to be the original rockabilly disc. Joining the Judd label (run by Judd Phillips, Sam's brother), Ray Smith & The Rock 'n' Roll boys made a national breakthrough with the hit 'Sweet Little Angel' in 1960 but, with Judd deciding to follow it with a series of nondescript ballads, it was to be their only major chart success.

Ray Smith remained in music for the rest of his days, but the continued lack of commercial acceptance clearly harmed him. Although he found brief success as a songwriter (composing a 1970 hit for Conway Twitty), Smith became a very quiet and reserved character, moving away from what little limelight there was, to Burlington, Ontario. It was there that he committed suicide by gunshot at his home.

DECEMBER

Saturday 15

Jackie Brenston

(Clarksdale, Mississippi,
15 August 1930)
The Delta Rhythm Kings
(Various acts)

Sam Phillips had a hand in Jackie Brenston's career as well – the Sun Records impresario maintaining that Brenston's 'Rocket 88' was the first bona fide rock 'n' roll record made. Brenston had been born and brought up in a musically fertile part of town, the local juke joints having hosted Son House and Robert Johnson – but it was sax, as opposed to guitar, that was Brenston's instrument of choice. A chance meeting with flamboyant teenage musician/DJ, Isaiah 'Ike' Turner (and his Kings of Rhythm/Delta Rhythm Kings) changed Brenston's fortunes: he joined the band Phillips would find so irresistible, and in 1951 the Sun head was beckoning them to his Memphis studio. With lead vocals split between Brenston and Turner, one of four resultant tracks, 'Rocket 88' – an ode to the group's preferred Oldsmobile – became a huge R & B number one for Chess. But because it featured Brenston's voice, the disc was subsequently credited to 'Jackie Brenston & His Delta Cats' – much to the annoyance of the rest of the band, especially Turner, and they turned their backs on the singer.

Finding success with another band proved hard, and Brenston drifted for many years from job to job (including both sax-playing and truck-driving), although Ike Turner forgave him enough to invite Brenston on tour with him and Tina during the seventies. But his health deteriorated through drink and lack of maintenance, and Jackie Brenston died of a heart attack at a Memphis army veterans' hospice.

Lest We Forget

Other notable deaths that occurred sometime during 1979:

Everton DaSilva (Jamaican percussionist/melodica-player, producer and head of the label Hungry Town; shot while recording with Horace Andy in New York)

Lester Flatt (pioneering US bluegrass singer with Flatt & Scruggs; born Tennessee, 19/6/1914; died following open heart surgery, 11/5)

Charles Mingus (peerless US jazz/R & B bassist/pianist; born Arizona, 22/4/1922; Lou Gehrig's disease, 5/1)

Tuza Mthethwa (South African guitarist with jive amalgamation The Soul Brothers; car crash – an unnamed sax-player also perished)

Bobby Napier (US bluegrass mandolin-player with The Lost Creek Boys; born Kentucky, 24/12/1933; crushed by a falling boulder, 21/11)

Norrie Paramor (top UK easy-listening bandleader turned producer of countless hits, also responsible for signing Cliff Richard & The Shadows to EMI; born London, 1913; unknown, 9/9)

Enrico Rosenbaum (US singer/guitarist with The Underbeats, who became Gypsy; born 18/6/1944; suicide, following long battle with drug addiction, 10/9)

Shelly Siegel (US head honcho of Mushroom Records who gave the world Heart and Terry Jacks; born California, 1946; brain aneurysm, 17/1)

Wayne Walker (US country/pop songwriter whose songs were covered by Elvis Presley, Patsy Cline, Eddie Cochran and Waylon Jennings; born Oklahoma, 13/12/1925; unknown, 2/1)

Vernon Wray (aka Ray Vernon, US guitarist with his brother Link Wray's band, The Raymen; perhaps bitter about his brother's extended success, he committed suicide by gunshot)

For a complete list of fallen artists, visit

www.numberoneinheaven.com

JANUARY

Wednesday 2

Larry Williams
(New Orleans, Louisiana, 10 May 1935)
The Lemon Drops

Possibly the first of music's several suicides in 1980, Larry Williams was found dead some days after apparently turning a gun on himself at his apartment in Los Angeles. The 44-year-old singer and keyboardist had grown up in a Creole community and taken his music/variety one-man act on the road from an early age (even employing a trained monkey at one stage). In his professional career, the largely underrated singer worked with a number of music legends such as Lloyd Price and the great Johnny 'Guitar' Watson, and finally made something of a name for himself on Lemon Drops hits like 'Bonie Moronie' (1957) and 'Dizzy Miss Lizzy' (1958) – songs that went on to become household favourites by better-known British stars.

Williams, who suffered deeply from a lack of confidence, did, however, become involved in narcotics dealing (which in 1959 had led Specialty Records to drop the young star) and, allegedly, prostitution; because of this, many still believe the singer may actually have been murdered by a cartel.

Sunday 6

Georgeanna Tillman
(Inkster, Michigan, 1944)
The Marvelettes

A founder member of the Michigan all-girl vocal group, Georgeanna Tillman was still at school when The Marvelettes found themselves signed to Motown having won a talent contest sponsored by the celebrated label. With the classic 'Please Mr Postman' (1961, augmented by a young Marvin Gaye on percussion), the group gained the not inconsiderable distinction of giving Motown its first million-selling record.

Tillman's health started to decline in the mid sixties; she married Contours singer Billy Gordon and left the spotlight to become a secretary at Motown. She died in Detroit, a victim of sickle cell anaemia and lupus.

Monday 7

Carl White
(Los Angeles, California, 21 June 1932)
The Rivingtons
(The Limelighters)

Carl White was, with Rocky Wilson, the co-composer of punchy pop classics 'Papa Oom Mow Mow' (1962, recorded by artists as diverse as The Crystals and Gary Glitter) and 'The Bird is the Word' (1963) – both of which were hits for his knockabout vocal troupe, The Rivingtons, an R & B act that drew much the same audience as The Coasters. White had found success with a number of incarnations of the band during the late fifties, initially as The Limelighters – fronted by charismatic lead singer Thurston Harris. Upon his departure, White took over lead duties (to lesser effect), fronting the band when it hit the revival circuit. Never a particularly healthy individual, Carl White died aged forty-seven of acute tonsillitis at his Los Angeles home. Another Rivingtons singer, Al Frazier, died in 2005.

FEBRUARY

Tuesday 19

Bon Scott

(Ronald Belford Scott – Kirriemuir, Scotland,
9 July 1946)

AC/DC

(Fraternity)

(The Valentines)

(The Spectors)

A former struggling musician briefly turned wild-living chauffeur to Australian rockers AC/DC, Bon Scott could have been the result of a comic writer's imagination, so regularly and with such panache did he role-play the lifestyle of a consummate rock 'n' roll frontman. With his new employers, Scott rapidly cemented a hard-drinking, womanizing reputation. So much so, that by 1974 (just a year into the band's career) he genuinely *had* replaced original singer Dave Evans – a performer considered too glam for the band's image. Scott was the ideal foil to fellow Scot guitarist Malcolm Young and his school-uniform-sporting brother Angus (lead guitar), as AC/DC's burlesque-infused rock 'n' roll took them from Aussie pubs to the world's stadia within the space of four years. Once a bagpiper with his father's band, the incendiary vocalist had fronted a variety of Australian pop-rock outfits since the early sixties (his family had relocated in the fifties), the best-known of which was perhaps The Valentines, who hit the Australian charts with 1969's 'My Old Man's a Groovy Old Man' and 1970's 'Juliette'. In 1973, a serious motorbike crash appeared to have curbed the singer's career in music. Not so: Bon Scott's ceaseless input into AC/DC's sound and songwriting, not to mention his own performance, was set to turn the band into one of the biggest-grossing

Bon Scott: His destiny was in his hands

rock acts by the end of the seventies. Piledriving albums *High Voltage* and *TNT* (1975), *Dirty Deeds Done Dirt Cheap* (1976), *Let There be Rock* (1977) and *Powerage* (1978) were to enjoy ever-increasing international sales as the decade ended. By 1980 the AC/DC juggernaut hit the USA.

Earlier in his music career, Scott and his Valentines bandmates had been arrested for possession of drugs – a heavily publicized event that coloured his reputation for the rest of his life and beyond. By the time AC/DC became a marketable concern, Scott was regularly indulging in many of the rock world's other forbidden pleasures.

> **'It's like losing a member of your family – that's the only way to describe it.'**
>
> Angus Young, AC/DC

The singer's lyrics for group standards like 'Go Down' and 'Whole Lotta Rosie' (both 1977) were not written from imagination: the former was inspired by a groupie known only as 'Ruby Lips', the latter a paean to a vast Tasmanian woman with whom Scott had frolicked in Melbourne. (Running into 'Rosie' again some time later, Scott was said to have been somewhat disappointed that she had slimmed down considerably from her former '42–39–56' dimensions.)

While the moral majority may have objected to these apparently misogynistic lyrics, fans saw the humour and lapped up AC/DC live; they achieved Billboard Top Twenty status for 1979's *Highway To Hell* as a result. With metal and hard rock enjoying something of a renaissance in the UK as well, the band found themselves sucked into a relentless schedule of touring and recording that further encouraged the drink/drug binges that had become synonymous with the band – and particularly Bon Scott. AC/DC were back in Britain in February 1980, celebrating *Highway to Hell* having been certified platinum. On the evening of the 19th, the unpredictable Scott eschewed his band's plans and sought instead the company of old friend and drinking buddy Alistair Kennear, the pair setting off on a bender to end all benders in London's Camden Town. Somehow finding their way back to Kennear's home in Dulwich, the pair continued the binge into the night, Scott eventually collapsing unconscious in his car. Believing his friend would sleep it off overnight, Kennear – in no fit state himself to take further responsibility – made the mistake of leaving Scott outside in his vehicle, where the temperature descended rapidly. The following morning, Kennear awoke to find Scott still apparently paralytic and, now fearing for his safety, drove him to hospital. It was to no avail – Bon Scott was pronounced dead on arrival,

believed to have died of alcohol poisoning – having 'drunk himself to death' according to a coroner's report. It was later proved, however, that not only had he twisted his neck in his sleep, asphyxiating himself, he had also inhaled his own vomit while unconscious. It was a fittingly rock 'n' roll death for a man who had lived the most rock 'n' roll life imaginable. Scott was flown home to his adopted city of Fremantle, Australia, where he was buried on 1 March 1980. (For its part, *Top of the Pops* – finger ever on the pulse – managed to play a tape of the band's recent performance of 'Touch Too Much' without mentioning the singer's death.)

Far from calling it a day, AC/DC called upon the services of singer Brian Johnson, formerly of British pub-rock hit-makers Geordie. He was no Bon Scott, but Johnson possessed a definite stage presence, and, like his predecessor, a voice that could strip paint at a hundred paces. He has fronted the band ever since, seeing world sales for AC/DC's albums exceed 150 million – the biggest seller by far being Johnson's first album, *Back In Black* (1980), a set dedicated to Scott's memory.

Thursday 21

Janet Vogel Rapp
(Pittsburgh, Pennsylvania, 10 June 1942)
The Skyliners

For many years a manic depressive, Janet Vogel Rapp committed suicide by carbon-monoxide poisoning at her home, leaving a husband and young family. The R & B harmony vocalist had enjoyed a measure of success with The Skyliners, for whom she'd registered a number of minor Billboard pop hits including 'Since I Don't Have You' (1959) – a record that reached number one in her home town. The

track had a more far-reaching impact in that Phil Spector cited it as a major influence on his 'wall of sound' production style during the sixties. Vogel – an original member of The El Rios before her time with The Skyliners – played little part in popular music after her second group disbanded.

Saturday 23

Jacob 'Killer' Miller
(Mandeville, Jamaica, 4 May 1952)
Inner Circle

In 1980, planning to search for his absentee father – the singer Desmond 'Sidney' Elliott – Jacob Miller made contact with a long-lost cousin, rising reggae star Maxi Priest, who resided in London (where Miller believed Elliott now lived). Part of a sprawling musical dynasty, Miller had known as a boy that his future was in reggae. Sent to live with his grandparents in Kingston at the age of eight, the young extrovert eventually befriended most of the music capital's leading musicians and producers, including Clement 'Coxsone' Dodd, King Tubby, Dennis Brown, Ken Boothe and Bob Andy, and began releasing records while still in his teens. At twenty-four, he joined Inner Circle – the group recruited this likeably imposing vocalist on the basis that he had been 'everywhere they had' – quickly scoring an international hit on Island with reggae singalong 'Everything Is Great' (1978).

In early 1980, ahead of Miller's planned trip to the UK, Island supremo Chris Blackwell took him and Bob Marley (his two leading reggae charges) to Brazil for the opening of the label's South American offices. Returning to his homeland on 21 February, Miller was in triumphant mood: a US tour opening for The Wailers was imminent, as was a new Inner Circle album, *Mixed-Up Moods*.

Two days later, however, celebration turned to grief. Driving his car along Kingston's Hope Road, Miller was killed instantly when the vehicle struck a pole and turned over, a death recorded as misadventure. The bereft Inner Circle broke up immediately – though a revived version of the band enjoyed its biggest hit more than a decade later with 'Sweat (a-la-la-la-la-long)'. Jacob Miller was just twenty-seven when he died. He never met up with Maxi Priest – and was never reunited with his father.

MARCH

Friday 14

Anna Jantar
(Poland, 28 January 1938)

The Polish nation went into mourning following the death of one of its most celebrated pop singers of the era, Anna Jantar. The vocalist, who racked up international hits with 'So Much Sun in the Whole Town' and her version of the Hank Williams tune 'Jambalaya' (called 'Baju Baju'), had won song festivals in Ljubljana, Sofia, Castlebar and Villach.

Jantar was killed when the Polskie Linie Lotnicze Ilyushin IL-62 aircraft taking her home crash-landed half a mile from Warsaw Airport. As the plane awaited clearance to land, indications were that its landing gear was not down. A surge of power then caused the freak disintegration of the second engine: later inspection revealed that its turbine disc showed severe metal fatigue. Among the eighty-six others who died in the disaster were twenty-two members of the US Olympic boxing team. Jantar was married to noted composer/songwriter Jaroslaw Kukulski; they had a daughter, Natalia

– just four when she lost her mother – who also enjoyed Eastern European success as a singer during the nineties. Her mother is commemorated by the Anna Jantar Award, created to honour musical prodigies at the annual National Festival of Polish Song.

Wednesday 26

'Jon-Jon' Poulos
(John Poulos – Chicago, Illinois, 31 March 1948)
The Buckinghams

John Poulos found himself a niche in US pop/rock before he had even reached his twentieth birthday, as The Buckinghams ran off a string of American chart hits during the heady period of 1967–8. Songs such as 'Don't You Care?', 'Mercy, Mercy, Mercy', 'Susan' and the chart-topping debut 'Kind of a Drag' (all 1967) were seldom off campus jukeboxes, while the group itself – Poulos (drums), Denny Tufano (vocals), Carl Giammarese (guitar), Nick Fortune (bass) and Martin Grebb (organ) – were constantly called on for television appearances.

As The Buckinghams' star began to flicker, Jon-Jon Poulos found himself more and more ensnared by drug abuse. The band split in 1970, and he spent the last ten years of his life managing other artists (including his former Buckinghams' colleagues Tufano & Giammarese), before a heroin-induced heart failure at his Chicago home ended his days less than a week ahead of his thirty-second birthday.

APRIL

Friday 4

Red Sovine
(Woodrow Wilson Sovine – Charleston, West Virginia, 17 July 1918)
The Singing Sailors
The Wandering Boys

Born Woodrow Wilson Sovine to particularly patriotic parents, the singer known as 'Red' had a career spanning 300 recordings over five decades with country acts The Singing Sailors and The Wandering Boys. Sovine was best known internationally for the excruciatingly sentimental 'Teddy Bear' (1976), a spoken-word 'song' about a crippled boy and his trucker buddy, which somehow also gave Sovine a posthumous Top Five hit in Britain – the nation's brief fascination with the Citizens' Band was mainly responsible for this lapse. However, when Red Sovine died at the wheel of his van, it was a heart attack – not CB distraction – that brought about his demise.

Monday 7

Nathaniel 'Buster' Wilson
(California, c 1945)
The (Fabulous) Coasters

Emerging out of Los Angeles during the mid fifties, the original Coasters were a vocal group that provided much-needed comic relief from the increasingly formulaic quartets dominating US doo-wop. After a fairly sober beginning, the group soon developed its own unique shtick, hits

like the Jerry Leiber/Mike Stoller-penned 'Yakety Yak' (1958), 'Charlie Brown', 'Poison Ivy' and 'Along Came Jones' (all 1959) becoming instant locker-room classics and eventual million-sellers.

When the original line-up dissipated, a number of cabaret versions of the legendary vocal clowns sprouted (some of which had little connection with the first line-up but adopted similar élan). One such was Cornell Gunter's Coasters, also known as The Fabulous Coasters. This incarnation was formed by long-time frontman Gunter who, having left The Coasters in 1961, overcame years of legal battles with former manager H B Barnum to front the only authorized version of the group during the sixties and seventies. The new band, initially a trio made up of ex-members of California vocal group The Penguins (plus occasionally Gunter's sister Shirley), was significantly bolstered by the addition of a new bass in the shape of Nate 'Buster' Wilson, a strong performer who took to his role with gusto. They also secured a new manager, high-profile business mogul Patrick Cavanaugh. Despite the existence of various other Coasters collectives (including a formidable rival built around Gunter's earlier colleagues Will Jones and Billy Guy), his band appeared to be the most popular. Cavanaugh's business practices were not all they should have been, however – nor were they particularly well hidden from his charges. As time passed, Wilson became all too aware of Cavanaugh's involvement in a series of fraudulent schemes in Southern California, and, as this latest incarnation of The Coasters planned to part company with its manager, was on the point of taking his evidence to the police. On 7 April 1980, Cavanaugh decided to take his own drastic action to avoid the probable custodial sentence . . .

Several weeks after his disappearance, parts of Nathaniel Wilson's body were found dumped near the Hoover Dam, while others were retrieved from a ravine near Modesto, California. These gruesome finds revealed that the singer had been shot in the head, before his hands and feet were cut off, presumably to prevent identification. On 8 December 1984, 53-year-old Cavanaugh was convicted in Clark County of first-degree murder and mutilation – and sentenced to death. His wife, a former stripper from Las Vegas, was the state's star witness, providing the evidence that was to link her spouse to the killing. In 1998, the incarcerated ex-manager attempted to clear his name, claiming that he had been undergoing treatment for haemorrhoids at the Martin Luther King Hospital in Los Angeles at the time of Nathaniel Wilson's murder. The evidence – at one point considered significant enough to warrant a new trial – was proven faked following an investigation by CBS current affairs show *60 Minutes*. Hospital employee Maurica Hawkins – who, it emerged, was an associate of another death-row inmate – was found to have falsified medical documents to substantiate Cavanaugh's declaration. In March 2005, his fourth appeal was refused as he awaited execution in Nevada – the venue for Gunter's murder ten years later (☛ *February 1990*).

See also *King Curtis (☛ August 1971); Bobby Nunn (☛ November 1986); Bob B Soxx (☛ November 2000). Original Coasters Will 'Dub' Jones (2000) and Billy Guy (2002) have also died, as have other touring members.*

Tommy Caldwell

(Spartanburg, South Carolina, 9 November 1949)

The Marshall Tucker Band

Formed in Spartanburg, South Carolina, in 1971, The Marshall Tucker Band (whose name derived from that on a mislaid key ring at their rehearsal studios) was widely hailed as one of the leading exponents of Southern rock, integrating country and jazz into their largely instrumental work. Joining his guitarist brother Toy's band (named Toy Factory), bass-player Tommy Caldwell was just twenty-three when the eponymous debut album by the renamed Marshall Tucker Band went gold in 1973. The band's reputation grew rapidly. *Carolina Dreams* (1977) shifted a million copies in the US, while lucrative touring slots with contemporaries Lynyrd Skynyrd and The Allman Brothers were a regular occurrence. But the connection with these rock giants extended beyond mere music: sadly, all three bands were to have similarly tragic histories.

The Caldwell brothers were understandably devastated by the death of younger sibling Tim, killed in a road crash in March 1980, so the news that Tommy Caldwell had been in a similar accident just one month later was utterly beyond belief. On 23 April, Tommy's new Toyota Landcruiser ploughed into a stalled jeep and rolled over in Spartanburg, leaving him with head injuries from which he would not recover. Toy died just thirteen years later (☛ *February 1993*), so the Caldwell parents suffered the rare heartbreak of having outlived all of their three sons.

Ian Curtis: Love tore him apart

'He cajoled us, nurtured us with his promises of success. After showing us what it looked like, he offered us a mere sip before he abandoned us on the precipice.' Deborah Curtis, 1995

Ian Curtis

(Manchester, 15 July 1956)
Joy Division

Nowadays looked upon with respect, Ian Curtis was always an outsider in his own lifetime: only his lyrics gave the world a small insight into the complexities of his mind. Then, on the eve of a debut US tour for Joy Division, the talismanic singer hanged himself at his Macclesfield home. It was a sudden, brutal climax to a short career starkly highlighted by a lethal combination of powerful performance, crippling illness and a need for control.

In their early career, Joy Division were frequently pulled up over trite flirtations with fascism (the name refers to the prostitutes' wing of a concentration camp in Karel Cetinsky's novel *House Of Dolls*), but on offloading this burdensome reputation, they sought to develop a sound that was both evocative and timeless. This, allied with Curtis's highly personal lyrics, made Joy Division one of the era's most influential British rock acts before the singer's death. But, far from the miserablist of the media's creation, Curtis was a visionary who found humour in the bleak and supreme beauty within the deeply unsightly.

With his awkward gait and sensible shirts, Curtis was never the embodiment of a rock icon – he was known locally as a loner who liked reading and history. He was always creative, writing and drawing his own books from a young age, but noticeably obsessive; within punk's rampant energy, Curtis discovered a physical outlet for his ideas and dreams. The founder members of Joy Division (then Warsaw) – Bernard Albrecht (guitar; occasionally 'Dicken', now 'Sumner') and Peter Hook (bass) – knew immediately on meeting him that they had their man. Finding an excellent drummer in Stephen Morris and attaching to alert media-player Anthony H Wilson (to whose Factory label the band was quickly signed), Joy Division set about surrounding themselves with other charismatic individuals in the shape of late gurus producer Martin Hannett (☛ *April 1991*) and manager Rob Gretton (☛ *May 1999*). It was Joy Division's live appearances for which they were best known, the singer's wild staring eyes and flailing limbs drawing the most attention. This was no gimmick, however: Ian Curtis had epilepsy, only discovering the condition in adulthood.

After a particularly severe fit, a hospitalized Curtis had been advised to take things easier if he were to enjoy a normal life. But 'a normal life' was *not* what the singer wanted – not part of his grand scheme and certainly not why he'd joined a band.

Curtis had begun to remove himself from the routine of his domestic life, his wife, Deborah, and their expected baby. Joy Division were a close-knit bunch who enjoyed one another's company and their 'focal point' found it increasingly hard to balance the demands of his professional life with the commitments of his home. Deborah Curtis says: 'Factory was like a family – they'd exclude anyone who wasn't what they were looking for.' Also, this being early 1979, loud jarring noise and strobe lighting were a fact of the live rock show: few concessions would be made for Curtis's condition. But although they could sound angular, stark and brutal, Joy Division were far from just another punk band. They had by now arrived at sounds that drove rock elsewhere, away from the saturated three-chord structures of the past few years. Their debut album, *Unknown Pleasures* (1979), with its shifting, contorting shapes and restless lyrics, confirmed all previous hyperbole. With critical acclaim secured and international fame impending, all kinds of opportunities began to open up for Joy Division. It was, however, the start of a difficult period for Ian Curtis's wife and their newborn daughter.

At the start of 1980, the group toured Europe. Ian Curtis, unbeknown to his wife, was continuing a fractured affair with Annik Honoré, a Belgian Embassy journalist and fan of his band whom he'd met late the previous year. Despite the emotional problems this was causing him, Curtis chose to take Honoré to the Continent with the band. On his return – consumed by guilt and self-doubt – Joy Division's frontman attempted suicide, collapsing after downing a bottle of duty-free Pernod and slashing pages from a Bible as well as his own wrists. (Or so he was to tell his bandmates: that he had actually cut only his torso was less self-destructive, if no less dramatic.) But Curtis's situation was having a detrimental effect on his physical health as well as psychologically. The traumas of this period in his life were documented in Joy Division's second album – their last work. If *Unknown Pleasures* was a compelling debut, follow-up *Closer* (1980) seemed sculpted in ice, and was probably the group's finest hour. With Deborah Curtis now aware of her husband's infidelity, the album was recorded when their marriage was at its most vulnerable. Honoré, who had attended the London sessions, recognized the guilt and despair in tracks like 'Isolation', 'Twenty-Four Hours' and 'Decades' once Ian had told her they had to break up. Following a frenetic series of concerts that played havoc with his physical routine and destabilized his condition, Curtis suffered a severe grand mal attack during a London gig, which saw him crash into the drum kit. His jilted lover waited backstage, wanting little to do with a situation she clearly found embarrassing. On returning home to Macclesfield, the depressed singer attempted suicide once more, consuming a lethal dose of his medication, phenobarbitone. This time Curtis was hospitalized and had left a note – there was now much more cause for concern, despite his protestations to his colleagues that he was 'just fucking around'. In late April, recording the single 'Love Will Tear Us Apart' and its accompanying video took his mind off matters. But only temporarily.

Just over a month later, divorce from Deborah imminent, Ian Curtis cancelled an (unlikely) afternoon's waterskiing with Bernard Sumner on the eve of Joy Division's first tour of the US. He chose instead to spend the evening alone in his house drinking coffee and whisky as he played Iggy Pop's *The Idiot* and watched Werner Herzog's *Stroszek* – an art-house film about a man who kills himself rather than choose between two lovers. In the early hours of 18 May, the confusion and hopelessness of his situation now too much to bear, Curtis scrawled a lengthy note to his estranged wife and hanged himself from a clothes rack in their kitchen. It was Deborah who found his body, returning from her parents' home the following midday, by which time any attempts to revive the singer were futile. Those around him were devastated by news they'd feared (suicide is, after all, five times more prevalent among epileptics than those in normal health). Deborah, however, was the hardest hit by Curtis's suicide: 'I felt angry with him because he'd had the last word. But how can you be angry with someone who's dead?' Honoré – whose affair with the singer had been briefly resurrected – reportedly sat in his temporary room at Anthony Wilson's home continually playing *Closer*. The album achieved UK Top Ten status on the back of the tragedy, while 'Love Will Tear Us Apart' has, of course, become a classic: a Top Twenty hit on three occasions, it was shortlisted for a Brit Award in 2005 – though was somehow pipped by Robbie Williams's 'Angels'.

The aftermath of Ian Curtis's death was almost as hard for the band as it was for his family, though the remaining members all knew early on that they *would* strive to continue. They adhered to an earlier band decision that a new name would be sought: the choice of 'New Order' was as unanimous as it was predictable. Dragging themselves away from their past, they went on to exactly the kind of international acclaim that Curtis had so desired. However, with this commercial acceptance for New Order's music came belated worldwide recognition for the brief, extraordinary work of Ian Curtis and Joy Division. The final weeks of Curtis's life were documented in the 2002 movie *24-Hour Party People*, while at the twenty-fifth anniversary of his death, at least two biopics were mooted.

JUNE

Charles Miller

(Olathe, Kansas, 2 June 1939)
War

Saxophonist/singer Charles Miller was a founding member of timeless funk/rock exponents The Creators – later Nightshift, then War. The band were initially signed to back former US football star turned soul hopeful Deacon Jones but found a higher profile as back-up band to ex-Animals lead Eric Burdon. Overcoming the 1969 death of bassist and prime mover Peter Rosen before an album was even cut, the group managed a steady stream of hits throughout the seventies including 'Me and Baby Brother' (1973), 'Why Can't We Be Friends?' (1975) and the excellent, much-borrowed 'Low Rider' (1976) before the rise of disco began to curtail their appeal.

Miller was shot dead, accidentally caught up in a Los Angeles street robbery that went tragically awry. The exact date of the incident remains unconfirmed, though had it been 1 June he would have been a day short of his forty-first birthday. War continued as a touring unit thoughout the decade.

See also *Papa Dee Allen (★ August 1988)*

JULY

Malcolm Owen

(London, 1955)

The Ruts

Frontrunners of the second wave of UK punk rock, The Ruts allied the powerful call-to-arms stance of The Clash with dynamic three-chord guitar thrash. The results – particularly the brilliant debut 'In a Rut' (1978) and Top Ten 'Babylon's Burning' (1979) – saw to it that the London band had really arrived by 1980. Also, like Strummer and co, The Ruts were ready to work with black artists (issuing a single via the label of UK reggae act Misty in Roots) and to adopt disparate musical styles. Indeed, so eclectic was The Ruts' following that their gigs probably heralded the first ever sighting of pogoing Pakistani fans – something that did not always sit well with a less welcome right-wing faction in their audience.

Singer Malcolm Owen had issues of his own, however – not least the break-up of his marriage and his subsequent return to the heroin habit he had acquired before forming the band. His death from an overdose abruptly ended a band with a great deal of potential – attempts to keep The Ruts alive proved futile.

Malcolm Owen: In a rut and couldn't get out of it

Monday 21

Keith Godchaux

(San Francisco, California, 9 July 1948)

The Grateful Dead

(Ghost)

(Dave Mason)

By the time 25-year-old keyboardist Keith Godchaux joined them full-time from Dave Mason's band, in 1972, Jerry Garcia's Grateful Dead were already legendary, true hippy survivors of the Haight-Ashbury scene – and fast becoming the biggest touring band in the USA. The departure of keyboard-player Ron 'Pigpen' McKernan had left a large hole and necessitated a change. Godchaux, while a more technically able musician, was not of the same calibre as the founder member in terms of presence or showmanship. This fact became something of an albatross to Godchaux – particularly after the pop-

ular McKernan's tragic death a year later (➟ *March 1973*). The new man made himself even less popular by installing his wife, Donna, as a back-up soprano vocalist: her inconsistent performances often alienated the hardcore fanbase. As a result, the couple's 1975 solo album took a critical and commercial panning. It was an uphill struggle that Godchaux couldn't win: after six years with The Dead, he and his wife were asked to leave in 1979.

Having just formed his new act with Donna – the pair now wisely renamed Ghost – Keith Godchaux was killed when he lost control of his car in Marin County, California. Just like his predecessor, Godchaux died the year after leaving Grateful Dead. It was to continue to be a fated position in the band: his replacement, Brent Mydland, also died prematurely (➟ *July 1990*), as did Vince Welnick in 2006.

See also *Jerry Garcia* (➟ *August 1995*). *Ghost briefly featured celebrated guitarist John Cipollina, another to die ahead of his time* (➟ *May 1989*).

John Bonham: Perhaps giving the bar staff his order?

SEPTEMBER

Thursday 25

John Bonham

(Redditch, Worcestershire, 31 May 1948)

Led Zeppelin
(Various acts)

If estimating the sales of the UK's biggest rock band of its generation is tricky, hazarding a guess as to how many shots of vodka the UK's biggest drummer, John 'Bonzo' Bonham, might have downed on his final night gives it a serious run for its money. Many believed that genial giant Bonham, a hell-raiser second perhaps only to good friend Keith Moon – whom he survived by just two years (➤❮ *September 1978*) – was always on course for an early grave.

Considered mature and good-natured, Bonham worked as a bricklayer before joining Birmingham-based act Terry & The Spiders at just sixteen years of age. With pub rockers The Band of Joy, he inadvertently teamed up for the first time with Led Zeppelin frontman-to-be Robert Plant. The classic line-up for Led Zep, though, only came together in 1968, virtuoso guitarist Jimmy Page recruiting the pair plus bass-player John Paul Jones to fashion a replacement roster for the defunct Yardbirds. (Page had originally wanted Procol Harum percussionist B J Wilson, who was unavailable, so Page had his manager, Peter Grant, inundate the phoneless Bonham's local pub with telegrams until their man was secured!)

The rest is history: Led Zeppelin went on to crash sales and attendance records left, right and centre as they dominated the European and US rock-album markets for well over a decade. And not undeservedly – Zeppelin's fusion of rock 'n' roll, blues, the 'newer' sound of heavy metal, plus good-time boogie, progressive and even (acceptable) stadium AOR, was not only innovative at the time, but brilliantly compelling and, needless to say, much copied since. With Page and Plant at the helm, the band could arguably boast rock's most dynamic frontline. Meanwhile, Bonham's primal drum style – occasionally playing with just his hands (see live solo 'Moby Dick') – coupled with Jones's throbbing bass provided a powerful 'engine'. Led Zeppelin's early US tours were perhaps the most excessive rock music has ever witnessed: what began as innocent food fights in hotels degenerated into marathons of drink, drugs and rampant debauchery. Tales of young women 'introduced' to marine life proliferate, but although mountains of substances and girls were made available to the drummer, stories about Bonham tend to be more drink than drug- or sex-related. By the late seventies, however, it had all become far too easy and the novelty was fast wearing thin. Bonham had now developed a fairly hefty heroin habit and had, by his own admission, replaced practical jokes with belligerence when drunk. In 1977, he was seldom out of the papers – a charge of aggravated assault against a San Francisco security guard was followed by a car crash at his home that luckily resulted only in broken ribs.

In the late summer of 1980, a largely exhausted Zeppelin had, after a prolonged absence, begun writing new material. The previous album – *In through the Out Door* (1979) – had not been well received and relations in the Zep camp had turned sour. Jimmy Page, feeling it was high time to put things right and celebrate the band's return from their hiatus, predictably decided to throw an impromptu bash at his new Windsor home, where Zeppelin had been rehearsing. Bonham chose to warm up by putting away four quadruple vodkas at a local inn. At Page's place, he continued his relentless imbibing until, having passed out on a sofa, he was removed to a bedroom by one of the band's assistants. By the following afternoon Bonham had still not emerged. It was only when John Paul Jones checked on him that Bonham's lifeless body was discovered: he had died some time that morning. Coroners ruled the death accidental, caused by pulmonary oedema – a waterlogging of the lungs resulting from that customary rock-star nemesis, 'inhalation of vomit'. Friends of Bonham maintain that his heroin problem accelerated the accident, while other Zeppelin members, despite explaining that his customary lack of sobriety made it hard to determine Bonham's level of inebriation that night, found themselves accused of some measure of responsibility. It was later estimated that the drummer had probably consumed in excess of forty measures of vodka in the space of an evening.

John 'Bonzo' Bonham was cremated and buried a few days later near his home, in front of eight local fans who had braved the driving rain. It was, for now, the end of a legendary rock act. Two months later, Led Zeppelin broke their silence with this statement: 'The loss of our dear friend and the sense of harmony felt by ourselves and our manager have led us to decide that we could not continue as we were.'

DEAD INTERESTING!

TAP INTO OBLIVION

In the hundreds of years since the dawn of history, no other rock institution has had such ill luck in the percussion department as Spiñal Tap. The British metal behemoths have seen numerous members come and go, but the weirdest departures have been reserved for the guys at the drum kit.

1969: John 'Stumpy' Pepys
The original Thamesmen drummer died the most infamous death in rock history, succumbing to a 'bizarre gardening accident' that authorities felt was 'best left unsolved'.

1974: Eric 'Stumpy Joe' Childs
Pepys's replacement choked on vomit five years later: in this case, there were no facilities to determine whose vomit it was.

1977: Peter 'James' Bond
Bond had joined Buddahead for an appearance at the Isle of Lucy Jazz & Blues Festival when he spontaneously combusted, leaving nought but a 'green stain' on his drum stool.

1992: Mick Shrimpton
Later sticksman Mick Shrimpton disappeared, never to be seen again, but was replaced by his brother Ric. (According to head Tap-man David St Hubbins, a further percussionist vanished after being packed into luggage ahead of a US tour.)

Friday 26

Auburn 'Pat' Hare

(Cherry Valley, Arkansas, 20 December 1930)

The Teen Kings

Born Auburn Hare to parents with a creative imagination, the aggressive blues musician took the name Pat in order to allay the frequent ribbing he received from colleagues. Hare was not one with whom to mess, however, his scorching fuzz-driven tone equally matched by his fiery temper. Working with Muddy Waters and Howlin' Wolf in 1948, he became a player rivalled only by Wolf's 'other' guitarist, Willie Johnson. Throughout his early career, Hare insisted on using the mail-order amp which he'd used when learning to play in his teens and which lent much to his trademark sound. His style was noted by Sun Records (yet again), who signed him for session work, notably his 1953 contributions to James Cotton's records, before running off a number of rough 'n' ready blues releases of his own. One of these – 'I'm Gonna Murder My Baby' (1954) – was to have a startling resonance a few years later: Hare's drink problem led to his ultimate fall from grace, when, in 1962, he actually *was* convicted of murdering his girlfriend (and an intervening policeman for good measure) by gunshot following a drunken domestic dispute. Pat Hare was imprisoned for life, which – it turned out – meant exactly that. His world in tatters, Hare died of cancer while still incarcerated in St Paul, Minnesota.

OCTOBER

Wednesday 15

Bobby Lester

(Robert Dallas – Louisville, Kentucky, 13 January 1930)

The Moonglows
(The Moonlighters)
(The Flamingos)

Bobby Lester was just twenty when he became tenor lead with Cleveland vocal troupe The Moonglows (originally The Crazy Sounds). The band – in its best incarnation, Lester, Harvey Fuqua (baritone lead/spokesman), Alexander 'Pete' Graves (tenor), Prentiss Barnes (bass) and Billy Johnson (guitar) – first recorded with Champagne (the label belonging to influential Ohio DJ Alan Freed), then with Chance. A flurry of singles was released over the next two years, though only 'I Just Can't Tell You No Lie' (1952) and 'I Was Wrong' (1954) were minor hits. Waiting for his payment, Lester worked by day in a coal yard, until the fortunes of The Moonglows – also recording as The Moonlighters – improved with a move to the Chess label. Several records placed on the Billboard charts, including 'Sincerely' (1955) and 'See Saw' (1956), though not Lester's own foray into songwriting, 'The Beating of My Heart' (1957). Money was still an issue. Lester believed that, as lead, he should earn more than his fellow singers; this could not be resolved, and he left the band soon after, Fuqua replacing him as permanent lead. In 1970, Lester – who now managed a nightclub – returned to the stage with The New Moonglows and re-formed Flamingos – but ten years later he was dead, having contracted lung cancer and pneumonia. He passed away in a Louisville hospital after a two-month stay.

See also *Billy Johnson (☞April 1987). Marvin Gaye (☞April 1984) was also briefly in The Moonglows, while no fewer than six Flamingos have since died, beginning with Nathaniel Nelson (☞June 1984).*

Monday 27

Steve Peregrin Took

(Stephen Porter – Eltham, London, 28 July 1949)

Tyrannosaurus Rex
(Shagrat)
(The Pink Fairies)

Although he had left before they hit commercial paydirt as T Rex, bongo-player/backing vocalist Steve Took was an original member of Marc Bolan's band, and was in situ as they began gathering critical plaudits at the end of the sixties. Took was persuaded to adopt his enhanced name to fit the group's image: it was, naturally, the star's idea – Marc Bolan was at that time influenced by *Lord of the Rings*-type imagery, effectively displayed in flowery Tyrannosaurus Rex hits like 'King of the Rumbling Spires' (1969). With the psychedelic reference points came the appropriate drugs, and Took was soon au fait with acid and was a heavy user by the time he left the band to elope with an American fan. It was not a good move: as T Rex reached the very top, the drummer's brief stints with The Pink Fairies and Shagrat were only marginally more successful than an attempted solo career under Bolan's manager, Tony Secunda.

When Secunda finally did manage to help Took in some way, it was to have tragic consequences. By 1980 the manager had somehow retrieved Tyrannosaurus Rex royalties believed lost for good. When the money came through, Took – still living the star lifestyle despite having fallen into relative obscurity – decided to blow a large proportion of it on drugs and drink. After the resulting party, his mouth numbed following a large intake of morphine and magic mushrooms, Steve Peregrin Took choked to death on the pit of a cocktail cherry in the early hours of the morning.

See also *Marc Bolan (◀ September 1977) plus the accompanying Dead Interesting! for a list of T Rex associates who have since died. Many other musical cohorts of Steve Took's have also passed on, including former Pink Fairies Dave Bidwell (1977) and Mick Wayne (☞ June 1994).*

NOVEMBER

Tuesday 4

Ronnie Goodson
(New Jersey, 2 February 1945)
Ronnie & The Hi-lites
(John Fred & His Playboy Band)

Ronnie Goodson was already showing great vocal potential in his regular role of Baptist choirboy at the age of twelve. With Frankie Lymon & The Teenagers paving the way for young black male vocal acts, he was snapped up for local quintet The Cascades. Despite one national hit with 'I Wish That We were Married' (1962), Goodson and the renamed Hi-lites found little success away from the East Coast. After the inevitable but vain stab at a solo career, Goodson sensibly returned to his studies – though he finally enjoyed a transatlantic Top Five hit in 1968 with the Beatles pastiche 'Judy In Disguise' as a member of John Fred & His Playboy Band. Goodson's health was poor, however, and the singer was diagnosed with brain cancer around this time. He died of a tumour at his home in Jersey City.

See also *John Fred (☞ April 2005)*

DECEMBER

Thursday 4

Ronnie Österberg
(Finland, 15 January 1948)
Wigwam
(Blues Section)

Drummer Ronnie Österberg was one of the leading protagonists of Finnish progressive rock during the late sixties and early seventies. He started out with the John Mayall-influenced jazz-rock outfit Blues Section in 1965, graduating to the more successful Wigwam three years later. With English singer Jim Pembroke at the helm, Wigwam proved a hit at UK music festivals for a number of years, although the band managed only modest commercial success outside their native land. Their best-known song was 1969's 'Luulosairas' – a number-fourteen hit in Finland (!) – though later album *Fairyport* (1971) is generally considered the group's best work by prog fans. Österberg died completely unexpectedly from heart failure at the age of just thirty-two.

Sunday 7

Darby Crash
(Jan Paul Beahm – Los Angeles, California, 1958)
The Germs

The seemingly condemned Darby Crash was on a collision course from the day he came into the world. Crash had an emotionally tough upbringing, losing an older brother to heroin at a very young age. At thirteen, when his stepfather passed away, he went in search of his natural father – only to discover that he, too, had recently

died. Music seemed a natural way out to Darby Crash (then 'Bobby Pyn'), who, on meeting guitarist Pat Smear through their drug dealer in 1976 while at school, formed the band that was to become influential punk-rock extremists The Germs. Despite the singer's destructive antics getting them banned from almost every venue they played, The Germs were opening for Devo and Blondie by 1979. (At one memorable performance, Crash smashed a glass into his face, dived headlong into the shards and still somehow managed to get himself stitched up in time to watch Blondie close the evening.)

Crash had forewarned his band that 'it would be over in five years'. Disbanding The Germs just when they looked to be breaking through, he took himself into his bathroom and, in a pact with his girlfriend, injected a lethal dose of heroin. Rumour has it that he was found emulating the shape of a cross, having written 'Here Lies Darby C' above his head, apparently dying before he could complete his name. Crash's partner survived – the singer had doctored the doses to ensure his death and her survival. As for Pat Smear, he famously went on to play with Nirvana – thus witnessing another volatile frontman's suicide first hand (☞ April 1994).

Crash's attempt at Sid Vicious-style rock immortality was, however, utterly scuppered by what took place just twenty-four hours later ...

John Lennon

(Liverpool, 9 October 1940)

The Beatles

(The Plastic Ono Band)

The killer often has much in common with his victim. In this case, both assassin and target had been outsiders from fractured family backgrounds, both had used drugs to enhance their visions – and, most crucially, both were unable to handle anonymity. But beyond these similarities, John Winston Lennon had everything that Mark David Chapman did not: unique talent, success, love and, above all, universal approval.

The young John Lennon was to become used to loss close at hand. His father, Alf, a merchant seaman, abandoned the family when Lennon was five. His mother, Julia, felt unable to care properly for their boy alone: under authority pressure, her sister Mimi became his surrogate mother, and brought up Lennon through his school years. Julia remained in close contact, and having learned banjo from her estranged husband, she encouraged her son in the *métier* at which he was to succeed so spectacularly. But Julia was never to witness her son's fame – she was killed by an off-duty police officer's car as she crossed a road near their homes when Lennon was seventeen. (Years later, the musician was to remember his mother in future songs and also in the naming of his first son, Julian.) Two years before this tragedy, Paul McCartney had also lost his mother – a factor that cemented the early relationship between the century's most potent songwriting partners.

Having failed academically, Lennon took a place at Liverpool College of Art (after some persuasion from Aunt Mimi), where the caustic young wit and general outspokenness so frowned upon in school seemed initially to be encouraged. Not especially gifted as an artist, Lennon used the opportunity to hang with cooler people, starting friendships with Cynthia Powell – his first major love – and the more artistically talented Stuart Sutcliffe, whom he encouraged to take up an instrument in the hope that they might play together the Elvis, Chuck Berry and Buddy Holly numbers he'd learned. By now a faltering guitarist, Lennon had already played in his own high-school skiffle combo, The Quarry Men. The addition of new acquaintances McCartney and the shy young George Harrison on guitars gave this unit an edge and, with Sutcliffe's rudimentary bass and Pete Best's drums, The Silver Beetles – later The

Beatles – were born. Lennon dropped out of the art school he felt held him back, fame as a musician now the only target in his sights.

Lennon suffered another major loss with the death of Sutcliffe from a cerebral haemorrhage in Hamburg (➤◀ *Pre-1965*), though his close ally had already left a band starting to make headlines. The German city had twice been home to The Beatles between 1960–62, with Lennon brandishing a shiny new Rickenbacker and McCartney now assuming bass duties, as they took up residencies at the Kaiserkeller, among other clubs – Lennon regularly reneging on his vow to remain faithful to Cynthia Powell (whom he nonetheless married, she having fallen pregnant soon after his return). During a remarkably busy 1962, Lennon also oversaw the recruitment of key manager Brian Epstein and drummer Ringo Starr, late of Merseybeat hopefuls Rory Storm & The Hurricanes, and The Beatles signed to Parlophone. But, if that year was eventful, the following few years were to take Lennon's breath away. Beginning with 'Love Me Do' (1962), 'Please Please Me' and 'From Me to You' (both 1963, the latter the first of eleven consecutive UK chart-toppers, and seventeen overall), each Lennon & McCartney song seemed to outdo the previous one. Beatles' record sales rocketed: 'She Loves You' (1963) went to number one twice inside two months at home, toppled only by 'I Want to Hold Your Hand' – a record reckoned to have sold a staggering 12 million copies worldwide. In the States, the group's acceptance was even more remarkable, The Beatles claiming the entire Top Five in the first week of April 1964, having drawn 40 per cent of the whole population to their earlier *Ed Sullivan Show* appearance.

By now the successful Lennon was showing some arrogance in his otherwise jocular stage presence. Consuming vast amounts of alcohol – and starting to experiment with drugs (both readily affordable and available) – the musician was already tiring of the write/record/tour merry-go-round. His first book, *In His Own Write* – an Edward Lear-esque collection he saw as an opportunity to express personal thoughts – gave him a diversion and was published early in 1964. Not all were in favour of what was admittedly a fairly indulgent piece of work: the MP Charles Curran described Lennon as 'in a state of *near-literacy*' having 'picked up bits of Tennyson, Browning and Stevenson, while keeping one ear on the football results'. No matter – the character-driven style he was nurturing bloomed in drug-fuelled Lennon songs like 1967's 'I am the Walrus', 'Lucy in the Sky with Diamonds' and 'Strawberry Fields Forever' (for many his masterpiece, though, almost unthinkably, the first Beatles single not to top the UK chart since 1963). Lennon's acerbic side was occasionally expressed without mere words: he was rumoured to have slapped Cynthia at least once and was not at this stage prepared to take fatherhood seriously – only the life-

Lennon makes up with Yoko following his 1974 binge. (In the foreground, Nilsson seems less willing to relent.)

'Life is what happens when you are busy making other plans.'

John Lennon

changing experience of his marriage break-up could prompt that. Powell described him as frequently tripping out on LSD on return from tours and spending hours in front of the television, and she believes that their relationship ended at this time. For his part, Lennon described 1966 as his 'fat Elvis' period.

The man most people see as the key figure in the world's most popular group made headlines with virtually every quote. After upsetting a few dignitaries with his extremely mild 'rattle your jewellery' gag at the 1963 Royal Variety Performance, Lennon's 'more popular than Jesus' remark was to create an international incident three years on. Again, the luxury of hindsight shows us that what he meant is as understandable now as the saying of it back then was

foolish. But the fact is that The Beatles probably *were* a bigger draw than Christianity at the time: US concerts were still inundated with screaming masses – to such an extent that Lennon, wishing to be seen as an artist as opposed to a figurehead, instigated their cessation after Candlestick Park in August 1966. And the other Beatles agreed with him. For Brian Epstein, this was a huge blow, possibly even a first step towards his tragic death the following year (➤◀*August 1967*) – another loss of a key figure in Lennon's life. His relationship with the manager was frequently a close one, though the persistent rumours about the nature of their friendship can be discounted.

On 9 November 1966 – five years to the day that he'd met Epstein – Lennon made the acquaintance that was to shape the remainder of his life. Although they were not to become lovers for another year, Lennon attended Yoko Ono's exhibition at London's Indica Gallery, and was blown away by both this mysterious Japanese artist and the highly conceptual work he felt elevated her to a higher plane than most of the women he'd met professionally. But before he could start any lasting liaison with Ono, three major relationships in Lennon's world had to give. The subsequent, predictable collapse of Lennon's marriage was echoed by that of his relationship with the press, who, with the new affair imminent, rounded scathingly on Ono as the spanner in The Beatles' works. McCartney was not far behind – his and Lennon's affiliation had soured during the intervening years. By 1968 Lennon and Ono were inseparable, considering themselves as 'one', to the chagrin of colleagues. The pair were vehement in their denouncing of US military presence in Vietnam, which caused further resentment in a country that still hadn't fully forgiven Lennon for 'Jesusgate'. Despite this – and the widespread belief that the Beatle was being tailed by the FBI – the couple remained in New York, Lennon's home for the last twelve years of his life.

One American less than happy with John Lennon's presence in his country was teenager Mark Chapman. A fan in his younger days, Chapman had now discarded the toy soldiers restyled as Beatles with guitars. The born-again Christian was irritated by the 'supercilious' comments of the central figure he'd once loved, whom he now saw as having betrayed his ideals. Chapman managed to quell his distaste. For a while.

Although producing the occasional record afterwards, The Beatles were effectively over by the end of 1969, all four managing one last joint gesture in the return of their MBEs. By now Lennon – who'd married Ono in April of that year – was already recording avant-garde work with his partner, including the notorious *Two Virgins* (1968), which gave the press even more ammunition with its full-frontal nude shot of the couple on the cover. His solo career was to be both less consistent and (understandably) less commercially viable than that with his earlier earth-shattering band. Under the banner of The Plastic Ono Band, Lennon and his wife – plus a variety of musicians who came and went – still produced challenging work; their songs usually carried a message, whether promoting global unity ('Give Peace a Chance', 1969) or warning of the dangers of hard drugs ('Cold Turkey', 1969). The couple's love was tested only once, by a 1974 split that caused Lennon to fall apart

'I'll probably be popped off by some loony!'

John Lennon, interviewed during the sixties

and spend most of his time on drinking bouts with pal Harry Nilsson. Pulling himself together, Lennon then scored a US number one with another old mucker, Elton John ('Whatever Gets You through the Night', 1974), having returned to Yoko, who then became pregnant with his second son, Sean. Replenished and content, Lennon happily took a back seat from professional life that was to last until 1980.

Early that year, Mark Chapman attempted suicide. The severely depressed 24-year-old had drifted through a number of jobs, his self-esteem was shot and his marriage (to, not uncoincidentally, a Japanese-American woman) a failure. As he fell into unconsciousness, Chapman had what he later described as a 'vision', which he believed – wrongly, as the world was to discover – had cured his ills. Although briefly invigorated, his good mood did not last. Chapman clearly had no idea how unwell he was. Living in Honolulu, in an alcoholic and drug-induced haze, and unable to work, he whiled away his hours at a library – where a book of photos caught his eye. The cover showed the man he had idolized as a boy, a man now living in *his* country, in luxury and in love. Angered by the picture, Chapman finally lost touch with reality and began plotting to kill John Lennon.

In October 1980, Lennon broke several years of silence to promote a new record that many had no idea was even planned, *Double Fantasy*. As a collection, the album fell short of past masterpieces but was held together by one or two pleasing moments, his and Yoko's continued devotion very much the main thrust, and its lead single '(Just Like) Starting Over' fared well on both sides of the Atlantic. During the first week of December, Lennon gave a last interview (an exclusive with DJ Andy Peebles, which Radio One delightedly aired over two days) showing him at his pithy and playful best. Just forty-eight hours after the final transmission, the most influential musician of his generation was gunned down at the doorway to his Manhattan apartment.

On 6 December, Mark Chapman had arrived in the city, and blown more money than he could afford on a room at the Sheraton and a hooker. The next day he laid low; in the early hours of 8 December, he called his estranged wife, knowing this was to be the day. That afternoon, Chapman staked his place among other Lennon fans outside the Dakota Building, securing his supposed hero's autograph at 5.30 pm before the musician left for the studio. For five hours, Chapman waited in turmoil, voices in his head repeating, 'He's mine! Let me kill him!' In his possession were the signed copy of *Double Fantasy*, a paperback of J D Salinger's novel *Catcher in the Rye* . . . and a .38. Lennon returned at 10.50 pm, following Ono out of their limousine. As he approached the main gate, he glanced at Chapman, vaguely recognizing the young man to whom he'd spoken earlier that day. Hearing his name called,

Lennon turned once more as Chapman – now in combat stance – unloaded five bullets in the legend's direction. Lennon was hit four times, in the back and neck, saying only, 'Help me!', before he collapsed. Rushed to Roosevelt Hospital in the back of a squad car, Lennon died shortly after arrival, his internal organs destroyed and having lost 80 per cent blood volume. Chapman remained where he was, reading.

The final loss in John Lennon's tale was for the world as a whole. While America broadcast the news live on television – ABC sports anchor Howard Cosell interrupted an NFL game to impart the 'unspeakable tragedy' – Britain awoke to hear the shocking news early on Tuesday morning. Mourning akin to that for JFK followed in Lennon's adopted home; in the UK, this was unprecedented. '(Just Like) Starting Over', which had slipped out of the Top Twenty, made a remarkable reversal to top the charts as the nation's grief placed a barrage of Lennon tunes back in the listings. The follow-up, 'Woman', also reached number one, as did the now iconic 'Imagine', with 'Happy Xmas (War Is Over)' close behind, the country's festivities muted. As distraught fans gathered in continued vigil across the world, a variety of tributes from other artists began with Roxy Music's cloying take on Lennon's 'Jealous Guy' (1981); other offerings emerged over the years from Elton John, Mike Oldfield, Queen and Paul McCartney – whose original reaction of 'It's a drag' had caused no small upset. For her part, Yoko Ono showed astonishing fortitude, protecting her young son and asking for forgiveness for a man now considered Public Enemy Number One.

Mark Chapman caused some surprise by pleading a straight 'guilty' in court, which saw him incarcerated for twenty years. With bail refused in 2000, he remains in jail – having on 8 December 1980 achieved the 'recognition' he'd believed was rightly his. By the final minute of that day, 100 million people across the globe knew his name.

See also *Harry Nilsson (☞ January 1994); George Harrison (☞ November 2001)*

Tim Hardin

(Eugene Hardin – New Jersey, 23 December 1941)

Like many of his contemporaries, American folk-rock singer Tim Hardin only really received the recognition he deserved posthumously. Eugene Hardin was brought up in Eugene, Oregon, where he had moved at an early age with his parents (both classically trained musicians). After giving up on performing arts, Hardin became a regular of Greenwich Village's burgeoning folk-rock scene during 1964, having served two years in the US marines.

Hardin's reputation was to soar following international hit versions of his now-classic song 'If I were a Carpenter' by Bobby Darin (1966) and the Four Tops (1968), though the singer had nurtured a drug habit from his early days (he had been a former room-mate of comedian Lenny Bruce, who was a heavy user at the time) and proved unreliable in the studio. Hardin was also deeply dissatisfied with his own recordings: according to reports, he was so unhappy with his first album that he broke down on hearing the master tape. Although his songs continued to be covered by names like Rod Stewart ('Reason To Believe') and Scott Walker ('Lady Came from Baltimore' – about Hardin's wife, actress Susan Moehr), the songwriter seemed constantly beset by health and psychological problems, developing drink and drug habits that not only consumed much of his income but culminated in his death – from an overdose of heroin and morphine in Hollywood, California.

Lest We Forget

Other notable deaths that occurred sometime during 1980:

Ray Cawley (US rock bassist with Nick Nasto then Bill Haley's Comets during the early seventies; car crash, which also killed his wife)

General Echo (Jamaican 'Slacker' DJ; mysteriously shot dead by the police – an incident recalled on Clint Eastwood & General Saint's *Two Bad DJ* album)

Bert Kaempfert (German bandleader and the first producer of The Beatles; born Hamburg, 1924; unknown, 21/6)

Bernie Mackey (US vocalist with The Ink Spots; born 29/7/1909; unknown, 5/3)

Mantovani (Italian orchestra leader/easy-listening giant; born Annunzio Paolo Mantovani, Venice 15/11/1905; unknown, 29/3)

Louis Neefs (Belgian pop singer who finished 7th in 1969's Eurovision Song Contest; born Ludwig Neefs, 1937; car crash, which also killed his wife, 25/12)

Jannie Pought (US soprano with vocal group The Bobbettes; born New York, 1941; stabbed on a New Jersey street by a complete stranger)

Professor Longhair (US blues/boogie-woogie pianist/vocalist – the 'grandfather of rock 'n roll'; born Henry Roland Byrd, Louisiana, 19/12/1918; natural causes, 30/1)

Carl Radle (US bass virtuoso who played with Eric Clapton/Derek & The Dominoes, Joe Cocker and George Harrison; born Oklahoma, 18/6/1942; kidney shutdown after years of alcoholism, 30/5)

David Whitfield (British pre-rock crooner who, during the fifties, managed 11 UK Top Ten hits, including #1s with 'Answer Me' and 'Cara Mia'; born Hull, 2/2/1925; died in Australia, 16/1)

. . . and one who didn't:

Martyn 'Segovia' Smith (British bassist with punk act UK Decay, was alleged to have died during the recording of his band's debut album: Smith is still alive, well and currently lives in Luton)

For a complete list of fallen artists, visit

www.numberoneinheaven.com

JANUARY

Friday 2

David Lynch
(St Louis, Missouri, 3 July 1929)

The Platters

Of the myriad black vocal bands working the circuit during the fifties, the most popular by some way was The Platters. Founder member David Lynch possessed a strong tenor, noticed while he was still at school in Los Angeles. Forming an embryonic version of The Platters (the name was then current slang for 'records'), Lynch entered endless talent contests before Svengali Buck Ram stepped in as both manager and voice tutor, signing them to Federal in 1953. The hits really started to come when The Platters – Tony Williams (lead tenor), Lynch (second tenor), Paul Robi (baritone), Herbert Reed (bass) and Zola Taylor (alto, and one of the few female singers in doo-wop) – moved to Mercury. No fewer than four of their singles – including the classics 'The Great Pretender' (1955) and 'Smoke Gets in Your Eyes' (1958, also a chart-topper in Britain) – took them to Billboard number one.

The bubble only burst for The Platters in 1959, when the group's males, including Lynch, were accused of having sexual relations with under-age white girls in a hotel room. (Taylor wasn't much more innocent herself, admitting years later to a 1956 relationship with 13-year-old Frankie Lymon of The Teenagers.) At a time of segregation, the public was outraged and the group struggled to place further records in the Top Ten. Powerful Platters lead Williams announced his plan to record solo in 1961; the group rallied with Sonny Turner as live lead until 1966, while the label continued to issue old Williams-fronted songs on record. David Lynch contracted cancer during the seventies, and succumbed to the disease at the age of fifty-one.

See also *Nathaniel Nelson (☞ June 1984); Paul Robi (☞ February 1989); Tony Williams (☞ August 1992). Completists may care to add early Platters Cornell Gunter (☞ February 1990) and Elsbeary Hobbs (☞ May 1996) who have since also passed on, plus manager/producer Buck Ram (1991) and later singer Randy Jones (2002).*

FEBRUARY

Monday 9

Bill Haley
(William John Clifton Haley Jr – Detroit, Michigan, 6 July 1925)

Bill Haley & His Comets (The Saddlemen)
(Various acts)

The kiss-curled 'great uncle of rock 'n' roll' was never really cool enough to be considered an icon of any movement, but he was, of course, instrumental in placing rock firmly on the map. Bill Haley was born blind in one eye, and found in music an outlet to help him overcome the shyness this impediment caused him as a boy. And overcome it he did: fascinated by the singing cowboys he encountered in his youth and taught to play guitar by his father, Haley fronted his own band at fifteen. After founding country acts The Downhomers and then the extravagantly named Four Aces of Western Swing, Haley – who also performed as a yodelling soloist – found work as a DJ at Pennsylvania pop/country station WPWA. He made his first inroads into recording his own music with The Saddlemen, an early fifties guitar band that specialized in 'cowboy jive'; this group hit regionally with 'Rocket 88'

(1951), the Jackie Brenston song considered by many to be rock 'n' roll's first. The Saddlemen became The Comets – and thus music history was duly made.

'Rock around the Clock' (1955) was actually the fourth single release by The Comets (the first hit had been 1953's 'Crazy, Man, Crazy', perhaps the first rock 'n' roll record to chart in America). 'Rock around the Clock' had been penned for them by writer James Myers and was only a moderate hit until licensed for the title sequence of Richard Brooks's 1955 teen-rebel movie *The Blackboard Jungle*; after this, the song topped Billboard's listings for two months and became the theme song of the young, who saw in rock 'n' roll a channel for their disaffection. The song became a worldwide smash, topping the charts in numerous countries; in Britain – where Haley was even bigger than at home – it re-entered the charts an impressive seven times. (The record is still the world's third-biggest-selling pop hit, behind Bing Crosby's 'White Christmas' and Elton John's 'Candle in the Wind '97'.) And there were many other hits: the rousing 'Shake, Rattle and Roll' – with its pre-equality demands for 'kitchen action' – had already given Haley and his band a million-seller in 1954 and 'See You Later, Alligator' came pretty close to doing likewise in 1956. But, for all this phenomenal success, Haley was never a rich man. His manager, 'Lord' Jim Ferguson, is believed to have squandered much of Haley's income over the years, to the degree that the singer, unable to meet the demands of the US tax inspectors, had to go into exile from his native land during the sixties. By this time, although he was still recording with Warners, Haley had been usurped by hipper, leaner creatures like Elvis Presley and Chuck Berry – he was always a big-set individual (not really designed for wall posters), and his health was to suffer accordingly. 1974 brought renewed interest in 'Rock

'I haven't done much in my life except give birth to rock 'n' roll. And I'd like to get credit for it.'

Bill Haley in 1968

Bill Haley (*top*), pictured in 1955 with 'rising' Comets Billy Williamson, Johnny Grande (who died in 2006), Joey Ambrose, Marshall Lythe and Dick Richards (Dick Boccelli)

around the Clock', which was back in both US and UK chart listings (the former because it was an early theme tune to the hit TV comedy *Happy Days*), but the death of his long-time friend and sax-player Rudy Pompilli (➤ *February 1976*) affected Haley enormously. The singer became withdrawn as a result, and his touring days ended with a 1979 performance in South America.

The circumstances surrounding Bill Haley's death are disputed to the degree that only the date can be agreed upon by all. Haley spent the last six years of his now-anonymous life at a modest home in Harlingen, Texas, shunning company and, according to the local police, becoming delusional to the extent that he would even deny who he was to occasional visitors. Haley was believed to be suffering from Alzheimer's disease – highly unusual for a man only in his fifties. He had also become a heavy drinker. Just hours after he had spoken on the phone to his two sons, he was found dead in his house, a bottle at hand: he is generally thought to have suffered a heart attack, although some insist he died of a brain tumour. He may have been no young buck when he hit the big time, but Bill Haley was a true rock 'n' roll pioneer. He was there before anyone else, pumping boogie into country and rockabilly while Elvis was still trying to sing gospel, while The Beatles were still just high-school rebels and before the blues had even reached the UK.

See also *Danny Cedrone (➤ Pre-1965)*

DEAD INTERESTING!

FALLEN COMETS

Attempting to unravel the ever-mutating history of Bill Haley's Comets – both during and after the big man's involvement – is near impossible. Below, however, is a brief guide to Haley's main protagonists now gone to rock around the celestial clock:

Ray Cawley (bass, d 1980)

Danny Cedrone
(guitar, 20/6/1920–18/6/1954)

Harold 'Curly' Chalker
(steel, 22/10/1931–30/4/1998)

Doles Dickens
(bass, c 1920–2/5/1972)

Dallas Edwards (guitar, d 11/1982)

Johnny Grande
(piano, 14/1/1930–3/6/2006)

Billy Gussak (drums, d 1994)

Ralph Jones
(drums, 1920–1/6/2000)

Arrett 'Rusty' Keefer
(guitar/bass/violin, d 1967)

Nick Masters
(Nick Nastos, steel, d 28/4/1995)

James E Myers
(drums/co-writer, 1919–9/5/2001)

Joe Olivier
(guitar, 10/12/1927–25/12/2001)

Rudy Pompilli
(sax, 16/4/1924–5/2/1976)

Paul Pruitt
(guitar, c 1943–14/5/2003)

David 'Chico' Ryan
(bass, 9/4/1948–26/7/1998)

Art Ryerson (guitar, 1913–10/2004)

Billy Williamson
(guitar, c 1925–3/1996)

Michael Bloomfield

(Chicago, Illinois, 28 July 1943)

The Paul Butterfield Blues Band
Bob Dylan
Electric Flag

A young Jewish blues fan who longed for stardom and the excuse to play before an audience, guitarist/singer Mike Bloomfield earned a reputation for jumping up on stage and hijacking club gigs on a regular basis years before he made his name with The Paul Butterfield Blues Band. So good was his playing that black players eventually accepted him and by the age of twenty Bloomfield was running his own blues club.

In fact, there was greater antagonism from the fans of Bob Dylan when the previously acoustic folk prodigy plugged in and went electric: Mike Bloomfield was Dylan's guitarist at this point, appearing on his *Highway 61 Revisited* album (1965). At the same time he had joined The Paul Butterfield Blues Band, (a move precipitated by the band's producer, Paul Rothchild), which was to cement Bloomfield's name as a major American blues player. Electric Flag was his own band, an unadorned though experimental blues combo formed in 1967 with long-time collaborator Nick Gravenites: the group played Monterey to some acclaim, but drug use and bad management made this a short project. Bloomfield's album with keyboardist Al Kooper and guitarist Stephen Stills – *Super Session* (1968) – was also well received, but the stop-start nature of his career ensured a low profile for this very gifted musician. Just months before he died there, Bloomfield rejoined Bob Dylan for a concert at the guitarist's home town of San Francisco.

The circumstances surrounding Mike Bloomfield's death are baffling.

Although he had clearly overdosed, it is disputed whether the drug in question was Valium or heroin. His body was found near his home, at the wheel of his Mercedes. All four of the car doors were locked.

See also *Paul Butterfield (* May 1987); John Kahn (* May 1996)*

APRIL

Sunday 5

Bob 'The Bear' Hite

(Torrance, California, 26 February 1945)

Canned Heat

The 300lb-plus scholar of blues discovered his passion while managing a California record shop called Rancho. Known as 'The Bear' for his vast proportions (he was also over 6' tall), Bob Hite discovered a fellow enthusiast in Alan 'Blind Owl' Wilson while at college in Los Angeles. The pair, both harmonica-players and would-be vocalists, formed Canned Heat – Hite took the name from a 1928 Tommy Johnson lyric – from the residuals of an earlier short-lived jug band, and electrified their sound for maximum R & B effect. Canned Heat – fleshed out with another blues fanatic in Henry 'Sunflower' Vestine (guitar), plus Larry 'The Mole' Taylor (bass) and (initially) drummer Frank Cook – wowed the massed throng at Monterey in 1967, Wilson's haunting, tremulous falsetto countering Hite's awesome bass growl and formidable bearded presence. The year after, the great 'On the Road Again' – Wilson's reworking of a blues standard – gave Canned Heat their first big international hit, inadvertently becoming something of an anthem for the hippy movement. This unlikely-looking band were suddenly huge, prompting a headline slot for The Heat at Woodstock. Hite and Wilson's influence did much to popularize the blues among white music fans as a result. 'To sing the blues, you gotta be an outlaw. Black guys are born outlaws, but we whites have to work for that distinction,' said Hite – not uncontroversially.

Despite considerable sales and mass critical acclaim, tragedy struck Canned Heat with the unexpected suicide of Wilson – the co-founder's body was found by a distraught Hite at his home (* *September 1970*). Canned Heat was a dispirited group after this, and their profile was to dip considerably in the aftermath. They did, however, continue to record and to tour unremittingly for the next decade. 'The Bear''s vast bulk finally gave out in 1981 – he collapsed between sets during a concert at Hollywood's Palamino nightclub. He'd been severely obese for two decades, but now sporadic use of cocaine and heroin was putting extra strain on an

On the road again, with 'The Heat' – Wilson, Hite, Vestine, De La Parra and Taylor

already ailing heart. (Like Wilson, Hite suffered from depression, though in his case it stemmed from his diminished fortunes and a bad marriage.) Taken from the venue by friends, Bob Hite died of a heart seizure at his home in Mar Vista later the same evening. Hite's staggering collection of some 60,000 blues discs was left to the United Artists archive.

By now largely a nostalgia-circuit blues band, Canned Heat suffered a third loss when Vestine died a rock 'n' roll death in France (☛ *October 1997*). Amazingly, The Heat *still* continued to burn after this, releasing albums into the new millennium. Their constantly morphing alumni have included Hite's bassist brother, Richard, who often played alongside 'The Bear'. He, too, died young – from cancer in 2001.

Tuesday 7

Kit Lambert

(Christopher Sebastian Lambert – 11 May 1935)

Born into a prolific line – his father was composer Constant Lambert, his grandfather the Australian painter George Lambert – the youngest Lambert was always likely to make a name for himself in one branch of the arts or another. Although his father was seldom around as he grew up, Lambert Sr's wilful reputation was to have some effect on the young man. While studying at Oxford, he discovered his sexual preferences – and did little to hide them. Kit Lambert first brushed with death in 1961: having left the army, he decided in a fit of bravado to become a jungle explorer, but a trip to the source of an uncharted Brazilian river ended in horror when a close friend was killed by a cannibalistic tribe. Shaken by this, Lambert relinquished this career, and moved into entertainment on his return. A lover of the cinema, he spent some time as a low-profile film director's assistant on such pieces as *The Guns of Navarone* and *From Russia with Love*.

Two years later, Lambert and film-making colleague Chris 'Chip' Stamp, searching for subject matter for a movie, chanced upon a British rock 'n' roll band. That group was The High Numbers – an early short-haired version of The Who. Abandoning the film project and ousting the manager, the inexperienced Peter Meaden (who died in 1978), Lambert and Stamp set about changing the band's fortunes. Lambert was key in encouraging Pete Townshend to write songs: his early gift to the guitarist of two tape recorders was reciprocated by a series of punchy pop classics and ambitious conceptual projects that made his and The Who's names over the next few years. (He also suggested Townshend's trademark 'windmill' guitar style.) By 1966 Lambert was assuming all production duties on the group's work. That same year, his and Stamp's new Track label landed a coup, signing Jimi Hendrix – and had several lesser successes such as Thunderclap Newman and The Crazy World of Arthur Brown. But by the mid seventies the relationship between Lambert and The Who had reached something of a natural cul de sac. Stamp returned to the film world, while Lambert produced a variety of styles of performer from Patti Labelle to a number of early punk bands, among whom he perhaps hoped to find a new Who.

In April 1981 – by which time he was spending much of his time living in and restoring an old Venetian palace – Lambert returned to London to stay with his mother for a few days, during which time he got himself into an altercation at a Kensington nightclub: a heavy drug user, Lambert reportedly fought with a dealer to whom he owed money. The next morning, Kit Lambert collapsed and fell down his mother's staircase, and died from a brain haemorrhage.

See also *Keith Moon (☛ September 1978); John Entwistle (☛ June 2002). Peter Meaden died a month before Moon.*

Tuesday 28

Steve Currie

(Grimsby, 20 May 1947)

T Rex

(The Rumble)

A former member of also-rans The Rumble, Steve Currie was the first bassist to join Marc Bolan's expanded line-up, answering a *Melody Maker* advertisement. He – along with other band stalwarts Mickey Finn (bongos/vocals) and Bill Legend (drums) – enjoyed the most potent period as T Rex hit pop superstardom. Between 1970 and 1973, there were few to touch the band in Britain as they marched forth with ten Top Five singles (including four UK number ones) and two chart-topping albums. But by the end of 1974 it had all started to unravel for T Rex, though Steve Currie remained at Marc Bolan's side (the frontman sacked everyone else), only leaving in 1976, by which time Bolan was enjoying only occasional successes.

Currie was immersed in session work with the likes of Chris Spedding and Wreckless Eric around the time of Bolan's car crash – but his own death a few years later was eerily similar. Just before midnight on 28 April, Steve Currie's car left the road near his home in Val da Parra, Portugal. The bassist died at the scene.

See also *Marc Bolan (☛ September 1977) plus the accompanying Dead Interesting! for a full list of T Rex acolytes now dead.*

MAY

Bob Marley

(Robert Nesta Marley – Nine Miles, St Ann's, Jamaica,
6 February 1945)

Bob Marley & The Wailers

Despite the best efforts of Bono and Bob Geldof, rock musicians are unlikely ever to have the spirituality and resolve to impact on the world's politics in the same way that Bob Marley did for Africans and Jamaican Rastafarians. That he did so while popularizing an erstwhile marginal form – and left behind such a vast, joyous reservoir of music – makes the achievement all the more remarkable.

Known mainly by his birth name of Nesta, Marley spent his childhood as something of an outcast, partly ostracized because of the lightness of his skin. His mother, Cedella, had been abandoned by her husband, a Welsh-born white quartermaster some thirty years her senior. Poverty necessitated a move to the neglected area of Trenchtown – so named for the sewage trench that ran through it from Kingston, but nonetheless significant as a spiritual home to the generation of Rastafarians who had made the area their own since the faith's inception in the thirties. Alienated by the bigotry outside, Marley sequestered himself, picking out tunes on a homemade 'sardine can' guitar with his close friend Neville 'Bunny' Livingston (later Wailer). The pair soon met another kindred spirit in Peter Tosh (Winston McIntosh), and formed The Wailers. Marley left school at sixteen, and briefly took a job as a welder at his mother's insistence, but quit when he almost lost an eye in an accident. He worked hard on his music, recording tunes like 'One Cup of Coffee' (1962) with Chinese/Jamaican producer Leslie Kong before Studio One picked up the group as a unit. Clement 'Coxsone' Dodd saw in The Wailers – in their early days the line-up also included Junior Braithwaite, Beverley Kelso and Cherry Smith – a Jamaican act that could potentially tap a similar market to that of Curtis Mayfield's Impressions in the USA: early recordings are very smooth and soulful. But Jamaican radio refused to play The Wailers' music, and *The Wailing Wailers* (1966) was the only album the group was to make with Dodd. Marley – with his new wife, Alpharita Anderson (Rita Marley, of Studio One vocal group The Soulettes, later of

The I-Threes) – left for the States to find employment as a migrant worker.

The Wailers regrouped in England, where label boss Chris Blackwell signed them to his forward-thinking Island label. With brothers Aston and Carlton 'Family Man' Barrett added as a rhythm section, the first record was *Catch a Fire* (1973), an album that remains just as potent more than thirty years after its release. Blackwell's enthusiasm in pushing Marley to the fore was detrimental to the group as a whole, however. After one further recording, *Burnin'* (1973), Tosh (who felt undersold) and Wailer (for financial reasons) left to persue solo careers: reggae purists will always question whether the Island Svengali's encouragement of Marley to find a wider audience was truly beneficial to the integrity of the music. But Marley's was a significant name by 1976, after 'No Woman No Cry' became an international hit the year before. Back in Jamaica, before a concert just ahead of the elections that year, the musician was the target of an assassination attempt, the first major political incident of his career. Assumed to be supporting progressive Prime Minister Michael Manley, Marley was shot in his home – allegedly by (paradoxically) conservative Jamaica Labour Party supporters – receiving minor injuries to his chest and arms; Rita Marley and, most seriously, manager Don Taylor were also injured, but recovered fully. (Those believed responsible were later 'intercepted' on the streets.) Displaying the iron constitution of the 'Lion in Zion' of which he sang, Marley rallied to enjoy his most commercial phase, the albums *Rastaman Vibration* (1976, a big US hit), *Exodus* (1977, perhaps his best work) and *Kaya* (1978) each outselling its predecessor. But his body was to prove weaker than his resolve: incurring what he thought was a football injury (Marley was a huge fan of the sport), the singer was advised in 1977 to have his big toe amputated for fear of infection. Marley refused, stating that this constituted bodily desecration – something a devout Rastafarian could never consider. Within a year the injury had turned cancerous, within three the disease had spread throughout his body.

With his melanoma kept firmly from the public, Bob Marley continued to tour throughout the next two years, the albums *Survival* (1979) and particularly *Uprising* (1980) suggesting that all was hunky dory in the singer's camp. In Britain, he enjoyed his biggest lifetime hit with 'Could You be Loved?', and another trip to America was arranged in order to promote the album and single there – at least that was the official story. In fact, Marley had travelled to Miami in order to receive specialist treatment for his condition. It became painfully apparent that Marley was unwell in September 1980 when, between shows with The Commodores at Madison Square Gardens, the singer collapsed while jogging in New York's Central Park.

Knowing his time was limited, Marley converted to

Bob Marley (*right*) and Wailers in ill-advised football moment

Christian Rastafarianism in Kingston and changed his name to Berhane Selassie (after the movement's father) in the process. After further treatment in Germany, Bob Marley was rushed back to Florida in May 1981; within three days he was dead – and a legend was instantly born. On learning the news it had gravely been expecting, the whole of Jamaica came to a standstill. Parliament acknowledged the passing of one the country's greatest children by going into recess for an entire week after his death. That summer, Jamaica's Reggae Sunsplash Festival was dedicated to the memory of the genre's most famous exponent – and featured The Melody Makers, a group comprising four of Marley's nine children. A statue of the singer, guitar in hand, was erected at Kingston's National Stadium, while his home has long been converted into a museum housing the late singer's sarcophagus. Marley himself was awarded a posthumous Order of Merit, the third highest Jamaican decoration available.

See also *Carlie Barrett (*☞ *April 1987); Peter Tosh (*☞ *September 1987); Junior Braithwaite (*☞ *June 1999); Clement 'Coxsone' Dodd (*☞ *Golden Oldies #19)*

> ## 'My music will go on for ever. Maybe it's a fool say that, but when me know facts, me can say facts. My music will go on for ever.'
> Bob Marley

JUNE

Monday 1

Mack Starr

(Julius McMichael – Brooklyn, New York,
25 November 1935)
The Paragons
The Olympics

Formed as a 'brother' group to the
legendary Jesters – New York's foremost vocal quintet of the mid fifties
– The Paragons were led by tenor/
lead Julius McMichael, a fine singer
from Brooklyn's Bedford/Stuyvesant
area who proved himself also as
a writer. McMichael attended the
Jefferson High School from whence
came most of his group – Ben Frazier
(second lead), Donald Travis (second
tenor), Ricky Jackson (baritone) and
Al Brown (bass). McMichael teamed
up with Paul Winley (of Winley
Records), with whom he co-wrote
the mini classic 'Florence' (1957), a
ballad that eventually sold well in the
US. Despite further memorable tunes
– some penned by McMichael – the
group could not match this early peak
and began to unravel in 1961. The
lead had, by now, reinvented himself
as the more swaggering Mack Starr,
and his band were less than thrilled
to have their releases billed as 'Mack
Starr & The Paragons'. By 1968 the
best Starr could manage was a slot
with a new version of The Olympics
– the vocal troupe that had lost tenor/
baritone Charles Fizer in the Watts
uprising three years before (➤ *August
1965*). Starr's sporadic solo career
found some following in the Northern
soul market of the seventies.

Mack Starr was killed when an
out-of-control automobile knocked
him off a motorcycle near his home
in Los Angeles. The Olympics still
recorded occasionally, the void left

by Starr filled by new lead William
DeVase.

Wednesday 3

Joe Santollo

(Jersey City, New Jersey, 23 July 1943)
The Duprees
The Elgins

The Duprees were in a minority of
white vocal acts competing with
their many black counterparts in the
saturated market of the early sixties. Emerging from New Jersey, the
group was put together from the
remnants of The Elgins – a vocal
unit that housed, among others, the
powerful tenor of Joe Santollo – and
The Utopians. Discovered by George
Paxton and Marvin Cane (president
and owner of Coed Records), the
renamed Duprees (originally The
Parisiens) went on to score nine
Billboard Hot 100 entries – no mean
feat for a white act that had until then
been a standards/covers unit. The
best-known hit was the first, 'You
Belong to Me' (1962) – a US gold-
seller. (The Duprees proved popular
elsewhere as well: their 'The Sand
and the Sea' was, perhaps unsurprisingly, number one for eight weeks in
Hawaii.)

The hits dried up at the time of
the British invasion, but The Duprees
continued to make records until the
mid seventies, although lead Joey
Vann (Canzano) left for a solo career
in 1964. Just as The Duprees were
preparing for a much-anticipated reunion tour, Joe Santollo suffered a heart
attack and died at Jersey City Medical
Center from subsequent internal
bleeding. He was only thirty-seven.

See also *Joey Vann (➤ February 1984).
Michael Arnone – another founder Dupree
– died in 2005.*

Sunday 28

Chuck Wagon

(Bob Davis – Los Angeles, California, 1957)
The Dickies
(The Quick)

Formed in 1977, The Dickies were the
first LA punk band to land a major
label deal. For a while back there, they
were America's clown princes of punk,
powering their way through breakneck
versions of rock (and other) standards
with a lack of ceremony that was as
admirable as it was disrespectful. The
band – at this time Leonard Graves
Phillips (vocals), Stan Lee (guitars),
Billy Club (Bill Remar, bass), drummer C(K)arlos C(K)aballero and
multi-instrumentalist Chuck Wagon
– were, almost unbelievably, originally
a jazz-tinged rock outfit, only choosing the new wave as their natural home
after watching The Damned play.
Wagon was by far the most insane of
this motley crew, sometimes wheeling
around the stage playing his electric
piano or, for some reason, donning
an Afro wig for the sax parts: hard to
imagine for those who'd known him as
plain old Bob Davis, bassist with The
Quick in the mid seventies. Signed to
A&M, The Dickies surprised many by
hitting big in Britain, their cover of the
'Banana Splits' theme (1979) making
UK number seven, while *The Incredible
Shrinking Dickies* was a Top Twenty
album. Perhaps the group's finest
moment was their Justin Hayward-
approved version of The Moody
Blues' 'Nights in White Satin' (1979)
– which still gives the original a not-
so-serious run for its money.

Their best days behind them, The
Dickies moved on by the early eighties
to embrace an embryonic California
punk scene that spawned Black Flag,
among others. Wagon had now taken
over the traps from Kaballero but was
showing signs of despondency. Early

in 1981, he quit The Dickies to record a follow-up to his own solo EP, *Rock 'n' Roll Won't Go Away* (1980). With a new Dickies album also in the offing, Wagon agreed to play some final local dates with his former bandmates – including one at Topanga Canyon. What happened on the night of 27 June remains largely a mystery, but it is known that Wagon had suffered a minor road accident on his way home, and returned to the venue to hitch a lift from a roadie. Back at his parents' San Fernando Valley home, Chuck Wagon took himself up to his bedroom and shot himself in the head with a .22 rifle. Although he survived the night, the drummer died in hospital the following morning. The surviving Dickies continue to release records (albeit with little exposure), making them the longest-running punk band still recording new material. The line-up has briefly included late ex-Smashing Pumpkins keyboardist Jonathan Melvoin (☞ *July 1996*).

JULY

Wednesday 1

Rushton Moreve

(John Russell Morgan – Los Angeles, California, 1948)

Steppenwolf
(Sparrow)

Steppenwolf weren't really a 'heavy metal' band, but may well have coined the expression in their best-known song. The band – John Kay (Joachim Fritz Krauledat, vocals), Goldy McJohn (keys), Jerry Edmonton (percussion) – all ex-Toronto folk-rock band Sparrow – Michael Monarch (guitar) and Rushton Moreve (bass) – were blues-based, though their seminal debut album paved the way for much-harder-edged music to follow.

A classic of its era, *Steppenwolf* (1968) was recorded in just four days and was the parent album to revved-up biker anthem 'Born to be Wild'. Its follow-up single, the psychedelia-drenched 'Magic Carpet Ride' emerged from a swiftly released second album. Both singles were million-sellers Stateside during the latter half of 1968, and Moreve became an important figure in the early (most successful) days of Steppenwolf. Indeed, he co-wrote with Kay most of the first two albums, The 'Wolf gaining deserved recognition for their thoughtful lyrics and, for the time, unusual values (they were vehemently anti-drug). The pair borrowed heavily from underground literature – the band's name itself came from Hermann Hesse's mystical novel.

Surprisingly, Moreve quit the band to return to session work after album number two, and was replaced by another former Sparrow-ite, Nick St Nicholas: over the years some forty-odd musicians came and went in Steppenwolf's history. In July 1981, Moreve jumped into his car, got his motor runnin' and headed out on the highway – and was killed in a head-on collision in Sun Valley, California. Oddly, drummer Edmonton died in almost identical circumstances twelve years on (☞ *November 1993*).

See also *Andrew Chapin* (☞ *December 1985*)

Saturday 11

Hubert Johnson

(Detroit, Michigan, 14 January 1941)

The Contours

Whether the phenomenal vocal ability of his cousin Jackie Wilson had anything to do with the depression Hubert Johnson was to feel in the latter part of his life remains unknown, but it was Wilson nonetheless who

Steppenwolf: Should've stuck with bikes ...

introduced The Contours to Motown head Berry Gordy – the supremo initially rejected the vocal five-piece. Two years on, a refreshed version of the band, including baritone Johnson, signed with the Motown head's own Gordy imprint, and gave the label a first million-selling record with 'Do You Love Me?' (1962); the song – originally intended for The Temptations – was a UK number one for Brian Poole & The Tremeloes the following year. Although further successes did not arrive so effortlessly, The Contours were always a hit on the R & B charts and in Britain's Northern soul casinos. But by the mid sixties Motown had lost interest in a band that didn't fit their smooth house style.

Johnson – who'd resigned from the band in 1964 – put a bullet through his head in mysterious circumstances at his Detroit home seventeen years later.

Thursday 16

Harry Chapin
(Greenwich Village, New York, 7 December 1942)

At the start of the seventies, there were as many musicians mourning the end of peace as there were others celebrating the start of noise. And there were those who just wanted to share a story or two: as hard-bitten as he was 'artsy', Harry Chapin was such a performer, eschewing the day's musical trends more through his very nature rather than by intention. Chapin was the son of Jim Chapin, a noted jazz drummer who, as well as heading his own sextet, had been a regular player alongside Woody Herman and Tommy Dorsey during the forties. As a teenager, Chapin Jr sang with a local boys' choir (with his friend Robert Lamm, later of the band Chicago) after his family

'Being a rock star is pointless. It's garbage. It's the most self-indulgent thing I can think of.'
Harry Chapin

Harry Chapin: More verity than balderdash

moved to Brooklyn Heights. With two more musical brothers in the family, the Chapins put together an on-off group which eventually recorded an album, *Chapin Music* (1966). While studying philosophy at Cornell University, Chapin had developed an interest in folk music so powerful that it caused him to drop his studies. After some years spent making film documentaries (one of which, *Legendary Champions*, was Oscar-

nominated in 1969), Chapin returned to music and to the Village – the place of his birth – where troubadours were making waves. Chapin's clever strategy of shunning the 'paid gig' roundabout and hiring himself a residency with his new band at the Village Gate – a venue frequented by industry types – was to pay off. Signed to the folk-loving Elektra label, Chapin scored a surprise US hit with 'Taxi' (1972), a song that blueprinted his distinctive style of emotive, 'real' tales of life's ironies, disappointments and occasional joys. 1974 saw a commercial peak for Harry Chapin: the heavy sentimental 'WOLD' – a song about a DJ estranged from his family – returned him to the US (and UK) singles Top Forty, before 'Cat's in the Cradle' gave him a US number one in December. This remarkably astute record – dealing with the selfishness of a career-obsessed father – has been a hit for many artists since. (Taking this success with a pinch of salt, Chapin's comment was: 'I suspect wives are buying it as zingers for their husbands.') 'I Wanna Learn a Love Song' (1974) recounted the preface to Chapin's own marriage and adoption of his wife's three children. (He was nothing if not a magnanimous individual: of the 200-plus concerts Chapin played a year, at least half were benefits or charity events.) Parent album *Verities and Balderdash* went gold in the USA, though Chapin wasn't to repeat the success; his only further hit was 1980's 'Sequel' (which was indeed just that, to his first chart entry).

Despite the commercial downturn, Harry Chapin was still a massive live draw, and, on the evening of 16 July 1981, had a hotly anticipated free show to attend at the Lakeside Theater, Eisenhower Park. Leaving his Huntington Bay home, Chapin was driving his 1975 VW Rabbit along the Long Island Expressway when he unexpectedly changed lanes and began to slow dramatically from a cruising speed of around 65 mph; his emergency lights were flashing, suggesting that the driver was experiencing difficulties – he had possibly suffered a heart attack. Hitting another vehicle side-on, Chapin swerved again, this time into the path of a long-bed truck unable to adjust its own speed in time to avoid collision. Chapin's VW was hit full-on, the fuel tank rupturing and bursting into flames as the car crumpled under the impact. The truck driver and another motorist managed to pull the badly injured singer clear but doctors working for half an hour at the Nassau County Medical Center were unable to save him. Thousands of fans learned the news as they awaited him at the venue.

Chapin's funeral at Huntington was attended by his parents, three brothers, widow and five surviving children. Elektra Records set up a memorial fund, which has raised some $5 million for charitable concerns in the years since its inception. Chapin's daughter, Jen – a respected singer/songwriter in her own right – maintains the charitable work for the WHY (World Hunger Year) Foundation, which her father founded three decades ago.

AUGUST

Friday 28

Ronnie Self

(Tin Town, Missouri, 5 July 1938)

How Ronnie Self didn't become a big star as rock 'n' roll kicked in during the late fifties is something of a riddle: he had all the charisma and attitude of a Gene Vincent and, some say, the voice of a white Little Richard – but he was known as something of a wild boy in the shit-kickin' town of his birth. The eldest son of a railroad worker, Self was frequently in trouble for what the press of the day loved to call 'juvenile delinquency' – assault and vandalism often high on the agenda. (He also once pursued a teacher with a baseball bat.) Somehow, the 18-year-old Self found it in him to land a songwriting/publishing deal in Nashville, and released a self-penned single, 'Pretty Bad Blues' (1956), with ABC. Perhaps he arrived fractionally too soon, as the record didn't hit. However, Self's ripped-up stage performance prompted Columbia to sign him up in 1957, so all was far from lost. Self then cut the track he is most readily associated with, the near-psychobilly 'Bop-a-Lena' (1958), which finally climbed the US charts, peaking at sixty-eight. Fittingly, he also recorded the original version of 'I Fought the Law' (1961). But Self surprised his small following by refusing a major all-star tour, which most artists would have jumped at, on the grounds that he had recently married and was expecting his first child. The decision proved costly: to Self's fans, this was about as un-rock 'n' roll as it came; to his label, it made him unreliable – thus Columbia dropped him. Although he was contracted by Decca shortly after, Self's recording career was on the decline. He remained a gifted songwriter, and several more hits were forthcoming, most notably for Brenda Lee, whose takes on his 'Sweet Nothin's' and 'I'm Sorry' were big sellers in 1960. At the same time, however, Self became self-destructive, complicating his personal life with addiction to booze, recreational drugs and tablets. Often called 'Mr Frantic', Self had long been known for his quick temper – now he was starting to lose control publicly. On one notorious occasion, Self burned his few gold discs in front of the offices of BMI in Nashville.

By 1980 Ronnie Self was pronounced unfit for any kind of work and his health deteriorated rapidly thereafter, to a sad, inevitable conclusion in August the next year. Ever a perfectionist, Self left a legacy of thirty-odd recordings, each a nugget of splintering rock 'n' roll with a tinge of country. Yet – except in Europe, where he's still viewed as something of a god – almost nobody remembers him.

Guy Stevens

(East Dulwich, London, 13 April 1943)

A major player in British rock in the sixties and seventies, Guy Stevens wasn't so much a manager, producer or musician as all three – which is perhaps why he does not figure as often in rock annals as his mentor Chris Blackwell or contemporaries like Andrew Loog Oldham. Record-junkie Stevens left school early to work as a journalist and disc jockey at the Scene Club, Soho – a nightspot that helped to start the careers of such bands as The Animals and High Numbers (ie, The Who) and was attended by various members of The Beatles, Rolling Stones and Yardbirds. Stevens later became an A & R executive at Island, where he ran the label's Sue subsidiary. In this capacity, he unearthed some highly influential acts, displaying an uncanny knack for naming them. Perhaps most famously, he named Procol Harum after his beloved pet cat. Unfortunately, Stevens was not around to enjoy that band's early success with 'A Whiter Shade of Pale' (for the title of which he is also rumoured to be responsible) in 1967 as he was serving a sentence in Wormwood Scrubs for drug possession. While inside, Stevens was taken with the title *Mott: The Hoople* – a novel by Willard Manus. During his time producing the band to whom he suggested the name, Stevens's drug- and alcohol-fuelled behaviour really began to show: on one occasion he destroyed a studio clock when it appeared that a session was running over, on another he filled a piano with beer to make it 'sound better'. Also producing Free, Traffic and Nirvana (the earlier band of that name), by the end of the 1970s Guy Stevens had embraced the new wave, working on The Clash's timeless *London Calling*.

Patrick Campbell-Lyons of Nirvana encountered a drunken Guy Stevens in 1980, and said later: 'A dishevelled figure mumbled something indistinguishable to me as I passed him. I recognized the person as Guy, and I knew it was near the end of his story.' And so it proved. His life apparently having fallen apart, Stevens suffered a heart attack in 1981 after overdosing on prescription tablets, dying at the age of just thirty-eight. Some reports have him falling down a flight of stairs, much like Kit Lambert earlier in the year (➤ *April 1981*); if this is true, he would be the second of three British rock managers to die in such a manner during 1981 alone – Michael Dempsey, of The Adverts, being the third, in December.

DECEMBER

Sonny Til

(Earlington Carl Tilghman – Baltimore, Maryland, 8 August 1925)
The Orioles

Tall and lanky, Sonny Til was an unlikely sex symbol, but once he opened his mouth and that true, mellow tenor issued forth, the female contingent of his audience were generally putty in his hands. Til (Tilghman, as was) had returned from the Second World War a hero, only to be thrown by an enthusiastic girlfriend into the lesser battlefield of talent contests. Til knew he could do it – he'd entertained the troops at many a USO show in his time.

In 1948, a vocal quintet named The Vibranaires – Til, Alexander Sharp (tenor), George Nelson (baritone), Johnny Reed (bass) and guitarist Tommy Gaither – finished a poor third in Arthur Godfrey's radio *Talent Scouts* contest but provoked such a reaction that they were asked back twice anyway. By July they were The Orioles and – managed by songwriter Deborah Chessler – and found themselves cutting sides for the Jubilee label. The first hit was 'It's Too Soon to Know' (1948), which rose to number one on the R & B listings and also became a sizeable pop hit. More hits arrived and, with Til's unique sound and natural stage presence, The Orioles were a sensation throughout 1949. But needless to say, it was all too good to be true. Sales slipped a shade during 1950, then The Orioles were beset by tragedy and drama. In November, the distinctive Tommy Gaither was killed and two other band members injured in a horrific car accident (➤ *Pre-1965*), while in 1951 another close call behind the wheel was followed by the attempts of a young (apparently suicidal) female fan to extort money from Til. Between then and 1955, most of the original line-up were to disappear, while Sonny Til remained in great demand, continuing to record as Orioles lead as well as solo and in duet with teenage prodigy Edna McGriff.

Keeping The Orioles' name alive proved a tough call for Sonny Til, though he did manage to perform under the name in some shape or form until 1980. Of the original Orioles, only Reed lived long enough to see the group inducted into the Rock 'n' Roll Hall of Fame in 1998: Nelson survived both car crashes only to die from an asthma attack aged thirty-three (1959), while Sharp – by then a member of The Ink Spots – passed away after a cardiac arrest (1970). A diabetes sufferer, Til died at Veterans' Memorial Hospital, Baltimore, also from a heart attack – though at just fifty-six, he was scarcely a 'veteran'.

Lest We Forget

Other notable deaths that occurred sometime during 1981:

Michael Dempsey (UK manager of punk band The Adverts who also edited the *Sniffin' Glue* fanzine; fell down a flight of stairs while changing a light bulb, and died of internal bleeding the next day, 6/12)

Carl Feaster (US doo-wop vocalist with The Chords, who hit US #2 in 1953 with 'Sh-boom' – one of the first black hits to gain a white audience; born 24/9/1930; cancer, 23/1)

Ernie Freeman (US pop/rock 'n' roll pianist who hit as lead with B Bumble & The Stingers – also worked with Duane Eddy and Bobby Vee and backed Frank Sinatra; born Ohio 16/8/1922; heart attack, 15/5)

Alan Malarowitz (US drummer with Sweetwater; born *c* 1950; falling asleep at the wheel, he crashed his car in the desert between LA and Las Vegas during the summer)

Dewey 'Pigmeat' Markham (US R & B/comedy singer, whose career spanned six decades crowned by the UK/US 1968 Top Twenty hit 'Here Comes the Judge'; born North Carolina, 18/4/1904; stroke, 13/12)

Hugo Montenegro (US composer/orchestra leader who scored a UK #1/US #2 with 'The Good, the Bad and the Ugly' in 1968; born New York, 2/9/1925; emphysema, 6/2)

Tommy Moore (UK drummer who toured Scotland in May 1960 with The Silver Beetles – ie, The Beatles – but left after a month because he despised John Lennon; born Liverpool, *c* 1924; unknown)

Doug Roberts (US drummer with The Fireballs, who made US #1 with 'Sugar Shack' in 1963; born 15/6/1941; unknown, 18/11)

Justin 'Jud' Strunk Jr (US country/comedy singer/banjo-player who hit with 'Daisy-a-Day' in 1973; born New York, 11/6/1936; piloting his own light aircraft, he crashed in a Maine forest, 15/10)

Joan Weber (US singer who topped the chart in January 1955 with 'Let Me Go, Lover' only to return to obscurity, depression and mental illness; born New Jersey, 12/12/1986; unknown, 13/5)

For a complete list of fallen artists, visit

www.numberoneinheaven.com

JANUARY

Friday 22

Tommy Tucker

(Robert Higginbotham – Springfield, Ohio,
5 March 1933)

(The Dusters)

Robert Higginbotham was an accomplished pianist before he had even mastered the longer words in his school reader. His family knew he was destined for success, but even *he* knew he'd have to lose the family name to get on. At school, he'd been named 'Tommy Tucker' after the pro-football great, and it stuck. His first live work was age sixteen with Bobby Wood's jazz-tinged band – but when this act suddenly became a vocal concern in the wake of the doo-wop craze, the newly renamed 'Tee' Tucker set up his own trio, The Dusters, with Welton Young (guitar) and Brenda Lee Jones (bass). After sessions with the Atco label, Tucker realized he had a fairly decent singing voice, and it seemed just a matter of time before the hits came (Young and Jones had already had success under their own steam, as Dean & Jean). A move to Herb Abramson's Atlantic finally placed Tucker high on the Billboard listings with the much-loved 'Hi-Heel Sneakers' (1964). The follow-up, Don Covay's 'Long Tall Shorty' (1964), was a lesser hit, but, like its predecessor, is still played today. Abramson stuck by his protégé, but no more hits were forthcoming. An irrepressible performer, Tucker still made a decent living from the club circuit and package tours, while working as a real-estate agent by day.

His demise is apocryphal: putting a high gloss on the wooden floors of his apartment in East Orange, New Jersey, the musician inhaled carbon tetrachloride, and his system was immediately poisoned by the noxious fumes. He died shortly after at College Hospital, Newark. His publicity people were quick to suggest that the musician had died from food poisoning – possibly to avoid the inevitable 'perfect finish' headlines.

Golden Oldies #1

Lightnin' Hopkins

(Sam Hopkins – Centerville, Texas,
15 March 1912)

The first of our over-age entries is a man rightly regarded as one of the greatest blues guitarists of all time. Lightnin' Hopkins was the real McCoy – a man who taught himself to play on a bizarre instrument fashioned from a cigar box and pieces of chicken wire at the age of eight. By the 1920s he was playing alongside Blind Lemon Jefferson, and the blues figurehead became a mentor during Hopkins's formative years. His big break was accompanying pianist Wilson 'Thunder' Smith, which, naturally, led to his nickname. Acquiring vices like trading cards, Hopkins was known for his love of alcohol, nicotine, gambling, fighting and womanizing, and – like many black blues players – he found himself down on his luck. He was imprisoned during his early twenties and scarred for the rest of his life by the leg irons used to restrain him while inside.

Amassing almost a hundred albums to his name, Hopkins enjoyed a Top Five pop hit in 1950 ('Shotgun Blues'), and later found a wide fanbase within the US psychedelic rock scene, opening for a slew of big names like Jefferson Airplane, Joan Baez and The Grateful Dead. Hopkins's live performances were unfortunately curtailed by a serious car accident in 1970, but he remained an incredibly skilled guitarist with a gift for writing songs with little preparation, whose music, whether acoustic or electric, would gain new followers as rock 'n' roll progressed. Lightnin' Sam Hopkins died on 31 January 1982 from cancer of the oesophagus; some 4,000 showed for his funeral in Harris County, Texas.

Alex Harvey: Rock 'n' roll's own Dennis the Menace

'Don't make, buy or shoot any bullets. And when you get your freedom, don't pish in the water supply.'

Alex Harvey gets oblique

FEBRUARY

Thursday 4

Alex Harvey

(Glasgow, 5 February 1935)

The Sensational Alex Harvey Band
(The Alex Harvey Big Soul Band)
(The Electric Cowboys)

It's hard to imagine that a hard-drinking rock 'n' roll stalwart like Alex Harvey was once groomed for pin-up stardom in the wake of acts like Tommy Steele, but then many don't realize that Harvey's musical roots were in Dixieland jazz and skiffle, or that he fronted a soul band during the early sixties. The unlikely winner of a 1957 Scottish newspaper talent contest, Harvey dined out on his win for a couple of years, the solidly built singer and guitarist forming The Alex Harvey Big Soul Band, an act which supported US rock 'n' rollers Gene Vincent and Eddie Cochran when they visited Scotland in 1960 (shortly before Cochran's death (➤ *Pre-1965*)). Harvey also landed a residency for his band in a Hamburg nightclub a couple of years after The Beatles. For the rest of the decade, he found irregular work as a session-player, and held down a succession of jobs, one of which is believed to have been as a lion-tamer. In 1972, Harvey's life was changed by two separate events. In one of pop music's most dramatic incidents, Harvey's younger brother, Les – also a musician, with whom he had recorded – was electrocuted on stage in Swansea while playing with his band, Stone the Crows (➤ *May 1972*). Just a few months later, promoter Bill Fehilly (then breaking another popular Scot-rock band, Nazareth) put Harvey in contact with Tear Gas, a crumbling group – namely Zal Cleminson (guitar), cousins Hugh and Ted McKenna

(keyboards and percussion) and Chris Glenn (bass) – and The Sensational Alex Harvey Band was formed. Here, finally, was an act to do some justice to a natural frontman – Cleminson, in particular, was a great foil to the hard man in the stripy shirt, with his Joker-style stage make-up and sequins. Over the next few years, SAHB, as they were mainly known, developed one of the most popular stage acts in the UK. They outgrossed (in every sense) most opposition, gigging almost constantly, putting out eight albums in five years and placing a series of hits in both album and singles charts. As a sort of shambling answer to Bowie's live shtick, Harvey also had his own 'alter ego', a stage creation known as 'Vambo' who was also the subject of many of SAHB's songs. The group's hilarious 1975 deconstruction of 'Delilah' was an improvised stage piece before it placed at UK number seven – while the band were in the USA having their equipment stolen by the Mafia! There was more tragedy for Harvey, though, with the plane-crash death of his manager, Fehilly, just as another hit, 'Boston Tea Party', was climbing the charts (1976). Clearly suffering from the loss, Harvey collapsed on tour in Europe. For the next few months, his live performances became more and more erratic as he depended increasingly heavily on alcohol and drugs. Also suffering from acute back problems, Harvey announced his retirement from live work in 1977. To all intents and purposes, The Sensational Alex Harvey Band were wound up when Cleminson joined rivals Nazareth after the *SAHB Stories* album (1976).

Ignoring medical advice, Alex Harvey went out on tour again early in 1982 with a new band, The Electric Cowboys – but his death just one day ahead of his forty-seventh birthday put paid to any further ventures. Harvey suffered a heart attack on a ferry heading back to England, and died in Zeebrugge, Belgium.

MARCH

Wednesday 17

Samuel George

(Detroit, Michigan, 1 October 1942)

The Capitols

Best known for their impressive dance routines and pumping, lurching 'Cool Jerk' single, The Capitols were one of Detroit's hottest acts as R & B moved into the mainstream. The band had begun as a five-piece around 1962, its main members being Samuel George (vocals/percussion) and Donald Norman Storball (guitar). Ollie McLaughlin's Karen label issued an early single, 'Dog and Cat' (1963), which garnered airplay but no sales; somewhat disillusioned, George and Storball split from the other members, eventually adding keyboard-player Richard McDougal. 'Cool Jerk' (1966) shot The Capitols into the US Top Ten – shifting almost a million copies in the process – but was the group's only significant hit. Later songs were just pale imitations of this dance-floor filler and the group split for good in late 1969.

Samuel George was stabbed to death with a kitchen knife in a family dispute at his home in Detroit. Storball had by this time become a policeman in the city, but it's not thought he was involved in any investigation of the murder.

Friday 19

Randy Rhoads

(Randall William Rhoads – Santa Monica, California, 6 December 1956)

Ozzy Osbourne's Blizzard of Ozz

Quiet Riot

To those with long memories, the events of 19 March 1982 read like another chilling, condensed version of 'the day the music died': a long journey, an overcrowded, broken-down tour bus, a Beechcraft Bonanza with a dubious pilot . . .

In an unlikely musical marriage, Randy Rhoads added his impressive classically trained guitar skills to the Brummie metal thrum of Ozzy Osbourne's Blizzard of Ozz. The youngest of three children, Rhoads was born into a musical heritage, and later taught guitar at his mother's music school. (There was little family snobbery about Rhoads choosing a rock career – he inherited his Gibson guitar from his grandfather.) Forming popular hard-rockers Quiet Riot at twenty – with Kevin DuBrow (vocals), Kelli Garni (bass) and Drew Forsyth (drums) – Rhoads made two albums with this band considered likely to be America's next big thing. As it was, their records were not even issued in the US and, despite hit status in Japan, Rhoads quit when asked by his musician friend Dana Strum to audition for Ozzy Osbourne late in 1979.

The former Black Sabbath leader now fronted Blizzard of Ozz, and by 1980 Rhoads was to be the Prince of Darkness's new lead guitarist. An instant hit in performance, Rhoads also contributed to Blizzard's first pair of albums, the eponymous debut (1980) and the (accurately titled) *Diary of a Madman* (1981). While touring this album, Rhoads's interest in classical guitar reawakened, and he spent much of the time on the road practising and taking tuition. It seemed to many that he might well give up rock 'n' roll and return to his roots – though it will never be known whether he would have.

On the evening of 18 March, the band and its entourage were heading towards Orlando for a slot supporting Foreigner at Florida's 'Rock Superbowl XIV' when it became apparent to driver Andrew Aycock that they would need to stop to replace some parts of the ailing tour bus. Aycock wasn't in the best frame of mind anyway: his ex-wife had showed up at Blizzard of Ozz's show and had insisted she be driven to Florida with the group. As Aycock – pumped up on cocaine – drove through the night, the couple bickered relentlessly at the front of the bus, much to the chagrin of Osbourne and his girlfriend, Sharon Arden, who were not best pleased at having another passenger in the already overcrowded vehicle. In the morning, the bus stopped at a depot in Leesburg, Florida, for repairs to be carried out. Spotting several Beechcraft light aeroplanes housed near by, Aycock boasted that he

'The day that happened is a day I'll never forget. It was the most horrific thing that has ever happened to me, because [Randy] was a sweet man.'

Ozzy Osbourne

could fly and suggested a quick spin while they waited. What the driver failed to mention was that his pilot's licence had been revoked following a recent accident. After keyboardist Don Airey and tour manager Jake Duncan had enjoyed a short flight, Rhoads and Osbourne's long-time costume designer, 54-year-old Rachael Youngblood, agreed, against their better judgement, to give it a go. Neither was a particularly comfortable flyer (especially Rhoads, who had something of a phobia), but perhaps they felt it would alleviate the tedium of the dragging journey. Exactly what happened while the craft was airborne will never be known, but it seems that Aycock, still very much under the influence of cocaine, decided to buzz the tour bus in order to put the frighteners on Osbourne and in particular the ex-Mrs Aycock. Diving four times, the Beechcraft clipped its wing against the bus on the final occasion, went into a mid-air spin and finally crashed in flames into a nearby house. All three on board were killed instantly. Some believe that Aycock may have deliberately attempted to hit his ex-wife who was standing yards from the bus.

Hearing the enormous crash, Osbourne and Arden leapt from their beds and ran to the scene. Learning that a deaf man lived in the house hit by the burning aircraft, Ozzy Osbourne heroically raced into the stricken building and pulled the stunned but grateful occupant to safety. Said Osbourne: 'Had I been awake I'd have been on that plane – probably sitting on the fucking wing.' But he was clearly distressed by the whole episode: although the guitarist was much younger, Osbourne considered Randy Rhoads a good friend and acted as a pall-bearer at Rhoads's funeral, even breaking with years of tradition to mark his respect for the deceased by showing up in a suit.

APRIL

Friday 30

Lester Bangs

(Leslie Conway Bangs – Escondido, California, 14 December 1948)

Probably the most 'out there' critic rock music has seen, Lester Bangs modelled his attacks on the leftfield stylings of beat writers like Hunter S Thompson and William S Burroughs rather than the largely sterile prose of many of his contemporary critics. Having already written an unpublished autobiographical novel, Bangs began his brief odyssey by responding to a 1969 small ad placed in *Rolling Stone* requesting reviews from its readers. Success at this brought him steady freelance work from the rock world's leading journal – until his somewhat confrontational style was considered too abrupt by editor Jann Wenner, who feared it might discourage major musicians from giving interviews. Thus Bangs was sacked, only to reappear within the pages of *Creem*, *Village Voice* and the UK's *NME* – his cathartic writing on a subject that was already beginning to take itself way too seriously would not be ignored. Among his other credits, it's widely believed that Bangs coined the term 'punk' (applied to rock music) – he certainly used it as early as 1970 when referring to the MC5.

Lester Bangs, despite not being a successful musician himself, fell into many of the scene's traps. By his thirties he'd become such a voracious amphetamine-user that when he was found comatose in his Manhattan apartment on 30 April 1982, it was first assumed that he had overdosed on something more sinister than the Darvon and Valium he'd taken to relieve the symptoms of influenza.

'Look at it this way: there are many here among us for whom the life force is best represented by the livid twitching of one tortured nerve, or even a full-scale anxiety attack.'

Lester Bangs offers his *raison d'être*, 1980

His death was, however, a complete accident. A wake was held for him at the legendary CBGB's club several days later. Kick-starting a vogue for fractured, stream-of-consciousness writing, Lester Bangs influenced an entire generation of music journalists – the majority pale imitations of the finest rock journalist at his emetic best.

JUNE

Thursday 3

Rusty Day

(Russell Edward Davidson – Detroit, Michigan, c 1944)

The Amboy Dukes
(Cactus)
(Detroit Wheels)
(The Midnighters)

An immense presence in every sense, Rusty Day was a white soul singer with a blistering vocal style who tipped the scales at around 350 lbs – when he was around, audiences pretty much took notice. With his backing band, The Midnighters, Day became something of a legend on the Detroit live circuit during the sixties, while a single, 'I Gotta Move #1' (1966), edged its way on to Michigan radio playlists. His reputation as a lover of wild living and the rawest whiskey – not to mention a fondness for recreational drugs – also caught fire at this time. Three years on, Day was selected to front The Amboy Dukes, Motor City's brashest new R & B band, recording with them on their third album, *Migrations*. But Day had competition in terms of personality: the band had been founded by no-nonsense guitarist Ted Nugent, a controlling leader who was vehemently anti-drugs. The probability is that Day, quite apart from his party-animal tendencies, was deflecting too much attention from self-styled 'wild man' Nugent – thus, after one further album, the aptly titled *Marriage on the Rocks* (1970), The Amboy Dukes were history as far as Day was concerned. He re-emerged with Cactus and later Detroit Wheels (taking over the helm from Mitch Ryder), but these spells would not capture the imagination in quite the same way.

Following the untimely death of AC/DC vocalist Bon Scott (☛ *February 1980*), it seemed probable that Day – with his appropriately raucous voice – might take his place as frontman for the good-time Aussie rockers. When this did not come to pass, Rusty Day relocated to Florida. Here, his hardcore lifestyle saw him shockingly murdered by heroin dealers when a transaction went badly wrong. Day was shot three times and died at the scene.

Thursday 10

Addie 'Micki' Harris
(Michelle Harris – Passaic, New Jersey, 22 January 1940)
The Shirelles

A founding member of one of the great girl groups, 'older sister' Micki Harris joined teenage school-friends – lead singer Shirley Owens, Beverley Lee and Doris Coley – to form The Poquellos in 1958. As luck would have it, another school-friend, Mary Jane, was the daughter of Tiara label-owner Florence Greenberg – who was sufficiently impressed with the quartet that she signed them immediately. With the group renamed The Shirelles, their own composition, the impressive 'I Met Him on a Sunday', was considered good enough for distribution by Decca – which put Harris and her colleagues into the R & B Top Fifty. It was obvious The Shirelles were set to be a major influence: with their marriage of doo-wop and upbeat pop, the group enjoyed an impressive string of hits, becoming the top act of Greenberg's new Sceptre label. Six of their records made the US Top Ten, with two – Goffin and King's 'Will You Love Me Tomorrow?' (1960) and 'Soldier Boy' (1962) – making it all the way to number one. A significant number of Shirelles songs were also covered by other groups: Manfred Mann took 'Sha La La' into the UK charts in 1964, while The Beatles' early sets included versions of 'Boys' and 'Baby It's You'; indeed, John Lennon professed them his favourite group in the early days of Beatlemania.

The British invasion took its inevitable toll on The Shirelles (as it did on so many acts), but the girls remained a popular draw on the oldies circuit during the seventies. In 1982, the group were again in the studio, back-up for the resurgent Dionne

Warwick (who had occasionally sung with the group in her early career), but, tragically, Micki Harris collapsed and died from heart failure following a performance in Atlanta, Georgia. Juggling various line-up changes, The Shirelles continued into the new millennium, and were inducted into the Rock 'n' Roll Hall of Fame in 1996.

See also *Doris Coley* (☛ *February 2000*)

Wednesday 16

James Honeyman-Scott
(Hereford, 4 November 1956)
The Pretenders
(Cheeks)

At just twenty-five one of the most versatile guitarists of his era, 'Jimmy' Honeyman-Scott's meaningless death seems no less of a waste two and a half decades on. He was another prodigy, playing with fully fledged rock musicians as a teenager. Like a lot of young boys, he'd been a fan of Eric Clapton and Hank Marvin, and he had mastered many of their tricks while his friends were still completing their railway layouts. Progressing to The Beach Boys, Honeyman-Scott found he was able to cope with the intricate fretwork here as well. While a member of Cheeks (alongside former Mott the Hoople keyboardist Verden Allen), Honeyman-Scott befriended local Hereford musicians Pete Farndon (bass) and Martin Chambers (drums), thereby sowing the earliest seeds of The Pretenders. The band was completed with the addition of Ohio-born singer Chrissie Hynde – in the UK pursuing a career as a music journalist. Any doubts Honeyman-Scott may have had were wiped out when Farndon and Hynde lined up one of his heroes, Nick Lowe, to produce a single for the group. The

The classic Pretenders line-up: Perhaps Chambers (*far left*) and Hynde knew what was to befall Farndon and Honeyman-Scott?

band, with no name yet, cut a cool version of The Kinks' 'Stop Your Sobbing' (arguably better than the original) at Regent's Park Studio in July 1978. Issued on the small imprint Real, this record put The Pretenders (as Hynde had now called them) into the Top Forty and on to *Top of the Pops* in January 1979. This was followed by the fabulous 'Kid', a self-penned item that showed the group's complete mastery of sixties hooks with sharp, confident new-wave leanings. The band – particularly Hynde and Honeyman-Scott, who had co-written it – were less keen on 'Brass In Pocket', but for once, label pressure proved decisive as this third single became the UK's first new number one of the eighties. The Pretenders were now one of the hottest acts in Britain – emphasized by a chart-topping debut album that went platinum around the world.

The depths to which The Pretenders were to plummet in the next eighteen months were truly disturbing. Things began well enough for Honeyman-Scott, who married Peggy Sue Fender (a US model well-named for a guitarist), but Farndon and Hynde split after a two-year relationship (she took up with The Kinks' Ray Davies), which caused tensions, and Farndon spent increasing amounts of time and money on hard drugs. After the critically snubbed *Pretenders II* – a record, in retrospect, dismissed very unfairly – Hynde and Honeyman-Scott both agreed that it was in the best interests of the band that Farndon should leave, setting a deadline of the return from an early 1982 world tour for his dismissal. After well-received shows in the Far East, Honeyman-Scott dashed off to the US with his wife to fulfil the dream of a lifetime by playing a series of shows with The Beach Boys – and returned buoyant, seemingly also having put paid to his own sporadic amphetamine use.

On 14 June, Hynde and Honeyman-Scott broke the news to Farndon that his escalating heroin use was no longer compatible with the band's plans. Relieved at having told the bassist of the decision, Honeyman-Scott spent the night of the 16th at a friend's London party, but the following morning, he was unrousable: with terrible irony, it was Honeyman-Scott who was dead from heart failure brought on by snorting cocaine. It seemed that having recently undergone detoxification, his body was no longer tolerant of the drug. Too devastated to attend Honeyman-Scott's Hereford funeral, Hynde took herself off to America to be with Davies, while the quietest Pretender, Martin Chambers, was left to contemplate the future. As for Farndon, he was living on borrowed time: he died following excessive drug use just ten months after Honeyman-Scott (☞*April 1983*).

JULY

Tuesday 6

Abrim Tilmon
(Little Rock, Arkansas, 12 January 1945)
The Detroit Emeralds

The Tilmon brothers – Abrim, Ivory, Cliophus and the rather less lyrically named Raymond – formed the silky-smooth Detroit Emeralds around 1968, the name surprising because they were all from Arkansas. The Emeralds – who'd trimmed to a three-piece by 1970 – rehearsed carefully executed singing and finely honed dance routines, distinguishing features of the records they placed on the US and UK charts two years on. Former postal worker Abrim 'Abe' Tilmon, with his gospel-trained voice, was clearly the group's leader; an accomplished musician, he wrote most of their material, including the excellent and much-covered 'Feel the Need in Me' (1973). This record punctured the UK Top Five, becoming by some way the biggest hit The Emeralds were to score. Various singers came and went (including future members of kitsch one-hit wonders The Floaters) until, in the eighties, two versions of The Detroit Emeralds started playing the clubs. Tilmon seemed happiest at this time to return to his gospel roots and sing in church once again.

Just ahead of a reunion tour, Abrim Tilmon collapsed and died from a heart attack at his home in Southfield, Michigan, having condensed both his life and career into an unusually brief period of time – he was just thirty-seven when he passed away. Tilmon is survived by his widow, two children and at least three grandchildren.

Tuesday 27

Daniel Beard
(4 November 1949)
The 5th Dimension

Long after their impressive run of hits – 'Aquarius', 'Wedding Bell Blues' (both 1969), 'One Less Bell to Answer' (1970) – had dried up, The 5th Dimension drafted in Daniel Beard to replace the popular Billy Davis Jr, who, with the band's female singer Marilyn McCoo, had moved on to work as a duet. Their moment clearly having passed, The 5th Dimension under Beard's leadership only managed one minor 1976 chart entry with 'Love Hangover' (which was utterly swamped by Diana Ross's hit version released at the same time). On Motown's payroll, though, the group went on to become a popular dinner-club act. Beard also made a small living as a studio engineer and had aspirations to become an actor.

Daniel Beard was in his sixth-storey (ie, top-floor) New York apartment one evening when a fire broke out – apparently started deliberately. The singer made it only as far as the fourth floor before being fatally overcome by smoke; his room-mate survived by climbing on to the roof. The arsonist was never caught.

Wednesday 28

Keith Green
(Brooklyn, New York, 21 October 1953)

A leading voice in the world of contemporary Christian rock, the distinctive, bearded Keith Green began his career in the secular world, despite having been born into a highly devout family – he was in his twenties when he was 'born again'. Aged eleven, Green had been the youngest-ever member of the American Society of Composers, Authors and Publishers (ASCAP), landing a simultaneous deal with Decca. He became a minister during the seventies, preaching the word on television as well as at the customary church meetings, while maintaining a career as a house song-writer (of both religious and secular songs) for CBS, where he met his wife, Melody. The pair founded the radical Last Days Ministries, through which they implored followers to purge themselves of all anti-Christian impurity. By the mid seventies Green was enjoying a successful solo career (in Christian rock terms), even attracting the born-again Bob Dylan to play harmonica on his 'So You Wanna Go Back to Egypt?' (1980).

Just two years after this career high, Keith Green died when the heavily overloaded Cessna 414 carrying him and eleven others nosedived shortly after take-off from an airfield in Lindale, Texas. Among the other fatalities were two of Green's four young children: Josiah, three, and Bethany, two.

AUGUST

Friday 13

Joe Tex
(Joseph Arrington Jr – Rogers, Texas, 8 August 1933)

At twenty-one, Joe Arrington was the landslide winner of an Apollo Theater talent contest, beginning in deceptively innocent fashion a career that would eventually see him blueprint funky, sleazy R & B. It took a while before the Joe Tex shtick caught on: his early releases with the King, Ace and Anna labels were not astounding. But it all worked out with maturity: as Joe Tex toured more and more, his voice took on a sandpaper rasp that was to set him apart from his contemporaries, and the huge R & B hit 'Baby You're Right' pretty much saved the singer's livelihood in 1962. (This self-penned number was also a substantial seller for James Brown.) Nevertheless, it was not until 1965 that a few cross-over hits emerged, when 'Hold What You've Got' gave Tex a Top Five US placing. Changing his given name to Yussuf Hazziez, Tex was to spend time lecturing as a Muslim minister. Simultaneously, he nurtured a 'preaching' style in his music, which often appeared to be promoting traditional values (as in 1965's 'A Woman (Can Change a Man)'), but by the next decade he was adopting a more flippant tone. The US Top Ten 'Skinny Legs and All' (1967) presaged a series of songs with less 'correct' values. 1972's million-selling 'I Gotcha' was a saucy though massively popular number, as was his final hit, 'Ain't Gonna Bump No More (with No Big Fat Woman)'. The latter took Tex as close as he would get to a pop chart-topper in another major market: it peaked at UK number two in 1977 and was his only British hit.

By now mainly dedicated to Islam, pro-football and his ranch home in Navasota, Texas, Joe Tex was by 1982 touring the oldies circuit with Wilson Pickett and Solomon Burke. He died at home from a heart attack less than a week before his forty-ninth birthday.

NOVEMBER

Friday 12

Patrick J Cowley

(Buffalo, New York, 19 October 1950)

Patrick Cowley began his love affair with music while still a student at the University of Buffalo, drifting from band to band until he met the outlandish Sylvester James – best known by his first name – who saw in Cowley's innovative synthesizer work something to which he could marry his band's funk-drenched songs. It took a few years before disco really began to kick in, but, during the explosion of mid 1978, Cowley and Sylvester's 'You Make Me Feel (Mighty Real)' became one of the genre's early classics, with its pounding rhythm and cyclical chorus. (The single was a much bigger hit in the UK, where it made the Top Ten.) This formula was to be repeated on a series of similar-feeling records, including 'Do You Wanna Funk?', a cut that charted just two months before Cowley's untimely death. Cowley – also co-founder of Megatone Records – made several solo albums and teamed up briefly with cult dance hero Paul Parker.

Patrick Cowley is thought to be the first-known major entertainer to have died from AIDS. His close friend and music partner Sylvester sadly died the same way just a few years later (☛ *December 1988*).

DECEMBER

Wednesday 1

David Torbert

(San Francisco, California, 7 June 1948)
New Riders of the Purple Sage
Kingfish (Horses)
(New Delhi River Band)
(Mescaline Rompers)

Briefly with The New Delhi River Band and Mescaline Rompers in the late sixties, Dave Torbert created his small page of rock 'n' roll history by meeting Jerry Garcia at the tail end of the Haight-Ashbury love-in and joining his New Riders of the Purple Sage (named after Zane Grey's novel), an offshoot of The Grateful Dead formed mainly to give Garcia an alter-ego group in which to experiment. Torbert was no also-ran, though; he was a more than decent bass guitarist who possessed a fine voice and could play blues harp. And it was plain that the New Riders were going to be more than just a sideline: often opening for The Dead, the band – sometimes Garcia and Torbert and always John Dawson (vocals/guitars/songwriting), David Nelson (guitars), Phil Lesh (bass) and Mickey Hart (drums) – became touted as the leading cosmic/psychedelic/country act of the time.

By 1971 the band had a recording contract and Torbert was a full-time member, taking over Lesh's duties. With New Riders, Torbert played on five albums in three years – taking lead vocal duty on most of the second album, *Powerglide* (1972), which, like its follow-up, *Gypsy Cowboy* (1972), also featured a couple of his own songs. But he had been playing simultaneously with Kingfish (who cut their first record under the name Horses), and joined them full-time in 1974.

Kingfish – which at one time also featured another 'Deadhead', guitarist Bob Weir – issued three albums before splitting; a fourth remained unreleased until years after Torbert's death, which came from a completely unexpected heart attack at the age of thirty-four.

See also *Spencer Dryden (* *January 2005)*

Thursday 2

David Blue
(Stuart David Cohen – Providence, Rhode Island, 18 February 1941)
Country Joe & The Fish
(Blues Project)

Another singer/songwriter with Robert Zimmerman connections, David Blue was part of the Greenwich Village set that had thrown up folk talents such as Phil Ochs. A mainstay of the area's clubs and bars in the early sixties, Blue, with his politically charged polemic, was popular with the Dylan crowd, but, veering towards rock, he headed for San Francisco to hook up with Country Joe & The Fish – a political/trip band on the verge of turning 'electric' – under his real name. Blue/Cohen was with the band for its most creative period but quit just ahead of their momentous performance at Woodstock. David Blue returned to New York and to his folk roots via a stint with the on-off Blues Project, but aside from a high-profile tour with Dylan in 1976, Blue featured less and less in the seventies music scene, becoming an actor instead (he appeared in the 1978 movie *American Friend* and on television). Like his contemporary David Torbert, Blue died young from a heart attack – while jogging through Washington Square Park in New York City.

Tuesday 21

Tomaz Hostnik
(Trbovlje, Ljubljana, Yugoslavia, 1961)
Laibach

Yes, hardline industrialists Laibach began as long ago as 1980, formed in Trbovlje by Hostnik and Miran Mohar – as the musical 'wing' of their 'New Slovenian Art' movement, known as NSK. As if this weren't enough, the pair were also currently serving with the Yugoslavian army. (The band's name was what Ljubljana was known as under Nazi occupation.)

Military obligations prevented much happening for Laibach until 1982, when the group experienced a great deal: they played their first live performances and recorded for the first time in a studio. Laibach's radical stance, however, provoked police scrutiny at a concert on 11 December in Zagreb; Yugoslavia was under communist rule and the group's pro-Stalinist stance had had authorities in a lather for some time. On this occasion they were under investigation for 'apparent use of military expedients' within their uncompromising stage act. It was to be Hostnik's last appearance with the band. He was found hanged from a hayrack just ten days later (the Hostnik song 'Apologia Laibach' is believed by many to be a suicide note). Laibach are now enormously popular, particularly in the US, where the band has been embraced by the industrial metal fraternity and Tomaz Hostnik is seen as something of a deity.

Lest We Forget

Other notable deaths that occurred sometime during 1982:

Joe Bauer (US jazz drummer and founder member of rock act The Youngbloods, who made US #5 with 'Get Together' in 1969; born Tennessee, 26/9/1941; brain tumour, 9/82)

Billy 'Butterball' Bowen (US vocalist with The Ink Spots; born Alabama, 3/1/1909; unknown, 27/9)

Tommy Bryant (US bass with a later incarnation of legendary vocal act The Ink Spots; born Pennsylvania, 21/5/1930; unknown, 3/1)

August Burns (US cellist with Sweetwater; having somehow survived a fall from a construction elevator while on a sabbatical in Germany, Burns contracted pneumonia and died after undergoing treatment)

Dallas Edwards (US guitarist who played in Joey Rand's touring version of Bill Haley's Comets; drowned in a Daytona hotel swimming pool while on tour, 11/1982)

John Felton (US bass singer/guitarist of California doo-wop combo The Diamonds; born *c* 1934; his light aircraft crashed into Mt Shasta, also killing his wife and two others, 17/5)

Murray 'The K' Kaufman (New York-based US rock 'n' roll DJ who became known as 'the fifth Beatle' following his friendship with the touring superstars; born 14/2/1922; cancer, 21/2)

Marty Robbins (US country/pop singer who charted many times, hitting US #1 with 1959's 'El Paso'; born Martin David Robinson, Arizona, 26/9/1925; heart attack, 8/12)

Warren Ryanes (US baritone with 'The Book of Love' hit-makers The Monotones, alongside his younger brother John (who died ten years earlier); born New Jersey, 14/12/1937; unknown, 6/1982)

Lynne Taylor (US folk singer who worked with Benny Goodman and Buddy Rich before topping the US charts with 'Walk Right In' (1963) as a member of The Rooftop Singers; unknown)

For a complete list of fallen artists, visit

www.numberoneinheaven.com

JANUARY

Wednesday 12

Reebop Kwaku-Baah
(Remi Kabaka – Lagos, Nigeria,
13 February 1944)
The Unknown Cases
Traffic
Can
(Various acts)

One of the first African musicians to enter European rock, Reebop Kwaku-Baah arrived in Britain during the sixties, where he taught his craft – percussion – and recorded with a number of African artists. While living in Sweden, Kwaku-Baah was contacted by Traffic's Steve Winwood, one of a number of contemporary musicians impressed with what they'd heard; initially brought in to tour with the top psychedelic-pop act, Kwaku-Baah remained with Traffic for most of the seventies. His first solo effort, *Reebop* (1972), was recorded with Swedish musicians and released while he was still playing with Winwood. Others followed, the stand-out universally acknowledged to be 1977's Moroccan-flavoured *Trance*. By now this influential rhythmist had featured on recordings by The Rolling Stones and Eric Clapton, though his best work was arguably with German progressive bands Can and Zahara.

An unusual character who did not believe in investment, Kwaku-Baah spent his not inconsiderable wealth, owning several expensive properties and automobiles by the time he died. His impetuousness did not end there, either: in 1973 Kwaku-Baah was imprisoned for three months for assaulting two police officers and a cab driver.

The drummer's death from a cerebral haemorrhage while on stage in Stockholm stunned the music world. Reebop Kwaku-Baah's final work had been the hypnotic, throbbing 1982 'ethno-dance-floor' favourite 'Masimbabele' with The Unknown Cases – a single that was only released posthumously with his family's permission.

See also *Chris Wood (*☞ *July 1983); Ric Grech (*☞ *March 1990); Michael Karoli (*☞ *November 2001); Jim Capaldi (*☞ *January 2005)*

Friday 21

Lamar Williams
(Gulfport, Mississippi, 14 January 1949)
The Allman Brothers Band
Sea Level (We Three)

Lamar Williams became the latest casualty in the long-running saga that was The Allman Brothers Band. The tragic – and remarkably similar – deaths of celebrated founder Duane Allman (☞ *October 1971*) and original bassist Berry Oakley (☞ *November 1972*) had etched the group's legacy deep in stone before the death of second bassist Williams added to the sad mystique of this truly original band.

Two months after Oakley's passing, long-time percussionist 'Jaimoe' Johanny Johanson recommended a friend of his for the new role – that friend was Lamar Williams, an ex-Vietnam veteran who specialized in traditional R & B. The album *Brothers and Sisters* (1973) was in mid-construction when Oakley rode out on his Triumph for the last time, and – with dark fortune – Williams's input gave the band's by-now-familiar sound a warmth it mightn't otherwise have possessed. September/October 1973 saw a commercial high for the bereaved band, with the album topping the US charts for five weeks and the culled single 'Ramblin' Man' very nearly emulating it, while another group standard, Dick Betts's 'Jessica' (yes, the *Top Gear* theme) seemed cut from much the same cloth. While middle America embraced the easier-going, more radio-friendly sound, hardcore Brothers fans felt the music was not true to the roots of the uncompromising unit they'd grown to worship.

It was an Indian summer: with Betts and Greg Allman beginning solo careers, the band had started to fragment by 1976. Williams and band members Johanson and keyboardist Chuck Leavell (already recording as We Three) formed Sea Level with guitarist Jimmy Nalls – eventually pitching four albums of well-crafted jazz/R & B-tinged rock to Capitol. Williams and Leavell then astonished everyone by refusing to return to The Allman Brothers when the group made its inevitable comeback in 1979. This was Lamar Williams's last major move: he had been diagnosed with cancer, believed to have been caused by exposure to Agent Orange while serving in Vietnam. He died at home in Los Angeles.

See also *Allen Woody (*☞*August 2000)*

Friday 28

Billy Fury
(Ronald Wycherley – Wavertree, Liverpool, 17 April 1941)

Billy Fury used his brief time well, particularly since bouts of crippling rheumatic fever (he was hospitalized at age six and again at sixteen) had damaged young Ron Wycherley's heart. He shrugged off illness at seventeen to work the tugboats on the Mersey – thus exposing himself to the music

arriving across the ocean as rock 'n' roll's fire began to spread from the USA. Already a decent musician – he had learned both piano and guitar – Wycherley attempted to copy the slurred vocal of Elvis Presley, somehow impressing pop figurehead Larry Parnes. The months between October 1958 and May 1959 were extraordinary: hoping to offload two compositions on Marty Wilde, Wycherley was instead given a slot on Parnes's 'Extravaganza Show', immediately electrifying the Birkenhead crowd and others with his dazzling appearance and his own songs – the latter something of a rarity then. The only aspect that jarred was his name, but Parnes had the solution to that: he already had Marty Wilde, Vince Eager, Duffy Power and Dickie Pride – so why not 'Billy Fury'?

Fury's enviable chart career began with his own 'Maybe Tomorrow' for Decca in February 1959, sparking a remarkable run of twenty-four Top Forty UK entries during the sixties – a figure matched only by The Beatles. (Oddly, Fury never managed a number one, though 'Jealousy' would miss by just one place.) But Fury's medical history could not be ignored. In December 1971, a second heart attack saw the singer undergo major bypass surgery at just thirty. His ill health had already caused appearances to be cancelled, which proved seriously detrimental to his career. By this time Fury was with Parlophone, the hits having pretty much deserted him along with his health – and a four-year marriage to model Judith Hall also faltered in 1973. But all was far from lost: a revival in rock 'n' roll kitsch that year saw the likes of David Essex and Alvin Stardust score hits – and landed Fury a part in the former's film vehicle, *That'll be the Day*. Five Fury tracks also adorned a chart-topping soundtrack album.

But none of this could prevent Billy Fury from declaring bankruptcy by the mid seventies, and the former

heart-throb eventually retired to a farm in Wales. In 1982, with TV appearances and a potential comeback tour likely, Fury collapsed again from his heart condition, this time exacerbated by kidney problems. Fury – now partially blind and paralysed – was recording a new album when he was found unconscious by his housekeeper; he died later that day at St Mary's Hospital, London, and was buried a few days later in Paddington Cemetery.

See also *Larry Parnes (*☞*August 1989)*

FEBRUARY

Karen Carpenter

(New Haven, Connecticut, 2 March 1950)

The Carpenters

In 1971, a large sector of the rock community was dismissing The Carpenters as lightweight, inconsequential, even 'muzak': to some, their music was a trite trinket box younger sisters or parents might be fooled into parting with money for once in a while. But the truth is that Karen Carpenter possessed one of the finest female voices pop music has ever heard, a lithe tenor that rolled across her brother's, and many others', words and melodies. So while it's true to say that the world's most successful family duo had descended into music barely worthy of their name by the late seventies, those early albums will always stand up to any amount of airplay. More sobering, though, is the fact that Carpenter's myth is augmented by her sudden death from a previously unrecognized eating disorder.

Richard Carpenter was the apparent musician of the family, but tomboy Karen became fascinated by rhythm while playing glockenspiel in the school band to avoid geometry classes. The family had moved to the sunnier climes of Downey, California, and somehow 'KC' (as she was widely called) persuaded her parents to invest in a drum kit, her attempts to learn the flute falling by the wayside. In the autumn of 1964, with her brother at California State University majoring in music, Karen, on drums, joined him and bass-/tuba-player Wes Jacobs in The Richard Carpenter Trio. This group placed in the Hollywood Bowl Battle of the Bands, winning a contract with RCA – but all their tracks were rejected and the trio had disbanded by 1966, when Karen herself cut solo records for Joe Osborn's Magic Lamp label, even trying out (unsuccessfully) for Kenny Rogers's First Edition. Here that unique voice was first revealed, suggesting to many that the 'group' concept wasn't one to which Karen and Richard Carpenter were especially inclined. They finally persuaded Herb Alpert to allow them to cut their own multi-tracked vocals and instrumentation: the A&M founder agreed that this might just work.

The Carpenters' first release was a ballad version of The Beatles' 'Ticket to Ride' – an atypical debut that nonetheless airplayed them to Billboard fifty-four in May 1970. But what followed was spectacular. Two months later, '(They Long to be) Close to You' – a Bacharach/David composition that had flopped for Dionne Warwick some years before – shot to number one in America, followed by the similarly titled second album, which blueprinted the style that was to make The Carpenters a household name around the world. Further hits followed: 'We've Only Just Begun' (1970, US number two), 'For All We Know' (1971, number three and winner of a soundtrack Oscar), 'Rainy Days and Mondays', 'Superstar', 'Hurting Each Other' (1971–2, all number two) and so it continued. Overjoyed at their success, the US's hottest brother-and-sister duo purchased twin condominiums in Downey that they (perhaps a little tritely) named after their first pair of hits. Snatching a host of Grammys, The Carpenters – considered square by the rock and hippy fraternities – were, between 1970 and 1980, the country's biggest-selling group.

But though 'Top of the World' returned her to the top of the chart in October 1973, Karen Carpenter was far from feeling the sentiment in her own life. Maintaining a smile for the cameras, she confided to her friend Olivia Newton-John that what she really wanted was something a little more humble: a house behind a white picket fence, a loving relationship, children – sadly, she was never to achieve any of this. Sales showed little sign of diminishing and The Carpenters were now in demand as a live act, their Vegas-style show a massive commitment. Although a 1976 tour of Japan was the largest-grossing of its kind in history, six solid years in the studio and on the road left their mark on both Carpenters: Richard took a year off after developing an addiction to Quaaludes and methamphetamine which temporarily damaged his concentration; Karen's problems were more sinister still. By 1978 her weight had dropped to below 80 lbs – she was slowly starving herself to death.

Little was known about the insidious disease anorexia nervosa before the eighties, but experts believed that few who had suffered for five years or more could make a full recovery. So it proved for America's purest songstress. Carpenter – who had had weight problems since she was seventeen – seemed to be on the mend. She took time out to make a solo album in 1979 (which, largely due to her brother's reaction to the project, remained unreleased until thirteen years after her death), then married property

Karen Carpenter: She'd only just begun ...

developer Tom Burris the year after. It was a false dawn: in 1982, her marriage already on the slopes, Karen sank into depression, and finally admitted herself to hospital in her temporary home, New York.

On 3 February 1983, Karen Carpenter had intended to meet Newton-John for a session of chat and retail therapy, but this plan was vetoed by her concerned mother, who insisted the singer spend a long weekend away from the city at the family home. Her daughter reluctantly obliged, driving from yet another home, her condo in Century City, LA, to Downey. That evening, as the clan dined at Bob's Big Boy, she proudly announced that she had gained 15 lbs. But Karen's large portion of prawns, Caesar salad and tacos cut little ice with a gathering who could see little real light within her sunken eyes. The following morning, she rose,

put on a red jogging suit (later reported to have contained five different types of prescription drugs in its pockets) and, as her mother had requested, went to her old walk-in closet to sort out her clothes. Hearing a thump from the room above her, Agnes Carpenter discovered her daughter slumped in the closet. The autopsy released later that year stated that Karen Carpenter had died of pulmonary oedema and cardiotoxicity exacerbated by anorexia nervosa and cachexia (abnormal weight loss). On 8 February, some 500 mourners attended her funeral at Downey Methodist Church, Alpert, Bacharach and Newton-John all acting as honorary pall-bearers. Five hundred more waited outside. Karen Carpenter's body was interred at Forest Lawn, Cypress, California, and moved by her brother, twenty years later, to the family plot at Westlake Village.

'You win – I gain.'

Karen Carpenter's cryptic crochet message
above her New York hospital bed, 1982

APRIL

Tuesday 5

Danny Rapp
(Philadelphia, Pennsylvania, 10 May 1941)
Danny & The Juniors

In the wake of 'street corner' vocal groups like Frankie Lymon & The Teenagers, The Four Lads and Dion & The Belmonts came Danny & The Juniors, a quartet formed at John Bartram High School as The Juvenairs. Comprising Rapp (lead), founder Dave White (aka Tricker, first tenor), Frank Maffei (second tenor) and Joe Terry (aka Terranova, baritone) – the group are better remembered for one phenomenal hit record than for their vocal virtuosity. The Juvenairs pestered producer John Madara until he took them to Singular Records label heads Larry Brown and Artie Singer, who in turn contacted Dick Clark (of *American Bandstand*) in order that he should hear the renamed Danny & The Juniors perform. Clark liked one particular track, 'At the Hop' (written by themselves as 'Do the Bop'). In December 1957, the group appeared on the show as a last-minute replacement for Little Anthony & The Imperials: within a month the record – issued by ABC-Paramount – spent the first of an extraordinary seven weeks atop the US charts. Radio fervently played the follow-up 'Rock 'n' Roll is Here to Stay' (1958, a virtual rewrite of the debut), but the song only briefly scraped into the Top Twenty. Although Danny & The Juniors avoided the stigma of the one-hit wonder, their only boast from hereon was that single number five, 'Somehow I Can't Forget' (1959), was the first stereo 45. The game was pretty much up: Rapp and Terry found respite in their own New Jersey radio show in the early

seventies, but the great days had gone for ever.

Rapp moved into more conventional employment thereafter, becoming the assistant manager of an Arizona toy factory, though he did lead one of two touring groups under the band name. Prone to occasional binge drinking, Danny Rapp had been in a belligerent mood before a performance at Phoenix's Pointe Tapatio Resort and was later found in his room at a Quartzsite motel, having apparently shot himself.

Thursday 14

Pete Farndon
(Hereford, 12 June 1952)
The Pretenders
(The Bushwackers)

Less than a year after the unexpected death of former bandmate James Honeyman-Scott (*June 1982*), bassist Pete Farndon's equally needless passing did little more than prove that Pretenders' frontwoman Chrissie Hynde was right to dismiss him when she did.

A brash and wilful character in every sense, Farndon was expelled from school and was working as a site labourer when his love of earthy rock 'n' roll saw him gravitate towards Hereford's pub-rock scene at the start of the seventies. Farndon was very much the drifting sort: after a spell in Australia touring with successful Sydney band The Bushwackers, he took himself off to Hong Kong – where his predilection for recreational drugs surfaced. Returning to the UK in 1978, Farndon was called up for bass duty (by mutual friend and early member Gas Wild) with the fledgling Pretenders, one of the soon-to-be-great bands to emerge out of Britain's punk movement. Almost at the same time, the leather-clad Farndon and his

apparent soulmate, Ohio-born singer Chrissie Hynde, began a two-year affair that was to coincide with The Pretenders' most successful period. At the start of 1980, the couple – plus Farndon's old pal guitarist Honeyman-Scott and drummer Martin Chambers – celebrated a double UK number one with the single 'Brass In Pocket' and the group's eponymous debut album. Despite two strong hit singles in 'Talk of the Town' (1980) and 'Message of Love' (1981), the second album felt a long time coming, which did The Pretenders – and particularly Pete Farndon – few favours, to say the least. Farndon's split from Chrissie Hynde in 1981 was fast-tracked by his escalating heroin use. After a physically exhausting tour of the US, the Far East and Australia, Farndon was eventually sacked on 14 June 1982 by the group's leaders elect, Hynde and Honeyman-Scott, for what they told the press was 'incompatibility' – obviously a cover for his increasingly wayward behaviour. Then, by a sick quirk of fate, Honeyman-Scott was found dead just two days later.

The devastated Hynde (now dating Ray Davies of The Kinks) briefly entertained the thought of allowing Farndon back into The Pretenders, though Chambers and manager Dave Hill were set against it. Instead, Farndon sought out old friends Topper Headon (The Clash) and Rob Stoner (Chris Spedding) in the hope of putting together a new band. However, even as this new group was working on their initial songs, Pete Farndon was found dead in the bathtub of his London apartment, drowned during a heroin-induced sleep. The catalyst to the bassist's demise was left in little doubt – the needle was still in his arm.

Sunday 17

Felix Pappalardi

(The Bronx, New York, 20 December 1939)

Mountain

A classically trained drop-out from the University of Michigan, musician Felix Pappalardi found a niche in pop music (via a short stint in the US army), hanging with the early folksters of Greenwich Village, which put him in touch with characters like Joan Baez, Richie Havens and Tim Hardin. Less interested at the time in performing rock himself, Pappalardi moved into production and cemented a serious reputation very quickly indeed. After work with Baez, The Youngbloods and The Lovin' Spoonful, Pappalardi found his greatest success in this capacity with British supergroup Cream. It is his fine input that sets *Disraeli Gears* apart from every other rock release of 1967 – with *Wheels Of Fire* (1968) and *Goodbye* (1969) not far behind it. By now Pappalardi had teamed with Gail Collins, a talented songwriter (with whom he co-wrote the Cream classic 'Strange Brew') who, significantly, became his wife. On the disbanding of Cream, Pappalardi finally lived his rock dream by forming the early hard-rock unit Mountain. Full of trickery and knowing bombast, Mountain – Pappalardi (bass), Leslie West (guitar), Steve Knight (organ) and Lawrence 'Corky' Laing (drums) – were a huge hit on the live circuit, and they were yet another act who found greater attention at Woodstock, even enjoying a hit single the following year with 'Mississippi Queen'. Perhaps it was a bridge too far: the battle to become the world's loudest rock act saw Pappalardi quit Mountain two years later with serious hearing problems. His career was significantly quieter thereafter.

At 6 am on the morning of 17 April 1983, the New York Police Department received a nervous call from Gail Collins Pappalardi. Detectives from the East 21st Street stationhouse travelled the seven blocks to the Pappalardis' elegant fifth-floor Waterside Plaza apartment above East River. Felix Pappalardi was found lying prone in his underwear, a single bullet wound in his neck and a .38 by his body; he was pronounced dead at the scene. Collins – who had refused to answer any questions until she'd consulted her attorney – was later that day charged with possession of a firearm and second-degree murder. She maintained throughout that the shooting was 'accidental', and was later found guilty only of criminally negligent homicide, a verdict which so appalled trial judge Justice James Left that he castigated the jury for their leniency before the court, sentencing Pappalardi's widow to a maximum four years. His dismay seemed well-placed when it came to light that Pappalardi's eleven-month affair with singer/groupie Valerie Merians had recently been discovered by his wife; he'd also recently bought Collins the piece, of which, according to friends, she was 'very proud'.

Golden Oldies #2

Muddy Waters

(McKinley Morganfield – Rolling Fork, Mississippi, 4 April 1915)

A key figure in the development of Chicago blues, Muddy Waters was brought up in Clarksdale by his grandmother after his mother died when he was young. He acquired his nickname as a boy because he was given to playing in the local creek. Running his own juke joint, Waters proved himself to be a magnificent slide-guitar-player and a highly gifted songwriter who took his lead from Delta greats like Son House and Robert Johnson. The ubiquitous Alan Lomax had spotted Waters's talent, offering him in 1942 the chance to contribute songs to the famed Library of Congress recordings. Waters left the Delta for Chicago shortly afterwards, recording behind Sunnyland Slim for Chess and eventually fronting his own band (sometimes known as The Headhunters) in the early fifties – a bewildering collection of talent that included at one time or another Little Walter Jacobs (blues harp), Jimmy Rodgers (guitar), Otis Spann (piano), Big Crawford (bass) and Elgin Evans (aka Elgar Edmonds, drums). This band were responsible for some great sides, including 'Hoochie Coochie Man', 'Mannish Boy' and 'I'm Ready'. Waters had 'plugged in' by now and paved the way for many other blues artists reluctant to use electric instrumentation.

Influencing a host of white blues-players during the sixties and seventies, Waters then reversed the trend by recording the bizarre near-psychedelic rock albums *Electric Mud* (1968) and *After the Rain* (1969), before a 1969 automobile accident left him unable to tour for three years. After collecting six Grammys during the seventies, Muddy Waters was eventually diagnosed with cancer in 1982, undergoing the removal of a lung and intensive radiation therapy. Suffering a relapse on 29 April 1983, Waters was rushed to hospital in Illinois, where he died in his sleep after a cardiac arrest.

JUNE
Thursday 5
Stan Rogers
(Hamilton, Ontario, 29 November 1949)

Standing 6'4", Stan Rogers cut an imposing figure as he growled his way through songs both political and anecdotal but always with a Canadian flavour. Rogers had made the rare move from rock 'n' roll to folk, playing as a bassist when still a teenager, then surprising many with his 1977 debut, *Fogarty's Cove*, an album of roots-flavoured vignettes that, although not a big seller, won praise from critics and peers alike. Rogers continued to chronicle the history of his native land in further well-received studio releases – *Turnaround* (1978), *Northwest Passage* (1981) and his final outing *From Fresh Water* – issued just after his premature death.

Frequently on the road, Rogers was returning from a folk festival in Kerrville, Texas, when disaster struck his Air Canada DC-9. A freak fire in one of the craft's toilet facilities spread quickly, forcing the pilot into an emergency landing. Although the aeroplane touched down safely, the crew had gravely underestimated the severity of the situation. Twenty-three passengers were killed either by flash fire or from smoke inhalation. Stan Rogers was among the latter.

Friday 20
Walter Jackson
(Pensacola, Florida, 19 March 1938)
The Velvetones

Distinctive-voiced R & B singer Walter Jackson suffered adversity from the very start: stricken with polio as a boy, he played his first clutch of live performances on crutches, some with vocal troupe The Velvetones. OKeh label record-producer Carl Davis saw potential in this plucky talent and invited Jackson to Chicago, where he put him together with the young Curtis Mayfield. This pairing resulted in a string of R & B hits such as 'That's What Mama Say' (1963) and Jackson's biggest-seller, 'It's an Uphill Climb to the Bottom' (1967). One record that did not chart for Jackson was 'My Ship is Comin' In', which was later a massive UK hit for The Walker Brothers. Throughout the seventies, the bespectacled singer recorded for a number of labels, including Brunswick and Chi-Sound, becoming popular among the UK's Northern soul audience – although his only notable seller elsewhere was a cover of Morris Albert's dinner-club favourite 'Feelings' in 1976. Walter Jackson died from an unexpected cerebral haemorrhage at the age of just forty-five.

JULY
Tuesday 12
Chris Wood
(Birmingham, England, 24 June 1944)
Traffic
(Various acts)

Entranced by jazz as a boy, Chris Wood was a young obsessive who counted the flute, archaeology and bird-watching among his many hobbies. Despite also being an aspiring painter – he had been placed at the Royal Academy – he eschewed this to return to his home town to play the local clubs with the likes of Christine Perfect (later McVie, of Fleetwood Mac) and Carl Palmer (later of Emerson, Lake & Palmer). Wood's sister Stephanie was costume designer for the up-and-coming Steve Winwood (already something of a local celebrity), who was instantly taken with this new face. The result was that Chris Wood played sax on ten Traffic albums as the band grew in stature, including the Top Ten-placing *Mr Fantasy* (1967) and *Traffic* (1968); there was also a clutch of hit singles such as 1967's massive 'Hole in My Shoe'. By 1968 he was already taking part in sessions with the then largely unknown Jimi Hendrix and toured with Dr John's band – marrying one of his singers, Jeanette Jacobs. Wood also became heavily dependent upon alcohol at this time, initially to deal with his fear of flying.

In 1970, Traffic re-formed after a sabbatical (Winwood had joined 'supergroup' Blind Faith for a year), but Wood's playing was suffering because of his addiction (he had now added substantial drug use to his alcohol intake). Traffic split in 1975, Wood's marriage likewise a few years after; nevertheless, he was shattered by the unexpected death of his ex-wife in January 1982. Though his own health was beginning to fail, Chris Wood managed to play a few sessions (including work with The Small Faces and John Martyn) and had his own project ready by the time he died from liver failure and pneumonia, at St Mary's Hospital, Birmingham.

See also *Reebop Kwaku-Baah (☞ January 1983); Ric Grech (☞ March 1990); Jim Capaldi (☞ January 2005)*

AUGUST

Tuesday 2

James 'Jamie' Jamerson
(Charleston, South Carolina, 29 January 1938)
The 'Funk Brothers'

The 'Funk Brothers' – with Jamerson *middle left*: Motown's backbone

Overcoming the stigma of a severe limp, Jamie Jamerson left home a nervous young guitarist to become one of the most revered bass-players soul music has yet known, inducted into the Rock 'n' Roll Hall of Fame in 2000.

After he moved to Detroit at fifteen, Jamerson's talent on the bass eventually drew the attention of Berry Gordy – who later dubbed the musician 'a genius of improvisation'. Among Motown's wealth of great talent it was hard to shine, but the house band known unofficially as the 'Funk Brothers' was all the richer for Jamerson's colossal input. Some of the hundred-plus hits to which he contributed include The Temptations' 'My Girl' (1965) and 'I'm Gonna Make You Love Me' (1968), The Four Tops' 'Standing in the Shadows of Love' (1966), Marvin Gaye's 'I Heard It through the Grapevine' (1968) and 'What's Going On?' (1971) and countless Miracles, Martha Reeves, Supremes and Stevie Wonder songs. Better still, name a favourite Motown classic and the chances are it's Jamerson's bass holding the piece together. However, since Jamie Jamerson's sad death from pneumonia exacerbated by alcoholism, there have been legal wrangles following the claims of bassist Carol Kaye to have played on many of these hits. A number of soul luminaries, including writing team Holland/Dozier/Holland, have come out in vehement support of Jamerson's extraordinary legacy.

See also *'Benny' Benjamin (☞ May 1969); Earl Van Dyke (☞ September 1992); Robert White (☞ October 1994). Other occasional 'Funk Brothers' Eddie 'Bongo' Brown (1984), 'Pistol' Allen and Johnny Griffith (both 2002) have also died.*

Wednesday 3

Jobriath
(Bruce Wayne Campbell – Pennsylvania, 14 December 1946)
(Pidgeon)

Today, Jobriath is spoken of as the first openly gay rock star: well, he may have been gay, but only a small minority of fans – Elton John and Morrissey among them, no doubt – could name one solitary song of his. To be fair to him, Jobriath (variously Jobriath Boone, Jobriath Salisbury) was a more talented performer than he is widely given credit for, but the level of management and label hype propelling him would probably have capsized the career of anyone – perhaps even David Bowie, to whose songs Jobriath's sagas of forbidden gay love and alien intervention were most often compared. Jobriath had, already, been a singer with late-sixties also-rans Pidgeon, and also appeared in an early cast of the musical *Hair*. But signed as a solo 'force' with Elektra in 1972, he was a dismal commercial failure: after two albums, *Jobriath* (1973) and *Creatures of the Street* (1974), Elektra ditched the singer – who subsequently moved into cabaret, re-emerging as Cole Berlin. One of rock's earliest AIDS-related casualties, Jobriath died a recluse in his apartment at the Chelsea Hotel – the scene of Nancy Spungen's death five years previously. The singer's body is believed to have not been discovered until several days after his passing.

Despite denial from its director Todd Haynes, many claim that Ewan McGregor's character in the 1998 movie *Velvet Goldmine* was based on a combination of Jobriath and Iggy Pop. Morrissey, meanwhile, attempted to hire Jobriath for a 1992 tour, unaware that the singer had been dead for almost a decade.

> **'Klaus Nomi was rock's queerest exponent.'**
>
> Rupert Smith, writer

Saturday 6

Klaus Nomi
(Klaus Sperber – Bavarian Alps, Germany, 24 January 1944)

An even more curious gender-bending performer than Jobriath was Klaus Nomi; by tragic coincidence, he died just three days later – his ultimate fate eerily similar.

Nomi began his working days as an usher at the Berlin Opera, his post-performance renditions of whatever had gone before proving popular

with colleagues. But the significant difference between Nomi and Jobriath was that he, unlike his US counterpart, was Bowie-approved. The pair had met after Nomi – now relocated to New York, where he worked as a pastry chef at the World Trade Center – was approached by the British star to back him on a 1979 television appearance. Dressed like a cross between a kabuki robot and a box of mid-price chocolates, Nomi straddled the parallel worlds of rock and disco, his voice similarly vaulting between counter-tenor and ear-splitting falsetto as he camped his way through covers of popular tunes and opera. Footage of one of his most distinctive

Klaus Nomi: A shadow of his former self

performances, 'Total Eclipse', was memorably broadcast by the BBC's *Old Grey Whistle Test* in 1980 – RCA saw fit to sign him up as a result.

But, following a 1981–2 world tour, Nomi's near-skeletal appearance shocked New York friends; it was clear all was not well. Doctors, not yet fully aware of the effects of AIDS, acknowledged that his immune system had all but broken down and diagnosed a malignant skin sarcoma. Confined to his apartment, Klaus Nomi passed away quietly. His funeral appropriately involved Wagnerian-style thunder at deafening pitch and a black-clad siren cavorting at his casket.

Wednesday 17

Mikey Smith

(Michael Smith – Jamaica, 1954)

Graduating in 1980 from the Jamaica School of Drama, reggae poet Mikey Smith had already issued the dub poem for which he would be best remembered, the powerful 'Mi Cyaan Believe It' (1978). The latter, released on Island in the UK, had been written shortly after the young and politically motivated performer had represented Jamaica at the 11th World Festival of Youth and Students. Smith was an able though headstrong poet, prepared to speak passionately about the struggle against poverty faced by many in his homeland. Which often caused friction with his opponents.

On 16 August 1983, Mikey Smith attended a political meet at Stony Hill where the Jamaica Labour Party Minister for Culture/Education, Olivia Grange, addressed the gathering. Smith – a fierce opponent of her views – allegedly heckled the speaker, for which he was greatly chastised. Twenty-four hours later,

he was set upon by JLP activists, who apparently attacked him with stones: one blow to the head proved fatal and the young reggae artist died later that day. Nobody has ever been brought to account over the slaying. In the words of fellow poet Linton Kwesi Johnson, 'Smith was one of the most interesting, original poetic voices to emerge from the English-speaking Caribbean during the twentieth century. His poetry was a means of giving hope, building awareness as a part of the whole process of liberation.'

SEPTEMBER

Thursday 15

Prince Far I

(Michael James Williams – Spanish Town, Jamaica, 1944)

In an increasingly dark year for reggae, Prince Far I became the latest Jamaican star to be murdered. Known as 'The Voice of Thunder', this genial giant of a DJ proved one of the most original stylists in seventies dub: although he was not much of a singer, his stream-of-consciousness rants were a marvel to behold. An imposing figure, Far I (then plain old Michael Williams) was employed by Clement 'Coxsone' Dodd as a bouncer at the fabled Studio One, only realizing his recording potential when veteran toaster DJ King Stitt failed to make a session. Far I stepped in and the result was one of his finest pieces of improvisation, 'Queen of the Minstrel' (1970). Taking a while to find his true voice, Prince Far I had to wait until 1976 to record a full debut album, *Psalms For I*, under the name by which he was to be known for the rest of his days. The year after, Far I's seminal 'Heavy Manners' single wryly

addressed Jamaica's overly stringent anti-crime policies. The powerful and widely felt diatribe divided Jamaican public opinion (the likes of Culture had already prophesied an upcoming apocalypse in their 'Two Sevens Clash') – but Prince Far I's polemic would nonetheless sound hollowly ironic just six years later. Far I established his own Cry Tough label – providing an outlet for himself and artists of similar standpoint – while also working with the notorious Roots Radics (aka Dub Syndicate). By the turn of the decade Far I was making considerable headway in Britain, where he was spending more and more time, his records regularly championed by John Peel and On-U label founder Adrian Sherwood.

In fact, all seemed well for this powerhouse of Jamaican culture until his death in 1983 at the hands of armed robbers who had broken into his Kingston home. Prince Far I – the latest victim of the Jamaican street crime that the government had singularly failed to quell – was shot twice in the stomach, and died at the scene.

NOVEMBER

Tuesday 8

Little James Booker

(James Carroll Booker III – New Orleans, Louisiana, 17 December 1939)

(Booker Boy & The Rhythmaires)

Players as diverse as Dr John, Allen Toussaint and Harry Connick Jr have all paid tribute to one jazz/blues pianist whose unique style inspired them: James Booker. Mastering the piano by the time he was eight years old, Booker ('JC' to his friends) was always likely to become one of the genre's more wayward characters. Aged ten, he was dragged thirty feet by a speeding ambulance in a horrific accident, and very nearly lost his leg; as it was, the eight fractures he received left him with a limp for the rest of his days, while the misplaced administration of painkilling morphine by the vehicle's paramedics prefaced a later drug dependency. A year on, The Piano Prince of New Orleans had his own gospel slot on WMRY, while at just fourteen, Booker – with his band, The Rhythmaires – became the youngest musician ever to record on Imperial. One of the prodigy's first jobs was to record Fats Domino's piano parts so that the constantly touring star need only add his own vocals. In fact, Booker's mimicking of the styles of top R & B pianists was so uncanny that Chess even employed him to tour as Huey 'Piano' Smith. Booker took time out from recording (after difficulties over his age and contracts) to enrol, in 1960, at university in Baton Rouge. However, his drug use became greater and he soon returned to work to support the habit. Throughout the sixties, James Booker recorded with a plethora of top-notch singers and musicians – Little Richard, Wilson Pickett and B B King among them – before a move to New York's Atlantic Records hooked him up with Jerry Wexler, King Curtis and Aretha Franklin, who recorded Booker's own 'So Swell When You're Well'. Much of the time, though, the pianist was far from 'well' – around this time, he lost an eye after getting a beating from some producers he had tried to defraud, though for the flamboyant and openly gay Booker, it was merely an excuse to wear a series of elaborate, glittery eyepatches on stage.

A promising partnership with Dr John was, however, curtailed by Booker's increasing drug use; the rogue musician then allegedly conned money from the bands of Fats Domino, Joe Tex and even Marvin Gaye before disappearing to New Orleans. Drugs were now a major part

Badfinger before tragedy: Gibbins, Mollard, Ham and Evans

of his life, and he was imprisoned for heroin possession for six months in 1971. Although he played sessions for big names like Ringo Starr and The Doobie Brothers, Booker's better days were slipping into the past. Live, he was still a wondrous experience, but his lifestyle promoted a seizure in 1982 that sounded alarm bells to everyone bar himself. Booker then took the unlikely step of taking a day job as a filing clerk to make ends meet, but he was already on borrowed time. Although doctors had told him that his liver had suffered irreparable damage, Booker took a critical dose of low-grade cocaine which prompted heart and lung failure. James Booker sat unattended for half an hour at Charity Hospital, New Orleans, before staff discovered that the one-time keyboard wizard was already dead.

Tom Evans
(Liverpool, 5 June 1947)
Badfinger
(The Dodgers)

Protégés of The Beatles, Badfinger must have felt in 1970 that they'd backed a winner signing to The Fab Four's new Apple imprint. Starting out as The Iveys, Tom Evans (rhythm/bass) and his co-founder, singer and pianist Pete Ham, issued a number of flop singles before Paul McCartney's 'Come and Get It' (1970) changed their fortunes, released under the new name of Badfinger. As The Beatles themselves fell apart, Badfinger appeared to slot into the gap they had left with a series of transatlantic hits, also supporting solo Beatles on their albums. The hits, however, did not last beyond 1972. Legal wrangles between

> **'There was no lasting nastiness in Tom, just an ever-growing sadness in the situation he found himself in. Just like Peter [Ham], he was quite a sensitive guy who was easily worn down by the negative pressures put on him.'**
>
> Bob Jackson, ex-Badfinger

Apple and Badfinger's management meant that royalties from chart success did not reach the writers, ie, Ham and Evans – the partners could only look on in disbelief as 'Without You' (a track from the group's second album) became an international multiplatinum success for Harry Nilsson. This situation became too much for Pete Ham: the group's founder first quit the line-up and then, tragically, committed suicide in his garage studio (➤ *April 1975*). Tom Evans was distraught at the death of his close friend and Badfinger disbanded, after which Evans and another bandmate, Bob Jackson, joined The Dodgers – though this was not to last. Having trained as an engineer years earlier, the guitarist cut his losses and returned for a few years to technical drawing – only to reform Badfinger with early collaborator Joey Molland, though two albums (around the turn of the eighties) were badly received.

Depressed by the continuing royalty disputes which had dogged the band's earlier career (and which had by now caused a massive rift with Molland), Tom Evans emulated his late colleague by hanging himself from a tree in his garden in Weybridge, Surrey. It is widely believed that Evans had also recently been diagnosed with a malignant throat tumour. Like Ham, he left a widow and child.

See also *Mike Gibbins (➤ October 2005)*

DECEMBER

Sunday 18

Jimmy Nolen

(Oklahoma City, Oklahoma, 3 April 1934)
James Brown
(The Johnny Otis Show)
(Maceo & All The King's Men)

An innovator of R & B/funk guitar, Jimmy Nolen, with his distinctive 'chopped' seventh and ninth chords, was an influence on many who followed, including Sly Stone, Chic's Nile Rodgers, most P-Funk practitioners and arguably even Jimi Hendrix, not to mention a slew of rock acts who adopted funk rhythms at the beginning of the eighties. Nolen – one of nine siblings brought up on an Oklahoma farm – grew up listening to T-Bone Walker, which persuaded him to ditch his violin lessons and take up the guitar instead. At nineteen, he joined blues singer Jimmy Wilson's band on tour, and then settled in Los Angeles. Nolen's work could be heard on The Johnny Otis Show Top Ten hit, 'Willie and the Hand Jive' (1958). The ambitious Nolen then fronted his own unit, eventually impressing James Brown sufficiently that the 'Godfather' recruited him in 1965. Perhaps the best-remembered example of Nolen's work is one of the first recorded with Brown – the classic 'Papa's Got a Brand New Bag' (1965). Despite a two-year break touring with sax-player Maceo Parker, Nolen stayed loyal to Brown and his various incarnations until he died from a heart attack at the age of forty-nine.

Tuesday 27

Walter Scott

(Walter Notheis Jr – St Louis, Missouri, 7 February 1943)
Bob Kuban & The In-Men

Here's an interesting one: lead singer of one-hit-wonder act from the sixties enjoys national hit about marital infidelity – only to fall foul of similar real-life scenario.

Bob Kuban's band The In-Men had been a going concern for a short while before the arrival of singer 'Sir' Walter Scott appeared to be the last piece of the jigsaw. His dynamic vocal style gave the band an edge, and, in 1966, the eight-strong St Louis pop act appeared to have cracked the big time with the infectious hit '(Look out for) The Cheater': the song, which warned of the dangers of having an affair, took the band high into Billboard's Hot 100. For some reason, Scott decided fame wasn't for him and walked away from it to front a local band, touring covers throughout the seventies. Success wasn't to be repeated for The In-Men, so perhaps it was the right move, though Scott and Kuban reconciled to perform once again for the TV cameras early in 1983 – which worked so well that the pair began planning for a twentieth anniversary reunion for the whole band the following June. By now Scott was divorced from his unfaithful wife, JoAnn.

At 7 pm two days after Christmas, Scott left his home in St Peters to purchase a car battery and mysteriously disappeared – his car was found abandoned at a local airport. Nothing was heard from or about Walter Scott for nearly four years – during which time his ex-wife and her lover, Scott's neighbour Jim Williams, were married. Then, on 10 April 1987, a grisly discovery was made in Williams's backyard: Scott's badly decomposed body – still hog-tied – face down in a concrete water cistern. On finding bullet wounds to his back, police rapidly accused Williams of his slaying – and began a double murder enquiry on discovering that Williams's former wife, Sharon, had also been killed. Despite the seemingly overwhelming evidence, the trial took nine years to reach court – largely due to the persistence of Scott's elderly parents, even then. Williams was given two concurrent life sentences without appeal, while JoAnn Notheis was sentenced to five years for hindering the investigation. Both parties continue to protest their innocence.

Dennis Wilson

(Inglewood, California, 4 December 1944)
The Beach Boys

'Maybe I just like a fast life – I wouldn't give it up for anything in the world. It won't last for ever either, though the memories will.' Dennis Wilson

Dennis Wilson only ever wanted freedom. It informed his life and, arguably, his death. The ocean offered him release and his ability to ride the waves, to his mind, made him the master of it. None of the other Beach Boys could surf, thus, in 1961, it was Dennis's favourite pastime that prompted The Beach Boys' great success. The extended freedom brought by this great success, however, encouraged pursuits of a more contentious nature.

The middle son of Murry and Audree Wilson, Dennis lacked the musical instinct of older brother Brian – rightly seen as the genius behind The Beach Boys' sound – but was game to learn the four-part harmonies his brother loved so much in the songs of The Four Freshmen. Under the regime imposed upon them by their father/manager, the brothers, Brian, Dennis and Carl – along with cousin Mike Love and college buddy Al Jardine – set about blueprinting the sound that would change the face of American pop music in the sixties. Dennis Wilson, happy to remain in the background as his brothers took the fore, taught himself the drums. Thus, The Pendletones became The Beach Boys (Dennis's suggestion), who became the top new group of the era with a series of hedonistic hits that focused on either the 'hot doggers' who graced the waves ('Surfin' Safari', 'Surfin' USA', 'Surfer Girl') or the hot rods that raced California's boulevards ('Little Deuce Coupe', 'Fun, Fun, Fun'). Behind the apparent joy of their music, though, The Beach Boys were subject to extreme discipline at the hands of frustrated songwriter Murry Wilson. For his part, Dennis quite literally had his hands burned as a boy for playing with matches. 'He beat the crap out of me,' the percussionist would much later admit. Another of his

The Beach Boys – Clockwise from top: Dennis Wilson, Brian Wilson, Al Jardine, Mike Love and Carl Wilson: Hang on to your tuxedo

father's punishments was to remove his glass eye, stand nose-to-nose with Dennis – and knock him across the room if he even flinched. The result for Wilson was not the heightened respect his father demanded but the escalation of an already troubled lifestyle as The Beach Boys' success grew and grew.

In 1966, The Beatles were cleaning up across America, their increasingly imaginative skewing of rock 'n' roll's original manifesto forcing the Wilsons to rethink much of their own output. The result was Brian Wilson's inspired *Pet Sounds*, an album believed by many to be a riposte to The Fab Four's *Revolver*, though it stands up as an epoch-defining record without any such comparison, as rich

in light as it is mellow in shade. Brian's increased use of hallucinogenics was apparent by now – but over the next eighteen months pretty much all of the band had gradually been drawn further and further into LA's hippy/drug scene. At a commune, Dennis befriended an apparently down-on-his-luck musician called Charlie, who swiftly moved himself and members of his 'Family' into Dennis's home on Sunset Boulevard and relieved the musician of some $100K. The Charlie in question was the demonic Charles Manson, who in 1969 committed a series of well-documented murders, including the infamous mass slaughter at the home of Sharon Tate, the then pregnant actress wife of film director Roman Polanski. Clearly, Dennis had no inkling of this a year previously, but was sufficiently concerned to have turfed The Family out of his house – though not before one of Manson's songs, 'Never Learn Not to Love' (originally written as 'Cease To Exist'), had been recorded by The Beach Boys. After the heavily amended track was issued (on 1969's *20/20*), an incensed Manson revealed his mania by pulling a .45 on Wilson and threatening to kidnap his sons. (On learning later of Dennis Wilson's death, the incarcerated but unrepentant Manson snarled: 'He was killed by my shadow because he took my music and changed the words from my soul.')

During the next few years Wilson's live work suffered and side projects foundered. One such was a duo with then unknown Daryl Dragon (later of Captain & Tennille fame), which fell apart in 1971 after the drummer severed several tendons putting his hand through a window. This also saw him bow out temporarily from The Beach Boys, who by 1974 were reduced to touring their hits to a new audience. In this decade, The Beach Boys managed only one Top Ten hit in their homeland (and even this was a cover – 'Rock 'n' Roll Music' by early influence Chuck Berry in 1976). Wilson, however, became the first Beach Boy to release a solo record in 1977, although neither of his two albums proffered much commercial return.

Dennis Wilson somehow found the confidence to return to the band during the late seventies and, briefly, the rough-hewn 'background Beach Boy' was perhaps the most popular with their female audience. Wilson's way with the opposite sex was widely known: he was to be married five times – twice to model/actress Karen Lamm in the seventies – and in 1979, after a brief affair with Christine McVie of Fleetwood Mac, he took up with 18-year-old Shawn Love. If the age gap didn't turn heads, the fact that she was widely believed to be the illegitimate daughter of Mike Love probably did. Wilson won support from some family members in his attempts to persuade her father to acknowledge his responsibility – something Love denies to the present day. The internal pressure between the two, allied with Wilson's continued reliance on alcohol and drugs, grew so intense that the only solution appeared to be to bar Wilson from concerts. Near-destitute, Wilson holed up on his 62-foot yacht, *Harmony* (his only real possession), until he had to sell it to meet debts – by now he was hitting the bottle as soon as the sun was up. With his situation becoming critical, the other Beach Boys somehow found it in themselves to pull him back on board in 1981 – but Wilson's world had become so enshrouded by his drinking that this merely postponed his fate.

Three days after Christmas in 1983, he frolicked on board *Emerald*, the yawl of his friend Bob Oster, at California's Marina del Rey. Here, Wilson boasted how he had lasted his latest detox course – perhaps not seeing the irony in giving out such information at the same time as tucking away several celebratory vodkas. Late in the afternoon, Wilson began diving off the slip where his own yacht had once been moored, retrieving a bizarre array of sea-corroded junk he had thrown from his craft years before, including a silver-framed photograph of Lamm. He was in a playful mood, so Oster and others gathered (including Wilson's latest girlfriend, Colleen McGovern) were unperturbed as he continued to plunge into twelve feet of murky, freezing water clad only in cut-offs and a face mask. When he failed to surface, his friends remained calm, believing the Beach Boy to be hiding – he was known for playing practical jokes. The penny dropped as they searched the local bars around the increasingly deserted marina. At about 5.30 pm, Dennis Wilson's lifeless body was retrieved from the water by passing harbour-patrol divers. Coroners put his death down to drowning, but a more thorough investigation suggested that, heavily under the influence, Wilson had hit his head on the underside of the slip, losing consciousness before he drowned. The 'endless summer' was over for the teenage hedonist who never really grew up.

A thirty-minute funeral three days later brought together many from Dennis Wilson's past and present, including his mother, brothers Brian and Carl, Wilson's first wife, Carol Freedman, and their daughter, Jennifer, second wife, Barbara Charren, and their two sons, Karen Lamm and Wilson's estranged teenage bride, Shawn Love, and their one-year-old son, Gage. With a special dispensation from President Reagan, non-serviceman Wilson was then given the burial at sea that he had always wanted.

See also *Carl Wilson (☛ February 1998)*

Lest We Forget

Other notable deaths that occurred sometime during 1983:

Winifred Atwell (Trinidadian pianist with an impressive series of 1950s UK hits – including chart-toppers 'Let's Have Another Party' and 'Poor People of Paris'; born Tunapuna, 27/2/14; unknown, 28/2)

Gene Bricker (US second tenor with integrated Pittsburgh vocal act The Marcels, who had a US/UK #1 with 1961's great 'Blue Moon'; born Pennsylvania, *c* 1941; unknown, 10/12)

Black Randy (US singer with LA punk outlaws Black Randy & The Metro Squad, whose set list included 'Idi Amin' and 'Loner with a Boner'; born John 'Jackie' Morris, California; HIV complications)

Larry Darnell (powerful early US R & B vocalist; born Ohio, 21/12/1928; lung cancer, 3/7)

Sidney Dunbar (US doo-wop bass with The Calvanes, a.k.a. The Nuggets; heart attack)

Richard Hughes (US rock drummer with Johnny Winter (1973–74); born 31/3/1950; suicide)

Hugh Mundell (gifted young Jamaican reggae artist/ producer; born East Kingston, 14/7/1962; shot dead after an argument over a stolen refrigerator while in a car with singer Junior Reid)

Clarence E Quick (US bass/founder of inter-racial vocal group The Del(l)-Vikings, also writer of their 1957 US Top Five hit 'Come Go with Me'; born New York, 2/2/1937; heart attack, 5/5)

Ray Tunia (US pianist/arranger with The Ink Spots; born 10/5/1916; unknown, 16/8)

Annelle Zingarelli (US punk vocalist with the oh-so-shocking NBJ; heroin overdose, 23/10 – two other band members, bassist Stain Farrington and drummer Mark Wills, have also died)

For a complete list of fallen artists, visit

www.numberoneinheaven.com

JANUARY

Sunday 1

Alexis Korner

(Paris, France, 19 April 1928)
CCS
Blues Incorporated
Alexis Korner's Blues Band
(Various acts)

One of the most significant names in the foundation of British blues, Alexis Korner arrived in the UK via France, Switzerland and North Africa – just in time for the London Blitz. He drowned out the swooping doodlebugs with a mix of American blues, learning to play along on piano and guitar. Preferring acoustic to the electric variant beginning to emerge, Korner joined Chris Barber's band at twenty-one and Ken Colyer's three years later, before playing London's circuit as a duo with harmonica-playing Cyril Davies. (By this time, Korner had accepted electric blues and was fast becoming one of its most respected white practitioners.)

The breakthrough came with the formation of the legendary Blues Incorporated, which also featured Ken Scott (piano), Dick Heckstall-Smith (saxophone) and a series of vocalists including John Baldry and Art Wood – the latter was the older brother of later Rolling Stone/Face Ron Wood, and members of both bands were frequently at Blues Inc's concerts. Ironically, the success of these blues-tinged rock bands, and others like The Animals, Yardbirds and Cream, was to deflect attention from the work of players like Korner. Nevertheless, he found a niche in broadcasting playing his favourite music until commercial success was finally forthcoming with CCS: the 25-strong mega-band enjoyed a series of hit singles between 1970 and 1972, among them a version of Led Zeppelin's 'Whole Lotta Love' and popular pub singalong 'Tap Turns on the Water'. Korner also took a speaking role on Hot Chocolate's 'Brother Louie' (1973). Korner's last supergroup, in the early eighties, was Rocket 88 – which at one time featured Jack Bruce on bass, Ian Stewart on piano and Charlie Watts on the drums. By 1982, though, his health was in serious decline and – a chain smoker most of his life – the 'father of British blues' died of lung cancer on New Year's Day 1984.

See also *Ian Stewart (☞ December 1985); Long John Baldry (☞ July 2005). Dick Heckstall-Smith died just months before Baldry (2004).*

Thursday 12

Stephen 'Tebes' Douglass

(Columbus, Ohio, 11 August 1950)
McGuffey Lane

McGuffey Lane's first hit was 'Making a Living's Been Killing Me' – a pertinent title, given their later history. Although their name might be forgotten now, this country-rock band seemed destined for major success at the start of the eighties, only to have their hopes dashed by a mixture of bad luck and tragedy. The band was formed by guitarist Terry Efaw and bassist Steve Reis, whose Athens, Ohio, address gave the act its unusual name. The group was swelled by Bobby Gene McNelly (vocals/guitar), John Schwab (guitar), Dick Smith (drums) and finally Stephen Douglass (keyboards/harmonica). Shifting 40,000 copies of their debut album (on their own label), McGuffey Lane were picked up by Atco, and – with tours alongside The Allman Brothers and The Charlie Daniels Band lined up – success seemed a fraction away. Radio hits such as 'Long Time Lovin' You' (1980) and 'Start It All Over' (1981) only strengthened this belief, though the band made it clear they had a specific audience in mind by shifting allegiance to Atlantic

American Records, a chiefly country label.

With the 1984 album *Day By Day* poised for release, Douglass died in a freak car accident returning from a gig. The record was subsequently dedicated to his memory, though McNelly was unable to continue, moving into songwriting before his own death in shocking circumstances almost exactly three years later (☞ *January 1987*).

eat Jackie Wilson: He's in heaven

Jackie Wilson

(Jack Leroy Wilson – Highland Park, Michigan,
9 June 1934)

(Billy Ward & The Dominoes)

For many decades his rich falsetto-tenor has been regarded as one of the greatest soul voices of all time, and his stage dynamism cited as an influence by singers as diverse as Elvis Presley, Michael Jackson and Levi Stubbs – yet behind Jackie Wilson's huge success lies a tale of unrelenting poverty, disloyalty, promiscuity and continued personal upset.

Wilson was not given the greatest start in life: his father was seldom employed, generally broke and had been an alcoholic since before his only child was born. This inevitably had an effect on the boy, who himself began drinking at the age of nine. And despite singing gospel with The Ever Ready Singers, Wilson – who lived in Detroit's problem North End district – was frequently in trouble and constantly skipped classes to hang with his 'Shakers' gang stooges. At sixteen he was placed in a correctional institute, where he lied about his age to join a boxing club – though after becoming a Golden Gloves welterweight champion, Wilson heeded his mother's wishes and gave up the sport to concentrate on singing.

Ubiquitous talent-show lurker Johnny Otis picked out 'Sonny' Wilson as having real potential – the singer was already displaying signs of the dynamic stage presence he was to become in time. After a couple of false starts, Wilson took a deserved place in Billy Ward's Dominoes, replacing Drifters-bound lead/tenor Clyde McPhatter in the process. With The Dominoes, Wilson experienced his first pop crossover success with 'St Therese of the Roses' (1956). The million-selling solo hit 'Lonely Teardrops' (1958) put the singer high into the US Top Ten, but the first hiccup in his career was the death of his manager, Al Green (no relation), with a deal with Brunswick on the table: this opened the door for the far less scrupulous Nat Tarnopol. This Greek businessman – rumoured to have mob connections – took Wilson to Decca instead, and saw fit to ditch his blossoming songwriting team, Berry Gordy and Roquel 'Billy' Davis, over a payment disagreement. Wilson trusted the man implicitly and foolishly handed over power of attorney to him. The hit records continued, but it was clear to most that intrusive arrangements were giving Wilson little space in which to express himself fully. Tarnopol misguidedly believed that rock 'n' roll was a mere fad and encouraged Wilson to spurn his own instincts and lean towards a more sterile supper-club audience.

However, if his songs lacked red blood, the singer himself did not: Jackie Wilson's reputation as something of a womanizer was becoming common knowledge. The now established singer – who'd been married to childhood girlfriend Freda Hood since 1951 – made another error of judgement in taking not one but two mistresses. The first was Harlean Harris, an aspiring *Ebony* model and former lover of the ill-fated Sam Cooke, the second an extremely volatile fan named Juanita Jones. When the latter eventually learned of the former, she followed Wilson and Harris home on 15 February 1961 and shot the singer twice in the stomach. Although Wilson fared better than Cooke (*Pre-1965*), he lost a kidney in intensive care and was to carry one of the bullets in his body for the rest of his days. Pressure from his management to fudge the story put Wilson in the bizarre position of defending his assailant's motives, suggesting that she was depressed and that he'd prevented her from committing suicide; Jones escaped all charges scot-free. In pain and temporarily unable to work, Wilson then suffered the humiliation of learning he was broke and having his home seized by the IRS. The reason for this was clear: Tarnopol had pocketed all his earnings while Wilson was incapacitated. *This* hurdle was overcome (by arrangement with the tax office), but Hood had understandably run out of patience with her wandering partner and filed for divorce.

With fewer hit records, Wilson remained in a dire financial situation which wasn't helped by a scandal involving him, his drummer Jimmy Smith and a pair of white girls (this was 1967) in a motel room. The agreed-on glue to mend Wilson's shattered public image was a hastily arranged marriage to Harris. Oddly, despite all this turmoil surrounding him, Wilson produced two dazzling soul gems at this time: '(Your Love Keeps Lifting Me) Higher and Higher' (1967) and 'I Get the Sweetest Feeling' (1968). Then, in 1970, the once-more-separated Wilson had to deal with the first of several tragedies involving his children: caught in the crossfire of a domestic argument, his eldest son, 16-year-old Jackie Jr, was shot and killed on a neighbour's porch. (Two of the singer's daughters were also to die young.)

In and out of drug rehabilitation, his career having spluttered for many years, Jackie Wilson was given a last opportunity by promoter and presenter Dick Clark on his 'Travelling Oldies Revue' – but what might have been looked upon as a sad conclusion to a glittering career was to prove heartbreaking and tragic. Having finally broken free of his management, a seemingly revitalized Wilson performed at the Latin Casino in Cherry Hill, New Jersey, on 25 September 1975. But, as he built up to a crescendo in the song 'Lonely Teardrops', Wilson suffered a massive heart attack and collapsed in front of hundreds of onlookers. His body dropped from the stage on to a concrete floor below, his head talking the full brunt of the fall. Although his breathing was restarted (reportedly by quick-acting Cornell Gunter of The Coasters), Wilson's career effectively ended there and then. He regained consciousness after three months (giving his family false hope), but Wilson was brain-damaged, and the last seven years of his life were spent in a vegetative state (in 1977, he was institutionalized at the Medford Leas Retirement Community). Wilson was just forty-one in 1975 – and would never utter another word. His distraught mother fell into a diabetic coma and died within a month of her son's accident. Many of his showbiz friends rallied around Wilson's bedside at this time. Barry White and The Detroit Spinners were said to have put $60K towards his nursing – though further rumour suggests that this money was swallowed up in back tax and also litigation. Tarnopol was finally collared and convicted on several federal charges regarding Wilson's royalties as the singer lay semi-comatose – though, after the manager's death (*December 1987*), Wilson's estate still awaited full backdated payments.

It was not until January 1984 that the one-time 'Mr Excitement' finally slipped away at Burlington County Hospital. His funeral was attended by Berry Gordy, The Spinners and The Four Tops. Gordy and Davis's 'Reet Petite' (1957) was reissued nearly thirty years later, giving Jackie Wilson a posthumous UK number one (and the top British single of 1986, with some 700,000 copies sold) – but it was three more years before his paltry Detroit plot could be marked with a stone befitting one of the greatest soul vocalists of all time.

Friday 27

Candy Givens
(Candy Ramey – Iowa, 9 December 1946)
Zephyr
(The Legendary 4-Nikators)

Born to a Colorado outlaw, the granddaughter of gamblers and train-robbers, it's perhaps unsurprising that rough-edged singer Candy Givens led the life that she did. Her unwieldy upbringing apparently took in some months on the run, living in a converted chicken coup, yet Givens excelled in her schooling and was earmarked in her Oklahoma high-school yearbook to make it as a major singing talent. With a bluesy vocal style reminiscent of the late Janis Joplin, Givens – then singing with a jug band from Aspen, Colorado – was snapped up by Boulder hard rockers Ethereal Zephyr, for whom she would contribute vocals, keyboard and harmonica to three albums (as the abbreviated Zephyr) during the seventies, alongside bassist David Givens – whom she had married in 1968 – and future Deep Purple guitarist Tommy Bolin. The band were unable to break into the charts though, and Bolin left to join The James Gang, but his death while on tour opening for Jeff Beck (◀ *December 1976*) prompted Givens and the rest of Zephyr to give it another shot.

Zephyr were still performing in 1984, although Givens – who had by now separated from her husband – was also moonlighting with The Legendary 4-Nikators. Ever seeking independence in one form or another, Givens had argued with her latest boyfriend on the night of 27 January 1984 and consumed a number of tequila shots with friends before locking herself into the bathroom with a clutch of Quaaludes. Having drawn a hot tub, the singer immersed herself and slowly lost consciousness – drowning in the hot water.

She was discovered much later by her concerned boyfriend, who had had to break down the door to reach her. One of Candy Givens's final performances had been for a rugby-club party, where she had stunned the massed hulks into silence with an improvised set of Motown covers.

FEBRUARY

Saturday 4

Paul Gardiner
(London, 1955)
Tubeway Army
(The Lasers)

Paul Gardiner was the quiet, unassuming bassist who seemed happy to remain in the shadow of frontman Gary Numan. The pair had been together since 1976 when they teamed up in The Lasers, an amateurish punk band which the two friends abandoned to form Tubeway Army a year later. Known early on as 'Scarlett', Gardiner was in place for Numan and Tubeway Army's spectacular success in 1979: the group – hitherto unknown – stormed to the top of the UK charts that summer with both 'Are "Friends" Electric?' and 'Cars' (which also hit the Billboard Top Ten in 1980), though by now Numan was happier to use just his own name. By 1981 the suddenly wealthy singer had disbanded his backing band, and Gardiner began work on solo material. That year, he just missed the Top Forty with 'Stormtroopers In Drag' (which seemed to feature Numan extremely heavily for a supposedly Gardiner-only affair). But the pair drifted apart somewhat over the next few years, Numan alienated by Gardiner's escalating drug use. The singer was nevertheless devastated by Paul Gardiner's death from a heroin overdose and posthumously issued the bassist's version of 'Venus In Furs' as the first release on his Numa imprint.

Tuesday 28

Joey Vann
(Joseph Canzano – Jersey City, New Jersey, 3 April 1943)
The Duprees
The Utopians

Joey Canzano and his Utopians appeared to be just one more set of melodic mouths until they combined their strengths with those of The Elgins, another popular Italian-American unit from the New Jersey area. Canzano – better known as Joey Vann – and co-singer Tom Bialoglow hooked up with the latter group's Joe Santollo and Mike Amato, and The Parisiens (as they were originally named) were born. Less a rock 'n' roll act than 'entertainers', the renamed Duprees' speciality was to remake oldies with their own flourishes – at which they became very expert. Under the guidance of Coed Records' George Paxton and Marvin Cane, the group notched up a series of US Hot 100 entries, including the Top Ten 'You Belong to Me' (1962).

Vann, the obvious focal point of the Duprees, had ambitions of his own, however, and broke free from the band in 1964. He issued a solo single on Coed, 'My Love, My Love' (1965 – ironically a bigger hit when issued by The Duprees, who'd replaced him with Michael Kelly), but failed to make much of an impact. Despite a reversal of fortunes with cabaret work during the seventies, Vann was largely forgotten by the time of his unexpected, early death from a heart attack.

See also *Joe Santollo (◀ June 1981). Another founder member, Mike Arnone, has also passed on.*

MARCH

Tom Jans

(Yakima, Washington, 9 February 1949)

We know few details about the life of folk musician Tom Jans, though his musical influences appear to be rich: his grandmother, for example, was a long-time member of a well-known Western jazz band called The Rocky Mountain Five. For his own part, Jans made his mark in the San Francisco folk scene, becoming as well known for his professional/personal relationship with Mimi Fariña (Joan Baez's sister) as for his music. Regardless, he produced four solid albums for recording giants A&M and CBS, two of which, *The Eyes of an Only Child* (1975) and *Dark Blonde* (1976), are widely considered gems. In his career, Jans also collaborated with several respected names, including Hoyt Axton, Lowell George and Kris Kristofferson. In more recent years, Tom Waits has paid homage to the singer.

In late 1983, however, Jans was involved in a serious motorbike crash that caused extensive damage to his kidneys – from which he never really recovered. Depressed, and more and more dependent on painkillers, he was found dead in his Santa Monica home, probably from an overdose.

See also *Mimi Fariña (☛ July 2001)*

APRIL

Marvin Gaye

(Marvin Pentz Gay Jr – Washington, DC, 2 April 1939)

(The Marquees)

Marvin Gaye was a keen chess-player. America's most celebrated soul artist of his era scrutinized each move to the nth degree – what he should do next, or indeed which route might bring him maximum reward. Throughout his life, though, Marvin Jr's main opponent was his namesake – the man who gave him life and the one individual who could second-guess his challenger's game. And at the end, Gaye made the fatal error of presenting his key adversary with the crucial piece with which to defeat him.

Starved of a normal father–son relationship, Gaye finally grew to despise Marvin Gay Sr, an apostolic minister whose main ambition appeared to be the control of the wife and household he believed were his possessions. Marvin Jr, the eldest of two sons, was the main focus of Marvin Sr's jealousy and wrath, considered a 'faggot' for choosing show business over non-secular music – and then resented for making a success of this choice. The flaws in his father were obvious: the God-fearing man who decreed hard work and decried indulgence privately drank to pass the many days he spent without employment. Gaye's love and affection for his long-suffering mother, Alberta, was therefore stronger than it might have been under other circumstances: he vowed to improve her life – particularly in light of her stories of family abuse as she grew up. As a child, she had witnessed *her* father pull a gun on her mother.

Rumours of his father's fascination with cross-dressing and his own struggle with his sexuality saw Gaye change the spelling of his name as he manoeuvred himself a discharge from the US air force in 1957. Soon after, Gaye abandoned the church choir to join DC doo-wop group The Marquees, his first non-secular foray. This vocal troupe were overseen by Gaye's friend guitar-great Bo Diddley, though soon appropriated by Harvey Fuqua as his new Moonglows unit.

'He wanted to die, but he couldn't do it himself. He got his daddy to do it.'

Andre White, Marvin Gaye's bodyguard

Singer and entrepreneur Fuqua became Gaye's first proper mentor, in 1959 taking a talent he felt had real potential out of the group and with him to Detroit, launching Gaye's extraordinary career. From this move another significant figure in Gaye's life emerged, in the shape of Motown founder Berry Gordy. Gordy initially used Gaye as a session man with the label's only real stars thus far, The Marvelettes (as back-up singer) and The Miracles (as percussionist). But he wasn't to wait long for a solo opportunity.

Gaye repaid Gordy by marrying his sister Anna – seventeen years the singer's senior. This relationship was troubled from the start – it became apparent that Gaye found liaisons with the opposite sex hard to maintain: by his own admission, he was 'old school', expecting women to serve him and always emphasizing that he was the 'provider'. As he became more and more in demand, though, Gaye's attitudes towards women in general deteriorated. At times he worshipped the women he loved, marvelling over them like fine wines, at others his sexism and philandering spilled over into murkiness and misogyny. He was a serial user of prostitutes and pornography, and spoke openly about his masturbatory fantasies at a time when, well, one didn't. Despite their having adopted a son, these extracurricular activities caused Gaye and Anna Gordy to split in 1975, and to divorce two years later.

Professionally, however, Marvin Gaye seemed to relate better to female partners. Marketed as the label's 'loverman', Gaye was now encouraged to perform duets, considered essential 'pop' by a label that was keen to appeal to both black and white markets. The singer thus scored a brace of 1964 hits with Mary Wells and recorded 'It Takes Two' (1967) with Kim Weston. Gaye was no stranger to the charts on his own, either. After some six years cutting middling US hits, he finally landed a transatlantic number one with the timeless 'I Heard It through the Grapevine' (1968, seven weeks on top in the US), and also had a series of successes with his favourite leading lady, Tammi Terrell. Little could halt Gaye at this stage – or so it seemed. Terrell's premature death (☞ *March 1970*) was the hardest buffeting Marvin Gaye had taken since the physical beatings he had received as a child. The devastated singer took a lengthy sabbatical from the public eye, vowing never to record another girl/guy duet. He did cut an album with Diana Ross in 1974, but something in the man's spirit had died along with Terrell. The record was not considered a success by Gaye, who felt threatened by the status of Motown and Gordy's top girl (also the boss's girlfriend), his mood and behaviour darkening further.

The short-term creative effect of his grief was perversely beneficial to Marvin Gaye: coupled with ongoing events in Vietnam and at home, it inspired the finest work of his career. He re-emerged with the breathtaking, self-written *What's Going On?* (1971), a classic album which revealed in songs like the title track and 'Mercy Mercy Me' Gaye's previously stifled love of God and his planet, shadowed by his despair for its inhabitants. Despite the enormous critical acclaim the record drew, Gaye fell deeper into paranoia, exacerbated by his relentless hoovering of cocaine – but yet again, this prompted good work. He viewed his competition with apprehension, but always managed to trump them with the sheer quality of his output. Fearful of losing his crown to a Teddy Pendergrass, a Lou Rawls or even a Barry White, Gaye followed the productive with the seductive: the steamily sexual *Let's Get It On* (1973) was inspired by new love Janis Hunter – this time a partner some years his junior, whom he'd woo in song for the last decade or so of his life. That Hunter aspired to a singing career herself was a nuisance to Gaye, who strove to prevent this (as he had done with his brother, Frankie, some years before). As the new record suggestively pronounced, he was to remain firmly 'on top' – a position he clearly relished.

Marvin and Tammi on US television in 1967: United – but not for long

Marvin Gaye: Let's get it on

'Did I love him? Let's just say I didn't dislike him.'

Marvin Gay Sr, interviewed in prison

But Gaye was to visit the darkest places of his life in the years that followed. Despite another US chart-topper with 'Got to Give It Up' (1977) – an extraordinary self-purging, disco-flavoured anthem – he was declared bankrupt the year after, with debts of several million dollars. An advance for two further albums with Motown held off the debt-collectors temporarily, but Gaye's affairs of both the heart and the pocket were out of control. Separated once again, he was shedding enormous amounts of cash on settlements, maintenance and court orders (the 1979 album title *Here, My Dear* is believed to be a direct reference to Anna Gordy's demands). This was topped by a heavy sprinkling of 'the white stuff' – Gaye himself said, 'I don't wanna know how much I spent on toot – several hundred thousand, I'd guess.' Gaye was more horrified, however, to learn that Motown – tired of waiting for their star to sort himself out – had issued an unfinished album in his absence. Gaye considered this a huge affront to his integrity and left Gordy and the label by mutual agreement almost immediately. He also left the US and the horrors it now held for him, living in secret European exile until the release of a first album for Columbia. *Midnight Love* (1982) was far from his most inspired work, though it spawned a huge international hit in 'Sexual Healing', the whole set produced by trusted friend Harvey Fuqua. By now, though, Gaye's behaviour was erratic and disturbing. His stage performance, once a peacock-like display of colour and poise, was now crass, little more than cheap sexual posturing with unwilling pawns. Another blow to his manhood was the loss of his home, which meant a return to the house he had purchased for his parents in 1965. Naturally, this also meant a return to the sick mother he loved and the sickening father he loathed.

Aware that he was distressed by his situation, Gaye's friends became concerned by his talk of suicide (plus at least one attempt), relieving him of a .38 revolver. The singer – almost goading his father into committing the crime – eventually gave the weapon to Gay Sr, his obsession with security seemingly causing him to lose his senses. On the morning of All Fool's Day 1984 (just one day ahead of his forty-fifth birthday), Gaye, now a bloated, drug-ravaged parody of a once-smooth prototype, sat quietly with Alberta in the darkened room he almost never left. As his father's rasping demands cut through the conversation in a manner the frayed singer could no longer tolerate, Gaye leapt up, stormed into Gay Sr's room and began hitting his father – an act that Gay Sr believed to be the utmost in disrespect: indeed, he'd vowed to his daughter Jeanne that should his eldest son ever attack him, he'd 'murder him'. So, Gay Sr retrieved the gun given him and fired into Gaye's chest. As his son slumped from the bed, Gay Sr shot again at point-blank range.

Marvin Gaye was pronounced dead at the California Hospital Medical Center just after 1 pm. Attendees at his funeral in Glendale included Stevie Wonder, Smokey Robinson, Gaye's favourite singer Dick Gregory, his two ex-wives and three children; some 10,000 onlookers viewed the casket before the singer was cremated. The only absentee was Gaye's father, busy displaying the bruises on his body and deflecting police questioning as though having prepared for that moment for decades. Following the November trial, Gay Sr – originally charged with murder – pleaded guilty to involuntary manslaughter, for which he received five years' probation. Having left no will, his son was unable to benefit his surviving children: all of his estate went to honour unpaid debts.

Friday 27

Z Z Hill

(Arzel Hill – Naples, Texas,
30 September 1935)

Z Z Hill amassed hits on the R & B
listings right through his illustrious
career, without ever achieving crossover success. A Texas-blues-drenched
soul singer, Hill named himself in
deference to his hero, B B King, and
served his time in lounge bars before
moving to Kent Records and gaining R & B hit status with songs such
as 'You Were Wrong' and 'Hey Little
Girl' during the mid sixties. His career
witnessed many dips in fortune, but
early cut 'I Need Someone to Love
Me' (1971) became a firm favourite
some seven years after its original
recording. And ten years later, Hill
– now well into his forties – was
signed with Malaco, enjoying a considerable revival not unlike that of
Millie Jackson, with whom he regularly
toured. His 1982 album, *Down Home
Blues*, remained in the chart until well
after his untimely death two years later.

Z Z Hill was injured in what
appeared to be a minor car accident in
February 1984 – within two months,
however, an undetected blood clot
provoked the heart attack that killed
him. But a trio of beardy Texan blues
rockers kept his name alive . . .

JUNE

Saturday 2

Nathaniel Nelson

(Chicago, Illinois, 10 April 1932)
The Flamingos
The Platters

A jewel in the crown of already-
glistering vocal troupe The Flamingos,
Nate Nelson was the magnificent
lead who somehow fitted snugly
within the R & B shuffle of this
pioneering group's songs. The group
– at its strongest with Nelson, Jake
Carey (bass), Tommy Hunt (tenor),
Terry Johnson (tenor) and Paul
Wilson (baritone) – has been widely
recognized as having influenced a
generation of soul and Motown acts,
with The Temptations, for example,
emulating their smooth choreography
as well as their predecessors' carefully-
constructed vocal parts.

Nelson – trained, like so many
black vocalists of his era, in gospel
– joined The Flamingos part-time in
1954, groomed to replace incumbent
lead Sollie McElroy. Under Nelson's
lead, the group enjoyed its most
prolific period, which included the
great ballad 'I'll be Home' (1956) and a
major national doo-wop hit – and recognized classic – in 'I Only Have Eyes
for You' (1959). As the group slowly
fragmented, Nelson fronted another
much-loved vocal troupe, The Platters,
the group managing to place a pair of
hits long after their most successful
period. Nate Nelson's sad death at the
age of fifty-two was hastened by his
hospital's inability to find a suitable
heart donor in time to save him.

See also *Bobby Lester (☙ October 1980)
– a later singer with The Flamingos.
Nate Nelson was the first of the original
group to shuffle off, since joined by Paul*

Wilson (1988), Sollie McElroy (1995)
and cousins Jake (1997) and Zeke Carey
(1999). Six Platters have passed away: see
David Lynch (☙ January 1981); Paul
Robi (☙ February 1989); Tony Williams
(☙ August 1992); also early Platters
Cornell Gunter (☙ February 1990) and
Elsbeary Hobbs (☙ May 1996). Manager/
producer Buck Ram (1991) and later singer
Randy Jones (2002) have also died.

JULY

Wednesday 4

Jimmie Spheeris

(New Orleans, Louisiana, 5 November 1949)

Poet/songwriter Jimmie Spheeris
was a well-recognized figure on the
California music scene, but died
before he could make a meaningful commercial breakthrough. His
Columbia debut, *Isle Of View* (say it
phonetically; 1971), gained critical
praise for the musician, though, and he
consolidated this success with strong
follow-up *The Original Tap-Dancing
Kid* (1973), after which 'The Venice
Minstrel' was much in demand for live
work, and able to attract Joni Mitchell's
producer Henry Lewy as a collaborator. After a fourth record, *Ports of the
Heart* (1976), Spheeris was, however,
without a record contract and facing
obscurity.

On the night he finished recording
his 1984 comeback album, Jimmie
Spheeris felt invigorated. He had
also recently completed a doctorate
in scientology (a tough shout for an
openly gay man) – and Independence
Day celebrations were just hours away.
Spheeris left the studio and jumped on
to his motorbike, speeding east back
home to Santa Monica; heading the
other way, though, was an inebriated
van driver, Bruce Burnside, who

collided with him. The musician was knocked from his bike and across the pavement – sustaining horrific head injuries. Spheeris was pronounced dead on arrival at Santa Monica Medical Center. His eponymous album would not see the light of day for a further sixteen years. The singer is survived by older sister Penelope – whose work as a film director includes *Wayne's World* and *The Decline of Western Civilization*.

Saturday 14

Philippe Wynne

(Philip Walker – Detroit, Michigan, 3 April 1941)

The Detroit Spinners
(Funkadelic)
(The Pacesetters)
(The JBs)
(The Afro-Kings)

A natural, fast-talking extrovert, Philippe Wynne was already in his thirties by the time his concert performances with The Afro-Kings raised awareness of his natural ability as both singer and showman. Meanwhile, as an act in the Motown stable, The Spinners ('Detroit' was added for the British market) found attention deflected from them on to more prosperous artists like The Miracles, The Temptations and The Four Tops. Wynne's defection to The Spinners was therefore a pretty good move for both parties.

The Spinners' fortunes really changed in 1971 when Aretha Franklin recommended them to Atlantic and the production mastery of Thom Bell – who saw in them the perfect vehicle for his smooth, soon-to-be-trademark 'Philadelphia' sound. Then, along came the ideal frontman in Philippe Wynne, a gospel-trained singer who had something of a pedigree, having worked with both

Bootsy Collins's Pacesetters and James Brown's JBs. The fans loved his dynamic, 'storyteller' delivery of the band's output, sending tunes like 'I'll Be Around' (1972), 'Could It be I'm Falling in Love' and 'Ghetto Child' (both 1973), 'Then Came You' (1974, a US number one with Dionne Warwick) and 'Rubberband Man' (1976) high into the charts on both sides of the Atlantic. Wynne stayed with the group until 1977 (missing out on later successes like 1980's reissue of 'Working My Way back to You'), then rejoined the P-Funk stable as a sometime member of George Clinton's Funkadelic, simultaneously conducting a solo career.

Although his greatest days were as the main man with The Spinners, Philippe Wynne was a tremendous performer to the very end – which came as he performed at the Jack London Square Club, Oakland. After leaping into the audience, Wynne suffered a fatal heart attack, collapsed and died.

Saturday 21

Michael Osborne

(California, 22 December 1949)

Axe

A melodic hard-rock band expected to clean up throughout the metal-friendly eighties, Axe came to prominence with one of the first MTV rock hits, 1981's 'Rock 'n' Roll Party in the Streets'. With tricksy guitarists Mike Osborne and Bobby Barth ever at the fore, they were much in demand, opening for Cheap Trick, Judas Priest, Mötley Crüe and The Scorpions, as well as selling a fair few copies of their *Livin' on the Edge* (1980) and *Offering* (1981) albums. Just as the band appeared to be breaking into the major league, the car in which Osborne and Barth were travelling home crashed on a

California highway. In that moment, Axe was finished: Osborne died at the scene, while the extremely fortunate Barth survived but needed several months to recuperate, eventually joining Blackfoot and Angry Anderson (Rose Tattoo). Axe made a comeback in 1997 with a new line-up.

AUGUST

Tuesday 7

Esther Phillips

(Esther Mae Jones – Galveston, Texas, 23 December 1935)

Another church-trained vocalist – and another protégée of Johnny Otis – Esther Mae Jones showed potential as an R & B performer as early as 1948, when she was entered by her sister into a talent show at one of the entrepreneur's clubs. 'Little Esther' (as she was billed) soon became a regular with Otis's California Rhythm & Blues Caravan, topping the R & B charts twice with her ballsy renditions of 'Double Crossin' Blues' and 'Mistrustin' Blues' (both 1950). The titles were perhaps apposite: the singer was clearly under age when working for Otis, and was also exposed to drugs while still a minor – allegedly to help this large-framed girl control her weight. Frustration with her mentor spilled over in 1951, when 'Little Esther' finally left Otis's show after one wage disagreement too many.

Esther Mae Jones was addicted to heroin before she was twenty – a sad fact that, along with her terminated employment, contributed to her regularly being broke. In 1962, however, young maverick Kenny Rogers signed the rechristened Esther Phillips to Lenox, his brother's country label, issuing the US Top Ten version of 'Release Me' (later a smash for Engelbert Humperdinck). Clearly demonstrating a talent far beyond the novelty of some of her earlier work, Phillips was picked up by Atlantic, for whom she recorded polished versions of classics – her 'And I Love Him' (1965), a take on The Beatles' tune, still stands tall – as well as some highly personal songs such as Gil Scott-Heron's heroin opus, 'Home is Where the Hatred is' (1972). Another cover gave Phillips her biggest latter-day hit, 'What a Diff'rence a Day Makes' (1975, UK number six), a dance-floor 'smoulderer', still arguably the definitive version of that standard.

But Esther Phillips's health had been seriously attacked by her earlier drug abuse. Confined to a bed at Harbor Medical Center in Carson, California, Phillips died from liver and kidney failure at the age of forty-eight.

Ann Christy

(Christiane Leenaerts – Antwerp, Belgium, 1945)

The world lost another fine chanteuse that day. Ann Christy isn't widely remembered outside her own country, yet this slight but powerful singer was deemed something of a goddess at home – and dubbed the 'female Brel'. A shop girl with no real musical background, Christy made a career singing in clubs; she was Flemish, but chose to sing in French, which (as Jacques Brel himself learned) was not considered the done thing among traditionalists. However, tenacious Christy was performing on television within a year of starting out, and in 1965 joined The Adams, a popular orchestra, which featured her friend, and later husband, drummer Marc Hoyois. Nurturing a distinctive look with hippy bell-bottoms and sandals, Christy hit big in Belgium with *Le Garçon que j'aimais* ('The Boy I Loved',

1971), and then represented her country at the Eurovision Song Contest in 1975, though she finished a miserable fifteenth. It was clear, though, that Ann Christy was better than this suggests. In 1978, she even attracted the interest of Bob Dylan, who penned two songs for the singer ('Walk out in the Rain' and 'If I Don't be There by Morning').

In 1980, Ann Christy secured another big hit with her version of 'The Rose' (from the Bette Midler movie vehicle) but was shortly thereafter diagnosed with cancer. With little payback for all her efforts, Christy died in relative poverty in a Brussels hospital.

Sunday 12

Lenny Breau

(Auburn, Maine, 5 August 1941)
Three
The Lenny Breau Trio

Although primarily known as a jazz-guitar improviser par excellence, Lenny Breau makes the cut here for his forays into blues, country and pop – and for the plainly mysterious nature of his death. Born to French-speaking country-performing Canadians, friend and mentor to rocker Randy Bachman (The Guess Who/Bachman-Turner Overdrive), who continues to champion Breau to this day, Breau nonetheless took a tangent into jazz, leading the acoustic act Three before cutting two albums of unique electric playing for RCA with his Winnipeg-based trio

'He knew more guitar than any guy that ever walked the earth.'

Chet Atkins

– completed by Ron Halldorson (bass) and Reg Kelln (drums). During the early seventies, Breau played largely as a sideman to Anne Murray (among others), before cementing his own fine solo work with a series of tours across Canada and the USA between 1974 and his death. Sometimes these were with former cohorts; at others alongside guitar greats like Chet Atkins, Buddy Emmons (pedal steel) and Phil Upchurch.

Lenny Breau's lifeless body was found in the swimming pool of his Los Angeles apartment complex on the morning of 12 August 1984. The initial verdict was drowning, but it soon became apparent that the musician had been strangled. At the time, it was widely believed that Breau may have had gambling or drug debts – or even domestic issues – though nobody has ever been brought to task for his murder in over twenty years. He is survived by his musician son, Chet Breau, also an accomplished guitarist.

Tuesday 14

Norman Petty

(Clovis, New Mexico, 25 May 1927)
The Norman Petty Trio

Although a musician of some merit in his own right, Norman Petty will probably always be remembered as the man who exploited the talent of Buddy Holly. Petty (via a stint as a local DJ) brought his small-time trio out of the tiny border town of Clovis – his wife, Vi, on the piano, Jack Vaughn on guitar, with Petty himself playing the organ. With little success forthcoming – bar the instrumental radio hit 'Mood Indigo' (1956) – Petty next concentrated on songwriting and helping to break local acts (such as Roy Orbison and The Rhythm Orchids) at his own studio. At this time, he was known for his magnanimity, charging musicians by the session as opposed to the hour. Between 1957 and late 1958, the young Buddy Holly – who had been dropped by Decca – recorded almost all his work at Norman Petty Studios. Petty was, after all, an innovative producer, and it was his reworked version of Holly & The Crickets' 'That'll be the Day' (1957) that went on to top the charts and sell a million copies. What rankles with folk nowadays is that Petty then demanded co-authorship of *all* The Crickets' further songs, working a deal very favourable to himself. Indeed, after Holly's untimely death (☞ *Pre-1965*) – by which time the pair had parted company anyway – Petty overdubbed a number of old Holly songs for rerelease. (Paul McCartney's securing of publishing rights from Petty in 1974 ensured that Holly's widow received overdue benefit from her late husband's success.)

Norman Petty had further success after the tragedy, and also returned to playing as keyboardist on hits by British group Brian Poole & The Tremeloes, before returning to the radio work of his youth. Petty died of leukaemia in a Lubbock hospital, just three months after the death of his former colleague Jack Vaughn. Violet Petty survived them by eight years.

SEPTEMBER

Wednesday 19
Steve Goodman
(Chicago, Illinois, 25 July 1948)

Prolific folk-rock musician Steve Goodman developed a following in both New York and Chicago – initially paying his bills by composing and singing jingles for radio commercials.

In Chicago, he met songwriting giant Paul Anka, whose contacts helped get Goodman signed to Buddah in New York. Success came in 1974, with singer David Allen Coe's recording of his 'You Never Even Call Me by My Name' becoming a sizeable country hit. Jingle-composing could now be shelved indefinitely.

Although his own musical achievements were more limited, Goodman – a folk musician in the storytelling tradition of Woody Guthrie – won acclaim for his songs, not least from Guthrie Jr (Arlo), who recorded Goodman's 'City of New Orleans' after reluctantly agreeing to listen to it in a bar. Having suffered from leukaemia for almost a decade, Goodman collapsed on stage in 1982 – his illness was now public. The artist still found time to make two final albums before his unavoidable death, at the University of Washington Hospital, Seattle.

NOVEMBER

Thursday 8
Tasha Thomas
(Jeutyn, Alaska, 1950)

Both a session vocalist and a rising star in her own right, New York-based disco diva Tasha Thomas worked with a broad array of talent, including Diana Ross, Stevie Wonder, Carly Simon, Cat Stevens, Kiss and Esther Phillips – the last of whom she survived by just three months. Thomas's early forays into music were as organist/singer with her mother's Pentecostal church choir; she was first recorded as part of the back-up choir for Louis Armstrong's 'Wonderful World' in 1968, and engaged more with the secular world throughout the

seventies, appearing on over a hundred recordings. Thomas moved into the spotlight singing the part of 'Auntie Em' in the Broadway musical *The Wiz* – her consistent performances winning her record deals with Orbit, then with corporate giant Atlantic. In January 1979, Thomas's 'Shoot Me (With Your Love)' became a radio hit, having caused a sensation across America's dance floors during the disco boom of 1978.

Sadly, just as her career was in the ascendant, Tasha Thomas was struck down with cancer – losing her battle at just thirty-three years of age in New York.

Tuesday 13
Don Addrisi
(Winthrop, Massachusetts, 14 December 1938)
The Addrisi Brothers

Cancer also took the life of 45-year-old singer/guitarist Don Addrisi, one half of songwriting/recording siblings The Addrisi Brothers. The boys had begun their entertainment careers in bizarre fashion – as members of their parents' flying trapeze team. They achieved a minor hit as a recording duo with 'Cherrystone' (1959) on Del-Phi, but Don and his younger brother, Richard (Dick), were to become better known as writers when their recording careers failed initially to ignite. In 1967, the Addrisis co-composed 'Never My Love', a US number-two hit for The Association – a song they had originally recorded themselves. In 1972, they scored a bona fide hit as singers with 'We've Got to Get It on Again' – though their second, 'Slow Dancin' Don't Turn Me On' (a Top Twenty single on Buddah), was a further five years in the making. (In 1977, they also enjoyed another writing success with Dorothy Moore's 'I Believe You'.)

By now Don and Dick Addrisi were on an unlikely excursion into the world of disco music, making inroads into the 12-inch market. Jumping labels like they were going out of style, the brothers had a final outing with Elektra in the early eighties – soon after which Don Addrisi succumbed to the pancreatic cancer he had been diagnosed with just months before.

Wednesday 14

Keith Hudson

(Trenchtown, Jamaica, 18 March 1946)

And the third major music personality to die from cancer within a week was Keith Hudson, known as 'The Dark Prince of Reggae' for his gutsy, uncompromising dub style. Another disciple of Clement 'Coxsone' Dodd, Hudson could count among his school friends pioneering future stars like Bob Marley and Ken Boothe. As a young employee with Dodd, Hudson was put in the unenviable position of being chief minder to Skatalite Don Drummond's saxophone, but this enabled him to record his first sides at Dodd's studio at just fourteen. Ever an enterprising individual, Hudson studied dentistry, which paid him a sufficient wage for him to practise his love of music in the evening. With the money he earned, he started his own label, Imbidimts, releasing tracks by the better-known Boothe, John Holt and Delroy Wilson, which enabled him also to issue his own output. The well-received debut album, *Furnace* (and strong follow-up *Class and Subject*, both 1972), allowed Hudson to emigrate first to the UK, then to the USA – reggae as a genre was beginning to pick up interest internationally. In America, he signed with Virgin, but the relationship was less than happy and after one album – almost a 'soul' record, completely out of keeping

with the artist's more far-reaching work – they parted company. Put simply, Hudson was too imaginative to fit within a major label's confines. He kept working, however, and while in New York he founded another label, Joint, putting out a series of impressive albums throughout the seventies and early eighties, including 1978's brilliant *Rasta Communication*. But, in August 1984, Keith Hudson was diagnosed with lung cancer. Although he appeared to rally, after responding well to radiation therapy the artist collapsed, complaining of stomach pains, on the morning of 14 November. Within an hour he was dead.

See also *Don Drummond (* 🗶 *May 1969) and Clement 'Coxsone' Dodd (Golden Oldies # 19)*

DECEMBER

Sunday 9

Razzle Dingley

(Nicholas Dingley – Royal Leamington Spa, 2 December 1960)

Hanoi Rocks

The adopted son of a haulage contractor and his wife, the young Nick Dingley relocated with his family to the Isle of Wight – where his love of drums and horseplay would first gain attention. Here, Dingley caught the rock 'n' roll bug, seeing Jimi Hendrix's legendary Isle of Wight Festival set while working as a site bottle-collector. The first among his friends to own both a moped and then a car, Dingley also developed a taste for speed as he raced the island's uncrowded roads. Razzle (as he became known) had a knack of charming those he met, and thus in 1982 he talked his way into the

drummer's seat in Hanoi Rocks – the Finnish glam-metal act whose picture he had seen in *Sounds* magazine – via stints with various low-rent punk acts in his new home of London. In truth, Hanoi Rocks – Dingley, Mike Monroe (vocals, piano, sax), Andy McCoy (lead guitar), Nasty Suicide (guitar) and Sam Yaffa (bass) – were never much more than a second-division New York Dolls-styled rock act who relied more on appearance than on great songs or musicianship; even the impressive hand of ex-Mott the Hoople frontman Ian Hunter as lyricist for 1984's *Two Steps from the Move* failed to raise them significantly above the mire. Yet their electrifying stage show made Hanoi Rocks one of the most popular rock draws in London at the time – and their version of Creedence Clearwater Revival's 'Up around the Bend' almost gave the group a UK hit single. Just a few months later, though, it was to prove a disturbingly unfortunate choice of cover.

Befriending fellow hair-metallers Mötley Crüe at that August's Donnington Festival, Hanoi Rocks took a break from their exhausting touring schedule to join their US buddies at Crüe singer Vince Neil's Redondo Beach home for a 'very metal' week-long party, organized to mark the notorious LA band's latest album release. With beer, cocaine and women as far as the eye could see, the party was already way out of control (Crüe's Mick Mars had nearly bought it by walking into the

'If I live through this, I'm going to settle down with a family and a nice house.'

Razzle kids himself in 1983

ocean high on Quaaludes) before Neil and Dingley decided to go and load up the singer's new 1972 Ford Pantera with more booze, blowing a couple of hundred dollars before driving back to the apartment. Just four blocks from home, encouraged by Dingley, Neil had built his speed up to 65 mph (in a 25 mph zone), braked and skidded out of control on the damp road. As he did so, the Pantera collided full on with an oncoming VW. While Neil was badly concussed with cracked ribs, Razzle Dingley took the full brunt of the impact: the 24-year-old drummer was driven to South Bay Hospital with excessive head injuries, from which he was pronounced dead at 7.12 that evening (the date on his headstone is 9 December, as per GMT). His body was flown to the Isle of Wight for cremation. Although Dingley was briefly replaced by ex-Clash drummer Terry Chimes, Hanoi Rocks split after a final gig in May 1985.

In the aftermath of the accident, Vince Neil was internationally castigated for his drunkenness and charged with vehicular manslaughter, though after a much-postponed trial, he escaped with a thirty-day sentence (reduced to eighteen for good behaviour) and 200 hours of community service; he was also ordered to pay the victims – the Dingley family plus the two badly injured passengers in the VW – $2.6 million. In 1992, the Mötley Crüe singer gave up music to become . . . a racing driver.

See also *Randy Castillo (☞ March 2002)*

Close!
Nikki Sixx
(Mötley Crüe)

Another hard-core drug-user of some years' standing, Mötley Crüe bassist Nikki Sixx has a history of odd heroin experiences – including once injecting neat Jack Daniel's when he'd run out of the real McCoy.

And the glam-metal band's 1989 track 'Kickstart My Heart' was not just a catchy title, either. Injected by a dealer on 22 December 1987, Sixx awoke some time later to discover that he'd overdosed and earlier 'died', according to the paramedics/police standing over him. A couple of shots of adrenalin had brought the metal showman back, but this seemingly horrifying experience had little effect on the dogged Sixx. He promptly hitchhiked home with two stunned female fans who – like his own band members – had heard of his supposed passing, left a message on his answering machine saying, 'I'm not home because I'm dead' – and shot up again. And overdosed again.

The Death Toll #3

I HATE MYSELF AND I WANT TO DIE

The following is a collection of songs on the tricky subject of suicide. Let's face it, listening to one or two of these might make self-destruction seem a preferable option . . .

1 'Ode To Billy-Joe'
Bobbie Gentry (1968)

The chilling yarn of Billy-Joe's leap from the Talahatchee Bridge – and the subsequent collapse of the narrator's family – took folk artist Bobbie Gentry all the way to number one in America. This classic song is also one of the few hits that prompted the making of a movie around its lyrics (Kenny Rogers's 'Coward of the County' being another).

2 'Suicide Is Painless (Theme From 'M*A*S*H')'
The Mash (1980)

Already for many years the title theme of a popular US sitcom, 'Suicide Is Painless' became a UK number one when it was finally issued as a single in 1980. Radio stations across the country spent the best part of two months fretting over whether they could legitimately play a ballad openly suggesting that death by one's own hand might be better than continuing a pointless war.

3 'Emma'
Hot Chocolate (1974)

The British pop/soul act's biggest hit at the time, 'Emma' told the tragic tale of a wannabe movie starlet who, despite everybody's belief in her, just couldn't get a break. Singer Errol Brown's shriek of despair as the record climaxes must rank as one of the rawest ever pieces of emotion on a hit record.

4 'Moody River'
Pat Boone (1961)

Perhaps the first 'suicide' ballad to become a major-league hit, Boone's tearjerker told the tale of a cheatin' girl who made the ultimate sacrifice to 'set her lover free'.

Which was all very noble, but the only thing her shattered boyfriend got out of it was one glove. (Useful only had he been friendly with Def Leppard's Rik Allen.)

5 'Someone Saved My Life Tonight'
Elton John (1975)
From Elton's mega-selling *Captain Fantastic & The Brown Dirt Cowboy* (1975) came this touching Bernie Taupin-penned account of intercepting the singer's somewhat flawed suicide attempt some years before. Confused about his sexuality, John had chosen to place his head in an oven rather than break off an engagement. What he hadn't realized was that the fumes wouldn't have been toxic anyway. Plus he'd left the kitchen window open.

6 'Jeremy'
Pearl Jam (1992)
Allegedly (loosely) based on vocalist Eddie Vedder's own troubled childhood, this Top Twenty single from the band's multi-platinum debut album *Ten* tells of a student outsider who kills his classmates and then takes his own life with his dad's gun. Like, heavy, dude.

7 'Asleep'
The Smiths (1985)
Well, it could only be a matter of time before Morrissey weighed in with his take on the dead. The song, a near-lullaby that makes eternity seem like a warm bath, was one of many great Smiths B-sides (in this case, to 'The Boy with the Thorn in His Side'). Asked his opinion on Kurt Cobain's suicide (➼ *April 1994*), The Smiths' singer surprised few by admitting he felt both 'sad and envious'.

8 'Dagenham Dave'
The Stranglers (1977)
Not to be confused with the Morrissey track of the same name, this tribute was released via the *No More Heroes* album, commemorating a hardcore fan of the black-clad new-wave artisans who chose to throw himself off a bridge.

9 'Teenage Suicide (Don't Do It)'
Don Dixon (1989)
Originally performed for the movie *Heathers*, this was the former REM-producer turned songwriter's only notable recording. The song was so dreadful that Dixon procured no further hits, and graduated to playing with Hootie & The Blowfish. Which sort of figures, really.

10 'Don't Jump off the Roof, Dad'
Tommy Cooper (1961)
Surely the most chilling suicide song of them all, Cooper's lament told the harrowing tale of domestic tension overspilling into frustration and finally desperation, as the father – badly neglected by his botanically obsessed wife and scornful children – took that last fateful walk to the highest point of the house. Or something.

DEAD INTERESTING!

VINYL SOLUTION?
On many occasions in US rock history, metal bands have been accused of having driven young listeners to commit atrocities on themselves – whether one played their records backwards, forwards or sideways. Way before those faintly ludicrous suggestions that Marilyn Manson's act might have prompted the 1999 Columbine massacre, a couple of cases involving suicidal British metallers caught the attention of *National Enquirer* readers across America.

Hard these days to envisage the patriarch of TV's least functional family putting out such challenging work as 'Suicide Solution' (1980), a cut from Ozzy Osbourne's debut album dealing with depression and alcoholism and reportedly about his friend Bon Scott of AC/DC (➼ *February 1980*). However, in 1986 the former dove-muncher was unsuccessfully sued by the parents of Californian youth John McCollum, who had taken it upon himself to end his own life two years earlier, having played the track to, well, death.

Further charges of subliminal messaging were levelled at Spiñal Tap-inspiring leather-lovers Judas Priest, whose *Stained Class* album (1978) – particularly the song 'Better by You, Better by Me' – was claimed to have provoked two Nevada youngsters into a suicide pact in 1985. The pair had felt driven to put shotguns to their heads: 18-year-old Raymond Belknapp died at the scene, while his 20-year-old friend James Vance was permanently disfigured, and died later from an overdose of medication. As for The Priest, they were found not guilty at the 1991 trial: in light of the violent previous histories of the two victims (one had attempted to choke his own mother), justice was seen to be done.

Lest We Forget

Other notable deaths that occurred sometime during 1984:

Eddie 'Bongo' Brown (US percussionist with the legendary 'Funk Brothers'; born 1932; heart problems, 28/12)

Rev C F Franklin (US gospel giant and father of Aretha Franklin; born Clarence LeVaughn Franklin, 22/1/1915; shot in the groin by burglars in June 1979, he lay comatose until he died of heart failure, 27/7)

Luke Kelly (Irish singer/banjo-player/founder of folk band The Dubliners; born Dublin (obviously), 17/11/1940; complications following a brain tumour, 30/1)

Wells Kelly (US drummer with rock band Orleans who also played with Meat Loaf, Bonnie Raitt and Ian Hunter; born 1949; choked on his own vomit, 29/10)

Patrick McAuley (Irish drummer/keyboardist with Them, later with Kim Fowley and rock band The Belfast Gypsies; born 17/3/1944; drowned in Co. Donegal)

Ron Tabak (Canadian singer with rock act Prism; born 25/9/1953; mugged the previous week, he was side-swiped by a car as he cycled to a friend's home – dying from a blood clot two days later, 26/12)

'Big Mama' Thornton (formidable US blues/R & B singer – the first to perform 'Hound Dog' – who was witness to the death of Johnny Ace; born Willie Mae Thornton, 11/12/1926; heart and liver problems, 25/7)

Jack Vaughn (US guitarist with The Norman Petty Trio – whose leader survived him by just three months – who also worked with Buddy Holly in 1957; unknown, 20/5)

Sonny Woods (US bass with vocal groups The Four Falcons, The Royals and The Midnighters who later moved into A & R work; heart attack)

Doug Wray (US rock drummer with country turned rock band The Raymen – brother of Link and the late Vernon Wray; born North Carolina, 4/7/1933; heart attack, 4/1984)

For a complete list of fallen artists, visit

www.numberoneinheaven.com

JANUARY

Wednesday 9

Paul Hewson

(Auckland, New Zealand,
25 October 1952)

Dragon
Cruise Lane
(Various acts)

A namesake of Bono, Dragon's Paul Hewson was, in his homeland, almost as revered as U2's frontman. Hewson was a strong keyboardist and songwriter who had already made a name for himself on the 'Down Under' rock scene with the bands (Marble) Arch – playing alongside his bassist brother, John – and the heavier Cruise Lane, whom he joined in 1970. Hewson flew to Sydney in 1975 to join Todd and Marc Hunter's melodic rock band Dragon, who had just relocated from Auckland; here, he was to experience a bizarre series of ups and downs. The first major event was that the cash-strapped band had all their equipment stolen, before CBS came in and offered a deal, helping to establish the group on Sydney's rock stations. Just as all seemed to be back on an even keel, drummer Neal Storey died from a heroin overdose, choking on his own vomit. Even then, the band rallied, with Hewson's songs very much the driving force, and scored a gold record with the album *Sunshine* (1977). In November of that year, the band's 'April Sun in Cuba' single was only kept from the Australian number-one slot by Paul McCartney's somehow all-conquering 'Mull Of Kintyre'; the following year, though, they reached the very summit with 'Are You Old Enough?' Dragon's appeal had now become broader, the band opening for big US acts like Boz Scaggs and Johnny Winter – but few lessons had been learned on the drug front. Along with singer Marc Hunter, Hewson had developed a serious habit of his own.

Dragon sold steadily until 1979, then imploded, largely due to the wayward behaviour of frontman Hunter. The group re-formed three years on, but with chart positions slipping by 1985, Hewson – who suffered from scoliosis – decided to call it quits. Returning to New Zealand for a break from the constant touring and partying, the keyboardist played live dates with local acts The Pink Flamingos and The All-Stars, which proved far less demanding. It was on a night out with members of The All-Stars that Paul Hewson fell victim to a final, fatal heroin overdose. Deciding to spend the night in a friend's car, he took one last hit and drifted into an endless sleep.

See also *Marc Hunter*
(☞ *July 1998*)

Friday 25

Bill Pickering

(Murchinson, Texas, 5 April 1927)

The Picks

Was 25 January 1985 'the day the music died'? Some might argue so, for it marked the passing of Bill Pickering who – unknown to many – sang backup on many of the original Buddy Holly & The Crickets recordings. While Holly's legacy lives on decades after his horrific death (☞ *Pre-1965*), the names of Pickering, his brother, John, and their friend Bob Lapham – The Picks – remain relatively obscure.

The brothers had begun singing with their parents as the Pickering Family Quartet during the forties, Bill encouraged to stand on an apple crate to help project his voice. Through their music, the brothers befriended the Holly family and Lubbock pianist Norman Petty. Bill Pickering later served in the navy and worked as a DJ – he was the first jockey to play Buddy Holly's solo release 'Blue Days, Black Nights' (1956). One year later, he made an unheralded reacquaintance with the singer. With The Crickets' 'That'll be the Day' ready to hit the market that July, Petty – now the group's producer/manager – decided that the backing vocals to another recently recorded future classic, 'Oh Boy!', needed a touch of 'pepping up'. Thus, in came The Pickering Brothers (now nicknamed The Picks) to provide overdubs – a favour they would also do for eight further songs (including 'Maybe Baby') the following October. By this time Holly and his band were the biggest name in town, and Petty saw no need to credit the boys for their vocals. With enough material in the bag for a first album and a series of hit singles, The Picks were never to work on Holly's songs again; when the legendary singer died, however, Pickering attended – and sang – at his friend's funeral. The Picks found it hard to forge a path on their own, separating into other lines of work before Bill and John reconvened as The Pickering Brothers and headed to Nashville in 1969. (In a strange twist, one of the A & R men they encountered there was Tommy Allsup, the former guitarist who had missed the Holly plane crash by the toss of a coin.) The brothers' career as a duo was effectively ended in 1974 by Bill Pickering's first aneurysm, which left him blinded for almost two years. Partially recovered, Pickering returned with his brother to the studio ten years on, after a chance conversation with Holly's widow, Maria Elena Santiago, revealed that her late husband had wanted to record with The Picks again. So, producing another set of overdubs, the brothers sang once more with their late friend. (This time, there was no Petty in attendance – long retired, he passed away at the beginning of the project (*August 1984*).) The resultant recordings were finally issued to the public as a 1998 Charly boxset, The Picks now inducted into the Rockabilly Hall of Fame for their part in Holly's legend.

Poignantly, the 1984 overdubs were Bill Pickering's last professional move. Suffering a further aneurysm, he died the following January in Lubbock, Texas, Holly's birthplace.

Monday 28

Dennis Parker

(New York, 28 October 1955)

A small-time porn-movie actor who went by the stage name of Wade Nichols, Dennis Parker was discovered by renowned disco producers Henri Belolo and Jacques Morali (The Village People, Ritchie Family), who saw in the moustachioed hunk a potential new star for the burgeoning gay market. In 1978, an album, *Like an Eagle*, emerged on Casablanca, and spawned two club hits the following year. This increased profile helped the singer/actor to land the part of Police Chief Mallory on CBS daily soap *The Edge of Night*. At the same time, Parker continued to work on adult films while attempting, unsuccessfully, to repeat his recording success.

Learning that he had AIDS in 1984, Dennis Parker became despondent, his depression preventing him from working for much of the time. To avoid the long-term ravages of the disease, Parker ended his own life by gunshot at his home.

Thursday 31

Barbara Cowsill

(Barbara C Russell – Newport, Rhode Island, 12 July 1928)

The Cowsills

Marketed as a sort of real-life Partridge Family (before the TV group emerged to steal their thunder), the whiter-than-white Cowsills enjoyed two years of US chart success during the last few years of the sixties. The band was made up of five brothers, Bill and Bob (both guitars), Paul (keyboards), Barry (bass) and John (drums), sister Susan (percussion) and mom Barbara (lead vocals) – the wife and children of naval officer/singer Bud Cowsill. Barbara Cowsill had been encouraged to join the group at thirty-eight by producer Artie Kornfeld, who promoted her

The Cowsills – with 'Mom' Barbara (*third right*): The family that played together *didn't* stay together

on the debut hit, 'The Rain, the Park and Other Things' (1967). The single was a smash, selling over a million copies in the States, and was only prevented from hitting number one by The Monkees. More hits came in the shape of 'We Can Fly', 'Indian Lake' (both 1968) and the theme from *Hair* – another million-seller (1969).

The Cowsills' career hit the rocks only when the group declined an offer from ABC to make a TV series of their activities – in the wake of the success of *The Monkees*. The company required younger singer/ actress Shirley Jones to play Barbara's role – which the family were understandably upset by. It cost them dearly: Jones took the part of 'singing mom' in *The Partridge Family* – and the David Cassidy-starring group took the Cowsills' place as pop music's top family act. Declaring bankruptcy, The Cowsills split in 1972. Barbara Cowsill took menial work to make ends meet. Her death from emphysema in 1985 remained a secret for years, though it now appears she passed away while working a shift at an Arizona nursing home.

See also *Barry Cowsill (* *September 2005). Bud Cowsill survived his wife by seven years, while Bill Cowsill died early in 2006.*

FEBRUARY

Thursday 7

Matt Monro

(Terence Parsons – Shoreditch, London, 1 December 1930)

Often dismissed as slight during his lifetime, MOR heart-throb Matt Monro has posthumously gained a credibility once thought unlikely – particularly in the USA where he was originally seen as a wannabe Frank Sinatra. Monro, a decent enough balladeer with a chocolatey-smooth voice, began his professional career as a club singer under the name Al Jordan, before pianist Winifred Atwell suggested the new moniker. It took a while to launch Monro's recording career, and the singer worked as a bus driver until an advertisement slot for Camay soap made the voice public at last. Fabled producer George Martin recorded Monro first, using him as a Sinatra soundalike on a Peter Sellers comedy album. On the week of his thirtieth birthday, Parlophone issued Monro's 'Portrait of My Love', a record that rose to UK number three and the first of several chart smashes over the next five years. Although he was less successful in the US, Monro chose to move there in 1965 to exploit the cabaret market. (That year, he also became the first artist – of several hundred – to cover The Beatles' 'Yesterday', securing another major UK hit.)

His reputation remained intact throughout the seventies, but Matt Monro's health dwindled during the next decade and he died from cancer at just fifty-two.

Thursday 28

David Byron

(David Garrick – Epping, Essex, 29 January 1947)
Uriah Heep
(Rough Diamond)
(Spice)
(The Stalkers)

Teaming with guitarist Mick Box, teenage vocalist David Garrick made his first foray into rock via the R & B-influenced Stalkers before spending three years as frontman of live favourites Spice. While this group enjoyed a residency at London's sweaty, boozy Marquee Club, Byron lived a twilight existence as a session-singer, recording a number of hit cover albums for the budget label Avenue. The group – now comprising Byron, Box, Paul Newton (bass) and Alex Napier (drums) – became Uriah Heep with the addition of keyboardist/guitarist Ken Hemsley and replacement drummer Nigel 'Ollie' Olsson, and a prog-rock legend was born. Debuting with the album *Very 'Eavy, Very 'Umble* (1970 – coincidentally the hundredth anniversary of Charles Dickens's death), Uriah Heep began a long career of album-orientated rock releases, negotiating some pretty serious critical disapproval along the way. The group juggled the usual predictable lyrical subjects, and also managed a sixteen-minute opening track on their second album, *Salisbury* (1971), which prompted a whole new craze among prog acts. (Having inspired Spiñal Tap's flirtation with Stonehenge, Uriah Heep might also be said to have blueprinted their drummer syndrome – Heep worked their way through at least five in their career.) As for Byron himself, he was every bit the star, usually taking the stage resplendent in a slashed jacket and other rock finery.

Although Heep charted a further eight albums over the next five years (unthinkable nowadays), the drug-related death of later bassist Gary Thain (*December 1975*) was followed by David Byron's professional decline – he gave a series of drunken performances that the band felt were compromising their own standing. He was sacked in July 1976, and joined metal band Rough Diamond. His health was by now in chronic deterioration (caused largely by a life dominated more and more by drugs and drinking) and, after the release of some indifferently received solo material on Arista, he succumbed to a premature heart attack.

MARCH

The Singing Nun

(Jeanine Deckers – Wavre, Belgium,
17 October 1933)

Jeanine Deckers was perhaps encouraged to dedicate herself to God as a result of a childhood devoid of love – and, after an unexpected spell in the limelight, was finally, fatefully, let down by the Church to whom she had devoted her life. Entering the Dominican convent of Fichermont in Waterloo (Belgium), Deckers, now known as Sister Luc-Gabrielle, entertained friends and students with songs composed on her guitar (itself named 'Sister Adele'); her superiors were so taken with her compositions, which they felt could be used in missions, that she was encouraged to record a selection in October 1961 at Philips Records' Belgium studios. Although Deckers was not an especially gifted vocalist (and her songs were not particularly inspired), the company was sufficiently impressed to press a thousand copies under the name Soeur Sourire ('Sister Smile') – these sold out across Europe almost immediately. Perhaps in response to the Kennedy assassination, the phenomenon of The Singing Nun then caught on once the album was issued in the US. The lead track, 'Dominique', was released as a single in November 1963, astonishing everyone – not least Deckers herself – by racing to the top of the Billboard charts that Christmas. As a result, the album followed suit and The Singing Nun found herself on television specials such as the hugely influential *Ed Sullivan Show* (to the chagrin of some of her superiors back in Belgium); a lucrative biopic, starring Debbie Reynolds, was also hastily

prepared – though Deckers herself was less than pleased with it, claiming it was not her life that was depicted.

But, despite all this media attention and the money-spinning ventures, The Singing Nun did not benefit: Deckers had taken a vow of poverty, so all of the royalties were reinvested into the Fichermont convent – which also owned her stage name. In 1967, Deckers decided to eschew the convent life and concentrate on a musical career under yet another new name (Sister Luc-Dominique, in deference to her hit record), producing unlikely songs such as 'Glory be to God for the Golden Pill' – a ditty celebrating birth control – which alienated all but a select few of her former sisters. The American market was equally sniffy, wanting more of the saccharine sweetness of earlier outings, and a follow-up hit was not forthcoming. A return to obscurity beckoned, and – infuriating her earlier colleagues further by beginning a lesbian relationship – Deckers, with her lover, Anne Pécher, turned her attention from music to the foundation of a school for autistic children.

There were those, however, who were not prepared to let her forget her past successes: the taxmen. Though her contract had almost completely cut Deckers out of any financial advantage, the revenue office still hit her with a bill of some £40,000 for past royalties; her objection that convent benefits were exempt went unheeded by the authorities. Plagued by depression, sexual confusion and

'We go now to God and hope he will welcome us – he saw us suffer.'

The suicide note of Jeanine Deckers and Anne Pécher

becoming more and more substance-dependent, Deckers and Pécher took their lives with a lethal mixture of alcohol and barbiturates in a suicide pact that shocked Belgium. The couple were buried together on consecrated ground in Wavre.

AUGUST

Kyu Sakamoto

(Kawasaki, Japan, 10 November 1941)

Kyu (pronounced 'cue') Sakamoto began in music as a jazz entertainer, playing Tokyo supper clubs before a transition to pop scored him hit records on the Japanese charts for Toshiba Records. The young singer's life was changed for ever by a business trip made to Japan by Pye label president, Louis Benjamin – who fancied Sakamoto's '*Ue O Muite Arukō*' ('I Look up When I Walk') as a potential hit for one of his British acts. Renamed 'Sukiyaki', the record reached the UK Top Ten, in a somewhat trad arrangement by Kenny Ball & His Jazzmen. Sakamoto's original then got airplay under the new title in the US, where it topped the charts for three weeks in June 1963 (similarly, the song once more climbed the UK charts, peaking at six). Like The Singing Nun, though, Sakamoto could not find a follow-up; his next single, 'China Nights', reached only fifty-eight in America, although mini classic 'Sukiyaki' achieved hit status again in 1981 for disco unit A Taste of Honey and later for R & B act 4PM.

At around 7 pm on 12 August 1985, Kyu Sakamoto was travelling to Osaka on Japan Airlines' flight 123 when the 747 – improperly repaired seven years previously – suffered bulkhead failure at 24,000 feet, crashing into Mount Osutaka near Ueno Village. The accident is considered among the worst-ever in aviation history, claiming the lives of 520 of the 524 passengers on board, the highest death toll for a single-plane accident.

OCTOBER

Saturday 12

Ricky Wilson
(Athens, Georgia, 19 March 1953)
The B-52's
(Black Narcissus)

From the musically fertile soils of Athens, Georgia, emerged the quirky, impertinent B-52's, a new-wave band with an enduring penchant for the kitsch and the flamboyant. The group was formed in essence by high-school pals Ricky Wilson (guitar) and Keith Strickland (drums), playing as Black Narcissus. On graduating, the pair travelled around Europe, after which they could only find work at a bus station – until a 1976 meeting with Kate Pierson (organ/vocals) and Fred Schneider (keys/vocals), late of local protest band The Sun-Donuts. The four joined forces – recruiting Wilson's sister Cindy (guitar/vocals) – naming their distinctive band after the girls' equally distinctive bouffant hairstyles. Quickly established as The B-52's' chief arranger, lead guitarist Wilson led the band to rapid success in their home town. A debut gig at New York's fabled Max's Kansas City was poorly attended, and only 2,000 copies of off-beat debut single 'Rock Lobster' were cut – but the group were making a loud enough noise to attract Chris Blackwell at Island Records. The reissued 'Rock Lobster' then caught sufficient attention to

send a debut album into the charts on both sides of the Atlantic, the single making the UK Top Forty in 1979 on the back of a great deal of radio play (reissued again to Top Twenty success in 1986); rumour even has it that John Lennon was encouraged to record again after hearing the band. Fuelled by Wilson's Dick Dale-esque guitar heroics, the group then put together a great second set in *Wild Planet* (1981), following this with *Mesopotamia* (1982) and *Whammy!* (1983). While recording the latter, though, Wilson made the distressing discovery that he was carrying the AIDS virus, and was forced into retirement during the sessions for The B-52's' largely ignored *Bouncing off the Satellites* album (1986).

By the time of Ricky Wilson's sad death from an AIDS-related illness, he was confined to a New York hospital bed; he was interred in Athens five days later. Though devastated, Wilson's surviving band rallied to score their biggest successes in the early nineties with international hits like 'Love Shack', 'Roam' and the 'Meet the Flintstones' theme.

Wednesday 23

Merle Watson
(Eddy Merle Watson – Deep Gap, North Carolina, 8 February 1949)

A huge fan of the blues, Merle Watson followed his father, Doc, into guitar-picking at the age of fifteen, touring the US with the country veteran, playing to packed houses. In more than twenty years as a duo, Doc and Merle Watson cut almost as many albums together, winning four Grammys along the way. By 1973 Watson had added slide guitar to his already impressive picking skills, giving the duo a further edge to their evocative country-tinged acoustic blues.

Merle Watson's untimely death

was the result of a combination of bizarre accidents. Rather oddly deciding to embark on some woodwork in the middle of the night, the guitarist suffered a bad muscle gash when a giant splinter spun off his bandsaw and embedded itself in his arm. Watson rapidly lost blood as he raced to a neighbour's home in his tractor. Safely patched up with the splinter removed, Watson – weakened but relieved – began the return journey. But as he negotiated a steep incline, the tractor's brakes froze, the vehicle flipped over and crushed him beneath it – killing him instantly. Doc Watson maintains that his son probably suffered a black-out or stroke at the wheel, the result of an inoperable brain tumour.

Friday 25

Gary Holton
(London, September 1952)
The Heavy Metal Kids
(The Damned)

They weren't especially 'heavy metal' – and the majority of them certainly weren't 'kids' – but pumped-up, over-amplified urchins The Heavy Metal Kids were, very briefly, one of London's hottest rock tickets. And about 80 per cent of their appeal was dynamic leader, Gary Holton, a singer who didn't need to be a star to lead a seriously rock 'n' roll life.

Holton had long desired to be an actor: he had already joined the Sadler's Wells theatre company by the time he left his Westminster public school, and later joined the Old Vic and Royal Shakespeare companies. His first performance break, however, was with The Heavy Metal Kids – Holton (vocals), Mick Waller (guitar), Danny Peyronel (keyboards), Ronnie Thomas (bass) and Keith Boyce (drums) – when they were discovered by former singer Dave Dee. The band

Gary Holton: Braced himself for a rough ride

'In the mid seventies,
the only thing I
remember listening
to was The Heavy
Metal Kids.'

Keith Richards,
The Rolling Stones

more pills to wake up, and harbouring a disturbing drink habit. Holton paid little heed to any warnings – not when he was believed dead after 'overdoing it', nor even when a girlfriend choked on her own vomit in 1977. The following year, the singer – whose behaviour had become erratic to say the least – was sacked and, even though he returned, the onset of punk meant that The Kids' moment had passed. Holton later spent a short time with The Damned, but he effectively left the music industry after The Heavy Metal Kids' split. He made a good name for himself, however, as a serious actor, winning parts on popular British television series such as *Shoestring* and rock-culture movies *Quadrophenia* and *Breaking Glass* before clinching the role for which he is best remembered: Wayne Norris in the massive ITV hit *Auf Wiedersehen, Pet*.

Although he had beaten an addiction to heroin, the press rounded on Holton – now, after all, a public figure – splashing tales of his former habit and bizarre private life (it transpired that Holton was living in a threesome with his lover, Jahnet McIllewan, and her boyfriend) across the front pages. The damage the revelations were doing to his son, Red, tore the actor apart. Desperate and confused, Holton – who also had spiralling debts – spent his last few weeks seeking solace with friends, one of whom, Paul Witta, invited the star to spend the night of 24 October at his Wembley flat. In the early hours of the morning, Gary Holton's body was discovered by McIllewan: a pathologist revealed that Holton had been drinking just half an hour before he died (his alcohol level was 199 mg), but was likely rendered unconscious by a shot of morphine – though no evidence of heroin use could be found. It was also believed by officials that his death had not been through misadventure. Although Holton had lately fallen out with most of the cast of *Auf Wiedersehen, Pet*, they all attended his funeral – and with the latest series incomplete, a stand-in was used for distant shots.

was formed when Holton was just twenty, securing a deal with Atlantic more for their onstage bravado than for any musical prowess. The nearest to a hit single the band managed was 'She's No Angel' (1976), which saw a shambling appearance on *Top of the Pops*, but they were something of a tonic live. The Kids were regulars at London's Speakeasy, and secured support slots for major acts: a 1975 show with Alice Cooper was memorable for Holton's stage-diving antics (in which he broke a leg), and the singer then won a £500 bet by sleeping with twenty-six girls in four weeks of a European tour. On top of all this, Holton was a keen imbiber of substances, taking pills to sleep,

DECEMBER

Thursday 12

Ian Stewart

(Pittenween, Scotland, 18 July 1938)

The Rolling Stones
(Rocket 88)

Ian Stewart's only 'crime' in life was not to have been blessed with the right look for a would-be rock star – at least according to Rolling Stones manager Andrew Loog Oldham. And thus his fate was sealed. Thick-set, with a dark 'throwback' quiff and protruding chin (the latter a result of a childhood calcium deficiency), 'Stu' Stewart looked, in the early days, like a cross between Desperate Dan and a prototype Morrissey as he slid, almost unnoticed, into position at his beloved piano.

Stewart was a few years older than the majority of The Stones: he'd played rhythm 'n' blues and boogie-woogie for years, his knowledge of these genres pivotal in the group's embryonic years. In the opinion of none other than Keith Richards, it was Stewart who was most significant in the assemblage of the band, risking his day job at ICI as he phoned round to land gigs. As the band gained notoriety, Stewart was there to drive, roadie, soundcheck and act as steadying influence to the boys who became the real stars – Jagger, Jones, Richards, Wyman and Watts. But Stewart, who had little truck with image issues, was seen, bizarrely, as a luxury by Oldham – an ambitious teenage manager who persuaded the others that Stu was *not* a Rolling Stone. Opinions on his reaction to his dismissal from the playing ranks – or, at least, the visible playing ranks – differ. Ex-wife Cynthia Dillane described him as 'devastated', while Richards talks only of his humility: 'All Stu did,' remembers the guitarist, 'was take a gentleman's

step back and say, "I understand that." That's the heart of a lion.'

The lion-hearted Stewart nonetheless held a position with the band for over twenty years, watching from the sidelines as The Stones became the second-biggest and then the biggest band in the world. He continued to play on many Stones classics, his robust piano audible throughout the group's oeuvre – notably on 'It's All Over Now' (1964), 'Star Star' (1973) and 'It's Only Rock 'n' Roll' (1974); Stewart also overdubbed the keyboard on Led Zeppelin's 'Rock and Roll' (1971). The keyboardist finally played with many of his heroes by forming blues supergroup Rocket 88 in 1979 with Watts, Jack Bruce, Paul Jones and Alexis Korner – the band often appearing for as little as £20 a night.

Warmly regarded as the conscience of The Stones, Ian Stewart – who had always preferred golf to the 'drugs and groupies' universe of the other members – died young, from a stroke as he sat in his Harley Street doctor's waiting room. His funeral was reportedly the first event at which Mick Jagger cried in public.

See also *Brian Jones (➤ July 1969)*

Ian Stewart: Stone alone

'He was the daddy of us all. He *made* the band.'

Keith Richards (again)

Sunday 22

D Boon
(Dennes Dale Boon – San Pedro, California,
1 April 1958)

The Minutemen

Rehousing California punk in a totally
different sector, guitarist D Boon
formed the great Minutemen (as The
Reactionaries) with bassist and former
school-friend Mike Watt in their home
town of San Pedro in 1979, the pair
having played together in some form
or another since they were ten. Punk
rock was fast disappearing back underground in the US, so Boon and Watt
looked towards jazz and funk influences to give The Minutemen a unique
take on 'hardcore' (as Americans were
now given to calling the genre). Boon,
unlike most punk guitarists, never
used distortion. One of the first bands
to record with the pioneering SST
label – sometime home to Black Flag,
Dinosaur Jr, Hüsker Dü and others –
The Minutemen issued a series of EPs
that featured Boon's leftist political
stance and Watt's surreal goof-outs.
(Few tracks exceeded sixty seconds in
length, explaining how the band came
by its name.) In five years, the group
put out some twenty releases, albums
What Makes a Man Start Fires? (1982),
Buzz or Howl under the Influence of Heat
(1983), the group's two-record masterpiece, *Double Nickels on the Dime* (1984)
and *Three-Way Tie (for Last)* (1985)
cementing their legacy.

For 'legacy' it would turn out to
be. Crossing Tucson, Arizona, after
a tour date, The Minutemen's van
– borrowed from The Meat Puppets
and driven by Boon's girlfriend, who
fell asleep at the wheel – spun out
of control, crashed and caught fire.
Boon, sleeping in the back, suffered
instant breakage of his spine, and died
without waking. It was the end for
The Minutemen, though a live album,

'Hacks can fawn over eighties albums by Springsteen and Prince, but *Double Nickels . . .* is the musical pinnacle of that wretched decade.'
Dave Lang, rock writer

Ballot Result, was released two years
later (by which time Watts had formed
Firehose). The group influenced many
that followed, among them Nirvana
and Sonic Youth.

Tuesday 31

Rick Nelson
(Eric Hilliard Nelson – Teaneck, New Jersey,
8 May 1940)

Andrew Chapin
(Massachusetts, 7 February 1952)

Ricky Intveld
(California, 1963)

Bobby Neal
(Missouri, 19 July 1947)

Pat Woodward
(California, 29 August 1948)

The Stone Canyon Band

Decades before *The Monkees* and *The
Partridge Family* (or, if you like, *The
Osbournes*, given the father's name),
the Nelson family played themselves
in *The Adventures of Ozzie and Harriet*,
a long-running radio/TV series based
around the musical family's world.
Father Ozzie Nelson was a noted
bandleader, mother Harriet Hilliard
a popular singer. Young Ricky played
himself from age eight, thereby catch-
ing the performing bug; and his popularity on the shows smoothed his path

into teen idolism, hit records just the
next step. If Elvis could do it, so could
he. Spurred on by adolescent jealousy
of a girlfriend's love for The King,
Nelson set about putting together an
impressive run of hit records of his
own towards the end of the fifties. But
although he was generally perceived as
teen pin-up material, Nelson fronted
a pretty decent rockabilly ensemble
(unnamed until they adopted the title
The Stone Canyon Band in 1970).
Helped greatly by some convenient
onscreen plugging, in just seven years
Nelson placed eighteen titles on the
Billboard Top Ten for Verve, Imperial
and Decca, with 'Poor Little Fool'
(1958) and 'Travellin' Man' (1961) producing number-one hits (an achievement uniquely matched by his father
and two sons).

In 1971, the now-mature Rick
Nelson – having long dropped the
'y' suffix from his name – returned
with a new Stone Canyon Band, a
country-flavoured update of his earlier
unit, and scored another US million-
selling hit with 'Garden Party' (1972).
By now considered a serious artist,
Nelson enjoyed accolades from the
likes of Johnny Cash and Creedence
Clearwater Revival's John Fogerty,
who often cited him as an influence.
By the eighties, however, Nelson's
tours were mainly nostalgia packages
with former contemporaries like
Bobby Vee and Del Shannon, which
nonetheless proved popular with a
fittingly older audience. The musicians
in his band were no slouches, though
– most had played major US venues,
while keyboardist Andy Chapin was a
veteran of both Steppenwolf and The
Association.

After a series of successful
Christmas dates, Rick Nelson and
The Stone Canyon Band flew from
Guntersville, Alabama, to Dallas for
a New Year's Eve show. Aboard the
DC-3 – purchased by Nelson from
Jerry Lee Lewis shortly before – were
the band, soundman Clark Russell,
Nelson's 27-year-old fiancée, Helen

Blair, and the pilot and co-pilot. With the door to the cockpit for some reason firmly shut, neither pilot had much inkling of what was going on in the rest of the aircraft, but four hours into the flight they noticed heavy smoke, which prompted them to radio the ground. The plane then swooped, clipping poles and severing power cables before hitting a tree and losing a wing. Barely missing a farm house, the DC-3, now ablaze, plunged to earth near DeKalb, Texas. Both pilots somehow scrambled, badly burned, from the wreckage, unable to do anything for their passengers, all of whom died, if not from the crash then from the inferno itself or from smoke inhalation. An inquest showed that a faulty gas heater at the rear of the craft was to blame for the onboard fire.

The funeral service for Rick Nelson six days later was no less eventful. In attendance were the singer's four children (including twins Gunnar and Matthew, who went on to US chart success just five years later) and – unexpectedly – his former wife, Kristin Harmon, who emerged from a limousine during the burial to demand inclusion in the singer's estate. Nelson and Harmon had been fighting a bitter divorce settlement that year, and, having recently been excluded from Nelson's will, his scorned ex-partner then sullied the occasion further by assaulting their daughter Tracy before crowds of astonished mourners. Litigation continued for months after – and also for Chapin's widow, Lisa Jane, who sued two aviation companies for his 'wrongful death'. The latter suffered another horrific tragedy eight years on, when her second marriage, to Steppenwolf drummer Jerry Edmonton, was ended by his death in an auto crash (☞ *November 1993*).

Lest We Forget

Other notable deaths that occurred sometime during 1985:

Ronnie Appoldt (US drummer with Georgia thrash-metal band Hallow's Eve; shot when an LA drug deal went awry – his replacement Rob Clayton died equally dramatically in 1992)

Tommy Blake (US rockabilly guitarist; born Thomas LeVan Givens, Louisiana, 14/9/1931; mysteriously shot dead by his wife Samantha, as he attempted to present her with a Xmas gift, 24/12)

Abel DeCosta (pioneering US lead tenor with doo-wop groups The Blenders and The Cues who also worked with many other R & B singers; born Abel DiCosta, 1929; unknown)

Lorraine Ellison (raw-edged US soul singer with The Ellison Singers and Golden Chords who later hit with 'Stay With Me' in 1966; born Pennsylvania, 1943; unknown, 17/8)

Fathead (Jamaican DJ foil to Yellowman, recognized for his 'oinks' and 'ribbits'; born Vernon Rainford, Kingston; murdered by gunshot, 22/12)

Brian Keenan (US drummer with Manfred Mann and black neo-soul act The Chambers Brothers; born New York, 28/1/1944; heart attack)

Mike Sund (US singer/guitarist with rock bands Little Joe & The Ramrods, The Redtops and The Mike Sund Combo; born Nebraska, 1944; unknown)

D'Marie Warren (US disco singer with Alton McClain & Destiny, who hit with 'It Must be Love' in 1979; born Delores Warren, California, 1953; car crash, 22/2)

Ricky West (UK funk keyboardist with Kool & The Gang (1969–78) who wrote their big-selling 'Hollywood Swinging' hit; born Richard Allen Westfield, Essex, 7/5/1943; long-term illness)

Tex Williams (US country/Western swing singer; born Sollie Paul Williams, 23/8/1917; having recorded such 'classics' as 'Smoke! Smoke! Smoke! (That Cigarette)', he succumbed to lung cancer, 11/10)

For a complete list of fallen artists, visit
www.numberoneinheaven.com

JANUARY

Phil Lynott

(West Bromwich, 20 August 1949)

Thin Lizzy
Grand Slam
(Various acts)

He was distinctive in many ways was Philip Parris Lynott – not least for his unique appearance. A dark-skinned Irish boy, Lynott was born out of wedlock to a Brazilian man (who played no part in his growing up) and an Irish girl, Philomena, living in the West Midlands. This being 1951, it was considered best for the boy to live with his grandmother Sarah – whose name would inspire a later hit record – in Dublin. Rock 'n' roll became Lynott's life during an adolescence toughened by frequent bigotry – the guitarist formed bands like The Black Eagles and Orphanage, both of which featured later collaborator Brian Downey. Lynott's characteristic bass style was nurtured in his third group, one of the many bands that have gone under the name Skid Row. But in 1969, having developed a decidedly Hendrix-esque swagger to go with his startling Afro and gypsy earrings, 19-year-old Lynott formed Thin Lizzy with Eric Bell (guitars) and Downey (drums).

Fancying himself as something of a poet, Lynott applied his folk-styled lyrics to Lizzy's first albums for Decca, an eponymous debut (1971) and *Shades of a Blue Orphanage* (1972) – though it was a traditional Irish drinking song that brought the band to the public's attention and put Phil Lynott on national television. 'Whiskey in the Jar' raced to UK number six early in 1973; Lizzy's interpretation, with its evocative intro, remains for many the definitive version of this standard. Various line-up changes ensued – hoary guitar hero Gary Moore came and went twice within four years – before the settled Lizzy frontline of Lynott (bass), Brian Robertson and Scott Gorham (both guitar) was established for the band's most fertile period. In 1976, a more hard-rock-friendly version of Lizzy was back in the UK singles Top Ten with the rowdy singalong 'The Boys are Back in Town' (the band's only American hit) and released a series of hit albums, the biggest of which was the concert recording *Live and Dangerous* (1978), which showed a band best enjoyed in performance. But while all was in order commercially, Phil Lynott was to endure, in 1977, the first of a number of serious health issues, contracting hepatitis while on tour. His abuse of heroin was

largely to blame. Nonetheless, Phil Lynott seemed to recover fully and all worries were forgotten. In 1980, he married girlfriend Caroline Crowther (daughter of late British TV presenter Leslie), and fathered a daughter, who shared his grandmother's name. One of the most popular characters on the music scene, Lynott even managed to straddle Britain's burgeoning new-wave scene: Thin Lizzy – and perhaps Motörhead – were the only heavy-rock bands considered cool enough for the post-punk generation, and this was reflected by a friendship with his countryman Bob Geldof (then of The Boomtown Rats) and a charity collaboration with former Sex Pistols Paul Cook and Steve Jones. (Unlikely covers of Lizzy hits include a Happy Mondays' deconstruction of 'The Boys are Back in Town' and the Smashing Pumpkins' take on 'Dancing in the Moonlight'.) The only downer at this time was the blanket ban of Lizzy's 'Killer on the Loose' single (1980), an ill-advised homage to serial murder (and not their first). But, ever a grafter, Lynott also juggled a solo career, with two early-eighties albums to his name – his biggest UK hit was the Moore collaboration 'Out in the Fields' (1985). By now, though, Thin Lizzy were fading, many – including Lynott himself – feeling the band had become a spent force. The frontman effectively split Lizzy in 1983, forming the short-lived Grand Slam (again with Downey) in their stead.

Phil Lynott was, unbeknown to many, himself a spent force. His body had withstood years of alcohol and drug abuse (which had somehow remained low profile for such a big star) but by the turn of 1986, it all came home to roost. On Christmas night 1985, Lynott (who had been attending rehab) fell into a drug-induced coma and was hospitalized in Salisbury for eight days; his wife and father-in-law were by his side as he passed away. The cause of death was officially recorded as heart and liver failure exacerbated by septicaemia. Phil Lynott – a statue of whom is planned in his beloved Dublin – was buried in Sutton, Ireland, overlooking Dublin Bay.

Tuesday 14

Daniel Balavoine
(Alençon, Normandy, 5 February 1952)
Présence
(Various acts)

A folk/pop singer, largely unheard of outside of his native France, Balavoine and his conscience were spurred by the 1968 student uprising, and he voiced his disquiet with a number of bands – none of whom reached a wide enough audience to make an impression. With the group Présence, however, Balavoine did enough to make himself heard, winning a solo contract with Barclay in 1975 – by which time he had ghosted vocals for up-and-coming disco star Patrick Juvet. Though he released a number of albums, Balavoine remained a cult figure, and it was only a role in rock opera *Starmania* (1978) that plucked him from obscurity, prompting a hit record at home with his own '*Le Chanteur*'. Always a controversial figure, Balavoine twice appeared

on television debates, on one berating presidential candidate François Mitterrand, and on another alienating many with some ambiguous comments about French war veterans.

Also interested in foreign concerns, Balavoine used the 1986 Paris–Dakar Rally to promote interest in providing water pumps for suffering African townships; it was one of these trips that ended in tragedy. Travelling with the rally's director, Daniel Balavoine was one of five on board killed when their helicopter flew into a sandstorm and, with no visibility, crashed into a dune.

Saturday 25

Albert Grossman
(Chicago, Illinois, 21 May 1926)

The son of Russian-Jewish immigrants, Albert Grossman graduated with an economics degree, which only hinted at the powerful position he was to hold in popular music in the decades that followed. Grossman was fired from his first notable position, in charge of a housing authority (he had led them to believe he possessed a business qualification). No matter: his next move, into music, proved to be key. Grossman and a colleague opened The Gate of Horn – a Chicago blues/folk club that booked acts like Big Bill Broonzy – while also inaugurating the Newport Folk Festival. Moving to New York, Grossman then assembled popular vocal trio, Peter, Paul & Mary in 1961, securing them a huge hit with 'Blowin' in the Wind', by Bob Dylan, whom Grossman then went on to manage. His later acquisitions included The Band, Janis Joplin and Paul Butterfield, as he became one of the most powerful men in the industry. It was to be short-lived, though: his sharp practices became widely recognized; and his and Dylan's partnership

had to be dissolved in court. During the seventies, Grossman nonetheless launched his own Bearsville label, home to Todd Rundgren and Foghat among others.

Albert Grossman was travelling to London from New York when he suffered a heart attack in his sleep. Even death couldn't keep Grossman out of the courts: without a will, the vast web of his empire took years to disentangle.

MARCH

Tuesday 4

Richard Manuel
(Stratford, Ontario, 3 April 1943)
The Band
(The Hawks)

Just over a month after the death of his former manager, pianist and singer Richard Manuel took his life in mysterious circumstances in Florida – perhaps as a result of his failure to kick a mounting drug and alcohol problem.

Manuel made the familiar leap from gospel to secular music as a boy, starting his own high-octane rock 'n' roll combo just as the genre was settling in around the US. A meeting with fellow performer Ronnie Hawkins (leader of The Hawks) proved a break, and Manuel joined this popular touring band until a falling-out saw the majority of the unit – Manuel (piano/drums/vocals), Robbie Robertson (guitar/vocals), Rick Danko (bass/vocals), Garth Hudson (organ) and Levon Helm (drums) – defect to become Bob Dylan's touring band in 1964. Contributing much to Dylan's transition from acoustic to electric folk by 1966, The Band (as they were generically rechristened) had to put up with a great deal of flack from

> **'[In 1975,] we both had the same problems – I felt insecure and he was *clearly* insecure. But he was incredibly gifted. Richard was the true light of The Band.'**
>
> Eric Clapton

audiences countrywide. Manuel and The Band were also present on Dylan's *Basement Tapes* (unreleased until 1975), on which Manuel's soulful voice could be heard properly for the first time. This series of songs was recorded at Dylan's esoteric Woodstock retreat, where The Band honed their own style – and the name of which prompted the title of a well-received debut album of their own, *Music from Big Pink* (1968). (Manuel's is the first voice to be heard on this set.) The highlight was 'The Weight', the most distinctive number from an album whose purism and reverence cut through rock's then obsession with psychedelia. For many, this was surpassed by the second album, *The Band* (1969), which showed the group of white gospel-inspired musicians at their very best. (Manuel, along with other members of The Band, continued to play on several of Dylan's releases throughout the seventies.) Manuel was perhaps best appreciated in a live environment, illustrated by his haunting solo vocal performances on *Rock of Ages* (1972). The Band's most notable concert was, however, the group's last of the period: supported by cameos from Dylan, Eric Clapton, Muddy Waters, Joni Mitchell, Van Morrison, Neil Young and Paul Butterfield, *The Last Waltz* (1976, released 1978) was to prove a fitting epitaph to this chapter of The Band's career as the group went their separate ways.

Manuel found work backing artists like Bonnie Raitt, but, having entered a rehabilitation programme in 1979, little was heard of him until The Band came together again (without Robbie Robertson, who was now enjoying the highest solo profile) for a series of ill-advised reunions in the mid eighties. It was during one of these tours that tragedy struck: having imbibed a post-show cocktail of alcohol and cocaine in his room at the Quality Inn in Winter Park, Florida, Richard Manuel hanged himself with his belt in the bathroom – just feet away from where his partner slept, unaware of any problem. No suicide note was left.

See also *Stan Szelest (↗ January 1991); Rick Danko (↗ December 1999)*

Saturday 22

Mark Dinning
(Max E Dinning – Drury, Oklahoma, 17 August 1933)

If he's remembered for nothing else, Mark Dinning will surely be recalled for presenting the world with one of the original death-ditty classics. Dinning was born into a musical family and grew up near Nashville; his father was an evangelical singer, his siblings, Lou, Ginger and Jeannie, found notoriety as The Dinning Sisters during the forties. It was his older brother, Ace, however, who gave Dinning his first break as a performer, encouraging the young guitarist to join him for live performances at his club. Dinning subsequently signed with MGM, soldiering on as a would-be country star until 1960, when he scored remarkable (and brief) pop fame with the controversial 'Teen Angel', a morbid classic, co-written with one of his sisters, involving a young girl killed in her car on the railroad track (↗ *The Death Toll #1*). This record sent the singer to number one in the US, shifting 3 million copies.

With no significant follow-up hit, Mark Dinning saw his career relapse into obscurity, and concentrated on the live circuit during the seventies and into the eighties. It was on his way home from such an engagement in Jefferson City, Missouri, that Dinning suffered a fatal heart attack – perhaps appropriately while at the wheel of his car.

Monday 31

O'Kelly Isley
(Cincinnati, Ohio, 25 December 1937)
The Isley Brothers

For over forty years the leader of his highly successful family band, O'Kelly Isley steered The Isley Brothers through numerous changes – both stylistic and line-up-based – beginning their career as a church vocal quartet in 1955. At this juncture, the group was O'Kelly Isley plus younger brothers Rudolph, Ronald and Vernon – but any early excitement was quelled by the tragic death of the last in a horrific cycling accident that year (↗ *Pre-1965*).

In 1959, O'Kelly Isley and his brothers – by now a fairly useful though as yet unsuccessful unit – were signed to RCA, and composed student favourite 'Shout', a million-selling R & B stomper that put the group on the map – although its crypto-religious call-and-response style was to infuriate some of the Isleys' church contemporaries. As though cursed by powers blasphemed, The Isleys then failed with their next few releases, winding up at Wand Records – while Scottish chanteuse Lulu later enjoyed the hit version of 'Shout'. For 'Twist and Shout' (1962), they added the latest dance craze to their earlier instruction, and finally crossed over to the pop Top Twenty, the song covered this time by The Beatles.

More label inconsistency meant they had no further hits until 1966 – more than ten years after O'Kelly had first brought his siblings together – despite using a young Jimi Hendrix on 1964's 'Testify'. With Motown, however, one single *did* make a significant impact: 'This Old Heart of Mine (is Weak for You)' (1966) once again ruptured the Billboard charts and climbed into the UK Top Three. Although relations with Berry Gordy's label were strained almost from day one, The Isleys went down a storm when touring in Britain, charting more hits, including the fabulous 'Behind a Painted Smile' (1969). (In the States, the funky 'It's Your Thing' gave them a Billboard million-seller for their new T-Neck imprint at the same time.) An almost neo-psychedelic Isley Brothers emerged during the seventies – now augmented by two more brothers, Ernie (guitar) and Marvin (bass), plus keyboardist cousin Chris Jasper (to keep it a family thing) – to bank more classic moments such as 'That Lady' (US/UK, 1973), 'Highways of My Life', 'Summer Breeze' (UK, both 1974), 'Fight the Power' (US, 1975) and 'Harvest for the World' (UK, 1976) and continue a consistent though differing run of hits on both sides of the Atlantic. A final dipping of toes into the murky reservoir of late-seventies disco seemed a touch unwieldy, but nonetheless kept the royalties drip-dripping into The Isleys' account. By the early eighties, however, the band had split into two factions, the newest acquisitions forming Isley Jasper Isley.

After cutting 1985's *Masterpiece* – a modestly titled final album of ballads – O'Kelly Isley suffered an unexpected heart attack and died from a cerebral haemorrhage at a New Jersey hospital. Thus – although the name was to be kept alive by Rudolph and Ronald – a thirty-year partnership for The Isley Brothers was ended.

JUNE

Friday 13

Dean Reed

(Wheat Ridge, Denver, Colorado, 22 September 1938)

At one point, Dean Reed might have been able to present a case for being the 'biggest rock star you never heard of'. His story is one of the most interesting in a decade that appeared to do its utmost to encourage the wannabe and discourage any form of conscience in rock 'n' roll. In truth, Reed was neither great singer nor great guitarist, but he possessed an extraordinary yearning to make a name for himself as a young man, no matter what path he was to follow. At seventeen, this 'path' was over 110 miles of rocky terrain that the headstrong youth, desperate to prove himself, chose to run for a bet: he won – a shiny quarter – beating a mule and rider. It was a typical response to challenge for a man who had had the need to win drummed into him by a strict father. Reed's relationship with his father, Cyril, somehow remained strong, despite the corporal punishment dished out to him and – most significantly – despite his father's right-wing views and support of the John Birch Society. The irony in this would become apparent when Reed hit his stride as a young singer. Having attended a military academy in deference to

'Dean Reed could laugh. A man that laughs doesn't kill himself.'

Phil Everly, long-time friend of Dean Reed

his father's wishes, Reed, disillusioned after graduation by the continuing Cold War, set about changing his world. And that of everyone else.

Dean Reed originally wanted to become a weather reporter, but he quit meteorological studies in Colorado to travel to Hollywood, fascinated by this new 'rock 'n' roll thing'. A chance meeting with a man on the road put him in touch with a Capitol Records boss – and he somehow got a recording contract. To his credit, Reed refused to rest on his laurels and enrolled in drama school, where he befriended the already famous Phil Everly (of The Everly Brothers) and also tutor Paton Price – a traditional liberal who was the first to encourage Reed's political ventures. With his records selling poorly in the US, Reed worked as an actor while he tried and tried again to make a musical breakthrough. In the end, his breakthrough came when one of his records, 'Our Summer Romance' (1959), became a massive hit in South America; Reed upped and left to visit Chile, Peru, Venezuela and Argentina, where, to his astonishment, he was greeted like a hero. And hero he was to many South Americans: the majority had yet to witness a young American prepared to criticize openly his country's leaders while befriending repressed performers and dissidents, happy to play prisons for free – even on a couple of occasions risking jail himself. His career barely out of the starting blocks at home, Reed stayed put. His South American experience showed the singer pretty starkly the injustices rife within these countries, while also exposing him to a large amount of ill-feeling towards his home nation. In 1966, a mistrustful Argentine government declared him persona non grata and packed him off back home.

But, delighted with the platform his fame had given him, Reed began to attend international peace conferences. Next, dubbed 'The Red Elvis', he became a sensation to Soviet youngsters force-fed Soviet music and starved of Western entertainment. Nobody behind the Iron Curtain had ever seen a singer in leathers and cowboy boots, and Reed was lapped up like the finest cream. According to Everly, who travelled there to play a series of shows as his old friend's guest, Reed 'couldn't leave his house without being mobbed'. By the time Reed reached East Germany he was already a megastar. His movie career – which had included a series of high-profile spaghetti Westerns while he lived in Italy during the late sixties – was refreshed here and, marrying for a third time (the beautiful actress Renate Blume), he settled now in Berlin. By 1985 the couple were planning to appear opposite one another in a Reed-penned movie called *Bloody Heart*.

Reed's career, however, began to unravel with the arrival of Glasnost in the early eighties. Young Russians now had a number of indigenous pop stars of whom they could be proud. Reed was suddenly seen as outmoded – a pawn for the establishment – and his sales plummeted spectacularly as a result. The man who had only wanted the world's different cultures to live in harmony was interpreted now as a mere panderer to controlling forces who, in the eyes of the young and forthright, had had their day. A severely disillusioned Reed felt a return to his native land would be the only way to save a career that had suddenly turned distinctly sour; he had, after all, always maintained his US passport and had made IRS contributions since his twenties. In October 1985, he visited the US to attend a Denver film festival – because it featured a piece about himself – and rediscovered a love for his country. While in the US, Reed played a low-profile concert in Loveland, Colorado; it was a stark contrast to all the adulation he had received in theatres across the world, and was to be the only performance he ever gave in his native country.

Back with Blume in East Germany, Reed was still determined to create something of a career in the US – and a final opportunity arrived in the shape of an interview with CBS flagship current-affairs show *60 Minutes*. The interview (shot in East Berlin and broadcast across the US in April 1986) began well enough, but Reed's apparent support for Mikhail Gorbachev and condemnation of Ronald Reagan was seen as 'pro-commie' to a middle America that hadn't moved on as much as he'd perhaps hoped. To top this, Reed then provoked a barrage of hate mail by appearing to come out in defence of the Berlin Wall; any musical comeback in his own land was effectively scuppered there and then. (This compounded the storm of protest that had greeted Reed's earlier references, on a KNUS Denver radio slot, to local broadcaster Alan Berg, assassinated by Aryan supremacists two years previously.)

A desperate Dean Reed, his career in tatters, now had only *Bloody Heart* left – and when this, too, began to suffer from funding problems, he disappeared, on the night of 12 June. Days of searching came to an end when the former star's body was found in a lake near his home in the Berlin suburb of Schmöckwitz on 18 June. Although no note was discovered, the coroner's verdict was suicide by drowning. But in the twenty years since his death, many have come out in support of a conspiracy – not least Everly and Reed's brother Dale, both of whom talk in terms of an assassination by the Stasi, KGB or CIA, though no evidence has ever been brought forward. Reed's mother – who passed away in 2001 – left money to her grandchildren specifically for investigative purposes.

His story has found a high profile across the States in the years since his passing, and Dean Reed was set to become the subject of a Dreamworks movie in 2005 – with new fan Tom Hanks mooted to play the central role.

JULY

Tracy Pew
(Melbourne, 19 December 1957)
The Birthday Party
(The Saints)

Tracy Pew, often described as 'Australia's Sid Vicious', only resembled the former Sex Pistol in one sense. In his homeland, at least, he was an iconic figure (and of course he died young) – but the main difference between them was that Pew could actually play bass a bit. Inspired by glam/schlock acts like Alice Cooper and The New York Dolls, The Boys Next Door were formed in Melbourne by Caulfield grammar-school friends Pew, Nick Cave (vocals), Rowland S Howard (guitar), Mick Harvey (various instruments) and Phil Calvert (drums). Changing their name, to that of a Harold Pinter play, The Birthday Party proceeded to become one of alternative rock's best-kept secrets before storming the UK in 1980. The band were not for the faint-hearted: driven by Cave's savage imagery (which continues within his work to this day), The Birthday Party became a huge draw, attracting art-rock lovers, punks and goths alike – though their highly original shtick fell in somewhere with contemporaries The Cramps, The Fall and Pere Ubu. A series of gut-wrenching albums, of which *Junkyard* (1982) is arguably the best, made the group's name, mainly in Europe. On stage, Stetson- and leather-clad Pew proved an excellent stooge to frontman Cave's stripped-to-the-waist posturing, his snaky basslines underpinning the Party sound. That is, when the genial musician's predilections would allow it – Pew often imbibed to the point of

OD off stage and in 1982 was arrested for drunk-driving. With other offences such as unpaid fines taken into consideration, Pew served two and a half months inside. The Birthday Party had run its course by the end of the next year, ending with a couple of great EPs, *The Bad Seed* and *Mutiny!* While Cave went on to form a band named after the former, Pew toured with top Aussie stalwarts The Saints.

Like Ian Curtis of Joy Division (*May 1980*), Tracy Pew was prone to epileptic seizures, in his case exacerbated by heavy drug use. In July 1986, the bass-player suffered a fit while lying in his bathtub; the resultant head injuries were so severe that Pew died from a brain haemorrhage. In bleak irony, the academic Pew had cleaned up considerably at the time of his death and re-entered university. (At least three different dates exist for Pew's death – this appears to be the accurate one.)

AUGUST

Wednesday 6

Michael Rudetski

(New York, 1959)
Culture Club

For years, Boy George convinced the world that his favourite indulgence was a cup of tea. The ebullient Mr O'Dowd may well have preferred Darjeeling to sex, but in 1986 his horrified fanbase watched agog as the Culture Club vocalist's previously hidden habits were exposed by the tabloids. However, the scandal's worst casualty was to be visiting American keyboardist Michael Rudetski.

With a seemingly firm grip on the UK's record-buyers having slipped in the past couple of years, Culture Club

had made a stuttering Top Ten comeback with the (appositely titled) 1986 album *From Luxury to Heartache* and a brace of moderate hit singles. On this album, New Yorker Rudetski – who had become a friend and acolyte of Boy George's – supplied keyboards. In return, somebody supplied the American with hard drugs. Later in the week that Boy George's own drug habit was revealed, Rudetski's body was found in the singer's London flat, where he had been staying on his own. A post mortem revealed that an overdose of heroin was the cause of death. With the British media going into meltdown over the frontman's disclosure, Rudetski as a person and musician was almost forgotten – and the band inevitably broke up amid the furore.

SEPTEMBER

Saturday 27

Cliff Burton

(San Francisco, California, 10 February 1962)
Metallica
(Trauma)
(Various acts)

A talented musician born to hippy parents, introverted Cliff Burton took an unlikely musical path – he is considered by metal fans to be one of the most innovative bassists of all time. Encouraged by his mother to study Bach and Beethoven, Burton rapidly grasped classical progressions; during his adolescence he was already applying this knowledge to his bass-playing. To his appreciation of classical and jazz (Burton namechecked bass virtuoso Stanley Clarke many times), the young musician added the aggression he'd found in the California and London punk scenes. Carrying this

formidable armoury, Burton met Big Jim Martin (later of Faith No More) and briefly formed Vicious Hatred, an experimental hard-rock act, which practised out in the wilds of northern California. Later, as bass-player with emerging Bay Area metal band Trauma, Cliff Burton was reluctant to up sticks and leave his beloved home town when Metallica's persistent drummer, Lars Ulrich, began urging him to join the LA-based thrash pioneers at the end of 1982. The solution was simple: Burton insisted that Ulrich and the rest of the band – James Hetfield (guitar/vocals) and Dave Mustaine (guitar, shortly thereafter replaced by Kirk Hammett) should relocate to San Francisco. So determined were Metallica to get their man that they did. It proved a wise move. With Burton on board, Metallica became an awesome proposition, making serious commercial inroads while sticking to their 'extreme' roots. The band's first albums, *Kill 'Em All* (1983) and *Ride the Lightning* (1984) showed a healthy distance from the metal posturing of the day – both featuring some great Burton cameos. Record number three, *Master Of Puppets* (1986), shifted half a million copies in the US alone (largely unheard of for a group snubbed by the production-line output of MTV et al). Burton became a fans' favourite: polite and reserved off stage, he was loved for his dextrous playing, wild performances and his informal T-shirt-and-flared-jeans appearance.

Without radio or television exposure, Metallica, like many extreme rock bands, relied on solid touring to get their message across. To support *Master Of Puppets*, the band embarked upon a gruelling schedule of European dates that took them into Scandinavia, where they were immensely popular (Ulrich being of Danish extraction). Following a well-attended gig at a cinema in Solna, Sweden, Metallica happily signed autographs before boarding the larger of their entourage's

Cliff Burton: Hair-raising capers

'Touring has become more pleasant now we have a better bus and stuff.'

Cliff Burton, interviewed the day before his death by writer Jörgen Holmstedt

two luxury coaches to head for the next destination, Copenhagen, where Ulrich's friends waited, having set up a post-concert party for the band. High spirits continued well into the journey, Burton and Hammett playing cards to see who would take the bigger bunk, much like the Tommy Allsup/Richie Valens gamble ahead of Buddy Holly's air crash (*Pre-1965*). This time, the fatal hand landed with Burton.

At around 6.50 am, Metallica's bus carried its sleeping passengers along the E4 motorway through the quiet region of Småländ, some fifteen miles from Ljungby. Possibly having fallen asleep at the wheel, the driver suddenly hit a ditch, pulling the coach sharply back up on to the road and attempting to regain control of the steering. At this point, the driver claimed that the vehicle hit a patch of black ice (which is disputed by Swedish press photographer Lennart Wennberg, among the first eyewitnesses at the scene), skidding across the road and then crashing violently into another ditch. Inside, most of those asleep had been thrown from their bunks, but Burton had been thrown clean through one of the windows. As the bus teetered and then tipped over, the bass-player was crushed beneath its vast chassis. Hetfield said: 'I saw our bus lying on top of Cliff, with his leg sticking out. I went to pieces.' The devastated band and crew – most escaping with superficial or short-term injury – soon got confirmation at a Ljungby hospital that Burton hadn't made it.

At Cliff Burton's funeral, the track 'Orion' – written mainly by the bassist – was played as the rest of the band offered their thoughts to the congregation. Burton's cremated remains were scattered around some of his favoured San Francisco haunts. A new bassist arrived just forty-one days later: former Flotsam & Jetsam member Jason Newsted, who remained with the band until 2001, though Hetfield and Ulrich continued to use Burton's material on later Metallica albums. In

2003, Hammett voiced the belief of the three longest-running members of Metallica that Burton could never be replaced: 'We still haven't got over the shock. We're still trying.'

OCTOBER

Wednesday 1

Andy McVann
(Liverpool, 1965)
The Farm

Years before they became the briefest of baggy sensations, The Farm (originally Soul of Socialism) were a grafting band of Scouse dance-rockers, formed by unemployed singer Peter Hooton and his pals to avoid having to get a job: the Liverpool music scene was then buzzing from the success of bands like Echo & The Bunnymen, Dead Or Alive and Frankie Goes to Hollywood. Like Hooton, drummer Andy McVann held strong socialist beliefs and loved his football. The pair – along with Steve Grimes (guitar) and Phil Strongman (bass) – saw the band as an outlet for their views, soon utilizing a horn section much like left-wing contemporaries such as The Redskins. A flurry of independent singles made little headway, however.

For McVann it was a particularly short-lived venture: he died in a crash after attempting to outrun a police car near his Liverpool home. The rest of The Farm persevered (Roy Boulter took over the vacant drummer's seat) until an unlikely breakthrough saw them enjoy major UK hits with 'Groovy Train' and 'All Together Now' (both 1990), as well as a number-one debut album issued eight years after the band's inception.

Wednesday 22

Jane Dornacker
(California, 1 October 1947)
The Tubes
Leila & The Snakes

The contributor of one of *Number One in Heaven*'s most dramatic tales, tall, vivacious singer turned comedienne turned traffic reporter Jane Dornacker began her varied performing and broadcasting career by befriending singer/guitarist Fee Waybill (John Waldo) during the mid seventies. His band, The Tubes, were creating something of a stir in both the US and UK with their over-the-top concert behaviour – chainsaws and wheelchairs featured prominently – and the leggy Dornacker somehow fitted the group's needs, both visually and vocally. She added the cod-seductive female voice to 'Don't Touch Me There' (which she also co-wrote), a brilliant *Rocky Horror*-style 'teen lust' parody from the band's 1977 hit EP, *White Punks on Dope*. At the same time, Dornacker was fronting Leila & The Snakes (as 'Leila'), a San Francisco glam act that also featured TV Dunbar (guitars), Pamela Wood (bass) and Scott Free (drums). Without much further musical success, Dornacker took to stand-up comedy and became a fixture of the San Fran comedy scene for some years, also appearing in the 1983 movie *The Right Stuff*.

Settling into a broadcasting career, Dornacker married and landed a job with New York's WNBC (later WFAN) as traffic reporter on board the station's N-Copter. Early in 1986, she and her pilot had survived a crash into New Jersey's Hackensack River during such a broadcast, which might well have put some off the job for good. Dornacker, however, took the experience in her stride and was in position again with a different pilot,

covering an afternoon accident slowing up New York's traffic on 22 October. In the middle of her live report, as Dornacker described the scenes below her, listeners heard the helicopter's engines strain dramatically; after a spine-chilling scream of 'Hit the water!', all sound went dead. Studio presenter Joey Reynold knew that something had gone badly wrong, but did his best to remain calm on air, suggesting that he and his audience 'say a little prayer'. The helicopter, its rotors having ceased to function, fell just seventy-five feet, and hit a chain-link fence before plunging into twenty feet of murky Hudson water. While her pilot Bill Pate survived with injuries, Dornacker died en route to hospital – throwing Reynold and his colleagues into deep shock. Another grim discovery was that the helicopter had been repaired using a military aircraft clutch wholly inappropriate for civilian use. Dornacker's daughter, Naomi, received $325K from the manufacturers as compensation.

'Hit the water, hit the water, *hit the water!*'

Jane Dornacker's last words, heard by thousands of radio listeners

Esquerita

(Eskew Reeder – Greenville, South Carolina, 1935)

Those who feel Little Richard was the real deal as far as rock 'n' roll is concerned might have done a double-take had they clapped eyes on Esquerita. The flamboyant pianist and singer predated the better-known artist's look by several years, but the resemblance is uncanny. A self-taught musician, Eskew Reeder was brought up in a God-fearing community, a near-neighbour of Jesse Jackson. Reeder gained his first singing experience with gospel troupe The Heavenly Echoes, cutting 'Didn't It Rain?' with them in 1953. He became 'Esquerita' when he signed as a solo artist with Capitol, prompted by fan Gene Vincent. On some of his early sides, Esquerita was accompanied by Vincent's Blue Caps and also the much-in-demand Jordanaires (for a time Elvis's backing band). Without much commercial success, however, the singer/pianist was reduced to label- and name-hopping for much of the next twenty-or-so years. (At one point, Esquerita – greatly under-appreciated while he was alive – was employed to augment the keyboard sound of some of Little Richard's records, which must have hurt.)

Little is known about Esquerita beyond his ostentatious stage persona, although he spent some years in jail at Riker's Island during the early eighties. His death from AIDS in 1986 went largely unnoticed.

Esquerita: The real deal

NOVEMBER

Wednesday 5

Bobby Nunn

(Birmingham, Alabama, 1925)
The Coasters
The Robins

Eager-to-please Bobby Nunn was an ambitious youngster set to become the full-throated, bluesy bass-baritone whose vocal illuminated the earliest work of The Coasters. In order to land his place in the group, Nunn (a former boxer) undertook odd jobs around the famous Barrelhouse Club in Watts, Los Angeles, which belonged to Johnny Otis. An opportunity to perform with Otis's A-Sharp Trio followed – this group was an embryonic version of the highly popular Robins. In 1951, The Robins split from Otis to work with Esther Phillips (Nunn had also issued solo records by this time) and then songwriting wizards Jerry Leiber and Mike Stoller – who set before them a series of great songs including Spark releases 'Framed' and 'Smokey Joe's Café' (1955). Nunn, along with tenor Carl Gardner, was encouraged by Leiber and Stoller to join them at Atlantic, where the writers were instrumental in creating The Coasters – the two former Robins vocalists now joined by Leon Hughes (tenor), Billy Guy (baritone lead, formerly of Bip & Bop) and Adolph Jacobs (guitar). There were to be many line-up changes as The Coasters became a sensation, with seemingly limitless variations to their comic/serious shtick.

Although he'd enjoyed a US Top Five pop hit with 'Searchin'' (1957 – the flipside to which, 'Youngblood', also independently gained Top Ten status), the now-married Nunn had tired of the touring that took up most of The Coasters' time, and he retired from the band. (His replacement, Will 'Dub' Jones, supplied the distinctive deadpan on massive hits like 'Yakety Yak' and 'Charlie Brown' the following year.) Bobby Nunn did, however, return to tour with a nostalgia version of the band (of which there were several) in the mid seventies, and he released two solo compilations albums before his premature death from a heart attack.

See also *King Curtis (* August 1971); Nathaniel Wilson (* April 1980); Cornell Gunter (* February 1990). 'Dub' Jones died in 2000, as did touring singer Bob B Soxx (* November 2000). Billy Guy died in near-destitution two years later.*

Saturday 15

Alec Murphy

(Boston, Massachusetts, *c* 1958)
Vivabeat
Human Sexual Response
(Audio-Vidiot)

Though much touted by British musicians, US band Vivabeat's history is littered with tragedy and misfortune – yet the story could have been so different. Despite receiving a fair amount of attention when they came to the UK in the early eighties, Boston's Human Sexual Response were eventually considered little more than an interesting name. The band's protagonist, guitarist Alec Murphy, had already jumped ship to form Vivabeat a year or so before (via the very short-lived US/German outfit Audio-Vidiot). Vivabeat, a new-wave/synth outfit in the style of early Roxy Music/Human League was completed by Murphy's old HSR bandmate Mick Muhlfriedel (bass), Buick heiress Consuelo de Silva (synthesizer), Marina del Ray (keyboards), Doug Orilio (drums) and British vocalist Terrance Robay. With assistance from early fan Peter Gabriel, Vivabeat were the first American band signed to London's Charisma Records. The group's 1980 debut featured the naggingly infectious 'The Man from China' – a song about a heroin dealer and the nearest they would ever get to a hit.

The label was (wrongly, in the end) keen to keep the band a well-kept secret until the album had picked up media interest. When this didn't happen, Murphy spent much of the downtime as a face on the LA punk circuit, producing some of the acts while sharing some of their habits. Legend has it that the guitarist (like the character in his song) was the dealer who sold Darby Crash of The Germs his fatal dose of heroin (* December 1980). With other band members also falling foul of the scene, Charisma dropped them soon after. Murphy and de Silva were both sacked, Orilio was paralysed in a 1982 car accident, and the band fell apart.

Alec Murphy was the first of no fewer than three former Vivabeat members to die from AIDS in under a decade – de Silva and Robay followed suit in 1991 and 1994 respectively. Marina del Ray says: 'That whole circle of people who were close to us is dead. The tragic thing is that by the time they died Connie and Alec had cleaned up and were finally getting their lives together.'

DECEMBER

Lee Dorsey

(Irving Lee Dorsey – New Orleans, Louisiana,
24 December 1924)

One of many future music stars with
boxing ambitions, mechanic-by-day
Lee Dorsey fought for light-heavy-
weight titles under the name Kid
Chocolate into his thirties. A promising rock 'n' roll singer with a soulful
R & B side, Dorsey was signed by
Allen Toussaint to Fury Records in
1960, hitting almost immediately with
the slight but catchy 'Ya Ya' the following year. This Billboard smash
was followed by a series of further
US chart entries, the biggest being
'Working in a Coalmine' (1966), which
he co-wrote for the Amy label. By this
time the singer had strong backing
from The Meters. (In Britain, Dorsey
also placed 'Holy Cow' in the Top Ten
that year.)

Contributing to a recording by
Southside Johnny & The Asbury
Jukes, Lee Dorsey enjoyed a resurgence of interest during the late
seventies – which even included opening for long-time fans The Clash. He
contracted emphysema, from which
he died in New Orleans at the age of
sixty-one.

Hollywood Fats

(Michael Mann – Los Angeles, California,
17 March 1954)
The Hollywood Fats Band
The James Harmon Band
The Blasters
(Various acts)

Revered by his friend and bandmate
Larry Taylor as 'the greatest electric-
blues guitarist ever', Hollywood Fats
played alongside many blues greats
as a young man. Fats's understanding
mother drove the guitarist to blues
joints when he was just thirteen,
ensuring the young prodigy received
an apprenticeship from the likes of
Magic Sam and Buddy Guy (who gave
Fats his nickname). During the seventies, Fats lit up the work of Muddy
Waters, John Lee Hooker, Canned
Heat and Albert King (the last of
whom sacked him for 'receiving too
much attention') with his dazzling
riffs. His own Hollywood Fats Band
(formed in 1978) was a very much
on-off affair, and perhaps his best
work was with guitarist Kid Ramos
in blistering Orange County blues act
The James Harmon Band. Despite
enormous accolades from the blues
fraternity, though, Hollywood Fats was
destined not to gain wider recognition
until he had passed on.

Joining The Blasters in 1985, Fats
was recording an album with the
California retro-rock band when he
suffered a heart attack – apparently
brought on by excessive heroin use
– and died in a Santa Monica hospital.

Tommy Kiefer

(Switzerland, 21 August 1957)
Krokus

Krokus emerged as Switzerland's
leading hard-rock exponents in 1974,
finding a sizeable fanbase in both the
UK and US by the turn of the eighties. The band's original line-up was
Tommy Kiefer (vocals/guitar), Chris
von Rohr (vocals/keys), Fernando
von Arb (guitar), Jurg Naegeli (bass)
and Freddy Steady (drums). A popular festival draw – particularly with
the addition of Maltese singer Marc
Storace – Krokus were to sell steadily
with a series of albums that moved
from the progressive to the generically metal during the early years of
their career: titles included the 1976
debut *Krokus*, *Painkiller* (1978) and
Metal Rendez-vous (1980). By 1981's
Hardware, however, Kiefer had
become yet another of rock's heroin
victims, and was kicked out of the
band when his habit became detrimental to Krokus; he was replaced by
roadie Mark Kohler.

Learning that he was dying from
AIDS, Kiefer became depressed and
withdrawn; his suicide by hanging,
though a horrific shock, was understood by his friends and former band
colleagues. The band, with their ever-
familiar logo adorning every sleeve,
continue to release albums into the
new millennium.

Lest We Forget

Other notable deaths that occurred sometime during 1986:

Everett Barksdale (US member of seminal vocal group The Ink Spots; born 28/4/1907; unknown, 8/1)

Linda Creed (top US songwriter who penned many hits for The Spinners and The Stylistics and 'Greatest Love of All', a hit for George Benson and Whitney Houston; born Philadelphia, 1948; breast cancer, 10/4)

Todd Crew (US bassist with California hard-rock acts The Drunk Fux and Jetboy, and friend of the young Axl Rose – which must have helped his cause no end; heroin overdose)

James Darroch (Australian punk singer/songwriter/bassist with The Celibate Rifles and Eastern Dark; born Sydney, *c* 1960; negotiating the 'deadly' Hume Highway, he died in a tour-van crash, 3/1986)

Coke Escovedo (US Latin/rock/funk percussionist with Santana and Azteca with his brother Pete – uncle of Sheila E; born Thomas Escovedo, California, 30/4/1941; unknown, 13/7)

Dick James (UK music publisher, who was the first to sign The Beatles – also worked with Elton John, Billy J Kramer and Gerry Marsden; born Reginald Leon Vapnick, 1921; heart attack, 1/2)

Cliff Leeman (US rock 'n' roll drummer who played sessions for The Comets; born Maine; unknown)

Charles Moffitt (US bass with doo-wop group The Velours; born New York, *c* 1932; murdered in an attack, 12/1986)

Dick Rowe (UK A & R man who famously turned down The Beatles while at Decca – though redeemed himself later by nabbing The Stones; born 1925; diabetes, 6/6)

Miki Zone (US guitarist with New York 'queercore' rock/disco band The Fast and Man2Man, who hit with 'Male Stripper'; AIDS – a decade before 'brother' Armand Zone suffered the same fate – 31/12)

For a complete list of fallen artists, visit

www.numberoneinheaven.com

JANUARY

Tuesday 6

Peter Lucia

(Peter Paul Lucia Jr – Morristown, New Jersey, 2 February 1947)

Tommy James & The Shondells (Hog Heaven)

A keen drummer since his pre-school years, Peter Lucia became, in December 1965, the third to hold down the position with Tommy James & The Shondells – a group set to sell 20 million records in the USA during the late sixties. Burgeoning heart-throb James and his band had already made a lot of progress, so Lucia didn't have to wait long for success. Within six months of his joining the band – now a definitive line-up of Lucia, James (vocals), Eddie Gray (guitar), Mike Vale (bass) and Ronnie Rosman (organ) – New York's Roulette Records issued the band's first single, 'Hanky Panky' (1966). The record, which had been a local chart-topper when issued as a bootleg on Michigan's Snap label, shot to number one across the nation, shifting a cool million copies in the process. This was just the first of a run of seventeen Top Forty hits for Tommy James &

The Shondells, including 'I Think We're Alone Now' (1967), 'Mony Mony' (1968, a UK number one) and the biggest-seller of all, 'Crimson and Clover' (1969), a classic song co-written and performed exclusively by James and Lucia.

These good times soured somewhat thereafter: James's health began to suffer during 1970, and he and The Shondells went their separate ways after the singer collapsed on stage in Alabama. Some months before, the band – or, at least, their management – had missed a huge trick, turning down the chance to play Woodstock. The booking agent had dismissed the festival as 'a stupid gig on a pig farm', which may or may not have had some bearing on Lucia and the remainder of The Shondells renaming themselves Hog Heaven in the wake of the split. In this guise, the group saw little success, while James also struggled to repeat The Shondells' success as a solo performer.

Still playing as a session man, Peter Lucia had been dining with friends after a round of golf when he collapsed while attempting to pay the bill. Lucia – who had been born with a hereditary heart problem – died at the scene from a massive coronary. Later in 1987, two Shondells covers, Tiffany's 'I Think We're Alone Now' and Billy Idol's 'Mony Mony', became back-to-back US number-one singles.

Wednesday 7

Bobby Gene McNelly

(Columbus, Ohio, 21 May 1950)

McGuffey Lane

Sadly, McGuffey Lane are a band likely to be remembered more for their tragic history than their music. Although they put infectious numbers such as 'Long Time Lovin' You' (1980) and 'Start It All Over' (1981) on to radio-station playlists, without much commercial success McGuffey Lane spent most of their time on the road. They did, however, pick up prestigious support slots with The Charlie Daniels Band and The Allman Brothers. A switch to more countrified sounds saw the band move to Atlantic American Records in 1983. Singer/guitarist Bobby Gene McNelly reacted badly to the shock death of the band's keyboard- and harmonica-player, Stephen Douglass (➤ *January 1984*), leaving the line-up to become a Nashville-based songwriter. McNelly's writing came to an abrupt end, though, in a scenario straight out of a C & W melodrama. In January 1987, he argued ferociously with his fiancée, pulled a gun on her and shot her dead. McNelly then turned the gun on himself.

FEBRUARY

Saturday 14

Wendy Holcombe

(Alabaster, Alabama, 19 April 1963)

Wendy Holcombe's is one of the more tragic stories in modern music. A talented singer and banjo-player, she developed an early penchant for the bluegrass favoured by her father (who had given up his own attempts to master the requisite instrument). At the age of twelve, Holcombe was playing the Grand Ole Opry, so greatly had she impressed veteran musicians Roy Acuff and Jim Ed Brown. Within months this flaxen-haired prodigy was appearing in a variety of country/ bluegrass shows and on local television specials. By then a multi-instrumentalist, her live performances took her across the world by the time she'd reached eighteen. Simultaneously, Holcombe, who had shown some talent as an actress, was courted by major networks for television drama work, appearing in a number of vehicles including the 1981 series *Lewis and Clark*.

Later that year, it was all over. Wendy Holcombe collapsed during a performance in Indiana. The teenager was diagnosed with an enlarged heart: this meant enforced retirement for a girl who should have been looking forward to her greatest years as a performer. Little was heard from Holcombe thereafter, the musician/ actress choosing to live quietly as a housewife. With no donor forthcoming, she died from heart failure at just twenty-three years of age.

Sunday 15

Jimmy Holiday

(Durant, Mississippi, 24 July 1934)

The following day, versatile soul/ R & B vocalist Jimmy Holiday died in a similar manner. The singer had come to some prominence with his self-penned 'How Can I Forget?' (1963), a song widely played when covered by former Drifter Ben E King. Although he'd made some fine records for the Minit label, Holiday was far more successful as a writer than singer, and retired from live work in 1969. His material was then covered and recorded by a slew of big names, including Ray Charles, Jackie DeShannon, Cher and even Annie Lennox. Unfortunately, he didn't live to see all of this success, yielding to heart failure in an Iowa hospital.

MARCH

Saturday 21

Norman Harris

(New York, 10 February 1938)

MFSB

His may be one of music's more anonymous names, but Norman Harris was, during the seventies, a significant figure in the all-dominating sound of Philadelphia soul. For almost all of the previous decade, Harris had been a working session guitarist, forming an enduring partnership with bass-player Ronnie Baker. Along with drummer Earl Young, the pair founded Golden Fleece, their own publishing company – the trio was also set to become the core of MFSB (Mother, Father, Sister, Brother). As the house band for Kenny Gamble and Leon Huff's Philadelphia International label, MFSB scored 1974's seventh-best-selling record in the US with 'TSOP (The Sound of Philadelphia)'. As a producer, Harris and his 'magic touch' created significant hits with First Choice, Gloria Gaynor, The Delfonics, Wilson Pickett and The Spinners – to name just a few.

Working in collaboration with the Salsoul label, Harris (who started his own Gold Mind imprint in 1979) made records of his own, but these were significantly lower key. He was still producing at the time of his death, from a heart attack at forty-nine.

See also *Roland Chambers (☞ May 2002). Ronnie Baker died just three years after Harris.*

Dino Martin

(Dean Paul Martin Jr – Santa Monica, California, 17 November 1951)

Dino, Desi & Billy

On the same afternoon, tragedy struck for one of America's favourite entertainers, Dean Martin, with the sudden death of his first son, Dean Jr – better known as Dino. It was a blow from which the former Rat Pack star never recovered.

As a teen, Dino Martin was a regular guest on his father's NBC variety show, and the close relationship Martin Sr had with Frank Sinatra proved helpful when Dino inevitably branched out into his own show-business career. Ol' Blue Eyes had been quick to have Martin – one-third of pop trio Dino, Desi & Billy – signed to his Reprise label in 1964. It couldn't fail, particularly as Desi was the son of another showbiz institution, Desi Arnaz and Lucille Ball. But the boys were not without talent, writing and producing their own material, some of which favoured The Beach Boys and The Byrds in sound. The only major surprise was that they were not more successful: only 1965's 'I'm a Fool', 'Not the Lovin' Kind' and 'Tell Someone You Love Them' impacted significantly on the Billboard Hot 100.

Martin's career was hampered by a 1974 arrest for the possession (and attempted sale) of two machine guns, but he continued in entertainment. He appeared sporadically in low-level television series and movies, including *Players* and *Made in USA* (the latter released after his death). By the eighties, however, Martin – who had gained his pilot's licence at just sixteen – was dedicating more time to the Canadian Air National Guard, and regularly offered to take his father flying. But Dean Martin Sr had never been entirely happy with his son's change of career and always refused. On the fateful day in March 1987, the on-duty Martin was making a near-vertical take-off climb in his F-4C Phantom jet when heavy cloud caused him to lose bearings in mid-air. The craft – travelling in excess of 550 mph – slammed against the snow-covered granite wall of Mount San Gorgonio on California's San Bernardino range, killing Martin and his co-pilot, Ramon Ortiz. The wreckage was not found for five days.

APRIL

Friday 17

Carlie Barrett

(Carlton Barrett – Kingston, Jamaica, 17 December 1950)

(Bob Marley &) The Wailers
The Upsetters

The self-styled 'Field Marshal' of the one-drop rhythm (emphasis on the fourth beat), Carlton Barrett, with his older bass-playing brother, Aston 'Family Man', provided the generator that was to keep The Wailers' machine rocking steady. Fascinated as a kid by the playing of The Skatalites' Lloyd Nibbs, Barrett constructed his own drum kit from a number of empty paint cans. In only a few years, the brothers impressed the Kingston clubs as The Upsetters (originally The Hippy Boys). Under the guidance of Lee 'Scratch' Perry, the group released the massive international hit 'Return Of Django' (1969), a national number one and, significantly, Top Five in a Britain suddenly very hip to new Jamaican sounds. More success came as The Upsetters teamed with Bob Marley, Peter Tosh and Neville 'Bunny' Livingston – The Wailers – who had been established for a good few years by then. With the departure of Tosh and Livingston in 1973, the Barretts remained with Marley (in the drummer's case, until his frontman's death (◂ *May 1981*)), laying down a solid foundation as The Wailers graduated from an open secret to one of the biggest touring bands in the world, in any given genre. Carlton Barrett's skills as a songwriter are evident on the songs 'Talkin' Blues' and 'Them Belly Full' from The Wailers' *Natty Dread* (1974).

After Marley's death, Barrett found himself in legal wranglings with Rita Marley over the use of the 'Wailers' name. In 1987, this looked to be no nearer resolution, and the stress of this was compounded by the fast disintegration of his marriage. On Good Friday that year, as Barrett strolled innocently out of his house on an errand to his local grocery store, he was hit twice in the head by gunshots from a car. Barrett died at his own front gate; his estranged wife, Albertine, and her cab-driver lover, Glenroy Carter, were charged with hiring hitmen.

See also *Peter Tosh (▸ September 1987); Junior Braithwaite (▸ June 1999); Olive*

'Senya' Grant (▸ *April 2001*) – all of whom were similarly murdered in Kingston.

Tuesday 28

Billy Johnson

(Hartford, Connecticut, 20 August 1928)

The Moonglows

In his mid twenties, versatile guitarist Billy Johnson – a former student of Hartford's Conservatory of Music – played behind Chicago R & B bandleader Sonny Thompson, before joining Louisville's Harvey Fuqua-led Moonglows in 1954. As the key musician among vocalists Fuqua (baritone lead), Bobby Lester (tenor lead), Alexander Graves (tenor) and Prentiss Barnes (bass), Johnson realized most success with The Moonglows' releases for Chess Records. Their biggest crossover was 1955's 'Sincerely', though a number of other records also became pop hits. On 'Ten Commandments of Love' (1958), Johnson can even be heard as a 'voice'.

Billy Johnson's post-Moonglows career included stints as a musician for Jackie Wilson, Brook Benton and even The Four Tops. He also spent time as a television producer before his death from heart failure in a Los Angeles hospital.

See also *Bobby Lester (◂ October 1980); Marvin Gaye (◂ April 1984)*

MAY

Sunday 3

Dalida
(Yolande Christina Gigliotti – Shoubra, Cairo,
17 January 1933)

Born to an Italian opera violinist and his wife, Yolande Gigliotti was a former Miss Egypt whose looks and voice helped her carve out a niche as both an actress and a singer. Almost as soon as she'd won the title, Gigliotti headed to France in order to exploit her sudden fame: inevitably, one branch of her twin-pronged career attack was to prove more successful than the other, and – despite having appeared on film with Omar Sharif – it was as a support singer to stalwarts Charles Aznavour and Gilbert Becaud that she made her mark. As 'Dalida', she was a huge hit from 1957, selling some 80 million records worldwide during her lifetime.

The flipside of this success and glamour was a personal life that beggared belief, so drenched was it in confusion and tragedy. Dalida left her first husband and original mentor, Lucien Morisse, for artist Jean Sobieski in 1961 – just months after the couple had married; Morisse, unable to cope with his grief, shot himself. In 1966, Dalida began a relationship with her RCA duet partner Luigi Tenco, a volatile man who desired success whatever the cost. Within months, Tenco too was dead from a self-inflicted gunshot wound after

Italy's San Remo Festival (*January 1967*). Dalida shortly thereafter tried to take her own life with sleeping pills. She recovered but, having put her life back into some sort of order after these events, then fell into a relationship with less-than-reputable playboy Richard Chanfray. The former convict – best known for his odd claim on French television to be the Count of St Germain – continued the macabre trend by killing himself in 1983, just as the couple planned to marry. Crushed beyond hope of any meaningful recovery, Dalida sought solace in Hinduism, but life now had little left for her. She returned to acting in the 1986 movie *Le Sixième Jour*, but it would be her last artistic statement.

In April 1987, Dalida sold her car, many of her belongings and, significantly, changed her will. She then lowered the blinds of her bedroom and swallowed a lethal dose of pills. Dalida was posthumously remembered by a monument in the Cimitière de Montmartre and on a French postage stamp issued ten years after her death.

Monday 4

Paul Butterfield
(Chicago, Illinois, 17 December 1942)
The Paul Butterfield Blues Band

Paul Butterfield's aptitude for the blues stemmed directly from Hyde Park, the predominantly black area in which he was born and brought up. A singer and musician, his mastering of the electric Chicago genre earned Butterfield respect from both black and white blues camps – and did much to interweave the two. Butterfield became a good friend to one of his heroes, Muddy Waters, the master occasionally allowing the novice to share stage space with him. The Paul Butterfield Blues Band was established properly when Butterfield befriended musician

and fellow university student Elvin Bishop, who shared Butterfield's fascination with the sounds of Chicago's South Side. It was on the North Side, though, that the band – Butterfield (harmonica/vocals), Bishop (guitar), ex-Howlin' Wolf backers Jerome Arnold (bass) and Sam Lay (drums), and eventually Michael Bloomfield (lead guitar) – began to find residencies. From here they were lured by producer Paul Rothchild to sign with Elektra Records in 1964. After an edgy beginning, with Butterfield and Bloomfield taking a while to warm to one another's styles, The Paul Butterfield Blues Band found themselves summoned by Bob Dylan for his first electric set at the 1965 Newport Folk Festival. The occasion is, of course, legendary: Dylan and the band were roundly heckled by the purists in the crowd – though there were many able to appreciate the breakthrough that was to come.

Although they made some great records, The Blues Band experienced too many defections and line-up changes ever to make a consistent impact. By the end of 1969 key players Bishop and Bloomfield had both left for pastures new, and the frontman tried out other musicians, most notably The Band's Levon Helm and Rick Danko. Butterfield performed on and off until the early eighties, when he was stricken with peritonitis, a painful stomach condition, which many feel led to his heroin addiction. At around the same time, he was shocked to learn of the drug-related death of former colleague Bloomfield (*February 1981*).

Returning to the stage early in 1987, Paul Butterfield looked to have beaten his twin health and drug issues – until he was found slumped in the kitchen of his Hollywood apartment by his manager. Butterfield was dead at forty-five from intestinal problems.

See also *John Kahn (* May 1996); Rick Danko (* December 1999)*

'Life has become unbearable – please forgive me.'
Dalida's suicide note

JUNE

Monday 1

Gary Driscoll
(New York, 1946)

Elf (Electric Elves)
Ritchie Blackmore's Rainbow
(Various acts)

A veteran of transatlantic hard rock, Gary Driscoll first took to the drums in the post-psychedelic late sixties, with the Ronnie James Dio-fronted Electric Elves. Driscoll and Dio struck up something of a friendship, augmented when – now known as Elf – they were approached by Deep Purple's Roger Glover, who offered to produce the group. Under his supervision, the band improved from a fairly pedestrian blues-rock combo to something nastier, going on to support Purple on their numerous world tours at the start of the seventies. At this time, Driscoll also became close to the headliner's singer, Ritchie Blackmore, who left Deep Purple in 1975, taking four of Elf's line-up – Driscoll, Dio, Mickey Lee Soule (keyboards) and Craig Gruber (bass) – to fashion his own band, Rainbow. The friendship did not last long: after just one debut album, Blackmore decided Driscoll was too set in his R & B ways, and replaced him with British percussion legend Cozy Powell. The heady days were never to be repeated for Driscoll, as none of his future bands (Dakota, Starcastle and Bible Black) matched the success of the earlier projects.

Since nobody has ever been brought to justice, the facts surrounding Gary Driscoll's murder remain murky almost twenty years after the event. It is known that he was killed at his New York home by more than one person, and the likelihood is that drugs were involved, but persistent rumour suggests that there was an occult or ritualistic aspect to Driscoll's death. The most disturbing allegation to emerge is that the drummer was flayed alive.

See also *Cozy Powell (* April 1998)*

Monday 8

Yogi Horton
(Lawrence Horton – Teaneck, New Jersey, 1954)
(Various acts)

He was one of the most respected session drummers in rock and R & B music, yet Yogi Horton was unhappy about the supposed lack of recognition he was receiving from those employing him, and this ultimately cost him his life. Throughout his long career, however, Horton seldom waited long for a big name to select him for recording. During the seventies and eighties, he added playing with Aretha Franklin, John Lennon, The Rolling Stones, Diana Ross, The B-52's, Deborah Harry and David Byrne to his CV, while touring for some years with Luther Vandross's band.

It was the last booking that was to cause him problems. Feeling undervalued (and underpaid), Horton sat staring out from his hotel room after a performance at Madison Square Gardens. Telling his wife he needed to do something, he then jumped from the seventeenth-floor window to the pavement below.

See also *Luther Vandross (* July 2005)*

Scott La Rock: First of the gang to die

AUGUST

Tuesday 25

Scott La Rock
(Scott Sterling – New York, 2 March 1962)

The first major death to occur in hip hop, Scott La Rock's murder set a grim marker for the gun-related violence witnessed within the genre over the next twenty years. Given the nature of his death, it's something of an irony that La Rock (then Sterling) had begun his career as an attorney, and met his musical partner KRS-One (Lawrence Krisna Parker) while a counsellor at the Bronx homeless refuge where the latter was a day visitor. As Scott La Rock, he operated as a DJ in the evenings, impressing KRS-One and another DJ, D-Nice, with whom he was soon to form Boogie Down

Productions. Alongside contemporaries Public Enemy, BDP added a cutting edge to existing hip-hop styles, encouraging young blacks to employ 'any means necessary' to realize their rights. Thus, *Criminal Minded* (1986), the debut album (produced in conjunction with fellow Bronx rappers Ultramagnetic MCs), steadily accrued sales and is now considered a landmark release in prototype gangsta rap.

Summoned for his experience in mediating stressful situations, Scott La Rock drove his pick-up over to a South Bronx housing project where D-Nice and an unnamed young rapper were embroiled in an argument over a woman. The 16-year-old attacker was, unbeknown to the DJ, armed with a handgun; La Rock was still seated in his pick-up when the fatal shots were fired. Following the murder, KRS-One (aka 'The Teacha') instigated the Stop the Violence campaign and modified his own stance in deference to the memory of his dead colleague; the rapper still regularly pays homage to Scott La Rock in his work.

SEPTEMBER

Friday 11

Peter Tosh
(Winston Hubert McIntosh – Grange Hill, Westmoreland, Jamaica, 9 October 1944)
(Bob Marley &) The Wailers

Just months after the killing of Carlie Barrett (☞*April 1987*), another Wailer, Peter Tosh ('The Stepping Razor'), was also senselessly cut down. A resilient youngster brought up by his aunt in Savanna-la-Mar (his minister father, whom Tosh did not meet until he was ten, sired many, many children, most of whom he neglected), Tosh made himself known as a musical talent in his remote but safe early home, playing guitar for a few shillings a time. This was fine until he was fifteen, when his aunt died and he was moved to the far more hostile environment of Trenchtown. There he met new friends Bob Marley and Neville 'Bunny' Livingston, also in their teens, the three fashioning an embryonic version of The Wailers. The guitarist maintained until his death that it was he who put a guitar in Marley's hand.

Under the combined watch of manager Joe Higgs and producers Clement 'Coxsone' Dodd and Lee 'Scratch' Perry, The Wailers became the hottest thing in Jamaica – yet the three band members barely saw a penny until they teamed up with Chris Blackwell at Island Records. Tainted by previous experience, Tosh was mistrustful of Blackwell, and very unhappy to be demoted to support once it was decided Marley would take a leading role ('I did not come on this earth to be a "background vocal",' he would often say). Despite seminal albums such as *Burnin'* (1973), Tosh knew he must go his own way in order to be heard properly. The first of several solid solo efforts, *Legalize It!*, was released on Capitol in 1976; the title track caused such consternation that it was banned from the radio in his homeland. Playing the 1978 One Love Festival alongside Marley, Inner Circle and others, Peter Tosh found himself in severe trouble after criticizing then-Prime Minister Michael Manley (and also his opposition, Eric Seaga) – the singer received a brutal beating at the hands of six policemen. (Tosh claimed that he only survived the ninety-minute attack because he knew how to roll his eyes back.) Some good was to come out of the appearance, however: Tosh was approached by admiring onlooker Mick Jagger – and a whole new professional chapter opened. Jagger signed Tosh to The Rolling Stones' label, contributing vocals to the song 'Don't Look Back' on Tosh's great album *Bush Doctor* (1978) and inviting Tosh to support The Stones on their American tour; on this occasion, the singer's criticisms of those in power were not met with violence. On the contrary, the shows did much to enhance Tosh's profile and two further albums were cut for the label, followed by two more for EMI – albums dubbed 'the Red X Tapes' for their inflammatory content. By the mid eighties, though, Tosh was happier at home with his wife and out of the limelight, the police beating – plus another he received from a drunk wielding a barstool, which left Tosh's left hand lacerated – sobering to the artist. Sadly, it was far from the end of the violence for Tosh.

Ever the humanitarian, Peter Tosh was to die a martyr. He'd befriended a street vendor known as Dennis Lobban, or 'Leppo' – a man with a long criminal record who had recently been incarcerated, but, Tosh believed, deserved an opportunity to get back on his feet. His belief was misguided. On the night of 11 September, Tosh was entertaining friends at his Kingston home when Lobban and two accomplices stormed the reggae star's house, all carrying guns. Pistol-

'Vampires don't come out and bite your neck any more. [Instead] they cause something destructive to happen. Blood will spill and those invisible vampires will get their meals.'

Peter Tosh ruminates

whipping Tosh, they demanded money – which Tosh didn't keep indoors. Following a needless and frenzied attack, Tosh's friend Winston 'Doc' Brown was shot dead, while the host and another guest, DJ Free-I, died later at Kingston's University Hospital from their wounds. Lobban – believed by some to have been a paid pawn, given that nothing was taken from Tosh's house – turned himself in soon after, and was convicted in just eleven minutes (a record for Jamaican justice). Neither of his accomplices has ever been captured.

See also *Bob Marley (◄ May 1981); Junior Braithwaite (►June 1999); Clement 'Coxsone' Dodd (►Golden Oldies #19)*

Monday 21

Jaco Pastorius

(John Francis Pastorius III – Norristown, Pennsylvania, 1 December 1951)
Weather Report
Word of Mouth
(Various acts)

A bass-guitar original, Jaco Pastorius developed his revolutionary style of fretless 'scattergunning' as a boy in Fort Lauderdale – going on to rival Stanley Clarke as the biggest influence in jazz/crossover playing. Until he was thirteen, Pastorius had played only percussion – his father was famed jazz drummer Jack Pastorius – but his bass craft soon made him a local wonder. Purchasing a 1962 Fender jazz bass, he removed the frets from it (to the horror of some) within the next four years Pastorius became Florida's finest exponent of the instrument.

His first spell with a 'name' band was with Wayne Cochran & The C C Riders, a Tampa Bay rock 'n' roll outfit very much a vehicle for its frontman. However, Pastorius was quickly fired for being far too prominent – or,

The peerless Jaco Pastorius, with his weapon set to stun

more likely, too good. Teaching music part-time at the University of Miami, Pastorius befriended a number of other notable musicians, including guitarist Pat Metheny and pianist Joe Zawinul of Weather Report, the seventies fusion pioneers, of whom he was already a fan. By now the bassist was much in demand: as well as producing his own stunning self-titled solo album (1976), Pastorius's nimble-fingered playing was much to the fore on releases by Metheny, Joni Mitchell, Ian Hunter, and Blood, Sweat & Tears – with whom he also toured. With the decks cleared, Pastorius finally hooked up with Weather Report (replacing the incumbent Alphonso Johnson), for whom he recorded six albums to 1981, and with whom his stage performances became legendary.

He was now dubbed 'The Greatest Bass-Player in the World', but alongside Pastorius's genius came severe mental and psychological problems, only intensified by his growing dependence on drugs and alcohol. Pastorius's final year with Weather Report saw some bizarrely distorted behaviour: he sometimes painted his face with marker pens, sometimes chose to appear naked in public. After quitting the band, he took his own project, Word of Mouth, out on the road, but that he was ill was clear to all. One of the more distressing episodes was an onstage eruption of violence at the 1983 Playboy Jazz Festival – one of several flashpoints that would ostracize him from his peers. By 1986 Pastorius was diagnosed manic depressive and committed to New York's Bellevue Hospital psychiatric unit. From this point on, the much-revered musician lived his life in the shadows, more often than not moving within low-rent drug circles, sleeping rough and jettisoning most of what his fame had bought him. On the night of 12 September 1987, Pastorius attempted to gain entry to Fort Lauderdale's Midnight Bottle Club – he was promptly refused entry

by security man Luc Havan because of his dishevelled appearance. In a fit of anger, Pastorius then tried to kick in the door, enraging Havan to the point where the bouncer, a martial-arts expert, beat him senseless, aiming a series of kicks at the musician's head. His skull fractured in several places – and his face battered beyond all recognition – Jaco Pastorius was admitted to nearby Broward Medical Center. He never emerged from a coma, and died in his father's arms nine days later. Although Pastorius was canonized within the music industry, his death went almost unreported by the media, while Havan – who'd initially blamed the musician's injuries on a fall – was released from jail after serving just four months of a two-year sentence.

DECEMBER

Saturday 5

Fat Larry James

(Philadelphia, Pennsylvania, 2 August 1949)

Fat Larry's Band
(The Delfonics)
(Blue Magic)

Short and very round, Larry James looked like neither a frontman nor a drummer, but he possessed a warmth that filtered through his bands' output over a relatively short career. James was first noticed by the public during his brief stints as a back-up man with The Delfonics and Blue Magic, but it was the formation of entertaining Philly funk unit Fat Larry's Band (sometimes FLB) that made his name. Oddly, the very US-centric band was far more successful in the UK, where they secured a radio hit in 1977 with 'Center City'. Even in his other capacity as manager of disco group Slick, James saw more action in the British

singles charts, where his first taste of Top Twenty success was with 1979's 'Space Bass'. Fat Larry's Band – who put out six albums before 1986 – finally hit paydirt with the smash 'Zoom' (1982), which was only kept from UK number one by Musical Youth; inexplicably, this very commercial disc failed to travel past number eighty-nine on the US R & B listings.

Within five years, though, James was dead: always a big man, he succumbed to a heart attack at just thirty-eight.

Monday 7

Richard Taylor

(Jersey City, New Jersey, 1940)

The Manhattans

The baritone singer with sweet soul/R & B outfit The Manhattans, Richard Taylor had seen the band emerge in 1960 out of the ashes of his US air force-formed Statesmen, a vocal quartet very much in the doo-wop tradition. After finding Florida-born lead George 'Smitty' Smith, The Statesmen located to New York to become The Dulcets, eventually plumping for the more geographical Manhattans in the early sixties. Throughout the rest of the decade, though, this crisp, well-drilled group performed and recorded in relative obscurity, waiting until the seventies for a major commercial breakthrough; by now, though, they had already lost frontman Smith to crippling illness (◀ December 1970).

After a host of releases on a variety of labels, The Manhattans sold over a million copies of the part-sung, part-spoken 'Kiss and Say Goodbye' (1976) – a tearjerker that stormed to US number one and was also a Top Five hit in the UK (as was the follow-up, a cover of Elvis's 'Hurt'). Already very ill, Taylor was forced to leave the group shortly after this burst of activity (though he'd rejoin for the occasional reunion). Converting to Islam, Richard Taylor preferred to be known as Abdul Rashid Talhah for the last ten years of his life. Exact details of his illness have been kept secret, although we know he died in Kansas City.

Wednesday 9

Will Shatter

(Russell Wilkinson – California, 10 June 1956)
Flipper
(Negative Trend)
(Any Three Initials)

As San Francisco recovered from the Sex Pistols' very public implosion during early 1978, a number of first-wave punk bands began to make themselves heard in the fall-out. One such were the largely forgotten Negative Trend, whose bassist/vocalist Will Shatter was still present as the band – Bruce Loose (second bass/lead vocals – already their third singer), Ted Falconi (guitar) and Steve de Pace (drums) – mutated into the wilful, crushing Flipper around 1979, with formerly institutionalized singer Ricky Williams briefly at the fore. Soon after, the band signed with underground label Subterranean. Their sound was primal, with much guitar feedback: a song like 'Sexbomb' (1982) was little more than a barrage of noise and some sound effects, with Shatter yelling over it. But they had something.

In 1982, *Album – Generic Flipper* was released (the group were later to take a dig at PIL for apparently lifting the idea) and two years later *Gone Fishin'* (1984) appeared. By now their sound was highly experimental, a kick against the thrash bands that surrounded them. Flipper, though, had already split, and Shatter was now issuing his avant-noise ruminations as one of Any Three Initials (A3I) in 1986. Just

a year later, the colourful bassist was dead from the disappointingly obvious method of a heroin overdose. Flipper re-formed some seven years after the original line-up had split (thanks in part to fan and Def American label boss Rick Rubin), with John Dougherty playing bass. Ten years after Shatter's untimely departure, he too died the same way (*October 1997*).

See also *Ricky Williams (** November 1992); Rik L Rik (** June 2000)*

Monday 21

John Spence

(Orange County, California, 2 February 1969)
No Doubt

Unlikely as it may now seem, No Doubt began life as a buzzing ska-influenced high-school band, put together by friends John Spence (vocals) and Eric Stefani (keyboards), while they sold burgers and desserts at an Anaheim Dairy Queen outlet. Their musical similarities became apparent – both were 2-Tone fans, not as rare in California as one might think – and before long, an eight-strong ska band was in place. 'No Doubt' was an expression used constantly by the hyperactive singer, so the name was never going to go away. The group soon trimmed down to become a very popular local draw with their quirky, arhythmic pop rock. By his own admission, Spence was not the strongest vocalist, but his onstage dynamics (backflips and jumps, mainly) captivated the audience so much that the introduction of Stefani's precocious 16-year-old sister, Gwen, on backing vocals initially went unnoticed.

But all was not well with John Spence. Having contemplated suicide at Thanksgiving, he carried out the deed just before Christmas in an

abandoned parking lot in Anaheim. A gun was found at his side. The rest of No Doubt were crushed by his death, but maintained that carrying on with Gwen Stefani as lead vocalist would be what the original singer would have wished. Well, perhaps.

Friday 25

Nat Tarnopol

(Detroit, Michigan, 26 January 1931)

A heavyweight player during the US soul explosion of the early sixties, the formidable Nat Tarnopol was feared and revered in equal measure. As underling to artist manager Al Green, Tarnopol – still in his mid twenties – found himself overseeing the affairs of emerging talent Jackie Wilson when his boss unexpectedly died. Tarnopol's management techniques were not uncommon in the music industry at this time: while he profited from the sales of Gene Chandler, Barbara Acklin and The Chi-Lites, the artists themselves seldom saw the money their modern counterparts now expect to receive. In his defence, it must be said that Tarnopol kept the wayward Wilson on the straight and narrow. However, Tarnopol spent the last fifteen years of his life fighting both legal charges and some fairly serious allegations from contemporaries. (Brunswick's vice president Carl Davis once claimed that Tarnopol and others had threatened to have him killed should he try to resign from the company – and Tarnopol was known to be acquainted with notorious music-industry 'insider' and alleged mob affiliate Gaetano Vastola.) Many of the legal issues were still unresolved when Nat Tarnopol died suddenly from heart failure on Christmas Day 1987.

See also *Jackie Wilson (** January 1984)*

Lest We Forget

Other notable deaths that occurred sometime during 1987:

Diane L Adams (US country singer who hit with 'I'm Little but I'm Loud'; born 4/10/1962; car crash, 4/4)

Hugh Bryant (US baritone with veteran vocal quartet The Delta Rhythm Boys; the fifth member of the group to pass on, he dropped dead on the spot after singing at Otha Lee Gaines's funeral, 7/1987)

Tony 'Stix' Destra (US rock drummer with Philadelphia-based 'hair metal' acts Cinderella and Britny Fox; born 20/9/1954; car accident, 8/2)

Joe DeZuniga (US singer/guitarist with California death-metallers Insanity; heart disease, 16/5)

Major Worries (Jamaican dancehall DJ; born Wayne Jones; shot dead near his Spanish Town home)

David Martin (US bassist with The Tom Toms and garage rockers Sam the Sham & The Pharaohs, who hit big with 'Wooly Bully' (1965) and 'Li'l Red Riding Hood' (1966); born Texas, 1937; heart attack, 2/8)

Adriel McDonald (US member of vocal group The Ink Spots; born 10/5/1905; unknown, 1/9)

Oliver North (not that one – US singer/guitarist with sharp new-wave trio The Comateens, formed with his brother Nic; born New York; unknown, 6/87)

Konrad 'Conny' Plank (noted German 'Krautrock' producer who introduced the world to Kraftwerk and also produced Devo, Brian Eno, Eurythmics, Killing Joke and Ultravox; born c1940; cancer, 12/1987)

Ted Taylor (US falsetto with vocal troupes Santa Monica Soul Seekers and The Cadets, who scored a 1956 Top Twenty hit with 'Stranded in the Jungle'; born Austin Taylor, Oklahoma, 16/2/1934; car crash, 22/10)

For a complete list of fallen artists, visit

www.numberoneinheaven.com

1988

MARCH

Monday 7

Divine

(Harris Glenn Milstead – Baltimore, Maryland,
19 October 1945)

The undisputed larger-than-life Queen
of High-NRG, cross-dressing Divine
stomped his way out of the closet
and into the discos of both the USA
and Europe, recording a number of
sweaty mini epics during the early to
mid eighties. He became infamous
twenty years earlier, however, as a high-
school friend of would-be film-maker
John Waters, and the latter was more
than happy to indulge this burgeoning curio's penchant for outlandish
women's clothing, selecting Milstead
(who had, to all intents and purposes,
already become 'Divine') for his first
pictures. Divine was – fittingly – still
working as a hairdresser when cast in
Roman Candles and *Eat Your Make-Up*.
As Waters's work flourished, Divine
found himself thrown into more and
more outrageous roles, such as the
'poodle-shit-eating' Babs Johnson
in *Pink Flamingos* (1972) and porno-
grapher's wife Francine Fishpaw in
1981's *Polyester*. Divine had a definite
comic talent, which was not tem-

Simply Divine, darling!

pered after he launched his recording career. While early disco-flavoured moments like 'Born to be Cheap' (1979) and 'Shoot Your Shot' (1982) had marginal appeal, 1983's 'Love Reaction' was a massive New York dance-floor favourite. The melody and rhythm were obviously borrowed from New Order's 'Blue Monday', but the Manchester band didn't mind and paid tribute to Divine thereafter. The following year saw the unlikely vision of Divine on *Top of the Pops* with the UK Top Twenty success of 'You Think You're a Man' – though the stilted Stock, Aitken & Waterman productions made the novelty pall somewhat by 1985; a brash cover of The Four Seasons' 'Walk Like a Man' was Divine's only significant further hit. But at the beginning of 1988, John Waters' *Hairspray* was released (Divine's performance as crass stage-mom Edna Turnbladt is generally considered his best) and all seemed back on course – particularly with a part in the popular mainstream US sitcom *Married . . . with Children* also set to start.

On the evening of 6 March, Divine had dined on pasta and treated those gathered at the Los Angeles Regency Hotel to an impromptu version of '*Arrivederci Roma*'. The following morning, however, he was expected on set and alarm bells began to ring when he didn't show. At noon, his manager, Bernard Jay, entered Room 261 to find Divine dead in his bed. The star, having ballooned to almost 370 lbs, had died in his sleep from an enlarged heart. Divine's Baltimore funeral was attended by many, and flowers arrived from a host of showbiz acquaintances (not least Elton John); his hearse was given police accompaniment. Divine had been reconciled with his mother, Frances Milstead, after a long period of estrangement, just before he died.

Andy Gibb

(Manchester, 5 March 1958)

Often mooted as a fourth Bee Gee, youngest Gibb brother Andy was undaunted by his brothers' staggering success, following impressively in their considerable wake. Both Gibb parents had been musicians, so it was unsurprising when their boys followed suit; Andy Gibb was just six months old when the family upped sticks to live in Australia, where all would perform regularly on the club circuit. In 1967, the sudden international success of older brothers Barry, Robin and Maurice was such that the family relocated themselves twice more, winding up on the Isle of Wight, where Gibb formed his first band in 1973. In 1975, he returned to Australia, where, like his brothers, one could say that he was something of a hit. An early single, 'Words and Music' became a local smash and was heard by entrepreneur Robert Stigwood, who flew Gibb to Miami to cut an album with (naturally) his brother Barry, then enjoying multi-

platinum success with The Bee Gees' *Saturday Night Fever* involvement. The response to Andy Gibb's soaring falsetto in America was phenomenal, and his first three singles all hit number one. That the songs bore a strong similarity to the work of his siblings mattered not – the Gibb brothers (in their various guises) were the hottest property of all and pretty much everything they touched turned platinum. Indeed, there were shades of Beatle-like US domination as Gibb bridged number-one hits by The Bee Gees with his own 'Love is Thicker than Water' (1978). Clearly this level of success could not continue indefinitely, and by 1980 Gibb's star was beginning to fade. (In his homeland, consistent success had been significantly harder to find from the start, though 1978's 'An Everlasting Love' had scraped the UK Top Ten.) After 1981, Gibb turned his attention to acting, but following a problematic and very public relationship with *Dallas* actress Victoria Principal, the previously married star dealt with their inevitable split by taking vast quantities of cocaine. As a result, he was relieved of the lead role in a Broadway production of *Joseph and the Amazing Technicolor Dreamcoat*; entering the infamous Betty Ford

Andy Gibb (*right*) with brother Barry: Blood is thicker than water?

Clinic in 1985, Gibb took two years to kick his habit. In early 1988, the singer – now apparently clean – learned he was close to bankruptcy and fled to the UK. Bailed out by a new deal with Island, Gibb was spurred on to write again (from the seclusion and comfort of brother Robin's Oxfordshire mansion), his new material supposedly revealing a new, 'mature' approach to pop music. But, frustrated by his inability to compose unaided, Gibb hit the bottle hard. Just after celebrating his thirtieth birthday, he complained of chest pains and was admitted to Oxford's John Radcliffe Hospital; he would not leave alive. Early on the morning of 10 March, Andy Gibb was awoken by an intern who wanted to take his blood. Gibb agreed, sighed and passed away. Although many were quick to blame his premature death on drug abuse, a post mortem revealed that Gibb – whose heart was dangerously enlarged – had died from the viral infection myocarditis. His body was flown back to Los Angeles for interment.

See also *Maurice Gibb (* January 2003)*

APRIL

Saturday 9

David Prater

(Ocilla, Georgia, 9 May 1937)
Sam & Dave

David Prater came by his musical partner and soulmate in an unusual way – he served Melionaires' singer Sam Moore breakfast for several months before the pair finally met properly at a talent show at Miami's King of Hearts Club in 1961. The club owner – feeling Prater's gruff baritone would work well with Moore's higher tones – eventually put them together. Sam & Dave were instantly popular on the R & B circuit, though it took the duo much longer to hit with the record-buying public. Spells at Roulette and then major label Atlantic were diluted by the act being 'leased' to Stax – a move that nonetheless proved pivotal. The Stax house band (ie, Isaac Hayes and various members of the MGs and the Memphis Horns) was the perfect backdrop to the singers' duelling voices and prompted a slew of hits, most notably 'Hold On! I'm a-Comin' (1966) and the million-selling 'Soul Man' (1967) – two of many songs penned by Hayes and Dave Porter.

With their higher profile, though, came glitches between the pair. Prater's penchant for drugs made him a highly volatile character and put the duo's relationship on hold for several years after 1970. (Attempts to reconvene in the early eighties were scuppered when Prater was exposed selling crack to an undercover cop.) Prater's launch of a 'fresh' Sam & Dave – featuring new partner Sam Daniels – was also thwarted when Moore understandably threatened legal action. Finally, David Prater was killed when his car crashed in Sycamore, Georgia, as he drove to his mother's house in Ocilla. A passenger survived with serious wounds, but Prater was thrown from the vehicle and died at the scene.

Brook Benton

(Benjamin Franklin Peay – Camden, South Carolina, 19 September 1931)
(The Sandmen)

Later the same evening, R & B lost another legend in the shape of silky baritone Brook Benton. Eventually a prolific hit-maker in the secular world, Benton began as a gospel vocalist, encouraged by his Methodist minister father. His CV included spells with notable gospel units The Golden Gate Quartet and The Camden Jubilee Singers, giants in worship music. Benton left non-secular music after moving to New York and working as a truck driver while singing with The Sandmen before a winning partnership was forged with noted songwriters Clyde Otis and Belford Hendricks. Benton was in his late twenties before the hits arrived – but arrive they did: US R & B chart-topper 'It's Just a Matter of Time' lived up to its title and took the singer into the Billboard Top Three in March 1959, and was followed by a run of hits – six of which were further R & B number ones. The biggest-selling hit was 'Boll Weevil Song' (1962), while duets with Dinah Washington also fared well (although the pair's personal relationship was reportedly occasionally hostile). Benton also managed to co-write major hits for Nat 'King' Cole, Clyde McPhatter and The Diamonds. His career in full sway, the casually good-looking pipe-smoker was also very much a pin-up of the day.

The inevitable lull came around 1964 (after the prophetic single, 'Going Going Gone'), although live work was still a highly lucrative outlet for the performer. Benton nonetheless managed another million-seller with 'Rainy Night in Georgia' (1970), before he returned to preaching by the end of the decade. Attempts to record again during the eighties were largely stymied by a legal wrangle with MGM over unpaid royalties. The case was settled in favour of Benton's estate just after his death. With many fans unaware he was suffering from spinal meningitis, the singer yielded to pneumonia while receiving treatment in New York for his condition.

See also *Dinah Washington (* pre-1965)*

Sandi Robison

(Barbara Jeanne Moyer – Las Vegas, Nevada,
14 October 1945)
**The Peanut Butter Conspiracy
(The Crosswinds)**

After losing her mother at a young age,
Barbara Jeanne Moyer was brought up
by her grandparents in Marin County,
San Francisco – an ideal location for
someone with folk-music ambitions.
On graduating from high school in
1963, the would-be singer came into
contact with local faces like David
Crosby, Robbie Robison (briefly her
husband) and Dino Valenti. Spotted
singing with her spouse in coffee
houses, Robison was soon invited to
join The South City Singers (later The
Crosswinds), for whom she cut her
first record in 1965. Robison moved
to Los Angeles – acquiring her new
first name after borrowing an ID card
to gain entry to a club – where, after
the birth of her son, Scott, the singer
formed psychedelic rock band The
Peanut Butter Conspiracy – with John
Merrill (guitar), Jim Cherniss (guitar), Alan Bracket (bass) and Spencer
Dryden (drums). A single for CBS, 'It's
a Happening Thing' (1967), made the
Hot 100 and the band slotted comfortably into the flower-power movement.

Their fame turned out to be very
much a local phenomenon, however,
and when PBC was discontinued in
1969, Robison took a lead role in the
stage musical *Hair*, by far her highest-
profile work. Around this time, she
also luckily survived an auto smash-up
on Ventura Highway. Playing the clubs
for the rest of her life, Robison became
ill and was admitted to hospital in early
April 1988, after a concert in Montana;
she died unexpectedly of toxic-shock
poisoning just two weeks later.

See also *Spencer Dryden (☛ January 2005)*

JUNE

Thursday 16

Kim Milford

(Richard Kim Milford – Glen Ridge, New Jersey,
7 February 1951)
**Moon
(The Jeff Beck Group)**

By macabre coincidence, Kim Milford
– another former cast member of *Hair*
– died just weeks after Sandi Robison.
Primarily an actor, he was born into
a performing family (his sister was
Oscar nominee Penelope Milford),
of whom he was arguably the most
widely talented. Apart from having
singing and acting skills, Milford was
also a composer, writer and dancer,
making his way into *Hair* at just seventeen. He also performed in *Jesus Christ
Superstar* and *The Rocky Horror Show*,
among a host of other credits. Milford
was a friend of Jeff Beck, fronting the
legendary guitarist's live band during
1972 (although he was fired shortly
before the end of a US tour). He also
recorded several albums under his
own name – including the interestingly
titled (for 1974) *Chain Your Lovers to the
Bedpost*, and formed the band Moon.

Despite suffering a severe injury to
his coccyx, Kim Milford continued to
perform as a singer and actor – perhaps unwisely, as his recovery was
very much impaired. Seldom healthy
thereafter, Milford passed away from
heart failure at just thirty-seven, following open heart surgery some weeks
before.

Jesse 'Ed' Davis

(Norman, Oklahoma, 21 September 1944)
**Taj Mahal
(Various acts)**

One of the most respected session
guitarists of all time, Jesse Davis – a
Native American of the Kiowa tribe
– was seemingly able to turn his hand
to any modern style, be it blues, country or rock. Little was expected when
Davis took a position, on graduating
from the University of Oklahoma, as
touring guitarist with Conway
Twitty, but after a move to California,
he became a full-time bottleneck-
player with Taj Mahal, recording three
albums with the country/blues giant
between 1967 and 1970. He even managed to release three albums of his
own in the early seventies.

Davis's later career matched him
with a variety of different artists, and
by the eighties he could boast stints
with various ex-Beatles, Eric Clapton,
Gene Clark, Joe Cocker, Bob Dylan,
The Monkees, Leon Russell and Rod
Stewart. Before his death, he began
a project with poet and activist John
Trudell. Unfortunately, Jesse Davis's
predilection for booze and heroin
culminated in a suspected overdose in
the laundry room of his Venice Beach
apartment.

Hillel Slovak

(Haifa, 13 April 1962)
**The Red Hot Chili Peppers
(What Is This?)
(Anthym)**

Israeli-born and of Czech descent,
Hillel Slovak was nonetheless

American, moving with his family to the US when he was just five. By the end of the seventies the young Kiss fan and budding guitarist had fallen into the company of drummer Jack Irons, and the pair emulated their heroes under the guises Anthym and later What Is This? A meeting at Fairfax High School with future bandmates Anthony Kiedis (vocals) and Flea (Michael Balzary, bass, who cites Slovak as the man who taught him to play) launched the band that today ranks as one of the world's biggest. For Slovak, the encounter was, however, to leave a darker imprint.

The Red Hot Chili Peppers' instantly recognizable meld of brash funk and thrash punk impressed fans at the LA bars and strip clubs in which they initially played. But, because of a contractual foul-up that left Slovak and Irons unable to play on the 1984 debut for EMI, session musicians were used alongside Kiedis and Flea – and the album suffered as a result. (Andy Gill of Manchester post-punks Gang of Four was the unlikely producer.) For the follow-up, The Chili Peppers headed for the vibe of Detroit and, with Slovak back in the mix and funk legend George Clinton at the desk, *Freaky Styley* (1986) was indeed something of a mini classic. This great record featured members of James Brown's band on brass, while the RHCP added their own semi-clad sleaze when touring the disc: Kiedis threw himself about on stage while Slovak sweated in tight underpants behind. By the third album the band were living their own lyrical blueprint of casual sex, balls-out rock 'n' roll, hard drugs and more casual sex. In 1988, the world was exposed for the first time to RHCP's 'socks on cocks' routine, for the *Abbey Road* EP, the band parodying The Beatles' sleeve image in such a way that if one never saw it, one might well imagine it.

For Hillel Slovak, it was, sadly, an epitaph. As The Chili Peppers prepared their fourth long-player, the gifted guitarist died from an apparently accidental heroin overdose while enrolled in detox. His body lay undiscovered for two days. (The slight possibility that Slovak had committed suicide was considered when it emerged that he had spoken to his brother James the night before his death, pointedly saying, 'I love you.') The death proved too much for Irons, who left almost immediately, while panic-stricken user Kiedis (who, shortly before, had had to be talked out of sacking the guitarist) also checked himself into rehab in Mexico. Said the singer later, 'Flea and I realized that we couldn't stop because of the death of our best friend. It was going to be a permanent source of sadness in our lives, but we wanted to keep going because it had become our lives.' And continue they did, returning after a year of inactivity with replacement guitarist John Frusciante, a gifted young man who also claimed to have learned everything he knew from watching and listening to Slovak. RHCP grew stronger (and more commercially viable) some time after, the band's million-selling 'Under the Bridge' (1992) an ode to the substance that had cost them so dearly.

JULY

Saturday 16

Nico

(Christa Päffgen – Cologne, Germany, 16 October 1938)

The Velvet Underground

She possessed one of the most distinctive looks and voices of her generation, yet died an ignominious death in the unlikeliest of settings. Christa Päffgen was raised in Nazi-controlled Berlin during the Second World War; she lived with her mother and grandmother, barely knowing her father, who was away on service duty and died in an Allied camp. After the war, Päffgen left school to work as a seamstress and lingerie salesgirl at thirteen, but her extraordinary beauty saw her plucked out as a fashion model and actress the year after. After living for a while in Paris and London, the renamed Nico (she was so named by a photographer) settled in New York in 1960, where, having made several notable appearances in movies (Fellini's *La Dolce Vita* among them) she joined Lee Strasberg's Method School – a classmate of Marilyn Monroe. By now Nico had adopted her almost-permanent black-clothes-pale-face look.

Possessing such presence, Nico was a natural networker: her relationship with Brian Jones of The Rolling Stones landed her a record deal with Andrew Loog Oldham's Immediate label, where she cut 'I'm Not Sayin'' (1964), penned by Gordon Lightfoot. The encouraging Bob Dylan also gave her a song – and introduced her to Andy Warhol. Nico gave up modelling to tour with the much-talked-about band he managed, The Velvet Underground. In this guise, she recorded her best-known songs, including Lou Reed's 'All Tomorrow's Parties' and '*Femme Fatale*' (both 1967). Her voice was now a hypnotic, narcotic drawl. This sojourn was short-lived though, as trouble frequently broke out between her and Reed. Back on the solo route, Nico found her stride with some extraordinary performances. Often playing the harmonium herself, she was also accompanied by some formidable names: Tim Hardin, Tim Buckley and mainly Jackson Browne, with whom she lived for some time. Her recorded output, however, remained too leftfield to make any commercial impact. And Nico's appearances in films were now likewise restricted to 'artistic' works with director Philippe Garrel.

Nico became something of an outsider during the latter half of the seventies, her physical appearance now extremely affected by her continued use of heroin: she became virtually down-and-out, living in basic accommodation in Prestwich, near Manchester. The limousines of the past were replaced – significantly – by a modest bicycle. Matters seemed to improve by 1985, with the John Cale-produced *Camera Obscura* bringing her back into the public eye. An apparently clean Nico toured the record and partially regained the fanbase that had deserted her over the past decade. For her final two years, Nico seemed content once more. Which made it all the more shocking when, in July 1988, she was found unconscious at the side of a road in Ibiza – her bicycle lying by her side. Having apparently suffered a massive head injury, Nico was rushed to Cannes Nisto Hospital, where she died of a brain haemorrhage at around 8 pm. The actual circumstances of the accident will doubtless never be ascertained – some fans expressed almost as much surprise at the fact that this erstwhile 'princess of darkness' might be visiting an island renowned for its constant sunshine as at her death. Nico was buried alongside her mother at Grunewald Forest cemetery park, Berlin.

Nico's life may have appeared doomed for some time, but at least she almost made it to fifty – unlike one or two previous lovers. In the space of just four years during the sixties, she had affairs with Brian Jones (☞ *July 1969*), Jimi Hendrix (☞ *September 1970*) and Jim Morrison (☞ *July 1971*) – all of whom died at the age of twenty-seven.

See also *Angus MacLise (☞ June 1979); Sterling Morrison (☞ August 1995)*

Close!
Ralf Hütter
(Kraftwerk)

Co-founder of enduring German electronica godfathers Kraftwerk, Ralf Hütter nearly anticipated Nico's tragic mishap with that most basic of machines back in 1983. With his cycle-race theme 'Tour de France' cleaning up across Europe, Hütter crashed his bicycle in the Dolomites, fracturing his skull and spending two days in a coma. His first words on coming to? *'Wo ist mein Fahrrad?'* ('Where's my bike . . . ?')

Friday 29

Pete Drake
(Roddis Franklin Drake – Atlanta, Georgia, 8 October 1932)

His $38 'talking' pedal steel gave self-taught Pete Drake a unique sound and selling point, and he is widely regarded as having introduced the instrument into the pop mainstream. Drake made his name in Nashville, over a relatively short period of time, recording countless country songs (working with names including George Jones and Tammy Wynette) while taking a permanent position as a sideman at the Grand Ole Opry in 1959. Backing Elvis Presley is probably how he is best remembered, but Drake also contributed to recordings by Bob Dylan (1967's *John Wesley Harding* and 1969's *Nashville Skyline* among them) as well as albums by George Harrison and Ringo Starr, without having any knowledge of The Beatles: 'The name didn't ring any bells – well, I'm just a hillbilly,' he once coyly explained.

After some years as a respected producer, Pete Drake died in his

Tennessee home at the age of fifty-five, having suffered for many years from a lung condition.

AUGUST
Sunday 14
Roy Buchanan
(Ozark, Alabama, 23 September 1939)
(The Heartbeats)
(The Hawks)

Another largely unsung giant of his instrument, Buchanan was for many the master of shimmering electric blues, his steel-guitar style emulated by many since his death. His family moved to Pixley when Buchanan was a boy; his father was a Pentecostal minister in the tiny Californian town. At seven, he had lessons from a teacher with the delightful name of Mrs Pressure, who broke down in tears whenever her charge hit a bum note. At fifteen, Buchanan and his Fender fronted The Heartbeats, but, despite his early promise, he would not earn wider attention until the seventies: by then, however, he had already played with rockabilly vocalist Dale Hawkins and had been a member of The Hawks (a precursor to The Band). Buchanan's talent was still known only by word of mouth by the time he featured on a 1971 PBS television special entitled *The Best Unknown Guitarist in the World*, a coup that won him a recording contract with first Polydor and then Atlantic, for whom – at last – he sold well. Before this, Buchanan had turned down opportunities to play with Eric Clapton and The Rolling Stones: fiercely protective of his work, Buchanan was frustrated by ever-more elaborate production of a sound he believed should remain primitive – in 1981, he dropped out of the recording process for four years. He was finally to have his way with *When a Guitar Plays the Blues* (1985), a record produced for Alligator. After two more well-received efforts, though, Roy Buchanan's world was to turn sour.

Struggling with alcohol addiction, Roy Buchanan had driven several blocks from his Virginia home, before – tipped off by his wife, with whom he'd had an altercation – police apprehended a man they believed was drunk and 'behaving strangely'. Placed in a cell at Fairfax County Jail, Buchanan was charged and left for half an hour to calm down. When officers checked on him, he was found hanged from the window grate. Some supporters of Buchanan believe that the verdict of suicide was trumped-up: the musician's injuries were consistent with a police 'choke hold' sometimes used to subdue aggressive inmates.

Robert Calvert

(Pretoria, South Africa, 9 March 1945)
Hawkwind
(Various acts)

On the same day, a heart attack took one of space rock's favourite sons, Bob Calvert. The self-styled poet/performance artist began his journey to marginal fame working on a London building site, though what any of his labouring cohorts made of this idiosyncratic individual is anyone's guess. Well-read and fascinated by the counter-culture of the period, in the late sixties Calvert met like-minded Dave Brock, guitarist of Hawkwind. The band was arguably the nearest Britain had to a 'scene', as famous for

their alternative lifestyle as for their music. Calvert's dramatic monologues became an occasional treat during Hawkwind's live shows, while in 1972, the Calvert-penned 'Silver Machine' gave the group an unlikely UK Top Five hit – although his vocals were overdubbed by Lemmy Kilmister's the year after. Perhaps Calvert's most inspired work had been that year's truly disturbing 'Sonic Attack', but he was to leave the band soon after (returning briefly for 1977's *Quark, Strangeness and Charm*). His solo work was quirkier still, including the concept album *Captain Lockheed and the Starfighters* (which featured some sizeable names in accompaniment, including Brian Eno and fellow weirdo Viv Stanshall), a drama about the life of Jimi Hendrix and a novel about the music business, *Hype*.

Hawkwind: Still in search of space, by the look of things . . .

Focusing more towards minimalist styles throughout the eighties, Bob Calvert died suddenly of a heart attack at just forty-three. Hawkwind reunited to play a benefit for his widow and children at the end of 1988.

Tuesday 30

Papa Dee Allen

(Thomas Sylvester Allen – Wilmington, Delaware, 19 July 1931)

War

By early trade a modern-jazz percussionist, Papa Dee Allen backed a variety of big names such as Dizzy Gillespie before heading to California, where soul, rock and R & B appealed more to the flamboyant musician. In 1967, he joined the ever-shifting and growing ranks of The Creators as a keyboardist and singer. The Long Beach funk/rock act became Nightshift – basically a backing unit for football/music hopeful Deacon Jones. When this didn't work out, the group was looked after by former Animals leader Eric Burdon. Renaming them War, Burdon set the band on the path to enormous popularity with the hit 'Spill the Wine' in 1970. For the rest of the decade, War enjoyed consistent success with a string of Allen-written international hit singles, including the million-selling 'Cisco Kid' (1973) and 'Why Can't We be Friends?' (1975). On the downside, the band also endured the deaths of early bassist Peter Rosen in 1969 and Charles Miller (➼ *June 1980*).

From the early eighties onwards, War were effectively a touring unit, their hit-making days behind them. While performing in August 1988 at the Talk of the Town nightclub in Vallejo, California, Papa Dee Allen suffered a cerebral haemorrhage, and died shortly afterwards.

OCTOBER

Sunday 9

Cliff Gallup

(Clifton Elwood Gallup – Norfolk, Virginia, 17 June 1930)

Gene Vincent & The Blue Caps

A lead guitarist of outstanding ability, Cliff Gallup lit up the early work of rock 'n' roll legend Gene Vincent with his fretwork. A member of Vincent's Blue Caps – alongside Willie Williams (guitar), Jack Neal (bass), Dickie Harrell (drums) and occasional pianist Max Lipscomb – Gallup was picked to play on the singer's debut single, 'Woman Love' (1956). It was, however, the B-side 'Be-Bop-a-Lula' that showed Vincent and the band at their best, and this quickly became a national smash. Gallup's performances adorned this and other Vincent classics like 'Blue Jean Bop' and 'Race with the Devil' (both 1956), by which time the group were far bigger in Europe than in the US. Despite recording a sizeable catalogue of songs with the heart-throb, Gallup was by Vincent's side for less than a year, finding the rigours of touring not to his taste. Replaced by Johnny Meeks, Gallup returned to his gospel-oriented roots and seldom strayed far from his home to play again. Vincent, who was disappointed to lose Gallup, did not enjoy the same level of success without him, and died in reduced circumstances some time after (➼ *October 1971*).

Following a 1988 booking at a Virginia Beach party, Cliff Gallup arrived home and promptly collapsed from a suspected cardiac arrest. He died later in hospital – almost seventeen years to the day after Vincent.

See also *Max Lipscomb (➼ March 1991); Willie Williams (➼ August 1999); Paul*

Peek (➼ *April 2001*). *Further Blue Cap musicians to have died are Grady Owen (1999), Jerry Lee Merritt (2001) and Juvenal Gomez (2002).*

Tuesday 25

Johnnie Louise Richardson

(Johnnie Louise Sanders – Montgomery, Alabama, 24 June 1940)

Johnnie & Joe
The Jaynetts

The daughter of J&S Records boss Zelma Sanders, Johnnie Louise Richardson was brought up in the Bronx by a musical family. She cut a number of doo-wop-styled ballads with R & B act Johnnie & Joe (the 'Joe' was Joe Rivers) during the late fifties – all for her mother's label. Many of their songs fared well on the R & B charts and seemed particularly popular with the Hispanic market: most notable was the extremely sentimental 'Over the Mountain; Across the Sea' (1957), which crossed over to Billboard Top Ten success for Chess. The duo's voices blended well, though it was quickly stressed that there was no romantic involvement between them. With no further success, Richardson set about forming her own label, Dice, though her fortunes were not to change until she joined The Jaynetts, an all-female trio. Richardson sang on their *Sally Go 'round the Roses* album (1963), though she missed out on singles glory with the hit title track, cut before she joined.

Johnnie Louise Richardson returned with a nostalgia version of Johnnie & Joe in 1982, releasing the acclaimed *Kingdom Of Love* album (1983). She died following an unexpected stroke at her label's premises.

DECEMBER

Roy Orbison

(Vernon, Texas, 23 April 1936)

(The Wink Westerners)
(The Teen Kings)
(The Traveling Wilburys)

Roy Orbison was perhaps the first great songwriter to merge country and rock 'n' roll, the man behind the Ray-Bans overcoming introversion and extreme personal tragedy to create a legend – only to die prematurely himself.

The future star was born to Orbie Lee and Nadine Orbison, and chose to take his mother's name as he embarked upon a career in music that would span three decades. Two long-standing myths about Roy Orbison are that he was albino or partially blind: neither is true, though Orbison's heavy-rimmed eye furniture was a necessity brought about by myopia – a condition that initially alienated him from friends. (The change to shades came about after the singer left his spectacles on a plane in 1963.) Brought up in the (aptly named) border oil town of Wink, Orbison picked up a guitar early, writing his first song, 'Vow Of Love', at just nine years old. His Wink Westerners gave an indication of a formidable talent, though the band broke up because the singer believed rock 'n' roll success was unlikely. The muse would return, however. Orbison left North Texas State College a qualified geologist who'd studied alongside Pat Boone, but, like his colleague, he was ready to return to music. With a new band, the more youth-friendly Teen Kings, Orbison cut the song 'Ooby Dooby' in 1956 under Norman Petty (Buddy Holly's producer) – and the track appealed to hot entrepreneur Sam Phillips. At Sun Records, though, the singer found himself way down in a pecking order that included Johnny Cash (who'd recommended him), Jerry Lee Lewis and Elvis Presley – and it became apparent that rockabilly was not suitable for his three-octave range. Orbison honed his songwriting skills at Nashville's Acuff-Rose Music (The Everly Brothers were to record his 'Claudette', dedicated to the singer's young wife), but it was at Monument that Orbison's career really took off. Though a first single failed to register, his now-classic 'Only the Lonely' (1960) shifted a million copies on both sides of the Atlantic. The

song – rejected by both Elvis and The Everlys – made US number two and UK number one, the first of a string of huge successes for an artist who quickly became one of the most popular in the world. 'Running Scared' gave Orbison his first US chart-topper the year after, while 'It's Over' and 'Oh, Pretty Woman' (both 1964) also did the trick in the UK, where he was by far the most popular singer that year, outselling even Presley. Back at home, 'Oh, Pretty Woman' broke The Beatles' stranglehold on the Billboard hit parade – just months after Orbison had toured Europe with Britain's biggest group.

With his career hitting a glorious high by the mid sixties, Roy Orbison's personal life paradoxically encountered an escalating series of catastrophes. In November 1964, the singer divorced Claudette Frady, whom he had learned was having an affair with their builder. Eighteen months later, Orbison remarried her, but the reunion was brief. The couple had long been motorcycle enthusiasts and, the star attraction at a Tennessee drag race meet, Orbison was left in shock when Claudette died in a collision with a truck. His 'Too Soon to Know' (1966), written as a tribute, subsequently became a big UK hit, though it strangely failed to sell in the US (presaging something of a downturn in his commercial fortunes). In 1968, when Orbison had just about come to terms with his grief, he was called home from a European tour: an explosion at the family home in Hendersonville, Tennessee had started a fire that killed two of his three sons; his older brother Grady Lee Orbison then died in a vehicle crash on the way to a Thanksgiving dinner with the singer in 1973. Somehow, Orbison managed to overcome such extreme personal loss, remarrying (German Barbara Wellhonen) and finding a new audience in the eighties as his records (and those with hoary supergroup The Traveling Wilburys – with Bob Dylan, George Harrison, Jeff Lynne and Tom Petty) began to shift units again. It was a welcome relief after a decade that had seen the singer play to audiences of fewer than 150 (and undergo triple heart-bypass surgery) By now, though, Orbison had received accolades from almost all of his peers, and befriended younger artists like Elvis Costello, Bruce Springsteen and k d lang, and was inducted into the Rock 'n' Roll Hall Fame in a 1987 ceremony.

With a new solo album, *Mystery Girl* (1989), ready for release, Roy Orbison took time out in December 1988 to visit his family in Nashville. While at his mother's house with his surviving children, Orbison excused himself to go to the bathroom, but he did not return. When the singer's son Wesley forced the door open, he discovered his father slumped on the floor. All attempts to revive him proved useless: 'The Big O' was dead at just fifty-two from a massive coronary. Posthumous tributes abounded, not least in the UK, where his greatest-hits package topped

Roy Orbison: It's over

> **'I once said to him, "Roy, you're probably the greatest singer in the world." And he said, "Probably."'**
>
> Tom Petty

the album chart and a single, 'You Got It', put the singer in the Top Three for the first time in well over twenty years; meanwhile, a monument was erected and museum for the singer opened in Wink. Orbison was, however, interred at Westwood Memorial Park in Los Angeles – at the wishes of his second wife. His songs have been covered by many artists including Buddy Holly, Don McLean, Linda Ronstadt and even Van Halen.

See also *George Harrison (☞ November 2001)*

Sylvester

(Sylvester James – Los Angeles, California,
6 September 1944)

(The Hot Band)
(The Cockettes)

Just a few months after Divine, disco's
previous 'reigning queen' also passed
away: African-American Sylvester
was perhaps the first on to the dance
floor with sequins and glitter where
previously we had only seen vest tops
or collars. The singer was exposed
to an eclectic range of music by his
grandmother, former blues singer
Julia Morgan, who had Sylvester listen
to gospel and jazz as well as her own
chosen field. Unfazed by his homosexuality though he was still being told
it was wrong, Sylvester was a natural
performer, moving to San Francisco in
1967 and setting up performance-art
(ie, drag) troupe The Cockettes – well,
it was never going to be anything else
– and adopting the stage moniker
Ruby Blue. Becoming familiar with
his take on show numbers, many were
surprised to learn that Sylvester also
had considerable talent as a ballad
singer; he landed a part in the musical *Hair* before, in 1973, forming The
Hot Band, a funk/dance conglomerate that predated disco – at one point
containing Izora Rhodes and Martha
Wash, later hit-makers as The Weather
Girls. Discovery by Fantasy Records
A & R man Harvey Fuqua – who
saw in the singer a star in the making
– prompted Sylvester to strike out
on his own, and a solo album was
released in 1977. With the exception
of his popular version of Ashford &
Simpson's 'Over and Over', the record
was largely ignored, but its follow-up
made Sylvester a big name. Boasting
the sizzling Patrick Cowley-produced
'You Make Me Feel (Mighty Real)' (a
UK Top Ten hit in 1978), the record

Sylvester: Even God couldn't save the queen

'One of the few truly gay celebrities never to have renounced his gayness on the ladder to success.'

Armistead Maupin

was a flag-bearer for the openly gay disco scene that blossomed at the turn of the eighties. (Sylvester was a considerable influence on ex-Bronski Beat/Communards singer Jimi Somerville, who took 'Mighty Real' back into the charts in 1990.) After appearing in the Bette Midler movie *The Rose*, Sylvester's appeal faded as the disco backlash kicked in. He did, however, team up once more with producer Cowley to create further high-energy gems – notably 'Do You Wanna Funk?' – on the album *All I Need* (1982).

Sadly, Cowley died within months of the record's release (☛ *November 1982*), one of the first showbiz victims of AIDS; in just three years, Sylvester himself had also been diagnosed with the condition, about which folk were still fairly ignorant. Refusing to denigrate his own sexuality, Sylvester continued to perform until shortly before his own passing; his final high-profile appearance was at the 1987 Gay Pride rally in San Francisco. He died from HIV complications a year later.

See also *Izora Rhodes-Armstead (☛ September 2004)*

Wednesday 21

Paul Jeffreys
(1955)
Cockney Rebel
Be-Bop Deluxe
(Chartreuse)

Bass guitarist with the original incarnation of Steve Harley's Cockney Rebel, Paul Jeffreys played on a string of hit singles during the mid seventies, including 'Judy Teen', 'Mr Soft' (both 1974) and the 1975 chart-topper '(Come up and See Me) Make Me Smile', as well as the albums *Human Menagerie* (1973), *The Psychomodo* (1974) and *Best Years of Our Lives* (1975).

After the group's 1977 split, Jeffreys joined occasional support act, the Bill Nelson-fronted neo-rock band Be-Bop Deluxe for live shows before forming his own group, Chartreuse, in 1979.

Just after 7 pm on 21 December 1988, Pan Am flight 103 began the second leg of its daily journey from Frankfurt to Detroit via London and New York. As the 747 flew over the small Scottish border town of Lockerbie, a device detonated in the forward cargo hold, causing the aircraft's chassis to disintegrate rapidly. In the horror that followed, 243 passengers and 16 crew lost their lives, as well as 11 people on the ground. Among the passengers was Paul Jeffreys – now working for a record company – and his new bride, Rachel, with whom he was travelling to the US on honeymoon. After much effort, the trial of Abdelbaset Ali Mohmed al-Megrahi was secured; the former Libyan intelligence officer was found guilty of mass murder and sentenced to life imprisonment. At a one-off gig shortly after the disaster, Harley dedicated the song 'Sebastian' – perhaps Cockney Rebel's finest moment – to the memory of his former colleague.

See also *Ian Parkin (☛ July 1995)*

Close!
John Lydon
(Sex Pistols/Public Image Ltd)

In February 2004, former Sex Pistol John Lydon revealed in an interview that he'd narrowly missed being on the 1988 Pan Am flight that exploded over Lockerbie – because his wife Nora had taken so long to pack. Said the singer, 'We had a big row and took the next flight out – the minute we realized what had happened, we looked at each other and almost collapsed.' Lydon also claimed that the incident prompted him to walk off the ITV reality show *I'm a Celebrity – Get Me out of Here!*, when staff would not tell him whether Nora's flight to the Australian set had arrived safely.

Lest We Forget

Other notable deaths that occurred sometime during 1988:

Fred Below (popular US R & B drummer with The Four Aces/Jukes, Moonglows, Drifters, Bo Diddley and John Lee Hooker, among others; born Illinois, 16/9/1926; cancer, 14/8)

Cathy Carr (US pop singer who hit US #2 with 'Ivory Tower' in 1956; born Angelina Helen Catherine Cordovano, New York, 28/6/1936; unknown, 1/11)

Janet Ertel (US bass with all-female 'barbershop' vocal act The Chordettes, whose biggest hit was 1958's 'Lollipop'; born Janet Buschman, Wisconsin, 1913; cancer, 22/11)

Son House (hugely influential US blues guitarist who'd been incarcerated and barely played before he was thirty; born Mississippi, 21/3/1902; Alzheimer's/Parkinson's disease, 19/10)

Gordon Huntley (UK pedal-steel guitarist best remembered for his sublime contribution to Matthews Southern Comfort's 1970 #1 'Woodstock'; born Berkshire, 1930; cancer, 7/3)

Howie Johnson (US drummer with instrumental surf-rock band The Ventures, scoring with 'Walk, Don't Run' in 1960; born Washington, 1938; unknown, 1/1988)

Memphis Slim (much-lauded and prolific US blues pianist; born John 'Peter' Chatman, Tennessee, 3/9/1915; kidney failure in his adopted home of Paris, 24/2)

Jimmy Soul (generically named R & B singer who topped the US charts with the novelty 'If You Wanna be Happy' in 1963; born James McCleese, New York, 24/8/1942; heart attack, 25/6)

Tenor Saw (distinctive Jamaican dancehall singer; born Clive Bright, Kingston, 1966; killed by a hit-and-run driver while allegedly selling cocaine in Texas, 8/1988)

Steve Walsh (larger-than-life UK DJ who hit the Top Ten with 'I Found Lovin'' in 1987; born 1959; after a car accident in Spain broke his leg, he suffered a massive coronary during surgery, 3/7)

For a complete list of fallen artists, visit

www.numberoneinheaven.com

JANUARY

Tuesday 17

Patti (McCabe) Barnes

(Patti McCabe – Lyndhurst, Ohio, c1940)

The Poni-Tails

The three Poni-Tails were from well-to-do backgrounds, Lyndhurst being one of Cleveland's better neighbourhoods. The original line-up of this early all-female vocal group – Toni Cistone (lead), Laverne Novak (high harmonies) and Karen Topinka (low harmonies) – were students at Brush High School; McCabe was from nearby Regina. In 1957, The Poni-Tails' likely first hit, 'Your Wild Heart', was effectively gazumped by Jay Layne's superior version, and Topinka's father pulled her out of the band in frustration. In stepped McCabe, and after a few further flops, the dream appeared to come true with 'Born Too Late' (1958) achieving transatlantic Top Ten status. But this memorable teen lament was to prove The Poni-Tails' only hit as other acts with perhaps stronger voices took over. With no royalty deal secured (as was commonplace at the time), the still-teenage Poni-Tails cut their losses and returned to cosy domestic lives and conventional employment.

Patti McCabe (now Barnes) died of cancer early in 1989. Cistone and Novak reunited for one last blast at a nostalgia convention in Cleveland eight years later.

Thursday 26

Donnie Elbert

(New Orleans, Louisiana, 25 May 1936)

(The Vibraharps)

Donnie Elbert was a guitarist/vocalist whose soaring falsetto made him popular with Northern soul audiences towards the end of the sixties. By this time he had performed with R & B vocal group The Vibraharps, though disagreement over the group's direction saw him leave in 1957, after just three releases. As a solo artist with the Deluxe and Vee-Jay labels, Elbert found himself in the frustrating position of selling large quantities of records in one area only: a prime example was 1960's 'Will You Ever be Mine?' which shifted a quarter of a million records in Philadelphia without ever breaking nationally. Finally, a remake of The Supremes' 'Where Did Our Love Go?' (1971) took him into the Billboard Top Twenty – a touch ironic for an artist who had once turned Motown down, particularly when his only other chart entry was a Four Tops cover. Having worked for five years as an A & R man with Polygram Canada, Elbert died after suffering a stroke.

FEBRUARY

Wednesday 1

Paul Robi

(New Orleans, Louisiana, 20 August 1931)

The Platters

Former choir leader Paul Robi's tenure as The Platters' baritone did not begin until Svengali (and former jazz-band manager) Buck Ram took the wet-behind-the-ears vocal group off the hands of rival entrepreneur Ralph Bass. The group – formed by Los Angeles high-school singer David Lynch (second tenor) – was groomed by manager/voice coach Ram into a fine unit that would sell over 50 million records in its career. For Robi, a 1953 move to California couldn't have been better timed; it was less lucky for previous baritone Alex Hodge, sacked by the group for allegedly attempting to sell marijuana to a policeman. Completed by Tony Williams (lead tenor), Herb Reed (bass) and female alto Zola Taylor, The Platters dominated the R & B vocal wars of the fifties, taking four of their songs to US number one – including the UK million-seller 'Smoke Gets in Your Eyes' (1958) – and enjoying considerable success the world over. The bubble only burst when various members of the group, including Paul Robi, were found in a compromising position with several under-age Cincinnati fans – after which they struggled to place on the charts, despite eventual acquittal. Robi was replaced by Nate Nelson in 1964.

Following this dip in fortunes, Paul Robi became very depressed and lost himself for some years to alcohol, before re-emerging with a 'new' Platters (one of at least four groups bearing the name) and touring successfully in New Zealand – much to the chagrin of Ram, who attempted to take out an injunction against the use of the name by former members of 'his' group. The singer, diagnosed with pancreatic cancer, won the dispute with Ram just before his death – and his widow was reported to have received $3.5 million.

See also *David Lynch (* January 1981); Nathaniel Nelson (* June 1984); Tony Williams (* August 1992). Early Platters Cornell Gunter (* February 1990) and Elsbeary Hobbs (* May 1996) have also died, as have manager/producer Buck Ram (1991) and later singer Randy Jones (2002).*

Saturday 4

Trevor Lucas
(Melbourne, Australia, 25 December 1943)
Fairport Convention
Fotheringay
(Eclection)

Severely dyslexic, Trevor Lucas was encouraged by his doctor (via his mother) to 'use his hands'. Obeying instruction, Lucas became a carpenter and, significantly, a first-rate guitarist, learning the folk standards that were to inform his later compositions. In Melbourne, Lucas was a popular live performer, and recorded his first solo record for East at just twenty. In 1965, the guitarist thought a short jaunt to check out the British scene would be interesting: he ended up staying for ten years, recording with some of the folk crossover scene's biggest names. After a second solo effort, Lucas joined Eclection for one eponymous album with Elektra, before guesting on Fairport Convention's album *Unhalfbricking* (1969) – the record the group was touring when young drummer Martin Lamble died (* *May 1969*). Lucas struck up a relationship with mercurial singer/musician Sandy Denny, which resulted in their 1973 marriage. The couple briefly set up Fotheringay, named after one of Denny's songs, after her departure from Fairport, but the commercial response did not match critical acclaim. The stand-out cut from their one 1970 album was Lucas's 'Ballad of Ned Kelly'.

Lucas played on Denny's solo records throughout the seventies, and also worked with a variety of other names, Al Stewart and The Strawbs among them. A Fairport Convention reunion proved a less than smooth ride, although two well-received records did come out of the re-formation – as well as some very

odd rock 'n' roll revival items. Tragedy hit Trevor Lucas and young daughter Georgia with estranged wife Denny's untimely death (* April 1978), after which the musician returned to Australia to produce indigenous acts. He died in his sleep from a heart attack, having remarried and fathered one further child.

Monday 6

King Tubby
(Osbourne Ruddock – Kingston, Jamaica, 28 January 1941)

King Tubby gained his earliest radio experience as a repairman, his fascination with sounds and gadgets the catalyst for his invention of a whole new genre, Jamaican 'dub' – the process of sound splicing within an instrumental break. With outdoor sound systems replacing a lot of conventional dancehall disc jockeying in the sixties, Tubby's tinkering found an outlet and he could leap up and fix a speaker if an event got out of hand – which happened frequently in Jamaica's most competitive pastime. Opening his own shop (Home Town Hi-Fi) and then a studio, King Tubby became the first name in Kingston for 'sound'. His ability to construct and deconstruct not just the hardware but the music that emanated from it was to make him the most sought-after producer in Jamaican reggae. Tubby's stripped-down tracks and strange sonic effects were used by producers Bunny Lee, Augustus Pablo and Lee 'Scratch' Perry, while he mentored Prince Jammy and The Scientist, two innovative dub artists who would wear Tubby's not-inconsiderable mantle after his death. In a production capacity, Tubby also oversaw more commercial work by the likes of John Holt, former African Brothers singer Sugar Minott and Delroy Wilson. A brilliant engineer, Tubby continued to make significant customizations, such as adding reverb facilities to mixing boards used by many DJs.

King Tubby's sudden death remains a mystery. Returning from his studio early in the morning, Tubby was approached by a lone man outside his Duhaney Park home. The dub pioneer was gunned down by the assailant in an apparently motiveless attack, for which nobody has ever been brought to justice.

Tuesday 14

Vincent Crane

(Vincent Cheesman – Reading, 21 May 1943)
The Crazy World of Arthur Brown
Atomic Rooster
Dexy's Midnight Runners

Growing up in Battersea, South London, Vincent Crane's first musical calling was as a classically trained pianist, graduating from Trinity College in 1964. His real love however was rock 'n' roll . . . Via a series of bands, Crane met the eccentric Arthur Brown in a Fulham house share, and the pair wrote the extraordinary 'Fire' (1968), a song that went on to top the UK charts, almost achieving the same in the US. Their album was also a major hit, and all appeared to be going well for the band, particularly as Crane's onstage antics were claiming almost as many headlines as Brown's well-documented pyrotechnics. But within a year the novelty was over and, escaping from a mountain of contract problems with Brown's group, Crane formed Atomic Rooster with drummer Carl Palmer (later of ELP). In this guise, he enjoyed hits with 'Tomorrow Night' and 'Devil's Answer' (both 1971).

Vincent Crane had been prone to psychiatric problems since boyhood, and the stress of a rock lifestyle sidelined him for long stretches with

depression. He saw numerous line-up changes within Atomic Rooster but few further sales, and in 1984 jacked it in to become an unlikely member of Dexy's Midnight Runners, playing on their third album, *Don't Stand Me Down* (1985). Rumours of an Atomic Rooster reunion were scotched by Crane's suicide at his Maida Vale home from an overdose of sleeping pills.

MARCH

Friday 10

Doc Green Jr

(New York, 8 October 1934)
The Drifters
The (Five) Crowns
(The Duvals)
(Various acts)

Harlem-born Doc Green Jr became, in 1958, the latest Drifters baritone in what was widely believed to be the definitive line-up of the many that fans would witness over the years. Green was a street singer, unfazed by confrontation and gifted with a rich voice. In 1952, he founded The Five Crowns (originally The Harmonaires) with close friend Wilbur 'Yonkie' Paul, who was eventually adopted by Green's family. From hereon, the group history becomes somewhat complicated. Suffice to say that six years and many recordings for Rainbow later, the final line-up was Green, James 'Papa' Clark (lead), Elsbeary Hobbs (bass), Benjamin Earl Nelson (soon to be Ben E King, lead tenor/baritone) and Charles Thomas (lead tenor). (Vocal singers often switched bands, and Green and Paul also offered their services to The Duvals at this time.) Approached by Drifters manager George Treadwell, The Crowns – with King at the front and minus heavy-

drinker Clark – became the 'new' Drifters. Within months, mainly spent on the road, the evocative Ben E King-written 'There Goes My Baby' (1959) shot to the top of the US R & B charts, stalling only at number two in the pop listings. (Meanwhile, The Duvals became the new Crowns and – well, there aren't enough hours in the day, frankly . . .)

The hits continued for The Drifters – including a Billboard number one in 'Save the Last Dance for Me' (1960) – but their fortunes dipped slightly with the loss of Ben E King to a solo career; he was eventually replaced by Rudy Lewis. Green left the line-up in 1962 to join a fairly unsuccessful imitation band named The Drapers, before forming The Floaters (not the 'Float On' hit-makers) with his old buddy Wilbur Paul and ex-Drifter Tommy Evans. Thereafter, Doc Green faded into obscurity as various touring incarnations of The Drifters underwent even more bewildering line-up changes. He was briefly a member of one such himself, led by Charles Thomas in the seventies. Green died of cancer at his home in New York State.

See also *Rudy Lewis (*✦ *Pre-1965) and the accompanying Dead Interesting! for a definitive list of the fifteen departed Drifters. Green's lifelong friend Wilbur Paul passed away in 1993.*

MAY

Friday 19

Ron Wilson

(Glendora, California, 9 March 1945)
The Surfaris

In the autumn of 1962, four Dick Dale fans figured they could and should form a band in the style of their surf-guitar idol: the result was The Surfaris – Jim Fuller (lead guitar), Bob Berryhill (guitar), Pat Connolly (bass) and Ron Wilson (drums). The group's impact was immediate and brief – and due to one tune. Beach-fanatic Wilson had had a dream about a mythical hero named 'Surfer Joe' – and thus the group had the subject for its first single, built around a Wilson drum solo from his school marching-band days. Unfortunately for the percussionist, it was to be the B-side, 'Wipe Out', that captured the rest of the country's imagination. According to legend, the tune was improvised in fifteen minutes – and within six months it had sold a million copies, rising to number two in America. From then on, the boys hit a series of snags: first, early saxophonist Jim Pash (who died in 2005) sued the group in order to be *removed* from record sleeves, then another 'Surfaris' issued a suit over the name; finally a group called The Impacts claimed they'd had the idea for 'Wipe Out' before Wilson and co. As if this weren't enough, the band failed to secure a significant follow-up hit ('Point Panic' made US number forty-nine) and received no performance royalties because they hadn't played on any further tracks on their album!

Major success in Japan saved their bacon; the band turned to non-instrumentals and Ron Wilson shortly thereafter also took on vocal duties. The group were to see 'Wipe Out' a hit again – a version by The Fat Boys, accompanied by The Beach Boys, went platinum less than a year ahead of Wilson's death from a brain aneurysm. Tragically, the former drummer was near-destitute by this time.

John Cipollina

(Berkeley, California, 24 August 1943)
Quicksilver Messenger Service
(Various acts)

One of the most original guitar stylists to emerge during the sixties, John Cipollina could probably have been a virtuoso on any instrument, so instinctive was his skill. As boys, he and his brother Mario (who would enjoy greater success than John as a member of Huey Lewis & The News) showed talent way beyond the norm before either had reached even ten years old. Cipollina lived a bohemian existence from a young age, smoking despite his asthma and living on a houseboat in Sausalito as he began his foray into the music business. San Francisco was certainly the place to be, and the guitarist found session work with The Deacons, before the band realized that with their new acquisition they could be something more than the covers act they had been content to be to date. Changing their name to Quicksilver Messenger Service in 1965, the group – Cipollina, Gary Duncan (guitar), David Freiberg (bass), Greg Elmore (drums) and later Nicky Hopkins (keyboards) – were punchier and more powerful than Haight-Ashbury contemporaries Jefferson Airplane and The Grateful Dead (or even Big Brother & The Holding Company, without Janis) but somehow failed to grasp similar commercial success. Cipollina and Duncan's twin-guitar assault was an acid-fried treat, however, making them perhaps the essential live unit of the era. Most of the group remained stubbornly anti-establishment (despite signing to Capitol), and returning singer Dino Valenti's urge to 'go folksier' was not met favourably by Cipollina, who left in 1970. After breaking away from QMS (who were

nonetheless to reconvene in 1975), Cipollina contributed his unique tones to a vast array of rock acts, his own Copperhead (not to be confused with the Southern rock band of the same name), Terry & The Pirates, Keith Godchaux's Ghost and Welsh prog act Man among them. Diagnosed with emphysema in 1988, John Cipollina died after being admitted into Marin General Hospital following a severe asthma attack.

See also *Keith Godchaux (◀ July 1980); Dino Valenti (▶ November 1994)*

JUNE

Pete de Freitas

(Port of Spain, Trinidad, 2 August 1961)
Echo & The Bunnymen

Pete de Freitas obtained his opportunity with Liverpool's most influential post-punk band for one of the least flattering reasons: the band's drum machine (allegedly the 'Echo' of their name, until the band later denied this) had broken. As a former public schoolboy from 'down South', attempting to place himself within one of 1979's most-likely-to Scouse rock acts might have proved tricky, but de Freitas was clearly the final piece of an impressive jigsaw. Already signed to WEA imprint Korova, the Doors-inspired Bunnymen – de Freitas, Ian McCulloch (vocals), Will Sargeant (guitar) and Les Pattinson (bass) – impressed with early singles such as 'Rescue' (1979) and the Top Twenty debut album *Crocodiles* (1980). Within three years the band was one of the UK's most popular live attractions, going on to chart strongly with stunning singles like 'The Back of Love' (1982), 'The Cutter',

'Never Stop' (both 1983) and 'The Killing Moon' (1984); their albums continued to sell well in Britain, but, after the release of *Ocean Rain* (1984) and a 1985 compilation, de Freitas decided to move on from Echo & The Bunnymen, and was replaced, improbably, by ex-Haircut 100 sticksman Mark Fox. De Freitas disappeared to New Orleans, where he lived a hedonistic existence on the money he had earned from the band – but it was quickly apparent that the situation was unsatisfactory to both parties, and the percussionist was reinstated by the end of 1986. The following year's eponymous album was considered water-treading by their British fanbase, but nonetheless finally broke the group in America. By the end of the next year, however, the death of his father prompted Ian McCulloch to split from the band himself.

Much to the chagrin of fans the world over, the remaining members decided to continue without their mercurial frontman – and rehearsals began for a 'Bunnymen Mk II'. It was on the way to one of the first of these rehearsals that Pete de Freitas's motorbike collided with a car in Rugeley, Staffordshire. The drummer died at the scene. Echo & The Bunnymen finally reunited successfully with McCulloch in 1997.

JULY

Monday 17

Paul C
(Paul McKasty, Queens, New York, c 1965)

He was one of the most unassuming, unsung characters to emerge from the New York rap community, but his influence is indelible. A key name among early hip-hop producers, white

'Paul C Lives'
Credit on the reverse of Main Source's *Breaking Atoms* (1991)

Irish boy Paul C's wild and innovative sonic mesh boomed out of a small Queens rehearsal space once rented by Metallica, the whiz of Studio 1212 making the most of basic analogue equipment. McKasty was likely the first to utilize drum-isolating sample techniques – highlighting the work of Ultramagnetic MCs, Stezo, Biz Markie and Mikey D – an innovation much copied since. His final major work was with Eric B & Rakim on *Let the Rhythm Hit 'Em* (1990); the album was co-produced with Large Professor (who gleaned most of the credit) – a man who would, to some degree, keep McKasty's vision alive.

Paul C was found by his brother in his Queens apartment, shot three times in the head as he lay in his bed. Sixteen years on, nobody is any the wiser to the identity of the killer, or indeed about any motive, though many have fallen under suspicion.

AUGUST

Friday 4

Larry Parnes
(Laurence Maurice Parnes – Willesden, London, 1930)

A hugely influential figure during Britain's rock 'n' roll infancy, Larry Parnes was the man who bestowed upon the public some of the most colourfully named stars of the era. Parnes's organizational awareness was apparent as early as his eighth birthday, for which he put together a children's entertainment; his undeniable shrewdness was not evident during his brief employment at the family's clothing business – he accrued debts and failed with shops of his own. However,

Mr 'Parnes, shillings and pence' with his most precious commodity, Billy Fury

moving into theatre, Parnes, with John Kennedy (a publicist who helped keep his business venture afloat in the early years), cottoned on to rock 'n' roll, and fortunes were set to change. Beginning with singer Tommy Steele, Parnes foisted on the market a series of replicas such as Vince Eager, Johnny Gentle (for whom he once employed The Beatles as back-up), Duffy Power, Dickie Pride and, the most successful, Marty Wilde. Although he apparently turned down Cliff Richard, Parnes then hit upon mega-heart-throb Billy Fury, whose career he guided for ten years, while also managing more conventional talent in The Tornados and the genial Joe Brown.

Knowing the pitfalls of pop stardom, Parnes advised and encouraged many of his charges, most notably Steele, to move into musicals – an area into which he himself effectively transferred during the late sixties. In 1981, Larry Parnes developed meningitis, which enforced his early retirement; his death eight years later is believed to have been as a direct result of the illness.

See also *Dickie Pride (* March 1969); Billy Fury (* January 1983); Heinz Burt (* April 2000); Alan Caddy (* August 2000)*

SEPTEMBER

Friday 8

Cowboy
(Robert Keith Wiggins – The Bronx, New York, 20 September 1960)
(Grandmaster Flash &) The Furious Five

Another New York hip-hop innovator, Keith Wiggins was among the first credited with rapping itself, joining DJ Grandmaster Flash (Joseph

Saddler) in the mid seventies as the latter – already getting attention for his fast-action craft of breaks and cuts – decided a vocal accompaniment would provide the hammer to knock in the nail. Wiggins came in to replace original choice Lovebug Starski (Kevin Smith), under the nickname 'Cowboy', becoming one of the first MCs as he delivered a series of rough 'n' ready rhymes to the beats: his call-to-arms phrases became rap staples within the next decade. With the addition of Grandmaster Melle Mel (Melvin Glover) and his brother Nathaniel, aka Kidd Creole, Flash's support troupe became The 3MCs. Operating much like Jamaican sound-system rivals, various posses would take one another on – with their equipment at stake. Grandmaster Flash and Melle Mel's careers were also developing separately – Mel had expanded his unit to become The Furious Five, with Rahiem (Guy Williams) and Scorpio (Eddie Morris) – and Joe Robinson Jr of Sugar Hill Records saw huge studio potential in what each was doing. After a few marginal offerings, the combined units gave the world the breakthrough hit 'The Message' (1982, penned by Robinson's wife, former hit-maker Sylvia). This record's extraordinary rumble was to change the face of black American music. But Flash was nonplussed by royalty policies, for which he would sue Sugar Hill (the subject of 1983's 'We Don't Work for Free'), and he left the label with Creole and Rahiem in 1984. Cowboy, Mel and Scorpio remained to score another massive international hit with 'White Lines (Don't Do It)' (in Britain, this track stayed on the charts for almost a year and was the thirteenth-biggest seller of 1984).

The subject matter of the record was to prove deeply ironic, though – Flash was now addicted to cocaine and Cowboy was slipping into the far darker world of crack. By 1987 he was serving time for possession, his career at an apparent standstill. With

drugs becoming the main focus of his last two years, Cowboy slipped off rap's radar to die in relative obscurity in a New York hospital. The cause of death was believed to be a heart attack brought on by his habit.

OCTOBER

Thursday 19

Alan Murphy
(Finsbury, London, 18 November 1953)
Level 42
Kate Bush
(Various acts)

A rebellious metalhead as a youngster, Alan Murphy survived expulsion from school to become one of the most respected British mainstream guitarists of the eighties. Blues-influenced Murphy spent his early career mainly in session mode, hopping from one act to another, in 1975 flying to Los Angeles to record with British band Ace only to join Long John Baldry when the sessions didn't work out. After three years of touring, Murphy returned to Britain to join the band of very 'happening' singer Kate Bush (despite never having heard of 'Wuthering Heights') for her *Never Forever* (1980) and *The Dreaming* (1982) albums – the singer apparently liked his 'whale sounds' and invited him back for later work. In the early eighties, work was more sporadic for Murphy, despite recording with Joan Armatrading, Go West, Nick Heyward, Mike & The Mechanics, Scritti Politti and Amii Stewart – as well as his own band SFX – but an opportunity with white soul/fusion act Level 42 arose early in 1988. By now Murphy had learned and accepted that he was HIV positive, so playing with the established British band perhaps represented a chance to end his days on a high: he contributed to the gold album *Staring at the Sun* (1988).

Although he kept the news of his condition to himself, many who saw Alan Murphy during his final year felt he hadn't long to live. Just three months after leaving Level 42, the guitarist passed away from pneumonia at the Westminster Hospital. Kate Bush's 1991 hit cover of Elton John's 'Rocket Man' was perhaps the last release to feature Murphy's work. The singer remembered him by featuring an empty chair with an acoustic guitar on it in the promotional video.

DECEMBER

Friday 1

Billy Lyall
(Edinburgh, 26 March 1953)
Pilot
(The Bay City Rollers)
(Various acts)

Billy Lyall: Dropped the Pilot

In the seventies, a young keyboard and flute-playing Scot was doing his best to extricate himself from the potential shackles of new teen group The Bay City Rollers. As someone who could actually play his instrument, Billy Lyall had no real place in a band that was effectively a pretty-boy front for a series of anonymous session men. Around the same time, another bunch of young Edinburgh boys were being touted as the next Rollers – but this band could play and had a tune (well, two) about them. Via a stint as an engineer at Craighall Studios, Lyall joined fellow ex-Roller David Paton (vocals/bass), Ian Bairnson (guitar) and Stuart Tosh (drums) in Pilot, and the group quickly secured a big transatlantic hit with the hopelessly optimistic but mightily infectious 'Magic' (1974).

Pilot had been signed to EMI at the same time as both Cockney Rebel and Queen – and the race was on to nail a number one. All three were to manage the feat during 1975, but Pilot, with the hopelessly optimistic but mightily infectious 'January', landed first.

However, after this blurt of huge success, they were unable to chart any further records higher than number thirty-one (1975's 'Just a Smile'), and Paton and Bairnson ran off to join The Alan Parsons Project. Lyall attempted a solo career with little success, during the eighties enjoying the dubious double honour of playing with Sheena Easton and Dollar. Diagnosed two years before, he, too, died of an AIDS-related illness in December 1989.

Thursday 14

Pattie Santos
(San Francisco, California, 16 November 1944)
It's a Beautiful Day
(Pharoe's Whistle)

She was working as – well, not a waitress in a cocktail bar – a check-out girl in a grocery store when It's a Beautiful Day's manager/promoter Matthew Katz decided that winsome teenager Patricia Santos was just the face to front the San Fran folk-pop band. As luck would have it, Santos had belonged to a school choir and possessed the voice to match the look. In IABD, she joined violinist and founder member David LaFlamme and his keyboardist wife, Linda; the group signed to Columbia (after a winning 1968 performance opening for Cream in place of Traffic) and issued their eponymous debut a year later. This record contained the band's best-known song in 'White Bird'. The LaFlammes' messy divorce probably dented the band's progress thereafter (Linda had already had enough, having been bottled at a gig), and numerous line-up changes followed. Santos was to be a permanent fixture, though, and It's a Beautiful Day issued four more albums to 1974; she also formed her own band, Pharoe's Whistle, and recorded with Bud Cockrell and Jaco Pastorius later in the decade.

In late 1989, an inebriated Pattie Santos was heading westwards through Santa Rosa at breakneck speed along a notorious stretch of Route 128 when she hit the kerb, then a fence, her car flipping up into the air and colliding with trees. The singer – who had not been strapped in – was pronounced dead at 1.20 am. Various members of IABD fell into protracted legal wrangles with Katz, and keyboardist Fred Webb also passed away just months later. Occasional vibraphonist Larry Blackshere was murdered in 2002.

See also *Jaco Pastorius (September 1987)*

Lest We Forget

Other notable deaths that occurred sometime during 1989:

Dean Beard (US rockabilly guitarist/pianist, leader of The Crew Cats and briefly a member of The Champs; born Texas, 1935; leukaemia, 4/1989)

Joseph Boatner (US vocalist with influential group The Ink Spots; born 27/9/1918; unknown – shortly before later members Cliff Givens and Stanley Morgan – 8/5)

Wick Larsen (US guitarist with oddly named Southern rockers Wet Willie; diabetic coma, 14/2)

Ewan MacColl (noted Scots folk stalwart who composed 'The First Time Ever I Saw Your Face' for wife Peggy; also father of the late Kirsty MacColl; born James Miller, Auchterarder, 25/1/1915; heart attack, 22/10)

Chris 'Biffa' McCaffrey (UK bassist with shamefully ignored Liverpool guitar band The Pale Fountains; brain tumour after a motorbike crash)

Ron Morgan (US guitarist with Three Dog Night and The Electric Prunes; born c 1945; hepatitis C)

Dámaso Pérez 'Prez' Prado (Cuban pianist/band-leader and 'Mambo King' who scored a 10-week #1 with 'Cherry Pink & Apple Blossom White' in 1955; born Mantanzas, 11/12/1916; stroke, 14/9)

D Lucifer Stele (US drummer with Colorado black-metal act Satan's Host; murdered, possibly by an anti-Satanist pressure group)

Nicky Thomas (Jamaican reggae singer who recorded the definitive version of 'Love of the Common People'; born Cecil Thomas, Portland, 30/5/1944; heart attack or suicide)

Steve Wahrer (US surf-rock drummer with The Trashmen, who nailed a Top Five hit with 1963's 'Surfin' Bird'; born Minnesota, 22/11/1941; oesophageal cancer, 21/1)

For a complete list of fallen artists, visit
www.numberoneinheaven.com

1990

JANUARY

Mel Appleby

(Melanie Susan Appleby – East London,
11 July 1966)

Mel & Kim

Remembered by most as the act that made the work of Stock, Aitken & Waterman just about bearable, Mel & Kim enjoyed brief UK chart domination with a run of house-flavoured pop hits between 1986 and 1988. In true Human League style, both girls were spotted dancing in a nightclub by the production team, who, for once, discovered something worth pursuing. It was only when massive success beckoned that Mel's previous *métier* as a nude model was inevitably unearthed by the tabloids.

The splendidly 'up' 'Showing Out' took Mel & Kim to UK number three at the end of 1986, its follow-up 'Respectable' reaching number one just three months later – the pair of singles shifted a combined 750,000 copies for the now-hot duo. The songs were also sizeable international hits and were followed by two further Top Ten singles and a 3-million-selling album, *FLM (Fun, Love and Money)*

Mel (*left*) & Kim: Fun, love, money and extravagant headgear

(1987). By now, though, the news that Mel Appleby had been diagnosed with spinal cancer was leaking to the outside world. The sisters, for some reason, continued to deny this in public, though Mel was shortly forced into retirement and the secret was thus out. Her death at the start of 1990 was met with many tributes. Kim Appleby pursued a briefly successful solo career thereafter.

Tuesday 23

Allen Collins
(Jacksonville, Florida, 19 July 1952)
Lynyrd Skynyrd
The Rossington-Collins Band

Beginning a career marked as much by personal catastrophe as it would be by international acclaim, guitarist Allen Collins left his school band The Mods, hooking up in 1965 with buddies Ronnie Van Zant (vocals) and Gary Rossington (guitar) to form an embryonic version of the future Southern rock megastars under the name My Backyard. After recording one 1968 single with a local label, the group – completed by early members Larry Jungstrom (bass) and Bob Burns (drums) – became Lynyrd Skynyrd, in commemoration of a former gym teacher who had given members a hard time years before. After various other line-up changes, Skynyrd scored their first hit album with *Pronounced Leh-Nerd Skin-Nerd* (1973), and quickly followed it with two more gold discs and million-sellers in the 1976 live double *One More for the Road* and the final, grimly prophetic *Street Survivors* (1977). By the last album, what is generally considered to be the definitive roster of Lynyrd Skynyrd was set at Collins, Van Zant, Rossington and newer boys Steve Gaines (guitar), Leon Wilkeson (bass), Billy Powell (keyboards) and Artimus Pyle (drums),

ahead of the much-anticipated 'Tour of the Survivors', which would also feature the band's back-up girl vocalists, The Honkettes. The tour ended in disaster with the light-aircraft crash that killed Van Zant, Gaines, his Honkette sister, Cassie Gaines, and road manager Dean Kilpatrick and injured Collins and the others (*October 1977*)

For Collins, the tragedy that ended an era for his band was merely a precursor to the heartbreaking concluding years of his own life. After forming The Rossington-Collins Band with his previous co-guitarist, the musician lost his wife, Kathy Johns, during her third pregnancy and immersed himself in his music, dedicating the new group's album *This is the Way* (1981) to her memory. As if this weren't enough, Collins drove his brand-new Thunderbird off the road in January 1986. The crash was so severe that the guitarist was left paralysed from the waist down; his girlfriend, Debra Jean Watts, was killed, and the crippled Collins was convicted of manslaughter and commanded to use his fame to warn the young against drinking and driving. Never fully recovering, Allen Collins appeared briefly with a 1987 tenth-anniversary re-formation of Lynyrd Skynyrd (playing in a wheelchair) but finally passed away after contracting pneumonia in 1989, the illness exacerbated by his decreased lung capacity, a product of his permanent disability.

See also *Leon Wilkeson (* *July 2001*)

Peter Sweval
(Piet Sweval – Toms River, New Jersey, 13 April 1948)
Looking Glass
Starz

On the same day, the field of commercial heavy rock lost Peter Sweval,

a bass-player who had found brief fame not once but twice during the seventies. Looking Glass was formed as a frat-house pastime while members Sweval, Elliot Lurie (vocals/guitar), Larry Gonsky (piano) and Jeff Grob (drums) prepared to graduate from Rutgers University, New Jersey. The musicians reconvened after leaving college and were stunned to find themselves signed to Columbia; heaven knows how they must have felt when their third single, the Lurie-penned 'Brandy (You're a Fine Girl)' – originally a B-side, topped the Billboard charts in the summer of 1972. Despite this mass acceptance of their work, Looking Glass were unable to repeat the success.

After Looking Glass, Sweval joined New York stadium pop act Starz (originally Fallen Angels, fronted by singer Michael Lee Smith) and enjoyed another brief flirtation with Billboard's Top Forty in 1977. Still touring with the band, Peter Sweval died of cancer in his late thirties.

Sunday 28

Sandra 'Puma' Jones
(South Carolina, 5 October 1953)
Black Uhuru
(Mama Africa)

Another cancer victim, 'Puma' Jones was a Columbia University graduate who became one of the most celebrated women in the predominantly male world of reggae. Raised in Harlem, New York, Jones migrated to Jamaica during the early seventies, where she worked as a social worker on housing projects, satisfying her love of reggae with the band Mama Africa in her spare time. Black Uhuru (originally just Uhuru, meaning 'freedom') had already released one album by the time Jones joined the ranks as a harmony vocalist – the ranks having been trimmed since the band's 1973 formation to just founder Derrick 'Duckie' Simpson and lead singer (Anthony) Michael Rose. The first album with Jones's vocal input was the excellent *Showcase* (1979, reissued later as *Guess Who's Coming to Dinner?*, named after the band's best-known song). Black Uhuru now signed with Island and, working with the fabled Sly Dunbar and Robbie Shakespeare, produced another great collection the following year: *Sinsemilla*. After the death of Bob Marley (☞ *May 1981*), the band became reggae's leading flag-bearers on the international stage – and the genre's first act to land a Grammy, for the 1984 album *Anthem*.

Rose had now left, and in 1987, a devastated 'Puma' Jones learned she had cancer and also bowed out of one of the second generation's best bands. For the first album without her unique voice (*Positive*, 1987), Black Uhuru brought in soundalike Ola Funke, but apparently felt her name should not appear on the credits. Jones passed away three years later and was buried in the town of her birth. Veteran Black Uhuru percussionist Sidney Wolfe also succumbed to cancer in June 1998.

FEBRUARY

Thursday 8

Del Shannon

(Charles Weedon Westover – Coopersville, Michigan, 30 December 1934)

(The Midnight Ramblers)

His tales of rejection and broken hearts spawning at least one bona fide classic, Del Shannon was one of the first pin-up idols to compose his own material. Always keen to promote his work, Charles Westover (as was) first found himself on the radio while

'The screaming kids when I got to number one . . . Lord, the fear was so great! I thought, what am I doing here?'

Del Shannon gives clues

Del Shannon: Here's Charlie

serving with the Special Services in Germany, hosting the *Get up and Go* show – but it soon became clear the keen guitarist would far rather be making the records than presenting them. On his return to Michigan, Westover sold carpets by day and cut rug by night with his Midnight Ramblers, a Hank Williams-influenced band formed with keyboardist Max Crook. Westover's 'carpet boss' heard an embryonic song called 'Runaway' and suggested they record it. Shortly after, a show at The Hi-Lo Club in Battle Creek was attended by local DJ Ollie McLaughlin, who signed the newly renamed Del Shannon to his label Embee – 'Runaway' gained instant hit status in the spring of 1961. At one point shifting over 80,000 copies a day, the record lived up to its title and topped the national charts for four weeks – six weeks in the UK, where the singer had The Beatles open for him on tour. The debut record's extraordinary falsetto and Musitron organ hook had captured the imagination of record-buyers the world over, and now Shannon – a reluctant star uncomfortable with all the sudden attention – was under pressure to follow it. Shannon managed another big seller in the US with 'Hats off to Larry' (1961), but, after this, his hit run was to yield just one more Top Ten entry (1964's 'Keep Searchin''), although in the UK he remained one of the most successful male solo acts throughout the early decade. Steadfastly hard-working, Shannon relieved the stress of constant touring (and the added strain of appeasing managers and labels who sought another 'Runaway') with alcohol. He admitted he didn't care for the taste – but he liked where it took him.

By 1966 Shannon's US fanbase had become concerned at the direction their favourite was taking: he was now working with Andrew Loog Oldham in London, and the resulting album, *Home and Away*, was refused release by his US label, Liberty. Similarly,

a bizarre psychedelic album issued under his real name was roundly ignored, presumably because his fans hadn't worked out that Del Shannon was behind the project. His work thus snubbed, Shannon developed a belligerent attitude towards recording and became aloof with his followers at home (although he found time to produce hits for LA girl band Smith and friend and fellow heart-throb Brian Hyland). The later years of his career were spent mainly in obscurity; Shannon was, however, to find friends among a new generation of rock musicians, not least long-time admirer Tom Petty, who guided his *Drop Down and Get Me* album in 1982, spawning Shannon's first Top Forty success at home for fifteen years with 'Sea of Love'. But the singer, despite having conquered his alcohol addiction, was descending into a self-destructive world of depression.

After consulting a doctor early in 1990, Shannon returned home to his wife, Beverley LeAnne Gutierrez, with a clutch of Prozac. His wife recognized immediate problems: Shannon began dieting drastically and eschewing all work commitments. Five days after appearing at the annual Buddy Holly memorial concert in Fargo, Del Shannon was found dead at his newly purchased home in California's Santa Clarita Valley, his bathrobe-clad body slumped in a rocking chair with a .22 rifle lying on the floor. He was cremated ten days later, and a monument was erected in his home town, Coopersville. Gutierrez fought back her devastation to sue pharmaceutical company Eli Lilly & Co for 'wrongful death, negligence and fraud', insisting that her dead husband had been 'a well-informed, healthy man' and had been using the drug for just two weeks.

George Suranovich
(Pittsburgh, Pennsylvania, 15 June 1944)
Love
The Eric Burdon Band
Blues Image
(Various acts)

The fourth drummer with Los Angeles rock band Love – following erstwhile percussionists Don Conka, Alban 'Snoopy' Pfisterer and Michael Stuart – George Suranovich already had an eclectic CV before he joined Arthur Lee's band, having played with Bo Diddley and even the military in Vietnam. Suranovich played – with Lee (vocals/guitar), Jay Donnellan (lead guitar) and Frank Fayad (bass) – on the 1969 albums *Four Sail* and *Out Here* (which included his vocals on his own composition 'Nice To Be') before regular disputes over money curtailed his time with the epochal four-piece. A proposed session with Jimi Hendrix then came to nothing when the legendary guitarist died suddenly (➤ *September 1970*). During the early seventies, Suranovich sat behind former Animals frontman Eric Burdon as he toured the US and drummed with Blues Image and, simultaneously, various other California-based bands. But a return to Love in 1977 for a live album didn't prevent Suranovich from pursuing his first calling as a jazz percussionist.

After a Sunday-evening performance, George Suranovich was rushed to hospital with chest pains and informed that he required bypass surgery. Although the surgery was routine, he collapsed from a massive heart attack a few nights later, and died at home. A number of bands played a concert in his honour some weeks later at Pittsburgh's Graffiti nightclub.

See also *Ken Forssi (➤ January 1998); Bryan MacLean (➤ December 1998).*

Early Love drummer Don Conka died in 2004.

Saturday 24

Johnnie Ray
(John Alvin Ray – Dallas, Oregon, 10 January 1927)

Poor old croonin' Johnnie Ray – he moved a million hearts in mono and rewrote the rulebook on how stars performed live. Often labelled 'The Prince of Wails', Ray was part Native American (Blackfoot), and thus cut quite a figure on stage. His wearing of a hearing aid was seen by more cynical folk as a 'prop' but in fact the singer had worn it most of his life, his deafness the result of a boyhood injury. Under the guidance of Al Green (not the singer but the entrepreneur who would later assist Jackie Wilson), Ray proved himself no slouch, writing his own material and working out his own inimitable stage routine. Backed by The Four Lads, Ray worked hard for a hit record and found one in spectacular style with the emotive 'Cry' (1951) – a record that spent eleven weeks at US number one. The heavy gospel influence of this record hoodwinked – accidentally it would seem – many black music fans into buying it at a time when markets were very split. 'Cry' clocked up a remarkable 2 million US sales. The gold records continued throughout the sixties, during which time the singer built up a massive European fanbase, and three of his singles – 'Such a Night' (1954), 'Just Walking in the Rain' (1956) and 'Yes Tonight, Josephine' (1957) – topped the British charts. The only blight on Ray's career was his incursion into movie acting, which suggested that his emoting was better kept to his musical performances.

With his star fading at home amid rumours of homosexuality and drug use, Ray refocused on Australia, which he toured more often than any other star of the era, and, of course, the UK, where he remained a major draw into the seventies (though by now strictly on the oldies circuit). Johnnie Ray's long affair with the bottle saw the singer succumbing to cirrhosis of the liver after a short stay at the Cedars-Sinai Medical Center in Los Angeles.

Monday 26

Cornell Gunter
(Cornelius Gunter – Coffeyville, Kansas, 14 November 1936)
The Coasters
The Flairs (The Hollywood Blue Jays)
The Platters
(Various acts)

The Coasters, those undisputed clown princes of R & B, must have upset someone somewhere along the way. Early lead Cornell Gunter might well have been watching his back after the murders of saxophone legend King Curtis (◀*August 1971*) and touring bass Nathaniel Wilson (◀*April 1980*), but to little avail: in the third unrelated shooting incident, Gunter was to follow suit – apparently a victim of mistaken identity.

With a professional blues singer for a mother, fine tenor Gunter was given all the encouragement he could possibly require, and a move to Los Angeles in his youth put him in touch with The Platters, the classic vocal group formed at Fremont High School with fellow singers 'Jody' Jefferson and brothers Alex and Gaynel Hodge. The apparently snail-like pace of The Platters' development, however, caused Gunter to jump ship to join The Flairs (a similarly styled doo-wop act that had begun as The Hollywood Blue Jays, taking the new name from the label that cut their first disc), on occasion drafting in his sister Shirley. The Platters, of course, went on to enormous success in Gunter's absence. Gunter finally teamed up with The Coasters in March 1958, via stints with several other acts. He replaced founder member Leon Hughes, and within four months the band enjoyed a US number one with the enduring 'Yakety Yak' (1958), one of several splendid Jerry Leiber- and

The Coasters – Guy, Jones, Gunter, Gardner and Jacobs: The drinks were on them

Mike Stoller-penned songs that the group made their own. The follow-up, 'Charlie Brown' (1959), sold almost as many copies, while 'Along Came Jones' and 'Poison Ivy' (both 1959), gave the quartet further riotous Top Ten entries. Gunter left The Coasters just at the point of decline to play with Dinah Washington; he would, however, return with a Coasters line-up of his own.

Despite legal threats from H B Barnum – manager of the 'original' Coasters – Gunter, who had already toured a renegade Drifters line-up, was fronting The Fabulous Coasters by 1980. It was nonetheless a rocky road, highlighted (or rather lowlighted) by manager Patrick Cavanaugh's murder of Wilson that year. Remarkably, Gunter's Coasters survived this horrific event and played throughout the decade to enthusiastic fans. In 1990, though, the group's catastrophic misfortune reared its head once more: after an engagement at the ill-named Lady Luck Hotel in Las Vegas, Gunter pulled up at an intersection in his 1978 Camaro. Witnesses reported a fierce exchange between the driver and a man waiting by the kerb. Suddenly, Gunter's car was showered with bullets. Struck twice, Gunter attempted to speed away but the severity of his injuries caused him to drive into a wall – by which time the singer was probably already dead. Although one suspect was detained and then released, Cornell Gunter's murderer has never been caught.

In the aftermath, big Coasters fans Sammy Davis Jr and Bill Cosby met funeral expenses. Gunter was laid to rest in Inglewood, California.

See also *Bobby Nunn (☞ November 1986); Bob B Soxx (☞ November 2000). Will 'Dub' Jones (2000) and Billy Guy (2002) have also passed away, as have offshoot members Randy Jones and Darrell Reynolds (both 2002), sometime drummer Gerald Baxter (2003) and five other Platters.*

MARCH

Saturday 17

Ric Grech

(Bordeaux, France, 1 November 1946)
Family (The Farinas)
Blind Faith
Ginger Baker's Airforce
Traffic
(Various acts)

A quiet but notable bassist, Ric Grech, who had been living in England since childhood, was just twenty when the Leicester-based soul/pop act The Farinas began to gain local notoriety. With the acquisition of 'distinctive' vocalist Roger Chapman in 1967, they became Family, earning a residency in London and a contract with Reprise. The line-up – Grech, Chapman, Charlie Whitney (guitar), Jim King (saxophone) and Rob Townsend (drums) – proved a popular draw across Britain and went on to enjoy significant album and singles chart success, although much of this was after Grech had left. He had, however, contributed several compositions to the albums *Music in a Doll's House* (1968) and *Family Entertainment* (1969). Grech then played the lesser star alongside Eric Clapton, Steve Winwood and Ginger Baker in that most notable of supergroups Blind Faith, to whose one album he also contributed violin. This, and his subsequent stints with Ginger Baker's Airforce and then Traffic, were not to last more than a year, the restless bass guitarist then also serving with The Bee Gees, Graham Bond, John Mayall, Gram Parsons and Rod Stewart throughout the seventies. Grech even played with a touring line-up of The Crickets in 1973.

Despite this constant work, Grech had a quiet eighties and was believed

near-destitute by the time he was hospitalized in Leicester. He died from combined liver and kidney failure.

See also *Reebop Kwaku-Baah (☞ January 1983); Chris Wood (☞ July 1983); Jim Capaldi (☞ January 2005)*

Monday 19

Andrew Wood

(Columbus, Mississippi, 8 January 1966)
Mother Love Bone (Lords of the Wasteland)
(Malfunkshun)

Probably regarded as the first notable grunge death, Andrew Wood actually began his brief career as a punk/glam crossbreed. Aged just fourteen, Wood was camping it up in a silver suit and slack-heeled motorbike boots as 'Landrew the Love Child', very much the focal point of Malfunkshun. With no real success, Wood somehow managed to keep this out-of-time unit a going concern for eight years – while acquiring the requisite drug habit. His time with his next band was much briefer, but of far greater importance in terms of rock's immediate development. As singer and occasional bassist with Lords of the Wasteland (soon to re-emerge as Mother Love Bone), Wood – with ex-Green River members Stone Gossard (guitar), Bruce Fairweather (guitar), Jeff Ament (bass) and Greg Gilmour (drums) – set about creating a blueprint for Seattle grunge. In 1989, MLB issued the acclaimed *Shine* EP for Polydor; an album, *Apple*, followed early in 1990.

At the urging of the rest of Mother Love Bone, Andrew Wood tried to wean himself off hard drugs, but it was too late: he was found semi-comatose by his girlfriend, having overdosed on heroin. Days later, Wood's life-support machine was switched off at the request of his family. Wood's contribution to music lived on to some degree in the Gossard/Ament project Temple of the Dog, a one-album mission that also featured future Soundgarden star Chris Cornell. Gossard and Ament then founded Pearl Jam – one of US rock's biggest-selling acts of the nineties.

JUNE

Monday 4

Stiv Bator(s)

(Steven John Bator Jr – Youngstown, Ohio, 22 October 1949)
The Dead Boys
Lords Of The New Church
(The Rockets)
(The Wanderers)

He was Punk-Rock America's loose cannon, a showman who bridged the gap between Iggy Pop and Sid Vicious, arguably (well, unarguably, in Vicious's case) possessing greater talent than either. And one of the genre's great characters was to have a fittingly self-destructive punk-rock demise . . .

As Stiv Bators (he added the 's' early in his career), the singer had reportedly given Iggy the infamous jar of peanut butter with which the proto-punkster smeared himself and made projectiles at a televized Stooges gig in 1970 – but Bators was very much a garage icon in the making himself. In 1975, he hung out with the lately touted Rockets (originally Rocket from the Tombs), the band that had housed Pere Ubu's David Thomas and the late Peter Laughner (☛ *June 1977*). But Bators's own 'great' band was to be The Dead Boys (aka Frankenstein), a sneering collective of oddballs formed after Bators (briefly 'Steve Machine') was sent packing from The Rockets, supposedly for his bizarre vocal delivery. The Dead Boys – Bators, Cheetah Chrome (ex-Rockets, guitar), Jimmy Zero (guitar), Jeff Magnum (bass) and Johnny Blitz (ex-Rockets, drums) – befriended their natural brothers The Ramones, who helped not only to place them at CBGB's but also to put out a couple of albums on the Sire label. The sophomore *We Have Come for Your Children* (1978) contained at least one punk classic in the minor hit 'Sonic Reducer'. However, it was their stage act that gained The Dead Boys notoriety. A skinny, emaciated specimen, Bators nonetheless possessed one of the largest penises in rock – an asset he was keen to display once in a while. Thus, live performances resulted in trouble – anti-punk gangs usually attempted to start fights with the band – which all in all gave The Dead Boys a rather brief shelf-life. On one occasion, Blitz almost died after being knifed in a post-concert fight, which resulted in the group's 1979 end.

After a move to the UK, a stint in a one-album band called The Wanderers and a bit part in the John Waters movie *Polyester*, Stiv Bators returned in style with Lords Of The New Church in 1981, the most commercially viable of any of his projects. The Lords – Bators, Brian James (ex-Damned, guitar), Dave Treganna (ex-Wanderers, bass) and Nick Turner (drums) – produced three strong albums, pulling in MTV interest and a goth/stadium-rock audience, though the punk theatrics were still very much a part of the performance. At one remarkable 1983 show, Bators set about his long-favoured onstage practice of throttling himself with a microphone cord – but his typically eager fans decided to join in, tightening the ligature around their waif-like hero's neck. As Bators began to turn blue, roadies pulled him backstage: in hospital, he was pronounced dead for two minutes, trumping pretty much all of *Number One in Heaven*'s Close . . . Closer! entrants. Returning from the other side, Bators's main emotion was disappointment that he couldn't recall how it felt to have snuffed it. How he felt when the moment *did* arrive is, of course, open to conjecture – but it was, perhaps unsurprisingly, just a matter of years before that eventuality. Bators was eventually sacked by Lords of the New Church (reportedly discovering his dismissal by reading a small ad for a new singer, which he then replicated on a T-shirt for his last performance), briefly returning to ignored solo work. Moving to Paris in 1988, Bator (once more 's'-less) attempted Dead Boys reunions, a supergroup with members of The New York Dolls and even a Lords re-formation – but the moment had passed for this unique performer, now very much yesterday's man.

On a Monday afternoon in June 1990, Stiv Bator was sitting on his motorbike at the kerb when a car sideswiped him, knocking him to the ground. Years of self-inflicted harm (and a few beatings) had left him immune to pain, so the singer merely walked back to his apartment and put himself to bed. This time, there was no second chance: the injuries were more serious than he realized, and Bator died from a blood clot as he slept. His ashes were dusted over the grave of another erstwhile Paris resident, Jim Morrison.

See also *Philip 'Taylor' Kramer* (☛ *February 1995*)

'I once died on stage. I mean, how do you top *that*, for Christ's sake?'

Stiv Bator - just before doing so for real

Tuesday 5

Richard Sohl
(1948)
The Patti Smith Group

In a bad week for US proto-punk, keyboardist Richard Sohl – for many years faithful sidekick to New York art-rocker Patti Smith – also passed away. Sohl had joined the singer and her guitarist, Lenny Kaye, in 1973, beginning a relationship with Smith and her innovative fusion of radical Dylanesque poetry and rock 'n' roll power that lasted well into the next decade.

The Patti Smith Group were one of the star attractions at New York's CBGB's, quickly signing to the MER label for their first single, 1974's hard-bitten 'Piss Factory'. A stunning album, *Horses* (1975), was then issued by Arista – and remains, thirty years later, one of the finest rock debuts of all time. Though Smith had vision, Sohl's input was also of supreme importance, so she was understandably disappointed when his persistent absenteeism saw him leave the group after the follow-up *Radio Ethiopia* (1976). Little was heard from the keyboardist as Patti Smith enjoyed her own commercial zenith towards the end of the decade, although he returned to her side for the solid comeback album *Dream Of Life* (1988). Richard Sohl died from heart complications – and not, as has been reported elsewhere, from either AIDS or a drug overdose. Four years later, Smith was to endure the deaths of her long-time partner, Fred 'Sonic' Smith of the MC5 (☞ *November 1994*), and her brother, Todd – both also from heart problems.

Jimmy Hodder
(Boston, Massachusetts, 17 September 1947)
Steely Dan
(Linda Ronstadt)
(Bead Game)

That same afternoon, drummer Jimmy Hodder also met his maker: the man who had made his name with East Coast rock/jazz titans Steely Dan was to die tragically at a swimming party.

Hodder began his music career with the little-remembered Boston hippy combo Bead Game, before joining the band whose smooth sound belied the origins of their name (to jog the memory, 'Steely Dan' was a steam-powered dildo from William Burroughs's cult novel *Naked Lunch*). Originally an accordion-player, Hodder took to the traps at the behest of The Dan's producer Gary Katz, contributing to their acclaimed first two albums, the gold-selling debut *Can't Buy a Thrill* (1972) and *Countdown To Ecstasy* (1973). With a pair of US hit singles, including the great 'Do It Again' (1972), the impact for the band – at this time centred around former Bard College buddies Donald Fagen (keyboards/vocals) and Walter Becker (bass/vocals), with Hodder, David Palmer (vocals), Jeff 'Skunk' Baxter (guitar) and Denny Dias (guitar) – was phenomenal, especially considering that they had been recruited purely for studio work. Hodder's stay with Steely Dan did not last much longer: with the band's main men increasingly reluctant to tour, he set off with Linda Ronstadt's band just as the third Steely Dan album, *Pretzel Logic* (1974), took off. While Steely Dan became the studio affair originally intended, Hodder disappeared into session oblivion.

Found by friends floating in the pool of his home in Point Arena, California, Hodder was rushed to hospital, where he died shortly afterwards. Coroners discovered that his blood alcohol limit was three times the recommended level.

See also *Jeff Porcaro (☞ August 1992)*

Saturday 23

Isaac Payton Sweat
(Port Arthur, Texas, 19 July 1944)
Johnny Winter's Black Plague Band
(The Crystaliers/The Coastliners)
(Various acts)

A bassist who made his name in both blues and rock, the colourfully named Isaac Payton Sweat actually began as a country musician – his father and uncles were well known for playing local hoedowns. 'Ike' grew up as rock 'n' roll came of age, eschewing the more conventional music of his family to play the new sounds on his banjo and guitar. He met Johnny Winter while they both attended Lamar College, and joined the future rock hero in his band The Crystaliers (later renamed The Coastliners), who became regional favourites. The relationship with Winter lasted through a number of bands, but Sweat was also keen to cut his own solo material – most notably a vocal version of Al Dean's 'Cotton-Eyed Joe' seen by many as definitive.

A lack of both further success and business nous – or even decent management – made Isaac Payton Sweat despondent with his lot, and he later returned to the safer shores of country music. After a performance in Houston, Sweat was found dead in the garage of his Richmond home, a gun by his left hand (he was right-handed), but no trace of gunpowder on either, suggesting suicide was unlikely. His death has remained a mystery ever since, as he was known to have neither enemies nor any particular drug dependency.

JULY

Sunday 1

Brent Mydland

(Munich, 21 October 1952)
The Grateful Dead
(Silver)

The history of The Dead – documented throughout *Number One in Heaven* – was already into its middle chapters by the arrival of Brent Mydland. The future keyboardist spent the first few years of his life in Germany, where his military father was stationed, but a move to California was the first step to shaping the young Mydland's career and lifestyle. As a boy, he was a fine pianist, and got into rock while at school. His first recording stint was at Arista, with his band Silver – a Bay Area trio comprising Mydland (vocals/keyboards), Greg Collier and John Batdorf (both guitar/vocals). This band's accomplishment saw them open for The Doobie Brothers and Three Dog Night: Grateful Dead guitarist/songwriter Bob Weir liked what he saw and promptly recruited Mydland for some side projects.

It was the dismissal of Keith and Donna Godchaux in 1979 that inducted Brent Mydland into the Dead fold. Little did he know what a precarious position keyboardist within it was to prove: perhaps the name of the first album to which he was to contribute – *Go To Heaven* (1980) – should have offered a clue? But Mydland settled well into the role, even donating his own 'Far From Me' to the track listing. Other than relentless performances before hordes of ravenous Deadheads, there was little further activity until *In the Dark* (1987). This commercial hit – the biggest of the band's lengthy career – crashed them into the singles charts for the only time with 'Touch

Of Grey' while seducing a whole new generation into the Dead vibe. Finally, *Built To Last* was released in 1989 – a collection that featured many of Mydland's compositions. But, at what seemed like rebirth, came death: the curse of the keyboardist hit The Dead once again. On return from a tour on the back of the record's success, Brent Mydland was found dead outside his home in Lafayette, having overdosed on a speedball (a cocaine/heroin cocktail). He left a wife and two daughters, eulogized by the keyboardist on the touching 'I Will Take You Home'.

Vince Welnick – Mydland's replacement – managed to stay alive in the risky position until the death of head honcho Jerry Garcia (☛ *August 1995*), although he, too, passed on in June 2006.

See also *Ron 'Pigpen' McKernan (☛ March 1973); Keith Godchaux (☛ July 1980)*

Sunday 15

Trouble T-Roy

(Troy Dixon – Mt Vernon, New York, 19 October 1967)
Heavy D & The Boyz

Heavy D & The Boyz were just one among a host of variable 'nu skool' rap acts that shifted the genre's focus to good women and good loving – ie, some distance from what earlier hip-hop exponents had been trying to achieve. Their frontman was the extraordinary but nonetheless likeable Heavy D (Dwight Errington Myers) – a man who tipped the scales at something like 250 lbs; The Boyz were dancers Trouble T-Roy and G-Whiz (Glen Parrish) and DJ Eddie F (Edward Ferrell). The first signing to Andre Harrell's Uptown label, Heavy D and co secured hits with their

albums *Livin' Large* (1987) and *Big Tyme* (1989).

Tragedy struck the quartet after a concert in Indianapolis: indulging in some post-show horseplay with touring companions Kid 'N' Play, T-Roy, fell from a balcony while dancing, hit his head and died later in hospital. The Boyz's platinum release *Peaceful Journey* (1991) was dedicated to their former colleague; T-Roy is also remembered in a number of rap songs, most notably Pete Rock & CL Smooth's 'They Reminisce over You (TROY)' (1992).

AUGUST

Thursday 9

Brandon Mitchell

(New York, 1971)
Wrecks-N-Effect

Wrecks-N-Effect were probably the posse that first introduced the rap world to the bling-and-booty-lovin' sound of New Jack Swing, their babe-laden promotional videos predating the likes of Sir Mixalot while proving influential to much of Snoop Dogg's work. Known as 'B-Doggs', Brandon Mitchell was a founder member of the trio assembled in 1987 with Aquil Davidson and Markell Riley. With a genre-defining single in 'New Jack Swing' (1988) and an eponymous album released on Atlantic two years later, global domination seemed on the cards for the group. For Mitchell, however, it was not to be. He was gunned down in New York, following a fierce argument over a woman. Davidson and Riley continued the project with Motown and RCA, achieving huge success with the 1992 hit 'Rump Shaker' (by now the act was spelt Wreckx-N-Effect).

Stevie Ray Vaughan

(Oak Cliff, Texas, 3 October 1954)

Double Trouble

(Various acts)

Even Eric Clapton admitted it – Stevie Ray was the best. Almost with just his Fender Strat, Vaughan captivated audiences across America and the world, becoming arguably the finest R & B/rock guitarist since his hero, Jimi Hendrix. He had much to thank his older brother, Jimmie, for – he taught him rudimentary chords at the age of eight, prompting Vaughan to play alongside him in the band Texas Storm and to unearth the blues that would colour his style.

Despite his obvious prowess, Vaughan was known for being under-confident about his playing, and this perhaps was why it took a little time for him to make his name. When his next band, Mark Benno & The Nightcrawlers, were dropped by A&M for being '*too* blues', a disheartened Vaughan made the short journey to Austin in 1975, where his brother was now fronting rockers The Fabulous Thunderbirds. A brief time with The Cobras marked Vaughan's real discovery by blues legend Albert King, who invited the band to open for him; again this was not to last, and before long Vaughan and his girlfriend, Lou Ann Barton, had formed yet another combo, Triple Threat. When they split in 1980, the guitarist put together the band with which he would be most associated, Double Trouble. By his side were Tommy Shannon (bass) and Chris Layton (drums), the group eschewing vocals to play a blistering instrumental blues. David Bowie was one of the many blown away by Vaughan's playing at this time, signing him up for his *Let's Dance* album (1983). Vaughan contributed to two

major hits – the title track and 'China Girl' and Double Trouble's own debut album, *Texas Flood*, (1983) became a hit on the back of this high-profile association (which was ended over a contract dispute). Vaughan was now a commodity in his own right, his distinctive long-coat-and-black-fedora-clad appearance only adding to the image. With further albums *Couldn't Stand the Weather* (1984) and *Soul To Soul* (1985), the only downside for Vaughan appeared to be an all-too-predictable slide into drug and alcohol addiction – although by the Grammy-winning *In Step* (1989) the guitarist appeared to have this licked as well. A further award-winner, *Family Style* (1990 – recorded with Jimmie Vaughan), was to enhance his by now global reputation, but sadly Vaughan had already died by its release.

The audience packed into the Alpine Valley outdoor theatre in Troy, Wisconsin, listened with relish as an

array of guitar talent entertained them long into the evening of 26 August 1990: on stage were headliner Eric Clapton, Robert Cray, Buddy Guy and the Vaughan brothers. An informal 'battle' had taken place between the guitarists, with Clapton graciously deferring to Stevie Ray Vaughan as the assembled musicians rattled through a twenty-minute encore of 'Sweet Home Chicago'. The mood was one of celebration and triumph; Vaughan, however, was not keen to party into the night and urged his brother to let him take the last seat on one of four chartered helicopters – despite the fact that conditions were worsening and chances were that the flight would be cancelled. With fog enshrouding the surrounding area, the pilot, Jeff Brown – who, unbeknown to his passengers, had been involved in previous crashes – ignored advice and took off over Wisconsin's hilly terrain. At 12.30 am, just a mile from the venue, the Bell

The burial place of Stevie Ray Vaughan: He took the blues some place else ...

206B Jet Ranger slammed into a man-made ski slope: Vaughan, Brown and three members of Clapton's entourage – agent Bobby Brooks, bodyguard Nigel Browne and tour manager Colin Smythe – were killed instantly. The search for the wreckage did not begin for a further four hours, and Clapton and Jimmie Vaughan were eventually given the heartbreaking task of identifying the bodies. Vaughan was buried in Dallas, next to his father, whom he had survived by just four years. Tributes to the electric-bluesman many believe to have been the greatest continue to be made to this day. In 1991, Texas Governor Ann Richards proclaimed 3 October 'Stevie Ray Vaughan Day', while a statue of the guitarist looms large in state capital Austin. Not to be outdone, Fender went on to issue their own 'Stevie Ray' limited edition stratocaster.

SEPTEMBER

Wednesday 5

Charlie Charles

(Hugh Glenn Mortimer Charles – Guyana, 1945)
Ian Dury & The Blockheads
(Loving Awareness)
(Various acts)

Charlie Charles was a pillar of British rock music for two decades, a session drummer par excellence who worked with everyone from Lulu to Arthur Brown; his reputation carried him to the US as well, where he sat behind a number of artists, including Link Wray. Originally in the British army, Charles returned to the UK in 1970, forming his own band, No Sweat, while honouring just about every session requirement going. In 1975, he teamed up with the Radio Caroline-promoted Loving

Awareness before meeting Ian Dury in 1977. The Blockheads were Dury's band, a hotchpotch of great musicians – including Chaz Jankel (guitar/keyboards) and Norman Watt-Roy (bass) – sympathetic to the singer's infectiously irreverent humour. In this capacity, Charles experienced huge success with the album *New Boots and Panties* (1978) and a series of great singles including 'What a Waste', the chart-topping 'Hit Me with Your Rhythm Stick' (both 1978) and 'Reasons to be Cheerful' (1979). Charles moved on to other projects during the 1980s, with less commercial success, and died from cancer in London ten years before his longtime friend and colleague Ian Dury (☞ *March 2000*).

Thursday 6

Tom Fogerty

(Berkeley, California, 9 November 1941)
Creedence Clearwater Revival
(The Blue Velvets/The Golliwogs)

After his ambitions of becoming a professional sportsman were crushed by a high-school injury, Tom Fogerty – the second eldest of five sons – took to music in earnest in the wake of the local popularity of his brother's band, The Blue Velvets. Already rhythm guitarist, Fogerty became lead singer of the band (soon adding his name to the credits), and helped move matters on apace in 1963 by landing the job of packing clerk at Fantasy Records – whom he soon persuaded to sign the brothers' band. Under the new, ill-chosen name of The Golliwogs, the band issued a few records for the label, but it was as Creedence Clearwater Revival that they began to take off. John Fogerty began to outflank his brother as the chief songwriter and architect of CCR's sound and socio-political stance – only one of Tom Fogerty's

songs ever made a Creedence album. Although they never enjoyed a US chart-topper, CCR sold over 10 million singles with John's compositions, hitting number two on no fewer than five occasions with 'Proud Mary', 'Bad Moon Rising' (number one in Britain) and 'Green River' (all 1969), 'Travelin' Band' and 'Lookin' out My Back Door' (both 1970). By 1971 his younger brother's increasing control of the group caused Tom to leave and CCR lasted just eighteen more months before imploding. For Tom Fogerty, the split would be costly to his sales. His self-titled solo debut (1972) only just scraped the US listings, after which his work was virtually ignored. A final album emerged in 1985, but Fogerty became unwell shortly thereafter, and finally succumbed to respiratory failure, a result of tuberculosis.

OCTOBER

Monday 8

B J Wilson

(Barrie James Wilson – Edmonton, London, 18 March 1947)
Procol Harum
(The Paramounts)
(Various acts)

Former Boys' Brigade drummer B J Wilson had played percussion with at least two bands before leaving his Southend school, so single-minded was he about his future *métier*. At sixteen, the confident Wilson answered a *Melody Maker* advertisement, replacing former sticksman Mick Brownlee in Parlophone R & B band The Paramounts, alongside student friends Gary Brooker (vocals/piano), Robin Trower (guitar) and Chris Copping (bass) – thus forming the core of classic UK rock band Procol Harum. The band's 1964 hit cover of 'Poison Ivy' was merely a precursor to the significant success most members would experience later in the decade. The key moment for Procol Harum was the first week of June 1967: not only did the group open for Jimi Hendrix but they also saw Brooker's and new songwriter Keith Reid's remarkable Bach-inspired 'A Whiter Shade of Pale' top the UK charts for the first of six weeks. As the record began to chart in America, Wilson and Trower rejoined Brooker for the hit follow-up 'Homburg', the drummer now gaining a fine reputation for his dynamic, imaginative fills. Mainly an albums band, Procol Harum released consistent material to lesser effect until a break in 1976, the albums *Shine On Brightly* (1968) and *A Salty Dog* (1969) perhaps housing their best work. 'Conquistador' (1972) and 'Pandora's Box' (1975) gave the band occasional hits, but, after a short-lived re-formation of Procol Harum, Wilson settled into session work with acts such as Joe Cocker, John Hiatt, Lou Reed and The Incredible String Band. Still enjoying his work, Wilson was famously described as 'like an octopus in a hot bath'.

B J Wilson's spiralling use of alcohol and drugs, however, left him open to illness and in 1987, an overdose at his Oregon home put him into a coma – attempts by Brooker to pull him out by playing their music proved fruitless. Finally, a bout of pneumonia had the better of him.

DECEMBER

Friday 7

Dee Clark
(Delectus Clark – Blytheville, Arkansas, 7 November 1938)
The Kool Gents (The Delegates/ The Goldentones)
(The Hambone Kids)

Dee Clark came by his vocal talent – and his unusual first name – via his mother Delecta, a singer of spirituals who encouraged her son to start recording in his early teens. This was with young upstarts The Hambone Kids, but it was as lead singer with The Kool Gents (originally The Goldentones, sometimes recording as The Delegates) that Clark found himself signed with the influential Vee-Jay label. But the full-throated singer's biggest successes by far were to come with his solo work: after a string of chart entries in the last couple of years of the fifties, he finally struck gold (literally) with 1961's catchy 'Raindrops', a record kept from the number-one slot only by Gary 'US' Bonds's 'Quarter To Three'. With no further hits in his homeland, Clark had to be content with a UK Top Twenty placing for the sprightly 'Ride a Wild Horse' – only his second British chart entry – some fourteen years later.

Without significant record sales for two decades, Dee Clark had to earn his crust touring the oldies circuit – a relentless duty for such a long period, and one which may have contributed to his early death from a heart attack.

Sunday 16

Jackie Mittoo
(Donat Roy Mittoo – Browns Town, Jamaica, 3 March 1948)
The Skatalites
(Various acts)

Jackie Mittoo remains one of reggae's unsung heroes – a virtuoso pianist who became a highly prolific songwriter during his short life. Mittoo, a musician before he even learned to write, had performed with a number of groups by the time he met Augustus Pablo at Kingston College, the pair becoming two-thirds of a trio rejoicing in the moniker The Jackie Mittree. It was as keyboardist with The Cavaliers Orchestra (originally The Sheiks) that Mittoo's prowess came to the attention of Clement 'Coxsone' Dodd, Jamaican reggae's top dog, who employed him as musical director at Studio One. With session regulars Roland Alphonso, Tommy McCook, Lloyd Brevette and legendary trombonist Don Drummond, Mittoo formed The Skatalites in 1964 – one of ska's most celebrated bands – surprisingly in existence for less than two years. Mittoo's solo output was mainly a series of excellent instrumental albums, but his prolific songwriting created hits for Alton Ellis, Marcia Griffiths and Freddie McGregor, while his 'Peanie Wallie' became The Wailers' early success 'Duppy Conqueror'. In the late sixties, Mittoo relocated to Canada, also spending time in the UK working with Bunny Lee, Sugar Minott and Musical Youth. Some time after rejoining the surviving Skatalites, Mittoo passed away from lung cancer in an Ontario hospital.

See also *Don Drummond (☛ May 1969); Tommy McCook (☛ Golden Oldies #6); Roland Alphonso (☛ Golden Oldies #8). Occasional singer Vic Taylor passed away in 2003.*

Lest We Forget

Other notable deaths that occurred sometime during 1990:

Floyd Butler (US singer with wholesome pop/soul combo Friends Of Distinction, who struck gold with 1969's 'Grazin' in the Grass'; born California, 5/6/1941; heart attack, 29/4)

Bobby Day (US R & B leader of The Hollywood Flames who also hit under numerous solo guises, including a 1958 #2 with the original 'Rockin' Robin'; born Robert Byrd, Texas, 1/7/1930; cancer, 27/7)

Jim Henson (noted US voice characterizer responsible for a slew of Muppets hits, including the UK Top Ten 'Halfway down the Stairs' (1977); born Mississippi, 24/9/1936; pneumonia, 16/5)

Kripp Johnson (US lead with noted inter-racial vocal act The Del(I)-Vikings; born Corinthian Johnson, Maryland, 16/5/1933; prostate cancer, 22/6)

Jo Ann Kelly (respected UK singer/guitarist with The Blues Band and Spare Rib; born London, 5/1/1944; brain tumour, 21/10)

Sean Oliver (Antiguan/British bassist with the excellent Pop Group and Rip, Rig & Panic – the band that launched Neneh Cherry – later with Float Up CP and Terence Trent D'Arby; sickle-cell anaemia, 3/1990)

Dave Prichard (US guitarist with metal act Armoured Saint; born California, 27/11/1963; leukaemia, 27/2)

Joel Rundell (US rhythm guitarist with New Orleans alt-pop band Better Than Ezra; suicide, 8/8)

Bert Sommer (US guitarist/vocalist with a later version of hippy/bubblegum band The Left Banke – and another cast member from *Hair* to pass on; born 1948; liver failure, 23/7)

Hal Worthington (US baritone singer with soul act The Unifics; born Harold Worthington, 1947; innocent victim of gangland crossfire in a Washington, DC, restaurant/ billiard parlour, 20/2)

For a complete list of fallen artists, visit

www.numberoneinheaven.com

1991

JANUARY

Tuesday 8

Steve 'Steamin'' Clark

(Sheffield, 23 April 1960)

Def Leppard

Although not an original member of Def Leppard, Steve Clark was the Sheffield metallers' most gifted musician. He learned classical guitar as a boy and attended Stannington College – to drop out in January 1978 when early Leppard Pete Willis booked the guitarist after hearing him play Lynyrd Skynyrd's 'Freebird' note-for-note. Clark's first contributions were on the debut EP *Getcha Rocks Off* (1979) – a statement of intent as the NWOBHM (New Wave of British Heavy Metal) began in earnest. The band soon fell into its familiar line-up – Clark, Joey Elliott (vocals), Willis (guitar, replaced by Phil Collen in 1982), Rick Savage (bass) and Rick Allen (drums) – signing with Peter Mensch (AC/DC's manager) and Mercury Records. Leppard's first album *On through the Night* (1980) was a moderate hit in the UK, and the band rubbed shoulders with a host of new British rockers like Iron Maiden, Saxon, Tygers of Pan Tang and Wychfynde – but it was in

Def Leppard as 'cubs': Clark, Collen, Elliot, Savage and Allen

the US that they really hit the big time. Consecutive albums *Pyromania* (1983) and *Hysteria* (1987) shifted a staggering 8 million copies *apiece* in America – the highest-ever sales for a band – where Leppard were easily (and a shade bizarrely) the biggest UK rock export of the era. Similarly, the extracted singles – of which 'Photograph' (1983) was probably the best – cleaned up across the Atlantic, 'Animal' finally taking the band into the Top Ten at home (1987), encouraging huge domestic sales for *Hysteria*. Despite this overwhelming success, Def Leppard still had something of a bumpy ride: in 1984, Allen lost an arm (☞ *Close!*) while Willis's sacking two years before

had been a direct result of his alcoholism, to which Clark appeared to pay little heed.

The guitarist, with his flowing golden locks and duck-walking stage performance, had long been the focal point of the band for groupies, and his relentless partying began to take its toll by the end of the eighties. Shortly after attending rehabilitation in London, Steve Clark died in his sleep from a combination of alcohol, barbiturates and anti-depressants taken during a party at his flat. The late guitarist was replaced by former Whitesnake axewielder Vivian Campbell, but, without the flamboyant Clark, Def Leppard lost much of their flair.

Sunday 20

Stan Szelest

(Buffalo, New York, 11 February 1942)
Ronnie Hawkins & The Hawks
The Band
(Various acts)

An associate of The Band since their early days as part of Ronnie Hawkins & The Hawks, pianist Stan Szelest was very much mentor to musicians such as guitarist Rick Danko. His first tenure with The Hawks was not a long one, Szelest choosing in 1960 to return to his engineering studies while playing sessions with various bands from his locale, including his own Ravens and also Bill Black's Combo. Before rejoining The Band in 1990, Szelest was constantly in demand as studio/touring musician, playing with a wide array of US artists including Captain Beefheart, Neil Diamond and Maria Muldaur. Just as the re-formed Band had won a four-album deal with CBS, Szelest died suddenly from a heart attack in New York. He was just forty-eight.

See also *Richard Manuel (*◀ *March 1986); Rick Danko (*▶ *December 1999)*

'Stan transmitted some powerful force to me.'

Rick Danko, The Band

Monday 21

Rob Graves

(Rob Ritter – California, *c* 1960)
The Gun Club
45 Grave
(Various acts)

The CV of bassist/songwriter Rob Ritter – more widely known by his witty pseudonym – reads like a glossary of Los Angeles punk and goth-metal during the early eighties. Ritter/Graves performed with many bands concurrently, his most prolific work probably that with 45 Grave, a California band (who began as Vox Pop) comprising the bassist, the delightful Dinah Cancer (Mary Simms, vocals), Paul Cutler (guitar), Paul Roessler (keyboards) and Don Bolles (ex-The Germs, drums). This visually arresting group cut at least one notable single, 'Black Cross' (1981). Simultaneously, Ritter was bassist with an early line-up of the Jeffrey Lee Pierce-fronted Gun Club, playing on that band's classic debut *Fire Of Love* (1981). Other appearances of this ubiquitous guitarist include The Nymphs, The Bags, Silver Chalice (with former 45 Grave buddy Bolles) and the brilliantly named Thelonious Monster. The scene's inevitable hotbed of drug culture, however, put Ritter in a precarious position, and the musician overdosed on heroin while in New York.

See also *Nigel Preston (*▶ *May 1992); Jeffrey Lee Pierce (*▶ *March 1996)*

Close!

Rick Allen

(Def Leppard)

After a punishing touring and recording schedule, Leppard's drummer Rick Allen was back in Britain to enjoy the 1984 Christmas and New Year break. Eager to show off his beloved Corvette Stingray, Allen took new girlfriend Miriam out to the Yorkshire moors – where he soon found himself in a game of cat-and-mouse with an Alfa Romeo. The percussionist put his foot down (as drummers do) and lost control of the left-hand drive; the car smashed through a dry stone wall and Allen was hurled through the sun roof – leaving his left arm in the vehicle. While his partner escaped with scratches, Allen was unable to have the limb reattached. Remarkably, the drummer was out of hospital within a month and back behind the traps a matter of weeks after that. By 1986 Allen's kit was almost entirely electronic; singer Joey Elliott has said, 'He's a better drummer with one arm than he ever was with two.'

FEBRUARY

Tuesday 12

Roger Patterson
(Florida, 1968)
Atheist

One of the most progressive and 'musicianly' of the Sunshine State's seemingly endless litany of death-metal acts, Atheist began life as RAVAGE (which hid the most contrived of acronyms: 'Raging Atheists Vowing A Gory End') before wisely settling on the name under which they developed a solid and – dare one say it – devout following. Beneath the blistering riffs adorning their debut album, *Piece Of Time* (1988), Atheist actually wove Latin and jazz elements into their sound. Before a second album could be issued, however, the group were involved in a horrific crash, returning in their van from a tour opening for Swedish band Candlemass. Although most of the band survived with severe bruising, bassist and founder Roger Patterson died at the roadside, apparently in the arms of singer/guitarist Kelly Schaefer.

Where he is now is anyone's guess, but being the first notable death-metaller to make the chronology, Roger Patterson should perhaps be dubbed 'number one in hell'. Ironically, his obituary was bumped down the pages of music papers that week by the passing of gospel pioneer the Reverend James Cleveland.

MARCH

Friday 1

Frank Esler-Smith
(London, 5 June 1948)
Air Supply

While musical director for the Australian stage production of *Jesus Christ Superstar*, keyboardist Frank Esler-Smith met singer Russell Hitchcock, who held a major role, and the pair began a relationship that was to culminate in multi-platinum album sales during the early eighties. Spending a couple of years writing together, Esler-Smith and Hitchcock founded Air Supply in 1976 – augmented by Graham Russell (vocals, also a *JCS* cast member), David Moyse (guitar), David Green (bass) and Ralph Cooper (drums) – and signed with Arista at the start of 1980. Air Supply's popularity in the US was particularly striking, their lushly orchestrated (if somewhat insipid) ballads spawning eight Top Five hits in three years – 'The One That You Love' (1981) gave them a number one. The group's best-known and biggest-selling record, however, was 1980's 'All out of Love', the only notable hit in a British market that otherwise remained stubbornly resistant.

After the emotionally draining 'Making Love out of Nothing at All' (1983) felt like one über-production too many, the USA also began to weary of Air Supply's rose-tinted outings and the group finally called it a day in 1988. Having returned to Australia, Esler-Smith passed away quietly from pneumonia three years later.

Saturday 2

Serge Gainsbourg
(Lucien Ginzburg – Paris, 2 April 1928)

One of the great characters of French popular music, Serge Gainsbourg was born to Jewish-Russian parents. His distinctive presence – in his final years he was most-often spotted in deliberately dishevelled state – helped him find frequent work as a director and actor, though this was secondary to his main loves of art and music. Gainsbourg had been classically trained as a pianist, but chose to move away from the traditional Boris Vian-styled '*chansons*' of his early work when popular music broke free of the naive mould during the sixties. The singer was already in his forties by the time he made his best-known recording, '*Je t'aime (moi non plus)*', which was issued to uproar in 1969, its supposedly sexually explicit content (one or two grunts and groans some seven years before Donna Summer turned 'faking it' into an industry) even provoking outrage from the Vatican. The song was actually a highly evocative piece, making a household name out of British singer/actress Jane Birkin, who later became Gainsbourg's wife. (Originally, '*Je t'aime*' had been recorded with Brigitte Bardot, who withdrew her vocal when the publicity became too much.) That summer, the song became the UK's first banned number-one single. Gainsbourg made a number of other records, including the critically acclaimed album *Histoire de Melody Nelson* (1971, dedicated to Birkin and based on Nabokov's novel *Lolita*) and some exceedingly off-the-wall offerings such as 'Rock around the Bunker' (1975, which echoed the black humour of Mel Brooks's *The Producers*) and even a hip-hop-flavoured collection, *You're Under Arrest*, his last release in 1987. (Well, why not hip

Serge Gainsbourg: A contemporary Baudelaire or Apollinaire – according to François Mitterrand

hop? Eight years earlier he'd reworked 'The Marseillaise' with reggae legends Sly Dunbar and Robbie Shakespeare – the record went to number one in France.)

As his work became increasingly idiosyncratic, Serge Gainsbourg himself became more of a handful in public: his most notorious moment was in 1988, when he told stunned US chanteuse Whitney Houston on a French Saturday-night chat show that he 'wanted to fuck her'. Nevertheless, the artist was much loved, and, following his death from a heart attack at his rue de Verneuil home, there was a huge outpouring of public affection. In 2003, the city of Clermont-Ferrand became the first to dedicate a *rue* to Gainsbourg's memory.

Saturday 16

Chris Austin
(North Carolina)

Kirk Capello
(Missouri)

Joey Cigainero
(Texas)

Paula Kaye Evans
(Texas)

Terry Jackson
(Missouri)

Tony Saputo
(Missouri)

Michael Thomas
(Tennessee, 1957)

The Reba McEntire Band

Well, this was it – the biggest single-band wipe-out *ever* in popular music history. And yet fate saw fit to ensure that the leader, country performer Reba McEntire, survived the carnage. McEntire, one of the most successful female singers of the last thirty years (sources suggest that only Barbra Streisand has outsold her), had enjoyed an unbroken run of hits that kept her and her nine-strong band in demand for live appearances. On the evening of Friday 15 March, the group had performed a private show in San Diego, with another scheduled the following night in Fort Wayne, Indiana. While McEntire stayed put in California for the night, her entourage split between two small Hawker-Siddeley aircraft to complete the journey before bedding down: one plane took off into the night sky towards Indiana, the other careered straight into Mount Otay within minutes of take-off. On board the latter were Chris Austin (vocals/guitar/mandolin), Kirk Capello (musical director/keyboards), Joey Cigainero (synthesizer), Paula Kaye Evans (vocals), Terry Jackson (bass), Tony

Reba McEntire: 'Ladies and gentlemen – tonight's set will be a cappella...'

Saputo (drums) and Michael Thomas (guitar). Also killed were McEntire's road manager Jim Hammon and two others, including the pilot.

The likeable balladeer was philosophical following what must have been a devastating, traumatic time: 'You can understand why God took 'em, 'cause they were so special – but, oh my gosh, how we missed 'em!' McEntire – who dedicated her 1991 *For My Broken Heart* album to the lost musicians – later found a niche in television and still fronts her own Fox sitcom.

Sunday 17

Max Lipscomb

(Dallas, Texas, 1937)

Gene Vincent & The Blue Caps

Max Lipscomb was no great shakes as a musician but possessed smouldering good looks, which prompted Gene Vincent's manager, Ed McLemore, to hire him. Lipscomb's position as Blue Caps pianist lasted long enough for him to appear with the group on *The Ed Sullivan Show* in 1957. With Vincent very much the focus, musicians came and went in the early days, and Lipscomb – under an alias, Scotty McKay – went solo at the beginning of 1958. His subsequent career was that of an amiable journeyman, the charming McKay/Lipscomb seemingly able to talk himself into a deal anywhere. With Ace Records, he even managed to work with Fats Domino, who presumably showed him how it *should* be done on the keys. Lipscomb turned to religion later in his life, and carved himself a small niche in Christian pop. He passed away from a heart attack, aged fifty-three.

Max Lipscomb – capped by Vincent

See also *Gene Vincent (* October 1971); Cliff Gallup (* October 1988); Willie Williams (* August 1999); Paul Peek (* April 2001). Other Blue Caps Grady Owen (1999), Jerry Lee Merritt (2001) and Juvenal Gomez (2002) are also dead.*

Wednesday 20

Dave Guard

(Honolulu, Hawaii, 19 November 1934)

The Kingston Trio

(The Whiskyhill Singers)

Warmly remembered as the man who helped move folk music from the coffee bars into the charts, Dave Guard (vocals, banjo) met fellow Kingston Trio founders Nick Reynolds (guitar/vocals) and Bob Shane (guitar/vocals) while attending Menlo College in Palo Alto, California ('Kingston' was chosen on a whim). The three, who had initially performed just to earn beer, became massively popular at their San Francisco residency and signed to Capitol in 1958: by the end of that autumn a stunned Kingston Trio sat proudly at number one in the charts with the million-selling 'Tom Dooley'. This worldwide hit prompted several lesser hit records (such as 1959's splendid 'MTA' – an ode to Boston authorities' sudden levying of subway taxes!) for an act whose pop status was to prove useful to the more leftfield exponents of folk. With a clutch of gold albums under their belts, The Trio were at their most potent before Guard left – to be replaced by John Stewart, with whom Guard would work in 1979 – forming his own less-successful Whiskyhill Singers in 1961.

Dave Guard fell victim to lymphoma while in Concord, New Hampshire. Having grown weary of the music business, he had previously emigrated to Australia.

APRIL

Dead

(Pelle Yngve Ohlin – Sweden, 1969)

Mayhem

(Morbid)

So to the grim stuff . . . Even his disturbing contemporaries admit that Pelle Ohlin was one weird individual: an outcast who found release in his beloved black metal, he became Dead, a self-reviling messenger from the other side who claimed to believe that everything 'normal' (including himself) deserved to die. With most, one might brush this off as lurid nonsense – with Dead, it was a manifesto eventually followed to its depressing conclusion.

Norwegian band Mayhem – Euronymous Øystein Aarseth, guitar), Necrobutcher (Jorn Stubberard, bass) and Kjetil Manheim (drums), who destroyed his reputation by running off, marrying and becoming a businessman – had a focus but no focal point. Until they found Dead. Original vocalist Maniac had attempted suicide and failed, bringing about his dismissal. A relocated Swede, Dead was much more the ticket and one could sort of tell he wasn't going to let them down. Having picked the new singer from the rotting remains of the band Morbid, Mayhem were soon on their way to becoming the most infamous Norwegian act of all time (and there was some pretty serious competition). Replacing Manheim with Hellhammer (Jan Axel Blomberg), Mayhem set about perfecting their live show, preparations for which were, shall we say, 'particular'. Dead – who now wrote most of the group's material – buried his stage gear ahead of concerts so that it would rot and become maggot-infested. Having already carried a dead guinea pig around in his pocket, Dead now tried the between-song ritual of inhaling from a plastic bag containing a decomposing raven, in order that he might have the 'essence of death' within him as he sang. And it didn't end there – one notable gig in Salpsborg in 1990 saw Mayhem take to the stage amid a display of impaled pig's heads, which they then hurled into the crowd in order to disperse 'wimps'. The singer's more regular habit of cutting *himself* on stage was possibly brought into relief by such stunts, for beneath all the posturing was a dark and deeply troubled individual. Informing an unconvinced Hellhammer that he intended to kill himself with a sharp knife, Dead disappeared to the band's shared house on the outskirts of Krakstad, where, by night, he carried out the deed, employing Euronymous's shotgun when the cutting of his veins took too long. As if this weren't enough, the rest of the story is the stuff of surreal myth.

Returning home, Euronymous found Dead's body in eponymous state, clad in an 'I Love Transylvania' T-shirt; his suicide note read simply, 'Sorry about all the blood!' Excitedly,

the guitarist raced back into town to buy film for his camera, the idea being – yes – to take photographs of Dead's bloodied corpse for use on Mayhem's next album cover (which he did). As the remaining band members sat around the body wondering what to do next, legend has it that someone – probably Euronymous – hit upon the notion of removing part of the dead singer's brain matter, which the group should then all eat, to inherit Dead's wisdom. And, incredibly, this they did: apparently – there's no way to disguise this – in some kind of ragout complete with paprika and vegetables. Fragments of the singer's skull were reportedly then removed and fashioned into necklaces for distribution among the leading death- and black-metal musicians of Scandinavia. The 'wisdom' duly inherited, it finally occurred to the surviving band some hours later that the suicide would probably have to be reported to the police. Mayhem were held and interrogated for some time, their supposed Satanic practices soon placing them among Norway's most (or least) wanted. And Dead's death was not the end of the story – as Euronymous was to discover (☞ *August 1993*) . . .

Thursday 18

Martin Hannett

(Manchester, 31 May 1948)

Having originally studied as a chemist, Martin 'Zero' Hannett played bass himself – with future Sad Café singer Paul Young – before turning his attention to co-founding Factory Records and producing the sound of Manchester sons The Buzzcocks during the early punk years – also working with Magazine, OMD, The Psychedelic Furs and U2 (his Rabid imprint was also the first to issue Jilted John's eponymous 1978 single). Hannett is, however, probably most recalled for his work in sculpting the timeless sound of Joy Division's two albums, his extraordinary techniques proving innovative to much that followed throughout the eighties. After the death of singer Ian Curtis (☞ *May 1980*), he turned his attention to surviving members, renamed New Order, kick-starting a new sound that brought them global success. Hannett had been friends with the group (and the broader Factory family, until litigation against owner Tony Wilson in 1982), unafraid to party hard and well known for his massive drink and drug intake.

Martin Hannett's death from a heart attack was unsurprising: he had ballooned to 26 stone (364 lbs) before his death. His coffin was initially unable to fit into his grave.

See also *Rob Gretton (☞ May 1999); Paul Young (☞ July 2000)*

'Death and black metal is something ordinary mortals should fear, not make into a trend! Those who don't like blood and rotten flesh thrown in their faces can *fuck off*!'

Dead, in 1990

Steve Marriott

(Bow, London, 30 January 1947)

The Small Faces
Humble Pie
(Various acts)

He became one of the most distinctive voices in early British rock, but had circumstances been different, Steve Marriott could have followed the acting path he started down as a boy. Dismissed from school, he found his way into the cast of Lionel Bart's stage version of *Oliver*, also making an appearance in the Peter Sellers film *Heaven's Above*. Association with the keen-eared Andrew Loog Oldham diverted Marriott towards music and, after some abortive solo work – and a few pub dates with future cohort Peter Frampton, as The Moments – he made the transition to front The Small Faces. The key line-up – Marriott (vocals, guitar), Ronnie Lane (bass), Ian McLagan (organ) and Kenney Jones (drums) – headed up the rising mod movement of early sixties London, though this seminal R & B/ pop act inevitably outgrew it. Of their twelve UK chart entries for Decca and Immediate – which included classics such as 'Sha La La La Lee' (1966), the number one 'All Or Nothing' (1966) and 'Tin Soldier' (1967) – only 'Itchycoo Park' (1967) broke America, rare at a time when most British acts were hitting constantly in the US. The group's dabblings with LSD produced the remarkable *Ogden's Nut Gone Flake* (1968), which presaged a psychedelic turn as it, too, topped the UK charts. Something of a wild boy, Marriott was The Small Faces' focal point, at one stage deemed a likely frontman for Led Zeppelin. Instead – partly in anger at Decca's release of 'Lazy Sunday' (1968), which he'd intended as a joke – Marriott left The Small

The Small Faces – McLagan, Lane, Marriott and Jones: Soon able to afford a jacket each

Faces in 1969 to create Humble Pie, a more progressive unit which featured his old sparring partner Frampton (ex-The Herd, guitar) as well as Greg Ridley (ex-Spookytooth, bass) and Jerry Shirley (drums). Marriott's only UK hit in this guise was 'Natural Born Bugie' (1969), though several albums made reasonable showings thereafter. While his former colleagues cleaned up as The Faces, Marriott subsequently recorded alone and with his seventies touring band, Packet Of Three. He also featured on recordings by a number of other artists; meanwhile, his dog can be heard on Pink Floyd's *Meddle*.

Settling for a lower profile during the next decade, Marriott made himself comfortable in his sprawling sixteenth-century home in Arkeston, near Saffron Walden in Essex (a venue for several episodes of BBC drama *Lovejoy*). Towards the end of 1990, Marriott and Frampton began writing together, the singer/guitarist visiting his friend's home in Los Angeles to set the project in motion. Apparently dog-tired after the lengthy flight home, Marriott consumed a few drinks and slumped, jet-lagged and asleep – with a lit cigarette in his hand. Fire authorities found his body the following morning, dead from smoke inhalation: the musician had attempted to escape, but – according to paramedics – owing to the vast amounts of alcohol, cocaine and prescription drugs in his system, he had been unable to. A treasure trove of rock 'n' roll relics and artefacts was also lost for ever.

See also *Ronnie Lane (☛ June 1997); Greg Ridley (☛ November 2003)*

Johnny Thunders

(John Anthony Genzale Jr – Leesburg, Florida,
15 July 1952)

The New York Dolls
Johnny Thunders & The Heartbreakers
(Actress)
(Various acts)

'The rock 'n' roll Dean Martin of heroin!'

Richard Hell – very much
Thunders' 'Joey Bishop'

New York prototype glam-punk
guitarist Johnny Thunders donned
women's blouses and dolled himself
up at a time when few US artists
dared to do so. Hard as it is to believe,
at school in New York he'd wanted
to pursue a career as a sportsman,
excelling in baseball far more than his
studies, but the long-haired outcast
was never going to fit in with the
jocks. Instead, the young Genzale,
adopting the name Johnny Volume,
fronted a rock band, The Jaywalkers,
creating the blueprint for his murky
blues-influenced rock guitar style.
Attracting like-minded friends in
Arthur 'Killer' Kane (bass) and Billy
Murcia (drums), he formed Actress,
which morphed into the seminal line-
up of The New York Dolls by 1971
– with the addition of school-friend
Sylvain Sylvain (né Mizrahi, guitar)
and highly distinctive vocalist David
Johansen. Record sales were never
huge, but with punk, metal and new-
wave luminaries admitting a substantial debt, The Dolls were to prove one
of the most influential acts of the
epoch. They put together a couple of
suitably murky albums too: *New York*

Dolls (1973) and *Too Much, Too Soon*
(1974).

The band's first of many encoun-
ters with the darker side, though,
occurred with the on-tour death of
Murcia (➤ *November 1972*) (the drummer was replaced by Jerry Nolan). Far
from pulling the band to its senses,
this loss heralded a public relationship
with drugs that would inform much of
their songs' subject matter and run to
some inevitable conclusions. Despite
later management by one Malcolm
McLaren and some very odd changes
in image, The Dolls never fully caught
on (at least, not at the time); Thunders
left during a 1975 tour to fashion the
popular Heartbreakers with Nolan and
Richard Hell (the former Television
bassist and future Voidoids frontman),
brushing with McLaren again as the
band frequently opened for The Sex
Pistols. Playing on Thunders's increasingly strung-out image, early publicity
for The Heartbreakers included
posters bearing the legend 'Catch 'em
while they're still alive!', but the group
somehow still came up with the excellent *LAMF* on Track Records (1977).
After the break-up of the band,
Thunders's further recorded work was
mainly in a solo capacity (1978's *So
Alone* is well worth digging up), though
he did link up with MC5 guitar-
ist/singer Wayne Kramer in Gangwar,
later fronting The Living Dead (with
Sid Vicious) and Oddballs, at one
point even playing with Steve Marriott,
whom he was to survive by just three
days (➤ *April 1991*). But Thunders's
addiction to heroin was critical now,
and the musician was effectively kept
going by his management and friends.
Throughout his life Thunders – who
was supposedly introduced to the
drug by Iggy Pop – must have spent
countless days wired: one waiter friend
at rock hang-out Max's Kansas City
described the guitarist once continuing
to hold a conversation with him while
his face was immersed in a fish dinner.

Just as plans were being made to
re-team with Nolan, Johnny Thunders

was found dead at a New Orleans
boarding house, his system reportedly
wracked with cocaine and methadone
(he'd been undergoing rehabilitation). A post mortem revealed that
the guitarist had also been suffering
from lymphatic leukaemia, of which
he was probably aware. A distraught
Nolan played in tribute to his
departed stooge shortly after the
event – unaware that within months
he would be the next Doll back in the
box (➤ *January 1992*).

See also *Arthur 'Killer' Kane (➤ July
2004)*

MAY

Will Sin

(Will Sinnott – Glasgow, 23 December 1960)

The Shamen

Before the addition of techno-boffin Will Sinnott, Aberdeen guitar band The Shamen – fronted by his friend Colin Angus – had been a fairly hit-or-miss psychedelic revivalist combo, with a couple of decent singles and a patchy debut album *Drop* (1987) to their name. Angus and Sinnott had met as trainee psychiatric nurses, which may or may not have influenced the group's subject matter or apparent obsession with drugs (admission of the latter did The Shamen out of a very lucrative McEwan's beer commercial). For the band's second album, *In Gorbachev We Trust* (1988), the renamed Sin's influence was apparent – the stop-start cod psychedelia was now replaced with synths, samples and riffing. By the third album, *En-Tact* (1990), the group had also recruited the rather-tiresome rapper Mr C, having fully embraced the rave culture of the era. Sin was now organizing a hectic tour schedule for the unit under the name 'Synergy'. A single from *En-Tact*, 'Pro-Gen' was remixed as 'Move Any Mountain' and considered a likely breakthrough hit for The Shamen, who began to draw serious attention in 1991. With this in mind, Angus and Sin departed to the Canary Islands to shoot a suitable promo for the group – an environment that couldn't have been more different from the overcast settings of their first recordings. With the film in the can, Angus returned to the UK without Sin, who fancied a few more days in the sun. An enthusiastic swimmer, Sin went diving off the island of Gomera; unaware of the water's strong currents, he was pulled under and drowned. The ever-subtle *NME* carried the story under a banner headline: 'Last Will and Testament'.

Encouraged by the musician's bereft family, Angus continued with The Shamen, and the band went on to clean up with a string of major UK hits. Indeed, 'Move Any Mountain' stormed into the Top Five that July, offering television audiences the sobering sight of a content Will Sin on location in Tenerife, captured just days before his untimely death.

Gene Clark

(Harold Eugene Clark – Bonner Springs, Kansas, 17 November 1944)

The Byrds

New Christy Minstrels

(Joe Meyers & The Sharks)

The son of an amateur musician, Gene Clark was raised in Tipton, Missouri, on country and bluegrass, aping Hank Williams's playing at just nine years old. Clearly set to become a significant talent, Clark played with many local bands and cut his first record at thirteen (with Joe Meyers & The Sharks), attracting the attention of Randy Sparks, whose popular folkies, New Christy Minstrels, he would join for a couple of albums in 1963. This only served to reveal to Clark that touting somebody else's material on the road was not for him – and meeting singer/guitarists Jim (later Roger) McGuinn and David Crosby at LA's Troubadour Club, they instantly formed a sympathetic trio. The addition of bass guitarist Chris Hillman and drummer Michael Clarke finally gave the world the first incarnation of the band that influenced two generations of folk and rock musicians, from The Beatles via Bob Dylan to REM: The Byrds. With McGuinn's twelve-string Rickenbacker taking precedence, Clark was by no means the foremost musician in the band but he swiftly took the singing and songwriting reins, penning timeless numbers like 'I'll Feel a Whole Lot Better' and 'The World Turns All around Her' for the band's critically acclaimed debut album for CBS. Despite this, their biggest early hits were interpretations of the songs of others – a couple of Dylan numbers, 'Mr Tambourine Man' (a US number one in 1965) and 'All I Really Want to Do', plus Pete Seeger's 'Turn! Turn! Turn!' (both also 1965).

One of his finest co-written Byrds tunes, 'Eight Miles High' – amusingly banned by authorities for a supposed drug connotation, became a hit after Clark left the band in March 1966 (ironically, 'fear of flying' was the main reason he cited). Solo attempts met with muted success, though albums with The Gosdin Brothers and Doug Dillard received a warm critical reception. The Byrds themselves entered a psychedelic countrified phase with the departure of David Crosby and the recruitment of Gram Parsons and Clarence White in 1968, but the line-up was inconsistent thereafter. Clark would rejoin various incarnations of The Byrds in the years to come, but his numerous solo outings were very much sidelined by the band's fans; in 1979, the imaginatively named McGuinn, Clark & Hillman earned a Top Ten album for Capitol (which nonetheless was followed by legal wrangles over use of The Byrds' name between Clark and McGuinn). The Byrds were inducted into the Rock 'n' Roll Hall of Fame just months before Gene Clark's death at home in Sherman Oaks, California, from natural causes after a stomach operation following years of drinking.

See also *Clarence White (➤ July 1973); Gram Parsons (➤ September 1973); Michael Clarke (➤ December 1993). Short-term drummer Kevin Kelley died in 2002.*

The great Temptations – Ruffin, Franklin, P Williams, O Williams and Kendricks. Of this line-up, Otis Williams is the only member still alive.

JUNE

Saturday 1

David Ruffin

(Davis Eli Ruffin – Meridian, Mississippi, 19 January 1941)

The Temptations
(Various acts)

Early failure proved the catalyst to turn budding gospel talent David Ruffin into a major soul star, leader of Motown's hottest male property, The Temptations. Having left for Detroit at the age of fourteen, Ruffin both sang and played percussion in a good number of acts (including The Dixie Nightingales) before Harvey Fuqua made the perhaps regrettable decision to turn him down as frontman for his new Moonglows in 1960. But the smart, diligent vocalist knuckled down after this setback, finding work first as a session drummer, then recording a well-received solo single, 'Mr Bus Driver Hurry', on Checkmate (1961). Ruffin had good family connections: his older brother was Jimmy Ruffin – soon to be a big-name singer himself – and his cousin Melvin Franklin was a member of Berry Gordy's fledgling Temptations. This link was to prove crucial. Replacing the seemingly unmanageable Elbridge 'Al' Bryant, Ruffin and his punchy baritone assumed lead position in a band that, over the next few years, set the standard for black vocal groups across America. Under the initial guidance of songwriter Smokey Robinson, The Temps proceeded to clean up with sixteen hits during Ruffin's tenure (most featuring his lead vocals), including the number one 'My Girl' (1965). Although the classic roster also boasted Franklin, Eddie Kendricks, Otis Williams and Paul Williams, Ruffin was the focal point, promoted to the position of soul royalty when he and singer Tammi Terrell became an item.

Ruffin's departure from The Temptations in July 1968 was officially put down to his desire to pursue a solo career, though it is widely known that he was dissatisfied with the label's payment policies and work demands on its artists. Put simply, Ruffin became resentful of the salary paid him and his colleagues when The Temps were pulling in tens of thousands of dollars per show. With this in mind, he bowed out (replaced by Dennis Edwards) that September, suing Motown for a reported $5 million. As a solo singer under the care of Fuqua, Ruffin enjoyed an early hit with 1969's 'My Whole World Ended (The Moment You Left Me)' – possibly written about Terrell – but otherwise only saw 'Walk away from Love' (1975, also a Top Ten hit in Britain) cross over to pop success. By now, Jimmy was the Ruffin scoring the greater hits.

In 1982 – after a spell in prison for tax evasion – David Ruffin returned to The Temptations for those hard-to-resist nostalgia tours, but his interests clearly now lay elsewhere. Juggling businesses outside music, Ruffin spent much of his cash on hard drugs and was arrested for possession of crack, which led to enforced detoxification. Tragically – though perhaps predictably – the singer could not overcome his addiction to the high-profile substance. Dropped anonymously by limo at the University of Pennsylvania Hospital, an unconscious Ruffin was discovered to have overdosed on the drug at a well-known crack house the previous night. He died in care at 3.45 am – tagged 'John Doe' until his identity was confirmed three days later. With the singer apparently near destitute, his friend Michael Jackson stepped in to cover funeral expenses. Despite this, it is also rumoured that he was checked into hospital holding a briefcase containing $40K in cash and cheques. The case later reappeared, minus the money . . .

See also *Tammi Terrell (*➼ *March 1970); Paul Williams (*➼ *August 1973); Elbridge 'Al' Bryant (*➼ *October 1975); Eddie Kendrick(s) (*➼ *October 1992); Melvin Franklin (*➼ *February 1995)*

AUGUST

Thursday 1

Vaughn Toulouse

(Vaughn Cotillard – St Helier, Jersey, 30 July 1959)

Department S (Guns For Hire)

Starting out as an occasional journalist (his credits include style-over-content culture magazine *The Face*), distinctive singer Vaughn Toulouse began to forge a small name for himself with Guns For Hire. The London ska combo's debut single, the intriguingly titled 'I'm Gonna Rough My Girlfriend's Boyfriend up Tonight', was issued by Korova in 1979. Performing this and a number of other songs by Toulouse and co-writer/guitarist Mike Herbage, GFH became an open industry secret long before their name change to Department S (after the cult sixties television series) in 1980. Under the new guise, Toulouse seemed to be heading for star status with the rerelease of fan favourite 'Is Vic There?' by RCA in April 1981. This unusual record – the B-side was a ludicrous cover of T Rex's 'Solid Gold Easy Action' with the then-unknown Bananarama – was played to the max on national radio and made UK number twenty-two, placing the band on *Top of the Pops* and threatening a complete album for Department S. But, with the next pair of singles, 'Going Left Right' and 'I Want', failing to deliver a similar impact, RCA shelved the project. Aside from a period signed to Paul Weller's Respond label, Toulouse's only other claim to notoriety was saying 'bollocks' to TV presenter/DJ Gary Crowley (formerly his manager) – a move that saw the latter sacked from his Saturday morning kids show.

Vaughn Toulouse died from an AIDS-related illness. His wake took place at London's Wag Club, which he had co-founded some years before.

SEPTEMBER

Wednesday 4

Dottie West

(Dorothy Marie Marsh – McMinnville, Tennessee, 11 October 1932)

Abject poverty, hunger, mental cruelty and sexual abuse – all staples for some solid C & W songwriting, but day-to-day reality for Dottie West, growing up in Tennessee, one of several children born to a workshy alcoholic who mistreated his family. The horror and anguish lingered around her into adulthood, but by then she had found an outlet for the torment. When her father was eventually imprisoned, Marsh (as she was born) and her family were able to thrive: her mother ran a couple of successful restaurants; Marsh herself became a singing sensation. But, with the cold sting of a country lyric pay-off, her life culminated in heartbreak and tragedy.

Marrying her college fiancé, Bill West (and taking his name), the singer found her way on to the books of Nashville's Starday Records, who cut her first single, 'Angel On Paper', within a week of meeting her. The record was a radio smash and put West on to the Grand Ole Opry. She befriended Patsy Cline and Jim Reeves (having advised Cline against flying beforehand, she then had to endure their remarkably similar deaths (➼ *Pre-1965*)) and, with her distinctive flame-red hair, became a part of the country glitterati within a year or so. Over three decades West would write and record more than 400 songs, the late sixties and early seventies especially good to her. Her records all showed strongly on the country listings, perhaps the best known being 'Country Sunshine', a tune picked up by Coca Cola for a lucrative jingle deal. She also recorded a duet album with the top male star of the day, Kenny Rogers, and when the pair played live, attendances were known to exceed 100,000. So where did it all go wrong? Despite a career that had embraced music, film and television, West publicly declared herself bankrupt in August 1990, with debts exceeding $3.5 million and a second divorce pending. After breaking down on a national talk show, the singer looked to religion as she attempted to piece together a world her now-extravagant lifestyle had destroyed. With an eerie prescience, she then told her pastor that 'Satan had come to steal happiness from her' and that she 'wanted to sing and dance with the angels'. Within months fate saw to it that she realized this wish.

On 30 August 1991, made late for a rare appearance at the Grand Ole Opry by her stalled car (a gift from Rogers), West flagged down a neighbour to drive her. 81-year-old George Thackston obliged, revving up to 55 mph (in a 25 mph zone) in an attempt to make the date – and lost control of his 1982 Plymouth. The car left the ground, remaining airborne for 75 feet and smashing into the Opryland exit ramp. The elderly Thackston somehow received just back and leg injuries while West suffered massive internal damage. She spent five days in intensive care, but as the hours marched on it became more and more apparent that the 58-year-old was not going to pull through. At 9.43 am on 4 September, Dottie West died from severe liver and spleen damage. Her Nashville funeral was attended by hundreds, with Rogers among those who offered words of tribute. West was portrayed by actress Michele Lee in the TV biopic *Big Dreams and Broken Hearts* (1995).

Rob Tyner

(Robert Derminer – Detroit, Michigan, 12 December 1944)
The MC5
(The Rob Tyner Band)
(Fireworks)

Involved with the band in a management capacity in the early sixties, Rob Tyner became singer with The MC5 (Motor City 5) in 1965, driving them from a cohesive covers unit into one of the most talked-about garage-rock acts in Detroit. The band's roster then featured the brilliant double-guitar assault of Wayne Kramer and Fred 'Sonic' Smith, with bassist Michael Davis and drummer Dennis Thompson providing the engine. Tyner was a politically driven performer – rare in rock music at the time – his lyrics and stage performance powerfully anti-government; the singer's other selling point (not that The MC5 'sold' at all) was his extravagant afro, which set MC5 even further apart from their contemporaries. The band became even more confrontational with the addition of the manifesto of new manager John Sinclair, a writer with radical White Panther party connections who believed in bringing the underground 'overground'. As a result, The MC5 found it hard to get their records either played or even stocked – the astonishing *Kick out the Jams* (1969) was banned by most stores/radio stations, who hadn't heard the word 'motherfucker' on a rock 'n' roll record until then.

But the MC5's anarchy spilled over to intra-band problems and, after two more albums, they called it a day in 1972. Tyner formed a couple of bands of his own during the decade (occasionally reviving the name of his best-remembered group). After the demise of his Rob Tyner Band in 1978, the singer spent some time promoting a host of new-wave bands (who all admitted a debt to The MC5), including Britain's Eddie & The Hot Rods, with whom he cut a record. He was still involved in solo work at the time of his death from a heart attack: Tyner was found at the wheel of his car, and passed away after removal to hospital in Michigan.

See also *Fred 'Sonic' Smith (☛ November 1994)*

Golden Oldies #3

Miles Davis

(Miles Dewey Davis III – Alton, Illinois, 25 May 1926)

A giant of the jazz trumpet, Miles Davis is included here for his undoubted influence over many soul and funk musicians – Prince, Herbie Hancock and Quincy Jones among them – who appeared in his wake. This was not merely as a musician, but as a modal composer and arranger of supreme innovation – and also as a presence.

Three years after stepping into the breach as a teenager with Billy Eckstine's band, Davis majored in theory at New York's Julliard, only to jack in his studies and move in with Charlie Parker. The upside was that Parker took him on in his quintet; the downside that Davis adopted his mentor's penchant for heroin. In partnership with arranger Gil Evans, Davis gave the world *Birth of the Cool* (1950) – because the musician was already regarded as an *enfant terrible* in the industry, the record was ignored until years later. Less so, *Kind of Blue* (1959), a set seen even then as a milestone in not just jazz but contemporary music per se. Davis issued countless long-players over the years, many with his world-famous quintet, many more under his own steam. By the seventies Davis was alienating some of his purist crowd by incorporating R & B and rock 'n' roll into his already eclectic sound.

In his personal life, Davis was seldom far from controversy: it is believed that for many years he was confused about his sexual orientation – despite the fact that he had countless affairs and fathered four children by different partners, tying the knot on at least three occasions. Seen sometimes as a difficult figure, Davis was also known for his outspoken opinions, occasionally bad-mouthing contemporaries in the press. His 'transfer' from heroin to cocaine left him in poor health; diagnosis of diabetes caused a five-year hiatus from playing. Around this time, Davis was at odds with the law – he was once beaten by racist New York police officers who tried to charge him with loitering. Written off as a has-been, the mercurial musician returned in 1981 with a series of innovative new recordings.

Miles Davis succumbed to pneumonia in conjunction with a stroke and respiratory failure in a Los Angeles hospital on 28 September 1991.

OCTOBER

Thursday 10

Gamble Rogers

(James Gamble Rogers IV – Winter Park, Florida, 31 January 1937)
The Serendipity Singers

A folk singer and writer in the traditional style, Gamble Rogers had already nurtured a reputation before taking on lead-guitar duties with The Serendipity Singers, a vast pop-folk ensemble formed at the University of Colorado. A popular booking on such enormously popular television showcases as *The Tonight Show* and *The Ed Sullivan Show*, the group enjoyed a big-selling hit with 'Don't Let the

Rain Come Down (Crooked Little Man)' (1964). Rogers left the group within two years, however, becoming something of a mainstay in the media, where his music and his dramatizations – including the PBS television screenplay *The Waterbearer* – continued to impress into the nineties.

Rogers was enjoying a day's rest at Flagler Beach near St Augustine, Florida, when his attention was drawn to a man apparently in difficulties in the water. Diving to his assistance, Gamble Rogers was sucked under by the heavy current, drowning before dozens of horrified onlookers. Following the incident, local recreation area Winter Park was renamed in his honour, while his protégé Jimmy Buffett dedicated an album, *Fruitcakes* (1994), to Roger's memory.

Friday 25

Bill Graham

(Wolfgang Grajonca – Berlin, Germany, 8 January 1931)

One of the few non-musician entrepreneurs to find his way into *Number One in Heaven*, Bill Graham was a celebrity in his own right, a significant figure whose business nous made it possible for some of America's most influential leftfield bands to play major venues. His father died in an accident just days after his birth, and Wolfgang Grajonca and his brother lived in an orphanage in Germany before emigrating to New York. Changing his name to Bill Graham, the young manager's success in raising funds for the defence of his San Francisco Mime Troupe (undergoing investigation for obscenity) by putting on a benefit music show started him off as a rock promoter. Further such benefits saw early performances by The Grateful Dead and Jefferson Airplane.

Graham's attempts to seize control of the Fillmore – San Fran's leading venue – saw him briefly incarcerated, but the entrepreneur was not to be denied. He relaunched the venue as 'Fillmore West' (simultaneously opening a New York counterpart, 'Fillmore East') and put on 'controversial' rock acts such as The Doors, Jimi Hendrix, Big Brother & The Holding Company, Santana and Frank Zappa's Mothers of Invention. Leaving the venues to concentrate on larger projects, he oversaw such events as Live Aid (1985).

The original Fillmore closed in 1989, following damage during the San Francisco earthquake. Then, with plans underway to revamp the classic auditorium, Graham was killed in a freak helicopter accident: the craft attempted to gain height during a severe storm, hit a transmission tower and exploded. The promoter (who had been attending a concert by that arch-rock 'n' roll rebel Huey Lewis) and two others on board, including the pilot, died in the crash.

NOVEMBER

Friday 8

Dave Rowbotham

(Manchester, 1958)
The Durutti Column
The Mothmen
(Pauline Murray & The Invisible Girls)

Dave Rowbotham had played with gifted Durutti Column founder Vini Reilly in The Invisible Girls, the late-seventies project of ex-Penetration singer Pauline Murray, a sort of new-wave supergroup that also featured Buzzcocks drummer John Maher. The guitarist/bassist recorded a number of discs with Reilly before the latter took the project forward as a solo affair. At a loss, Rowbotham and other Column-ites formed The Mothmen, releasing *Pay Attention* (1981) on On-U Sound. The sophomore record *One Black Dot* appeared a year later, but the band split acrimoniously shortly after. The remainder of the band enjoyed success with Simply Red, while the rest of the decade was quiet for Rowbotham, apart from playing several sessions with Factory. He managed to find his way into some fairly dubious company.

At the end of a traumatic year for Factory, Dave Rowbotham's body was discovered at his Burnage flat some time after his death: the guitarist had been murdered with an axe. Although no one has ever stood trial for his killing, a clue came to the surface in the otherwise-impenetrable lyrics of 'Cowboy Dave', a track on the album *Yes, Please!* (1992) by former Factory cohorts Happy Mondays. It was widely suspected that an S&M-loving former companion of Rowbotham's was responsible for the atrocity: frantically seeking drugs – or the money to score them – the anonymous woman is thought to have taken out her desperation on the hapless musician.

Freddie Mercury

(Farrokh Bulsara – Stone Town, Zanzibar, 5 September 1946)

Queen

'I've had more lovers than Liz Taylor. I've tried relationships on both sides, male and female. And all of them were wrong.' Freddie Mercury

A year punctuated by a spate of AIDS-related demises saved the biggest name to succumb to the disease until last. Yet, until just two days before his death, Queen's outlandish figurehead had, for reasons that remain undisclosed, kept his condition a secret from the world. The grief that followed Mercury's passing was, however, quickly replaced by a cascade of celebration of his time in the spotlight; in an industry increasingly dependent upon background figures, Mercury was considered by most to have been rock 'n' roll's last consummate showman.

Mercury was originally Farrokh Bulsara, a Zanzibar-born boy who had seen something of the world, having attended boarding school in Panchgani, India, before his parents took him and his younger sister to England in 1964. Turning down the suggestion that he might attend music school, the grade-four pianist earned instead a diploma in illustration at Ealing College of Art in 1969. Nonetheless, Bulsara took his first steps into the music business, his remarkable multi-octave voice developing as he fronted a succession of small-time groups (including school-band The Hectics, Sour Milk Sea, Wreckage and Ibex) before running a market art-and-fashion stall with drummer Roger Taylor, whose band Smile recruited him as singer. Joining guitarist Brian May and bass-player John Deacon, the pair founded Queen (the now-renamed Freddie Mercury's choice, over Taylor's Build Your Own Boat), signing with EMI in 1971. (Already recognized as a potential star in the making, Mercury simultaneously recorded The Beach Boys' 'I Can Hear Music' as Larry Lurex.) It was not until the album *Queen II* (1973) that the band broke through. In 1974, they accepted a last-minute *Top of the Pops* slot when a David Bowie promo failed to materialize, and the public had its first real glimpse of the long-haired, spandex-donning Mercury as Queen's terrific 'Seven Seas of Rhye' climbed into the UK Top Ten.

Freddie Mercury: . . . and there were indeed one or two 'cocktails' over the years

The song branded Queen and Mercury to record-buyers; its follow-up, 'Killer Queen', was only held from number one by David Essex that autumn. The next year, Queen cracked open the international market in spectacular style. In November 1975, they topped the UK charts for nine weeks with the extravagant, sprawling 'Bohemian Rhapsody' (far from the group's best record, but these days frequently voted the UK public's favourite single), simultaneously heading the albums chart with *A Night at the Opera*, replete with its Mercury-designed group crest: both would also find Top Ten placings in the USA. Much of their work was starting to skirt a prog-rock arena that was technically efficient but soulless, though Queen – and especially Mercury – appeared to retain an intelligence and humour not always found in British album rock during the seventies. The singer's pomp, pose and semi-operatic warbling made him the supreme foil for the band's cod-classical musicianship. The 'humour' only started to pall with 1978's grim *Jazz* album; its paean to 'Fat Bottomed

Girls' and the like not especially well received by Mercury's growing gay fanbase. There are one or two other horrors among their *oeuvre* (one tries hard to forget 1982's *Hot Space*), but Queen and Mercury showed they were able to survive critical panning while effortlessly straddling the least likely musical trends: 'Crazy Little Thing Called Love' (1979) pre-empted a rockabilly revival to top the US charts; the throbbing 'Another One Bites the Dust' (1980) somehow headed America's *black* music chart before giving the band a second Billboard number one; 'Under Pressure' (1981), a strong duet with Bowie, showed Queen could stay relevant in a clinical eighties pop market.

It was probably the group's appearance at Live Aid in 1985 that cemented their position as a UK institution. Freddie Mercury – hair cropped, decked in his uniform of leathers, or vest and jeans, and possessing the now-trademark moustache – stole the charity show with a performance of typical bravado and camp deprecation. He was the complete entertainer, yet he kept his private life a closely guarded secret. Although his hedonistic lifestyle and numerous male/female affairs were well known, Mercury never officially came out as bisexual to his fans. Long after a 1980 split with 'public' girlfriend Mary Austin, the couple appeared together in what now seems to have been an arrangement for the press. The moving 'Who Wants to Live Forever?' – issued on *A Kind of Magic* (1985) – suggests that the singer may have learned he was HIV positive as early as 1984 (when little was known about AIDS). Having confided his bad news to Austin, Mercury's sudden reversion to monogamy with a final partner, Jim Hutton (later his carer), was also perhaps a clue to his worsening condition. A final concert at Britain's Knebworth Festival in 1986 announced his retirement from public life, but Mercury and Queen continued to record, with no lessening of sales. In January 1991, the band achieved their third UK number-one single with 'Innuendo' (a disquietingly epic production even longer than 'Bohemian Rhapsody'), although no one was any the wiser as to his illness. Mercury's filmed appearances to promote the record showed him gaunt and frail, beginning a flurry of rumour. The record's parent album was similarly littered with clues in the shape of tracks such as 'I'm Going Slightly Mad', 'These are the Days of Our Lives' and the stirring 'The Show Must Go On'.

On 23 November, Mercury finally revealed to the press that he had AIDS and was close to death. The singer had already told friends that he must now dispense with his increasing regime of essential medication and face up to the end. He was now partially sighted, bed-bound and virtually immobile; the last task his friends had to perform was to help Mercury to the bathroom and back. At 7.45 the next evening, Freddie Mercury, the King of Pomp, was dead. With him were several friends, including Hutton, and his beloved pet cats. Mercury was cremated the following day, and his ashes are widely believed to have been scattered at Lake Geneva (a place of which the Queen frontman had been extremely fond and one where his statue was shortly to be unveiled) – though apparently only Austin knows the truth of this matter. To the chagrin of his family, Mercury left 50 per cent of a multi-million-pound inheritance and his Georgian mansion in Kensington – the home in which he died – to Austin in his will; Hutton, by contrast, was left £500K. Much also went to AIDS charities.

Having had a solo career for some years in tandem with his Queen recordings, Mercury secured a posthumous UK number one with 'Living on My Own' (1993). Various Queen records have also (unsurprisingly) fared favourably since his death, but the Mercury legacy has in truth become something of a licence to print money, his undoubted craft now diluted to the nth degree following relentless outings by (and with) boy bands, nostalgia-based compilation albums and dubiously conceived musicals featuring his songs.

Eric Carr

(Paul Charles Carravello – Brooklyn, New York, 12 July 1950)

Kiss

(Creation/Mother Nature/Father Time)

Although latterday Kiss drummer Eric Carr's death was overshadowed by that of Freddie Mercury, it nonetheless proved a difficult twenty-four hours for lovers of stadium glam. Like Mercury, Carr had displayed early promise as an artist before switching to music: his father bought him a Ludwig kit and he soon joined Salt 'n' Pepper, a badly named black/white combo that went on to become Creation. This New York-based funk act kept a loyal fanbase, although they were not to make any kind of breakthrough nationally. Tragedy struck in 1974, when two members of the group died in the notorious Gulliver's nightclub fire in Westchester (➤ *June 1974*); Carr not only survived, but also pulled band members John and Sarita Henderson to safety. (In deference to the deceased, Creation was renamed not Cremation but Mother Nature/ Father Time.)

Eventually returning to his day job repairing gas stoves, Carr learned that long-time Kiss drummer Peter Criss had left the band and he auditioned to be the schlock-rockers' new percussionist. Carr inherited not only Criss's position, but also his 'fox' face make-up, as the new-look Kiss went on to even greater success than the original line-up had experienced in the seventies. With them, Carr helped cut eight albums, and a few hit singles including 'Crazy Crazy Nights' (UK, 1987) and 'Forever' (US, 1990).

A final cover of Argent's 'God Gave Rock 'n' Roll to You' reached the British Top Five in the wake of Carr's death, though the drummer appeared only in the record's promo, having by this time been replaced for recordings

– somewhat crassly, given his open-heart surgery in April 1991. Eric Carr succumbed to a cerebral haemorrhage while in hospital in New York.

DECEMBER

Tuesday 10

Headman Tshabalala

(Ladysmith, KwaZulu-Natal, South Africa, 1947)

Ladysmith Black Mambazo

One of four brothers who founded the celebrated a cappella 'isicathamiya' group Ladysmith Black Mambazo in 1964, Tshabalala gained international prominence when the ten-strong troupe contributed harmonies to Paul Simon's multi-platinum *Graceland* album (1986). LBM's performance on the record may have been well received by Simon's huge fanbase, but it sat uncomfortably with many others in light of the anti-apartheid boycott of South African musicians imposed by the UN.

Finding himself involved in a roadside scuffle with an off-duty highway security guard – who was later charged with his murder – Tshabalala was fatally shot in Pinetown, near Durban. It is widely believed that the murder was racially motivated. Since his passing, Ladysmith Black Mambazo have become one of the biggest-selling African groups in the world, receiving a Grammy and numerous commissions for endorsement work – though other members of the family, Nellie Shabalala and Ben Shabalala, also died in shooting incidents during the next decade.

Lest We Forget

Other notable deaths that occurred sometime during 1991:

Jerome Brisch (US singer, aka Alex Deluxe/Presley Haskell, with rated new-wave bands The Haskells and In a Hot Coma; born Wisconsin, 29/2/1952; murdered while out walking his dog, 16/5)

Terry 'Tex' Carson (UK bassist with Merseybeat band The Dennisons; multiple sclerosis – singer Eddie Parry died of a heart attack three years later)

Roger Christian (US DJ, actor and prolific 'surf' songwriter; born New York, 3/7/1934; suicide, 11/7)

Odia Coates (US soul/gospel vocalist with The Edwin Hawkins Singers who also scored major hits in duet with Paul Anka; born Mississippi, 1942; breast cancer, 19/5)

'Tennessee' Ernie Ford (hugely popular US country/pop singer who topped the UK charts with 'Give Me Your Word' and 'Sixteen Tons', the latter also a US #1; born – guess – 13/2/1919; liver failure, 17/10)

Jacques Morali (US disco writer/producer who created The Village People; born 1947; AIDS, 15/11)

Paula Pierce (distinctive US guitarist/songwriter with garage punks The Pandoras, Direct Hits and Rage; born California, 23/6/1960; aneurysm, 10/8)

Buck Ram (formidable US R & B manager/songwriter who penned classics like 'The Great Pretender' and 'Only You' for The Platters; born Samuel Ram, Illinois, 21/11/1907; natural causes, 1/1)

Vince Taylor (noted UK rockabilly singer/guitarist who was somehow bigger in France; born Brian Holden, London, 14/7/1949; a recluse for most of his later years, he succumbed to cancer, 28/8)

J Frank Wilson (US singer with rock band The Cavaliers, who hit #2 with 'death disc' 'Last Kiss' in 1964; born John Frank Wilson, Texas, 11/12/1941; diabetes, 4/10)

For a complete list of fallen artists, visit

www.numberoneinheaven.com

The Death Toll #4

ACCIDENTS WILL HAPPEN

The following are ten tales of cataclysm and disaster, real and fictitious, committed to disc. Come on, what were *you* doing when you heard the news about the *Edmund Fitzgerald*?

1 'New York Mining Disaster 1941'
The Bee Gees (1967)

What chance the grinning Manx brothers would open their distinguished career with this fictional tale of tragedy? But, fair's fair, the song's opening gambit still sounds as haunting today as it did four decades ago. Harrowing it may have been, yet it was nowhere *near* the disaster that the brothers Gibb would experience when they made that *Sgt Pepper* movie a decade or so later . . .

2 'Dust Storm Disaster'
Woody Guthrie (1936)

The first folk figurehead and daddy of the 'devastation ditty' was surely Guthrie, who in his time wrote many songs dealing with dust blizzards, plus various others documenting massacres, plane wrecks and floods. In this truly choking piece of work, Arlo's dad tells of the Great Plains dust storm of 1935 that swept from Oklahoma to the Rio Grande, destroying hundreds of homes, lives and acres of cropland as it wended its perilous way.

3 'Wreck of the Edmund Fitzgerald'
Gordon Lightfoot (1976)

Gifted Canadian writer Gordon Lightfoot emerged with this tale of watery peril via his deceptively cheery-sounding 1976 album *Summertime Dream*. In its lyrics, Lightfoot commemorated the twenty-nine brave men lost on Lake Superior the previous November, when their 26,600-tonne freighter came a cropper in severe gales. Lightfoot himself was made of far sturdier stuff: in 2002, he survived a coma brought on by abdominal haemorrhaging – and then topped even that by chancing an appearance on *Canadian Idol*.

4 'When the Levee Breaks'
Led Zeppelin (1971)

Blues-obsessives Led Zep updated this Memphis Minnie/Kansas Joe 1929 flood epic for their fourth album, layering it with as much ooze and sexual innuendo as they could muster. (Well, as much as a blues dirge describing the homeless migrant workers' struggle to escape catastrophe could take before it was submerged completely.) Appropriately, John Bonham recorded his drum part down in a well.

5 'Black Diamond Bay'
Bob Dylan (1976)

'Black Diamond Bay' was the venue for Bob Dylan's surreal tale of natural disaster, inspired by a Joseph Conrad novel. A volcano, it seemed, had belched forth lava and fire, engulfing a hotel and leaving nothing but a Panama hat and a pair of shoes. Luckily for Zimmy, he wasn't there: he'd heard about it via a Walter Kronkite news report and hadn't wanted to go there anyway. For Dylan's closest shave with Ma Nature, try the truly baffling 'Talking Bear Mountain Picnic Massacre Blues' (1961).

6 'The Lubbock Tornado'
Terry Allen (1980)

Much-respected contemporary roots/country singer Terry Allen recalled the force 5 tornado that swept through the late Buddy Holly's home town – Lubbock, Texas – in May 1970, killing twenty-six and injuring over fifteen hundred. In the long run, Allen himself did better out of it than most: he's now enjoying a belated career resurgence with alt-country fans while signed to the highly credible Sugar Hill label.

7 'St Francis Dam Disaster'
Frank Black & The Catholics (2000)

The former Pixies leader always had a penchant for songs about those who suffered. From his *Dog in the Sand* album, this track documented a tragic event that had occurred in Los Angeles nearly four decades before he was born. The dam in question had been completed only two years before the calamity; when it burst in 1928 under the pressure of 12 billion gallons

of water, there were nearly 500 human casualties. Engineer William Mulholland escaped a manslaughter charge – but human remains were still being unearthed well into the fifties.

8 'America's Still Standing Tall Tonight'
The Front Porch Country Band (2001)

No prizes for guessing the theme here: The FPCB were among the quickest off the mark with their tribute to those who survived 9/11 – the lead track from an EP of three songs dedicated to the tragedy. The otherwise little-known Front Porchers piledrive their way into our Top Ten by also having released a song about the meteorite that struck north-east America earlier the same year.

9 'Fifteen Feet of Pure White Snow'
Nick Cave & The Bad Seeds (2001)

It's barely a surprise that Australia's Bard of the Scarred might feature here either. In this upbeat tune, Cave calls out for Mona, Mary, Michael – well, a whole host of characters whose names begin with 'M' – as an avalanche covers the area and everyone, it seems, bar the singer. With all this death around him, Nick can think only of the icicles hanging from his knees and the fact that there's nothing worth stealing in the house.

10 'Black Hole Sun'
Soundgarden (1994)

This sneaks in on the 'speculative' ticket. 'Black Hole Sun' – like the band's name – references a Seattle sculpture. Chris Cornell and his band of doom-mongers were never far from talk of impending disaster and this huge transatlantic hit was arguably the definitive word in post-grunge apocalypsos. What's more, it was accompanied by a Howard Greenhalgh promo of grinning rednecks being sucked up into the sky.

1992

JANUARY

Tuesday 14

Jerry Nolan

(Brooklyn, New York, 7 May 1946)
The New York Dolls
(Johnny Thunders &) The Heartbreakers
(Various acts)

Just nine months after the death of figurehead guitarist Johnny Thunders (➻ *April 1991*), a third New York Doll was to go unexpectedly. An avid rock 'n' roll fan as a kid, Jerry Nolan was taught drums by a serviceman (his father was in the military), going on to play with a varied array of acts that included Cradle (featuring a pre-UK-success Suzi Quatro) and trans-sexual schlock artiste Wayne County. Finally, the death by misadventure of sticksman Billy Murcia (➻ *November 1972*) – who had been using Nolan's kit – created an opening for him within the US's most talked-about glam act, The New York Dolls. Nolan was in the chair as The Dolls were signed to Mercury in March 1973, his distinctive powerhouse drumming pulling their two albums above the mundane, but it was all about attitude with this group – and Nolan possessed it in spades. Although the sound of the

band was liberating, they did not shift units as anticipated, soon finding themselves dropped by the label and under Malcolm McLaren's charge by 1974. The band's image-change under the future Sex Pistols manager – to Red Chinese-styled leather garb – was not to Nolan or Thunders's taste, and the pair cut loose from singer David Johansen and guitarist Syl Sylvain during a 1975 tour of Japan. The departing twosome formed possibly the druggiest of all proto-punk bands, The Heartbreakers. With this classic group, Nolan and Thunders opened for The Sex Pistols (at the time of his death (➻ *February 1979*), Sid Vicious had been living at Nolan's apartment) and cut a great debut in *LAMF* (1977) – but they had always had a love-hate relationship and split the year after.

Nolan nonetheless crossed paths many times with the guitarist in his subsequent work, and he was visibly shattered by Thunders's death. Nolan was already unwell and receiving treatment for bacterial meningitis by the time he played his last gig, a tribute to Thunders, late in 1991. Suffering a stroke, the drummer fell into a coma, spending his final weeks on life support.

See also *Arthur 'Killer' Kane (➻ July 2004).*

Wednesday 15

Dee Murray

(David Murray Oates – Gillingham, Kent, 3 April 1946)
The Spencer Davis Group
The Elton John Band
(Various acts)

'Dee Murray made huge musical and personal contributions to my life.'
Elton John (despite firing him in 1975 and 1984)

A British bassist with a remarkable CV, Dee Murray began his professional career with Mirage and then UK one-hit wonders Plastic Penny ('Everything I Am', 1968). In the latter, he encountered drummer Nigel Olsson, and the pair graduated through the latter phases of the declining Spencer Davis Group to join Elton John's set-up in the early seventies. It was an exciting time for the still-young Murray, playing around the world with the new star: John was particularly huge in America, where at least four of his singles went to number one during the period Murray was playing. After 'Philadelphia Freedom' (1975), the latest hit to do so, Murray and Olsson were let go by John – but Murray rallied to secure session work with more big names such as Procol Harum, Alice Cooper, Kiki Dee and Yvonne Elliman. Murray reconvened with John for a further four years – but was again dismissed in 1984, soon after which he learned he had skin cancer. Suffering a stroke during chemotherapy, Dee Murray was taken to hospital in Memphis and died four days later.

APRIL

Sunday 19

Rob Clayton
(Georgia, 1968)
The Jody Grind
Hallow's Eve

Robert Paul Hayes
(Georgia, 1966)
The Jody Grind

Deacon Lunchbox
(Timothy Tyson Ruttenber – Georgia, 1951)

With rock heading towards grunge meltdown in 1991, the sound of The Jody Grind was unusually mellow and jazz-tinged, claiming fans with the hypnotic performance and vocal of a strong frontwoman, Kelly Holmes. The band's debut, *One Man's Trash Is Another Man's Treasure* (1990), garnered plaudits left, right and centre for the Atlanta-based four-piece – Holmes, Bill Taft (guitar), Robert Hayes (bass) and drummer Walter Brewer. By the release of *Lefty's Deceiver* (1991), Brewer had left and been replaced by new boy Rob Clayton, a versatile percussionist who had previously served at the other end of the rock spectrum with thrash-metallers Hallow's Eve

(whose previous drummer, Ronny Appoldt, had been murdered in 1985), playing on their *Monument* album (1988) before the group fell into disarray and disbanded.

Just months after Clayton joined The Jody Grind, the band hit the road for yet another tour. As they completed a show in Pensacola, Florida, the new drummer – known for some reason as 'Angel Boy' – informed the hard-drinking older members of the band that he wished to return to Georgia to attend Easter service with his family (something of a turnaround, given his previous band's interests). Fending off their ribbing, he and Hayes jumped into the band's hired van and set off into the fog. Travelling back with them was local Atlanta singer/performance artist Tim Ruttenber – better known to his public as Deacon Lunchbox, a bearded, chainsaw-wielding, cross-dressing poet who had opened for The Jody Grind. As the van reached the brow of a hill on Interstate 75 in Alabama, a 48-foot truck approaching from the other direction began veering erratically, before crossing right into the van's path. All three were killed instantly; Clayton was decapitated as the van slid under the truck. The negligent driver of the truck was found to have been drunk, asleep at the wheel and at least 10 mph over the speed limit; he survived to receive a superficial prison sentence. While The Jody Grind finished there and then, Holmes continues her solo career to this day.

Saturday 25

Brian 'Too Loud' MacLeod
(Halifax, Nova Scotia, 25 June 1952)
Headpins
(Chilliwack)
(Various acts)

Brian MacLeod had been a stalwart of the Canadian and Northern California rock scenes since the early seventies. The drummer began in earnest at the softer end of the pomp-rock scale with Chilliwack, a Vancouver band signed to Mushroom Records – home of future stadium types like Heart. In his first band, MacLeod met guitarist/vocalist Bill Henderson and bassist Ab Bryant, with whom he formed Headpins after the label went into stasis following the 1979 death of boss Shelly Siegel. Recruiting photogenic singer Denise McCann (wife of The Guess Who's Randy Bachman) and drummer Matt Frenette, MacLeod took the unusual step of giving up percussion for guitar as the band readily embraced the 'hair metal' vogue of the time. Despite a substantial live following (and tours with Whitesnake), Headpins were unable to find more than token success, and a number of line-up changes lead to a split in 1986. Eventually moving into production, MacLeod won a prestigious Juno award in 1983, before succumbing to bone cancer nearly a decade later.

MAY

Friday 1

Sharon Redd
(Norfolk, Virginia, 19 October 1945)

Tiny but flamboyant eighties disco diva Sharon Redd seemed destined for global stardom. For a start, she had some pretty serious musical connections in her immediate family: her sister is Snap vocalist Penny Ford, her brother Gene Redd Jr, a producer/arranger with Kool & The Gang; her stepfather was a member of Benny Goodman's band. Redd was also a terrific performer in her own right and the purveyor of one or two sizzling disco epics. Openly gay, Redd was warmly accepted into the late-seventies scene, having previously performed in *Hair*, backed Bette Midler and gained recognition as 'the Schaeffer beer girl' on US television. She signed with Epic, then Prelude, giving the world a great second album, *Redd Hott*, and such hits as 'Can You Handle It?' (1981), 'Never Give You Up' (1982) and 'In the Name of Love' (1983).

As Sharon Redd prepared a comeback, the DNA-remixed 'Can You Handle It?' (1992) became her biggest hit in the UK (where Redd had most successfully crossed over) – yet three months later she was dead. Her passing is generally attributed to pneumonia, though it is widely believed she was carrying the AIDS virus, making Redd the highest-profile female singer at the time to fall to the disease. (Unsubstantiated rumour suggests, however, that, performing barefoot, Redd stepped on broken glass and eventually succumbed to a staph virus.)

Monday 4

Dudu Zulu
(Dudu Mntowaziwayo Ndlovu – Zululand, South Africa, 25 December 1957)
Johnny Clegg & Juluka/Savuka

Dudu Zulu – who had recently re-embraced his birthname (above) – did not live to see the reintegrated South Africa of which he and his band had dreamed. A noted supporter of black South Africa's cause, popular white singer Johnny Clegg had employed Dudu as percussionist/dancer with first Juluka (who almost managed a UK hit with 1983's 'Scatterlings Of Africa') and then Savuka, to whom Dudu also contributed vocals.

The musician was returning from a neighbour's to his home in Esiphongweni when he was shot at close proximity in what was believed to have been a case of mistaken identity. During this time of destabilization, local 'taxi wars' had flared up between drivers desperate to maintain their patches: Dudu was thought to have been killed erroneously, or in crossfire. A family man orphaned himself as a young boy, Dudu Zulu left nine children, his shooting coming less than six months after that of Ladysmith Black Mambazo's Headman Tshabalala (➤ *December 1991*).

Thursday 7

Nigel Preston
(London, 1959)
The (Southern Death) Cult
Sex Gang Children
The Gun Club
Theatre of Hate
(Various acts)

A drummer on the fertile British post-punk scene of the early eighties, Nigel Preston was as well known for his party-animal image as for his short-lived tenures with some of that era's top leftfield bands. Beginning his career with Kirk Brandon's Theatre of Hate, Preston found himself on *Top of the Pops* with the excellent Top Forty-scraping 'Do You Believe in the Westworld?' (1982). His career levelled off with art-goth scenesters Sex Gang Children during 1983, but the journeyman drummer was soon to bed down with much-touted Bradford rockers The Southern Death Cult – who could boast their own 'Glimmer Twins' in singer Ian Astbury and guitarist Billy Duffy (bassist at the time was Jamie Stewart). Gradually trimming their name down to The Cult (via Death Cult), the band placed two albums on the UK charts during 1983 and 1984. However, just prior to The Cult's 1985 Top Twenty singles break-through, Preston was sacked because of his increasingly wayward lifestyle.

Unperturbed, the percussionist formed his own punk band, Baby Snakes, and also joined Jeffrey Lee Pierce – a punk- and blues-obsessed Californian now living in London – and his band The Gun Club for a European tour in the late eighties. The two musicians were both strong personalities and constantly at one another's throats, Preston finding Pierce's rigid work ethic hilarious. Tellingly, both were also heroin users. Although exact details are not known, Nigel Preston appears to have died from an overdose of the drug while staying in Brixton. Pierce apparently refused to contribute to a tribute record for the late drummer.

See also *Rob Graves (☜ January 1991); Jeffrey Lee Pierce (☞ March 1996)*

Friday 15

Barbara Lee Jones

(Barbara Lee – The Bronx, New York,
16 May 1947)
The Chiffons

The Chiffons – 14-year-olds Judy Craig (lead) and Sylvia Peterson, with 13-year-olds Barbara Lee and Patricia Bennett – were the consummate girl group, forming while at New York's James Monroe High School. Their first manager was Ronnie Mack, who gave the group their name and in 1960 put the girls up against New Jersey rivals The Shirelles with a recording of the latter's 'Tonight's the Night': although they lost this particular battle (to a pretty formidable opponent), The Chiffons' day would come two years later. Topping the chart with 'He's So Fine' (1963), the group was now part of a wave of East Coast female acts – which also included Brooklyn's The Crystals – cleaning up in the US. 'One Fine Day' was hastily released after the *real* follow-up stiffed, and also sold shedloads, though the group had to wait until 1966 for a third and final Top Ten entry with the Motown-esque 'Sweet Talkin' Guy'. In the seventies, the group – by then without their own deal – were caught up in a plagiarism case against George Harrison, who, it was ruled, had taken the melody for his 1971 number one 'My Sweet Lord' from the girls' Mack-penned chart-topper. Which set the ex-Beatle back over $500K.

The Chiffons: Please pleat me

With hits and television work drying up for the quartet, Barbara Lee settled into married life and a more regular existence. The former teen star died suddenly from a heart attack the night before her forty-fifth birthday. After her death, Craig – who had left in 1969 – returned to the Chiffons for tours and public appearances with Patricia Bennett.

Friday 29

Ollie Halsall

(Peter Halsall – Southport, England,
14 March 1949)
Timebox/Patto (Take 5)
Boxer
(Various acts)

Ollie Halsall was very much an unsung hero – a British guitarist who played left-handed, his fluid style lighting up many a recording over two decades. As a child, he showed promise on piano and drums as well as the instrument for which he would become best known, and even joined his first band, Take 5, as vibes-player. Changing the band's name first to Timebox – under which they managed a Top Forty single with The Four Seasons' 'Beggin'' (1968) – the group then became Patto, in deference to singer/guitarist Mike Patto. By now Halsall was wielding his familiar white Gibson, and also moonlighting as instrumentalist Rusty Springs. Nonplussed by Patto's musical direction, Halsall left to become singer (and now also synth-player!) with hard-rock band Tempest, though this too was to prove unsatisfactory. Over the next few years he played with some great British names – Kevin Ayers, John Cale, Brian Eno and Viv Stanshall – and for a while in the band Boxer, again with Patto. In 1977, Halsall hooked up with another Bonzo Dog member, Neil Innes, to record the Beatle spoof *The Rutles*, his musicianship and speeded-up vocal aping Paul McCartney (*Monty Python*'s Eric Idle played the onscreen character).

Ollie Halsall was back playing with Kevin Ayers when he died suddenly from an unexpected heart attack in his Madrid apartment. It later emerged that the musician had become hooked on heroin around 1989, while attempting to assist a member of the band Radio Futura who was an addict.

Although unsullied by any association with drugs throughout his career, Halsall had blown the last of his earnings on a fix that was to kill him in his sleep. His ashes were scattered at Cala Deià in Mallorca, and Halsall's dedicated fans positioned a volume control on his headstone.

See also *Mike Patto (**March 1979); Greg Ridley (**November 2003)*

JUNE

Saturday 27

Stefanie Sargent

(Seattle, Washington, 8 June 1968)
7 Year Bitch
(Barbie's Dream Car)

Often lumped with two post-punk movements, the Seattle grunge scene and the Foxcore/Riot Grrl movement, 7 Year Bitch were in fact closer to a band like L7 in their distinctly 'rock' outlook. The band – formed in 1990 by ex-Barbie's Dream Car members Stefanie Sargent (guitar), Selene Vigil (vocals) and Valerie Agnew (drums) – recruited Elizabeth Davis (bass) and immediately hit censorship problems, first and foremost for their name (this *was* the US, remember), and also for song titles such as 'No Fucking War' (1992), written at the start of the first Gulf conflict. Opening for happening Seattle punks The Gits, 7 Year Bitch put out *Sick 'Em* (1992), a debut album, on small imprint C/Z Records – but tragedy was to occur before the record hit the shelves. After also drinking heavily, Sargent was found dead from an apparent heroin overdose: a needle was found next to her body.

With new guitarist Roisin Dunne on board, the band produced a second album, *¡Viva Zapata!* (1994), which

understandably expressed more personal sentiments than its predecessor, and featured the song 'Rockabye', written in Sargent's memory. The record title itself alluded to murdered friend and Gits singer Mia Zapata. As a result of the appalling crime that brought about Zapata's death (*July 1993*), members of 7 Year Bitch were instrumental in setting up Home Alive – an anti-violence project promoting self-defence for young women. After a move to Atlantic proved unrewarding, however, 7 Year Bitch ended in 1997.

JULY

Sunday 5

Paul Hackman

(Kitchener, Ontario, 1953)
Helix

Helix came into being as early as 1975, and guitarist Paul Hackman joined the Ontario-based band three years later, after they had become quite a local attraction. Built around the vocals of Brian Vollmer and the guitar and drums of twins Brian and Brent Doerner, Helix peddled a familiar brand of late-seventies pomp metal, pulling in a loyal fanbase without ever really breaking into the upper echelon. Hackman became a core figure in the line-up, playing on eight albums over the next decade or so as the band toured the world with just about every major metal name of the day.

Returning from a Vancouver show at around 8 am, one of two Helix tour vans failed to negotiate a hairpin bend and left the road near Kamloops on the Coquihalla Highway, rolling forty feet down an embankment. Sound engineer Al Craig and crew members Alan Russell (who had fallen asleep while driving) and Mike Palmer suffered minor injuries; Paul Hackman, however, had been thrown clear of the van and was badly hurt. Bassist Daryl Gray attempted to flag down help – apparently, some twenty vehicles ignored the injured musician before a doctor pulled up. (The second Helix van was unaware of the accident.) Hackman later died in hospital from severe internal injuries. The shattered band issued a single, 'That Day is Gonna Come', in honour of the late guitarist, with a promotional video featuring Super-8 footage of him on tour with Helix. Said Craig, 'The guy was the most harmless human being. It's hard to fathom that he's not here any more.'

Sunday 26

Mary Wells
(Detroit, Michigan, 13 May 1943)

Mary Wells: 'Miss Motown' in 'Gordy' attire

Mary Wells's success as Tamla Motown's first solo chart-topper almost never happened: born into a single-parent household, Wells was stricken with spinal meningitis which left her temporarily crippled, partially sighted and semi-deaf. Despite this disability, she sang regularly at her local church, and taught herself to walk again at the age of five. Just over a decade later, the young singer so impressed Berry Gordy with a vocal rendition of her own song 'Bye Bye Baby' (apparently composed for her hero, Jackie Wilson) that the wily Motown head signed her on the spot. Wells recorded the tune herself and scored a Top Ten R & B hit in 1960; the record also managed a very respectable forty-five on the pop listings. Another of her songs, 'I Don't Want to Take a Chance', then made the US Top Forty. It was under Smokey Robinson's guidance that Wells became Queen of Motown, however. She had a string of major

US hits, penned by the star, over the next four years; the biggest by some way was 'My Guy' (1964) – a number one that stopped just short of the million mark in America and also took her to number five in Britain (her only significant hit this side of the Atlantic). Her business friendships blossomed, with Marvin Gaye selecting her for duets and The Beatles naming her as their favourite US chanteuse, offering her a number of songs for an album – in return for which she dedicated the record to the Liverpool foursome. Wells was prolific in other ways, too: she produced six children with second husband Cecil Womack (and later married his brother, Curtis). She had previously tied the knot with songwriter Herman Griffin, who, believing she was being exploited by Motown, encouraged her to sue Gordy in 1965. Although she

was successful in this action, Wells found scoring hits on other labels difficult, and left the business during the seventies to concentrate on her by now substantial family.

In 1990, Mary Wells – enjoying something of a revival on the tour circuit – learned the devastating news that she had cancer of the larynx, promoted by a forty-a-day cigarette habit. Without major health insurance, she then suffered the ignominy of having to sell her vast home. An array of music stars, led by Martha Reeves, former Supremes Diana Ross and Mary Wilson (with whom Wells is often confused), plus Bonnie Raitt, Bruce Springsteen and Rod Stewart, offered assistance to this popular performer. But Wells's health was weakening: yielding to a bout of pneumonia, she died two years later at the Kenneth Norris Jr Cancer Center at UCLA.

AUGUST

Wednesday 5

Jeff Porcaro
(Hartford, Connecticut, 1 April 1954)
Toto
Steely Dan
(Various acts)

If a *Number One in Heaven* award existed for most apocryphal death tale, then that of drummer Jeff Porcaro would likely give Cass Elliot (➤*July 1974*) a close run. Porcaro was born into a musical dynasty: his father Joe was a traditional percussionist and brothers Mike (born 1955) and Steve (born 1957) – with whom he would later play in Toto – were a bassist and keyboardist respectively. Jeff was probably the most widely respected Porcaro, however. While still at Grant High School in California, he landed a job as in-house drummer on CBS's *Sonny & Cher* television show – a position that caused him to abandon his studies but put him in touch with some of the top names in music. When he was just nineteen, Porcaro was recruited by Steely Dan for a lengthy tour; the New Yorkers then kept him on for three big-selling albums, *Pretzel Logic* (1974), *Katy Lied* (1975) and *Gaucho* (1980). His reputation had flourished by now and as FM rock's most sought-after session drummer, Porcaro added the names of Boz Scaggs, Barbra Streisand and Warren Zevon to his address book by the end of the seventies. With Toto, Porcaro moved into US music's major league, the band soon becoming one of those select 'logo' acts (see Chicago, Foreigner, Journey, REO Speedwagon, Styx, etc) who can shift dinosaur-sized units of AOR confection with nary the twitch of the eyelid. Their best-selling album was *Toto IV* (1983),

with offerings like 'Rosanna' and the admittedly rather engaging 'Africa' (a US number one) likewise doing pretty smart business on the world's singles charts. And it didn't end there: during the decade Porcaro rubbed shoulders with most blue-chip names, contributing to records by Dire Straits, Hall & Oates, Madonna, Paul McCartney, Randy Newman, Pink Floyd, Lionel Richie and Michael Jackson, with whom he co-wrote 'Human Nature'.

Continuing his session work into the nineties, Porcaro was all set to unleash the latest Toto meisterwerk *Kingdom Of Desire* on the public: it proved a swansong. After his body was found at his Hidden Hills, California, home rumour spread like knapweed that the drummer, a keen gardener, had died from an allergic reaction to the pesticide Dursban. It transpired, though, that Porcaro had no traces of the chemical in his body whatsoever and had suffered a heart attack brought on by the far-more-routine catalyst of long-term cocaine abuse.

See also *Jimmy Hodder (➤June 1990)*

Friday 14

Tony Williams
(Elizabeth, New Jersey, 5 April 1928)
The Platters

Part-Native American singer Tony Williams already had a following before his selection for the fifties' best-selling vocal group. His smooth, swooping tones were much in evidence during time spent with the New Jersey Baptist gospel choir, where Williams was first noticed. After a spell with the US air force, Williams trained his voice diligently and relocated to Los Angeles, where The Platters – a struggling quartet fronted by future-Coaster Cornell Gunter

– were transformed by his vocal input. The crucial break came with the close tutoring of new manager Buck Ram, who launched the group big time, initially via the Federal label. Although The Platters became the first black vocal band to outsell rival white versions of their songs, Tony Williams-led classics such as 'Only You' and 'The Great Pretender' (their first US number one in 1955) were actually initially disliked by a group keen to fit in with rock 'n' roll – the records' huge sales made them think again. The hits continued – 'My Prayer' (1956), 'Twilight Time' and 'Smoke Gets in Your Eyes' (both 1958) remarkably all scaled the pop listings – with Williams contributing much to the songwriting, though if anyone could find evidence of this on the heavily Ram-doctored credits, they'd be doing well. After acquittal for a 1959 misdemeanour involving four of The Platters and a hotel room full of under-age girls, it became tougher to place the once pure-as-snow group on radio stations anywhere – and by 1961 'The Voice of The Platters' had had enough. The mercurial lead left his group behind (he was replaced by Sonny Turner) to attempt a solo career, but success without his group was virtually impossible to find. As focal point of The Platters' sound, Williams's voice still appeared on subsequent releases by the group, the Mercury label suing Ram over the lead's departure. It was the start of much litigation that was to follow as The Platters splintered into various touring line-ups: Williams found himself the subject of another lawsuit when attempting to use the Ram-owned name during the early eighties. With his life disappearing into a black hole of alcohol abuse and financial difficulty, Williams was forced to join an authorized Platters line-up shortly before his death.

Like Mary Wells, Tony Williams had – despite his profession – been a heavy smoker in the years before enlightenment, paying a hefty price when stricken with emphysema and diabetes.

See also *David Lynch (January 1981); Nathaniel Nelson (June 1984); Paul Robi (February 1989). Early members Cornell Gunter (February 1990) and Elsbeary Hobbs (May 1996) have also died, as has the later singer Randy Jones (2002). Buck Ram passed away eighteen months before Williams.*

SEPTEMBER

Earl Van Dyke
(Detroit, Michigan, 8 July 1930)
The 'Funk Brothers'

He was dubbed 'The Chunk of Funk' – and Earl Van Dyke was certainly no shrinking waif. The traditionally trained pianist and arranger had originally seen his future in the classical sector. His father had played violin but, when money was needed, had taken a job at the local Ford plant: for Van Dyke, moving into R & B was his way of making ends meet. While touring with Lloyd Price, he met bassist Jamie Jamerson, who was backing Jackie Wilson; the pair teamed up with 'Benny' Benjamin in 1961 to form Motown's much-loved studio band, nicknamed the 'Funk Brothers'. In this guise, the musicians backed many of the label's top acts, among them The Four Tops, Marvin Gaye, The Supremes and The Temptations. The downside of this was that Van Dyke and his buddies were on call 24/7 – and really weren't properly remunerated (or even credited) for their efforts. A disgruntled Van Dyke lead a musicians' strike in 1965, which brought about a change in pay structures and an eventual opportunity for

Van Dyke to cut his own records at the label.

The hits continued into the seventies, but Van Dyke had become weary of a music business that was leaving him behind. By the end of the next decade he was diagnosed with carpal tunnel syndrome. After the deaths of Benjamin (May 1969) and Jamerson (August 1983), Van Dyke's passing from prostate cancer brought a remarkable story to an end.

See also *Robert White (October 1994). Occasional 'Funk Brothers' Eddie 'Bongo' Brown (1984), Richard 'Pistol' Allen and Johnny Griffith (both 2002) have also since passed on.*

OCTOBER

Harry Ray
(Hackensack, New Jersey, 15 December 1946)
The Moments
(Ray, Goodman & Brown)
(The Voltaires)

During the sixties, bass baritone Harry Ray was regularly spotted singing at the corner for a few pennies, but his hit-making status as lead with soul/ R & B act The Moments only began *after* they'd hit with 1970's 'Love on a Two-Way Street'. At this stage, Ray was singing with The Voltaires, an also-ran vocal group that lacked his ambition. It was Moments singer William Brown's throat disorder that opened the door for Ray, The Moments – now Ray, Brown, Al Goodman and distinctive falsetto Mark Greene – running off a series of major hits, particularly in Britain, where 'Girls' (1975, with The Whatnauts), 'Dolly My Love' (1975) and 'Jack in the Box' (1977) all achieved Top Ten status.

The most sublime cut, 'Look At Me (I'm in Love)' (1975), surprisingly fared indifferently. In the US, a further big hit – 'Special Lady' (1980) – was secured as the group trimmed down to become Ray, Goodman & Brown. Harry Ray's attempted solo career was largely scuppered by a return of his lifelong problem with hypertension – resulting in the stroke that cost the singer his life just short of his forty-sixth birthday.

Eddie Kendrick(s)
(Union Springs, Alabama, 17 December 1939)
The Temptations

The life of young Edward James Kendrick was changed for ever by a move to Birmingham, Alabama, which put him in contact with Paul Williams, a fellow singer who was also to become his best friend. The pair enthralled audiences with their choir performances, and in 1955 formed a doo-wop trio with Kell Osbourne and relocated to Ohio. Kendrick earned a pittance by day as a dishwasher, drifting between an assortment of night-time vocal duties until he and Williams reunited as The Primes (originally The Cavaliers) – the group that caught the attention of manager Milton Jenkins. The latter had a second band under his wing – The Distants – with whom Kendrick and Williams amalgamated to form The Elgins, later The Temptations. Under Berry Gordy's guidance, The Temptations eventually became Motown's – and soul music's – biggest act. The gentle, considered manner of Kendricks (now with added 's') balanced well with Williams's earthier appeal and the voices of Elbridge 'Al' Bryant, Melvin Franklin and Otis Williams, but the group proved hard to break until a significant change in 1964. Issues between Bryant and Paul Williams saw the former sacked as lead and the latter shifted back, with new boy David Ruffin drafted to the fore: the substitution was inspired, elevating The Temps to superstardom. A series of massive US pop hits ensued – including the number ones 'My Girl' (1965) and 'I Can't Get Next to You' (1969) – with Kendricks adding his light falsetto and smoothly executed dance moves to the mix. The encompassing of pop-psychedelia to keep The Temps in synch with the zeitgeist was less to Kendricks's taste, though, and this – along with the dismissal of his friend Williams (whose health problems worsened throughout his life) – prompted him to leave the group behind in 1971. Ironically, just weeks before, the Kendricks-led 'Just My Imagination' had given The Temptations a third American number one.

As a solo commodity, Kendricks surpassed even his own expectations. After a number of flops, among the hit records he scored on his own were the tremendous 'Keep On Truckin'' (1973), a US chart-topper that became a funk classic, and another strong dance-floor filler, 'Boogie Down' (1974). This success was tempered somewhat by the suicide of his lifelong friend Williams (*August 1973*), and he could not sustain the standard of his output. Kendrick, who reverted to his birth spelling to overcome Motown's ownership of his name, was, following litigation with his former employers, to fade from the public gaze by the end of the seventies. In 1982, he rejoined Ruffin and another on-off Temptations lead, Dennis Edwards, for revival slots, but within a decade his performing career was ended by cancer. Eddie Kendrick – who had a lung removed in 1991 – was unable to defeat the disease he attributed to a lifetime of smoking, and passed away in Birmingham the following year. Like many of his former colleagues,

he died in poor health and relative poverty.

See also *Elbridge 'Al' Bryant (* *October 1975); David Ruffin (* *June 1991); Melvin Franklin (* *February 1995)*

Saturday 10

Lennie Peters
(Leonard Sergeant, London, 1933)
Peters & Lee
The Migil Five

That the male partner in Peters & Lee achieved brief but notable success during his career is remarkable, given the extraordinary misfortune and ill health that afflicted him throughout his life. His blindness was not, as many believe, a birth defect: Lennie Sergeant's parents may have felt lucky that their 5-year-old son lost only the sight in his left eye when knocked down by a careless driver. Ten years later, though, Sergeant – an uncle to The Rolling Stones' Charlie Watts – got into an argument with some stone-throwing thugs as he attempted to sunbathe: the ringleader resolved the disagreement by lobbing a brick at the hapless teenager, permanently damaging his right eye.

Overcoming his disability to master the piano, the renamed Lennie Peters began his music career as a soloist, playing with The Migil Five, though he left before the quintet's Top Ten hit 'Mockingbird Hill' (1964). A panel-

pleasing performance with singer Dianne Lee on ITV's *Opportunity Knocks* talent show in 1972 changed the musician's fortunes for ever. In 1973, the duo topped the UK charts with the million-selling 'Welcome Home', the first of a number of schmaltzy hits that included the near-identikit 'Don't Stay Away Too Long' (1974) as well as a series of gold albums. The duo were never romantically inclined – Lee married Rick Price of glam-rockers Wizzard – but overcame a brief hiatus to remain together recording and touring until Lennie Peters's death from bone cancer in Enfield, London.

Sunday 25

Roger Miller
(Fort Worth, Texas, 2 January 1936)

The future King of the Road had a difficult start: when just a baby, Roger Miller lost his father to spinal meningitis and was sent with his two older brothers to live in the C & W-drenched state of Oklahoma, his only real companion his radio and the weekly broadcasts from the Grand Ole Opry it offered. A break for the young music-lover came unexpectedly when he stole a guitar at seventeen; he confessed to the theft and chose military service over a custodial sentence. Miller honed his playing skills while on duty in Korea, and entered the field of songwriting

'What do I do with unused songs and lyrics? I smoke 'em.'
Roger Miller

in Nashville when he returned home. At the age of twenty-three, he penned his first country chart-topper, Jim Reeves' 'Billy Bayou', but it wasn't until the mid sixties that Miller hit paydirt with his own hit records. The biggest, of course, was 'King of the Road' (1965), a warm account of hobo life that became a US million-seller and went to number one in the UK: this song now boasts countless cover versions by artists as diverse as Dean Martin, The Proclaimers and REM. Miller's other hits included 'Dang Me' (1964), the somewhat rose-tinted 'England Swings' (1965) and the unexpectedly tender 'Husbands and Wives' (1966) (Miller himself was to marry three times). Though he won numerous Grammys during the sixties, Miller's crowning achievement in his own eyes was a 1985 Tony award for his score to the *Huckleberry Finn*-inspired Broadway musical *Big River*.

Like many of his generation, Miller had known little of the dangers of cigarettes, and succumbed to lung cancer at California's Century City Hospital – the fourth big name to die of a smoking-related disease in 1992.

NOVEMBER

Friday 13

Ronnie Bond
(Ronald Bullis – Andover, Hampshire, 4 May 1942)
The Troggs

Ronald Bullis had been a bricklayer before he became Ronnie Bond, the engine behind the garage-inspired Troglodytes (earlier Ten Foot Five) – Reg Presley (Reginald Ball, vocals), Chris Britton (guitar) and Pete Staples (bass). Signed by Kinks manager Larry Page, The Troggs – sensibly having

abbreviated their name – quickly became the latest sensation in Britain, where their second single 'Wild Thing' (1966) shot to number two (behind The Stones' 'Paint It, Black'). The record – which the group had originally resisted as 'corny' (it was probably closer to dumb genius) – went on to top the US charts, shifting a million copies and becoming a standard. Its follow-up, 'A Girl Like You', gave The Troggs a domestic number one and 'I Can't Control Myself' completed a reasonably good year for the band by reaching number two. (The only black spot was a small amount of radio blanking of the third hit due to its supposedly overt sexual content.) The hits continued to a lesser extent throughout the next year – Bond occasionally adding songs or vocals to albums – with the drummer and Presley later recording solo material, by which time The Troggs were on a sabbatical: Bond's first single, the oddly matched 'Carolyn'/'Anything For You' (1969), stiffed – as would all further releases. In 1972, Bond and Presley reconvened The Troggs, but the magic had gone. During the rest of the decade, the group toured the oldies circuit and issued a series of rather embarrassing covers. During this time a studio argument rich in foul language was stored and later issued as 'The Troggs Tapes'. By the next decade even this kind of novelty had worn off, Bond and Presley falling out for ever.

After Ronnie Bond's death from a lengthy illness, Presley happened upon untold wealth with Wet Wet Wet's point-missing-but-fifteen-week-chart-topping cover of 'Love is All Around' (1993), a Troggs hit from 1967. He reportedly spent much of it on crop-circle research.

John Cascella
(New York, 29 April 1947)
John Cougar Mellencamp
(The Faith Band)

John Cascella is best remembered as instrumentalist with Indiana-based mainstream rocker John Mellencamp, but the musician was close to thirty before he eschewed his jazz roots for rock 'n' roll. Cascella had previously played with The Faith Band, scoring a radio hit with 'Dancin' Shoes' (1978). Like him, Mellencamp – then using the name 'Cougar' – was a late starter in popular music. Mellencamp had already crashed the US charts with million-sellers like 'Hurts So Good' and 'Jack and Diane' (both 1982) before the pair got together on the singer's 1984 album *Uh Huh*. During his nine-year spell with Mellencamp's band, Cascella contributed keyboard and saxophone, but it was his accordion-playing which inspired most – best demonstrated on the 1987 hit 'Paper and Fire'. The musician also played sessions with many other performers including Bob Dylan and Kim Carnes.

On the night of 14 November 1992, John Cascella returned from the Evander Holyfield–Riddick Bowe Heavyweight Championship fight in Indiana. He suffered a massive coronary while driving his car, lost control and veered off into a cornfield – where the vehicle, with Cascella's body still at the wheel, was later found by a passing motorist. The musician, who was buried in Indianapolis, has a playground named in his honour at the city's Rhodius Park.

Ricky Williams

(Richard Williams – San Francisco, California, 1955)
Flipper
(The Sleepers)
(The Toiling Midgets)
(Crime)

A mainstay of San Francisco's throbbing underground punk scene, Ricky Williams had already spent time in an institution for his disturbing behaviour before taking up drums with Palo Alto band Crime, who, for some reason, renamed him 'Ricky Tractor'. As singer with The Sleepers, Williams began to sculpt a style that saw him (briefly) recruited as lead with ground-breaking nihilists Flipper. The singer's near-demented performance camouflaged lyrics of some intensity and were thought to be a significant influence on Kurt Cobain and Nirvana. Williams also recorded 1982's engaging *Sea Of Unrest* album with The Toiling Midgets (who replaced him with Mark Eitzel, later of American Music Club). Contrary to widespread belief that Williams died from a heroin overdose, he in fact suffered a rare respiratory condition that finally accounted for him in his late thirties.

See also *Will Shatter (* December 1987); John Dougherty (* October 1997)*

Paul Ryan

(Leeds, 24 October 1948)
Paul & Barry Ryan

Pre-dating Bros by some twenty-five years, Paul and Barry Ryan were pop's original pin-up twins, the sons of fifties chanteuse Marion Ryan (*née* Sapherson), who enjoyed a major UK hit with 'Love Me Forever' (1958), by which time her sons were already showing signs of following in her footsteps. The pair began steadily with a series of modest hits for Decca in the UK – starting with 'Don't Bring Me Your Heartaches' (1965) – before the more introverted Paul Ryan began to feel the strain of their teenybop status and requested to move more into the background. The reshuffle reaped instant dividends: Barry Ryan's reading of his brother's composition 'Eloise' (1968) soared to number two in the UK, earning a gold disc. Although this was to prove a career zenith, Ryan was happy in his new role, also penning hits such as Frank Sinatra's 'I Will Drink the Wine'.

Leaving music, Paul Ryan opened a small chain of hair salons during the eighties, which earned the already wealthy songwriter a decent living until his early death from cancer. Marion Ryan survived her son by seven years.

DECEMBER

Eddie Hazel

(Brooklyn, New York, 10 April 1950)
Parliament/Funkadelic

A disciple of Jimi Hendrix, teenager Eddie Hazel sat on the porch of his home in Plainfield, New Jersey, honing his craft on a guitar given him for Christmas by an older brother. Hazel had a distinct style of his own, however, and impressed Billy 'Bass' Nelson and legendary frontman George Clinton, who were at this point touring as The Parliaments. Eventually persuading Hazel's slightly over-protective mother – who had moved her sons to New Jersey in order to avoid 'gangs and drugs' – the pair secured the young guitarist for their line-up. As the group morphed into the multi-tentacled funk monster known as Funkadelic, Hazel's extravagant solos became a trademark of the group's sound. Much of his (and the band's) adopted psychedelia could be attributed to their massive substance intake. Hazel's was fairly well documented in the elaborate ten-minute jam he contributed to the defining 'Maggot Brain' (1971), his mother's opinion of which remains undocumented. The guitarist became friends with original drummer 'Tiki' Fulwood (whom he had been instrumental in placing), and at one point their LSD-partying became so consuming that Clinton – in a rare moment of hierarchical convention – suspended their wages (and subsequently fired Fulwood). The normally affable Hazel then found himself in serious hot water after an assault on an airline stewardess, and was incarcerated for some time. In the event, Clinton welcomed his tremendous playing (and some back-up vocals) back into the P-Funk fold – Hazel contributed to 1975's *Let's Take It to the Stage* – but by now the ever-expanding set-up was leaving him behind.

Devastated by the death of Fulwood (* *November 1979*), Hazel dropped out of the project for some years, pursuing a solo career and also contributing to the work of others, including The Temptations. His own health had deteriorated alarmingly during the eighties, but Hazel snubbed medical advice and returned to a 'P-Funk All-Stars' tour package early in 1992. Suffering severe internal bleeding and liver failure – possibly the result of his activities in his younger days – Eddie Hazel died at home in New York just months after the shows.

See also *Glen Goins (* July 1978); Raymond Davis (* Golden Oldies #27)*

Bobby LaKind

(California, 1945)

The Doobie Brothers
(Various acts)

A drummer with seventies rock behemoths The Doobie Brothers, Bobby LaKind stayed in place as the band moved seamlessly from blues-flavoured offerings through FM rock to the AOR-stylings of the late seventies. While Keith Knudsen hammered away on a regular kit, LaKind was by his side playing congas – a treat first heard on the band's *Taking It to the Streets* album (1976). In 1979, The Doobies enjoyed a chart-topping album with *Minute By Minute* and a massive-selling (and Grammy-winning) US number-one single with the very radio-friendly 'What a Fool Believes'. As well as his work with The Doobies, LaKind also provided studio drums for Nicolette Larson, The Nitty Gritty Dirt Band and Linda Ronstadt.

For Bobby LaKind, The Doobie Brothers effectively ended in 1990, though the band reconvened for benefit shows in 1992. By now LaKind had been diagnosed with colon cancer, which, despite treatment, was to claim his life that Christmas. LaKind was the first of four former Doobie Brothers to pass away.

See also *Cornelius Bumpus (*➤* February 2004); Keith Knudsen (*➤* February 2005). Bassist Dave Shogren also passed away in 1999.*

Lest We Forget

Other notable deaths that occurred sometime during 1992:

Roy Claxton Acuff (celebrated US honky-tonk musician dubbed The King of Country Music – mainly for his nurturing of others; born Tennessee, 15/9/1903; congestive heart failure, 23/11)

William 'Hank' Mizell (US rockabilly singer/guitarist best known for the 1976 smash 'Jungle Rock'; born Florida, 9/11/1923; unknown, 23/12)

Jackie Edwards ('Jamaica's Nat "King" Cole' – a singer/songwriter whose credits include two Spencer Davis Group chart-toppers; born Wilfred Gerald Edwards, 1938; heart attack, 15/8)

Steve Gilpin (popular New Zealand new-wave singer with Mi-Sex; born Wellington, 28/4/1950; car crash returning from a gig, 25/11)

Herb Kenny (US bass with the pioneering Ink Spots; born Pennsylvania, 12/6/1914; natural causes, 11/7 – two months ahead of lead tenor Jimmie Nabbie)

Randy Laire (US bassist with Bay Area thrash-metallers Heathen; car accident, which also killed his girlfriend, who'd fallen asleep at the wheel, 9/1)

Charlie Ondras (US drummer with Jon Spencer-led alt-rockers Boss Hog and his brother Chris's industrial-noise act Unsane; born New York, 1965; heroin overdose, 6/1992)

Brenda Payton (US R & B leader of Brenda & The Tabulations; born Pennsylvania, 1949; illness, 14/6)

Fleming Williams (US tenor vocalist with soul/disco act The Hues Corporation – he left just after their 2-million-selling 1974 #1 'Rock the Boat'; born Michigan, 1953; drug-related, 9/1992)

Ozaki Yutaka (Japanese rockabilly singer/'pin-up'; born Tokyo, 29/11/1965; pulmonary oedema – found naked in an alleyway, he is believed to have been force-fed alcohol/amphetamines, 25/4)

For a complete list of fallen artists, visit
www.numberoneinheaven.com

1993

JANUARY

Friday 22

Helno
(Noël Rota – Paris, c 1965)
Les Negresses Vertes

One of the more arresting French musical exports of the post-punk era, Les Negresses Vertes ('The Green Negresses' – an insult apparently thrown their way by French bouncers) fused cabaret, street performance, ska and flamenco to create a unique sonic and visual experience. Head of this vast troupe – sometimes fifteen-strong in the studio – was vocalist Helno Rota de Louracqua, generally referred to by his (assumed) first name. Formed in 1987, the band debuted with the striking, anarchistic '*200 Ans d'Hypocrisie*', and proved an unlikely hit at British festivals. A debut album, *Mlah!* (1988), similarly gained much critical praise this side of the channel and has since shifted half a million copies worldwide.

Helno's life and career were curtailed, however, by his vast appetite for alcohol and particularly hard drugs. Although a second album, 1991's *Famille Nombreuse*, found its way on to 1FM's playlist, Helno was now under-going rehabilitation, his heroin habit seriously out of control and detrimental to his writing and performance. Just as it appeared Helno had beaten his addiction, the singer was found dead, apparently from an overdose, at his home. Les Negresses Vertes rallied to issue further records in their figurehead's absence, but much of the original charm of their work was sacrificed to the input of producers and remixers.

FEBRUARY

Thursday 18

Patrick Waite
(Jamaica, 16 June 1969)
Musical Youth

Bass-playing Patrick Waite – like his cohorts in happy-go-lucky reggae scamps Musical Youth – was brought up in Birmingham, England; he was the son of Techniques vocalist Frederick Waite and alongside his brother Freddie Jr (drums), Waite joined Duddeston Manor school-friends the Grant brothers – Kelvin (guitar) and Michael (keyboards) – plus vocalist Dennis Seaton to form the band in 1979. A locally released single 'Political'/'Generals' emerged the following year, and, after being championed by DJ John Peel, Musical Youth found themselves in the unlikely position of being signed to MCA while still at school. In 1982, the group's bouncy cover of The Mighty Diamonds' 'Pass the Koochie' (altered to 'Pass the Dutchie' to avoid any career-stymieing drug references) stunned the pop world by shooting to number one in Britain within two weeks of release, then propelling Musical Youth into the US Top Ten. A strong album and three further Top Twenty hits in their homeland (including a pleasing-enough 1983 collaboration with Donna Summer on 'Unconditional Love') kept The Youth in the public eye for another year or so, before their fortunes – and especially those of Patrick Waite – took something of a downturn. Following a poor-selling second album and Seaton's departure, Musical Youth split in 1985.

For Patrick Waite it was a disaster: the former child star moved into petty crime before the decade was out. The ex-bassist had already spent time inside and was awaiting a court appearance for drug possession when he suffered a freakish domestic accident. Waite collapsed at a friend's house, hitting his head and dying instantly from the impact: a post mortem revealed that not drugs but an undiagnosed viral infection had caused the initial black-out. In 2003, Seaton took surviving members of Musical Youth – who surely by then barely fitted the description – back out on tour.

Toy Caldwell

(Spartanburg, South Carolina, 13 November 1947)

The Marshall Tucker Band

(Various acts)

'There's a big space in the world only Toy could fill.'

Charlie Daniels

Steeped in Southern values, guitarist Toy Talmadge Caldwell Jr went against the grain by playing covers of 'British invasion' tunes in a band called The Rants. His father was a known local musician, so it was unsurprising when both Toy and his bassist brother Tommy – previously in a Spartanburg band called New Generation – joined forces in Toy Factory, the first incarnation of what would become The Marshall Tucker Band. After a spell in the marines – during which time he was badly injured – Caldwell returned to South Carolina and his music. Expanding the line-up in 1971, the band – now the Caldwells, Doug Gray (vocals), George McCorkle (lead guitar), Jerry Eubanks (sax) and drummer Paul Riddle (there was no 'Marshall Tucker') – blended country and rock to fashion their own brand of the deep-fried Southern rock made popular by other acts such as The Allman Brothers. With Toy Caldwell's writing driving the project, an eponymous debut album on Capricorn turned gold in 1973, and all appeared rosy for a group that appealed to two generations of music lovers. Indeed, the seventies were very kind to the band:

their numerous albums performed well, tours sold out and the odd hit single – such as 'Heard It in a Love Song' (1977) – kept the coffers nicely topped up.

In 1980, though, matters were to take a tragic turn with the deaths of both of Caldwell's brothers in quick succession. In March of that year, a younger (non-musician) brother, Tim, died in a car crash, and Tommy was killed in *his* car just a month later (☞*April 1980*). The affairs of The Marshall Tucker Band were understandably lower key following this traumatic period, with Caldwell going on to session work after the group's eventual split in 1985. In the last years of his life, the guitarist suffered profoundly from bronchial problems exacerbated by his predilection for cocaine: this eventually came home to roost with a complete respiratory collapse. Caldwell, who'd been suffering from influenza, returned from a visit to his doctor and died in his sleep. Married with two daughters, Caldwell had just finished his second album. On the day of his death, he'd been due to play a fundraiser in honour of his late friend Ronnie Van Zant (☞*October 1977*), of fellow Southern rockers Lynyrd Skynyrd.

MARCH

Jeff Ward

(Chicago, Illinois, 28 November 1962)

Nine Inch Nails

Ministry

(Various acts)

Jeff Ward had been a mainstay of Chicago's industrial-rock scene for some years before he took to the road with Trent Reznor's Nine Inch Nails

for the first Lollapalooza package tour in 1991. A drummer with leading acts such as Ministry and Lard, he also played with Ministry singer Al Jourgensen in industrial supergroup Revolting Cocks, and at the time of his death was percussionist with the prophetically named Low Pop Suicide.

Ward had been struggling with heroin addiction for a while before his inner demons finally had the better of him in 1993. His death from self-inflicted carbon-monoxide poisoning prompted the Nine Inch Nails song 'Downward Spiral', while Ward's friend (and former NIN guitarist) Richard Patrick also dealt with the issue in 'It's Over' by his next band, Filter.

See also *E William Tucker* (☞*May 1999*)

APRIL

Mick Ronson

(Hull, 26 May 1946)

David Bowie (& The Spiders from Mars)

Ian Hunter/Mott the Hoople

(Various acts)

He was quite simply the leading lead guitar in UK glam rock. Mick Ronson, having immersed himself in the violin and piano as a youngster in unfashionable Hull, rose to become the snarling-yet-sensitive foil to both David Bowie and Mott the Hoople's Ian Hunter, while arranging and recording with many other gargantuan names of the era.

Ronson's family were practising Mormons – a fact that had some resonance in his adult life – and the young musician broke away from their restricting lifestyle to play in

Mick Ronson: All eyes on the lead guitarist ...

Yorkshire-based pub-rock acts such as The Rats and The Hullabaloos. Ex-Rat John Cambridge recommended the guitarist to the emerging Bowie, who soon recognized in Ronson a sympathetic character possessing no small ability. The eager-to-please Ronson then moved into the stairwell of the former David Jones's London flat! A prolific musical relationship with Bowie (he struck up a more personal one with the singer's hair stylist, Suzy Fussey) resulted in five of The Thin White Duke's best albums: *The Man Who Sold the World* (1970), *Hunky Dory* (1971), *The Rise and Fall of Ziggy Stardust and The Spiders from Mars* (1972), *Aladdin Sane* and *Pin Ups* (both 1973). Much of the sound employed in the group's work can be attributed entirely to the inspiration of Ronson. Never one to upstage his frontman, Ronson nonetheless engaged in some oft-recalled 'heavy electric petting' with Bowie on an *Old Grey Whistle Test* performance, enraging a British television audience that, at the time, felt *The Black & White Minstrel Show* to be more

appropriate evening entertainment. Ronson, decked in slashed-open jumpsuit, also complemented the singer's sartorial style. When Bowie killed off Ziggy in 1973, Ronson embarked on his own projects, producing two well-received albums, *Slaughter on 10th Avenue* (1974) and *Play Don't Worry* (1975), as well as Lou Reed's classic *Transformer* (1973), and playing with Bowie-protégé Ian Hunter. Hunter's band, Mott the Hoople, were very much on the decline commercially by the time Ronson jumped on board, but the two remained close after the inevitable 1974 disbanding: indeed, Ronson played lead on Hunter's excellent solo hit, 'Once Bitten, Twice Shy' the following year. Another year on, and the seemingly inexhaustible Ronson was producing an album for former Byrds' leader Roger McGuinn (*Cardiff Rose*). Over the next decade and a half, the guitarist worked with Bob Dylan, Elton John, ex-New York Doll David Johansen, Van Morrison and Glen Matlock's post-Pistols band, The Rich Kids.

By 1991 Mick Ronson – having recently separated from Fussey, with whom he had a teenage daughter – was diagnosed with liver cancer and told fairly bluntly that his days were numbered. Rather than disappear into a black hole of self-pity, Ronson went back to the studio to work on his third solo album (some sixteen years after the second) and also produced Morrissey's *Your Arsenal* (1992). Ronson's last live performance was as part of an April 1992 tribute to the recently departed Freddie Mercury (◀ *November 1991*), the only occasion on which he, Bowie and Hunter all played together. Ronson, who had recently rediscovered his faith and joined the Church of Jesus Christ of Latter-Day Saints, died at his home in London just over a year later. His final solo set, *Heaven and Hull* (featuring contributions from Bowie, Def Leppard's Joey Elliott and John Mellencamp), was issued posthumously.

JUNE

Saturday 5

Conway Twitty

(Harold Lloyd Jenkins – Friars Point, Mississippi,
1 September 1933)

Country music's most prolific hit-maker was known by a variety of nicknames, his preferred being 'The Best Friend a Song Ever Had'. Conway Twitty (the name derived from two small towns in Arkansas and Texas respectively) was raised on a houseboat and made his radio debut at just twelve years old – but he would juggle career opportunities in baseball and the armed forces before he took to music full time. At Sun Records, Twitty appeared to be heading in a rockabilly direction, sharing studios with the likes of Elvis, Johnny Cash and Jerry Lee Lewis, but it was a country-flavoured ballad that made the man a star across the genres: 'It's Only Make Believe' (1958) took Twitty to number one in both America and Britain. And it was in the C & W listings that the singer cleaned up most: it's reckoned that he charted some fifty-five songs, including an astonishing thirty-plus solo country number ones. In the seventies, Twitty was to duet with country legend Loretta Lyn, at the same time opening up other business interests – a fast-food chain ('Tweet yourself to a Twittyburger!') and his own music theme park, the somewhat opulent Twitty City in Tennessee. (The park was sold on to a Christian foundation following Conway Twitty's death.)

The singer – who had complained of stomach pains the previous week – was found unconscious on the floor of his tour bus and died later from an abdominal aneurysm. Conway Twitty's estate shortly thereafter became the subject of a distasteful and very public dispute between members of the families of his three ex-wives.

Monday 28

G G Allin

(Kevin Michael Allin – Lancaster, New Hampshire,
29 August 1956)
The Murder Junkies
(Various acts)

A motley collection of punks, thrill-seekers and deadbeats gathered at East Village's Gas Station venue on the night of 27 June, eagerly anticipating the return of the world's most notorious underground rock act (after a three-year custodial sentence for the onstage stabbing of a female fan). The converted service-station venue was a fitting one for a unique 'artist' like Allin: vast sculptures of car parts stretched upwards towards the damp ceiling, the pervading odour was of sweat, alcohol and stale gasoline. Then, there he was – naked as a jaybird and aching to corrupt yet another gathering of onlookers. Once again, Allin – gnashing and reeling after consuming a bag of cocaine that afternoon – uttered his infamous promise of four years earlier that he would commit suicide by gunshot before them on stage, but repeated that his audience must wait until a suitable Halloween night for such a spectacle. No, tonight, they would just have to make do with a compilation of Allin's greatest hits – obscenity, vomiting, self-mutilation, onstage nudity and defecation, and a no-holds-barred physical assault on those attending. Within twenty minutes, when the soundman pulled the plug on the show (as was standard procedure), several audience members had been attacked with the microphone, a photographer knocked unconscious and a woman smeared in Allin's excrement. The show ended in pandemonium; Allin then threw himself at a door, shattering the glass, lacerating his body and sending shards everywhere. A riot ensued, patrons smashing furniture and windows, bouncers attacking the protagonists with rocks – and the soundman setting his pit bull on anyone and everyone within reach. Minutes later, armed police added to the chaos. A bloodied, messed-up Allin somehow skulked away unnoticed along with his entourage, none of whom batted an eyelid at this all-too-familiar scene. Back at the apartment of his pal Johnny Puke, Allin – thanks largely to a vast quantity of heroin – calmed down at last. Leaving him to sleep off the effects of the drugs and his injuries, Puke, his girlfriend and Liz Mankowski, Allin's 17-year-old fiancée (yes, somehow he had one), left the singer to sleep. By morning his wretched body was very cold – and very dead.

A character who could almost have been contrived for *Number One in Heaven*'s rumination, G G Allin always claimed his shocking act was 'situationist' and not a result of his frankly bizarre upbringing. Originally

> **'He was all purple. He had snot coming out of his nose and blood coming out of his mouth – and a big fucking scowl on his face. Typical G G really.'**
>
> Merle Allin, G G's brother, on discovering his corpse

christened Jesus Christ Allin by his over-zealously religious father, the future shock-rocker and his brother and mother were forbidden by Allin Sr to speak after dark – some rumours even suggesting that the man had dug graves for his family in the basement, threatening their execution and his suicide if they refused to comply with his pious order! Needless to say, Allin's mother eventually filed for divorce and changed her son's name (his brother had already shortened 'Jesus' to 'G G'), but by then Allin was already behaving in a disturbed manner. He was to find some outlet for his anger in the primal rock 'n' roll of The Stooges and New York Dolls – though the performances of these bands were far from sufficiently extreme in Allin's eyes. As a young adult, there appeared every chance he might revert to a normal life (Allin married and fathered a daughter) but by 1980 he left this domesticity behind, emulating early hero Jerry Lee Lewis by taking up with a girl of thirteen. Allin's music at this stage still just about fitted the description: with The Jabbers, he performed a hybrid of early Stones and Sex Pistols-styled rock 'n' roll, though the singer learned before long that it was not his music that attracted attention but his snarling stage performance – which, accordingly, became more and more alarming (as would his deeply violent and misogynistic lyrics). Apart from a stint recording with former MC5 members Wayne Kramer and Dennis Thompson, Allin fronted more ludicrously offensive bands by the year, bearing names like Afterbirth, The Drugwhores, Sewer Sluts, Scumfucs and, finally, The Murder Junkies. Allin – whose motto was 'My mind is a machine gun, my body the bullets and the audience my target' – recorded some twenty albums in his lifetime, though none of these bears much revisiting. He'll always be better remembered for countless performances such as the one described above – and a long history of incarceration,

usually for drug possession, public obscenity, violent conduct or parole violation.

So, instead of the dramatic spectacle he had envisaged, G G Allin's passing was more a pitiful echo of so many rock 'n' roll deaths of the past. That he ever managed to impress respected names in US alternative music is frankly remarkable, yet among his supporters can be found Dinosaur Jr's J Mascis and Sonic Youth's Thurston Moore – both of whom claimed they'd wanted to work with the lunatic vocalist – as well as older-schoolers like Dee Dee Ramone (☞ *June 2002*) and Allin's shock-rock contemporary Wendy O Williams (☞ *April 1998*), both of whom have also since died.

JULY

Thursday 1

Dave Insurgent
(David Rubinstein – Queens, New York, 1964)
Reagan Youth

An even grimmer tale would affect New York's punk scene soon after. Influential punk band Reagan Youth had been formed by Jewish-American singer David Rubinstein (who later became Dave Insurgent) and his guitarist friend Paul Bakija (Paul Cripple) while the pair were still at high school in Rego Park. The band never made it big, but they were for many years a hot live attraction on Manhattan's punk scene. Their ironic use of Nazi/Ku Klux Klan get-up notwithstanding, Reagan Youth graduated to regular appearances at CBGB's with their songs about peace politics. A lack of commercial acceptance was frustrating to Reagan Youth, who appropriately disbanded at the end of President Reagan's term of office. The group

– mainly Insurgent – actively dealt in smack, but more serious was the fact that the singer's fiancée, Tiffany Bresciani, had moved into prostitution to fund her own addiction.

On the evening of 24 June, she and Insurgent made their usual trip to Houston Street to meet a regular client, the singer waiting near by until Bresciani reappeared. On this occasion, however, she did not return. Four days of apprehension were finally ended when Bresciani's body was found in the back of a truck that had been pulled over by police. The driver was Joel Rifkin – Long Island's most notorious serial killer, whose prime target was prostitutes, of whom he murdered seventeen. For Dave Insurgent, the horror and despair proved too much. Just one month before, his mother had died in a car accident; now the atrocity that befell his lover (and his own spiralling heroin problem) pushed the singer over the edge. Although the exact date is unknown, he died by his own hand the following month.

Wednesday 7

Mia Zapata
(Louisville, Kentucky, 25 August 1965)
The Gits

All she wanted from life was 'a cabin in which to live, a Jeep to drive and a sheepdog to ride shotgun'. Mia Zapata's was a powerful voice of conscience breaking out of an increasingly indulgent Seattle underground scene; many thought she had the stamina to make it big – but, as the above suggests, her aspirations tended more to the spiritual. The figurehead of bluesy punk-rockers The Gits – alongside Matt Fred Dresdner (with whom she formed the band in 1986 at college in Ohio, bass), Joe Spleen (guitar) and Steve Moriarty (drums) – Zapata was frequently categorized as a part of the burgeoning grunge and Riot Grrl (or 'Foxcore') movements, though the singer was always quick to distance herself from what she considered a fad. But, regardless of her dismissal of the music business, in 1993 – with a strong debut album, *Frenching the Bully* (1992), released on C/Z and a second, *Enter the Conquering Chicken* (1993), near completion – The Gits seemed on the verge of a major breakthrough anyway.

The socially adept Zapata enjoyed frequent nights out with friends and fellow musicians, and on the evening of 6 July 1993, she spent some hours doing what she enjoyed most – drinking into the night at Seattle's Comet Tavern. At around 2.30 am, Zapata bade farewell to a friend she had briefly visited on Capitol Hill and went in search of a cab home. Mia Zapata's body was discovered dumped in a dead-end street about an hour later by a streetwalker named Charity, who described the singer as lying in a cross formation with arms splayed. Zapata, it transpired, had been viciously assaulted, raped and then strangled with the drawstrings of her own sweatshirt.

Zapata's murder was the thirty-third recorded during an appalling year for Seattle homicides, but having left almost no evidence, the perpetrator eluded the authorities for almost a decade. The singer's death sent a huge shockwave around the area's thriving music community, and a string of fundraising events featuring huge Seattle bands Nirvana (for whom The Gits had often opened), Pearl Jam and Soundgarden drew much money but no further clues. Meanwhile,

fellow locally based female musicians such as Bikini Kill, 7 Year Bitch and former Runaways/Blackhearts singer Joan Jett started Home Alive, a self-defence programme for women. Finally, trace evidence matched saliva retrieved from Zapata's body to the DNA profile of 50-year-old Cuban immigrant Jesus C Mezquia, a transient construction worker and fisherman. Mezquia was a serial criminal with a history of violence towards women – and at the time of his apprehension had recently served a sentence in his home state of Florida for a separate felony. A verdict of first-degree murder was finally passed on 25 March 2004, and Mezquia was sentenced to thirty-six years in prison – effectively the remainder of his life. While the sentence at last brought justice, Zapata's former boyfriend Robert Jenkins described the emptiness still felt by all those connected to Mia Zapata: 'It brings something – but nothing like closure.' Recordings of Mia Zapata's remarkable voice and lyricism, of which none of the original band had ever been aware, came to light, preserved on tape, in the late nineties. These have now been issued on the compilation *Seafish Louisville*.

In interview, detective Richard Gagnan had described to Seattle radio station KUOW the prescience felt by him and his colleagues when flying to Miami to follow up the Florida lead. The flight tag – which he has kept to this day – read simply 'MIA'.

For information on Home Alive, visit www.homealive.org

'Mia was the best of our family. She had a complete and total social conscience – she cared about people.'

Richard Zapata, Mia's father

Don Myrick

(Chicago, Illinois, 6 April 1948)

Earth, Wind & Fire
(The Phenix Horns)

Although overshadowed by figureheads Maurice White and Philip Bailey, saxophonist Don Myrick was nonetheless an integral part of Earth, Wind & Fire – the giant Chicago-formed funk/R & B amalgamation that shot to stardom in the early seventies. Myrick had previously played with White in a jazz unit called, imaginatively, The Jazzmen (later The Pharaohs). His Phenix Horns [*sic*] – Rahmlee Davis, Michael Harris and Louis Satterfield (who died in 2004) – became EWF's back-up in 1975, the group presenting spectacular live shows to promote their music. One such concert performance was captured on *Gratitude* (1975); at this point, White, Bailey and co had achieved their first peak with 'Shining Star', a US number one and perhaps EWF's finest moment. Myrick – who stayed with EWF for seven years – developed a broader reputation within the industry and added his sax solos to the work of mainstream artists like Phil Collins, The Emotions, Heaven 17 and Deniece Williams.

It is often reported that Don Myrick was murdered: the fact is that he was shot accidentally by an LAPD officer searching for drugs. The officer had a warrant to search Myrick's apartment, but was too fast to react when he saw what he thought was a pistol in the musician's hand. There had been considerable drug paraphernalia on the premises – but the 'weapon' turned out to be a long cigarette lighter. The family of Don Myrick (who, it transpired, was using crack cocaine to alleviate the pain he had been suffering since his diagnosis with leukaemia) settled with the police department out of court for a rumoured $500K.

See also *Wade Flemons (☛ October 1993)*

Saturday 31

Bass Thing
(Rob Jones – Kingswinford, Dudley, 1964)
The Wonder Stuff
(The Bridge & Tunnel Crew)

A fan of British goth and metal as a young man, Rob Jones always wanted a career in rock 'n' roll but, sadly, he was not ready for success when it came knocking. Moving to London, Jones became a small-time roadie, involved in the underground thrash scene. A decent bass-player, he worked his way through a number of acts before leaving the capital to return home – where Stourbridge band The Wonder Stuff were seeking a final member. Assuming the nickname Bass Thing, Jones – with his trademark mop of black hair and his eyeliner – became a firm favourite among The Wonder Stuff's growing legion of fans, and the band's intelligent mix of folk and garage-style rock propelled them into the charts with debut album *The Eight Legged Groove Machine* (1988). Being in one of the UK's most promising rising bands, however, was not for Jones. With a second album, *Hup!* (1989), and a clutch of singles like 'Don't Let Me Down Gently'

'I always knew that bastard would make me cry.'

Miles Hunt, leader, The Wonder Stuff

performing well in the UK, The Wonder Stuff – Jones, Miles Hunt (vocals/guitar), Malcolm Treece (guitar) and Martin Gilks (who died in April 2006 – drums) – were in constant demand for photo shoots and television, which was all alien to Bass Thing, who sought solace in the bottle. He left the band for America that Christmas (to be replaced by Paul Clifford). In the States, Jones married and divorced in quick succession, he and his partner, Jessica Ronson – a former friend of his idol, Sid Vicious – having formed a short-lived band, The Bridge & Tunnel Crew.

While The Wonder Stuff became arguably the biggest leftfield band in Britain, Rob Jones was found dead in his New York apartment, having apparently suffered a heart attack. It is widely believed that he had been using heroin at the time.

AUGUST

Thursday 5

Randy Jo Hobbs
(Randolph County, Indiana, 22 March 1948)
The McCoys
Johnny Winter
Edgar Winter's White Trash
(Various acts)

Already fronting his own band, The Coachmen, 17-year-old bassist Randy Jo Hobbs joined brothers Rick (later known as Rick Derringer, vocals/guitar) and Randy Zehringer (drums), and Ronnie Brandon (keyboards) just as Union City garage-pop act The McCoys (originally Rick & The Raiders) were about to top the US charts with 'Hang On Sloopy' (1965). This record shifted some 6 million copies worldwide, opening up support slots for The McCoys with big

names like The Rolling Stones. With succeeding singles making diminishing returns, the group had a shelf-life of only a few years, though Hobbs was set for a prolific career in US rock 'n' roll for another two decades. The McCoys became Johnny Winter's backing band in the seventies, Hobbs then donning his Stetson and playing bass with the giant guitarist's brother Edgar Winter's band White Trash. Having also become close to Jimi Hendrix before his untimely death (☛ *September 1970*), Hobbs cultivated a mammoth drug habit that would finally kill him in 1993. By this time – despite a prolific career – Randy Jo Hobbs was reported to be flat broke and living on the breadline in Dayton, Ohio.

See also *Bobby Ramirez (☛ July 1972)*.

Tuesday 10

Euronymous
(Øystein Aarseth – Norway, 15 April 1968)
Mayhem

... and so, with much trepidation, *Number One in Heaven* steps once more into the warm and welcoming arena of Norwegian black metal, returning to the continuing drama of the genre's most notorious band. Their singer Dead having, yes, died (☛ *April 1991*), Mayhem were found not guilty of his killing but were thereafter labelled public enemies in Oslo – a position the remaining members clearly relished. Founder and guitarist Euronymous was soon revealed as leader of a group known as The Satanic Terrorists, a unit supposedly formed to crush Christianity in Norway, thereby returning the nation to its glorious Viking past; there were even reports that this faction had been behind the torching of a number of Norway's churches. But if the actions of some followers were clearly a very serious issue, then

'Euronymous is dead! And now I'm going to piss on his grave!'

Count Grishnackh calls his UK record label, Candlelight, just hours after the killing

Ian Stuart

(Ian Stuart Donaldson – Blackpool, 11 August 1957)

Skrewdriver

the unfolding story of Mayhem was to be almost blackly comic by contrast.

In 1992, the group were in need of a facelift. With bass-player Necrobutcher (Jorn Stubberard) leaving the line-up, Euronymous and drummer Hellhammer (Jan Axel Blomberg) sought new members with whom to complete *De Mysteriis Dom Sathanas*, an upcoming album, already written. Euronymous recruited singer Attila Csihar (ex-Tormentor) and, most significantly, a bassist called (ironically) Christian 'Varg' Vikernes, formerly of Burzum and better known by his stage moniker, Count Grishnackh. The events surrounding the making of 'the most over-rated record in black-metal history' were to become a dark landmark in music. During the recording and promotional touring (in one incident a watching fan was injured when struck by a severed lamb's head), relations between Euronymous and Grishnackh reached freezing point. The Count, who had idolized Euronymous in the past, attempted to curry favour with Mayhem's leader by presenting him with cartridges he claimed were from the gun that had killed Dead: the guitarist – who was not keen to keep Grishnackh in the band – was unimpressed, knowing that the gun in question had been his. Grishnackh, his head permanently filled with sick new concepts of Satanism, anarchy and racial purity, became obsessed

with the notion that Euronymous and other characters on the scene such as Faust were perceived as more evil than he was – and thus put a fairly blunt plan into action to change folks' acuity a little.

Arriving at Euronymous's Oslo flat at 5.15 am on 10 August 1993, Grishnackh produced a large knife and proceeded to stab his 'enemy' twenty-three times. The guitarist's body was found an hour later, clad only in underpants and covered in blood. From his prison cell (which the bassist often described as 'too comfortable and not violent enough'), Grishnackh recalled his earlier actions with glee: 'I hit him directly in his skull! His eyes went "boing!" and he was dead!' Sentenced to a maximum term, The Count continued to extol his fascistic views from his cell and issued further music under his electronic guise, Burzum. It was not the end for Mayhem, who – now officially the blackest metal band in the world – still record and tour to this day, which says much for their stamina and sheer nerve, if not for the judgement of record labels. But if these incidents did any good at all, they drew attention to a scene fast losing control of itself, flushing out a few serious wrong-doers in the process.

The notorious leader of right-wing punks Skrewdriver, Ian Stuart actually began his rock 'n' roll career as singer with Rolling Stones tribute act Tumbling Dice (although he should by no means be mistaken for *Number One in Heaven* entrant Ian Stewart (☛ *December 1985*)). The original Skrewdriver formed after seeing The Sex Pistols play in 1977, and were signed by Chiswick Records – the label nurtured the band's skinhead look, though later vehemently claimed to have had no notion whatsoever of the singer's neo-fascist leanings. The truth is, however, that Skrewdriver always attracted a violent faction within their audience. (Fairly good authority has it that unlikely fan Bob Geldof was knocked unconscious at one of their early gigs.)

The hardcore really moved in once Stuart had re-formed the band in 1982 (by which time they could only release material via German label Rock-o-Rama), Skrewdriver allying themselves with extreme groups like the National Front and Combat 18. Ian Stuart died in a car crash in Derbyshire that some of his supporters still believe was 'arranged' by Special Branch.

OCTOBER

Wednesday 13

Wade Flemons
(Coffeyville, Kansas, 25 September 1940)
Earth, Wind & Fire (The Salty Peppers)

Just months after the shock slaying of Don Myrick (🕮 *July 1993*), Earth, Wind & Fire's Maurice White learned of the death of another of his early acquaintances. Wade Flemons – already a veteran of the music business, having formed his first band at just thirteen – was signed to VeeJay as a solo vocalist when he encountered White in 1967. Both artists were founders of The Salty Peppers, a fairly basic act that somehow flourished and became EWF. During their time together, Flemons backed White's vocals as singer and keyboardist, witnessing the band's transition to stardom in 1972. White's power within Earth, Wind & Fire was such that he sacked the entire group just one year later – and Flemons was not exempted. Wade Flemons's career in music was thus curtailed, although he made some income from songwriting. He died from cancer at the age of fifty-three.

Sunday 31

River Phoenix
(River Jude Bottom – Madras, Oregon, 23 August 1970)
Aleka's Attic

Although primarily a cult actor, River Phoenix merits his place in *Number One in Heaven* for his numerous connections to the music world. Phoenix was the eldest of five children (the equally esoterically named Rain, Joaquin, Liberty and Summer, who are all also actors) born to Children of God devotees John and Arlyn Bottom, who (understandably) changed their surname by deed poll. With much encouragement from these proactive if unorthodox parents, ten-year-old River displayed his acting gift on national television before his movie debut in 1985's *Explorers*. A number of increasingly impressive parts were to follow: his role in *Running On Empty* (1988) earned Phoenix an Oscar nomination, while his best performance was in *My Own Private Idaho* (1991). Phoenix had also been a reasonably talented guitarist since childhood, forming the Florida-based band Aleka's Attic with his sister Rain; an album, the palindromically titled *Never Odd or Even*, was recorded, though it has never been released. The band's song 'Across the Way' can be heard on an album for PETA, one of many charities supported by the strict vegan – while Phoenix also sang on a 1992 album by his friend John Frusciante, of The Red Hot Chili Peppers.

At the end of October 1993, Phoenix was in Los Angeles for the shooting of his latest picture, *Dark Blood*. Evenings spent at Sunset Boulevard's Viper Room (a club then owned by actor Johnny Depp) were a given for any upwardly mobile face – but one was to end tragically. Phoenix, who had been partying heavily there, was, at around 1 am, offered some supposedly high-grade Persian coke by an acquaintance: immediately the substance had an adverse effect on the 23-year-old actor, who went into spasms before fleeing the men's room in search of his girlfriend, Samantha Mathis, and siblings Rain and Joaquin, who were at the bar. Phoenix was taken outside, where he collapsed, going into seizure and then cardiac arrest on the pavement in front of the club. Rushing Phoenix to the Cedars-Sinai Medical Center, paramedics inserted a pacemaker, but were unable to bring the actor back. He was pronounced dead at 1.54 am. The autopsy revealed ephedrine, marijuana and Valium in his system, as well as lethal levels of cocaine and morphine.

River Phoenix – whose coffin was tampered with by a press intruder the night before his cremation – wore a T-shirt bearing his band's name as he lay in state. Boasting many friends in the music business, the young star has been remembered in songs and albums by Anastacia (a former school-friend), Belinda Carlisle, Natalie Merchant, Brazilian musician Milton Nascimento, REM, Rufus Wainwright and The Chili Peppers, whose 1995 *One Hot Minute* collection contains tributes to deceased friends Phoenix and Kurt Cobain (🕮 *April 1994*), among others. Frusciante became massively depressed following Phoenix's overdose and was even presumed dead himself by those with whom he then lost touch. The musician had also witnessed the similar death of his guitarist hero, early Chili Pepper Hillel Slovak (🕮 *June 1988*). Frusciante finally re-emerged in January 1997 to play – you guessed it – The Viper Room.

NOVEMBER

Sunday 28

Jerry Edmonton
(Jerry McCrohan – Edmonton, Alberta, 24 October 1946)
Steppenwolf
(Sparrow)
(Various acts)

Twelve years after the car-crash death of Steppenwolf co-founder and bassist Rushton Moreve (🕮 *July 1981*) his long-time buddy, Canadian drummer

Jerry Edmonton, was killed in remarkably similar circumstances.

As The Sparrows (who originally recorded future Steppenwolf classic 'The Pusher'), Edmonton and Moreve recruited singer John Kay, kick-starting the career of Steppenwolf – the blues-rock band produced their barnstorming 1968 debut album in under a week. In terms of singles, Steppenwolf also appeared set for a long stay with the million-sellers 'Born to be Wild' – written by the drummer's brother Denny, aka Mars Bonfire – and 'Magic Carpet Ride' (both also 1968). The band remained popular through US rock's post-Woodstock period, but many line-up changes saw them split by the mid seventies. Edmonton served with other rock bands, including Manbeast and Unicorn, before his death in Santa Barbara, California, at the wheel of his car.

See also *Andrew Chapin (◂ December 1985)*

with former Rainbow drummer Bobby Rondinelli, so had something of a pedigree in top-division hard rock. Whether Gillen ever mentioned he'd auditioned for a part in Andrew Lloyd Webber's *Cats* is not recorded, though his tenure of just eighteen months suggests his secret might have leaked out. (To be fair, Sabbath as a band were falling apart around the time of 1987's *Eternal Idol* album.) Gillen began his own group, Badlands, a supergroup of sorts, which also featured Sabbath drummer Eric Singer, guitarist Jake E Lee (ex of Dio) and bassist Greg Chaisson – but a fractured career saw this band also break up, in 1992.

Although he was to form yet another act, Sun Red Sun, there were more sinister reasons for Ray Gillen's departure from Badlands. He had become very unwell, and depressed as a result of diagnosis with HIV, which he kept from family and friends until close to the end. Gillen died at home in New Jersey on 3 December – by coincidence, a date now recognized as World AIDS Day.

DECEMBER

Friday 3

Ray Gillen
(Cliffside Park, New Jersey, 12 May 1959)
Black Sabbath
Badlands
(Various acts)

Painfully good-looking and athletically lean, Ray Gillen would have seemed an unlikely vocalist for Black Sabbath ten years before, but once the metal pioneers took a more stadium-friendly stance, he appeared to fit the bill for their mid-eighties incarnation. The high-pitched vocalist jumped into the breach following the departure of Glenn Hughes; he'd already worked

'If we can't be free, at least we can be cheap.'
The wisdom of Frank Zappa

Frank Zappa

(Baltimore, Maryland, 21 December 1940)

The Mothers of Invention

(Various acts)

Few musicians took to the supposedly serious matter of music-making with the humour and panache of Frank Zappa. A genuine contender in the 'farthest out' stakes, Zappa displayed such sheer ingenuity in his vast output that he was always going to ruffle the feathers of a society unequipped to deal with his art and irony. But this was surely the catalyst for the man and his work – until his death, Zappa remained several steps ahead of an industry never his intellectual equal.

The part-Sicilian Zappa moved from Baltimore to California when he was just ten years old; Zappa Sr (yes, it was his real name) was a meteorologist studying poisonous gases. The headiness of the tarnished West Coast air clearly had some influence on his son, who, despite a chequered school career (he was once suspended for an impromptu display of homemade pyrotechnics), managed to graduate from the somehow appropriate-sounding Antelope Valley High. At fifteen, he was hanging with the likes of fellow maverick Don Van Vliet (the future Captain Beefheart), both fans of disparate musicians such as bluesman Howlin' Wolf and experimentalist Edgar Varèse. Together, they featured in an eight-piece R & B act called The Black-Outs, though neither showed much indication of things to come. Zappa's further education foundered and he ensconced himself in music theory and B-movie scoring. In 1962, though, he clashed with authority in an incident that was to inform much of his future direction: framed by an over-zealous vice squad, he was imprisoned for ten days after selling a fake porn tape to an undercover officer for just $100. (Unfazed, Zappa reminded them on his release that his subsequent probation would help him avoid the draft.)

Zappa fashioned a number of bands, many of which

Frank Zappa: Despite many scrapes over the years, no one dared park on his head ...

'Sometimes he sings. Sometimes he talks to the audience. Sometimes there is trouble.'

The sleevenotes for *Freak Out!* (1966)

featured Van Vliet and most of which bore odd names such as Captain Glasspack & The Magic Mufflers (probably informing Beefheart's later choices). The latter became The Mothers (originally spelled 'Muthers') on Mother's Day 1964, to be renamed – quite effectively in the event – 'The Mothers of Invention' by nervous Verve record executives. With the 1966 debut *Freak Out!* (the world's first double album), Zappa at last exhibited to any member of the public open-minded enough to listen his skills as social commentator as well as wordsmith and, of course, those of a damn fine guitarist. At this point, Zappa's lyrics were built around sexual punning (when he wasn't dedicating entire sides to Varèse) but his delivery was so gauche his songs could barely be considered offensive. Further great recordings followed (with the MOI line-up mutating, and disappearing, frequently): *Hot Rats* (1969) is still the most celebrated Zappa long-player, and even found the man a Top Ten position in Britain, where his shtick – initially appealing to fans of The Bonzos or Syd Barrett – began to pull in a wider audience. Throughout the seventies, the artist was either reinventing himself, his sound or The Mothers, or nurturing newcomers such as the extremely grateful Alice Cooper. And when he wasn't quite so busy, Zappa found time to father four children by his second wife, Gail Sloatman, esoterically naming them Moon Unit, Dweezil (a nickname legally adopted by his son), Ahmet Emuukha Rodan and Diva Muffin – thereby starting a whole new 'thing' among rock dads. When quizzed about this by Joan Rivers, Zappa's typically spot-on response was: 'Consider for a moment any beauty in the name "Ralph".'

Hugely prolific in the studio despite two bizarre incidents in 1971 (☛ *Closer!*), Zappa parodied – or completely attacked – a number of US institutions in his time, in 1979 turning his attention to disco with *Sheikh Yerbouti*, a thinly veiled slur against the trend. This record contained the tremendous 'Dancing Fool', one of two close shaves Zappa had with Billboard. (The other, 1982's 'Valley Girl', featured 14-year-old Moon Unit 'like, totally grossing out' on vocals.) Zappa showed undeniable prescience that same year with the issue of *Joe's Garage*, an album imagining a future in which music was outlawed: just six years later, he confronted the PMRC (Parents' Music Resource Center) at Capitol Hill, to justify his work, accusing the group, whom he dismissed as 'bored housewives', of promoting censorship. The entire hearing was made public via the brilliantly titled 1985 album *Frank Zappa Meets the Mothers of Prevention* and is transcribed in the autobiography he finished shortly before his untimely death.

In January 1990, Frank Zappa – who had suspected he was ill for a while – learned he was suffering from prostate cancer, and doubled his efforts to do justice to the countless ongoing projects he felt he might not have time to complete. Zappa soon became unable to perform live, and his two eldest children went public with news of their father's condition; he died at his Laurel Canyon home three years later, leaving some fifty albums in his wake. While it took until 1995 to install Zappa into the Rock 'n' Roll Hall of Fame (a move he would have in any case rebuked), the unique performer has since had a mollusc, a jellyfish, an Intel motherboard, a gene and at least two asteroids named in his honour.

See also *Henry 'Sunflower' Vestine (☛ October 1997).*

Close!
Frank Zappa
(The Mothers of Invention)

How Zappa made it into his fifties is remarkable when one takes on board the events that befell him in early December 1971. The Mothers were in Switzerland for a concert in Montreux when it all kicked off: an overexcited devotee chose to show his appreciation for Zappa by firing a flare into the ceiling, the resulting inferno destroying not only the venue, but also every last scrap of the musicians' equipment – save one cowbell. Zappa was upset by this (even rumoured to be suicidal) but opted to abandon further Continental dates for a couple of shows at London's Rainbow Theatre. At the end of the first of these, a jealous fan – 24-year-old Trevor Howell, whose girlfriend had a crush on Zappa – decided to attack the singer. In front of hundreds of onlookers, Zappa plunged ten feet into the orchestra pit, breaking his leg, injuring his spine and damaging his larynx. The artist (briefly rumoured to be dead by those gathered outside) was confined to a wheelchair for nine months and never sang the same way again. Howell served just one year of stir for his trouble.

The Swiss incident had a silver lining for Deep Purple, watching from the audience that night. The British rock behemoths sensibly evacuated the premises, watched the blaze from their hotel and promptly wrote a song about it – 'Smoke on the Water'.

Sunday 5

Doug Hopkins

(Tempe, Arizona, 11 April 1961)

The Gin Blossoms

(Various acts)

He might have had it all. Singer and guitarist Doug Hopkins was one of the more gifted of the new breed of US songwriters, but he took his own life just months before a major breakthrough saw The Gin Blossoms – the Arizona band he had helped form – become serious contenders. Hopkins had dabbled in music for many years, initially fronting Moral Majority with school-friend Bill Leen, whom he had taught to play bass. Various bands, such as The Psalms and Ten O'Clock Scholars, came and went before The Gin Blossoms (apparently named in honour of W C Fields's complexion) began in earnest in 1986, Hopkins and Leen eventually joined by singer Jesse Valenzuela, rhythm guitarist Robin Wilson and Philip Rhodes, already the band's third drummer. A tight, popular unit, The Gin Blossoms signed to A&M early in 1990, and a number of Hopkins-composed tunes made up the strong second album, *New Miserable Experience* (1992). The band thus became a staple of radio and MTV rotation. But by now Doug Hopkins was no longer in the band. From an early age he had suffered spells of severe depression, all too readily deflected with binge drinking – something with which his bandmates could no longer deal: by 1992 they had replaced the guitarist with

Scott Johnson. A bitter wrangle over future royalties ensued, the rest of the band attempting to buy Hopkins out for $15K. A year on, the musician – now with struggling band The Chimeras (whom he dramatically quit on stage) – could only stand and watch as two of his contributions, 'Hey Jealousy' and the fabulous 'Found out about You' became international hits, while the parent album shifted 3 million copies.

Increasingly embittered by both his former band's success and a split from his live-in girlfriend, Doug Hopkins – who had attempted suicide on six previous occasions – left rehabilitation, purchased a .38 from a pawn shop and ended his life at home in Tempe. Although they were to enjoy Top Ten success with a third album *Congratulations . . . I'm Sorry* (1996), The Gin Blossoms clearly lacked something without Hopkins, and disbanded in 1997.

Sunday 19

Michael Clarke

(Michael James Dick – Spokane, Washington, 3 June 1944)

The Byrds

The Flying Burrito Brothers

Firefall

Drummer with the legendary West Coast country-rock band The Byrds at the very height of their success, Michael Clarke remained in the seat throughout the group's best years. Having met singer/guitarist Roger (then Jim) McGuinn and early member David Crosby while playing the bars and coffee houses of San Francisco, Clarke was *in situ* for The Byrds' breakthrough cover of Dylan's 'Mr Tambourine Man' (1965) (but was not to hear his work on the chart-topping version, session men having been brought in to rerecord pretty much the whole song, bar McGuinn's trademark playing). For the next year or so, The Byrds – Clarke, Crosby, McGuinn, singer/writer Gene Clark and bassist Chris Hillman – were the top rock act across the USA, but the spectre of the session drummer was to return to haunt Clarke. After a flurry of excellent albums, the percussionist became disillusioned with a band that – unsurprisingly, given the wealth of talent therein – was pulling in different directions. He quit during the recording sessions for the 1967 album *The Notorious Byrd Brothers* (for which he co-wrote 'Artificial Energy'), much of his work rerecorded before the album's issue.

After a spell with Hillman in The Flying Burrito Brothers, Clarke founded soft-rockers Firefall with fellow Burrito, vocalist Rick Roberts. This mellow band – who scored a number of US hits starting with 'You are the Woman' (1976) – were ideally suited to the soft-rock excesses of the decade, and Clarke enjoyed a lifestyle of some wealth and hedonism. Although publicly anti-drugs, he was an infamous drinker. Re-forming The Byrds during the eighties, Clarke won a court battle with Crosby, Hillman and McGuinn, and joined Gene Clark on tour until the latter's death (➤ *May 1991*). Working until his own death from liver failure two years later, Clarke cut a sorry figure, years of alcohol abuse leaving him an emaciated shadow of his former self. He died at home in Treasure Island, Florida.

See also *Clarence White (*➤ *July 1973); Gram Parsons (*➤ *September 1973). Another former Byrds drummer, Kevin Kelley, died in 2002.*

'The first record was really Doug. It's a beautiful record and Doug was an intricate part of it.'

Jesse Valenzuela, singer, The Gin Blossoms

Lest We Forget

Other notable deaths that occurred sometime during 1993:

Bingy Bunny (Jamaican reggae guitarist with The Morwells and Roots Radics who also played with many big dancehall names; born Eric Lamont, 1954; prostate cancer, 1/1993)

Charizma (US MC who partnered producer Peanut Butter Wolf; born Charles Hicks, California, 1973; shot attempting to resist an unprovoked assault, 12/1993)

Nigel Dixon (UK rock/rockabilly singer with Whirlwind and Havana 3am; born Middlesex, 1956; cancer, 3/4 – just months ahead of Whirlwind drummer Phil 'Foghorn' Hardy's similar passing)

Marv Johnson (noted early Motown singer who scored a transatlantic Top Tenner with 1959's 'You Got What it Takes'; born Michigan, 15/10/1938; stroke at a backstage party, 16/5)

Criss Oliva (US metal guitarist who formed Savatage with his vocalist brother Jon; born New Jersey, 3/4/1963; car crash, 17/10 – his widow survived but was found dead at home 12 years later)

Panhead (Jamaican reggae DJ; born Anthony Johnson, St Mary, 1966; murdered, 10/1993)

Root Boy Slim (notorious singer with Washington politico-punks The Sex-Change Band; born Foster Mackenzie III, North Carolina, 9/7/1945; natural causes, 8/6)

Andy Stewart (jovial if stereotypical Scots entertainer who hit the UK Top Five in 1989 with his reissued 'Donald Where's Your Troosers?'; born Glasgow, 1933; heart condition, 11/10)

Sun Ra (ground-breaking pianist who influenced many jazz/funk acts; born Herman Sunny Blount, Alabama – or Saturn, as he liked to insist – 22/5/1914; stroke, 30/5)

Ray Williams (UK bassist with Welsh rockers Man; born Merthyr Tydfil, 1943; lengthy illness, 12/1993)

. . . and another who didn't

Hewhocannotbenamed, US guitarist with East Coast punks The Dwarves. Angered that the band had circulated an 'April fool' rumour that the musician (aka Peter Konik, proving that he *can* be named) had been stabbed to death in Philadelphia, their label – the increasingly influential Sub Pop – gave the band its marching orders.

For a complete list of fallen artists, visit

www.numberoneinheaven.com

1994

JANUARY

Saturday 15

Harry Nilsson

(Harry Edward Nelson III – Brooklyn, New York,
15 June 1941)

Wishing to follow in the footsteps of his mother, Harry Nilsson was principally a songwriter at the beginning of his career, working at a bank and submitting material to the likes of The Monkees, Ronettes and Yardbirds (who cut his 'Ten Little Indians'). Back then, Nilsson's three-octave range was undiscovered, until a spate of commercial jingles gave the singer wide exposure and won him a contract with RCA in 1967. His debut album, the curiously titled *Pandemonium Shadow Show*, was no commercial giant, but – largely because of a Beatles medley, 'You Can't Do That' – drew the attention of The Fab Four, of whom John Lennon would become a close friend. By 1969 Nilsson was enjoying a long-overdue hit with the reissued (and Grammy-winning) Fred Neil tune 'Everybody's Talkin'' (best known from its inclusion in the movie *Midnight Cowboy*) but by far his biggest was to be the Badfinger classic, 'Without You', a worldwide number

one and a song that outsold all others in 1972. Nilsson made no secret of his frustration that few of his own compositions matched the success of these. The fact that his singles choices were often trite, joky affairs never likely to sell (see 1976's 'Kojak Columbo') didn't alter this perception.

During 1974, while Lennon was apart from Yoko Ono, he and Nilsson were regularly ejected from Los Angeles bars for their behaviour – what had initially been planned as a 'lost weekend' lasted almost an entire year: the musicians worked together, played together, but most of all got perpetually hammered together. Nilsson's own misuse of alcohol was to cost him dearly twenty years later. Although his voice had been irreparably damaged by years of drinking, Nilsson was putting the finishing touches to a comeback album when he suffered a massive coronary in 1993 – from which he was never to recover.

DEAD INTERESTING!

HIGH-RATIO NILSSON

Set to die young himself, Harry Nilsson had a connection to an eerie number of high-profile rock deaths. The writers of his biggest hit, 'Without You', Pete Ham (➤ *April 1975*) and Tom Evans (➤ *November 1983*) both committed suicide in otherwise unrelated circumstances. Meanwhile, among his many music acolytes were 'Mama' Cass Elliot (➤ *July 1974*) and The Who's Keith Moon (➤ *September 1978*) – both of whom died at Nilsson's London flat.

Having been closely involved after the death by shooting of occasional Beatles collaborator Mal Evans (➤ *January 1976*), a shocked Nilsson was provoked by the assassination of his very close friend John Lennon (➤ *December 1980*) into speaking for the campaign against gun ownership in the US.

Saturday 22

Rhett Forrester

(Tucker, Georgia, 22 September 1956)

Riot

(Mr Dirty)

Rhett Forrester was tall, blond and good-looking, shaping up well as a tennis pro and brave enough to graduate from his mother La Fortune's ballroom-dance class. But with a voice reminiscent of Free's Paul Rodgers and the position of frontman for New York hard-rockers Riot, he was surely set for superstar status in rock music. (Forrester even threw a few handy 'bad boy' points into the mix by serving time for a gas-station robbery.) The singer had taken vocal lessons and auditioned for Riot, his natural charisma winning him the slot as the band opened for The Scorpions in 1982. For a while, the metal group were among the US's most popular live attractions, but after two consistent (if predictable) studio albums with Forrester, *Restless Breed* (1982) and *Born In America* (1983), they split amid disagreements with their management. Forrester took himself off to France, where he recorded his own album, *Gone with the Wind* (1986), Riot's fanbase switching allegiance to Forrester's solo career. A new project, Mr Dirty, was underway by January 1994.

Early on the morning of 22 January, Rhett Forrester was sitting at the wheel of his car at a north-west Atlanta intersection. According to a witness, he was approached by two men and an argument ensued; one of the men then produced a gun and shot the singer in the back, the bullet piercing his heart. Although Forrester was able to drive a few blocks before flagging down a police cruiser, he died as he tried to explain what had happened. More than ten years on,

no motive for the killing has ever come to light, and the perpetrators are apparently still at large. Original Riot singer Guy Speranza died in 2003.

MARCH

Friday 18

Ephraim Lewis

(Birmingham, England, 1968)

A soul/R & B vocalist of whom much was expected, Ephraim Lewis had been recording for four years by his tragic demise in 1994. Lewis was the youngest of eight children, who were prompted by their father, Jabez, to form a Jackson Five-style vocal/gospel act. Some of the kids – Ephraim included – acted on this, but the venture fell apart with the death of their mother in 1984. The 16-year-old Lewis then left home, to be discovered by Sheffield's Axis Studio, whose owners, Kevin Bacon and Jon Quarmby, believed that they might have hit upon the 'British Michael Jackson'. Elektra Records agreed that this young singer had something, signed him and issued a debut album, *Skin*, in 1991 – which then didn't perform as anticipated. Aside from sluggish album sales, Ephraim Lewis had one or two unresolved personal issues: splitting with a long-term girlfriend, he began an affair with student Paul Flowers, whom he had met by chance at (appropriately) Sheffield Botanical Gardens. They were apparently very happy, until

Lewis left the country. To improve his commercial potential, Elektra had sent Lewis to work with new songwriters in Los Angeles – but pretty much as soon as he'd touched down, the singer fell in with some questionable company. Now openly gay, Lewis wanted to use his incipient fame to promote a positive image to other young black gays (of whom there are precious few in the music industry). The downside of all this, however, was Lewis's increased use of drugs, particularly methamphetamine (speed) – the substance of choice in the West Hollywood gay community. On the day he died, Lewis, it seems, experienced a delayed reaction to the drug he had taken earlier in the week, and the young prodigy's behaviour degenerated into what was widely described as very public psychosis. When his naked antics at his apartment were reported to the police at 7 am, Lewis apparently descended into deep paranoia, attempting to escape arrest by scaling the tenement building's outside wall and leaping from balcony to balcony. At the top floor, he tried to break into a room by smashing a window, inflicting injuries on himself as he did so. Then the inevitable happened: Lewis missed a jump and fell, hitting the courtyard below via an ornamental ficus tree. He suffered extensive – and ultimately fatal – head injuries.

For years afterwards, his family pursued the possibility that Lewis's label – or the police – might be responsible for their boy's death, but to little avail. Of his seven siblings, a brother, Sylvester, also died in his twenties, while two others have had extensive treatment for psychiatric disorders.

'The music that guy had in him. He was as good as Sam Cooke.'

Richard Hawley, formerly of Lewis's labelmates The Longpigs

Tuesday 22

Dan Hartman
(Harrisburg, Pennsylvania, 8 December 1950)

The Edgar Winter Group

Keyboard/bass wizard Dan Hartman
played with his first band, The
Legends, at just thirteen – but his
prodigious talent didn't see any real
return for another decade. By then,
Hartman was a fully paid-up member of The Edgar Winter Group,
alongside other young rock luminaries like Rick Derringer and Ronnie
Montrose. The band scorched to US
number one with the largely improvised opus 'Frankenstein' in 1973.
'Free Ride', a follow-up hit later that
year, was penned by Hartman himself. But as the decade progressed,
Hartman – perhaps to the chagrin of
his R & B/rock buddies – developed
an interest in dance music, leaving
EWG in 1976 and signing with Blue
Sky. Two years later, gold-selling single
'Instant Replay' caused a sensation in
the discotheques and penetrated the
Top Ten in Britain, where the record
was on permanent radio rotation and
became one of that year's top sellers.
Hartman's biggest US hit was 1984's
catchy 'I Can Dream about You', also
a Top Twenty success in the UK,
where Hartman's 'Relight My Fire'
became a chart-topper for Take That
& Lulu just before his death.

Although he was diagnosed
with AIDS in the late eighties, Dan
Hartman continued working, producing records for artists of the calibre
and diversity of Foghat, Tina Turner,
Muddy Waters and Paul Young at his
own Schoolhouse Studios. The much-
respected musician died from a brain
tumour in Connecticut.

APRIL
Tuesday 5

Kurt Cobain
(Hoquiam, Seattle, 20 February 1967)

Nirvana

Maybe some are just too pure for success. Dubbed 'The
Voice of a Generation' when he was alive and 'The Last
Great Rock Star' after his death, Kurt Cobain – so he
claimed – never really wanted it. Behind those searching
blue eyes was the mind of a victim, a reluctant star who
despaired at the thought of mass acceptance. But if, as
Liam Gallagher might have it, Cobain was a 'fuck-up who
couldn't handle it', there are countless reasons for the
Nirvana frontman's slide into grunge hell – and not all are
directly related to the man's status as the top dog in rock's
pound. By the time grunge had become a 'brand' Cobain
was already streets ahead of the designer turmoil adopted
by his rivals. Through the brilliant, intuitive medium of
Nirvana's music, he made a difference; that his position
as number one was utterly deserved only goes to make
Cobain's tale more stirring.

Any two-bit psychologist will tell you that the kind of
dysfunctional upbringing endured by Cobain is likely to
encumber an individual's development, no matter how
outwardly happy or talented he or she may appear. As a boy
growing up in the logging-town backwater of Aberdeen,
Seattle, Cobain spent as many nights on the sofas of kindly
neighbours and schoolmasters – or even under a local
bridge – as he did at home. The busted-up relationships
of his parents (either together or apart) and the resultant
triangle of anger enveloping them and their young son
were what coloured the future star's lyrics. That so many of
his songs mention firearms is no coincidence either: when
the confrontational Cobain had 'gotten bored of throwing
shit at cars', he fished all his father's guns from the muddy
waters of the Wishkah – where they had been thrown by
his frustrated mother – and traded them for his first amp.
He discovered the power of the chord, first through Led
Zeppelin and then through British punk rock. Although he
was disappointed by the paucity of riffing in, for example,
The Clash's *Sandinista!*, it taught the young guitarist that
powerful needn't mean violent. Cobain started creating
his anthems as a teenager: he hung with Seattle heroes and
'godfathers of grunge' The Melvins, inspiring his own

Kurt Cobain: *Swore* that he didn't have a gun

band, Skid Row (who also went by various other names). Cobain learned both to play properly and to present himself, his music and his very original thoughts. But until they became Nirvana, nobody gave this band too much of a shout; eventually Sub Pop did, in 1989, allowing Cobain (vocals, guitar), Krist Novoselic (bass) and Chad Channing (percussion) to cut their first album, *Bleach*, for a bargain $600 (coughed up by temporary guitarist Jason Everman). The 'bargain' was, of course, Sub Pop's. *Bleach* surprised alt-rock fans by throwing a few melodies into the post-punk stew: one of Cobain's finest tunes, 'About a Girl' (allegedly written for his live-in girlfriend, Tracy Marander), had its first outing here.

Few bands find themselves the orchestrators of a seismic change in rock music: with *Nevermind* (1991), Nirvana – albeit unknowingly – became just that. For this album, the group had signed to Geffen for more than $250K and had established the classic line-up, with cheery drummer Dave Grohl the final piece of the jigsaw. The record's production (courtesy of pre-Garbage guitarist Butch Vig) was cleaner than anticipated, but it gave songs like 'Come as You Are' and 'Lithium' a defined edge that brought Cobain's work crashing into the mainstream. The tune that made the most impact was 'Smells Like Teen Spirit', a massive US/UK Top Tenner that the singer defiantly admitted was based on Boston's 1976 FM-anthem 'More than a Feeling'. 'Teen Spirit' (inspired by Bikini Kill guitarist Kathleen Hanna's graffiti on Cobain's bedroom wall) became – to its writer's chagrin – the era's defining moment. Astonishingly, *Nevermind* toppled Michael Jackson's *Dangerous* from Billboard's pole position on its way to estimated worldwide sales of more than 15 million. But Cobain and his band's disaffection with their sudden idolization was apparent. Nirvana's success had opened the door for a number of other Seattle bands, most notably the far-more-corporate Pearl Jam, whom Cobain hated (prime-movers Mudhoney, his friends, were surprisingly left behind), while shows attracted legions of Guns n' Roses-loving 'metal kids' – 'fuckheads who don't get it', according to the singer, who now kissed his bandmates and wore dresses on stage to infuriate the jock contingent. Many felt that such moves were a deliberate attempt by the band to self-destruct while at the top.

More self-destructive, though, was Cobain's predilection for hard drugs. While the Nirvana leader admitted to occasionally using, he promptly justified this by claiming heroin relieved an undiagnosed stomach condition from which he'd suffered since childhood. Now, his much-publicized relationship with Hole singer Courtney Love – a known user – prompted questions about addiction. The couple's marriage in Waikiki in February 1992 changed the dynamic of Nirvana for ever: regardless of her talent, Love was generally regarded as at best manipulative, not to mention highly jealous of any female in the singer's company (one of her main targets was Hole bassist Kristen Pfaff, who died in mysterious circumstances just two months after Cobain (☞ *June 1994*)) – and, initially at least, as riding Cobain's coat-tails to further her own career. To say that she didn't love the man would be unfair, though, and the couple were clearly delighted with the arrival of their daughter, Frances Bean, in August 1992. But within a week of the child's birth the Cobains' bliss had all but dissipated: a *Vanity Fair* article suggesting that Love – dismissively boastful of her drug proclivities – had used heroin while pregnant sent their world into cataclysm. The weight of responsibility was now on Kurt Cobain. Clearly aware of the glaring errors his wife had made in interview with Lynn Hirschberg, he found himself under fierce pressure to back her regardless. When the interview tapes were then made available to UK biographers Britt Collins and Victoria Clarke, the threats from both Cobain and (mainly) Love, towards Clarke particularly, were shocking in their violence and ferocity. In early 1993, they suffered the humiliation of having to win a court battle in order to regain custody of their daughter.

Around the time of Nirvana's third album, it became clear to both Grohl and Novoselic that their friend and colleague was now someplace else. (Grohl in particular was vociferous in his dislike of Courtney Love's interference, referring to her as 'Yoko' – as opposed to the '[Sid and] Nancy' comparison, which, for some reason, the couple preferred.) It could be debated for ever whether Cobain

'The worst crime is ... for you to continue to be a rock star when you *fuckin' hated it!*'

Courtney Love's voice addresses the issue and the crowd, 10 April 1994 had actually begun to show suicidal tendencies by the release of the remarkable Steve Albini-produced *In Utero* (1993, originally to be entitled, flippantly, *I Hate Myself and I Want to Die*) – but the singer's increasingly wilful behaviour, plus frequent drug stupors and disappearances, were starting to tear Nirvana asunder. In the light of Cobain's death, the record is painful to listen to, a damaged, disturbed rampage through everything he and Nirvana had created – though this is not to say that *In Utero* isn't still hugely powerful and compelling, achieving what the band had intended, not to mention light-years ahead of the output of their main rivals. Even if Geffen hated it.

In the last year of his life, Cobain attempted to kick heroin, which he claimed made his stomach problems unbearable once more. Then, by some miracle, a doctor came up with a diagnosis, scoliosis – temporarily relieving the delighted singer from one of his major burdens at least. The burden of coming off heroin was, however, one he seemed less able to accommodate. During 1993, police made many visits to his home, usually to investigate either drugs or firearms possession (Cobain claimed his guns were purely for protection). Cobain was also banged up for several hours after an alleged assault against Love. By the start of 1994 he was talking of divorce. Then in early March 1994, a distraught Courtney Love called for help from a Rome hotel room, where Cobain had apparently overdosed. Nirvana's tour had been postponed because of the singer's throat infection, and he, Love and Frances Bean had attempted to spend some quality time in the Italian capital – though even this seemed beyond Cobain now.

On 8 April, Gary Smith was fitting security lighting when he made the discovery that so many in Cobain's world had dreaded. Despite a major search for the AWOL singer, the maintenance man was the only one who had thought to enter a room called 'the greenhouse' above the garage at the musician's Seattle home. Cobain's body was found slumped with a 20-gauge Remington shotgun resting on his chest – he had been dead for three days, killed by a single bullet wound to the mouth. By his side was an open wallet and driver's licence, presumably for identification; as well as Cobain's well-publicized suicide note, there was also drug paraphernalia near by. Within the hour the shocking news flashed across the world. A verdict of suicide was passed with little ado, and the media circus epilogue for a rock great began in earnest. Tributes came and went as expected, with Courtney Love leading a wake on 10 April that was undermined by a number of Cobain's friends choosing to retire to Krist Novoselic's house afterwards. In Seattle's Space Needle Park, 5,000 Cobain followers held their own vigil, singing Nirvana songs and burning their flannel shirts in what *Spin* magazine described as 'an awesome moment of pagan catharsis'. Inevitably, sales of Nirvana records thereafter went through the roof – and at least sixty-eight

copycat suicides were reported. (As for the other musicians, Courtney Love and Hole enjoyed brief fame (before the singer attempted various reinventions of herself, most notably as a Versace-clad movie starlet), Grohl still enjoys rock superstardom with Foo Fighters, while Novoselic saw two projects, Sweet 75 and Eyes Adrift, bite the dust before becoming politically active.)

Although the external signs point to an open-and-shut suicide, twelve years on there are an increasing number of dissenting voices. Leading a crusade that has spawned countless books and websites (and an intriguing documentary by British film-maker Nick Broomfield) is private investigator Tom Grant, hired by Love to investigate Cobain's earlier disappearance. Grant has since turned against his former employer, who, in his view, stood to lose everything had the couple divorced. Grant has run an ongoing campaign for the case to be reopened. (Among his claims are that, at his death, Cobain was loaded up with so much heroin that it would have been impossible for him to fire a gun and that there were no fingerprints on the weapon.) Furthermore, both Cobain's best friend, Dylan Carlson, and Frances Bean's nanny, Jackie Ferry (who had resigned a week before Cobain's passing), have stated that most of the couple's rows towards the end seemed to involve money – and, most crucially, Cobain's will. Remarkably, another dissenting voice is that of Love's father, Hank Harrison, a former manager of The Grateful Dead. Less convincing, though nonetheless intriguing, was the claim of Washington schlock-rocker Eldon 'El Duce' Hoke that Love had offered him money to kill her husband – before he died in mysterious circumstances himself (☛ *April 1997*). But the authorities apparently remain satisfied by the suicide verdict, while what little evidence coming to the fore tends to be snuffed by Love's lawyers.

Wendy Cobain – Kurt's mother – memorably talked of her son 'going and joining that stupid club' on learning of his untimely suicide. 'Stupid', perhaps, but 'exclusive' undeniably: dying at twenty-seven, the Nirvana singer joined the ranks of such figureheads as Robert Johnson (☛ *Pre-1965*), Brian Jones (☛ *July 1969*), Jimi Hendrix (☛ *September 1970*), Janis Joplin (☛ *October 1970*) and Jim Morrison (☛ *July 1971*).

Lee Brilleaux

(Lee Green – Durban, South Africa,
10 May 1952)

Dr Feelgood

(Pigboy Charlie)

A family man fascinated by history, country life and travel, Lee Brilleaux once said that he'd rather attend a dog race than go clubbing – all of which pretty much sums up the unspoiled attitude of a man whose quiet personal life ran at odds with his intense stage image. Young Lee Green pitched up in the unlikely setting of Canvey Island in Essex, exposing himself to a subculture of R & B, blues and pub rock. Splitting from their jug band, Pigboy Charlie, in 1971, Green (soon to become Brilleaux, vocals) and Sparko (John B Sparks, bass) melded with Wilko Johnson (John Wilkinson, guitar) and The Big Figure (Johnny Martin, drums), who were members of the Southend-based Roamers. The genesis of their name, Dr Feelgood, varies depending on the source, but the most likely derivation – given Brilleaux's love of the blues – is the 1962 Piano Red song of that name. With the snarling Brilleaux and bug-eyed Johnson holding court, Dr Feelgood became essential live viewing, and were the most incendiary group in a scene populated by up-and-coming bands like The Kursaal Flyers and Eddie & The Hot Rods. Nobody was especially surprised when the band signed with United Artists in 1974. Although a great debut single, 'Roxette' (1974), and mono-recorded album *Down by the Jetty* (1975) were slow sellers, it was only a matter of time before the British public caught on. The next three albums all made the UK Top Twenty – the chart-topping live *Stupidity* (1976) was a career high. (Unashamedly British

Lee Brilleaux: Despite this picture, he did it right

about their R & B, Dr Feelgood were obviously going to be a harder sell in the US: the 'jetty' of their first album was situated in Canvey as opposed to America's Deep South.) After Johnson left, Brilleaux and his band experienced a drop in commercial fortunes, although the sinister and infectious 'Milk and Alcohol' (1979) gave them a deserved Top Ten hit. By the mid eighties Brilleaux was the only surviving original member, but steadfastly ploughed on, even issuing a self-titled solo album in 1986.

Dr Feelgood, in one form or another, played 200-plus gigs most years, a tribute to the stamina of their great frontman. Even with his health clearly failing him, Brilleaux played up until January 1994 – his death from lymphoma sadly all but obliterated by the events of a couple of days before, which were only just reaching the rock press.

MAY

Baron Frederik van Pallandt

(Copenhagen, 4 May 1934)

NINA & Frederik

Born into wealthy Danish aristocracy, Frederik van Pallandt didn't really need the royalties from big-selling hit records, but he managed a few nonetheless, with his partner, Nina Magdalene Møller. The duo recorded quaint folk songs as Nina & Frederik, and gained popularity in Europe with a series of hit singles – the best known, the lullaby 'Little Donkey', took them to number three in the UK during Christmas 1960 (the year in which they married). The couple's act, however, became obsolete with the onset of the beat boom, and they ceased recording, eventually splitting in 1969. While Nina van Pallandt went on to some fame as a movie actress, her estranged husband lived in seclusion on a farm in Ibiza. His murder in 1994 remains unresolved, though stories of a contract killing abounded at the time. More likely is that he was shot dead by robbers trying to steal his boat.

Monday 23

Jimmy Fernandez

(Los Angeles, California, 1965)

The God Machine

Nestled somewhere between the twin plateaux of metal and industrial rock, The God Machine's brooding work was to prove influential to a number of late-nineties bands in both the US and UK, where the band had relocated in 1990. Comprising school-friends Jimmy Fernandez (bass), Robin Proper-Sheppard (his real name, vocals/guitar) and Ronald Austin (drums), the trio developed a following in their home city of San Diego. Eventually picked up by the London-based Fiction label, TGM recorded a pair of well-received albums, and were compared to Jane's Addiction, Smashing Pumpkins and Soundgarden – but it was clear to most that theirs was an altogether darker muse.

Sadly, the second God Machine long-player emerged just months after the death of Fernandez, in September 1994. Complaining of a migraine, the bassist had slipped into a coma and died three days later of a brain haemorrhage at London's Royal Free Hospital. The posthumous album was released under the title *One Last Laugh in a Place of Dying* – after which, Sheppard and Austin called it a day. Their tribute to Fernandez was simple, yet touching: 'He believed that no matter what tragedy should befall one or what pain lies hidden beneath the surface, you are never alone.'

JUNE

Saturday 4

Derek 'Lek' Leckenby

(Leeds, 14 May 1943)

Herman's Hermits

(The Wailers)

Although regarded as somewhat lightweight in comparison with The Beatles, Kinks or Rolling Stones, Herman's Hermits, it should be remembered, shifted a phenomenal 10 million records in the US alone during 1965. The Manchester-formed quintet – eldest member Leckenby (guitar), former child actor Peter Noone (vocals), Keith Hopwood (guitar), Karl Green (bass) and Barry 'Bean' Whitham (formerly with Leckenby in The Wailers, drums) – had already stormed to number one in the UK with the Carole King/Jerry Goffin-penned debut single 'I'm into Something Good' (1964). Consistent hit-makers at home, Herman's Hermits became an absolute sensation in America after an appearance on the influential *Ed Sullivan Show*, giving The Fab Four a serious run for their money the following year. Perhaps the most important musician in the group, Leckenby added innovative playing to tracks like 'Mrs Brown, You've Got a Lovely Daughter' (1965), a song the band felt too corny for UK release but one of several gold records Stateside. By 1971, the moment had pretty much passed for a group that had done well to retain impetus for that long. Noone's attempt at an only briefly successful solo career forced Herman's Hermits to consider a different approach – Leckenby and his remaining colleagues recruited a new singer (Peter Cowap, who died just three years after Leckenby) and took a country direction.

Diagnosed with non-Hodgkins lymphoma, Leckenby ignored medical advice and continued to play with the latest incarnation of Herman's Hermits during 1992. His condition worsening, he died in his adopted home town, Manchester.

Thursday 16

Kristen Pfaff

(Amherst, New York, 26 May 1967)

Hole

Janitor Joe

Just two months after the death of her husband, Courtney Love was hit by another loss – and *Live Through This*, the choice of title for the second Hole album, appeared more prophetic by the day. University of Minnesota graduate Kristen Pfaff took to the bass quite late on, but her attitude and sass with rock band Janitor Joe prompted Hole guitarist Eric Erlandson to offer her the space left by departing bassist Jill Emery. By the start of 1993 Hole – now Pfaff, Love, Erlandson and Patty Schemel (drums) – were enjoying some serious hype, helped by the emergence of a number of strong female-founded bands, not to mention Love's relationship with Kurt Cobain. The band, with a debut album, *Pretty on the Inside* (1991), behind them, had been taken on by the big boys at Geffen (yep, Nirvana's label), strong tracks like 'Violet' and 'Doll Parts' auguring well for the second record in 1994.

Cobain's suicide (➤ *April 1994*) put on hold Hole's plans for promoting *Live Through This*, and an immediate hiatus seemed the best way of dealing with a situation that, aside from widespread grief, had created a great deal of suspicion. Just before his death, Cobain had made little secret of his 'admiration' for Hole's bass-player and the breakdown of his relationship with Love led Kristen Pfaff to feel threatened by the Hole leader. Pfaff – herself just out of a relationship with Erlandson – decided to cut loose from the misery of Seattle and hook up again with Janitor Joe, who were leaving for a brief tour. Her friend Paul Erickson hired a haulage van and prepared to drive the bassist out of Washington on the morning of 16 June, though how permanent an arrangement this might have been will never be known. When Erickson called on her at 9 am, there was no reply. He allegedly let himself into her apartment and broke into the bathroom to find Pfaff's body slumped in the bathtub, an array of drug paraphernalia by her side. Because she had recently undergone rehabilitation for heroin use, a verdict of accidental death was passed, but Pfaff's family, among others – who maintain the position to this day – were adamant that there had been foul play here, as well as in Cobain's case; Courtney Love was instructed not to attend Pfaff's funeral in Buffalo, New York.

> **'I think she's a fucking talented musician. I think she's so beautiful, but if I told her that and Courtney found out, it'd be hell.'**
>
> Kurt Cobain on Kristen Pfaff

Friday 24

Mick Wayne

(Hull, 1945)

The Pink Fairies

David Bowie

(The Hullabaloos)

(Various acts)

Basing their name on that of their home town, The Hullabaloos were formed around 1965, while guitarist Mick Wayne also played with bands like The Outsiders (with whom he cut the Jimmy Page-penned single 'Keep on Doing It'), Bunch Of Fives, The Tickle and Junior's Eyes – before a major break came his way via the initially unheralded David Bowie. Wayne backed the young singer on 1969's hit 'Space Oddity' – further royalties came his way when a 1975 reissue topped the chart – and Junior's Eyes continued to back Bowie on tour. Wayne's next band were infamous hippies The Pink Fairies, whom he joined in 1972, staying with the band for just a few months before all concerned realized it wasn't likely to work. So Mick Wayne's legacy as one of rock's greatest journeyman guitarists was cemented: he spent the next couple of decades as a session musician before relocating to Michigan, where he also became a well-respected producer. Wayne had been working on a solo album and in conjunction with Phil Collins shortly before his shocking demise. Trapped in a friend's house, Wayne burned to death in a freak fire.

See also *Steve Peregrin Took (➤ October 1980). Early Pink Fairies drummer Dave Bidwell died in 1977.*

Monday 27

Deah Dame

(Debra Jean Hurd – Houston, Texas,
20 September 1958)

Damian Dame

Briefly a sensation in New Jack Swing, Damian Dame – Deah Dame and Damian Broadus – were a tight, competent duo whose career was cut short by a double tragedy. Damian Dame were the first act to record for LaFace (who a couple of years later hit the jackpot with TLC), Deah Dame's strong writing and cool vocals the focal point of their output. An R & B chart-topping single 'Exclusivity' and self-titled debut album (both 1991) showed promise, the production duo of Babyface and Reid lifting the music above the mundane. Before a follow-up could be completed, however, Dame – who at thirty-six was a mite older than most of her peers – died in a car accident. In the wake of the tragedy, Broadus continued as a producer until his own early death (☛ *June 1996*). By chilling coincidence, this occurred exactly two years to the day after the passing of Deah Dame.

JULY

Sunday 17

Chuck Valle

(Charles G Valle – Queens, New York,
10 July 1965)

Murphy's Law
Ludichrist
Dripping Goss

Emerging from New York's hardcore punk scene in the early eighties,

Murphy's Law appealed to fans of both metal and the new wave with their trashy, uncompromising sound. Sneery Chuck Valle – one of many bassists employed by the band – stood out from the rest: he was a decent musician who acquired studio and production skills throughout his career. He played concurrently with the similar-veined Ludichrist (formerly Intestinal Militia) and Dripping Goss. Before his untimely death, Valle engineered a number of punk and rap artists' recordings.

Murphy's Law had something of a following on the West Coast, and were touring in Los Angeles when tragedy struck. After a successful show, the band were queuing for hot dogs outside the venue when Chuck Valle was approached by a man who took exception to him. After a brief argument, the assailant pulled a knife and, in an apparently motiveless attack, stabbed the bassist, who died at the scene.

SEPTEMBER

Saturday 3

Major Lance

(Winterville, Mississippi, 4 April 1939)

A childhood friend of Curtis Mayfield – they were brought up in the same Chicago housing project and both attended Wells High School – Major Lance developed into a fine Midwestern soul singer, Mayfield providing him with ammunition in some strong compositions. Lance had signed first to Mercury, then, in 1962, to OKeh Records, giving up earlier ambitions of becoming a boxer. The singer hit almost immediately with Mayfield's popular 'The Monkey Time' (1963), a song that elevated Lance into the pop Top Ten and, like so

many other tunes of that era, spawned a brief but impacting dance craze. Further hits were to follow; the biggest by far was 'Um Um Um Um Um Um' (1964). This was the only one of his songs to make any impression on the British charts, though a UK tour the following year saw Lance backed by the as-yet-unknown Elton John.

Those early US hits were very much the pinnacle of Major Lance's career, though he did find a willing audience during the UK Northern soul boom of the seventies. The rest of Lance's career was dogged by misfortune. A return to the US in 1974 presaged the start of a promising business career, with the launch of his Osiris Records with friend and producer Al Jackson Jr (of Booker T & The MGs), but Jackson's shocking murder (☛ *October 1975*) put the project in jeopardy. Major Lance's world all but collapsed in 1978, however: a conviction for supplying cocaine resulted in three years' detention; the once-popular vocalist's audience had all but disappeared by his release. The nostalgia circuit provided a small safety net, but by 1987 Major Lance's health was failing him. Suffering fading vision and a first heart attack, he was forced to take life more easily, and although his August 1994 performance at the Chicago Jazz Festival was well received, Lance died from heart failure at his Georgia home just weeks later.

Tuesday 27

Ken 'Dimwit' Montgomery

(Vancouver, British Columbia, 1958)

DOA
(Various acts)

One of the most notable aspects of the Vancouver underground scene was the band–instrument trading that seemed to take place ad infinitum. A former member of fondly remembered band The Skulls, Ken Montgomery was one of a number of drummers to pass through the ranks of Canadian punks DOA (Dead On Arrival). 'Dimwit' – as he was widely known – joined the band at the suggestion of his younger brother Charles (aka 'Chuck Biscuits'), himself a founder percussionist of the band. The two brothers – a third brother was DOA's roadie – spent time behind the traps of several Vancouver punk bands, The Pointed Sticks, Subhumans and Victorian Pork among them. By far the leaders of the scene, though, were DOA, who could claim fans in Nirvana, who opened for them at a 1989 Seattle gig.

'Dimwit' Montgomery had a couple of spells as DOA's drummer before turning down the opportunity to join thrash-rockers Slayer to form his own band, The Four Horsemen. He was no junkie, but had developed an escalating heroin habit by the time of his death. Having purchased a near-100-per-cent-pure batch of China White, the drummer overdosed almost immediately in his bedroom. 'Dimwit' was apparently buried with his favourite sweater, his drumsticks and a cookie. Within months, though, DOA – who had already seen early bassist Simon Wilde die of a brain tumour – were dealing with a third tragedy: the appalling death of yet another drummer, Ken Jensen (➤ January 1995).

OCTOBER

Thursday 27

Robert White

(Harrisburg, Pennsylvania, 19 November 1936)
The 'Funk Brothers'
(Various acts)

An early member of Motown's classic in-house band, guitarist Robert White had started as a touring musician with Harvey Fuqua's pioneering vocal line-up The Moonglows. Poached by Berry Gordy, White soon fell in with a host of great musicians as the 'Funk Brothers', the band essentially formed to back groups like The Four Tops. He was never to achieve the status of 'Benny' Benjamin, 'Jamie' Jamerson and Earl Van Dyke, but White was a feature of the set-up until 1972, when Gordy shifted Motown's offices to Los Angeles. Like most of his fellow musicians, White remained very much in the background, only emerging for a Temptations reunion several years before his death during open heart surgery.

See also *'Benny' Benjamin (*➤ *May 1969); James 'Jamie' Jamerson (*➤ *August 1983); Earl Van Dyke (*➤ *September 1992). Other occasional 'Funk Brothers' Eddie 'Bongo' Brown (1984), 'Pistol' Allen and Johnny Griffith (both 2002) have also died.*

NOVEMBER

Friday 4

Fred 'Sonic' Smith

(West Virginia, 13 September 1949)
The MC5
Sonic's Rendezvous Band

An undisputed prime architect of punk's visceral noise, MC5 founder Fred 'Sonic' Smith traded licks with Wayne Kramer, the pair creating one of the most dynamic guitar partnerships rock has seen. Arriving in Detroit – to the awakening strains of Motown – the rebellious Smith was soon kicked out of the very junior high at which he and Kramer first planned their musical diversion. They were tight musicians, but as The Bounty Hunters the pair ploughed few original lyrical avenues until the recruitment of bassist/lead singer Rob Tyner; as The MC5 the band gelled into a unit most still call 'the best band you never saw'. Adopted as mascot by the vehemently anti-government White Panther Party (their influence on punk was not purely in sound), The MC5 developed a distinct reputation as underground rock bad boys, their milestone first record, *Kick out the Jams* (1969), putting the polemic on to vinyl. But, with stage stunts such as the burning of the US flag, they found it hard to secure gigs anywhere – and record sales suffered accordingly. A less militant second record, *Back in the USA* (1970), unfortunately presaged a split within the ranks. Smith had now become the main songwriter, the subject matter shifting to the less cerebral. After one further collection, The MC5 disbanded. The post-MC5 'Sonic' Smith was altogether quieter, but put together a new act, The Rendezvous Band, which, although

'It's a lesson to people who might think heroin is a fun thing. It's a stupid, bloody horrible thing.'

Joey 'Shithead' Keithley, singer, DOA

nowhere near as influential as his first, was still a pretty decisive unit. This was very much a Detroit supergroup, comprising The Rationals' Scott Morgan, former Stooges drummer Scott 'Rock Action' Asheton and bassist Gary Rasmussen of Up. The guitarist then chanced upon rising new-wave poet Patti Smith at a party in Coney Island in 1976 – 'The Smiths' went on to become one of rock's cooler married couples in 1980, then surprised many by retiring from music to raise two children. Smith did, however, write most of his wife's quiet 1988 comeback album, *Dream Of Life*, though by now the harder living of his youth was beginning to take its toll on the guitarist's health. He was not alone: Rob Tyner's unexpected passing (➤ *September 1991*) prompted Smith and other former MC5ers to perform in tribute to their former singer.

But within three years Smith too was dead. Patti Smith was utterly devastated by the death of her husband from heart failure in a Detroit hospital; the grieving singer relocated to New York.

Wednesday 16

Dino Valenti

(Chester Powers – Danbury, Connecticut, 7 November 1943)

Quicksilver Messenger Service

Cusping the hippy scenes of both East and West coasts, singer/guitarist Dino Valenti was a colourful figure critical to the formation of acid-rockers Quicksilver Messenger Service. The young Valenti and his sister were born to variety entertainers, and spent most of their childhood travelling from town to town; Valenti was labelled 'the magical brat', owing to his act and general demeanour. Although he suffered a broken marriage, early experiences left Valenti unfazed by

strong personalities, which was to his advantage as he moved west into a houseshare with David Crosby (of The Byrds), Paul Kantner (of Jefferson Airplane) and bassist David Freiberg, who joined him at the birth of QMS – alongside the brilliant John Cipollina and Gary Duncan (guitars), Greg Elmore (drums) and later Nicky Hopkins (keyboards). Previously a 'minstrel' with a few solo sides for World Pacific, Valenti's first achievement on the signing of Quicksilver to the ubiquitous Elektra was to get himself banged up for drug possession. At a time when the authorities were making examples of young people (Mick Jagger, Brian Jones, etc), Valenti was, to his horror, given a custodial sentence, and had to sell the rights to his finest song, 'Get Together', to bust himself out of jail. 'At the time, I figured I could always write another,' claimed Valenti after his release. Cipollina, who had previously befriended the singer, was distinctly put out by Valenti's return, QMS having cut a couple of long-players without their renegade frontman – and promptly left the band. In Valenti, he, like many others, saw a confrontational character; most put this trait down to the frontman's previous 'gypsy' lifestyle. The truth was, however, that Valenti had a rare brain condition, undiagnosed until it became life-threatening.

With QMS a distant memory (the band never recovered without Cipollina), Dino Valenti underwent major surgery around 1983 – but it was clear he was living with a condition that was in effect something of a time bomb. Valenti died a decade later in Santa Rosa, leaving a legacy of many fine songs to the Library of Congress. The Jimi Hendrix hit 'Hey Joe', however, was not written by Valenti, despite many claims to the contrary.

See also *John Cipollina (➤ May 1989)*

Tommy McManus

(Enniskillen, Northern Ireland, 1966)

Mama's Boys

On the same day, another childhood illness resurfaced to claim its victim. Plucky drummer Tommy McManus had been diagnosed with leukaemia at just nine years old, and stunned doctors by apparently defeating the disease within a couple of years. Growing up in rural County Fermanagh, McManus and his brothers Pat (guitar) and John (bass) followed a heritage of traditional Irish music before a career in soft metal beckoned, with support slots to Irish rockers Horslips and Thin Lizzy in the early eighties. A contract with Jive gained proper distribution for the band's fourth album (no less), but it was in America that Mama's Boys attracted most attention. McManus suffered his first relapse as the band's Slade cover 'Mama Weer All Crazee Now' (1985) was breaking across the Atlantic. A second relapse occurred in 1992, when the hard-working four-piece were on a tour of Europe, this time more serious, and the young drummer was advised to undergo a bone-marrow transplant. Tommy McManus waited a year for a donor to be found, but sadly passed away during the operation. His two brothers – having composed a eulogy to their sibling called 'Brother's Lament' – closed the book on Mama's Boys and re-entered the world of more traditional Irish rock as Celtus in 1996.

Wednesday 23

Tommy Boyce
(Sidney Thomas Boyce – Charlottesville, Virginia,
29 September 1939)

Tommy Boyce was one of the most prolific US songwriters in the sixties. After a fruitless recording career as a teen pin-up, Boyce's first successful tune was 'Be My Guest', a Top Ten hit for Fats Domino in 1959 – further compositions for Curtis Lee ('Pretty Little Angel Eyes' and 'Under the Moon of Love') got Boyce invited to work at the fabled Brill Building in New York, where he was partnered with Bobby Hart. The pair really hit paydirt with the million-selling 'Come a Little Bit Closer' (1964) for Jay & The Americans and, moving to Screen Gems, a number of songs for the Monkees, for whom they shared songwriting duties with another young product of Brill, Neil Diamond. Boyce finally realized the dream of his own Top Ten hit with his and Hart's 'I Wonder What She's Doing Tonight?' (1968), and, during the seventies, the duo toured with Mickey Dolenz and Davy Jones. As a quartet, they regularly performed The Monkees' 'Last Train to Clarksville' – Boyce and Hart's only Billboard chart-topping composition.

Tommy Boyce suffered a severe brain aneurysm at the age of forty-three, which had a hugely detrimental effect on the demeanour of this previously 'up' individual. Attempting to deal with depression, he appeared on US chat shows and revealed his worsening condition to millions. Boyce – writing his autobiography at the time – committed suicide in strangely similar circumstances to his long-time friend, singer Del Shannon, who also died at the age of fifty-five (◄ *February 1990*). Just as he appeared to have overcome the worst of the affliction, Boyce was found by his wife on the morning of 24 November 1994. The songwriter had apparently shot himself in the head.

DECEMBER

Saturday 10

Garnett Silk
(Garnett Smith – Manchester, Jamaica,
2 April 1966)

Beginning his career as a juvenile 'toaster', Garnett Smith was known as Little Bimbo before choosing the smoother moniker that would complement his adult vocal style. Silk made his first recordings as an 18-year-old DJ – under the guidance of natural mentor Tony Rebel – though his first bona fide release was 'Problems Everywhere' (1987), which earned him the respect of fellow artists such as Sugar Minott, who worked with him as a result. Silk was shortly to convert to Rastafarianism, a transition marked by the album *Garnett Silk Meets the Conquering Lion* (1988), something of a hidden classic until its 2000 reissue. Still known by many as Little Bimbo, Silk recorded with a variety of other artists, most notably Rebel and veteran singer Derrick Morgan, who mostly oversaw the singer's graduation from the dancehall of his younger days. The next five years were a somewhat inconsistent period in Silk's career, though his studio output remained phenomenal and sprinkled with occasional gems. This remarkable work rate also saw the singer collapse on stage in New York around this time. In 1994, however, it seemed Silk was set for the big time as he finalized a deal with Atlantic Records.

Before he'd even had time to complete a first album for the high-profile label, disaster struck. Returning to Jamaica to visit his mother, Garnett Silk asked friends to show him how to use a pair of guns he'd purchased following a recent burglary at his Mandeville home. As the others watched, one weapon was discharged accidentally, hitting a propane tank, which in turn set the house ablaze. Silk and his friends made haste for the door, before the musician realized his mother lay asleep upstairs: he tried to save her but both were overcome by smoke – and perished.

Friday 23

Dan Hamilton
(Spokane, Washington, 1 June 1946)
Hamilton, Joe Frank & Reynolds
The T-Bones

Guitarist Dan Hamilton started out as a songwriter/composer, a skilled musician from a young age. At nineteen, he found himself with a hit on his hands, having formed LA-based studio trio The T-Bones. Hamilton's gut-busting 'No Matter What Shape (Your Stomach's In)' (1965) – an instrumental based on an Alka Seltzer commercial – reached Billboard's Top Five. With fellow T-Bone Tommy Reynolds and a third vocalist, Joe Frank Carollo, Hamilton then enjoyed another big-selling hit with 'Don't Pull Your Love' (1971). Hamilton, Joe Frank & Reynolds (the band) then traded Reynolds for Alan Dennison – oddly keeping the original group name – and returned with the swooning soft-rock ballad 'Fallin' In Love' (1975). This American number one was quickly followed by the similar-veined 'Winners and Losers', though after this, Dan Hamilton faded somewhat from the scene, co-writing low-profile songs with his wife. He died during abdominal surgery in California.

Sunday 25

Eugene 'Bird' Daughtry
(Philadelphia, Pennsylvania, 29 October 1939)

The Intruders

A native of Philadelphia, Eugene Daughtry was a member of one of the key groups to inform the 'Philly' sound of the seventies. The Intruders – Daughtry, lead singer Sam 'Little Sonny' Brown, Robert 'Big Sonny' Edwards and Phil Terry – had been around for some seven years before securing a major US hit with 'Cowboys To Girls' (1968). The group's smooth stylings gave them several R & B chart entries thereafter, but few pop successes other than the rather trite '(Love is Like a) Baseball Game' (1968) and the 1973 airplay smash 'I'll Always Love My Mama'. In the UK, The Intruders scored a surprise final Top Twenty hit with 'Win, Place or Show (She's a Winner)' during the summer of 1974.

Eugene Daughtry had been unwell for many years before his death on Christmas Day 1994 from liver and kidney failure.

Lest We Forget

Other notable deaths that occurred sometime in 1994:

Papa John Creach (veteran US violinist who joined Jefferson Airplane at the age of 53; born Pennsylvania, 28/5/1917; suffering a coronary during the LA earthquake, he then died of pneumonia, 22/2)

Yvonne Fair (powerful Motown diva who backed James Brown, later making UK #5 with 1976's 'It Should Have Been Me'; born Virginia, 1942; unknown, 6/3)

Eric Gale (US guitarist with R & B/funk unit Stuff; born New York, 20/9/1939; lung cancer, 25/5 – just a year on from bandmate Richard Tee)

Danny Gatton (gifted, multi-styled US session guitarist; born Washington, DC, 4/9/1945; suicide by gunshot – without explanation, 4/10)

Deborah Glasgowe (UK-based reggae vocalist who recorded the original 'Mr Loverman'; born 1965; cancer/brain haemorrhage, 25/1)

Henry 'Raleigh' Gordon (Jamaican musician with much-loved trio Toots & The Maytals; born Clarendon, 1942; unknown)

Nicky Hopkins (revered UK session pianist who played with Jeff Beck, John Lennon, Paul McCartney, The Rolling Stones and Bob Seger; born London, 24/2/1944; heart/abdominal problems, 6/9)

Dave Mulchin (US bassist with unlikely New York punks The Sturgeon Riverbottom Nightmare Band; suicide, 6/1994 – just one month after keyboardist Kevin Toby had also taken his own life)

Donnie Owens (US country/pop guitarist who hit in 1958 with 'Need You'; born 30/10/1938; threatened by an attacker, he was accidentally shot by his intervening motel-manager girlfriend, Chato D'Rea, 27/10)

DJ Train (US MC to rappers JJ Fad and former NWA member MC Ren; born Clarence Lars, c 1971; killed in a fire at his mother's home, 25/6)

For a complete list of fallen artists, visit
www.numberoneinheaven.com

1995

JANUARY

Tuesday 24

David Cole
(Tennessee, 3 June 1962)
C&C Music Factory

David Cole lived up to his billing as 'the boy most likely to', leading and voice-training a choir in his teens, then landing a DJ position as he hit his twenties. The beginning of the nineties looked more than promising for Cole and his project partner, Robert Clivillés. As C&C Music Factory the duo – having survived on the underground circuit throughout the late eighties – rode the crest of a wave with a pulsating series of dance-floor smashes featuring the dynamic vocals of Freedom Williams. The US 2-million-selling number one 'Gonna Make You Sweat (Everybody Dance Now)' (1990) was a radio mainstay, as were the follow-up 'Here We Go' and the next summer's 'Things That Make You Go Hmmm...', which also placed Top Five in the UK. Cole's reputation was now such that he subsequently produced major singles and albums with Aretha Franklin, Richard Marx, Martika and Mariah Carey.

However, as his hits continued,

David Cole was diagnosed with spinal meningitis at the age of thirty-one. The news came only weeks after C&C Music Factory had been awarded a Grammy for their production work on the Whitney Houston movie *The Bodyguard*. Within months Cole's condition had deteriorated; Clivillés ended the act as a going concern on his partner's death.

Sunday 29

Ken Jensen
(Vancouver, British Columbia, 1962)
DOA
(The Four Horsemen)

Vancouver punk stalwarts DOA (Dead On Arrival) had been formed in 1978 by the stylishly named trio of guitarist and singer Joey 'Shithead' Keithley, bass-player Randy Rampage and original percussionist Chuck Biscuits. In the event, Keithley was the only permanent member of a band whose roll-call otherwise reads like a police 'missing' file: DOA had already seen four drummers come and go before Ken Jensen joined up for their 1992 album, *Thirteen Flavors of Doom*. Jensen was killed when a fire swept through his East Vancouver home on the afternoon of 29 January 1995; much of the

band's equipment was destroyed at the same time, though four friends of the band were believed to have escaped the blaze. Keithley issued the DOA album *The Black Spot* (1995) in Jensen's memory: 'He was the nicest of young guys – full of enthusiasm and getting better all the time. I've worked with a lot of musicians, man, and Ken didn't have any dislikeable angles.' Just four months previously, DOA had lost previous drummer Ken 'Dimwit' Montgomery to a far more conventional rock 'n' roll death (➨ *September 1994*), while the first major tragedy for the band had been the 1991 passing of early bassist Simon Wilde. Jensen, like Montgomery, had also played with the hapless Four Horsemen.

FEBRUARY

Sunday 12

Philip 'Taylor' Kramer
(Ohio, 1952)
Iron Butterfly
(Various acts)

Physics genius cum prog bassist gets psychobabble and drives into oblivion, anyone? When he disappeared early in

Richey Edwards

(Blackwood, South Wales, 22 December 1967)

The Manic Street Preachers

Former Manic Street Preachers guitarist Richey James Edwards has still to be declared dead (his family eschewed this option in 2002). In terms of striking a chord, Edwards's disappearance ahead of an imminent US tour seemed to echo the final days of Joy Division singer Ian Curtis (➧ *May 1980*); in this case, however, there has never been closure.

In his youth, Edwards shunned the conventions of education – though he emerged from Cardiff University with a degree – burying himself in literature, which stirred within him a desire to write. The young Edwards read widely (including the complete works of Shakespeare by his sixteenth birthday), his predilection for hiding himself away for days while his contemporaries played football precursory to the dysfunctional public image fans later came to worship. With a history of mental problems, Edwards would in his adult and professional life undergo treatment for a variety of physical disorders: most disturbingly, he showed signs of the self-harm that was to cause sensation in 1991. With The Manics sometimes ridiculed for the sloganeering that accompanied much of their early output, Edwards took it upon himself to suggest that he, at least, was genuine, carving the words '4 REAL' into his arm in front of stunned journalist Steve Lamacq. Thus, the eyeliner-wearing rhythm guitarist cemented a reputation that his lyrics about prostitution, the Holocaust and his own eating disorders could only augment. The Manic Street Preachers' *The Holy Bible* (1994) is considered by many the most harrowingly personal UK rock album since Joy Division's *Closer* – a catharsis via Edwards's notebooks – the song '4st 7lb' in particular a reminder of the worsening condition of its author. Just days after the album's release, he'd checked himself into The Priory; in the months that followed, he shaved his head and dressed as a concentration camp victim.

Then, on 1 February 1995, Edwards (who'd briefly gone AWOL from tour duty the previous summer) checked out of London's Embassy Hotel at 7 am, ahead of the band's flight to America. All that was left behind was a note reading simply: 'I love you.' Although there's evidence that he returned to his Cardiff flat, Edwards's whereabouts from this moment cannot be ascertained. Unconfirmed sightings of the musician occurred regularly over the next fortnight, while nearly £3K was withdrawn from his account – and, significantly, the majority of his notebooks were thrown into a river. David Cross, a young man with a mutual friend,

Richey Edwards: Out there?

'It does not enter my mind – and never has done. I am stronger than that.'

Richey Edwards, on suicide

claimed to have held Edwards in conversation at Newport bus station and cab-driver Anthony Hatherhall later told how a young man fitting the guitarist's description took a random journey with him through the Welsh valleys. Hatherhall supposedly dropped his passenger at the Severn Bridge, where Edwards's silver Vauxhall Cavalier was discovered on 14 February. Since then, identification of dredged-up remains as his has been dismissed, as have the majority of reported sightings as far afield as Brighton and Fuerteventura.

Richey Edwards once spoke of the perfect disappearance – perhaps as escape, perhaps because he wanted to be sought or at least talked about. Whether he's alive or not, he has achieved these objectives quite spectacularly.

1995, 42-year-old Philip Kramer had just forty cents in his pocket – but in his head harboured an arsenal of analytical information worth millions. A computer executive, Kramer had designed revolutionary compression software in the past; a student of theoretical physics, he knew equations that he believed would be of critical significance in the future; and as an aerospace engineer, he knew how to configure the flight path of a nuclear missile in the present. And somehow this genial six-foot-five giant still found time to play bass with prog legends Iron Butterfly.

Kramer was the son of Ohio scientist Ray Kramer, a professor of electrical engineering at Youngstown State. It was clear he had inherited his father's prowess when, at the age of twelve, Philip Kramer won top prize at a local science fair, having built a laser powerful enough to burst a balloon. Kramer taught himself guitar at much the same time, quickly forming a garage band (the appropriately named Concepts) and then a Carpenters-style duo with his sister Kathy before he was twenty. When this did not yield the interest the young musician craved, he hit the alternative scene with a rock group called Max with then-unknown Ohio native Stiv Bators (later of The Dead Boys) – during which time he was occasionally living rough. By 1973 a job as a prop builder with Warner Brothers had eventually put Kramer in touch with Ron Bushy – drummer and founder member of Iron Butterfly. Although the band had been defunct for two years, Bushy, Kramer and erstwhile Butterfly guitarist Erik Braunn decided to take them on the road once more. The response was so impressive that for two years Kramer's bass and gruff vocal tones delivered Iron Butterfly standards like the 1968 enormo-hit 'In-a-Gadda-da-Vida' to appreciative fans who'd never really gone away. Kramer whiled away time on the tour bus by scribbling illegible equations on hotel stationery – and,

unlike most rock musicians, maintained fitness by completing 1,000 push-ups a day. After a couple of lukewarmly received new albums, however, the band split for a second time. When Gold, another band with Bushy, failed to ignite, Philip Kramer cut his losses and returned to scientific study.

Kramer had not completely finished working with rock stars: in 1990 he founded Total Multimedia, a computer company that pioneered compression software with his friend Randy Jackson (of The Jacksons). Despite early promise, the company was on shaky ground before it brought in former IBM executive Peter Olson to help turn its fortunes around. Olson, a proven name in the world of business technology, was also a huge subscriber to the then vastly popular *Celestine Prophecy*, James Redfield's lifestyle compendium which spoke of 'energy fields' and 'intuitive vibrations'. Those who did not buy into it dismissed the book as a hotchpotch of new-age clichés, but Olson believed in them wholeheartedly – and soon convinced Kramer, a man apparently grounded in hard scientific fact, about 'beings of spiritual energy'. However, the more of this information the former musician assimilated, the more unsound his work practices became. By the beginning of 1995 colleagues were concerned by Kramer's habit of working late and coming in to the office overflowing with some new hypothesis or other. By now he was concentrating on fractal and light-speed theories – his father's speciality; although the work was revolutionary in itself, Kramer had begun speaking in tongues, almost as if attempting to write his own sequel to Redfield's thesis. The whole episode caused considerable unrest at Total Multimedia and the company fell into a downward spiral; eventually, Kramer's co-directors convinced him that he would have to fire Olson. On the morning of 12 February, Kramer climbed into his 1993 Ford Aerostar van and, leaving

his home near Thousand Oaks, drove to meet one of the directors at Los Angeles Airport to discuss a final resolution to the growing problem. Kramer failed to arrive. There was no sign of the van – and, as days and weeks passed by, no sign whatsoever of Philip 'Taylor' Kramer.

It was Philip Kramer's immersion into the world of defence technology that led to the most serious conjectures about his disappearance. Kramer – who had found a niche in radar technology – had knowledge which was key to the design of the MX missile in Northrup, a project that he was working on at the time of his disappearance. Displaying the kind of glee normally reserved for tales of alien abduction or 'Elvis is alive' stories, the US media went into meltdown over this one – the way they saw it, kidnapping by a hostile foreign government was the most likely cause. There was a lot of support for this thinking: Ohio Democrat Representative James Traficant Jr requested FBI intervention – he believed Kramer and his father had hit upon a mathematical breakthrough and that the former could have been kidnapped in order for his extraordinary knowledge to be used for nefarious purposes. However, one or two clues that emerged soon after hinted at a more personal crisis. It transpired that Kramer had made seventeen cellphone calls that morning to his family and friends – an unusually high number for a businessman preparing to attend a routine meeting. Some messages expressed love, particularly that to his wife, Jennifer, and two children; a further message to Bushy spoke of 'meeting again on the other side'. Finally, a noon 911 call surreally relayed how he believed O J Simpson was innocent – and, more significantly, how the musician himself planned to commit suicide.

For almost four and a half years, no evidence turned up. Finally, on 29 May 1999, amateur photographers chanced upon the well-hidden wreck of a Ford van and some skeletal remains at the foot of a ravine in Malibu, California – the vehicle and its occupant having plunged some 400 feet from the road above. Although it did not take long to ascertain that the bones were those of Philip Kramer, it was hard to fathom how this tragedy could have gone unnoticed in broad daylight – and whether Kramer actually took his own life remains unconfirmed.

See also *Stiv Bator(s) (* *June 1990); Erik Braunn (Brann) (* *July 2003). Original Iron Butterfly singer Darryl DeLoach died in 2002.*

Tony Secunda
(London, 24 August 1940)

The noted pop entrepreneur began his music-business career (after a brief stretch in the navy) as an early rock 'n' roll booker who found slots for acts like Georgie Fame and Johnny Kidd & The Pirates. After a spell working with the circus and as a wrestling promoter, Secunda made a vast amount of money through Beatles' merchandise, which he then invested in his management business. Secunda seemingly had something of a Midas touch: he discovered The Moody Blues and The Move, the latter of whom he managed until sacked in spring 1968 following the band's odd legal set-to with then Prime Minister Harold Wilson, who'd been featured on one of their sleeves. Secunda still had the touch, however, then looking after Procol Harum and, most significantly, T Rex, who, under his wing, became the biggest UK pop sensation of the early seventies. In semi-retirement, Secunda died of a heart attack at his home in California.

See also *Marc Bolan (* *September 1977) and the accompanying Dead Interesting! for links to all T Rex-related deaths. Various other charges of Secunda's have*

died, including The Move's Carl Wayne (*August 2004).*

Saturday 18

Bob Stinson
(Mound, Minnesota, 17 December 1959)
The Replacements
(The Bleeding Hearts)

Bob Stinson was a founder member of US cult pop-punks The Replacements, the Paul Westerberg-fronted band that burst on to the US alternative scene in 1980. Stinson had been given his first guitar at age eleven, forming the earliest incarnation of the band (then named Dogbreath) with his younger brother, Tommy, while in their teens. Wowing fans with an 18-track 35-minute debut LP (1981's great *Sorry Ma, Forgot to Take Out the Trash*), The Replacements quickly carved a niche alongside their natural 'fathers', The Ramones, while paving the way for contemporaries like Hüsker Dü and REM. Indeed, Peter Buck (of REM) recorded with them during the mid eighties, as did Alex Chilton of band heroes Big Star. The manic Bob Stinson was the band's early focal point, wearing dresses or diapers on stage – predating Kurt Cobain by almost a decade. But by 1986 Stinson's substance abuse had wearied the rest of the band, who voted to let him go (his replacement Replacement was Slim Dunlap). Although Stinson fashioned a new outfit, The Bleeding Hearts, he was soon diagnosed manic depressive, and was put on medication by the turn of the decade. On 18 February 1995, Stinson's body was found at his girlfriend's Minneapolis apartment: according to the Hennepin County coroner's office, his death was as a result of natural causes, exacerbated by prolonged drug and alcohol use. By the end, the guitarist was near destitute.

Thursday 23

Melvin Franklin
(David English – Montgomery, Alabama, 12 October 1942)
The Temptations

Among the first of Motown's classic vocal groups, The Temptations were, in 1961, essentially a combination of two previous Detroit-based acts, The Primes and The Distants. The former was to provide two new members – Eddie Kendricks and Paul Williams – when a break-up of the latter quintet left Otis Williams, Elbridge 'Al' Bryant and Melvin Franklin. Franklin provided the extraordinary basso profundo to complement the harmonies of his bandmates. After a barren three years, the hits started happening for The Temptations with the introduction of lead singer David Ruffin – and the meticulous attention of Motown hero Smokey Robinson. His 'My Girl' (1965) became in their hands an enduring masterpiece – while just as memorable were The Temps' much copied but never equalled dance routines. As an act, they were peerless between 1968 and 1971; as the most distinctive voice, Franklin was soon immortalized on international smashes like 'I Can't Get next to You' (1969) and 'Ball Of Confusion' (1970).

By the early seventies a rift in the band left only Franklin and Otis Williams from the original line-up. Although Franklin's throbbing vocal was never better presented than on the US number one 'Papa was a Rollin' Stone' (1972), the decline had set in. The Temptations toured consistently into the nineties, but by then it had become a circuit trawl for this once-great vocal troupe. Suffering from diabetes and rheumatoid arthritis, Franklin ceased touring in 1994. Within six months he was dead: admitted to the Cedars-Sinai Medical Center

in Los Angeles suffering from seizures, he died a week later from heart failure.

See also *Paul Williams* (☛ *August 1973); Elbridge 'Al' Bryant* (☛ *October 1975); David Ruffin* (☛ *June 1991); Eddie Kendrick(s)* (☛ *October 1992). Franklin's nephew was later funk star Rick James, who also died prematurely* (☛ *August 2004).*

MARCH

Sunday 5

Vivian Stanshall

(Shillingford, Oxfordshire, 21 March 1943)

The Bonzo Dog (Doo Dah) Band

One of music's best-remembered oddballs, Viv 'Ginger Geezer' Stanshall was the man who introduced the world to 'Adolf Hitler on vibes', among a host of other strange characters inhabiting the songs of The Bonzo Dog (Doo Dah) Band. Stanshall fled a strict upbringing (his father forced him to speak BBC English while his mother taught him to knit) to hone his extensive talent at London's Walthamstow Art School. The first, and most successful, result was the Bonzos, a collective of like-minded weirdos, including *Monty Python* collaborator Neil Innes. The group – who scored an unlikely UK Top Five hit with 'I'm the Urban Spaceman' (1968) – specialized in the surrealist British humour prevalent at the time, with Stanshall frequently referred to as 'music's Tony Hancock'. The group's creative peak was arguably the single's parent album, *The Doughnut in Granny's Greenhouse* (1969), and a residency on the cult ITV series *Do Not Adjust Your Set*. The Bonzos' quirkiness somehow never quite caught on in the US, though, and it was following a 1970 American tour that its members went their separate

Viv Stanshall withstands investigation from Germaine Greer in this 1969 *Oz* photoshoot

ways. Stanshall went on to enjoy cult success with Bonzo Freaks and Big Grunt (who were visually even stranger than the Bonzos), became a close friend of lunatic *sympathique* Keith Moon, and saw his *Sir Henry at Rawlinson's End* creation become first an album, then a book and finally a movie starring Trevor Howard. Stanshall had long been fascinated with the nineteenth-century peer and Assyriologist Rawlinson and his ground-breaking work in deciphering cuneiform: this project was a prime opportunity for the writer to meld his own undeniable eccentricity with that of the hard-drinking anthropologist. (By strange coincidence, Stanshall's death came one hundred years to the day after that of his hero.) But the politically correct eighties were not so tolerant of Stanshall's whimsicality. The writer became less visible as time marched on, his alcohol and tranquilizer addiction picking up more column inches than his work, although a play, *Stinkfoot*, gathered favourable reviews in 1988. In the mid nineties, Stanshall emerged from institutional convalescence a confused, shuffling character in slippers, venturing only occasionally out of his third-floor Muswell Hill flat to buy groceries. However, he managed to find it in himself to play a popular resident slot at The Angel, Islington, with a few old Bonzo friends, and had an album *in situ* in 1995. Stanshall – in spite of his well-documented problems with booze – also made a lucrative series of TV commercials for Ruddles beer.

Just as he appeared to have overcome his addictions and to be on the brink of a major revival, the last year of Viv Stanshall's life was beset by a series of cruel events. A violent mugging by attackers with knives was followed by the theft of his hi-fi equipment by a homeless man to whom he'd offered shelter. Finally, Stanshall was found dead by firemen after a freak blaze at his home, details of which remain sketchy to this day.

Tuesday 7

David Loucks

(Seattle, Washington, 8 December 1960)

Racer

Tin Ear

David Loucks was a bass virtuoso and journeyman singer/producer who'd played with US soft-rock act Racer (formerly Yourself) and was a highly respected face on the Pacific North-West rock scene during the early eighties. He moved on to front his own electronic band, Tin Ear, with his multi-instrumentalist brother Allan. Loucks's best-known song, 'Chemical Imbalance', featured on the posthumously issued album *Tin Ear* (1996).

On 5 March 1995, Loucks was duped into recording a bogus rap track with a 25-year-old man calling himself 'Paul Waller' and an accomplice (later identified as Shawn Swenson and Joseph Gardner) at his Seattle recording studio, Alternative Productions. When the time came to pay for studio use, Waller/Swenson claimed to have mislaid their wallets and another appointment was made for two days' hence, when Loucks would release the recordings. On the night in question, however, several men appeared at the studio intending to steal the musician's valuable digital equipment; the attempted heist went badly awry.

David Loucks was found by his distraught father the following morning, having been repeatedly shot with a stun gun, then gagged and bound by the gang – and finally brutally strangled. Following considerable efforts by Loucks Sr, a Seattle attorney – and a positive identification by the deceased's brother – Swenson and Gardner were eventually sentenced to fifty-five and twenty-nine years' imprisonment respectively for the murder, their courtroom pleas that

the sole intention had been to steal Loucks's equipment falling on deaf ears.

Wednesday 8

Ingo Schwichtenberg

(Hamburg, 18 May 1965)

Helloween

Manic depressive Ingo Schwichtenberg had not really recovered from his sacking as percussionist with German power-metallers Helloween when he took his own life by leaping in front of a train near his home town.

All had begun well for Helloween – Schwichtenberg, Kai Hansen (vocals/guitar), Michael Weikath (guitar) and Marcus Grosskopf (bass) – but twelve years of only moderate success left the members in an almost constant state of friction. In 1993, the founder drummer's worsening mental state had reached a critical point as far as his fellow band members were concerned, when, ahead of a gig in Japan, he collapsed in a compulsive crying fit. Schwichtenberg's excessive cocaine use did not help, the euphoria it produced drawing his condition into stark relief when Helloween were on tour. The poor performance of their latest album, *Chameleon*, and their subsequent dropping by EMI, effectively sealed Schwichtenberg's fate with the band, and the percussionist struggled to find work thereafter. Although former colleagues were badly shaken by his unexpected death, a very different line-up of Helloween has continued to record since.

Alan Barton

(Cawley, Yorkshire, 16 September 1953)
Black Lace
Smokie

Black Lace were among the more reviled acts of the early eighties. This odd duo – Alan Barton and Colin Routh, who originally represented the UK at Eurovision in 1979 – chalked up almost an entire year on the British charts in 1983–4. Their biggest hits, Brits-abroad favourites 'Superman' and the truly hideous 'Agadoo', saw to it that the group would be on the playlist at weddings across the country for ever. Displaying a marginal improvement in artistic judgement, singer Barton joined seventies hit-makers Smokie (replacing pin-up Chris Norman) in time for a comeback tour in 1986. Despite UK indifference to a sound now considered *passé*, the revitalized group went on to clock up unlikely platinum albums in Scandinavia, Russia and South Africa.

Constantly on the road, tragedy struck for Smokie when their minibus plunged into a ravine on their return to the airport after a gig in Düsseldorf. While other group members escaped with minor injuries, Barton died from a severe head wound in a Cologne hospital the following week, never having regained consciousness.

Alan Barton (*second left*) with Black Lace: 'Superman' *doesn't* return . . .

Close . . .

Agnetha Fältskog
(Abba)

In 1983, notoriously phobic Swedish ice-maiden Agnetha Fältskog – having pretty much left the all-conquering Abba behind her – felt she could never overcome her fear of flying and decided to hire a coach for future touring. Negotiating treacherous Swedish weather conditions late at night, her driver braked suddenly, causing the singer's vehicle to skid on the icy road and topple over. Fältskog somehow survived being thrown through a window with little more than concussion – but refused thereafter to use the roads.

Closer!

Mike Nolan
(Buck's Fizz)

Just what is it about Eurovision types and tour buses? In December the following year, another former winner's coach was also involved in a calamitous accident. After the collision with an articulated lorry in Newcastle, it was believed Buck's Fizz pin-up boy Mike Nolan might never walk or indeed speak again, the head injuries he'd incurred putting him in a coma. Good fortune prevailed, however, and the singer recovered to return to the studio within six months. For the Fizz, though, all fell flat with a split coming after just one further hit record.

Eazy-E

(Eric Wright – Los Angeles, California,
7 September 1963)

NWA

There are many who see Compton-born Eric Wright as the true godfather of gangsta rap. As the notorious Eazy-E, he kick-started the brief but brilliant life of NWA (Niggaz With Attitude), building his independent label, Ruthless, on previously ill-gotten gains. Teaming up with DJs Dr Dre (Andre Young) and Yella (Antoine Carraby), Eazy-E refined an originally sprawling roster to the classic NWA line-up – himself, Dre, Yella plus Ice Cube (O'Shea Jackson) and MC Ren (Lorenzo Patterson). Although Eazy's own album, *Eazy Duz It*, was released the same year, it was NWA's *Straight Outta Compton* (1989) that really shocked a nation with its thinly concealed illustrations of the brutality of LA street life. The album, NWA's second, contained such rap flashpoints as 'Gangsta Gangsta' and, most notably, the incendiary 'Fuck tha Police'. This pivotal track was written as a direct response to the violent treatment E and Dre had received at the hands of the LAPD as a result of an ill-advised drive-by paintballing the pair had dished out to some innocent bystanders one afternoon. An FBI attempt to block the record's distribution gained enormous publicity for NWA, ensuring that the album thereafter went platinum – and that its main architects, including E, would pocket six-figure salaries the following year. Another of the group's biggest hits was 'Express Yourself', a stirring call to arms to the black underclass that echoed closely a song written by Eazy-E's own musician father, Charles Wright, in 1970. Said his manager, Jerry Heller, '[E] was the most Machiavellian guy I ever met.

NWA: No one dared drop the 'E' (*second left*)…

He instinctively knew how to control people – and his musical instincts were infallible.'

An eventful, if short, career for E was to follow: after two further albums, NWA split acrimoniously in 1990, fuelling a highly public power struggle between Eazy and Dr Dre, who teamed up in 1992 with the notorious 'Suge' Knight to form Death Row Records. (The new label's roster included new rap heavyweights Snoop Doggy Dogg and Tupac Shakur.) Beginning a hip-hop trend for dissing the enemy on records, Dre cast the first stone; Eazy's reaction to what he

clearly saw as treachery was to issue an entire full-length LP, *It's On (Dre) 187um Killa* (1993) – little more than a prolonged fantasy involving the shooting of Dre plus one or two of his new charges, including the rising Snoop. This pretty grievous dissing of his former friend was full of bitter vitriol (see 'Real Muthaphukkin Gs'), on top of which E included doctored images of Dre wearing lipstick and eyeliner on the sleeve – the ultimate insult in the gangsta fraternity. The legions of fans who had been faithful since NWA days, however, loved this very open spat between their two idols.

In the aftermath, E kept followers on their toes, to say the very least, by orchestrating a brief but extraordinary pact with President George Bush, donating money to the Republican Party. He then issued a startling endorsement of the LAPD officers involved in the notorious 1993 Rodney King trial, dining with one of the accused, Tim Coon, and baldly stating, 'They was jus' doin' their job!' Ruthless meanwhile continued as a going concern, and E showed his ability to spot raw talent by discovering Bone, Thugz & Harmony, whose debut album for the label also went platinum.

A natural showman, and always in love with the notion of being rap's bad boy, Eazy-E fathered seven children by six partners before learning he was carrying the AIDS virus. E only went public with his condition a few weeks before he succumbed to it, marrying girlfriend Tomika Wood and finally reconciling with first Cube, then Dre at the Los Angeles Medical Center as he awaited death. A typically brash open letter from the dying star read: 'I would like to turn my own problem into something good that will reach out to my homeboys and their kin, because I want to save their asses before it's too late.' On the day of E's funeral, then Mayor of Compton, Omar Bradley, declared him 'Compton's favourite son' and even announced an 'Eazy-E Day' in recognition of the artist's immortalization of the LA suburb. Given Bradley's stark denouncement of NWA two years before (for portraying Compton as 'a gang-ridden cesspool'), it was a remarkable climb-down – and very much cemented Eazy-E's improbable acceptance by Californian authorities.

Selena

(Selena Quintanilla – Lake Jackson, Texas, 16 April 1971)

US popular culture more than occasionally throws up stories that test the credulity of all but the most avid made-for-TV-movie fan, surreal episodes like those involving sporting heroines Tonya Harding or Monica Seles that seem constantly to overshadow news of genuine world significance. One of the more puzzling tales of this nature was the pointless death of young Tejano singer Selena Quintanilla Perez – better known to her legions of young fans simply by her first name. Selena was born to celebrated Tex-Mex vocalist Abraham Quintanilla, who was to mould her career from an early age, putting her on stage at his newly opened restaurant when she was just nine, at the front of a hastily assembled band, Selena y Los Dinos ('Selena & The Guys'). Selena – revamped as a bustier-clad sex siren – then re-emerged at the tail end of the eighties with a string of carefully manufactured crossover pop recordings. Despite the plainly sterile nature of her music, Selena's major label debut, *Entre a Mi Mundo*, topped the Tex-Mex charts, while she also smashed a non-sport attendance record at the Houston Astrodome in 1992. It was at this stage in her career that Selena's father figured that his daughter would need a fan club to sate the seemingly unquenchable enthusiasm of her followers. One of the most vociferous of these was an otherwise dour 32-year-old woman called Yolanda Saldivar.

Selena: Someone came into her world

A registered nurse from San Antonio, Saldivar wore Abraham's resistance down until he agreed to let her manage the club and organize some of the star's business interests. Well, it made perfect sense: things were hotting up for Selena, who was now married and had a huge Latin crossover hit with 'Como La Flor' (1992), topping off a triumphant year with a Grammy. Tejano (a mix of Texan and Mexican stylings) was big business, and the media was soon talking of Selena as a 'Latina Madonna' set to usurp the convalescing Gloria Estefan in her absence.

All seemed fine for the first year or two of Saldivar's 'organization' – at least superficially. She had built up the fan club sufficiently to warrant ditching her day job, and was soon allowed to oversee the running of one of Selena's two boutiques. But Saldivar's business methods – which clearly should have been monitored more closely by the star and her family – were far from sound. Her obsessive, over-protective supervision of Selena brought complaints from fans across the USA: some believed her to be driving a wedge between the singer and her audience, while, more prosaically, many more claimed to have received nothing for their $20 administration fee. Which is where the story takes its sinister turn.

Perturbed, Selena – who naively thought well of Saldivar – questioned her about the increasing allegations of fraud. This was met with howls of protest from her employee, who bizarrely used a trumped-up claim of rape to conceal her guilt. A legally enforced hospital examination made the tearful Saldivar change her story, but before any kind of proper financial investigation could commence, Saldivar fled to Mexico – taking with her some fairly damning documentation. With the situation fast spiralling out of control, she agreed to meet the singer and her guitarist husband, Chris Perez, at a Days Inn motel in

Corpus Christi, Texas. After a frantic argument in the unlikely surroundings of this tiny hostelry, Saldivar locked herself in her room, refusing to relinquish the crucial documents. With her spouse rapidly losing his patience, Selena agreed to leave her distressed employee for the night, to return home and then attempt to speak to her the following morning alone. It was to prove a costly decision. On the morning of 31 March 1995, catering manager Ruben De Leon described hearing the ring of a single shot from a .38, followed by the jaw-dropping sight of the famous young singer staggering badly injured into his lobby. As he dialled for police and ambulance assistance, 23-year-old Selena – nursing a horrific injury to her right shoulder – bled to death from a severed artery right in front of him. She was officially pronounced dead at 1.05 pm.

Predictably, US television audiences tuned in to watch the ensuing stand-off, while hordes of fans arrived to scream for Saldivar's blood. The tragic farce ended ten hours later when Saldivar was dragged away by police, after having pointed her gun at her own head for almost all this time. The extraordinary aftermath included 16 April (which would have been the singer's twenty-fourth birthday) being declared an official holiday by Governor George W Bush – unprecedented for a recording artist who had had just one Billboard pop hit and was scarcely known outside her own country. Soon, her followers were able to buy a commemorative Selena doll from a new fan club, not to mention various posthumous albums and books. More extraordinarily still, they could draw tickets from a lottery to attend the trial of her killer, who, in September 1995, was sentenced to thirty years' imprisonment, despite her pleas that the shooting was accidental and that the bullet had actually been intended for herself. As a postscript, it was revealed in 1998 that the dying

Selena – displaying remarkable loyalty, even in her final moments – had been clutching a fourteen-carat gold ring that was supposedly a gift from Saldivar. In the event, her killer was discovered to have charged the ring to the star's credit account.

JUNE

Sims Ellison

(Austin, Texas, 10 March 1967)

Pariah

An impressive hard-rock bass-player, Ellison formed Pariah with his brother Kyle (guitars) and drummer Shandon Sahm in the late eighties; the band quickly developed something of a local following before an opportunity to record an album with Geffen Records came knocking. Having recorded *To Kill a Mockingbird*, however, Pariah had to wait three years for the material to be released: when it eventually surfaced late in 1993, their moment had already passed – and the record bombed. By early 1995 Pariah were treated exactly thus and had been dropped from Geffen's roster.

Depressed, Ellison ended his life by gunshot; his distraught ex-manager, Wayne Nagle, was sufficiently moved by the suicide to form the support foundation SIMS, which offers counselling to musicians suffering from mental illness.

Wednesday 14

Rory Gallagher

(Ballyshannon, Republic of Ireland,
3 March 1948)

Taste

Emerging as an international force in
late-sixties blues rock, Rory Gallagher
was perhaps the only guitarist to marry
the skiffle he had loved as a boy with
the blues of Muddy Waters – he would
later realize the dream of playing with
Waters. Gallagher had learned much
of his craft in local amateur showband
The Fontanas, before turning his
attention to the musical phenomenon
sweeping the UK. He formed the
three-piece Taste, who were signed up
by Polydor on relocating to London
and secured a Top Twenty album, *On
the Boards* (1970). Following this success, Gallagher surprisingly split the
group, becoming a solo act during the
seventies. By now a recognized virtuoso, he also played on a number of
records by other artists.

An unlikely star, Rory Gallagher
dressed down for his performances
and suffered from intermittent stage
fright throughout his career. To
combat this, the nonetheless popular
guitarist regularly indulged in drinking
bouts: as a consequence, he underwent liver surgery more than once.
However, after a transplant appeared
to have saved his life, Gallagher failed
to recover from a resultant chest
infection, and died at London's King's
College Hospital a month after his
operation.

Friday 30

Biggie Tembo

(Rodwell Marasha – Chinhoyi, Mashonaland,
30 September 1958)

The Bhundu Boys

The Bhundu Boys burst on to the
scene from the Zimbabwe capital
of Harare, a city whose name – with
an irony not lost on those who have
followed the career of this otherwise most uplifting of musical acts
– translates as 'death everywhere'.
When their native country (formerly
Rhodesia) gained independence in
1980, opportunities improved for
musicians oppressed by the previous
regime. Indeed, 'Bhundu Boys' refers
to the guerrillas who fought to make
such liberation a possibility: as a boy,
singer and guitarist Biggie Tembo, like
hundreds of other youngsters, served
as a runner to these soldiers. An early
member of the band, Tembo joined
group founder Rise Kagona on the
nightclub circuit, frequently performing their hypnotic brand of 'jit jive'
on borrowed equipment. This state
of affairs changed dramatically following the release of '*Hatisi Tose*', a
record that spent three months atop
the Zimbabwe charts in the mid eighties. The Bhundus soon became one
of the first non-Western acts to tour
Europe – culminating in an unlikely
support slot for Madonna at Wembley
Stadium. Tembo was clearly the main
man, turning in performance after
performance that had the most retiring of observers jumping to their feet.
(Influential British DJ John Peel allegedly broke down in tears during one
show at London's Dingwalls club.)

The Bhundu Boys were seldom far
from more serious issues, however,
and tragedy struck three times in quick
succession for them with the AIDS-
related deaths of band members
David Mankaba (1991), Shepherd

Munyama (1992) and Shakespear
'Shakie' Kangwena (1993). Biggie
Tembo (who had mysteriously been
voted out of the band in 1990) was
clearly affected by all this, pursuing a
solo career which took in some deeply
religious music. Before his own death,
Tembo had, like his mother before
him, taken up preaching. Clinically
depressed, this once-irrepress-
ible performer ended his days in a
Zimbabwean mental institution, where
he hanged himself in his bedroom.
Rise Kagona continues to perform
with a new line-up of the band.

Phyllis Hyman

(Pittsburgh, Pennsylvania, 6 July 1949)

Phyllis Hyman had a distinct philosophy on life: she believed that just as
she had the right to choose how to
live, she possessed the same entitle-
ments regarding her death. In short,
Hyman believed that suicide was a justifiable solution for those who could
not manage the spiritual, emotional or
physical pain of their lives.

Hyman, deep-voiced and statu-
esque, was a distinctive talent. Her
career began to flourish in earnest
when she graduated from Buddah
Records to the esteemed Arista label in
1978. She'd scored hits with Buddah,
but this move elevated her to the
level of contemporaries like Chaka
Khan and Melba Moore. Plans were
afoot for this exciting new singer:
Arista allegedly even told her that she
would be 'the next Diana Ross'. She
(possibly unintentionally) cracked
the burgeoning gay market with the
highly praised album *Can't We Fall in
Love Again?* (1981), while impressing Broadway audiences with her
performances in the Duke Ellington
tribute show, *Sophisticated Ladies*. But
progress internationally was slow for
Hyman, and her continued annoyance
at Arista's impatience boiled over

when Whitney Houston arrived at the label in 1984. The company's obsession with a younger, supposedly fresher talent caused artist and label to go their separate ways. Many believe Hyman failed to move on from this setback, although her career briefly revived at Philiadelia International – during which time Arista chose to delete several earlier releases.

Just hours before a scheduled performance at Harlem's Apollo Theater, Hyman told a friend this would be the final concert she would play. In truth, she had already sung her last. Apparently depressed by the recent loss of both her mother and grandmother – and traumatized by the Oklahoma bombing – Hyman felt that her own time had come. Discovering her unconscious, Hyman's live-in assistant, Lennice Malina, contacted police, whose reports listed a multitude of pills and suicide notes at her Manhattan apartment. Phyllis Hyman died two hours later at New York's Roosevelt Hospital. In her adult life, Hyman had been diagnosed as bi-polar (suffering from manic depression), but, refusing to accept conventionally prescribed drugs, had chosen to self-medicate – distorting her mental state even further.

Her manager and close friend, Gloria Gracia, talked also of her 'empathic' nature, which supposedly caused her to feel the physical pain of others and experience premonitions: 'Phyllis never considered herself to be "psychic" per se, but her sensitivity was such that she experienced telepathy, precognition and, generally speaking, the paranormal environment in a way that did not allow her to be easily understood by others.' The posthumous *I Refuse to be Lonely* (1995) – much of which deals with her personal struggle – tells us that Phyllis Hyman was a very complex character indeed.

JULY

Saturday 1

Ian Parkin
(Wakefield, 1950)
Be-Bop Deluxe

Ian Parkin was rhythm guitarist with singer Bill Nelson's cult seventies rock act Be-Bop Deluxe – the pair became friends during the early/mid sixties, forming the nucleus of the band (as The Strangers) while still at school in Wakefield. Parkin played on only one Be-Bop Deluxe album, 1975's critically acclaimed debut, *Axe Victim*, before an acrimonious split later that year saw a change of line-up; the band became history in 1978. Indeed, Nelson hadn't stayed in touch with Parkin – who, still involved in music, was married with two children – but was moved by his untimely death, believed to have been from cancer: 'This brings great sadness to my heart. His companionship during my teenage years and early twenties will always be fondly remembered.' Just months later, Nelson learned of the death of another former Be-Bop Deluxe colleague, bass-player Charlie Tumahai, who unexpectedly died from heart failure in Auckland on 21 December.

See also *Paul Jeffreys (◀ December 1988)*

Charlie Rich
(Colt, Arkansas, 14 December 1932)

An undisputed giant of popular country music, the distinctively side-burned Charlie Rich's lesser-known prior career had included farm labouring and a stint with the US air force, before a slew of rockabilly-flavoured early recordings with the Judd label made him a radio staple by the early sixties. Nevertheless, it took 'The Silver Fox' (as Rich became affectionately known) a dozen more years to top the US hit parade. Rich is probably best remembered for the US platinum-selling 'The Most Beautiful Girl' (1973), a Billboard chart-topper that also rose to number two in the UK the following year), alongside a host of other sentimental standards such as the title cut from the *Behind Closed Doors* album (1973) and 'A Very Special Love Song' (1974). In 1973, Rich walked away with The CMA's Male Vocalist and Album of the Year honours.

Coming from humble beginnings, Charlie Rich found fame difficult to accommodate, seeking relief from its pressures in alcohol. With fewer chart successes during the eighties and nineties, Rich withdrew from the spotlight, though his few live performances remained sell-outs. The singer was en route to Florida on such a tour when a blood clot on his lung claimed his life; he died at a hospital in Hammond, Louisiana.

AUGUST
Wednesday 9

Jerry Garcia

(Jerome John Garcia – San Francisco, California,
1 August 1942)

**The Grateful Dead
(Various acts)**

Five-year-old Jerome John Garcia could only stand and watch as his father, jazz musician José Garcia, was swept to his death on a fishing trip. This and a number of other sobering early events proved a catalyst to the future Grateful Dead legend as he sought the spiritual. What he found was more a way of life than the mere vocation chosen by others.

Brought up by his grandmother, 'godfather of freaked-out Americana' Jerry Garcia was exposed early on to the music of the Grand Ole Opry, an acquired taste for country and folk enhanced by his older brother's collection of Chuck Berry and T-Bone Walker recordings. His brother Clifford owed him that much: during an eventful childhood, he'd accidentally severed one of Garcia's fingers while chopping wood in 1948. Despite what to some might seem an insurmountable setback, Garcia still learned guitar and banjo, forming jug bands until an unspecified misdemeanour in 1959 caused him to join the army rather than go to prison. Perhaps unsurprisingly, Garcia's inconsistent disciplinary record brought him the discharge that he probably in any case desired. The following year, the musician claimed that a spiritual awakening, after he was thrown from a rolling car, 'began his life in earnest'.

Returning to San Francisco, Garcia – who was otherwise spending time playing bluegrass and teaching acoustic guitar – teamed up with poet Bob Hunter

(Robert Christie Burns). The pair played together in a series of coffee-house groups, their collision significant in that, later on, Hunter contributed most of the lyrics to Garcia's Grateful Dead guitar musings. The early sixties saw the murky beginnings of the folk counterculture, a scene that also attracted rhythm guitarist Bob Weir and his friend keyboardist/vocalist Ron 'Pigpen' McKernan; the latter became Garcia's right-hand man through the first years of The Dead. Folk, blues and jug developed into a fertile scene that eventually gave the world proto-psychedelic rock acts like Jefferson Airplane, Big Brother & The Holding Company, Country Joe & The Fish and Quicksilver Messenger Service – but the daddies were undeniably The Dead. Garcia finally saw their first single 'Stealin'' appear on Scorpio in 1966, his band now fleshed out by Phil Lesh (bass), David Grisman (mandolin) and Bill Kreutzmann (percussion, augmented by Mickey Hart in 1967). For three years, Garcia and his Deadheads were hugely creative for a supposedly stoned-out bunch of hippies: *The Grateful Dead* (1967), *Anthem of the Sun* (1968) and *Aoxomoxoa* (1969) cemented a reputation for organic music that grew out of the plethora of Merry Pranksters 'Acid Test' parties at which the band and its improvising were generally centre stage. But, though it had been a necessary replacement for the already-taken Warlocks, the choice of name was also strangely prescient – the shadow of mortality followed Garcia throughout his career. The trauma of losing his father had made him withdrawn as a boy; the death of Garcia's mother in a car crash would be emotionally reflected in arguably The Grateful Dead's finest work, the album *American Beauty* (1970), a collection that contains some genuinely touching songs (such as 'Box of Rain') which shortly elevated The Dead to rock's top table.

The deaths of close friends Janis Joplin (•✿ *October 1970*) and McKernan (•✿ *March 1973*) – the latter just a year after McKernan had left The Dead – would also hit Garcia hard, though the head Deadhead continued to lose himself in what had now become an ideology rather than a means of paying the bills (which he was scarcely doing anyway). But he was nothing if not prolific in his art: in addition to turning out a couple of albums a year, Garcia recorded and issued The Grateful Dead's live shows obsessively, and

> '**The lame part of the sixties was the political part, the social part. The *real* part was the spiritual part.**'
> Jerry Garcia

also found time for a host of elaborate side projects – one of which spiralled into New Riders of the Purple Sage, for whom Garcia and Hart guested on their debut album. But with the juggernaut-like Dead becoming the biggest touring unit in the USA, a bewildering array of musicians came, rocked and tuned out. Somehow, Garcia ploughed on through setback after setback, despite his own narcotics dependency. Falling into a diabetic coma in 1986 was his own closest call at this stage, though even after this, the revitalized Grateful Dead enjoyed their biggest commercial success with the US Top Ten *In the Dark* (1987). The album's accompanying single, 'Touch Of Grey', also became a major hit – finding an unlikely new market in the MTV generation. But perhaps this was to be expected: through adversity and a constantly changing musical environment, Garcia always seemed to rise from The Dead to take whoever was in his latest pack of stooges up to the next level.

But even Captain Trips – as he was often labelled – couldn't go on indefinitely. Despite having embraced to some degree the US vogue for healthier living and diet, Jerry Garcia's earlier lifestyle finally called time on him at the Serenity Knolls Chemical Dependency Center in California on 9 August 1995. Found unconscious on the floor of his room by a nurse, who attempted CPR, Garcia was pronounced dead by paramedics at 4.23 am, having suffered a heart attack in his sleep. Remaining members of The Dead saw fit – finally – to end the group after thirty years as a going concern in December 1995.

A legend within more conventional US popular culture for some time, the former figurehead of the underground has been commemorated in a number of ways (including the posting of his image on bottles of wine), though of the many tributes paid to the singer, the Ben & Jerry's ice-cream flavour Cherry Garcia seems to be the most enduring, raking in over $400K a year profit for its makers and Garcia's estate. For a month after Jerry Garcia's death, the dessert was prepared with black cherries (instead of the usual Bings) as a token of respect for the legend that inspired it.

See also *Keith Godchaux (☙ July 1980); Brent Mydland (☙ July 1990); John Kahn (☞ May 1996)*

Bobby DeBarge

(Robert Louis DeBarge – Ohio,
5 March 1956)
Switch
(DeBarge)

Led by Bobby DeBarge and Phil Ingram, Switch were protégés of Jermaine Jackson when they first came to prominence in 1978. Signing to Motown, the band made serious inroads into the US R & B/pop charts with 'There'll Never Be'. The DeBarge family was much like that of Jacksons: among its ten children were brothers Tommy (bassist with Switch) and the younger Eldra, who, under Bobby's guidance, fronted disco favourites DeBarge. Switch continued on Total Experience records, while DeBarge went on to enormous success on Motown, with Bobby playing mainly a production role on hits like their infectious, million-selling 'Rhythm of the Night' (1985). Success, however, was fleeting: by 1987 Eldra was concentrating on a solo career while Bobby, perhaps ill-advisedly, fronted a new line-up of DeBarge.

Suffering without the vast income of his earlier career, DeBarge, and another musician brother, Chico, found themselves imprisoned in Michigan for cocaine trafficking in 1988. Then, soon after the release of his own solo album, *It's Not Over*, Bobby DeBarge added to the proliferation of AIDS deaths during the nineties; it is widely thought that he contracted the disease while in jail. DeBarge's devastated family subsequently ditched pop music to return to their gospel roots.

Wednesday 23

Dwayne Goettel

(Vancouver, British Columbia,
1 February 1964)

Skinny Puppy

Canadians Skinny Puppy were hard-core industrial experimentalists par excellence well before it was a fashionable genre in which to immerse oneself. Their music a fusion of electronica and metal riffs, Puppy were a band obsessed with issues of inhumanity and the darker side of the human psyche: the name was appropriate in that their infamous live shows often featured traumatizing images of vivisection. Never a likely commercial unit-shifter, Skinny Puppy were nevertheless picked up by Columbia in 1987, even finding time for various side projects Download, Duck and Pigface (which featured members of Revolting Cocks). Keyboardist and sample wizard Dwayne Rudolph Goettel had begun as a trumpeter in his high-school band; he was in the middle of working on the band's ninth studio album when he was found dead from a suspected heroin overdose in his parents' bathroom.

Saturday 26

Ronnie White

(Detroit, Michigan, 5 April 1939)

The Miracles

A founding member of one of Motown's most cherished acts, Ronnie White first encountered singer Smokey Robinson as his family's paper boy; the pair then formed an embryonic Miracles – The Five Chimes – during their time together at Northern High School. The Chimes became The Matadors and eventually The Miracles, and were picked up by Nat Tarnopol (Jackie Wilson's manager) and then Berry Gordy, who managed the band as it gave Motown an early number-two smash with Robinson's sharp pop composition 'Shop Around' (1961). The hits – 'You've Really Got a Hold on Me', 'Mickey's Monkey' (both 1963) and 'Ooh Baby Baby' (1965), among others – flowed; Robinson and White began to clean up, also writing tunes for The Temptations, Marvin Gaye and Mary Wells. Working so closely caused frequent arguments between lead Robinson and bass baritone White, and the former eventually left The Miracles in 1972. Early disco favourite 'Love Machine' (1976) was one of the few chart hits the once-great act enjoyed without its talismanic former frontman, and they disbanded for good two years later. After a far-quieter later career, Ronnie White died in retirement from leukaemia at his Detroit home.

Wednesday 30

Sterling Morrison

(Holmes Sterling Morrison – East Meadow,
Long Island, New York, 29 August 1942)

**The Velvet Underground
(Various acts)**

Guitarist Sterling Morrison was a student at Syracuse University when he befriended literature major and basic musician Lou Reed. Having lost touch, the pair met once again in New York, where the mythology surrounding the Velvet Underground began in earnest. Wilfully anti-establishment, the band – completed by multi-instrumentalist John Cale and (eventually) androgynous percussionist Moe Tucker – built its reputation around seventeen-minute noisefests like 'Sister Ray' (1967).

The influence of The Velvets was always at a polar opposite from their commercial success; part of the legend was the patronage of iconic pop-artist Andy Warhol, who financed the band's first (self-titled) album, and also introduced them to funeral vocalist Nico (Christa Päffgen). Warhol's 'banana' design became (like The Rolling Stones 'lips') a powerful visual emblem. Despite one or two attempts at a more commercial sound, there was no mainstream breakthrough for a band destined to remain the most famous cult-rock act of all time. Morrison, earning extra money as both an English teacher and later a tugboat captain in Houston, parted company with Reed in 1971, their relationship having soured. Despite these unlikely career paths, Morrison's music didn't die completely: he is known to have played with several acts in Texas during the eighties, one of which was The Bizarros.

Despite Nico's sudden death (⏴ *July 1988*), The Velvet Underground attempted a brief reunion, opening for U2 in 1993. The guitarist's performances were well received, but the group had fallen out (yet again) by the end of the tour. Two years on, Sterling Morrison succumbed to a nine-month battle with non-Hodgkin's lymphoma in Poughkeepsie, New York – the day after his fifty-third birthday – ending this truly revolutionary band for ever. Cale, who had handed over all VU guitar duties to Morrison in 1968, performed two specially written pieces at his memorial.

See also *Angus MacLise (⏴ June 1979)*

SEPTEMBER

Friday 1

Damon Edge
(San Francisco, California, 1950)

Chrome

Guitarist and synth-player Damon Edge formed cult San Francisco hard-rock act Chrome in 1977. Somewhat averse to playing live, Edge would not take Chrome on the road, bar one 1981 date in Italy, where the band had a considerable following. This caused conflict with outspoken (and impressively named) frontman Helios Creed, who contested any decision to remain cooped up in the studio; the pair went their separate ways – never to reconcile – when Edge moved to Berlin with his musician girlfriend, Fabienne Shine. By the time of his death Edge was described as an obese shut-in who drank heavily, a distressing break-up with Shine the main cause of his self-neglect. Tragically, he lay dead in his LA apartment for nearly a month before discovery.

Friday 8

Jack Vigliatura VI
(Palm Harbor, Florida, 1974)

Bill White
(Clearwater, Florida, 1972)

For Squirrels

The young, up-for-fun members of Florida thrash-rockers For Squirrels had finally got their act together: singer Jack Vigliatura, bass-player Bill White and guitarist Travis Tooke grew up together in Clearwater, playing for themselves, all the while believing their music was 'for squirrels'. In truth, a series of early, shambolic performances obscured the fact that this band had genuine promise. Sony thought so: they invested in For Squirrels, backing an impressive debut album, *Example*, and airplay hit, the Kurt Cobain tribute 'Mighty KC', in 1995, even paying to record their hedonistic charges in the enviable environment of Compass Point in the Bahamas. But the band had improved immeasurably in a short space of time – and an equally enviable showcase at the legendary CBGB's in New York, set up by friend and tour manager 21-year-old Tim Bender, was the next test. For Squirrels passed this with flying colours and the stage seemed set for stardom.

As the triumphant band made the long journey back to Florida on Interstate 95, disaster struck. Some fifty miles south of Savannah, Georgia, a rear tyre blew, causing their tour van to lurch violently and overturn several times. According to Georgia State Patrol, Vigliatura, White and Bender all died from massive head injuries at the scene, while drummer Jack Griego was lucky to survive with smashed vertebrae and ribs. Tooke suffered a broken elbow and lacerations, but, like Griego, pulled through in Liberty Memorial Hospital, Georgia. The funerals of Vigliatura and White were held five days later in Palm Harbor, while Bender's memorial took place in Cary. It was a tragic end for a band that had just wanted to play music for fun: indeed, one of Bill White's early stage antics was to perform seated – and wearing a crash helmet.

Saturday 16

Dougie Palompo
(St Andrews, Scotland, 1969)

The Flying Medallions

Just a week after the For Squirrels disaster, a bus carrying chaotic South London punks The Flying Medallions from a Belgian festival skidded on a motorway and crashed, instantly killing bassist of two years, Dougie Palompo. Having been together for some years, the band were finally enjoying moderate success touring their latest album, *We Love Everybody and Everything's Great* (1994). The Medallions (some of whom mutated into the band Flicknife Rickshaw after the tragedy) were known for their cryptic sleeve notes; this latest release had featured the enigmatic phrase: 'The conquest of death should be the central concern of science. Death should be snuffed.'

OCTOBER

Saturday 21

Shannon Hoon
(Richard Shannon Hoon – Lafayette, Indiana, 26 September 1967)

Blind Melon

LA-based alt-rockers Blind Melon were at the height of their powers when they played David Letterman's high-profile talk show. Earlier that day, the death of Nirvana's Kurt Cobain had been announced (◀*April 1994*): for Melon's performance, lead singer Shannon Hoon daubed a symbolic question mark on his forehead as a 'tribute'. Whether anyone chose to reciprocate the gesture after Hoon's

Blind Melon – Shannon Hoon ever at the centre: No rain, but copious tears …

NOVEMBER

'Country' Dick Montana
(Daniel Monty McClain – Carmel, California, 1955)
The Beat Farmers

Following the recent trend set by Big Sugar drummer Walter 'Crash' Morgan (who had died on stage in Iowa that October), 'Country' Dick Montana suffered an onstage aneurysm at the Longhorn Saloon in Whistler, British Columbia. A wild-styled leader of San Diego alt-rock band The Beat Farmers, the vocalist/percussionist collapsed into his drums, passing away there and then. Montana – who also had a recent history of thyroid cancer – had just completed his band's eighth record, *Manifold*, and solo effort *The Devil in Me*. According to long-time friend and admiring musician Mojo Nixon, among the inimitable frontman's legendary stunts were the drinking of beer with his feet and the selling of songs he didn't even own to a record company.

Friday 17

Alan Hull
(Newcastle-upon-Tyne, 20 February 1945)
Lindisfarne
(Various acts)

Woody Guthrie-influenced singer/guitarist/pianist Alan Hull fast became a local hero to North-Easterners as his folk-rock band Lindisfarne became a popular festival draw in the late sixties. A songwriter rated by many at the time as one of Britain's finest, Hull had to wait for ten years to taste real success. Having played the clubs with

sad heroin-related death eighteen months later has not been recorded.

Hoon left his home town with the intention of emulating fellow Lafayette native W Axl Rose – coincidentally, one of Hoon's first brushes with fame would be to appear on the Guns n' Roses promo for their 1991 hit 'Don't Cry'. But Shannon Hoon was far from a cameo performer: Blind Melon – Hoon, Roger Stevens (guitar), Christopher Thorn (guitar), Brad Smith (bass) and Glen Graham (drums) – signed a $500K contract with Capitol, and Hoon's reputation as both songwriter and rock 'n' roll bad boy began to grow. An eponymous debut album (1992) – which went on to sell 4 million copies – and a major hit single, the exquisite 'No Rain' (1993), brought the singer to the forefront of the industry. Hoon upset Vancouver authorities with a display of nudity at a show that year – though *Rolling Stone* saw the humour in this and had the entire band strip off for a cover shoot that November. But this early burst of publicity proved the zenith for Blind Melon. An appearance at the ill-fated Woodstock II Festival in 1994 (coupled with Hoon's tangle with security at that year's Grammy awards) preceded

a follow-up album, *Soup* (1995), that divided the critics and failed to sell in similar quantities to its predecessor. By now Hoon's zealous use of psychedelic drugs was causing consternation among his Melon colleagues; their decision to bring in a drug therapist for the group's 1995 tour was met with derision by the lead singer, who, finding the counsellor intrusive, promptly fired him. Two weeks later, Hoon was dead, found slumped in the back of the band's tour bus by Blind Melon's sound engineer, just before a show in New Orleans. This event was voted 'Third Most Depressing Moment of 1995' by the readers of the UK metal paper *Kerrang!*

Said Stevens, 'It sometimes got to the point where I was expecting that call. But when he died, he was fresh out of rehab and was really healthy. I really don't think there was anything anyone could have done. I believe people learn from example and experience. We had him go to rehab a few times, but eventually we knew it was up to him to quit.' Stevens issued a posthumous collection of Blind Melon songs, *Nico* (1996, named after the singer's daughter, Nico Blue) before disbanding the group in 1999.

an assortment of bands, the break-through occurred in 1972 with two UK Top Five singles for Lindisfarne – now Hull, Simon Cowe (guitar/mandolin), Ray Jackson (mandolin/banjo), Rod Clements (bass/violin) and Ray Laidlaw (drums). 'Meet Me on the Corner' and the whimsical reissue 'Lady Eleanor' charted concurrently to three hit Lindisfarne albums within a year, of which the first, *Fog on the Tyne* (1971), gave the group a once improbable chart-topper. Despite this unexpected national acceptance, Lindisfarne split soon after, and the new line-up had to wait a further six years for a third Top Ten single (1978's 'Run For Home', also a US hit), and a further twelve for a fourth – the less-welcome 'Fog on the Tyne (Revisited)' (1990), featuring a vocal 'performance' by footballer Paul Gascoigne.

By the late eighties Lindisfarne had become little more than a perennial Christmas knees-up act. Hull then became active in Labour politics before his death from a heart thrombosis in November 1995. Having released solo albums for over two decades, Alan Hull completed work on his final record on the night that he died.

See also *Kenny Craddock (*➤ *May 2002)*

Tuesday 21

Peter Grant
(London, 5 April 1935)

A former wrestler from a deprived background, Grant tagged himself first with The Yardbirds, then The Pretty Things and Led Zeppelin, becoming arguably the most successful rock manager since Brian Epstein. Far from keeping his bands in order, Grant was widely recognized as the protagonist in Led Zeppelin's much-reported touring debauchery

during the seventies. But the 250 lb-plus Grant – who had been known to use strong-arm tactics to land gigs – was not a character with whom to mess: on one notable occasion, he single-handedly (and very publicly) 'dispatched' a pair of US marines who had been mocking Robert Plant and Jimmy Page's extravagant haircuts, uttering the immortal phrase 'What's your fucking problem, Popeye?' as he removed them from the scene. After another fracas in 1977, Grant received a suspended sentence for an attack on an employee of US promoter Bill Graham.

The accidental death of Led Zep drummer John Bonham (➤ *September 1980*) saw a devastated Peter Grant finally distance himself from the music industry. Grant himself died of a heart attack in the back of a friend's car while travelling to his Eastbourne home.

Matthew Ashman
(London, 1962)
Bow Wow Wow
Adam & The Ants
Agent Provocateur
(The Chiefs of Relief)

A 'puppet' (in name only) of Malcolm McLaren, Matt Ashman was actually a versatile musician who switched from the jazz leanings of his youth to hit the sharp end of UK glam punk by the eighties. A teenage member of Adam & The Ants, Ashman contributed keyboards and guitar to the band's debut album *Dirk Wears White Sox* (1979), enjoying a belated Top Ten hit with 'Young Parisians' (1981) as Adam's new brood hit paydirt. By this time Ashman was a key member of equally tribal-sounding pop act Bow Wow Wow, a band that courted controversy by somewhat brazenly parading its under-age singer, Annabella Lwin. A couple of 1982 hits notwithstand-

ing, Bow Wow Wow didn't match the success of McLaren's earlier charges – he had, of course, also overseen the career of The Sex Pistols – and split after two albums.

Matthew Ashman then teamed up with ex-Pistols drummer Paul Cook for the largely unsuccessful Chiefs of Relief, before working as a session-player. His dance project, Agent Provocateur, looked more likely to succeed, with a well-received single 'Kicks' (1995). However, Ashman fell into a coma and died of complications arising from a diabetic condition before the debut album could be completed.

Friday 24

Junior Walker
(Autry DeWalt II – Blytheville, Arizona, 14 June 1931)
Junior Walker & The Allstars
(The Jumping Jacks)

Saxophonist Junior Walker was the third Motown giant to pass away in 1995 and possibly the first of the Detroit music factory's instrumental players to have made a worldwide name for himself. Walker's earliest band was The Jumping Jacks, a troupe that played Indiana clubs during the fifties. The Allstars formed on his relocation to Michigan, and were discovered by singer Johnny Bristol in 1961. After their first US R & B hit with 'Shotgun' (1964), a stream of chart entries ensued, most notably the international smash '(I'm a) Roadrunner' (1969). Although hits were fewer towards the end of the seventies, Walker enjoyed an unlikely guest slot on Foreigner's US Top Five song 'Urgent' (1981).

Diagnosed with cancer six years before, Junior Walker died at his adopted home of Battle Creek, Michigan. Allstars drummer Billy 'Stix'

Nicks continued to tour the band, while Walker's son kept his father's name alive by pursuing a career as a percussionist in his own right. Long-time Allstars saxophonist Willie Woods survived his boss by just two years.

Saturday 25

Wildchild

(Roger McKenzie – Southampton, 1971)

'Wildchild' was the alter ego of the dance-mix practitioner who otherwise conducted business under the less flamboyant moniker of Roger McKenzie. Born in Southampton, at the age of twenty McKenzie made the exhausting journey to Brighton – ie, the future home of 'big beat' – where he worked as an underground house DJ and set up his own Dark & Black label. The single 'Renegade Master' (1995) was, however, issued on Norman 'Fatboy Slim' Cook's label, and became a club and Top Twenty hit that September, putting Wildchild on *Top of the Pops*.

By now, though, Wildchild had relocated to New York, where his tragic death from an unspecified heart condition one short month later came as a complete shock to the many who had recently worked with him. Sensing its unfulfilled potential, Cook excellently restyled the single in 1998, presenting Roger McKenzie's estate with a posthumous number-two hit in the UK and nearly 2 million worldwide sales.

DECEMBER

Sunday 10

Darren Robinson

(New York, 10 June 1967)
The Fat Boys

A unique act, Brooklyn's The Fat Boys – first known as The Disco 3 – won a recording contract as a result of their performance at a 1983 talent contest at New York's Radio City Music Hall. The band had a combined weight of over 750 lbs (54 stones/340 kilos), thus manager Charles Stettler and producer Kurtis Blow suggested the change of name.

An astonishing 60 per cent of this mass belonged to Darren 'Buffy the Human Beat Box' Robinson, who, with his size and uncanny repertoire of vocal effects, was clearly the group's focal point. Alongside rapping compadres Mark 'Prince Markie Dee' Morales and Damon 'Kool Rock-Ski' Wimbley, Robinson enjoyed notable crossover pop success – particularly with the covers 'Wipe Out!' (1987, with The Beach Boys) and 'The Twist (Yo Twist)' (1988, with Chubby Checker), US Top Twenty hits, both of which came within an ace of topping the UK singles charts. A series of smaller hits and a couple of movie roles followed, but – as with the novelty doo-wop acts their shtick echoed – The Fat Boys were to have only a brief shelf-life. The album *On and On* (an abortive 1989 attempt to harness the growing gangsta-rap vogue) harmed the group's credibility, while even more damaging was Robinson's charge of being accomplice to an under-age sexual liaison. This blew up when a video, made at a party he'd attended, was seized by police following a girl's complaint; although Robinson hadn't been directly responsible for the occurrence, it led to The Fat Boys' dissolution in 1992.

Ten days after a surprise reunion for the group, Darren Robinson sat on a couch entertaining friends again with his unwavering portfolio of sound effects. As he attempted to climb on to a stool, Robinson lost first his balance, then his breath, falling heavily and finally going into cardiac arrest. Attempts to revive him via mouth-to-mouth and CPR proved fruitless, and paramedics pronounced him dead at around 3 am. New York's outsized clown prince of rap had passed away

The Fat Boys – Robinson (*left*), Morales and Wimbley: May have had health issues

at just twenty-eight: never the fittest of human beings, Robinson had been suffering from respiratory influenza and was diagnosed lymphoedemic just weeks before.

Saturday 30

Clarence 'Satch' Satchell

(Cleveland, Ohio, 15 April 1940)

The Ohio Players

Originally the instrumental Ohio Untouchables, The Ohio Players were a seventies R & B group who embraced the burgeoning disco scene with relish, filling US dance floors with a number of mid-seventies smashes such as the number ones 'Fire' (1974) and 'Love Rollercoaster' (1975). (The latter became the centre of some controversy when the scream of a woman in the mix was rumoured to be the result of a genuine murder; it wasn't, of course, but The Players waited until the record had run its course to explain this!)

Known by his stage moniker, 'Satch', Clarence Satchell survived polio as a boy to become the band's main saxophonist and flautist. As The Players grew in stature, it was on Satchell's insistence that the record sleeves featured lurid images of sparsely clad women – in spite of this, they still earned themselves a number of Grammy nominations. Clarence Satchell passed away in Dayton, Ohio, one of many 1995 victims of aneurysm, leaving five daughters and a son, and at least six grandchildren. Fellow Ohio Players founder-member Ralph 'Pee Wee' Middlebrooks survived Satchell by only two years.

Lest We Forget

Other notable deaths that occurred sometime during 1995:

Baltimora (UK Europop singer best known for 1985's 'Tarzan Boy'; born Jimmy McShane, Derry, 23/5/1957; AIDS, 28/3)

Louise Dean (UK singer with dance act Shiva, who'd just scored with 'Work It Out'; born Yorkshire, 1971; hit by a drunk, uninsured driver in Huddersfield, she died from massive head injuries, 8/7)

Kenny Everett (notorious UK DJ and TV comedian who hit the Top Twenty in 1983 with 'Snot Rap'; born Maurice Cole, Liverpool, 25/12/1944; AIDS, 4/4)

Stephen David Harle (British punk drummer with UK Decay; born 1961; died backpacking in India, 1/3)

Billy Jones (US country-rock guitarist with The Outlaws; born Michigan, 20/11/1949; suicide, 9/2 – three weeks before the overdose death of his bassist Frank O'Keefe)

Sean Mayes (illustrious UK keyboardist with Fumble who then played with David Bowie – he wrote *We Can be Heroes*, a revealing account of the latter's 1978 tour; born London, 1945; AIDS, 12/7)

Paul A Rothchild (revered US rock producer who shaped the sound of The Doors, Janis Joplin and Love, among others – father of Grant Lee Buffalo bassist Dan; born New York, 18/4/1935; cancer, 30/3)

Pete Walli (Finnish acid-rock singer/guitarist with Kingston Wall; born Petri Walli, Helsinki, 25/2/1969; he threw himself from the tower of the beautiful church at Töölö, 28/6)

Delroy Wilson (noted Jamaican reggae vocalist; born Kingston, 5/10/1948; alcohol-related illness, 6/3)

Wolfman Jack (legendary US DJ, originally 'Daddy-Jules'; born Robert Weston Smith, Brooklyn, 21/1/1938; heart attack, 1/7)

For a complete list of fallen artists, visit
www.numberoneinheaven.com

1996

JANUARY

Tuesday 16

Richard Kermode
(Lovell, Wyoming, 5 October 1946)
Janis Joplin's Kozmic Blues Band
Santana
(Various acts)

Richard Kermode was a jazz pianist who adopted rock 'n' roll, having mastered a number of instruments while he grew up in Buffalo. One of the many who took notice of this very gifted musician was Janis Joplin, who recruited Kermode ahead of her marvellous performance at Woodstock in 1969. Inevitably, The Kozmic Blues Band ceased to be after Joplin's death (➤ *October 1970*), but the keyboardist and soprano sax-player found session work with other San Francisco bands such as The Grateful Dead, before playing on three albums with Santana. He also recorded with Labelle and Malo. By the time of his early death from cancer, Kermode was living in Denver, having returned to his jazz roots.

See also *Leone Thomas (➤ May 1999); David Brown (➤ September 2000)*

Sunday 21

Edem Ephraim
(London, 1 July 1959)
Dennis Fuller
(Jamaica, 19 June 1960)
The London Boys

Loved and ridiculed in equal parts, The London Boys were, at their peak in 1989, the last word in Eurodisco kitsch. Edem Ephraim and Dennis

Fuller chanced upon one another working lowly-paid jobs in Germany during 1980, going on to pack the floors of Hamburg's gay clubs as rollerskating duo The Roxy Rollers. In this guise, they were unearthed by producer Ralf-René Maué, who turned them into the (briefly) all-conquering London Boys. Somehow, Ephraim and Fuller's blend of old-school Hi-NRG disco and Eurovision camp smashed them into the Continental charts – shifting nearly 5 million records in the process. Britain had had its first tantalizing glimpse of the pair some

The London Boys – Ephraim and Fuller: Kitsch 'n' synch

years before, dancing in Kate Bush's 'Sat in Your Lap' promo; now, their own singles 'Requiem' (1988) and 'London Nights' (1989 – only kept from the top by Liverpool's own gift to European culture, Sonia) hit big in the UK, while a London Boys album, *The Twelve Commandments of Dance*, was also a surprise smash.

Then, some time after their huge triumph, there was tragedy. By the mid nineties Ephraim and Fuller were working as a touring novelty. Following some dates in Austria, the duo were travelling across the Alps with Ephraim's wife, Bettina, and a Hamburg DJ friend. As they negotiated a particularly treacherous section of mountain road, a drunk Swiss driver attempted to pass on the opposite side. The resultant collision killed both London Boys – plus the two passengers and the other driver. Ephraim and Fuller both left young children.

Friday 26

Stevie Plunder

(Anthony Hayes – Canberra, 1963)

The Whitlams
(Various acts)

With a smile on his face, a cold beer in his hand and a fistful of amphetamines, Anthony Hayes became his alter ego, 'Stevie Plunder', guitarist and very-much-frontman of The Whitlams – in the early 1990s, Australia's 'band most likely to'. Graduating from earlier bands such as The Plunderers and Hippy Dribble, Plunder formed The Whitlams in 1992 – on Australia Day, naturally – with Tim Freedman (piano) and Andy Lewis (bass), using studio drums until they could find a suitable percussionist. The band, named after their favoured Prime Minister, set about recording a debut EP, *Introducing the Whitlams* (1993). A full-length

album emerged the following year, and with the single 'I Make Hamburgers' afforded much airplay, all seemed very promising for the band.

However, four years to the day of his band's formation, Stevie Plunder's body was found at the foot of a cliff – an apparent suicide that shocked a music industry celebrating another Australia Day. No motive has ever been ascertained. Although the band continued under Freedman's guidance, a second suicide – that of Lewis in 2000 – was to horrify The Whitlams' fanbase once more.

MARCH

Saturday 2

Dinho Alves

(Guarulhos, São Paulo, 4 March 1971)

Bento Hinoto

(Guarulhos, São Paulo)

Julio Rasec

(Guarulhos, São Paulo)

Samuel Reoli

(Guarulhos, São Paulo)

Sergio Reoli

(Guarulhos, São Paulo)

Mamonas Assassinas (Utopia)

With a name meaning 'killer melons' (or 'mammaries', if you like) and a swathe of dubious poetry, Mamonas Assassinas may have appeared to be little more than a South American equivalent of California's Bloodhound Gang, but they were the biggest new rock band out of Brazil during a triumphant 1995. That year, the band's eponymous first album had shifted 2 million copies in their homeland – and, having upset parent groups with hits like '*Vira-Vira*', '*Pelados Em Santos*' and 'Robocop Gay', Mamonas

Assassinas were now looking to conquer the rest of the Americas. It was all a far cry from the serious rock of the band's beginnings (as Utopia), when they sold just fifty copies of their debut EP. By the start of 1996 an appearance by the riotous, irreverent Mamonas – Dinho Alves (vocals), Bento Hinoto (guitar), Julio Rasec (keyboards) and brothers Samuel (bass) and Sergio Reoli (drums) – was suddenly worth $50K a throw. Then, after one of the shortest spells in rock's spotlight, it was all over: the group's rise was suddenly, shockingly curtailed by a multiple tragedy eerily foreseen by more than one.

Set to record a second album in Portugal, the band left Brasilia after the last of some 200 live performances since June 1995. The normally chirpy members seemed quiet and strangely apprehensive, as though aware of the events about to unfold. Having his hair dyed red ahead of the final show, Rasec had told hairdresser Nelson de Lima of a premonition he'd had the night before, in which he saw a plane crash – perhaps prompted by young Sergio Reoli, who collected air-disaster clippings as a macabre hobby. Then, as visibly nervous singer Alves boarded the band's chartered Lear jet that evening, he was accosted by a runway worker who wished him 'a smash success in Portugal': the singer wryly replied that the only likely 'smash' would be his head, in an accident. Almost unbelievably, just an hour later he – and all of his band colleagues – were dead. Having left Brasilia at 11 pm, after thirty minutes the craft had begun its descent into São Paulo when it somehow dipped and smashed into a mountainside, cutting a 200-yard path through the trees as it disintegrated. In the carnage, all nine on board perished: as well as Mamonas Assassinas, their stage manager, their bodyguard, the pilot and co-pilot were also killed. The following morning, Brazilian teenagers awoke to the harrowing sight of television pictures relaying the live rescue attempt – and gruesome pictures of the scene were *not* being censored. Horrifyingly, especially given the band's earlier predictions, Alves's body was missing the upper half of his head when discovered, while Rasec had been completely decapitated; other band members' bodies were mutilated beyond recognition. (With no black box on board the craft, crew negligence can never be proven, though rumour suggests one of the *band* may have been trying to fly the plane when it crashed.)

Two days later – on what would have been singer and pin-up Alves's twenty-fifth birthday – troops were called in to control the inconsolable young followers of Brazil's hottest band, who'd gathered in their tens of thousands outside the morgue in São Paulo. The kids calmed themselves as best they could with impromptu renditions of the Mamonas' biggest hits (which in itself must have made for bizarre listening, given the band's preferred subject areas). Sympathies, however, were rather more muted elsewhere in the community. Many devout Christians who *didn't* care for the band's sometimes profane and often sexually explicit lyrics genuinely believed that divine retribution had been carried out there and then – the grim tale of Mamonas Assassinas was from then on exploited as a cautionary sermon for Brazil's young and reckless. One such detractor may have been noted Brazilian psychic Mother Mae Dinah, who had described 'dark shadows' around the band and – extraordinarily – predicted their passing in an air crash some months before the event.

Saturday 16

Joe Pope

(Atlanta, Georgia, 6 November 1933)
The Tams

From poverty-stricken backgrounds, The Tams formed as early as 1952 (as The Four Dots), four ghetto buddies – Joseph and Charles Pope, Robert Lee Smith and Horace Kay – with a song to share. With no funds to back them, the gang decided on the gimmick of wearing colourful tam o'shanters with their beachwear to gain attention. Thus they had a name as well as a collection of fine and soulful voices – of which Joe Pope's was readily pushed to the fore. It wasn't until 1960 that The Tams managed to secure a publishing and recording deal, scoring a US hit (of sorts) with 'Untie Me' (1962). In January 1964, the quartet – now signed to ABC-Paramount – stormed the Top Ten with 'What Kind of Fool (Do You Think I Am)'. While this was by far their biggest US seller, seven years later the group raced to the top of the UK charts with 'Hey Girl, Don't Bother Me' on Probe, Britain's ninth-best seller of 1971. Two other Tams' standards, 'Be Young, Be Foolish, Be Happy' (1970) and 'There Ain't Nothing Like Shaggin'' (1987 – obviously about the sixties dance craze of that name as opposed to anything else) also made inroads into the UK listings.

With a career spanning more than fifty years, The Tams join that elite collection of vocal groups still performing into the millennium. Smith, however, is the only original member treading the boards, former lead Joe Pope having died from heart failure.

Friday 22

Don Murray

(Glendale, California, 8 November 1945)
The Turtles

The Turtles confounded all those who'd dismissed them as bandwagon-jumpers by achieving huge success in America between 1965 and 1969. Initially members of surf instrumental bands styled after the likes of The Surfaris, The Turtles – Don Murray (drums), Howard Kaylan (Howard Kaplan, vocals/saxophone), Mark Volman (vocals/saxophone), Al Nichol (piano/guitar), Jim Tucker (guitar) and Chuck Portz (bass) – found inspiration in the achievements of local boys made good The Byrds. Briefly (and ill-advisedly) changing the spelling of their name to 'Tyrtles', the group also followed Roger McGuinn and company's lead by covering a Bob Dylan song, taking 'It Ain't Me Babe' into the US Top Ten in the autumn of 1965. When the public appeared to be tiring of their somewhat slavish copying of The Byrds' blueprint, The Turtles reinvented themselves as a crypto-psychedelic pop unit. In this guise, the band were much more the ticket, running off a series of memorable hits such as the 1967 million-seller 'Happy Together'. Murray, however, missed out on the band's most glorious period: tired of constant touring, he had quit The Turtles in June 1966, and was replaced by percussionist John Barbata.

Don Murray was to leave the music industry far behind him. Kaylan and Volman briefly joined Frank Zappa's Mothers of Invention, and The Turtles were a distant memory by Murray's untimely death. He passed away following heart surgery. Later Turtles keyboardist Bob Harris died in 1993.

Jeffrey Lee Pierce

(Montebello, California, 27 June 1958)

The Gun Club

Jeffrey Lee Pierce was one of the great unsung heroes of rock 'n' roll. Whether better management could have brought this anti-hero amalgam of Brando, Monroe, Morrison and Howlin' Wolf to the masses will never be known – but for those who bought into the ethic of The Gun Club, his like will never be seen again. In his late teens, Pierce became a devotee of Deborah Harry and Blondie, going on to run the New York power-popsters' fan club and befriending guitarist Chris Stein, who produced a couple of early eighties albums for this unusual young man's band (originally called Creeping Ritual) via his Animal label. The Gun Club had already exploded on to the scene with a fabulous debut, *Fire Of Love* (1981), which offered a powerful combination of howling blues and dead-end punk rock – the songs set alight by the singer's extraordinary performances, both on stage and in the studio. Pierce loved the music of the Delta, adopting slide-guitar techniques for his songs and reworking blues standards like Tommy Johnson's 'Cool Drink of Water'. The Gun Club – originally Pierce (vox/guitar), long-term sidekick Kid Congo Powers (Brian Tristan, guitar), Rob Ritter (bass) and Terry Graham (drums) – saw numerous changes in personnel over the years, the reckless, self-destructive Pierce disbanding and regrouping them almost wilfully. But that was pretty much the man: if he wasn't learning Haitian voodoo, he'd be getting himself beaten up or sectioned. That's if he hadn't shot up a load of heroin first.

After a brief solo outing, 1985's *Wildweed*, a refreshed Pierce surprised

Jeffrey Lee Pierce: Join his Club

'Jeffrey felt a certain pressure to live up to the idea he was going to die for rock 'n' roll. He'd play up to it sometimes – and ultimately it killed him.'

Nick Sanderson, drummer, The Gun Club

fans by re-forming The Gun Club with a whole new line-up that included his Japanese girlfriend, bassist Romi Mori – revealing a lusher variant of his previous garage stylings on the excellent *Mother Juno* (1987), a record produced in Britain by The Cocteau Twins' Robin Guthrie. Further recordings emerged into the nineties, including the fine solo album *In Exile* (1992). Pierce was literate and widely read, and also took to the stage as a spoken-word artist at this time.

The singer's habits did not, however, refine themselves: after years of drug and alcohol abuse, Pierce was diagnosed with cirrhosis of the liver when he suffered a severe nosebleed while on tour in Germany. He would never be in good health again. Those who recognized the shambling character while he resided in London recall incidents such as a fight in a Kensington pub when Pierce pulled a samurai sword on shocked assailants (which saw him deported at the end of 1995). Jeffrey Lee Pierce – who had an assortment of new projects underway (including a biography and yet another Gun Club) – fell into a coma at his father's home in Los Angeles on 28 March 1996 from which he was not to emerge. Tragically, a fatal clot on the brain resulting from his cirrhosis finally robbed the world of this genuine original; Pierce was laid to rest some days later in a Buddhist ceremony in Los Angeles. Since his passing, numerous artists have cited Pierce and The Gun Club as a huge influence, most notably distinguished US acts The Pixies and The White Stripes.

See also *Rob Ritter (* January 1991); Nigel Preston (* May 1992)*

APRIL

Thursday 18

Bernard Edwards

(Greenville, North Carolina, 31 October 1952)
Chic
(Outloud)
(The Power Station)

Bernard Edwards – who had relocated to New York with his family as a boy – had the most significant meeting of his life at just seventeen years of age. Befriending fellow guitarist Nile Rodgers, he made the first tentative steps towards greatness as a house bassist at the city's Apollo Theater. The pair, plus drummer Tony Thompson, fashioned The Big Apple Band – a club unit eventually forced to change their name (under pressure from Walter Murphy's identically named disco combo) to become the dance aggregation Chic. The addition of first Norma Jean Wright, then Alfa Anderson and Luci Martin as vocalists gave Edwards and Rodgers's band the lift it needed – and a flurry of great singles placed Chic at the pinnacle of the disco boom at the tail end of the seventies. The first was 1977's 'Dance, Dance, Dance (Yowsah, Yowsah, Yowsah)', which went Top Ten on both sides of the Atlantic; the biggest was 'Le Freak' (1978) – a remarkable 4-million-selling supernova smash that rewrote the rules as regards funk basslines. Between 1977 and 1982, Edwards and Rodgers could do no wrong, also producing smash hits for the revitalized Diana Ross and Sister Sledge.

With Chic's studio output laid to rest for a decade in 1982, Edwards released his own collection a year later (with the band Outloud) and remained in demand as a producer, instrumental in the success of work by ABC, Deborah Harry and Robert Palmer – and Palmer's Duran Duran collaboration, The Power Station. A regrouping of Chic – for the poorly received *Chicism* (1992) – was followed by that of The Power Station in 1996. Edwards had to join the latter when bassist John Taylor (who has often cited Edwards as his primary influence) walked out of the group. But it became clear that Bernard Edwards was taking on too much when he fell ill while reuniting with Nile Rodgers and a host of other stars for a showcase in Tokyo. Although showing no outward signs of ill health, Edwards took to his bed, where his condition became grave: his death from pneumonia shocked fans the world over (not least in Japan, where both Chic and The Power Station were still big news).

See also *Robert Palmer (* September 2003)*

Mike Leander

(Michael Farr – London, 30 June 1941)

That same day, a very different but nonetheless influential character passed away from cancer at his London home. Realizing he was unlikely to make the big time as a musician, Mike Leander abandoned the skiffle group of his teens to study music and law, earning himself the role of musical director at the Decca label in 1964. In this guise, Leander coaxed out the best in Marianne Faithfull, overseeing a number of hits for Mick Jagger's girlfriend. He was also responsible for producing singles by Lulu and Billy Fury, simultaneously composing for a variety of other UK artists. Although his best work is probably the arrangement he offered The Beatles' 'She's Leaving Home' (George Martin was unavailable), Leander will be remembered by most as the man behind the overwhelming seventies success of Gary Glitter, although this might be a source of some embarrassment to his family now. Leander – fascinated by African tribal rhythms – co-wrote several of the glam superstar's massive hit singles, including 'Rock 'n' Roll Parts I & II' (1972), 'Do You Wanna Touch Me? (Oh Yeah)' and 'I'm the Leader of the Gang (I Am)' (both 1973). Leander was also responsible for broader musical works, such as the London productions of the musicals *Jesus Christ Superstar* and *Matador*.

Tuesday 30

Beatmaster V
(Victor Ray Wilson – Los Angeles, California, 20 February 1959)
Body Count

With all the members having attended South Central LA's Crenshaw High during the seventies, the 1989 formation of uncompromising rap/metal crossover act Body Count appeared to be something of a school reunion. This was to be no 'jolly', however: Body Count – Ernie C (guitar), D-Roc (Dennis Miles, guitar), Mooseman (Lloyd Roberts, bass) and Beatmaster V (drums) – were not backward in coming forward on matters of social and political injustice. Although they were barely competent musically at the outset, with snarling rapper Ice-T fronting the onslaught, Body Count were in the public eye immediately with the song 'Cop Killer', from the band's self-titled debut album (1992). This notorious track was a direct attack on LA's allegedly corrupt law unit, and had to be pulled by Warner Brothers from later pressings.

It was to be the most notable achievement of the band's career. Later records had to be issued elsewhere when Ice-T fell out with Warners, sales suffering accordingly. From hereon,

the biggest headlines created by Body Count were for a series of tragedies that began with the sad death of Beatmaster V from leukaemia. The original line-up has since seen two others pass on: Mooseman fell in yet another drive-by shooting in 2001, while D-Roc was a second victim of cancer in 2004.

MAY

Kevin Gilbert
(Sacramento, California, 20 November 1966)
Giraffe
(Toy Matinee)

Although a very talented musician, songwriter and producer, Kevin Gilbert's progress was possibly blighted by the greater success of Sheryl Crow; the fact that Crow was his girlfriend filled far more column inches than the musician's own work did. In his early career, Gilbert fronted a number of his own bands, of which the best known were progressive-rock acts Giraffe and Toy Matinee, but the shelving of the latter's album in 1990 saw the multi-instrumentalist concentrate more on Crow's material. Her massive 1994 breakthrough record *Tuesday Night Music Club* – the title referred to an unofficial group of musicians, of which Gilbert was one – featured no fewer than seven of Gilbert's songs (or co-compositions), including the huge hit 'All I Wanna Do'. By the follow-up, though, Crow had ditched Gilbert, along with pretty much all of the other musicians who helped create the first album. Gilbert went on to build his own studio and produce Keith Emerson and ex-Bangle Susanna Hoffs, and record a brace of low-key solo albums.

An upturn in Kevin Gilbert's fortunes seemed likely after a Giraffe reunion, when Gilbert's tapes were given to Genesis, who were looking for a new lead singer to replace Phil Collins. On 17 May, Gilbert's manager arrived at his client's Eagle Rock home to bring him news of an audition with the British prog giants. Spotting the musician slumped by the stairs, he broke in to discover Gilbert dead, apparently *Number One in Heaven*'s only victim of accidental auto-erotic asphyxiation (the risky practice in which thrill-seekers deprive themselves of oxygen until they reach orgasm) – which, despite rumours, was *not* the cause of INXS star Michael Hutchence's death a year later (☛ *October 1997*). Gilbert was also believed to have been dabbling heavily with drugs at the time.

Johnny 'Guitar' Watson
(Houston, Texas, 3 February 1935)
(The Mellotones)

Later that evening, Japanese fans of Texas funk pioneer Johnny 'Guitar' Watson were shocked when their hero collapsed on stage at a gig in Yokohama. One of the most underrated performers of all time, Watson was encouraged to play music by his pianist father and preacher grandfather, who bought him the guitar that was to give him the nickname for his last forty years. When the family shifted to Los Angeles, 'Young John Watson' (as he was then known) found himself back at the keys again, however, as the teenage pianist with Chuck Higgins's Mellotones. By the mid fifties Watson had picked up the guitar again and sought to emulate the music of his hero and fellow Texan T-Bone Walker: as it turned out, this vibrant performer had his own sound and a unique onstage manner. Audiences were warming to

'They call Elvis "The King" – but the sure-enough "King" was Johnny "Guitar" Watson!'

Etta James

Johnny 'Guitar' Watson: A real mother for ya

the electrification of the blues, but they had yet to see the likes of Johnny 'Guitar' Watson, a personable, humorous presence one minute, whipping up a storm the next. One aghast young onlooker, Jimi Hendrix, was the first name to admit the influence of this vibrant talent, noting particularly the method by which the guitarist played with his teeth. For twenty years, Watson made his living recording for a variety of labels (even as a jazz-styled pianist when it was called for), before the funk boom of the seventies brought him a whole new audience. The DJM albums *Ain't That a Bitch* (1976) and *A Real Mother for Ya* (1977) both sold half a million worldwide, Watson's bass-centric deep funk finally having pushed him on to mainstream radio with great cuts like 'I Need It' (1976). The musician's influence swept broadly through music in the eighties and nineties – the likes of Prince, Ice Cube and Snoop Dogg have all paid homage in their recorded work. His own *Bow Wow* album (1994) achieved a long-overdue Grammy nomination for Watson.

Johnny 'Guitar' Watson remained a huge live force into his sixties; the 1996 tour of Japan drew even more devotees than before. The musician's performances had thrown up the usual mix of dynamism and good humour, with no suggestion of what was to befall him at the Ocean Boulevard Blues Café on the night of 17 May. During a rendition of his 1975 hit 'Superman Lover', Watson dropped to the stage. Though many initially thought this part of the performance, it soon became clear he was in trouble. His heart had stopped before he even reached hospital, and Watson was declared dead at 9.15 pm. While a sense of shock reverberated, a member of Watson's band took the stage some nights later to tell fans that it was 'kind of what he would have wanted'.

Saturday 25

Brad Nowell

(Long Beach, California, 22 February 1968)
Sublime

Ever a hyperactive character, Brad Nowell was a teenage surfing enthusiast who embraced punk rock, reggae and ska. Nowell was blond, tanned and ripped – a look that was starting to return to vogue following the wasted appearances of many grunge heroes. He was a natural frontman for Sublime, a band with a powerful sound reminiscent of Nowell's favourite LA punk acts from the eighties. The buzzing Long Beach circuit readily accepted Sublime, but the scene was rife with drugs – a fact not missed by the band's first album, *40 Oz to Freedom* (1996), nor indeed his Skunk label, upon which it was released. Nowell – who, considered a gifted child, had been prescribed Ritalin to stave off Attention Deficit Disorder – experimented, and became a heroin addict in his twenties. Nonetheless, Sublime appeared to be hitting the big time and in 1996 began work on a major-label debut for MCA.

Tours and publicity abounding, Nowell still found time to marry his girlfriend, Troy Bendekker (the mother of his year-old son, Jake), on 18 May – but a week later the singer was dead. Despite trying to stick to a rehabilitation regime, Nowell was found dead from an overdose on the floor of his hotel room the morning after a concert at Petaluma, California. The sessions for the album were released two years later as *Second Hand Smoke*.

Close... Mark Linkous

(Sparklehorse)

Enigmatic US songwriter Linkous's 1995 debut album was almost his last. Following a triumphant performance in London in March 1996, the Sparklehorse frontman unwisely mixed his prescription drugs, and fell awkwardly in his hotel room, trapping his legs beneath him. The resultant suspension in blood flow caused muscular damage and momentary cardiac arrest. Fast, intensive surgery at London's St Mary's Hospital saved Linkous's life. The grateful singer (who performed live several times in a wheelchair) went on to dedicate tracks from his second album to the folk who pulled him through. Said Linkous of his ordeal: 'It fucked me up! I was so pumped up on morphine and having operations all the time, I didn't know where I was for two months!' He added, 'I don't think doctors and nurses in the US are as compassionate.'

Closer! David Gahan

(Depeche Mode)

'New Life' was Dave Gahan's first major hit, and it was to resonate as doctors pulled the singer back from the other side in 1996. Once a bumfluff-sporting pretty boy of UK synthpop, the Depeche Mode singer had amazed fans by re-emerging in the early nineties as a tattooed rock god with a host of new pals like hard-rock figurehead Axl Rose. On 28 May, Gahan took his new tag a little too seriously, overdosing on a 'speedball' of heroin and cocaine at LA's Sunset Marquis Hotel – just months after a failed suicide attempt at his home. Confirmed dead for several minutes, the Mode-man was revived by astonished paramedics – and was then promptly arrested by somewhat less-astonished law-enforcement officers.

Thursday 30

John Kahn

(California, 13 June 1947)
The Jerry Garcia Band
The Paul Butterfield Blues Band
(Various acts)

Musician and artist John Kahn worked with some of the best-known San Francisco musicians of his era, including Jerry Garcia, whom he met in 1972. Kahn became a mainstay of Garcia's various side projects while never quite graduating to Grateful Dead status (allegedly because band members felt he encouraged the leader's drug usage) – although he was to work with them as a producer in 1978. As a bassist, Kahn also recorded with Elvin Bishop, Michael Bloomfield, Al Kooper and Maria Muldaur, then joined a later line-up of The Paul Butterfield Blues Band. John Kahn's own habit finally caught up with him in 1996 when he was found dead from a cardiac arrest at his home in Mill Valley – a combination of heroin, cocaine and antidepressants was found in his system.

See also *Michael Bloomfield (* February 1981) Paul Butterfield (* May 1987); Jerry Garcia (* August 1995)*

Elsbeary Hobbs

(New York, 4 August 1936)

The Drifters
The (Five) Crowns

The big break for throaty bass vocalist Elsbeary Hobbs came when notorious Drifters manager George Treadwell sacked the original line-up and recruited The Crowns – a similarly styled troupe waiting in the wings. With super-soulful Ben E King (lead tenor) at the front, Hobbs, Doc Green (baritone), James 'Papa' Clark (lead) and Charles Thomas (lead tenor) finally broke The Drifters on to the national pop charts. In the summer of 1959, 'There Goes My Baby' – featuring Hobbs's prominent tones – came within an ace of topping the pop listings; the following year 'Save the Last Dance for Me' went to number one, but for The Drifters' bass vocalist, time in the spotlight was all too short. After Ben E King left over a financial dispute, the group struggled with a series of new lead singers (which came to a dramatic head in 1964 when the latest, Rudy Lewis, was found dead (☛ *Pre-1965*)). By now Hobbs had been drafted (himself replaced by a number of hopefuls before the returning Tommy Evans took the position) – which effectively ended his singing career for a decade.

Finding work as a hospital therapist in the interim, Elsbeary Hobbs had rejoined one of many touring versions of The Drifters by the end of the sixties, which kept him busy for most of the rest of his life. The singer died from lung cancer in New York – one of some fifteen former Drifters now passed on (☛ *Pre-1965/Dead Interesting!*).

JUNE

Saturday 1

Alan Blakely

(Bromley, Kent, 1 April 1942)

The Tremeloes

Cancer was also to take a founder member of one of Britain's most successful sixties pop acts, The Tremeloes. Guitarist/keyboard-player Alan Blakely was one of a group of Essex school-friends – Ricky West (Richard Westwood, lead guitar), Alan Howard (bass) and Dave Murden (drums) – who'd formed the fledgling band behind singer Brian Poole in 1959. Signed to Decca – who foolishly sidestepped The Beatles in order to lay claim to the band – The Tremeloes nonetheless gave the label a great start with the UK number one 'Do You Love Me?' (1964), making them the first southern group to top the chart during the beat era. Although he was a reasonable singer himself, Blakely stood back to let Len 'Chip' Hawkes replace Brian Poole (and Howard on bass) when Poole left for an attempt at solo stardom in 1966. This move appeared a good one – The Tremeloes scored a second number one with the classic 'Silence Is Golden' (1967) and a decent run of other hits to 1970 – but the group's dismissal of its past and attempted prog direction proved to be a huge error of judgement. (At one point, The Tremeloes passed up the song 'Yellow River', which gave Blakely's brother Mike a number one with Christie.) The group had been all but forgotten by the record-buying public when Blakely left the line-up in 1975.

The inevitable nostalgia tours followed, but Alan Blakely had all but left the music industry by the time of his death.

Mathew Fletcher

(London, 5 November 1970)

Heavenly
Talulah Gosh
(Bugbear)

His associations with two of the UK indie scene's most 'innocent' bands perhaps make the death of drummer Mathew 'Fat Mat' Fletcher all the more incongruous. As reviled by the press as they were loved by their not-insubstantial fanbase, Talulah Gosh – an Oxford-based five-piece formed by Fletcher and his sister Amelia (aka Marigold, vocals/guitar) – emerged after the 'C86' movement instigated by the *NME*. The band's songs were lightweight and sometimes painfully twee, but occasionally touched upon the sublime (early tune 'The Day She Lost Her Pastels Badge' and 1991 sessions album *They've Scoffed the Lot* showed the humour lying beneath the surface of their work). Perhaps inevitably, it was to be something as innocuous as 'university commitments' that brought an end to the band in 1988, but the Fletchers (and guitarist Peter Momtchiloff) were not to be floored, and re-emerged as the much-touted Heavenly in 1989. Recording for Scotland's Sarah Records label (alongside such fey wonders as Even as We Speak and The Field Mice), Heavenly put out some unexpectedly strong albums in the nineties, much of the material written by Mathew Fletcher, who was also recording with his own punk outfit, Bugbear. However, by the issue of the final album, *Operation Heavenly* (1996), on Wiiija, the band was under something of a pall following Fletcher's shock suicide. There seemed to be little forewarning of the drummer's hanging, and those associated with the band have remained tight-lipped about the event ever since.

Amelia Fletcher continues to play with her current band, Tender Trap.

JULY

Friday 12

Jonathan Melvoin
(Los Angeles, California, 6 December 1961)
Smashing Pumpkins
The Dickies
(The Family)

The son of a noted jazz pianist, Jonathan Melvoin learned drums as a small boy and mastered a wide variety of other musical skills that were to see him flit between rock genres during his short career. The brother of Prince & The Revolution's Susannah and Wendy Melvoin (the latter of Wendy & Lisa fame), he began, at their behest, with the Prince-endorsed The Family, then played drums on the purple musician's *Around the World in a Day* (1985). A 1994 spell as drummer and road manager with original gonzo punks The Dickies gave Melvoin, who somehow juggled this role with his career as a paramedic, a complete change of musical direction. Then, in 1996, the musician was recruited as second keyboardist with alternative-rock giants Smashing Pumpkins, leader Billy Corgan being keen to augment his line-up as they toured the newly platinum album *Mellon Collie and the Infinite Sadness* (1995).

Following a triumphant show in New York, the band returned to their hotels – in Melvoin's case, to the Regency in Park Avenue. The vehemently anti-drug-and-alcohol Corgan and other band members James Iha and D'Arcy Wretzky retired to another hotel several blocks away. Unbeknown to them, Melvoin and regular drummer Jimmy Chamberlin dallied on the street, scoring what they believed to be high-grade heroin from a dealer. Despite having avoided an earlier sacking from the band by the skin of his teeth, Chamberlin, with Melvoin, drank into the night, then shot up back at the hotel. Having fallen into a haze, the drummer – a more seasoned user than his bandmate – awoke at around 3.30 am to find Melvoin comatose. Putting Melvoin in the shower, on the advice of 911 services, proved fruitless: when officers arrived at 4.15 am, the 34-year-old keyboardist was pronounced dead. The following day, all the members of the Chicago-based band were detained in New York for questioning, and five days later, Chamberlin was given his marching orders from the band (though he was later rehired).

Smashing Pumpkins – already enduring a difficult year, after the death of a fan at a Dublin show – were not invited to Jonathan Melvoin's funeral, though they later agreed to pay $10K to his widow, Laura, and baby son. Ironically, the dead musician's father, Michael Melvoin – for many years the chair of the National Academy of Recording Artists and Sciences – had long been a campaigner to rid the music world of drugs, in particular the heroin that was to kill his son.

See also *Chuck Wagon (* *June 1981)*

Tuesday 16

John Panozzo
(Chicago, Illinois, 20 September 1948)
Styx

With his twin brother, the bass-playing Chuck, drummer John Panozzo was determined to emulate the extravagant stylings of his favourite prog bands: in the event, it proved to be bombastic ballads that drove his band to the very top as the seventies came to a close. The twins played together from age fifteen, growing up as US rock gained confidence in the face of the UK's beat boom. By 1970 Styx (then the rather anonymous TW4) had recruited a strong vocalist/instrumentalist/songwriter, Dennis DeYoung, and guitarists John Curulewski (who was replaced by Tommy Shaw in 1976 and died in 1988) and James Young. It was not until 1975 that Styx unlocked the Billboard charts, however, with the DeYoung-penned single 'Lady', which sold a million copies. Momentum grew with a series of platinum albums – the peak for Styx was surely 1979's *Pieces Of Eight* and its number-one single, the orchestrally driven 'Babe' (their only noteworthy UK hit, a year later). The band showed more resilience than most of their stadium rivals, scoring hits into the nineties – 'Show Me the Way' (1991) was picked up as a chest-beating Gulf War anthem.

Heavy drinking taking its toll on his health, John Panozzo at this point began to take a sidelined role in Styx's activities: to his chagrin, the drummer – suffering an arm injury – was eventually replaced by Todd Sucherman for a reunion tour in 1996. Within days he was dead, discovered at his Chicago home, the victim of a series of bleeding ulcers resulting from cirrhosis of the liver. Styx continued into the millennium (legal wrangles replaced the recording of new material); Chuck Panozzo, meanwhile, was diagnosed HIV positive in 2001.

Wednesday 17

Chas Chandler
(Bryan James Chandler – Heaton, Northumberland, 18 December 1938)
The Animals

Chas Chandler couldn't really have done a lot more to secure his place in pop folklore. The genial six-foot Geordie was first of all bassist with an internationally successful beat group, then discovered and managed one of the finest talents rock music has ever seen (Hendrix, as opposed to Slade), and finally used his experience and clout as a music ambassador for his beloved Newcastle. Befriending pianist Alan Price, Chandler played with the latter's blues trio in 1962 before they discovered charismatic vocalist Eric Burdon – and renamed the band The Kontours. Completed by Hilton Valentine (guitar) and John Steel (drums), the band were then renamed The Animals – and the big time was just around the corner. According to late producer Mickie Most, they recorded the transatlantic number one 'House of the Rising Sun' (1964) in less than twenty minutes. The single was the biggest of eight Top Ten hits the band enjoyed in the UK, including 'Don't Let Me be Misunderstood' and 'We Gotta Get out of This Place' (both 1965), but ferocious internal squabbling caused Chandler to follow Price's lead and leave The Animals in 1967: 'We toured non-stop for three years and hardly saw a penny,' Chandler revealed in 1994. (Even a reunion tour twenty years later had to be cancelled because of an outbreak of onstage brawling between the musicians.)

In 1968, Chandler chanced upon a young musician named Jimi Hendrix playing in a bar in Greenwich Village; he knew immediately that this young man was going to cause a sensation. Wasting no time, Chandler took Hendrix to England, introducing him to guitarist Noel Redding and drummer Mitch Mitchell – the remaining pieces of The Jimi Hendrix Experience. Having produced the prodigy's first two albums, Chandler later said on record that he wished he hadn't left the job unfinished: falling out with the star before the release of *Electric Ladyland* (1968), the manager never had the chance to make up with Hendrix before he died (**◄** *September 1970*). In terms of out-and-out

Chandler and Hendrix: Listen, Jim – you run through 'Voodoo Chile' as many times as you want. I'm just gonna nip out for some tabs ...

commercial return, though, Chandler's most successful period was surely his dozen or so years as manager of Slade, supervising the Wolverhampton good-time boys as they topped the British charts no fewer than six times between 1971 and 1974.

In his later life, the former Animal began his own label and helped develop the 10,000-seat Newcastle Arena. The project was completed just a year before Chas Chandler's death from an aortic aneurysm.

See also *Noel Redding (◄ May 2003)*

Monday 22

Rob Collins

(Sedgley, West Midlands, 23 February 1963)
The Charlatans

A decade after Rob Collins's death, many still feel that, despite his increasingly wilful behaviour while a member of the band, The Charlatans were at their best when he was about. A pianist since his teens, Collins developed a swirling organ sound that set the music of The Charlatans apart from their immediate peers (Stone Roses, Inspiral Carpets, etc). The band – fronted by photogenic singer Tim Burgess, who joined Collins, John Baker (guitar – soon replaced by Mark Collins), Martin Blunt (bass) and John Brookes (drums) – hit the jackpot first time, their debut album, *Some Friendly*, topping the UK listings in 1990, while evocative hits such as 'The Only One I Know' (the *NME*'s Single of the Year) meant that their faces were seldom far from *Top of the Pops*. Perhaps Collins's own most distinctive moment was his jarring Hammond intro on the 1992 Top Twenty hit 'Weirdo'. Then, in November 1993, Collins was suddenly imprisoned for four months for his supposedly unintentional part in the armed robbery of an off licence; while he waited at Her Majesty's pleasure, The Charlatans built an entire album (1994's *Up to Our Hips*) around the swathes of organ Collins had already created.

The Charlatans were close to finishing yet another album, *Tellin' Stories*, at Monmouthshire's Rockfield Studios in 1996 when another, far worse incident occurred. Expecting the roads to be quiet, Collins had decided to drive himself and Charlatans sound engineer Richard Peet back to the studio after a session at a local pub. Collins miscalculated a bend, and his BMW flipped up and off the road, throwing the driver through the sunroof and fifty feet into a cornfield. While Peet escaped unhurt, Rob Collins was confirmed dead at the scene from massive head injuries; his blood alcohol level was found to be twice the legal limit. Collins, who left an estranged wife and young daughter, was remembered on the next single 'One To Another' (issued just two weeks after his death) and its parent album – the biggest hits of The Charlatans' career.

The Charlatans, with Rob Collins (*left*): Just lookin'

Sunday 28

Margie Ganser Dorste

(Marguerite Ganser – Queens, New York, 4 February 1948)

The Shangri-Las

Like her identical twin sister, Mary Ann, Margie Ganser seemed to live out a tragic life not dissimilar to those of the heroines of The Shangri-Las' many mini soap operas. Two of five New York siblings, Margie and Mary Ann lost their father when very young, finding in music an outlet for their creative desires – and in high-school friends Mary and Liz 'Betty' Weiss some near neighbours who shared their dreams. The four girls stumbled almost accidentally upon a sound of their own (unique in that their somewhat nasal singing voices seemed to harmonize perfectly) – not missed by Kama Sutra boss Artie Ripp when he caught a performance by the then Bon Bons in 1963. Nor was their potential overlooked by production genius George 'Shadow' Morton, who assembled two classic 1964 hits for the repackaged Shangri-Las in 'Remember (Walkin' in the Sand)' and 'Leader of the Pack' (☛ *The Death Toll #1*). Aged sixteen and seventeen, the four girls were all minors, so contracts with Red Bird had to be signed by the three surviving parents, which somehow saw The Shangri-Las – like so many other sixties groups – miss out on a small fortune in royalties in the years to come. Although the stark, melodramatic 'I Can Never Go Home Anymore' (1965) gave them a third Top Ten hit, the Shangri-Las subsequently found it harder to chart their records. Nonplussed by the lack of funds coming her way, the studious Margie Ganser left the Shangri-Las in 1966 to return to college.

The death of her twin sister (☛ *March 1970*) inevitably hit Margie Ganser hard and, blaming the industry for the tragedy, she turned her back on music for ever. Ganser finally found happiness in her marriage to Bill Dorste in 1972, and later worked with the telecommunications giant Nynex. She died from breast cancer in hospital in New York: as per her wishes, her ashes were buried with those of her beloved twin.

Jason Thirsk

(Hermosa Beach, California,
25 December 1967)

Pennywise

Named after the demonic clown in Stephen King's novel *It*, California punks Pennywise – high-school pals Jason Thirsk (bass), Jim Lindberg (vocals), Fletcher Dragge (guitar) and Byron McMackin (drums) – emerged in 1989. Following a slow-burning 1991 debut album, Lindberg left to get married and Thirsk assumed vocals. Staunch believers in the 'no sell out' and 'DIY' ethics of punk rock, Pennywise, unlike many of their peers, refused to join a major label and thus missed out while bands like Green Day and The Offspring hit the big time. Thirsk had long had a problem with alcohol, which appeared to be exacerbated by his demotion when Lindberg returned. With fourth album *Full Circle* (1997) imminent, the bass-player upped sticks and left, committing himself to rehabilitation. Though he seemed to have beaten his addiction, Jason Thirsk relapsed and was found by his girlfriend in his yard, having apparently died from a self-inflicted gunshot wound. Pennywise continued with Randy Bradbury, who had played bass on the album.

Seagram Miller

(Oakland, California, 1970)

One of the most widely touted of the Bay Area's new rap freestylers, Seagram Miller based many of his lyrics on his experiences in Oakland's notorious East Side – the area he had grown up in and seen ripped apart by gang culture since the early eighties. Miller signed with the RapaLot label, and his debut, *Reality Check* (1995), was just beginning to place the rapper on a national platform when tragedy struck him down. In the early hours of the morning of 31 July, he and colleague Gangsta P were approached by a masked gunman who seemed to be tracking the latter. When the assailant opened fire, Miller threw himself across his friend – taking the full onslaught of the bullets. Gangsta P survived the attack, but Seagram Miller was mortally wounded. Understandably, hundreds showed up to pay their respects at the heroic artist's Oakland funeral some days after the tragedy.

SEPTEMBER

Lee Baker

(Joseph Lee Baker – Memphis, Tennessee, 1944)
Lee Baker & The Agitators
Moloch
(Mudboy & The Neutrons)

Uncompromising singer/guitarist Lee Baker was a powerhouse of the Memphis-blues scene, playing on Beale Street with the likes of Mississippi Fred McDowell and Furry Lewis as a young man. His lengthy career included stints with late-sixties blues-rockers Moloch (who released one 1970 album on Enterprise), Alex Chilton, Rufus Thomas and even country stalwart Charlie Rich. Baker formed the much-loved Mudboy & The Neutrons in 1972 – the band that really should have been the making of him – finally playing the clubs with his own Agitators during the eighties and nineties.

In August 1996, a freak fire all but destroyed Baker's home; the musician was philosophical and optimistic about it when he learned nobody had been hurt. However, by dark coincidence, just one month later, on the night of 10 September, Baker – as much through necessity as neighbourliness – was staying with his aunt, Sally McKay, at her nearby home in Horseshoe Lake, Arkansas, when a pair of teenage boys attempted to break into the house, believing it empty. Disturbed first by McKay and then Baker, the boys panicked and pulled guns on their victims. When Baker attempted to intervene, he was shot in cold blood – as was his aunt, just moments later. Abandoning their dying victims, the criminals then set fire to the house before making their getaway. Baker left a wife and three sons.

2Pac

(Lesane Parrish Crooks – Brooklyn, New York, 16 June 1971)

Fast becoming rap's highest-profile act, 2Pac as a character had few equals within the genre as the nineties reached their halfway mark: he seemed more concerned with enhancing his own legacy than diminishing that of his so-called rivals. But 2Pac found himself recast as hip hop's new 'bad boy' and became embroiled in what many believe to have been an entirely orchestrated feud with The Notorious BIG – the rivalry seemingly nurtured by idle words and the cunning of others.

Tupac Amaru (it's Inca for 'shining serpent') Shakur was renamed by his single mother, Afeni – a former Black Panther who had served time for terrorism while pregnant with him – who told him falsely that his absent father was dead. Her son quickly proved that he was a talented, if wayward soul; indeed, he showed such range in his days at the Baltimore School for the Arts that his tutors believed the young man going by the name 'MC New York' could have played Shakespeare. Because of his turbulent family life, though, Shakur was moved to Oakland before he could complete his studies. As he morphed into his alter ego, 2Pac, it became apparent to the young extrovert that music, in particular rap, was the main market for him. After all, he had much material for his lyrics: his stepfather was a wanted narcotics dealer (eventually jailed for sixty years), his mother a confessed addict whose dedication in bringing him up inspired 2Pac's early career. Alongside the gangsta staples of corrupt cops and 'booty', the rapper included veiled references to literature and, particularly on the debut album *2Pacalypse Now* (1991), lyrics that appeared to empathize with subjugated women, which set him apart from the posturing of most of his rivals. Shakur was still keen to prove that he was red-blooded, however, and his numerous girlfriends included actress Salli Richardson, Keisha Morris (to whom he was married for reasons of convenience while in prison) and finally Kidada Jones – daughter of

black-music legend Quincy Jones – his room partner on the fateful final night in LA.

While recording his own work – and also with critically acclaimed unit Digital Underground – Shakur gained broader notoriety for his role in the street movie *Juice* (1992), several light years away from the roles hoped for by his Baltimore tutors. But this was who the man now was – a savvy, sharp-tongued operator with fewer scruples but the charisma to elevate him to the pinnacle of his chosen field. (A year on, he featured in *Poetic Justice* alongside Janet Jackson – the actress/singer insisted that her opposite number took an AIDS test before shooting; he refused.) Around this period, Shakur had a notable pair of his many, many altercations with the police: the first saw him win a $42,000 lawsuit after being beaten up for disrespecting Oakland officers; the second was a bizarre incident in which the rapper raced to the rescue of a black motorist in Atlanta, shooting two officers he believed were harassing the young man. In the event, the policemen involved were found to be intoxicated – and all charges against Shakur were dropped. This, of course, elevated him to the position of God among his peers. Shakur's subsequent incarceration for a sexual-abuse felony – which he denied until his death – did little to undermine their thinking. But, before he could even face the sentence, events took another strange turn: Shakur was shot outside a nightclub during an apparent robbery. He only just escaped with his life (Bad Boy artists renamed him '1Pac' after he lost a testicle) but was imprisoned nonetheless in February 1995. Serving eight months inside Clinton Correctional Facility, Shakur kept busy: he read widely, married Morris and earned the dubious distinction of being the first ever artist to boast a Billboard number-one album while inside (*Me against the World*). The FBI were equally busy, it seems. They had long seen the gangsta movement as a national menace, perhaps even Black Panther-affiliated. It was (allegedly) FBI policy to place undercover officers with jailed felons from the hip-hop community in order to create dissension within their ranks. 2Pac's followers believe that he was encouraged to think that his erstwhile friend Christopher Wallace (aka rapper The Notorious BIG/Biggie Smalls) had been involved in his attempted murder the previous November. 2Pac – who had countless feuds with fellow artists – created a further rift with his former cronies by switching allegiance from the East Coast to the West, joining Death

'Suge' Knight: **'You OK, Pac?'**
2Pac: **'Me? You're the one shot in the motherfuckin' head!'**

Row Records in California at the behest of formidable head honcho Marion 'Suge' Knight, who was prepared to pay the artist's bail in return for three albums for his label. Shakur perhaps saw in this man the father figure he had missed in his youth; Knight clearly saw something beyond this kind of relationship. He himself had a long-running feud with Bad Boy (the New York label owned by Puff Daddy, for whom The Notorious BIG recorded), and was believed to have used Death Row (now Tha Row) as an outlet for less-than-legal pursuits. However, while Knight involved himself with these underground activities, Shakur recorded an astonishing amount of material for him – certainly more than three albums' worth, as would become apparent in the years that followed. Just before his death, the rapper (who had famously predicted his short lifespan) recorded the single 'I Ain't Mad Atcha' and shot a premonitory video depicting himself in heaven jamming with a number of his dead heroes.

So, with all that had gone on before, the events of the night of 7 September had an eerie and depressing inevitability about them. 2Pac and Knight, dressed to the nines, were special ringside guests of former heavyweight champion Mike Tyson at his Las Vegas fight with Bruce Seldon. After the fight, Shakur got into a skirmish of his own in the lobby of the MGM hotel, the venue for the spectacle. Recognizing Orlando 'Baby Lane' Anderson, who had recently beaten up and robbed one of his bodyguards, Shakur flew at the Compton 'Crip' (ie, a gang member affiliated more with Bad Boy than with Death Row, whose protection came from the 'Bloods'). He was joined by Knight, who, breaking the terms of his own parole, weighed in with some convincing kicks. Within an hour the smell of revenge was in the air. 2Pac travelled to Knight's Club 662 (where the artist was apparently due to perform with Run DMC) in the boss's Sedan, leading a convoy of friends. At an intersection just half a mile from the club, the Sedan was joined by a white Cadillac, from which an occupant aimed a gun at Knight's car and issued thirteen shots into the vehicle. While Knight suffered only a graze to the head, Shakur, who had attempted to dive into the back, was hit four times – in the chest, arm and thigh. He had not been wearing the regulation bulletproof vest issued him by Death Row. After a series of operations, including one to remove a lung, Tupac Shakur was pronounced dead at 4.03 pm on 13 September – a black Friday that would be long commemorated by his legions of fans.

The Notorious BIG (who had apparently been in Vegas that evening) and Puff Daddy expressed no real surprise at Shakur's shooting but great shock and regret when he didn't pull through. The copycat murder of Biggie just months later (☞ *March 1997*) blew the whole scenario wide open once more, with accusations flying all over. Yet ten years on, the truth remains unconfirmed – and will likely remain so,

given the number of those involved protected or running scared. Or indeed dead. 2Pac's long-time pal rapper Yafeu 'Kadafi' Fula had been in the convoy and offered to testify to what he saw – but was shot before he could utter a word. Baby Lane was similarly gunned down in 1998. Knight's detractors maintain that he orchestrated the entire fracas at the MGM, though the huge risk to himself (and his parole terms) make this unlikely; he was, however, known to be concerned by rumours that Shakur wished to return to New York, maybe into the arms of Bad Boy – perhaps out of the rap industry altogether. When interviewed by the ubiquitous Nick Broomfield in San Quentin (where he was serving time for the parole violation), Knight's emphasis seemed to be more upon the 'crime' of snitching than on the proliferation of gun murders within the rap community. (Now released, Knight remains close to controversy: as recently as August 2005, he was shot in the leg at a party for rapper Kanye West.)

2Pac's mother continues to release her son's material (some under the alias of Makaveli), and his sales have quintupled since his death. To his mother's credit, much of the royalty money has been used to found Georgia's Tupac Amaru Shakur Center for the Arts. In 2005, 'Ghetto Gospel' gave the star a first UK number one – in the company of the still-very-much-alive Elton John.

OCTOBER

Thursday 17

Chris Acland
(Lancaster, 7 September 1966)
Lush
(Panik/Infection)

The tragic suicide of drummer Chris Acland offers perhaps the ultimate cautionary tale to those seduced by the idea of a career in a rock band. In 1996, Lush had finally graduated from stalwart indie also-rans into a bona fide chart-bothering pop unit, yet Acland was earning barely £150 a week when he died. Acland had played in a number of other guitar bands before he and Miki Berenyi formed Lush – Acland, Berenyi (vocals/guitar), Emma Anderson (ditto) and Steve

'Getting in the charts and having your face in the papers doesn't mean you'll be up to your eyeballs in cash. If you're lucky enough to sell millions, then it'll be record companies, publishers, managers, agents, licensees and PRs that take their slice before any money finds its way to you.'

A sobering warning from Lush's Miki Berenyi

Rippon (bass, replaced by Phil King in 1991) – at North London Polytechnic in 1988. The band had an ethereal sound owing much to the likes of The Cocteau Twins, and indeed shared the latter's 4AD label. Although Lush had a loyal-enough following, it was clear that it would wane once the shoe-gazing movement of the early nineties had run its course. The gut-punch Britpop gave UK music seemed to change the band's fortunes for the better: in the mid nineties, they returned with the hit album *Lovelife* (1996) and a run of Top Thirty singles including the sneering, Camden-centric 'Ladykillers' – a far cry from the fey soundwashes of yore.

But despite these successes, Lush were unable to break the US, and the constant touring and promotion came at a price. With Anderson set to quit, all plans were put on hold by the appalling news that followed. Spending a week at his parents' home in Kendal, Cumbria, Chris Acland was found hanged in their barn. Apparently depressed by his financial and domestic situations (including a distressing split with a girlfriend), Acland had been on prescription sedatives for some time before he took

his life. Said Berenyi, 'Chris's death finished Lush. He was one of my best friends ever and there was very little else I wanted to do without him.'

NOVEMBER

Saturday 2

Eva Cassidy

(Oxon Hill, Maryland, 2 February 1963)

(Chuck Brown & The Soul Searchers)

With little interest in academic studies, Eva Cassidy – who, as a child, sang and played guitar in a band with her father and brother – planned a career as an artist until her near-flawless crystalline soprano was discovered. In 1986, music producer Chris Biondo overheard her voice when mixing a record for one of her friends. Biondo, who had a relationship with Cassidy, had the foresight to nurture her talent over a period of a few years before exposing her to some of the significant figures with whom he worked – one such being the very impressed

soul balladeer Roberta Flack. For Cassidy, though, mass critical and commercial acceptance was to arrive after her death.

In 1993, Cassidy began touring as singer with Chuck Brown & The Soul Searchers (also, briefly, with the band Pieces of a Dream) and recording with Blue Note records. It was also around this time that she had outpatient surgery for a malignant lesion on her back, treatment she and most around her believed to be routine. A year or so later, however, increasing pain in her hip forced Cassidy to abandon touring (as well as her work as a mural artist) and seek further tests: the news was bad. In the summer of 1996, Cassidy was diagnosed with advanced melanoma and given only months to live. Weakened, she was admitted to hospital, emerging just once to sing a touching rendition of 'What a Wonderful World' at her own tribute concert, some six weeks before her death. Her ashes were scattered at Chesapeake Bay, Maryland.

Remarkably, it wasn't until 2000 that Eva Cassidy's work passed into the greater public consciousness. Unearthed by the BBC (particularly by veteran DJ and fan Terry Wogan), a large back catalogue of her songs – most notably those on Cassidy's fourth album, *Songbird* – were reissued on a series of CDs. Her albums shifted over 4 million copies, and in 2003, Eva Cassidy, who had never played in the country, became the only artist with three posthumous number-one albums in Britain.

'All I want to do when I get well is sing and travel with my music.'

Eva Cassidy, 1996

Tiny Tim: Pushing up the tulips

Saturday 30

Tiny Tim
(Herbert Khaury – New York, 12 April 1932)

'From the sublime . . .' etc. Often referred to as 'Master of the Disturbing', part-Lebanese, part-Jewish Herbert Khaury toyed with a number of aliases before settling on the Dickens character's identity in the late fifties. The singer's big break came after some appearances on cult American TV comedy hour *Rowan & Martin's Laugh-In* in 1967, whereupon he was offered a recording deal with Reprise and the deranged falsetto of his 'Tiptoe Thru' the Tulips' (1968) vaulted into the US Top Twenty; the debut album *God Bless Tiny Tim* then went Top Ten. His onscreen marriage to GTO Miss Vicki on *The Johnny Carson Show* similarly garnered much publicity (and the couple's daughter, born in 1971, was honoured with the name 'Tulip'). Tiny Tim was no slouch, however – an educated man,

his live performances were liberally sprinkled with erudite song references and historical nuggets.

By his later shows, Tiny Tim had all but dropped his quavering high pitch for a more natural baritone, but audiences still – for some reason – clamoured for the voice of old. In September 1996, he suffered a coronary at the Massachusetts Ukulele Festival and was warned by his GP to take things more easily. Instead, Tiny Tim kept up the live appearances. At a charity function at the Women's Club of Minneapolis, Tiny Tim completed a rendition of his biggest hit, then collapsed at the side of the stage, finally succumbing to that year's second heart attack. Khaury was buried alongside his trusty ukulele and – of course – a single tulip. His work was kept alive by its strangely fitting inclusion in the pilot episode of anarchic kids' show *Spongebob Squarepants*.

DECEMBER

Monday 9

Patty Donahue
(Akron, Ohio, 29 March 1956)
The Waitresses

Emerging from an Ohio new-wave scene that gave the world Devo, Chrissie Hynde and Pere Ubu, The Waitresses were a sassy, self-aware outfit just made for the pose of singer Patty Donahue. The song that first gained the group some attention was 'I Know What Boys Like' (reissued 1982 – an Australian Top Ten hit), an anthem of tease penned by Donahue's partner in the band, guitarist Chris Butler. This resulted in a deal with Ze Records, who issued the first Waitresses album, *Wasn't Tomorrow Wonderful?* (1982). The debut fared well, missing the US Top Forty by only one place, but The Waitresses – Donahue, Butler, Dan Klayman (keyboards), Mars Williams (sax), Tracy Warmworth (bass) and Billy Ficca (drums, ex-Television) – were destined to remain a cult phenomenon. That said, their 'Christmas Wrapping' remains an annual 'jolly' far more welcome than the usual Slade/Wizzard/Wham fare.

After the recording of a second album, Patti Donahue was replaced in The Waitresses by Holly Vincent (ex-Holly & The Italians). Donahue – once a backing singer for Alice Cooper – briefly rejoined the band in 1984 before taking up a more background role as an MCA music publisher, a position she held until shortly before her untimely death in New York from lung cancer.

Faron Young

(Shreveport, Louisiana, 25 February 1932)

Considered by some to be a cuter, slighter Hank Williams, Faron Young was discovered by hawkish talent-spotter Webb Pierce, who placed the novice singer on his local *Louisiana Hayride* radio programme at the start of the fifties. Young had fronted his own country group as a teenager – initially to while away the time at high school, from which he inevitably dropped out – and picked up more than a few of Williams's onstage trademarks. But Young was to become a better singer and songwriter than most of the Nashville elite cared to admit. His first country chart hit was the almost rock 'n' roll-sounding 'Live Fast, Love Hard, Die Young' (1953) – Young appears to have achieved most of these objectives during his lifetime (persistent rumours connect him with a number of partners, including Patsy Cline). A star of several movies and very much a heart-throb of his generation, Young also

managed a couple of crossover hits with 'Hello Walls' (1961) and 'It's Four in the Morning' (1972), a huge UK hit that put the singer on *Top of the Pops* alongside Slade and Alice Cooper. (The song and its protagonist were then further immortalized by British songwriter Paddy McAloon of Prefab Sprout in 1984).

Young's later career, though, was blighted by poor sales, alcoholism and the singer's increasingly cantankerous behaviour. He discharged firearms in public places and, on one notorious occasion, proffered corporal punishment to a young girl in his audience who stuck her tongue out at him. It seems sad that a figure as significant as Faron Young should feel that the industry had snubbed him, but it became apparent during the nineties that the singer – whose health was rapidly deteriorating – had given up not just on music but on life itself. Hugely depressed by the emphysema that had affected him since 1990, Young put a shotgun to his own head at his home on the night of 9 December, and died in hospital the following morning.

Faron Young: When he wasn't lovin', he wasn't livin' ...

'I'm not an alcoholic. I'm a drunk.'

Faron Young

Ruby Murray
(Belfast, 29 March 1935)

Ruby Murray's trademark hoarse vocal style was not, in fact, a gimmick – as a child, she underwent an operation to correct her vocal chords, giving her the characteristic voice that would enchant millions. Having taken her first tentative steps as a 12-year-old entertainer in Belfast, Murray made her mark on BBC television's *Quite Contrary* while still a teenager (and gained a fan in guest Frank Sinatra). The response to her was extraordinary: Murray's remarkable feat of charting five simultaneous UK Top Twenty hits early in 1955 is unlikely ever to be bettered. The biggest of these was the schmaltzy 'Softly, Softly', a number one that sold over 750,000 copies.

By her twenty-fifth birthday, however, it was pretty much all over. As many were to find out (Helen Shapiro among them), longevity was more difficult for female singers to achieve during this era. In Murray's case, the seismic shift created by rock 'n' roll dated her sentimental ballads overnight, but she was now married . . . and there was always cabaret. Enduring at least two nervous breakdowns, alcoholism and a painful divorce (after which she remarried), Ruby Murray finally passed away from liver cancer at a Torbay hospital. Her instantly recognizable name lives on via her songs – and, of course, its rhyming-slang adoption. Mine's a king prawn bhuna.

Lest We Forget

Other notable deaths that occurred sometime during 1996:

Les Baxter (US 'exotica' orchestra leader who topped the charts with both 'Unchained Melody' and 'The Poor People of Paris' in the fifties; born Texas, 14/3/1922; kidney failure, 15/1)

Dawn Crosby (hard-living US singer with thrash-rockers Détente, aka Fear Of God; born California, 1963; liver failure exacerbated by alcohol and drug abuse, 15/12)

Vinnie Daze (US drummer with thrash-metal band Demolition Hammer; born Vincent Civitano, New York; while travelling in Africa, he contracted and died from 'globefish poisoning' – apparently, 11/3)

Jim Ellison (US rock singer/guitarist with Material Issue who also played with members of Blondie, Guns n' Roses and Urge Overkill; born Illinois, 18/4/1964; suicide by carbon monoxide asphyxiation, 20/6)

Curtis Hairston (US R & B singer with The BB&Q Band who enjoyed an international solo smash with 1985's 'I Want Your Lovin' (Just a Little Bit)'; born North Carolina, 10/10/1961; kidney failure, 18/1)

Gus Hardin (US country balladeer; born Carolyn Ann Blankenship, Oklahoma, 9/4/1945; head-on car collision, 17/2)

Kenny Hillery (one-time US metal bassist with Quiet Riot; born *c* 1970; suicide, 5/6)

Nicodemus (Jamaican DJ/reggae artist; born Cecil Wellington, 1957; diabetes, 26/8)

Arthur 'T-Boy' Ross (US songwriter for many big names including Marvin Gaye and Madonna – sibling of Diana Ross; born 1949; he was found murdered in his basement along with his wife, Patricia, 22/6)

Johnny Sandon (UK singer with Merseybeat band The Remo Four – originally a soloist backed by The Searchers; born Bill Beck, 1941; suicide by hanging, 23/12)

For a complete list of fallen artists, visit
www.numberoneinheaven.com

1997

JANUARY

Wednesday 1

Townes Van Zandt

(Fort Worth, Texas, 7 March 1944)

Townes Van Zandt has been described posthumously as 'The Van Gogh of Songwriting', so admired was his technique by some of folk and rock's recent greats. As college drop-out and son of an oil tycoon Van Zandt strolled proudly from coffee shop to bar in his early years, the title of 'Texas Troubadour' came more readily to the lips of his followers – who included Merle Haggard. A gnarly, dry humour pervaded the singer's early songs, though it was heart-wrenching ballads such as 'For the Sake of the Song' (1968) that brought him to a wider audience. That said, Van Zandt's wares were destined to remain unfamiliar to most, although Willie Nelson's cover of his 'Pancho and Lefty' was a country chart-topper in the early eighties. Numerous country/folk acts recorded versions of his songs thereafter, including Emmylou Harris, Lyle Lovett and The Cowboy Junkies. Lack of broader appeal for his own output, though, depressed Van Zandt, who began to drink heavily, his physical condition deteriorating to the point that he stopped recording completely during the eighties.

Around Christmastime in 1996, Townes Van Zandt underwent hip surgery, which triggered the heart attack that was to cost him his life. His own idol had been country pioneer Hank Williams, whose way with a melody and ability to extract so much from a lyric was to inform Van Zandt's own work throughout his career. Ironically, the singer died forty-four years to the day after his mentor (➡ *Pre-1965*).

'Townes Van Zandt was the best songwriter in the whole world – and I'll stand on Bob Dylan's coffee table in my cowboy boots and say that!' Steve Earle

Thursday 2

Randy California

(Randolph Craig Wolfe – Los Angeles, California, 20 February 1951)
Spirit
(Jimmy James & The Blue Flames)

Young Randy Wolfe founded the embryonic Spirit (then jazz/fusion group The Red Roosters) with his stepfather, jazz drummer Ed Cassidy, when he was just sixteen – creating one of the few credible 'father and son' partnerships in rock. While Cassidy had previously played with Ry Cooder, for his own part, California, as he'd been dubbed by Jimi Hendrix, had already accompanied Jimmy James & The Blue Flames. With Jay Ferguson (vocals/bass), Matt Andes (bass/slide guitar) and John Locke (piano) completing the line-up, the band continued under the somewhat unwieldy name of Spirits Rebellious, until, as Spirit, they claimed an early radio hit with 'I Got a Line on You' (1969), which made it to number twenty-five in America. Unfortunately, the band committed a faux pas that year by not taking up Hendrix's offer to play Woodstock. Despite Spirit delivering their best album in *Twelve Dreams of Dr Sardonicus* (1970), the

Kenny Pickett

(Kenneth Lee – London, 3 September 1942)
The Creation
(The Kennedy Express)

The Creation – originally The Mark Four – were the short-lived band touted as 'the next cultural phenomenon' by Tony Stratton-Smith's equally short-lived Planet Records. With his penchant for spray-painting the stage, Kenny Pickett was certainly a notable frontman – but it just didn't happen, though The Creation – Pickett, Eddie Phillips (guitar), Mick Thompson (rhythm guitar), Bob Garner (ex-Merseybeats, bass) and Jack Jones (drums) – were actually better than the hype might have had folk believe. Their biggest hit (well, it made thirty-six in November 1966) was the catchy, guitar-driven 'Painter Man' (Top Ten when demolished by Boney M in 1979), but few other Creation ditties caught the public's attention. Pickett nevertheless enjoyed a varied and unusual career in music. Leaving The Creation in 1967, he became road manager for Led Zeppelin and Steppenwolf, before composing the biggest hit of his life – yes, Clive Dunn's 'Grandad', a UK number one in 1970.

Kenny Pickett re-formed The Creation in the mid nineties (after a brief tenure as singer of The Kennedy Express), the band gaining something of an audience from the Britpop crowd, signing with (aptly) Alan McGee's Creation label. Then, at a gig in Mortlake, South London, the singer collapsed and died during a rendition of Chuck Berry's 'Johnny B Goode'. He is believed to have suffered a coronary, though the post mortem failed to confirm a definite cause of death.

Randy California: Still here in spirit

displeased Ferguson and Andes ran off to form Jo Jo Gunne a year or so after. A trimmed-down Randy California & Spirit turned out eclectic albums by the year, while retaining their West Coast following. (In the early nineties, the original line-up regrouped for tours.)

California always had a recklessness about him. His career almost ended early on when he fractured his skull when thrown from a horse, while in 1973, after the band's van and equipment was stolen in London, an already fragile California plunged into the Thames and had to be rescued. His reputation as a loose cannon only escalated after this strange precursor to his tragic passing. On holiday with his mother, Bernice, the guitarist

and his 12-year-old son, Quinn, encountered treacherous waters while swimming off the coast of Molokai, Hawaii. Axe-hero California became folk-hero as he pushed his boy to safety: sadly, strong undercurrents overcame the musician. His body was never recovered, and Randy California was declared lost at sea just a day later. Bernice Cassidy continues to preserve her late son's heritage – not least with her claim that Led Zeppelin's 'Stairway to Heaven' was, in fact, lifted from 'Taurus', one of California's earliest compositions.

Golden Oldies #4

Colonel Tom Parker

(Andreas Cornelius van Kuijk – Breda,
The Netherlands, 26 June 1909)

A significant figure in rock 'n' roll history, Tom Parker earns his position here more genuinely than he did his military title: an illegal alien who arrived in the USA aboard a merchant ship, Parker took on an assumed identity in order to join the US army. He only began his forays into show business on his return to civilian life, a move to Louisiana opening up opportunities as a C & W music promoter – and it was here, as opposed to in the army, that Parker became 'Colonel', the epithet given him by state governor Jimmie Davis. Parker chanced upon singer Elvis Presley, whom he persuaded Sun to offload to RCA for a remarkable $35,000 – a vast figure for a relative unknown. From hereon, Parker controlled Presley's career closely. While many of his methods were highly questionable, there's little doubt that The King would not have taken his throne without the Colonel's guidance. Parker's method, so he claimed, was based around the 'less is more' principle, the manager keeping his star away from the public eye to maximize interest. Elvis, for example, never played in Europe – though many believe the reason behind this Parker decision was that the Svengali himself wouldn't have been readmitted into the US. Meanwhile, Parker pocketed nearly half Presley's earnings from record sales, publishing, residuals or profits from the movies the star was roped into making during the sixties. In the early seventies, Parker sold the rights to Presley's back catalogue to RCA for an undisclosed amount – but on terms that were unfavourable to the singer. To his credit, Parker had masterminded such strokes as Elvis's triumphant comeback shows in Vegas around this time, which fans still hold in greater affection than any early performances. On balance, though, his cosseting of Presley was greatly damaging to the singer, who lived a life of crass indulgence behind the scenes: the legend's death (➤ *August 1977*) is still considered by many an inevitable result of such a lifestyle.

Parker outlived his protégé by almost twenty years, finally agreeing to sell many of Presley's master recordings to RCA in 1983. After finding a lower-profile position as entertainments consultant for Hilton Hotels during the nineties, Parker died from a stroke on 21 January 1997 – appropriately, perhaps, in Las Vegas, in whose casinos he is thought to have spent much of his fortune.

Wednesday 22

Billy Mackenzie

(Auchterhouse, Dundee, 27 March 1957)
The Associates

A headstrong teenager, Billy Mackenzie travelled extensively and even married in Las Vegas to avoid deportation; his desire to sing only manifested itself on his return to the British Isles – though not everyone cared for the cheery Scotsman's four-octave range. When The Associates – Mackenzie, plus multi-instrumentalist Alan Rankine – came out of Edinburgh with a cover of 'Boys Keep Swinging' (1979), the critics were ready to dismiss another David Bowie copyist (this was the year of Gary Numan, after all). A year on, *The Affectionate Punch*, a shimmering, original debut album for the Fiction label, changed all that. By 1982 The Associates had jumped at an offer from Warner Brothers and soon became chart regulars – for that year at least. Second album *Sulk* (1982) raced into the Top Ten – as did the very distinctive single 'Party Fears Two' (a tale of student gatecrashing, somehow plucked as the theme to BBC Radio Four's *Weekending*), and sprightly follow-up 'Club Country' almost followed suit. Mackenzie seemed born into the spotlight, weaving and grinning his way through live shows and television slots alike. This was a time of silver lamé and white teeth: with a third chart success, '18 Carat Love Affair', Mackenzie easily looked the part. The first problems, however, came with the delay in releasing further material; Rankine had been less happy with all the attention lapped up by Mackenzie, and the pair parted soon after. Returning in 1984 with some new Associates – Steve Reid (guitar) and Howard Hughes (keyboards) – the singer found the locks had been changed while he'd been away. Thereafter, none of Mackenzie's albums or singles (which included 1985's lovely 'Breakfast') registered on the charts.

With a solo set, *Outernational* (1991), dismissed by both critics and punters alike, Mackenzie was declared bankrupt three years later. Although he'd landed a further deal with Nude (Suede's label) in 1996, the singer had already moved back to his parents' Dundee home – and was succumbing to serious depression as he approached his forties. It seems that the death of his mother that year proved the straw that broke the camel's back: four days after sealing his contract, Mackenzie took himself into his father's garden shed and swallowed a combination of prescription tablets. Shortly after the removal of his son's body, the singer's bereft father burned the shed and everything in it.

Billy Mackenzie's work for Nude was issued via the touching and highly personal posthumous collection *Beyond the Sun* (1997).

The Sweet – Scott, Tucker, Connolly and Priest: Better watch out if you've got long blond hair

FEBRUARY

Brian Connolly

(Brian McManus – Hamilton, Scotland,
5 October 1945)

The Sweet

Set to become the prettiest boy in British glam rock, Brian Connolly went by the name of McManus until leaving home and opting for his birth mother's name when he discovered his adopted status at eighteen. Connolly was already a seasoned guitarist by the time he formed Wainwright's Gentlemen in 1966 (once boasting Deep Purple's Ian Gillan as vocalist),

a serious rock band that changed its name to Sweetshop two years later. As the shorter, cuter The Sweet, Connolly – with Andy Scott (guitar), Steve Priest (bass) and Mick Tucker (drums) – rose steadily to the fore of UK popular rock. Conceding that they would sell more under the songwriting team of Nicky Chinn and Mike Chapman ('Chinnichap'), The Sweet went on to fight regular chart battles with Gary Glitter, Slade and T Rex as *Top of the Pops* became fun again. The band's enormous singles sales between 1971 and 1975 peaked with the number one 'Blockbuster' (1973), but this was surrounded by an impressive tally of other bubblegum hits, including five records at number two, of which 'Ballroom Blitz' (1973) was also a very healthy US seller. (The Sweet also managed eight number ones in Germany.) The dimpled Connolly

was clearly the focus for teen worship, but he was happy to share the limelight with bass 'tart' Priest, whose fluttering interjections became a band gimmick, copied by many. A split with Chinnichap (who had plenty of other big-name artists to cater for) preceded a dip in fortunes for The Sweet, however, although they did write 'Fox on the Run' (1975), another big US hit that also pushed new pin-ups The Bay City Rollers all the way in the UK.

Connolly left the band after a final Top Ten entry with the introspective 'Love is Like Oxygen' (1978). Drinking heavily, the singer attempted a solo career, having fallen out with his bandmates of many years. His health declined dramatically in the years that followed, not helped by serious problems in his personal life and near-bankruptcy. Connolly had little to fall back on financially – most of the hit royalties had landed at the feet of the writers. Thus, in the early nineties, the singer took his own line-up of The Sweet out on the road (in direct competition with Andy Scott's version of the band, though the pair settled their differences prior to Connolly's death) but his continued abuse of alcohol rendered many performances non-starters. Connolly even had plans to follow a country direction, feeling this would be better for his voice, but by now it was too late – he had already suffered a series of heart attacks due to his addiction. Partially disabled, Brian Connolly died of renal failure at his home in Slough. It was a grim, unflattering end for one so clearly associated with glamour – though the singer managed the rare feat of being surrounded by three of his former partners (plus his two daughters and young son) on his deathbed.

See also *Mick Tucker (☛ February 2002)*

Thursday 13

Michael Menson

(Michael Tachie-Menson – London, 1967)

Double Trouble

With partner Leigh Guest, Michael Menson made up Double Trouble, the rap/dance duo operating mainly as back-up to The Rebel MC (Michael West). Although Ghanaian diplomat's son Menson enjoyed several hits in the UK – most notably the Top Five 'Street Tuff' (1989) – it was the appalling racially driven circumstances of his murder which, sadly, most will recall first.

After his short time in the spotlight was over, 30-year-old Menson began to suffer severe delusional episodes that resulted in his being moved into supported accommodation in London by the start of 1997. Then, on the night of 28 January, in Edmonton,

North London, a lost and disorientated Menson was set upon by three men, who attacked him twice, first stealing his personal stereo and then throwing white spirit over him and setting his clothes alight. Michael Menson died sixteen days later from horrific burns to his back. No statement or evidence had been taken by police – who assumed the former artist had attempted suicide. Menson's family were distraught at what they felt was a botched inquiry, and it took two years to bring his killers to justice. Of the attackers (who were found to have racist motives for the killing), Mario Pereira was found guilty of murder, while Harry Constantinou and Ozguy Cevat – who had to be pursued to Cyprus for trial – were both convicted of manslaughter. One of Britain's highest-profile atrocities in years, the case came hot on the heels of the Stephen Lawrence murder trial.

MARCH

Sunday 9

The Notorious BIG

(Christopher Wallace – Brooklyn, New York, 21 May 1972)

And so the squabble went on. And so another life was needlessly wasted. With titles like 'Ready To Die', 'Machine Gun Funk' and 'You're Nobody ('Til Somebody Kills You)', Christopher Wallace – aka The Notorious BIG (or sometimes Biggie Smalls) – was either remarkably prescient or, more likely, had the measure of his market's glorification of gang culture. Either way, his envelopment in the East–West rap wars was only ever going to have one result.

The Notorious BIG (it stands for 'Business Instead of Game',

apparently) earned his soubriquet well before he'd signed a deal with Bad Boy Entertainment. Biggie was a known narcotics dealer who gained 'respect' in the Bedford/Stuyvesant hood where he had been brought up mainly because of his formidable six-foot-three, 350-lb-plus presence. With a served conviction behind him, the man had the perfect credentials for gangsta rap and was snapped up by Sean 'Puffy' Combs for his label, releasing a million-selling debut album in 1994. *Ready To Die* might have had depressingly predictable subject matter, but whatever – Biggie was the newest folk hero, offering the East

---

DEAD INTERESTING!

LURCH OF THE POISONED MIND

Gangsta rappers involved in actual gangsta crimes is hardly a new thing these days, but in 2002, 'Suge' Knight's Tha Row stable found itself at the centre of the genre's most horrific story yet. Supposedly up-and-coming Texas-born rapper Big Lurch (real name Antron Singleton) had just recorded his first album for the label when police found him covered in blood on a South Central LA street on the morning of 10 April. In a scenario more reminiscent of the Norwegian black-metal scene, Singleton had murdered and mutilated his flatmate Tynisha Ysais . . . and eaten a section of her lung.

The prosecution alleged that Singleton – who was believed to have a history of mental illness – had been 'plied with drugs' by the label and encouraged to go forth and 'commit a crime that would make him more marketable as a gangsta artist'. On 7 November 2003, he was sentenced to life behind bars. Knight, meanwhile, testified that he had never even met Big Lurch, let alone heard him rap.

Biggie: Notorious, big and ready to die ...

Coast its most convincing challenge yet to the West Coast elite. One of those who appeared a touch peeved by Wallace's success was Tupac Shakur, who allegedly believed his former friend was adopting his style: perhaps Shakur was prompted to make these accusations because, though Biggie might have had an aura about him, he wasn't in the same league in terms of talent. A series of inevitable spats via record and video developed, 2Pac claiming he'd slept with Wallace's wife, singer Faith Evans. The accusation that Wallace was involved in Shakur's near-fatal shooting in November 1994 merely iced the cake.

In 1995, Biggie swept the awards to the chagrin of all at Death Row Records: but things were about to become more intense. After Shakur's highly publicized assassination (➤ *September 1996*), although no arrests were ever made, Biggie knew he was living on borrowed time. On the evening of 9 March, seemingly

unfazed by an assault charge hanging over him and appearing pumped and preened, The Notorious BIG attended the annual *Soul Train* awards in Los Angeles. Then, as he was driven to the after-show party at LA's Petersen Automotive Museum, the rapper was murdered in a drive-by shooting frighteningly similar to that of 2Pac six months before. As the GMC Suburban carrying Biggie waited at a stoplight, a 'dark car' (no better description was ever given) pulled up alongside and a passenger unloaded between six and ten bullets into the Suburban: The Notorious BIG was declared dead at 1.15 am at the Cedars-Sinai Medical Center. Following a suitably outsized funeral in New York, his ashes were shared between his mother (who featured prominently in his lyrics, as Shakur's mother did in his), Evans and his high-profile ex rapper Lil' Kim. The inquest met with an inevitable silence. Indeed, so short of answers were the

police that at one point they couldn't even identify the driver of Biggie's car. Nearly a decade on, the identity of the perpetrators remains a mystery – though certain names have been mentioned frequently, including that of a former LAPD officer. Although nobody has yet been brought to justice, in the spring of 2006, the City of Los Angeles was held responsible for withholding information during a botched civil case, and BIG's family was awarded over $1 million in compensation.

The Notorious BIG's final album was chillingly titled *Life After Death*; predictably, it sold bucketloads in the wake of his death, as did Puff Daddy and Faith Evans's somewhat turgid tribute, 'I'll be Missing You' (1997). Which – conversely – owed a small amount to The Police.

Jermaine Stewart

(William Jermaine Stewart – Columbus, Ohio, 7 September 1957)

(Shalamar)

A former piano student, Jermaine Stewart – owing a small debt to Michael Jackson – developed his dance and vocal style on arriving at the 'happening' scene in Chicago. As a dancer, he toured with The Chi-Lites and Staple Singers, joining successful disco unit Shalamar in 1980. But, with few opportunities to be much more than a shadow to the group's obvious star, Jeffrey Daniels, Stewart became disillusioned and left for a solo career. His break came at the hands of Culture Club – the British pop group used the singer's backing vocals on the US hit 'Miss Me Blind' (1984); bassist Mikey Craig then financed Stewart's own demo, and solo recognition was at last on its way. Stewart scored his biggest hit with the club singalong 'We Don't Have to Take Our Clothes Off', a record that made the Top Five on both sides of the Atlantic, becoming the UK's fourteenth-biggest hit of 1986. Generally speaking, he was a bigger star in Europe than at home: the single 'Say It Again' gave him another UK Top Ten hit in February 1988, while 'Don't Talk Dirty to Me' was a million-seller in Germany the same year. But his distinctly eighties performances appeared dated by the start of the next decade: Stewart had a much lower profile and slower record sales. Unbeknownst to his loyal fan-base, he was also battling AIDS – the disease that cost him his life in 1997. Some sources cite liver cancer as the cause of Stewart's death, though this was probably a complication.

Harold Melvin

(Philadelphia, Pennsylvania, 25 June 1939)

Harold Melvin & The Bluenotes

The father of smooth Philly soul began his journey to legend as the teenage singer of impromptu 'street corner' ballads; at sixteen, he was already fronting The Blue Notes (two words back then), at that time a fairly uncomplicated doo-wop ensemble. But until 1970 – ie, for a very long time after the group's foundation – they had to make do with revenue from live performances, their records for some reason largely failing to register with R & B consumers. Then, Melvin (who had steered his troupe – Roosevelt Brodie, Jesse Gillis Jr, Franklin Peaker and Bernard Williams – thus far) hit upon the idea of employing a second lead voice – that of soul schmoozer Teddy Pendergrass, who'd also played drums with The Bluenotes. The latter, under the guidance of Melvin and the essential songwriting team of Kenneth Gamble and Leon Huff, created a timeless, near-forlorn sound that at last made an impact. After one or two chart flirtations, the group enjoyed its biggest worldwide hit with 'If You Don't Know Me by Now' (1972), following this with a sequence of similar-paced tearjerkers such as 'The Love I Lost' (1973) and 'Don't Leave Me This Way' (1977) – The Bluenotes' biggest UK hit. When Pendergrass left to pursue a solo career in 1976, Melvin employed other lead singers, but the Bluenotes' moment appeared to have passed. Throughout his career, Melvin had also guided other noted vocalists such as mid-period Bluenote Billy Paul, and also Sharon Paige, whom he'd employed on the group's studio work.

Harold Melvin continued to perform until his death: the singer suffered a series of strokes, dying in his sleep at home in Mount Airy, Pennsylvania. The Bluenotes carried on, keeping the name alive in tribute to the man at the helm.

APRIL

Laura Nyro

(Laura Nigro – The Bronx, New York, 18 October 1947)

Her father being a jazz trumpeter and her mother an opera aficionado was unfortunately still not enough to lift Laura Nyro to the heights that she had hoped for as a young girl. Nyro proved herself time and time again to be a talented songwriter, but found little success with her own recordings. Debuting at the Monterey Pop Festival as a 19-year-old, she was barracked mercilessly by the crowd, who were there to see and hear The Byrds, The Grateful Dead, Hendrix, Joplin and The Who – Nyro's odd choice of an 'angel' outfit also did her few favours. This was a shame, as her debut album, *More Than a New Discovery* (1966), contained some nice moments, not least 'Stoney End' – later a Top Ten hit for Barbra Streisand. Others to have recorded her songs include Blood, Sweat & Tears, Peter, Paul & Mary (both recorded 'And When I Die'), Three Dog Night ('Eli's Coming') and The Fifth Dimension, whose cover of Nyro's 'Stoned Soul Picnic' was a 2-million seller in 1968. Despite management by a young David Geffen, Nyro failed to make a commercial breakthrough, and retired from performing at just twenty-four;

she nonetheless continued to put out sporadic albums.

Although touring once more during the late eighties (to great acclaim), staunch pacifist Laura Nyro was happier with more domestic pursuits, such as bringing up her son, Gil. Diagnosed with ovarian cancer, she died just short of her fiftieth birthday.

Saturday 19

El Duce

(Eldon Hoke – Seattle, Washington, 24 March 1958)
The Mentors

The notorious beer-loving drummer and (if one stretches one's imagination) singer with schlock-rockers The Mentors, El Duce will always be better recalled as the man who claimed Courtney Love offered him money to kill Kurt Cobain just before the latter's death (➤ *April 1994*). Alongside guitarist Eric Carlson (aka 'Sickie Wifebeater'), Hoke had fronted The Mentors since 1978, their repertoire coming up against moral crusaders with its themes of sexual proclivity, drinking and violence (indeed, the recital of some of Hoke's ludicrous poetry caused hoots of laughter at the Tipper Gore-led Congressional Hearings in 1985). Fast-forward twelve years: El Duce famously told film-maker Nick Broomfield that Love had, in 1993, offered him $50K (and a blow job, which he turned down, if other sources are to be believed) outside a Hollywood record shop to blow her husband's head off. He concluded that someone else had actually carried out the deed; in 1996, a polygraph lie-detector test astonishingly suggested he was telling the truth.

Although few were likely to miss his music, Eldon Hoke's death just

a week after the interview was shot came as a shock to a lot of people – not least to the Cobain murder theorists. Hoke's body was found by a railway track in Riverside, Los Angeles; authorities – having ascertained the high volume of alcohol in his blood – put his death down to 'misadventure'. Hoke's friend and music journalist Al Bowman said, '[El Duce] was excited about his upcoming tour – he didn't kill himself. I'm convinced this has something to do with Kurt Cobain.' And so the conspiracy theories proliferated.

MAY

Friday 23

Tim Taylor

(Dayton, Ohio, 1969)
Brainiac

Tim Taylor was the unlikeliest of punks. Though singer, guitarist and chief songwriter with Brainiac, he liked nothing more than to dabble with vintage synthesizers (especially anything bearing the Moog name), many of which ended up being used in his recorded output. His band, the raffish but intelligent Brainiac, were just as eclectic. Clearly inspired by fellow Ohio-ites Devo, they looked to be heading places by 1997, having put out four albums in as many years, with wondrous titles like the chaotic *Hissing Prigs in Static Couture* (1996).

However, after a tour of the UK, supporting Beck, tragedy brought this interesting band's career to an abrupt halt. Just ten days after his return to Dayton, Taylor lost control of his car, most likely because of a broken accelerator – the vehicle slammed into first a fire hydrant and then two

telegraph poles. Before he could be pulled from the wreckage, the car burst into flames. Taylor, rumoured to have been decapitated in the crash, was presumed to have been killed by the impact.

Jeff Buckley

(Orange County, California, 17 November 1966)

(Gods & Monsters)

Jeff Buckley – his was a parallel world of contradiction: his behaviour kind and caring, yet wilful; his notions naive, optimistic, yet wise. And his death, like his music, was a direct product of these paradoxes. Like his father before him, Buckley functioned as he played, on instinct. Both maverick musicians, they made a startling father-and-son double, Jeff Buckley also removing himself accidentally from a world that didn't always understand. Like Buckley Sr, he died in a manner dramatic, rash and unnecessary.

Throughout his brief career, Buckley shunned comparison with the father who had left him and his mother when Jeff was still in the womb. To say that he didn't enjoy, or assimilate, Tim Buckley's music would be untrue, however. Brought up by his mother, Mary Guibert, and (for a time) her partner, Ron Moorhead, Buckley was eight years old when his father finally relented and met his son for the first time after a concert in Huntington Beach. Just a few months after father and son had spent a week together, Jeff Buckley learned of Tim's freakish death (*June 1975*). Despite the breakthrough in their relationship, Buckley (who had excitedly adopted the surname as a result of the holiday) did not receive an invitation to his father's funeral, nor was he referred to in any of the many obituaries (his half-brother, Taylor, was mentioned by name).

As he grew up, Buckley embraced his father's remarkable work – he stunned the audience at a 1991 tribute to Tim Buckley – as he would those of many other musicians right across the spectrum. A vinyl junkie, he consumed The Smiths, The Cocteau Twins, Edith Piaf, Led Zeppelin, hair metal and *qawwali* vocalist Nusrat Fateh Ali Khan in equally voracious quantities, and assimilated them all to produce a unique product of his own. His rounded, soaring vocals (and remarkable physical resemblance) meant that comparisons with his father were inevitable; these became an irritation to a talent who only wanted to be recognized for himself. (DJ Mark Radcliffe, during a live 1FM session: 'Your father had a similar sense of abandon . . .' Jeff Buckley: 'Yeah – he abandoned *me*.') With his early performances in New York plagued by 'Tim hippies', it was only in the last year of his life that Buckley publicly acknowledged his father's influence – at least on a professional basis. 'It should be known that I have great admiration for Tim. Some things he did embarrass me to hell, but the things that were great I would hold up against anything. But that's respect as an artist – because he wasn't my father. My father was Ron Moorhead,' he told a television interviewer, before adding sagely, 'Each of us will stand on his own – in time.'

In 1992, that time was fast approaching for Jeff Buckley. After a spell in New York's Greenwich Village with avant-garde combo Gods & Monsters (leader and former Captain Beefheart guitarist Gary Lucas was said to be 'crushed' when Buckley called it a day), the emerging artist, who could already boast many column inches in hungry music journals, was snapped up by Columbia on a reported million-dollar signature. The first recorded results were issued on the *Live at Sin-é* mini album (1993), four strikingly different yet somehow connected pieces (two originals, two covers) taken from a performance at the cult East Village venue. It was Buckley's full-length debut, however, that sent a chill down the industry's collective spine. *Grace* (1994) featured Buckley plus his band – Michael Tighe (guitar), Mick Grondahl (bass) and Matt Johnson (drums, replaced eventually by Parker Kindred) – but it was the main man whose voice, guitar, harmonium and organ, writing and arranging set the album head and shoulders above most others that year. Tracks such as the vast, soaring title cut, space-shifting 'So Real' and exquisite radio hits 'Last Goodbye' and 'Lover, You Should've Come Over' could only attract converts to the growing throng who felt Buckley was already surpassing his father's work. Yet the record shifted just 100,000 or so copies. Buckley was much bigger in the UK and Australia than at home, where *Grace* largely remained an undiscovered masterpiece until after its maker's death.

Buckley himself was dissatisfied, not with sales so much as finish. He had fast gained a reputation as a perfectionist and this was to cause problems with his second long-player, provisionally entitled *My Sweetheart, the Drunk*. For this, Buckley hired his hero Tom Verlaine (of New York art-rockers Television) as producer, to the chagrin of his label, who didn't see this as part of the essential commercial forward shift. As rehearsing at the Memphis studio stretched on and on – running up a bill of some $350K – Buckley became despondent. He was hyperactive, and found relationships difficult (among the 'lovers who came over' were Joan Wasser of alt-rock band The Dambuilders and Elizabeth Fraser of Scottish post-punk favourites The Cocteau Twins), but was shattered once it became apparent that his working association with Verlaine was not functioning. Desperate for headspace, Buckley allowed his band time off while he stayed put in Memphis, working without the pressure of others present.

By the end of May 1997 Jeff Buckley felt ready to nail the album once and for all – to the huge relief of his

Jeff Buckley: Everybody here wanted him

'I have a love of misadventure.'

Jeff Buckley, in interview with *Q Magazine*, 1994

label and band. On the 29th, as he awaited the return of his musicians, Jeff Buckley and a new friend, New York hairdresser Keith Foti, took themselves off to the rehearsal space, getting lost on the way and diverting to the Wolf River, which intersects with the Mississippi just short of Memphis. On the bank, Buckley cranked up his friend's boom box and sang raucously along to Led Zeppelin as Foti played his guitar. The next Foti knew, Buckley had jumped into the river fully clothed – and continued to sing, floating on his back. Foti shook his head and grinned, until a pair of boats passed by. Despite his shouts to Buckley that he should get out of the water, the star kept swimming, careful to evade a 100-foot barge. Momentarily relieved, Foti went to move the tape deck from the lapping waves at the water's edge. When he looked up again, Buckley was gone. Taken by the undertow created by the vessels, the singer had drowned.

Buckley had died almost as he'd lived, ever pushing boundaries to a natural conclusion. His body was – perhaps appropriately, given the eulogies that were to come – recovered six days later at the base of Memphis's famed Beale Street, the home of so much great musical heritage. One such eulogy was by Led Zeppelin's Jimmy Page, who, upon learning that his band's was the last music heard by Buckley, was moved to describe the late artist he'd grown to love as perhaps the finest singer of the previous twenty years. Jeff Buckley's second album was issued posthumously as *(Sketches for) My Sweetheart the Drunk*.

Friday 30

West Arkeen

(Aaron West Arkeen – Neuilly-sur-Seine, Paris, 18 June 1960)

The Outpatience

Songwriter West Arkeen had an enviable address book of friends from music's hierarchy: the quiet, unassuming guitarist had been close with the not-so-quiet Guns n' Roses – of whom he is posthumously regarded as the unofficial fifth member. Arkeen contributed songs such as 'It's So Easy' and 'Patience' as the band rose to global domination. His own band, The Outpatience – Arkeen (guitar), Mike Shotton (vocals), brothers Joey (guitar) and James Hunting (bass), Greg Buchwalter (keyboards) and Abe Laboriel (drums) – were less well known, but received good reports for their first album, *Anxious Disease* (1996). Arkeen had also collaborated with Sly Stone, Johnny Winter – and Jeff Buckley, whom he survived by just one day.

In early 1997, West Arkeen suffered second-degree burns to a third of his body when an indoor barbecue set exploded. To alleviate the pain and distress caused by this bizarre accident, Arkeen was taking prescription medication – an overdose of which is believed to have killed him.

JUNE

Wednesday 4

Ronnie Lane

(Plaistow, London, 1 April 1948)

The Small Faces
The Faces
Slim Chance
(Various acts)

It's impressive to think that rhythm guitarist turned bassist Ronnie Lane was just twenty when he laid down the distinctive tones that backed The Small Faces' *Ogden's Nut Gone Flake* (1968). The affable young Eastender befriended another, singer Steve Marriott – the pair were most integral to the rise of the mod movement's earliest heroes. Lane was as significant a contributor as the vocalist/guitarist, sharing songwriting duties as The Small Faces – Marriott, Lane, Ian McLagan (organ) and Kenney Jones (drums) – enjoyed well-documented singles-chart success during the mid to late sixties (1966 number one 'All Or Nothing' was the high spot). Some of the band's most impressive, idiosyncratic material lay in their album output, however, and with the chart-topping *Ogden* they proved they could compete with The Beatles and Stones as far as homespun psychedelia was concerned. The album also performed admirably in the US, spawning The Small Faces' only American hit, 'Itchycoo Park' (1968). Lane stayed put after the departure of his sidekick in 1969, the band becoming The Faces, now with still-wet-behind-the-ears Rod Stewart as singer. Commercial success continued as the band veered down a seventies pub-rock avenue, songs such as 'Last Orders Please' (1971) and 'Pool Hall Richard' (1973) suggesting where the new band would be happiest spending a lazy Sunday

afternoon. But, with Stewart becoming the focal point – he was concurrently cleaning up in both the US and UK as a solo act – Lane found his input compromised, and embarked upon his own folk-rock project, Slim Chance, which earned modest approval with Top Forty hits in 'How Come?' and 'The Poacher' (both 1974). By now Lane was living a maverick lifestyle, making a caravan his home as he further busied himself on projects with top-table associates Marriott (as Majik Mijits), sometime-Face Ronnie Wood and that other mod guru Pete Townshend – their *Rough Mix* (1977) was one of the best-received records of Lane's career.

Ronnie Lane had been advised that he had multiple sclerosis as early as 1976 (the condition had occurred previously within his family). This news shocked many of his contemporaries such as Jeff Beck, Eric Clapton and Jimmy Page, who, in 1983, rallied to raise money for both Lane and MS research (as would natural successors Paul Weller, Oasis and Ocean Colour Scene at the time of his death). Lane continued much of his professional life from the confines of a wheelchair, relocating to the USA – the harrowing death of his old friend Marriott (☛ *April 1991*) was another hard psychological burden with which he had to deal. Although he continued to perform and record as much as he was physically able, Lane finally succumbed to his debilitating condition in hospital near his home in Trinada, Colorado. His third wife, Susan, buried the guitarist on the day of his death – apparently an Apache tradition.

The Four Tops – Fakir, Payton, Benson and Stubbs: They just couldn't help themselves

Friday 20

Lawrence Payton

(Detroit, Michigan, 2 March 1938)

The Four Tops

For the extraordinarily enduring Four Tops, the death of Lawrence Payton was the first time the group were forced to alter their roster; bearing in mind that they first came together in 1953, this is some achievement.

High-school track-and-field star Payton met his group – Renaldo

'Obie' Benson (his colleague at Northern High), Abdul 'Duke' Fakir and lead singer Levi Stubbs (both from Pershing High) – as 14-year-old Detroit students at a birthday party. As The Four Aims, they found little success, but having replaced 'intent' with 'target', the renamed Four Tops signed first to Chess, then Motown on the way to becoming a much-loved institution. Ten years had passed by the time Berry Gordy persuaded the group to sign, and a first hit arrived in the shape of 'Baby I Need Your Loving' the following summer. Stubbs's far-reaching vocal on 'Baby . . .' thereafter became the norm as the group hit the heights with out-and-out classics such as the number-one pop hits 'I Can't Help Myself' (1965) and 'Reach out I'll be There' (1966 – also a UK chart-topper). These and a host of other Tops chartbusters were penned by the near-faultless team of Holland, Dozier and Holland, as Motown became the world's leading music factory. Without HDH – who left the stable in 1967 – Payton and his cohorts found hit-making tougher, but they still troubled the listings into the seventies, recording for a number of labels, and The Tops remained a big draw. They rejoined Motown in 1983, but by now greatest-hits packages were more the order of the day. (Payton had pursued a less-successful solo career in the mid seventies, which spawned just one album.)

Lawrence Payton fathered nine children by his wife, Elizabeth, before his death from a heart attack prompted by recently diagnosed liver cancer. The Four Tops continued to tour, making their first line-up change in four and a half decades with the introduction of Theo Peoples of The Temptations.

See also *Renaldo 'Obie' Benson (* *Golden Oldies #26)*

JULY

Howard Pickup

(Howard Boak – London, 1951)

The Adverts

The short, interesting career of London punks The Adverts was kick-started when young guitarist Howard Boak answered singer/guitarist Tim Smith's small ad in *Melody Maker*. Like many UK bands of their era, The Adverts – the renamed TV Smith and Howard Pickup, Gaye Advert (Gaye Black, bass) and Laurie Driver (Laurie Muscat, drums) – made a virtue out of their lack of musical proficiency, releasing the 45 'One Chord Wonders' on Stiff in 1977. Indeed, a poster campaign publicizing the band's imminent tour proclaimed: 'The Adverts know one chord. The Damned know three. See all four.' Within months, a second single, the dark classic 'Gary Gilmore's Eyes' (based on the tale of the executed US murderer (◀ *Death Toll #2*)) vaulted the band into the Top Twenty and on to *Top of the Pops*. Although debut album *Crossing the Red Sea with The Adverts* (1978) was also a moderate success, the group could muster no further hits (despite some kicking singles like 'No Time to be 21' and 'Television's Over') and, after an ignored second album, went their separate ways at the end of 1979. For Pickup, there was to be no further involvement in the music world. He died at his London home just weeks after having been diagnosed with brain cancer.

AUGUST

Fela Anikulapo Kuti

(Fela Ransome Kuti – Abeokuta, Nigeria, 15 October 1938)

Koola Lobitos/Africa 70/Egypt 80

The man mainly responsible for the international expansion of 'Afrobeat', Fela Kuti spread his words of protest despite actually coming from a relatively comfortable middle-class background – but, in the event, against considerable provocation. Kuti went against his parents' wish for him to study medicine, opting instead for a place at London's Trinity College of Music, where his social aware-

ness – not to mention his methods of expressing it – came to life. In the early sixties, Kuti's style of music was far more marginalized, usually referred to by the slightly misleading tag of 'High Life'. His band, Koola Lobitos – who became Africa 70 at the turn of the decade (and Egypt 80 ten years later) – were among the first to expose Afrobeat to a European audience. Kuti relished the opportunity to take swipes at the corrupt Nigerian establishment – as much for what he saw as their Westernization as for their apparent disregard for the poorer classes. Back in his homeland, Kuti was arrested for condoning marijuana; his house was virtually destroyed by the army in 1974. With Kuti making a huge deal of this event in his next recorded works, three years later, his new home was also burnt to the ground, far more brutally this time: the singer himself received a fractured skull while his

Marital bliss with Fela Kuti

elderly mother was thrown bodily from a bedroom window, sustaining appalling injuries from which she was to die months later. Despite this quite outrageous breach of his human rights, Kuti received little support in Nigeria, and was also deported from Ghana when he attempted to escape further punishment. His life continued to be eventful – in 1978 he married twenty-seven women simultaneously, in a traditional ceremony.

In 1984, Kuti was imprisoned for what appears to have been a trumped-up charge of currency smuggling. After more than two years in prison, he toured the USA and then recorded further diatribes against the corrupt Nigerian leadership that had incarcerated him, such as the near-orchestral 'Teacher Don't Teach Me Nonsense' (1987). Diagnosed with AIDS, Fela Kuti died ten years later from heart failure.

SEPTEMBER

Friday 19

Rich Mullins

(Richmond, Indiana, 21 October 1955)

From the other end of the pop-music spectrum came Rich Mullins, a very popular contemporary Christian songwriter whose compositions were covered by many and whose modern beliefs often challenged the religious hierarchy. Mullins produced his first self-titled album for Reunion Records in 1986, finding time to follow it with eight more over the next decade while also teaching the underprivileged and involving himself in charitable causes. He received considerable accolades when his 'Sing Your Praise to the Lord' was covered by popular Christian singer Amy Grant. Rich Mullins died in unusual circumstances in a car accident in LaSalle County, Illinois. While his passenger, musician Mitch McVicker, survived serious injuries, Mullins was thrown clear from the vehicle to be hit and killed by a passing tractor.

Sunday 21

Nick Traina

(Nicholas John Steel – San Francisco, California, 1 May 1978)

Link 80
(Knowledge)

The son of bestselling romance authoress Danielle Steel, Nick Steel (aka Traina) had begun to make a name of his own with his teenage punk/ska band. Traina was a singer with a great deal of attitude, seeming perfect for the lead role in Link 80, who took him on in 1995. Early gigs were apparently very impressive, club-goers witnessing the unlikely sight of the famous novelist and her entourage rubbing shoulders with Mohawks and skins alike. However, it was apparent to anyone who read his lyrics that Traina was suffering from severe depression. Just as the band was signed with the Asian Man label, Traina walked out to begin a new group, Knowledge, in August 1997. This project had barely begun when the singer was found dead at his mother's home from an apparently self-inflicted morphine overdose. A distraught Danielle Steel remembered her son in the biography *His Bright Light: The Story of Nick Traina*.

OCTOBER

Sunday 12

John Denver

(Henry John Deutschendorf Jr – Roswell, New Mexico, 31 December 1943)

(The Chad Mitchell Trio)

These days, country boy John Denver is mentioned almost as often for his dramatic death as he is for his impressive record sales. The man who arrived in Roswell soon after those pesky aliens was – in the first of a series of grim ironies – the son of a US air force officer, encouraged to play guitar by his grandmother, who bought him a vintage acoustic Gibson when the young Deutschendorf was just twelve. Dropping out of his studies, the budding musician became John Denver in 1965, when he joined folksters The Chad Mitchell Trio, replacing the lead singer. His cheery, down-home style proved popular, giving him the confidence to embark on a solo career four years later. As a songwriter, Denver had few peers in popular country during the seventies, the songs 'Sunshine on My Shoulder', 'Annie's Song' (both 1974, the latter his only UK hit), 'Thank God I'm a Country Boy' and 'I'm Sorry' (both 1975) all topping Billboard's pop listings and all certified as (at least) gold discs. Apart from his many other hits – Denver scored eight platinum albums – he also saw his songs covered with great success by, for example, Peter, Paul & Mary ('Leaving on a Jet Plane', 1969) and Olivia Newton-John ('Take Me Home, Country Roads', 1973). And the singer was by no means inactive in other areas either: as well as earning some acclaim for his acting in such movies as 1977's *Oh God!*, Denver was a valued supporter of many causes, including his own environmental group, The Windstar Foundation. Perhaps more surprisingly, the apparently cosy Denver saw fit to speak out alongside some of rock's more outlandish characters against increased censorship in music during the eighties.

So, what to do with all those millions in the bank? The tidy sum that didn't have to be given up in either of his admittedly messy divorces was put to use by John Denver to finance his second great love – flying. An experienced pilot, he had owned a Lear Jet in the past and was even said to have flown fighter aircraft. On 11 October 1997, Denver purchased a Rutan Long-EZ, a two-seater fibreglass aircraft that had been modified, it seems, once too often. As the plane flew above Monterey Bay, onlookers were horrified to see it dip and descend at speed, crashing headlong into the ocean: John Denver was killed instantly, his body – or what remained of it – rendered unrecognizable by the impact. Investigation into the crash found that the craft had failed when, attempting to access the reserve fuel tank, Denver had been unable to locate its switch, which had been moved by the previous owner to a somewhat awkward position behind

John Denver: Left us on a jet plane

the pilot's left shoulder. In order to activate it, Denver would have had to turn completely around, thus losing control of the plane. It also transpired that Denver, serving a suspension for multiple drunk-driving, had had his pilot's licence revoked and should never have been airborne in the first place. It was then later revealed that two previous pilots of the craft had had problems with the reserve-tank switch – and had narrowly avoided death themselves.

Denver's funeral in Aspen, Colorado, five days later was attended by thousands and – yes – there was a fly-past organized for the occasion. Sure, he was a keen pilot, but it seems almost painful to report that among the songs chosen for Denver's funeral were 'On the Wings of a Dream', 'High Flight' and 'The Wings That Fly Us Home'.

Glen Buxton

(Akron, Ohio, 10 November 1947)

Alice Cooper

In 1965, few thought that The Spiders – a high-school band fronted by a preacher's son – had much of a future. But when lead singer Vincent Furnier adopted the alias 'Alice Cooper' (the identity was unearthed during a Ouija-board session), fortunes changed for ever for him and his band. Furnier's henchman, guitarist Glen Buxton (aka 'The Blond Bomber') was almost as essential to the group as the leader. As Alice Cooper the band, they – plus Mike Bruce (guitar), Dennis Dunaway (bass) and Neal Smith (drums) – set about 'driving a stake through the heart of the Love Generation', signing to Frank Zappa's Straight label and effectively inventing the shock-rock genre. Critical acclaim was decidedly muted until 1971, however, when their theatrical, riff-heavy music started to make sense to a US audience coming to terms with metal and glam. Although they hit first in America ('I'm Eighteen', 1971), Alice Cooper became a bigger act in Britain, where the great 'School's Out' was a number-one single in 1972. Touring back-to-back gold albums in *School's Out* (1972) and *Billion Dollar Babies* (1973), Cooper, Buxton et al employed dolls, snakes, chickens, guillotines – you name it – as one of the world's hottest live acts.

Although the hits continued (particularly in the UK), Alice Cooper (the singer) fired the entire band in 1974. This was a huge blow to Buxton, who attempted projects of his own to lesser effect. (Interestingly, Cooper's star likewise faded considerably without Buxton – at least for a while.) The guitarist began to indulge heavily in drugs and alcohol and is believed to have attempted suicide at least once

as he struggled to maintain anything like a career. Although he eventually made a living teaching music, Buxton – who had moved to a ranch in Iowa – died from pneumonia ineffectually combated by his damaged immune system.

Henry 'Sunflower' Vestine

(Washington, DC, 25 December 1944)

Canned Heat
The Mothers of Invention
(Various acts)

The last survivor of Canned Heat's great triumvirate, Henry 'Sunflower' Vestine found his spiritual home when he joined the band shortly after their 1966 creation by fellow blues aficionados Al 'Blind Owl' Wilson (guitar/harmonica) and Bob 'The Bear' Hite (vocals/harmonica). A former guitarist with Frank Zappa's Mothers of Invention, Vestine was also fairly adept on the accordion, an instrument he'd been encouraged to learn as a child. Canned Heat were something of a revelation to white rock audiences: after an eye-opening performance at Monterey in 1967, their hits 'On the Road Again' and 'Going Up Country' (both 1968) cemented them as the band that would popularize blues-boogie. The Heat underwent their share of tragedies, though, notably the deaths of Wilson (➥ *September 1970*) and Hite (➥ *April 1981*). The group was never much more than a name after these losses, but continued manfully with Vestine still in the line-up, the guitarist also playing with a series of local bands in his adopted home of Oregon.

It was in Paris, at the end of a Canned Heat tour, that Henry Vestine was found dead by his bandmates as

---

Close! John Denver

The boyish country star could, it seems, have met his maker a decade previously. Apparently desperate to become the first civilian in space, John Denver took NASA's physical and mental examination, passing convincingly, and then lobbied the administration to include him on the space-shuttle programme in 1985 – only to be refused. The shuttle met with disaster on 28 January the following year; all seven on board were killed. As a tribute, Denver penned the song 'Flying For Me', dedicated to those who perished.

they prepared to check out of their hotel: after celebrating into the night, Vestine's body had apparently given out; the guitarist passed away from respiratory failure. The band continue to record and perform.

See also *Frank Zappa (▶︎ December 1993)*

Friday 31

John Dougherty

(Oakland, California, 20 April 1961)
Flipper

Their undoubted resonance at odds with any commercial success, San Francisco punks Flipper carried out their own sonic crusade against the music of the early eighties. Spectacularly crude live, Flipper purveyed what they called PET Rock, warning audiences that this was 'not a joke, and if it were it wouldn't be funny'. Prime mover Will Shatter's death from a heroin overdose (▶︎ *December 1987*) did not halt the band's progress. Bass-player John Dougherty was a later member of a group of alumni that was eventually to read like a battle memorial. He joined Flipper around 1991, the band having been re-formed at the behest of Def American head Rick Rubin; within a (largely unsuccessful) year, however, sometime singer Ricky Williams had died from a rare disease (▶︎ *November 1992*) while long-term bassist/vocalist Bruce Loose was lucky to suffer only vertebrae damage after a car crash. Emulating Shatter, Dougherty was later found dead from a heroin overdose at his home. His band had nonetheless proved a great influence on others: Concrete Blonde, The Melvins, Mudhoney and Sebadoh have all covered their music, while late grunge icon Kurt Cobain wears a Flipper T-shirt on Nirvana's *In Utero* packaging.

NOVEMBER

Thursday 6

Epic Soundtracks

(Kevin Paul Godfrey – Croydon, Surrey, 23 March 1959)
Swell Maps
(Various acts)

Although never a huge star, in his later years the extravagantly named drummer must have enjoyed the power he had to enforce Epic Records' change of name to Soundtrax for their film-music division. Epic Soundtracks formed early UK punk band Swell Maps in 1974 with his brother, Nikki Sudden (Nick Godfrey, who died in March 2006), while the pair were looking after their parents' home in Solihull, Birmingham. While Soundtracks was studying at art school, Swell Maps recorded their classic 'Read About Seymour' single (1977), followed by two albums and two sessions for omnipresent DJ John Peel. Too arty for the punk set, the group split in 1980, though Soundtracks rejoined his brother later in the decade in his band The Jacobites, and also contributed to records by Crime & The City Solution, Red Crayola and latterly These Immortal Souls. While working at London's Record & Tape Exchange, voracious music hound Soundtracks produced material for three solo albums, beginning with *Rise Above* (1991), which is regarded by many as his best work.

By the time of his death Epic Soundtracks had grown frustrated by the authorities' unwillingness to allow him to work in the USA, where he had something of a following – Evan Dando of The Lemonheads, with whom he had recently co-written material, was a noted fan. He had also recently split with a long-term girlfriend, and this weighed heavily on his mind. Having apparently overdosed on prescription drugs, Soundtracks had been dead for some weeks before his landlord discovered the body. Although no note was left, a verdict of suicide was returned.

'Don't you get depressed? I can't understand that.'

Epic Soundtracks, to his brother, Nikki Sudden

Michael Hutchence

(Lain Cove, Sydney, 22 January 1960)

INXS

He was frequently described as the 'lovechild' of Mick Jagger and Jim Morrison – a portrayal that certainly captures the pose and definitely the lifestyle and predilections, if not the character or musical output. At the time of his death, though, Michael Hutchence was a hollow impression of the rock god he'd originally aspired to be, famous for little more than *being* famous, his world shrunk by constant tabloid pressure.

Hutchence spent much of his upbringing in Hong Kong, the financial centre where his father gained and lost most of his fortune. Less concerned with money in those days, Hutchence was bereft when his parents subsequently separated, a move that also split him from his older brother, Rhett. In his place, Hutchence found three new brothers back in his native Sydney – Andrew (keyboards), Tim (guitar) and Jon Farriss (drums) – and the four created the embryonic band that would become INXS. Garry Morris, manager of Australian stadium agitpropsters Midnight Oil, saw potential in the band – and particularly in leather-clad Hutchence; INXS recorded their self-titled debut album in 1980. It took a further two years for the band to go global, but they did so with *Shabooh Shoobah* (1982) and *The Swing* (1984), which housed the Australian number one 'Original Sin' – and finally in some style with *Kick*, the dance-tinged 1987 album that spawned the band's largest worldwide hit, the very fetching 'Need You Tonight' (US number one, UK number two). A band completely at home with multi-formatting, INXS also picked up five MTV awards for the single's promotional video.

By now the willowy Hutchence had morphed into a much cooler 'Jon Bon Jovi' look, with feathered, highlighted hair and designer garb on request. For the singer, these were his salad days: all his wildest dreams of rock success had been achieved many times over (9 million times, if you rack up the sales of *Kick*), a succession of seemingly endless A-list beauties queuing up to take his arm. Hutchence's relationships with first fellow Aussie Kylie Minogue and then model Helena Christensen gave the singer a taste of the paparazzi furore to come. But this was nothing compared to the tabloid frenzy occasioned by his relationship with former model, TV presenter and rock-biz socialite Paula Yates. The pair had begun an affair allegedly half an hour after she interviewed the INXS singer on Channel 4's *The Big Breakfast*, and London's gutter press turned Hutchence into Public Enemy Number One for ending the marriage of 'Saint' Bob Geldof – while Hutchence's mother, Patricia, turned *her* wrath on the substance-fuelled Ms Yates. It would be unfair to place all the blame for Hutchence's sudden downturn in fortunes on Yates, but it did seem to coincide with her arrival. Since 1992's *Welcome to Wherever You Are*, INXS's sales had fallen (particularly in America, where their distinctly eighties amalgam of dance and rock was now considered passé) and the press were quick to jump all over *Elegantly Wasted*, the band's 1997 'twentieth-anniversary comeback' album. The target of the hacks' wrath was not just the patchy musical content, but also Hutchence himself, whose appearance, most felt, was *less* than 'elegantly wasted'.

The pressure finally got to rock's erstwhile least flappable man, it seems. Although he was delighted by the birth in 1996 of his first child – Heavenly Haraani Tiger Lily, Yates's fourth exotically named daughter – friends described Hutchence as distracted, over-imbibing and profligate with his money, leading to the (unproven) suggestion that his partner was draining his resources to fund her drug habit and increasingly protracted legal proceedings. The couple were keen to win custody of Yates's other three children (with Geldof) and bring them to Australia for an INXS tour; in the early morning of 22 November, the dispute was to come to a head. Hutchence had begun the previous evening happily enough – after all, he was back in Sydney, booked into the Ritz-Carlton Hotel on the beautiful Double Bay – spending quality time with first his father and then British actress Kym Wilson (another Hutchence 'ex') and her boyfriend, Andrew Rayment, the trio spending considerably on the hotel bar's champagne and beer. The party continued in room 524, Hutchence's suite, the singer drinking vodka by now, until almost 5 am, when his guests left. Some hours later, a series of calls to and from Britain altered his mood considerably. A tearful Yates, in London, explained that Geldof was not prepared to allow the children to travel with him; Hutchence then flew into a rage, telephoning their father and yelling, 'Your children fucking hate you. *I'm* their father – when are you going to realize that?' The last person to hear from the singer was another ex-girlfriend, Michelle Bennett, who received his answerphone messages some time after they were left. She described him as 'sounding drunk and very upset'. Bennett raced to the hotel: when there was no reply from his room, she placed a note at reception and left.

At around midday, a hotel maid made the grim discovery of Michael Hutchence's body, naked and prone by the door of his room. He had hanged himself, it seems, with his belt from the door, the weight of his body having broken the buckle. The room was reportedly littered with empties – alcohol, tablets, you name it. A coroner confirmed that as well as alcohol and cocaine, the INXS star's system contained Prozac. Auto-erotic asphyxiation was ruled out early on and his death filed as a suicide. But the lack of any explanation to his friends, fans or even his family left enduring questions unanswered – perhaps most mysterious is the fact that his estate left no more than $50K to his daughter.

Hutchence's memorial was relayed like a state funeral on live television in his homeland on 27 November. Attendees included Diana Ross, Kylie Minogue, the rest of INXS and a distressed Paula Yates, who had flown in from the UK with their daughter on hearing of his death. It's said that relations between her and Hutchence's family were so bad (his mother blamed her indirectly for his death) that the ashes of the singer – who had stated in his will that he did not want to be cremated – had to be divided up in order to maintain the peace. The family continues to fight over the remainder of his assets, much of which is tied up in discretionary trusts.

A person with the possibly apt name of Peter Hore briefly became Australia's Most Hated Man when he performed an extraordinary mock hanging at Hutchence's televized funeral: shouting, 'This is how he did it, Paula!', the sick individual – well known for disrupting major events – threw himself from a balcony with a dog-collar and leash around his neck. None of this helped Yates, who never recovered from her lover's death. She allegedly kept Hutchence's ashes under her pillow and a giant poster of the singer on her bedroom wall until her own tragic death from an overdose on 17 September 2000. (In a remarkable though gratifying twist, Geldof became legal custodian of the orphaned Tiger Lily, now able to grow up with her three half-sisters.)

'How do I keep sane? I am barely doing it.'

Michael Hutchence in his last major interview, September 1997

Paula and Michael: Paying for an 'original sin'?

Friday 28

Michael Hedges
(Enid, Oklahoma, 31 December 1953)

Michael Hedges was a virtuoso guitarist who described his music as 'violent acoustic', 'new edge' or 'heavy mental', so infused was it with different influences. Hedges was classically trained, having also learned cello and piano, but discovered in rock music the space for the experimentation he craved. Employing a two-handed picking style, Hedges – who recorded eight albums for his own Windham Hill label, including the Grammy-nominated *Taproot* (1990) – became renowned for his highly original techniques and sound. He worked with Crosby, Stills & Nash, Bob Dylan, John Lennon, Paul McCartney and Frank Zappa, among many, many others.

On the night of 28 November 1997, Michael Bridges was travelling home to Mendocino, San Francisco, following a Thanksgiving visit with his girlfriend in New York, when his car spun out of control and rolled down an embankment on Highway 128, near Boonville. The guitarist's body lay undiscovered in the wreckage for four days.

DECEMBER

Sunday 14

Kurt Winter
(Winnipeg, Manitoba, 2 April 1946)
The Guess Who
(Brother)

The Guess Who were already the biggest pop band to have emerged from Canada by the time Brother guitarist

Kurt Winter stepped into the breach left by Randy Bachman, who departed to form Bachman Turner Overdrive in 1970. Soon after he joined the band, Winter was chuffed to see his composition 'Hand Me Down World' become The Guess Who's latest hit. He went on to contribute to three albums by the band, co-composing other hits including the Top Ten 'Clap for the Wolfman' (1974), a song featuring the vocals of disc jockey Wolfman Jack.

Known as 'The Walrus', the moustachioed Winter developed a liking for the indulgences of the day – which was to have a devastating effect on his system in later years. Sacked from The Guess Who in late 1974, he died from combined liver failure and a bleeding ulcer at a hospital in his home town of Winnipeg. Sometime guitarist Domenic Troiano – who also played with The James Gang and Bush (not the British band) – died of prostate cancer in 2005.

Thursday 18

Nicolette Larson
(Helena, Montana, 17 July 1952)
Commander Cody & His Lost Planet Airmen
(Various acts)

Diminutive singer/guitarist Nicolette Larson developed her unique singing and playing styles as a girl, her family constantly on the road because of her father's work commitments with the US Treasury. A move to San Francisco after some difficult high-school years put Larson into the vibrant musical environment that she craved, and she attracted the attention of Commander Cody & His Lost Planet Airmen. Leader Cody (aka George Frayne) employed Larson as a singer, the celebrated good-time band suddenly massively popular after a major hit with 'Hot Rod Lincoln' (1972). Adding

her touch to a number of the band's records over the next three years, Larson also played with Hoyt Axton and Emmylou Harris, whose guitarist, Hank DeVito, she briefly married. The contacts she made established Larson as a solo act, and she scored a Top Ten Billboard hit with Neil Young's 'Lotta Love' (1978). Her subsequent debut, *Nicolette*, sold well for Warner Brothers, and Larson went on to show her remarkable diversity by also singing with Young, Linda Ronstadt, The Doobie Brothers and even Van Halen. But despite a Country Music Award for Best New Act (oddly, as late as 1984), Larson couldn't repeat the success of her debut album. A move to MCA, then to CGD, didn't alter her fortunes greatly, spawning only one major country hit with 'That's How You Know When Love's Right' (1986).

Nicolette Larson maintained a reasonable media profile with occasional record releases and a number of movie roles during the late eighties and nineties (including a part in the 1989 comedy *Twins*); she also married drummer Russ Kunkel and gave birth to a daughter, Elsie May. Her unexpected death following complications from a cerebral oedema stunned many in the pop, country and film industries.

Sunday 21

Amie Comeaux
(Brusly, Louisiana, 4 December 1976)

If Nicolette Larson's death was a blow to the world of country music, the tragically young passing of singer Amie Comeaux came as an even greater shock. Clearly a gifted performer, with a golden-girl image, Comeaux issued *Moving Out*, her debut album for Polydor, in 1994. In the next couple of years, the young prodigy toured

Europe and prepared for her second album, but the Polygram organization dropped her before its issue. The record, though, became a tribute release: travelling from Nashville to her parents' home near Baton Rouge, Louisiana, Amie Comeaux's Dodge Avenger skidded off a wet road, slamming her into a tree. While her passengers – her grandmother and a god-daughter – survived the crash, the singer was killed outright.

Wednesday 31

Floyd Cramer

(Shreveport, Louisiana, 27 October 1933)

An inductee into both Rock 'n' Roll and Country Halls of Fame, Floyd Cramer was a self-taught pianist who made his name initially on the popular *Louisiana Hayride* radio shows, where he was often placed alongside huge stars such as Patsy Cline, Jim Reeves and Hank Williams Sr. Moving to Nashville – the home of country music – Cramer diversified to play sessions with up-and-coming popular stars such as The Everly Brothers, Roy Orbison and a young Elvis Presley, whom he accompanied on the singer's first classic sides. Cramer was no stranger to chart success himself, either. A trio of his records made the US pop Top Ten, one of which, 'On the Rebound' (1961), gave him a surprise UK number one. Perhaps his biggest payday, though, came with his recording of the theme for the enormously popular television soap *Dallas* in the late seventies. Passing away from lung cancer at a relatively young age, Floyd Cramer nonetheless survived almost every one of the great stars he accompanied.

Lest We Forget

Other notable deaths that occurred sometime during 1997:

LaVern Baker (revered US R & B diva; born Delores Williams, Illinois, 11/11/1929; diabetes, 10/4)

Richard Berry (US doo-wop vocalist with The Flairs and Robins who finally earned writing royalties on his greatest composition, 'Louie Louie', just before his death; born Louisiana, 11/4/1935; aneurysm, 23/1)

Jo Bruce (UK keyboardist with world music mavericks The Afro-Celt Sound System – son of Cream's Jack Bruce; born 9/2/1969; asthma attack, 8/10)

Chris Burmeister (Danish guitarist with rock band The Bushpilots; born 1969; shot by a Palestinian gunman while visiting the Empire State Building – US singer Matt Gross survived the attack – 23/2)

Keith Ferguson (US blues-rock bassist with the hugely popular Fabulous Thunderbirds, who finally went Top Ten with 1986's 'Tuff Enuff'; born Texas, 23/7/1946; liver failure promoted by drug abuse, 27/4)

Louis 'Tony' McCall (US drummer with mighty funk unit Con Funk Shun; born California, 28/12/51; shot by an intruder at a friend's Stone Mountain home, 25/6 – the case is still unsolved in 2006)

Ben Raleigh (US songwriter who penned mawk classic 'Tell Laura I Love Her' and, uh, the *Scooby Doo* theme; born New York, 16/6/1913; he died in a kitchen fire after his bathrobe caught alight, 26/2)

Jimmy Rogers (celebrated Chicago-blues guitarist who played with Sunnyland Slim, Otis Spann, Muddy Waters and all the best guys; born Mississippi, 3/6/1924; emphysema/colon cancer, 19/12)

Wally Whyton (UK leader of skiffle band The Vipers, who scored two Top Ten hits in 1957 – later a popular BBC radio and TV broadcaster; born London, 23/9/1929; cancer, 22/1)

John Wolters (US soft-rock drummer/vocalist who tasted international success as a member of Dr Hook – with and without The Medicine Show suffix; born New Jersey, 28/4/1945; liver cancer, 16/6)

For a complete list of fallen artists, visit

www.numberoneinheaven.com

1998

JANUARY

Monday 5

Sonny Bono

(Salvatore Phillip Bono – Detroit, Michigan, 16 February 1935)

Sonny & Cher

With no obvious vocal talent, Sonny Bono nonetheless made the most out of his career, achieving his main successes in pop music and beyond after his thirtieth birthday. This, though, was only after many attempts at stardom: an A & R with Los Angeles label Specialty Records, Bono – working as a butcher's boy by day – recorded under a variety of names including 'Ronny Summers' and 'Prince Carter'. Under the gaze of producer Phil Spector, success arrived in the shape of 'Needles and Pins', a song co-written by the singer with Jack Nitzsche – which was taken to number one in the UK by The Searchers in 1964. By now Bono had met Cherilyn Sarkisian LaPierre – Cher, for short. Divorcing his wife, Bono and his new love began a striking partnership with the all-conquering 'I Got You Babe' (1965, written by Bono). A series of lesser hits proved mainly that the public liked Cher, and, while she went

Sonny and Cher keep up the public profile through gritted teeth

on to a remarkable solo career that continues to this day, Bono's one and only solo album died. Despite their relationship foundering, 'Sonny & Cher' proved a marketable-enough brand for a CBS television series to outlive their romance by some years.

Not to be outdone by his second ex-wife's impressive further career, Bono (who seemed happy to be the butt of Cher's rather crass alimony wisecracks on their show) found himself a niche in film acting, though his television work was generally restricted to mini series such as *Fantasy Island*. A contretemps with one of the actors in the latter caused Bono to reassess his career and, for the staunch Republican, a move into politics followed. Somehow, the former singer – only moved to stand for election when red tape prevented him from increasing the size of a restaurant sign – was voted Mayor of Palm Springs in 1988, a far cry from his bohemian lifestyle of old. Six years on, the man who claimed he'd never voted until in his fifties was elected into the US House of Representatives as Congressman for the State of California. Many doubted his credentials, but, as Bono himself pointed out, 'You can't be a dummy and have the achievements I've had in my life.'

Sonny Bono was holidaying at the Heavenly Ski Resort, Lake Tahoe, with his fourth wife, Mary Whitaker, and their two children when he failed to show after a solo run. Bono's body was discovered in woods off piste. He had apparently lost control and hit a tree, dying from head injuries. His distressed widow – who replaced him in Congress – later blamed her husband's death on his addiction to prescription medication, claiming that ingesting twenty tablets a day had greatly impaired Bono's judgement. Despite the claim, an autopsy had shown no evidence of pills or alcohol in Bono's system.

Ken Forssi
(Cleveland, Ohio, 1943)

Love
The Surfaris
(The Buffalo Springfield)

Later the same day, a less-vaunted hero of California's pop counterculture died from brain cancer. Ken Forssi was a dynamic, beach-loving bass guitarist who had begun his career with The Surfaris as the group was issuing its final album. With that group well past its sell-by date, Forssi was to find high-level critical acclaim – if not massive commercial acceptance – as a member of the seminal psychedelic rock group Love (originally The Grass Roots). The bassist was in place as the group issued three albums for Elektra – *Love* (1966), *Da Capo* and *Forever Changes* (both 1967) – whose radiance is perhaps only fully appreciated today.

Forssi and the other band members, however, were often at loggerheads with authority, abusing drugs to a greater degree than singer Arthur Lee claimed to approve of. Briefly standing in for Buffalo Springfield's Bruce Palmer while the latter was in trouble with the law, Forssi was then incarcerated himself in 1968 (as was Love guitarist John Echols shortly after). Upon his release, the bass-player discovered he no longer had a place in Love. Long having left the music business, Ken Forssi died at his home in Florida.

See also *George Suranovich (* February 1990); Bryan MacLean (* December 1998). First Love drummer Don Conka passed on in 2004.*

Golden Oldies #5

Carl Perkins
(Carl Lee Perkings – Tiptonville, Tennessee, 9 April 1932)

The Perkins Brothers

Unarguably a giant of rock 'n' roll, Carl Perkins pioneered the fusion of country and R & B to create rockabilly. The young guitarist overheard crop workers singing gospel and spirituals, which encouraged him to master his instrument – initially a converted cigar box. Perkings's father was unable to work through illness and the family were living on the breadline, so Carl and his brothers, Jay and Clayton, performed for pennies as the (renamed) Perkins Brothers. Perkins's composition 'Movie Magg' won him a talent contest when he was just thirteen, and ten years later became his first side for Sun Records. This record may have died, but his next didn't. Legend has it that Perkins wrote 'Blue Suede Shoes' on an old potato sack in his kitchen at 3 am: his recording of the song delighted Sam Phillips by scaling the charts to peak at number two in May 1956. Then, travelling with his brothers to New York's *Perry Como Show*, Perkins was involved in a serious car crash, fracturing his skull and neck. Elvis took his place on the show, and the rest, as they say, is history.

Thereafter, Perkins's career was biased more towards the country market, where he was a consistent hit-maker. Among the many notable fans of Perkins's work were Johnny Cash – who took the guitarist with him as a touring member of his band for almost ten years – and The Beatles – who covered a number of Perkins tunes prior to their global success. However, following the tragic deaths of Jay Perkins (* *Pre-1965*) and then Clayton (* *December 1973*), Perkins became hugely despondent and dependent on alcohol. His attempted comebacks met with mixed reactions. He continued to record with old acquaintances such as Cash, Paul McCartney and Willie Nelson until his passing on 19 January 1998. After a series of strokes, Carl Perkins died from throat cancer in hospital in Jackson, Tennessee.

FEBRUARY

Thursday 5

Joe Stubbs

(Joseph Stubbles – Detroit, Michigan, 1942)

The Falcons
The Originals
(The Four Tops)
(The Contours)
(101 Proof Aged in Soul)

The younger brother of The Four Tops' Levi Stubbs, Joe Stubbs was lead singer with The Falcons – which meant being sandwiched between legends Eddie Floyd and Wilson Pickett. Stubbs was never to reach the heights these contemporaries did, but he was a strong vocalist nonetheless and often hired by Motown as cover: with his brother's help, this occasionally included live work with The Four Tops themselves. Joining The Falcons in 1957, Stubbs's voice was at the centre of their biggest hit, the pop Top Twenty entry 'You're So Fine' (1959). Stepping down as lead in 1962, Stubbs re-emerged with his own group under the somewhat unwieldy name of 101 Proof Aged in Soul, scoring his only Top Ten hit with 'Somebody's Been Sleeping' (1970) – though this featured Clyde Wilson on lead duties. Joe Stubbs had long been suffering the heart condition that eventually killed him. (Wilson Pickett died in January 2006.)

Tim Kelly

(Trenton, New Jersey, 13 January 1963)

Slaughter
(Various acts)

A massive fan of made-up metal-lists Kiss, guitarist Tim Kelly realized a dream when Slaughter supported Gene Simmons and his glam dinosaurs on their first tour after he signed up. He'd been invited to join the band – Mark Slaughter (vocals/guitar/keyboards), Dana Strum (bass) and later Blas Elias (drums) – after meeting them at a friend's barbecue. Kelly had been a solid guitarist since his teens, gaining a good deal of experience with other bands, including his older brother's group, Allegiance. With the approval of Kiss, Slaughter cleaned up with the glossy 3-million-selling debut album for EMI, *Stick It to Ya* (1990), which, while not the most ground-breaking listen, certainly pushed all the necessary buttons. Similarly, power ballad 'Fly to the Angels' punted the band into the Billboard Top Twenty and was an MTV mainstay. Although *Wild Life* (1992) kept things bubbling, promotion to metal's premier league was scuppered by a number of events: a falling-out with EMI (they left for CMC), Elias's motorcycle accident, which shut up shop for a year; and Kelly's continuing problems with drugs. A third studio album, *Fear No Evil* (1995), did not fare as well as its predecessors.

On 5 February, Tim Kelly was travelling along Highway 96 when an 18-wheeler tractor/trailer crossed the middle lane and struck his car head on, before ploughing into another vehicle. Kelly survived until arrival at a clinic in Baghdad, Arizona, whereupon he was pronounced dead from severe head injuries. The truck driver – who was sentenced to three years in prison and fined $20K – was discovered to have had at least three types of drug in his system, including amphetamines. A memorial service near Kelly's former home in the outskirts of Las Vegas drew a huge crowd; local authorities also declared a 'Slaughter Day'.

Carl Wilson

(Hawthorne, California, 21 December 1946)

The Beach Boys

Dennis and Carl Wilson – before the tide went out for ever

Life's a beach and then you die, it seems. Not that Carl Wilson would have had many regrets. Ever the mediator, the great leveller, he hadn't perhaps the inspiration of older brother one, Brian, nor the presence of older brother two, Dennis, but what Wilson had – apart from a fine voice and more than a few decent licks on his Fender Strat – was an uncanny ability to contain disaster when it threatened.

While Brian Wilson was hypnotized by the perfect arrangements of The Four Freshmen, it was Chuck Berry fan Carl who suggested the boys 'went rock 'n' roll'. The three brothers' musical aspirations began under the name Carl & The Passions – a small, early nod, perhaps, to the pivotal role the 15-year-old was to play in the years to follow. The moniker was quickly changed to The Pendletones – reminding Carl of his position – with the addition of their cousin Mike Love and school buddy Al Jardine; the band then became the more generic Beach Boys – a brand that would outlive at least two of the Wilson brothers. The Beach Boys signed with Capitol (via the regional Candix) in 1962, scoring a rapid spate of feel-good California surf hits, Carl Wilson's faultless backing to Brian's sensitive lead voice an essential ingredient – his own time in the spotlight would come later. By the end of 1963 The Beach Boys were pretty much the biggest thing in US music, but by the time they'd scored their first number one with 'I Get Around' (1964) the cracks were already beginning to show. After the group's first world tour, Brian Wilson's partial breakdown and subsequent retirement from live performing proved a huge watershed for The Beach Boys – unexpectedly instigating their finest work. With the leader spending more time perfecting their sound in the studio (as well as more time under the influence of psychedelics), Carl's angelic vocal was given greater prominence. This was most notable on the 1966 hit 'God Only Knows' – written especially for him by his brother. This dedication proved inspiring to the youngest Wilson, whose touching falsetto elevated the tune to one of the finest of the band's career – and, for many, one of the best of the entire decade. Even more impressive was worldwide number one 'Good Vibrations' (1966), at that time the biggest hit of The Beach Boys' history. Again Carl's vocal complemented Brian's extraordinary musical arrangement and the group finally seemed to be giving

The Beatles a run for their money. The following year, Carl Wilson successfully avoided both the draft and then 'civilian duties' (ie, community service) by refusing to take the Oath of Allegiance.

With Brian Wilson fading from view during the seventies (or, more accurately, ballooning out of sight), his younger brother took on songwriting responsibilities but – with the exception of the wry and critically acclaimed *Surf's Up* (1971) – The Beach Boys were no longer the force of old. In 1972, an album, *Carl and The Passions*, re-emphasized the singer/guitarist's standing in days gone by, but it really wasn't up to the standard of previous outings. Realizing that, without the main man, their best bet was to tour as a nostalgia act, The Beach Boys then put original material on to the back burner. Internal squabbling and disappointment at the band's apparent loss of ambition saw Wilson issue his own solo albums, *Carl Wilson* (1981) and *Youngblood* (1984), to almost universal indifference (a third was released after his passing). The musician's disappointment in these relative failures had, however, been put into some kind of perspective by the death of his brother Dennis (◀ *December 1983*).

Carl Wilson returned to the fold to sing lead on 'Kokomo' (1988), a fairly inconsequential Beach Boys workout (for the equally inconsequential Tom Cruise movie *Cocktail*), which astonishingly sold over a million copies in America on its way to becoming the group's biggest smash of all time. This prompted The Beach Boys' induction into the new Rock 'n' Roll Hall of Fame, and prompted Carl – now very much the leader of the band ('I haven't spoken to Brian in a while – I don't even know his telephone number . . .') – to resume touring. This he continued to do despite learning he had lung cancer in 1996. Having undergone chemotherapy, Wilson played with The Beach Boys throughout their 36th Annual Tour in 1997, even introducing his doctors on stage at one concert. Believing he would make a full recovery, his family, friends and bandmates were devastated by Carl Wilson's death in early 1998 – the cancer had spread to his brain. He was survived by his wife and two sons. With the peacemaker dead, the surviving Beach Boys split, re-formed, split again and generally argued about everything, litigation flying left, right and centre.

'There was no one more spiritual than Carl.'

Marilyn Rutherford,
Brian Wilson's first wife

Falco

(Johann Holzel – Vienna, 19 February 1957)

(Drahdiwaberl)

Although his death was overshadowed by that of a genuine legend, Austrian singer Falco could, unlike Carl Wilson, claim one or two international solo hits that outsold anything by his former band. As bassist with punk band Drahdiwaberl (no, nor us), the former Vienna Music Conservatory student remained an undiscovered talent. While singing with a jazz-rock band, he became Falco Sturmer, shortening the name for his solo debut, '*Ganz Wien*' (1978), a controversial early single that documented Vienna's heroin scene. Five years passed before Falco began to find any sort of international acceptance, his '*Der Kommissar*' becoming a surprise dance smash in the US. Any possibility of a pop hit was thwarted, however, by British band After the Fire's remarkably rapid cover, which sold a million copies in America in 1983. A disgruntled

Falco: Hopefully not buried in that jacket

Falco returned powerfully to the spotlight in 1986 with his album *Falco 3* – which contained the ambitious slice of eighties pop that was 'Rock Me Amadeus'. This track did the business for him, topping the charts in sixteen countries including the US and UK. But after one more hit, (the not dissimilar) 'Vienna Calling', Falco was gone again . . .

Not a poor man after this burst of success, Falco remained popular in German-speaking countries but took himself off to live in the Dominican Republic for tax purposes. It was here that the singer was killed, when his Jeep collided with a bus near Puerto Plata.

MARCH

Wednesday 11

Stacey Guess
(Efland, North Carolina,
21 November 1964)
**Squirrel Nut Zippers
(Various acts)**

Among the more unusual musical styles emerging during the nineties was 'alternative swing', a genre almost entirely the property of one band – namely Squirrel Nut Zippers, the unlikely unit formed by Jim Mathus (vocals/guitar/trombone) and Katharine Whalen (vocals/banjo). A former member of Pressure Boys and Sex Police, Stacey Guess, a talented trumpeter with an ear for the unusual, joined SNZ in 1993, contributing to the band's sprightly debut, *The Inevitable Squirrel Nut Zippers* (1995). (The hyperactive Guess had a number of other projects on the go simultaneously.)

His previous musical experiences had led Guess into hard drug use, however, and he was not to enjoy the huge success the group had with the follow-up. While the million-selling *Hot* (1996) was being recorded, the trumpeter was away receiving treatment for heroin addiction. After taking an accidental overdose, Stacey Guess died in hospital, four days after falling into a coma.

DEAD INTERESTING!

NOT-SO-SUPER FURRY ANIMALS . . .
When choosing a name for their act, musicians might do well to avoid the word 'squirrel'. During the nineties, the bushy-tailed varmints – in one way or another – claimed at least six lives in popular music. Just weeks after Stacy Guess's death, punk high-priestess Wendy O Williams – latterly known as 'The Squirrel Lady' – also died (➤ *April 1998*). A year on, cult French MC Squirrel AKA lost his life in an accident. Some years before, two members of promising young Florida band, For Squirrels, plus their tour manager had been killed after a high-speed blow-out (➤ *September 1995*).

. . . And a Couple That Got away?
The late Bobby Lester of The Moonglows (➤ *October 1980*) is often confused with Robert 'Papa Squirrel' Lester – who sang with The Chi-Lites and remains very much alive. Meanwhile, dicing with titles like 'Skag Heaven', raging Kentucky youngsters Squirrel Bait did the sensible thing by going their separate ways in 1987, members enjoying rodent-free success with such seminal acts as Slint, Bastro and The Palace Brothers.

Friday 13

Judge Dread
(Alexander Minto Hughes – Snodland,
Kent, 1945)

It was never going to be 'high art' with Judge Dread. A former wrestler ('The Masked Executioner'), Alex Hughes carved himself an enviable niche in British music with his adaptations of 'rude reggae' hits and enjoyed a run of nine Top Forty hits in Britain during the seventies – not one of which received radio airplay. A huge fan of ska, Dread had taken his name from a Prince Buster song, and offered himself up as a bouncer at the music clubs he loved in London's West End. Here, he befriended many of those he'd go on to emulate – among them legends Bob Marley and Clement 'Coxsone' Dodd, for whom he even acted as bodyguard. Dread's own hits began with 'Big Six' (loosely based on Buster's 'Big Five'), one of three discs that spent a remarkable fifty-five weeks on the UK charts in 1972–3.

Whatever his merits as an artist, he holds two records: he was the first white act to land a hit in Jamaica, and he accrued the most banned songs (eleven), with later titles such as 'Up with the Cock' (1978) suggesting that rather than being toned down, his work was becoming even more explicit. Apparently, Dread was even snubbed by *Top of the Pops* when he requested a ten-second slot on the show just to thank his fans. More bizarrely, one of his more innocuous songs, 'A Child's Prayer', was selected by Elvis Presley for recording – though the latter's death (◀ *August 1977*) unfortunately prevented this almost inconceivable occurrence.

Judge Dread went the way he might perhaps have chosen – on stage, before his faithful audience of many years. At the end of a performance at Canterbury's Penny Theatre, Dread (a Kent native), dressed in a Superman T-shirt, turned to salute his band and slumped as he walked offstage. In hospital, the singer was pronounced dead from a massive coronary. According to those present, Dread's journey there was almost as 'comic' as one of his songs: reportedly, the St John's ambulance broke down and needed to be bump-started; then police pulled the vehicle over for some minutes when locals alleged 'a bunch of skins' (ie, the singer's friends) had stolen it.

> ## 'I've never been unhappy. It's not about fame or money – it's about getting the most out of life.'
> Judge Dread, 1997

Judge Dread: Doubtless preparing to get laid in his grave?

APRIL

Wednesday 1

Rozz Williams
(Roger Alan Painter – Pomona, California, 6 November 1963)
Christian Death
(Various acts)

Satanism, industrial noise, facial white-out, onstage horror – Rozz Williams caught that particular Californian wave way before the likes of Marilyn Manson. Although they didn't release any material until 1982's genuinely disquieting *Only Theatre of Pain*, Christian Death – Williams (vox), Rikk Agnew (guitar), James McGearly (bass) and George Belanger (drums) – had existed since Williams, born into a strict Baptist family, was fifteen. The band, originally inspired by British glam acts like T Rex and David Bowie, began with crass stage antics (such as allegedly eating a dead cat), before going on to fashion dark attacks on the organized religion Williams knew all too well. In particular, Williams singled out the corruption he felt inherent in modern Christianity, emphasizing the US Church's some-times shady links with politicians. After two further albums, Williams (who was also involved in other projects, like Premature Ejaculation with performance artist Ron Athey) left the band and Christian Death promoted more-theatrical guitarist Valor Kand to the front. From this moment, the group's output descended from an occasionally well-conceived agenda into badly executed Nazi imagery-by-numbers and self-parody. In 1989, Williams's rival Christian Death line-up somehow lost out to Kand's version.

Rozz Williams remained an interesting performer, constantly juggling ideas, but with his increased dependency on heroin and his manic depression, many could foresee only one end for him. This was sadly borne out in April 1998, when Williams was found hanged, by his room-mate Ryan Gaumer at their West Hollywood apartment. The singer, who had appeared happier in recent days, left no note.

Rob Pilatus
(Munich, 8 June 1965)

Milli Vanilli

Girl, you know it's fake. One might have thought it couldn't get much worse for Milli Vanilli – the pop sen-sation of 1989 exposed as a sham, a ventriloquist act par excellence who suckered the public long enough to see their debut album turn multi-platinum. So how did they manage to let it slip? The simple answer is that by accepting a Grammy award in 1990 Milli Vanilli and the act's perpetrators became too greedy – having shifted all those records, they just didn't know when to let it go. Once exposed, their personal humiliation resonated years longer than any of the hits.

But, compared with much that had gone before, Milli Vanilli – Euro dancers Fabrice Morvan and Rob Pilatus – wasn't *that* bad an idea: two reasonably good-looking guys who could pull one or two moves and appear to mouth a few girl-pleasing platitudes when the moment called. The US lapped them up – *fourteen* million record sales in one year hasn't

been achieved by many. The duo had arrived in style: 'Girl You Know It's True', 'Baby Don't Forget My Number', 'Girl I'm Gonna Miss You' and 'Blame It On the Rain' (all 1989, all million-selling singles) gave them the best US starting run since The Beatles – except that it wasn't Morvan and Pilatus singing on the records but session men Charles Shaw, John Davis and Brad Howe. On reflection, it's odd that so much fuss was made once the truth was out. The supremo behind Milli Vanilli was Frank Farian, who had duped some 10 million Britons into believing that Boney M (or most of them, at least) were responsible for *their* own output ten years earlier. So Milli had to return their Grammy. Then, in one of the most cringingly awful moments in pop history, the pair attempted to prove in a press conference that they *could* sing – which gave the world the unique scenario of photographers clamouring to escape.

In the aftermath, the always slightly wayward Rob Pilatus fell apart. Morvan had something of a voice after all, it seemed, and a solo career looked likely for him – but former model Pilatus now had nothing but a growing cocaine problem and a lorry-load of debts. Still living in Los Angeles, he'd threatened suicide as early as 1990, falling into petty

'The only disgrace is how Rob died, all alone. Where were the ones that pushed us to the top, who made the millions?'
Fabrice Morvan (who maintains Pilatus's death was unintentional), 1998

Morvan and Pilatus of Milli Vanilli: The trophies were replicas, too

crime by the middle of the decade to support his habit (Farian apparently then bailed him out of jail). Just weeks before his death, Pilatus was interviewed in rehab by a German television channel and shocked viewers with both his appearance and the bald statement that he wished to die.

Then, on the morning of 3 April, the inevitable happened. Pilatus's body was discovered in a hotel room; he had overdosed on alcohol and prescription medication. For Rob Pilatus, the sad story was finally over. Even in death, he received little respect – jokes along the lines of 'was it him in the casket?' abounded. But it was a genuine tragedy, for in pop music there have been far worse 'crimes' than the naked ambition of a regular young guy offered the chance of a lifetime. The continued greed and opportunism of faceless executives who can always hide behind something – or someone – else when caught out might just be one.

Cozy Powell

(Colin Flooks – Cirencester,
29 December 1949)

Rainbow
The Jeff Beck Group
Cozy Powell's Hammer
Black Sabbath
(Various acts)

In the house of British hard rock, Cozy Powell represents the mortar that holds the whole structure together, so regularly do his contributions seem to recur. Quite apart from the above list of name acts for whom he manned the traps, Powell can also claim to have drummed with stadium shakers like Roger Daltrey, Gary Moore, Robert Plant, ELP, The Michael Schenker Group and Whitesnake – and his own act,

Bedlam. Powell, a technical musician, began as a journeyman with The Sorcerers in the late sixties, until Jeff Beck called upon his services for a pair of albums in 1972. Working sessions with Mickie Most at RAK proved pivotal, the industry guru suggesting Powell cut some records of his own. The first was the hypnotic 'Dance with the Devil' (1973), a record completely of its time that sold almost half a million copies in Britain. Other hits followed, such as 1974 football chant 'Na Na Na', but within another year the drummer was conscripted by Ritchie Blackmore for his post-Deep Purple

project, Rainbow – Powell remained with them for five albums. Although his subsequent career was more fragmented, Powell had now accrued some considerable wealth – much of which he invested in his greatest love, fast cars. So great was his obsession that, in the eighties, the drummer had briefly planned to quit music for motor racing.

By 1998 the percussionist shared the grounds of his Bristol home with a fine collection of automobiles and motorbikes – one of which he crashed, breaking his ribs and injuring his foot. Even as he recovered

'Oh *shit*!'
Cozy Powell bids his girlfriend farewell

Cozy Powell puts his foot down

from this, the insatiable Powell was involved in another crash in his Saab 9000: while speaking to his girlfriend, Sharon Reeve, on a mobile phone (before such activities were outlawed), the drummer suffered a high-speed blow-out and collided with a guard rail on the M4. Rushed to hospital, he was pronounced dead on arrival. It seems Powell was not only driving at 104 mph but was also found to be over the limit and not wearing a seat belt. It is thought that Cozy Powell – who had yet another new project on the way at the time of his death – contributed to at least sixty-five rock albums during his career.

Monday 6

Wendy O Williams

(Wendy Orlean Williams – Webster, New York, 28 May 1949)

The Plasmatics

The Queen of Shock Rock started as she intended to continue, a child-performer turned high-school rebel who seemed happiest either making as much noise as possible or disrobing in public – two traits she was to use to some effect in her career. Small-time entrepreneur Rod Swenson (aka 'Captain Kink') liked what he saw when Williams showed up at his New York strip club in 1976, suggesting a marriage with the punk-rock vogue of the time. The Plasmatics were pure theatre – the band signed with UK label Stiff and debuted at CBGB's to some response. With music very much taking a back seat, the band proceeded to blow up cars and take chainsaws to television sets in their low-concept stage act – Williams sported a Mohican, her breasts covered only by duct tape. Songs like 'Butcher Baby' and 'Monkey Suit' were largely an irrelevance, although the parent album, *New Hope for the*

Wendy O Williams: Taped before a live audience

Wretched (1980), sold initially. But once it became apparent that The Plasmatics were not likely to sell many more records, their act descended into low-rent pornography, and Williams was frequently arrested on obscenity charges. Post-Plasmatics, the singer found it harder to place herself, though she still somehow earned a Grammy nomination for the solo effort *WOW* (1985) and managed to land a few film roles.

Changing tack completely, Williams became an animal carer – an unlikely role that earned her the nickname 'The Squirrel Lady'. But her career had been full of such anomalies and oddities; the ability to lead a normal life seemed beyond her. Finally, she was found in woods near her Connecticut home by lover Swenson, having shot herself in the head with a pistol. Williams's long-time partner claimed that the former singer had been ready to die, having planned her suicide well in advance.

One of the singer's better-known recordings was an unusual cover of 'Stand by Your Man', a 1982 duet with Motörhead's Lemmy Kilmister. The song was, of course, the biggest hit of Tammy Wynette's career – and, by remarkable coincidence ...

Tammy Wynette
(Virginia Wynette Pugh – Itawamba County, Mississippi, 5 May 1942)

... from the disputed First Lady of Punk, to the undisputed First Lady of Country. Enduring a life of seemingly relentless pain – both emotional and physical – Tammy Wynette touched the lives of millions with her songs of feminine suffering. Brought up by her grandparents on a farm without electricity (her father had died of a brain tumour when she was an infant), the future star made her own entertainment, learning guitar and piano as well

as taking singing lessons. Then, at the age of just seventeen, Wynette found herself in the first of five abusive marriages – to Euple Byrd, who dismissed her ambitions of being a singer with a curt 'Dream on, baby!' Their marriage lasted only six years but produced three children. A year after her divorce, Wynette graduated as a beautician before recording her first country tracks for Epic. By 1968 she had already cut her three best-known songs: 'I Don't Wanna Play House', 'DIVORCE' and then, paradoxically, 'Stand By Your Man' – a song that apparently recommended that women forgive their philandering partners. Two more marriages – to Don Chapel in 1967 and singer George Jones two years later – saw her suffer further at partners' hands (fists, in the case of the hard-drinking Jones), although she and Jones collaborated in the studio as the 'King and Queen of Country'. Divorced again in 1975, Wynette then witnessed the irony of 'Stand By Your Man' being reissued to top the UK charts. And the soap opera of her personal life didn't stop there. In 1976, the singer wed Nashville businessman Michael Tomlin. This time, the marriage (which had been hastily arranged, in any case) lasted less than two months; Wynette then found a fifth husband in songwriter and producer George Richey in 1978 – a union that was, somehow, to last the rest of her life. Aside from the rollercoaster ride of her love life, Wynette was also frequently unwell, filed for bankruptcy at least once and even suffered an abduction – which many, including her surviving daughters, believe may have been staged by Richey in order to conceal yet more signs of abuse.

In her career, Tammy Wynette recorded some fifty albums, enjoying seventeen country number ones. After a final, extraordinary crossover hit single with The KLF in 'Justified and Ancient' (1992, UK number two, number one in many other

countries), Wynette withdrew from music, preferring to market her own jewellery. Having undergone some twenty operations in her time, she probably knew she was nearing the end. Surviving four days in a coma during 1994, Wynette's body finally gave out in April 1998: the singer died lying on her sofa in the Nashville home that once belonged to Hank Williams Sr. Her memorial – televised live in the USA – was jam-packed with country luminaries, many of whom performed, including Merle Haggard, The Oak Ridge Boys and Dolly Parton.

Unhappy with the verdict of a blood clot as the cause of their mother's death, Wynette's daughters requested an exhumation of their mother's corpse – buried without an autopsy – a year after her death. When this was refused, they hit both her physician (for over-prescribing strong medication) and Richey (for continuing to administer it, despite the chronic damage it was doing to her system) with $50 million lawsuits. Richey himself then filed for the body to be exhumed, in order to clear his name. With lawyers satisfied that the original verdict was correct, Richey then asked to *re-exhume* the body in 2004, in order to move it to the mausoleum that would contain his own remains on his passing. Even in death, Tammy Wynette may not rest in peace, it seems.

Friday 17

Linda McCartney
(Linda Louise Eastman – Scarsdale, New York, 24 September 1941)
Paul McCartney & Wings

A much-maligned figure in popular music, Linda McCartney was an accomplished rock photographer when she first encountered Paul at

Linda McCartney: Her produce has been sampled by many — even if her music hasn't ...

'The best tribute you can pay Linda? Go veggie.'

Paul McCartney, 1998

London's Bag o' Nails nightclub in 1967. One detail should be cleared up: McCartney was not, as is often misreported, any kind of heiress to the Eastman photographic dynasty, though she did have a privileged upbringing; her father (who oddly had changed his name from Epstein) was a successful business attorney. Marrying Paul McCartney in 1969 (he was her second husband, after geophysicist John Melvyn See, with whom she had one daughter), she was taught by him to play keys and joined Wings, the band Paul formed after the break-up of The Fab Four. Linda McCartney's musical contribution to one of the seventies' biggest bands is perhaps better left to one side, but she did co-write some of the group's songs, and went on to record her own material, much of which appears on a post-humous album, *Wild Prairie* (1998). On top of this, McCartney kept her-self busy with a series of photography books, as well as the campaign to en-courage vegetarianism that prompted her ubiquitous frozen-food range.

Mother to three more children, with the ex-Beatle (including renowned fashion designer Stella), Linda McCartney apparently never spent a night apart from her husband in twenty-nine years of marriage – save that brief spell while he was under investigation in Tokyo for marijuana possession. She learned of her breast cancer in 1997. Although it appeared at first that the disease was controllable, a recurrence early in 1998 suggested that the cancer had spread to her liver, and McCartney died soon after on her family's ranch in Tucson, Arizona. Her memorial service in London drew the three surviving Beatles together for the first time in thirty years.

See also *Jimmy McCulloch (* September 1979)*

MAY

Golden Oldies #6

Tommy McCook
(Cuba, 4 March 1927)
The Skatalites
The Supersonics

Saxophonist Tommy McCook had the best start in life, attending the Alpha Cottage School in Kingston – a breeding ground for great musical talent as Jamaica began to find its feet in the industry. Originally a more jazz-influenced player who had mastered tenor sax and flute while living in the Bahamas, McCook became a pioneer in the world of ska as leader of Jackie Mittoo's new band The Skatalites (the name suggested by McCook, apparently) in 1964. The Skatalites were inspired by the extraordinary work of trombonist Don Drummond but broke up as an indirect result of the latter's incarceration (which preceded his dramatic death (May 1969). McCook went on to front the more rocksteady-influenced Duke Reid session band The Supersonics, before recording mainly as a solo artist throughout the seventies. McCook then surprised the ska community by reuniting the surviving Skatalites in the US in 1983, issuing a brand-new album, *Return of the Big Guns* (1984).

Ten years later, The Skatalites embarked upon their first ever world tour – but by now Tommy McCook's health was beginning to fail him. A heart attack having curtailed his live work, McCook eventually died on 4 May 1998 from a combination of pneumonia and heart failure at his home in Atlanta, Georgia.

See also *Jackie Mittoo (December 1990); Roland Alphonso (Golden Oldies #8). Singer Vic Taylor died in 2003.*

Thursday 7

Eddie Rabbitt
(Brooklyn, New York, 27 November 1941)

What the Judge never managed, the Rabbitt pulled off: the career of singer/songwriter Eddie Rabbitt really took off when Elvis recorded his 'Kentucky Rain' in 1970. He'd struggled as an artist since 1964, finally moving to Nashville, where he became a favourite on the country scene. Rabbitt's own crossover success began as late as 1979 when he contributed the languid 'Every Which Way but Loose' to the Clint Eastwood movie of that name, but the following year he earned his biggest success with the Billboard number one 'I Love a Rainy Night' (1980), and scored another five Top Twenty hits over the next two years. Eddie Rabbitt's subsequent career was lower key, and his heavy smoking eventually caused the lung cancer that was to shorten his life.

Saturday 9

Lester Butler
(Virginia, 12 November 1959)
The Red Devils
13

Here's an odd one. Lester Butler was a white-hot guitarist/harmonica-player making his name on the circuit of his adopted LA with The Red Devils, the blues combo who gained sufficient notoriety to back R L Burnside, Johnny Cash and Mick Jagger (who, at one point, rated them as his favourite band). When The Devils folded in 1994, Howlin' Wolf fan Butler began another, arguably even better combo called, simply, 13. The band – Butler (vocals/blues harp), Alex Schultz

(ex-Mighty Flyers, guitar), Mark Goldberg (ex-Canned Heat, bass) and James Intveld (mainly drums) – looked set to outdo Butler's previous group.

But it was not to be. On the night of 8 May, Butler was due to play a Hollywood gig with 13 when he dropped by the house of sometime drummer Bill Bateman with friends Glenn Demidow and April Ortega. The latter gave him a shot of heroin – too much, it transpired – and Butler's friends then injected him three times with cocaine in a bizarre effort to reverse the effects. Without contacting emergency services, they then drove the now-comatose Butler to his gig – and proceeded to watch the rest of his band play without their leader, left 'asleep' in a van! The story gets stranger: the trio then removed Butler to Bateman's home, from where, the following evening under cover of night, they took him to his own bed. Lester Butler's body was discovered by another friend early on Sunday 10th. Demidow and Ortega were found guilty of manslaughter, and served five years between them.

See also *Johnny Cash (Golden Oldies #16); R L Burnside (Golden Oldies #29)*

Thursday 14

Rudy West
(Newport News, Virginia, 25 July 1933)
The Five Keys

The Five Keys were the result of many months of practice by two sets of Virginian brothers – Ripley Ingram (octave tenor); Raphael Ingram (second tenor); Bernie West (bass/baritone); and Rudy West (first tenor). The quartet had begun as the gospel-flavoured Sentimental Four, landing a contract with Capitol (via Aladdin), and changed the name to something more upbeat as they converted to a more secular style with the addition of another tenor, Edwin Hall. A hit in live performance, The Five Keys – who then lost Raphael Ingram to the draft, gaining occasional lead Maryland Pierce, baritone/second tenor James 'Dickie' Smith and guitarist Joe Jones – managed numerous R & B chart entries, including three crossover hits, beginning with 'Ling Ting Tong', between 1954 and 1957. At the end of this period, Rudy West left the group to marry, and his subsequent recording career faltered. West, employed as a US postal worker until retirement, underwent cancer treatment before dying from a heart attack at home in Chesapeake. The day's other big event meant that he received only a small notice in the newspapers.

Ripley Ingram died three years before West, while occasional singer Ulysses Hicks collapsed and died as early as January 1955, as the group went on tour.

Golden Oldies #7

Frank Sinatra

(Hoboken, New Jersey, 12 December 1915)

There's little one can say that hasn't been said several thousand times over about Ol' Blue Eyes. The son of a part-time abortionist, Frank Sinatra grew up to become the western world's most touted singer/actor/music entrepreneur and eventually a character larger than any of his chosen *métiers*. Sinatra first recorded in 1939, joining Tommy Dorsey's band before embarking on his illustrious solo career in 1942. In the US, Sinatra racked up twenty-six gold albums (for a soloist, a record surpassing even that of Elvis Presley); in Britain, his signature tune, 'My Way', spent 122 weeks on the listings. As a solo artist with Columbia, Sinatra appealed to the bobby-soxer pre-rock 'n' roll set; his movies then afforded him

the tack-on bad-boy image as he grew in stature and began hanging with the infamous Rat Pack. Sinatra's sometimes wild private life led to many murmurings about connections to the Mafia – a detail not missed in Kitty Kelley's unauthorized 1986 biography.

Frank Sinatra continued to perform live until just three years before his death from a heart attack on 14 May 1998. He was reportedly buried with a miniature of Jack Daniel's, a pack of Camel cigarettes and an assortment of US candy.

JULY

Friday 17

Marc Hunter

(Taumarunui, New Zealand, 7 September 1953)
Dragon

With his bass-playing younger brother Todd, Kiwi Marc Hunter founded Dragon – a melodic rock unit which became one of Australia's biggest acts during the late seventies. Singer Hunter was just twenty years old when his band signed to Vertigo, the prog label issuing two records in quick succession. In the progressive field, Dragon were swamped by bigger international names, the albums *Universal Radio* (1974) and *Scented Gardens for the Blind* (1975) somewhat ignored, prompting the Hunter brothers to relocate from Auckland to Sydney. With the line-up now stable – Hunter, Hunter, Paul Hewson (keyboards), Robert Taylor (guitars) and Neal Storey (drums) – (or so they thought), Dragon signed with CBS and acceptance seemed just a fiery breath away. But theft of the band's equipment was followed by the harrowing drug-related death of Storey in 1976 – and Dragon appeared to be back at square one. The group rallied,

though, scoring big-selling albums and huge domestic hits such as 'April Sun in Cuba' (1977, number two) and 'Are You Old Enough?' (1978, number one). With success came the downside: despite the sobering experience of a few years before, both Marc Hunter and Hewson developed crippling heroin habits. The increasingly volatile lead singer then pretty much blew Dragon's position as Australia's biggest band during a 1978 US tour, expected to break the act there. A well-built frontman, claiming to have little fear of hostile audiences, he almost caused a riot when the band opened for Johnny Winter in Texas, calling the crowd 'faggots' (Winter reportedly bet with his band on who would shoot Hunter first). The following year, Todd Hunter was put in the embarrassing position of having to sack his wayward brother.

Hunter trod a solo path for a while after, racking up moderate Aussie hits with 'Island Nights' (1979) and 'Big City Talk' (1981), until, in order to stave off debts, Dragon re-formed in 1982, to lesser effect. The band overcame a second heroin-related death – that of departed songwriter Hewson (➤*January 1985*) – to continue in a more AOR vein into the nineties, the irrepressible Hunter ever at the fore. Unlike Storey and Hewson, Marc Hunter survived his years of heroin abuse, but in 1997 was diagnosed with throat cancer, which rapidly took over his system. After a final live appearance at his own benefit concert, Hunter died in July, leaving a widow and three children. Some 700 mourners attended his Sydney funeral.

Sunday 26

'Chico' Ryan

(David Allen Ryan – Boston, Massachusetts,
9 April 1948)
Sha-Na-Na
The Happenings
(Bill Haley & His Comets)

Sha-Na-Na were a well-established
rock/doo-wop revival act well before
the arrival of singer and bassist 'Chico'
Ryan in 1973. His credentials were
impressive: apart from playing with
hit-making New Jersey beat group
The Happenings in the early seventies,
Ryan had also toured with rock 'n'
roll pioneer Bill Haley on one of the
kiss-curled singer's many nostalgia
tours – frequently upsetting the
main man by refusing to wear official
Comets gear. During the seventies and
beyond, Sha-Na-Na almost became
a caricature of themselves, a novelty
act par excellence. Biker-jacketed,
slick-haired Ryan had the requisite
look as the group became Johnny
Casino & The Gamblers for mega-
movie *Grease*; they then secured their
own television variety series in the US
(a sort of brilliantined *Hee Haw*). At
the age of fifty, 'Chico' Ryan suffered
a mysterious accident in Nevada, and
died in a Boston nursing home.

See also *Vinnie Taylor (*⚹*April 1974)*

SEPTEMBER

Friday 4

Lal Waterson

(Elaine Waterson – Hull, 15 February 1943)
The Watersons

With her sister, Norma, and brother,
Michael, Lal Waterson made up the
folk trio The Watersons, the three
siblings beginning their singing career
while very young indeed. The group
cut its first album proper, *Frost and
Fire*, in 1964, following it with three
others – at a time when folk was
beginning to give way to the beat
boom. Nonetheless, The Watersons's
oeuvre is considered core to the development of later UK folkies such as
Fairport Convention and Steeleye
Span. With the group suspended
by the end of the decade, Lal and
Michael Waterson returned in 1972
with an album featuring contributions
from many future folk luminaries.
The Watersons regrouped for further recordings, and Lal Waterson's
compositions were covered by many,
including June Tabor. A later incarnation of The Watersons included
celebrated folk instrumentalist Martin
Carthy, Lal Waterson's brother-in-law.

Shortly after completing the record
Once in a Blue Moon with her son Oliver
Knight, Lal Waterson passed away at
home from the cancer diagnosed just
days before.

Monday 21

Oz Bach

(Paul Bach – Huntington, West Virginia,
24 June 1939)
Spanky & Our Gang
(Tarantula)
(Wings)

Without the quality of songwriting of
their closest rivals, The Mamas & The
Papas, Spanky & Our Gang are often
overlooked in US pop history – but
the act still managed five Top Forty
hits between 1967 and 1969. Hatted,
moustachioed bass-player Paul 'Oz'
Bach had studied music in Florida,
attending the University of Miami
while finding slots backing some of
the era's best-known local names.
Bach relocated again – to Chicago this
time – after he met founder musician
Malcolm Hale and quirky Illinois blues
singer Elaine 'Spanky' McFarlane
during a three-day Florida 'hurricane'
party. The group – completed by guitarist Nigel Pickering – scored their
first major hit with the catchy 'Sunday
Will Never be the Same' (1967). For
Oz Bach, though, it would be a brief
spell in the spotlight: he quit the band
before a second album the year after;
Spanky & Our Gang were then left
reeling by the sudden deaths of Hale
(⚹ *October 1968*) and Bach's replacement, Lefty Baker (⚹ *August 1971*).

Although his post-Spanky band
projects, Tarantula and Wings (not
Paul McCartney's group, obviously),
were not to take off, Oz Bach went on
to work with a variety of musicians
(including Steve Miller and Linda
Ronstadt) and was also a respected
music arranger for theatre and film.
For a short while, Bach even fronted
his own television talk show. Bach's
long battle with cancer finally came
to an end shortly before his sixtieth
birthday.

OCTOBER

Sunday 11

Raymond Myles

(New Orleans, Louisiana, 1957)

An R & B-influenced gospel singer, Raymond Myles was expected to emulate his lifetime hero Al Green, so profound was the effect he had on those who listened to him. In 1969, Myles enchanted many with his heartfelt 'Prayer from a 12-Year-Old Boy', a record that called for an end to both segregation and the Vietnam War. But, instead of jumping ship to the secular market he clearly loved, Myles maintained his gospel standing, touring with his own Raymond Anthony Myles Singers and also performing with genre heavyweights such as The Mighty Clouds of Joy and, yes, even the Reverend Al Green. Then, with cruel irony, the singer who had first made his name with a call for peace was gunned down by a car-jacker in his home town of New Orleans. His assailant has never been brought to justice.

NOVEMBER

Sunday 8

Lonnie Pitchford

(Lexington, Mississippi, 8 October 1955)

Young blues pretender Lonnie Pitchford modelled himself very much on the legacies of Robert Johnson and Elmore James, learning his craft from Delta practitioner Eugene Powell (whom he survived by just four days).

Guitarist Pitchford's unique selling point was his utilization of the African single-stringed diddley-bow, an instrument otherwise unheard of in blues. As a teenager, he wowed the audience at 1974's National Folk Festival, going on to tour the world and play with an assortment of musicians, including Johnson's stepson Robert Junior Lockwood and even rock singer John Cougar Mellencamp. Despite this, the musician only ever cut one album himself, 1994's *All Around Man*. Diagnosed HIV positive, Pitchford died prematurely from complications arising from pneumonia and is buried in Ebeneezer, Mississippi.

Golden Oldies #8

Roland Alphonso

(Havana, Cuba, 12 January 1931)

The Skatalites
(The Soul Vendors)
(The Ruinaires)

Just months after the passing of founder and fellow sax-player Tommy McCook (◄ *Golden Oldies #6*), the world of ska lost another key member of the genre's first real stars, The Skatalites. Alphonso, born to a Cuban father and Jamaican mother, got his break when the jazz-trained tenor saxophonist encountered Clement 'Coxsone' Dodd at the latter's Studio One complex, becoming an in-house musician by the end of the fifties. With ska being Jamaica's first indigenous musical creation, the country embraced The Skatalites to such an extent that it's hard to believe that the group effectively existed for just a year and a half. Nevertheless, the band line-up read like a hall of fame – Alphonso, McCook, Don 'Cosmic' Drummond (trombone), 'Ska' Campbell (tenor sax), 'Dizzy Johnny' Moore and Baba Brooks (both trumpet), Lloyd Brevett (bass), Jackie Mittoo (piano) and Lloyd Knibbs (drums) among

them. In their career, Alphonso and The Skatalites also played as back-up to The Wailers – and Alphonso sometimes jumped ship to record with Dodd's rival, Duke Reid. The Skatalites, however, were not afforded the respect they should have been and ended as a going concern after the incarceration of Drummond in 1965, though the band's signature tune, 'Guns Of Navarone' became an international success two years later. Alphonso was elsewhere by then, playing with his own set-up, The Soul Vendors (initially The Soul Brothers), and then club band The Ruinaires until his first mid-performance stroke in 1971. After a dozen years in the shadows, Roland Alphonso, now residing in New York, re-formed The Skatalites; this time, the band toured the world and finally received the acclaim they deserved.

Roland Alphonso suffered a second stroke as he played with The Skatalites at The Key Club, West Hollywood – a blood vessel in his neck burst during his performance. This time, though, the hospital-bound sax-player fell into a coma some two weeks later, and died on 20 November 1998. Now considered something of a legend, Alphonso was one of four select musicians to be awarded the Jamaican government's Order of Merit – the others being Dodd, McCook and, of course, Bob Marley.

See also *Don Drummond (◄ May 1969); Jackie Mittoo (◄ December 1990). Sometime Skatalite Vic Taylor died in 2003.*

Friday 27

Barbara Acklin
(Oakland, California, 28 February 1943)
(The Chi-Lites)

Leaving her Baptist choir beginnings, Barbara Acklin – having moved to Illinois at the age of five – studied classical music at Dunbar Vocational High before her cousin, keyboard-ist/arranger Monk Higgins, helped place her as a secretary at St Lawrence Records, where her melodic voice was heard for the first time. Guided by Higgins, Acklin moved to Chess, where she sang back-up to the likes of Fontella Bass and Etta James. A budding songwriter, Acklin penned 'Whispers (Gettin' Louder)', a big hit for Jackie Wilson in 1966; her own singing career was slow, however, and though a few songs would trouble the R & B charts, only one record, 'Love Makes a Woman' (1968), gave her a crossover hit. Moving labels several times, Acklin wound up at Chi-Sound, where she married Eugene Record, lead vocalist with The Chi-Lites. Her own hits having dried up, she co-wrote a pair of the group's standards, 'Stoned Out of My Mind' and the enduring 'Have You Seen Her?'

Barbara Acklin had long retired from music by the time of her death in 1998. From her home in Omaha, Nebraska, the singer had been inter-viewed by a Chicago cable television station – and had complained of contracting a bad cold. One week later, Acklin was rushed to hospital as she visited a friend for Thanksgiving. There, she was diagnosed with pneu-monia, from which she died shortly thereafter.

See also *Eugene Record (☛ July 2005)*

DECEMBER

Friday 11

Lynn Strait
(James Lynn Strait – Manhasset, New York, 7 August 1968)
Snot
(Lethal Dose)

The media-baiting LA hardcore rock band Snot was formed by singer Lynn Strait in 1995, after his original band, Lethal Dose, split. Amazingly, Snot drew the attention of Geffen Records, who signed the band up for a debut album, *Get Some* (1997). (The singer had not been able to sign his contract in person, as he was serving a thirty-day jail sentence at the time.) Strait then incurred the wrath of his pres-tigious label after some onstage sex-ual activity with a dancer at the 1998 Ozzfest. Snot 'got blown' for a second time when the label then dropped them. Lynn Strait was on his way from his home in Santa Barbara to Los Angeles when his Ford Tempo struck another vehicle, resulting in a three-car pile-up on Freeway 101. Strait – who was discovered to be dosed up on cocaine at the time – died at the scene, as did his faithful dog, Dobbs, a mas-cot who'd graced the cover of Snot's debut album.

Tuesday 15

Orion
(Jimmy Hodges Ellis – 26 February 1945)

An even more curious performer was Jimmy 'Orion' Hodges, one of the few tribute acts to feature in *Number One in Heaven*. Originally performing under his own name as an early sixties rock

'n' roll hopeful, Hodges re-emerged as Orion in 1978, an Elvis-impressionist second to none. His act was consid-ered so convincing that, after Presley's death (☛ *August 1977*), Orion not only performed (masked) at least once with The Jordanaires, but his vocals were used on a series of Jerry Lee Lewis sides in order that the gullible might believe them to be genuine duets.

Back to being plain old Jimmy Ellis, the former 'star' died in very dramatic circumstances at the pawn store he ran with his former wife, Elaine Thompson, in Salma, Alabama. Confronted by desperate small-time criminal Jeffrey James Lee, both Ellis and Thompson were killed, blasted at point-blank range by the assailant's sawn-off shotgun; store assistant Helen King was left injured. Lee and two teenage accomplices were later charged with the double murder.

Tuesday 22

Chris Galvin
(Bristol, 1959)
The Experimental Pop Band
The Brilliant Corners

Starting out as The Hybrids, Bristol's Brilliant Corners became one of the leading guitar bands in Britain's post-'C86' scene. Bass-player Chris Galvin started the band with his friend guitarist Davey Woodward, and The Brilliant Corners carved a small niche for themselves, particularly with spar-kling single 'Brian Rix' (1987) and third album *Somebody up There Likes Me* (1988) on their own SS20 label. Attracting no real attention – save one appearance on Radio One's John Peel Show – Woodward and Galvin folded the project after no fewer than seven studio albums. The pair went on to create 'skewed boho-pop' (according to the *NME*) with The Experimental Pop Band in 1995, issuing an acclaimed debut album, *Discgrotesque* (1997). It was to be Galvin's only contribution. Terminally ill with cancer, he passed away at the end of the following year. Davey Woodward pays tribute by continuing with the band to the present day.

Friday 25

Bryan MacLean

(Los Angeles, California, 25 September 1946)
Love
(The Bryan MacLean Band)

The first rock band signed by the influential Elektra label, Love were the brainchild of charismatic singer Arthur Lee – though there are many who still believe the real magic was in the playing of guitarist Bryan MacLean. A fan of folk and rock, MacLean had escaped his privileged upbringing to befriend fellow guitarist and Byrds-founder David Crosby, the latter inviting him to join the fledgling band as a roadie. Also emerging were The Grass Roots, Lee's precursor to Love, whom MacLean was to join by the end of 1965. Initially, the latter found it hard to force his writing on to Lee, who had a very distinct vision of where Love were headed. After a great self-titled first album (1966), Love returned even more impressively with the wondrous *Da Capo* and *Forever Changes* (both 1967) – the second of these featured many MacLean compositions, most notably the classic 'Alone Again Or'. Strangely, the sessions for this last album had witnessed extreme band disharmony, and MacLean decided to make his own way after its release. It proved a bad move: MacLean's substance abuse snowballed and the errant guitarist found himself falling increasingly foul of the law. By 1970 he had all but jacked in music.

A Christian convert, Bryan MacLean re-emerged with a more religious strain of pop music until launching his own side project, The Bryan MacLean Band, in the early eighties. This group contained an up-and-coming singer/guitarist in the shape of his half-sister, Maria McKee, who would go on to record MacLean's 'Don't Toss Us Away' as leader of the excellent Lone Justice. Bryan MacLean – who had released his final solo album, *Ifyoubelievein*, just a year before – was enjoying a Christmas lunch with his friend Love biographer Kevin Delaney when he collapsed and died from a heart attack.

See also *George Suranovich (☞February 1990); Ken Forssi (☞January 1998). Original Love drummer Don Conka died in 2004.*

Wednesday 30

Johnny Moore

(Selma, Alabama, 15 December 1934)
The Drifters
(The Three Hornets)

Enduring vocalist Johnny Moore learned his trade as tenor with The Hornets, a doo-wop group from Cleveland, Ohio, whose popularity stretched little further than their home state. The Drifters, on the other hand, formed a year earlier, were at the point of huge stardom by the time manager George Treadwell hired Moore at the end of 1954. The singer's recruitment was an effort to bring wayward lead singer Little David Baughan into line: Moore, who had been given just B-sides to sing at this stage, was actually briefly dismissed three months later when this odd plan appeared to be working. He was installed as an official singer soon after, when Baughan reverted to his earlier ways. Moore spent most of his time on the road with The Drifters for the next few years, the group on a strict wage with record sales barely affecting their personal wealth.

In 1957, the singer was drafted, but on his return to civilian life tried his hand as a soloist under the name Johnny Darrow (to avoid confusion with singer Johnny Moore of The Blazers) before returning to The Drifters' fold (via The Drapers, an offshoot) in 1963. Moore was thus a veritable senior by the time he was installed as lead in 1964. Previous lead Ben E King had left the line-up, and The Drifters – by now regular hit-makers – had struggled to find a suitable replacement; Moore was only offered the 'permanent' role after the shocking death of then-current lead Rudy Lewis (☞Pre-1965). The day after Lewis's passing, Moore sang vocals to 'Under the Boardwalk', the first major hit to showcase him. With sales beginning to dip, The Drifters exploited their European popularity, nurtured during the mid sixties, eventually relocating to England, where Moore fronted their hugely successful seventies incarnation. Although Drifters aficionados tend to see this version of the group as slighter than the early R & B line-ups (some songs were now written by the British partnership of Roger Cook and Roger Greenaway), there is little arguing with the parade of UK hits they accumulated, such as the 350,000-selling 'Kissin' in the Back Row' (1974) and 'There Goes My First Love' (1975). In 1978, Moore again attempted a solo career, but still found success easier to come by as a Drifter. After some wrangles over ownership of the name, the singer teamed with Ben E King for the first time ever during the eighties, and The Drifters brand became a staple of the oldies circuit. Johnny Moore appeared on British television with The Drifters just days before his death from respiratory failure.

Johnny Moore is one of fifteen dead Drifters (☞Pre-1965/Dead Interesting!)

Lest We Forget

Other notable deaths that occurred sometime during 1998:

Gene Autry (enduring country singer; born Orvon Gene Autry, Texas, 29/9/1907; cancer, 2/10)

Damita Jo (US R & B singer with The Red Caps who became queen of the 'answer record'; born Damita Jo DeBlanc, Texas, 5/8/1930; respiratory failure, 25/12)

Karl Denver (pre-Beatles-era UK hit-maker whose biggest of four Top Ten entries was 'Wimoweh' in 1961; born Angus McKenzie, Glasgow, 16/12/1933; brain tumour, 21/12)

Tony De Vit (noted UK dance producer who also remixed pop kids East 17 and Louise; born Worcestershire, 12/9/1957; bronchial pneumonia/bone-marrow failure, 2/7)

Charlie Foxx (US R & B guitarist/singer/songwriter who partnered his younger sister Inez to some success; born Charlie Fox, North Carolina, 23/10/1939; cancer, 18/9)

Johnny Funches (US R & B lead tenor with Hall of Fame inductees The Dells; born Illinois, 18/7/1935; emphysema – possibly induced by his later position as a steel-mill worker – 23/1)

David 'Junior' Kimbrough (noted US blues singer/songwriter/ guitarist; born Mississippi, 28/7/1930; heart failure – barely surprising, given that he supposedly fathered 36 children – 17/1)

Antoine 'TCD' Lundy (US vocalist with doo-wop-styled hip-hop act Force MDs; born New York, 3/2/1964; Lou Gehrig's disease, 18/1 – just three years after the death of bandmate Mercury Nelson)

Patty Russell (US singer with soul troupe Patty & The Emblems; born New Jersey; leukaemia, 9/1998 – her death came two months ahead of that of baritone Alexander Wilde)

J D Summer (US gospel singer with Elvis Presley, The Blackwood Brothers and Stamps Quartet – possessor of the world's deepest bass; born Florida, 19/11/1924; heart attack, 16/11)

For a complete list of fallen artists, visit

www.numberoneinheaven.com

The Death Toll #5

ROVER'S NON-RETURN

You've guessed it: the following is a veritable pet cemetery of songs dedicated to much-loved – and now departed – furry friends. (Well, dogs, mainly.)

1 'Old Tige'
Jim Reeves (1961)

Arguably the 'daddy' of all dead-pet anthems, 'Old Tige' tells of the young soldier whose faithful hound had seen him through trial after trial as a kid. Not only had Old Tige saved the boy from drowning in the creek, the remarkable pet had also pulled him to safety from 'that chargin' bull that gored ma dad to death'. Returning home from Korea, the young storyteller was reunited with Old Tige, who negotiated him dutifully through the storm past a newly built dam of which the soldier had previously been unaware. On arriving back to his momma, the young man learns the chillin' truth: lonely Old Tige had died three years before.

2 'Shannon'
Henry Gross (1976)

An AOR smash for former Sha-Na-Na founder member Gross, this ditty was, strangely, not about his own dog called Shannon. Nope, that would have been way too obvious; this tune was penned in memory of an Irish setter belonging to close friend Beach Boy Carl Wilson – also called Shannon – that had recently gone to the great kennel in the sky. The cloying lyrics and Gross's shrill delivery somehow gave him a US gold disc – a feat he'd never achieve again.

3 'Wildfire'
Michael Murphey (1975)

A pony this time, Wildfire was the loyal companion to Murphey's ghostly heroine, a nameless young rider who died in a blizzard searching for her missing hoofed friend. Panicked by the brewing storm, Wildfire had busted loose from his stall to disappear without trace – until the unwitting Murphey began hearing the girl and her pony as he lay in his bed. Spooky stuff.

4 'Ali Baba's Camel'
The Bonzo Dog Doo Dah Band (1969)
Whether a camel constitutes a pet as such is perhaps open to debate, but the relationship between The Bonzos' Ali Baba and his talking, shorts-wearing mount was certainly more than merely professional. Having stolen the camel from a zoo, the rider then enters them into a desert race, which they win 'by a camel's hair' – laughing themselves to death in the process.

5 'So Long'
The Handsome Family (2002)
An Albuquerque husband-and-wife team, The Handsome Family (aka Brett and Rennie Sparks) upped the dead-pet ante considerably with this lo-fi track from their 2002 album *Twilight*. Lyricist Rennie reels off an extraordinary list of former pets of hers that met untimely ends: they include tinsel-eating Snickers (a dog); Mr Whiskers, a cat that leapt from a window; a brown rabbit run over by accident and a family of gerbils who escaped from their cage. The couple are now banned from all local pet stores.

6 'Big Ted'
Incredible String Band (1969)
Scotland's Incredible String Band were fast becoming known for their bewildering repertoire of animal tunes by the time this opener for their *Changing Horses* LP arrived. 'Big Ted' was a prize boar that, growing long in the tooth, had to be sold to the butcher by its impoverished owner. The group – who also sang of a 'Good Dog' and 'Cousin Caterpillar' – mused in the song that Ted might one day return as a milking cow. LSD had been available in Britain for a while by 1969.

7 'Old Shep'
Elvis Presley (1957)
The King's faithful hound surprisingly *didn't* meet his maker in the litter tray with a mouth full of Kennomeat and flea tablets. The disturbing lyrics here suggest that Elvis himself was going to put the ageing pet out of its misery with a shotgun. Didn't they give injections in those days?

8 'Jeremy is Innocent'
Rex Barker & The Ricochets (1979)
A genuine event this time: this strange record (made by *That's Life* TV presenter Doc Cox, also of 'Ivor Biggun' fame) was a dig at the previous summer's scandal involving outed British politician Jeremy Thorpe. Boasting barking hound and shotgun as accompaniment, the minimal lyrics referred to the cruel shooting of Rinka, a dog belonging to Thorpe's former lover, model Norman Scott. Thorpe was acquitted of any involvement the following year, though he lost his seat (as it were) at the general election. Rumours that The Ricochets were asked to contribute royalties to animal charities remain unsubstantiated. There wouldn't have been a great deal, either way.

9 'Poor Old Horse'
The Albion Band (1978)
Rising from the ashes of Steeleye Span, The Albion Band were main players in the British electro-folk scene of the seventies. In this traditional dirge, the singer talks of 'tanning the beast's hide' if it popped its clogs and 'going for another ride' if it, erm, didn't. Never a likely hit, the record limped to a knacker's yard finish of number seventy-eight in the UK chart, despite ever-reliable DJ Simon Bates seeing fit to make it his Record of the Week during a heady summer of post-punk and *Saturday Night Fever*.

10 'Put the Bone In'
Terry Jacks (1974)
Fast becoming the undisputed 'king of maudlin', Terry Jacks topped charts across the world with 'Seasons in the Sun'. Lesser known, but no less mawkish, was the B-side – a eulogy to a fictitious pet mongrel who, having come to a sticky end on the road, had to be buried with a favourite bone. For some reason, the track was a big hit in its own right in France.

DEAD INTERESTING!

CHRISTMAS CRACKLER ...
Jim and William Reid of celebrated East Kilbride noiseniks The Jesus & Mary Chain originally named their band Death Of Joey after the demise of a pet budgerigar one Yuletide. The brothers' father, mistaking the pet for a piece of wrapping paper, unceremoniously booted him into the fire. One question remains: how much was left for Boxing Day sandwiches?

... at Alice's restaurant
Meanwhile, in June 1977, Detroit shock-rock godfather Alice Cooper suffered the distressing loss of the beloved pet boa constrictor frequently seen in his stage show. The reptile, it seems, was bitten and killed by a rat intended for its lunch.

JANUARY

Monday 11

Barry Pritchard

(Birmingham, England, 3 April 1944)

The Fortunes

Starting as an acoustic trio called The Clifftones, The Fortunes were Birmingham's answer to the higher-profile sixties beat groups of Liverpool, London and Manchester. The three originators of the distinctive Fortunes sound were Glen Dale (Richard Garforth, vocals/guitar), Barry Pritchard (vocals/guitar) and Rod Allen (Rodney Bainbridge, vocals/bass). Turning electric, the band bolstered itself with keyboardist David Carr and drummer Andy Brown to win a local talent show (in which they had been pitted against at least one other band called The Fortunes). The prize was a deal with Decca and – after a few false alarms – a spate of infectious singles, beginning with the UK number-two hit 'You've Got Your Troubles' (1965), which also broke the group into the US Top Ten. Perhaps the best was the band's interpretation of Lynsey de Paul's 'Storm in a Teacup' (1972), by which time Dale and Carr had left. As a founder, Pritchard led The Fortunes throughout the seventies and eighties and, while hits dried up, saw to it that they remained a decent live attraction. Retiring from the group through ill health in 1995, the singer passed away following a heart attack.

Friday 15

John Baker Saunders

(Montgomery, Alabama, 23 September 1954)

Mad Season

(The Walkabouts)

The fact that short-lived Seattle post-grunge supergroup Mad Season was conceived in a rehab facility won't come as much of a shock to anyone who recalls the group, its members and their one 1995 album, *Above*. Bassist Saunders had rallied Pearl Jam guitarist Mike McCready, who in turn called upon Alice In Chains singer Layne Staley and Screaming Trees drummer Barrett Martin for the project. US radio picked up on the remarkably commercial-sounding 'River Of Deceit', but Staley's disappearance brought the band to an abrupt halt. Saunders had had a murky past with blues bands in Minneapolis, and also toured briefly with Seattle mainstays The Walkabouts. The bass-player was found dead in his Seattle apartment from an apparent heroin overdose, having battled addiction to the drug for some time.

See also *Layne Staley (*➤ *April 2002)*

Sunday 31

Jose Angel 'Pepe' Farias

(Monterrey, Mexico, 1975)

Silvestre Rodriguez Jr

(McAllen, Texas, 1971)

Intocable

The last day of January 1999 saw Tejano's fastest-rising unit lying shattered on a highway, having been on their way to a concert in Monterrey.

The sprawling Intocable – Jose Angel 'Pepe' Farias (MC/percussion), Silvestre Rodriguez (bass/vocals), Ricardo Muñoz Solis (lead vocals/accordion), René Martinez Santos (drums), Sergio Serna (various percussion) and Daniel Sánchez (guitar) – integrated contemporary styles to win over a new generation of fans to the splinter genre of Norteno, a traditional North Mexican folk style. In just five years, the group, whose name means 'Untouchable', seemed just that, accruing four gold albums (starting with 1994's *Fuego Eterno*) and in 1998 playing to 65,000 at Houston's Astrodome. Then just months later, it all seemed to be over: Intocable's speeding station wagon blew a tyre and skidded off the highway near Reynosa at around 11 am. While each member of the act suffered injuries of varying degrees, Farias and Rodriguez were confirmed deceased at the scene. The band's newly appointed manager, Joe Angel Gonzales, died on his way to hospital. Although the tragedy didn't shake the Tejano world in quite the same way as the death of Selena (◀ *March 1995*), it came as a huge shock to the many fans who gathered at the scene within hours to pay their respects. But who says adversity shouldn't make you stronger? With new MC Juan Hernandez and replacement bassist Felix Salinas, the seemingly unflappable Intocable survivors re-emerged with their biggest-selling album yet, *Contigo*, just months after the accident.

Gwen Guthrie: 'Rent' asunder

FEBRUARY

Tuesday 2

David McComb

(Perth, Australia, 17 February 1962)
The Triffids
(The Blackeyed Susans)
(Co-star)

Echoing the sparse terrain of their homeland, the music of Western Australia's Triffids offered vast open spaces and often quite beautiful detail. A fan of The Velvet Underground and Leonard Cohen, musician and vocalist David McComb relocated to Sydney after graduating from university to realize his vision during the eighties. He'd originally recruited his talented multi-instrumentalist brother

Robert while the siblings were still at school – the band, then known as Dalsy, inspired by drummer/vocalist Alsy McDonald. Completed by bassist Martin Casey and (eventually) Jill Birt on keyboards, The Triffids drew attention with the impressive debut album *Treeless Plain* (1983) – but it was a move to London and the splendid third record, *Born Sandy Devotional* (1986), that cemented their reputation. The languid but compelling mood continued with *Calenture* (1987), though the lack of a commercial breach saw the band's magnum opus 'Bury Me Deep in Love' later licensed to Aus-soap *Neighbours* (perhaps the only black mark against McComb in his entire career, though one can see why he allowed it). After the dissolution of this perennially underrated band at the back end of 1989, McComb embarked on a variety of ventures, including his acclaimed solo album, *Love Of Will*

(1994), which stood up to most of The Triffids' out-put, as well as the lower-key bands The Blackeyed Susans and Co-Star, a band he formed after re-enrolling at college.

On 30 January 1999, McComb was involved in a traffic accident and had to spend a night in St Vincent's Hospital, Melbourne, after which he was released, believed to be OK. In a sad twist, reminiscent of the death of Stiv Bator (◀ *June 1990*), David McComb died suddenly three days afterwards. It transpired, however, that McComb had suffered for many years from a heart condition – undergoing a transplant in 1995 – but was still experimenting occasionally with drugs. While a combination of these factors would seem to have been responsible for his passing, a verdict of heroin toxicity is now the generally accepted reason.

Wednesday 3

Gwen Guthrie
(Gwendolyn Guthrie – Okemah, Oklahoma,
14 July 1950)
(The Ebonettes)
(The East Coast Band)

Best remembered for her hypnotic
UK Top Five hit 'Ain't Nothin' Goin'
on But the Rent' (1986), sultry-voiced
New Jersey resident Gwen Guthrie
was a well-respected singer for many
years before and after this moment
of fame. Guthrie began singing with
a pair of groups, The Ebonettes and
The East Coast Band (later The New
York City Players, boasting future
Cameo star Larry Blackmon among
their ranks), at other times singing
jingles for television commercials and
also co-writing songs with Patrick
Grant for the likes of Sister Sledge
and UK singer Linda Lewis. She
crashed the US music scene on a bigger scale during the early seventies as
support vocalist to Billy Preston and
Steely Dan, and in 1974 toured with
her friend Aretha Franklin. With help
from reggae luminaries Sly Dunbar
and Robbie Shakespeare, Guthrie
launched her own recording career,
culminating in her huge 1986 success
– she would not enjoy another hit of
the calibre of 'Rent'.

A tireless campaigner for AIDS
and other charities, Gwen Guthrie
– whose husband had also died
prematurely – lost her own battle with
uterine cancer in hospital in Orange,
New Jersey.

Monday 15

Mc Big L
(Lamont Coleman – Harlem, New York,
30 May 1974)
Diggin' in the Crates Crew
(Children of The Corn)

Changing his identity to MC Big L,
Lamont Coleman was the latest in
a long line of street rappers who
seemed to be breaking out of the
underground. The ebonics-employ-
ing freestyler was originally a member
of Children of the Corn (with future
stars Ma$e and Cam'ron), before he
teamed up with DITC (Diggin' in the
Crates Crew) alongside such cohorts
as Fat Joe, Lord Finesse, Diamond D,
Showbiz and AG. Big L's first album
was *Lifestylez ov da Poor and Dangerous*
(1995), an album of well-executed if
predictable streetwise fare. This eventually created enough of an impact
for Jay-Z's label Roc-a-fella to come
beckoning – but the artist hadn't long
to live.

Just a few blocks from his Harlem
apartment, Big L was cornered and
shot nine times by 29-year-old gunman Gerard Woodley. The attacker,
it appeared, had an ongoing dispute
not with Coleman but with his older
brother, Lee. With the latter serving
time in prison, Woodley – who was
already wanted for drug trafficking
– presumably felt Big L to be the next
best thing. A posthumous DITC
album featured much material by the
late MC.

MARCH

Tuesday 2

Dusty Springfield
(Mary Isabel Catherine Bernadette O'Brien
– Hampstead, London, 16 April 1939)
The Springfields

Believed by many to be the finest
white female blues singer of her
generation, convent-educated Dusty
Springfield is often overlooked as the
singer who also introduced Britain
to Motown back in 1961 – although
her later productions perhaps owed
more to Phil Spector's influence
than Berry Gordy's. These sounds
were little known in Britain at the
time, but were stylishly replicated
by a singer destined to become the
nation's favourite during the decade.
Eschewing her given name for that of
the folk-flavoured trio for whom she
sang early in her career, Springfield
enjoyed a short run of hits with The
Springfields – with her brother Tom
and friend Tim Field – including the
US-flirting 'Silver Threads and Golden
Needles' (1962). (The singer had
earlier polished her vocal skills with
MOR three-piece The Lana Sisters.)
Dusty Springfield was close to being
a household name by the time 'I Only
Wanna be with You' (1963) positioned
her as the UK's brightest new female
singer. This Burt Bacharach-penned
standard – which also achieved hit
status in America – was the first of
sixteen Top Twenty hits in Britain.
While Springfield's career high was
undoubtedly the 1966 chart-topper
'You Don't Have to Say You Love Me',
other hits trip off the tongue in a litany
of familiarity – 'I Just Don't Know
What to Do with Myself' (1964),
'In the Middle of Nowhere' (1965)
and 'I Close My Eyes and Count to
Ten' (1968) among them. The *New*

'Let's have lunch.'
Dusty Springfield deals with the news
of her illness, 1994

The peerless Dusty Springfield: New threads and an old needle

Musical Express awarded Springfield the honour of Best Female Vocalist pretty much every year between 1964 and 1969, while her own UK television series established her as a cross-generation celebrity.

But, disenchanted with her homeland, her career faltering after ten years of almost unbroken success, Dusty Springfield moved to Los Angeles in 1972. Despite having received critical acclaim for her *Dusty In Memphis* album (1969), commercial acceptance began to elude Springfield, who even spent time working as an anonymous session vocalist to make ends meet towards the end of the seventies. An unlikely call from Neil Tennant and Chris Lowe of The Pet Shop Boys brought her out of semi-retirement, and the huge hit 'What Have I Done to Deserve This?' (US/UK number

two, 1987) encouraged her to move back to London. The record's triumph prompted further UK hits (some written by The Pet Shop Boys) as the magic of Dusty Springfield unexpectedly caught on again, presumably with the offspring of her original fanbase, who lapped up old standards such as 'Son of a Preacher Man' (1969), now rebranded by its inclusion in Quentin Tarantino's *Pulp Fiction*.

A known recluse, Springfield fought many public battles in her time: there was her refusal to play for segregated South African audiences in the early sixties, her dismissal of fame and glamour, her struggles with drink and drug addiction and the apparent contradictions of her sexual identity. In 1994, she was to have a new fight on her hands: true to form, Springfield's reaction to her breast

cancer was as unbending as had been her attitude to most other matters. Springfield was awarded the OBE in recognition of her achievements early in 1999, but by then she was too unwell to collect her accolade; she died from the disease weeks later. Just two months short of what would have been her sixtieth birthday, Dusty Springfield's funeral procession drew thousands to the streets of Henley-upon-Thames, where their heroine made her final journey in a glass-sided hearse, surrounded by floral tributes. Yet in her final interview only months before, the singer they called an icon had expressed her wish 'to die as Mary O'Brien'.

Freaky Tah

(Raymond Rodgers – Queens, New York,
14 May 1971)

The Lost Boyz

Yet another rapper born and killed in the same neighbourhood, Freaky Tah, with his 'permanent childhood' pals The Lost Boyz, was an artist who embraced different styles and issues, finding far more to talk about than the glorification of the gangs that had polluted hip-hop music for so long. Sadly, this did not prevent Tah's own death by violent means.

The Lost Boyz – gravel-voiced MC Tah joined by Mr Cheeks, Pretty Lou and Spigg Nice – created an unusual look, complete with dreadlocks and nappies on their heads. A gold-selling debut album on Universal, *Legal Drug Money* (1996), emphasized its protagonists' anti-chemical stance, a point of view taken on board by the many who propelled the batch of singles that preceded it into the chart – underground anthems such as 'Lifestyles of the Rich and Shameless' and 'Renee'. A self-deprecating follow-up, *Love, Peace and Nappiness* (1997), seemed to further The Lost Boyz' growing reputation as they won applause from further afield for denouncing the criminal activity of their youth. (The group were to make even more friends by channelling much of their profit back into the local community.)

To celebrate the birthday of Mr Cheeks, Freaky Tah and The Lost Boyz headed to a party at New York's Four Points Sheraton Hotel – where a sadly familiar scenario was to be played out. As he left the event at around 4 am, Tah was approached from behind by a ski-masked gunman (who presumably wouldn't have looked out of place among the revellers). His attacker unloaded one fatal shot into the back of the rapper's head, then fired into the air as he made good his escape. Freaky Tah was declared dead on arrival at Jamaica Hospital. The killing appeared motiveless, but in the days that followed several suspects were pulled in by police – at least two claiming to be the triggerman, which suggests that the taking of a life is still seen very much as a badge of honour on the street. For a while, NYPD looked into a possible connection with the assassination of MC Big L just a few weeks before (◄ *February 1999*), he and Freaky Tah having recently recorded together.

> **'I will miss him – he was the thunder and I was the rain. This black-on-black crime needs to stop.'**
>
> Mr Cheeks, The Lost Boyz

Freaky Tah (*top*): Not just another lost boy

APRIL

Friday 9

Colin Manley
(Liverpool, 16 April 1942)
The Remo Four
The Swinging Blue Jeans

Once upon a time, guitarist Colin Manley was a classmate of Paul McCartney and George Harrison at Liverpool Institute Grammar School, the three musicians often grouping in empty classrooms to play Duane Eddy and Chet Atkins numbers. Manley was the first to make some kind of an impact, at sixteen years of age forming The Remo Quartet (later The Remo Four) – described by the young Beatles as the band to whom they had to aspire in order to make it themselves. In the next few years, it was, of course, to be the Beatles who made waves, The Remo Four nonetheless proving a popular act as they toured with the rising superstars in 1964. During the rest of the decade, the Brian Epstein-managed Remos found work backing solo stars like Billy Fury and Billy J Kramer, before disbanding in 1970 – though not before Manley had crossed paths once more with Harrison, playing on his *Wonderwall Music* soundtrack album (1968).

On his own, Manley backed a number of unlikely characters (including his friend comedian/singer Freddie Starr), becoming absorbed into variety. In 1977, he joined a later incarnation of sixties favourites The Swinging Blue Jeans – and remained with them until his death from cancer twenty-two years later.

Friday 16

Skip Spence
(Alexander Lee Spence Jr – Windsor, Ontario, 18 April 1946)
Jefferson Airplane
Moby Grape

So – was he misunderstood, or just plain fried? The story of Alexander 'Skip' Spence is one of many cautionary tales from the LSD-addled sixties – the gifted though impressionable son of a jazz musician was a casualty of prolonged hallucinogenic use. In the end, Spence was left to fend for himself – a sad and all-too-familiar example of a musician with much to give somehow slipping through life's net. Spence was, somewhat bizarrely, originally cast as drummer with Jefferson Airplane, his wayward, unkempt look appealing to former folk singer Marty Balin, who selected his man at a club where Spence was supposed to be auditioning for Quicksilver Messenger Service. (This kind of confusion and opportunism was to punctuate the guitarist's career.) Despite contributing four songs to a debut album, *Jefferson Airplane Takes Off* (1965), Spence became disenchanted with the band's direction, not to mention the length of time it was taking to issue the record, so he took off himself, to Mexico, before returning to start his own band. Now wielding his beloved guitar, Spence unleashed Moby Grape, a group of psychedelic blues warriors boasting four songwriters in their ranks. This band – Spence (guitar/vocals), Peter Lewis (ditto), Jerry Miller (ditto, but lead guitar), Bob Mosley (bass) and Don Stevenson (drums) suited Spence far more but was ultimately capsized by a series of odd events. Massively publicized by Columbia Records, Moby Grape's first album was hyped by the simultaneous issue of its tracks on five singles,

a crazy ploy which backfired – as did a band member's decision to 'flip the bird' on the sleeve photo, which saw the record pulled from some stores. A series of drug busts, squabbles with management and Spence's increasing LSD- and alcohol-promoted paranoid schizophrenia ended any real interest in the project. In 1968, while working on a follow-up album, he attacked his cohorts with a fire axe – resulting in his incarceration in a secure unit at Bellevue for six months. It was not the last time the guitarist would be institutionalized.

On his release, Spence launched a solo career. Although often dismissed as impenetrable, his 1969 album *Oar* (all of which he wrote and played) is actually a very touching work, albeit as addled as one might expect. A fine talent who could, and should, have been a major star, Spence existed only in the shadows, his mental condition deteriorating to the degree that he wound up in care once more, at other times living either reclusively or on the streets. Although he had reportedly managed to kick his alcoholism by 1999, a bout of pneumonia destroyed his already weakened constitution. He died at the Dominican Hospital in Santa Cruz.

See also *Spencer Dryden (☞ January 2005)*

Sunday 25

Larry Troutman
(Hamilton, Ohio, 12 August 1944)
Roger Troutman
(Hamilton, Ohio, 29 November 1952)
Zapp

'He ain't breathin', he's my brother.' The dramatic demise of both Larry and Roger Troutman is likely to remain enshrouded in mystery for ever – a tale of double-crossing, jealousy or perhaps just desperation. The real catalyst to their band Zapp's fame was 'Little' Roger, a multi-instrumentalist who liked to be known purely by his first name and had fashioned his first group at the age of ten. Involving two further brothers (Lester and Terry), Roger & The Human Body was the group's first incarnation in the mid seventies; older brother Larry played the congas, but seemed happier as manager when the renamed Zapp began to gain recognition. Roger was very much the focal point and recognized contributor of the bulk of the ideas and musicianship, with cheeky, Kid Creole-meets-Prince pin-up looks. With the help of P-Funk guru Bootsy Collins, Roger & Zapp – as they were later to be billed – had a major radio hit with the single 'More Bounce to the Ounce' (1980), a voco-der-driven slice of electro-funk that took them to the top of the R & B charts. With the super-confident younger brother also taking on solo recordings, Larry took a back seat, overseeing Troutman Enterprises, the business side of Zapp's affairs. Or not, as the case may be …

Roger Troutman's best year was 1987 – his solo hit 'I Want to be Your Man' was all over the US airwaves as it climbed into the Billboard Top Five. Although not all his releases sold as well, his subsequent reputation put the musician in demand with a number of rap acts during the nine-ties, and Roger continued to put out his own material at quite a rate. For his part, Larry had pushed Troutman Enterprises into real estate and even transport hire – yet something was wrong. On the night of 25 April 1999, Larry Troutman let his younger brother know that the company's financial situation was critical and that this was likely to affect Roger's record-ings. A fierce argument then broke out between the pair in an alleyway behind their studio in Dayton, Ohio. Suddenly pulling a gun, Larry shot his brother several times, leaving him for dead as he jumped into his Sedan and

sped away; he then turned the pistol to his own head as he drove, pulled the trigger and crashed the car into a wall some blocks from the studio.

Some 4,000 mourners joined the Troutman family at a combined service a few days later. Perhaps the most unusual tribute that day was a rendition of 'Amazing Grace' by young Rufus Troutman (a nephew of the deceased siblings) using Roger's vocoder – the machine that had driven his last hit, the US number one 'California Love' (1996). This track had been a collaboration with Tupac Shakur, who'd also died by the bullet, just months after its success (◀ *September 1996*).

The Troutman family's grim his-tory continued just four years later with the death of Roger's son, singer Roger T Lynch – who had performed with Zapp as a kid.

Monday 26

Kemistry
(Kemi Olusanya – Birmingham, England, 1964)

A collaborator with other DJs like Goldie (Clifford Price) and Storm (Jane Connelly, a former college friend), Kemistry operated at the sharp end of the UK's blossoming drum 'n' bass/jungle scenes, her involvement in the Metalheadz organization attracting such ground-breaking talents as Adam F, Grooverider and Photek to the label. Despite her pioneering work, few other personal details are known about Kemistry – save for the tragic and freakish way in which she died. Travelling back with Storm from a club night they had co-hosted, Kemistry was killed just outside Winchester when a lorry's wheel threw up a loose cat's eye from the motorway – the missile smashed

through the windscreen and fatally wounded the DJ as she sat in the passenger seat.

Adrian Borland
(London, 6 December 1957)
The Sound
(Various acts)

Equally sad was the suicide of Adrian Borland – a musician destined to remain unrewarded by his industry – on the same night. Beginning as punk also-rans The Outsiders, The Sound morphed from a group often unfairly dismissed as Joy Division clones into a very original psychedelic act. Guitarist/singer Borland – plus Graham Green (bass – later replaced by Graham Bailey), Colvin Mayers (keyboards – who died in 1993) and Michael Dudley (drums) – issued a string of interesting singles (including the much-played 'Hothouse' (1981)) and a pair of solid albums for the indie imprint Korova but, with no breakthrough, had to sit back as con-temporaries like U2 and labelmates Echo & The Bunnymen took the spoils. Borland – who also recorded as the experimental Second Layer and, after the dissolution of The Sound in 1988, as Adrian Borland & The Citizens, as well as the lesser-known Honolulu Mountain Daffodils – also made an income as a producer.

Borland, disillusioned after visit-ing an ex-girlfriend, was taken home from a Kennington restaurant by police, believed delusional. Frightened of being sectioned, he then let himself out of his parents' house and threw himself under a London Underground train at Wimbledon station early in the morning. The musician, who was in the process of recording a new album, *Harmony and Destruction*, had recently discontinued his prescription medication.

Friday 30

Darrell Sweet
(Bournemouth, 16 May 1947)
Nazareth

A key cog in the well-oiled machine that was Nazareth, percussionist Darrell Sweet moved to Glasgow as a boy – putting him in the middle of a burgeoning rock scene. With The Shadettes, Sweet found himself in what may have seemed an unambitious covers band; as Dunfermline favourites Nazareth, however, the group shortly displayed impressive songwriting skills, realized by a born-to-do-it front duo: hoary singer Dan McCafferty and slide-guitar maestro Manuel Charlton. Bankrolled by the ubiquitous bingo entrepreneur Bill Fehilly (who had also overseen the making of Alex Harvey), Nazareth set about putting together a debut album, which paved the way for a run of great hit singles – three of which, paradoxically, were covers: 'This Flight Tonight' (1973, written by Joni Mitchell), 'My White Bicycle' (1975, Tomorrow) and 'Love Hurts' (1977, Boudleaux Bryant).

With the hits drying up at the end of the seventies, Nazareth's downfall was confirmed after the unexpected death of Fehilly in 1976; the band were allegedly swindled out of a lot of money by his replacement. Nazareth maintained a sufficient international following, however, to operate as a touring unit on their own. It was on such a tour in the US that the genial, unassuming Darrell Sweet passed away from a sudden backstage heart attack before a concert in New Albany, Indiana. The venue has since unveiled a plaque in the drummer's honour.

MAY

Saturday 8

Leon Thomas
(Leon Thomas – East St Louis, Illinois, 4 October 1937)
Santana

Multi-instrumentalist Leon Thomas was best known as a practitioner of 'kosmigroov', the experimental jazz/spiritual style he virtually made his own. After studying in Tennessee, Thomas wound up in New York in the late fifties, an out-an-out blues/jazz singer with an uncanny ability to break into yodelling. As a musician, Thomas worked mainly in the jazz field, though he joined Carlos Santana's Latin-tinged rock band in the early seventies. The 1973 album *Welcome* featured Thomas's lead vocals on a number of tracks, but his problems with narcotics curtailed his career far too soon. After a couple of years of near-constant touring, Leone Thomas (as he now chose to spell his name) left Santana to perform smaller venues and gradually slipped off the radar. Thomas died in the Bronx, New York, from a heart attack brought on by the leukaemia he had suffered from for a number of years.

See also *Richard Kermode (☛ January 1996); David Brown (☛ September 2000)*

Friday 14

E William Tucker
(New York, 1961)
Ministry
(Various acts)

A guitarist whose dalliances were mainly in the field of US post-punk/industrial, E William Tucker was a respected tutor of the instrument who otherwise worked mainly as a session-player. His short-lived Swinging Pistons had sufficient impact to encourage Ministry leader Al Jourgensen to hire Tucker's services for an upcoming album, *The Mind is a Terrible Thing to Taste* (1989). The result attracted virtually every other industrial big-hitter, and Tucker then went on the road with Foetus, KMFDM, My Life with the Thrill Kill Kult, Pigface and Revolting Cocks – with whose Chris Connelly he would later collaborate in the studio.

On the eve of yet another tour with Ministry, E William Tucker's body was found in his apartment by a room-mate, accompanied by a suicide note that ran to ten pages. In a gesture as uncompromising as much of the music he made, Tucker had apparently swallowed a bottleful of pills, before slitting his throat. Like Nirvana's Kurt Cobain five years previously (☛*April 1994*), Tucker was believed to have been suffering a mystery stomach illness that caused him considerable pain.

See also *Jeff Ward (☛ March 1993)*

Saturday 15

Rob Gretton

(Wythenshawe, Manchester,
15 January 1953)

Larger-than-life Rob Gretton was
a key figure in the development of
Manchester's post-1977 music scene.
Gretton was twenty-five when he discovered Joy Division (then known as
Warsaw) at the Rafters Club, where he
worked as a DJ, and offered to manage the band. Sagely, Gretton kept
them away from major labels, issuing
their records on Anthony Wilson's
Factory label; under his guidance, the
band, despite its short life, became
one of the most influential the country has ever produced. After singer Ian
Curtis's death (◄ *May 1980*), Gretton
encouraged surviving members to
relaunch as New Order (the choice of
name was perhaps the only questionable decision he ever made). The band
went on to further critical acclaim
– and this time global stardom.
Gretton later launched the legendary
Haçienda Club as well as his own

label, Robsrecords, which enjoyed a
major 1993 hit with 'Ain't No Love
(Ain't No Use)' by the band Sub Sub
(now better known as members of
The Doves).

After the death of producer Martin
Hannett (◄ *April 1991*), hard-living
Rob Gretton – who died from a
sudden heart attack at his Manchester
home – became the third Factory
figurehead to pass on.

Tuesday 18

Augustus Pablo

(Horace Swaby – Kingston, Jamaica, 1953)

A huge presence in the development
of reggae and the diversification of
its sound, Horace Swaby gave himself to Rastafarianism as a teenager,
using his music to express his beliefs.
Swaby was a self-taught pianist, often
called upon by Bob Marley for early
Wailers sessions, and joined a house
band at Randy's Studio, thereafter
becoming known as Augustus Pablo.
Before he was even out of his teens,
the ambitious Pablo had recorded his

own material, including 'Iggy Iggy'
(1969) and 'Java' (1972). He was
soon running four of his own labels
and producing the work of Junior
Delgado, Jacob 'Killer' Miller and
Hugh Mundell (all of whom also died
prematurely). Although the impact of
Pablo's 'Far Eastern' dub stylee was
lessened by the rise of dancehall during the eighties, the genre effectively
permeated British dance and rock during the early part of the next decade,
and Pablo found himself in demand
by bands such as Primal Scream.

Augustus Pablo suffered from
myasthenia gravis – a rare condition
that attacks the central nervous system. He left a partner and two young
children.

JUNE

Wednesday 2

Junior Braithwaite

(Franklin Delano Alexander Braithwaite
– Kingston, Jamaica, 4 April 1949)
The Wailers

The pointless killing of Junior
Braithwaite in June 1999 was the latest
death to befall the world's best-loved
reggae outfit. Braithwaite was born
in Kingston's notorious Trenchtown
ghetto, just a street away from Bob
Marley's house. As youths, Braithwaite
and Marley – along with Peter Tosh
(Winston McIntosh), Bunny Wailer
(Neville Livingston) and backing singers Beverley Kelso and Cherry Smith
– formed the earliest vocal version of
The Wailers, emulating top harmoniz-
ers Higgs & Wilson. Eventually super-
seding their heroes, The Wailers cut
their first records when Braithwaite
was only fourteen, the cheery young
singer taking lead vocals on a number

Minsk – 29/5/99

The deaths on this day of fifty-four young fans of Russian dance act
Mango Mango represented the worst ever toll in rock concert history. In
this case, those who died had been attempting to enter a tube station as
they left the gig but, in common with most other major-event tragedies,
the victims were crushed or asphyxiated when crowd movement could
no longer be controlled. The events brought to mind the deaths of young
fans Bernadette Whelan (crushed at a London David Cassidy show in 1974)
and Dubliner Bernadette O'Brien (who died watching Smashing Pumpkins
in 1996) – and, most significantly, the loss of eleven lives when The Who
played Cincinnati, Ohio, on 3 December 1979.

These scenes were sadly to be repeated on 30 June 2000 at Sweden's
Röskilde Festival. As grunge behemoths Pearl Jam started playing the
popular festival's Orange stage, nine devotees were killed in a similar
manner.

of songs such as 'Habits' and 'It Hurts to be Alone' – his was considered the best voice by no less an authority than Jamaican recording giant Clement 'Coxsone' Dodd. Braithwaite had other ambitions, however, and left his band and country for the US just months later to pursue a career in medicine in Chicago. The death of his close ally Bob Marley (*May 1981*) prompted Braithwaite to return to Jamaica in 1984; Bunny Wailer was keen for him to join the surviving band members for a *Never Ending Wailers* album (finally issued in 1994). After the deaths of Tosh (*October 1987*) and Braithwaite, one particular song – 'Together Again' – stands out from this poignant set, the last the singer was to record with The Wailers. An attempted solo comeback by Braithwaite faltered, although there are unreleased tracks that may someday see the light of day.

In an all-too-familiar scenario, Junior Braithwaite was visiting a friend's Kingston home when three anonymous gunmen broke into the house. In the fracas that followed, the singer was killed with a single shot, as was his host, musician Lawrence 'Chadda' Scott. It was the second shooting at the address that year, and among the differing statements made by police were that the crime had been related to stolen weapons kept at Scott's – and that Braithwaite had simply been in the wrong place at the wrong time.

'I don't have any animosity towards anyone. I love, because love is the greatest thing. Love is the key to eternal life.'

Junior Braithwaite, interviewed by Roger Steffens, 1985

Screaming Lord Sutch

(David Sutch – Kilburn, London, 10 November 1940)

Screaming Lord Sutch & The Savages

The original long-hair and first name in comic rebellion, Screaming Lord Sutch's musical career dates back to the fifties – though he'll always be best known for his askew political persona. Sutch was a man whose antics infuriated as many as they delighted, his complex history culminating in severe depression and eventual suicide. Perhaps the most appropriate way to set out his obituary is as one might for the kind of statesman Sutch parodied throughout his career.

1941: The policeman father of the infant David Sutch is killed during the London Blitz.

1960: Screaming Lord Sutch emerges as a rock 'n' roller with The Savages. His 'My Big Black Coffin' and 'Jack the Ripper' singles (1962) – produced by fellow maverick, the late Joe Meek (*February 1967*) – are snubbed by the BBC for being 'too shocking'. The Savages' stage act at the time predates Alice Cooper by a decade, with its inclusion of coffins, severed heads, knives and other Sutch obsessions. The group will never have a UK hit.

1961: Sutch falls foul of the law by attempting twice to elope with (different) teenage girls.

1963: Sutch runs for Parliament for the first time, with the appropriately named – in light of his previous misdemeanour – National Teenage Party.

1964: The singer founds pirate station Radio Sutch, in order to get his records played.

1966: Lord Sutch stands against Prime Minister Harold Wilson at Huyton. Wilson, who at first refuses to shake his hand, eventually relents and offers Sutch a cigar. Among Sutch's many policies over the years are one or two that came to fruition, including an end to discrimination against long hair, the abolition of the 11-plus exam and all-day drinking in pubs – though how much of this was down to Sutch's influence is open to debate. Perhaps his most sage observation was: 'Why is there only one Monopolies Commission?'

1968: Despite having no connection to nobility, Sutch changes his name by deed poll to 'Screaming Lord Sutch, Earl of Harrow'.

1970: His album *Lord Sutch and Heavy Friends* features such luminaries as Keith Moon, Jimmy Page and Noel Redding. Despite this, it is ranked 'The Worst Album of All Time' in a 1998 BBC poll.

1983: Sutch founds the infamous Monster Raving Loony Party – and will become the longest-serving British party leader, standing for election some forty times. His latest attempt to change his name, this time to 'Mrs Thatcher', is thwarted, however.

1990: The Monster Raving Loony Party poll 418 votes in Bootle, Liverpool – some 263 more than David Owen's SDP. Sutch's offer to merge with Owen's party is politely declined.

1999: Sutch is found dead at his home by his girlfriend, Yvonne Elwood,

having hanged himself. Diagnosed bi-polar, Sutch had been down since the death of his mother two years previously – and was also addicted to anti-depressants. Prime Minister Tony Blair says: 'Our elections will never be quite the same without him.'

Sunday 27
Brian O'Hara
(Liverpool, 12 March 1942)
The Fourmost

Several days after Sutch, another British early sixties hero took the same drastic measure as The Savages frontman. Lead singer/guitarist of Merseybeat front-runners The Fourmost, O'Hara and his band – Mike Millward (guitar), Billy Hatton (bass) and Dave Lovelady (drums) – were one of Brian Epstein's early discoveries, picked up around same time as Gerry & The Pacemakers and Billy J Kramer. This association assisted them in landing a deal with Parlophone and a brief succession of UK hits, of which 'Hello Little Girl' (1963, written by Lennon and McCartney) and 'A Little Loving' (1964) breached the Top Ten. The band were popular, but issued just one album (1965's *First and Fourmost*); their chart career faltered after Millward contracted the illness that eventually cost him his life (⏪ *March 1966*). Brian O'Hara continued to front The Fourmost as they settled into regular nightclub work, somewhat clunky comic routines now replacing their earlier image. Despite regular band reunions into the eighties, little had been heard from the singer when his body was discovered by police at his Waverley home. O'Hara had hanged himself in his bedroom.

Screaming Lord Sutch: One final return in the box ...

JULY

Thursday 1

Dennis Brown

(Kingston, Jamaica, 1 February 1957)
(Byron Lee & The Dragonaires)

An increasingly dark year for reggae continued with the death of the genre's 'Crown Prince', 42-year-old Dennis Brown. Throughout its history, the reggae scene has always been open to youngsters, and Brown was no exception. Despite losing his mother, the genial singer – often known by his second name, Emmanuel – had begun singing at nine, an under-age performer in Jamaica's clubs, scoring homeland hits at just eleven. Nurtured by Studio One, Brown saw a couple of songs – The Impressions' 'No Man is an Island' and 'If I Follow My Heart' (both 1969) – become radio favourites. And he did follow his heart, switching between studios as he built up an enviable collection of mainly Joe Gibbs-produced albums and singles over the years; British pop followers will remember the classic 'Money in My Pocket' (1979), which took Brown on to *Top of the Pops*. Brown also found time to sing with The Dragonaires and run his own Yvonne's Special label (named after his wife of many years), and during the eighties managed to ride the dancehall revolution with some aplomb.

A tremendous artist who recorded almost seventy albums in his brief time, Dennis Brown was taken far too young. He apparently died from upper respiratory failure brought on by a severe bout of pneumonia, addiction to crack cocaine having weakened his immune system. Unsubstantiated rumour, however, suggests Brown may have had AIDS: two previous girlfriends of the star had been diagnosed HIV positive, and one was already dead.

Saturday 3

Mark Sandman

(Newton, Massachusetts, 24 September 1952)
Morphine
(Treat Her Right)

Look up the word 'undersold' and then ask yourself why your dictionary doesn't just display a picture of Mark Sandman, incandescent lead singer and two-string bassist with Morphine. Sandman, a veteran of several Massachusetts also-rans including the bullish, bluesy Treat Her Right, was already approaching forty by the time Morphine got their act together as a fascinating new addition to the fertile Boston alt-rock scene. The band eschewed guitars to offer an atmospheric, faux-beatnik sound – created by Sandman, Dana Colley (tenor sax) and Jerome Deupree (drums, shortly replaced by THR's Billy Conway). Morphine were prolific from the off, issuing three albums in almost as many years: *Good* (1992), *Cure For Pain* (1993) and their finest work, *Yes* (1995). In these three releases, chief songwriter Sandman painted bluesy scenes of broken romances and seedy motels, inviting comparison with Tom Waits. The fourth album, *Like Swimming* (1997), perhaps over-egged the pudding, but by 1999's (in the event, posthumously issued) *The Night* collection Morphine were back in full majestic swagger.

But, unfortunately, that was it. At the start of a European tour, which was to include Britain (where the band had become most popular), Mark Sandman collapsed two songs into a concert in Palestrina, thirty miles outside Rome. Attempts to revive the singer – who'd once survived a brutal stabbing as a cab driver – proved fruitless: Sandman died from a heart attack as he was taken by ambulance to hospital. One of three brothers who all died at relatively young ages, Sandman was survived by both parents, a sister and his partner, writer/agent Sabine Hrechdakian.

'One of the sexiest bands around.'

P J Harvey rates Mark Sandman and Morphine

Tuesday 6

Michael Wallace

(London, 6 June 1956)
Chalice
Third World

Originally a member of seminal Jamaican band Chalice, Michael Wallace – who preferred to spell his name 'Mikel' in those days – enjoyed several years of fame with the band; their 'I Still Love You' (1981) topped the national charts for almost four months. Third World were a renowned reggae band with a number of international hits to their credit, most notably The O'Jays' 'Now That We've Found Love' (1978) and 'Dancing on the Floor' (1981); Wallace didn't join this group until 1998, when he became a touring player.

The motive behind his killing remains unclear, but it seems Wallace was driving his Nissan Sunny at around 11.30 am when he was approached by unknown individuals, one of whom shot him in the neck before escaping. He died shortly after at Kingston's University Hospital.

Wednesday 14

Gar Samuelson

(Dunkirk, New York, 1958)

Megadeth
Fatal Opera
(The New Yorkers)

A veteran of the New York jazz-rock scene, Gar Samuelson changed tack completely to play drums with the Dave Mustaine-led speed-metal unit Megadeth between 1983 and 1987. A persuasive character, Samuelson led the San Francisco band (briefly) down a more interesting route than the standard three-chord metal that had gone before, perhaps the first musician to add swing to extreme rock. The percussionist was in place as Megadeth issued the huge-selling *Killing is My Business . . . and Business is Good!* (1985) and *Peace Sells, But Who's Buying?* (1986), before being unceremoniously dumped by the former Metallica man, who presumably found Samuelson's style too cheery. Samuelson had relocated to Florida to run a studio in Orange City and was performing with his own band, Fatal Opera, at the time of his death from liver complications.

Saturday 17

Kevin Wilkinson

(Swindon, 1958)

(Various acts)

Kevin Wilkinson must have possessed one of the most enviable CVs in British pop music, yet by the end he was clearly overcome by depression. Turning professional in 1979, Wilkinson began drumming with US new-wave group Holly & The Italians, coming very close to a UK hit with 1980's 'Tell That Girl to Shut

Up'. Graduating to The Waterboys, Wilkinson could be heard on most of the group's albums, also working with Robert Fripp and China Crisis. A versatile musician, he could also claim contributions to the recordings of American acts, most notably Bonnie Raitt and Joey Ramone. During the nineties, the percussionist toured with Squeeze, Howard Jones and The Proclaimers – but found the commitment detrimental to the home life he craved.

While it was known that Kevin Wilkinson occasionally suffered mild depression, the discovery of his dead body came as a huge shock to his wife, Marilyn, and the couple's three children. The drummer had hanged himself at their Swindon home.

AUGUST

Wednesday 18

Johnny 'Guitar' Byrne

(Liverpool, 4 December 1939)

Rory Storm & The Hurricanes

One of just a handful of professionals who can claim to have played alongside a future Beatle, rhythm guitarist Johnny Byrne was a founder member of Merseybeat nearly-men Rory Storm & The Hurricanes. Byrne adopted the name 'Guitar' as the band became popular on Merseyside. Somehow, though, they were to suffer the frustration of never having a hit – while all the other Liverpool bands around them seemed to do it in their sleep. The Hurricanes could, however, claim a number of firsts, one being that they played The Cavern before anyone else, another that Brian Epstein's earliest production credit was on one of their many flop singles. The Beatles connections inevitably continue – The

Hurricanes travelled to Hamburg with them, and then finally relinquished their drummer, Ritchie Starkey, to The Fab Four in 1962 as the latter's greater chances of success became apparent.

On top of the pain of failure, Rory Storm & The Hurricanes also endured their share of tragedies through the years. In 1967, guitarist Charles 'Ty' Brian died following a post-concert collapse, and lead singer Alan Caldwell ('Rory Storm') passed away five years after this (➤ *September 1972*). Johnny Byrne – who had made many attempts to reunite The Hurricanes over the years – was in the process of completing the band's biography when he succumbed to the crippling motor-neurone disease that had stricken him a few years before.

Friday 20

Bobby Sheehan

(Brooklyn, New York, 12 June 1968)

Blues Traveler

The Grateful Dead-inspired Blues Traveler came together back in 1988, the brainchild of Bobby Sheehan and his close friend singer/harmonica-player John Popper – the band completed by Chan Kinchla (guitar) and Brendan Hill (drums). They were a hot live attraction and issued six albums to 1998, mainstay Sheehan playing on each of them. By 1994's *Four*, Blues Traveler were starting to make serious inroads into Billboard's charts; the single 'Runaround' was an unexpected smash the following year, racking up a near-record-breaking run on Billboard's hit parade. The group went through difficulties, however, particularly Popper, who suffered an injury that confined him to a wheelchair for most of 1993.

Worse was to come for the frontman in 1999: recovering from angioplasty to clear a blocked artery, he learned of his friend's death. Bobby Sheehan's body was discovered by friends; it transpired that the bassist's system contained traces of cocaine, heroin and Valium.

Wednesday 25

Rob Fisher
(Cheltenham, 5 November 1959)
Naked Eyes
Climie Fisher

The great outdoors was of much importance to Rob Fisher's farming family, but a near disaster in his father's yacht 'changed everything' for the young wannabe musician. Fisher left the wilds a few years later to study music and electronics – which pretty much shaped his future. Naked Eyes – Fisher (keys/synth) and singer Pete Byrne – began as Neon, working with Peter Gabriel towards an EMI deal; they made it in 1983, but in America as opposed to Britain. That year, the duo rode in with the second British invasion (Culture Club, Duran Duran, etc), scoring hits with 'Always Something There to Remind Me' and the catchy 'Promises Promises'. This high didn't last long, however, and, with no success back home, Naked Eyes split at the end of 1984. The following year, Fisher met singer Simon Climie while working with Scritti Politti, and thus a new duo was formed. This time, there was, conversely, greater success in the UK than the US, Climie Fisher scoring Top Ten entries with 'Rise to the Occasion' (1987) and 'Love Changes Everything' (1988). They also managed several lesser hits and penned songs for many major artists – Five Star, Fleetwood Mac, Jermaine Jackson, George Michael, Milli Vanilli and Jermaine Stewart among them.

By the end of the nineties, Rob Fisher had moved on from his part-

nership with Climie and was looking to reunite with Pete Byrne. Before their album could be completed, though, Fisher was rushed to hospital with a mysterious illness, rumoured to be cancer. He was admitted for emergency surgery – but did not recover. It could be argued that recording Climie's songs is a bad omen. Fisher, Stewart (➤ *March 1997*) and Rob Pilatus of Milli Vanilli (➤ *April 1998*) have all died, while Five Star and Michael have since experienced high-profile scrapes with the law . . .

Saturday 28

Willie Williams
(Ervin Williams – Millinocket, Maine, December 1935)
Gene Vincent & The Blue Caps
(The Virginians)

Beginning with high-school band The Northern Lights, 'Wee' Willie Williams embarked on his career at the birth of rock 'n' roll, graduating via The Virginians (he was from New England) to Gene Vincent & The Blue Caps. The rhythm guitarist had the right 'cheeky chappie' look to complement Vincent's lean, mean moodiness, but the relationship didn't last long. Although he played on one or two genuine classics (1956's 'Be-Bop-a-Lula' among them), Williams made way for guitarist Teddy Crutchfield, going on to a good career as a DJ with Virginia's WCMS radio station and later as director of Tree Music Publishing.

Willie Williams was a keen shooter, often arranging target practice with his many friends. It was just before one of these occasions that tragedy struck in the most freakish of manners in the driveway of his Florida home. Williams was rummaging through a duffel bag on the back seat of his car when a rifle inside it fired

accidentally. The former rocker was hit by a single shot just below the chest and confirmed dead on arrival at Blake Medical Center.

See also *Gene Vincent (➤ October 1971); Cliff Gallup (➤ October 1988); Max Lipscomb (➤ March 1991); Paul Peek (➤ April 2001). Other deceased Blue Caps are Grady Owen (1999), Jerry Lee Merritt (2001) and Juvenal Gomez (2002).*

SEPTEMBER

Ed Cobb
(California, 1938)
The Four Preps

A marked influence on The Beach Boys, vocal harmony quartet The Four Preps – Ed Cobb (bass), Bruce Belland (lead tenor), Glen Larson (baritone) and Marvin Inabnett (high tenor) – formed at Hollywood High School in 1955. After a slow start, the group racked up several hits through Capitol; the best remembered are probably '26 Miles (Santa Catalina)' and 'Big Man' (both 1958), which earned them gold discs. Cobb, who had simultaneously co-arranged and produced the moderately successful British instrumental band Piltdown Men, left the fresh-faced group in 1966. Thereafter, he went on to further success as a producer (earning thirty-two gold records) and as a songwriter – his 'Tainted Love' was a massive success for that pair of crash-survivors Gloria Jones and Marc Almond (Soft Cell). Ed Cobb had formed a New Four Preps by the time he died from leukaemia while vacationing in Honolulu.

Stephen Canaday

(Springfield, Missouri, 12 September 1944)

The Ozark Mountain Daredevils

Arkansas's Ozark Mountain Daredevils were among country rock's more inventive practitioners during the seventies, and their easy-going smash 'Jackie Blue' became one of 1975's most played records on AM radio. Drummer Stephen Canaday joined the band two years later, by which time the Larry Lee-fronted six-piece were on the decline, though still a popular touring attraction. Recording one album, *Modern History* (1989), with the band, Canaday then moved to Nashville and operated primarily as a tour manager for a number of country acts, including at one point Tammy Wynette.

Canaday was also making a decent living as a photographer, and on the morning of 25 September 1999, he and aircraft-owner Rick Loudermilk took to the skies over Nashville to grab some aerial shots of the area. At around 11 am, residents and workers in the area became concerned when Loudermilk's vintage single-engine aircraft appeared to be struggling to make a turn. Buildings emptied as the plane plummeted into trees before crashing into a derelict office block; fast-acting locals doused its chassis with water to quench any fire. Loudermilk was already dead and the unconscious Stephen Canaday was losing blood from a severe wound to his leg. Despite all attempts to save him, the former drummer died on his way to hospital. Since the WW2 craft was controllable from the rear seat, it can never be ascertained exactly which of the two deceased men was the pilot that morning.

See also *Bill Brown* (☛ *July 2004*)

OCTOBER

Friday 1

Lena Zavaroni

(Rothesay, Isle of Bute, 4 November 1963)

Lena Zavaroni's archetypal fairy tale turned tragedy will always strike a chord with the British public – and the irony of her parents running a fish-and-chip shop won't be lost on the more cynical, either. In 1973, Zavaroni's 'pigtails and pinafore' act enchanted viewers of ITV's *Opportunity Knocks*, her five-week winning run catapulting the precocious 10-year-old to childhood stardom. In reality, her music-hall shtick was only marginally more palatable than that of contemporary Bonnie Langford, but the Lucille Ball-approved Zavaroni nonetheless shot into the UK Top Ten with 'Ma He's Making Eyes at Me' early the following year. Her variety style was perhaps too dated to sustain a chart career beyond this though, and Zavaroni (who undoubtedly had talent) found her way into theatre and television, still the youngest performer ever to top the bill at the London Palladium.

As the years passed, however, it was Zavaroni's weight issues that courted attention, as opposed to her singing. Always a small-framed girl, less than five feet tall, she was diagnosed anorexic at the age of thirteen (at a time when little was known about the disease) and her weight dropped to an alarming 35kg while she was at London's Italia Conti stage school. This psychological problem was to dog the artist for more than two decades, her health and confidence suffering to the extent that she retired from show business at just twenty-five. An increasingly tragic figure, Zavaroni was further jolted by divorce, then

The tragic Lena Zavaroni: Stages of decline

a fire that destroyed much of her showbiz memorabilia and, most devastatingly, the apparent suicide of her mother in 1989. In the years before her own death, the performer lived on state benefits in a council home, the press making much of a charge of the alleged theft of a fifty-pence packet of jelly early in 1999 (which was later thrown out of court). An indication of her deteriorating mental state was Zavaroni's explanation that 'stealing food doesn't count as eating it'.

In a sad finale echoing the higher-profile death of Karen Carpenter (☛ *February 1983*), Lena Zavaroni was admitted to a Cardiff hospital on 7 September, where it was hoped a last, drastic brain operation would provide a cure; within two weeks she had returned, a blood infection having caused her heart to fail. The autopsy put Zavaroni's death down to bronchial pneumonia.

Wednesday 13

Lord Ulli
(Ullrich Günther – Hamburg, c 1940)
The Lords

Hamburg's The Lords were one of the few German beat groups to make any kind of impact outside their homeland, the band aping British acts of the early sixties, right down to the haircuts. What set them apart was good-looking lead singer Lord Ulli and his unique microphone and floor technique. Less memorable were the band's songs, of which only '(Over in the) Gloryland' (1966) stands up to much repeated listening. The Lords' later work appeared to draw on skiffle and US folk rock.

With a fortieth anniversary approaching, The Lords put together a grand concert for the many fans who had remained loyal to the band since the beginning. As they launched into yet another favourite, Lord Ulli suddenly slipped, fell heavily and cracked his skull on the side of the stage. Thus Ulli very nearly received his 'ideal death', though he held on for a week before dying from a brain haemorrhage in hospital.

Tuesday 26

Hoyt Axton
(Duncan, Oklahoma, 25 March 1938)

A successful musician, songwriter and actor, Hoyt Axton was encouraged by his mother (who herself had co-written such pop standards as 'Heartbreak Hotel') to learn classical piano, until his preference for blues and boogie-woogie became apparent. In his twenties, Axton had his first break with the song 'Greenback

'When I die, I'd like to drop dead from the stage.'

Lord Ulli

The Lords, with Ulli (*centre*): A hard act to follow

Dollar', a moderate hit for The Kingston Trio in 1963; this success led to a deal with Horizon and then Vee-Jay, for whom Axton recorded four albums. Axton, like his mother, will likely be best remembered for the songs he wrote for others, the biggest of which was 'Joy to the World', taken to US number one for six weeks in 1971 by Three Dog Night, the band for whom he had been opening. The nearest Axton came to a crossover hit in his own right was 1979's 'Della and the Dealer', from his highly rated *Rusty Old Halo* album. A much-loved performer who also appeared in over thirty movie and television roles, Axton died from a coronary on his Montana ranch.

Thursday 28

Wes Berggren
(Dallas, Texas, 3 April 1971)
Tripping Daisy

Taking their lead from Led Zeppelin at their riffing best and The Beatles at their most psychedelic, Tripping Daisy – Tim DeLaughter (vocals/guitar), Wes Berggren (guitar), Mark Pirro (bass) and Mitch Marine (drums) – burst out of Dallas in 1991. A first album, *Bill* (1992), was enough to secure a deal with Island, for whom this prolific band recorded four albums over the next six years. The most impressive was *Jesus Hits Like the Atom Bomb* (1998) – but within a year of its issue the band were no more: Wes Berggren, a long-time drug-user, was found dead of an overdose of cocaine, propoxyphene and benzodiazepine. DeLaughter finally achieved deserved international recognition a few years on as leader of the excellent Polyphonic Spree.

NOVEMBER

Saturday 13

R J Vealey

(Charleston, West Virginia, 1962)

Atlanta Rhythm Section
(Various acts)

A drummer in the classic rock style, R J Vealey joined Southern-rock journeymen Atlanta Rhythm Section in 1995, the band then a touring unit (ARS had scored seven US Top Forty hits – including the sultry 'So Into You' (1977) – during the late seventies). Although just thirty-seven when he died, Vealey was a well-respected figure in the industry with a lengthy CV of projects by the time he joined the Ronnie Hammond-fronted band. They were promoting their first album in a decade at a concert at the campus of Florida's Central University when the percussionist collapsed backstage from a massive heart attack. Vealey's death – on his daughter's first birthday – was entirely unexpected.

Saturday 27

I Roy

(Roy Samuel Reid – St Thomas, Jamaica, 28 June 1942)

'I Roy was Jamaica's greatest ever DJ.'
Producer Harry Mudie

Young Roy Reid, better known to the music world as I Roy, started out in unlikely fashion as a government accountant, making his name by evening as the DJ in front of most of Spanish Town's resident sound systems. An impressed Harry Mudie invited this young mic artist to toast on a series of great singles at his Dynamic Sounds Studios, until a disagreement over, of all things, touring arrangements ended their partnership in 1971. Thus I Roy's first album, *Presenting I Roy* (1973), was delayed – it was released on Trojan and, produced by Augustus Clarke, did not disappoint. At this point, I Roy was working under a number of different producers as he found his voice, most notably Lee 'Scratch' Perry; the prolific artist put out no fewer than thirteen singles in 1975! In a spat that predated the reciprocal tongue-lashings of Eazy-E and Dr Dre, I Roy's success briefly raised the ire of rival Prince Jazzbo and the pair chose to air their differences on vinyl.

These disagreements seemed to have dissipated by the late eighties, with the much lower-profile I Roy then recording on Jazzbo's label, Umoja. But with fewer record sales, I Roy's life fell into disarray, the artist spending his final years on the streets. Although his death from heart failure was met with little ceremony by the world's music press, I Roy should always be recalled as a significant character for his multitude of seventies recordings.

DECEMBER

Friday 3

'Scatman' John Larkin

(El Monte, California, 13 March 1942)

The creator of surely the nineties' most irritating pair of hit singles, John Larkin developed his scat style to mask a stutter that he had had since his youth. What on earth Scatman John got up to for the first fifty-odd years of his life is anyone's guess, but for the last five he must have had a ball: from early 1995, Scatman shifted some 3 million copies of his brace of albums, the singles 'Scatman (Ski-Ba-Bop-Da-Dop-Bop)' and 'Scatman's World' were huge hits in the UK, while pretty much all his releases – perhaps unsurprisingly

– charted strongly in Japan. A long-time smoker (which probably didn't do his voice much good, either), Scatman John died from lung cancer at his home in Los Angeles.

Saturday 10

Rick Danko

(Richard Clare Danko – Simcoe, Ontario, 29 December 1942)
The Band
Ronnie Hawkins & The Hawks

The quavering falsetto that highlighted such classic moments as 'The Weight' (1968) and 'Stage Fright' (1970) was the latest heritage voice to be silenced as rock hurtled towards 2000. Inspired by his musical older brother Maurice, Rick Danko was a frail young singer with multi-instrumental flair who left school at fourteen to emulate his heroes Hank Williams and Sam Cooke. His achievements as a key member of The Band were perhaps even broader than either's. Danko's professional work began, however, with Ronnie Hawkins's classic band The Hawks, most of whom continued with this later manifestation. The limitations of life with a rockabilly unit were apparent to Danko; by 1966 The Band had moved on sufficiently to line up behind Dylan as he plugged in, to a barrage of catcalls. But folk rock now existed, and *Music from Big Pink* (1968) set out the Band's stall as roots musicians with potentially vast influence. Their music celebrated the disintegration of Middle American values during a time of cultural revolution (and, of course, life on the road) – but now with the added power of an electric chord or two.

Rick Danko's input to the group was utterly essential, and never better illustrated than in The Band's celebrated *Last Waltz* performance at the San Francisco Winterland Ballroom in 1976. His fragility and musical prowess were displayed in rawer form on a solo effort for Arista, *Rick Danko* (1978) – which is often overshadowed by the momentousness of *The Last Waltz*. Although Danko was to re-form The Band in the early eighties, it was largely to please followers and to secure the band's induction into the Rock 'n' Roll Hall of Fame (which they managed ten years later). The re-formation was hugely damaged, however, by the after-show suicide of Danko's long-term friend Richard Manuel (*March 1986*).

Having moved to Woodstock, with its atmosphere and legacy, the singer/guitarist/violinist became a workaholic, never happier than when involved in projects with others. Among his collaborators were Paul Butterfield, ex-Band member Levon Helm and folk legend Eric Andersen. Rick Danko's quiet passing in December 1999 seemed somehow to befit this outwardly passive yet inwardly impassioned player. Danko was found by his wife, his heart having given out as he slept.

See also *Paul Butterfield (* *May 1987); Stan Szelest (January 1991)*

Rick Danko: The last waltz was called too soon

Saturday 17

Grover Washington Jr

(Buffalo, New York 12 December 1943)
(The Four Clefs)

Grover Washington bridged the gap between R & B and modern jazz in much the same way as artists like Herbie Hancock and Wynton Marsalis (with both of whom he was to record) would in his wake. His love affair with the saxophone began as a child (both his parents were musicians), though it was not until he was in his late twenties that Washington created a stir with the album *Inner City Blues* (1971). Originally touring with Ohio band The Four Clefs, Washington and his honed style appealed to a younger generation of music lovers – although one or two purists were quick to describe his work as commercial and oversmooth. He nonetheless managed crossover hit records – one of which, 'Just the Two of Us' (1978) with Bill Withers, might just be the theme tune for pretty much every easy-listening radio station in the free world.

Washington collapsed at around 6.30 pm during a pause at a New York recording of CBS television's *The Early Show*. The musician, who was administered CPR in his dressing room, died at the scene from a heart attack.

Sunday 18

Joe Higgs
(Kingston, Jamaica, 1940)

The last major reggae life snuffed during a sad pre-millennium was that of the genre's most unsung father figure, Joe Higgs. A songwriter to Toots & The Maytals, Peter Tosh and Delroy Wilson, Higgs cut a few tunes in his own right, the most notable being 'Oh Manny Oh' (1960), which shifted a creditable 50,000 copies in Jamaica. A guitarist who was noted for his ability to impart his gift to others, Higgs tutored the likes of Bob Marley, while also helping to arrange early Wailers' songs. His own recordings were fewer and farther between, though *Triumph* (1988) was a late-on album that was just that.

Joe Higgs had been undergoing treatment for cancer for some time by his death just ahead of his sixtieth birthday. But despite dying relatively young, Higgs still managed to outlive three of the original Wailers, Marley (⚓ *May 1981*), Tosh (⚓ *October 1987*) and Junior Braithwaite (⚓ *June 1999*).

Curtis Mayfield: Somehow held it together right to the end ...

Monday 26

Curtis Mayfield
(Chicago, Illinois, 3 June 1942)
The Impressions

Curtis Mayfield's distinctive soul voice seemed as at home with tales of the street as it was handling a love song. Also a fine guitarist, Mayfield was arguably the most significant of the first breed of black American singers to branch out beyond the confines of doo-wop – although he, too, found an initial outlet through a vocal group. Mayfield had co-founded The Impressions (originally The Roosters) – with Jerry Butler (replaced by Fred Cash) and Sam Gooden – as early as 1956, though he was not to lead the group until after their Top Ten-flirting debut hit 'For Your Precious Love' (1958). With small jealousies leading to Butler's departure, Mayfield was centre stage for the trio's biggest hit, 'It's All Right' (1963). Around this period, the singer's burgeoning social conscience was beginning to show itself – Mayfield was composing a number of Impressions tunes, filling the distinct gap left by the death of Sam Cooke (◀ *Pre-1965*). With songs like 'This is My Country' (1968) and 'We People Who are Darker than Blue' (1970), Mayfield picked up the baton of Cooke's 'A Change is Gonna Come'. His 'We're a Winner' effectively became the anthem of Black Power – a musical echo to the salutes of Tommie Smith and John Carlos at the 1968 Olympics. At the turn of the decade, Mayfield left The Impressions to forge a solo career that would expose the underbelly of black American culture in his most noted works. *Superfly* (1972) was a treat, the anti-drug soundtrack of the Gordon Parks-directed movie of the same name and the high point of the early-seventies 'blaxploitation' vogue that also made the name of Isaac Hayes. Destined to define Mayfield's legacy, the score – which won the artist four Grammy nominations and an impressive amount of further work – has dated infinitely better than the film.

A period of lesser activity was brought to a dramatic halt at an outdoor concert in Brooklyn during August 1990. In front of thousands, a horrific accident involving a fallen lighting rig left Curtis Mayfield paralysed from the neck down. Although this appeared to have ended Mayfield's composing ('I can't just reach over and grab my guitar – that's the worst thing!'), the artist found it within himself to forge ahead. In 1996, he returned with the enjoyable *New World Order* – his vocals were painstakingly recorded before diabetes added to escalating health complications. Already quadriplegic, Mayfield had to have a leg amputated a year before his death. Finally, having slipped into a coma, he passed away the day after Christmas 1999. A twice-inducted member of the Rock 'n' Roll Hall of Fame (both with The Impressions and solo), Mayfield was survived by his mother, his wife and no fewer than ten children and seven grandchildren.

Lest We Forget

Other notable deaths that occurred sometime during 1999:

Boxcar Willie (much-loved US country 'hobo'; born Cecil Travis Martin, Texas, 1/9/1931; leukaemia, 12/4)

Bob Herbert (UK impresario who helped put together Bros, then The Spice Girls with his son Chris, later topping even this by managing Five; born Essex, 4/2/1942; car crash in bad weather, 9/8)

William 'Hammy' Howell (largely unsung UK keyboardist with rock revivalists The Darts, who remarkably scored three #2 hits during 1978; born London, 24/10/1954; heart failure, 13/1)

Buddy Knox (admired US rockabilly singer with The Rhythm Orchids, who hit #1 in 1957 with 'Party Doll'; born Texas, 20/7/1933; cancer, 14/2)

Eddie Kurdziel (US guitarist with cult new-wave survivors Redd Kross, also with Fuzz Bubble; born Pennsylvania, 25/9/1960; accidental heroin overdose, 6/6)

Guy Mitchell (hugely popular US pop crooner who went to #1 four times in Britain, most notably with 'Singin' the Blues' in 1956; born Al Cernik, Michigan, 27/2/1927; complications following surgery, 1/7)

Anthony Newley (consummate UK singer/entertainer who scored numerous pop hits including two 1960 chart-toppers, 'Why' and 'Do You Mind?'; born London, 24/9/1931; renal cancer, 14/4)

Doug Sahm (wily singer/guitarist who posed as British nobility to land The Sir Douglas Quintet the US/UK hit 'She's about a Mover' – father of Meat Puppet Shandon; born Texas, 6/11/1941; heart attack, 18/11)

Frankie Vaughan (much-loved UK pop/cabaret heart-throb who scored hits including 1956's 'Green Door' and 1957's 'Garden Of Eden'; born Francis Abelsen, Liverpool, 3/2/1928; heart condition, 17/9)

Christopher Zimmermann (German touring bassist with industrial-metal act Rammstein; the DC-9 in which he was a passenger exploded on take-off in Mexico, 9/11)

For a complete list of fallen artists, visit
www.numberoneinheaven.com

2000

JANUARY

Saturday 8

Joe Dan Petty
(Macon, Georgia, December 1947)
Grinderswitch

Grinderswitch are probably best known in the UK for their 'Pickin' the Blues' (for three decades the theme music for BBC disc jockey John Peel's influential radio show) but in the States the Southern rockers have a further history. But, despite recording seven albums between 1972 and 1982, the group – Dru Lombar (vocals/guitar – who died in 2005), Larry Howard (guitar), Joe Dan Petty (bass), Stephen Miller (keys) and Rick Burnett (drums) – were never premier leaguers like Lynyrd Skynyrd, though they had connections with The Allman Brothers, for whom Petty later worked as a guitar technician.

Unfortunately, the misfortune and catastrophe long associated with the latter bands were to afflict Grinderswitch in 2000. Petty, who had received his pilot's licence just a year before, was airborne in his Beechcraft 23 with fellow pilot Ronald Turpin when a dodgy fuel line caused them to seek a premature landing.

On attempting this, the craft collided with a Cessna 172 as it approached Georgia's Herbert Smart Airport: Petty and Turpin were killed at around 2.45 pm when the Beechcraft then careered into foliage before bursting into flames. As with Stephen Canaday some months before (◀ *September 1999*), it was unclear which man had been piloting the aircraft.

Thursday 20

Ray Jones
(Oldham, 22 October 1939)
(Billy J Kramer &) The Dakotas

The Dakotas were originally Ray Jones's band, not Billy J Kramer's: the bassist had formed the four-piece in Manchester during 1960, their guitar-led style reminiscent of The Shadows, or perhaps the surf music just beginning to emanate from across the Atlantic. The Dakotas – Jones, Pete Maclaine (vocals), Mike Maxfield (guitar), Robin McDonald (guitar) and Tony Mansfield (Tony Bookbinder, drums – brother of Elkie Brooks) – scored an early hit with 'The Cruel Sea' (1963), before a meeting with the influential and persuasive Brian Epstein changed the course of events for the band. With Maclaine sidelined (he

formed his own less successful unit The Clan some time thereafter), The Dakotas were relocated to Liverpool as backing musicians to upcoming star (and British Rail worker) Kramer. Despite immediate success in this formation, Jones was impressed neither by Kramer nor the disparity in earnings between star and band. After a remarkable run of hits during 1963–4 – which included UK number-one hits 'Bad To Me' and 'Little Children' – the bassist's time with the group was finally called by Epstein in July 1964.

Ray Jones quit the industry in 1967, turning to psychiatric nursing for the remainder of his career. He is believed to have passed away from a heart attack.

FEBRUARY

Friday 4

Doris Kenner-Jackson
(Doris Coley – Goldsboro, North Carolina, 2 August 1941)
The Shirelles

Although they weren't the first to be formed, The Shirelles were undeniably the earliest girl group to create waves in an erstwhile male-dominated pop industry. The four teenagers who made up The Poquellos (as they were initially called) were Doris Coley (who had recently moved with her family from North Carolina), Addie 'Micki' Harris, Beverley Lee and Shirley Owens (later Alston-Reeves), a quartet of high-school friends from Passaic, New Jersey, who had penned a prize-winning ditty, 'I Met Him on a Sunday', which so impressed local label owner Florence Greenberg that she became the girls' manager. Within two years, The Shirelles had topped the US charts with 'Will You Love Me Tomorrow?' (1960), clearing a route for The Chiffons, Crystals, Ronettes and Shangri-Las to follow. After repeating the feat with 'Soldier Boy' (1962), The Shirelles turned to more mundane matters, such as marriage and, in Coley's case, raising a family – which led to her departure from the group in 1967.

Doris Kenner-Jackson (as she was now known) reunited with various Shirelles for two nostalgia tours during the seventies and eighties, but by the end of the following decade she'd become gravely ill with breast cancer. She died in hospital in her adopted home of Sacramento, California.

See also *Addie 'Micki' Harris (* *June 1982)*

Monday 7

Big Pun

(Christopher Lee Rios – The Bronx, New York, 9 November 1971)

Formidable Christopher Rios – who, like many rappers, operated under a variety of pseudonyms – is widely credited as the man who gave Puerto Ricans a voice in the otherwise black-dominated world of New York hip hop. Although his handle was 'Big Punisher', Rios was actually a genial sort, a family man with three children and a little more to his shtick than dealing and gunslinging. Before his death, Big Pun's career had barely started, but he'd managed to cash in on the vogue with a double-platinum, Grammy-nominated debut album, *Capital Punishment* (1999), on Loud. By his own admission, Pun ate ''til he couldn't tie his shoelaces', addressing his weight problem through his lyric-writing – hence self-deprecating song titles such as 'I'm Not a Playa, I Just Crush a Lot'. Widely respected within the field, Pun had worked with Wyclef Jean, Busta Rhymes, Wu-Tang and long-time collaborator Big Joe – whose 350 lb girth he utterly dwarfed.

Pun's almost inevitable coronary took him just ahead of the release of a second album, *Yeeeah Baby!* (2000): he was enjoying hit status as a guest vocalist with Jennifer Lopez when his increasing mass (rumoured to have reached an astonishing 700 lb) finally floored him.

Big Pun: Don't get up . . .

'Lonesome' Dave Peverett

(Dulwich, London, 16 April 1943)

Foghat

(Savoy Brown)

Dulwich-born Dave Peverett made the unlikely transition from the London blues circuit to the American mainstream by the mid seventies. Dubbed 'Lonesome' by his early bandmates, Peverett graduated from blues journeymen Savoy Brown, taking with him bassist Tony Stevens and drummer Roger Earl, and picking up guitarist Rod Price, to form the band Foghat (the name derives from a Scrabble session he had as a boy), which became an FM mainstay during the seventies. With Bearsville Records, the band's boogie-fuelled rock appealed to an entire generation of early air-guitarists, the band achieving an instant hit with 1972's *Foghat*. From this, the prolific Peverett et al logged a series of popular albums with suitably 'rawk' titles like *Energized* (1974), *Rock 'n' Roll Outlaws* (1974, containing the Top Twenty single 'Slow Ride') and *Fool for the City* (1975). (A 1977 live album showed this group at their best, however, and accordingly sold 2 million copies.)

Foghat's popularity diminished with the onset of disco and new wave, though both Peverett and Earl toured with versions of the group into the nineties. 'Lonesome' Dave Peverett was diagnosed with kidney cancer in 1998, but after much chemotherapy he was able to keep touring until shortly before his death.

See also *Rod Price (☞ March 2005)*

Saturday 12

Oliver

(William Oliver Swofford – North Wilkesboro, North Carolina, 22 February 1945)

(Good Earth)

In 2000, Oliver Swofford became the latest victim of the remarkable 'curse of *Hair*'. During the folk boom of the mid sixties, Swofford had fashioned his own college-based bluegrass band The Virginians, set to make something of an impact with a debut album as Good Earth. The undoubted star was Swofford: manager and Four Seasons producer Bob Crewe recommended him to record Lionel Bart's 'Good Morning Starshine' (it was also the work of Bart that prompted the stand-alone name of 'Oliver'). The song was a runaway success, soaring to Billboard number three in 1969, and closely followed by an even bigger hit in 'Jean', the theme from *The Prime of Miss Jean Brodie*.

But though there was a hit album to accompany these big-selling singles, Oliver couldn't repeat the trick: attempts by United Artists to relaunch him as a 'serious' artist also failed miserably. By 1982, in his new career as a builder's rep, Oliver Swofford was about as far removed from stardom as he could possibly be. He had been living in Shreveport, Louisiana, for four years at the time of his death from cancer.

Golden Oldies #9

Screamin' Jay Hawkins

(Jalacy Hawkins – Cuyahoga County, Ohio, 18 July 1929)

A wild blues-based performer at a time when 'clean cut' seemed the norm, Screamin' Jay Hawkins never really sold records, but utterly wowed the faithful at live dates – not to mention fellow artists like Fats Domino and Tiny Grimes, who were to book him regularly on their shows. With the possibly unique claim of having borne six children by different fathers, Hawkins's mother encouraged her son to study classical piano – with a career in opera a distinct possibility. His noted aggression, however, was evident even before Hawkins picked up the guitar in his early twenties, the artist having been a Golden Gloves middleweight champion in his teens. What was key to Hawkins's work, though, was the inherent humour lacking in that of most of his contemporaries: his demented 'I Put a Spell on You' (1956) was accompanied by

Screamin' Jay Hawkins: Out of his head?

a highly theatrical borderline-voodoo stage show in which he appeared brandishing a flaming skull known as 'Henry' as he was wheeled on in a coffin.

Later in his career the much-admired guitarist opened for lifetime fans The Rolling Stones, his act influencing many high-profile rock groups such as Black Sabbath, Arthur Brown and Alice Cooper, and his songs covered by, among others, Creedence Clearwater Revival. Screamin' Jay Hawkins had decamped to Paris by the time of his death from complications following an aneurysm. The guitarist passed away from multiple organ failure on 12 February 2000 at a clinic in Neuilly-sur-Seine.

Tuesday 22

Matty Blag
(Matthew Roberts – 1964)
Blaggers ITA

Ten years after the British punk scene became caught up with undesirable far-right movements, along came Blaggers ITA – a no-nonsense group of anti-fascists who mixed rap and rock during their brief flirtation with fame. At the helm was Matty Blag (occasionally aka Matt LaCoste), a man unafraid to boast of 'hunting down' neo-Nazis in his songs – one of which, 'Abandon Ship' (1994), very nearly gave Blaggers a Top Forty hit on EMI. Almost always at odds with a press that couldn't see a difference between the Blaggers' behaviour and that of the political groups they opposed, Blag reached the height of infamy when, in 1993, he was quizzed about his methods by *Melody Maker* journalist Dave Simpson. Not one to suffer those he considered fools, Blag beat *him* up, too. With success seemingly around the corner, this misdemeanour effectively cost the band, Blaggers

ITA struggling to remain with any UK label thereafter. A performer who engaged in dangerous onstage antics such as leaping from amp stacks into what would have been a pretty sparse crowd, Blag clearly also took many risks in his personal life, dying from a heroin overdose.

Wednesday 23

Ofra Haza
(Hatikva, Tel Aviv, 19 November 1959)

From the other end of the pop-music spectrum came Ofra Haza, an Israeli singer whose notable appearance as runner-up in the 1983 Eurovision Song Contest (with '*Chai*') did not reflect her true talent. She was already a huge star in her homeland before a sample of her voice exposing the fullness of her range made her a household name in Western music. Haza's sinuous '*Im Nin'Alu*' ('If the Gates of Heaven are Locked') is probably the only recording to feature on three major UK hits within two years: originally placed in Eric B & Rakim's 'Paid In Full' (1986), the sample was then picked up by 4AD studio group MARRS for the chart-topper 'Pump Up the Volume' (1987) before Haza's own version landed her in the Top Twenty in 1988. Further to this, Haza is likely the only purveyor of Yemenite poetry to appear on a goth record: her additions to The Sisters of Mercy's 'Temple Of Love' (1991) similarly gave Andrew Eldritch's band their biggest UK hit. Showing remarkable versatility, she also contributed to Paula Abdul's 'My Love is Real' (1995).

Ofra Haza's family hid news of her suffering from AIDS, considering it shameful despite the fact that she had contracted HIV via a blood transfusion twenty years before. Haza had been married just three years before her death from the disease.

Ian Dury
(Upminster, Essex, 12 May 1942)
Ian Dury & The Blockheads
(Kilburn & The High Roads)

He was undoubtedly the warmest performer to emerge from the UK's new-wave scene – a poet, writer and actor given to role-playing both on screen and, most significantly, via his songs. And yet, for Ian Dury, it might never have happened. Despite his poor health and early deprivation, Dury made many friends throughout his life due to his humour and expansive optimism. After a bout of polio left him partially paralysed at the age of seven, Dury spent several years in a home for disabled children – where he was seldom happy. But his style and talent were readily displayed, at first during the sixties in his days as an art teacher at various schools around London – a profession he'd entered after graduating from the Royal College of Art. Dury's first forays into music took place during this time: in 1970 he became singer with the peripatetic pub-rock band Kilburn & The High Roads, who cut albums with Pye and WEA, though were more popular as a live act. Not so the next band, Ian Dury & The Blockheads, a splendid collision of new wave, jazz, music hall and rock 'n' roll – with jaunty wordsmith Dury the perfect person at the helm. With punk holding centre stage in the UK, the seemingly anomalous Blockheads somehow fitted right in, signing with one of the new wave's coolest labels, Stiff, in 1977 – by which time Dury was already thirty-five years old. The debut single 'Sex and Drugs and Rock 'n' Roll' (1977) set

> **'I don't spend my time shaking my fist at the moon. It doesn't make you feel any better. Fifty per cent of any battle you're in is your spirit.'**
>
> Ian Dury, in 1999

Ian Dury: From Essex – in case you couldn't tell ...

the stall for one of the great British albums of the era, *New Boots and Panties* (1978) – a scrapbook of bawdy verse, fly-by-night characters and no shortage of killer licks. Although this represented an artistic peak for Dury, his commercial zenith was to arrive with 'Hit Me with Your Rhythm Stick' (1978), a UK number one at the start of the next year – and then 'Reasons to be Cheerful' (1979), which wasn't far short. Subsequent albums were inevitably patchier than *New Boots*, with Dury having to settle for respect as opposed to the fan worship to which he'd grown accustomed. This more middling profile provided the opportunity to air a few grievances about the treatment in the media of the disabled (of which he was one), which Dury did with some aplomb in the single 'Spasticus Autisticus' (1981) – though nobody heard it, thanks to the double irony of a BBC ban.

With interest in his work waning on the radio (and therefore in the charts), Ian Dury turned to acting – for which the world had already seen he possessed a natural gift – and also screen-writing. After some deserved success in this field – Dury found roles in a number of movies, including Peter Greenaway's 1989 film *The Cook, the Thief, His Wife and Her Lover* – he then returned in 1998 with the acclaimed album *Mr Love Pants*, followed by the rather less welcome news of his deteriorating physical condition. Having become a goodwill ambassador for the disease that had crippled him as a child, Dury now revealed he had cancer of the bowel, which was fast spreading to his liver. His death in 2000 robbed the world of entertainment of a true original. Although Dury's Cockney brogue limited his success mainly to his homeland, characters like 'Billericay Dickie', 'Clevor Trever' and 'Plaistow Patricia' say more about Britain in the last century than much of the country's contemporary literature. The singer is survived by four children, including his son, Baxter, who – having featured as a boy on the cover of his father's most famous album – had issued two well-received records of his own by 2006.

See also *Charlie Charles (* ☙ *September 1990)*

Friday 31

Adrian Fisher
(England, c1950)

Sparks
Boxer

A respected guitarist, Adrian Fisher joined US brothers Ron (keyboards) and Russell Mael (vocals), plus fellow Britons Martin Gordon (bass) and Dinky Diamond (drums) in the second line-up of Sparks – one of the most visually arresting pop bands of the seventies. Fisher added the key riffs that enhanced the group's splendid series of sub-operatic staccato hit singles, including 'This Town Ain't Big Enough for Both of Us' (UK number two, 1974), 'Amateur Hour' (1974) and 'Something for the Girl with Everything' (1975). A member of the band for two years, Fisher re-emerged with UK rock band Boxer in 1977, later also playing with Paul Rodgers. Although his death was put down to myocardial infarction, it is believed Fisher's exuberant lifestyle of alcohol and drugs may have contributed more than a little to his demise.

See also *Mike Patto (➤ March 1979)*

APRIL

Thursday 6

Eugene Pearson
(Joshua Leviston – New York, 1935)

The Rivileers
The Drifters
(The Cleftones)

The latest member of The Drifters in our survey to pass away (see Rudy Lewis (➤ *Pre-1965* and the accompanying *Dead Interesting!*) was baritone Eugene Pearson – who, as 18-year-old Joshua Leviston, had begun his singing career with New York's Rivileers. The young man was an avid songwriter whose fervour impressed small-time entrepreneur Sol Rabinowitz: his subsequent investment in the group was sufficient to record an EP of Pearson's songs headed by the schmaltzy 'A Thousand Stars' (1954). Despite being of high quality – and sufficiently commercial to retain radio airplay – this sadly did not lead to the expected breakthrough for the group. A disillusioned Pearson, having signed away the rights to his tunes, left music for the armed forces – where he learned that a group called The Innocents had successfully rerecorded 'A Thousand Stars'. Frustrated but determined to restart his career as a singer, Pearson then joined The Cleftones and finally The Drifters as the troupe's baritone during the highly successful years of 1962–6. Thereafter, Pearson juggled appearances as part of a Drifters touring unit with far less stressful shifts with the New York transit police. His death in 2000 was due to lung cancer – though just five years earlier, Eugene Pearson had been present when The Rivileers played their first concert in over forty years.

Friday 7

Heinz Burt
(Hargin, Germany, 25 July 1942)

The Tornados

As a 19-year-old bacon-slicer in unfashionable Southampton (having arrived from equally unfashionable Hargin), blond-haired Heinz Burt cut an unlikely figure. Good-looking and magnetic, Burt found that his life underwent dramatic changes when he arrived as a young rock 'n' roll-obsessed bassist in London: the unfaltering attention of one Joe Meek saw to that. The UK's first independent producer saw a role for Burt in his studio-based instrumental band The Tornados, alongside Alan Caddy (lead guitar), George Bellamy (rhythm – father of current rock hero Matt Bellamy, of Muse), Roger Lavern (keyboards) and Clem Cattini (drums). Among the first results was the magnificent 'Telstar' (1962), an evocative piece of zeitgeist pop that, having reached number one at home, also saw The Tornadoes (as they were spelled in the US) become the first UK band to reach the summit in America. Despite being recorded in ninety minutes – and dismissed as 'crap' by the wilful Burt on first hearing – the record stamped itself indelibly into world culture with 5 million global sales. After a follow-up, 'Globetrotter' (1963), also fared well in the UK, Meek began to see solo possibilities for the boy, who was fast becoming something of a favourite of his. There's little doubt that Meek had a major crush on Burt, pushing the young musician forward to the detriment of one or two other charges – and, with the promise of gold records, moving him into the now-famous Holloway Road flat that was the focal point of Meek's working life (and, indeed, his death). No matter that Burt – now renamed simply 'Heinz' – didn't really possess much of a voice; he had the requisite pose and looks, while with the Eddie Cochran tribute 'Just Like Eddie' (1963) Meek had given Burt an admittedly quite good tune to kick-start his solo venture. (The producer also gave him a bottle of peroxide, thus emphasizing his blondness to the max.)

Things started to go downhill when it became apparent that Burt was not going to reciprocate Meek's feelings. Over the next few years, Burt was handed hectic tour schedules (quite possibly as punishment by Meek): during one performance, sharing the stage with his heroes Gene Vincent and Jerry Lee Lewis, the out-of-his-depth 'Heinz' was pelted with baked beans by witty rockers in the audience. His records also began to slip dramatically in the charts. Cutting his losses, the former star decided on a diversion into cabaret – while his mentor's life ended in the shocking and sensational episode in which Burt was briefly implicated (☛ *February 1967*). Without Meek to enhance his work, Burt was reduced to doing the panto circuit by the seventies. The last stages of Heinz Burt's life were distressing: crippled by motor neurone disease, he played his final gig just two weeks before his death, from a wheelchair at a club in Hampshire. His funeral attracted 150 guests – who celebrated the erstwhile heart-throb's life with a ghostly rendition of 'Telstar'. It is said that Burt had just £18 to his name at the time of his passing.

See also *Kim Roberts (☛ July 2000); Alan Caddy (☛ August 2000)*

Thursday 27

Vicki Sue Robinson
(Harlem, New York, 31 May 1954)

For an all-too-brief moment, she was a star: if not the queen of disco (that position was clearly taken by Donna Summer), Vicki Sue Robinson seemed a princess in waiting – her vibrant 'Turn the Beat Around' (1976) a Top Ten realization of the girl's aspirations. Brought up in Philadelphia by artistic parents (her mother was folk singer Jolly Robinson, her father Bill a respected black actor), the young singer had returned to New York just ahead of her teens, her ebullience winning Robinson starring parts in *Hair* and *Jesus Christ Superstar* in 1970, while her strong cabaret-style vocals eventually brought her backing work with a number of fellow artists, among them Cher, a young Michael Bolton and – unlikeliest of all – Japanese noodlers The Sadistic Mika Band. Robinson's solo success, surprisingly, was limited to her one major hit and its parent album, a collection of upbeat dance numbers – though she remained in demand as an actress and performer, while also warbling one or two memorable jingles for TV commercials.

The nineties vogue for all things retro gave Robinson a new lease of life in her later career: her earlier hit was revamped by Gloria Estefan and she herself returned to the studio to cut a new album. This revival was unfortunately sent crashing by the news in 1998 that she had cancer, but Vicki Sue Robinson showed her tenacity, performing until the final curtain. She died at her home in Connecticut.

MAY

Wednesday 31

Johnnie Taylor
(Crawfordsville, Arkansas, 5 May 1937)
The Soul Stirrers
(The Highway QCs)
(The Melody Makers)
(The Five Echoes)

Brought up by his grandparents, the hugely influential Johnnie Taylor trained his voice as a boy by singing in church near his Arkansas home. His rich tones gained Taylor a place in local gospel quartets, most notably the Chicago-based Melody Makers and Soul Stirrers – the latter the celebrated unit that featured a young Sam Cooke in its roster. Taylor and Cooke became close friends, Taylor taking over as lead vocalist when Cooke switched to secular music. Taylor made a similar move in 1961, recording for Cooke's SAR record label – but his friend's death (☛ *Pre-1965*) resulted in a devastated Taylor needing to find another label. With Stax, Taylor was an R&B sensation, four of his singles attaining number one in the chart – though it wasn't until the disco boom of 1975–6 that he reached the summit of Billboard's pop listings. 'Disco Lady' was an extraordinary, haunting record that earned the first ever platinum disc, eventually shifting over 2 million copies.

Known as 'The Soul Philosopher', Taylor showed great diversity in his career, covering gospel, soul, R & B, disco and even a touch of blues in his later recordings for Mississippi label Malaco. Johnnie Taylor's extravagant lifestyle was probably mainly to blame for his death, from a heart attack at Charleton Methodist Medical Center, Dallas.

JUNE

Friday 30

Rik L Rik
(Richard Brian Elerick – Los Angeles, California, 1961)
F-Word
(Negative Trend)
(Electric Frankenstein)
(The Celestials)

Yet another member of the early California punk alumni to die young, Rik L Rik had blazed his own personal trail, aged sixteen, as singer with F-Word back in 1977. The group's main claim to fame was that their live album *Like It or Not* (1978) could be said to be the first LA punk album to be released. When this project inevitably imploded, Rik joined Negative Trend – the group that were to become the fabled Flipper. Unfortunately, the singer left before this, working his way through a number of new-wave units, including Electric Frankenstein, for whom he was performing as late as 1997: Rik was due to record with The Celestials at the time of his death, from brain cancer. Rik L Rik was apparently working for a funeral director at the end of his life.

See also *Will Shatter (☞ December 1987)*

JULY

Saturday 1

Cub Koda

(Michael Koda – Detroit, Michigan, 1 October 1948)

Brownsville Station

(The Del-Tinos)

Now remembered for a rock standard, the versatile Cub Koda was cutting records as early as 1963. Having learned drums as a boy, he graduated to the guitar, forming high-school trio The Del-Tinos when just fifteen. The group recorded a few singles (mainly covers) during their three-year lifespan, after which Koda moved on to a couple of other units before emerging in Brownsville Station at the end of the decade. This next three-piece – based in Ann Arbor – also featured vocalist Michael Lutz and drummer Henry Weck. Within a few years, Station's brand of over-driven rock had become popular (think BTO, Steppenwolf, etc). Their national breakthrough came at the start of 1974 with the singalong 'Smokin' in the Boys' Room' – a Billboard Top Five hit that earned them a gold disc and charted in most countries across the world. One of the classic bad-boy anthems, the song has been covered many times – a 1985 mangling by Mötley Crüe is one of the better-known examples. Interestingly, this was not the direction desired by Koda, who preferred to tone down his band's output – until the lack of hits prompted a disbanding in 1979. Koda was well respected for his awesome knowledge of rock 'n' roll, R & B and the blues. He was also a much-published writer who contributed to *Discoveries* music magazine for more than two decades. After a sabbatical from music, Koda returned in 1995 with a solo album that finally produced another hit in 'Random Drug Testing'.

Just three months before his death, Cub Koda was still working, a further solo disc was out and the usual merry-go-round of promotion and touring meant that his calendar was chock-full until the end of 2000. However, all of this came to an abrupt halt when Koda died due to complications arising from kidney dialysis at around 2.45 am on 1 July.

> ## 'A short white kid makes a record that gets played on the radio and sells a million. How can *that* be a curse?'
> **Cub Koda**

Saturday 15

Paul Young

(Wythenshawe, Manchester, 17 June 1947)

Sad Café

Mike & The Mechanics

The SAS Band

(Various acts)

Although less recognizable than his namesake, Paul Young probably enjoyed more critical acclaim and almost certainly possessed the better white soul voice. But, until the last few weeks of the seventies, Young's first 'name' act, Sad Café – Ian Wilson (guitar), Ashley Mulford (guitar), Vic Emerson (keyboards), John Stimpson (bass) and David Irving (drums) – were best known for the lurid sleeve photographs for their albums *Fanx Ta-Ra* (1977) and *Misplaced Ideals* (1978). Prior to success, Young could have been spotted as early as 1962, fronting Johnny Dark & The Midnights before spending time with beat unit The Toggery Five and then Gyro, the band in which he met Wilson. However, after what seemed an eternity in the pub-rock doldrums, it finally happened for Young with Sad Café's winsome (and 250,000-selling) 'Every Day Hurts' (1979). Further hits followed, including 'My Oh My' (1980) – a tune that out-Stoned even Jagger and Richards. Their time in the spotlight lasted little more than a year, though, as various attempts to re-create the drama of 'Every Day Hurts' fell on deaf ears. After disbanding Café, Young took a couple of years away from the business before returning as one of several singers to front Mike & The Mechanics, the AOR side project of former Genesis guitarist Mike Rutherford – which went on to outsell much of his previous band's work. Although the albums *The Living Years* (1988), *Beggar on a Beach of Gold* (1995) and *Greatest Hits* (1996) all went gold,

Young had some pretty stiff competition for lead voice from ex-Squeeze and Ace vocalist Paul Carrack – but nonetheless crooned the US Top Five 'All I Need is a Miracle' (1986). Young also briefly re-formed Sad Café and sang with The SAS Band.

Paul Young was in semi-retirement when he collapsed from an apparent heart attack at home in Cheshire: the singer died on arrival at Wythenshawe Hospital.

Saturday 22
Kim Roberts
(Rosemary Ann Cottnam – Halifax, Yorkshire 11 April 1945)
Limehouse
Rusty & The Renegades
(The Settlers)
(Gilbert O'Sullivan)

Kim Roberts, whose demise was the latest in a run of deaths related to Joe Meek, was first discovered by the producer's protégé, Tornados bassist Heinz Burt, who thought the teenage singer had something special when he saw her perform back in 1963. Meek gave Rosemary Ann Cottnam her new name and identity, slapping her vocals on to a backing track by The Outlaws (a band that featured a young Ritchie Blackmore) for her first single, 'Prove It' (1963). Although her solo career didn't really take off, Roberts nonetheless found her way into show business, albeit elsewhere in the world, fronting a television show in South Africa, where she was extremely popular. Thereafter, Roberts sang with pop-folk also-rans The Settlers and then as backing to Gilbert O'Sullivan as he cleaned up in Britain and America. Her later career was more stop-start, the vocalist working with blues bands Rusty & The Renegades and the all-female Limehouse; Roberts also appeared on stage with old friends Screaming Lord

Sutch & The Savages (she later married the drummer, Jack Irving). Her final live performance was at a memorial concert for Sutch in June 2000. Just weeks later, Kim Roberts passed away after complaining of a heart murmur.

See also *Joe Meek (☛ February 1967 and the accompanying Dead Interesting!); Screaming Lord Sutch (☛ June 1999); Heinz Burt (☛ April 2000)*

AUGUST
Wednesday 2
Jerome Smith
(Miami, Florida, 18 June 1953)
KC & The Sunshine Band
The Divinyls
Blowfly

Here's a nasty one. The life of Jerome Smith, original rhythm guitarist with disco heavyweights KC & The

Sunshine Band, came to an unfortunate end in an accident at his new workplace – a construction site at Florida's West Palm Beach.

Smith was at founder Harry 'KC' Casey's side when The Sunshine Band came bouncing out of Florida to enjoy unrivalled global success during the seventies. The hits seemed to arrive at the snap of Casey's fingers: the group enjoyed five number ones in the USA alone, including three on the trot with the funky 'Get Down Tonight', 'That's the Way (I Like It)' (both 1975) and '(Shake, Shake, Shake) Shake Your Booty' (1976). Jerome Smith's trademark playing had been present on all these chartbusters, as it had been on George Macrae's worldwide chart-topper 'Rock Your Baby' (1974) – the song that convinced Casey that this was indeed his man. While Casey was in no doubt about Smith's guitar work, he was less happy with the musician's increased drug intake – a sore point that eventually cost Smith his place in the group during 1979. Having cleaned himself up, Smith returned to music with outrageous disco artiste Blowfly, for whom he played on many albums: he was also to work with the

KC and the Sunshine Band, with Jerome Smith standing to leader Harry Casey's right shoulder: Sound your family horn!

excellent Australian pop band The Divinyls.

By the summer of 2000, Smith was sufficiently rehabilitated to rejoin Casey and his latest line-up of The Sunshine Band some twenty years after the pair had gone their separate ways. Now a 47-year-old construction worker, Smith was excited by this prospect and dreamed of re-creating the good old days with his former friend. Sadly, it wasn't to be: one morning, as Smith attempted to operate a bulldozer at the work site, the sometime musician fell from the machine. As he landed, the vehicle continued to trundle forwards, trapping Smith beneath it and crushing him. He was killed instantly. His death followed that of later Sunshine Band keyboardist Ernest 'Snuffy' Smith, who died after an asthma attack in April 1997.

Wednesday 16

Alan Caddy

(Chelsea, London, 2 February 1940)

The Tornados
Johnny Kidd & The Pirates (The Five Nutters)
(The Alan Caddy Orchestra)

Hot on the heels of the passing of bassist Heinz Burt (➤ *April 2000*) came news of the death of the more talented Alan Caddy, lead guitarist with The Tornados. Caddy's background was one of some musical expertise: his father was a dance-band drummer who ran a jazz club; Caddy himself had been head chorister and orchestra leader at his Battersea school. It came as some surprise to his family when Caddy developed a love for skiffle and beat that saw him playing most nights of the week at clubs, while he worked by day as an estate agent. As guitarist with The Five Nutters, he became friends with Johnny Kidd (aka singer Frederick Heath), playing with the

band on their transformation into Johnny Kidd & The Pirates, thus giving Caddy his first taste of rock 'n' roll stardom. Donning extravagant stage gear with a piratical theme, The Pirates – completed by Brian Gregg (bass) and Clem Cattini (drums) – proved to be one of the UK's best pre-Beatles rock 'n' roll bands: this was reflected in tunes such as 'Please Don't Touch' (1959) and 'Shakin' All Over' (1960), the latter of which shifted half a million copies in Britain. Despite this, Caddy and Cattini left the group (after a disastrous tour of Italy in 1961) to sign over to wunderkind producer Joe Meek's home-based studio, forming the basis of the Tornados. This group – originally vaunted as backing for Billy Fury – then experienced what none of them would have believed possible a few years before: their 'Telstar' (1962) topped the charts in both the UK and US (and pretty much everywhere else) on its way to becoming the biggest-selling instrumental piece of all time. For Caddy, this was his major triumph. With Meek being tone-deaf, it had been down to the guitarist to arrange the piece – as he would further tunes by The Tornados.

The phenomenal success of 'Telstar' couldn't be repeated, however, the quiet Caddy eventually moving on to arrange for a slew of sixties and seventies artists, including: Elkie Brooks; Dave Dee, Dozy, Beaky, Mick & Tich; Kiki Dee; The Pretty Things; Spencer Davis Group; and Dusty Springfield. Caddy also worked more anonymously for Polydor and was behind a series of budget cover albums for Avenue. His final appearance was at a 1991 Joe Meek memorial concert in Lewisham. Despite being a heavy drinker throughout his life, Alan Caddy is believed to have died from natural causes.

See also *Johnny Kidd (➤ October 1966); Joe Meek (➤ February 1967)*

Saturday 26

Allen Woody

(Douglas Allen Woody – Nashville, Tennessee, 2 October 1956)

The Allman Brothers Band
(The Artimus Pyle Band)
(Gov't Mule)

Signing up with the ill-fated Allman Brothers Band mightn't seem the wisest decision to some, but bassist Douglas Allen Woody could see only greatness in the heroes of his youth. By the time he joined the restyled band in 1989, The Allmans' history was already strewn with casualties, guitarist Duane Allman having led the way in a motorbike accident (➤ *October 1971*), Woody's antecedent bassists Berry Oakley (➤ *November 1972*) and Lamar Williams (➤ *January 1983*) following the co-founder to that great jam session in the sky. Woody was perhaps already dicing with death: he'd previously played with The Artimus Pyle Band – the group knocked together by the former Lynyrd Skynyrd drummer who had escaped the carnage of his band's 1977 air crash by the skin of his teeth (➤ *October 1977*). Allen was a decent musician, though, having learned guitar and bass by his fifteenth birthday, his father encouraging him to get into blues and country as well as the rock 'n' roll he loved. With this in mind, he and fellow Allman Brothers guitarist Warren Haynes eventually jumped ship to form the offshoot rock act Gov't Mule in 1997, a hard-rocking band that had begun to acquire much good press by the turn of the millennium.

But the extraordinary curse of the Southern bands was set to continue. At 10.30 am on 26 August 2000, the body of Douglas Allen Woody was found seated in a chair in his room by a shocked chambermaid at the Marriott Courtyard Motel in Queens.

Woody, who was set to fly back to Nashville after a New York concert, was believed to have suffered a heart attack in his sleep.

SEPTEMBER

Monday 4

David Brown
(New York, 15 February 1947)
Santana
(Various acts)

An early bass guitarist with globe-conquering Latin rock legend Santana, David Brown joined The Santana Blues Band, as it was known, in 1966. After shortening the band's name, Mexican-born guitarist and singer Carlos Santana settled his classic line-up of Brown, Gregg Rolie (keyboards/vocals), Jose Chepito Areas (timbales), Mike Carrabello (congas) and Michael Shrieve (drums), ahead of their memorable Woodstock Festival appearance in 1969. The effect of the band's live show was potent, with the eponymous debut album vaulting into the American Top Five. Its follow-up, *Abraxas* (1970), is widely considered Santana's finest work (at least by pre-millennial fans), this album spawning big hit singles in 'Black Magic Woman' and '*Oye Como Va*' (both 1971). After the recording of *Santana III* (1971), Brown left the group: the album topped the charts in his absence. The bassist's immediate replacement was jazz virtuoso Stanley Clarke, with whom Santana went on to pursue more experimental styles. Brown – who was also a flautist – briefly rejoined Santana during the seventies, but spent more time on other projects for the remainder of his career, such as sessions with Greg Allman and Boz Scaggs. Little was heard of the bass-

player in the years prior to his death in 2000 from liver and kidney failure. By this time, of course, his former boss had found a whole new audience with the 20-million-selling *Supernatural*.

See also *Richard Kermode (►◄ January 1996); Leone Thomas (►◄ May 1999)*

Saturday 9

Victor Cross
(London, 21 June 1960)
The Robotics
(The Twinkle Brothers)

The Robotics was the unlikely name for a group of accomplished reggae musicians employed to back some of the biggest names in Jamaican music when on tour in Europe, including Horace Andy and Mad Professor. Forty-year-old keyboardist Victor Cross was one of the best-loved members, an experienced musician from a prolific family (which included his sister, singer Sandra Cross) who had also played with Norman Grant's Twinkle Brothers group. One artist frequently associated with The Robotics was 'Wet Dream' hit-maker Max Romeo, by 2000 a veteran performer still much loved on the continent. As the Romeo/Robotics tour bus wended its way towards an engagement in Orléans, France, the vehicle was struck by another. Following the horrendous collision, Romeo pulled through unscathed, though several members of the party were badly hurt – in particular, guitarist Jerry Lions. Victor Cross was even less fortunate – he died at the scene from multiple internal injuries.

Close!
Brad Roberts
(Crash Test Dummies)

From our 'It Had to Happen' vault: Crash Test Dummies frontman, Canadian singer/songwriter and 1994 'Mmm Mmm Mmm Mmm' hit-maker Brad Roberts rolled his prized 1989 Cadillac on 28 September 2000. Roberts – who was later fined for possession of marijuana – survived this Nova Scotia 'crash test', breaking his arm in ten places. He was pulled from the wreckage by a passer-by only minutes before the stricken vehicle burst into flames.

OCTOBER

Tuesday 3

Benjamin Orr
(Benjamin Orsechowski – Cleveland, Ohio, 8 September 1947)
The Cars
(The Grasshoppers)
(Big People)

A high-school drop-out with one ambition in mind, young Benjamin Orsechowski (who thankfully shortened his name upon turning professional) was to achieve success well beyond his adolescent hopes. It was a slow process, however. As leader of Ohio rock band The Grasshoppers, the renamed Orr proved a versatile musician, filling most band roles at one time or another. Shortly after the split

'If I fall down one day and can't get up – that's when you'll know it's over.'
Benjamin Orr takes it on the chin

of this band owing to the demands of the Vietnam call-up, Orr encountered vocalist/guitarist Rik Ocasek at a party in 1968, the pair fashioning a rock duo which eventually became The Cars.

By 1976, the band – who had wisely dropped their original name, Cap'n Swing – were finally complete: Orr took up the bass, as Elliot Easton (guitar), Greg Hawkes (keyboards) and David Robinson (ex-Modern Lovers, drums) completed the familiar Cars line-up. Initial success was greater in Europe, with 'My Best Friend's Girl' (1978, featuring Orr's vocal) climbing into the UK Top Five (mainly because it was Britain's first-ever picture disc), but when the US cottoned on to the group, it cottoned on in some style. The best of The Cars shiny new-wave hits were arguably 'Let's Go' (1979) and 'Shake It Up' (1982), though it was to be the ballad 'Drive' (1984) that was to provoke the strongest reaction – particularly in the UK when applied to the harrowing scenes of the Ethiopian famine. In a 12-year career, The Cars racked up more than 20 million sales. Just prior to their split, Benjamin Orr issued his own solo album, *The Lace* (1986), giving him a hit under his own name. Post-Cars, he was quieter, but did re-emerge with a supergroup called Big People, which featured Pat Travers, Jeff Carlisi (.38 Special), Derek St Holmes (Ted Nugent) and Liberty DeVito (Billy Joel).

In May 2000, fans and former bandmates were shocked to learn of Benjamin Orr's hospitalization due to pancreatic cancer. Although Orr continued to play with Big People late into the year, his condition was deemed inoperable: the prolific and hard-working musician died at his Atlanta home just weeks after his band's final show.

Sunday 22

Bobby Soxx

(Robert Glenn Calverley – Dallas, Texas, 29 December 1954)
Stickmen with Ray Guns
Teenage Queers
(The Enemy)

He was so hard-drinking and wild-living that the biggest surprise for most who knew of him was that Dallas punk-figurehead Bobby Soxx hadn't died years ago. Indeed, rumours had been bandied about for years that Soxx (Calverley, to his folks) had perished this way or that – but he somehow bounced back, whether with The Enemy, Texas punk legends Teenage Queers or his later band, the excellently named Stickmen with Ray Guns. Some tales about him had substance (though not as much as Soxx's system): he'd been in countless fights, had been shot at and even stabbed by burglars on one occasion. Soxx himself had spent time incarcerated, or – if he was lucky – in a secure unit. Some of his behaviour was, it's true, completely unacceptable (wife-beating, vandalism, you name it), the singer's only excuse being that he could remember none of it. His self-purging was a key component of The Stickmen's songs – best evoked on the album *Some People Deserve to Suffer* (2002).

But, as for death, well, that seemed to be reserved for others – such as his

'Death couldn't touch Bobby. He was bulletproof.'

Barry Kooda, guitarist with Dallas punks The Nervebreakers

pal Mike Vomit, who died on Soxx's porch back in 1984 (the Vomit Pigs' singer had passed on after a furious bout of eating and drug-taking). By the late nineties, Soxx appeared to have beaten his demons: he had found regular employment as a cook and had stayed out of chokey for some years. In 2000, however, he was still claiming 'drinking's all I got' – and early in the morning of 22 October, he had his final, fateful date with the bottle. It was no surprise to see the singer drink himself into a stupor – but this time his liver finally surrendered and he was never to wake up.

Friday 27

Winston Grennan

(Duckenfield, Jamaica, 16 September 1944)
Toots & The Maytals
The Ska Rocks
(Various acts)

Winston Grennan was the drummer whose one-drop rhythms informed the rocksteady sound that was to emerge in ska during the sixties and seventies. Grennan, whose family had a background in jazz, began in that genre, but made the move over to reggae and ska as the new styles grew in Jamaica. Recording at the studios of Duke Reid, Grennan played with The Caribbeats and The Supersonics, his percussive techniques taught to the likes of Sly Dunbar and The Wailers' Carlton Barrett. He also played with Roland Alphonso and Jackie Mittoo, later of The Skatalites. By the time he left Jamaica, Grennan – who had seen something of the world as a member of Toots & The Maytals – had accompanied virtually every big name on the island. Based in the USA, the drummer inevitably became more invisible to Jamaican audiences, but nonetheless worked at his craft and led his own band,

The Ska Rocks. He had moved to Nantucket, Massachusetts, by the time of his death from bone cancer.

See also *Jackie Mittoo (☞ December 1990); Roland Alphonso (☞ Golden Oldies #8)*

NOVEMBER

Thursday 2

Al Grierson
(New Westminster, British Columbia, 1948)

Tales of floods are generally the stuff of folk singers' tunes (☞ *Death Toll #4*): for Al Grierson, it was just such an occurrence that was to claim his life. Relocated to Texas, Canadian-born Grierson became known as 'The Poet Laureate of Luckenbach' – the celebrated one-horse town where he lived, outside of Austin. State-wide, he was loved, a regular performer at the Kerrville Folk Festival with an enormous cache of songs, both traditional and original, at his fingertips. Despite having written and played for many years, Grierson – a lifelong wanderer (and former Buddhist monk) – did not release his first album until 1995.

Five years on, with flash floods washing through Texas, he made the fatal error of alighting from his stalled pick-up: at around 5.45 pm, the singer was swept two miles to his death – one of several people killed in the disaster.

Thursday 16

Joe C
(Joseph Calleja – Taylor, Michigan, 9 November 1974)
Kid Rock's Twisted Brown Truckers

Known in respectable circles as 'the man who's three foot nine with a ten-foot dick', Joseph Calleja had been afflicted with coeliac disease – a condition preventing his small intestine from absorbing nutrients – since his childhood. By the age of twenty, Calleja still maintained the appearance of a child, his growth stunted by the disease, which required him to take seventy pills a day by the end of his life. Rock/rap crossover artist Kid Rock saw something in the diminutive fan ever at the front at his gigs: after sharing a joint with Calleja, Rock invited him to join his tour as a dancer and freeform rapper. When Kid Rock became a huge star in the US, Joe C (as Calleja dubbed himself) shared some of the fame. His recorded contributions included 'Kyle's Mom is a Big Fat Bitch' from the *South Park* soundtrack, while no shortage of humour was evident in a promo for Rock's 'Cowboy' (1999), in which Calleja duelled with pint-sized actor Gary Coleman – himself afflicted with nephritis.

That Joe C wouldn't live into his thirties was perhaps inevitable, but his death at twenty-six still prompted impressive eulogies from those who had known him and observed his brave acceptance of his condition. Kid Rock himself was not slow in paying tribute: 'We have lost part of our family. He brought a smile to everyone who has ever known or seen him. In a world full of confusion, Joey made all of us laugh.'

Friday 17

Bim Sherman
(Lloyd Jarrett Vincent – Westmoreland, Jamaica, 2 February 1950)

Going by a vast number of pseudonyms – Jarrett Tomlinson, Bim Shieman, Lloyd Tomlinson, J L Vincent, etc – Bim Sherman did what he had to in order to stay ahead of the game in Jamaican music: the tactic was widely employed, reggae musicians finding it easier to make a living under a variety of labels, which also

Winston Grennan, with 'Toots' Hibbert and 'Raleigh' Gordon: Good to the last 'drop'

Bim Sherman: Loved forever

meant a variety of names. Formerly a fisherman, Sherman's talent prevailed, however, the singer's sweet voice finally leading to an album release with *Love Forever* (1978). Sherman's popularity in Britain – much of which was due to the championing of his work by DJ John Peel – resulted in his being signed by cutting-edge label On-U Sound, who issued a number of great albums, beginning with *Across the Red Sea* (1982) and ending with *What Happened* (1998), by which time the artist had been diagnosed with cancer. Bim Sherman died from the disease at his home in London.

Thursday 23

Bob B Soxx
(Bobby Sheen – St Louis, Missouri, 17 May 1941)
Bob B Soxx & The Blue Jeans
(The Coasters)
(Various acts)

Just a month after his namesake, the better-known Bob B Soxx also passed over to the other side. Moving from Missouri to Hollywood as a boy, Bobby Sheen developed a taste for the glamour he felt was within his grasp. He was, after all, a decent singer who

fashioned his voice and clean-cut looks on those of Clyde McPhatter of The Drifters. In his early career, Sheen joined touring versions of The Robins and The Coasters; he also lent backing vocals to the first Crystals hit, 1962's 'He's a Rebel' (Sheen had the range to cope with a higher register), under the auspicious direction of Phil Spector and his burgeoning 'Wall of Sound'. From the same session came 'Zip-a-Dee-Doo-Dah' (from the soundtrack of *Song of the South*), which proved so popular with those present that Spector released it. This time, Sheen's voice was up front, the singer becoming 'Bob B Soxx', leader of the non-existent Blue Jeans vocal group who were actually former 'Blossoms' Darlene Love and Fanita Barrett. The record was a Top Ten smash, with Soxx/Sheen an immediate hit with teenage girls. All of which begs the question, why did Spector then mess with the formula? The follow-up singles featured lead vocals by Love – who was still, after all, on Crystals duty – and flopped badly.

Bobby Sheen attempted to pursue a solo career after this, but the moment seemed completely to have passed him by: his subsequent records were good, but only really appealed to the UK Northern soul crowd. Sheen died in relative obscurity, from pneumonia, at his home in Los Angeles.

See also *King Curtis (☙August 1971); Nathaniel Wilson (☙April 1980); Bobby Nunn (☙November 1986); Cornell Gunter (☙February 1990). Will 'Dub' Jones (2000) and Billy Guy (2002) have also passed away, as has Darrell Reynolds (also 2002).*

Thursday 30

Scott Smith

(Donald Scott Smith – Vancouver, British Columbia,
13 February 1955)

Loverboy

Canadian group Loverboy were the rock band your girlfriend liked: the epitome of eighties soft-metal excess, they were a blow-waved bunch of pretty boys with a nice line in topped-up tans, toned torsos and titillating Top Twenty tunes. Comprising Mike Reno (vocals), Paul Dean (guitar), Scott Smith (bass), Doug Johnson (keyboards) and Matt Frenette (drums), Loverboy burst out of Vancouver with a series of radio-friendly albums and a goodly batch of Billboard hits. 'Working for the Weekend' (1982) is perhaps their best-known song – featuring on countless teen movie soundtracks – though it was 'Lovin' Every Minute of It' (1985) and 'This Could be the Night' (1986) that took them into the US Top Ten, alongside a raft of gold albums between 1980 and 1997.

A lover of sailing for almost as long as he had been of women, Scott Smith frequently blew his considerable wad on massive yachts. On 30 November 2000, Smith, his 'lovergirl' Yvonne Mayotte and friend William Ellis took the bassist's 37-foot craft out on to the water just off San Francisco's Ocean Beach: Smith planned to moor it in Southern California for the winter. About four miles off the coast, strong winds caused gigantic, powerful waves to begin battering the craft, at which point the experienced Smith banished Mayotte and Ellis below deck. It was some time before the pair realized that both Smith and the boat's steering wheel were missing, wrenched from the deck into the turbulent waters. Unhurt, they contacted coast guards, but a search for the musician's body proved fruitless.

DECEMBER

Monday 18

Kirsty MacColl

(Croydon, Surrey, 10 October 1959)

One of the finest British pop song-writers of her generation, Kirsty MacColl conversely enjoyed her biggest hits with the songs of others, though in truth only flirted with the fame that should have been hers. Depressed as a child, MacColl suffered from asthma and was subsequently placed in a special school by authorities who seemed to want to brush a fairly common medical condition under the carpet. Her ability, though, was spotted as early as 1966 when the future star and her mother – choreographer Jean Newlove, by then separated from MacColl's father, the noted folk musician Ewan MacColl – appeared on a BBC television series on gifted children, and she was already writing songs by the age of eleven. MacColl attended Croydon Art College and briefly became Mandy Doubt, singer with best-forgotten punk band The Drug Addix. Her future songwriting was inspired more by Phil Spector than The Sex Pistols, however, and a shimmering Stiff Records debut, 'They Don't Know' (1979), surprised many. The record should, of course, have been a huge hit for MacColl, topping airplay charts during the summer, but a distribution strike prevented this – the first in a series of unfortunate events that hampered her career. (Some parity was restored when singer/comedienne Tracey Ullman's somewhat saccharine rendition of the song earned MacColl a gold disc in 1983.) MacColl spent time with five different labels during a turbulent recording history; her first bona fide hit, 'There's a Guy Works Down the Chip Shop Swears He's Elvis' (1981), was issued by Polydor, who then rejected a second album, which they felt was non-commercial. Returning to the label she had left three years before, MacColl reached the Top Ten in 1985 with Billy Bragg's 'A New England' Shane McGowan: 'She turned a good song into a great song'), before the company went bankrupt. Now a mother, MacColl – who suffered from extreme stage fright in any case – took a sabbatical. After much-needed time off, her *Kite* (1989) and *Electric Landlady* (1991) albums for Virgin weren't the vast successes they'd anticipated, despite top-dollar songs like the singles 'Free World' and 'Walking Down Madison' pulled from each (a later *Best of* compilation for the label then went platinum, proving a point or two somewhere). A spell with ZTT similarly failed to alter the course of history. During her career, the massively respected MacColl recorded with a vast array of British and American artists, including Simple Minds, Happy Mondays, Talking Heads, The Wonder Stuff, Evan Dando and, of course, MacGowan and The Pogues – for whom she illuminated the near-chart-topping 'Fairytale of New York' in 1987, for many the best Christmas hit ever.

In January 2000, Kirsty MacColl seemed finally to have found contentment in her life. She had signed with Virgin subsidiary V2, releasing the witty, critically acclaimed *Tropical Brainstorm*, an album of Cuban-influenced songs. Most importantly – with her failed marriage to producer Steve Lillywhite long behind her – she had a new partner in saxophonist James Knight. Invigorated by these significant upturns in both her personal and professional lives, she planned a scuba-diving vacation for her lover and her two sons, Louis and Jamie, at the end of the year in a part of the world she'd grown to love.

Cozumel is Mexico's largest island, a 28-mile stretch of white sand and clear reef-strewn water off the Yucatan peninsula that – after some endorsement from world-famous diver Jacques Cousteau – developed from a quiet fishing community into a thriving tourist and recreation centre during the sixties. For an enthusiast like MacColl, it was the ultimate divers' paradise. On 18 December, she took her sons to experience the underwater world with diving instructor Ivan Diaz and a number of other divers in an area specifically designated for the sport. As MacColl and her sons prepared to surface, Diaz spotted a large speedboat approaching rapidly within the restricted area. The vessel was travelling too fast for any significant action to be taken, however: as she pushed her sons to safety, Kirsty MacColl was struck and killed instantly, her body mutilated by the impact (her eldest son, Jamie – who remained astonishingly composed in the aftermath – even spoke of 'swimming in his mother's blood'). It was a wicked, violent end to a life of such creativity.

After the tragedy, the problems of seeking justice became apparent to all connected with MacColl. Although clearly not responsible for the accident, 26-year-old Juan José Cenyam took (or was instructed to take) responsibility for it, the untrained boat hand being ordered to pay £1,500 to MacColl's sons, a sum related to his paltry salary. It became apparent, however, that the man in charge of the speedboat was wealthy businessman Guillermo Gonzalez Nova, who years later has still not been brought to any kind of justice, nor made any kind of public statement of culpability or indeed proffered any kind of apology to the bereft family. For Kirsty's octogenarian mother, Jean (who chooses to

From Croydon to Cuba – There'll never be anyone else like Kirsty

employ the name MacColl to publicize her 'Justice For Kirsty' campaign), it has clearly been a distressing process: in 2004, she was confounded yet again when the Mexican Federal Prosecutor refused to re-open the case. (At the time of writing, the campaign had succeeded in obtaining a commitment from the Attorney General that a new criminal investigation will be opened and has secured implementation of greater security for divers in designated areas. Full details of the ongoing campaign can be found at www.kirsty-maccoll.com.)

Back in Britain, MacColl's passing has prompted continued tributes for the artist, her music and her beliefs. Given the manner of her death, the sleeve design for *Tropical Brainstorm* offers a poignant reminder of a part of the world that had become important to the singer at the end of her life: ironically, she had become actively involved in the Cuban Solidarity Movement, which pursued justice in its attempts to bring an end to US economic sanctions.

Tuesday 19

Rob Buck
(Jamestown, New York, 1 August 1958)

10,000 Maniacs

The band's name a corruption of a largely forgotten B-movie title, 10,000 Maniacs first offered their new-wave folk to the public around 1981. Singer Natalie Merchant and bassist Steven Gustafson had met at Jamestown Community College where they co-ran a campus radio station. Rob Buck and John Lombardo (guitars) were among six of a huge original line-up to make the final cut. Signed to Elektra, the Maniacs were mainly an outlet for Merchant's musings and unorthodox stage presence, songs like 'My Mother the War' (1982) piquing the casual listener. Despite a loyal following in New York, the band were most popular in the UK, where their albums sold steadily (as opposed to spectacularly), with *Blind Man's Zoo* finally breaching the Top Twenty on both sides of the Atlantic in 1989. Buck, who had played the guitar since he was a kid aping Jimi Hendrix, went on to write a good number of the group's songs, including their most popular, 'Hey Jack Kerouac' (1987). Merchant's departure from the band in 1993 effectively ended interest in 10,000 Maniacs, though they did continue throughout the nineties with singer Mary Ramsey. Rob Buck had been hospitalized at the University of Pittsburgh Medical Center for some weeks by the time of his death from liver failure, his health having deteriorated too rapidly to allow a transplant.

Sunday 31

Eddy Shaver
(John Edwin Shaver – Texas, 20 June 1962)

Shaver

The son of Texan country singer Billy Joe Shaver – who nearly named the boy 'Electric' – Eddy Shaver couldn't have cut a more diametrically opposed figure, either in looks or style. True, he wielded a guitar like his father (and he had performed with artists like Kris Kristofferson, Willie Nelson and Dwight Yoakam), but Shaver Jr was a more 'out there' performer than Billy Joe, his long, lank hair, brooding stage presence and (appropriately) razor-like riffs becoming trademarks by the end of 2000. During the seven previous years, the family's band Shaver had released five albums of gritty road-house honky-tonk. Shaver's dynamism in performance belied a a quiet nature, although he latterly developed a taste for one or two rock 'n' roll pleasures. Following a strenuous gig in Austin, Shaver died from an accidental heroin overdose – the guitarist had been married for just two months. For his father it was to be the third bereavement within two years, both his wife and mother also having passed on.

'If he wasn't my kid, I couldn't afford him.'

Eddy Shaver's father

Close!
Bryan Ferry

As head honcho to the suave and sophisticated, Bryan Ferry generally steers clear of the headlines, leaving any public dramas either to ex-partners or his bloodsport-loving son. On 29 December 2000, however, the former Roxy Music frontman had little choice in matters, when a deranged passenger decided to attempt a hijack of the aircraft carrying him from London to Nairobi. The man – 27-year-old Paul Mukonyi – burst into the cockpit and began tussling with the flight crew, causing the jet to plummet 10,000 feet.

Ferry, his family and the other passengers (who included socialite Jemima Khan) were briefly in considerable danger, but the pilots managed to subdue Mukonyi, who remained bound until the aircraft could be safely landed.

Lest We Forget

Other notable deaths that occurred sometime during 2000:

William Martin Bennett (US rock drummer with Sam the Sham & The Pharaohs, who hit #2 with 'Wooly Bully' in 1965 and again with 'Li'l Red Riding Hood' a year later; born New York, 12/7/1944; heart attack, 25/10)

Russ Conway (hugely popular UK pianist/composer who was 1959's biggest-selling act in Britain with the chart-toppers 'Side Saddle' and 'Roulette'; born Trevor Stanford, Bristol, 2/9/1925; cancer, 16/11)

Tony Flaim (Canadian blues singer with Downchild; born 1947; heart attack, 10/3 – just weeks after Richard 'Hock' Walsh, the man he'd once replaced)

Geoffrey Goddard (UK composer/songwriter of the Joe Meek-produced 'mawk' classic 'Johnny Remember Me' who also ghosted keyboards on The Tornados' 'Telstar'; born 1938; heart attack, 15/5)

Ralph Jones (legendary US rock 'n' roll drummer with Bill Haley's Comets; born Pennsylvania, 1920; following heart surgery, 1/6)

Will 'Dub' Jones (US vocalist with madcap R & B legends The Coasters, who also sang with The Cadets and Mighty Travelers; born Louisiana, 14/5/1928; diabetes, 16/1)

Julie London (sultry US singer/actress loved for classic hits like 1955's 'Cry Me a River'; born Julie Peck, California, 26/9/1926; lengthy illness following a stroke suffered five years previously, 18/10)

Nick Massi (US pop/harmony singer/bassist who enjoyed 17 hits including 4 chart-toppers with the legendary Four Seasons; born Nicholas Macioci, New Jersey, 19/9/1927; cancer, 24/12)

DJ Screw (US hip-hop producer who innovated the art of 'screwing down' samples; born Robert Earl Davis Jr, Texas, 1970; overdose of codeine – the drug that inspired his work – 16/11)

Bobby Warren (US touring singer with The Drifters; shot while driving his car, 29/4)

For a complete list of fallen artists, visit

www.numberoneinheaven.com

JANUARY

Tuesday 2

Jimmy Zámbó

(Imre Zámbó – Budapest, 1958)

Although unknown to most of the world, Jimmy Zámbó was a rags-to-riches hero to millions in his home country. In Hungary they called him 'The King', this medallion-wearing, mullet-headed rock balladeer who'd been named Singer of the Year in 1993 before picking up a series of platinum records – plus two Golden Giraffes (it says here) – on his way to national stardom. By the end of 2000, he had his own weekly RTL television slot and was number one once again with the schmaltzy *Christmas With Jimmy* album. So what better way to thank his loyal fans than by giving them something they'd never forget?

After a riotous New Year's Day spent drinking with his wife and friends, the singer decided he needed to take a nap. As it turned out, next door's cockerels decided that the party was far from over, their crowing causing Zámbó to see red. An avid hunter, he owned a collection of firearms including a 9 mm Beretta, which he aimed at the offending birds, much to

the consternation of his wife, who had come to investigate the noise. Calming down, Zámbó explained that no harm had been done and that he was now out of bullets. He then chose the Terry Kath method of proving this (☛ *January 1978*). Cocking the gun, Zámbó pulled the trigger and unloaded the last remaining bullet – into his own skull. The singer was rushed to hospital, but pronounced dead at around 5 am. A vast throng of candle-bearing fans gathered outside his home the next day, the nation descending into collective disbelief.

Sunday 7

James Carr

(Clarksdale, Mississippi, 13 June 1942)

You may not recall his name, but those who loved him refuse to believe that James Carr possessed anything other than a voice up there among soul's very best. A gospel-quartet singer brought up in Memphis, Carr was taken under the wing of Quinton Claunch, who felt his new Goldwax label needed an 'Otis Redding' of its own and detected pure gold in the voice of this unimposing young man. With the label, Carr finally scored a hit with 'Love Attack' (1966), but further

songs – such as the searching 'Dark End of the Street' (1967) – were not to secure any kind of lasting position. While touring with Redding, audiences were quick to dub him a 'copyist' of the bigger star: he had simply arrived on the scene too late. Developing a taste for marijuana and alcohol, Carr found himself slipping into despondency as the big break continued to elude him – even after Redding's untimely death (☛ *December 1967*).

A split from his manager had an even worse effect on the falling star: suffering from manic depression, his songs grew ever darker. His singing career virtually over, Carr spent many of the remainder of his days in and out of institutions. He returned to perform in the early nineties, but, though there were fleeting moments, his voice was not what it had been in his prime. Carr, having been plagued by lung cancer for many years, died in a nursing home.

> **'You have people all around, but you can still be alone – like James was. He was tryin' to be a star, but he didn't know how.'**
>
> Roosevelt Jamison,
> James Carr's manager

The Cramps *c* 1979: Bryan Gregory at the feet of 'two-headed' Lux Interior and 'Poison' Ivy, with long-term drummer, Nick Knox

Theophilus Beckford
(Trenchtown, Kingston, Jamaica, 1935)

Credited by many as one of the key originators of ska, Theophilus Beckford honed his craft practising on the family grand piano, aping his favourite Roscoe Gordon jump-blues records as he did so. Beckford is probably best remembered for the Clement 'Coxsone' Dodd-produced 'Easy Snappin'', a 1956 hit later revived for a nineties jeans commercial. Beckford received few royalties, however: despite working with the likes of the late Desmond Dekker, Lord Flea and Toots & The Maytals, he led a life of poverty in Trenchtown.

His time came on 19 February 2001, following a violent dispute with an acquaintance in the neighbouring district of Callalew Mews. The furious row had continued for some time before the man attacked Beckford with a machete while his back was turned. His assailant planted the weapon into the musician's skull, killing him in an instant.

MARCH

Wednesday 10

Bryan Gregory
(Greg Beckerleg – Detroit, Michigan, 20 February 1955)
**The Cramps
(Various acts)**

An original guitarist with Ohio-formed psychobilly shockers The Cramps, 'proto-goth' Bryan Gregory cut a striking figure alongside band mainstays the imposing Lux Interior (Erick Purkhiser, vocals) and vampish 'Poison' Ivy Rorschach (Kristy Wallace, guitar). The voodoo-obsessed axeman had met Interior at a New York record store and joined the band in 1976 (with his sister Pam Balam, the first of many drummers), lured by the promise of his very own Flying 'V'. The Cramps had decamped to the Big Apple where they felt pickings might be richer. And they were right. Miles Copeland – manager of The Police, for whom the band opened several European dates in 1979 – signed the group to his Illegal label, issuing an EP and first-album-proper, the Alex Chilton-produced *Gravest Hits* and *Songs the Lord Taught Us* (1980), in quick succession. Gregory was only around for this first album, but Ivy is quick to suggest that he didn't even contribute much to the recording of that, either: instead, the guitarist just *looked* the part, turning heads wherever he went – and even pulling a switchblade on a group of besuited businessmen who dared to laugh at him in a restaurant. Unhappy with their musical direction, Gregory left The Cramps in 1980 – apparently disappearing with the van and most of the group's equipment! While his former colleagues went on to greatness in his absence, Gregory turned up again with the faintly desperate Beast a couple of years on, later joining two further acts, The Dials and Shiver, before fading from the underground rock scene. Bryan Gregory suffered a heart attack after a long period of ill health, finally dying from pneumonia at California's Anaheim Memorial Medical Center.

Sunday 4

Glenn Hughes
(New York, 18 July 1950)
The Village People

They could have been The Spice Guys – six costumed cockerels manufactured by producer Jacques Morali to cash in on New York's blossoming

'People' get ready: Jones, Willis, Hodo, Briley Hughes and Rose prepare to take on the big boys

gay disco scene. The recruitment was simple; the small ad, specific: 'six singers and dancers, must be good-looking, gay and sporting moustaches'. Thus, in 1977, the phenomenon that was The Village People was born. The group couldn't fail with its outlandish East Village stereotypes: the naval serviceman (Alex Briley); the construction worker (David Hodo); the cowboy (Randy Jones); the Native American (Felipe Rose); the cop (Victor Willis). The eldest, and perhaps most outrageous, was Glenn Hughes, a former toll-collector now dressed as little more than a leather enthusiast whose get-up summed up pretty much where these People were coming from. And, boy, did it work – and not just at home: 'YMCA' topped the UK charts in late 1978, also selling over a million in the US, 'In the Navy' (1979) not falling far short of the same mark. There were other rollicking hits as well: 'Macho

Man' (1978), 'Go West' (1979 – the tune that also led to the outing of The Pet Shop Boys some years after) and 'Can't Stop the Music' (1980) – the latter from the largely forgettable musical of the same name.

The hype was over by the mid eighties (lead singer Willis even blowing his gay cred by marrying *Cosby Show* actress Phylicia Rashad), although The Village People continued to tour, hanging up their gear for the last time shortly before Glenn Hughes's death. By the time Hughes had been diagnosed with lung cancer, it was too late to save him: at his funeral in Manhattan his fellow Village People acted as pall-bearers.

Wednesday 7

Michael 'Smitty' Smith
(Beaverton, Oregon, 27 March 1941)
Paul Revere & The Raiders
(Brotherhood)

Michael 'Smitty' Smith was such a popular member of Oregon pop-rockers Paul Revere & The Raiders that the pin-up drummer had his own fan club. After a slow start with the lone 1961 hit 'Like Long Hair', The Raiders – Smith, Mark Lindsay (vocals), Paul Revere (keyboards), Drake Levin (guitar) and Mike Holiday (bass, replaced by Phil Volk) – became something of a sensation as America began to bite back at the British invasion. Between 1965 and 1969, the group scored a formidable run of hits, including 'Kicks', 'Good Thing' (both 1966) and

'Him or Me – What's It Gonna Be?' (1967), though Smith jumped from the bandwagon briefly to start a new project, Brotherhood, with Levin and Volk, before returning to The Raiders for their only US number one, 'Indian Reservation', in 1971. Retiring a couple of years later, Smith could only be tempted from his Hawaiian idyll by a Raiders reunion gig in 1997, three years after which he passed away from natural causes.

Golden Oldies #11

John Phillips
(Parris Island, South Carolina, 30 August 1935)
The Mamas & The Papas
(The Journeymen)

The principal songwriter for The Mamas & The Papas, John Phillips was the man behind such classic pop moments as 'California Dreamin'' and the US number one 'Monday Monday' (both 1966). A former member of The Journeymen, Phillips married singer (Holly) Michelle Gilliam, the pair joined by Denny Doherty and Cass Elliot as they moved from New York's Greenwich Village to join the beautiful people in Los Angeles. After a chart-busting two years, internal problems caused the group to split: a later reunion was hampered by Elliot's refusal to become involved and, of course, her subsequent death (-◄ *July 1974*). A perhaps ill-advised 'mark II' of the group then emerged in 1992, Phillips being joined by his actress daughter Mackenzie (another daughter, Chynna, found fame with Wilson Phillips around the same time).

Phillips – who also penned Scott Mackenzie's flower-power anthem 'San Francisco' and organized the 1967 Monterey Festival that propelled Janis Joplin and Jimi Hendrix to stardom – died from heart failure on 18 March 2001.

See also *Tim Rose (*❧ *September 2002).*

The Mamas & The Papas: John Phillips shares his last life-saver with Cass Elliott, Denny Doherty and Michelle Gillian

APRIL

Tuesday 3

Paul Peek

(High Point, North Carolina, 23 June 1937)
Gene Vincent & The Blue Caps
The Peekaboos

The Blue Caps were a bunch you really wouldn't want to take home to Momma, and Paul Peek, the gum-chewing, red-haired replacement for guitarist 'Wee' Willie Williams, looked every bit the part in Gene Vincent's gang. It was a far cry from his musical family's other affairs: his parents were both country musicians, while The Peek Sisters (his three older siblings) were a vocal troupe far too nice to be mixing with the likes of Vincent and co. Although he was not to last long in the singer's ever-changing line-up, Peek wrote a few songs before becoming one of The Blue Caps' posing 'Clapper Boys' with Tommy Facenda. After two years of relentless touring, Peek, a lover of the steel-pedal guitar, pursued a solo career, but met with less recording success on his own. His band – The Peekaboos – were a popular draw locally, however, and there was even time to reconvene with surviving members of The Blue Caps in the early nineties, before Peek passed away from cirrhosis of the liver.

See also *Gene Vincent (*✒ *October 1971); Cliff Gallup (*✒ *October 1988); Max Lipscomb (*✒ *March 1991); Willie Williams (*✒ *August 1999). Other Blue Caps Grady Owen (1999), Jerry Lee Merritt (2001) and Juvenal Gomez (2002), have also died.*

Friday 6

Charles Pettigrew

(Philadelphia, Pennsylvania, 12 May 1963)
Charles & Eddie
(Down Avenue)

Much was expected of sweet soul duo Charles Pettigrew and Eddie Chacon after a triumphant first year in 1992. As Charles & Eddie, their initial hit, 'Would I Lie to You?', was a Top Twenty success in their homeland, making it all the way to number one in Britain, as well as in fifteen other countries. The pair had met accidentally over a mutual love of Marvin Gaye's *Trouble Man* album, which Chacon was carrying on a subway train. Former jazz student Pettigrew, new to New York City, had previously been singing with a minor Pennsylvania act called Down Avenue. The huge success of Charles & Eddie's debut single and album, *Duophonic*, was misleading, however, since further hits proved surprisingly elusive. A second album, *Chocolate Milk*, inexplicably took three years to arrive – and bombed. The duo split soon after, Pettigrew going on to work with former Talking Heads/Tom Tom Club stalwarts Chris Frantz and Tina Weymouth. Having returned to Philadelphia, Pettigrew fought cancer for some time before dying at home.

Sunday 15

Joey Ramone

(Jeffrey Hyman – Forest Hills, New York, 19 May 1951)
The Ramones

'Hey ho! Let's go!' – and so they did . . . Beginning in 2001, the cartoon men of punk-rock cool began shuffling off into the afterlife as quickly as one of those two-minute wonders that bewitched us all back in 1976.

As The Ramones skulked off, the myth of the band was duly established: seen as something of a joke a quarter of a century back, the band are now looked upon as gods by the outsiders who followed their stumbling career. First away was Joey, the man who perhaps most epitomized the ethic of The Ramones: awkward-looking, a skinny misfit – and at six foot six a target for the other kids at Forest Hills High School. The former Jeffrey Hyman grew up in the tough township near Queens, New York, a big fan of those original UK 'punk rockers' The Rolling Stones, The Who and, uh, Herman's Hermits. A major hero was Keith Moon, this fact placing Hyman in the traps as The Ramones began to come together in 1974. Since his height clearly made it impossible for Hyman – now Joey Ramone – to sit behind the drums, the budding musician was offered centre stage by school/bandmates Johnny Ramone (John Cummings, guitar), Dee Dee Ramone (Douglas Colvin, bass – originally the band's studio manager) and Tommy Ramone (Thomas Erdelyi, drums – the second of many Ramones percussionists). The group had really arrived once word escaped of their twenty-minute residency sets at New York's legendary CBGB's. Where longer shows were demanded, The Ramones would merely repeat the set. (Joey: 'First time I went, there was sawdust over the floor and dogshit everywhere . . .')

Accompanying the punchy sets, the band's leathers, ripped denims and sneakers made for a disquieting look, even among the likes of contemporaries David Byrne, Deborah Harry, Richard Hell, Patti Smith and Tom Verlaine. Sire Records stepped in anyway and signed the band, who recorded their debut album, *The Ramones*, for just $6,000 early in 1976. The tunes were more 'garage' than 'punk', but the ethic was there in early standards like 'Now I Wanna Sniff Some Glue' and 'Beat on the Brat' (at 2'30", the second-longest track on the album). Remarkably, the record made

its way to US number 111! The band were nothing if not prolific: two further albums emerged in 1977, *Ramones Leave Home* and *Rocket To Russia*, the latter containing a first UK Top Forty hit in 'Sheena is a Punk Rocker' (the best they ever managed at home was sixty-six with 'Rockaway Beach'). Joey, in particular, was a huge believer in pop, encouraging a more classic sound for *Road To Ruin* (1978) and the Phil Spector-produced *End of the Century* (1980), crystallized in the latter's standout track '(Do You Remember) Rock 'n' Roll Radio?' (Indeed, Joey was the only Ramone to get along with the unpredictable producer – who was said to have pulled a gun on the band when

they attempted to walk out!) Ramones records after this were far less essential, though *Too Tough to Die* (1984) showed a solid understanding of the USA's new hardcore movement. By now, a rift between long-time members Joey and Johnny had dampened matters more than they'd realized: it seems Johnny stole Joey's girlfriend Linda in the early eighties – and then married her. This was not 'brudderly love', and the pair were never to make up.

As though somehow emphasizing his standing as a 'one-off', Joey Ramone never married nor sired any children. Always of questionable health, he'd been born sterile and was also susceptible to many other

The Ramones: Johnny, Tommy, Joey and Dee Dee – Gabba's greatest hits

'The closest I can describe is Jerry Lewis in *The Nutty Professor.'*

Mitchell 'Mickey Leigh' Hyman recalls watching his brother on stage for the first time ailments (the band's 'I Wanna be Sedated' (1978) was supposedly written after the singer's collapse from exhaustion following a strenuous tour). Joey's idiosyncratic behaviour was later put down to obsessive-compulsive disorder, bandmates often remarking upon his many quirks and rituals. Then, as The Ramones wound down, Joey Ramone was diagnosed with lymphoma in 1994, treatment for which remained hidden from the public eye but hampered much of his planned solo work. (The album *Don't Worry about Me* did emerge posthumously (2002), the bravery of its title enhanced by a touching version of Louis Armstrong's 'What a Wonderful World'.) Although known to have been a drug-user in his younger days, Joey's unexpected death on Easter Sunday 2001 in a New York hospital (supposedly after listening to U2) made him punk's first major icon not to die from an overdose or commit suicide.

Between The Bowery and 2nd Street – just behind the venue that used to be CBGB's – now lies 'Joey Ramone Place', officially renamed in November 2003.

See also *Dee Dee Ramone (*☛ *June 2002); Johnny Ramone (*☛ *September 2004)*

See also *Dee Dee Ramone (*☛ *June 2002); Johnny Ramone (*☛ *September 2004)*

Thursday 19

Olive 'Senya' Grant
(Kingston, Jamaica, 1958)
(The Wailers)

Olive Grant was a talented singer/songwriter with a melodic voice that led to her being taken under the wing of bass-player Aston 'Family Man' Barrett, the famed associate of Bob Marley & The Wailers, The Hippy Boys and Upsetters. Recording as 'Senya', her early songs were full of well-intentioned, conscience-pricking sentiment, as in 'Children of the

Ghetto' (1975), but were nonetheless well performed. Grant's best work is probably to be found on the ultra-rare 1980 album *Juvenile Delinquent*, where her maturity was now starting to show. She then made her first major stage appearance at the 1981 Reggae Sunsplash concert in London, re-jigged as a tribute to the recently departed Bob Marley (☛ *May 1981*).

Without ever really breaking through commercially, Olive Grant also worked as a restaurateur and raised a family, while involving herself in many charitable concerns throughout her life. All of which begs the question, who would want to take her life? In April 2001, this is exactly what happened: the singer was back at home in Kingston, planning further recordings, when she was attacked and stabbed to death in the street – a crime for which no one has ever been held accountable.

MAY

Friday 11

Marlon Brando
(Marlon Bryant – The Bronx, New York, 1978)
Sporty Thievz

The creative force behind New York rap unit Sporty Thievz, Marlon Bryant (who, for reasons best known to himself, adopted the name Brando) founded the group with ex-Wreckin' Crew members King Kirk and Big Dubez in Yonkers, New York, during 1997. The trio first gained notoriety for the 1998 album *Street Cinema*, but it was the TLC-baiting anthem 'No Pigeons' (a direct riposte to the girl group's hit 'No Scrubs') that attracted wider attention. Sporty Thievz were working on a second album when Brando was killed in what appeared to

be a deliberate hit as he left a late-night delicatessen. A minivan – which had already jumped a red light – mounted the kerb, ploughing into the artist and crushing his legs, before speeding away. Brando was pronounced dead upon arrival at South Bronx's Lincoln Medical Center. The rapper – whose assailants were never caught – had recently fathered his first child.

Friday 25

Brian Pendleton
(Wolverhampton, 13 April 1944)
The Pretty Things

It all began so well for The Pretty Things, the band courting even more media controversy than their musical and geographical rivals The Rolling Stones, that a comparable run of hits appeared to be a formality. Indeed, founder member Dick Taylor (guitar) was a close friend of Mick Jagger's, and had even played with the fledgling Stones until leaving to attend art school. Their former Dartford schoolmate Brian 'Yeti' Pendleton (rhythm guitar) was, meanwhile, already earning a crust at his father's insurance firm – but was only too glad to quit and grow his hair long (The Pretty Things were arguably the first band to make a point of doing this). The group was completed by the addition of Phil May (vocals/harmonica) and John Stax (John Fullegar, bass), a succession of drummers keeping the band on its toes. In early 1964, Fontana signed up one of the hottest new acts of the period, The Pretty Things breaking into the Top Ten with their second single, 'Don't Bring Me Down' (1964) and a debut album (1965). The band's sound and attitude was probably too 'punk' for the times, however, and they eventually lost out to the bluesier Stones. The group became big on the Continent, but thanks to poor management, they missed out on the British invasion of the USA. As the UK hits diminished in stature by 1966, Brian Pendleton decided to jump ship, returning to his job in the City as an underwriter. He passed away from lung cancer at the age of fifty-seven, but had managed to maintain sufficient contact with The Pretty Things (a going concern in one form or other well into the seventies) to benefit from the occasional royalty.

Monday 28

Tony Ashton

(Edward Anthony Ashton – Blackburn, 1 March 1946)

Ashton, Gardner & Dyke
The Remo Four
(Various acts)

Another respected British rock musician to succumb to cancer was Tony Ashton, a vocalist, musician and songwriter who served his apprenticeship as a member of The Remo Four. Ashton performed for many years as both singer and organist with the group as they supported The Beatles in Hamburg (where they were briefly to become the resident band). The nearest he came to stardom, however, was with bassist Kim Gardner and drummer Ron Dyke as the imaginatively named Ashton, Gardner & Dyke, who scored a one-off chart smash with 'Resurrection Shuffle' (1971). This trio was to last for three albums, Ashton also finding time to work with Deep Purple mainstays Jon Lord and Ian Paice, as well as assisting with solo work by both Paul McCartney and George Harrison. Ashton later turned his talents to painting and jingle-writing.

See also *Kim Gardner (☞ October 2001)*

JUNE

Wednesday 13

Marcelo Fromer

(São Paulo, 3 December 1961)

Titãs

Rhythm guitarist Marcelo Fromer was a co-founder and key member of Titãs, one of Brazil's foremost rock bands since the early eighties. Although the band – who wrote and recorded in Portuguese – found it hard to sell in English-speaking countries, they were multi-platinum artists at home and created enough interest for an MTV *Unplugged* session, the results of which became one of the band's biggest albums in 1996.

On 11 June 2001, Fromer, a keen jogger, left his São Paulo home for an early evening run. Because of an energy crisis, Brazil had at that time been restricting the use of electricity – and street lights were in the front line for cutbacks. As night descended, a motorcycle appeared from out of the gloom, hitting the guitarist, who cracked his head on the pavement; the motorcylist fled the scene seconds later. Two days on, Marcelo Fromer died, never having regained consciousness. A man of no small talent, he had recently been working on a biography of his friend the noted Brazilian international footballer Preto Casagrande.

Golden Oldies #12

John Lee Hooker

(Clarksdale, Mississippi, 17 August 1917)

He was the Delta-bluesman who quite literally showed two fingers to those who had gone before, his picking style becoming a trademark. John Lee Hooker was the Baptist minister's son who learned to play in the house of the Lord, before cashing in his chips with the music of the Devil. It's probably fair to say that Hooker crafted a style to which most major white rock artists owe something: he cut his first single in 1948 ('Boogie Chillen'), but was as influential – if not more so – in his final years. In 1999, Hooker celebrated his fiftieth year as a recording artist (having released over a hundred albums), the musician cited by the likes of Keith Richards, Van Morrison, Bono and Robert Cray as he picked up virtually every accolade/award going. Not bad for a guitarist who seldom strayed from two chords.

John Lee Hooker died from natural causes at his home in the Bay Area of San Francisco on 21 June 2001.

JULY

Tuesday 10

James 'Chuck' Cuminale

(Oswego, New York, 1952)

The Colorblind James Experience
(The Whitecaps)

As homage to his favourite blues guitarist, Blind Willie McTell, James Cuminale adopted the epithet 'Colorblind' when he played the coffeehouses of New York during the mid seventies. Cuminale – an accomplished vibraphonist as well as guitarist and singer – relocated to San Francisco where he made his first record with the short-lived Whitecaps in 1980. He was then on the move again, shifting back to the East Coast with the newly formed Colorblind James Experience for the release of a critically acclaimed debut album in 1987. Contrary to popular belief, Cuminale (for some reason now known as 'Chuck') never actually made his best-known relocation: the wonderful, John Peel-championed 'Considering a Move to Memphis' was merely speculation about how things might have turned out had he made his home in the town he'd already dismissed as unimpressive.

The Colorblind James Experience issued three further albums but never quite made the breakthrough, although popularity in Europe encouraged them to give up day jobs briefly for a tour in 1988. Cuminale died suddenly from a heart attack in the swimming pool of his home in Rochester, New York, in the company of his wife and sons.

Wednesday 11

Herman Brood

(Zwolle, The Netherlands, 11 May 1946)

Herman Brood & The Wild Romance
Long Tall Ernie & The Shakers
(Various acts)

One of Holland's most outlandish musicians, Herman Brood was a drug-dealer turned rock phenomenon who found success with a variety of acts – his main priority being to stay in the papers as long as possible. And this didn't stop at his death . . .

A distinctive art-school figure with his shock of black hair, pianist Brood joined The Moans, later to become rock-revival act Long Tall Ernie & The Shakers, before going on to sing with no lesser musicians than Van Morrison and John Mayall, until his dealing in LSD led to his imprisonment in 1968. Once back in the outside world, Brood's subsequent projects put him in the esteemed company of a post-Focus Jan Akkerman, and new-wave *femme fatales* Nina Hagen and Lene Lovich, with whom he starred in the 1979 movie *Cha Cha*. His main band were The Wild Romance, who found some commercial success, although even this was hampered by the singer's wayward behaviour with narcotics and prostitutes. Excluding time out by Brood for solo work, there were at least three line-ups of The Wild Romance.

Brood's death did not come as much of a surprise to those who knew the extremes to which this wilful artist was prepared to go. Even as late as 1999, he was still using drugs – the hard variety this time – and was charged with firearms offences. Then,

John Lee Hooker: The pick of Delta-bluesmen

on 11 July 2001, the singer took himself up to the roof of the Amsterdam Hilton and plunged to his death. It was no less than the media expected from a man who'd always sought that extra thrill and pursued publicity to the finish.

Sunday 15

Too Poetic

(Anthony Berkeley – Trinidad, 1966)

Gravediggaz

Also going by the name of Grym Reaper, Too Poetic was one of the main guys with hip-hop supergroup Gravediggaz, a New York-based unit comprising lead producer Prince Paul (Paul Huston), Frukwan (Arnold Hamilton – aka The Gatekeeper) and The Wu-Tang Clan's notorious RZA (Robert Diggs). The group were a part of the mushrooming horror/rap genre of the mid nineties that also threw up acts like The Flatlinerz and Insane Clown Posse. Poetic was born the son of a minister in Trinidad, growing up in Brooklyn, where he befriended the sprawling Stetsasonic unit in 1987 – from which the contacts that lifted the one-time homeless musician into rap's upper echelons were to accumulate. A first Gravediggaz album, *Six Feet Deep*, emerged in 1995: it sold well, unlike the second, *The Pick, the Sickle and the Shovel* (1997), which led to the act being dropped by Gee Street.

Too Poetic and his crew continued without a label, working on a third album, *Nightmare in A Minor* – but the artist's health was already worsening. With doctors virtually giving up on colon cancer they considered too aggressive for treatment, Poetic did admirably to survive as long as he did. Even as his body was losing the battle, Poetic managed a fourth album with Gravediggaz and a solo joint before his death.

Wednesday 18

Mimi Fariña

(Margarita Mimi Baez – Palo Alto, California, 30 April 1945)

Richard & Mimi Fariña

Mimi Baez – the youngest of three daughters born to Quakers, a Mexican scientist and his Scots wife – trained as a dancer and musician. One of her elder sisters was Joan Baez, whose more prominent career saw Mimi fall in with many of the folk artists of the early sixties – most notably Bob Dylan, who worked closely with Joan. Mimi's own musical career began in earnest when she started a relationship with noted author/musician Richard Fariña, whom she married at just eighteen, the pair embarking on a relatively successful career as a folk duo. For the next three years, the two partnerships almost rewrote the book on bohemia, their lifestyles much envied by folk's new followers. The pivotal moment for the Fariñas was a triumphant performance in the rain at the 1965 Newport Folk Festival – just hours before Dylan was heckled for plugging in. It all came crashing down on Mimi's twenty-first birthday, however, when her husband was suddenly killed in a motorcycle accident during her party (➤*April 1966*). After this unexpected tragedy, Fariña's career was fractured: moving to San Francisco, her varied interests led the singer into a variety of projects. In the early seventies, she became briefly involved, both musically and emotionally, with folk singer Tom Jans, but her increasing contributions to Richard Fariña tributes coupled with Jans's own desire to break into the mainstream caused them to part company. (It is widely believed that Jans found the constant references to a deceased legend intimidating and thus chose to branch out alone. Ironically, his own premature death was also

a result of a motorcycle accident (➤*March 1984*).)

A performance with her sister Joan and bluesman B B King at Sing Sing Prison awoke an interest in humanitarian affairs, leading to the creation of Fariña's Bread & Roses organization. Seeking to help those isolated by society, the foundation won a great deal of support from other artists and earned Fariña a good number of accolades. For twenty-five years, her life was largely dedicated to this cause. Fariña died at her home in California's Mill Valley, having fought lung cancer for two years.

Thursday 19

Judy Clay

(Judith Guions – St Paul, North Carolina, 12 September 1938)

(The Drinkards)

The day after the death of Mimi Fariña, the R & B world said goodbye to Judy Clay, a fine but ultimately ill-fated vocalist whose career was initially hampered by the USA's sluggishness in coming to terms with the race issue. Originally a gospel singer with The Drinkards, Clay teamed up with white artist Billy Vera, the pair becoming the first integrated act to make any kind of impact. Despite their fine records, because of some pretty backward decision-making in 1968 the duo could not be seen together on television and sales foundered. The same year, Clay did achieve a major hit with the classic 'Private Number', her version with William Bell riding into the UK Top Ten. Although she gained many credits as an anonymous backing singer to the likes of Ray Charles, this success was to be a one-off. As a solo artist, Clay was not to flourish as many of her contemporaries did, leading her to become embittered and her marriage to fail. In 1979, Judy Clay's career hit rock bottom when an album that had taken some considerable time to complete remained unreleased, added to which the singer was then diagnosed with a brain tumour which almost ended her life.

Perhaps understandably, Clay then returned to the gospel singing of her youth, where she would remain until her death from injuries sustained in a major car accident near her home.

Friday 27

Leon Wilkeson

(Jacksonville, Florida, 2 April 1952)
Lynyrd Skynyrd
The Rossington-Collins Band
(Various acts)

The bizarre life of Leon Wilkeson took its first unlikely turn when the 14-year-old bassist was approached by the sister of singer Ronnie Van Zant, who needed a new man for his fledgling blues rock band, The Collegiates. However, Wilkeson's parents were not keen for him to continue what was fast becoming a full-time hobby, to the detriment of his studies. After a stint with a local band, King James Version, Wilkeson – by now one of the state's best bass guitarists – once more took the call from Van Zant, as Lynyrd Skynyrd were signed to MCA. Wilkeson eventually became a fully fledged member of Southern rock's fastest-rising band, his stage gimmick of wearing outrageous headgear leading to his nickname 'the Mad Hatter'. By 1977, Lynyrd Skynyrd had reached their critical and commercial zenith, a series of gold albums now in their wake – but tragedy was just around the corner. As they prepared for the tour based on their album *Street Survivors*, band members Steve and Cassie Gaines, plus among those road manager Dean Kilpatrick, were killed in a horrific air crash that stands as one of rock's most significant. For Wilkeson,

a very fortunate survivor himself, the death that hit him hardest, however, was surely that of his old buddy Van Zant (☛ *October 1977*).

For the next few years, Leon Wilkeson (and other surviving Skynyrds) turned to other projects as they attempted to rebuild their lives. In 1980, three of the group reunited to form The Rossington-Collins Band (why the bassist's name didn't feature isn't known), although this failed to last beyond one album, the band members clearly still burdened by the effects of the tragedy. Amazingly, a new Lynyrd Skynyrd then emerged for the tenth anniversary of the crash, with Johnny Van Zant replacing his elder brother on vocals. Resultant tours were, according to Skynyrd diehards, fairly hit-and-miss affairs, although not without drama. During the early nineties, Wilkeson was allegedly woken by guitarist Ed King one night on the tour bus to find himself drenched in his own blood, an assailant having attempted to slit his throat as he slept. In the aftermath of this incident accusations flew between King and Wilkeson's wife Rhonda, with whom he had had something of a turbulent relationship. No charges were ever pressed, and this latest grisly chapter in Lynyrd Skynyrd's history remains unsolved. But, for Wilkeson, his time was running out: back at home during a swift break from a lengthy tour, the bass legend was found dead in his Ponte Verdra Beach hotel room. His death was put down on this occasion to natural causes.

Due to a legal agreement made with Ronnie Van Zant's widow on her husband's death that the band *must* contain at least three original members to be able to perform under the name, suddenly, in mid-tour, 'Lynyrd Skynyrd' were no longer viable! The solution came forward, however, in the shape of replacement bassist Evan Evans, who had at least played a few times in the band's earlier incarnation.

See also *Allen Collins (☛ January 1990).*

AUGUST

Thursday 2

Ron Townson

(St Louis, Missouri, 20 January 1941)
The Fifth Dimension
(Wild Honey)

At a time when black recording artists in the USA were trying to make serious political points, the biggest-selling popular soul act was, by contrast, the bright 'n' breezy Fifth Dimension. Formed as vocal troupe The Versatiles in 1966, the group – Ron Townson, Marilyn McCoo, Florence LaRue, Billy Davis Jr and Lamont McLemore – swept out of St Louis to international fame with a consistent run of Billboard hits between 1967 and 1973. Many dismissed their output as muzak, finding the heavily orchestrated harmonies a little trite, but there was no denying the commerciality of songs like 'Up, Up and Away' (1967), Laura Nyro's 'Stoned Soul Picnic' (1968) or the brace of 1969 chart-toppers, 'Aquarius' and 'Wedding Bell Blues'. By the seventies, the group concentrated more on placing one voice to the fore (usually McCoo's), which prompted Townson to work on his own project, Wild Honey, at the same time. Eventually, McCoo and Davis left to work as a duo, Townson, LaRue and McLemore keeping The Fifth Dimension alive on the tour circuit. The original roster was in place for a nineties reunion, but due to his failing health Townson dropped out permanently in 1999. For two years, he had battled kidney disease: two years on again, renal failure was to claim his life.

Aaliyah's wall: Speaks for itself

Saturday 25

Aaliyah

(Aaliyah Dana Haughton – Brooklyn, New York,
16 January 1979)

She was the teen star whose death
– not unlike her early history – will
continue to be at the centre of wild
rumour and speculation. Aaliyah was
the latest big name in music to be
killed in a light-aircraft crash, at just
twenty-two, her sudden passing a real
loss to the glamorous end of R & B in
the US.

Aaliyah is Arabic for 'highest, most
exalted one', and indeed the young
singer appeared to be something
beyond the ordinary. Brought up in
Detroit, Michigan, the spirit of Motor
City appeared to have brushed off on
the singer at a young age, although

a small amount of nepotism hadn't
gone amiss, either: Aaliyah opened a
Las Vegas show for her aunt, Motown
star Gladys Knight, aged just eleven
and within three years had a record
deal with her uncle's Blackground
label. But, before there could be
success, there was significant scandal:
a debut album, the aptly titled *Age
Ain't Nothing but a Number* (1994), was
produced by notorious R & B lothario
R Kelly, who was to face accusations
regarding his relationship with the
singer, then only fifteen. The rumours
had begun to spread when *VIBE*
magazine printed what it alleged was
a marriage certificate binding Aaliyah
(who it was claimed had falsified
her age) to the 27-year-old Kelly.
Significantly, neither party denied the
accusations and an annulment was
reportedly sought soon after. The
damage had been done, however,
Aaliyah changing labels and never
again working with Kelly (who faced

further charges of conducting under-
age liaisons a few years later). Finally,
Aaliyah's music became of greater
interest to the public than her personal
life, a sophomore album, the Missy
Elliott- and Timbaland-produced
One in a Million (1996), proving her
maturing talent. This much-improved
Atlantic release sold an impressive
8 million copies worldwide (although
admittedly a significant percentage
of these sales were posthumous),
Aaliyah now able to take her place at
R & B's top table unassisted. Within
the next three years, the photogenic
star could add modelling (for Tommy
Hilfiger) and movie acting (in the
martial arts flick *Romeo Must Die*)
to her increasingly impressive CV.
That year, Aaliyah also scored her
first US number-one single with 'Try
Again' (2000) from the film's soundtrack – which also made the UK's Top
Five – but a hungry public were now
awaiting Aaliyah's third album.

The self-titled record released at the end of July 2001 was certified gold after just two weeks on the shelves. A flagship single, 'We Need a Resolution', had surprisingly stuck at fifty-nine in the US, however, which prompted the singer's advisers and her label to arrange some glamorous promos for further singles culled from the album; with 'Rock the Boat' the next song selected, the belief was that any 'boat' was going to need some seriously blue water beneath it. The following month, Aaliyah and her entourage travelled with director Harold 'Hype' Williams for a location shoot on Abaco Island in the Bahamas. With some suitable footage in the can, the nine-strong entourage had a small party to celebrate before heading back to Miami. Just before 6.50 pm on the evening of 25 August, the small Cessna 402B took to the air – but something went wrong immediately. Within minutes, the plane began to plummet, crashing into a forest near Marsh Harbour and bursting into flames upon impact. The singer was one of six on board who were killed instantly, the remaining three dying shortly thereafter in hospital.

Back at home, the news of Aaliyah's death began to break. Fellow artists stopped performances to pay respect, while a giant billboard poster in Los Angeles promoting her album was transformed into a 'speaking wall' for tributes from desolate fans. Following the singer's funeral in New York six days later (during which twenty-two white doves were released into the sky), investigation into the crash began in earnest. In the aftermath of the disaster, two major facts came to the fore: the Cessna was overloaded by as much as 1,120 kg, with both luggage and passengers, the aircraft being designed to a carry a maximum of eight people. Most significantly, the pilot (who had a previous conviction for drugs offences) was found to have traces of cocaine and alcohol in his system.

(Luis Antonio Morales Blanes had allegedly also obtained his licence from Blackhawk Airways by deceptive means, having claimed hundreds of hours never actually flown. Aaliyah's parents finally came to an out-of-court settlement with the plane's operators in September 2003.)

Thus, with a sick irony, Aaliyah's sales *did* receive the boost they needed – though not for a reason anyone would have chosen or anticipated. Her eponymous album rallied to number one in America, while the single 'More than a Woman' gave her a posthumous chart-topper in Britain early in 2002.

Wednesday 29

Graeme Strachan

(Malvern, Melbourne, 2 January 1952)
Skyhooks

Just a few days on from the Aaliyah tragedy, a similar tale was dominating headlines Down Under. Graeme Strachan had formed rock band Skyhooks as a teenager with pals from Mount Waverly, guitarist and songwriter Greg Macainsh and drummer Freddy Strauks, in a group then called Frame. Although Strachan then dropped out to complete a carpenter's apprenticeship, the others tracked him down when Melbourne's Mushroom Records showed an interest in signing the band. In 1975, the glammed-up Skyhooks were Australia's biggest indigenous rock band, their first pair of albums both topping the charts (the first for a mind-boggling sixteen weeks), while their racy singles were often denied airplay by conservative Australian radio.

Then, after two years of solid touring, Strachan – nicknamed 'Shirley' for some reason – left in 1978 for a solo career and television work. An acknowledged 'rock god', his many fans were astonished to see the singer

reappear with first his own children's series about an animal pop group, then a popular lifestyle show on home improvements. The Australian media nonetheless went into meltdown after his tragic death in 2001. Strachan died when the Bell 47 helicopter he was learning to pilot was caught in a strong wind and crashed into Mount Archer near Kilroy West, Queensland. Original Skyhooks singer Steve Hill died from cancer four years later.

SEPTEMBER

Thursday 6

MC Carl Crack

(Karl Böhm – Swaziland, 1971)
Atari Teenage Riot

'Carl Crack' was the *nom de plume* of Karl Böhm, one of the founding members of critically acclaimed German techno activists Atari Teenage Riot. Born in Africa, Crack had been brought up in Berlin, where the music scene appealed greatly. But, with neo-Nazis seeming to have taken over the genre, ATR founder and former punk guitarist Alec Empire (Alexander Wilke) came up with a new strain in 1992 – which he called 'digital hardcore' – to combat the extreme right. With distinctive singer Hanin Elias, experimental-noise artist Nic Endo and MC Carl Crack by his side, ATR began to make waves beyond their homeland during the nineties. A large advance proffered by recording giants Phonogram was apparently duplicitously used by the band to set up Empire's DHR label, enabling Crack to issue his solo album *Black Ark* (1998). With all appearing to be running according to Empire's plan, disaster struck. A persistent drug-user, Carl Crack was beginning to suffer illusionment with the music industry, his career thereafter consisting mainly of television jingles and co-writing credits.

Doyle had married and settled into a life breeding dogs and cultivating a vineyard by the time of his diagnosis with throat cancer in 1999. He died two years later.

Thursday 24

Kim Gardner

(London, 27 January 1948)

Ashton, Gardner & Dyke
Pacific Gas & Electric
The Creation
The (Thunder)Birds

Journeyman rock bassist Kim Gardner was best remembered as an early cohort of future Faces/Rolling Stones guitarist Ronnie Wood. The duo were art-school pals who formed blues-based band The Thunderbirds with Alistair Mackenzie (vocals), Tony Munroe (guitar) and Pete McDaniels (drums). The group were signed by Decca, who, feeling that 'Thunderbirds' was too common a name in rock 'n' roll, decided in their infinite wisdom to rename them The Birds. Poor chart showings were exacerbated by legal threats from The Byrds regarding the name, and The Birds – who then tried 'Birds Birds' – split. Similar misfortune was to ensue when Gardner joined the over-hyped Creation in 1966, a band that also imploded two years on. With Ashton, Gardner & Dyke – a jazzier combo Gardner formed with keyboardist Tony Ashton and drummer Roy Dyke – the bassist at least enjoyed a major hit with 'Resurrection Shuffle' (1971).

Kim Gardner later toured with a number of acts, including US band Pacific Gas & Electric, before starting his own business as a restaurateur.

extreme health problems, both physically and mentally, his body finally giving out after a fatal overdose taken at his Berlin apartment. Atari Teenage Riot – who had taken a break while Crack received medical help – were now on hold indefinitely, Elias joining US industrial band Pigface.

OCTOBER

Saturday 13

Peter Doyle

(Abbotsford, Melbourne, 28 July 1949)

The New Seekers
(The Virgil Brothers)

A product of the talent-show boom of the early sixties, Peter Doyle was already a chart regular in Australia by the time he'd turned seventeen, a teen pin-up with cover hits such as Conway Twitty's 'Speechless' (1965). International success was not immediate, however, although his label

Sunshine had high hopes for The Virgil Brothers, the band Doyle joined in 1968. This act was marketed as an Australian Walker Brothers, but it was clear that they did not possess the charisma of their US peers. Despite making it on to British television (on a show hosted by Joe Brown), the trio broke up, leaving Doyle high and dry. Staying in Britain, he then joined The New Seekers, perhaps the UK's purest pop act, and success was to be spectacular, if brief, for Doyle. The two-girl (Eve Graham and Lyn Paul), three-guy (initially Doyle, Marty Kristian and Paul Layton) line-up scored 25 million worldwide sales, the biggest hits, 'I'd Like to Teach the World to Sing' (1971) and 'You Won't Find Another Fool Like Me' (1973), both topping the UK charts and selling a million apiece. (Their 1972 Eurovision offering, 'Beg, Steal or Borrow', tantalizingly finished runner-up, also stalling at UK number two.) But Doyle had left The New Seekers by the time 'Fool' reached the top, the restless singer already fed up with the fame game. Attempting a career back home as a singer/songwriter, Peter Doyle's lyrics suggested complete dis-

Gardner died in LA from cancer just months after former band member Tony Ashton (*May 2001*).

NOVEMBER

Saturday 17

Michael Karoli
(Straubing, Germany, 29 April 1948)
Can
(Sofortkontakt)

At nineteen, guitarist Michael Karoli was a decade younger than his colleagues when he joined influential German experimentalists Can in 1968. Karoli was then a music student in a class run by the band's leader, bassist and electronics whiz Holger Czukay, who, alongside Can keyboardist Irmin Schmidt, had himself studied under noted avant-garde composer Karlheinz Stockhausen (other members at this stage were woodwind player David Johnson and drummer Jaki Liebezeit). Karoli's playing was much more 'grounded' than that of his bandmates, creating something of a heady mix of styles. To many, Can never bettered their 1969 debut album, *Monster Movie*, but this was just the first of a hugely uplifting legacy of work. Primarily an album band, Can issued twelve studio collections for seven labels in just ten years, and even managed a token UK hit single with 'I Want More' (1976). With group personnel chopping and changing throughout the decade, Karoli – known as 'Miki' – found himself contributing vocals for *Soon Over Babaluma* (1974).

By 1977 Czukay, Can's Mentor, had left, but the band's output continued to be interesting, if no longer as ground-breaking as it had been. Attempted reunions were thereafter largely unsuccessful, though in 1999 the four original members regrouped to play an evening of solo material. Karoli – who had already issued a well-received solo album, *Deluge* (1983) – used the occasion to showcase his latest project, Sofortkontakt. Now living in France, Karoli yielded two years later to the cancer against which he had been battling bravely for some time. His influence is continually cited by musicians as diverse as former Teardrop Explodes leader Julian Cope and Monster Magnet frontman Dave Wyndorf.

See also *Reebop Kwaku-Baah (January 1983)*

Sunday 18

Scott Murray
(Melbourne, 16 January 1979)
28 Days

As nu metal and rap metal became the prominent commercial styles in rock during 2001, Australia's 28 Days had come through as something of a surprise package in a market dominated by the likes of US bands Limp Bizkit and Linkin Park. Although not sonically ground-breaking, 28 Days were rare in that they injected humour into an increasingly angst-ridden genre – a point reasonably well illustrated in the band's self-titled (and Australian chart-topping) first album proper (2001). Before the group could complete a second record, however, they lost drummer and founder member Scott Murray, who died from injuries sustained after he was struck by a speeding car as he returned from a group rehearsal. The percussionist – who had been engaged to be married – was remembered by his colleagues, who stated: 'Everything 28 Days do from now on and for ever is dedicated to Scott Murray.'

Saturday 24

Melanie Thornton
(Charleston, South Carolina, 13 May 1967)
(La Bouche)
Maria Serrano-Serrano
(25 November 1973)
Nathaly van het Ende
(The Netherlands, 1974)
Passion Fruit

In a year littered with aircraft disasters, one of the worst (although receiving relatively little coverage by the disaster-fatigued press), occurred near Zurich at the end of November. Young German-American singer Melanie Thornton had shaken off the Europop mantle of her past and was currently embarking on an independent career that had already seen an album reach the Top Twenty, while one song, 'Wonderful Dream', had been selected by Coca-Cola for their 2001 Christmas television campaign. During the previous decade, Thornton – discovered by Frank Farian while working in Germany – had been part of manufactured pop act, La Bouche (with partner Lane McCray), scoring a number-one single in Italy with 'Sweet Dreams' (1994). This 'dream' had lasted for five years but had been something of a disappointment to Thornton, who now found herself in Switzerland to promote her 'maturer' solo album – entitled *Ready To Fly* . . .

After a successful performance in Leipzig, Thornton drove to Berlin where she boarded Crossair Flight LX3597 to head back towards Zurich, where a further round of publicity, including a slot on TV3 show *Die Bar*, awaited her. Also on board were Maria Serrano-Serrano, Debby St Marteen and Nathaly van het Ende – a Dutch/German dance trio known as Passion Fruit.

With snow beginning to fall, visibility had become poor as the 97-seater Avro RJ100 aircraft circled to land in Zurich. Shortly after 10 pm, the plane lurched and hit the ground some five miles short of the runway, before crashing into woodlands. Of the thirty-three on board, twenty-four were killed in the accident – among them Thornton, Serrano-Serrano (whose birthday was to have been the following day) and van het Ende. A shocked St Marteen somehow walked away from the scene. Investigators into the crash described the aircraft as 'flying too low' and the pilot as being 'overtired'. Crossair shortly thereafter became Swiss International Airlines.

'Love one another.'

George Harrison's final words

George Harrison

(Hunt's Cross, Liverpool, 24 February 1943)

The Beatles
(The Traveling Wilburys)

Had he found himself in any band other than The Fab Four, George Harrison would surely have been the stand-out musician. A versatile and inventive guitarist, Harrison's less forceful personality meant that his public had to wait until his later career for his own voice to emerge. He was the quietest and probably the most genteel of The Beatles, and the first to find fulfilment away from music – his spirituality serving him until his final hour.

Harrison's start in life was suitably humble: he was the son of a Liverpool bus driver and was brought up in a terraced house with an outside lavatory. At school in the fifties, he was a surprisingly mediocre student, music replacing studies when Harrison turned fourteen. By now, Paul McCartney was a friend and, making one of his sager suggestions, recommended his pal purchase a guitar. Harrison became a huge fan of US rock 'n' roll (in particular Chuck Berry and Carl Perkins), easily mastering his £3 instrument to join John Lennon and McCartney's Quarry Men a year on. At the turn of the decade, the rise of the renamed group enabled the guitarist to give up his job as an electrician's apprentice: by 1962, The Beatles – now with Ringo Starr and Brian Epstein in their respective roles – were the most exciting thing happening in British music.

There are many music fans who maintain that it was George Harrison – despite notable competition from Clapton, Jones et al – whose distinctive lead riffs most informed rock music in the mid sixties. But in the studio, the quietest Beatle had constantly to bend to the wills of Lennon, McCartney and producer George Martin (who later admitted, 'I was beastly to George'). Harrison, buzzing with suppressed creativity, described the situation as 'like having diarrhoea and not being allowed to go to the toilet'. So, wedged between the twin behemoths of the band, Harrison was perhaps fortunate that *any* of his songs made the final cut. There were some great moments nonetheless, with 'Here Comes the Sun' (1969), which remains a much-covered pop standard; 'Taxman' (1966), Harrison's wittily ironic take on where the group's phenomenal success had left them financially; 'Love You To' (1966); and 'Within You Without You' (1967), which showed his burgeoning interest in Eastern mysticism. The most sublime, though,

George Harrison: Something in the way he moved us ...

was 'Something' (1969) – supposedly written for Harrison's first wife, Pattie Boyd (and originally offered to Joe Cocker). The song was described by John Lennon as 'the best on *Abbey Road*' while Frank Sinatra went as far as to call it 'the greatest love song of the last fifty years'. But, as though to remind Harrison of his status in the group, it stalled at number four in the UK charts as The Beatles as a unit slowly began to unravel.

Harrison came out of the split well: his acclaimed album *All Things Must Pass* (1970) was the first a solo Beatle was to issue, Harrison having stockpiled many songs during his time in the band. At the start of the following year, his 'My Sweet Lord' single (later the subject of a plagiarism suit) topped the charts for a month on both sides of the pond. Over the next few years, more compositions were to become major hits for others (Starr's 'Photograph', 1973) as well as himself ('Give Me Love (Give Me Peace on Earth)', 1973), while his 1971 concert in Bangladesh initiated the concept of staging music events for charity. Harrison's circle of friends at this stage was considered the epitome of cool, Eric Clapton, David Crosby and Bob Dylan being among his closest. Indeed, it had been Crosby who had introduced Harrison (and the other Beatles) to Ravi Shankar in 1966: while Lennon went on drinking binges with Harry Nilsson, his former bandmate adopted fully the spiritual, meditative lifestyle of the Maharishi Mahesh Yogi. It was then that Harrison experienced his first major health problem – he contracted hepatitis in 1976 – provoking a legal furore with A&M (who owned his Dark Horse imprint) when an album, *Thirty Three and 1/3*, could not be completed as a result. Having taken no part in the post-Beatles squabbling, the murder of John Lennon (◀ *December 1980*) shocked and saddened Harrison a great deal, his 'All Those Years Ago' hit (1981) instantly modified as a tribute to his departed friend. (Almost two decades after Lennon was shot, Harrison nearly suffered the same fate when crazed Michael Abram, thirty-four, invaded his Henley-on-Thames home on 30 December 1999. The intruder believed that he was 'on a mission from God' when he attacked the singer and his wife: unlike Mark Chapman, who had made a similar claim, Abram was acquitted of attempted murder on the grounds of insanity. Harrison – who apparently warded off his intruder with mantras – displayed great courage and humour, adding, 'I don't think he was auditioning for The Traveling Wilburys.')

During the eighties and nineties, George Harrison was to keep a lower profile, having remarried – Olivia Arias, in 1978 – and fathered his only son, Dhani. One of his other successful co-productions during this time was *Life of Brian*, the film made by his *Monty Python* friends for which Harrison's profitable film company, Handmade, provided financial backing. At the end of the eighties, Harrison

broke his musical silence with an album, *Cloud Nine* (1987), and its huge UK/US hit single 'Got My Mind Set on You'. As 'Nelson Wilbury', he was now also a member of supergroup The Traveling Wilburys, alongside Dylan, Tom Petty, Jeff Lynne (ex-ELO), and Roy Orbison, until the latter's death (◀ *December 1988*).

Although the singer remained philosophical about his condition, it came as a shock to Harrison's family, friends and followers when he revealed that he was suffering from throat cancer in 1998, growths shortly thereafter occurring in his lung. Despite going into remission, he suffered further metastasis two years later. But, armed with great faith and no fear of death, George Harrison bravely accepted his fate at the Los Angeles home of his friend Gavin de Becker, his last wish that his ashes be spread by the River Ganges. A final album, *Brainwashed*, emerged a year after the singer's death.

DEAD INTERESTING!

NUMBER ONES IN HEAVEN

When George Harrison's remastered 'My Sweet Lord' toppled Aaliyah's 'More than a Woman' in January 2002, it represented the first-ever example of one dead artist following another to number one in the UK.

For twenty-four years, his old buddy John Lennon had been the only artist to have had a posthumous chart-topper replaced by another of his own songs – when 'Woman' knocked 'Imagine' from the top – until a flurry of reissued Elvis hits bombarded the charts at the beginning of 2005 to mark what would have been Presley's seventieth birthday. The replacement of 'One Night' by 'Jailhouse Rock' thus repeated the feat.

DECEMBER

Saturday 15

Bianca Butthole
(Bianca Halstead – The Bronx, New York,
5 May 1965)
Betty Blowtorch
Butt Trumpet
(Various acts)

In 2001 the multi-tattooed Bianca Butthole – whose name was perhaps not the most glamorous of pseudonyms – appeared to be making something of a late bid for alternative stardom. During her early career the singer – formerly Bianca Halstead – had experienced a number of disappointments with other bands in her adopted Los Angeles before joining amusingly named punkettes Butt Trumpet in the early nineties. When this too went pear-shaped, the singer/bassist and bandmates Blare N Bitch and Sharon Needles (both guitarists) formed Betty Blowtorch, with drummer Judy Molish, in 1998. But, with a first album, *Are You Man Enough?*, just out on the Foodchain label, this band also began to fall apart. Butthole rallied, recruiting notorious L7 guitarist Jennifer Finch and a stand-in drummer and continuing to promote the record.

Following a gig with Nashville Pussy at the New Orleans El Matador Club, Butthole left the venue after partying into the small hours with brothers Brian and William McAllister. The trio jumped into Brian McAllister's 1986 Corvette and sped off into the night. Shortly after 5.30 am, the car reached a speed of 100 mph, spinning out of control across lanes on St Louis Route 110 near Kinner, before being hit full on by a car travelling in the other direction. The Corvette was nearly ripped in two and Butthole,

travelling in the passenger seat, was killed instantly. Brian McAllister – discovered to be more than three times over the legal alcohol limit – was found guilty of reckless driving and sentenced to twenty years in prison. One particularly sad footnote was that Butthole herself had been sober for ten years.

Sunday 16

Stuart Adamson
(William Stuart Adamson – Manchester,
11 April 1958)
Big Country
The Skids
(The Raphaels)

Almost a decade before grunge emerged, Stuart Adamson and his Big Country pals seemed single-handedly responsible for keeping the plaid-shirt industry afloat. Born in Manchester, the future guitar hero's family moved to the Crossgates area of Dunfermline, Scotland, where his fascination with rock 'n' roll began. Adamson had grown up listening to pomp and prog groups, but when punk and new wave came along, it gave him the impetus he needed to do it himself. In 1977, the dream because reality when The Skids – the band he'd formed with writer/singer Richard Jobson (plus bassist William Simpson and drummer Tom Kellichan, replaced by Rusty Egan in 1980) – received a call from Virgin following the release of their self-financed EP, *Charles*. Richard Branson's label then signed

the band to a hopelessly optimistic eight-album deal. By the third single, 'Into the Valley' (1979), the band was climbing the charts and appearing on *Top of the Pops*. With further records making the listings ('Masquerade' and 'Working for the Yankee Dollar' also hit the Top Twenty that year), it seemed perhaps the deal wasn't so far-fetched after all . . . until a rift between Adamson and Jobson caused the guitarist to leave after three albums to set up on his own. This, of course, proved a good move.

By the mid eighties, Big Country – Adamson (now on vocals as well as guitar), Bruce Watson (guitar), Tony Butler (bass) and Mark Brzezicki (drums) – were one of the UK's most successful bands. The first two albums, *The Crossing* (1983) and *Steeltown* (1984), both went platinum, while the singles chart was bombarded with anthemic hits like 'Fields Of Fire', 'In a Big Country' (also a US smash), 'Chance' and 'Wonderland' over a triumphant two-year period. But it was in performing live that Big Country's meshing of new wave and stadium rock was shown to best advantage, and their tours were always sold out. The cracks began to show with hackneyed third album *The Seer* (1986), however, which nonetheless still sold well (a single, 'Look Away', also gave the band their highest UK chart position). It was then that the workaholic frontman experienced the first of his break-downs: subsequent recordings were only to sell to Big Country's steadfast fanbase as the brush cuts and sleeve-less checked tops started to look very dated indeed.

'Back by noon Sunday.'
The note left by Stuart Adamson for his son Calum on 7 November 2001

Stuart Adamson (*right*) with Big Country pals Watson, Butler and Brzezicki: Checked out

Despite worldwide record sales of more than 10 million, Stuart Adamson descended into alcoholism, racked with manic depression even when he was off the bottle. In 1999, it appeared that Big Country might yet have something to offer when the band headlined Kosovo charity events in Scotland (where they were always welcome) and Kosovo itself. But this was a false dawn: after some time on the wagon, Adamson returned to drink and split the group – after eighteen years as a going concern. Despite forming a new act, The Raphaels, the singer – now living in Nashville, Tennessee – found that his world was falling apart. With his second marriage close to collapse, Adamson went missing twice in 1999 and 2001: on the second occasion, the mystery of his disappearance ended in tragedy. With his wife, Melanie Shelley, filing for divorce and a drink-driving charge hanging over him, Stuart Adamson decamped to Hawaii without informing friends or relatives. After over a month away, his body

was discovered in his room at the Best Western Plaza Hotel in Honolulu. The musician – heavily under the influence of alcohol – had died by his own hand, the verdict given as asphyxiation by hanging. Despite his success in America, no one involved in Adamson's inquest recognized the former star, although a wealth of international tributes soon followed news of the singer's death.

Tuesday 18

Clifford T Ward
(Kidderminster, 10 February 1944)
(Cliff Ward & The Cruisers)

His was the sunnier face of British folk, a lighter Nick Drake, perhaps. Clifford T Ward was an amiable Bromsgrove school teacher momentarily turned pop star when his ballad 'Gaye' surged into the UK Top Ten

during the summer of 1973. It had been something of an uphill struggle for the musician before his brief flirtation with fame: in 1963, his beat group Cliff Ward & The Cruisers won a Midland band contest and expectations were high. When success didn't happen, the singer held down a number of clerical jobs before taking up his post teaching English and divinity. Still working as a teacher, Ward then recorded for John Peel's Dandelion label. A debut album, *Singer-Songwriter* (1972), did not set any bells ringing but did enable Ward to graduate to the Charisma label. Already a substantial hit in Britain, 'Gaye' (1973) took him into the Top Five in, of all places, Brazil. A follow-up, 'Scullery', boasted an equally attractive melody but failed to have the same impact, mainly owing to its somewhat optimistic lyrical stereotyping at a time when the Women's Liberation movement was making waves. Changing fashions in general were to make it hard for Ward to sell further records.

Clifford T Ward embarks on perhaps the most 'DIY' promotional campaign ever seen in pop music

In 1984, his output (now mainly songwriting) was curtailed by the distressing news that he had multiple sclerosis. As the musician's condition deteriorated, friends such as Elton John and Sting raised money to finance his treatment, but it became clear that extending his life, rather than improving his condition, was the most that could be achieved. By the nineties Ward was effectively confined to his Worcestershire home: it is reported that the creation of his final album, *Julia and Other New Stories* (1994), had entailed the singer crawling to his home studio to work on it. To his many followers, Clifford T Ward's death from pneumonia, after years of suffering, arrived as something of a blessing.

Despite only ever achieving a fraction of the acclaim or success of the recently departed George Harrison (➤ *November 2001*), Ward could at least claim one thing in common with the ex-Beatle – his songs were also recorded by Ringo Starr and Art Garfunkel. Added to which, Ward's fine 'Home Thoughts from Abroad' (1973) was, remarkably, voted fourth in a 2002 BBC Radio poll of the best songs of the last half-century.

Lest We Forget

Other notable deaths that occurred sometime during 2001:

Chet Atkins (influential US country guitarist who worked with The Everly Brothers, Elvis Presley and Hank Williams Sr, among countless others; born Tennessee, 20/6/1924; lung cancer, 30/6)

Perry Como (much-loved US pop crooner whose 'magic moments' spanned more than five decades; born Pierino Ronald Como, Pennsylvania, 18/5/1912; lengthy illness, 12/5)

William Cooper Glenn (US founding musician of distinctive alt-rock acts The Rain Parade and Mazzy Star; born California, 1957; cancer, 16/3)

Ronnie Hilton (UK pop singer probably best known for his 'Windmill in Old Amsterdam' and its infestation of rodents – though he had far bigger hits; born Adrian Hill, Yorkshire, 26/1/1926; stroke, 21/2)

Tony Howard (UK journalist/manager of Jeff Beck, Hawkwind, The Pretty Things and T Rex; born London, 12/6/1939; he died after three weeks in a coma, 26/11)

Ernie K-Doe (popular US R & B vocalist who made #1 with 1961's 'Mother-in-Law'; born Ernest Kador Jr, Louisiana, 22/2/1936; liver failure, 5/7)

Jerry Lee Merritt (US rock 'n' roll lead-guitar great who played with many of the big names, in particular Jerry Lee Lewis, Carl Perkins and Gene Vincent & The Blue Caps; born 1934; heart attack, 4/5)

Fred Neil (highly regarded US folk/pop singer/guitarist/songwriter; born Ohio, 16/3/1936; cancer, 7/6)

O C Smith (popular US R & B/pop singer who had 1968 #2 hits in the US with 'Little Green Apples' and in the UK with 'Son of Hickory Holler's Tramp'; born Ocie Lee Smith, Louisiana, 21/6/1932; heart attack, 23/11)

Gareth Williams (UK singer/bassist/keyboardist with John Peel-favoured rock mavericks This Heat; born Cardiff, 23/4/1953; cancer, 24/12)

. . . and yet another who didn't

Rachela Williams, former US rock singer with Rock Solid, was widely reported to have died in a Los Angeles motorcycle crash in January 2001; she is, in fact, still working as an actress and fashion model.

For a complete list of fallen artists, visit
www.numberoneinheaven.com

2002

JANUARY

Wednesday 2

Zac Foley

(Zachary Sebastian Rex James Foley – Gloucester, 9 December 1970)

EMF

(Carrie)

Manchester may have had the lion's share of baggy talent, but it was an unlikely bunch of scallywags from the Forest of Dean who were to take the spoils in America. Formed in Cinderford in 1989, the 'Epsom Mad Funkers' were to become a household name within a year thanks to the infectious 'Unbelievable' – a single that just maybe defines the then musical landscape in the UK more succinctly than any other. EMF – James Atkin (vocals), Ian Dench (guitar), Zac Foley (bass), Derry Brownson (keys) and Mark Decloedt (drums) – followed this with the even better (though not as successful) 'I Believe' and an album, *Schubert Dip* (1991). But the biggest prize came from the US: 'Unbelievable', issued six months later

EMF, with Zac Foley (*third from right*): A band of substance

in America, stormed to number one, offloading nearly 2 million copies in the process. But, as with contemporaries Jesus Jones, who also conquered the States that summer, it was a never-to-be-repeated moment.

Foley was an integral part of the band in its eight-year history, a loud character who chugged out the chords – when he wasn't performing interesting party tricks with his foreskin and various pieces of fruit. A textbook hedonist, the bassist claimed to have been 'pumping himself full of any-

thing' by the time of the band's all-but-ignored second album *Stigma* (1992); by then, he'd have been oblivious to the fact that it wasn't happening any more for EMF. Despite one more theme-continuing hit with 'I'm a Believer' (successful mainly for the appearance of comics Reeves & Mortimer on the record) in 1995, the band ended as a going concern two years later. Foley's usage of substances did not, however.

After some particularly exuberant New Year celebrations, Zac Foley

'He was dicing with death.'

Dr Stephen Chan, coroner at St Pancras Hospital

failed to emerge from a paralytic state. A friend at whose house he'd been recovering had to kick the door in to reach him – but it was already too late. Foley – who had recently formed a new band, Carrie – was found deceased, the empty cans, vodka bottle and crack paraphernalia around him illustrating all too graphically the manner of his death.

Jon Lee

(Newport, Wales, 28 March 1968)

Feeder

(Temper Temper)

It just didn't make sense. After years on the periphery picking at scraps, Feeder had finally crashed British rock's executive dining rooms – and the future looked to be fine cuisine as far as the eye could see. Both their third album, *Echo Park* (2001), and its lead single, the shoutalong 'Buck Rogers', had taken the band into the UK Top Five, the album having sold close to 150,000 copies by the end of the year. As for founder member Jon Lee, he'd recently moved to Miami (ie, a far cry from Newport) and he and his wife were looking forward to the imminent arrival of a second son. Life surely couldn't have been better?

Former sprinter Lee had met fellow Feeder mainstay and pin-up Grant Nicholas (vocals/guitar) many years before, the pair bonding immediately and forming the band Temper Temper back in 1987 before playing together in London-based Reel – the group that would become Feeder. Via the small-ads magazine *Loot*, the pair found Japanese bassist Taka Hirose and slowly began to make inroads on the London rock scene. Recording on the small Echo label, the band rose to score their first bona fide hit with 'High' (1997): by the end of 1999, Feeder were chart regulars, their second album

'**Jon had such a taste for life – which makes this whole thing such a mystery to us all. But I obviously didn't know him as well as I thought.'**

Feeder frontman, Grant Nicholas

Jon Lee (*centre*), with fellow Feeders Grant Nicholas and Taka Hirose: The comedown after the high

proper hitting the Top Ten. As fame beckoned, the band travelled the world and Lee met Brazilian model Tatiana Englehart while touring America in 1998. The romance blossomed; the couple wed and planned a family – but the pressure, like Feeder's fame, was gradually building a head of steam. With Feeder about to make it big, Lee barely had time to spend with his wife and baby son: when he discovered that Englehart was pregnant with their second child late in 2001, the drummer began to find it impossible to balance the needs of his young family with his commitment to the band. Lee hid his anxieties from virtually everyone – until it was too late. Shortly after 6 am on 7 January 2002, Grant Nicholas

took the call from Jon Lee's brother: his friend and bandmate of seventeen years was dead, having hanged himself at his Florida home.

Three years later, Nicholas – whose band remains highly successful, now with Mark Richardson on drums – told the *Sunday Times*, 'There are things I know, gruesome details of how he did it. At first I couldn't sleep, or do anything. I worked so intensely, the engineers thought I was having a breakdown . . . But Jon's death has made me more focused, more confident. Maybe more grateful.'

Tuesday 8

David McWilliams
(Cregagh, Belfast, 4 July 1945)

Northern Irish singer/songwriter David McWilliams gave the world at least one classic song but his career was to be hampered by one crucial factor: his manager was a shareholder of Radio Caroline.

McWilliams was born in Belfast, a keen footballer who might have made it professionally had he not become obsessed with music, and especially with the songwriting of Buddy Holly. Despite his background, McWilliams more closely resembled an outlaw from the Wild West, with his three-quarter beard and dusty Stetson, when he first created a stir in 1967. While a debut album, *David McWilliams Sings Songs by David McWilliams*, fared well on Major Minor, its follow-up reached UK number twenty-three – largely because of the inclusion of the genuinely haunting 'The Days of Pearly Spencer', a song about a homeless man McWilliams had befriended. This would surely have been a major hit if it hadn't have been for a ban by the sniffy BBC, who – despite having poached half their DJs from Radio Caroline – didn't want to be seen associating with the pirate radio station that was playing the track incessantly. McWilliams had to wait a quarter of a century to see Marc Almond's version of the song claim its rightful place in the UK Top Five.

As it was, McWilliams's songs were to remain a little-known treat, the nearest he came to a hit single thereafter being with 'By the Lights of Cyrian' in 1977. Almost unheard from in his last years, David McWilliams died from natural causes in County Antrim.

David McWilliams: In the days of pirate sponsors ...

FEBRUARY

Saturday 2

Paul Baloff
(Oakland, California, 25 April 1960)
Exodus
(Piranha)

Singer Paul Baloff can hold a serious claim to be a pioneer of thrash metal – although, ultimately, it was others who were to collect on his investment. Forming Exodus in 1981, Baloff found himself at the core of California's burgeoning Bay Area metal scene, alongside bands such as Testament and Death Angel. Exodus – Baloff (vocals), Gary Holt (guitar), Kirk Hammett (guitar), Geoff Andrews (bass) and Tom Hunting (drums) – began solidly but were to lose out when Hammett left to join the band that was to become the biggest of the genre, Metallica. After recording the acclaimed first album, *Bonded by Blood* (1985), Baloff became worn down by infighting and left Exodus to form Piranha, but the glory days were now behind him. Exodus, with Baloff, reunited to tour in 1997 and issue the group's final offering, *Another Lesson in Violence*.

Paul Baloff's sudden death from a stroke came as an enormous blow to the thrash community as a whole, although his health had never been particularly good. His life support was switched off when he failed to emerge from a coma.

Waylon Jennings

(Littlefield, Texas, 15 June 1937)
(The Outlaws)
(The Highwaymen)
(Old Dogs)

Had he not passed away in 2002, Waylon Jennings would undoubtedly have earned the *Number One in Heaven* award for rock 'n' roll's closest ever call. While he certainly shouldn't primarily be remembered for his role in the passing of a legend, the careers of Waylon Jennings and Buddy Holly will always be inextricably linked in other ways. Jennings was born during the Texas 'Dust Bowl' storms of the thirties (documented closely by one of his heroes, Woody Guthrie), his singing and guitar-picking appealing to local radio producers, who were keen to give him airtime. The early rock 'n' roll circuit saw him interchange slots with Holly and Roy Orbison as the state's key emerging talents. Holly was the first to make it big; after his own flurry of successes, the bespectacled rocker then became the first to produce Jennings. Although this didn't provide the latter with any gold discs, Holly was keen to invite him along as touring bass (despite the fact that it was not his instrument), The Crickets having gone their separate ways: the tour in question was the Winter Dance Party of 1959. As the weather worsened and the tour bus gradually began to fall apart, Holly, Jennings and others decided to fly on to the next venue in North Dakota. With the Big Bopper suffering

particularly badly, Jennings gave the hefty star his seat on the hired Beechcraft – and the rest, as they say, is rock 'n' roll history.

It was to take many years for Jennings to come to terms with the horrific accident that took the life of Holly, Richardson and Richie Valens (*Pre-1965*) – particularly in light of that infamous pre-flight joke he shared with Holly. But Jennings was to return in some style a few years later, having ditched rock 'n' roll for an 'outlaw' sound set to become his trademark (as it would for empathetic performers Johnny Cash, Kris Kristofferson and Willie Nelson, with whom Jennings was to form The Highwaymen in later years). Relocating to Phoenix, Arizona and then Nashville, Tennessee, the guitarist steeped himself in good country vibes and began to churn out the hits on A&M (most of which appeared on the 1970 album *Don't Think Twice*), although his insistence on having his own band was not looked upon well by the labels of Nashville who presumably didn't like paying other musicians. Despite his relative success, Jennings's life at this time seemed permanently hampered by problems: the musician was addicted to amphetamines and in enormous debt, with various of his marriages collapsing around him (he had four wives in all). In 1972, a bout of hepatitis almost ended his life.

The turning point came shortly after his recovery with a new contract that satisfied Jennings's desire to tour properly. With Nelson, Jennings formed the semi-permanent Outlaws (with singer/producer Tompall Glaser), the duo issuing some great,

rough-hewn country recordings during the seventies and eighties. Waylon Jennings managed sixteen country chart-toppers over the years and also picked up a pair of Grammys into the bargain – something even he might not have expected at the start of the seventies. Throughout his career the hugely respected Jennings was to befriend musicians from across the genres: during the nineties, for instance, he became close friends with thrash-metal heroes Metallica (in whose music he discovered a similar integrity to his own) and also recorded with Los Lobos. In a final foray into supergroupdom, he recorded an album, *Old Dogs* (1998), with country pals Bobby Bare, Jerry Reed and Merle Tillis.

Several months after his worsening diabetes required the amputation of his left foot, Waylon Jennings breathed his last in his sleep and the world whispered goodbye to one of country music's wildest, wittiest exponents. Presumably, Jennings and Holly can at last see the funny side of that throwaway comment all those decades before.

Mick Tucker

(Harlesden, London, 17 July 1949)
The Sweet

He wasn't the main attraction in Britain's most glamorous pop act of the early seventies, but perhaps that's the way Sweet drummer Mick Tucker preferred it. The band, in which the characters of the other members were more readily identifiable – Brian Connolly (vocals/silver stack heels), Steve Priest (bass/'ladyboy' make-up) and (finally) Andy Scott (guitar/spooky glances) – had been Wainwright's Gentlemen and Sweetshop before settling on the

'I hope your plane crashes!'

Waylon's cheery banter of 2 February 1959

shortened name that was to serve them so well between 1971 and 1978. As part of the classic band line-up, Tucker enjoyed massive UK hits from the poppy 'Co Co' (1971) and 'Little Willy' (1972) to the anthemic, Chinnichap-composed metal bubblegum of 'Ballroom Blitz' and the number one 'Blockbuster' from an all-conquering 1973 in which they also cracked the US market.

An acrimonious split with singer Connolly in 1979 was a crippling blow from which The Sweet were not to recover. Relations became so bad that two versions of the band toured the nostalgia circuit during the mid nineties.

But, with Priest now a session player in the United States, Scott continues to use The Sweet's name, some years after Connolly's tragic death (➤ *February 1997*) and now that of Mick Tucker. Always the quiet one, Tucker passed away after fighting leukaemia for some years and in spite of a bone-marrow transplant it was hoped might save him. In the words of Priest – in a piece of overstatement that might just have caused his friend of thirty years to blush – 'He was the best drummer England ever produced.'

MARCH

Friday 1

Do'reen

(Doreen Waddell – Southend, Essex, 1966)
Soul II Soul
The KLF

Around 1990, all looked rosy for young British soul singer Doreen Waddell – better known in the music world as Do'reen. The vocalist had been plucked from relative obscurity to work with two of the UK's big-

Marc Moreland (*right*) with Wall Of Voodoo: The 'mess' was calculated

gest-selling acts. With the Jazzy B-led London dance collective Soul II Soul, Do'reen shared lead vocals with Caron Wheeler on the international chart-topping album *Club Classics Volume 1* (1989), although it was Wheeler who sang on the number-one single 'Back To Life'. Then there was The KLF, the Bill Drummond/Jimmy Cauty project that spawned a number of huge hits worldwide, including 'Justified and Ancient' (1991) – the album version of which also featured Do'reen's voice.

Doreen Waddell – who had reverted to her given name – was to experience harder times, however, the vocal sessions having dried up as mainstream tastes moved away from the club sound during the nineties. On the morning of 1 March 2002, the former star was apprehended at a Sussex branch of Tesco on suspicion of shoplifting: Waddell panicked and ran from the supermarket's fire exit on to the A27 Shoreham bypass where she was struck three times by speeding vehicles. The singer died that afternoon in hospital, but it took a further three days before her body could be identified. Goods from the store, including clothes intended for Waddell's 4-year-old son, were found strewn across the tarmac.

Marc Moreland

(West Covina, California, 1958)
Wall Of Voodoo
(Marc Moreland Mess)
(Various acts)

Marc Moreland was a child of rock's sexual revolution; he loved Alice Cooper and Iggy Pop with their giant, spiked hair and extravagant make-up. That he was also a damn fine guitarist as well was a bonus to all those who loved his look as he stalked about on stage. Moreland had played in a number of California schlock bands before he and his bass-playing brother Bruce formed the near-legendary Wall Of Voodoo with equally charismatic singer/keyboardist Stan Ridgway, Charles Gray (synth) and Joe Nanini (drums – who died in December 2000). Over the course of a decade, the band released several studio albums for IRS, but never quite achieved the impact they deserved, despite coming mighty close with *Call of the West* (1982): the 1983 hit single 'Mexican Radio' was a Moreland composition. WOV disbanded in 1989.

A big fan of Johnny Cash, Moreland emulated more than just his hero's guitar-playing. According to his brother, the musician drank heavily throughout his life, enjoying the rock 'n' roll lifestyle to the full: 'Everyone thought *I* was going to die, but I came through – and Mark just continued drinking . . .' Eventually, the guitarist required a liver transplant, but the operation was not successful: without health insurance, he had travelled to Paris in order to seek treatment, but his body rejected the liver soon after, shutting down five days later. By the end of his life, Moreland had been recording again (his own solo album, as Marc Moreland Mess), his Fender Flying 'V' never far from his side.

Friday 15

Marshall Leib
(Marshall Leibovitz – Northridge, California, 26 January 1939)
The Teddy Bears
The Hollywood Argyles
The Moondogs

It requires a stern constitution to take on Phil Spector, as many have found to their cost over the years: Marshall Leib was one of the few who came away successfully. Back in the fifties, the athletic, good-looking Leib – formerly a member of short-lived rock 'n' rollers The Moondogs – was the guitarist with teen-pop fly-by-nights The Teddy Bears, along with Phil Spector (multiple instruments) and singers Carol Connors (Annette Kleinbard) and Harvey Goldstein. Inspired by the epitaph on Spector's father's gravestone, the group came up with 'To Know Him is to Love Him' (1958), funding the recording themselves. Astonishingly, the record was picked up by the Dore label, and rocketed to the top of the charts. By Christmas, it had sold over a million copies. Due to

contractual failings The Teddy Bears issued only two more records with Dore, but it was revealed years later that Leib and Connors (by then a successful songwriter) were owed a great deal of money in royalties by Spector. They sued him in 1996 – and won.

Leib had gone on to play with The Hollywood Argyles (the band hastily formed by singer Gary Paxton when his 'Alley Oop' hit number one in 1960) and also recorded with Duane Eddy before setting up his own Marsh label. He died from a heart attack at the age of sixty-three.

Tuesday 26

Randy Castillo
(Albuquerque, New Mexico, 18 December 1950)
Ozzy Osbourne
Mötley Crüe
(Various acts)

Mötley Crüe's worst days of excess were well behind them by the time drummer Randy Castillo joined the ranks in 1999. The departure of Tommy Lee (and his huge kit) may have ended an era for a band synonymous with mayhem, but there were still notorious Vince Neil (vocals), Mick Mars (guitar) and the legendary Nikki Sixx (bass) to hold the fort for all things debauched. Castillo offered something more spiritual to the band, although he could hammer out a rhythm or two as well, having served time with Crüe's natural mentor Ozzy Osbourne for eight years – Lee having introduced the pair in 1985. Castillo played with many other hard-rock acts, including The Wumblies (his first group), The Motels and also the band of former Runaway Lita Ford. Crüe had just issued their first album in some time, *New Tattoo* (2000), when Castillo fell seriously ill with a stomach complaint and had to pull out of a

major tour. While the band promoted the album without him, Castillo began working on a project with Alice In Chains bassist Mike Inez. As this began to gain momentum, the drummer started to experience swellings and pain in his neck: he was diagnosed with a carcinoma, from which he was not to recover. Despite aggressive radiotherapy, Randy Castillo went into relapse: he died in his sleep at the Cedars-Sinai Hospital.

See also *Razzle Dingley (* *December 1984)*

Joe Schermie
(Madison, Wisconsin, 12 February 1946)
Three Dog Night

Between 1969 and 1974, they were America's biggest-selling singles band. Originally produced by Beach Boy Brian Wilson, Three Dog Night eventually pulled away on their own to shift more than 50 million records in a career that took in three different lead singers, Danny Hutton, Cory Wells (Emil Lowendowski) and Chuck Negron. The band mainstays were Mike Alsup (guitar), Joe Schermie Jr (bass), Jimmy Greenspoon (keyboards) and Floyd Sneed (drums) – all in place as Three Dog Night racked up eighteen consecutive Top Forty hits, including number ones with 'Mama Told Me Not to Come' (1970), 'Joy to the World' (1971) and 'Black and White' (1972).

Exhausted by all the touring, Schermie left the band in 1973, going on to play with KATT but refusing to join a TDN reunion in 2000. It transpired he had been extremely unwell, news of which only reached his former colleagues on his death from a heart attack, on the same day as Castillo.

APRIL

Fad Gadget

(Frank Tovey – London, 8 September 1956)

'Fad Gadget – is it a group? Is it a person?' His was a name to conjure with while perusing the *NME*'s indie charts during 1981 and 1982. In reality, Gadget was plain old Frank Tovey, a musician, synth-player and perform-ance artist revered by many within the industry, yet barely known by the world at large. Arriving at around the same time as fellow electronica enthusiasts Cabaret Voltaire, Clock DVA and the pre-pop Human League, Gadget gave a London slant to a genre for some reason dominated by acts from Sheffield. Gadget's first single, 'Back to Nature' (1979), emerged on the Mute label, whose owner Daniel Miller was a huge fan of the musician's off-beat work, as indeed were later, more famous stablemates Depeche Mode and Yazoo. There were no hits, but milestones in Tovey's *oeuvre* include the singles 'For Whom the Bells Toll' (1983), 'Collapsing New People' and 'One Man's Meat' (both 1984). He issued eleven albums in twelve years with the label, titles like *Easy Listening for the Hard of Hearing* (1984, after which time he reverted to his given name) illustrating that the man didn't really take himself as seriously as some may have thought. Frank Tovey died suddenly from a heart attack.

Fad Gadget: Bound to entertain

'I'm currently writing new material, so be patient my little rodents!'

Frank Tovey's message to his fans, 2 April 2002

Layne Staley

(Kirkland, Washington, 22 August 1967)

Alice In Chains

(Mad Season)

Layne Stanley: The lead 'Chain' proved the missing link

Unbeknownst to anyone, Layne Staley – for more than a decade a legend of grunge/metal – died alone at his home.

Obsessed with glam rock since he was a kid, drummer turned singer Staley sought the most outlandish glam-metal name for his band, regardless of what kind of music they were set to make. Having met guitarist and principal songwriter Jerry Cantrell, Staley began Alice In Chains in 1987, recruiting bassist Mike Starr and drummer Sean Kinney as the band became something of a hot ticket on the Seattle grunge circuit. Early EPs *Sweet Alice* (1989) and the prophetic *We Die Young* (1990, by which time AIC had signed to Columbia) created a sound a good deal more metal-affiliated than the punkier Nirvana or Mudhoney, but proved before long that there was indeed sensitivity in their work. *Dirt* (1992) was, on the surface, a heavily guitar-based album, yet Staley's lyrics touched on the alienation and severe drug addiction that were to affect his life irreparably. In America, Staley and Alice In Chains were cleaning up (at least in a commercial sense), wowing rock fans with their performances at the Lollapalooza Festival and then scoring a pair of number-one albums in the reissued *Sap/Jar Of Flies* (1994) and *Alice In Chains* (1995 – often called 'Tripod' in deference to the distinctive three-legged dog that adorns its sleeve); in Britain, the band achieved hit singles with the deeply introspective 'Would' and 'Them Bones' (1993). At around the same time, Staley played with grunge supergroup Mad Season and was also the artist behind the striking sleeve design for their *Above* album

(1995). But, by 1996, Staley's regular disappearances and on/off problems with heroin had reached the point where his main band were unable to tour to support their records: the only live work undertaken at this point was an MTV *Unplugged* session that showed Staley to be in very poor condition indeed. Finally, four gigs at which the band opened for glam giants Kiss proved to be the last in which Staley was to appear with Alice In Chains, or indeed anyone . . .

Recording just two more songs with his group, Layne Staley began to fall apart after the death of his girlfriend Demri Parrott from a drug-related bacterial infection on 29 October 1996. Many of his acquaintances believe that the singer gave up after this tragedy, his world spiralling into overwhelming depression and worsening addiction. The final five years of Staley's life were spent mainly as a recluse, his death in

2002 a sad, degrading end for a man who had achieved a great deal. With his neighbours complaining of a smell emerging from his condominium around 19 April, authorities broke in to find the former singer's body in a state of considerable decomposition and surrounded by drug paraphernalia – he had died from an injection of heroin and cocaine. Staley could be identified only by his dental records.

The singer was remembered by his loyal friend Cantrell, who dedicated a solo album to Staley shortly after his death: similarly, the band Staind included the track 'Layne' on their *Fourteen Shades of Grey* album (2003). Grunge fans were quick to link the supposed date of his death to that of Kurt Cobain (➤ *April 1994*) – believed to be eight years to the day earlier.

See also *John Baker Saunders (➤ January 1999)*

Lisa 'Left Eye' Lopes

(Philadelphia, Pennsylvania, 27 May 1971)

TLC

With US R & B fans still mourning the death of Aaliyah, the sudden loss of another female icon came as perhaps an even greater blow. The life of Lisa Lopes, filled as it was with great success, came to an end when she visited Honduras on missionary work, her new image a far cry from that of the tough cookie seldom out of the papers during the previous decade.

In 1991, Lopes answered the call from Atlanta teenager Crystal Jones who wished to start a hip-hop/R & B unit she was calling 2nd Nature. Iowa singer Tionne Watkins had been the first to respond, with Lopes – having arrived from Philadelphia with little more than a keyboard and a few dollars – soon joining them. Jones had to suffer the indignity of being sacked from her own project at the behest of early manager Peri 'Pebbles' Reid and record label LaFace, to be replaced by former Damian Dame dancer Rozonda Thomas. The name TLC (an acronym for 'tender loving care') was selected to reflect the girls' nicknames, respectively T-Boz, Left Eye and Chili. (Lopes's sobriquet derived either from an admirer's comment on the beauty of her left eye, or the suggestion that she habitually replaced the left lens of her stage glasses with a condom – you can decide.) As the group became an instant smash in the US, it became obvious that Lisa 'Left Eye' Lopes was very much the creative talent, her sassy songwriting and self-performed raps making her the focus of TLC. Their sound inevitably dubbed 'New Jill Swing', TLC's first album, *Ooooh ... On the TLC Tip* (1992), sold impressively, but *CrazySexyCool* (1994) broke new records, shifting an astonishing

11 million copies in the US alone and earning one of the RIAA's first diamond awards. On top of this, TLC enjoyed an unbroken run of hit singles, the second album spawning the number ones 'Creep' and 'Waterfalls', as they rose to become the biggest female group since The Supremes. But, thanks mainly to Left Eye, keenly protected by TLC's management, the girls were soon in debt to the tune of $3.5 million.

On 2 September 1993, Lopes filed a lawsuit against boyfriend Andre Rison (wide receiver with the Atlanta Falcons) for alleged assault. Rison denied the allegations and the couple attempted to make up, but matters were about to grow more serious.

During another squabble in 1994 the singer – who had been battling alcoholism since her teens and was inclined to mood swings – took Rison's designer sneakers and set fire to them in the football star's bath. Within an hour, Rison's entire $2-million mansion was ablaze: firefighters called to the scene could do nothing to save the property. Lopes was charged with first-degree arson, ordered to undergo rehabilitation and serve five years' probation. TLC's huge debts came about because of her spiralling insurance payments, though, remarkably, she and Rison were reunited later in the decade.

But none of these events seemed to faze Lopes, as she and TLC rallied to score another multi-platinum album,

Lisa Lopes: She had her eye on many during her time

Fanmail (1999), which once again bore two Billboard chart-toppers with the familiarly man-baiting 'No Scrubs' and 'Unpretty'. But the increasingly wilful Lopes (who had by now started her own production company) was feeling the restrictions of life within a group. In November, such was her belief that she was carrying TLC, Lopes penned a letter to *Entertainment Weekly* challenging both of her bandmates to record solo albums which they would then issue as a three-CD set. An interesting idea but, needless to say, one that didn't get off the ground – not helped by Lopes's disappearance without trace the following summer. She re-emerged with a new boyfriend in tow (though this was not to last) and a UK number one with Mel 'Sporty Spice' C, 'Never Be the Same Again', drawn from her solo album *Supernova* (2001), which was not issued in the US. As though to distance herself further from TLC, Lopes then sought a tougher image, signing with Suge Knight's Death Row label as NINA ('New Identity Non-Applicable', apparently).

Lopes had just begun work on both a second solo album and a new set with the partially reconciled TLC when she was killed in a road accident in Jutiapa, Honduras. The Mitsubishi sports vehicle, driven by Lopes, had been carrying eight passengers (including her sister) from the jungle to a natural-medicine compound. As Lopes attempted to pass another car, a truck approaching from the other direction caused the singer to veer drastically to avoid a collision. According to eyewitnesses, the van hit two trees and flipped several times before coming to rest. While no one else suffered more than superficial injuries, Lopes was killed outright, having suffered blunt trauma to her skull and chest. Her label's spokesperson described the singer – who had recently adopted a young girl called Snow – as having recently undergone something of a spiritual epiphany and enjoying the

best time she'd known for some years. Her funeral in Atlanta inevitably drew fans in their thousands. A shattered TLC carried on as a two-piece, though the dramatic downturn in their commercial fortunes perhaps tells its own story.

MAY

Saturday 4

Juliette Valentine
(Juliette Williamson – California, 1952)
The Chicago Brother & Sister Blues Band

It was a classic, macabre tale of jealousy and murder, yet it all took place in 2002 – and in broad daylight. Juliette 'Valentine' Williamson was the gritty-voiced black singer/bassist of San Francisco blues trio The Chicago Brother & Sister Blues Band. The group hadn't recorded a great deal, but remained massively popular in live performance. A regular feature of such gigs was the friction between Valentine and her boyfriend, guitarist/multi-instrumentalist Bruce 'The Judge' Brooks. The latter had been in love with Valentine from the day he had met her – when she had been working as a secretary – wooing her into dating him by teaching her to play bass, but the relationship was to prove volatile, violent and ultimately

tragic. Fuel to the fire was provided by Brooks's heavy drinking: by 2002, he was downing a gallon of red wine a day. Although many guest musicians came and went from the ranks of Chicago Brother & Sister, the man usually caught in the middle of the constant infighting was veteran drummer Francis Clay.

On the evening of 4 May 2002, a performance at Frisco's famed Pier 41 was brought to an abrupt halt by a fearsome fracas in which Valentine took a hammer to her lover's in-car stereo, destroying a prized gospel tape in the process. Most who witnessed the event laughed it off: after all, this was small fry compared to some of their spats – following a recent ding-dong Brooks had informed the police that his girlfriend had bitten him and set her dog on him. But this time, the guitarist was truly incensed: retrieving the hammer tossed out of his car, he sped off with Valentine, the pair still hollering at one another. That was the last anyone heard from the singer. Juliette Williamson's severely decomposed body was recovered from the water nearly three weeks later near Yerba Buena Island. Further investigation revealed that she had received eight blows to the head and was then dumped in the water by Hunters Point shipyard. Brooks – who had served time once before – threw himself on the mercy of the court and escaped a murder conviction on the grounds that his actions had not been premeditated: the guitarist was sentenced on a charge of manslaughter.

> ## 'I always loved Juliette. I feel like I cut myself in half.'
> Bruce Brooks

Wednesday 8

Roland L Chambers III

(Philadelphia, Pennsylvania, 9 March 1944)

MFSB

(The Dells)

Roland Chambers was a key figure in the rise of Philly soul throughout the seventies, achieving significant credits in composing, production and performance with a galaxy of major-league stars. As lead guitarist with The Romeos, Chambers played alongside his brother Karl (drums), but it was the meeting with singer Kenny Gamble and the group's creator, Leon Huff (who in 1971 co-founded the Philadelphia label with Gamble), that was to prove the most significant in his career. Apart from placing the musician into sessions with, among others, Archie Bell, Phyllis Hyman, The O'Jays, Teddy Pendergrass and Lou Rawls, Chambers was also to clinch a prestigious tour with Marvin Gaye. Label owners Gamble and Huff then recorded Chambers's own band MFSB (Mother Father Sister Brother), and watched open-mouthed as the latter's 'TSOP (The Sound of Philadelphia)' soared to number one across America in 1974, becoming the recognized theme tune to US television's R & B showcase *Soul Train* thereafter. Roland Chambers retired from the studio in the 1990s, but continued occasional live dates with Philly-soul survivors The Dells. He passed away from heart failure just weeks after his younger brother.

See also *Norman Harris (* ◀ *March 1987)*

Thursday 16

James Dewar

(Glasgow, 1942)

The Robin Trower Band

Lulu & The Luvvers

Stone the Crows

Originally a near-anonymous bass-player with the backing band for Scots teenage sensation Lulu, James Dewar graduated to become one of the most recognizable voices in rock. Dewar only began to gain recognition after the shy musician was approached to be both singer and bassist by blues chanteuse Maggie Bell for her band Stone the Crows. By far his best work, though, was with the band of ex-Procol Harum guitarist, Robin Trower, with whom his soaring vocals can be heard on several big-selling albums. The band were particularly huge in America, where the stadium concerts that so suited Dewar's voice were always sold out. The 'little guy with the big voice' found that his health was beginning to let him down by the mid eighties, however; Dewar's days in the limelight were far behind by the time of his death from a massive stroke.

See also *Les Harvey (* ◀ *May 1972)*

Thursday 30

Kenny Craddock

(Wrekenton, Gateshead, 18 April 1950)

Lindisfarne

Ginger Baker's Airforce

(Various acts)

To list all Kenny Craddock's credits would take a book in itself. He was 'high priest of the Hammond', a versatile musician whose best work was on recordings by better-known names. Craddock began as a club-hopping musician who followed his own heroes (such as British blues giant Graham Bond) before finding a footing with the Alan Price-approved Happy Magazine in the mid sixties. By 1970, Craddock was performing with a post-Cream Ginger Baker and his Airforce, as well as participating in early ex-Beatle projects such as George Harrison's *All Things Must Pass* (1970). Thereafter, it was Craddock's collaborations with Alan Hull that drew most attention, the musician contributing to his friend's solo albums as well as attempted comebacks by Hull's formerly successful Lindisfarne. He was in fact working with Hull when the latter passed away during the making of his final album (◀ *November 1995*).

For Kenny Craddock, the end came after moving with his second wife to his beloved Portugal: while working on a solo album, he was involved in a horrific car crash, dying from his injuries soon after.

JUNE

Wednesday 5

Dee Dee Ramone

(Douglas Colvin – Fort Lee, Virginia, 18 September 1952)

The Ramones

(Various acts)

It was perhaps unsurprising that Dee Dee died the way he did: he'd been 'using' since he was plain old Douglas Colvin, a shit-kicking teen roaming the streets of Queens, New York, in search of something to do. Having moved from Virginia to Berlin as the son of a US soldier and his German wife, Colvin found himself a bit of an outsider when he returned to America at the age of sixteen. The first 'brudders'

to hook up with Colvin were similarly 'alienated' guitarist John Cummings and as-yet-undecided musician Thomas Erdelyi, two guys with whom he played bass in The Tangerine Puppets, a sort of pre-pubescent Ramones that shared a love of sixties music as well as cheap drugs. The first genuine Ramones tunes came from early sessions at Cummings's Forest Hill home. Finding themselves unable to master cover versions of songs, bassist Colvin (shortly to become Dee Dee Ramone) was prompted to write early numbers like 'Loudmouth' and 'I Don't Wanna Walk around with You'. With the ungainly Jeff Hyman joining in 1974 as first drummer then singer (Tommy picked up the sticks), the final piece of this perverse jigsaw was now in place and the myth around what became for many the greatest punk-rock band of them all could begin to unfold. Just who were these 'punk Monkees' who dressed the same, talked the same and even took the same identity? Well, none other than Dee Dee (Colvin), Joey (Hyman), Johnny (Cummings) and Tommy (Erdelyi): The Ramones had blasted away rock's cobwebs in just two and a half minutes flat.

Dee Dee Ramone guided the band's music for fifteen years, sometimes with clarity, more often through a drug-fuelled haze. As The Ramones became figureheads of the punk establishment, Dee Dee's continued dabbling with heroin irritated the hell out of his colleagues (especially Johnny and the cleaned-up Joey) but it was to inform many of their best-loved songs, such as 'Glad to See You Go' (1977, written about his junkie ex-girlfriend), 'I Wanna be

Sedated' (1978) and 'Chinese Rocks' (1980, co-written with fellow user and ex-New York Doll Johnny Thunders), while '53rd & 3rd' (1976) fuelled some speculation that the bass-player might have worked as a rent boy at the infamous New York pick-up point referred to in the title. Feeling the strain of a long-term relationship with both his Ramones buddies and the needle, Dee Dee left the band in 1989 (replaced by Chris 'C J' Ramone), although he was to reunite with the group in the nineties. A brief, bizarre stint as rapper Dee Dee King on the *Standing in the Spotlight* album (1987) was followed by the formation of two very short-lived acts, The Chinese Dragons and Sprockett. The bassist's final recorded work was to be with California post-punks Youth Gone Mad in 2002, while The Ramones themselves were finally inducted into the Rock 'n' Roll Hall of Fame that March. On collecting the band's gong, Dee Dee commented: 'I would like to thank, uh, myself. Thank you, Dee Dee, you're very wonderful.'

At about 8.25 on the evening of 5 June, Dee Dee Ramone's wife Barbara Zampini found the musician lying face down on the sofa in a pool of his own vomit – with heroin balloons and other impedimenta within reach. Within a quarter of an hour, the former Ramone was confirmed dead, from an accidental overdose. His autobiography – which had woven a lurid tale of borderline insanity and chemical dependence, with little emphasis on the music – had suggested that Dee Dee had been completely clear of drugs by 2001.

See also *Joey Ramone (* April 2001); Johnny Ramone (* September 2004). Dee Dee also collaborated with Sid Vicious (* February 1979), Stiv Bator(s) (* June 1990), Johnny Thunders (* April 1991) and even G G Allin (* June 1993) – the first three of whom featured as 'ghosts' in his 'completely fictional' 2001 novel,* Chelsea Horror Hotel.

Robbin Crosby

(Robbinson Lance Crosby – San Diego, California, 4 August 1959)

Ratt

Guitarist with Ratt since 1979, Robbin Crosby threw off the poses and pulled out the riffs as the metal idols shifted a million copies or more of their first four Atlantic albums. The band – Crosby, Steve Pearcy (vocals), Warren DeMartini (guitar), Juan Croucier (bass) and Bobby Blotzer (drums) – were originally known as Mickey Ratt when they impressed the label with their first, self-released album in 1983. Melodic hit 'Round and Round' (co-written by Crosby) helped their Top Ten debut album *Out of the Cellar* (1984) top the triple platinum mark by 1985, while the band's tongue-in-cheek masquerading foreshadowed much of the California hair-metal scene of the next decade.

Ratt split up in 1992 amid considerable animosity, while Robbin Crosby's dependence upon drugs caused his health to collapse in the years that followed. The big-built guitarist was pronounced HIV positive in 1995, his weight ballooning to over 400 lb as a pancreatic condition threw his metabolism irreparably out of balance. And although Ratt had re-formed toward the end of the decade, it took Crosby's death in 2002 to see the group finally reconciled.

Daniel Langlois

(St Albert, Alberta, 1982)

Jordan 'The Judge' Wodehouse

(Edmonton, Alberta, 19 August 1982)

Compromise

At the time of their deaths, guitarists Daniel Langlois and Jordan Wodehouse were still in their teens, halted at the point of major success with straight-edge rockers Compromise – Langlois having been a member of the Canadian band for just two months. For his part, Wodehouse wrote and produced most of their music, also serving as the group's driver.

Having already conquered home territory, Compromise looked to strengthen their growing fanbase while on tour in the US, a series of shows providing an exciting challenge for the young band. After a well-received gig in Birmingham, Alabama, Wodehouse drove his band to the next destination at around 2 am, unaware of the impatient driver of a 1994 Nissan Pathfinder tailing Compromise's 1985 Ford van. The more nimble Nissan accelerated to an approximate speed of 90 mph to the van's 75 mph, suddenly rear-ending the Ford with a massive impact that sent both vehicles hurtling in opposite directions. The van struck a tree, which virtually ripped it in half, all five band members being thrown from the vehicle. Wodehouse, who was ejected from the front window, was killed instantly, while Langlois, asleep in a bunk when thrown from the rear window into the path of another car, died on arrival in hospital. Singer Jesse Zaraska, bassist Braden Sustrik and drummer Ryan Kittlitz survived the collision, as did the culpable Nissan driver, Ricky Nolen. In a tribute to the band's fast-rising status, Wodehouse's funeral was attended by nearly 800 mourners.

John Entwistle

(Chiswick, London, 9 October 1944)

**The Who
(Various acts)**

With the classic rhythm section now gone, it was an altogether quieter time for the erstwhile World's Loudest Band. In truth, John Entwistle could probably have done without the battering his right ear took from Pete Townshend's maxed-out guitar amp every night; in later life, the musician suffered more from deafness than the rest of The Who put together. Entwistle had himself been a man of few words, anyway: as an artist though, he was a true pioneer of his instrument and preferred to do his talking via his bass guitar.

The Who were just the band for a serious musician like Entwistle – raucous, untamed and energetic when they were young, defiantly ambitious as they became an established name, loved and revered elder statesmen by the time they had passed three decades in the game. Entwistle and Acton County Grammar School pal Townshend were first off the mark, teaming up in bluesy rock 'n' roll band The Confederates, while Entwistle moonlighted with the jazz band for whom he'd played for a while. Such was the bassist's gentle demeanour that colleagues at his Civil Service tax department job hadn't even realized he'd left when The Who went full time. Joined by the strident Roger Daltrey (vocals), Entwistle and Townshend had furthered the legend as The Detours (then with Doug Sandon on drums), before performing as The High Numbers under image-obsessed manager Peter Meaden. The Who as we know them really began with the sudden arrival of a new percussionist (Keith Moon) and a fresh manager/producer, Kit Lambert, who could see longer-term possibilities for the band than merely being mod-pacifiers. By the end of 1965 and following the release of the timeless 'My Generation'

John Entwistle: Anyway, anyhow, anywhere ...

(both album and single, the latter of which boasted an Entwistle bass solo), The Who were one of the biggest new groups in the UK. In the band's moody bassist, fans could look to a stoic presence amid all the mayhem that Daltrey, Moon and Townshend were to create. Thus he became known affectionately as 'The Ox', immortalized as such on the final track of that first album.

Entwistle maintained his image throughout the great Who years of the late sixties and seventies, adding his flourishes to the band as they graduated from the spiky pop of their earliest guise to the sprawling rock statements of *Tommy* (1969), *Quadrophenia* (1973) and beyond. Entwistle's own songwriting within The Who was limited to a few songs – among them 'Boris the Spider' (1966) and the great 'Heaven and Hell' (1970) – though his gifts extended beyond what was generally assumed of him. As a boy, he'd sung at just two years of age; he also learned the piano and was also highly proficient on trumpet and tenor horn. In adult life, Entwistle was also a reasonably accomplished painter, widely known for his love of the countryside, dogs and cars (although he never learned to drive). But, although he enjoyed a drink or three in the company of Moon, what Entwistle *wasn't* noted for was the kind of wild living associated with his bandmates.

The way he went, therefore, came as a bolt from the blue to his many admirers. In 2002, the reunited Who (well, the three survivors from the early days, plus well-connected drummer Zak Starkey) embarked upon a number of live shows in the US,

'I drink in them.'

the multi-date tour beginning in Las Vegas on 28 June. The evening before the first concert, John Entwistle had clearly decided a little entertainment was required before the hard slog ahead. The musician disappeared to his room at the Hard Rock Hotel at around 3 am after a session drinking with his band. Daltrey and Townshend were concerned, however, when their bassist failed to appear the following morning. Their fears were confirmed: Entwistle – who had also been due to open an exhibition of his artwork in Vegas the following day – was found dead of a heart attack, induced by cocaine use and the rigours, it seems, of a session with an obliging Las Vegas call-girl, who had described her companion as unresponsive when she awoke that morning.

A devastated Roger Daltrey nonetheless had to admit that it might just have been the way The Ox would have wanted to go: 'If John could have planned his death, he would have written it almost the way it happened. The only thing that would have been different would be that he'd want his body to be mummified and placed in the bed, the room filled with his beloved fish and his guitars. He'd have wanted a glass door to seal the room, with a notice saying "Hard Rock Exhibit". It would have been The Entwistle Suite – he'd have loved that.' With Italian-born bassist Pino Palladino replacing him on the tour, The Ox was finally put out to grass in Stow-on-the-Wold, Gloucestershire.

Entwistle's extensive collection of effects – including bass guitars, costumes and his own works of art – fetched in excess of $1 million at a Sotheby's auction in 2003. One guitar, a 1958 Gibson Explorer, went for close to £100K, while Peter Hook of New Order was understood to have been the recipient of another. Ironically, given his original employment, some of the money raised was used to offset tax demands against his vast Cotswolds mansion.

See also *Keith Moon (◀ August 1978). The Who's first managers, Peter Meaden (1978) and Kit Lambert (◀ April 1981), both also died prematurely.*

AUGUST

Friday 2

Nathan Maddox

(Japan, 1977)

Gang Gang Dance

One of the project's two vocalists, Nathan Maddox was a founder member of little-known experimental unit Gang Gang Dance. The Brooklyn-based quintet had released one self-titled CD via the Fusetron label, their music primal and penetrative, drawing from Ethiopian influences. The history of this interesting band was, however, to be diverted in an unexpected direction.

Maddox, being the type of guy who did that kind of thing, decided to dance on the rooftop of his girlfriend's Chinatown apartment during a severe lightning storm. As he cavorted, the singer was struck by a stray bolt and killed instantly, becoming *Number One in Heaven*'s only such victim. Gang Gang Dance continued as a band, dealing with this tragedy by refusing to accept that Maddox had left them and continuing to use his voice. Synth-player Brian DeGraw summed it up thus: 'The idea of him not being involved in the music after his departure from Earth is just absolutely impossible. The last thing we recorded with him was the final scream at the end of side two of the Fusetron LP, and I think the sound of that scream says quite a lot.'

Dave Williams: Mild-mannered and unassuming to the end

Dave 'Stage' Williams

(Texas, 29 February 1972)

The Drowning Pool

Howling and angry on stage, Drowning Pool singer Dave Williams was, by all accounts, considered to be among metal's nicest guys behind the pose. His band were one of the new breed of hard-rock outfits, designed to be enjoyed live and – alongside US contemporaries Coal Chamber and Sevendust (with whom Drowning Pool landed their first touring break) – offering a real alternative to nu metal's 'designer' angst. Within six weeks of its release, the band's first album, *Sinner* (2001), was certified platinum. A year on, a follow-up was scheduled for recording, with hair-metal legend and fan Nikki Sixx set to produce.

The Drowning Pool – Williams, C J Pierce (guitar), Stevie Benton (bass) and Mike Luce (drums) – were once again on tour with Ozzy Osbourne's Ozzfest that summer, with hordes of followers looking forward to Williams's visceral stage act. The band were travelling by tour bus to Bristow, Virginia, for the latest leg of the tour when Dave Williams failed to appear from his bunk during a stopover at Manassas. Found by members of the crew, the singer had died in his sleep, coroners later confirming his death as a result of cardiomyopathy – a disease of the heart muscle. Although it was suspected that Williams's previously undiagnosed condition might have been exacerbated by cocaine, no traces of any drug were found in his system. As the rock 'n' roll machine trundled on regardless, Drowning Pool returned in 2004 with a new singer, Los Angeles tattoo artist Jason 'Gong' Jones – though he, too, was replaced by Ryan McCombs a year on.

Paul Samson

(4 June 1953)

Samson

(Various acts)

Paul Samson was the axe-wielding warrior chief of the British rock act that bore his name, but Samson were never to match the international achievements of contemporaries like Def Leppard and Iron Maiden. Formed in 1977, the band was an integral part of the UK's new heavy-metal scene ('NWOBHM', to resurrect its snappy acronym), in their earliest incarnation boasting Maiden's future frontman Bruce Bruce (Dickinson) as singer, before he saw the light and shifted allegiance. The line-up also included demented drummer Thunderstick (Barry Graham), whose decision to play in an executioner's mask drew more than the occasional raised eyebrow.

Paul Samson himself was a decent enough guitarist who had come through the ranks of a number of bands since his teens, to remain leader of Samson for over seventeen years and more than a dozen box-ticking albums. The musician and long-time partner in crime Nicky Moore (vocals) had just completed yet another Samson collection, *Brand New Day* (2002), when Samson – who had been battling cancer for some years – died at his home in Norfolk.

SEPTEMBER

Saturday 7

Erma Franklin

(Shelby, Mississippi, 13 March 1938)

(The Cleo-Patrettes)

In another existence, she'd have been one of the world's most respected singers – her effortless, gospel-trained voice made for the soul standards she would surely have mastered. But when Erma Franklin wasn't in dispute with record labels, she was spending her career in the shadow of her younger sister Aretha. A singer who, of course, *is* the world's most respected.

Erma, having found her voice in her father's church choir at just five years of age, later sang with Aretha and a third sister, Carolyn, as the trio The Cleo-Patrettes. As Aretha was being discovered, Erma rejoined her father to tour with his gospel group. She'd had the opportunity to record with Chess, but Reverend Franklin wanted his eldest daughter to go to college. She complied – and the first of a number of missed opportunities disappeared into the ether. Returning to music on graduation, Erma was taken up by Epic but, despite the thrill of a debut album, *Her Name is Erma* (1961), constant disagreements between singer and label caused this also to end in disappointment. Next, Atlantic beckoned and, for the first time, Erma Franklin was being promoted to her satisfaction. But with the exception of an R & B Top Ten hit, 'Piece of My Heart' (1967 – and even this a song now more readily associated with Janis Joplin), her records refused to sell. Joining Aretha, now a superstar, on tour was Franklin's only real option after this. Following yet another failed stint, this time with Brunswick, she stepped away from the music industry altogether – with just a Grammy nomination as reward for all her hard work.

With both her father and Carolyn passing away during the eighties, little was heard from Erma Franklin until she – like her sister fourteen years earlier – died from cancer at her Detroit home.

Tuesday 24

Tim Rose

(Washington DC, 23 September 1940)

(The Smoothies)
(The Big Three)

Respected folk troubadour Tim Rose very nearly eschewed his career in music for one in the priesthood, his ecclesiastical ambitions scuppered by his supposedly inappropriate behaviour, details of which are now thankfully lost to history.

Instead, he hooked up with fellow 'heathens' John Phillips (later of The Mamas & The Papas) and Scott 'San Francisco' Mackenzie – both of whom of course went on to enjoy greater commercial success than Rose – in a group called The Smoothies. The songwriter was nonetheless very much a part of the DC folk/pop scene. In 1962, he and Cass Elliot made up two-thirds of The Big Three (completed by James Hendricks), the group putting out two albums in a busy year, before the relationship soured. With CBS on the lookout for the next Bob Dylan, Rose embarked upon a solo career. Receiving little commercial recognition for his first album, *Tim Rose* (1967), he became very much a musician's musician, his career putting him in the studio with the likes of John McVie (of Fleetwood Mac), Aynsley Dunbar and even John Bonham. Before his death – following surgery for bowel cancer – Rose had left music for a number of years to work as, among other things, a geography teacher, but had returned with the acclaimed albums *Haunted* (1997) and *American Son* (2002).

See also *'Mama' Cass Elliot* (☙ *July 1974*); *John Phillips* (☙ *Golden Oldies #11*)

OCTOBER

Friday 18

Steve MacDonald

(Quebec, 1971)

Gorguts

Don't let the name fool you: Gorguts could claim to have catapulted death metal to stratospheric heights with their extraordinarily complex 1998 album *Obscura*. The French-Canadian band – formed by vocalist Luc Lemay and Sylvain Marcoux (guitar), Eric Giguere (bass) and Stephane Provencher (drums) – had been around for almost a decade before they released the record. When Provencher disappeared around 1993, Steve MacDonald replaced him but, always a troubled individual, the percussionist's career with the band was fitful, to say the least. He had been battling bouts of severe depression long before his suicide in 2002. MacDonald was found hanged at his home, Gorguts ending as a band two years later.

DJ Jam Master Jay

(Jason Mizell – Queens, New York,
21 January 1965)
Run-DMC

Run-DMC were the rap act of the people – outwardly peaceful, good-humoured and keen to promote hip hop far beyond its racial and musical core. From the outset, Jam Master Jay – though not apparent in Run-DMC's name – was a key figure.

Jason Mizell spent his entire life in Hollis, Queens, the three members of Run-DMC coming together in this neighbourhood around 1981. Leader Joseph 'Run' Simmons came through the ranks as a DJ with early rap success Kurtis Blow, pulling on board child-hood buddy Darryl 'DMC' McDaniels and finally 'DJ Jam Master Jay' – the former garage bassist and drummer whose musical talents formed the backdrop to Run-DMC's old-skool joints. In turn, the others adopted Jam Master's black sweatsuits, Fedora and laceless Adidas sneakers, and the impact of the slick trio was immediate. In 1983, the group signed with Rush Productions – conveniently owned by Run's brother, rap figurehead Russell Simmons – to release a hit album a year later that exposed Jay's twin-deck skills to the public. Run-DMC really broke into the mainstream after their appear-ance at Live Aid (1985), but it was their triple-platinum third set, *Raising Hell* (1986), that pushed the group into the premier league. The chief catalyst for this was the reworking of the Aerosmith oldie 'Walk This Way', a Top Ten hit on both sides of the Atlantic – the first rap track to achieve this status in America and to break into the previously 'safe' MTV playlist.

Success at this level was not to be sustained over the next pair of albums – particularly in the wake

DMC, Run and Jam Master take their trainers for a work-out

'This is not a person who went out looking for trouble. He is known as a person that builds, creates and tries to make the right things happen.'

Dr Dre, the voice of the West Coast

of competition from the emerging West Coast gangsta scene – but, after a hiatus, the band once more found major success with a track from the vaults, this time their own 'It's Like That' (1998), remixed by friend Jason Nevins. The record shot to number one in Britain within a week of release, easily the group's biggest single, with sales of over a million. Mizell spent any down time there was wisely, setting up his own JMJ Records, which scored an instant hit with rap act Onyx: later, the label could boast 50 Cent as having been in their ranks as a novice. Like the other members of Run-DMC, Jay – who also opened an academy for budding MCs – developed a reputation for his encouragement of new talent in general. Sadly, this goodwill was to be exploited.

After a well-received latest rap/rock fusion album, *Crown Royal* (2001), and a tour with old buddies Aerosmith, Jay took himself back to the studio. On the afternoon of 30 October 2002, he was working at Merrick Street, Queens, with a companion, Urieco Rincon, when two unnamed men were buzzed into the second-floor studio at around 7.30 pm. Details remain sketchy to this day, but what is undeniable is that a violent argument broke out in the studio's lounge area, in the aftermath of which both Jay and Rincon were shot. The latter escaped with an injury to his ankle, but tragically, Jam Master Jay – who had publicly denounced the gangland culture he felt was killing rap as a genre – took a bullet in the head at point-blank range. He was dead before an ambulance could reach the building, by which time his assailants were long gone. Within the hour, local performances by top names including Russell Simmons and Big Daddy Kane were halted as news of Jay's death reverberated around New York. No one could quite believe that the 37-year-old father of three, whose hip-hop battles had, it was thought, *always* been restricted to the grooves, had gone in such a manner.

Four years on, his murder is still enshrouded in mystery. Though Jay had been the victim of a shooting incident in the nineties, it was not believed to be connected with his death. Other unproven rumours suggested that he may have owed back taxes (which wouldn't account for a shooting) or perhaps even drug money (which would). In 2003, it was then alleged that the incident might have had a direct connection with 50 Cent, who was said to have recorded a track taunting Murder Inc Records associate Kenneth McGriff over his drug convictions – a slur apparently punishable by death. When the former survived shooting in 2000 (to which he frequently refers in interview), Jay, having defied the boycott imposed upon 50 Cent by recording him, might thus have been shot in retaliation. (Three days after Jay's death, 50 Cent promoter Kenneth Walker was found in his van on a New York backstreet having been shot eight times – though authorities were unsure whether this incident was in any way related.)

Run-DMC's tributes to their DJ had already been set in place via the cuts 'Jam Master Jay', 'Jay's Game' (both 1984) and 'Peter Piper' (1986), and these were among the many anthems played out as Jam Master Jay was laid to rest four days after his death. As his car rolled slowly along a packed Linden Avenue, Jay could be seen in stoic repose and decked out, as ever, in brand-new – and laceless – Adidas sneakers.

NOVEMBER

Golden Oldies #13

Lonnie Donegan
(Anthony James Donegan – Glasgow, 29 April 1931)

If his music may seem to some a touch pedestrian nowadays, 'King of the Skiffle' Lonnie Donegan was, to budding musicians such as John Lennon, once as cutting-edge as Eminem in his reinterpretation of black American styles.

In the pre-rock 'n' roll era, Donegan – who chose his name in homage to blues guitarist Lonnie Johnson – was the first to cross over with a Leadbelly tune ('Rock Island Line', 1956), going on to

Lonnie Donegan: Long lost Lon

enjoy shedloads of UK hits including the number ones 'Cumberland Gap', 'Gamblin' Man' (both 1957) and 'My Old Man's a Dustman' (1960). Donegan's passing from a long-term heart problem came on 3 November 2002 in nearby Peterborough while he was on tour in Nottingham. The news drew a flurry of tributes from the likes of Elton John, Paul McCartney, Van Morrison and Queen axeman Brian May.

DECEMBER

Wednesday 4

Bernie Dwyer
(Manchester, 11 September 1940)
Freddie & The Dreamers

Another big fan of Lonnie Donegan was young Freddie Garrity, who began his own skiffle group – a predecessor to the chart-bothering Freddie & The Dreamers formed by the chirpy ex-milkman in 1960. The band – Garrity (vocals – who died in May 2006), Derek Quinn (lead guitar), Roy Crewsdon (rhythm), Pete Birrell (bass) and Bernie Dwyer (drums) – were as much a comic turn as they were a musical act, their onstage dance routines more than competition for The Shadows'. The only non-dancer was drummer Dwyer, who deadpanned from the back as the frontman grinned through a series of major UK hits, including 'If You Gotta Make a Fool of Somebody', 'I'm Telling You Now' (a US number one two years later) and 'You Were Made for Me' (all 1963). As with many of the era's pop acts, success was to be short-lived for The Dreamers; they were reduced to performing on children's TV by the early seventies. Bernie Dwyer had left the music business behind some decades before his death from lung cancer.

Monday 9

Mary Hansen
(Maryborough, Queensland,
1 November 1966)
Stereolab
(Various acts)

A supposed shrinking violet, Mary Hansen supported her early forays into music at the box office of the Scala Cinema in London. Onstage, however, there was no lack of confidence: tall and elegant, the guitarist's counterpoint to main singer Laetitia Sadier's lyrics about space-age furniture or modern Marxism (usually sung in French) gave Stereolab the possibly unique tag of avant-garde MOR. In truth, this band were much more, the Krautrock/Bacharach inspirations providing just a fraction of their overall sound. In 1992, Australian-born Hansen joined Sadier,

Tim Gane (various instruments), Duncan Brown (bass), Sean O'Hagan (keyboards) and Andy Ramsay (drums), as the 2-year-old band began to break from the confines of late-night radio. Two years on, Stereolab made a huge splash in the US at Perry Farrell's Lollapalooza Festival, while seeming to close in on chart action at home with the singles 'French Disko' and the truly wondrous 'Ping Pong'. Now they were making arguably their best albums in *Mars Audiac Quintet* (1994), *Emperor Tomato Ketchup* (1995), *Dots and Loops* (1997) and *Cobra and Phases* (1999). Although the breakthrough never came – which was unlikely in any case to have bothered Hansen and co – the ever-morphing Stereolab remained one of the decade's most striking acts, enjoying sell-out shows despite their apparent status as unknowns.

As she travelled to rehearsal at a London studio, Mary Hansen was struck from behind and knocked from her bicycle by a reversing truck. Despite bystanders coming to her aid,

Stereolab's Mary Hansen: Creating sonic delight in a better place

Hansen died before she could be taken to hospital. The music industry as a whole was shocked to learn of the passing of the singer/musician, who also contributed to recordings by the bands Brokeback, Chicano, Moonshake, Mouse On Mars, The Wolfhounds and The High Llamas (O'Hagan's other project). Although she had lived in Britain since 1988, Mary Hansen's funeral took place at her home town of Maryborough near Brisbane. *Hybrid*, a collection of Hansen's recordings, was issued in 2004, while Stereolab continue to pay tribute to one of their key players.

Friday 13

Zal Yanovsky
(Toronto, Ontario, 19 December 1944)
The Lovin' Spoonful
(The Mugwumps)
(Various acts)

Restless musician Zal Yanovsky dropped out of college in his native Toronto to become a key figure in the Greenwich Village pop explosion of the mid sixties, his band responsible for some of that era's brightest music. Initially collaborating with singer and multi-instrumentalist John Sebastian as The Mugwumps (with future Mamas & Papas duo Cass Elliot and Denny Doherty), Yanovsky believed a career in music might never take off when he was passed over for a role in the television pop series *The Monkees*. But success was not long in coming for the guitarist: his and Sebastian's 'Do You Believe in Magic?' (1965) was picked up by producer Erik Jacobsen, who rerecorded it with the pair, plus Steve Boone (bass) and Joe Butler (drums) – and The Lovin' Spoonful were born. Between September 1965 and December 1966, The Spoonful racked up seven Top Ten hits in America, 'Daydream' being the biggest

seller worldwide, the US number one 'Summer in the City' perhaps the most evocative. Yanovsky was certainly the most distinctive member of the band onstage, his Davy Crockett gear much imitated by other stars of the day. The wheels began to come off the wagon for the guitarist, however, when he found himself at the centre of a marijuana bust in San Francisco in 1967. A native of Canada, his only real choice was to head back home to Ontario to avoid possible incarceration. Although he was to return to The Lovin' Spoonful the year after, Yanovsky had lost much credibility with his contemporaries, having failed to testify in the court cases of various friends. On top of this, while he'd been away a third album had stiffed, causing Yanovsky to jack the band in for good. Back once again in Canada, he attempted a solo career with the album *Alive and Well in Argentina (and Loving Every Minute of It)* (1971), which no one bought.

The erstwhile musician went on to open Chez Piggy (despite his Jewish roots), a restaurant in Quebec, and produce a spin-off book of recipes. Zal Yanovsky was still quite a notable figure in and around Toronto at the time of his death, at home, from congestive heart failure.

See also *'Mama' Cass Elliot (* July 1974)*

'I am not Che Guevara.'

Joe Strummer, 1980

Clash city rockers: Mick Jones, Topper Headon, Paul Simonon and the extraordinary Joe

Joe Strummer

(John Graham Mellor – Ankara, Turkey, 21 August 1952)
The Clash
(The Mescaleros)
(The 101ers)
(Various acts)

If The Sex Pistols took all the headlines at the time, then The Clash won the longer campaign, succeeding in taking their potent blend of agitprop and great tunes from punk's smallest clubs to the masses. Of the band, Joe Strummer was clearly the creative core, a man originally dismissed as too privileged for punk rock, now revered as perhaps the most honest British voice to emerge from the movement.

The son of a diplomat, Joe Strummer was originally 'Woody Mellor' (after folk legend Woody Guthrie) – a name perhaps betraying his musical traditionalism – while a member of Welsh rockers The Vultures. A late starter on the guitar ('I was like a gorilla with three fingers!'), the 21-year-old musician was taught the rudiments of his instrument by Tymon Dogg, a friend he'd met at one of the many squats he'd inhabited on arrival in London. Basic accommodation and lack of employment were behind the dissatisfaction fuelling the energy of seminal pub-rockers The 101ers – the band Strummer formed at 101 Walterton Road – who developed a reputation as 'a great free night out'. And it was in the dole queue that Mick Jones and Paul Simonon first thought about approaching the man who was to change their lives.

Unlike many UK punks, Strummer loved American rock 'n' roll and made no bones about the fact that he wanted to crack the States when The Clash came into being. He may have been against all-pervading US culture (viz 1977's 'I'm So Bored with the USA'), but American music informed the band Strummer was to make his own. The potency of his rock 'n' roll was also to be infused with other influences previously unheard in British punk, such as reggae, rockabilly and folk. (His new moniker also displayed a self-deprecating humour previously unencountered in the new wave.) With CBS, the label that wised-up to the potential greatness of The Clash – Strummer, ex-London SS guitarists Jones and Simonon (who took up the bass), plus drummer Nicky 'Topper' Headon – the band really made their mark as they duelled with The Pistols et al on the 1976 'Anarchy in the UK' tour. Not that Strummer and The Clash espoused anarchy, or indeed any of punk's nihilism: their message – contained within the lyric of first single 'White Riot' (1977) – was one of activism against exploitation, authority and control. Strummer, with his trademark stance, was just the man to carry this off. A first album, *The Clash* (1977), performed well at home, though nearly didn't receive a release in the States (and what a mistake that would have been, given its subsequent US acclaim). To the dismay of some of their fans, the band then employed Blue Oyster Cult producer Sandy Pearlman to craft the follow-up, *Give 'Em Enough Rope!* (1978) – weaker than the debut album, despite its number-two peak in Britain and a couple of great minor hits in 'Tommy Gun' and 'English Civil War'. The band were still unsettled at this point (Headon left and returned at least twice, to be replaced briefly by Terry 'Tory Crimes' Chimes and even, at one point, future Culture Club drummer Jon Moss) and Strummer was still derided by his Pistols rivals ('Agitprop out of the back of *Time Out*,' in the words of ex-member Glen Matlock). The biggest trouble he could find for himself was a £100 fine for stealing hotel pillowcases. But the music was improving.

The best Clash record – and to many, one of the best rock albums of all time – was 1979's *London Calling* (1980, US), a set that confirmed Strummer's complete understanding and assimilation of other musical cultures (already conveyed in great earlier cuts like 'Police and Thieves' and 'White Man in Hammersmith Palais'). For a punk band, a double album was almost unthinkable, but if there was a duff track among the nineteen dished up, then it has still to make itself apparent a quarter of a century later. *London Calling* also gave Strummer and co that elusive American breakthrough – it made Billboard number twenty-seven, while culled track 'Train In Vain' also became a hit. The

Clash then compromised their position a tad with the 36-song *triple* set *Sandinista!* (1980), though this too contains some Strummer/Jones gems such as 'The Call-Up' and 'Magnificent Seven' – which is cited by some as the first British rap single (if you don't count 'Captain Beaky'). To cement their American popularity, the record became the second Clash effort in succession voted *Village Voice* magazine's Album of the Year.

But Strummer was becoming restless. During the making of *Combat Rock* (1982), the singer went AWOL, causing a crucial tour to be postponed and leading British fans to believe that he was by now 'bored of the UK'. The record fared well, even providing a US Top Ten hit with Headon's tremendous 'Rock the Casbah' and – eventually – the band's only UK number one, 'Should I Stay or Should I Go?' (1982 – reissued to sell jeans, 1991), though it was apparent that The Clash in their first, greatest guise were starting to fall apart. Although they opened a number of shows for The Who – surely one of the most incendiary double-bills ever – Headon (for his drug habit) then Chimes were both dismissed in 1983, to be followed by Jones (who re-emerged a couple of years later with Big Audio Dynamite). Strummer and Simonon – who by now was barely in the band – just about kept the Clash flame alight for a while longer, though the less said about *Cut the Crap* (1986) the better.

'I'm one of those people that pick up small and interesting bits of wood and don't want to let go of them. I'm fascinated with the wrapper on a sardine can. A little "cuckoo"': Joe Strummer thereafter resembled something between a free spirit and a lost soul, frequently described as delusional by those who met him during the early nineties. His solo music career was fitful but the singer took on with some panache a couple of film roles (most notably in Jim Jarmusch's 1989 *Mystery Train*). Suddenly in 1999, Strummer re-emerged with the very enjoyable Mescaleros, joined on stage impromptu by Jones in 2002 for the pairing's first live appearance together since Clash days (Strummer's later response to this was a good-humoured 'Bloody cheek!'). But it was to be the last.

Jones, Simonon and Headon all stated that plans for a full Clash reunion had been put in motion by the time of Joe Strummer's passing: he was just fifty when he died at his

'Joe is as huge an inspiration to me now as he was in 1977. He taught a whole generation of us more about politics than any number of teachers or politicians. I *desperately* wish reports were untrue.'

Iggy Pop, on learning of Strummer's passing

Somerset home, having apparently suffered a heart attack during his sleep. Homages flowed for months after, with Headon even quoted as saying: 'If any of us should've gone prematurely, it shouldn't have been Joe. It should've been me.' The legend of the man's work remained intact, however, tributes arriving from the many rock stars – among them The Manic Street Preachers and U2 (Bono having recently worked with Strummer) – who happily conceded a substantial debt to punk's most eclectic voice.

Among the legacies left by Strummer were the Future Forests ecology campaign, now supported by major current artists such as Coldplay and The Foo Fighters (www.futureforests.com). A music foundation has been set up in honour of Joe Strummer and a very impressive Class 47 locomotive engine bears his name.

Saturday 28

Meri Wilson Edgemon
(Mary Edna Wilson – Nagoya, Japan, 15 June 1949)

Meri Wilson will most likely always be known as a one-hit wonder. By the end of her life, however, she had become president of Georgia's Americus Arts Council – a far cry from her 'single-entendre' past as the flirtatious voice behind 1977's sauciest hit record. In the days before female orgasms were spoken of in such terms, Wilson – she became 'Meri' to avoid confusion with the former Supreme – hit the US Top Twenty and UK Top Ten with the single 'Telephone Man'. This record single-handedly started a trend in which 'ringing a bell' became the euphemism of choice, notably continued by Anita Ward in 1979. Wilson's follow-up 'Rub-a-Dub-Dub' (1978) was, frankly, rubbish, and that was pretty much the last that was heard of her. Well, up until her sudden death, at any rate. Meri Wilson – who had married and taken up more serious musical pursuits – was killed after she lost control of her car on Sumpter County's Highway 377.

Tuesday 31

Kevin MacMichael
(Dartmouth, Nova Scotia, 7 November 1951)
The Cutting Crew
(Various acts)

Kevin MacMichael could, contrary to Ms Wilson, boast a couple of major hits for his band, eighties fly-by-nights The Cutting Crew. In the seventies, the keen guitarist had found broader attention harder to come by as a member of Beatles tribute act Spice. And there were other bands, the most notable being Fast Forward, who also had suggestions of The Fab Four in their sound – before MacMichael headed for the UK, where success was finally to beckon. The Cutting Crew were formed in 1985, MacMichael joined by Nick Van Eede (vocals), Colin Farley (bass) and Martin Beedle (drums). The band's smooth shtick fitted snugly into the transatlantic AOR scene (though heaven knows why they chose a name that made them sound like a B-Boy outfit). A first single, the tepid '(I Just) Died in Your Arms' (1986), was a Top Five UK hit before making it all the way to the top slot in America and beyond in 1987; a further US Top Ten hit 'I've Been in Love Before' then emerged from the band's debut album *Broadcast*. When the second album, well, 'died on its arse tonight', the game looked to be up for The Cutting Crew, who, after their next album failed to sell, were dropped by Virgin in response to changing fashions. Before calling it a day, Kevin MacMichael worked with a hero of his, Led Zeppelin's Robert Plant, on the well-received album *Fate of Nations* (1993). But eight years on, the guitarist learned he had lung cancer: he died from the disease within a year of diagnosis.

Lest We Forget

Other notable deaths that occurred sometime during 2002:

Richard 'Pistol' Allen (prolific US drummer with Motown's 'Funk Brothers' house unit – who therefore played on countless top hits; born Howard Richard Allen, Tennessee, 12/8/1932; cancer, 30/6)

Peter Bardens (UK rock/prog singer/keyboard stalwart with Them and Camel; born London, 19/6/1945; lung cancer, 22/1)

Rosemary Clooney (big-selling US light-pop singer who scored a transatlantic #1 with 1954's 'This Ole House'; born Kentucky, 23/5/1928; lung cancer, 29/6)

Cesar Diaz (Puerto Rican rock eccentric with Frijid Pink – known in the industry as 'The Amp Doctor' – who went US/UK Top Ten in 1970 with 'House of the Rising Sun'; born 13/7/1951; liver failure, 26/4)

Gus Dudgeon (renowned UK producer whose work made Elton John an international star; born Surrey, 30/9/1942; car crash, which also killed his wife, 21/7)

Doug Ferguson (noted US experimental keyboardist with Vas Deferenz Organization, Ohm and Yeti; born Texas, 25/9/1970; pancreatic infection, 23/2)

Juvenal Gomez (US drummer with Eddie Cochran and Gene Vincent's Blue Caps – when he was just fifteen; born Texas, 1942; heart attack, 12/9)

Billy Guy (kiss-curled US baritone with Bip & Bop and the original Coasters; born Frank William Phillips, Texas, 20/6/1936; heart attack – he died impoverished in Las Vegas, 5/11)

Peggy Lee (much-loved US singer whose biggest song was 1958's 'Fever'; born Norma Delores Egstrom, North Dakota, 26/5/1920; heart attack, 21/1)

Billy Ward (US lead singer with classic vocal group The Dominoes – alongside Clyde McPhatter and Jackie Wilson; born Robert Williams, California, 15/9/1921; natural causes, 16/2)

For a complete list of fallen artists, visit

www.numberoneinheaven.com

JANUARY

Saturday 11

Mickey Finn

(Thornton Heath, Surrey, 3 June 1947)

T Rex

(Various acts)

According to Marc Bolan, Mickey Finn 'couldn't sing, but looked superb'. Finn's role in T Rex? To take over the departed Steve Peregrin Took's bongos. Finn's predecessor had alienated Bolan with his songwriting ambition, but the new man had no such aspirations. No matter – it was the best decision Finn was ever to make: he was in place as Bolan made the transition from flower-child folkie to glam superstar. Mickey Finn began as a painter, but was booted out of his Croydon art school despite no small talent – certainly more than he'd shown as a musician with bands such as The Blue Men and Hapshash & The Coloured Coat. It was Finn the artist to whom Bolan was initially drawn. The nature of their relationship has always remained a closely guarded secret, though the singer made little secret of his fondness for the percussionist's Triumph. Likewise, Finn fancied the idea of a career in rock 'n'

Bolan and Finn: The 'glamour twins'

roll. He was in luck: starting with the infectious 'Ride a White Swan' (1970), T Rex took root at the business end of the UK charts for the first four years of the seventies with a series of shimmering hit singles, of which 'Hot Love', 'Get It On' (both 1971), 'Telegram Sam' and 'Metal Guru' (both 1972) all went to number one (a host of others came pretty close, too) – their market equally split between art-rock fans and screaming teenyboppers. With Bolan the central figure, Finn didn't really say a lot – but he had a nice line in silk blousons.

By 1975, with T Rex no longer the country's biggest pop act and Bolan's forays into US electric funk and disco making him more or less redundant, Finn left the band, Bolan's death (➤ *September 1977*) hitting him hard as he vainly attempted to find further projects to follow the glory years. Finally, in 1997, there emerged Mickey Finn's T Rex, a hotchpotch of musicians (including ex-T Rexites 'Dino' Dines and Paul Fenton, plus Bolan's son Rolan on occasion) approximating Bolan's best tunes. In September 2002 – the twenty-fifth anniversary of Bolan's death – the group played to some 2,000 fans, but just three months later the ailing Mickey Finn was also dead, losing his battle with liver and kidney disease at Croydon's Mayday Hospital. He was interred in nearby Norwood, fans celebrating his life at a memorial service the same afternoon. And, yes – Mickey Finn *was* his real name.

See also *Steve Peregrin Took (➤ October 1980); Steve Currie (➤ April 1981); 'Dino' Dines (➤ January 2004).*

Maurice Gibb

(Douglas, Isle of Man, 22 December 1949)

The Bee Gees

By the time it all came to a close in 2003, The Bee Gees could almost make a claim for three careers, so definitive were their different incarnations. Yet, had matters worked out even slightly differently early on, it might never have happened for pop's most famous falsettos. Of the three brothers, Maurice Gibb – younger than his twin, Robin, by just fifteen minutes – was the polite, quiet boy who disapproved of the misbehaviour of his elder brothers which often landed all three in trouble with the police in Chorlton-cum-Hardy (where they'd moved from the Isle of Man). The ambition that was to take them to the very top only began to reveal

itself after a move to Brisbane when Maurice was just eight years old.

Having sung together in public in Lancashire, the trio – Maurice, Robin and eldest brother, Barry – found themselves on Australian television by 1960, their barbershop-style harmonies thrilling middle-class audiences across the country. (And they were still breaking the law at this stage, in the sense that Queensland had strict child-labour policies.) The roles were already set out at this stage: Barry, three years the senior, led (naming the band 'Bee Gees'); Robin was in place as co-lead; the taciturn Maurice played guitar and keyboards, offering occasional vocals by the time the group were signed to Festival Records (Polydor in the UK). After some minor Australian singles, the three headed back to Britain, where a first proper hit arrived in the shape of the haunting 'New York Mining Disaster 1941' (1967, US/UK Top Twenty), a disquieting fable nobody had anticipated from three fresh-faced young men barely

The Bee Gees – Maurice, Robin and Barry: Too much hair then?

into shaving (*Death Toll #4*). After a stutter with the non-charting 'To Love Somebody', The Bee Gees exploded internationally with another stirring effort, 'Massachusetts' (1967), which took them to number one in the UK. The hits continued unabated and a second British chart-topper arrived with 'I've Gotta Get a Message to You' (1968, US Top Ten), Maurice quietly enjoying the band's fame as his two brothers bickered about where The Bee Gees should go next. Having met her in a BBC canteen, the musician married singer Lulu in 1969 in a hotly covered media wedding. Now that the group's two leads had fallen out, all three brothers attempted badly received solo recordings. Despite his part in the first of nine US number ones by the Bee Gees, 'How Can You Mend a Broken Heart?' (1971), Maurice was to suffer major crises in both his personal and professional life over the next few years, including a divorce from Lulu (allegedly due to his increased drinking). After a break, the group returned some years on, and Maurice's work was key to the sound of the albums *Main Course* (1975) and *Children of the World* (1976), which – with hits like 'Jive Talkin'' and the great 'You Should Be Dancing' – pres- aged The Bee Gees' new and totally unexpected 'funky/streetwise' style that was to blossom two years later. Although fans of their earlier sound were sceptical, The Bee Gees smashed records everywhere with their remark- able soundtrack to disco movie *Saturday Night Fever* (1977), the 30 million copies sold making the album one of the all-time top-sellers. And, as well as a slew of US number-one singles in 'Staying Alive', 'Night Fever', etc, the Gibb sound was in demand from other singers as well. For the next three years, Yvonne Elliman, Olivia Newton-John/John Travolta, Samantha Sang, Barbra Streisand, Tavares and Frankie Valli were all to top the charts with Bee Gees compositions – as was younger brother Andy Gibb, with a run of

remarkably similar-sounding power ballads. (The only 'down' at this time was the brothers' involvement in the truly grim *Sgt Pepper's Lonely Hearts Club Band* movie.)

During the eighties, Maurice Gibb admitted to alcohol dependence. Via Alcoholics Anonymous, he conquered the addiction, but some believe the damage to his liver was to prove critical in the years to come. Despite the thrill of an unexpected number one in 1987 (the indifferent 'You Win Again'), it was a difficult time for The Bee Gees in general: Barry had his own medical problems, as did Andy, who died aged only thirty (*March 1988*). Maurice responded by throwing himself into the role of musical director for the final few Bee Gees albums, but it was obvious by the end of the millennium that his health was also failing. Maurice Gibb died from complications during surgery to mend a twisted intestine – believed to be a birth defect – a recently awarded CBE accepted in 2004 on his behalf by his beloved son Adam.

Perhaps one of Gibb's most telling quotes came when walking off UK television host Clive Anderson's live show in 1997: abandoned on set by his infuriated brothers, Maurice baldly stated, 'I'm sorry, I don't do impres- sions!' before making his exit.

FEBRUARY

Thursday 20

Ty Longley

(Sharon, Pennsylvania, 4 September 1971)

Great White

It was rock's biggest disaster – ever. For the families of those who perished in the Station nightclub, Rhode Island, the nightmare that occurred

on 20 February 2003 will continue indefinitely; for veteran metal act Great White, it represents a macabre legacy with which none of the band's music can ever compete.

Great White were a hard-rock/hair- metal outfit formed by singer Jack Russell back in 1981, but the band had to wait almost a decade for mainstream success. After a series of lukewarmly received albums, the band – Russell, Mark Kendall (guitar), Tony Montana (bass), Michael Lardie (keyboards) and Audie Desbrow (drums) – finally achieved a hit with their cover of the Ian Hunter tune 'Once Bitten Twice Shy' (1989). This and its parent album *Twice Shy* gave them a boost: although Great White were not to repeat the success, association with the album was to increase future concert attendances tenfold. By the end of the next decade, the band had a greatly different line-up, now featuring a new lead guitarist in Pennsylvanian-born Ty Longley. At the start of 2003, Longley had extra reason to be excited, as he looked forward to the birth of his first child.

A concert at the 300-capacity Station nightclub, West Warwick, Rhode Island, would not normally be considered a major event, but with Great White having wound things down a fraction, it was to be their last show for the foreseeable future. By 9.30 pm, the first band of the evening, hard-rockers Fathead, had finished their set and the expected surge to see the main event, Great White, had begun. By the time the band took to the stage, The Station was almost 50 per cent over capacity. As the group struck up chords and poses before their eager crowd, a series of 'gerbs' (small indoor pyrotechnics in 'flashpots') ignited around the stage – a typical rock-concert side attraction. The effect seemed more impressive than had been expected, until the audience began to realize that this firework display was *not* what had been planned. Within seconds, the band's backdrop was ablaze, soundproofing foam used within the wall cavities proving highly flammable. Within minutes, the entire venue was engulfed in flame and smoke visible for miles. Attendees turned and fled, but with so many exiting so small a venue, it was never going to be possible to prevent casualties, many being trampled in the crush. Emergency services were fast to the scene and worked hard to clear the club. By morning, the extent of the disaster became harrowingly clear to all: more than eighty were confirmed dead (a figure that was to increase), with over 150 injured, ranging from the slight to twenty listed as critical.

Ty Longley was one of those confirmed deceased on Monday 24th, his shattered girlfriend and family travelling to the site along with four hundred other relatives of the dead. In the aftermath, a fierce argument blew up between representatives of Great White and the club owners, brothers Jeffrey (who'd been present and had assisted in the evacuation of the building) and Michael Derderian – both of whom maintained that no provision for a pyrotechnic show had been requested by the band nor indeed been granted. Great White inevitably testified otherwise, Russell telling CNN that 'obviously there (had been) some sort of miscommunication'. As the legal row raged on, it was revealed that the rider in Great White's contract made *no* reference to the use of fireworks in their show. Another nightclub owner, Dominic Santana, confirmed that the band had also failed to gain permission before using pyrotechnics at *his* club (New Jersey's popular Stone Pony) just a week before – though it should be added that other club owners were equally quick to support the band, claiming permission had been both sought and granted. (Remarkably, a film crew had been on location at the Station to make a documentary about club safety, following a stampede that had led to twenty-one deaths at a club in Chicago earlier the

same week. The cameramen managed to capture vital footage as the fire began to burn out of control.)

That December, the Derderians were charged on two hundred counts of involuntary manslaughter (two per death) – though this would have been only small comfort to bereft Heidi Peralta, who'd given birth to 'Acey' Ty Longley Jr that August. Despite this ruling, at the end of 2005 the case still remained unresolved, lawyers for the Derderian brothers asking for new information to be taken into consideration.

Sunday 23

Howie Epstein

(Norman Howard Epstein – Milwaukee, Wisconsin, 21 July 1955)
Tom Petty & The Heartbreakers

One of the most respected bass-players in American rock for two decades, Howie Epstein was best

remembered as the foil to US guitar hero Tom Petty, with whose vocals he was to harmonize on The Heartbreakers' biggest songs. Originally, Epstein had played mandolin, one of the younger exponents of the instrument during the seventies folk boom – an attribute that also drew him to the attention of Bob Dylan, upon whose albums he played during the following decade. Epstein joined forces with Petty in 1982 – by which time The Heartbreakers were well established – first contributing bass to the Top Ten album *Long After Dark* (1982). While working with Petty, Epstein also began a relationship, both professional and personal, with country singer Carlene Carter (Johnny Cash's stepdaughter), for whom he produced two albums, including the Grammy-nominated *I Fell in Love* (1990). The couple remained lovers for fifteen years, the relationship ending only after a heroin bust in 2001, as a result of which Carter was sentenced to a year's probation.

With no small irony, it appears to have been heroin that put paid to

Exactly 100 people were killed in what has since been confirmed as the US's fourth-deadliest nightclub inferno. Apart from the Great White guitarist, a number of other members of their extended fraternity were killed as a result of that fateful evening on Rhode Island.

Forty-year-old DJ and WHJY radio presenter Mike 'Dr Metal' Gonsalves (who had been hosting the show) was one of the first confirmed deceased; cousins 34-year-old Keith Mancini (bass) and 39-year-old Steven Mancini were members of opening band Fathead, while the latter's bandmate from another rock act, Nightfall, guitarist Scott Griffith, thirty-one, was in the audience and perished. Guitarist Thomas Marion, 45-year-old Dale Latulippe – drummer with Rhode Island band Ball & Chain – and 17-year-old Shryne guitarist Nicky O'Neill also died as onlookers. Among the crew who perished were Jeff Rader (who had toured with Alice Cooper) and Bob 'Hairball' Roger.

Howie Epstein. The bassist had been in poor health, suffering from influenza, stomach problems and a leg abscess (probably exacerbated by his status as a user). Rushed to hospital by his latest girlfriend, who described the comatose Epstein as 'under distress', the musician died from a suspected heroin overdose in hospital near his home in Santa Fe. 'I'm devastated,' commented his former lover Carter, adding, 'My kids thought of Howie as their father.' (Carter was to suffer further losses just months later with the deaths of her mother June Carter Cash, stepfather Johnny Cash (☛ *Golden Oldies 6*) and half-sister Rosey Nix Adams (☛ *October 2003*).)

MARCH

Thursday 6

Alice Martineau

(London, 8 June 1972)

Her moving story posthumously revealed in a BBC television documentary, Alice Martineau appeared outwardly to have had it all: she was a talented musician/songwriter, with striking looks and many acquaintances in the business (her father had produced rock giants Def Leppard and Judas Priest). But Martineau was born with cystic fibrosis, the genetic disorder that hampers the functioning of vital organs such as the pancreas and lungs.

Though her chances of survival were written off time and again, the aspiring Martineau conquered goals as though routine: despising tags such as 'brave', she graduated from university against expectation, achieved her first ambition of becoming a model, and then defied the odds further by getting herself signed up to Sony Music in 2001. The corporate giant then faced flack from media cynics who accused the label of cynically seeking a 'British Eva Cassidy' (☛ *November 1996*). The attitude of those around Martineau was best summed up by promoter Phil Long: 'If they don't sign Alice, it's because she's ill – if they do, they're exploiting her. Her music stands up on its own.' Indeed, the singer's work was (rightly) compared favourably with multi-platinum artists like Dido, her debut 'If I Fall' (2002) chosen as Single of the Week by 1FM disc jockey Jo Whiley, who also supported the rising star in her documentary – a television special intended to chronicle Martineau's rise to commercial acceptance.

With a sad inevitability, Alice Martineau passed away during its making as she awaited a triple organ transplant, an operation that would in any case have entailed huge risk. Working at home in Kensington, she suffered massive internal haemorrhaging too sudden to allow transport to hospital, and the programme thereafter took on the tone of a tribute.

> ## 'I can make believe that I am fit and healthy. It's the thought of what I might be able to achieve after my transplant that will help get me through it. I get quite carried away sometimes – and then I wake up.'
> Alice Martineau, writing for the *Telegraph* in 2002

Saturday 8

Adam Faith

(Terry Nelhams-Wright – Acton, London, 23 June 1940)

(The Worried Men)

For a while, Adam Faith represented the only real challenge to Cliff Richard as pop's heart-throb wars began to hot up in late 1959. If his music tended to be dismissed as slight, the versatile Faith was no slouch himself in a career that encompassed acting, music production and even financial journalism before his unexpected death. Terry Nelhams was widely regarded as a strong communicator who disregarded class barriers: originally from a council estate, he was discovered working as a film-studio assistant having rapidly climbed the ladder from messenger boy. With skiffle all the rage (thanks largely to Lonnie Donegan), the singer had formed his own group, The Worried Men, attracting the interest of television producer Jack Good who recorded the band for an edition of the BBC's *Six Five Special*. It was clear to him that the singer could make it with a change of image and he even offered the would-be star a book of names from which to choose a suitable moniker. As the restyled Adam Faith, he was pushed forward by John Barry (the future movie-score composer) who provided the fledgling singer with some sure-fire hits – all delivered in Faith's post-Buddy-Holly-hiccough style. Of these, the first two releases, 'What Do You Want?' (1959) and 'Poor Me' (1960), both made UK number one and a series of further smashes kept Faith at the top for the next three years. Critics derided some of the record choices (in the case of 1960's 'Lonely Pup (in a Christmas Shop)', they had a point) and it became clear with the emergence of The Beatles and Stones that the shelf-life of a pop crooner was now not a long one. With this in mind, Faith began a second career as an actor, which initially paid dividends as he began to pick up high-profile drama roles, the best remembered probably his television portrayal of ex-con *Budgie* or the tough rock manager in the movie *Stardust* during the early seventies. Remarkably, Faith found time to manage a chart-topping star in real life, as he took on responsibility for Leo Sayer, producing both him and Roger Daltrey (to whom he'd recommended Sayer's 'Giving It All Away', the Who frontman's biggest solo hit). A near-fatal car crash in 1973 resulted in Faith's autobiographical single 'I Survive', but after the record failed to break into the charts he retired from singing for good.

During the 1980s, Faith fell out with Sayer, the latter suing him for unpaid earnings. Whether this prompted his foray into the world of financial journalism is uncertain, but *Daily Mail* readers were not the only ones to be astonished by this dramatic u-turn. Faith, now considered something of a guru to the money-makers of the eighties, also invested in satellite TV's *The Money Channel* – though, with sobering irony, this proved an enormous flop, bankrupting the former singer in 2002 and saddling him with debts reportedly approaching £32 million.

It's uncertain whether this disappointing television experience inspired the now-famous last words with which Adam Faith has regularly been credited. The former singer had a history of heart problems that had led to emergency surgery in 1986. Then, after a performance in a play at Stoke-on-Trent, Faith was suddenly taken ill in his hotel room, dying shortly afterwards from a heart attack. Showing he'd lost none of his, shall we say, 'charm', Faith died in the arms of Tanya Arpino – a waitress some forty years his junior with whom he'd been having an affair. Faith's widow Jackie was understandably upset by this,

the couple only recently having been reconciled after seven years apart. The split had followed a series of previous misdemeanours including a 'love match' with tennis star Chris Evert. Jackie Nelhams subsequently banned Arpino from the funeral. (In another ironic twist, Faith had been appearing in the Donald Churchill play *Love and Marriage*.)

Adam Faith: 'Poor me', indeed

'Channel 5 is all shit, isn't it? Christ – the crap they put on there! It's a waste of space!'

Adam Faith wins *Number One in Heaven's* 'Finest Last Words' award

Teemu 'Somnium' Raimoranta

(Helsinki, 1977)
Finntroll
Impaled Nazarene

If you'd been wondering when you might see the first Finnish folk-metal entry in this book, well, the wait is over. Teemu Raimoranta was a versatile guitarist from Helsinki who could play bass, rhythm and lead guitar, thus making him ideal for black-metal act Impaled Nazarene, a unit seemingly obsessed with black magic and, especially, goats. The somewhat limited *oeuvre* encouraged Raimoranta – stage name 'Somnium' – to form his own band, Finntroll, in 1997. This time, the influences incorporated black metal, Finnish folk and even polka, the lyrics now extending to include goblins and trolls, for maximum effect all sung in Swedish! By 2003 Raimoranta was back working with Impaled Nazarene, however, after the enforced retirement of Finntroll singer J 'Katla' Jamsen.

Early one morning in March 2003, the guitarist had apparently been drinking heavily with friends when he suffered a fall on his way home. The story ran that Raimoranta had fallen from a Helsinki bridge, breaking his spine, though later interviews with friends present at the time (including Impaled Nazarene singer Mika Luttinen) suggest that he had little alcohol in his system and had deliberately thrown himself off. The reliability of Luttinen's testimony was questioned, however, following this 'generous' tribute to his close friend: 'We didn't miss him in rehearsal – he was always off saying he had to meet his mum or something. We're a better band, now. We have a better guitarist.'

APRIL

Wednesday 2

Edwin Starr

(Charles Edwin Hatcher – Nashville, Tennessee, 21 January 1942)
(The Future Tones)

As the world reverberated to reports of war in Iraq, the man whose anthem did so much to rally opposition to an earlier conflict passed away at his home near Nottingham. For Edwin Starr it was an ignominious end to a vibrant career in which in the space of a decade the singer bridged the gap between full-throated soul and bass-heavy disco. Starr began recording with the largely forgotten doo-wop outfit The Future Tones, before military service beckoned, pulling the fledgling singer away for two years. His take on The Temptations' 'War' was a milestone in soul-music history, and certainly the most incendiary song ever issued by Motown. The singer had already breached Billboard's Top Ten with the raunchy '25 Miles' (1969) by the time 'War' took him to number one in August 1970, the stirring dance-floor packer a timely reminder of the disapproval felt by America's youth at their country's continued occupation of Vietnam. Suddenly, Starr was a spokesman (his presentation many years later of a BBC radio series on the civil rights movement was well conceived), and the song was destined to re-emerge as a soundtrack staple throughout the next three decades. For Starr, the seventies were noticeably quieter after this resounding success, a move to the UK then seeing the singer reinvent himself once more. In 1979, his singles 'Contact' and 'H.A.P.P.Y. Radio' were

Edwin Starr: 'War' resulted in victory

both big UK disco hits, a gruff but pleasing antidote to the falsetto shrieks that seemed to occupy every other available second of airspace at the time following the success of *Saturday Night Fever* and the like. His sales thereafter faltering, Starr turned to a number of other luminaries (given that this includes Stock, Aitken & Waterman, the term is used advisedly) to reverse the trend. However, his only other notable hit was 'Funky Music Sho Nuff Turns Me On' – revamped by Leeds dance-collective Utah Saints in 2000.

A long way from his birthplace of Nashville, Edwin Starr died of an apparent heart attack in his adopted home of Beeston, Nottinghamshire.

Thursday 10

Little Eva

(Eva Narcissus Boyd – Bellhaven,
North Carolina, 29 June 1943)

Her aunt was 'Big Eva', so she, at less than five feet tall, was 'Little Eva' – simple as that. Like Edwin Starr, Eva Boyd was known primarily for one massive hit. Her unique voice was first chanced upon by the vigilant and influential songwriting couple Carole King and Gerry Goffin, who'd employed the young unknown as a nanny in 1961, having met her when she was working as a maid at the legendary Brill Building. Eva had already sung as a prominent member of her family's gospel choir, and she herself devised the dance moves that were to accompany 'The Loco-motion', the astonishingly successful first release that shot her to number one in America in the fall of 1962. With 'new dance' ditties something of a phenomenon at the time, 'The Loco-motion' sold millions worldwide (number two in the UK), though fame was to be fleeting. After a couple of further US Top Twenty entries, the novelty of Little Eva's

shrill tones began to wear thin, her best outlet thereafter proving to be as a backing singer for acts like The Drifters. When she quit the business in 1971, Little Eva – who had earned just fifty dollars a week when she was at number one in an era when performance royalties were rarely paid – emerged as penniless as she'd been a decade earlier. Indeed, the former star was forced to return to menial work. When 'The Loco-motion' re-entered the UK charts in 1972, it's said that Eva wasn't even aware of the fact.

Kylie Minogue's successful reigniting of Eva's biggest song did, however, bring her out of retirement in the late eighties, the star recording a gospel album that performed better than was expected. She returned to the UK with Little Richard in 2001, but diagnosis with cervical cancer – from which she died two years later – was to curtail any longer-term plans of career revival.

Golden Oldies #14

Nina Simone

(Eunice Kathleen Waymon – Tryon,
North Carolina, 21 February 1933)

Critics found her cold and aloof: she was simply 'better'. As much a legend of soul and the blues as she was a jazz singer, Nina Simone's effortless tremolo seemed to weave in and out of the delicate melodies with which she accompanied herself, her voice an amazingly sophisticated and versatile 'instrument' in its own right. Like so many others, Simone was inspired by religious music; she also studied piano at New York's prestigious Juilliard Academy. She then suddenly became involved in the civil rights movement, in direct response to the fact that her parents had been moved from their front-row seats when watching her perform for the first time.

Nina Simone: Little girl blue

This association – which later landed her in trouble for withholding income tax as protest – informed a number of her recordings, not least 'To be Young, Gifted and Black', though her biggest hits were 'Ain't Got No (I Got Life)' (1968) and the reissued 'My Baby Just Cares for Me' (1987), both of which made the UK Top Five. Nina Simone had relocated to Provence, France, at the time of her death from cancer on 21 April 2003.

MAY

Tuesday 6

Gerry Shephard
(28 December 1951)

The Glitter Band

He was never going to upstage Gary, but Gerry Shephard still cut a memorable seventies pop figure with his customized 'star' guitar – a prop he used until just months before his death. From 1972, The Glitter Band epitomized a working-class glam-rock ethic: they were a pretty basic-looking bunch underneath it all, but poured into their glittering suits they were, if not essential, a visually arresting addition to *Top of the Pops* for a couple of years. Although never likely to match the success of original leader, Gary Glitter, the group built upon his trademark yelps and handclaps to run off seven sizeable hits of their own, including 'Angel Face', the admittedly brilliant 'Just For You' (both 1974) and 'Goodbye My Love' (1975). Beach Boy fan Shephard – very much the talent of The Glitter Band – died following a lengthy illness.

Sunday 11

Noel Redding
(Folkestone, 25 December 1945)

The Jimi Hendrix Experience
(The Noel Redding Band)
(Various acts)

He was the quiet man with the giant hair, the ideal counterpart to perhaps the greatest rock guitarist ever known. Noel Redding was partially given the gig for his look, the abundant Afro offset by the granny-style glasses made famous by John Lennon. At nine, the reticent Redding had played violin in front of his school, but with the mandolin becoming all the rage in the early sixties, the young musician took it up and formed several bands of his own: names such as The Strangers and The Lonely Ones hinting at his taciturn nature. In 1966, he was selected by Chas Chandler for the role of bassist in the happening Jimi Hendrix Experience – a three-piece fronted by a mercurial musician who couldn't even get himself arrested back at home. But even this was an accident: Redding had originally applied to become a guitarist with Chandler's band, The Animals.

Despite many treasured memories, such as the Monterey Pop Festival of 1967, the musician revealed afterwards that his 'experiences' were not all happy ones while with Hendrix and John 'Mitch' Mitchell (drums). Creative in his own right, Redding found Hendrix to be fairly controlling, something he'd expected at first but of which he grew weary as time went by. After the release of the timeless *Electric Ladyland* (1968), he left the band; the main issue was that old chestnut: royalties. Although he was to remain friends with Hendrix until the latter's untimely death (◄ *September 1970*), by 1974 Redding had been forced to sign away considerable

Gerry Shepherd (*right*) with The Glitter Band: Showed much flare

Noel Redding (*left*), with Jimi Hendrix: A vital part of The Experience

future earnings from the three major hit albums (and several singles) issued by The Experience. (Financial problems in the eighties obliged the bassist to relinquish his prized Fender Jazz – the machine upon which he'd written many of his Experience bass lines – for £10K.) Redding's own later bands, Fat Mattress – formed in 1969 with Neil Landon (vocals), Jim Leverton (guitar) and Eric Dillon (drums) – US rockers Road and finally The Noel Redding Band (an Irish-based act that also featured Thin Lizzy guitarist Eric Bell), were not commercially viable and the bassist's financial situation became ever more precarious, prompting him to leave the UK.

Since the mid eighties, Redding had maintained a lower profile in his adopted Ireland, but visitors to the De Barra pub in County Cork would have heard the man play most Friday evenings. It was the owner of this establishment, Bobby Blackwell, who found Noel Redding's body in the bathroom of his home in Ardfield, Clonakilty, on the evening of Monday 12 May 2003, the musician having failed to show for two nights. His death ascribed to 'shock haemorrhage due to oesophageal varices in reaction to cirrhosis of the liver', Redding was cremated a week later in west Dublin.

'Take away his role as the bass-player in the largest rock trio of all time and strip away all the glory of his musical career. As a human being, he was a fabulous guy.'

Ian Grant, Redding's manager

Monday 19

Camoflauge

(Jason Johnson – Savannah, Georgia, 1981)

As he walked to the building of his Savannah-based label, Pure Pain Records, accompanied by his young son (who thankfully remained unhurt), rapper Camoflauge became the latest to take the bullet as hip hop's rollcall ticked off another name.

Already on his third album, Camoflauge was for some reason seen as a role model in his township, the only one of Savannah's 'sons' to have achieved success in hip hop. Despite managing to pull himself some way out of the ghetto of his childhood to a Billboard-charting album, *I Represent* (2000), the rapper appeared to have few aspirations beyond the usual tiresome litany of guns, bling and 'bitches'. He could also lay claim to that other 'must-have' of the self-respecting rap artist, a prison sentence. The year his first album was launched, Camoflauge spent two months inside under suspicion of murder, although he was released when a grand jury failed to indict him. The rapper really must have felt he'd hit the big time when Universal issued his second album – boasting the inspired title *Strictly 4 Da Streets: Sex, Drugs and Violence Vol 1* (2002) – but Camoflauge was dropped soon afterwards and signed to Pure Pain instead. Perhaps displaying how desperate Savannah was to promote one of its own, he was thereafter invited to speak at local schools and act as 'Santa' for the children of the housing project where he was brought up.

Despite being shot at the previous year, Camoflauge's death in hospital was met with the usual mixture of shock and tributes to a martyr by his homeboys. Various suspects were interviewed, but with no further information forthcoming, nobody, by 2005 at least, could be charged with the artist's murder.

Sunday 25

Jeremy Michael Ward
(California, 1976)
The Mars Volta
DeFacto

In 2003, The Mars Volta was one of the most interesting – and certainly most visually arresting – new bands to emerge from America. The group had risen from the ashes of strident So-Cal politicos At the Drive-In, whose Cedric Bixler Zavala (vocals) and Omar Rodriguez-Lopez (guitar) had teamed up with Ikey Isaiah

Owens (keyboards) and sound manipulator Jeremy Michael Ward, with whom both had worked in the band DeFacto. Ward was one of rock's unsung heroes, an offstage performer and former repoman whose sonic inspirations guided much of each band's output. In 2003, The Mars Volta promoted a full-length debut CD, the curiously titled *De-Loused in the Crematorium*, an album which (presciently) tells the story of a man in a drug-induced coma. To promote the record, they embarked upon a hectic schedule of dates with The Red Hot Chili Peppers across Europe where the band's never-less-than-intriguing mix of psychedelics, pop and hardcore rock was particularly popular.

On their return from the other side of the world, The Mars Volta learned of the sudden death of Ward from a suspected heroin overdose. His body was found by his room-mate in Los Angeles. Picking themselves up from the tragedy, the band recruited former ATDI member Paul Hinojos to replace the late soundsmith.

Friday 30

Mickie Most
(Michael Peter Hayes – Aldershot, Hampshire, 20 June 1938)
(The Playboys)

Mickie Most was one of the most prominent non-musician faces during the UK's glam-rock era – a clear-thinking, decisive presence amid a sea of glitter and decadence. While never possessing the maverick tendencies of a Joe Meek or Tony Visconti, Britain's most prolific pop producer is still said to hold the record for the most number-one singles worldwide. If this comes as a surprise, then even more remarkable is the statistic of his own band, The Playboys, running off eleven

Mickie Most: 'If that's The Arrows again, tell 'em I'm busy ...'

straight number-one singles in South Africa with covers of US rock 'n' roll standards! Most, though, will chiefly be remembered for his engineering of so many stars' careers. In the sixties he handled the records of Donovan, Herman's Hermits, Brenda Lee and Lulu, beginning with the biggest hit of them all, The Animals' 'House of the Rising Sun' (1964 – a track reportedly recorded in fifteen minutes for just £1 1s), which took his work to the top of the charts in twelve countries. Consolidating on this, Most then set up his own label, RAK (initially in conjunction with future Led Zeppelin manager Peter Grant), scoring further chartbusters with Hot Chocolate, Suzi Quatro and Smokie during a seemingly unstoppable period throughout the seventies. This unbroken triumph continued some way into the 1980s, Most discovering Kim Wilde when she was just a teenager, as well as collaborating with his son Calvin Hayes's briefly successful band, Johnny Hates Jazz.

In 2000, Mickie Most – who also made a name as the 'voice of reason' on ITV's *New Faces* – contracted mesothelioma, a rare, inoperable form of lung cancer, from which he died at his London home. He was believed to be worth at least £50 million at the time of his death.

JUNE

Friday 6

Dave Rowberry
(Nottingham, 4 July 1940)
The Animals
(The Mike Cotton Sound)

Well before he joined the chart-topping Animals, keyboardist Dave Rowberry gained experience backing some of pop music's biggest names on the club circuit. With The Mike Cotton Sound, Rowberry accompanied The Four Tops and even a young Stevie Wonder, before Eric Burdon came knocking to find a replacement for the departing Alan Price, who had grown weary of his band's constant travelling abroad. Already a major band, The Animals had been to the top with 'House of the Rising Sun' (1964), but enjoyed further major international hits once Rowberry joined the following year: the keyboardist proved himself more than adept as backing vocalist to Burdon on several of these songs, including the insistent 'We've Gotta Get out of This Place' (1965). With The Animals falling apart after a US tour in 1967, it was a short stint for Rowberry, who was a far better player than often credited.

Dave Rowberry returned to the relative anonymity of session work for the remainder of his career, appearing on stage in 1994 with Burdon and 'The Animals II' before his unexpected death from heart failure some years later.

Thursday 19

Ethan James
(Ralph Burns Kellogg – Pasadena, California, 1946)
Blue Cheer
(Various acts)

He may have had a conventional end but Ethan James was a highly unconventional musician. Extremely proficient at the piano, guitar, bass and drums, James was a founder member of Blue Cheer, the cult West Coast band believed by many (mainly US fans) to be the world's original heavy-metal band. A member of Cheer for six years and three albums, James was revered by fellow musicians and even played with fellow Haight-Ashburians Janis Joplin and Jerry Garcia before joining Mint Tattoo. Believing two forenames were essential for a musician, James legally ditched his birth name in his thirties, by which time he'd set up the prolific Radio Tokyo studios in Los Angeles, the perfect home for California's burgeoning post-punk scene. Among the acts James produced there were the future platinum-toting Bangles and Red Hot Chili Peppers, while significant alternative names such as Black Flag and The Minutemen were also regular clients. Fascinated by medieval music, James was able to add the nyckelharpa and hurdy-gurdy – which he often played as a Los Angeles busker – to his impressive repertoire. A man of deep faith, the musician was also a church-goer for three decades up until his death from liver cancer. Blue Cheer co-founder Jerry Russell survived James by just two years.

Wednesday 25

Orion Satushek
(Portland, Oregon, 1976)
Reeks & The Wrecks
The Spooky Dance Band

It was a textbook drunk-driver scenario: a van disappeared into the night, leaving three popular young people shattered on the tarmac, two dead, one seriously injured. The victims were Orion Satushek, singer and keyboardist with Portland rock bands Reeks & The Wrecks and The Spooky Dance Band; his collaborator in the latter, 23-year-old Caroline Buchalter; plus visiting artist Angela Leazenby, aged twenty-six.

Satushek was eagerly anticipating the release of The Wrecks' latest album, *Knife Hits*, at the time that the three friends and a fourth companion, Larry Needham, took to the streets on their bicycles around midnight on 25 June. As they travelled at leisurely pace, van-driver Lindsey Llaneza (already charged with a recent drink-driving offence) approached rapidly from the opposite direction; the man, who was discovered to be three times over the limit, swerved past the first cyclist, Needham, but struck the remaining three. Of the group, Satushek and Leazenby (having only recently arrived in the area) were killed outright: the musician was hurtled through the windscreen of a parked Chevy, while his friend was thrown a reported 400 feet by the impact. The 'lucky one', Buchalter, was taken into intensive care, her pelvis smashed, but she eventually recovered. The incident galvanized an extraordinary number of Oregon cyclists, who took to the streets several days later to protest against the dangers of drink-driving. For his part, Llaneza – dubbed a murderer by the mob – faced charges of first-degree assault and manslaughter. In April 2004, he received twenty years' imprisonment.

JULY

Friday 4

Barry White

(Barry Eugene Carter – Galveston, Texas, 12 September 1944)

(Love Unlimited)

(The Upfronts)

He may have been the first of his kind, he might well be the last – and, at eighteen stone, he was almost certainly 'everything' – but the sultan of steaming, sexual soul was actually a devout Christian. Accompanying his single mother and siblings, Barry Eugene Carter left Texas for Los Angeles' tough East Side when he was a boy, his choir singing merely a cover-up for a tearaway lifestyle that could have resulted in the future superstar spending his entire life on the wrong

side of the tracks. At seventeen, Carter was locked up for his part in the theft of $30,000 dollars' worth of tyres (he obviously had plans to become a Michelin man even then): this came on the back of lesser felonies. This was a wake-up call and from then on the renamed White's priorities were clearly delineated. He found some work backing small-time vocal group The Upfronts (two of whom were reform-school friends), which brought

him to the attention of their label. Subsequently, he managed to sell a few songs (one of which was recorded by Bobby Fuller) while playing various instruments on many small-label sessions, something White had done since playing the piano on a Jess Belvin record when just eleven years old. The major break for White came with his backing of post-Supremes Philly girl group Love Unlimited from 1969, by which time White had already

Barry White: Qualified to satisfy

married, separated and sired four children. The singer stamped his authority on proceedings to the extent that he married lead singer Glodean James (supposedly the focus of his later lyrics) and soon had the group backing *him*.

For a few years, White was to be lord of soul's steamy jungle, swatting away the opposition (Billy Paul, Teddy Pendergrass, etc) like so many flies – and even giving Marvin Gaye a run for his money for the very top position. In one sense, he was *definitely* the bigger star, his awesome stage presence seducing an entire generation of female admirers, who dubbed the neatly bearded White 'The Walrus of Love'. Albums and singles flew from the shelves – nearly 100 million in all. Principal among his many snappily titled hits were the sultry 'Can't Get Enough of Your Love, Babe' (1974, US number one), 'You're the First, the Last, My Everything' (1974, UK number one, US number two) and the near-faultless 'You See the Trouble with Me' (1976, UK number two). Despite his devout background, White's albums at this stage featured some seriously moist moments, though White cited his religious convictions when later turning down the opportunity to parody his former character as Chef in television's *South Park* – a job that then went instead to his friend Isaac Hayes.

In 1983, White was given a stark reminder of his criminal past when his older brother Darryl was shot dead in a needless dispute with a neighbour over just twenty dollars. There was little solace in music either: a climate change restricted White's later successes to the occasional hit, 1994's US/UK Top Twenty comeback 'Practice What You Preach' a notable example. Barry White's immense bulk, however, meant that he suffered greatly from high blood pressure as he grew older and, relying more and more heavily on his forty-strong Love Unlimited Orchestra who had supported him for almost

thirty years, he was advised to stop touring in 1999. His final months were believed to have been spent in a great deal of pain as his vital organs began to fail him; White's death from kidney failure was therefore seen by many as a blessing. He may have retired to that velvet-lined boudoir in the sky, but posthumously White retains the love of a generation of fans who just ain't never, *never* gonna give him up . . .

Sunday 20

Adam Cox
(Portland, Oregon, 1980)

Matthew Fitzgerald
(Portland, Oregon, 1983)

Jeremy Gage
(Portland, Oregon, 1981)

The Exploding Hearts

US indie rock had mourned the lost lives of members of For Squirrels (◂ *September 1995*) and Compromise (◂ *July 2002*) in highway crashes, before another such incident took place in Oregon in July 2003. The details were depressingly similar. Garage punks The Exploding Hearts were buzzing from the great reception to their first record, *Guitar Romantic* (2002) – described by *Rolling Stone* as 'a cross between The Ramones and Big Star' – when the band met their untimely end on Interstate 5 near Eugene, Oregon. The Exploding Hearts had spent the weekend partying in San Francisco after two triumphant headlining gigs, but late that Sunday it was clear that bassist Matthew 'Matt Lock' Fitzgerald was over-tired and in no state to drive as the band made its way back home through the night. Over-compensating after the van drifted from the road, Fitzgerald caused the vehicle to hit a kerb and flip over. As it rolled, he, singer/guitarist Adam 'Baby' Cox and

drummer Jeremy 'Kid Killer' Gage were thrown out and killed by the impact. A fourth member, Terry Six, aged twenty-one, escaped with minor scratches, as did 35-year-old manager Rachelle 'Ratch Aronica' Ramos – the only passenger wearing a seatbelt.

Friday 25

Erik Braunn (Brann)
(Erik Keith Braunn – Pekin, Illinois, 11 August 1950)

Iron Butterfly

Guitarist Erik Braunn wasn't in the original line-up of San Diego's most outlandish psychedelic-progsters, but he could easily have been. Only a teenager when he was snapped up by Iron Butterfly, he was already an experienced musician, having played the violin since he was just four. In 1966, Braunn (or Brann, as he was sometimes known) completed the classic Butterfly roster of Doug Ingle (vocals/keyboards), Lee Dorman (bass) and Ron Bushey (drums). The band had toured with major names like The Doors and Jefferson Airplane before they unleashed a debut record, *Heavy*, and the extraordinary seventeen-minute epic 'In-a-Gadda-da-Vida' (both 1968), the latter selling millions of copies in various formats over the years. Braunn left Iron Butterfly after the next album, *Ball* (1969), to be replaced by Mike Pinera of Blues Image, but he was to make frequent returns to the group which, despite folding in 1971, seemed to maintain a fanbase regardless. Braunn stayed in music, working as a session musician and producer until shortly before his death from a cardiac arrest.

See also *Philip 'Taylor' Kramer* (◂ *February 1995*). *Early member Darryl DeLoach passed away just nine months before Braunn.*

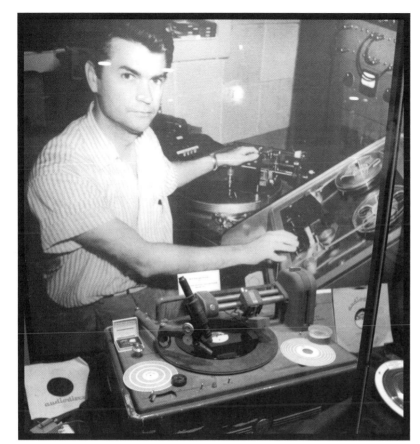

Sam Phillips at the cutting edge of recording technology

Sam Phillips
(Florence, Alabama, 5 January 1923)

Just two days before his twenty-seventh birthday, producer Sam Phillips opened the door to what was to be rock 'n' roll's first real home – 706 Union Avenue, Memphis, better known as Sun Records. Recording mainly black artists for the first five years or so, Sun welcomed names like Jackie Brenston, B B King and Rufus Thomas into its studios, before Elvis Presley walked in and changed the face of popular music for ever. Then, to stave off a debt, Phillips offloaded his biggest asset to RCA for just $35K. Nevertheless, for his shrewd scouting of these great musicians, plus the likes of Johnny Cash, Roy Orbison and Carl Perkins, Phillips was rightly one of the first names inducted into the Rock 'n' Roll Hall of Fame. He died from respiratory failure on 30 July 2003.

AUGUST

Monday 18

Tony Jackson
(Liverpool, 16 July 1938)
The Searchers
(The Vibrations)

Famously drunk when the band auditioned for an unimpressed Brian Epstein, Tony Jackson nonetheless fronted The Searchers as they rose to become one of the most significant bands of the Merseybeat explosion. The Searchers were just a duo – singer/guitarists John McNally and

Eric Braunn of Iron Butterfly: A metal moth-er?

Mike Pender – when Jackson signed up, the line-up completed by drummer Chris Curtis. Like fellow upstarts The Beatles, the group trod the usual round of Liverpool nightclubs, even emulating them by playing Hamburg in 1962. The Searchers were quick to follow The Fab Four to number one with 'Sweets for My Sweet' (1963), almost turning the trick again with the similar-sounding follow-up 'Sugar Spice'. By the time of the group's biggest seller, 'Needles and Pins' (1964), Jackson had been

removed from his post as singer, though he continued as bassist for a third number one, 'Don't Throw Your Love Away' (1964). Unhappy with the move towards soft rock (as opposed to 'beat'), Jackson left The Searchers that July, after which the band's sales dipped significantly.

Unfortunately, so did Jackson's. His next band, The Vibrations, barely scraped into the charts, the singer more concerned about refining his features with expensive cosmetic surgery than honing his tunes. Jackson

left the music industry for more conventional employment a couple of years later, increasingly embittered by his lack of personal success. He played with Mike Pender's Searchers during the nineties, but the onset of arthritis was to curtail even this. Suffering from diabetes as well as alcohol-related diseases, Tony Jackson was apparently penniless when he died in a Nottingham hospital.

See also *Chris Curtis (☛ February 2005)*

SEPTEMBER

Sunday 7

Warren Zevon
(Chicago, Illinois, 24 January 1947)

Unassuming though he may have looked, part-Jewish part-Mormon songwriting legend Warren Zevon nurtured a darker side in his work. But this remained hidden for some time, while the fresh-faced Zevon toured the USA with The Everly Brothers, who were keen on his piano-playing. The musician – who'd made a good living penning jingles and songs for high-profile bands like The Turtles – found that his own first album, *Wanted Dead or Alive* (1969), barely caused a ripple, its follow-up not even meriting release by his label One Way. The breakthrough came when Zevon moved to Los Angeles, putting him in touch with major artists such as Jackson Browne (who produced his 1976 major label debut) and Linda Ronstadt (who hit with his 'Poor, Poor Pitiful Me' in 1978) and seeing the introduction of his trademark glasses. The next album, *Excitable Boy* (1978), contained what would become Zevon's best-known song,

Warren Zevon: Reached the heights via some twisted stares

Johnny Cash: 'The one on the right is (also) on the left'

'Werewolves Of London', his only US hit and a staple for movie soundtracks for ever after. *Bad Luck Streak in Dancing School* (1980) continued the upward trend for Zevon, the songs 'A Certain Girl' and 'Gorilla, You're a Desperado' both international airplay hits. However, the decadent side of the Californian scene affected Zevon to the extent that his career was hampered for some years by serious alcohol- and drug-related problems, the songwriter merely regarding these as fuel for his creativity, despite the toll they would take on his health. The musician dedicated his 1980 album to author Ross McDonald (one of many writers to befriend him), who it is believed counselled Zevon through some heavy times. He also became acquainted with the up-and-coming REM, who, as major fans of his work, were delighted to collaborate with Zevon on their Hindu Love Gods project in 1990. Zevon's self-confessed phobia of doctors and hospitals were to hit back

at him in his fifties when the singer learned that he had mesothelioma in 2002: his days were by then clearly numbered. Thankfully, Zevon lived long enough to see the birth of his twin grandsons.

Although Warren Zevon made numerous comebacks in the final decade of his life, his work is always likely to remain an acquired taste – a shame, given that he was one of the most original, imaginative and concise songwriters to emerge from an environment that produced much that was hackneyed and overblown.

Golden Oldies #16

Johnny Cash
(Kingsland, Arizona, 26 February 1932)

Classed as a country artist throughout his career, Johnny Cash was clearly much more than this, frequently voicing publicly his distaste for the Nashville mainstream. Sure, like those of his nemeses, Cash's lyrics of sin and redemption were informed by a rockily eventful personal life, but they also possessed a sardonic humour unique to the genre, displayed prominently in lighter numbers like 'A Boy Named Sue' (1969) and 'One Piece at a Time' (1976).

The frankness of 'Folsom Prison Blues' (1968) drew a huge fanbase among inmates, though Cash never served a sentence himself, even if there were, of course, several 'one-night stands'. Given his upbringing, this was probably a remarkable achievement – the abuse of an alcoholic father and the death of his older brother Jack in a horrific sawmill accident (the boy living on in agony for a week before he died) only steeling Cash to succeed. As his career took off, he did, however, cultivate an outlaw image and became addicted to booze and amphetamines (sharing an apartment with Waylon Jennings wouldn't have helped), his first marriage collapsing in 1966. His second marriage, to June Carter, a singer who helped Cash kick his addictions, was altogether more harmonious and the couple were still together at Carter's death, just four months before his own.

Johnny Cash died on 12 September 2003 from complications of the diabetes diagnosed six years previously. An admirer of many styles of music, his ability as an interpreter of the writing of new artists became especially noted by a third generation of listeners drawn by chilling renditions of Nick Cave's 'The Mercy Seat'; Depeche Mode's 'Personal Jesus'; U2's 'One'; and, perhaps most significantly, Trent Reznor's 'Hurt' – which won Cash his final Grammy, just days ahead of his death.

Wednesday 24

Matthew Jay
(Plymouth, 10 October 1978)

In an apparently impulsive manner, young singer/songwriter Matthew Jay ended his life in a gesture that nobody will ever fully be able to interpret. Although he was born in England, Jay was brought up by his Beatles-, Stones- and folk-loving parents in Abergavenny, South Wales, playing in the family's semi-professional band. Eager to learn as much as he could from those who had preceded him, the guitarist became a disciple of seventies artist Nick Drake (☜ *November 1974*), though none

of his colleagues had any idea that Jay's life would conclude in such a similarly unfulfilled and tragic way. In 1999, Jay signed with Parlophone subsidiary Food Records, despite never having played live before. Jay's first full-length record, *Draw*, arrived in 2001 to some acclaim, the singer landing high-profile support tours with Dido, Doves, Starsailor and The Stereophonics as he began to work on material for a second set. With minimal sales – and there were clearly many reasons for that – Jay felt under pressure from EMI to deliver with the next record, but in 2003 the label decided not to continue with the artist when suitable collaborators could not be found.

The next move, though, was one that nobody expected. Shortly before midnight on 24 September, Matthew Jay fell to his death from the seventh-storey window of a friend's apartment in Harrow, north London. The authorities were quick to confirm that the singer had been alone at the time (although since the event, it has become apparent that this was *not* the case, when an unnamed girlfriend and another acquaintance were discovered to have been present around the time). Beneath the shock and upset, family and friends were mystified: although frustrated by the hiccough in his career, Jay was not believed to have been depressed, having spoken cheerfully to his family that same evening. Was it suicide? Was it an accident? Followers of Nick Drake felt they'd heard this one before . . .

Friday 26

Robert Palmer
(Robert Allen Palmer – Batley, Yorkshire, 19 January 1949)
Vinegar Joe
The Power Station
(The Alan Bown Set)

Regarded as something of an old-school gent, clean-cut Robert Palmer spent many years working the circuit with a variety of bands before his huge multi-platinum successes of the 1980s. The first decade of Palmer's life was spent in Malta where his serviceman father was stationed, but the would-be singer was to be quick off the mark once his family returned to the UK. Palmer joined his first band at fourteen, polishing the style that led to his being picked up as a replacement for Jess Roden in The Alan Bown Set in the late sixties. Better known were Vinegar Joe, a bluesy pop band in which Palmer sang alongside the throaty Elkie Brooks (the pair having sung previously in Dada) and which enjoyed a reasonably high profile in 1972–3, recording three albums. Although Brooks was also to enjoy solo success, Palmer clearly had the edge in star potential. After an acrimonious falling-out with his co-star, he left to record *Sneakin' Sally through the Alley* (1974) in the USA, with no less than The Meters as backing band and Lowell 'Little Feat' George at the desk. This, and *Pressure Drop* (1975), both sold steadily, but it wasn't until 1978's *Double Fun* that Palmer achieved a US hit single in the light, optimistic 'Every Kinda People'. Record sales at this stage were no indication of his eighties dominance, however, and even *Clues* (1980) – possibly Palmer's best album – required assistance from the unlikely hand of Gary Numan to furnish him with a UK hit. More collaborations followed, including the truly wretched Power Station project with Andy Taylor and John Taylor of Duran Duran, which found favour for Palmer with the teenies in 1985 (and again, to somewhat better effect, ten years later). Absolute paydirt was hit, however, with the platinum album *Riptide* (1985), which confirmed Palmer as pop's number-one 'Lothario' with its brace of million-selling US singles, 'Addicted To Love' and 'I Didn't Mean To Turn You On' (both 1986 – also UK Top Ten hits). Some gratuitous model-heavy promo work from late director Terence Donovan didn't go amiss here, either.

So, what to do once you've made your millions from AOR pop music? Simple: set up a studio in Switzerland (closer to the bank account, one might imagine) and then strip it all back down to the gritty, blues-influenced material of your early work. To his credit, Palmer did this with some aplomb with his final recording, *Drive* (2003), though admittedly not before a couple of reworkings of *Riptide* to keep the management and label happy. Robert Palmer had lived in exile for fifteen years when the news filtered back home of his sudden and unexpected death from a heart attack while spending a weekend in Paris with his partner. He was interred in his adopted city of Lugano.

See also *Bernard Edwards (* April 1992). The death in November of drummer Tony Thompson meant that three sometime members of The Power Station had died by the end of 2003.*

OCTOBER

Tuesday 21

Elliott Smith

(Steven Paul Smith – Omaha, Nebraska, 6 August 1969)

(Heatmiser)

(Stranger Than Fiction)

Hot on the heels of Matthew Jay's mysterious death came the apparent suicide of a more established singer/songwriter whose tender and deeply introspective songs similarly echoed the work of Nick Drake. Yet, despite his widely acknowledged tendency towards the morose, the circumstances surrounding Smith's death remain unclear.

The young Smith was not yet a year old when his parents divorced, the boy growing up in Texas with his mother and a reportedly abusive stepfather (whom he'd later threaten to pursue), which eventually resulted in his moving to Oregon to be with his father. Before he was out of his teens, the singer, not wanting to sound like a 'jock', had changed his first name, and fronted his first rock band, Stranger Than Fiction, at high school. Smith – who'd graduated from university in Massachusetts with a degree in philosophy – was at this stage a fan of thrashier music than the kind that would make his name, forming the Fugazi-esque Heatmiser with Neil Gust (guitar), Brandt Peterson (bass, replaced by Sam Coomes, who played with Smith throughout his career) and Tony Lash (drums) while living on benefits. This band displayed for the first time Smith's clever juxtaposition

Elliott Smith: Mr Misery?

'Yeah, like Kurt, he was making music for the sad kids.'

Mary Lou Lord, friend of Elliott Smith (and former girlfriend of Kurt Cobain)

'[Smith's was] the best suicide I ever heard of!'

Tact, as ever, from another of Cobain's exes, Courtney Love

of sophisticated, lyrical ideas against an uncommercial backing, and lasted until 1996, by which time the singer was already acknowledged as being greater than the sum of the band's individual parts. Elliott Smith solo was a different beast: his songs were oblique, well crafted and endlessly haunting. A first album, *Roman Candle* (1994), now sounds awkward compared to what the man achieved over the next decade, but reveals a sensitivity with which Smith was to become synonymous. While friends of Ian Curtis (for example) were quick to talk of his 'laddish' joking, Smith was habitually portrayed by his contemporaries as wilfully morose, always ready to suggest that 'this would be the last time they saw him alive'. So the signs were in place – but the music was remarkable. Wonderful albums like *Either/Or* (1997) and major-label debut *XO* (1998) seemed to pluck from (and perhaps even improve on) the finer moments of Simon & Garfunkel. The singer/songwriter had spent two years in a drug-fuelled haze, though, rumours of his inability to remain *compos mentis* during live shows perhaps suggesting that Smith was now using crack. He cleaned up for a while – long enough to collect a 1998 Academy award for the song 'Miss Misery', one of several chosen for the Gus Van Zant movie *Good Will Hunting* – but was clearly using again following the 2000 album *Figure Of Eight*, which, presumably by reason of its smoother production, had disappointed certain critics.

Elliott Smith, although now 'clean', talked openly of increasing depression before his death in 2003. He was not

lonely, however, at least not in the more literal sense of the word. He now had a live-in girlfriend, Jennifer Chiba, singer with the paradoxically named Happy Ending, a Los Angeles guitar band Smith had nurtured and taken on the road with him when promoting his latest album. It is believed that Smith's production input into the band's work was causing resentment, however. As a producer, he was known to be a perfectionist, which led to a huge row when an impatient member of Happy Ending waltzed off with the master tapes for their first single. His input was also causing tension with Chiba, a factor that increased the pressure on her when Smith died. The pair had endured the mother of all domestics when Smith finally cracked. Infuriated by her boyfriend's threats of self-harm, Chiba locked herself in their bathroom – only to emerge when she heard the guttural scream that could only mean that Smith had actually carried out the threat he'd made more than once before. She rushed to him to discover a kitchen knife embedded in his chest, the singer/songwriter collapsing before her: Smith died in hospital just over an hour later. The music world was stunned: despite knowing him to be a depressive, the authorities – and indeed many of the singer's fans – weren't convinced it was suicide. Certain factors seemed highly suspicious: the singer's name had seemingly been misspelled on a Post-It note that had served as his suicide missive (though this has since been cleared as a transcription error in the coroner's report), while self-stabbing is of course almost

unheard of as a suicide method. For Chiba, it was the beginning of a nightmare. Although abuse (and even death threats) from Smith's fans on her band's website forced its closure – and, eventually, the break-up of Happy Ending – she was never questioned by the authorities, having apparently refused all such requests. Investigations are still ongoing.

All outstanding work on Elliott Smith's unfinished final album, *From a Basement on a Hill* (2004), was resolved with a great deal more ease than have been the inquiries surrounding its perpetrator's grim departure.

Friday 24

Rosey Nix Adams
(Rozanna Lea Adams – Tennessee, 13 July 1958)

James Campbell
(1963)

(The Sidemen)

Another mysterious possible suicide – in this case, an apparent pact between two musicians – emerged just days later, this time in the world of country and bluegrass. Although never as successful as her mother, June Carter Cash, or legendary stepfather, Johnny Cash, Rosey Adams had made a living as a songwriter, as well as playing guitar and providing back-up vocals on many of Carter's releases. As a child (her father was Carter's previous husband, Edwin Nix), Adams apparently used to help her mother by hunting out Cash's stash of pills.

For his part, James Campbell had played fiddle with timeless bluegrass acts such as Bill Monroe as well as his own group, The Sidemen; he'd enjoyed a level of success, but had undergone numerous courses of treatment for drug addiction. At the time of the pair's death, friends had remarked that Campbell had seemed 'worn out by life'. Rosey Nix Adams had also recently seemed distracted: those who saw her at the recent funerals of her mother and stepfather (*Golden Oldies #16*) had described the musician as depressed beyond the normal response to a loved one's passing. Nevertheless, the discovery of her and Campbell's bodies (apparently made by Adams's husband) in a disused tour bus just a month later came as a further shock to grieving relatives. The pair had worked together for some years and were in the process of recording a new project. It was established that they had died from carbon-monoxide poisoning, faulty gas heaters being blamed. Authorities were thus quick to pronounce the death 'accidental'. Although the exact nature of their relationship isn't known, the presence of drug paraphernalia hints of other possibilities.

NOVEMBER

Wednesday 5

Bobby Hatfield

(Beaver Dam, Wisconsin, 10 August 1940)

The Righteous Brothers
(The Variations)

The soaring voices of Bobby Hatfield and Bill Medley – The Righteous Brothers – gave the world its first real taste of blue-eyed soul. Known as 'The Blond Bomber', Hatfield had recorded with Anaheim vocal group The Variations and on his own (with little success) by the time he met ex-Paramours singer Medley in 1961. The name 'The Righteous Brothers' was apparently coined by an African-American marine who watched an early performance of theirs in Santa Ana. The pair obviously possessed both range and vocal control, a fact not lost on Phil Spector, who offered to produce them. Following a series of modest hits, the duo – who had already opened for The Beatles – scored with a record destined to become the most-played radio hit of all time. In January 1965, the duo's *twelfth* single, 'You've Lost That Lovin' Feelin'', went to number one in both America and Britain (where Andrew Loog Oldham took out a press ad to ensure that the song beat Cilla Black's version to the top) on its way to sales of several million. Those who didn't believe The Righteous Brothers could pull off the trick again were then forced to eat their words as their rendition of 'Unchained Melody' climbed the world's charts that autumn. (In the UK, the record only went to number one after its inclusion in the sappy 1990 movie *Ghost*.)

After another US chart-topper with '(You're My) Soul and Inspiration' (1966), a sudden collapse in sales induced Hatfield to attempt another

Righteous Brothers Bill Medley and Bobby Hatfield: Rediscovered that lovin' feelin'

solo career – again with little success. Following a couple of different Righteous Brothers line-ups in which Medley and Hatfield linked up with other singers, the pair reunited for a number of albums in the seventies and enjoyed another big US-seller with the slightly cloying (though very *Number One in Heaven*-friendly) eulogy to dead rock stars, 'Rock 'n' Roll Heaven' (1974). The Righteous Brothers continued to tour until Hatfield's death late in 2003. As they prepared for a concert in Kalamazoo, The Blond Bomber died in his sleep – apparently from a cocaine-induced heart attack.

Wednesday 19

Greg Ridley

(Cumberland, 23 January 1947)
Humble Pie
Spooky Tooth
Boxer
(Various acts)

Introducing himself to the music industry as the 'Dino' of Dino & The Danubes, bassist/guitarist Greg Ridley became a well-known figure in British rock with his twin stints in major groups Humble Pie and Spooky Tooth. The latter band came about after Ridley created The VIPs with school-pal singer/keyboardist Mike Harrison, the pair of them recruiting Luther Grosvenor (guitar, later of Mott the Hoople), Gary Wright (organ, later solo) and Mike Kellie (drums). This band made several albums, though Ridley was to leave after 1969's *Spooky Two*: that year, the bassist received an offer he couldn't refuse – to join ex-Small Faces legend Steve Marriott in a new supergroup called Humble Pie. The band – Ridley, Marriott (vocals/guitar), Peter Frampton (guitar) and Jerry Shirley (drums) – scored an immediate smash with 'Natural Born Bugie' (1969) but weren't to achieve further hits. After the break-up of Humble Pie in 1977, Ridley took a break from music, a return to the game with the band Boxer not proving satisfactory. Greg Ridley died after a stroke on holiday in Spain had left him comatose.

See also *Mike Patto (March 1979); Steve Marriott (April 1991); Ollie Halsall (May 1992)*

Wednesday 26

Soulja Slim

(James Tapp – Gentilly, Louisiana, 9 September 1977)

Soulja Slim's brief career – which saw him work with major names in the hip-hop world, including Snoop Dogg – was at a low ebb at the time of his death. After success with a gold debut album, *Give It to 'Em Raw* (1998), Slim faded from the scene somewhat, though a lengthy spell behind bars for armed robbery didn't help matters.

Outside the rapper's mother's duplex in Gentilly, Soulja Slim – who had survived a shooting back in 1995 – was ambushed and shot four times as he emerged from his car shortly before 6 pm: he collapsed and died on the front lawn, the car's engine still running. Just before the shooting, Slim had been in an altercation at a gas station, though it is more widely believed that the killing was connected to a major falling-out Slim had over finances with his previous record label, No Limit. An investigation led New Orleans police to a suspect who was not charged (due to lack of evidence) but was then fingered for the killing of another Louisiana rap artist a month later. Perhaps unsurprisingly, the star himself also became a posthumous suspect in one or two recent murders in the area, including that of Robert Lee Paige, who had been shot and thrown into a City Park lagoon that September. Slim's mother was vehement in the defence of her late son. It has since been revealed that a substantial price had been put on Slim's head by the New Orleans gangsta fraternity.

Saturday 29

K-Rupt

(Carlton Williams Bongo Juma – Nairobi, November 1979)

Doubtless many will find the completely unprovoked murder of Kenyan rapper K-Rupt more tragic than that of Soulja Slim. During the previous two years, K-Rupt had been enjoying national success with various hit records, including his latest dub 'Dada Njoo', which was on the charts at the time of his death. The day after a show with fellow Kenyan hip-hop star Nameless, the rapper was riding a matatutu (two-man taxi) to his next performance when the vehicle was commandeered in an apparent car-jacking. As K-Rupt argued with the attackers, one pulled a gun on him and killed him with a single shot. His body was found dumped in Laikipia Forest. 2003 was an extraordinarily hard year for Kenyan rap music, with the deaths of K-Rupt's sometime collaborator E-Sir in March and Wicky Mosh the following month.

David Mathenge

He may be known as Nameless (and, to most, still remains faceless), but Kenyan hip-hop musician David Mathenge deserves a mention in *Number One in Heaven* for having survived what looked like certain death. Twice. Within six months.

On 18 March 2003, having appeared the previous evening as a special guest alongside rapper E-Sir at a Nakuru beauty pageant, the rising star returned to his native Nairobi in a tour vehicle. Apparently distracted by the splendour of Lake Elementaita, the driver of the Mitsubishi lost control, the vehicle careering off the motorway and down a bank. In all, three passengers were thrown out and killed – including E-Sir – but 'Nameless' Mathenge, who remained conscious the whole time, was released from hospital with merely a fractured ankle. Then, in August the same year, Mathenge was the survivor of an eerily similar car crash that resulted in another two fatalities. Understandably, the artist has said: There is nothing that makes you feel the value of life more than when you have come so close to death.'

Lest We Forget

Other notable deaths that occurred sometime during 2003:

June Carter Cash (popular US country singer/musician who co-wrote her husband's 'Ring Of Fire' hit; born Valerie June Carter, Virginia, 23/6/1929; after heart surgery – and four months before Johnny, 15/5)

Arthur Conley (US singer who scored a million-seller with the Otis Redding co-written 'Sweet Soul Music' in 1967; born Georgia, 4/1/1946; intestinal cancer, 17/11)

Dino Conner (US vocalist who lined up alongside his twin brother, Shazam, in briefly popular R & B vocal trio H-Town; born Keven Conner, Texas, 1974; car crash, 28/1)

Slim Dusty (Australian country legend who scored an international pop hit in 1959 with 'Pub with No Beer'; born David Kirkpatrick, New South Wales, 13/6/1927; cancer, 19/9)

Jinny Janis (US member of a cappella vocal act The Chordettes, who went to #2 with the million-seller 'Lollipop' in 1958; born Virginia Osborn, Washington, 25/4/1927; cancer, 19/5)

Rana Ross (formidable 'chick rock' bassist with metallers Sinboy and Vixen; born Rana Langer, New York, 20/10/1961; AIDS, 3/5)

Dick St John (US pop songwriter with Dick & Dee Dee, who hit US #2 with 1961's 'The Mountain's High'; born Richard Gosting, California, 1940; head injuries after slipping from a ladder, 27/12)

Vic Taylor (Jamaican reggae/ska singer with pioneering acts Tommy McCook & The Skatalites and Byron Lee & The Dragonaires; born 1946; heart failure, 23/6)

Claude Trenier (US final surviving member of pioneering lounge rock 'n' rollers The Treniers after his brother Buddy passed away in 1999; born Alabama, 14/7/1919; cancer, 17/11)

Sheb Wooley (US actor/singer responsible for massive 1958 novelty #1 'The Purple People Eater'; born Oklahoma, 10/4/1921; leukaemia, 16/9)

For a complete list of fallen artists, visit

www.numberoneinheaven.com

JANUARY

Monday 12

Randy Vanwarmer

(Randall Van Wormer – Indian Hills, Colorado, 30 March 1955)

His name will live on longer in the memory than his short-lived solo career, but Randy Vanwarmer remained a successful songwriter well after his short flirtation with fame back in 1979. Vanwarmer had lost his father in a car crash in 1967 and was subsequently raised in Cornwall, England. He returned to the US to join the New York music scene in the late seventies. Vanwarmer wrote the schmaltzy ballad 'Just When I Needed You Most' when he was only eighteen, his rendition of the song going on to

'If I could find a "randy van warmer", I'd go out and buy a transit tomorrow morning.'

John Peel, 1979

sell 2 million copies at the end of the decade, a Top Ten hit in both the US and UK. With rock and disco all the rage, further efforts like this one were less successful, but Vanwarmer soon found an outlet for his songwriting in country music, where his composi- tions scored major hits for, among others, Alabama and Dolly Parton. Vanwarmer continued to generate impressive songwriting credits before leukaemia took him at just forty-eight years old.

Wednesday 14

Valfar

(Terje Bakken – Sogndal, Norway, 1978)

Windir

Finally, a Norwegian black-metal death due to misfortune rather than criminal activity. Formed around 1995, Windir donned the garb and growled the tunes convincingly enough as the latest in a long line of Scandinavian satanists, singer Valfar – who'd begun the project as a one-man enterprise – the suitably striking frontman with his straggly hair, white-out make-up and stage blood. Needless to say, once the band had become established around 2001, titles like 'Dance of Mortal Lust' and the grimly prophetic 'Journey to the End'

Close!
Ted Nugent
(Amboy Dukes)

From the 'He Had It Coming' Department: the ASPCA's least- favourite rock dinosaur very nearly 'got his' on 11 January 2004 – on the set of his own reality TV series. As the cameras rolled for VH1's *Surviving Nugent: The Ted Commandments,* the notorious right-wing hunting enthusiast lost control of the chainsaw he was wielding, very nearly turning himself into one of the fillet steaks he so dearly loves. The bad news for deer and mountain lions everywhere was that although Nugent lost an enormous amount of blood, the 55-year-old's injuries were not sufficient to have him put down – and the show (which, appropriately for many reasons, was filmed at his ranch in Waco) continued within hours.

also gained Windir a strong following in the USA.

Under his given name of Terje Bakken, Valfar was, in fact, a family man still close to his parents. On 14 January 2004, he headed into the Sogndal Valley in Norway's frozen west to visit the family cabin. With snow falling heavily and the road even more treacherous than usual, Valfar soon realized his car would not be able to make it, and attempted to turn and head back. Sadly, the singer's body was found three days later near Reppastølen. He had died from hypothermia.

Thursday 15

Jimmi Lawrence

(Chichester, 25 January 1977)
Hope of the States
(Screwpitch)

Chichester hadn't been especially noted as a hotbed of British rock talent until the earnest, powerful Hope of the States emerged in 2002. The young six-piece quickly found themselves in the unlikely position of rubbing shoulders with S Club 8 as their conscience-pricking second single, 'Enemies/Friends' (2003), vaulted them into the charts and on to *Top of the Pops*. Hope of the States – Sam Herlihy (vocals/guitar/piano), Anthony Theaker (guitar/piano/organ), Jimmi Lawrence (guitar), Mike Siddell (violin), Paul Wilson (bass) and Simon Jones (drums) – had proved themselves as a live act and now sought recognition for their first album. With almost no prior warning, they were hit by tragedy just as success beckoned.

At the start of 2004, the album *The Lost Riots* was near completion at the Wiltshire-based Real World Studios (owned by Peter Gabriel). Around 4 am on 15 January, members of the group found the body of co-founder

'**Our last days with Jimmi were the happiest we have ever shared together. He was immensely proud of his work on the record and could not wait for others to hear it.**' Hope of the States

and former Screwpitch guitarist Jimmi Lawrence hanging from rafters at the building. His friends then had the distressing duty of trying to revive the musician – to no avail. There had been no indication that Lawrence – just a week or so from his twenty-seventh birthday – was considering taking his life. The progress of Hope of the States has been understandably subdued in the time since his death: the debut album was well received, however, and further singles, 'The Red, the White, the Black, the Blue' and the touching 'Nehemiah' (both 2004), charted strongly. A new album, *Left*, was released June 2006.

Wednesday 28

'Dino' Dines

(Peter Dines – Hertfordshire, 17 December 1944)
T Rex
(Various acts)

Marc Bolan and T Rex had waved their best days goodbye by the time 'Dino' Dines joined the depleted line-up in 1974. A respected session keyboardist with bands such as P P Arnold and The Hollies, Dines had been recruited after the singer's close friend David Bowie – who needed musicians for his 'Diamond Dogs' tour in 1974 – had asked Bolan to audition band members for him. Learning that this supposed unknown had also once backed The Beach Boys, Bolan kept Dines for

himself. Although Dines was a decent enough musician, he was to face enormous amounts of critical flack as T Rex fell out of favour with the press (who'd described his work as 'end-of-the-pier tinklings'). There were still hits to be had – 'New York City' (1975) and 'I Love to Boogie' (1976) both made the Top Twenty – but the glory days of 1971–2 were well gone. Bolan's death (☙ *September 1977*) then brought an abrupt and unexpected end to Dines's latest venture. In his later years, 'Dino' crossed the risky line between musician and fan by playing with T Rextasy – one of several Marc Bolan tribute bands. Before his death from a heart attack, Dines had lost count of the times he'd heard: 'So what was he *really* like?'

See also *Steve Peregrin Took (☙ October 1980); Steve Currie (☙ April 1981); Mickey Finn (☙ January 2003)*

FEBRUARY

Wednesday 4

Cornelius Bumpus

(Dallas, Texas, 7 May 1945)
The Doobie Brothers
Steely Dan
(Various acts)

A voluminous figure in every sense, Cornelius Bumpus made the move from jazz to rock, in which guise he was to enhance many big-selling US acts during his career. His first experiences of playing live occurred when he was a 10-year-old alto saxophonist in the school band, Bumpus making the instrument his own in the years to come. As a solo artist, the musician's commercial appeal was limited to a small but loyal fanbase, but his early dalliances with bands were to change all that. Among others, he played with Moby Grape and Boz Scaggs in the seventies, joining The Doobie Brothers during their 'Michael McDonald' phase, though relations turned sour in the late nineties when original Doobies sued Bumpus and others over use of the name. His time with Steely Dan, on the other hand, was highlighted by a Grammy for the comeback album *Two Against Nature* (2000). Indeed, Bumpus remained with Steely Dan until his death from a coronary in 2004. The sax-player suffered the attack while on a flight from New York to California.

See also *Bobby LaKind (December 1992); Keith Knudsen (February 2005). Original Doobie Brother Dave Shogren passed away in 1999.*

Saturday 21

Les Gray
(Carshalton, Surrey, 9 April 1946)
Mud
(The Mourners)

Amid the spangly garb of rivals The Sweet, T Rex and Gary Glitter, the feather-cut hair and Foster Grant eyewear looked, initially, clunky and misplaced. But, by the end of 1974, Les Gray and Mud – earring-fancier Rob Davis (guitar), Ray Stiles (bass) and Dave Mount (drums) – were outselling all of them.

More unlikely still was the support tour with Jack Jones as the band

began making its name after winning a 1968 talent contest – by which time Gray had already played jazz and fronted his younger brother's skiffle band, The Mourners. It took a few more years to hone the style that won Mud a legion of fans, the Nicky Chinn/Mike Chapman-composed 'Crazy', 'Hypnosis' and 'Dynamite!' establishing the band in the charts during 1973. The following year was, however, Mud's finest: in 1974, the group began and ended the year at number one, 'Tiger Feet' (the year's biggest-selling UK single) and the fairly dismal Elvis pastiche 'Lonely This Christmas' each shifting more than 500,000 copies. And there were many other hits to which to dance 'the angel' (that notorious hands-on-hips boogie preferred by hod-carriers in Boots No 7): Mud's third chart-topper was to be an update of Buddy Holly's 'Oh Boy' (1975), which enhanced their appeal to the nation's ageing Teds. By 1976, Gray's pose had begun to wear thin as the glam era died away, Mud choosing to ditch both the Chinnichap composing team and their label, RAK, for Private Stock. Promoting a supposedly maturer sound, the group had become something of a laughing stock by the end of 1975 ('Show Me You're a Woman', anyone?). Gray's attempts at a solo career also foundered after the Top Forty-bothering 'Groovy Kind of Love' (1977), and the nostalgia circuit beckoned. While Gray – who was in debt up until his death – was forced to take 'Les Gray's Mud' out on the road in the nineties, Stiles had joined The Hollies, and Davis cashed in many times over as co-writer (with former dance chanteuse Cathy Dennis) of the million-sellers 'Groovejet' (Spiller, 2000) and 'Can't Get You out of My Head' (Kylie, 2001). What Dave Mount is up to is anyone's guess.

For Les Gray, a coke habit would have been *far* too glamorous: it was his fifty cigarettes a day that led to his demise – from a heart attack while battling throat cancer – at his home in

Portugal. Feeling the operation would end his career, Gray had even turned down the voice-box surgery that might have saved his life. He'd intended to appear that weekend at a Glasgow glam revival show that became a memorial to one of pop's more distinctive frontmen.

MARCH
Friday 5

John McGeoch
(Greenock, Renfrewshire, Scotland, 28 May 1955)
Magazine
Siouxsie & The Banshees
Visage
PIL (Public Image Ltd)
(Various acts)

Guitarist John McGeoch was a guiding light who showed British punks that virtuosity was far from being a dirty word, and his startling and original contributions to so many groundbreaking new-wave bands spoke for themselves. McGeoch had moved down from Scotland to Manchester in his teens, becoming fascinated by the town's burgeoning new-wave scene that produced bands such as The

'I learned to play copying all John McGeoch's stuff in Magazine and The Banshees.'
Revelation from John Frusciante, guitar legend and sometime Red Hot Chili Pepper

Buzzcocks, The Fall and Joy Division. Ditching his position as co-leader of the first band, Howard Devoto (Howard Trotter) had started Magazine in early 1977, McGeoch then joining as an ideal player for this more progressive band. The pair wrote together, many of the early songs appearing on the acclaimed Virgin Records album *Real Life* (1978). The guitarist remained with Magazine for two further albums, *Secondhand Daylight* (1979) and *The Correct Use of Soap* (1980), before commitments with other bands (including Steve Strange's Visage, with whom he enjoyed his first Top Ten single) meant that he no longer had room for Devoto's project. The main catalyst for his departure, though, was Siouxsie & The Banshees – the most commercially viable of all McGeoch's bands. Many of his fans believe that the guitarist's best work emerged in his two years with Siouxsie. Albums like *Kaleidoscope* (1980) and *Juju* (1981) exploited McGeoch's swirling style, while perhaps inspiring a few future goth axe-wielders.

McGeoch's heavy workload inevitably took its toll in 1982; suffering nervous exhaustion (not assisted by the guitarist's taste for fine wine and heroin), he was hospitalized and out of the band, to be replaced temporarily by The Cure's Robert Smith. A break of several years (some of which was wasted in former Skid Richard Jobson's abortive Armoury Show project) preceded the musician's time with John Lydon's PIL, the group shedding much of its experimental, leftfield image under his influence and enjoying success on the Continent (though less so in the UK). In his time, McGeoch was also to find space in his diary to work with Generation X, Heaven 17 and Spandau Ballet's John Keeble.

Possibly rock's purest definition of a workaholic, John McGeoch even made time to retrain as a nurse once he'd hung up his guitar. He died in his sleep from an unspecified illness, leaving a wife and daughter.

Tuesday 9

Rust Epique
(California, 1968)
Crazy Town
Pre)Thing

Although little more than a manufactured rap/rock hybrid created as the genres cross-pollinated, Crazy Town – Shifty Shellshock (Seth Binzer, vocals), Bret 'Epic' Mazur (vocals/production), Rust Epique and Antonio 'Trouble' Valli (guitars), Doug 'Faydoedelay' Miller (bass), Adam Goldstein (DJ) and James 'JBJ' Bradley (drums) – made an immediate impact on a market that had recently made stars of the more 'metal' Linkin Park and the funnier Bloodhound Gang. The band's third single, 'Butterfly' (2001), scored them a Billboard number one while scaling the charts worldwide as the hype machine went into overdrive. Then, as debut album *The Gift of Game* (2001) was slammed by some sectors for its retrograde sexism, Epique was slung out for being 'too crazy' for The Town.

Returning with his harder-rocking new band – named Pre)Thing – the singer/guitarist became disillusioned at what he believed was a lack of promotion for the group's first album, *22nd Century Lifestyle* (2004). There was little coverage at all, until Rust Epique's sudden death from a heart attack at his Las Vegas home. It seems that, during 2003, Epique had apparently done little other than make a complete nuisance of himself at V2, the label that had signed his band. In fact, staff at the company had become so fed up with his rudeness via phone and email that they resorted to the imaginative solution of informing the press that he was mentally ill (even forging documentation, to prevent any embarrassing interviews) and

then created 'Bob Rubinstein' – an entirely fictitious publicist to whom the unknowing Pre)Thing could send emails and voicemails. Some months after Epique's sudden death, *Rolling Stone* received an email from 'Rubinstein' explaining that he had resigned from V2 after bringing in a psychic to enable the musician to conduct interviews from beyond the grave. Thus the ruse came full circle. Even though the band no longer existed, Pre)Thing were starting to gain airplay and column inches that they couldn't have *bought* earlier on.

Wednesday 10

Dave Blood
(Dave Schulthise – Philadelphia, Pennsylvania, 16 September 1956)
The Dead Milkmen

Picking up the 'gonzo' baton from California's The Dickies, The Dead Milkmen emerged from the Philly punk scene around 1983. A whole bunch of breakneck paeans to girlfriends, UFOs and laundromats spilled out of The Milkmen's *oeuvre* over the next few years, their albums rejoicing in great titles like *Big Lizard in My Backyard* (1985) and *Metaphysical Graffiti* (1990) – the latter featuring the nearest the band was ever to come to a hit in the MTV-favoured 'Punk Rock Girl'. Grade A student Dave 'Blood' Schulthise (bass) had formed the band, in lieu of a PhD in economics, with singer/synth-player Rodney 'Anonymous' Linderman, adding guitarist 'Joe Jack Talcum' Genaro and drummer Dean 'Clean' Sabatino. The band were very close-knit and toured incessantly, clocking up thousands of miles in a converted ambulance.

The Dead Milkmen's split in 1995 left Blood at something of a loss. Still an academic, he studied Serbo-Croat – even moving to Serbia to teach

English (until hostilities there drove him back to the States in 1999) – but, without his band, he became despondent. At the start of the millennium, the former bassist was beset by seemingly unshiftable tendonitis (perhaps as a result of his playing). Finally, the death of his mother from cancer in January 2004 pushed Blood over the edge: one night at his sister Kathy's house, he took his own life. She told the press: 'David has been "away" for a long time. Maybe he's happy now – finally released from a life that only gave him conflict and turmoil.'

> **'Every time I consider picking up the four-stringed love axe again, I hear this voice in the back of my head asking me, "Do you really want to have to take Darvocets in order to be able to tie your shoe laces or twist the lids off of juice bottles?"'**
>
> Dave Blood, shortly before his death

Thursday 11

Edmund Sylvers

(Memphis, Tennessee, 25 January 1957)

The Sylvers

Ten-strong family vocal group The Sylvers appeared to be the 'biggest new thang' as the US celebrated its bicentennial. Brother-and-sister groups were no new concept of course, but The Sylvers were the first to stick a disco beat behind their permanent smiles. In 1976, Angelia, Charmaine, Foster, James, Jonathan, Leon Frank, Olympia-Ann, Pat, Ricky and lead singer Edmund (count 'em) went to number one with the slight but catchy 'Boogie Fever', followed by another million-seller, 'Hot Line', before the year was out. The group had been a going concern for four years by now, Edmund Sylvers's high tenor integral to the sound. But, by 1980, the 23-year-old leader decided he wanted that solo career. Sculpting the regulation 'Michael Jackson' hair, he issued a less-crafted album, *Have You Heard?*, for Casablanca, drawing something of a blank thereafter. Many years after moderate success as a producer for Freda Payne, Sylvers – who once provided the voice of Marlon on US TV's *Jackson 5* cartoon – died from lung cancer at his home in Richmond, Virginia.

Golden Oldies #17

Johnny Bristol

(Morganton, North Carolina, 3 February 1939)

It was hard to believe that the hit-maker of 'Hang on in There Baby' had reached the golden age of sixty-five, let alone passed on. Johnny Bristol was to become a member of the Motown family in more senses than one: in his early career, he'd been an in-house songwriter (with cohort Jackie Beavers) and producer for Berry Gordy, later marrying the founder's niece Iris. Bristol's own solo successes were fewer and farther between than his hits for Gordy, though in the last week of September 1974 he enjoyed two simultaneous UK Top Five hits with the aforementioned title track from his album of the time, plus The Osmonds' take on another, 'Love Me for a Reason'.

As a writer/producer, Bristol polished up the songs of Marvin Gaye, David Ruffin, Tammi Terrell and Junior Walker – with all of whom he can once again compare notes in some heavenly studio. Johnny Bristol died after an apparent seizure on 21 March 2004.

Friday 26

Jan Berry

(William Jan Berry – Los Angeles, California, 3 April 1941)

Jan & Dean

If The Beach Boys were the kings of surf, then Jan Berry might have been the genre's mischievous knave. In fact, Jan & Dean dodged studies to trawl hits some years before their California friends/rivals introduced them to the wonders of saltwater recreation. The kids at University High, Los Angeles, all seemed to have captured a spirit of the time and appeared destined for success in music or the movies. Fellow alumni of Bel Air 'bad boy' Berry were future musicians Kim Fowley, Beach Boy Bruce Johnston, Nancy Sinatra and would-be actors James Brolin and Ryan O'Neal. An 'A' student, Berry often bunked off lessons to smoke cigars, race hotrods around the school area – and indeed father an illegitimate son, Stevie. (Remarkably, the latter was raised as Berry's *brother* to avoid embarrassment for his 'society' parents. He died from AIDS during the nineties – just one of a host of tragedies to afflict the Berry family. In 1973, the singer's younger brother Bruce fatally overdosed at a party while acting as a roadie for Crosby, Stills, Nash & Young; even more tragically, their infant sister Carol had drowned in the family's pool many years earlier.)

Berry began harmonizing with Dean Torrence alongside 'lost' third man Arnie Ginsberg as The Barons (formerly The Internationals). But with Torrence about to serve his country in the Reserves, it was Jan & Arnie who were signed up first: Berry's garage was the venue for the recording of first hit 'Jennie Lee' (1958) – a simple melody, on the unlikely subject of a burlesque performer, which stunned the pair by reaching US number eight that summer. Ginsberg then joined the navy, making way for the returning Torrence – who rerecorded what was to become a second chart entry, 'Baby Talk' (1959) – now Berry's permanent partner as the hits arrived as regularly as California rollers. 'Surf music' was all the rage – and to prove everybody was your friend at the beach, Brian Wilson even helped out with the lyrics to 'Surf City' (1963) to give Jan & Dean their only chart-topper, which infuriated his manager father. Indeed, there are still many who think of it as a Beach Boys hit – though Wilson has been quick to point out that Berry always impressed *him* in terms of his stage presence and studio skills.

Like the Wilsons, Berry and Torrence also had an obsession with automobiles that was to inform much of their output. This culminated with the near-prescient 'Dead Man's Curve' (1964), a heavily produced melodrama that spoke – in so many words – of the dangers of high-speed dragster racing. Two years on, this song was set to resonate eerily: preoccupied with his own imminent draft, a medical-school examination (yes, he studied by day and recorded all night), plus a heartbreaking split with songwriter girlfriend Jill

Gibson (later of The Mamas & The Papas), Berry was involved in a near-fatal car crash. As he took his brand-new Corvette Stingray for a spin along LA's Whittier Boulevard on 12 April 1966, Berry lost control, hitting the kerb and slamming into the back of a stationary gardener's truck. Paramedics arriving on the scene believed he was already dead – until they detected breathing. His brain partially exposed by the impact, Berry underwent emergency surgery at UCLA Hospital, remaining in a coma for days – and in a state of paralysis for several months. It would take the singer a decade to regain full speech and the ability to sing. In an extraordinarily eventful and mishap-ridden year, Berry had already escaped having his leg amputated after an accident on a movie set, and had also testified in court following the attempted abduction of Frank Sinatra Jr. (Three years earlier, Berry had lent his best friend Barry Keenan $500 to carry out the abduction, assuming his pal to be broke and/or joking – only to discover twenty-four hours later that Keenan had indeed carried out his plan. The latter – who was jailed along with two accomplices – then went on to become a property millionaire.) Shortly after the car crash, Torrence issued an ill-advised crypto-'Jan & Dean' album. Columbia Records refused to support *Save It for a Rainy Day*, and dropped the act soon after. (Torrence then wisely moved into record-sleeve design.)

With questionable taste and logic, CBS television welcomed the phoenix-like duo back in 1977 with the

lurid biopic *Dead Man's Curve*, which included many of Berry and Torrence's friends (including one or two Beach Boys) in its cast. Jan Berry was, of course, to be admired for his refusal to succumb to his disabilities: he married in 1991 (with Torrence as best man), the pair continuing to record as Jan & Dean, although their appeal was now restricted to the fans that had grown up with the band in the first place. Berry finally passed away in the spring of 2004, just a week ahead of his sixty-third birthday, the seizure that finally claimed his life a direct result of the car accident almost forty years earlier. A man who had once boasted an IQ of 185, Berry had specified that his body be donated to science before cremation.

APRIL

Thursday 1

Paul Atkinson

(Cuffley, Hertfordshire, 19 March 1946)
The Zombies

It was cancer that felled original Zombies guitarist Paul Atkinson, a lesser-vaunted member of the band who nonetheless went on to develop his own identity in his later music career. With British guitar bands absolutely cleaning up across the pond, The Zombies – Atkinson,

'Jan wasn't a very nice or gracious person, but he did it first. He succeeded in putting a pretty face on LA ghetto doo-wop music.'

Kim Fowley, rock producer and high-school colleague of Jan Berry

Colin Blunstone (vocals), Rod Argent (keyboards), Chris White (bass) and Hugh Grundy (bass) – had far greater success in America than in their native Britain. Their timeless first hit 'She's Not There' (1964 – only kept from number one by Bobby Vinton's insipid 'Mr Lonely') was followed by further big sellers in 'Tell Her No' (1965) and the reissued 'Time of the Season' (1969). While Blunstone, White and, particularly, Argent went on to further successes, Atkinson moved behind the scenes and built up a solid reputation as a CBS record executive, signing a wide variety of rock/pop acts, among them Abba, Bruce Hornsby and Judas Priest. Paul Atkinson had moved to Los Angeles in the eighties, reuniting with Argent and Blunstone on stage just weeks before his death from kidney and liver problems.

Golden Oldies #18

Niki Sullivan

(South Gate, California, 23 June 1937)
Buddy Holly & The Crickets
(Various acts)

A distant cousin of Buddy Holly, Niki Sullivan played rhythm and sang backing vocals as part of the classic Crickets line-up with Holly, Joe Mauldin (bass) and Jerry Allison (drums) – contributing to more than twenty of the group's ground-breaking songs. His own ambition fired by working with an innovator of the stature of Holly – alongside the feeling that the latter didn't really need a second guitarist – Sullivan left The Crickets at the end of 1957 while the group were still on the crest of a wave. Although Sullivan was to find little success with his own bands The Plainsmen and The Hollyhawks, at least he wasn't on the flight that ended his former leader's life (☜ *Pre-1965*). Instead Niki Sullivan died from a heart attack in his sleep on 6 April 2004.

Monday 26

Scott Williams

(James Scott Williams – New Orleans, Louisiana, 1965)
Soilent Green
(New Religion)

Incorporating a variety of styles including black/death metal, speed, thrash and stoner rock, Soilent Green – described by *Rolling Stone* as one of the ten most important hard-rock bands in the US – were Louisiana's hardest, nastiest ride for some years. Their lyrics covering the usual subjects associated with extreme metal, perhaps Soilent Green shouldn't have anticipated a smooth passageway to success: whether they did or not, they certainly weren't to get it.

In December 2001, the band – Ben Falgoust (vocals, also of Goatwhore), Brian Patton (ex-Eyehategod/Nuclear Crucifixion, guitar), Tony White (guitar), Scott Williams (ex-New Religion, bass) and Tommy Buckley (ex-Christ Inversion/Crowbar, drums) – almost ended prematurely. Involved in a tour-van crash on an icy East Washington freeway, each member suffered injuries, in particular Patton and Williams, who both had extensive fractures to their shoulders. Just four months later, in *another* van wreck, this time in Chicago, replacement bassist Jonny Modell suffered an almost identical injury to that which had sidelined Williams. In this accident, Falgoust was also hospitalized for months.

For Scott Williams, who'd joined the band in 1992, the accidents were merely a precursor to his own violent and dramatic death. Unknown to many of his fans (some of whom would probably have disowned him for it), Williams was gay and having a relationship with Tracey Terry at the start of 2004. At a restaurant on the night of Monday 26 April, two friends

of the pair were startled by Terry's apparently jealous exit when he saw Williams talking to another man. The two friends took an upset Williams to his mother's home where it was anticipated he and Terry might resolve their differences. Not so, however: – just before midnight, neighbours overheard arguing, followed by gunshots. Pat Williams found her son dead from a bullet wound to the head. The police then located Terry's body, an injury to the chest and a nearby .38 telling officers all they needed to know. Despite his history, those who knew Williams described the bassist as 'a quiet man who liked barbecues'. But the misfortune dogging Soilent Green did not stop here: sometime singer Glenn Rambo was found dead just eighteen months later, a victim of Hurricane Katrina.

MAY

Golden Oldies #19

Clement 'Coxsone' Dodd

(Kingston, Jamaica, 26 January 1932)

The most influential producer that reggae has yet seen first became fascinated with rhythmic music when spinning records for customers at the Kingston shop owned by his parents. American blues and R & B drew former farm labourer Dodd to the US, where he'd stock up on rare 45s to bring back and play on one of the five sound systems he operated back home. His early production work helped nurture the careers of Lee 'Scratch' Perry, The Skatalites and Toots & The Maytals. Then, in 1963, Dodd opened the fabled Studio One on Brentford Road, Kingston – a building that was to attract some great early exponents of reggae, including Bob Marley & The Wailers, who cut their first sides under the supervision of its owner. Other great names passed through Studio One's portals, including Horace Andy, Dennis Brown, Burning Spear, Sugar Minott and Delroy Wilson, the studio becoming more synonymous with rocksteady and dancehall by the seventies. Dodd received Jamaica's Order of Distinction in 1991.

Ever the perfectionist, Clement '(Sir) Coxsone' Dodd – whose unusual nickname apparently derived from his boyhood skill as a cricketer – died 'at the controls' from a heart attack on 4 May 2004.

Tuesday 11

John Whitehead

(Philadelphia, Pennsylvania, 2 July 1948)
McFadden & Whitehead
(The Epsilons)
(Talk of the Town)

The shock murder of John Whitehead proved once more that gun crime knows no boundaries in the multi-genre world of popular music. Formerly a young buck hoping to make a name in the industry, Whitehead had played with high-school vocal group The Epsilons with his pal Gene McFadden, the pair touring with soul legend Otis Redding before reaching their twenties. In 1970, McFadden & Whitehead recorded with Talk of the Town before being taken on as writers by the Philadelphia International label to create a series of major soul hits over the next few years. Between them the prolific duo composed The O'Jays' 'Backstabbers', 'I'll Always Love My Mama' for The Intruders and 'Bad Luck' and 'Wake Up Everybody' for Harold Melvin & The Bluenotes, among countless other hits. McFadden & Whitehead only returned to the studio at the end of the seventies to record the huge international hit 'Ain't No Stopping

Us Now' (1979, US number thirteen, UK number five) – a song improvised in the studio by Whitehead – and an album of similarly paced disco standards.

Despite a Grammy nomination, there were no other hits for the duo and in the eighties John Whitehead spent time in prison for tax evasion. Worse was to follow, however. During the evening of 11 May 2004, Whitehead and a 20-year-old friend, mechanic Ohmed Johnson, were working on his SUV in the West Oak Lane area when approached by two armed men, who began arguing with Johnson. The men then drew their weapons and fired a dozen times before disappearing without trace. Johnson survived after being struck on the buttocks, but Whitehead died almost at once from a bullet wound to the neck. Among the first to the scene were the musician's wife Eleanor, daughter Dawn (one of his eleven children) and his long-time colleague McFadden who, according to television reporters, stood trembling by his dying friend. Police have been unable to determine any motive and indeed no suspect has been apprehended, though it is widely believed that Johnson was the intended target.

Gene McFadden – who shortly afterwards learned that he had liver and lung cancer – passed away in January 2006.

Saturday 15

Clint Warwick

(Albert Eccles – Birmingham, England, 25 June 1940)
The Moody Blues
(The Rainbows)
(Danny King/Gerry Day & The Dukes)

In the end, he was more an 'Albert Eccles' than a 'Clint Warwick'. Warwick joined The Moody Blues

– a band of two very different and distinct manifestations – just as they conquered the British then American markets, when 'beat' became the by-word in music. If there *was* a Birmingham scene, then they were certainly at its head: bassist/singer Warwick (named by his bandmates after Clint Walker and Dionne Warwick) was recruited in May 1964, after stints at Butlins with local blues/skiffle dead-enders The Dukes and The Rainbows. For The Moodys – Warwick, Denny Laine (vocals/guitar), Ray Thomas (vocals/harp/flute), Mike Pinder (keys) and Graeme Edge (drums) – it was instant success, with the UK number one and worldwide smash 'Go Now' (1964). Follow-ups didn't stick as readily, however, and, with pressure from his wife (who had just borne the couple's first child), Warwick quit early in 1966. With The Moody Blues soon calling it a day, it appeared he had made the right decision – until Justin Hayward (guitar) and John Lodge (bass) gave the band the facelift that was to make them the darlings of the psychedelic/prog brigade. Despite encouragement to return to music from big northern pop names Chas Chandler (ex-Animals) and Muff Winwood (ex-Spencer Davis Group, now a big-name producer), Clint Warwick returned to his trade as a carpenter. In later life, he suffered the heartbreak of losing a son in 1996 before his own death eight years later from a liver condition intensified by alcohol abuse. But, despite his short career in the music business, he could at least boast having jammed many times with The Beatles and Rolling Stones – not a bad epitaph.

JUNE

Saturday 5

Robert Quine

(Akron, Ohio, 30 December 1942)

Richard Hell & The Voidoids
(Various acts)

Robert Quine was as much a progressive- as punk-rock musician, influenced greatly by The Velvet Underground, the band that merged the experimental with the most stripped-down rock 'n' roll in town. This was when he wasn't listening to Miles Davis or Link Wray. Or Richie Valens. And the former law graduate was a fine student of music, knowing when to leave influence behind and embrace innovation as he paved the way for a more cerebral kind of punk music. Just *don't* call him a session musician . . .

For a start, Quine was clearly too good a player for the likes of the ramshackle Richard Hell & The Voidoids, but the uneasy marriage spawned some memorable work as the guitarist – already in his mid thirties and going bald – outshone all the spike-tops on stage at CBGB's. The Voidoids – Hell (vocals/bass), Quine (guitar/noise), Ivan Julian (guitar) and Marc Bell (ex-Wayne County & The Electric Chairs, drums) – were not to last long in this incarnation, but nonetheless gave the world a definitive punk album in *Blank Generation* (1977), highlighted by Quine's input. With Hell seemingly losing the battle with heroin, though, other members became bored: 'He couldn't decide whether to be a rock star or just go die' was a typically acerbic observation from Quine, who once claimed to have been put off hard drugs by watching *Dragnet* on television. The guitarist was not one to suffer fools gladly, so future work was always going to be selective. In Lydia Lunch, Quine found a kindred spirit and a similar refusal to compromise: he added his idiosyncratic sonic slashes to the New York art-punk's album *Queen Of Siam* (1979). From here on, Robert Quine's resumé offers a bewildering array of collaborations, from popular songwriters Lloyd Cole and Green Gartside (Scritti Politti) to avant-garde jazz saxophonist John Zorn, taking in Tom Waits, Matthew Sweet and Ikue Mori on the way. Quine also spent four years recording and touring with hero-turned-buddy Lou Reed during the early eighties, while dishing out a few albums of his own material.

Robert Quine's suicide was a touch baffling, the contents of a note left behind remaining undisclosed, though friends had described him as unhappy, even angry, in the year following the death of his wife Alice. The guitarist's body was found at his New York apartment by friend and guitar-maker Rick Kelly during the Memorial Day holidays. It was confirmed that, yes, a heroin overdose was the cause of death. Richard Hell was unavailable for comment.

'Robert Quine was . . . an original and innovative tyro of the vintage beast.'

Lou Reed extols Quine's guitar talent as a guitarist

Golden Oldies #20

Ray Charles

(Ray Charles Robinson – Albany, Georgia, 23 September 1930)

Frank Sinatra called him 'the only genius in the business' and it would be hard to contradict this tribute to a man whose inner vision shaped soul, R & B and perhaps the whole popular culture of his day. Ray Charles's blindness was not a birth defect: his sight diminished in childhood – possibly as a result of glaucoma. The future musician then tragically lost both parents and his baby brother within a couple of years while still an infant himself. As a young man, he learned Braille and music at the Florida School for the Deaf and Blind, moving to Washington at sixteen, where his talents as a soulful singer and pianist flourished quickly. Mastering country, swing and jazz, the former gospel singer then courted controversy by composing his own secular lyrics to songs of worship.

Having performed with several bands, Charles signed as a solo artist first with Atlantic then ABC, as his hit R & B tunes began to cross over to the mainstream pop listings: he logged over thirty US Top Forty hits, including the number ones 'Georgia on My Mind' (1960 – the Hoagy Carmichael song appropriated by Charles's home state as its official anthem in 1979), 'Hit the Road Jack' (1961) and the near-spiritual 'I Can't Stop Loving You' (1962). Despite his hero status, Charles had frequent brushes with the authorities: on the up side, drawing huge attention to the issue of racial segregation (despite a baffling agreement to play in South Africa in 1981); on the downside, through his well-documented heroin addiction. The singer was also a notorious womanizer – he fathered twelve children by seven different ladies.

The great Ray Charles: Hit the road for the last time ...

His death from a persistent liver complaint on 10 June 2004 robbed the world of a man as charismatic as he was urbane – but Ray Charles nevertheless left behind a vault of priceless treasures.

Thursday 10

Graeme Kelling
(Paisley, Scotland, 4 April 1957)
Deacon Blue
(Tune Cookies)

A band with a fervent following at home, 'The Blue' – Ricky Ross (vocals/guitar), Graeme Kelling (ex-Tune Cookies, guitar), James Prime (keyboards), Ewan Vernal (bass) and Dougie Vipond (drums) – emerged from the Glasgow area with perhaps more ambition than artistic integrity, early critics dismissing them as 'Prefab Sprout lite'. They were, however, set for far greater commercial success than Paddy McAloon's group: after a few aborted attempts at chart domination, Deacon Blue (it's a corruption of the Steely Dan song title) cracked things with the platinum album *Raintown* (1987) and hit singles 'Real Gone Kid' (1988), 'Wages Day' and 'Fergus Sings the Blues' (both 1989). By the end of the decade, the band had a million-selling album with the smugly titled *When the World Knows Your Name* (1989), despite committing the cardinal sin of inviting Ross's girlfriend Lorraine McIntosh in as full-time singer. To their credit, Deacon Blue did well in America and continued the trend of big-selling albums and the odd hit single until a split in 1994.

Deacon Blue re-formed in 1999 for a series of well-attended dates, but sadly for family man Graeme Kelling, diagnosis with pancreatic cancer a year later kept further projects to a minimum. He made a final appearance with the band, however, three months before his death from the disease. Deacon Blue continue.

Monday 28

Ryan Noel
(New York, 1975)
ARE Weapons
(Clikatat Ikatowi)

ARE Weapons were the hottest new band to emerge in 2001 from the rock movement known as 'electroclash': the sound was intense and visceral, with little attempt made to disguise its ramshackle approach. Signed to Rough Trade on the recommendation of ex-Pulp man Jarvis Cocker, the band – Brian McPeck (vocals), Paul Sevigny (synth/manager – brother of actress Chloe Sevigny), Ryan Noel (guitar) and Matthew McCauley (bass) – made short work of placing themselves into every available press column. A couple of decent albums, plus singles such as 'Street Gang', 'New York Muscle' (both 2001) and 'Hey World' (2003), suggested that ARE Weapons would live up to their potential. Ryan Noel – who was also a semi-pro skateboarder – divided his time between this band and New York scenesters Clikatat Ikatowi. A premature end arrived, though, when the guitarist's body was found at his band's Soho studio. Noel, who was believed to be 'clean', had died from a heroin overdose.

JULY

Tuesday 6

Syreeta
(Syreeta Wright – Pittsburgh, Pennsylvania, 3 August 1946)

Known more for her higher-profile partnerships than for her solo work, former Motown secretary Syreeta (known as 'Rita') was nonetheless a decent singer and songwriter who contributed lyrics to first husband Stevie Wonder's album *Talking Book* (1972), having married him in what appeared to be a dream union back in 1970. In the event, the couple lasted less than two years before separating. Syreeta – who'd originally been described as 'promising' by Brian Holland of the Holland/Dozier/Holland partnership – saw her own recording career pick up after the split and was even, at one stage, considered as a replacement for Diana Ross in The Supremes, until Mary Wilson vetoed the idea. In the US, she struggled to score crossover hits, though reggae bubblegum moment 'Your Kiss is Sweet' took her into the UK Top Twenty in 1975 (the much better 'Spinning and Spinning' (1974) and 'Harmour Love' (1975) also made token chart showings). Syreeta duetted with other major artists in her time – most notably Billy Preston (who died in June 2006), for the smash ballad 'With You I'm Born Again' (1980), and Jermaine Jackson. She later backed Michael Bolton, by which time her options had clearly become more limited.

Her career quieter as she concentrated on her family, Syreeta returned in 1994 to tour in the stage musical *Jesus Christ Superstar*. She'd spent much time in Britain by the time of her death from bone cancer, after a two-year battle with the disease.

Tuesday 13

Arthur 'Killer' Kane
(The Bronx, New York, 3 February 1952)
The New York Dolls
(Various acts)

Despite being the fourth of them to pass on to that trashy grotto in the sky, Arthur Kane was the New York Doll who was 'saved'. Less rock 'n' roll than Johnny Thunders or Jerry Nolan, and certainly less flamboyant than David Johansen, Kane somehow rode the band's rollercoaster of bad luck and hard drugs to find religion and then re-emerge on stage with the other survivors just a month before his death.

Unassuming bassist Kane – known throughout his career as 'The Killer' – began with guitarist Thunders and early Doll Billy Murcia (drums) in the hard-rock band Actress before the trio

merged with Johansen (vocals) and Syl Sylvain (guitar) in a cycle shop in New York. The first notable achievement of The New York Dolls was to lose Murcia after a drugs binge while on tour in Britain (☞ *November 1972*), which at least put the band a few pages nearer the front of the tabloids. With Jerry Nolan taking the late drummer's place, the band completed more costume changes than they did albums under the watchful gaze of punk Svengali Malcolm McLaren, The Dolls' reputation only really taking off once they'd disbanded, following the departures of Thunders and Nolan to form The Heartbreakers in 1975. By now, Kane had given himself over to the bottle and was 'miming' his bass lines as the rest of the group argued around him at live shows. Two years on, the remaining Dolls went their separate ways, Kane forming the largely unsuccessful Killer Kane (with a pre-WASP Blackie Lawless). Ten years on, Kane arrived at another crossroads: it is widely believed that, at breaking point, he attempted suicide at the end of the eighties before finding apparent sanctuary in religion and devoting his life to Mormonism.

It took former Smiths frontman Morrissey (an unknown and president of The Dolls' UK fan club in the seventies) to reunite the group – or, at least, the three left after the deaths of Thunders (☞ *April 1991*) and Nolan (☞ *January 1992*) – for his Meltdown Festival on 18 June 2004. The show was believed by some to be the best The Dolls had played (which wouldn't have been that tall an order) but sadly proved to be the last gig in which

Kane was to take part: unknown to Johansen and Sylvain, the bassist was suffering from leukaemia, dying from the disease just three weeks after The New York Dolls' triumphant comeback. The two survivors – who later suggested that Kane himself may have been unaware of his condition – vowed to continue The Dolls in some form, with a new album issued in 2006.

Friday 23

Bill Brown
(Fayetteville, North Carolina, 21 March 1960)
The Titanic Blues Band
The Ozark Mountain Daredevils
The Misstakes

Don Shipps
(Springfield, Missouri, 1953)
The Titanic Blues Band
(Granny's Bathwater)

Don Shipps had been widely considered Missouri's top blues/jazz-player, his style allowing him into the crossover acts and bringing some commercial acceptance. Beginning in the interestingly named fusion band Granny's Bathwater, bassist Shipps had witnessed the group, which had once backed Martha Reeves, fall apart after the death of leader Mike Bunge in a 1975 car crash. He'd rallied to play as a sideman until forming the very popular Titanic Blues Band in 1991. For his part, guitarist Bill Brown had come closer to national success with the rock band The Misstakes during the late seventies, opening for big names like U2 and The Eurythmics over the next few years. Then, having played one gig with The Ozark Mountain Daredevils – best known for an earlier hit, 'Jackie Blue' (1975) – he ended up joining the re-formed act full time and stayed for fifteen years until his death. But, lured by a great musi-

'I will always remember the look of bashful happiness on Arthur's face as people in the audience constantly called out his name.'

Lifelong Dolls fan Morrissey

cian like Shipps, Brown also found space in his diary for The Titanic Blues Band.

The TBB were set to play their home town of Springfield as a precursor to the multi-date Greater Ozarks Blues Festival on the evening of 23 July 2004 when a catastrophe befell Brown and Shipps early that same morning. Staying at Brown's duplex, the two musicians were unaware that a fire had begun elsewhere, spreading to entrap them inside the building. With no means of escape, the pair died from smoke inhalation and severe burns. It was the second major disaster to hit The Ozark Mountain Daredevils after the death of earlier drummer Stephen Canaday five years before (☞ *September 1999*). The remaining Titanic members, renamed The Back Alley Band, played at the festival in tribute to their late friends.

AUGUST

Friday 6

Rick James

(James Ambrose Johnson Jr – Buffalo, New York, 1 February 1948)

(The Mynah Birds)
(Various acts)

How he lived to be fifty-six remains a source of amazement to many: a self-styled rebel who carried his anti-establishment stance to outrageous lengths both on and off stage, Rick James became funk's campest 'black knight' in a career spanning over thirty years. James – one of eight children – dropped out of school and then the US navy; all par for the course, he felt, if he were to emulate his successful uncle, Melvin Franklin of The Temptations. The singer moved to Toronto to form The Mynah Birds

(they'd wisely dropped the name 'Sailor Boys') with a roster that at various times included Goldie McJohn (later of Steppenwolf) and James's room-mate – none other than Neil Young. Briefly with Columbia, the band then joined Motown, where, though they weren't to release any of their own records, James was later to find a lot of work as a producer. (A spat with his manager then led to James being arrested and briefly incarcerated for draft evasion.)

In 1977, following several false starts with Salt 'n' Pepper, Heaven & Earth and the London-based Main Line, James finally formed The Stone City Band, a unit heavily influenced by the P-Funk that was to shape his future sound. The singer also identified with the ostentatious stage garb of George Clinton and co, and this was a major factor in the success of the single 'You and I', which finally earned James a gold disc in 1978, as did 'funk 'n' roll' albums *Come Get It!* (1978) and *Bustin' out of L Seven* (1979). Around this time, the darker side of James's world began to manifest itself publicly: quite open about his recreational drug use ('Mary Jane', his ode to pot, had been a minor hit in 1979), the singer was hospitalized many times for overindulging. For a third album, *Fire It Up* (1979), James was accompanied on tour by his 'close friends' The Mary Jane Girls and a young singer called Prince. James was now at his most hedonistic, tales of cocaine and sex parties far outstripping the number of critiques of the man's music for the next decade or so. It helped sell records, though: 1981's *Street Songs* and its flagship single, 'Superfreak' (with The Temptations as backing singers!), became the biggest-selling hits of James's career, the latter also being sampled by cod-rapper MC Hammer on 'U Can't Touch This' (1990 – for which James sued him to hell and back, clearing a reported $30 million in royalties).

If the eighties were something

of a topsy-turvy ride in the life of Rick James, the next decade was even worse. The singer's coke habit now cost him close to $15K a week (which eventually took care of any royalty money), the first signs of 'the beginning of the end' displaying themselves in 1991–2, when James and his dancer partner, Tanya Hijazi, were arrested and charged with the imprisonment and assault of young women at the singer's Hollywood Hills home. Later revelations led to the even more serious charges of 'possession of deadly weapons', 'torture' and 'enforced oral copulation' (plus 'aggravated mayhem', whatever that might entail). With James out on bail of $1 million, he and Hijazi disappeared for a year, only to be re-arrested in December 1992, after which James served two years in Folsom Prison. In 1997, he married Hijazi (although his publicist suggested otherwise after his death) and, having suffered a first stroke while on stage in Colorado, effectively pensioned off his alter ego, and all it entailed, for good.

Rick James was found dead at his apartment by his personal assistant in August 2004. Although he'd slowed his life down to a more manageable pace, James was still found to have nine different substances (including Valium and methamphetamine) in his system at the time of his death. The original verdict of 'natural causes' was thus scrapped in favour of 'accidental toxicity', in addition to pulmonary and cardiac failure, plus complications of diabetes and stroke: in short, the guy didn't have a chance. James – who had been working on his autobiography, *Confessions of a Superfreak*, when he died – was interred in his home town of Buffalo, New York.

See also *Brian Palmer (☞ October 2004)*

Saturday 7

Paulette Valenzuela
(20 June 1970)
The Abuse

A hard-rock band that had opened for multi-platinum angst-merchants Korn, The Abuse were considered one of San Diego's most promising alternative acts. Despite her leather-clad, tough-girl stage image, singer Paulette Valenzuela worked as a legal secretary by day and was widely known as a humanitarian. In 2004, the band was looking to consolidate on their success when everything ground to a sudden halt.

On 6 August, the outgoing Valenzuela was hosting an impromptu get-together at her Ocean Beach apartment, when at around 3 am three strangers arrived and asked whether they could crash the party. Her friendly nature getting the better of her common sense, the singer invited them to join her and her friends. Later, as the three latecomers were taking their leave, a frozen steak fell to the floor from the jacket of 21-year-old Samuel Horn, who had clearly attempted to steal it from Valenzuela's freezer. As she confronted him over the theft, Horn pulled a gun on the singer, announcing that he was robbing everyone and that they should hand over all their valuables. Astonishingly, Valenzuela – who was known for her take-no-shit attitude – then attempted to call his bluff by pressing the gun in his hand to her own head: the startled attacker withdrew the weapon sharply, unloading a bullet into her chest, which penetrated her heart, killing her instantly. A 100-strong wake was held for the singer just two nights later. On 15 July 2005, Horn – who had been hiding out in Rosarito, Mexico, since initial questioning – was found guilty of the shooting of Paulette Valenzuela and sentenced to life imprisonment.

Friday 13

Jak Airport
(Jack Stafford – Catford, London)
X-Ray Spex
(Classix Nouveaux)
(Various acts)

Despite his decidedly glam-rock looks, Jak Airport was the guitarist/writer that flamboyant singer Poly Styrene (Marion Elliot) wanted for her colourful punk outfit, X-Ray Spex, signed to EMI as the corporates bought into the new wave during 1977. Airport was an unlikely choice for a punk band, numbering among his eclectic influences both Kraftwerk and Debussy, though it was with his power chords that he lit up X-Ray Spex. The line-up – completed by noted saxophonist Lora Logic (Susan Whitby), Paul Dean (bass) and B P Hurding (drums) – came together after Styrene's *Melody Maker* advert drew them from all corners of the UK. And a terrific band they were. X-Ray Spex banged out the hits – 'Oh Bondage up Yours!' (1977), 'The Day the World Turned Dayglo', 'Identity' and 'Germ Free Adolescence' (all 1978) – before punk's implosion saw them disband in 1979. (Just one album, *Germ Free Adolescents* (1978), pulled together Poly and Jak's musings about the plastic age before it was over.) Post-Spex, Airport formed his own partnership with Dean before joining new romantic also-rans Classix Nouveaux (with Hurding) for live work.

Jack Stafford was believed to have been in his forties when he died from cancer; he'd left music to become a well-respected figure in the unlikely surroundings of the BBC's corporate and public relations department.

Thursday 26

Laura Branigan
(Brewster, New York, 3 July 1957)

She mightn't have been the most obvious choice to play Janis Joplin on Broadway, but leg-warmer-toting Laura Branigan surely had all the brashness and self-belief needed for the part. Of Irish/Italian ancestry, Branigan found her natural home at New York's Academy of Dramatic Arts, where she began to polish the style that was to hand her the fame she craved. It was in Italy that the singer made her first impact, with the single 'Gloria' (1982), a strident, Euro-friendly pop stomper that was not to be an international hit for another year. When the remastered song *did* hit back at home, it *really* hit: a million-seller in the US, 'Gloria' impacted around the world, reaching number six in Britain. Further smashes like 'Solitaire' (1983) and particularly 'Self Control' (1984 – her other major UK hit, which also spent seven weeks at number one in Germany) showed that Branigan was right at the fore of a dance/stage-school collision that had also foisted on an unsuspecting world the the dubious delights of Toni Basil, *Flashdance* and The Kids from Fame. An MTV ban on 'Self Control' that was never explained to the singer may well have prevented her from topping the charts at home. With her US popularity cooling, the former waitress then concentrated more on dramatic parts, which eventually led her to the starring role in the musical *Love, Janis* (to the evident horror of Joplin's surviving fanbase). Branigan – who had once backed Leonard Cohen – maintained a lower musical profile, but was to duet with other more complementary singers in her time, including the equally melodramatic Michael Bolton, Aussie favourite John Farnham and, yup, David Hasselhoff.

Laura Branigan – who had lost her husband to cancer just eight years before – was caring for her sick mother in East Quogue when she failed to rise one morning: the singer had died in her sleep from an undetected brain aneurysm. Branigan had complained to friends of headaches for a fortnight before her death, but had failed to seek medical attention.

Tuesday 31

Carl Wayne

(Colin David Tooley – Birmingham, England, 18 June 1943)
The Move
(Carl Wayne & The Vikings)
(The Hollies)

A vital cog in Birmingham's early pop machine, Carl Wayne saw his first band, The Vikings, record three flop singles with CBS before hitting the big time. Wayne (vocals), Ace Kefford (bass) and Bev Bevan (percussion) teamed with Roy Wood (ex-Mike Sheridan & The Nightriders, guitar) and Trevor Burton (ex-Danny King & The Mayfair Set, guitar/vocals) to spring The Move upon a startled public in 1966. The next year was something of a whirlwind for the band, with three of their singles – 'Night Of Fear', 'I Can Hear the Grass Grow' and 'Flowers in the Rain' (insert your own 'first record on Radio One' reference here) – reaching the UK Top Five. By the end of 1967, The Move were also making headlines for their wild publicity stunts: fuelled by wayward manager Tony Secunda, Wayne and co were successfully sued by Harold Wilson for a promotional campaign that incorporated the then prime minister in a mocked-up nude bedroom photograph. Wayne himself became known for stage antics that

included demolishing everything in sight with an axe and, on at least one occasion – pre-dating The Plasmatics, Tubes, Eminem, etc – chainsawing a Cadillac in half, the crazy tyke.

But, despite continued UK success – unlike many of their contemporaries, The Move didn't crack America – the band was fragmenting. Kefford left in 1968 (due to illness), with Burton (opposed to 'commercial' material) and finally Wayne (to follow a solo career) departing soon after, despite the fact that The Move had now scored a number-one single, 'Blackberry Way' (1968). Suffice to say that Wayne did *not* repeat his band's success on his own, though he was for several years to appear on television, singing theme tunes and ad jingles; he was also offered stage roles, including that of the Narrator in the long-running London show *Blood Brothers*. In 2000, the singer returned to formal band work, replacing Allan Clarke when he retired as frontman for The Hollies. Within months of his diagnosis with what was thought to be a controllable cancer of the oesophagus, Wayne deteriorated and died in hospital following a routine check-up.

See also *Tony Secunda (• February 1995)*

SEPTEMBER

Wednesday 15

Johnny Ramone

(John Cummings – Long Island, New York, 8 October 1948)
The Ramones
(The Tangerine Puppets)

So, finally, we lost dear old Johnny . . . While Joey, Dee Dee and Tommy were sniffing it, Johnny Ramone had used that infamous glue to hold the band

together. This was the man who'd kept his fellow Ramones on the straight and narrow – suddenly, like Joey (• *April 2001*) and Dee Dee (• *June 2002*), another 'brudder' was no more.

Despite regarding him as something of a taskmaster, The Ramones couldn't have survived without the clear thinking and business sense of Johnny, many within the band's orbit believing that the creativity of Dee Dee and Joey (alongside whom he was to stay the course in The Ramones) could not have flourished otherwise. As young Johnny Cummings, the guitarist was affiliated with various gangs and briefly addicted to heroin – perhaps getting all his tearaway tendencies out of his system back then. In his first band, The Tangerine Puppets, Johnny resembled a young biker, his regulation long hair, leathers and tennis shoes informing The Ramones' 'uniform' – adherence to which he was to insist upon in the following years. Johnny was already twenty-five when The Ramones came together, his friendship with fellow outsiders Dee Dee (Douglas Colvin), Tommy (Erdelyi) – both ex-school buddies/fellow Puppets – and Joey (Jeff Hyman – who shared Johnny's love of sixties garage pop) finalizing the seminal line-up of Ramone (vocals), Ramone (guitar), Ramone (bass) and Ramone (drums). Let's face it, a record-buying public that had contented itself with Bread and The Eagles was never going to get *this*; thus the wonder of The Ramones was to remain an open secret for – well – virtually the band's entire career. Shame really, because, aside from the group's obvious, if unacknowledged, brilliance even back in 1976, Johnny was a fine guitarist who improved dramatically as The Ramones developed (he was nominated *Rolling Stone*'s 17th Greatest Guitarist in 2003 – ahead of John Frusciante, Bo Diddley and even Pete Townshend). But whatever one's view of his technical prowess, the significance of his

'Gander gander hey!': The late, legendary Johnny still attracting new fans ...

contributions to timeless albums like *Ramones* (1976), *Leave Home* (1977), *Rocket To Russia* (1977) and *Road To Ruin* (1978) cannot be denied.

But if their two-minute anthems came together easily enough, The Ramones' personal history was far from harmonious. Johnny and Joey fell out early on, mainly as a result of the former 'stealing' the latter's girlfriend (an event supposedly documented in 1981's 'The KKK Took My Girlfriend Away'), but also – almost unbelievably – owing to a clash in political colours. Johnny was a closet Republican who finally made his allegiances known when The Ramones were inducted into The Rock 'n' Roll Hall of Fame in 2002. He and Joey continued to work together but they never made up. In the great Ramones documentary *End of the Century*, Johnny explained how he felt their estrangement was so insurmountable that he couldn't even bring himself to make up with the singer when he lay dying in hospital in 2001.

By contrast, Johnny Ramone's own death bed was attended by a broad range of rock (and associated) celebrity friends. The guitarist had been suffering from prostate cancer for five years, although he was believed to be on the point of pulling through when he passed away in his sleep. Lisa Marie Presley was by his bedside, as was guitarist Pete Yorn and musician/actor Vincent Gallo, plus 'heavy' friends Rob Zombie and Pearl Jam's Eddie Vedder, and their wives. Although he never reconciled with Joey, Johnny was to be reunited posthumously with Dee Dee – in the corm of the magnificent statue that sits near the latter's graveside at the Hollywood Forever cemetery. So, RIP Joey, Dee Dee, Johnny: we may only just have started the millennium, but it sure feels like the end, the end of the century ...

'The band was a family
– and Johnny was Dad.'

C J Ramone (Dee Dee's replacement in 1989)

Weather Girls Izora Rhodes-Armstead and Martha Wash: Anticipated quite a deluge

Bruce Palmer

(Liverpool, Nova Scotia, 9 September 1946)
The Buffalo Springfield
(Crosby, Stills, Nash & Young)
(The Mynah Birds)
(Various acts)

Bruce Palmer has sometimes been passed off as a mere journeyman musician who happened to play with some of the era's best rock artists: the truth is that the quiet spirit who dusted melodic bass lines with his back to the audience was more crucial a player than many of the bigger names about him. Toronto-raised Palmer served his apprenticeship with a variety of the city's bands before recognition came his way. Among these were Robbie Lane & The Disciples (a band who later backed Ronnie Hawkins after he'd sacked The Hawks) and the legendary Mynah Birds. Playing in the latter placed him alongside the young Rick James (whom Palmer survived by just two months (➤*August 2004*) and, for the first time, singer and guitarist Neil Young.

It was for his work with The Buffalo Springfield that Palmer is most noted, however. Palmer and Young – heading for Los Angeles in the latter's black hearse – were shortly to encounter Stephen Stills (vocals/guitar), Richie Furay (vocals/guitar) and Dewey Martin (drums).

Thursday 16

Izora Rhodes-Armstead

(Texas, 1942)
The Weather Girls/Two Tons o' Fun

Likely always to be associated with just the one hit record, Izora Armstead and her (aptly named) partner, Martha Wash actually recorded three albums for Columbia before their brand of Hi-NRG disco went out of fashion in the late eighties. A couple of strapping ladies, it must be said, Armstead and Wash originally backed Sylvester in 1976, the former already in her thirties: their shtick drew a huge fanbase, giving rise to Two Tons o' Fun, a part music, part slapstick affair. From this came the song that was to change things ... As The Weather Girls, the double act looked to have broken through with 'It's Raining Men' (1984, a song rejected by Donna Summer), which was only kept from UK number one by Lionel Richie's dreary 'Hello' (though Geri Halliwell's otherwise pointless cover was to make the leap seventeen years later). Without a follow-up, The Weather Girls went their separate ways, Armstead reviving the act some years on with her daughter Dynell Rhodes. A victim of her size, Armstead died of heart failure at home in California.

See also *Sylvester (➤December 1988)*

'Bruce was the soul of the whole thing. His bass-playing was like nothing I'd ever heard before.' Neil Young

Although steeped in folk, the band's guitar-harmony-heavy approach came as a refreshing change to American rock fans tiring of the British sound by 1966. The Buffalo Springfield's first two albums are gems, though Palmer almost didn't get a look-in on the second: deported back to Canada after a marijuana bust in 1967, the musician sneaked back across the border disguised as a businessman to save his band from the more mundane contributions of bass sessionists. With his drug intake (and obsession with mysticism) on the rise, however, Palmer's second deportation proved the last straw for members of The Buffalo Springfield, who then replaced him with the less gifted but more reliable Jim Messina (later of Poco). Bruce Palmer's history after this becomes more chequered: still favoured – as a musician, at least – by past bandmates, he played bass briefly as an unnamed member of Crosby, Stills, Nash & Young, issuing a solo album, the mystical *The Cycle is Complete* (1971), after further drug problems caused him to be ditched a second time. Long-time admirer Young later plucked Palmer from obscurity for his *Trans* project ten years later – though this time, it was alcoholism that dogged his work. Inducted into the Rock 'n' Roll Hall of Fame in 1996, Palmer died from a heart attack at his home in Toronto.

Golden Oldies #21

Cordell Jackson

(Cordell Miller – Pontotoc, Mississippi, 15 July 1923)

Affectionately known in her latter years as 'The Rockin' Granny', Cordell Jackson was the remarkable woman who played the men at their own game during rock 'n' roll's earliest days. Describing herself

– correctly – as 'the first female to write, arrange, accompany, record, engineer, produce and distribute her own music', Jackson had striven for some time to get her guitar tunes recorded at Sun Records, eventually founding her own label in 1956. The company (pointedly named Moon Records) didn't generate many million-sellers, but became a good stable for smaller country and rockabilly acts.

After languishing for many years in obscurity, Cordell Jackson gained new recognition via cover versions of her music performed by Alex Chilton and Tav Falco. Pretty soon, a new generation was to witness the unlikely combination of Jackson duelling with former Stray Cat Brian Setzer in a Budweiser commercial. Aged eighty-one, she died following a lengthy illness on 14 October 2004, but not before having started her own website.

Golden Oldies #22

John Peel

(John Ravenscroft – Heswall, Cheshire, 30 August 1939)

When the news broke of the death of John Peel, the outpourings of grief weren't *quite* in the same league as those for Princess Diana, but, suffice to say, the old dame didn't fare badly. And rightly so – he was probably the most significant figure over the past few decades when it came to the development of contemporary music. After National Service, his early career had taken the then John Ravenscroft to the USA where he brazened his way into the courtroom for the arraignment of Lee Harvey Oswald following the assassination of JFK. Peel gained entry in the guise of a reporter for the *Liverpool Echo*, the court authorities seemingly buying his borderline Scouse accent, which also came in handy in

landing 'Mr Ravencroft' [*sic*] the role of 'official Beatles correspondent' for first KLIF radio in Dallas, then KOMA in Oklahoma City. Further exploits (and a short-lived marriage) preceded Peel's return to Britain and pirate Radio London, where, as host of *Perfumed Garden*, he acquired the name that was to last for the remainder of his days.

Being one of the original disc jockeys on Radio One's roster in 1967 was pretty much all Peelie shared in common with the likes of Tony Blackburn and Pete Murray. While the daytime gang dictated the placing of the average and the asinine in the nation's charts, Peel's late-night show proudly championed Captain Beefheart, Tyrannosaurus Rex, Kevin Ayers, The Sex Pistols, Joy Division/New Order, Billy Bragg (who, in 1983, famously bribed the DJ with a mushroom biriani to play his tape), Napalm Death and The White Stripes – alongside the most obscure reggae sides and, of course, The Fall, who were to record some twenty-four of the man's legendary sessions.

John Peel also made numerous shows for other BBC stations, becoming, as he grew older, something of a genial curmudgeon, the witty spokesman for middle-class family woe. Then, in a 2002 countdown, Peel was remarkably (or perhaps unsurprisingly, depending upon one's standpoint) voted in at forty-three in the BBC's '100 Greatest Britons' poll. Despite this, the constant reshuffling of his 1FM show was to cause Peel considerable stress, according to his great friend and fellow presenter Andy Kershaw – who broke down when interviewed on television following Peel's passing on 25 October 2004. The latter had been holidaying with his wife Sheila in the Inca city of Cuzco in Peru when he suffered a sudden heart attack while dining – all a far cry from Peel's own prediction that he'd perish in a car crash while trying to read an artist's name on the back of a cassette.

Many of those artists – now, of course, successful musicians – were among the thousand or so attending

John Peel: 'See, even the great hang posters of their heroes ...'

Peel's funeral, among them Jack and Meg White (The White Stripes), Jarvis Cocker (Pulp) and Feargal Sharkey, formerly of The Undertones, whose 'Teenage Kicks' had remained Peel's favourite track since its release in 1978. But, now that Peel is gone, just how the next breed of mavericks is to make itself heard remains anyone's guess ...

'Perhaps it's possible John can form some kind of nightmarish career out of his enthusiasm for unlistenable records.'

R H J Brooke, Peel's oh-so-perceptive housemaster at Shrewsbury School, 1956

NOVEMBER

Monday 1

Mac Dre

(Andre Hicks – San Francisco, California,
5 July 1970)

Since he was around nineteen years of
age, Andre Hicks – better known to
his small but so-solid fanbase as Mac
Dre – had issued over a dozen albums
without ever breaking out of the
underground circuit, as well as setting
up his own Thizz Entertainment label.
Mac Dre's lyrics – like those of so
many of his contemporaries – echoed
his violent, outlaw lifestyle. The artist
was believed to have been a member
of the notorious Vallejo Romper
Room Gang, a group responsible for
pizza-parlour stick-ups and even a
bank robbery, his connection to which
led to Dre spending five years in jail.

Bearing all this in mind, Dre's death
due to a drive-by shooting might seem
par for the course, but police remain
uncertain of any motive. Mac Dre was
apparently the passenger in a white
van travelling through Kansas when he
was attacked from a car that pulled up
next to the vehicle as it waited at traffic
lights. The van swerved across two
lanes of the highway, crashing down
an embankment – though Dre was
already dead from the bullet wound by
the time it came to rest.

Terry Knight

(Richard Terrance Knapp – Flint, Michigan,
9 April 1943)

(Terry Knight & The Pack)

A rather different murder that
occurred the same day shocked locals
in the quiet town of Temple, Texas.

Throughout a long and productive
career in rock 'n' roll Terry Knight had
earned praise as a disc jockey, musician, producer and manager, enjoying
a measure of success in each guise.
At twenty-one, Knight was believed
to have been the first US presenter to
play music by The Rolling Stones, his
ground-breaking show on Detroit's
CKLW ahead of the game when it
came to playing British pop artists in
general. Knight's enthusiasm for the
music from across the pond informed
much of his own output: the Stones-
influenced Terry Knight & The Pack
were one of those bands of whom
more was expected than was delivered,
but their local fame was enough to
make the would-be singer and guitarist a decent living for a few years.
The Pack's cover of The Yardbirds'
'Mister, You're a Better Man than I'
(1966) gave Knight a (small) national
hit, while Brownsville Station returned
the favour with a cover of one of his
tunes on their hit album *Yeah!* After
an aborted solo career, Knight moved
into production before finding real
success as manager of Michigan multi-
million-selling arena-rock trio Grand
Funk Railroad. When sacked from the
position in 1972, Knight responded by
denouncing the group's output, thereby echoing the sentiments of a press
that had savaged GFR's offerings
with clockwork regularity. (Before
this, one of Knight's favourite axioms
had been that, in 1970, Grand Funk
Railroad sold him 'a record every four
seconds'.)

By 2004, Terry Knight had long
been retired from the music business,
addiction to cocaine and heroin having
consumed much of his creativity
(and most of his money) in the eighties. Sharing an apartment with his
daughter Danielle and her partner
Donald Alan Fair, Knight arrived back
on the evening of 1 November to
discover a drugged-up Fair attempting
to attack his daughter with a knife.
Neighbours reported a fracas and the
police arrived to discover the former

musician dead from a series of knife
wounds. Knight, it seems, had stepped
in to prevent the assault, Fair then
turning his wrath on his girlfriend's
father. In November 2005, Fair was
finally sentenced to life imprisonment
for Knight's murder.

Thursday 4

Rob Heaton

(Knutsford, Cheshire, 6 July 1961)

New Model Army

Straddling the twin markets of
punk and neo-folk, Bradford's New
Model Army emerged in 1983, voicing the growing discontent of anti-
Thatcherites, their name borrowed
from that of Cromwell's revolutionary
troops, who had opposed the culture
of greed pervading Britain at the time
of the Civil War. Formed in 1980 by
Justin 'Slade the Leveller' Sullivan
(vocals/guitar), Stuart Morrow
(bass/vocals) and Rob Heaton
(drums/guitar/various), NMA
offered an unpolished manifesto
never better displayed than on their
debut album, *Vengeance* (1984). For his
part, although primarily a drummer,
Heaton was a strong all-round musician who wrote or co-wrote many of
New Model Army's standards over
sixteen years with the band. Seven of
the band's singles made the Top Forty,
perhaps the best known being 'No
Rest' (1985), the lead song from their
second LP.

Rob Heaton, who had undergone
brain surgery, left New Model Army
in 1998, concentrating on Fresh
Milk, his project to encourage and
nurture young musical talent. His
death – following a fall at his Bradford
home – revealed pancreatic cancer
of which he'd been unaware. At the
musician's funeral, Sullivan played the
1989 NMA song 'Green and Grey' in
tribute, Heaton's finest composition.

Monday 8

Roger Johnston
(Texas, 26 December 1939)

The Monks

Formed by five American GIs stationed in Germany, The Monks (who certainly shouldn't be confused with the UK band of 'Nice Legs' fame) became a cult draw in the mid sixties. Their heads shaven into monastic tonsures, Gary Burger (vocals/guitar), Dave Day (rhythm guitar/vocals), Larry Clark (organ), Eddie Shaw (bass) and Roger Johnston (drums) caused no little upset to religious groups keen to expose their apparent blasphemy. Far from being put off, The Monks (back in America after discharge in 1965) added black cassocks to the look, as well as miniature nooses instead of neckties; as for the music, it was primitive and mantra-like, Johnston's jazz-influenced drumming broken down to a minimal tribal beat. The band returned to Germany to record their first and only album, *Black Monk Time* (1966). But although their existence was brief, the group's sound influenced a great number of later acts, including the otherwise original Velvet Underground.

Ironically, after The Monks had long dispersed, Roger Johnston became custodian for his local Methodist church. He was, however, still playing, the band having made several recent comebacks by the time of his passing from a lengthy illness.

Saturday 13

Ol' Dirty Bastard
(Russell Tyrone Jones – Brooklyn, New York, 15 November 1968)

The Wu-Tang Clan

Ol' Dirty Bastard ... The Professor ... Big Baby Jesus ... Dirt McGirt ... Joe Bannanas ... Osirus ... or just plain old ODB – whatever one chose to call him, the troubled Russell Jones stood out as one of the true mavericks of hip hop for a decade up until his unexpected death. But the man who'd made rap his escape from the impoverishment of his childhood became as much press fodder for the extremes of his personal life as he did for an impressive body of work.

Drawing together Staten Island's sprawling Wu-Tang Clan with his cousins RZA (Robert Diggs, also of Gravediggaz) and GZA (Gary Grice), ODB developed a unique vocal style that veered from the almost melodic to the slurred and, on a couple of occasions, to the nigh-on incoherent. By the time of The Clan's debut, *Enter the Wu-Tang: 36 Chambers* (1993), the 'family' had grown to include further members – Cappadonna, Ghostface Killah, Inspector Deck, Masta Killa, Method Man, Raekwon and U-God. Although much of their subject matter covered, shall we say, familiar territory, The Clan – and especially ODB – had a highly original take, their imagery steeped in Chinese folklore and martial arts (on which they had certainly done their homework). The map of the East Coast was thus restructured to suit their ends, with Staten Island, their patch, being renamed 'Shaolin'. As many Clansmen were to do, ODB also established his own solo career with the albums *Return to the 36 Chambers* (1995) and *Nigga Please* (1999 – which featured the hit 'Got Your Money', accompanied by Kelis), his main band having cleaned up with a platinum-selling second album, *Wu-Tang Forever* (1997, a US and UK chart-topper), in between.

At the 1998 Grammys, ODB stormed the stage during singer Shawn Colvin's acceptance speech with his notorious (and baffling) 'Wu-Tang is for the children!' outburst – prompted by Puff Daddy's victory over The Clan in an earlier rap category. It's likely that this was the moment that his audience learned all was far from well in Dirtyland. For, having built himself up into something of a celebrity in hip-hop circles, ODB had also been busy elsewhere. He was alleged to have fathered no fewer than thirteen children by a variety of women before his thirtieth birthday, in 1997 running into trouble with the authorities for (perhaps

Ol' Dirty Bastard – with just about the only Liberty he didn't take ...

heart problems in the Jones family, paramedics were baffled, and it was to take another month before the cause of death was revealed. Traces of the painkiller Tramadol and cocaine (plus a sealed wrap of the drug) had been found in ODB's stomach, the lethal combination causing his system to shut down completely. Cause of death was thus ruled an accidental overdose. Five days later, the deceased artist (who also had his own computer games and clothing range) was eulogized by fans and fellow artists alike at his funeral in Brooklyn.

Friday 19

Terry Melcher
(Terry Jorden – New York, 8 February 1942)
Bruce & Terry/The Rip Chords

The son of actress Doris Day and her first husband, trombonist Al Jorden, Terry Melcher went on to become a major entertainment figure in his own right, shaping the sound of Californian pop during the sixties and early seventies. Melcher, who barely knew his father, was brought up by Day's mother before being adopted by the actress's third husband (though neither could tolerate the other). Already a producer at Columbia, Melcher – under the name Terry Day – formed the duo Bruce & Terry with future Beach Boy Bruce Johnston, the pair scoring a Top Five hit with 'Hey Little Cobra' (1964) as The Rip Chords. Melcher's main work, however, was to oversee the output of The Byrds (for whom he produced 1965 chart-toppers 'Mr Tambourine Man' and 'Turn! Turn! Turn!') and Paul Revere & The Raiders.

A name familiar to many on the California scene was that of Charles Manson. By deigning to turn down the would-be singer and writer at his audition, Melcher had transgressed

understandably) falling behind with maintenance payments. And this was revealed to be far from ODB's only misdemeanour: there were several arrests for assault, shoplifting, driving without a licence and possession of Class 'A' drugs (supposedly in fear for his reputation, ODB had famously told arresting officers to 'make the rocks disappear'), possession of an offensive weapon, making terrorist threats and the possibly unique charge of 'wearing a bullet-proof vest as a convicted felon'. In true gangsta style, he'd also twice taken bullets. (In the interests of balance, it should also be pointed out that in 1998 ODB saved the life of a girl trapped under a car.) Escaping from state-ordered

detox in 2000, ODB went AWOL for some weeks before being traced and arrested – just days after stunning fans by appearing onstage with The Clan. During his subsequent incarceration this clearly disturbed man attempted suicide at least once.

Just two days short of his thirty-sixth birthday, Ol' Dirty Bastard had been working on his comeback project at Wu-Tang's New York studios on West 44th Street when he collapsed in the lounge. The artist, who had complained of breathing problems and chest pains during the afternoon, was pronounced dead at just after 5 pm: within minutes the studio was teeming with inconsolable Wu-Tang fans. As there was no history of an unwritten law. The producer and his girlfriend – actress Candice Bergen – had been living at 10050 Cielo Drive, Los Angeles, when they decided to move on. Just months later, the home was the venue for one of the era's most shocking crimes, new owner Sharon Tate being one of five (six, if you include her unborn baby) victims of a brutal killing by Manson and his followers. At the trial, it had been widely reported that Melcher was the intended victim: Manson denied this, chillingly stating that he knew the musician's current address – but suggesting that his intention had been to 'send Melcher a message'.

Melcher recovered from this sobering experience but his future in music was less secure, though he was to act as executive producer for four years on his mother's television series. Melcher continued to make records, with Gram Parsons and Ry Cooder – and a couple on his own – though his biggest latter-day success was probably as co-writer of The Beach Boys' chart-topper 'Kokomo' (1988). The musician had been battling melanoma for some years by the time of his death in 2004.

DECEMBER

Thursday 2

Kevin Coyne
(Derbyshire, 27 January 1944)
(Siren)

Although championed by John Peel, singer/songwriter Kevin Coyne had a quiet career with only occasional bursts into the spotlight – this despite a remarkable output of some thirty-five albums. Coyne's idiosyncratic lyrics of pain and human fallibility were largely based on his experi-ences as a London-based therapist working with the mentally ill, a job he'd held down while recording two albums for Peel's Dandelion label with guitarist Dave Clague under the group name Siren. Poor commercial response then obliged Coyne to look for other outlets; bizarrely, he was in the frame as The Doors sought a new singer after the death of Jim Morrison (◀ *July 1971*). How that might have panned out is certainly fodder for the imagination.

Instead, Coyne settled for a series of variable solo albums with a number of different labels. The best was *Marjory Razorblade* (1973), his first effort for Virgin (Richard Branson was, apparently, a huge fan), sadly swamped by Mike Oldfield's simultaneously issued *Tubular Bells*. Broad-minded and keen to absorb all forms of music, Coyne was to work with a number of distinguished names over the years, including Andy Summers (later of The Police), Zoot Money, The Ruts, Robert Wyatt and ex-Slapp Happy singer Dagmar Krause. But success continued to elude him and, follow-ing a stint with Cherry Red, Coyne relocated to Germany in 1985. Here, he was far better accepted, and not just as a musician: previous problems with alcoholism and depression were

'When people are in the turmoil of breakdown, they become more direct.'
Kevin Coyne

kicked into touch as Coyne exhibited paintings, took on acting roles and published two books of short stories. Having issued several new records (his two sons now featuring as musicians), Kevin Coyne was believed to have been at his most contented in 2004 – which makes his death from fibrosis of the lung somehow all the sadder. The story has it that Coyne spent his last few months lugging an oxygen tank around Europe with him while on tour, his final performance in Vienna taking place on the night of his death.

Wednesday 8

'Dimebag' Darrell Abbott

(Dallas, Texas, 20 August 1966)

Pantera
DamagePlan

They called it the 'day the metal died'. A rock night that wouldn't normally have seen any greater carnage than the usual mosh-pit bruising accelerated into an onstage holocaust that shouldn't have been possible. In the middle of the mayhem was former Pantera guitarist 'Dimebag' Darrell Abbott, the target of the first and only onstage assassination to be recorded in this book.

The son of country musician and songwriter Jerry Abbott, the young guitarist found himself banned from virtually all Texas contests simply for winning too often. His fretboard skills led to the originally monikered 'Diamond' Darrell Abbott and his drummer brother Vinnie Paul joining the fledgling Pantera when the guitarist was only seventeen. A band of Black Sabbath fans that developed to encompass both thrash and power metal, Pantera (the name derives from the members' home town of

'Dimebag' Darrell: Ultimately, there was no 'DamagePlan'

'Bottom line: you've got Jimi Hendrix, you've got Eddie Van Halen, you've got Randy Rhoads – and you've got "Dimebag" Darrell.'

Zakk Wylde, guitarist with Ozzy Osbourne/ Black Label Society

Pantego as well as being Portuguese for 'panther') were musically far more adept than many of their peers, the line-up of Abbott, Abbott and Rex 'Rocker' Brown (bass) getting into their stride when vocalist Phil Anselmo replaced Terry Glaze in 1988. The band were always full on, angry and challenging, peaking with fearsome albums *Vulgar Display of Power* (1992) and *Far Beyond Driven* (1994, a US chart-topper). Some critics contended that Pantera at their best were one of the finest metal acts ever. (Those who didn't rate the band suggested that their sound was derivative of the more established Metallica or perhaps obscurer Louisiana groove-metal merchants Exhorder.) Something of a hero among air guitarists, Abbott also found time for the more sedate pastime of writing a monthly column for *Guitar World*.

The break-up of Pantera in 2003 was one of considerable acrimony, though, indirectly resulting in the tragedy of December 2004. Having fallen out with the volatile Anselmo, the Abbott brothers worked with veteran country rebel David Allan Coe, before embarking on their next metal project, DamagePlan, with Patrick Lachman (vox) and Bob Zilla (bass). This band's first album, *New Found Power* (2004), made a decent showing on the Billboard charts and 'life after Pantera' seemed likely. But it was not to be, the ghastly events of 8 December effectively ending DamagePlan as a going concern. As the band began a low-key performance before 250 devotees at the Alrosa Villa nightclub in Columbus, Ohio, an armed fan named Nathan Gale beat security to scale an eight-foot fence, enter the club in haste and approach stage left – 'Dimebag' Darrell's usual spot. Grabbing the guitarist, Gale put a Beretta pistol to his head – and shot him twice at point-blank range; Abbott died instantly. In the pandemonium that followed, DamagePlan security guard Jeff

'Mayhem' Thompson was also fatally shot, as was employee Erin Halk and audience member Nathan Bray, as they attempted to assist the stricken musician. Gale – said to have been uttering disparaging remarks about the break-up of Pantera as he carried out his attack – then held the weapon to the head of drum technician John Brooks, before James Niggemeyer, a police marksman, finally took the assailant out with a single bullet from afar as concert-goers fled for their lives. In this jaw-dropping scenario, Gale (who had previous convictions for petty crimes) had somehow had time to reach the stage and unload fifteen bullets before security were even close enough to apprehend him. All of which naturally prompted Abbott's family to take legal action against the venue in 2005.

Within hours, the Alrosa Villa was to become a shrine to the memory of 'Dimebag', two generations of metal fans joining forces to howl both their sadness and outrage at the events of the previous night as the forecourt became swathed with yellow roses and makeshift inverted crosses. Some days later, one of the most extraordinary eulogies arrived in the form of an online video from Phil Anselmo, who, having publicly denounced Abbott for breaking up Pantera, was now seen choking with grief upon his words.

Alex Soria

(Montreal, Quebec, 1966)

The Nils

(Chino)

The brilliance of Alex Soria won't ever be known to the world in general – after all, he was a small-time guitarist in a small-time punk band who were never likely to make it out of their locale – but even so The Nils were cited by no less than Bob Mould of Hüsker Dü. Taught to play three chords by his older brother Carlos, Soria had mastered his instrument in days and became the band's chief songwriter when they began back in 1979. Within a few years, the group had been signed and were working with producers such as Brit stalwart Chris Spedding – and an EP, *Sell Out Young* (1985), did just that. But problems with personnel, management and distribution prevented what many thought should have been an inevitable graduation to the big league.

Perhaps if The Nils – or Chino, the band Soria then formed in the late nineties – had been American, things might have been different. In the event, the lack of musical progress was just one setback too many for Alex Soria: forced into unreliable menial employment and succumbing to drug abuse, he took his life one night. After a major row with his partner, Soria raced to a nearby railway line, waited for a train and then saluted the driver before leaping to his death.

'Nobody played an SG [guitar] like that little fucker!'

Sean Friesen, The Asexuals

Frank 'Son' Seals

(Osceola, Arkansas, 14 August 1942)

As a novice artist brought up on a diet of Earl Hooker and Albert King – with both of whom he'd eventually tour – 'Son' Seals played Chicago blues like he really meant it. The youngest of thirteen kids born to musician Jim 'Son' Seals, the guitarist emulated his father by playing at his juke joint and inheriting his nickname (then going on to better Seals Sr by siring *fourteen* offspring of his own). Soon known for the sheer intensity of his playing, Seals recorded several albums of material that blended Delta roots music with the rock 'n' roll with which he'd grown up. The latter years of 'Son' Seals's life were the *real* stuff of the blues, however: having been unwell since the seventies, in 1999 he lost a leg to amputation, already having lost much of his face to a psychotic ex-wife who'd shot him in the head as he slept. On completion of his reconstructive surgery, Seals then lost his mobile home to a fire and his prized custom guitar to a thief. His death from diabetes may perhaps be seen as a kind release after a decade in which his authenticity as a bluesman was sorely tested.

Lest We Forget

Other notable deaths that occurred sometime during 2004:

John Balance (UK singer/performer with experimental, occult-obsessed duo Coil; born Geoffrey Burton, Nottinghamshire, 16/2/1962; belying his stage name, he fell fifteen feet from a balcony, 13/11)

Johnny Bragg (US vocalist with various vocal groups – the world's best-known 'incarcerated' singer, with The Prisonaires; born Tennessee, 26/2/1925; cancer, 1/9)

Ritchie Cordell (US pop songwriter whose smashes included #1s 'Mony Mony', 'I Think We're Alone Now' and 'I Love Rock 'n' Roll'; born Richard Rosenblatt, New York, 10/3/1943; pancreatic cancer, 13/4)

Norma Nicole 'Skeeter' Davis (hugely popular US country singer who recorded for four decades, originally with The Davis Sisters; born Mary Frances Penick, Kentucky, 30/12/1931; breast cancer, 19/9)

Willem 'Mouth' Duyn (Dutch Europop singer with Maggie MacNeal who scored Top Ten hits in the US with 1972's 'How Do You Do?' and in the UK with 1974's 'I See a Star'; born 31/3/1937; heart attack, 3/12)

Thomas 'Quorthon' Forsberg (Swedish black-metal pioneer who fronted Bathory; born 1966; heart failure, 7/6)

Dick Heckstall-Smith (revered UK jazz/blues saxophonist who worked with numerous artists including Graham Bond and Alexis Korner; born Shropshire, 26/9/1934; cancer, 17/12)

Rudy Maugeri (founding Canadian baritone/arranger for vocal group The Crew-Cuts, who scored nine US Top Forty hits including 1955's 'Earth Angel'; born Ontario, 27/1/1931; pancreatic cancer, 7/5)

Mel Pritchard (respected UK rock drummer with Barclay James Harvest; born Lancashire, 20/1/1948; heart attack, 28/1)

George Williams (US lead vocalist with R & B act The Tymes, who went to #1 at home with 1963's 'So Much in Love' and in the UK with 1974's 'Ms Grace'; born Pennsylvania, 6/12/1935; cancer, 28/7)

For a complete list of fallen artists, visit
www.numberoneinheaven.com

2005

JANUARY

Wednesday 5

Danny Sugerman
(California, 11 October 1954)

Danny Sugerman – just twelve years old when he snuck out to watch The Doors perform at Long Beach – was to live a remarkable story of juvenile achievement. Sugerman for his part was not content with just the two-dimensional version of the hero his pals tacked to their bedroom walls, while Morrison for his was clearly impressed with the boy who hung around after hours and at The Doors' offices during school time. The singer suggested fanmail-answering then associate management roles for Sugerman when he was still just fourteen. Sugerman's love of the band, coupled with natural administrative and negotiating skills, proved him equal to these tasks; indeed, he went on to manage the post-Morrison Doors, replacing Bill Siddons. The downside to this extraordinary backstage pass was that Sugerman (who'd even begun *looking* like the singer) became a heroin addict while still in his teens. The death of his 'brother' Morrison

(➡ *July 1971*) having hit him hard, most of Sugerman's memories of this era are nonetheless documented in the acclaimed 1980 Doors biography *No-One Here Gets Out Alive* and *Wonderland Avenue*, his autobiography of 1989.

As though these previous exploits weren't enough, Sugerman then went on to manage the equally wilful figures Iggy Pop (albeit briefly) and 'super-groupie' Bebe Buell. Later, Sugerman perhaps even topped this by marrying Oliver North's former shredder-happy secretary Fawn Hall, with whom he stayed until his death after a long and painful battle with lung cancer. He may have conquered heroin and alcohol via stints in rehab units, but it was Sugerman's lifetime addiction to cigarettes which claimed his life in the end.

> **'Danny's standing side by side with his great friend Jim Morrison – and the two of them will now be laughing into eternity.'**
>
> John Densmore, drummer, The Doors

Tuesday 11

Jimmy Griffin
(Cincinnati, Ohio, 10 August 1943)
Bread
The Remingtons
(Black Tie)

Growing up in a neighbourhood where rock 'n' roll abounded, guitarist Jimmy Griffin eventually took the 'softer' option, forming the definitive AOR band Bread with songwriter David Gates. Early on, his musical proficiency had been noted by local wild boys Dorsey and Johnny Burnette, who lived just across the road; their connections eventually led Griffin to Los Angeles and a music community swept away by the new sounds emerging. The guitarist cut a solo album for Reprise in 1963 (*Summer Holiday*), but although his songs were recorded by high-profile stars such as Bobby Vee, major success for Griffin was still six years away.

Bread began in 1969, Griffin and his new pal Gates (vocals/guitar/keyboards) accompanied by Robb Royer (bass) and Jim Gordon (drums – replaced by Mike Botts after the first album). With beat music now replaced in the US by the smoother sounds of Blood, Sweat & Tears and The Carpenters (for whom Griffin later wrote the Grammy-winning 'For All We Know'), Bread were to fit right in, topping the Billboard chart with the seductive 'Make It with You' (1970). A series of similarly paced Gates tunes followed, some of which – 'If', 'Baby I'm-a Want You' (both 1971) and 'Everything I Own' (1972) – went on to become MOR classics. Griffin was away from the band for three years after several artistic disagreements with Gates, although he returned for the evocative *Lost without Your Love* (1977). After this album, Bread called it a day, however, Griffin returning to solo work. Black Tie emerged in the late eighties, the guitarist teaming with Billy Swan and former Eagles bassist Randy Meisner, though this seemingly infallible line-up was unable to achieve the success of Griffin's earlier band. The next venture, The Remingtons, propelled him back into the US Top Ten with 'A Long Time Ago' (1992), but there were no further hits and subsequent work for Jimmy Griffin was restricted to sessions and songwriting, plus a Bread reunion in 1997. Griffin had been receiving treatment for a year when he died from cancer at home in Nashville.

See also *Mike Botts (☞ December 2005)*

Spencer Dryden

(New York, 7 April 1938)
Jefferson Airplane
New Riders of the Purple Sage
The Peanut Butter Conspiracy
(Various acts)

On the same afternoon, cancer took another stalwart of American rock music in the shape of psychedelic-rock percussionist Spencer Dryden. The drummer – who boasted Charlie Chaplin as an uncle – came from a jazz background, his syncopated rhythms largely unheard in pop music before he formed the Los Angeles band The Heartbeats with noted guitarist Roy Buchanan. This was a full ten years before Dryden replaced the errant Skip Spencer as drummer of hippy leading lights Jefferson Airplane. By 1967, the band – Dryden, Grace Slick (vocals), Paul Kantner (guitar), Jorma Kaukonen (guitar) and Jack Casady (bass) – were at the height of their powers with Top Ten signature tunes in 'White Rabbit' (complete with Dryden's distinctive snare) and 'Somebody To Love' remained at the frontline of the counterculture alongside The Grateful Dead et al for three years. Most remember Monterey, Woodstock and Altamont as the decade's trio of key festivals; fewer recall that The Airplane were the only band to play all of them, Dryden in place as musical history was made. After leaving the band in 1970, Dryden found himself a niche with the equally influential (if not as commercially viable) New Riders of the Purple Sage and The Peanut Butter Conspiracy. In the eighties, he emerged from a brief sabbatical from music to perform with the ultimate hippy supergroup The Dinosaurs – comprising members of The Dead, Country Joe & The Fish, QMS and Big Brother & The Holding Company – though he played no part in the metamorphosis of Jefferson Airplane into Starship during that decade.

Spencer Dryden's final years were highly distressing. After a botched hip operation left him permanently crippled, a fire in September 2003 then destroyed his home and most of the memorabilia from those golden years of the sixties. Finally, he was diagnosed with colon cancer in October 2004, a benefit concert held by his high-profile friends raising just about enough for the vast medical bills he was now accruing. Dryden, however, lasted only three months after diagnosis, dying from the disease at his home in Penngrove, California.

See also *Sandi Robison (☞ April 1988); Skip Spence (☞ April 1999)*

Tuesday 25

Ron Kersey

(Tyrone Kersey – Philadelphia, Pennsylvania, 7 April 1949)
The Trammps
The Salsoul Orchestra
(Various acts)

A keyboardist with a good line in dramatic fills, Ron 'Have Mercy' Kersey became part of the fixtures and fittings at Philadelphia International – the label that blended soul and dance to such fine effect during the seventies. Kersey developed his nickname while a member of the Massachusetts air force band, the audience loving his stage presence and relentless energy. A meeting with Philly legend-to-be Norman Harris elevated the musician to a higher plane, however: having played mainly in the studio with the largely faceless Salsoul Orchestra, Kersey then produced his finest work – and found an outlet for his exuberant personality – with The Trammps (formerly The Volcanos/Moods). Most US fans remember this great band solely for the *Saturday Night Fever*-housed 'Disco Inferno' (1977), but there were other pulsating hits such as 'Zing Went the Strings of My Heart' (1974) and 'Hold back the Night' (1975 – a UK Top Five hit). But such was the glut of black dance acts at the time, The Trammps – Kersey, Earl Young (vocals), Jimmy Ellis (vocals), Dennis Harris (guitar), Stan Wade (bass), John Hart (organ) and Michael Thompson (drums) – were never to achieve the level of fame that they clearly should have.

Ron Kersey maintained a sizeable income afterwards by writing, arranging and producing the likes of Gloria Gaynor, Grace Jones, B B King, Gladys Knight and even Stevie Wonder. His days were numbered, however, following a stroke in 1997. Kersey's final years were spent under the care of his sister Toni, before being carried off by a bout of pneumonia.

Golden Oldies #23

Ray Peterson

(Denton, Texas, 23 April 1935)

'The Golden Voice of Rock 'n' Roll' was, in truth, more balladeer than rocker – but a pretty impressive one, boasting a four-and-a-half-octave range. Ray Peterson overcame the polio that killed some of his classmates to become a respected singer and even a golf pro in his later life, the future star developing his voice by entertaining fellow patients as he received treatment for his condition. Hit status was not quick in arriving but, with his seventh release, Peterson took 'The Wonder of You' (1959) into the US and UK charts in a rendition that prompted Elvis Presley to record the song himself and score a 1970 UK chart-topper. Peterson's best-known hit was Jeff Barry's classic death ditty 'Tell Laura I Love Her' (1960) (➤ Death Toll #1), though yet again, the song – subject to a ban by some US states – was destined to be better recalled as a British number one for Welshman Ricky Valance. Working with Phil Spector, Peterson achieved another US Top Ten hit that year in 'Corinna Corinna', but future recordings under the young maverick producer were less noteworthy – and failed to impact upon the business end of the hit parade.

Peterson founded his own Dunes record label with agent Stan Shulman in

Ray Peterson perhaps finds another way of telling Laura . . .

1961, but the cabaret circuit became his performing environment for the next two decades, with 'Laura' remaining a staple in Ray Peterson's act until his retirement. On 25 January 2005, the much-admired star died from cancer at home in Smyrna, Tennessee.

Jim Capaldi: Caught up in Traffic

Jim Capaldi

(Nicola James Capaldi – Evesham, Worcestershire,
2 August 1944)

Traffic
(The Hellions/The Revolutions/Deep Feeling)
(Various acts)

The son of an Italian music teacher, Jim Capaldi probably felt his given name wasn't 'rock 'n' roll' enough to suit his own forays into the business. His father encouraged Capaldi in his attempts to master the drums, although it was clear the young boy had considerable talent even at the age of twelve. As a teenager, Capaldi became a well-established though still very fresh face on the Worcester music scene, forming his first band, The Sapphires, in 1961; two years on, he met guitarist Dave Mason and started

up The Hellions – an oft-renamed band that was to form the basis of Traffic. The major breakthrough for Capaldi arrived as The Hellions went to Hamburg – a noted destination for would-be British stars – as backing musicians to singer Tanya Day. (Also in tow were The Spencer Davis Group – months away from their brief but spectacular success in the UK – Capaldi and Mason befriending the band's wunderkind singer, Steve Winwood.)

The Hellions (later The Revolutions/Deep Feeling) becoming something of a local legend, Capaldi – who had also tried his hand successfully as vocalist – played with another friend, Jimi Hendrix, before reconvening with Winwood to fashion Midlands-based psychedelic supergroup Traffic at the start of 1967. The band (completed by flautist/saxophonist Chris Wood) achieved instant success with the great Top Five singles 'Paper Sun'

and 'Hole in My Shoe', plus the hit debut album *Mr Fantasy*. The group was forever wracked by personnel upheaval, however, with pretty much all members leaving at one point or another to start other projects. In Capaldi's case, it was Wooden Frog, an aborted sideline affair that occurred only when Winwood disappeared to work with Blind Faith in 1968. Somehow, the nucleus of Traffic rallied to release two of their best albums, *John Barleycorn Must Die* (1970) and *The Low Spark of High-Heeled Boys* (1971), by which time the hit singles had dried up. Simultaneously, Capaldi embarked on a reasonably successful solo career that spawned the acclaimed album *Oh How We Danced* (1972) and later even included a couple of UK chart hits in 'It's All up to You' (1974) and, most notably, a Top Five cover of Roy Orbison's 'Love Hurts' (1975). Over the course of the next three decades, Capaldi issued twelve albums of his own, recording with some serious names, including Eric Clapton, George Harrison, Bob Marley and Carlos Santana. Traffic – *sans* Wood, who had died ten years before (☞ *July 1983*) – even joined in with the fine comeback, *Far From Home* (1994), that saw Capaldi tour once again with Winwood.

Jim Capaldi will always be remembered as a selfless individual, unspoiled by rock fame and ever ready to assist others. The environmentally conscious musician had married his Brazilian girlfriend Aninha in 1977, moving to South America where he became active in ecological issues and also his partner's Jubilee campaign to assist Brazil's thousands of street children. Capaldi remained involved with these projects (as well as another prospective Traffic reunion following the band's 2004 induction into the Rock 'n' Roll Hall of Fame) until struck down by the stomach cancer that was to claim his life early on the morning of 28 January 2005.

See also *Rebop Kwaku-Baah (☞ January 1983)*

Saturday 29

Eric Griffiths
(Denbigh, North Wales, 31 October 1940)
The Quarry Men

Despite a potentially great start in music, Eric Griffiths is destined to be remembered as 'John Lennon's school-friend', an original member of The Quarry Men who never graduated to the world's best-loved pop group. A keen though distracted guitarist, Griffiths dropped conventional lessons to learn a few chords via Lennon's mother. Griffiths didn't have the natural ability of his friend, but was invited to join The Quarry Men because he had a new guitar and essential amplification. Following the arrival

of first Paul McCartney, then George Harrison – whose lead-guitar skills effectively put paid to Griffiths's interest in a music career – the guitarist was sacked over the phone during the band's very next rehearsal. Thereafter, Griffiths worked for the merchant navy and prison service while The Beatles became . . . well, you know the rest.

Just eight years before his death in Scotland from pancreatic cancer, Griffiths joined 'John Lennon's Original Quarry Men' – Rod Davis (banjo/guitar), Len Garry (tea-chest bass/guitar), Colin Hanton (drums) and Pete Shotton (washboard) at an emotional reunion for The Cavern Club's fortieth anniversary, the group also going on to record the album *Get Back Together* (1997).

See also *John Lennon (☞ December 1980)*

FEBRUARY

Tuesday 8

Keith Knudsen
(LeMars, Iowa, 18 February 1948)
The Doobie Brothers
Southern Pacific

Primarily a drummer, Keith Knudsen joined The Doobies at the band's commercial peak, arriving just in time to see songwriter Tom Johnston's 'Black Water' reach number one in the US at the start of 1975. The otherwise quiet Knudsen had learned how to pummel out a rhythm in eighth grade, going on to play with beat groups as he sought to emulate his heroes The Beatles as a teenager. Just as it appeared Knudsen's career might never evolve beyond that of journeyman session player, the musician met

The Doobies' manager Bruce Cohn, who hinted that the band would need a replacement for the departing Michael Hossack. The result was a tenure that lasted until the band split in 1982, Knudsen maintaining a position within the line-up of Johnston (vocals/guitar), Pat Simmons (vocals/guitar), Jeff 'Skunk' Baxter (the erstwhile Steely Dan guitarist) and Tiran Porter (bass). The most significant change in the seventies was the temporary retirement of Johnston from fatigue, another former Steely Dan member, Michael McDonald, then joining as full-time singer/keyboardist from 1975. Although Doobie Brothers purists weren't overly enthused by the smoother sound afforded by McDonald's voice, the band nevertheless secured another multi-platinum album, *Minute By Minute*, in 1979.

Following The Doobies' split, Keith Knudsen formed the successful country-rock unit Southern Pacific with singer/musician John McFee (another former Doobie Brother), while also arranging charity events to benefit Vietnam veterans, for which he received widespread acclaim. This culminated in a fully fledged Doobies reunion in 1987 (including Johnston) and a notable performance in Moscow, where the band were still huge. An album, *Sibling Rivalry* (2000), was widely thought to contain the strongest Doobies material in two decades. Although it was far from their biggest seller, Knudsen realized a personal ambition by singing lead on selected tracks, despite having been diagnosed with cancer back in 1995. Knudsen eventually died from pneumonia ten years later.

See also *Bobby LaKind (☞ December 1992); Cornelius Bumpus (☞ February 2004). Early Doobie Brother Dave Shogren died in 1999.*

Monday 28

Chris Curtis
(Christopher Crummey – Oldham, 26 August 1941)
The Searchers
(The Flowerpot Men)
(Roundabout)

Well, the name was going to have to go first – and it did, when Chris Crummey was just nineteen, Searchers leader Tony Jackson suggesting 'Curtis' during an interview. The drummer/singer had lived in Liverpool since the age of four, developing a love of American rock 'n' roll (particularly Fats Domino), skiffle and his city's indigenous Merseybeat. Within this nascent scene, The Searchers – Curtis, Jackson, Mike Pender (Mike Prendergast) and John McNally (both vocals/guitar) – became second only to The Beatles in popularity, although unlike their more illustrious peers they were more content to cover US standards than write their own material. For a couple of years, however, The Searchers couldn't fail: 'Sweets for My Sweet' (1963), 'Needles and Pins' and 'Don't Throw Your Love Away' (both 1964) all made number one in Britain, with an assortment of other hits not far behind. For his part, Curtis wrote much of the band's original material, such as it was, though this was generally confined to album tracks. It became apparent, however, that the drummer – a devout churchgoer who shunned the rock 'n' roll lifestyle – was unhappy in the spotlight and he quit The Searchers in 1966. Stories vary, but it seems that Curtis – who was known as 'Mad Henry' by various Beatles – may have hastened his departure by some wilful drug abuse and general unreliability while on a world tour that year. The official reason was given as 'nervous exhaustion', Curtis being replaced by percussionist John Blunt.

Thereafter, Chris Curtis toured briefly with the manufactured Flowerpot Men (who'd scored a surprise 1967 smash with 'Let's Go to San Francisco'), having become a producer of some note, working with Alma Cogan and Paul & Barry Ryan. Later attempts as an artist were less successful, though the rock band formed with his brother Dave – Roundabout – was a direct precursor of Deep Purple, featuring as it did Jon Lord and Ritchie Blackmore in the line-up. By the seventies, Curtis had kicked music into touch and joined the Civil Service as a tax inspector, though he was occasionally to perform as a folk musician in later years. Curtis died at his home following a lengthy illness: the date above represents when his body was discovered; he died perhaps as much as two days before that.

See also *Tony Jackson (* *August 2003)*

MARCH

Wednesday 9

Kurt Struebing
(Seattle, Washington, 1965)
NME (New Messiah Emerging)

Guitarist Kurt Struebing's brand of metal might have been too extreme even for the recently departed Tommy Vance, but it's not so much the music that draws the attention with this story. In April 1986, Washington police received a garbled 911 call from a young man who claimed to have murdered his mother with a hatchet and a pair of scissors. Which, apparently, he had. Struebing was guitarist with Federal Way metal act NME (or New Messiah Emerging, the name usually punctuated with swastikas), an alleged neo-Nazi act 'at war with the world'. Suffering from severe psychosis, Struebing had attempted to cleanse his body with carpet shampoo the day before he committed the crime. He'd become obsessed with the belief that all humans – including his family and friends – were robots, the singer feeling that if he tried killing himself and his adoptive mother, 53-year-old Darlee Struebing, it would somehow prove his theory. In the event, Struebing was sentenced to twelve years for second-degree murder in a high-security institution (later reduced to eight, due to his disorder), where he attempted suicide at least once. By 1994, the musician was released, re-forming NME and reissuing the band's 10-year-old album, *Unholy Death*, the following year to a new audience of metal thrill-seekers. And it doesn't end there . . .

Amazingly, Kurt Struebing had turned his life around by 2005 to such an extent that reliable sources claimed he was now a successful graphic artist who was only too ready to help others by playing benefit concerts (he'd recently raised money for the bereaved family of a soldier shot in Iraq) – and on top of this a quiet, doting family man who loved his wife and son. Which makes Struebing's death in his home town in 2005 all the more baffling. Approaching the Spokane Street bridge, raised to allow a tug to pass below on the Duwamish Waterway, the guitarist failed to slow down in his Volkswagen Jetta, crashing through two barriers and careering off the edge of the draw span. The car plunged fifty feet to the road below; Struebing was killed by the impact.

Thursday 10

Jackie Neal
(Baton Rouge, Louisiana, 7 July 1967)

An equally dramatic tale emerged from the US just twenty-four hours later, with the shocking murder of pop/blues singer 'Jazzy' Jackie Neal, the victim of an apparent crime of passion. Neal was one of ten siblings born to noted Baton Rouge blues-man Raful Neal. Though she was not as internationally recognized as her father, the singer had made sufficient headway to play a series of high-profile dates in Europe, for which she had purchased her own tour bus. Neal's four albums had sold stead-ily, and there were many who felt that, despite her age, she could still crack the big time: one of these was her boyfriend, James White. Neal, however, had ended their relationship at the end of 2003, after which White's behaviour had become increasingly disturbed. Weeks after threatening the singer and smashing her car windows, White made his way to the crowded T'Nails beauty salon, Baton Rouge, where he pulled out a gun and fired four bullets into Neal before turning the gun on himself. Neal's friend Angela Myers was critically injured during the shooting, while the intended victim died within seconds of the attack. In the outpouring of grief that followed, the hospitalized White was apprehended: on 11 May 2005, despite a plea of 'not guilty', he was charged with first-degree murder (plus attempted murder) and faced execution.

It had been a particularly difficult year for the Neal family, with the deaths of father Raful and brother Ronnie occurring just before that of the singer, who had three children of her own.

Danny Joe Brown
(Jacksonville, Florida, 24 August 1951)

Molly Hatchet
(The Danny Joe Brown Band)

Later that same day, the death was announced of singer Danny Joe Brown, a long-time member of Southern rockers Molly Hatchet. The former coastguard joined the popular band (named after a murderous seventeenth-century prostitute) at the age of twenty-four, Molly Hatchet then securing a deal with Epic, who issued the band's eponymous, platinum-selling first album in 1978. The second, *Flirtin' With Disaster* (1979), surprised even the band by shifting in excess of 2 million copies worldwide as Hatchet – Brown, Dave Hlubek, Steve Holland and Duane Roland (guitars), Banner Thomas (bass) and Bruce Crump (drums) – became much-sought-after festival headliners. Brown suffered constant health problems, however, and, following the onset of diabetes in 1980, was obliged to retire from Molly Hatchet's punishing tour schedule. Following a short-lived sojourn with his own band, Brown felt compelled to return to his first group for the album *No Guts . . . No Glory* (1983), by which time hard rock was back in vogue. Although record sales never matched those of the early days, Molly Hatchet remained a going concern until 1998, when the singer finally pulled the plug on the band following a stroke.

Danny Joe Brown died at home in Davie, Fort Lauderdale – just half an hour after returning from a four-week stay in hospital. The cause of death was given as 'complications arising from diabetes', including renal failure and pneumonia.

Wednesday 16

Justin Hinds
(Steertown, Ocho Rios, Jamaica, 7 May 1942)

Justin Hinds & The Dominoes

Justin Hinds – who arrived in Kingston aged seventeen – was to become one of the great names of early Jamaican ska, a Rastafarian, Bible-toting main-stay of Duke Reid's Treasure Isles label, whose band The Dominoes never gained the recognition they deserved. The group – named after the main man's favourite R & B singer Fats Domino, and consisting of Hinds plus backing singers Junior Dixon and Dennis Sinclair – made numer-ous records for Reid after Clement 'Coxsone' Dodd turned them down in 1963. But, over the next decade, Hinds became extraordinarily prolific, his best-known songs perhaps 'Carry Go Bring Come' (1963), 'Botheration' (1964, rerecorded 1967) and 'Mighty Redeemer Part I & II' (1968). Hinds continued recording into the seventies and eighties, working with producers of the calibre of Jack Ruby (Burning Spear, etc), though, by this time, Justin Hinds was more active in Europe than he was at home. Although slow-ing down as he grew older, the singer continued to tour tirelessly until 2004. His death came just weeks after diag-nosis with lung cancer.

Tuesday 22

Rod Price
(London, 22 November 1947)

Foghat

Respected UK-born slide-guitarist Rod Price was to become the fulcrum of boogie rockers Foghat during the band's most prolific years. Alongside fellow Londoner and ex-Savoy Brown singer/guitarist 'Lonesome' Dave Peverett, Tony Stevens (bass) and Roger Earl (drums), Price enjoyed remarkable commercial success in the US with Foghat, who ran off five gold records and a double-platinum live set between 1972 and 1981. Known as 'The Magician of Slide', Price was a mainstay of the band until its split at the start of the eighties (though Foghat were to reconvene for later recordings). Thereafter, the musician's fine traditional style saw him play with a variety of artists, including Champion Jack Dupree, John Lee Hooker and Muddy Waters; he also issued a couple of albums of his own, *Open* (2000) and *West Four* (2003).

Rod Price's untimely death followed an accident at his New Hampshire home. It appears that the musician suffered a coronary before falling downstairs, sustaining head injuries from which he died shortly afterwards. In recent years, the rock 'n' roller had developed a reputation as a family man and loving father to his five kids.

See also *'Lonesome' Dave Peverett (↦ February 2000)*

Paul Hester: Simply crowded out?

Paul Hester

(Melbourne, 8 January 1959)
Crowded House
Split Enz
(Various acts)

His mother a jazz drummer, Paul Hester didn't need much encouragement to pick up the sticks himself. Disillusioned by the menial work he felt he'd never escape, Hester began his own band, Cheks (later Deckchairs Overboard), within which he began to receive recognition in his native Australian music scene. It was Midnight Oil drummer Robert Hirst who suggested Hester to Neil and Tim Finn of the internationally successful New Zealand band Split Enz in 1983, the percussionist then remaining with the brothers as from the dying embers of this band rose the better-known Crowded House. The group scored an immediate hit with an eponymous debut record that spawned the international smash 'Don't Dream It's

Over' (1987, US number two), which has since become a semi-standard, and covered by many artists. Although their second album had a more modest reception, Crowded House nonetheless became one of Europe's biggest draws with their third, *Woodface* (1991), and its clutch of hits, including 'Fall at Your Feet' and the catchy 'Weather With You' (the band's biggest UK seller). But, following the *Together Alone* set (1993), Hester felt increasingly uncomfortable in a set-up now largely under the guidance of Neil Finn, and abandoned a US tour to spend time with his baby daughter.

Paul Hester found post-House work with bands such as Tarmac Adam, but became far better known as a music presenter on television back in Australia. Despite a successful career, though, the musician had, for many years, hidden a painful battle with depression from his family and colleagues. Tragically, this secret was to be revealed in the most shocking manner when the former star's body was found in a Melbourne park early one Saturday morning: Hester had apparently taken his own life by hanging.

APRIL

Monday 11

Junior Delgado
(Oscar Hibbert – Kingston, Jamaica, 25 August 1958)
(Time Unlimited)

The young singer of Jamaican harmony sensations Time Unlimited, Junior Hibbert – as he was known – formally adopted his nickname 'Delgado' (Spanish for 'skinny') once it became apparent he'd not be able to shake it. Delgado had been a frequent prizewinner in talent showcases (Lee Perry then producing Time Unlimited's early recordings) before the singer decided to turn solo while still a teenager. Delgado was immediately in demand with some of the great names in reggae, including Bunny Lee, 'skanga' maestro Rupie Edwards in his heyday, and Dennis Brown, whose 'Tition' he was to record in 1975 – a song that presaged the thought-provoking, conscience-stirring work of Delgado's later career. At the age of twenty, Delgado issued the solo set *Taste of the Young Heart* (1978), his 'low-moan' delivery a definite selling-point. Further albums, the limited-edition *Dance a Dub* (1978) and *Effort* (1979), brought 'Jooks' (as he was also affectionately known) to the attention of producers such as Augustus Pablo and, most significantly, Sly Dunbar and Robbie Shakespeare, with whom he worked closely in the early eighties. In 1981 Delgado enjoyed a Jamaican chart smash with the Dunbar/ Shakespeare-produced 'Merry-Go-Round'; but within a year, the singer was arrested following a drugs bust and imprisoned for eighteen months. On his release, Delgado split his time equally between his homeland and Britain, where he had a loyal following. Here he wrote 'Broadwater Farm', his prescient diatribe against the crime-ridden north London estate that was then to make front-page news after the murder of a police constable there in 1985 (when the record was banned as a matter of sensitivity). Another area of political interest to Delgado was apartheid in South Africa, a subject featuring on his *Ragga-muffin Year* album (1986), his most successful record. Later releases in a hugely prolific career included 1998's *Fearless* (featuring, among many collaborators from across the pop world, Faithless's Maxi Jazz and former Special, Jerry Dammers) and Delgado's tribute to a late friend, *Sings Dennis Brown* (2000) (➤ *July 1999*). Junior Delgado himself received numerous tributes from fellow artists following his death from natural causes.

Golden Oldies #24

Johnnie Johnson
(Fairmont, West Virginia, 8 July 1924)

One of the great blues/rock 'n' roll pianists, Johnnie Johnson apparently learned musical timing by listening for trains from his room; later, he honed his craft in the company of musicians from Count Basie and Lionel Hampton's jazz bands while serving with the Marine Corps. Though he was subsequently to play with names such as Eric Clapton, Bo Diddley and Buddy Guy, it was Johnson's work with Chuck Berry that is most readily recalled. Such was his impact upon Berry (whose 'Maybellene', 'Roll Over Beethoven' and 'Sweet Little Sixteen' were just three Johnson collaborations) that the singer was inspired to compose the standard 'Johnnie B Goode'. Despite this, Johnson spent the best part of his career as a relative unknown, credits seldom offered to 'backline' musicians in pop music's early years.

Although he clearly had a very strong case, there was to be no remuneration for Johnson when, in 2002, authorities threw out a 2-year-old royalty claim by the pianist on the grounds that too much time had elapsed since his contributions to the hits of Berry and others. Johnnie Johnson died from natural causes at his home in St Louis, Missouri, on 13 April 2005.

'It is a gift from God almighty!'
Johnnie Johnson's mother, upon hearing her son play for the first time in 1928

Friday 15

John Fred
(John Fred Gourrier – Baton Rouge, Louisiana, 8 May 1941)
John Fred & His Playboy Band

Perceived as the classic US one-hit wonder, John Fred actually fronted his first band, The Playboys, as early as 1956, the hyperactive frontman scoring a US number eighty-two 'smash' with 'Shirley' (1958) – and in those days, 100,000 or so copies would have been required to achieve that status. The record performed admirably given that no one had heard of Fred, its success perhaps down to the fact that The Playboys were none other than Fats Domino's backing group. The Playboy *Band*, on the other hand, issued six flop singles before conquering all about them with the number one 'Judy In Disguise' (1967). The song – which also made the UK Top Five – was a semi-successful parody of Lennon & McCartney's 'Lucy in the Sky with Diamonds', but hit through its own catchiness as opposed to the wit of its lyrics. The irony was complete when Fred and his cohorts supplanted The Beatles themselves at the top of the US charts – but, aside from the near-hit 'Hey Hey Bunny' (1968), they were not to trouble the stat men again. Instead, the musician tried his hand, very successfully, at producing, going on to become vice-president at RCS Records.

John Fred was the son of Detroit Tigers baseball legend Fred Gourrier, and a fair player himself, teaching the sport at high-school level before his death from kidney failure. Passing away three weeks before his birthday, the singer never *quite* had the chance to record that parody of 'When I'm 64'.

See also *Ronnie Goodson (* November 1980)*

Tuesday 19

Bryan Ottoson
(Hennepin County, Minnesota, 1978)
American Head Charge

It's perhaps no coincidence that American Head Charge began life at a rehab clinic, where 'inmates' H C Banks III (Chad Hanks, bass) and Martin Cock (Cameron Heacock, guitar/vocals) discovered a mutual love of intense industrial metal. Their first major-label album, *The War of Art*, emerged in 2001, after which the 'band' needed to expand in order to play that year's Ozzfest. Finally settling on members Bryan Ottoson (guitar), Justin Fouler (keys) and Chris Emery (drums), American Head Charge then set off on a rampage through the US, the band fast becoming as synonymous with its violent on- and offstage antics as their music. In their time, AHC have been known to fire shotguns and scrap with their fans during gigs.

Despite the band's aggressive substance abuse, the death of the distinctively coiffured guitarist Ottoson while touring their latest album, *The Feeding* (2005), was accidental – and the result of a surfeit of prescribed medication. AHC were set to open for fellow 'nihilist clowns' Mudvayne at North Charleston's Plex Club when the accident occurred. Knowing him to be a heavy sleeper, Ottoson's bandmates had left him in his bunk ahead of the performance. When his lifeless body was later discovered, the authorities also removed from his bunk a bottle of pills prescribed for the guitarist's severe strep throat. It was empty.

Golden Oldies #25

Hasil 'The Haze' Adkins
(Boone County, West Virginia, 29 April 1937)

He didn't sell many records, nor was he even especially well known outside rockabilly circles, but guitarist Hasil Adkins earns his place in *Number One in Heaven* for sheer exuberance – and a good line in songs about decapitation. An act best enjoyed live, 'The Haze' wowed fifties rock 'n' roll fans with numbers such as 'We Got a Date' – one of some *7,000* songs the man claimed to have written. In this, Adkins talks of meeting his girl and, you guessed it, cutting off her head: crass, perhaps – distasteful, definitely: hence the interest of eighties psychobillies The Cramps, who covered his 'She Said'. But whatever his lyrical subject matter, Adkins was also well thought of at New York label Norton, who were still putting out his musings in 1999.

Just ahead of his death three days before what would have been his sixty-eighth birthday, Hasil Adkins was run down outside his home by a demented driver who claimed at least one other victim. Despite this, it still remains uncertain whether The Haze's death on 26 April was as a direct result of the injuries he sustained.

MAY

Tuesday 10

David Wayne
(David Wayne Carnell – Renton, Washington, 1 January 1958)
**Metal Church
(Reverend)**

Formed in 1980 as Shrapnel, Metal Church was the somewhat generic dark-metal brainchild of guitarist Kurdt Vanderhoof, whose San Francisco apartment apparently inspired the band's name. The group – who veered towards the satanic without ever immersing themselves completely in it – returned to the guitarist's home town of Washington, where they were completed by Craig Wells (guitar), Duke Erickson (bass), Kirk Arrington (drums – preferred for some reason to Lars Ulrich, who instead joined Metallica and experienced sales of which MC could only dream) and rasping vocalist David Wayne, who replaced the incumbent Mick Murphy in 1983. The first pair of albums, *Metal Church* (1984) and *The Dark* (1986), surprised many by becoming commercial successes, containing the live favourites 'Metal Church' (naturally), 'Gods Of Wrath' and 'Watch the Children Pray'. Unhappy with his band's next project, Wayne left The Church in 1989 to set up his own spin-off act, Reverend (in keeping with the crypto-religious theme). Vanderhoof had also flown the nest by this time, though both were to make an 'emotional' return ten years later for the comeback album, *Masterpeace* (1999). David Wayne was recording with his final, self-named band when his car was involved in a head-on collision early in 2005. He was to die from his injuries some months later at his Tacoma home.

Monday 23

Mike 'Yaz' Jastremski
(California, 16 March 1963)
Heathen
(Pigs)

Metal's run of bad luck continued, however, with the death of Mike Jastremski, a former member of San Francisco thrashers Heathen. The wayward bassist joined the band – David Godfrey (vocals), Lee Altus ex-Angel Witch, guitar), and Darren Minter (drums), plus a host of musicians who came and went – for their acclaimed Ronnie Montrose-produced debut, *Breaking the Silence* (1987), though he had left temporarily to form his own band, Pigs, before Heathen issued their follow-up album in 1996. The far-from-prolific Bay Area group retained popularity despite constant upheavals in their line-up – and the death in 1992 of replacement bassist Randy Laire. Heathen finally welcomed Jastremski back in 2001 for a tour and recording, which eventually produced the comeback/remasters album *Recovered* (2004).

It soon became apparent that Jastremski was far from 'recovered', however. A lifelong drinker and drug abuser, he was expelled from the band a second time just ahead of the album's release. The following year, his erstwhile Heathen colleagues learned of the bassist's death from a heart attack in a clinic while undergoing detox.

Karl Mueller: Soul brother

JUNE

Friday 17

Karl Mueller
(Minnesota, 27 July 1963)
Soul Asylum

Rising from the ashes of Minneapolis rockers Loud Fast Rules, Soul Asylum enjoyed brief but notable success as one of the first acts to emerge from the post-grunge *mêlée*. The former, though, had been founded by easygoing bassist Karl Mueller, guitarist Dan Murphy and drummer/guitarist Dave Pirner back in 1981, new percussionist Grant Young joining for the earliest Soul Asylum release in 1984. The group signed first with A&M

(who issued two albums up to 1990), before a deal with Columbia prevented what might have been an early split. Thus rejuvenated, the group issued *Grave Dancer's Union* (1992), a double-platinum set of earnest rock songs, including the hit 'Runaway Train' – a tune that, thanks to the highly effective use of its promo, became an international anthem for missing youngsters. In Britain, the band sold steadily, placing five singles in the Top Forty before 1996 (including the twice-released 'Somebody to Shove'), though follow-up collections, *Let Your Dim Light Shine* (1995) and *Candy from a Stranger* (1998), suffered as a result of the genre falling out of fashion.

When, in May 2004, Karl Mueller learned the devastating news that he was suffering from throat cancer, Soul Asylum rallied other bands (including a re-formed Hüsker Dü) to raise funds for his treatment. Despite going into remission, Mueller was to die from his condition a year later. The bassist is best remembered via the exotically titled Soul Asylum album *Say What You Will, Clarence – Karl Sold the Truck* (1984). The band returned with a new album, *Crazy Mixed Up World*, in 2006, the last record to feature a man who had given this enduring Twin Cities group almost twenty-five years' loyal service.

JULY

Golden Oldies #26

Renaldo 'Obie' Benson
(Detroit, Michigan, 14 June 1937)
The Four Tops

Best recalled as the bass within the legendary Four Tops, Renaldo 'Obie' Benson was perhaps the most talented member of the group; as well as possessing that great voice, he was also a fine songwriter and choreographer for The Tops – or The Four Aims, as they were originally known. Benson and high-school buddy Lawrence Payton met Levi Stubbs and Abdul 'Duke' Fakir at a party in 1953, the four dropping the name 'Aims' (for fear of confusion with The Ames Brothers) as they signed with Chess Records. Failure here was perhaps a happy accident: it took until 1964 for The Tops to bed themselves in at Motown, the group then presenting Berry Gordy with a series of sparkling hits – particularly between 1964 and 1970 – including the classic chart-toppers

'He put a smile on everybody's face.'
'Duke' Fakir, a surviving Top

'I Can't Help Myself' (1965) and 'Reach out I'll be There' (1966 – also a UK number one). His distinctive nickname no more than the combination of the final syllable of his first name with the first of his surname, 'Obie' Benson achieved a major critical triumph with 'What's Going On?' the song he co-wrote with Marvin Gaye, now widely regarded as one of the greatest of all time.

The Four Tops maintained an unbroken line-up until the death of Lawrence Payton (◀ *June 1997*), which proved something of a watershed for a group still performing regularly. 'Obie' Benson made his final appearance with The Four Tops on the *Late Show with David Letterman* just months before his death from cancer on 1 July 2005. The bass singer was replaced by Payton's son, Roquel.

Friday 1

Luther Vandross
(New York, 20 April 1951)

The first day of July 2005 saw another, rather different legend of R & B pass away. For his part, Luther Vendross seemed more about style than passion, his recordings epitomizing the smooth, high-production values foisted upon soul music in the eighties. Vandross spent most of his childhood in the Bronx, one of a musical family that had also produced his elder sister Patricia, a singer with The Crests of 'Sixteen Candles' fame. Inspired by his sibling – whose record almost reached number one at the time of their father's death in 1960 – Vandross vowed to make music his world as well, joining a group while still at high school, and earning vocal and production credits as a teenager. Mainly a backing singer in his early career, Vandross – when he wasn't making jingles for Kentucky Fried Chicken – recorded with a number of impressive names, including Quincy

Jones, Roberta Flack, Carly Simon and, perhaps surprisingly, David Bowie, who invited the singer to tour with his 1974 'Diamond Dogs' show and back him on the *Young Americans* album (1975). A major breakthrough came when the group Change invited Vandross to sing the international hit 'Searching' (1980), but the singer was in his thirties before he could boast a platinum album of his own. The age factor was clearly one that Vandross turned to his advantage, however, his audience largely middle-class, thirty-something couples who lapped him up, as they did rivals like Al Jarreau, Alexander O'Neal and particularly Freddie Jackson, with whom Vandross was said to have had a somewhat terse relationship. (The singer himself regularly ducked questions regarding his sexuality: he never married, nor sired any children, and was seldom paired with anyone.) It was in a live environment that Vandross was to thrive, since remarkably, although he sold 25 million records, he never managed a number-one hit in either America or Britain – his biggest singles being the duets 'The Best Things in Life are Free' (1992) with Janet Jackson, and 'Endless Love' (1994) with Mariah Carey. One of his last studio albums, the highly personal *Dance with My Father* (2003), reached the summit at home, however. From this came a 2004 Song of the Year Grammy for the title track (co-written by Richard Marx, another favourite with women of a certain age).

This triumph, one of eight Luther Vandross earned in his time, was to be his last. Suffering from hereditary diabetes that caused his weight to fluctuate dramatically, the singer experienced the deaths of several family members ahead of his own. A stroke in 2003 having weakened him, the singer developed pneumonia and underwent a tracheotomy. Finally, surrounded by his family at the John F Kennedy Medical Center in New Jersey, he passed away. Vandross was interred near by, at George Washington Memorial Park.

'A boy so mellow, so powerful; a boy of rare, rare vintage.'

The Reverend Jesse Jackson

Luther Vandross: Presumably the aunt who bought him the sweater was in the audience

Raymond Davis

(Sumter, California, 29 March 1940)

The Parliaments/Parliament/Funkadelic
(Zapp)
(The Temptations)

The youngest of twelve kids, Ray Davis was an original bass vocalist with harmony group The Parliaments, who scored a Top Twenty hit with '(I Wanna) Testify' (1967) – inadvertently contributing to one of the great musical phenomena of the last fifty years. The group was fashioned by the irrepressible George Clinton, who oversaw their transition into 'Parliament' (and the overlapping Funkadelic), a larger-than-life funk amalgamation that produced some of the most blistering and futuristic sounds/images black music had yet witnessed (a clear influence upon current acts like OutKast). Davis's smouldering tones can be heard on P-Funk greats like 'Tear the Roof off the Sucker' (1975) and 'One Nation under a Groove' (1978).

After taking a sabbatical from the relentlessness of Parliament life in 1984, Davis threw himself back into work by joining another funk unit, Zapp, before touring with a revised line-up of The Temptations. Before succumbing to illness, Davis rejoined Clinton and fourteen of his old pals to take 'The Original P' back on the road once more. Despite dying from respiratory complications on 5 July 2005 at the relatively young age of sixty-five, Ray Davis still outlived a number of his contemporaries.

See also *Glen Goins (⚰ July 1978); 'Tiki' Fulwood (⚰ November 1979); Eddie Hazel (⚰ December 1992); Roger and Larry Troutman (⚰ April 1999)*

Wednesday 6

Denis D'Ell

(Denis James Dalziel – Chigwell, Essex,
14 October 1943)

The Honeycombs
(Various acts)

Truck-driver's son Denis Dalziel was told 'he could sing a bit' by his workmates while earning a crust as a railway signalman, so he took their advice and stormed a local talent contest, winding up as singer with an embryonic version of The Honeycombs – D'Ell, Martin Murray (lead guitar), Alan Ward (guitar) and John (bass) and Ann 'Honey' Lantree (drums) – as they trawled the spit 'n' sawdust of London's pub scene. The genesis of this band's (brief) success was one of supreme good fortune, the renamed Denis D'Ell seen as possessing an ideal voice by songwriters Ken Howard and Alan Blaikly, who'd already penned the song that was to become The Honeycombs' signature tune. Produced in his inimitable way by maverick Joe Meek, 'Have I the Right?' – complete with floor-stomping percussion – raced to UK number one in the summer of 1964, having survived an indifferent response from national radio. The real gimmick of The Honeycombs was female drummer Lantree, and it was she, as opposed to D'Ell, who was the main focus when the group took the record into the US Top Five later that year. Further hits proved harder to come by (impossible, in America) and The Honeycombs were effectively just D'Ell and Lantree when one finally arrived in the shape of 'That's the Way' (1965).

His subsequent solo career was a huge disappointment to D'Ell, the singer contriving a thirtieth anniversary get-together for The Honeycombs before eventually fronting unknowns like The Southside Blues Brothers. The singer – whose voice was occasionally compared to the late Gene Pitney's – died from cancer.

Thursday 14

Michael Dahlquist

(Seattle, Washington, 22 December 1965)
Silkworm

John Glick

(Boston, Massachusetts, 1970)
The Returnables

Douglas Meis

(Montana, 1975)
The Dials

A creative and avid 'hobbyist', Michael Dahlquist counted mountaineering and puppetry among his preferred pastimes, though he was surely most admired for his percussion skills with the Seattle rock band Silkworm, an outfit formed in 1987. Without ever cracking a scene that almost literally blew up around them, Silkworm impressed listeners with albums like *L'aire* (1992 – now considered a collector's item) and *Libertine*, one of two albums issued in 1994. The band

The Honeycoms, with Denis D'Ell (*foreground*) – taken during their 'insurance salesmen' period

were signed to the forward-thinking Matador label thereafter (the splendid *Firewater* (1996) the first album to be issued) but proved unable to make an impact on the scale of contemporary labelmates such as Guided By Voices, Pavement and Yo La Tengo. By the turn of the millennium, Silkworm had been signed by Touch & Go, the band's last album, *It'll Be Cool*, arriving in 2004.

Just months ahead of his fortieth birthday, Michael Dahlquist was one of three musicians to become the unwitting victims of a bizarre incident. After lunch with good friends and fellow rockers John Glick (guitarist with the highly rated Returnables) and Doug Meis (drummer with otherwise all-female punks The Dials), the three – all employed at an Illinois audio-equipment manufacturer – were returning to work by car. As the Honda Civic waited in line at a red light, 23-year-old model/exotic dancer Jeanette Sliwinski rammed them from behind at 70 mph in her Ford Mustang. The Civic was crushed between the Mustang and the car ahead, all three musicians being killed by the impact. It appears the crash was intentional. Sliwinski, who survived the collision with minor injuries, had been using her mobile phone at the time, having had a 'serious fight' with her mother following events in her life that left her 'suicidal'. While local music fans mourned the loss of three great talents, Sliwinski was charged with three counts of first-degree murder. Surviving Silkworm members Tim Midgett (guitar/vocals) and Andy Cohen (guitar/vocals) went on to form Bottomless Pit.

Golden Oldies #28

Laurel Aitken
(Cuba, 22 April 1927)

Whether known as the 'godfather of ska' or just 'Boss Skinhead', the popularity of singer Laurel Aitken seemed to transcend the genre and cross generations. Having begun his singing career in the forties, Aitken bagged an eleven-week chart-topper in Jamaica with 'Little Sheila/Boogie in My Shoes' (1958), widely regarded as the first ska hit – and certainly the first release on Island Records. His output in the West Indies continued to sell, though Aitken was to receive little commercial reward elsewhere in the world; despite this, he became a popular cult figure in Britain, having moved there in 1960. Adopted by the skinheads in the late part of that decade, Aitken was once more in favour during the ska revival at the turn of the eighties, touring with bands such as The Beat, while harder-core punks The Ruts also played as his backing band.

Laurel Aitken performed late into his life, continuing even after diagnosis with throat cancer some time ahead of his death from a heart attack early on the morning of 17 July 2005.

Laurel Aitken: The 'Godfather' dressed for business

Thursday 21

Patrick Sherry

(Bradford, 1976)

Bad Beat Revue

> **'I accept his death was a tragic accident doing something he loved.'**
>
> Charlotte Sherry,
> Patrick's widow

Up-and-coming Yorkshire rockers Bad Beat Revue – whose 2003 debut album *Still Cheating* had impressed many – only stepped in to play a Club *NME* night at The Warehouse, Leeds, on 20 July after the anticipated band had pulled out hours before. His group having something of a reputation for rip-roaring shows, singer Patrick Sherry – who formed BBR with his guitarist brother Brendan – was known for his onstage highjinks; unfortunately, on this night, his grande finale was to end in disaster. Attempting to reach a mid-air lighting rig, Sherry threw himself into the air but failed to make full connection with the gantry, arcing into a somersault instead, due to the force of his momentum, and landing on his head before his shocked audience. Sherry was rushed to Leeds General Infirmary but died the following morning from severe head and neck injuries. A shopfitter by day, the charismatic frontman and his wife of two years had been expecting a child. (The event mirrored somewhat the blunt-trauma death of German metal singer Gunther Dietz, whose Hamburg audience moved to one side as he took his final stage dive in August 1997.)

Long John Baldry

(Haddon, Derbyshire, 12 January 1941)

Bluesology
Steampacket/The Hoochie Coochie Men/
 Cyril Davies Allstars
Blues Incorporated

On the same day, British blues lost a singer revered as one of its genuine 'giants', in both senses of the word, a vast number of top names – including Eric Clapton and Elton John – having honoured the man as an inspiration to their own careers. It's easy to see how Long John Baldry – at six foot seven – came by his nickname, but this formidable performer was also blessed with a rich baritone to augment his image. Alexis Korner was one of the first to take a shine to Baldry, inviting him to join his Blues Incorporated line-up in 1961 after hearing the young man exercising his lungs with the combos of Cyril Davies and Ramblin' Jack Elliott. Blues Incorporated became a legendary name, nurturing the talents of, among others, Jack Bruce and various future Rolling Stones. Returning to Davies's group, Baldry took over after the sudden death of its leader in 1964, refashioning the band as The Hoochie Coochie Men, who thereafter became Steampacket. This remarkable blues conglomerate boasted both Baldry and an edgy young man called Rod Stewart providing the male vocals, while Julie Driscoll supplied the female voice. (Jimmy Page had been a guitarist with the unit as well.) Baldry's shoulder-rubbing with the great and good didn't end there: after the demise of Steampacket, he formed Bluesology with Reg Dwight, aka Elton John. (Dwight created his own moniker from those of sax-player Elton Dean and Baldry himself – while the latter is credited as the person who talked him out of committing suicide, as documented in John's 1975 song 'Someone Saved My Life Tonight' (☛ *Death Toll #3*).)

Long John Baldry adopts the pose most others reserved for him ...

Baldry enjoyed his greatest success as a solo artist with the Pye label, taking the swoonsome ballad 'Let the Heartaches Begin' all the way to UK number one at the end of 1967. Further singles were also hits as the singer became an unlikely pin-up towards the end of the decade. Baldry's career was halted by mental-health problems, causing him to be institutionalized in the early seventies. Though he made a spirited comeback – the album *Baldry's Out!* (1979) showed a considerable sense of humour – he was not to enjoy the same level of acceptance again. (A fluke Australian hit with 'You've Lost that Lovin' Feeling' – performed with US singer Kathi MacDonald – did, however, come his way later that year.)

For the last twenty-five years of his life, John Baldry took citizenship in Canada, where he settled into a lucrative second career as a voice-over artist, for which he gained a Grammy nomination in 1998 for his work with Disney. Failing to shake off a severe chest infection contracted early in 2005, Baldry was admitted to Vancouver General Hospital – but doctors were unable to save him.

See also *Alexis Korner (◄ January 1984). Blues Incorporated saxophonist Dick Heckstall-Smith died just months before Baldry (2004).*

Friday 22

Eugene Record

(Chicago, Illinois, 23 December 1940)

The Chi-Lites

Originally confusing everyone as one of two vocal troupes called The Hi-Lites, Marshall & The Chi-Lites – renamed in 1960 after lead singer Marshall Thompson – flitted from label to label until a new leader brought a change in their fortunes. Thompson's school-friend Eugene Record had steadily been making a name for himself as a songwriter of no small merit, and by the end of the decade, his contributions saw The Chi-Lites – Record (lead), Thompson (baritone), Robert 'Squirrel' Lester (tenor) and Creadel 'Red' Jones (bass) – transformed into their best-known guise as smooth soul operators. Early hits, such as '(For God's Sake) Give More Power to the People' (1971), contained something of a political message, but it's with ballads like 'Have You Seen Her?' (1971, reissued in the UK, 1975), 'Oh Girl' (1972, a US number one), 'Homely Girl' (1974) and the much-underrated 'It's Time for Love' (1975) that The Chi-Lites are most readily associated. Record's work for others on the Brunswick label – including his first wife Barbara Acklin, who died seven years before him (◄ *November 1998*) – caused him to move away from the group in 1976 to concentrate on solo recordings.

Although he was to spend most of the remainder of his days singing gospel as a born-again Christian, Eugene Record – who composed some 300 songs in his lifetime – found time to rejoin The Chi-Lites between 1980 and 1988. The band remained particularly popular in Britain where they'd charted many more hit records than at home. Record had battled cancer for months before his death

at his Hazelcrest home in Illinois – the state where he had lived for his entire life.

AUGUST

Close!
Marc Cohn

Known worldwide for his 1991 hit 'Walking in Memphis', Grammy-winning musician and songwriter Marc Cohn didn't otherwise see much headline action until events on 7 August 2005 put him back on the front page. Following a show at the Botanic Gardens in Denver, Cohn and his driver Thomas Dube pulled out of a garage, only for their van to be confronted by carjacker Joseph Yacteen, who fired at the windscreen. Remarkably, the bullet was slowed by the glass, grazing the driver (who was also Cohn's tour manager) before glancing off the musician's head.

Miraculously, Cohn was not killed by the point-blank shot, remaining lucid and talking on his way to hospital. 'Frankly, I can't tell you how he survived,' commented police spokesman Sonny Jackson.

Wednesday 10

Rock Halsey

(Charles Hand – Los Angeles, California, 8 February 1956)

Rock Bottom & The Spys

Born to a B-movie actor and a former Miss Germany, Rock Halsey – aka 'Rock Bottom' of Los Angeles punks The Spys – was going to find his way in showbiz somehow. However, other than from their loyal fanbase, the band were starved of attention, despite one very good EP that contained their signature tune, 'Rich Girl' (1978), and a few other hummable songs – all lost as punk struggled to make any impact on America's airwaves.

However, fan Ryan Richardson's attempts to reunite the former Spys more than twenty years later unearthed a series of events so grim they almost defy belief. Drummer Blank Frank was reported to have been killed in a house fire, followed by news that another percussionist, Joel Martines, had also died (no date being available for either death); bassist Ian Icon then committed suicide in August 2001 after the death of his son; while another member, Guillermo Libutti, was allegedly wanted for questioning following the murder of a flatmate during a botched cocaine deal at his LA home. Finally, when it appeared there could be no further bad news, Halsey was himself reported murdered while serving a long sentence for drugs and firearms offences. In a final twist of fate the former leader – poised for transfer to a less secure unit where parole was a distinct possibility – had been beaten to death by a fellow inmate.

Sunday 21

Stevo
(Steven Ronald Jensen – California, 1959)
The Vandals

The original singer with Long Beach punks The Vandals, Steven 'Stevo' Jensen was as well known for his frequent spats with other band members as he was for the actual product. Formed in 1981 by guitarist Jan Nils Aukerman (who quit the band three years later), The Vandals underwent so many line-up changes in their first half-decade it's barely worth enumerating them. A first EP,

Peace Thru Vandalism, arrived in 1982, followed by the Restless Records debut *When in Rome Do as the Vandals* two years later. Jensen's inability to get along with his bandmates saw to it that his stay at the front of this much-talked-about band was not to be a long one. He quit music to become a masseuse in 1984, but arguments and lawsuits rumbled on, most notably with former Vandals bassist and figurehead Joe Escalante. Jensen was staying in Maui when he died from an overdose of prescribed medicine. The Vandals remain an institution, however, and exist with a roster completely different from the one that began a generation back – even boasting Keanu Reeves as a guest guitarist at one show.

Denis 'Piggy' D'Amour
(Montreal, Quebec, 1959)
Voivod

The month was to end with the deaths of two Canadian cult rock legends. Guitarist Denis D'Amour got together with Denis 'Snake' Bélanger (vocals, later replaced by Eric Forest), Jean-Yves Thériault (bass) and Michel Langevin (drums) to form Voivod in the early eighties, the thrash-metal band breaking much new ground with their experimental sound,

Voivoid – Langevin, D'Amour, Thériault and Bélanger: Piggy not quite in the middle

unconventional time-signatures and apocalyptic lyrical matter. The band were to undergo many changes in line-up and label, but garnered critical acclaim for albums such as *War and Pain* (1984), *Rrrooooaaarrr!* (1987) and *Nothingface* (1989). In 2004, Voivod – now complete with former Metallica guitarist Jason Newsted on board – signed with The End to record their eleventh album in two decades. Denis D'Amour had been working on the record when diagnosed with colon cancer early in 2005. By August, the disease had spread to the guitarist's liver and other vital organs. Surrounded by his family, D'Amour fell into a coma on 25 August, slipping away less than twenty-four hours later.

Jim Bescott

(Vancouver, British Columbia, 1953)

The Young Canadians (The K-Tels)

'Basically the guy really could play – he truly was great.'

Joey 'Shithead' Keithley of Canadian punk stalwarts DOA

Just five days on, Vancouver punk 'godfather' Jim Bescott died under very strange circumstances in a grocery-store car park. The former film-maker became bassist with The Young Canadians (originally The K-Tels, until the record and gadget company served papers during a gig), building up an impressive onstage relationship with singer/guitarist Art Bergmann, the trio completed by drummer Barry Taylor. Pre-dating The Jesus & Mary Chain by several years, The Young Canadians ripped into surf rock with an expletive-ridden tune called 'Hawaii' (1979), which was to remain their best-known record, though Bescott was to write a couple of their classics, 'No Escape' and 'Automan'. Inevitably, the group lasted no longer than a couple of years, but remain pioneers in Canadian new wave.

It seems Jim Bescott died when he was backed over by a semi-tractor trailer as he stood waiting in a Safeway parking lot in Kitsilano: the musician was crushed beneath the vehicle's rear wheels as it reversed in to make a delivery.

SEPTEMBER

Thursday 1

Barry Cowsill

(Newport, Rhode Island, 15 September 1954)

The Cowsills

As the toothsome young bassist with America's most wholesome family act, Barry Cowsill appeared the perfect antidote for parents 'concerned' by the activities of bands such as The Grateful Dead. When ambitious father Bud Cowsill bought him his first instrument, Barry – one of six siblings – made his first tentative move towards stardom playing with his brothers in the earliest incarnation of The Cowsills when ten years old. Between 1967 and 1970, the group could do little wrong: two singles, 'The Rain, the Park and Other Things' (1967) and 'Hair' (1969) both raced to US number two, selling over a million apiece. The group had been touted as the next TV sensation after The Monkees, but the refusal of The Cowsills to play alongside actress Shirley Jones (as opposed to their own mother, Barbara, the erstwhile singer) brought their moment of fame to an abrupt halt. It's reported that MGM label boss Mike Curb dropped the group for its association with 'a musical that promoted drug use'.

Barry Cowsill's later life could not have been in starker contrast to that of his childhood. Divorce alienating him from his children, he slipped into depression and (genuine) drug abuse. Although he'd recorded a solo album in 1998 and six years later had reunited for a one-off performance with his family (minus both parents, who had passed away some years before), the musician had clearly not shaken his problems, having been charged with making nuisance calls to a former partner. Cowsill had been due to re-enter rehab in September 2005 when his New Orleans home was among the thousands struck by Hurricane Katrina. While other noted musicians – Fats Domino and Alex Chilton among them – were found alive and well, Barry Cowsill's drowned body was finally identified by dental records on 28 December 2005. The date of his death can thus only be approximated – as can that of metal singer Glenn Rambo, the other noted musician killed in the cataclysm.

See also *Barbara Cowsill (* January 1985). Bill Cowsill died in February 2006.*

Golden Oldies #29

R L Burnside

(Robert Lee Burnside – Harmontown, Mississippi, 23 November 1926)

Most of his life Delta-bluesman R L Burnside worked as a sharecropper and commercial fisherman, his music merely a weekend diversion for his many Mississippi friends; the expressive singer and guitarist only turned professional at an age when most are thinking of jacking it in. Burnside's early adulthood was eventful, to say the least. In the fifties he relocated to Illinois where his search for work brought the guitarist into contact with other blues players. Following the murder of his father and two of his brothers, the grief-stricken Burnside returned home, only to be incarcerated for the shooting of a man he claimed was trying to commandeer his house.

Burnside's distinctive slide and multi-range vocal style was brought to wider attention in the late sixties, though it was not until 1991 that the ageing guitarist's work was 'discovered' by Fat Possum Records, a Mississippi label specializing

R L Burnside: A style of his own

in artists of his generation. Among his new fans were younger blues lovers such as Jon Spencer (of Blues Explosion), who recorded the album *A Ass Pocket o' Whiskey* (1996) in a log cabin with the veteran musician. His health was already in decline by the end of the decade, though, Burnside suffering a heart attack in 2001 that curtailed live performances. On 1 September 2005, in a Memphis hospital, the musician passed away from his heart condition, to be survived by a wife and several children – two of whom followed him into the blues game.

OCTOBER

Tuesday 4

Mike Gibbins

(Swansea, 12 March 1949)

Badfinger
(Various acts)

Drummer Mike Gibbins discovered his talent for percussion during his time as a cadet with the sea scouts, his father encouraging the young musician by buying him a kit at thirteen. In the early sixties, Gibbins – like many around him – became fascinated with the beat music emanating from nearby Liverpool, joining a number of local bands, including rock 'n' roll covers act The Misfits, from whom he was poached by Ron Griffiths for his mod band, The Iveys. This band (minus the singer) became Badfinger, the biggest British pop music hope to emerge from the disbanding Beatles' Apple stable. Indeed, all looked good as Badfinger cleaned up at home and in the States with a series of catchy pop singles, including 'Come and Get It' and 'No Matter What' (both 1970). Global success did not mean vast royalties, however, a cripplingly bad management deal eventually culminating in the suicides of both songwriters, Pete Ham (☛ *April 1975*) and Tom Evans (☛ *November 1983*). Mike Gibbins was understandably crushed by this double tragedy – Ham in particular had been a close friend – but pulled himself together to continue in music, playing on the hits of others, one of which was 'It's a Heartache' (1977) by fellow Welsh artist Bonnie Tyler.

Gibbins was living in Florida at the time of his sudden death from natural causes during his sleep. Guitarist Joey Molland remains as the only surviving member from Badfinger's early line-up.

Monday 10

Nick Hawkins

(Luton, Bedfordshire, 3 February 1965)

BAD II (Big Audio Dynamite)
(Dusk Til Dawn)

An enthusiastic guitarist from boyhood, Nick Hawkins realized a major ambition by teaming with his old Clash hero Mick Jones in the latter's second band, Big Audio Dynamite. Hawkins joined the band in 1990, contributing to several albums, including the gold-selling *The Globe* (1991). By now, the group were past their UK heyday of the mid eighties, re-forming as BAD II, and later recording simply as Big Audio. Hawkins remained in the line-up until 1997. The guitarist's parents had been told that their son was diabetic at just nine years of age and that he was unlikely to survive beyond thirty: in the event, he lived ten more years, to be taken by a stroke. Hawkins, who had been working on an album with Dusk Til Dawn at the time of his death, was survived by his wife, R & B singer Jo Beng. The couple had lived in Las Vegas for some years.

Nick Hawkins: BAD boy in better days

Saturday 22

Franky Gee
(Francisco Gutierrez – Havana, Cuba, 19 February 1962)
Captain Jack

A former US soldier based in Germany, Francisco Gutierrez customized his uniform to become first 'Westside', then 'Franky Gee', the camp DJ turned Europop artiste who somehow captured the imagination of his adopted continent as one half of Captain Jack from 1995. Gutierrez had come to despise the military and, ably accompanied by female counterpart Sunny (Lisa da Costa), donned his jacket and red cap to satirize much of the lifestyle he'd been forced to adopt when money was short. Many of Captain Jack's songs were based on marches, a gimmick that clearly worked as the duo shifted millions of records across Europe, their music often lifted for arcade games. Each of the act's seven albums was declared at least gold during the frontman's short lifetime, Gutierrez accompanied by three further Sunnys.

While out walking with his son Francisco Jr (an aspiring rap artist) during a holiday in Mallorca, Gutierrez collapsed and fell into a coma on 17 October, doctors citing a cerebral haemorrhage. The man who to all intents and purposes *was* Captain Jack passed away in hospital five days later.

Saturday 29

David Townsend
(California, 1955)
Surface

His father a soul producer and the co-writer of Marvin Gaye's 'Let's Get It On', David Townsend had much to live up to. But, around the turn of the nineties, he appeared to have done just that, his band Surface giving New Kids on the Block a run for their money as the US's number-one pin-ups. With younger bandmates Bernard Jackson and lead singer David 'Pic' Conley, Townsend saw his compositions start to shift units with the Top Twenty 'Happy' (1987), a fairly upbeat tune that suggested good things ahead. Instead, the Columbia act trod the familiar path of saccharine R & B, nonetheless selling records in their millions: 'Shower Me with Your Love' (1989) was an airplay staple, its follow-up, 'The First Time' (1990), topping the national charts as Surface frenzy hit meltdown. Fame was not to last for the trio, however, more polished acts (Boys II Men, etc) stepping in to usurp them soon after. Despite this, Townsend had his lyric-writing to fall back on, penning tunes for Sister Sledge and New Edition, among others.

Just months after announcing a reunion tour, David Townsend – who outlived his father by just two years – was found dead at his home in Northridge, California, on 2 November; it was thought he'd lain undiscovered for three days. Though foul play was ruled out, his death remains a mystery at the time of writing.

NOVEMBER

Friday 4

China Nishiura
(Mana Nishiura – Hiroshima, 11 October 1975)
Shonen Knife
DMBQ
(Various acts)

The highlight of Mana 'China' Nishiura's career was surely as drummer with internationally enjoyed pop-punk princesses Shonen Knife – though she'd joined noise-metal act DMBQ by the time she lost her life in dramatic circumstances while on tour in the USA. Nishiura had been a top session drummer in Japan for many years, sitting in for alternative bands such as Jesus Fever and Teem before joining sisters Naoko

Shonen Knife: sharp and steely to the point

(vocals/guitar) and Atsuko Yamano (bass, formerly drums) in the John Peel and Kurt Cobain-approved band in 2001. Shonen Knife had been around for some twenty years by this time, their records appearing on many labels, including Sub Pop.

China Nishiura remained with the Yamanos until 2004, when she joined DMBQ, which, like the previous act, pulled interest in the US. The group were on an American tour when their Econoline van was involved in a highway accident on the New Jersey Turnpike. The vehicle was struck from behind by a Mitsubishi Eclipse and rolled down an embankment. While other band members were hospitalized, the drummer was tragically thrown to her death.

Golden Oldies #30

Link Wray

(Frederick Lincoln Wray – Dunn, North Carolina, 2 May 1929)

He believed he was 'too slow' to play the guitar properly, so instead Link Wray invented the power chord, in so doing fathering punk and heavy rock. Wray – who was three-quarters Shawnee Native American – was very much a musician's musician, cited as a key influence by almost every major rock star from David Bowie to Bruce Springsteen via Pete Townshend and John Lennon. Initially joining the family band The Palomino Ranch Gang, Wray began his solo career in 1956 as 'Lucky' Wray. He was to channel much of his natural aggression into music, writing the classic 'Rumble' in 1956 (Top Twenty, 1958 – later covered by The Dave Clark Five and Duane Eddy) after witnessing a fight at one of his shows. Wray – now fronting The Ray Men – was also known to punch holes in his amp to create the first 'fuzz guitar' effect. Despite one or two further hits, Wray

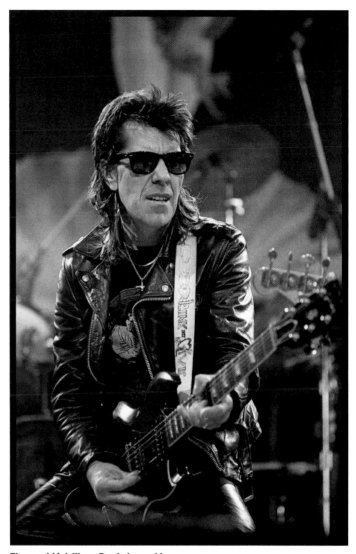

The great Link Wray: Ready to rumble

was to suffer from a bad management deal and received few royalties.

After the wilderness years of the seventies and eighties, Link Wray returned to favour during the nineties after the inclusion of his work in the soundtrack of movies such as *Pulp Fiction* and *12 Monkeys*. Dying from a heart attack on 5 November 2005 (at his home in Copenhagen where he'd lived for twenty-five years), the guitarist nonetheless outlived many contemporaries and bandmates, including his brother Vernon, who committed suicide in 1979.

Saturday 19

Mr Pit

(Steven Zorn – St Paris, Ohio, July 1983)

A remarkable story emerged from Ohio to make national headlines across America. Steven Zorn had spent a few years on the sidelines of rap, a decent enough performer who went by the name of Mr Pit, such was his affiliation with pit bulls. After something of a struggle, the 22-year-old white hip-hop artist – hotly tipped by Aaliyah/Will Smith producer Lemoyne Alexander – was finally to have his CD *Raw Meat* released through Koch Records in Atlanta. On the night of 18 November 2005, Zorn was intent on celebrating.

Together with high-school friends Shane Hanes and Cody Cornette, Zorn drank steadily into the night and, once the subject of his deal had been exhausted, drew their attention to a 'zip' pen gun he'd acquired the previous week. Although fascinated by the slimline weapon, Zorn expressed frustration that it appeared jammed: as though to prove his point, the rapper placed the piece against his head and popped the trigger three times. On the third occasion, the zip gun fired. Bleeding profusely, Zorn was flown by helicopter to hospital in Dayton, but was declared brain dead on arrival. Mr Pit's album was still expected to be released in 2006, while the deceased's mother launched a campaign to draw attention to the dangers of the weapon.

Monday 28

Tony Meehan

(Daniel Joseph Anthony Meehan – Hampstead, London, 2 March 1943)

(Cliff Richard &) The Shadows
Jet Harris & Tony Meehan
(The Tony Meehan Combo)
(The Vipers)

Although they were never to register a US Top Forty hit, The Shadows were by far and away Britain's most distinctive and successful instrumental band, dominating the UK listings at the turn of the sixties – and drummer Tony Meehan was there at the very start of it all. Already having played drums for five years, Meehan was, in December 1958, coaxed away from his studies by the lure of £25 a week to tour with the band then known as 'The Drifters'. The backing band to the largely unknown Cliff Richard, The Drifters – then Meehan, Hank Marvin (lead guitar), Bruce Welch (rhythm) and Jet Harris (bass) – were (for obvious reasons) forced to seek a name-change, beginning in earnest the legend of The Shadows. The projected dates did not materialize until the following year, Meehan gaining experience playing with Harris's other band, skiffle favourites The Vipers, in the meantime. Aided by the magnetism of the pouting Richard, The Shadows became the number-one pre-Beatles attraction on the UK circuit. Having topped the charts three times with the singer, they then began to show that they could be equally adept at rattling off the hits under their own steam. After a couple of flops, the classic 'Apache' – the first of sixteen Top Ten hits – stayed at number one for five weeks in 1960, supplanting Richard's 'Please Don't Tease', upon which The Shadows also played; the record later took the *NME* Record of the Year award. Meehan, however, was to grow tired of constant touring before the group's most dominant period of 1961–2. With a second record now in pole position ('Kon-Tiki', 1961), the drummer made the decision to quit at the very top, pulling out of a UK tour in order to pursue new ambitions as an A & R man with Decca. Brian Bennett assumed the kit as The Shadows went on to greater strengths. But – continuing a remarkably consistent chart return – Meehan still found time to reunite with Harris (who'd left The Shadows just two months after he had) for the number-one single 'Diamonds' (1963 – featuring Jimmy Page on guitar), a tune that gave the pair the added satisfaction of deposing their former band at the top spot. The duo almost turned the trick twice more that year with further massive hits in 'Scarlett O'Hara' and 'Applejack' – but the drummer's own Tony Meehan Combo was less successful.

Known as 'The Baron', Tony Meehan had a taste for the better things in life, using his career to fund his lifestyle of choice. Over the subsequent years, the drummer continued to play sessions for a number of top artists, occasionally rejoining the enduring Shadows over the decades and, most notably, Richard for his 1989 arena shows. In later life, Meehan pursued an interest in psychology, but his main devotion was to his wife and seven children. It was as the result of a domestic accident that the otherwise healthy musician lost his life: hitting his head during a bad fall at home, Meehan died from his injuries later that afternoon at a Paddington hospital.

See also *John Rostill (*☙ *November 1973)*

DECEMBER

Sunday 4

Tre' Stylez

(Richard Normand Michaud III – North Carolina,
2 November 1982)

Tre' Stylez

From North Carolina came the story of yet another rap shooting, although this time the victim seemed only to be attempting to do good by his fellow man. Richard Michaud had an unusual take on hip hop, blending street styles with the industrial metal of bands like Skinny Puppy to create a different flavour. A rap fan all his life, Tre' Stylez – or simply 'Trey' – had a good-humoured attitude to the genre that pulled fans from a variety of local boroughs.

With his latest CD doing the rounds, Stylez, dressed in his finery, hung out with friends at an all-night party in Greensboro; by 7 am most of the alcohol had been polished off and just a handful or so guests remained. Rumour later circulated that, at some point, two brothers who had not long arrived began arguing violently. Fearful that the situation was getting out of hand, the rapper apparently intervened – to have a gun pulled on him for his trouble. The weapon was discharged at point-blank range and Stylez died on the spot. Some days later, the usually disparate hip-hop community was united at a benefit for the dead artist. The story of Stylez's killing was then thrown into some doubt by a local retired policeman, who, having called at the apartment, suggested that the killing was the result of a fierce poker game – and nobody present was prepared to confess to having fired the gun. In March 2006, the suggestion came forward that the artist may even have fired the weapon himself.

DEAD INTERESTING!

NUMBER ONE IN HEAVEN – OFFICIAL!

So, who is the 'deadest' group? It might sound like a fun pastime for lengthy car journeys or slow parties, but few have the gen on which act takes the spoils. Well, now it can be revealed: The Drifters finish third with fifteen departed members; the passing of original pianist Johnny Grande in June 2006 pushes The Comets further ahead with seventeen; but runaway leaders of the Deceased Members Hit Parade are doo-wop stalwarts The Ink Spots, with no fewer than *twenty-seven* of their ever-changing personnel gone to croon with St Peter. They are:

Everett Barksdale (28/4/1907–8/1/1986)
Joseph Boatner (27/9/1918–8/5/1989)
Billy 'Butterball' Bowen (3/1/1909–27/9/1982)
James O Bradley (15/6/1923–13/12/2002)
Jerry Daniels (14/12/1915–7/11/1995)
Bill Doggett (16/2/1916–13/11/1996)
Charlie Fuqua (20/10/1910–21/12/1971)
Kurt W Geisler (1/1/1925–23/8/2002)
Cliff Givens (17/1/1918–6/6/1989)
Asa 'Ace' Harris (1/4/1910–11/6/1964)
Orville 'Hoppy' Jones (17/2/1902–18/10/1944)
Bill Kenny (12/6/1914–23/3/1978)
Herb Kenny (Bill's twin: 12/6/1914–11/7/1992)
Ramon Loper (25/11/1935–16/10/2002)
Bernie Mackey (29/7/1909–5/3/1980)
Adriel McDonald (10/5/1905–1/9/1987)
David McNeil (1932–7/1/2005)
Stanley Morgan (1922–21/11/1989)
Gene Mumford (24/6/1925–10/5/1977)
Jimmie Nabbie (1920–15/9/1992)
Simon 'Pico' Payne (28/7/1925–26/7/2002)
Al Rivers (1927–17/2/1993)
Alexander Sharp (1919–1/1970)
Judge 'Fletcher' Smith (22/9/1913–15/8/1993)
Ray Tunia (10/5/1916–16/8/1983)
Lloyd Washington (1920–22/6/2004)
Ivory 'Deek' Watson (18/7/1909–4/11/1969)

Completists may like to add the following 'spin-off' Ink Spots: Billy Byrd, Lorenzo Conyers, Artie Dicks, Charles Gray, Grant Kitchings, Gene Miller, Charles Owens and Ray Pollard. Dates here are, however, harder to ascertain – and the likelihood is that there are others who have passed on. (Incidentally, pianist Johnny 'Ace' Harris – who died in 2000 – often presented himself as an *official* Ink Spot, but was actually an imposter.)

Original Ink Spot Huey Long – born in Sealy, Texas, on 25 April 1904 – was still performing in 2005 and celebrated his 102nd birthday in Houston.)

Friday 9

Mike Botts
(Oakland, California, 8 December 1944)
Bread
(Various acts)

Although not an original member of Bread, Mike Botts was in the drummer's seat for the band's most prolific period between 1970 and 1972. Botts had already made something of a name for himself as touring percussionist with Hoyt Axton and Righteous Brother-on-leave Bill Medley, but made the decision to join Bread when 'Make It with You' (1970) began to make significant progress in the US charts. Under the seemingly unerring guidance of songwriters David Gates and Jimmy Griffin, the band produced a series of massive international hits with some genuinely touching soft-rock ballads, the melodies of which still come readily to mind. With the two main characters often at loggerheads, Botts remained the smiling face of the band, even when Bread twice split. After the final separation, the drummer found much session work with other soft-rockers like Eric Carmen, Dan Fogelberg and Linda Ronstadt, and later as a key member in Tina Turner's band. In 2002, Botts issued his only solo album, *Adults Only*.

Mike Botts had celebrated his sixty-first birthday just hours before succumbing to cancer of the colon – his long-time bandmate Griffin having also died from the disease at the start of the year (*January 2005*).

Tuesday 13

Jason Bachiller
(Dorchester, Massachusetts, 1984)
Edwin 'EJ' Duncan
(Dorchester, Massachusetts, 1984)
Chris 'Fat Boy' Vieira
(Reading, Massachusetts, 1986)
Graveside

An up-and-coming Boston rap unit, Graveside perhaps had an idea of the irony within their name, such was the stereotypically violent world within which they lived and worked. That three members were slain in the very basement where much of their material was mixed is just one more grim coincidence.

But, despite their absorption of the more dismal prerequisites of gangsta rap, Graveside were popular boys who, according to local followers, 'just used harsh words as an outlet' and were known to be friendly and helpful. Something must have gone badly awry, however. On the evening of 13 December, Jason Bachiller, Edwin Duncan and Chris Vieira, plus another friend, Jihad Chankhour, were waiting for the fourth member of the band, Jelani Haynes, downstairs at Duncan's Dorchester apartment – home to the makeshift recording studio built by his mother. It seems that, at some point after midnight, a lone gunman entered the building, shooting all four in an execution-style killing, before making a speedy escape in Vieira's car. It was Boston's worst multiple homicide in ten years. Needless to say, because of Graveside's apparent fascination with firearms, the press was shortly brimming with 'I told you so' editorials.

The young Brazilian woman from whom Duncan rented his rooms was alleged to have disappeared within hours of the murders – though, at the time of writing, the killer remains unidentified and at large.

Lest We Forget

Other notable deaths that occurred sometime during 2005:

James Austen Jr (US baritone with The Platters; born Tennessee, 1937; lung cancer, 24/12)

Les Braid (UK pop bassist with Merseybeat stars The Swinging Blue Jeans, of 'Hippy Hippy Shake' and 'You're No Good' fame; born Liverpool, 15/9/1937; lung cancer, 31/7)

Tyrone Davis (popular US soul singer who scored Top Five pop hits with 1969's 'Can I Change My Mind?' and 1970's 'Turn Back the Hands of Time'; born Mississippi, 4/5/1938; stroke, 9/2)

Hal Kalin (much-loved US pop singer with duo The Kalin Twins, who topped the UK chart with 'When' in 1958; born New York, 16/2/1934; car accident, 23/8)

Pierre Moerlen (noted French prog multi-instrumentalist with Gong; born Alsace-Lorraine, 23/10/1952; natural causes, 3/5)

Johnny Reed (US bass with vocal legends The Orioles; born Maryland, 16/8/1923; natural causes, 18/6 – he was the fifth original Oriole to pass on following Tommy Gaither's death over fifty years before)

Wayne Southworth (UK death-metal singer with Doom; born 1977; epileptic seizure, 18/3)

Jakson 'Thunderfoot' Spires (US drummer/song-writer with Southern rockers Blackfoot; born North Carolina, 12/4/1951; aneurysm, 16/3)

Ryan Summer (US drummer with fêted alt-rockers The Brian Jonestown Massacre and Cocaine Unicorn; born Oregon, 9/9/1978; genetic blood disorder, 14/8)

Tommy Vance (ever-popular UK rock DJ/presenter; born Richard Anthony Crispian Francis Prew Hope-Weston – no word of a lie – Oxfordshire, 11/7/1941; stroke at the wheel of his car, 6/3)

... and the latest hoaxes?

Metal guitarist **Rob Arnold** of Chimaira was reported via internet and US radio to have died on 8 February 2005 after a man's body was found in an abandoned car. If there was a corpse, it wasn't his – the musician was amused by the stories. Arnold's family, meanwhile, were happy to continue accepting tributes and donations in his name.

Taking matters to a natural plateau, Californian death-metal band Blood Freak issued a spoof report that all three members – **Jason Grinter** (vocals/bass), **John Sellier** (guitar) and **Pete Dobbins** (drums) – had perished in a road accident in Anaheim on 12 August 2005. Yep – it was a publicity stunt. The band returned as flesh-eating zombies within weeks.

For a complete list of fallen artists, visit

www.numberoneinheaven.com

Acknowledgements

Many thanks to the following for their support in this vast project:

Gloria Simmonds, Caroline and David Hammond, Bill Matthews, designer Richard Marston, Tony Lacey, Zelda Turner and Emma Horton (Penguin), and Patrick Walsh (Conville & Walsh).

... and the many others who doubtless feel they've been hearing about this for years.

Thanks also to the authors of so many great rock biographies, encyclopaedias and websites.

Picture Credits

The publishers wish to thank the following agencies for their permission to reproduce copyright material in this book. Every effort has been made to trace the copyright holders. We apologize for any unintentional omission and would be pleased to insert the appropriate acknowledgement in any subsequent impression.

Empics: pp. 108, 111, 134, 173, 385, 396

Getty Images: pp. 28, 73, 80, 99, 107, 183, 232, 266, 273, 392, 525

Redferns: pp. vi, ix, xi, xiii, xv, 1, 7, 8, 9, 12, 16, 18, 20, 27, 37, 40, 48, 51, 53, 54, 65, 87, 95, 113, 115, 125, 143, 150, 153, 155, 156, 177, 202, 206, 218, 241, 249, 251, 255, 262, 269, 270, 290, 299, 307, 311, 326, 329, 331, 373, 378, 389, 391, 393, 406, 423, 433, 437, 438, 440, 444, 448, 459, 462, 463, 471, 473, 477, 494, 501, 504 505, 507, 529, 533, 551, 539, 559

Retna: pp. 49, 71, 98, 102, 119, 122, 130, 137, 138, 147, 161, 165, 178, 180, 187, 192, 207, 216, 226, 228, 233, 238, 253, 314, 317, 332, 333, 341, 343, 345, 351, 348, 355, 361, 367, 369, 375, 376, 382, 388, 394, 408, 409, 415, 419, 422, 426, 427, 429, 454, 465, 503, 509, 547, 557, 558